ESSENTIAL X-MEN

VOLUME 10

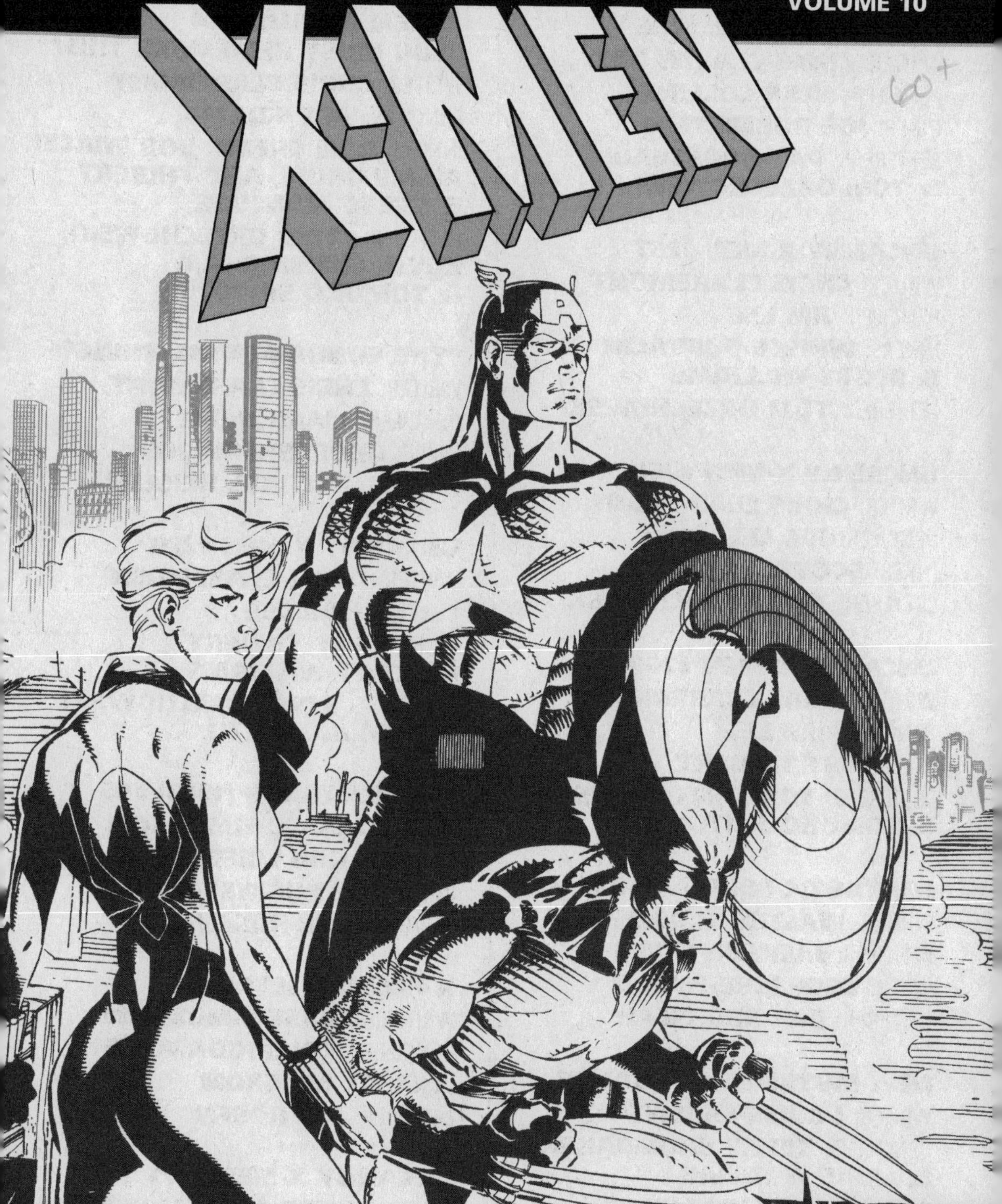

60+

UNCANNY X-MEN #265-272 & ANNUAL #14, NEW MUTANTS #95-97 AND X-FACTOR #60-62; AND MATERIAL FROM FANTASTIC FOUR ANNUAL #23, NEW MUTANTS ANNUAL #6 AND X-FACTOR ANNUAL #5

UNCANNY X-MEN #265
WRITER: **CHRIS CLAREMONT**
PENCILER: **BILL JAASKA**
INKER: **JOE RUBINSTEIN**
LETTERER: **JOE ROSEN**

UNCANNY X-MEN #266
WRITER: **CHRIS CLAREMONT**
PENCILER: **MIKE COLLINS**
INKER: **JOE RUBINSTEIN**
LETTERERS: **PAT BROSSEAU
& TOM ORZECHOWSKI**

UNCANNY X-MEN #267
WRITER: **CHRIS CLAREMONT**
PENCILER: **JIM LEE**
INKERS: **WHILCE PORTACIO
& SCOTT WILLIAMS**
LETTERER: **TOM ORZECHOWSKI**

UNCANNY X-MEN #268
WRITER: **CHRIS CLAREMONT**
PENCILER: **JIM LEE**
INKER: **SCOTT WILLIAMS**
LETTERER: **TOM ORZECHOWSKI**

UNCANNY X-MEN #269
WRITER: **CHRIS CLAREMONT**
PENCILER: **JIM LEE**
INKER: **ART THIBERT**
LETTERERS: **TOM ORZECHOWSKI
& TOMOKO SAITO**

FANTASTIC FOUR ANNUAL #23
WRITER: **WALTER SIMONSON**
PENCILER: **JACKSON GUICE**
INKER: **GEOF ISHERWOOD**
LETTERER: **PAT BROSSEAU**

NEW MUTANTS ANNUAL #6
WRITER: **LOUISE SIMONSON**
PENCILERS: **TERRY SHOEMAKER
& CHRIS WOZNIAK**
INKERS: **SCOTT WILLIAMS,
AL MILGROM, ART THIBERT
& HARRY CANDELARIO**
LETTERER: **JOE ROSEN**

X-FACTOR ANNUAL #5
WRITER: **LOUISE SIMONSON**
PENCILER: **JON BOGDANOVE**
INKER: **AL MILGROM**
LETTERER: **JOE ROSEN**

**X-MEN ANNUAL #14
"YOU MUST REMEMBER THIS"**
WRITER: **CHRIS CLAREMONT**
PENCILER: **ART ADAMS**
INKERS: **DAN GREEN, BOB WIACEK,
AL MILGROM, ART THIBERT
& STEVE MANCUSE**
LETTERERS: **TOM ORZECHOWSKI,
KEVIN CUNNINGHAM
& TOMOKO SAITO**

"THE FUNDAMENTAL THING"
WRITER: **CHRIS CLAREMONT**
PENCILER: **MARK HEIKE**
INKER: **GEOF ISHERWOOD**
LETTERER: **MICHAEL HEISLER**

UNCANNY X-MEN #270
WRITER: **CHRIS CLAREMONT**
PENCILER: **JIM LEE**
INKERS: **ART THIBERT
& SCOTT WILLIAMS**
LETTERERS: **TOM ORZECHOWSKI
& TOMOKO SAITO**

NEW MUTANTS (1983) #95
WRITER: **LOUISE SIMONSON**
PENCILER: **ROB LIEFELD**
INKER: **JOE RUBINSTEIN**
LETTERER: **JOE ROSEN**

X-FACTOR (1986) #60
WRITER: **LOUISE SIMONSON**
PENCILER: **JON BOGDANOVE**
INKER: **AL MILGROM**
LETTERER: **JOE ROSEN**

UNCANNY X-MEN #271
WRITER: **CHRIS CLAREMONT**
PENCILER: **JIM LEE**
INKER: **SCOTT WILLIAMS**
LETTERER: **TOM ORZECHOWSKI**

NEW MUTANTS (1983) #96
WRITER: **CHRIS CLAREMONT**
PENCILER: **ROB LIEFELD**
INKERS: **ART THIBERT
& JOE RUBINSTEIN**
LETTERERS: **TASK FORCE Z**

X-FACTOR (1986) #61
WRITER: **LOUISE SIMONSON**
PENCILERS: **JON BOGDANOVE
& JOHN CAPONIGRO**
INKER: **AL MILGROM**
LETTERER: **JOE ROSEN**

UNCANNY X-MEN #272
WRITER: **CHRIS CLAREMONT**
PENCILER: **JIM LEE**
INKER: **SCOTT WILLIAMS**
LETTERER: **TOM ORZECHOWSKI**

NEW MUTANTS (1983) #97
WRITER: **LOUISE SIMONSON**
PENCILER: **GUANG YAP**
INKER: **JOE RUBINSTEIN**
LETTERER: **JOE ROSEN**

X-FACTOR (1986) #62
WRITER: **LOUISE SIMONSON**
PENCILER: **JON BOGDANOVE**
INKER: **AL MILGROM**
LETTERERS: **TASK FORCE Z**

REPRINT CREDITS

MARVEL ESSENTIAL DESIGN:
RODOLFO MURAGUCHI

FRONT COVER ART:
JIM LEE & SCOTT WILLIAMS

FRONT COVER COLORS:
CHRIS SOTOMAYOR

BACK COVER ART:
ANDY KUBERT

BACK COVER COLORS:
JOHN KALISZ

COLLECTION EDITOR:
NELSON RIBEIRO

ASSISTANT EDITOR:
ALEX STARBUCK

EDITORS, SPECIAL PROJECTS:
**MARK D. BEAZLEY
& JENNIFER GRÜNWALD**

SENIOR EDITOR, SPECIAL PROJECTS:
JEFF YOUNGQUIST

SENIOR VICE PRESIDENT OF SALES:
DAVID GABRIEL

SVP OF BRAND PLANNING
& COMMUNICATIONS:
MICHAEL PASCIULLO

RESEARCH:
JEPH YORK

PRODUCTION:
DAMIEN LUCCHESE

BOOK DESIGNER:
MICHAEL CHATHAM

EDITOR IN CHIEF:
AXEL ALONSO

CHIEF CREATIVE OFFICER:
JOE QUESADA

PUBLISHER:
DAN BUCKLEY

EXECUTIVE PRODUCER:
ALAN FINE

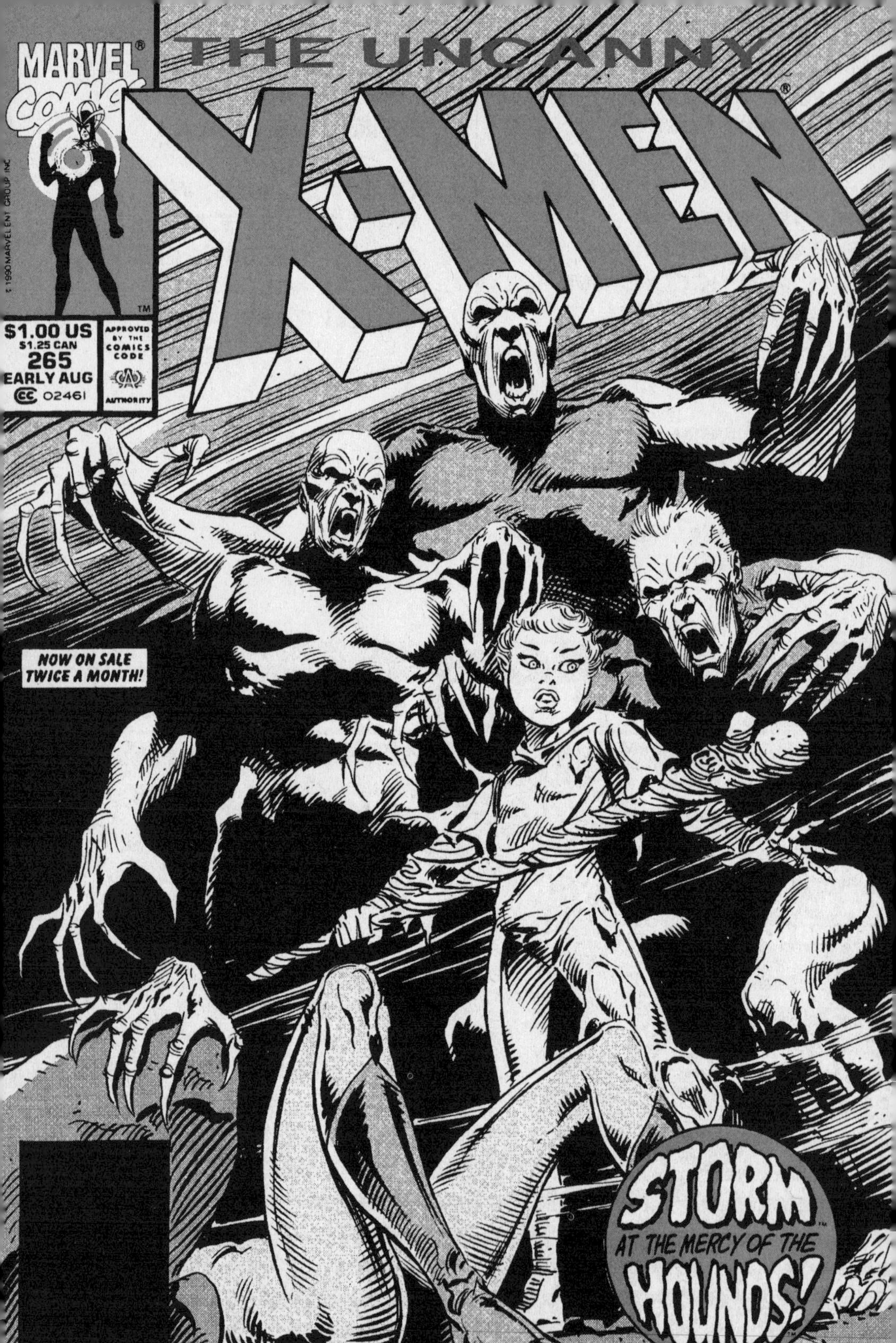
MARVEL COMICS
THE UNCANNY X-MEN
$1.00 US
$1.25 CAN
265
EARLY AUG
02461
APPROVED BY THE COMICS CODE AUTHORITY
© 1990 MARVEL ENT GROUP INC
NOW ON SALE TWICE A MONTH!
STORM AT THE MERCY OF THE HOUNDS!

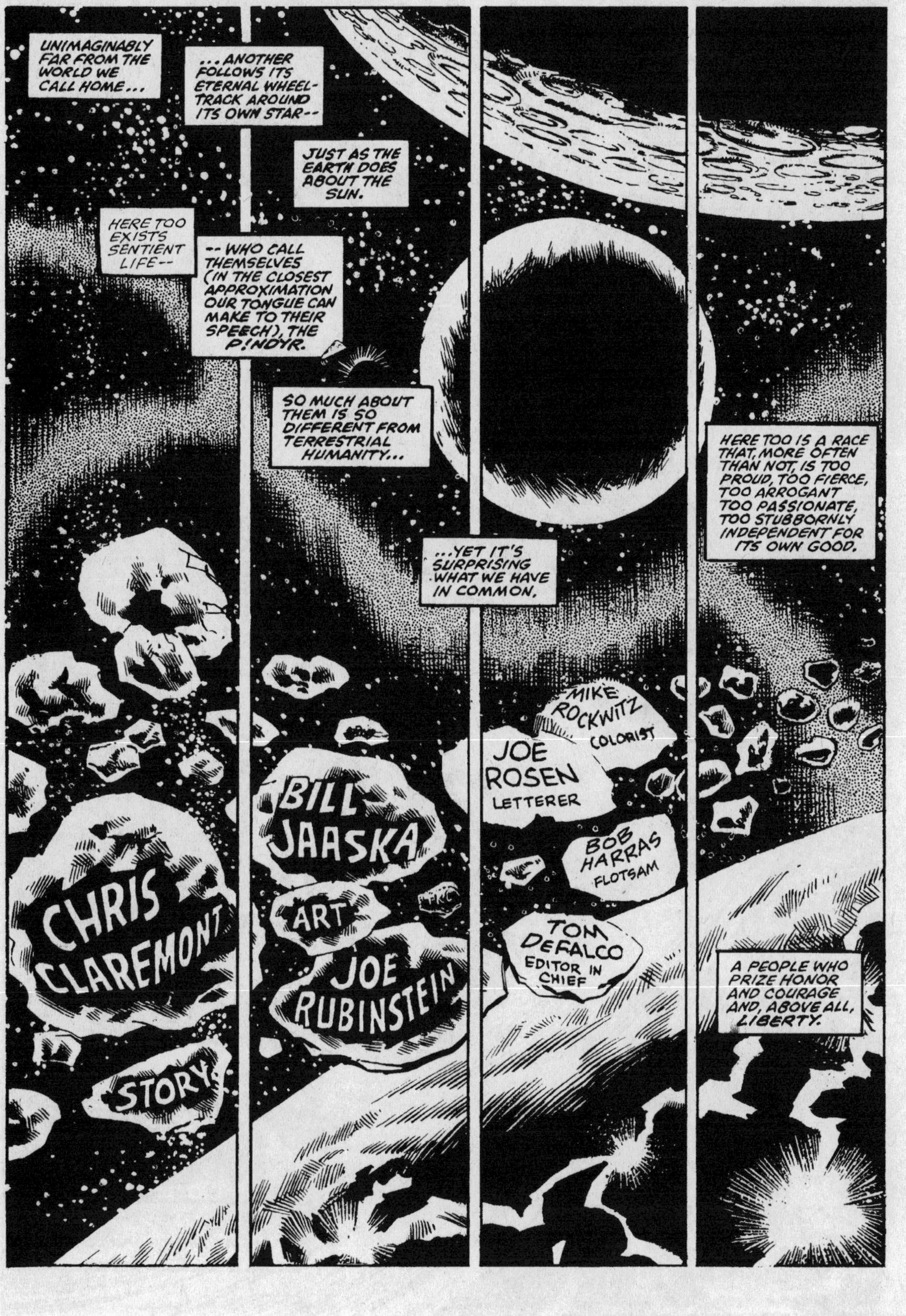
UNIMAGINABLY FAR FROM THE WORLD WE CALL HOME...
...ANOTHER FOLLOWS ITS ETERNAL WHEEL-TRACK AROUND ITS OWN STAR--
JUST AS THE EARTH DOES ABOUT THE SUN.
HERE TOO EXISTS SENTIENT LIFE--
--WHO CALL THEMSELVES (IN THE CLOSEST APPROXIMATION OUR TONGUE CAN MAKE TO THEIR SPEECH), THE P!NDYR.
SO MUCH ABOUT THEM IS SO DIFFERENT FROM TERRESTRIAL HUMANITY...
...YET IT'S SURPRISING WHAT WE HAVE IN COMMON.
HERE TOO IS A RACE THAT, MORE OFTEN THAN NOT, IS TOO PROUD, TOO FIERCE, TOO ARROGANT TOO PASSIONATE, TOO STUBBORNLY INDEPENDENT FOR ITS OWN GOOD.
A PEOPLE WHO PRIZE HONOR AND COURAGE AND, ABOVE ALL, LIBERTY.
CHRIS CLAREMONT
STORY
BILL JAASKA
ART
JOE RUBINSTEIN
MIKE ROCKWITZ COLORIST
JOE ROSEN LETTERER
BOB HARRAS FLOTSAM
TOM DEFALCO EDITOR IN CHIEF

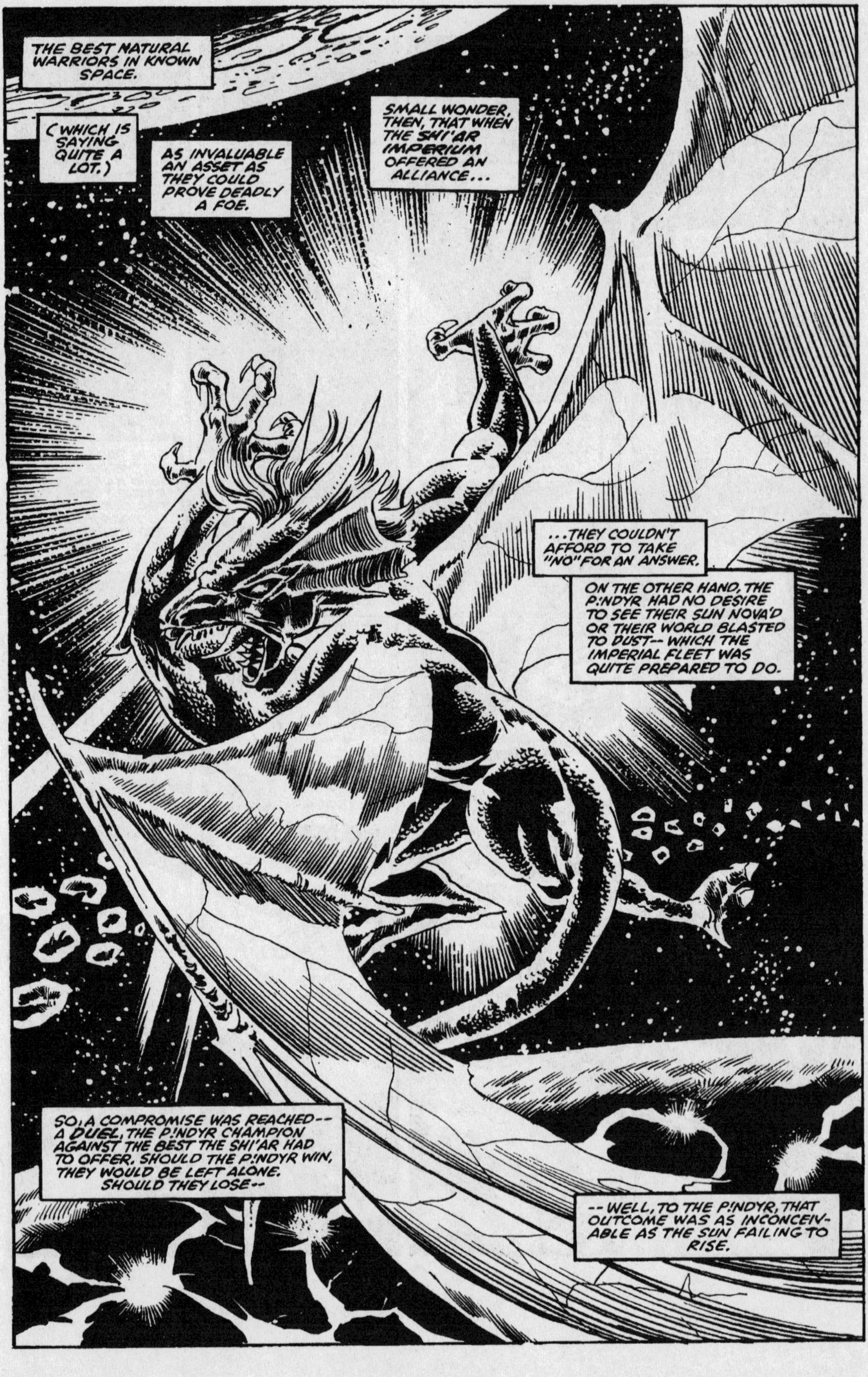
THE BEST NATURAL WARRIORS IN KNOWN SPACE.
(WHICH IS SAYING QUITE A LOT.)
AS INVALUABLE AN ASSET AS THEY COULD PROVE DEADLY A FOE.
SMALL WONDER, THEN, THAT WHEN THE SHI'AR IMPERIUM OFFERED AN ALLIANCE...
...THEY COULDN'T AFFORD TO TAKE "NO" FOR AN ANSWER.
ON THE OTHER HAND, THE P!NDYR HAD NO DESIRE TO SEE THEIR SUN NOVA'D OR THEIR WORLD BLASTED TO DUST-- WHICH THE IMPERIAL FLEET WAS QUITE PREPARED TO DO.
SO, A COMPROMISE WAS REACHED-- A DUEL, THE P!NDYR CHAMPION AGAINST THE BEST THE SHI'AR HAD TO OFFER. SHOULD THE P!NDYR WIN, THEY WOULD BE LEFT ALONE. SHOULD THEY LOSE--
--WELL, TO THE P!NDYR, THAT OUTCOME WAS AS INCONCEIVABLE AS THE SUN FAILING TO RISE.

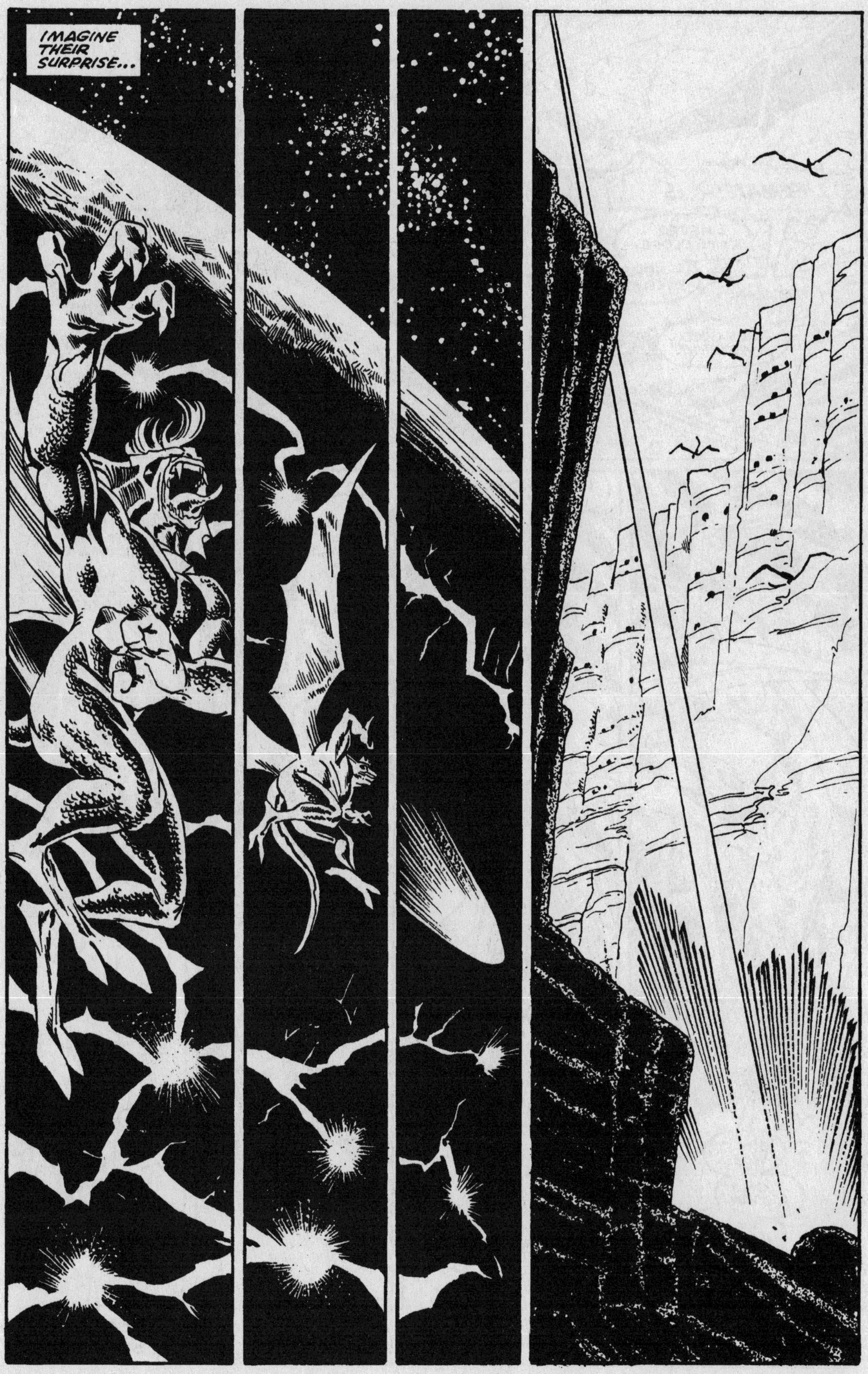
IMAGINE THEIR SURPRISE...

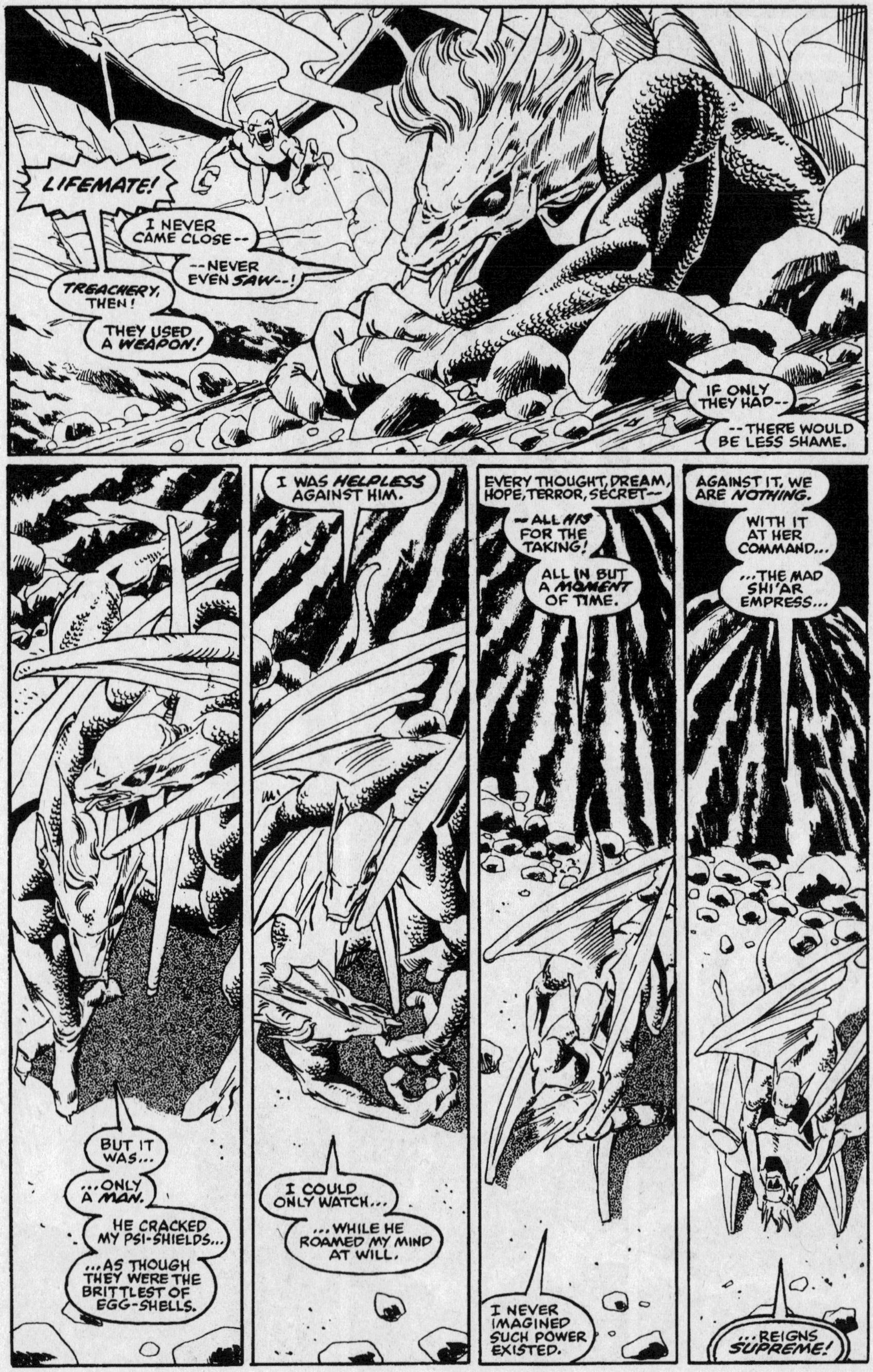
LIFEMATE!
I NEVER CAME CLOSE--
--NEVER EVEN SAW--!
TREACHERY, THEN!
THEY USED A WEAPON!
IF ONLY THEY HAD--
--THERE WOULD BE LESS SHAME.
BUT IT WAS...
...ONLY A MAN.
HE CRACKED MY PSI-SHIELDS...
...AS THOUGH THEY WERE THE BRITTLEST OF EGG-SHELLS.
I WAS HELPLESS AGAINST HIM.
I COULD ONLY WATCH...
...WHILE HE ROAMED MY MIND AT WILL.
EVERY THOUGHT, DREAM, HOPE, TERROR, SECRET--
--ALL HIS FOR THE TAKING!
ALL IN BUT A MOMENT OF TIME.
I NEVER IMAGINED SUCH POWER EXISTED.
AGAINST IT, WE ARE NOTHING.
WITH IT AT HER COMMAND...
...THE MAD SHI'AR EMPRESS...
...REIGNS SUPREME!

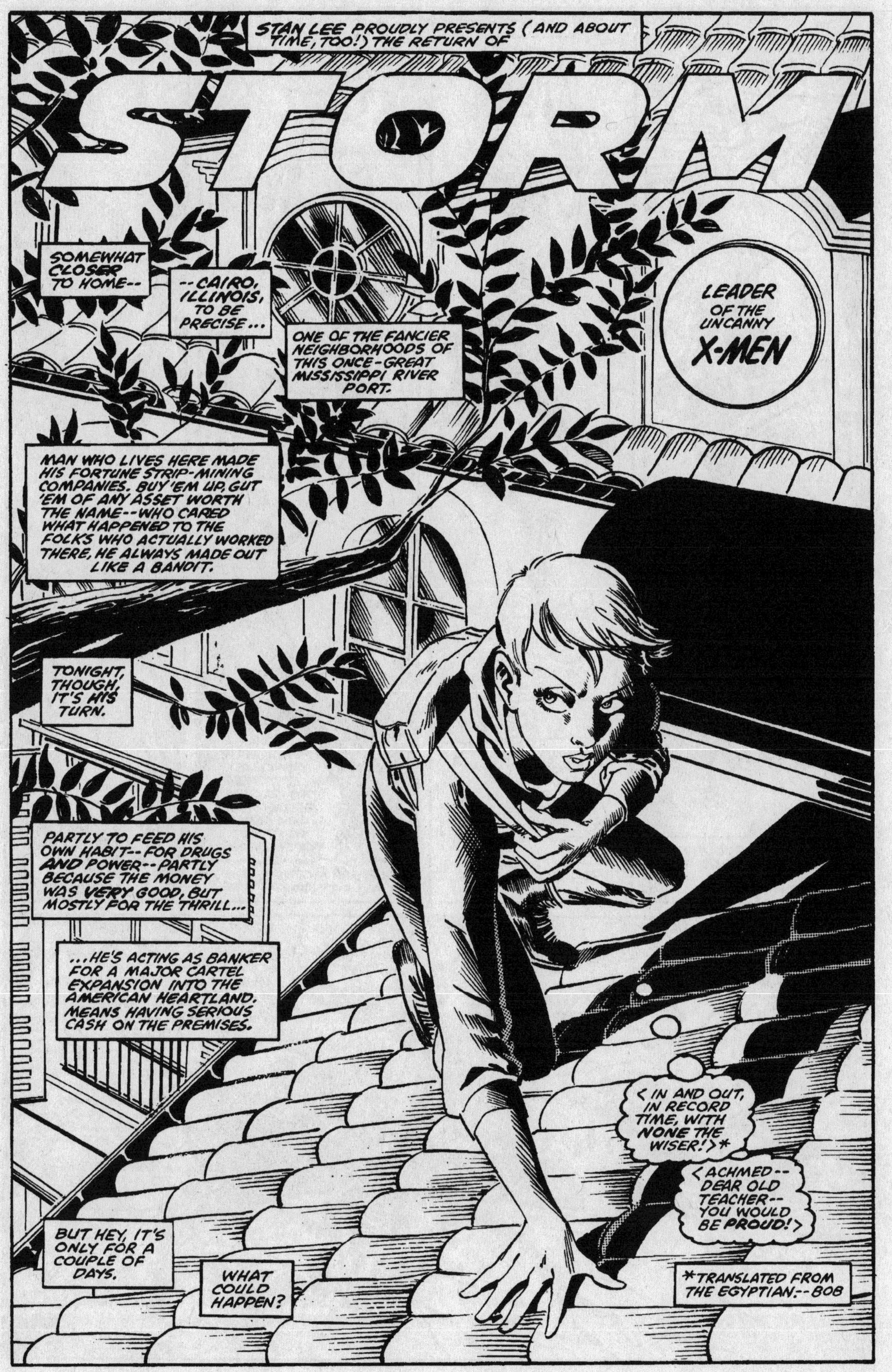
STAN LEE PROUDLY PRESENTS (AND ABOUT TIME, TOO!) THE RETURN OF
STORM
LEADER OF THE UNCANNY X-MEN
SOMEWHAT CLOSER TO HOME--
--CAIRO, ILLINOIS, TO BE PRECISE...
ONE OF THE FANCIER NEIGHBORHOODS OF THIS ONCE-GREAT MISSISSIPPI RIVER PORT.
MAN WHO LIVES HERE MADE HIS FORTUNE STRIP-MINING COMPANIES. BUY 'EM UP, GUT 'EM OF ANY ASSET WORTH THE NAME--WHO CARED WHAT HAPPENED TO THE FOLKS WHO ACTUALLY WORKED THERE, HE ALWAYS MADE OUT LIKE A BANDIT.
TONIGHT, THOUGH, IT'S HIS TURN.
PARTLY TO FEED HIS OWN HABIT-- FOR DRUGS AND POWER-- PARTLY BECAUSE THE MONEY WAS VERY GOOD, BUT MOSTLY FOR THE THRILL...
...HE'S ACTING AS BANKER FOR A MAJOR CARTEL EXPANSION INTO THE AMERICAN HEARTLAND. MEANS HAVING SERIOUS CASH ON THE PREMISES.
<IN AND OUT, IN RECORD TIME, WITH NONE THE WISER!>*
<ACHMED-- DEAR OLD TEACHER-- YOU WOULD BE PROUD!>
BUT HEY, IT'S ONLY FOR A COUPLE OF DAYS.
WHAT COULD HAPPEN?
*TRANSLATED FROM THE EGYPTIAN.--BOB

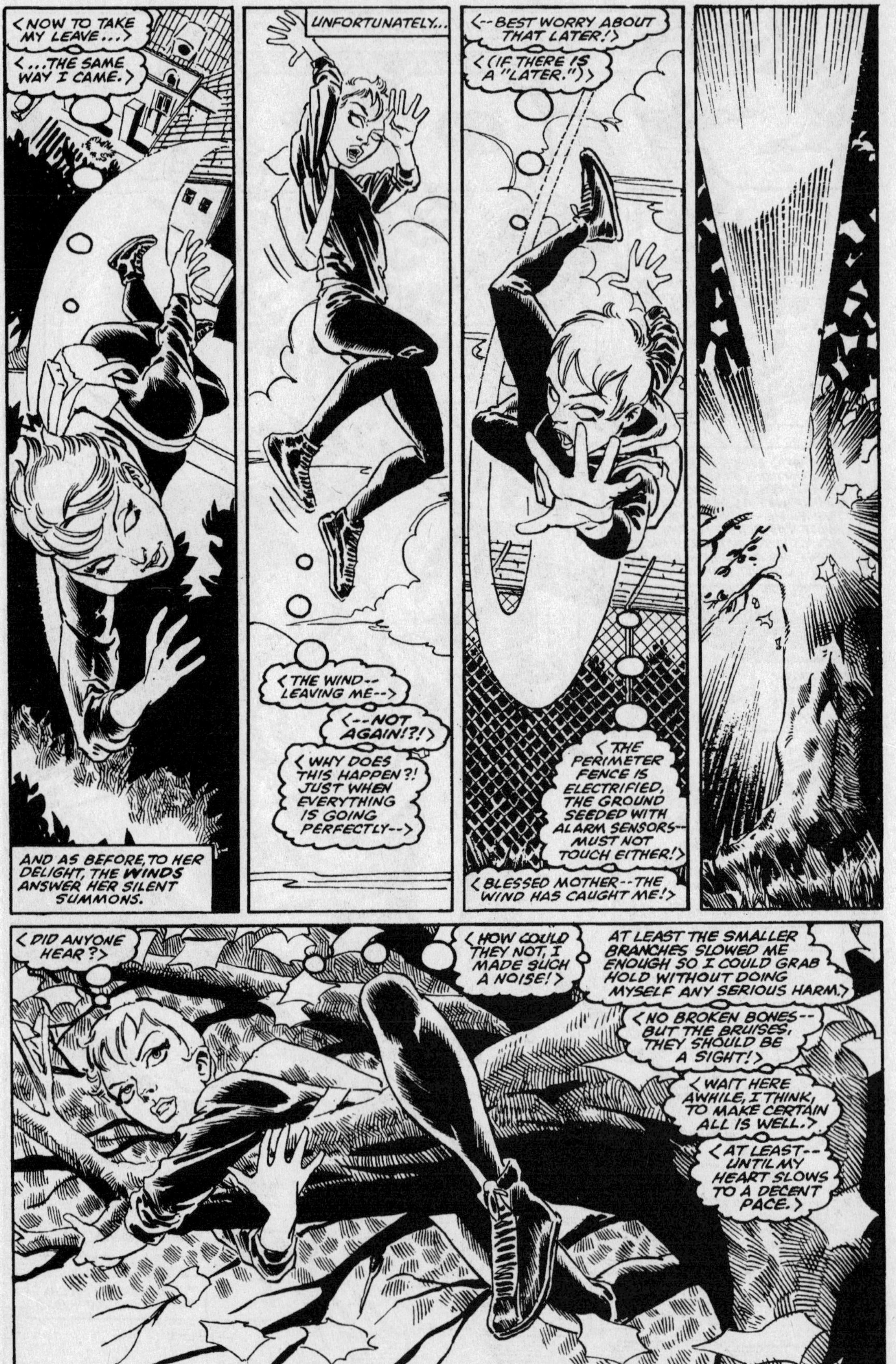

< NOW TO TAKE MY LEAVE... >
< ...THE SAME WAY I CAME. >
AND AS BEFORE, TO HER DELIGHT, THE WINDS ANSWER HER SILENT SUMMONS.
UNFORTUNATELY...
< THE WIND-- LEAVING ME-- >
< --NOT AGAIN!?! >
< WHY DOES THIS HAPPEN?! JUST WHEN EVERYTHING IS GOING PERFECTLY-- >
< --BEST WORRY ABOUT THAT LATER! >
< (IF THERE IS A "LATER.") >
< THE PERIMETER FENCE IS ELECTRIFIED, THE GROUND SEEDED WITH ALARM SENSORS-- MUST NOT TOUCH EITHER! >
< BLESSED MOTHER--THE WIND HAS CAUGHT ME! >
< DID ANYONE HEAR? >
< HOW COULD THEY NOT, I MADE SUCH A NOISE! >
AT LEAST THE SMALLER BRANCHES SLOWED ME ENOUGH SO I COULD GRAB HOLD WITHOUT DOING MYSELF ANY SERIOUS HARM. >
< NO BROKEN BONES-- BUT THE BRUISES, THEY SHOULD BE A SIGHT! >
< WAIT HERE AWHILE, I THINK, TO MAKE CERTAIN ALL IS WELL. >
< AT LEAST-- UNTIL MY HEART SLOWS TO A DECENT PACE. >

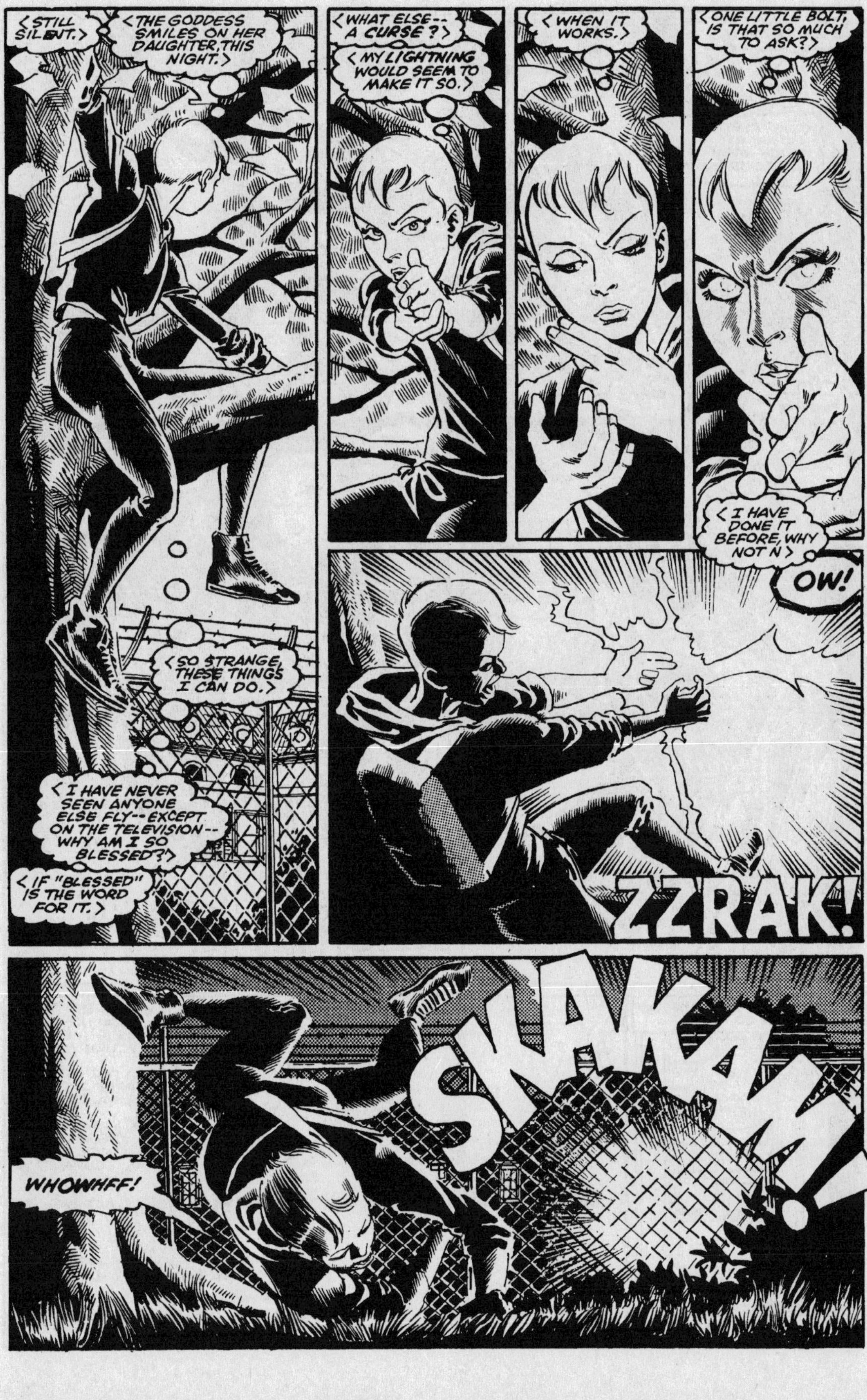
<STILL SILENT.>
<THE GODDESS SMILES ON HER DAUGHTER, THIS NIGHT.>
<SO STRANGE, THESE THINGS I CAN DO.>
<I HAVE NEVER SEEN ANYONE ELSE FLY--EXCEPT ON THE TELEVISION--WHY AM I SO BLESSED?>
<IF "BLESSED" IS THE WORD FOR IT.>
<WHAT ELSE--A CURSE?>
<MY LIGHTNING WOULD SEEM TO MAKE IT SO.>
<WHEN IT WORKS.>
<ONE LITTLE BOLT, IS THAT SO MUCH TO ASK?>
<I HAVE DONE IT BEFORE, WHY NOT N>
OW!
ZZRAK!
SKAKAM!
WHOWHFF!

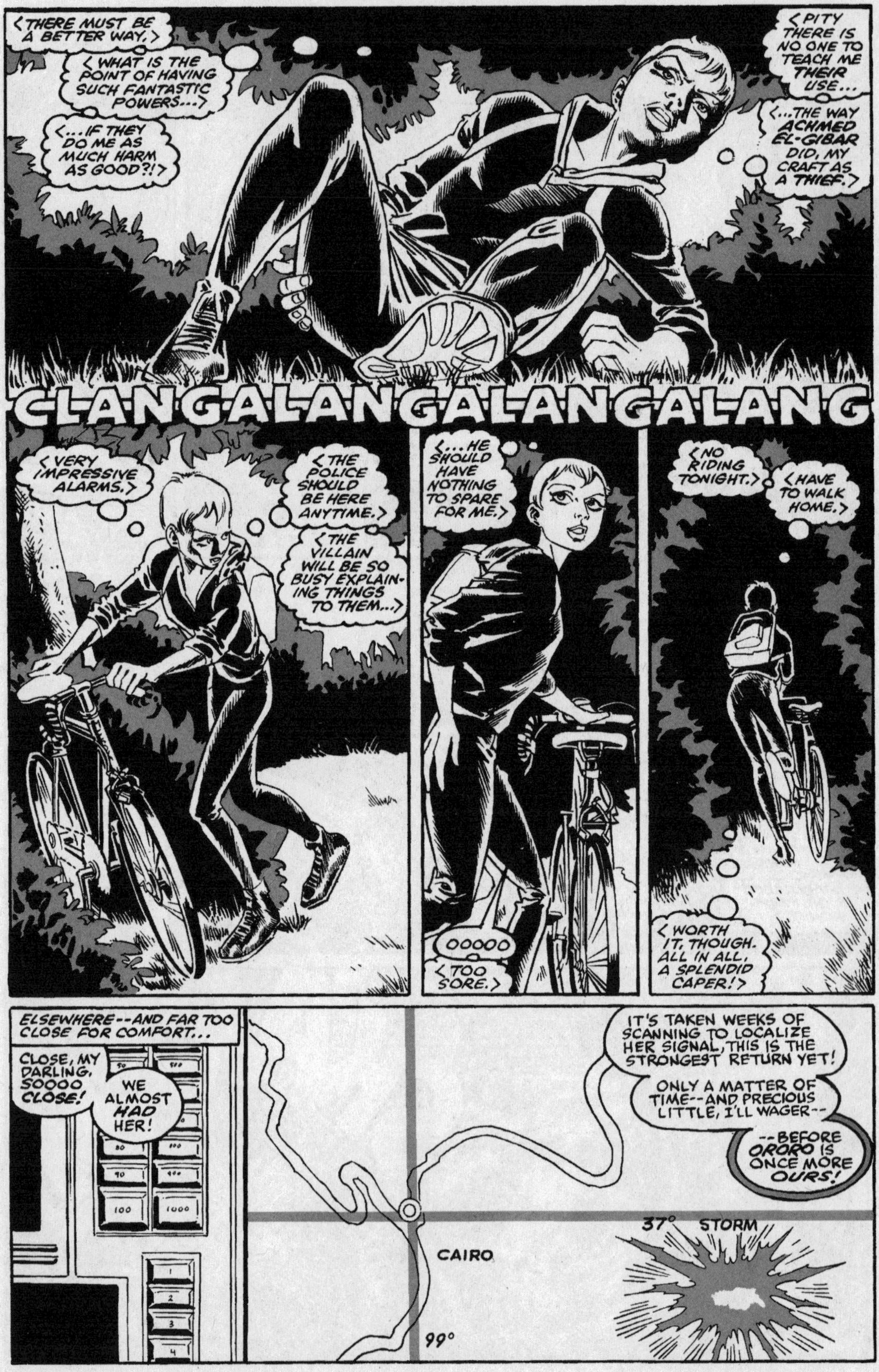

<THERE MUST BE A BETTER WAY.>
<WHAT IS THE POINT OF HAVING SUCH FANTASTIC POWERS...>
<...IF THEY DO ME AS MUCH HARM AS GOOD?!>
<PITY THERE IS NO ONE TO TEACH ME THEIR USE...
<...THE WAY ACHMED EL-GIBAR DID, MY CRAFT AS A THIEF.>
CLANGALANGALANGALANG
<VERY IMPRESSIVE ALARMS.>
<THE POLICE SHOULD BE HERE ANYTIME.>
<THE VILLAIN WILL BE SO BUSY EXPLAINING THINGS TO THEM...>
<...HE SHOULD HAVE NOTHING TO SPARE FOR ME.>
OOOOO
<TOO SORE.>
<NO RIDING TONIGHT.>
<HAVE TO WALK HOME.>
<WORTH IT, THOUGH. ALL IN ALL, A SPLENDID CAPER!>
ELSEWHERE--AND FAR TOO CLOSE FOR COMFORT...
CLOSE, MY DARLING, SOOOO CLOSE!
WE ALMOST HAD HER!
IT'S TAKEN WEEKS OF SCANNING TO LOCALIZE HER SIGNAL, THIS IS THE STRONGEST RETURN YET!
ONLY A MATTER OF TIME--AND PRECIOUS LITTLE, I'LL WAGER--
--BEFORE ORORO IS ONCE MORE OURS!
37°
STORM
CAIRO
99°

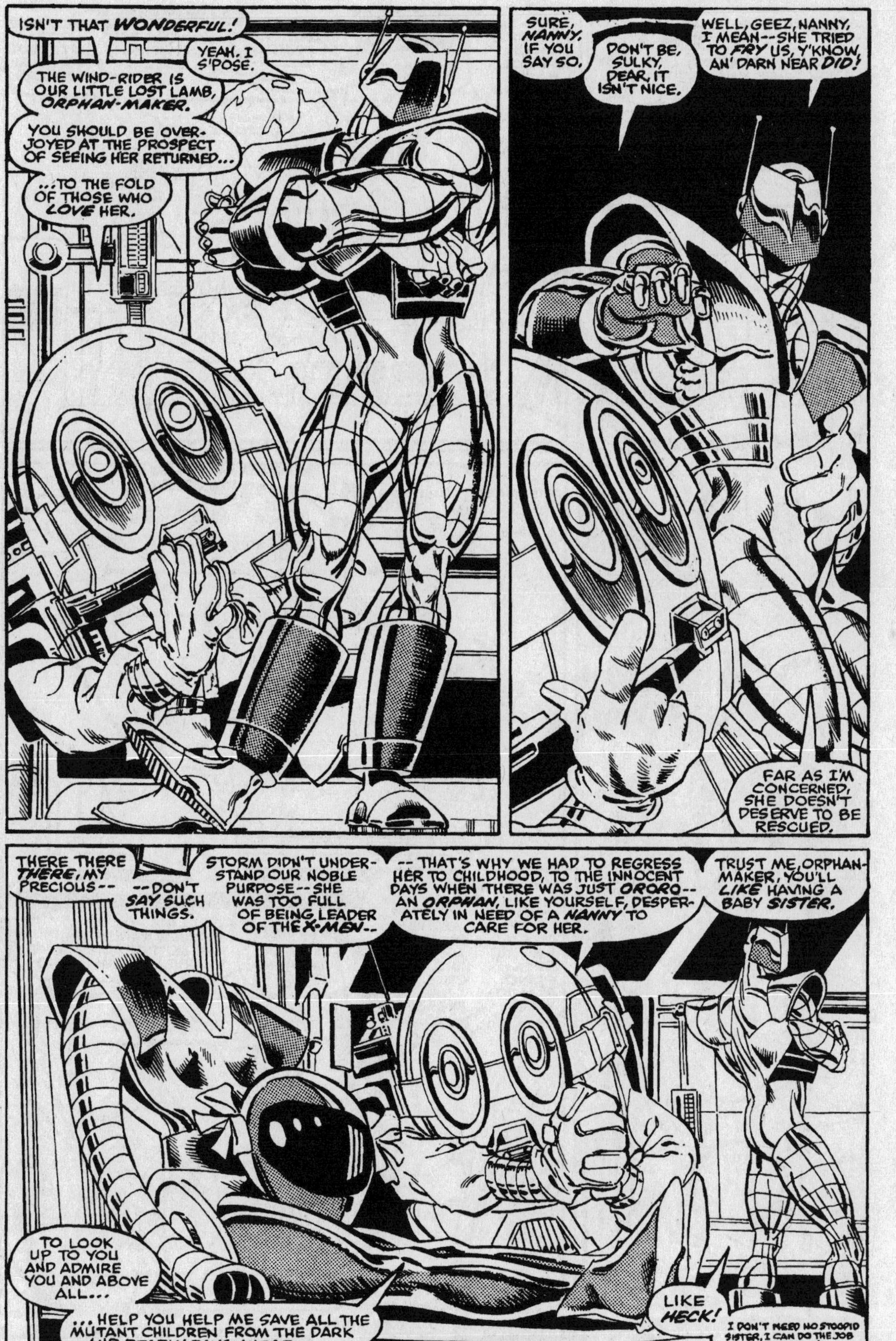
ISN'T THAT WONDERFUL!
YEAH. I S'POSE.
THE WIND-RIDER IS OUR LITTLE LOST LAMB, ORPHAN-MAKER.
YOU SHOULD BE OVER-JOYED AT THE PROSPECT OF SEEING HER RETURNED...
...TO THE FOLD OF THOSE WHO LOVE HER.
SURE, NANNY. IF YOU SAY SO.
DON'T BE, SULKY, DEAR, IT ISN'T NICE.
WELL, GEEZ, NANNY, I MEAN--SHE TRIED TO FRY US, Y'KNOW, AN' DARN NEAR DID!
FAR AS I'M CONCERNED, SHE DOESN'T DESERVE TO BE RESCUED.
THERE THERE THERE, MY PRECIOUS--
--DON'T SAY SUCH THINGS.
STORM DIDN'T UNDER-STAND OUR NOBLE PURPOSE--SHE WAS TOO FULL OF BEING LEADER OF THE X-MEN--
--THAT'S WHY WE HAD TO REGRESS HER TO CHILDHOOD, TO THE INNOCENT DAYS WHEN THERE WAS JUST ORORO--AN ORPHAN, LIKE YOURSELF, DESPER-ATELY IN NEED OF A NANNY TO CARE FOR HER.
TRUST ME, ORPHAN-MAKER, YOU'LL LIKE HAVING A BABY SISTER.
TO LOOK UP TO YOU AND ADMIRE YOU AND ABOVE ALL...
...HELP YOU HELP ME SAVE ALL THE MUTANT CHILDREN FROM THE DARK AND DEADLY DAYS AHEAD.
LIKE HECK!
I DON'T NEED NO STOOPID SISTER, I CAN DO THE JOB MYSELF!

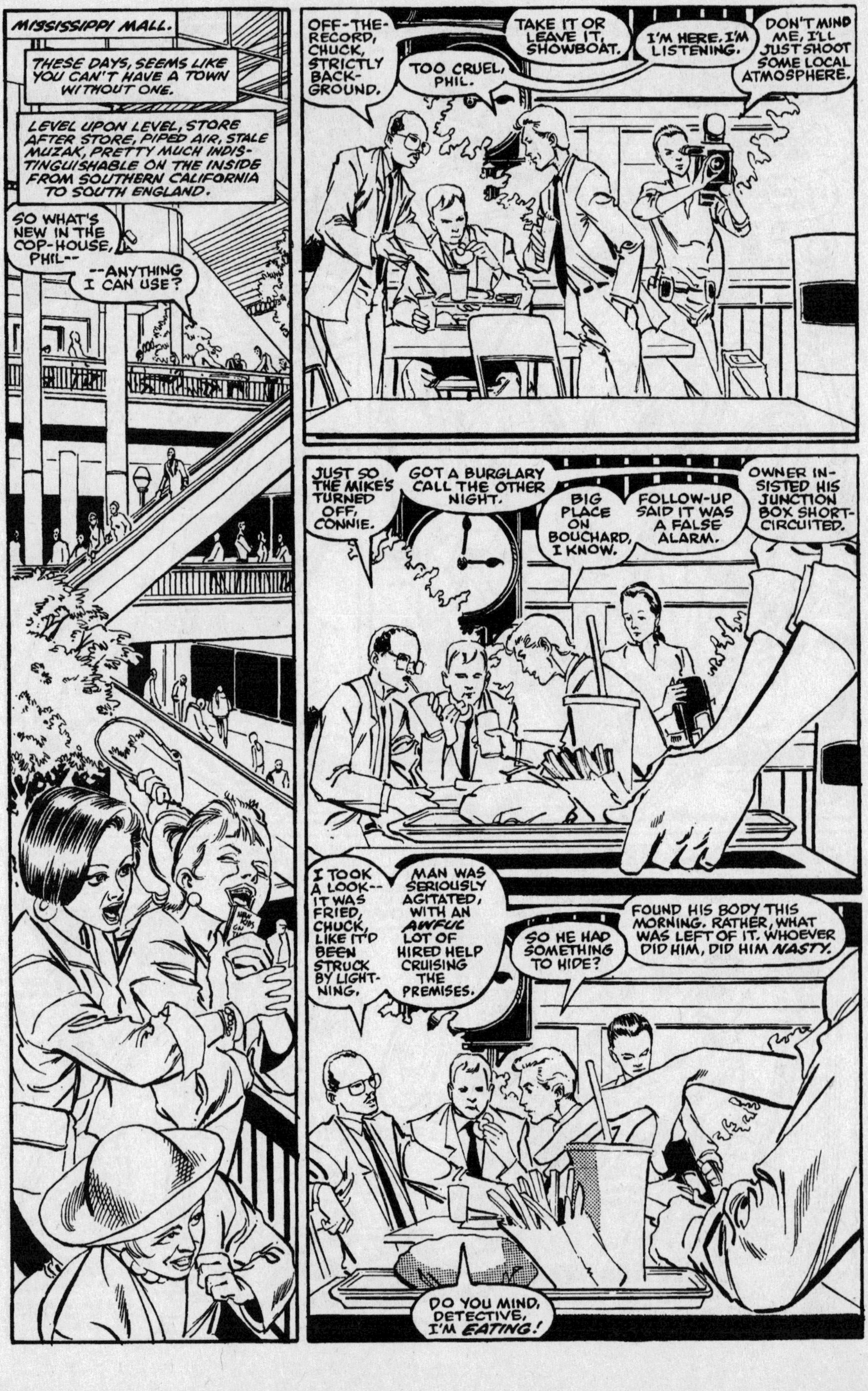
MISSISSIPPI MALL.
THESE DAYS, SEEMS LIKE YOU CAN'T HAVE A TOWN WITHOUT ONE.
LEVEL UPON LEVEL, STORE AFTER STORE, PIPED AIR, STALE MUZAK, PRETTY MUCH INDISTINGUISHABLE ON THE INSIDE FROM SOUTHERN CALIFORNIA TO SOUTH ENGLAND.
SO WHAT'S NEW IN THE COP-HOUSE, PHIL--
--ANYTHING I CAN USE?
OFF-THE-RECORD, CHUCK, STRICTLY BACKGROUND.
TOO CRUEL, PHIL.
TAKE IT OR LEAVE IT, SHOWBOAT.
I'M HERE. I'M LISTENING.
DON'T MIND ME, I'LL JUST SHOOT SOME LOCAL ATMOSPHERE.
JUST SO THE MIKE'S TURNED OFF, CONNIE.
GOT A BURGLARY CALL THE OTHER NIGHT.
BIG PLACE ON BOUCHARD, I KNOW.
FOLLOW-UP SAID IT WAS A FALSE ALARM.
OWNER INSISTED HIS JUNCTION BOX SHORT-CIRCUITED.
I TOOK A LOOK-- IT WAS FRIED, CHUCK, LIKE IT'D BEEN STRUCK BY LIGHTNING.
MAN WAS SERIOUSLY AGITATED, WITH AN AWFUL LOT OF HIRED HELP CRUISING THE PREMISES.
SO HE HAD SOMETHING TO HIDE?
FOUND HIS BODY THIS MORNING. RATHER, WHAT WAS LEFT OF IT. WHOEVER DID HIM, DID HIM NASTY.
DO YOU MIND, DETECTIVE, I'M EATING!

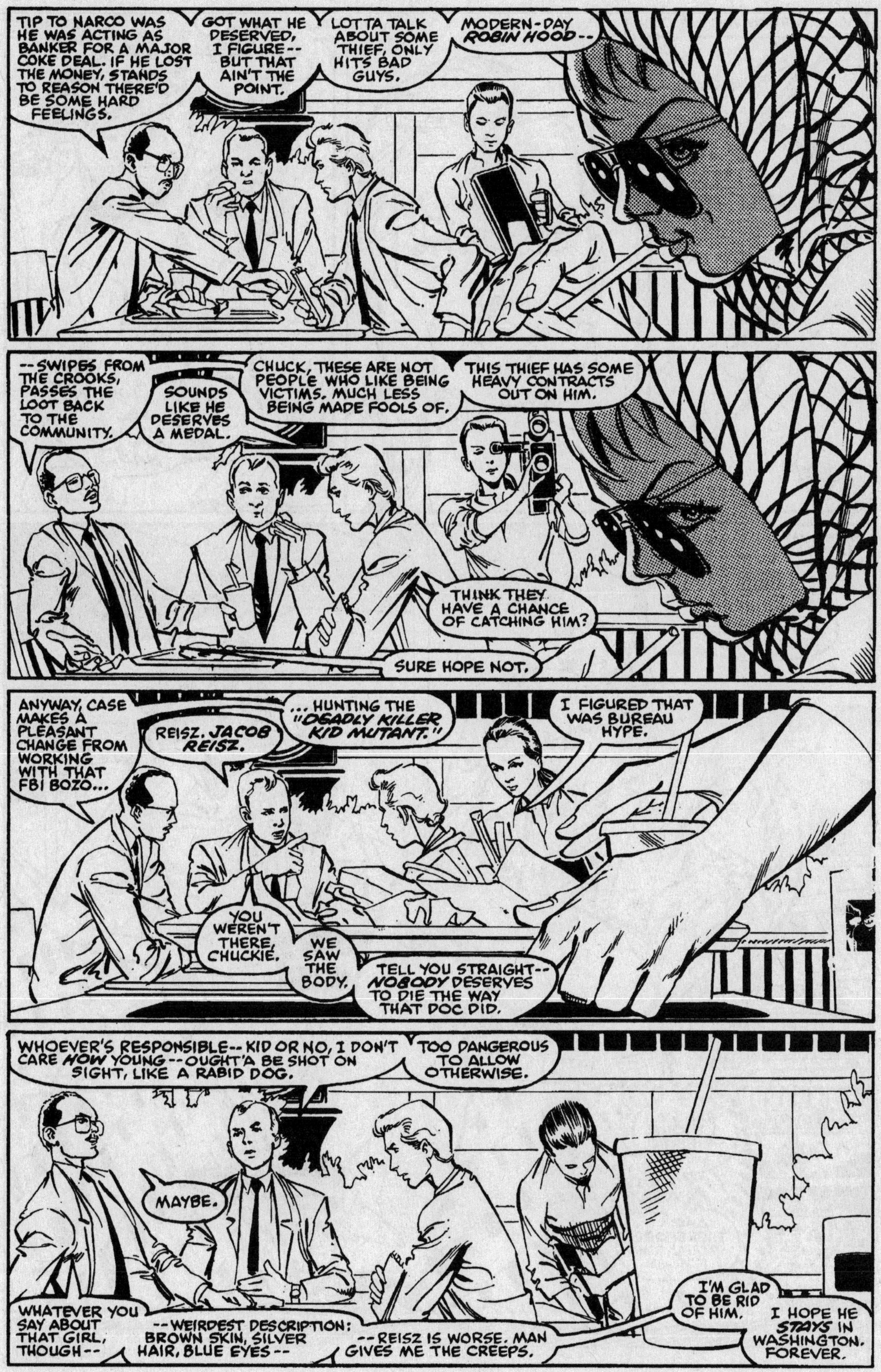
TIP TO NARCO WAS HE WAS ACTING AS BANKER FOR A MAJOR COKE DEAL. IF HE LOST THE MONEY, STANDS TO REASON THERE'D BE SOME HARD FEELINGS.
GOT WHAT HE DESERVED, I FIGURE-- BUT THAT AIN'T THE POINT.
LOTTA TALK ABOUT SOME THIEF, ONLY HITS BAD GUYS.
MODERN-DAY ROBIN HOOD--
--SWIPES FROM THE CROOKS, PASSES THE LOOT BACK TO THE COMMUNITY.
SOUNDS LIKE HE DESERVES A MEDAL.
CHUCK, THESE ARE NOT PEOPLE WHO LIKE BEING VICTIMS. MUCH LESS BEING MADE FOOLS OF.
THIS THIEF HAS SOME HEAVY CONTRACTS OUT ON HIM.
THINK THEY HAVE A CHANCE OF CATCHING HIM?
SURE HOPE NOT.
ANYWAY, CASE MAKES A PLEASANT CHANGE FROM WORKING WITH THAT FBI BOZO...
REISZ. JACOB REISZ.
...HUNTING THE "DEADLY KILLER KID MUTANT."
I FIGURED THAT WAS BUREAU HYPE.
YOU WEREN'T THERE, CHUCKIE.
WE SAW THE BODY.
TELL YOU STRAIGHT-- NOBODY DESERVES TO DIE THE WAY THAT DOC DID.
WHOEVER'S RESPONSIBLE-- KID OR NO, I DON'T CARE HOW YOUNG--OUGHT'A BE SHOT ON SIGHT, LIKE A RABID DOG.
TOO DANGEROUS TO ALLOW OTHERWISE.
MAYBE.
WHATEVER YOU SAY ABOUT THAT GIRL, THOUGH--
--WEIRDEST DESCRIPTION: BROWN SKIN, SILVER HAIR, BLUE EYES--
--REISZ IS WORSE. MAN GIVES ME THE CREEPS.
I'M GLAD TO BE RID OF HIM.
I HOPE HE STAYS IN WASHINGTON. FOREVER.

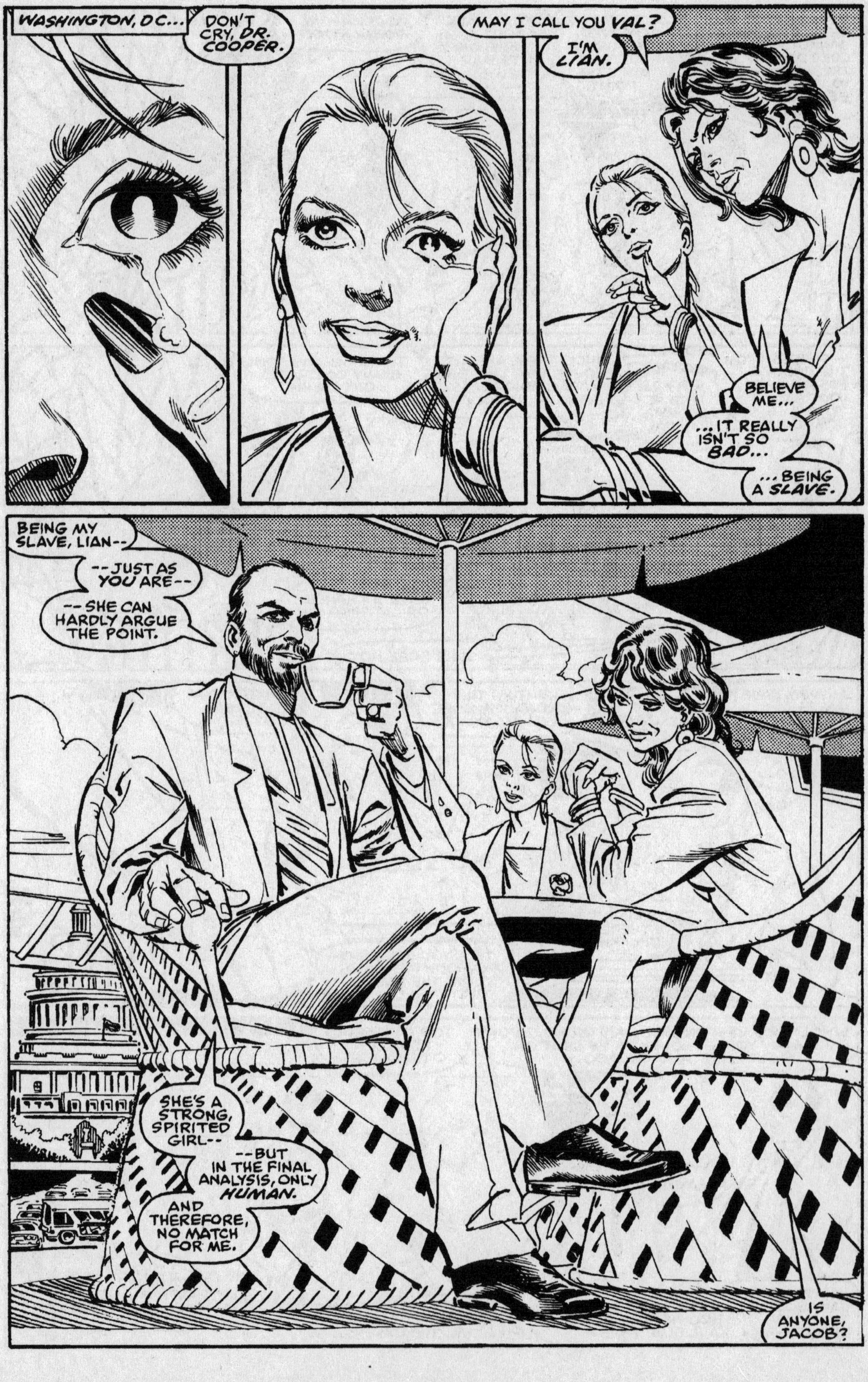
WASHINGTON, DC...
DON'T CRY, DR. COOPER.
MAY I CALL YOU VAL?
I'M LIAN.
BELIEVE ME...
...IT REALLY ISN'T SO BAD...
...BEING A SLAVE.
BEING MY SLAVE, LIAN--
--JUST AS YOU ARE--
--SHE CAN HARDLY ARGUE THE POINT.
SHE'S A STRONG, SPIRITED GIRL--
--BUT IN THE FINAL ANALYSIS, ONLY HUMAN.
AND THEREFORE, NO MATCH FOR ME.
IS ANYONE, JACOB?

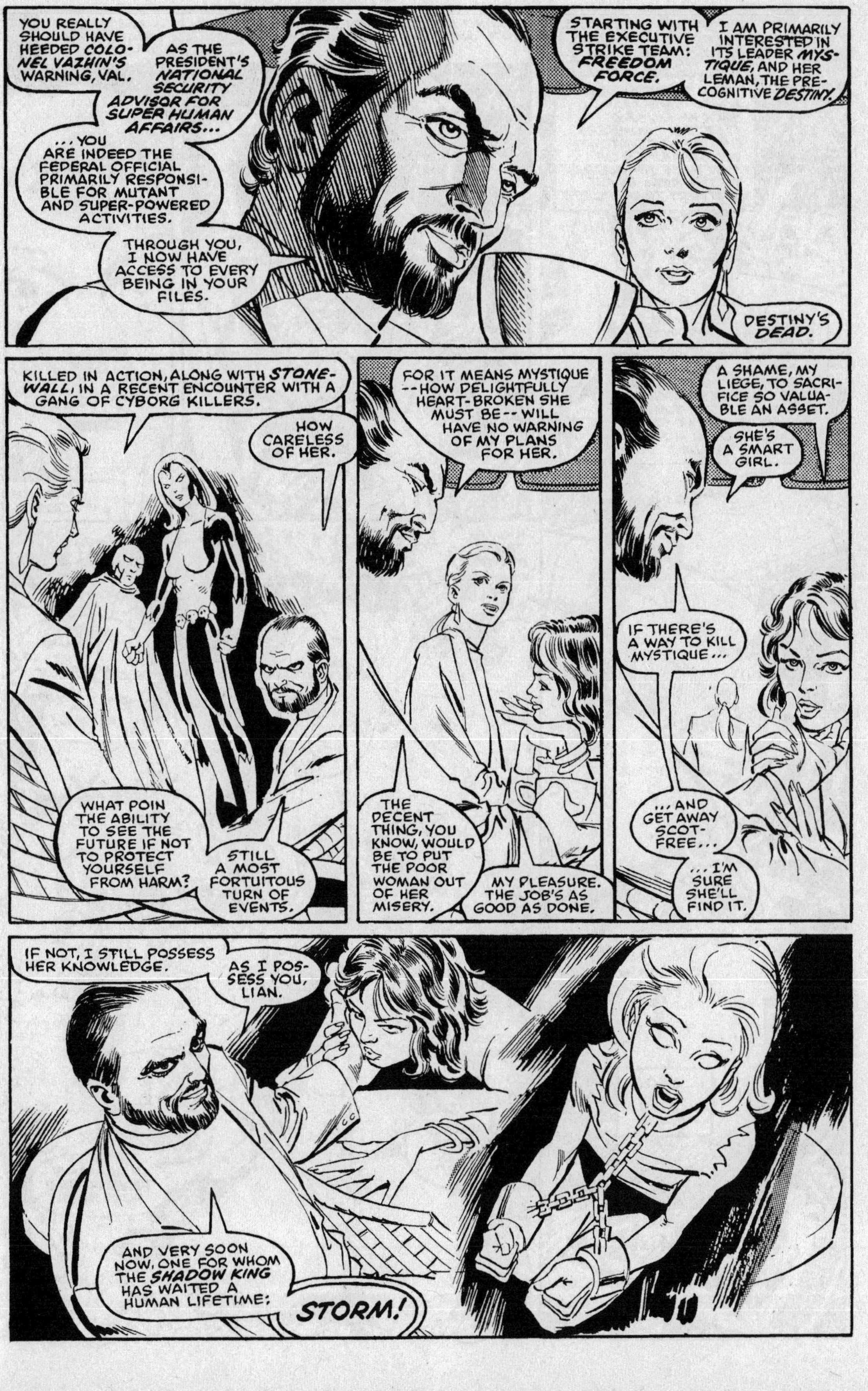
YOU REALLY SHOULD HAVE HEEDED COLONEL VAZHIN'S WARNING, VAL.
AS THE PRESIDENT'S NATIONAL SECURITY ADVISOR FOR SUPER HUMAN AFFAIRS...
...YOU ARE INDEED THE FEDERAL OFFICIAL PRIMARILY RESPONSIBLE FOR MUTANT AND SUPER-POWERED ACTIVITIES.
THROUGH YOU, I NOW HAVE ACCESS TO EVERY BEING IN YOUR FILES.
STARTING WITH THE EXECUTIVE STRIKE TEAM: FREEDOM FORCE.
I AM PRIMARILY INTERESTED IN ITS LEADER MYSTIQUE, AND HER LEMAN, THE PRECOGNITIVE DESTINY.
DESTINY'S DEAD.
KILLED IN ACTION, ALONG WITH STONEWALL, IN A RECENT ENCOUNTER WITH A GANG OF CYBORG KILLERS.
HOW CARELESS OF HER.
WHAT POIN THE ABILITY TO SEE THE FUTURE IF NOT TO PROTECT YOURSELF FROM HARM?
STILL A MOST FORTUITOUS TURN OF EVENTS.
FOR IT MEANS MYSTIQUE --HOW DELIGHTFULLY HEART-BROKEN SHE MUST BE-- WILL HAVE NO WARNING OF MY PLANS FOR HER.
THE DECENT THING, YOU KNOW, WOULD BE TO PUT THE POOR WOMAN OUT OF HER MISERY.
MY PLEASURE. THE JOB'S AS GOOD AS DONE.
A SHAME, MY LIEGE, TO SACRIFICE SO VALUABLE AN ASSET.
SHE'S A SMART GIRL.
IF THERE'S A WAY TO KILL MYSTIQUE...
...AND GET AWAY SCOT-FREE...
...I'M SURE SHE'LL FIND IT.
IF NOT, I STILL POSSESS HER KNOWLEDGE.
AS I POSSESS YOU, LIAN.
AND VERY SOON NOW, ONE FOR WHOM THE SHADOW KING HAS WAITED A HUMAN LIFETIME:
STORM!

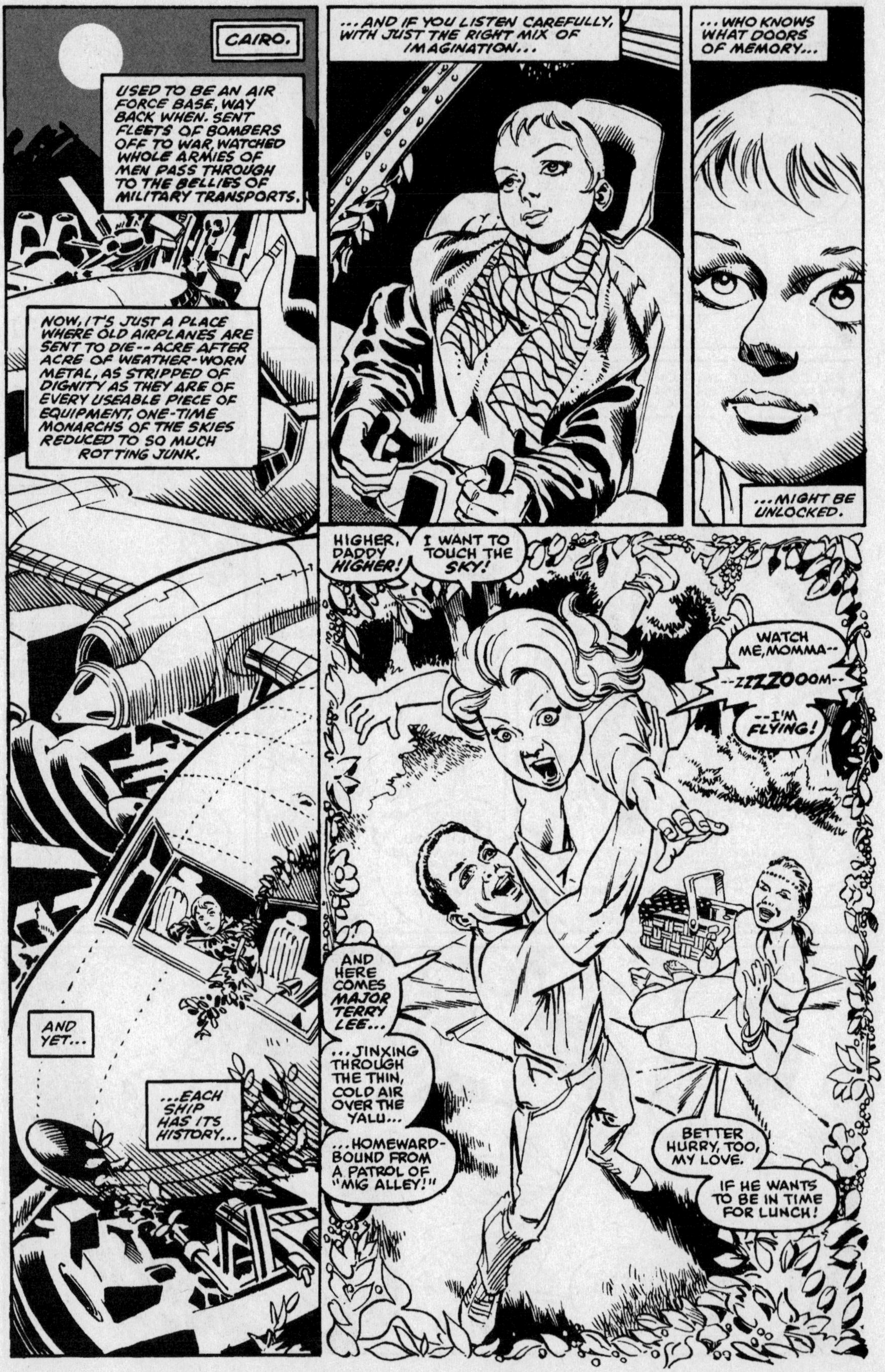
CAIRO.
USED TO BE AN AIR FORCE BASE, WAY BACK WHEN. SENT FLEETS OF BOMBERS OFF TO WAR, WATCHED WHOLE ARMIES OF MEN PASS THROUGH TO THE BELLIES OF MILITARY TRANSPORTS.
NOW, IT'S JUST A PLACE WHERE OLD AIRPLANES ARE SENT TO DIE-- ACRE AFTER ACRE OF WEATHER-WORN METAL, AS STRIPPED OF DIGNITY AS THEY ARE OF EVERY USEABLE PIECE OF EQUIPMENT, ONE-TIME MONARCHS OF THE SKIES REDUCED TO SO MUCH ROTTING JUNK.
AND YET...
...EACH SHIP HAS ITS HISTORY...
...AND IF YOU LISTEN CAREFULLY, WITH JUST THE RIGHT MIX OF IMAGINATION...
...WHO KNOWS WHAT DOORS OF MEMORY...
...MIGHT BE UNLOCKED.
HIGHER, DADDY HIGHER!
I WANT TO TOUCH THE SKY!
WATCH ME, MOMMA--
--ZZZZOOOM--
--I'M FLYING!
AND HERE COMES MAJOR TERRY LEE...
...JINXING THROUGH THE THIN, COLD AIR OVER THE YALU...
...HOMEWARD-BOUND FROM A PATROL OF "MIG ALLEY!"
BETTER HURRY, TOO, MY LOVE.
IF HE WANTS TO BE IN TIME FOR LUNCH!

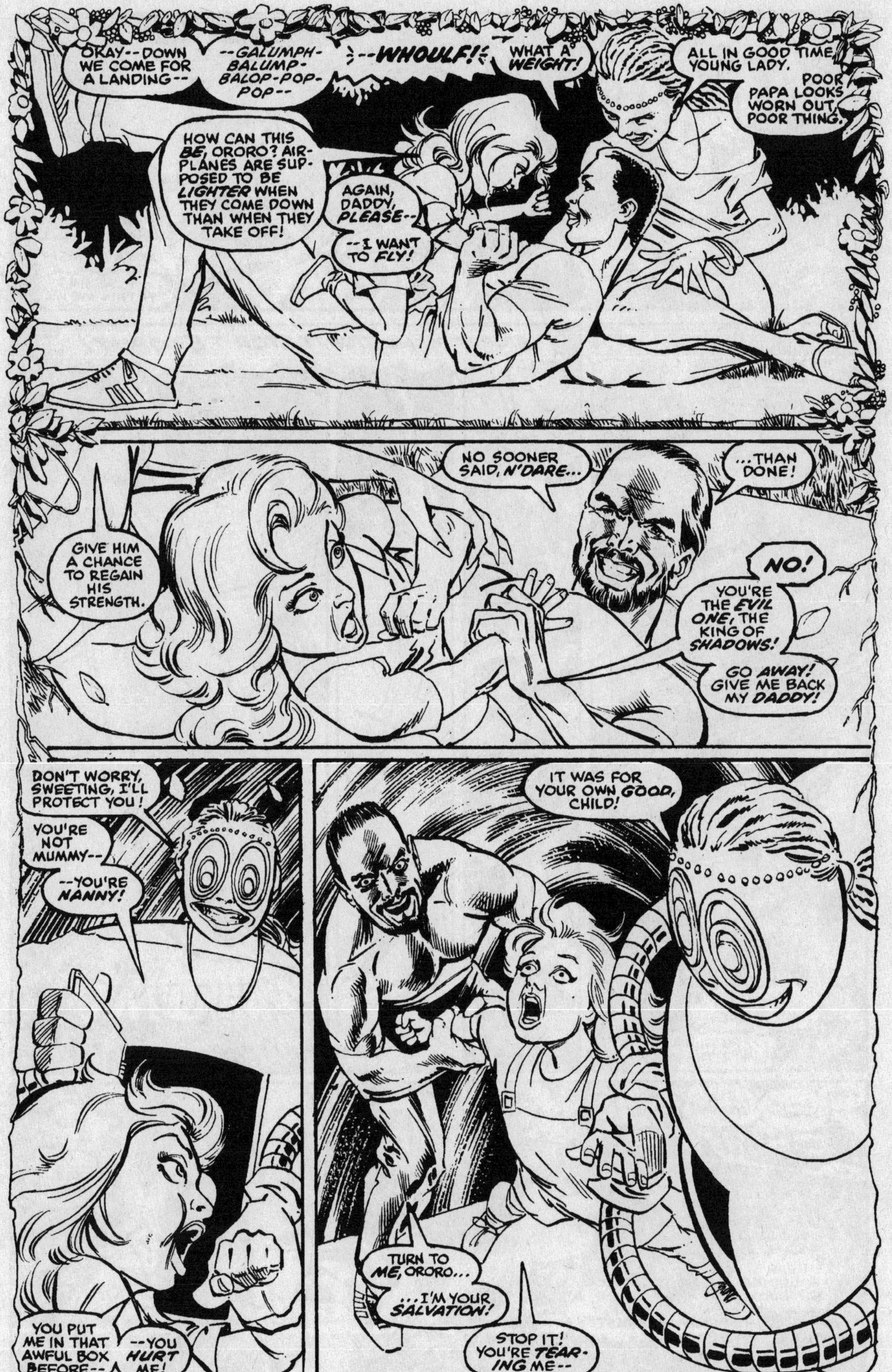
OKAY--DOWN WE COME FOR A LANDING--
--GALUMPH-BALUMP-BALOP-POP-POP--
--WHOULF!
WHAT A WEIGHT!
ALL IN GOOD TIME, YOUNG LADY.
POOR PAPA LOOKS WORN OUT, POOR THING.
HOW CAN THIS BE, ORORO? AIRPLANES ARE SUPPOSED TO BE LIGHTER WHEN THEY COME DOWN THAN WHEN THEY TAKE OFF!
AGAIN, DADDY, PLEASE--
--I WANT TO FLY!
GIVE HIM A CHANCE TO REGAIN HIS STRENGTH.
NO SOONER SAID, N'DARE...
...THAN DONE!
NO!
YOU'RE THE EVIL ONE, THE KING OF SHADOWS!
GO AWAY! GIVE ME BACK MY DADDY!
DON'T WORRY, SWEETING, I'LL PROTECT YOU!
YOU'RE NOT MUMMY--
--YOU'RE NANNY!
YOU PUT ME IN THAT AWFUL BOX BEFORE--
--YOU HURT ME!
IT WAS FOR YOUR OWN GOOD, CHILD!
TURN TO ME, ORORO...
...I'M YOUR SALVATION!
STOP IT! YOU'RE TEARING ME--

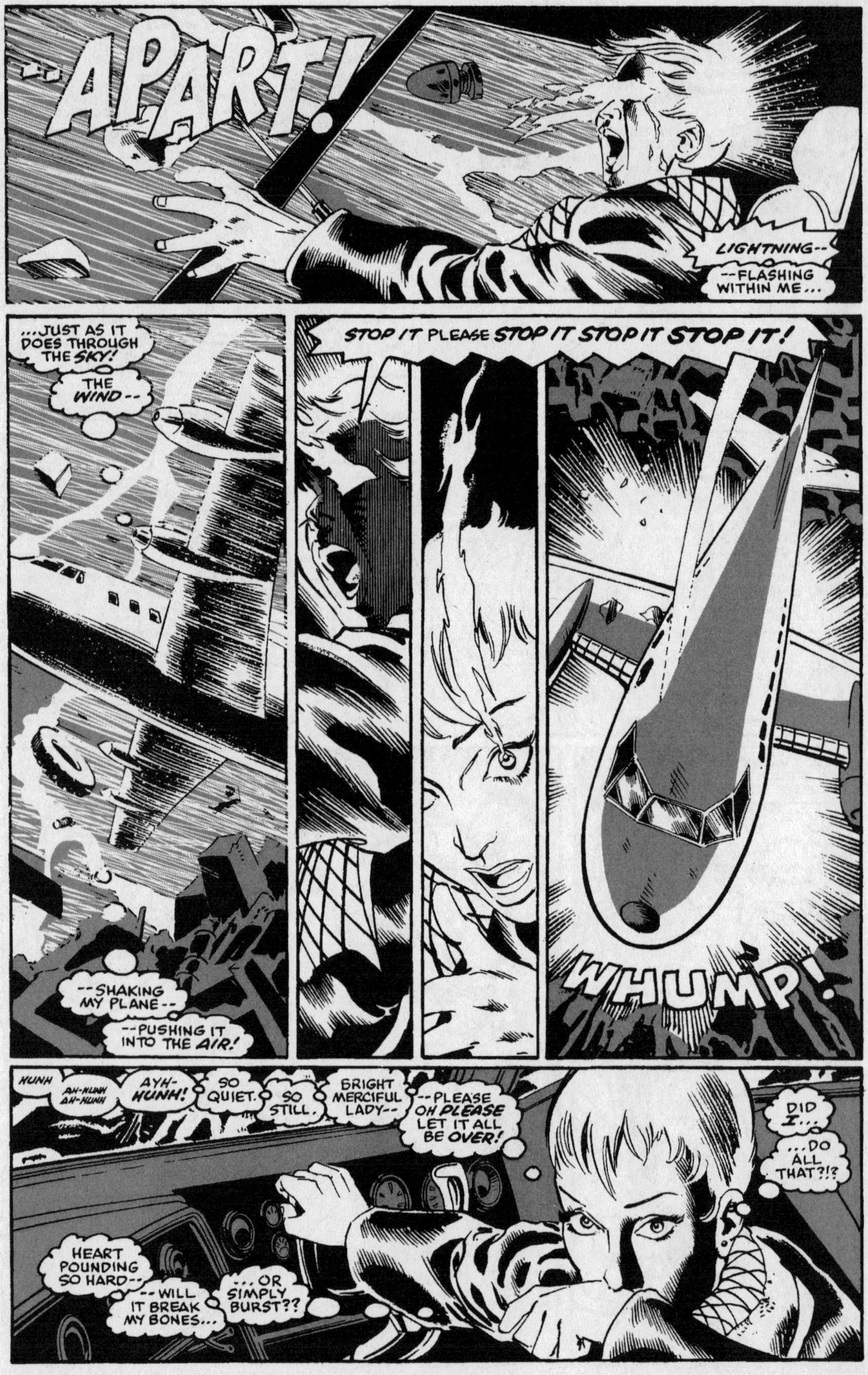

--APART!
LIGHTNING--
--FLASHING WITHIN ME...
...JUST AS IT DOES THROUGH THE SKY!
THE WIND--
--SHAKING MY PLANE--
--PUSHING IT INTO THE AIR!
STOP IT PLEASE STOP IT STOP IT STOP IT!
WHUMP!
HUNH
AH-HUNH AH-HUNH
AYH-HUNH!
SO QUIET.
SO STILL.
BRIGHT MERCIFUL LADY--
--PLEASE OH PLEASE LET IT ALL BE OVER!
DID I...
...DO ALL THAT?!?
HEART POUNDING SO HARD--
--WILL IT BREAK MY BONES...
...OR SIMPLY BURST??

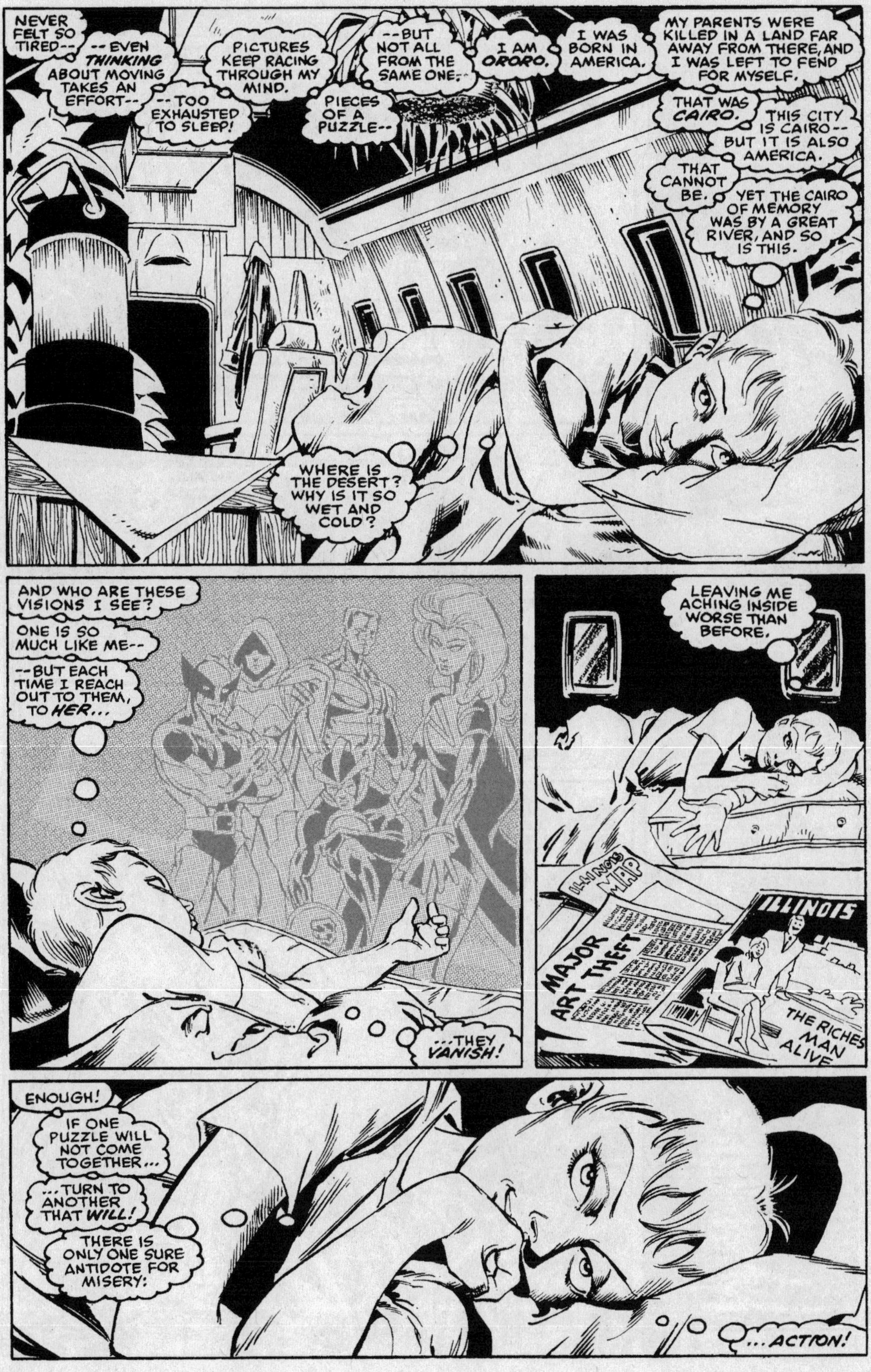
NEVER FELT SO TIRED--
--EVEN THINKING ABOUT MOVING TAKES AN EFFORT--
--TOO EXHAUSTED TO SLEEP!
PICTURES KEEP RACING THROUGH MY MIND.
--BUT NOT ALL FROM THE SAME ONE.
PIECES OF A PUZZLE--
I AM ORORO.
I WAS BORN IN AMERICA.
MY PARENTS WERE KILLED IN A LAND FAR AWAY FROM THERE, AND I WAS LEFT TO FEND FOR MYSELF.
THAT WAS CAIRO.
THIS CITY IS CAIRO--BUT IT IS ALSO AMERICA.
THAT CANNOT BE.
YET THE CAIRO OF MEMORY WAS BY A GREAT RIVER, AND SO IS THIS.
WHERE IS THE DESERT? WHY IS IT SO WET AND COLD?
AND WHO ARE THESE VISIONS I SEE?
ONE IS SO MUCH LIKE ME--
--BUT EACH TIME I REACH OUT TO THEM, TO HER...
...THEY VANISH!
LEAVING ME ACHING INSIDE WORSE THAN BEFORE.
ILLINOIS MAP
MAJOR ART THEFT
ILLINOIS
THE RICHES MAN ALIVE
ENOUGH!
IF ONE PUZZLE WILL NOT COME TOGETHER...
...TURN TO ANOTHER THAT WILL!
THERE IS ONLY ONE SURE ANTIDOTE FOR MISERY:
...ACTION!

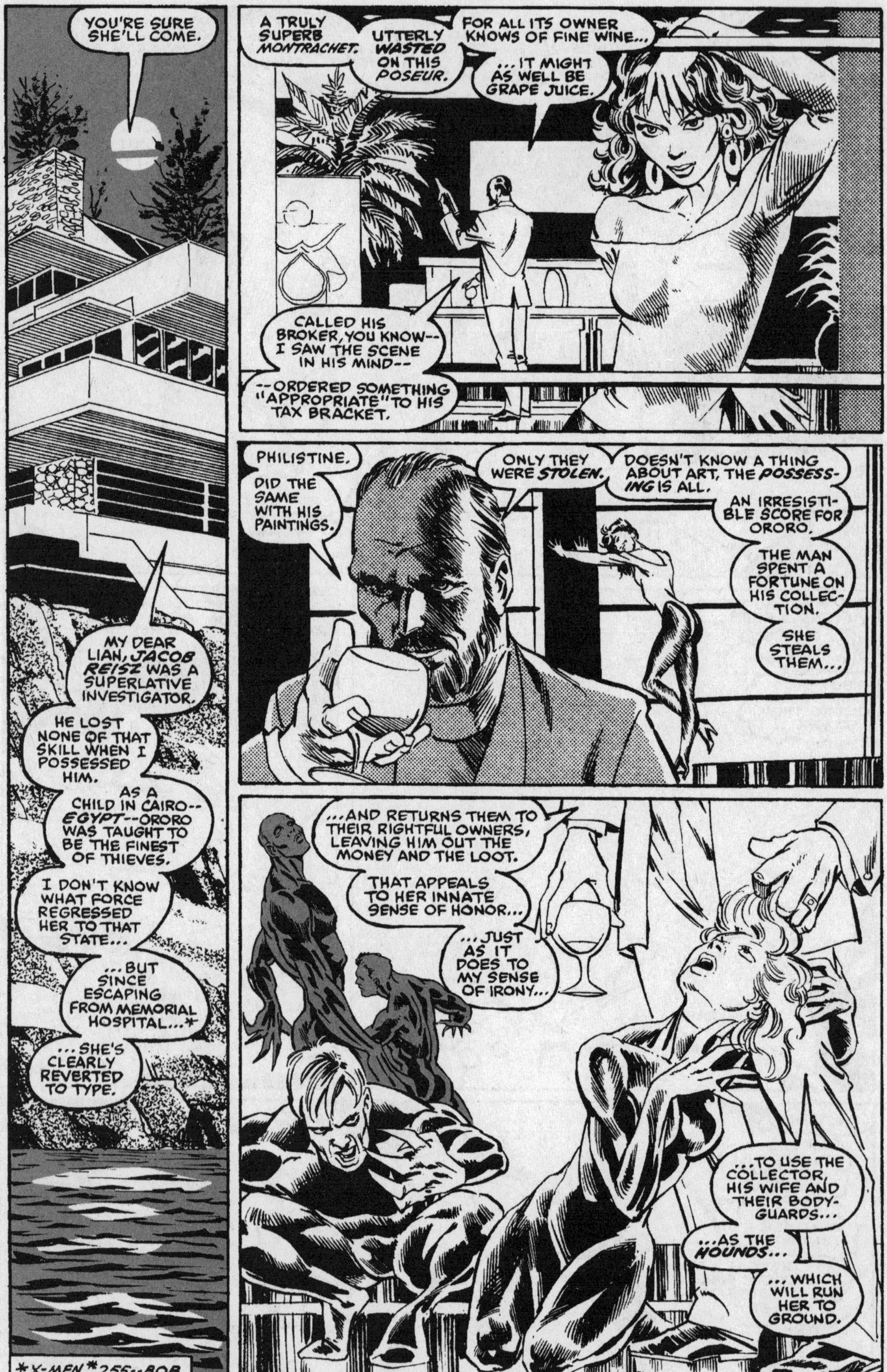

YOU'RE SURE SHE'LL COME.
A TRULY SUPERB MONTRACHET.
UTTERLY WASTED ON THIS POSEUR.
FOR ALL ITS OWNER KNOWS OF FINE WINE...
...IT MIGHT AS WELL BE GRAPE JUICE.
CALLED HIS BROKER, YOU KNOW-- I SAW THE SCENE IN HIS MIND--
--ORDERED SOMETHING "APPROPRIATE" TO HIS TAX BRACKET.
PHILISTINE.
DID THE SAME WITH HIS PAINTINGS.
ONLY THEY WERE STOLEN.
DOESN'T KNOW A THING ABOUT ART, THE POSSESSING IS ALL.
AN IRRESISTIBLE SCORE FOR ORORO.
THE MAN SPENT A FORTUNE ON HIS COLLECTION.
SHE STEALS THEM...
MY DEAR LIAN, JACOB REISZ WAS A SUPERLATIVE INVESTIGATOR.
HE LOST NONE OF THAT SKILL WHEN I POSSESSED HIM.
AS A CHILD IN CAIRO--EGYPT--ORORO WAS TAUGHT TO BE THE FINEST OF THIEVES.
I DON'T KNOW WHAT FORCE REGRESSED HER TO THAT STATE...
...BUT SINCE ESCAPING FROM MEMORIAL HOSPITAL...*
...SHE'S CLEARLY REVERTED TO TYPE.
*X-MEN*255:--BOB
...AND RETURNS THEM TO THEIR RIGHTFUL OWNERS, LEAVING HIM OUT THE MONEY AND THE LOOT.
THAT APPEALS TO HER INNATE SENSE OF HONOR...
...JUST AS IT DOES TO MY SENSE OF IRONY...
...TO USE THE COLLECTOR, HIS WIFE AND THEIR BODYGUARDS...
...AS THE HOUNDS...
...WHICH WILL RUN HER TO GROUND.

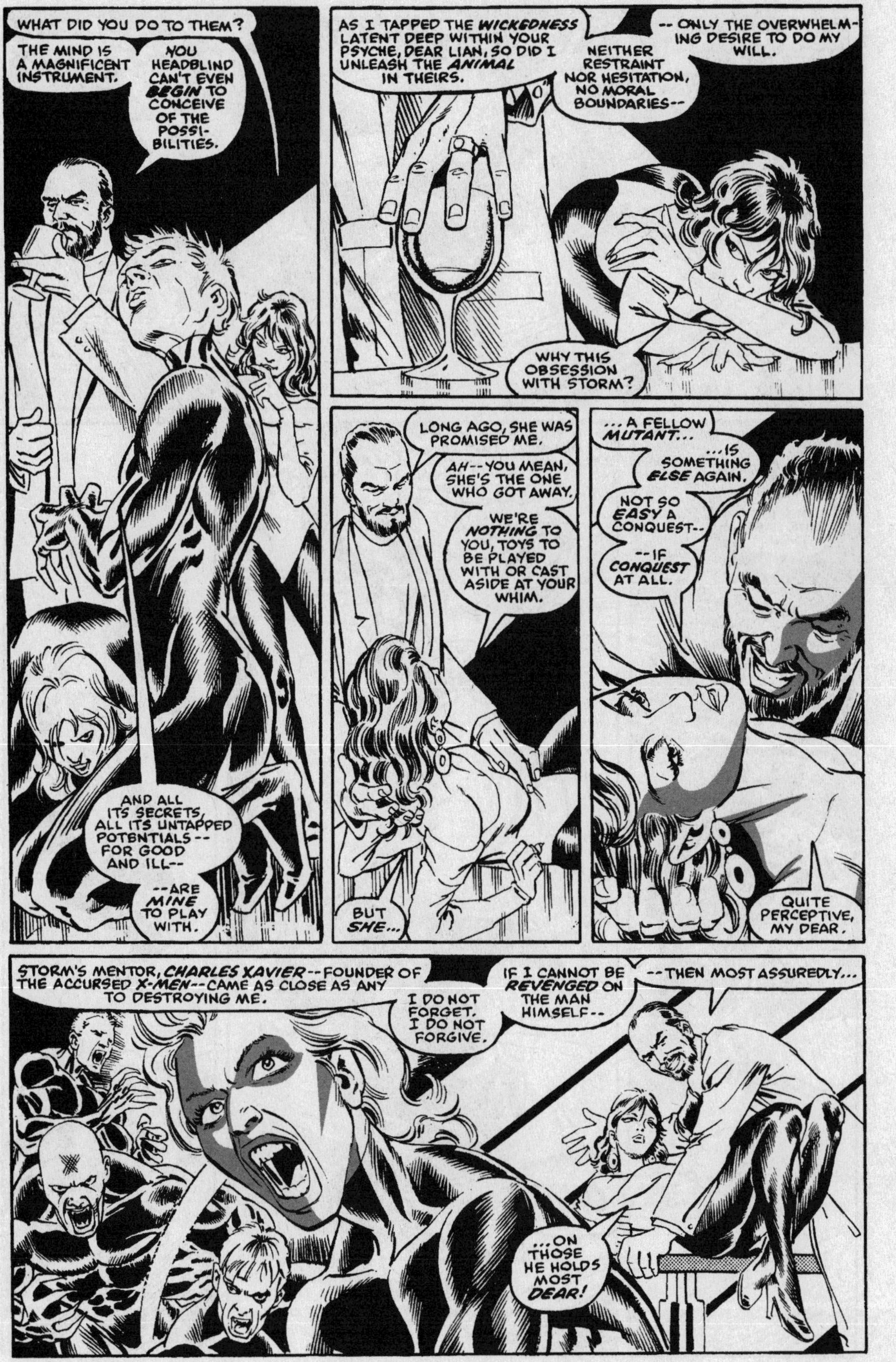
WHAT DID YOU DO TO THEM?
THE MIND IS A MAGNIFICENT INSTRUMENT.
YOU HEADBLIND CAN'T EVEN BEGIN TO CONCEIVE OF THE POSSI-BILITIES.
AND ALL ITS SECRETS, ALL ITS UNTAPPED POTENTIALS-- FOR GOOD AND ILL--
--ARE MINE TO PLAY WITH.
AS I TAPPED THE WICKEDNESS LATENT DEEP WITHIN YOUR PSYCHE, DEAR LIAN, SO DID I UNLEASH THE ANIMAL IN THEIRS.
NEITHER RESTRAINT NOR HESITATION, NO MORAL BOUNDARIES--
-- ONLY THE OVERWHELMING DESIRE TO DO MY WILL.
WHY THIS OBSESSION WITH STORM?
LONG AGO, SHE WAS PROMISED ME.
AH-- YOU MEAN, SHE'S THE ONE WHO GOT AWAY.
WE'RE NOTHING TO YOU, TOYS TO BE PLAYED WITH OR CAST ASIDE AT YOUR WHIM.
BUT SHE...
... A FELLOW MUTANT...
... IS SOMETHING ELSE AGAIN.
NOT SO EASY A CONQUEST--
--IF CONQUEST AT ALL.
QUITE PERCEPTIVE, MY DEAR.
STORM'S MENTOR, CHARLES XAVIER-- FOUNDER OF THE ACCURSED X-MEN-- CAME AS CLOSE AS ANY TO DESTROYING ME.
I DO NOT FORGET. I DO NOT FORGIVE.
IF I CANNOT BE REVENGED ON THE MAN HIMSELF--
-- THEN MOST ASSUREDLY...
...ON THOSE HE HOLDS MOST DEAR!

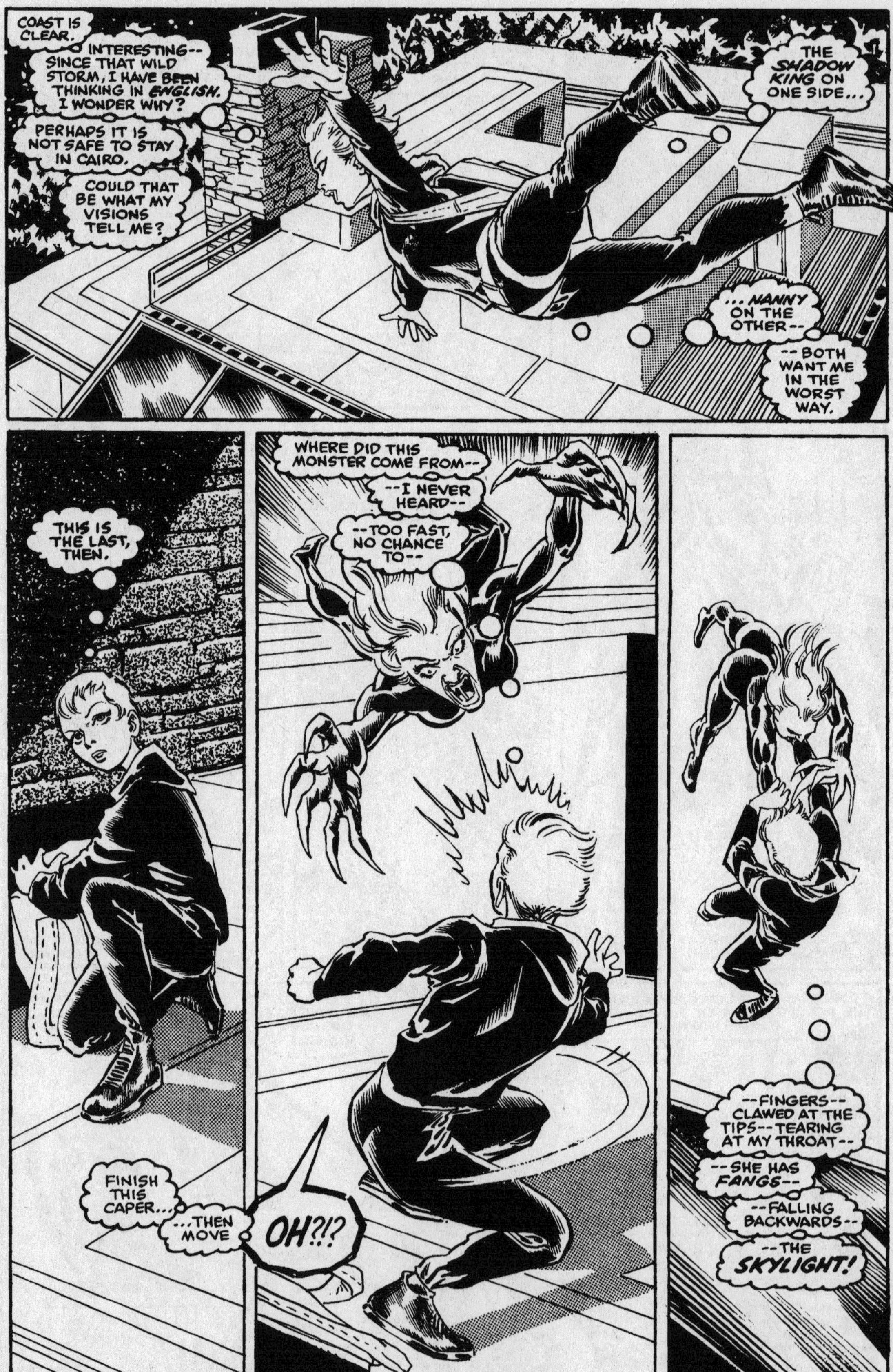
COAST IS CLEAR.
INTERESTING-- SINCE THAT WILD STORM, I HAVE BEEN THINKING IN ENGLISH. I WONDER WHY?
PERHAPS IT IS NOT SAFE TO STAY IN CAIRO.
COULD THAT BE WHAT MY VISIONS TELL ME?
THE SHADOW KING ON ONE SIDE...
...NANNY ON THE OTHER--
--BOTH WANT ME IN THE WORST WAY.
THIS IS THE LAST, THEN.
FINISH THIS CAPER...
...THEN MOVE
OH?!?
WHERE DID THIS MONSTER COME FROM--
--I NEVER HEARD--
--TOO FAST, NO CHANCE TO--
--FINGERS--CLAWED AT THE TIPS--TEARING AT MY THROAT--
--SHE HAS FANGS--
--FALLING BACKWARDS--
--THE SKYLIGHT!

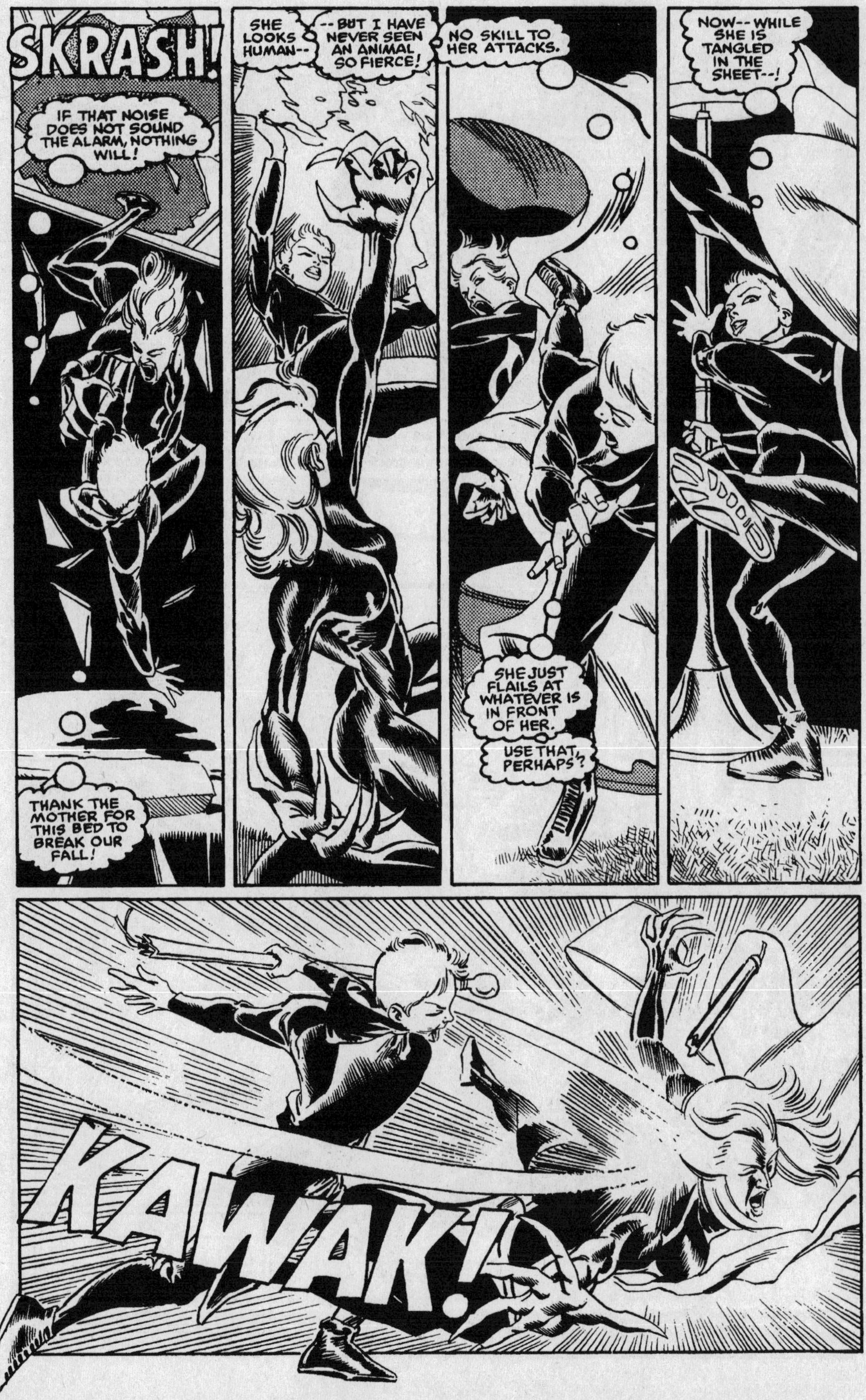
SKRASH!
IF THAT NOISE DOES NOT SOUND THE ALARM, NOTHING WILL!
THANK THE MOTHER FOR THIS BED TO BREAK OUR FALL!
SHE LOOKS HUMAN--
--BUT I HAVE NEVER SEEN AN ANIMAL SO FIERCE!
NO SKILL TO HER ATTACKS.
SHE JUST FLAILS AT WHATEVER IS IN FRONT OF HER.
USE THAT, PERHAPS?
NOW--WHILE SHE IS TANGLED IN THE SHEET--!
KAWAK!

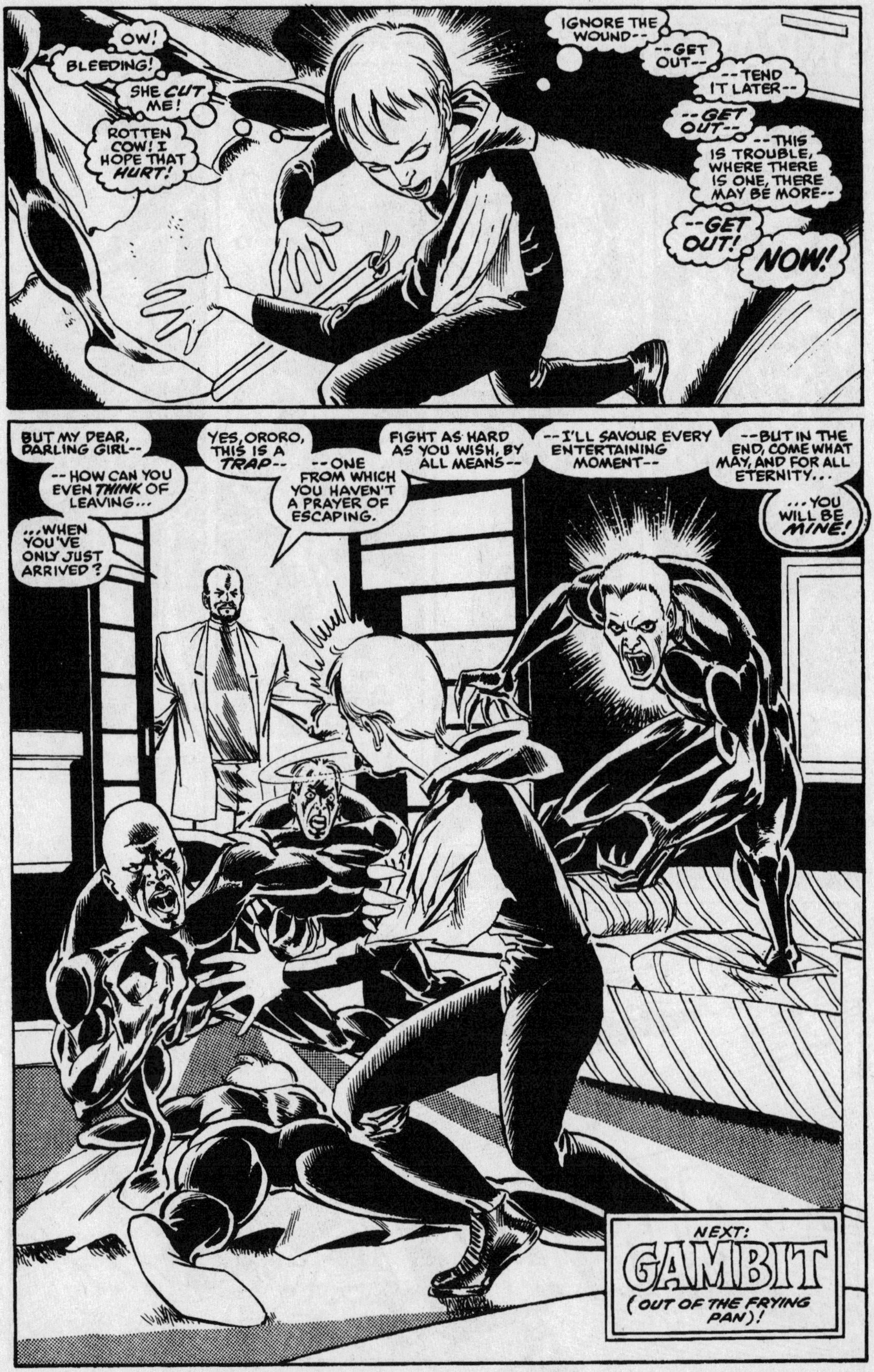
OW!
BLEEDING!
SHE CUT ME!
ROTTEN COW! I HOPE THAT HURT!
IGNORE THE WOUND--
--GET OUT--
--TEND IT LATER--
--GET OUT--
--THIS IS TROUBLE, WHERE THERE IS ONE, THERE MAY BE MORE--
--GET OUT!
NOW!
BUT MY DEAR, DARLING GIRL--
--HOW CAN YOU EVEN THINK OF LEAVING...
...WHEN YOU'VE ONLY JUST ARRIVED?
YES, ORORO, THIS IS A TRAP--
--ONE FROM WHICH YOU HAVEN'T A PRAYER OF ESCAPING.
FIGHT AS HARD AS YOU WISH, BY ALL MEANS--
--I'LL SAVOUR EVERY ENTERTAINING MOMENT--
--BUT IN THE END, COME WHAT MAY, AND FOR ALL ETERNITY...
...YOU WILL BE MINE!
NEXT:
GAMBIT
(OUT OF THE FRYING PAN)!

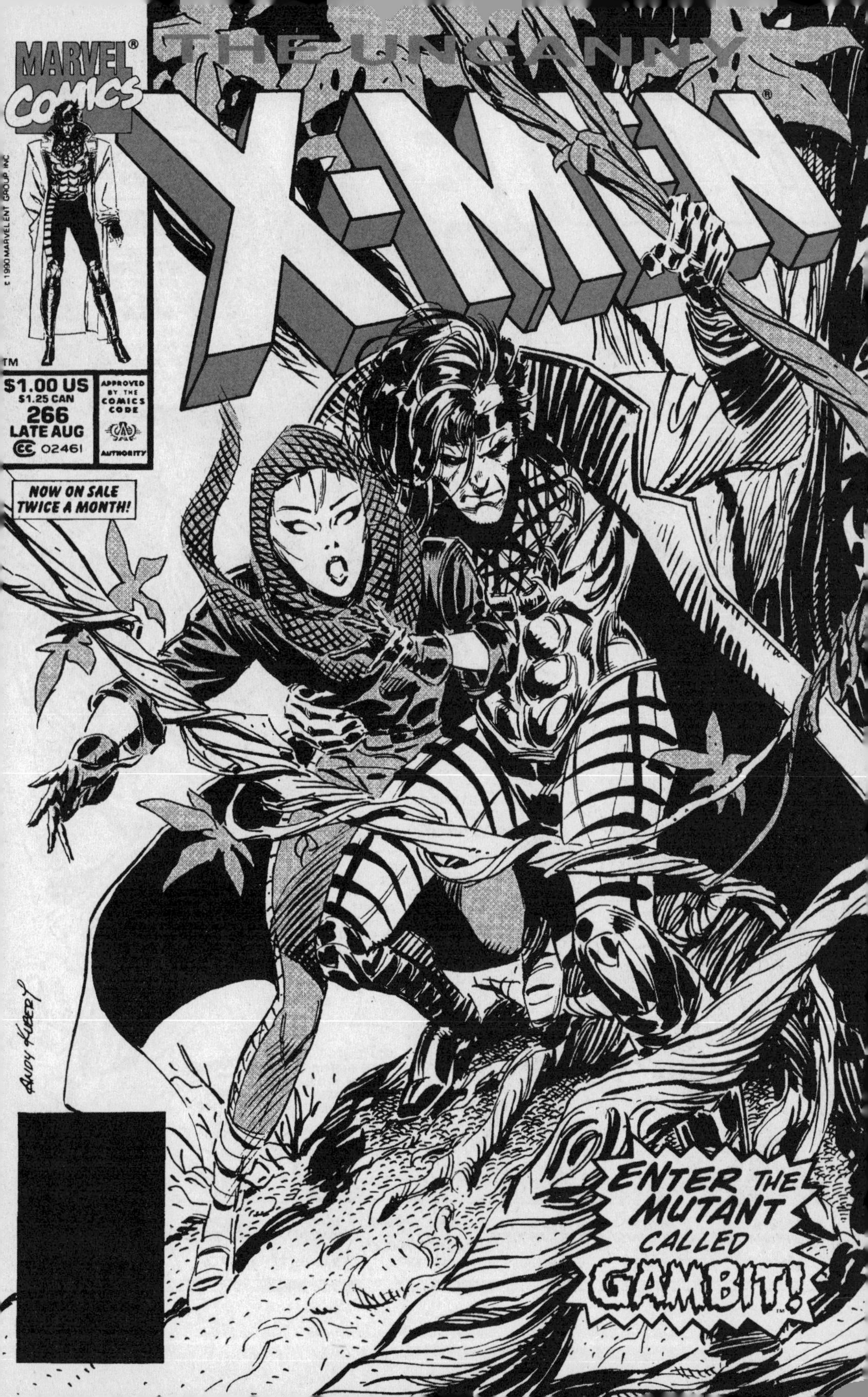
MARVEL COMICS
THE UNCANNY
X-MEN
© 1990 MARVEL ENT GROUP, INC
$1.00 US
$1.25 CAN
266
LATE AUG
02461
APPROVED BY THE COMICS CODE AUTHORITY
NOW ON SALE TWICE A MONTH!
ENTER THE MUTANT CALLED GAMBIT!

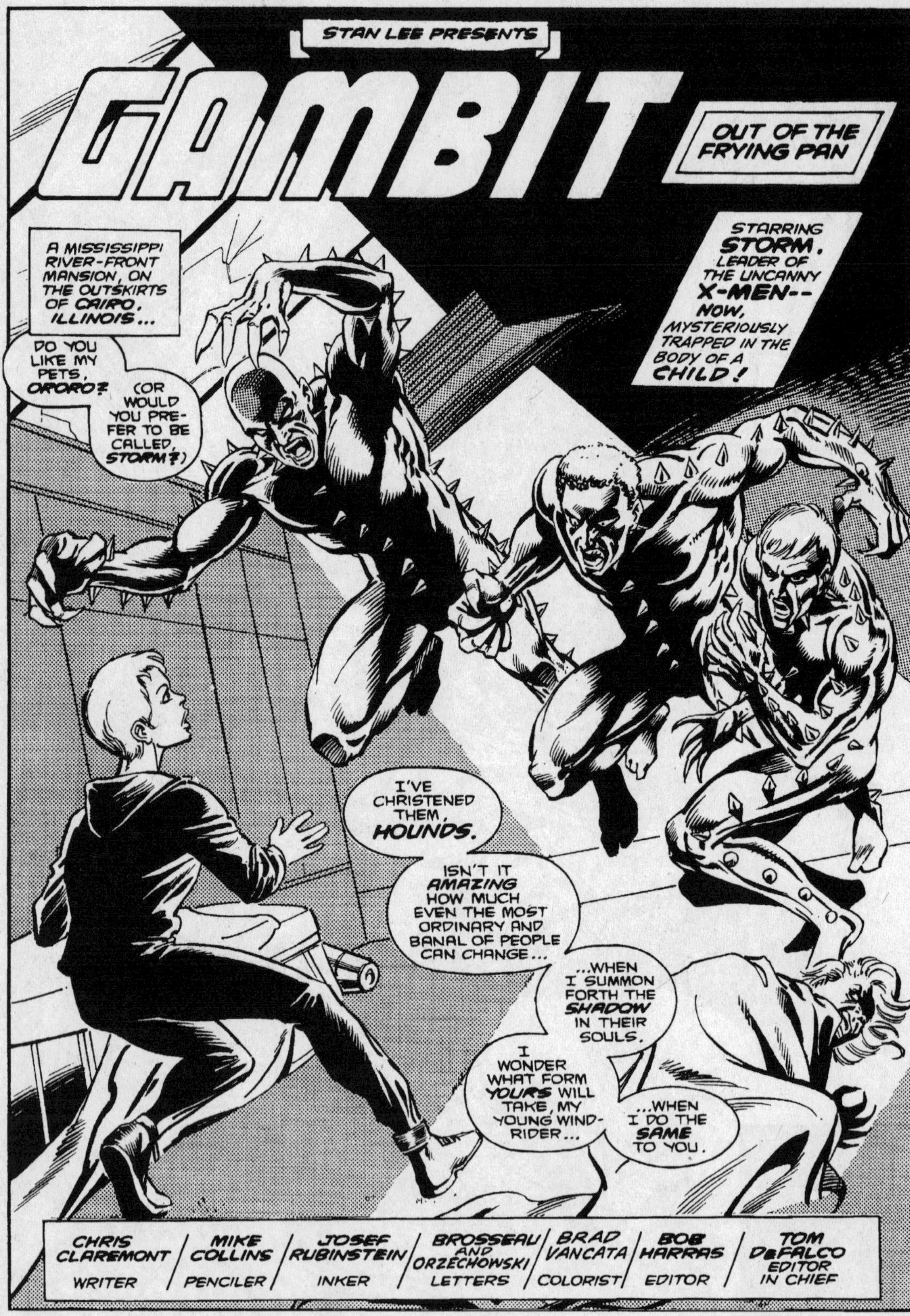
STAN LEE PRESENTS
GAMBIT
OUT OF THE FRYING PAN
A MISSISSIPPI RIVER-FRONT MANSION, ON THE OUTSKIRTS OF CAIRO, ILLINOIS...
STARRING STORM, LEADER OF THE UNCANNY X-MEN-- NOW, MYSTERIOUSLY TRAPPED IN THE BODY OF A CHILD!
DO YOU LIKE MY PETS, ORORO?
(OR WOULD YOU PREFER TO BE CALLED, STORM?)
I'VE CHRISTENED THEM, HOUNDS.
ISN'T IT AMAZING HOW MUCH EVEN THE MOST ORDINARY AND BANAL OF PEOPLE CAN CHANGE...
...WHEN I SUMMON FORTH THE SHADOW IN THEIR SOULS.
I WONDER WHAT FORM YOURS WILL TAKE, MY YOUNG WIND-RIDER...
...WHEN I DO THE SAME TO YOU.
CHRIS CLAREMONT WRITER
MIKE COLLINS PENCILER
JOSEF RUBINSTEIN INKER
BROSSEAU AND ORZECHOWSKI LETTERS
BRAD VANCATA COLORIST
BOB HARRAS EDITOR
TOM DeFALCO EDITOR IN CHIEF

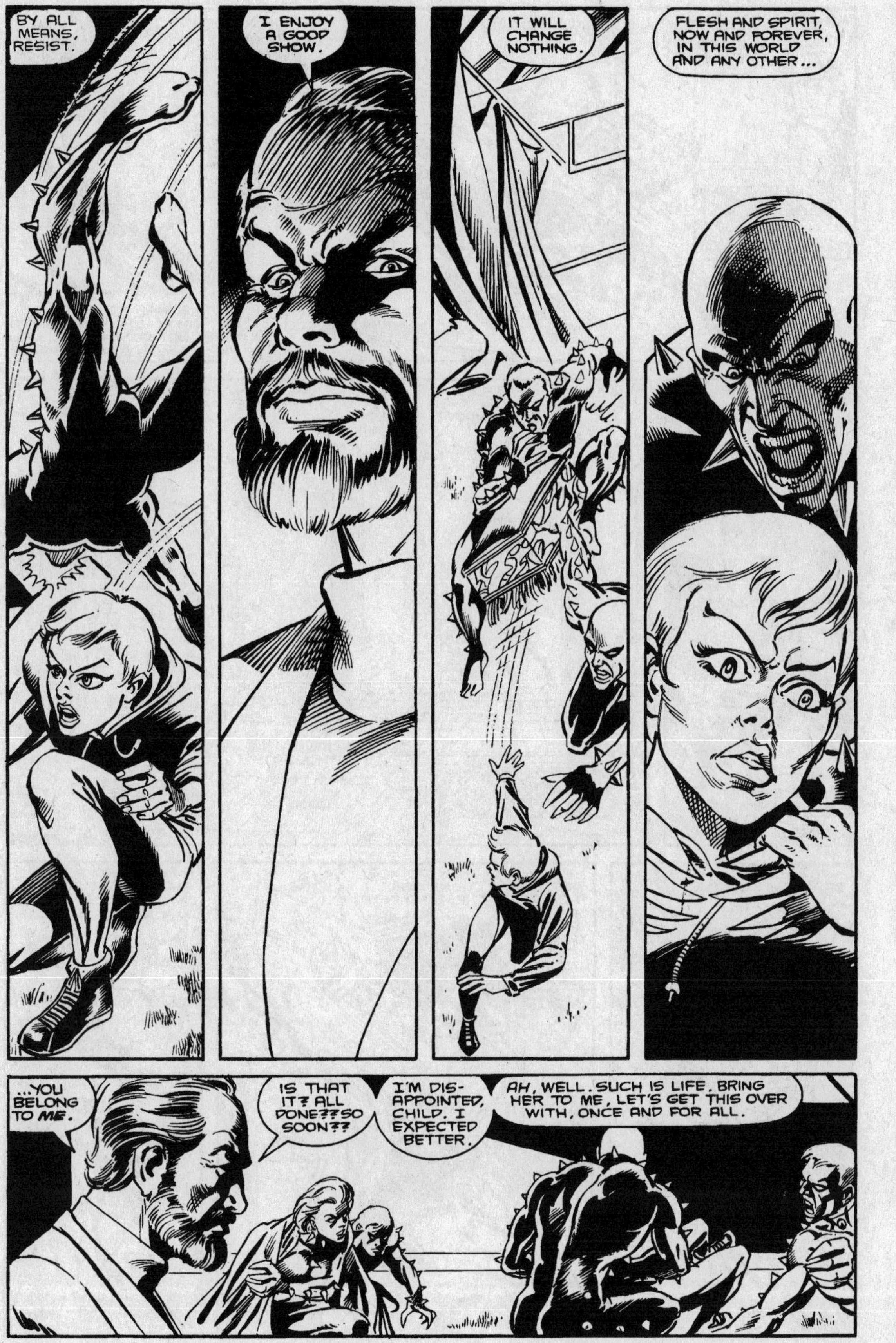
BY ALL MEANS, RESIST.
I ENJOY A GOOD SHOW.
IT WILL CHANGE NOTHING.
FLESH AND SPIRIT, NOW AND FOREVER, IN THIS WORLD AND ANY OTHER...
...YOU BELONG TO ME.
IS THAT IT?? ALL DONE??SO SOON??
I'M DIS-APPOINTED, CHILD. I EXPECTED BETTER.
AH, WELL. SUCH IS LIFE. BRING HER TO ME, LET'S GET THIS OVER WITH, ONCE AND FOR ALL.

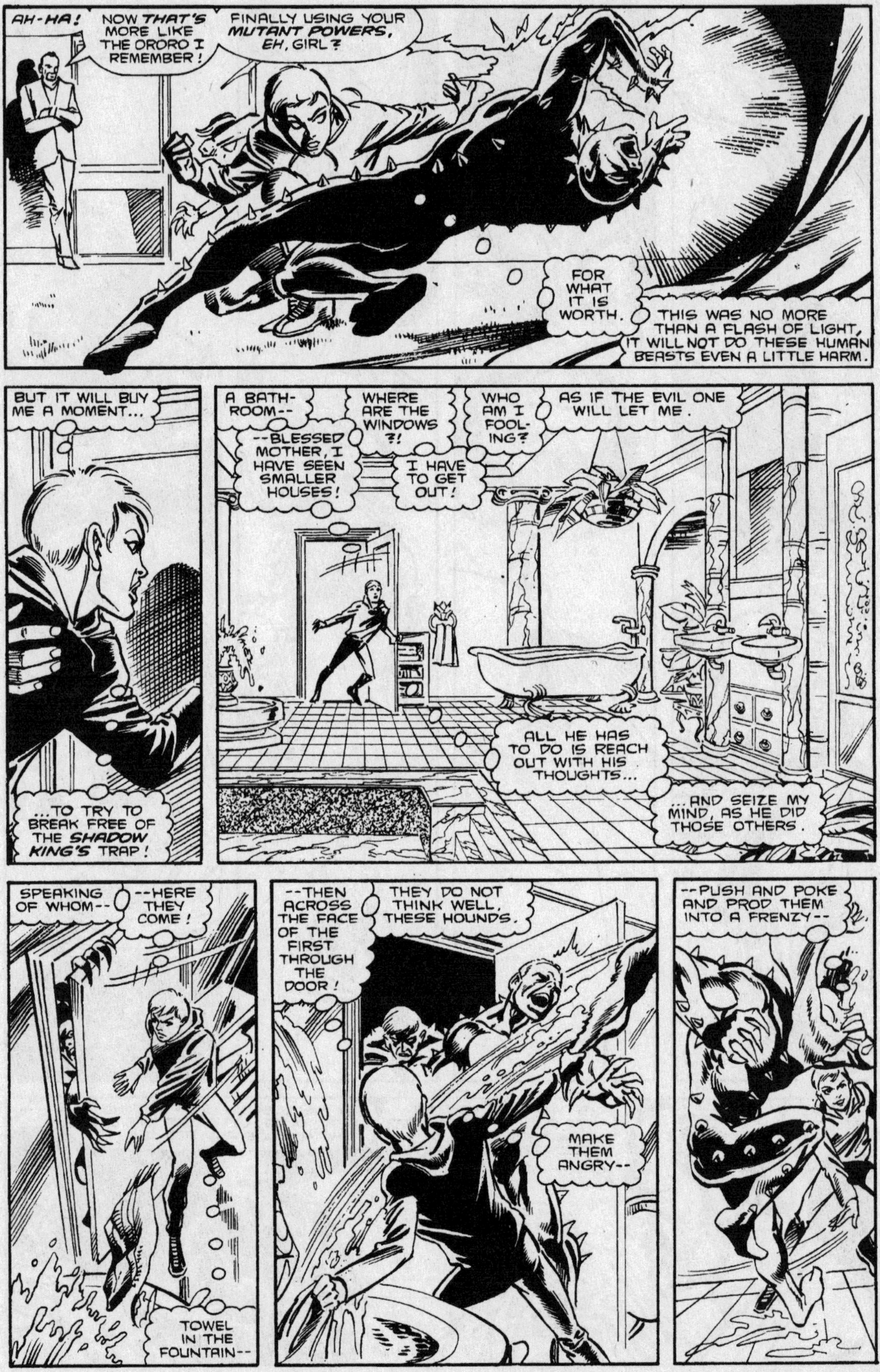
AH-HA!
NOW THAT'S MORE LIKE THE ORORO I REMEMBER!
FINALLY USING YOUR MUTANT POWERS, EH, GIRL?
FOR WHAT IT IS WORTH.
THIS WAS NO MORE THAN A FLASH OF LIGHT, IT WILL NOT DO THESE HUMAN BEASTS EVEN A LITTLE HARM.
BUT IT WILL BUY ME A MOMENT...
...TO TRY TO BREAK FREE OF THE SHADOW KING'S TRAP!
A BATH-ROOM--
--BLESSED MOTHER, I HAVE SEEN SMALLER HOUSES!
WHERE ARE THE WINDOWS?!
I HAVE TO GET OUT!
WHO AM I FOOL-ING?
AS IF THE EVIL ONE WILL LET ME.
ALL HE HAS TO DO IS REACH OUT WITH HIS THOUGHTS...
...AND SEIZE MY MIND, AS HE DID THOSE OTHERS.
SPEAKING OF WHOM--
--HERE THEY COME!
TOWEL IN THE FOUNTAIN--
--THEN ACROSS THE FACE OF THE FIRST THROUGH THE DOOR!
THEY DO NOT THINK WELL, THESE HOUNDS.
MAKE THEM ANGRY--
--PUSH AND POKE AND PROD THEM INTO A FRENZY--

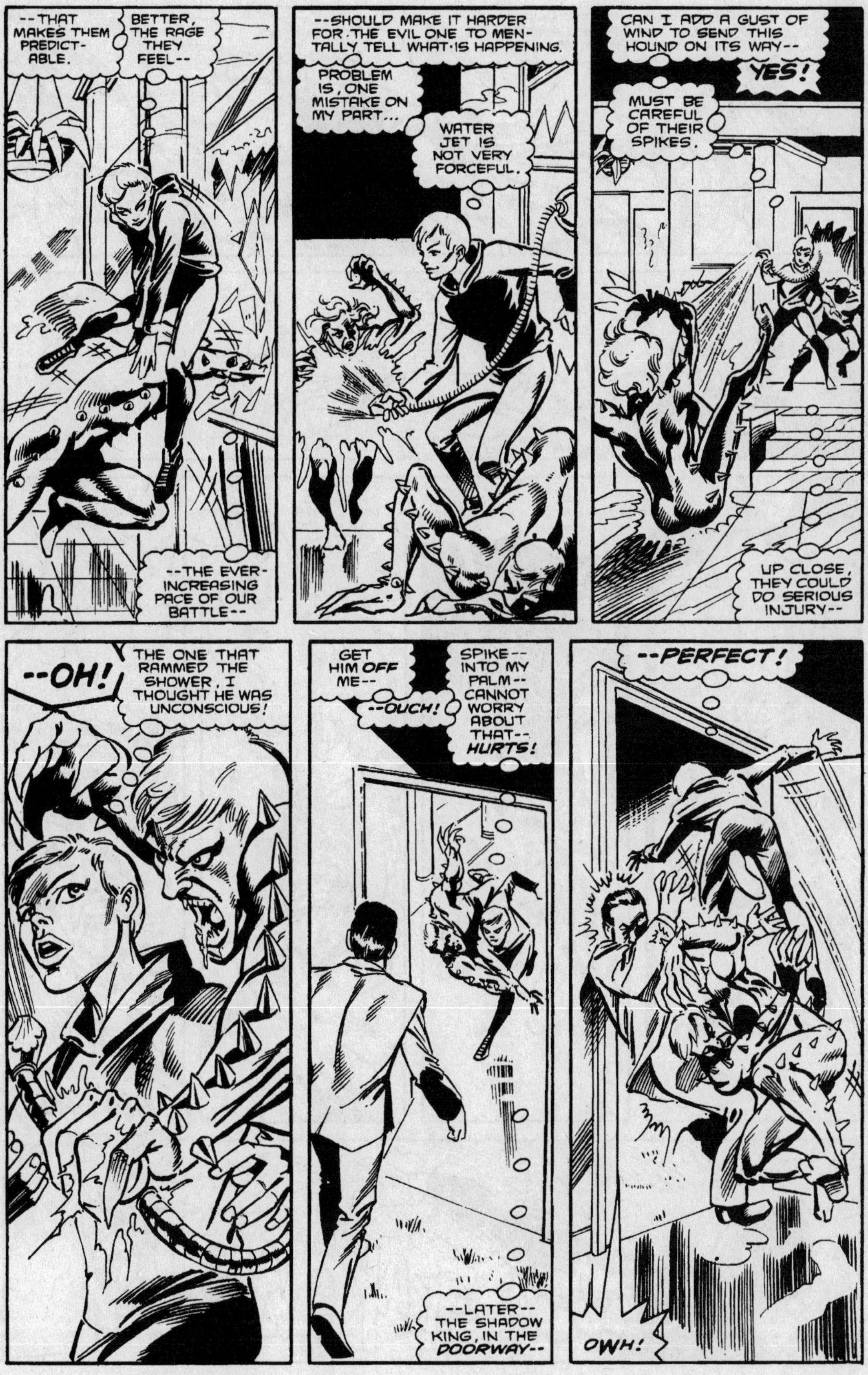
--THAT MAKES THEM PREDICT-ABLE.
BETTER, THE RAGE THEY FEEL--
--THE EVER-INCREASING PACE OF OUR BATTLE--
--SHOULD MAKE IT HARDER FOR THE EVIL ONE TO MEN-TALLY TELL WHAT IS HAPPENING.
PROBLEM IS, ONE MISTAKE ON MY PART...
WATER JET IS NOT VERY FORCEFUL.
CAN I ADD A GUST OF WIND TO SEND THIS HOUND ON ITS WAY--
YES!
MUST BE CAREFUL OF THEIR SPIKES.
UP CLOSE, THEY COULD DO SERIOUS INJURY--
--OH!
THE ONE THAT RAMMED THE SHOWER, I THOUGHT HE WAS UNCONSCIOUS!
GET HIM OFF ME--
--OUCH!
SPIKE--INTO MY PALM--CANNOT WORRY ABOUT THAT--HURTS!
--LATER--THE SHADOW KING, IN THE DOORWAY--
--PERFECT!
OWH!

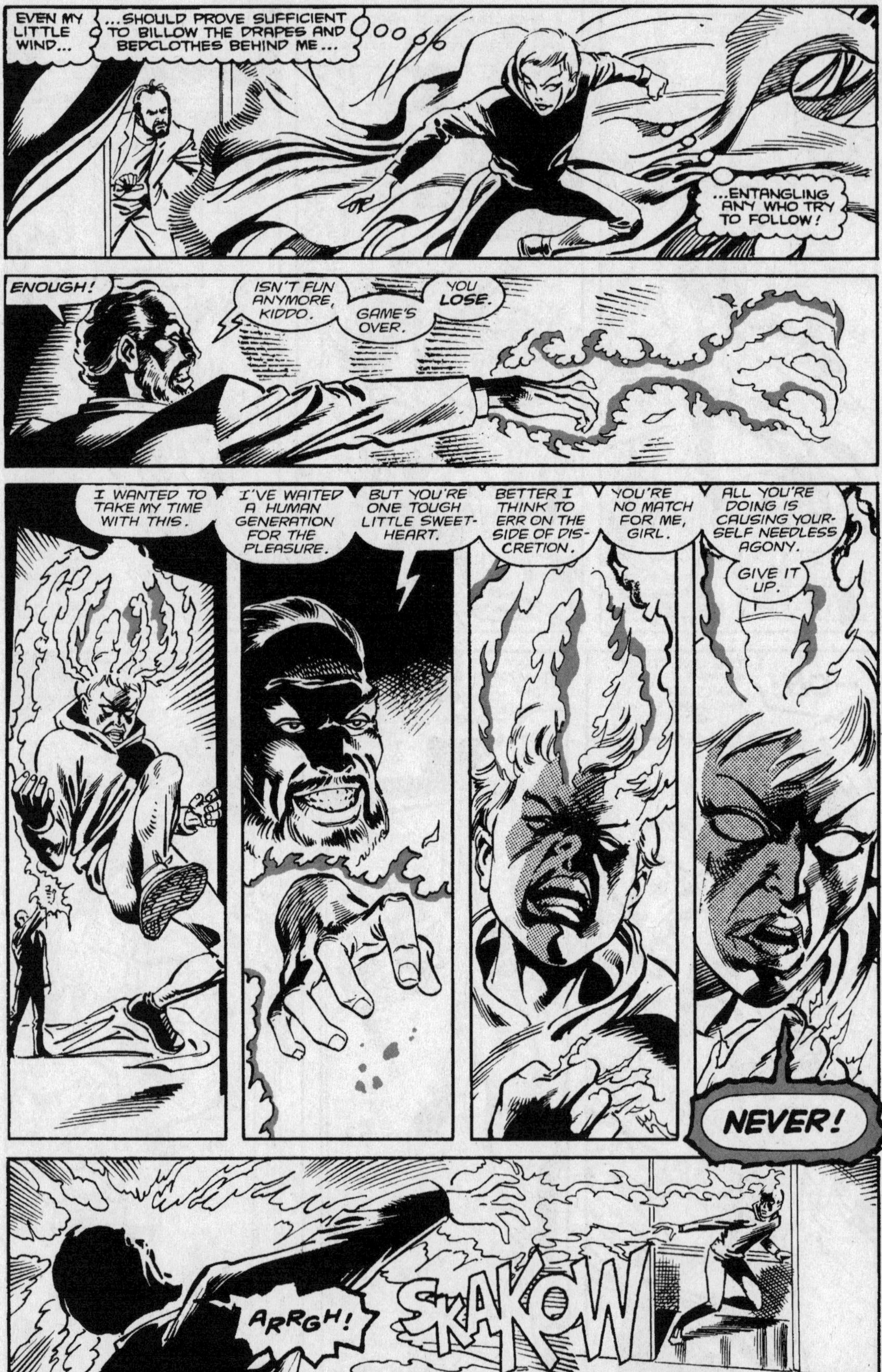
EVEN MY LITTLE WIND...
...SHOULD PROVE SUFFICIENT TO BILLOW THE DRAPES AND BEDCLOTHES BEHIND ME...
...ENTANGLING ANY WHO TRY TO FOLLOW!
ENOUGH!
ISN'T FUN ANYMORE, KIDDO.
GAME'S OVER.
YOU LOSE.
I WANTED TO TAKE MY TIME WITH THIS.
I'VE WAITED A HUMAN GENERATION FOR THE PLEASURE.
BUT YOU'RE ONE TOUGH LITTLE SWEET-HEART.
BETTER I THINK TO ERR ON THE SIDE OF DIS-CRETION.
YOU'RE NO MATCH FOR ME, GIRL.
ALL YOU'RE DOING IS CAUSING YOUR-SELF NEEDLESS AGONY.
GIVE IT UP.
NEVER!
ARRGH!
SKAKOW

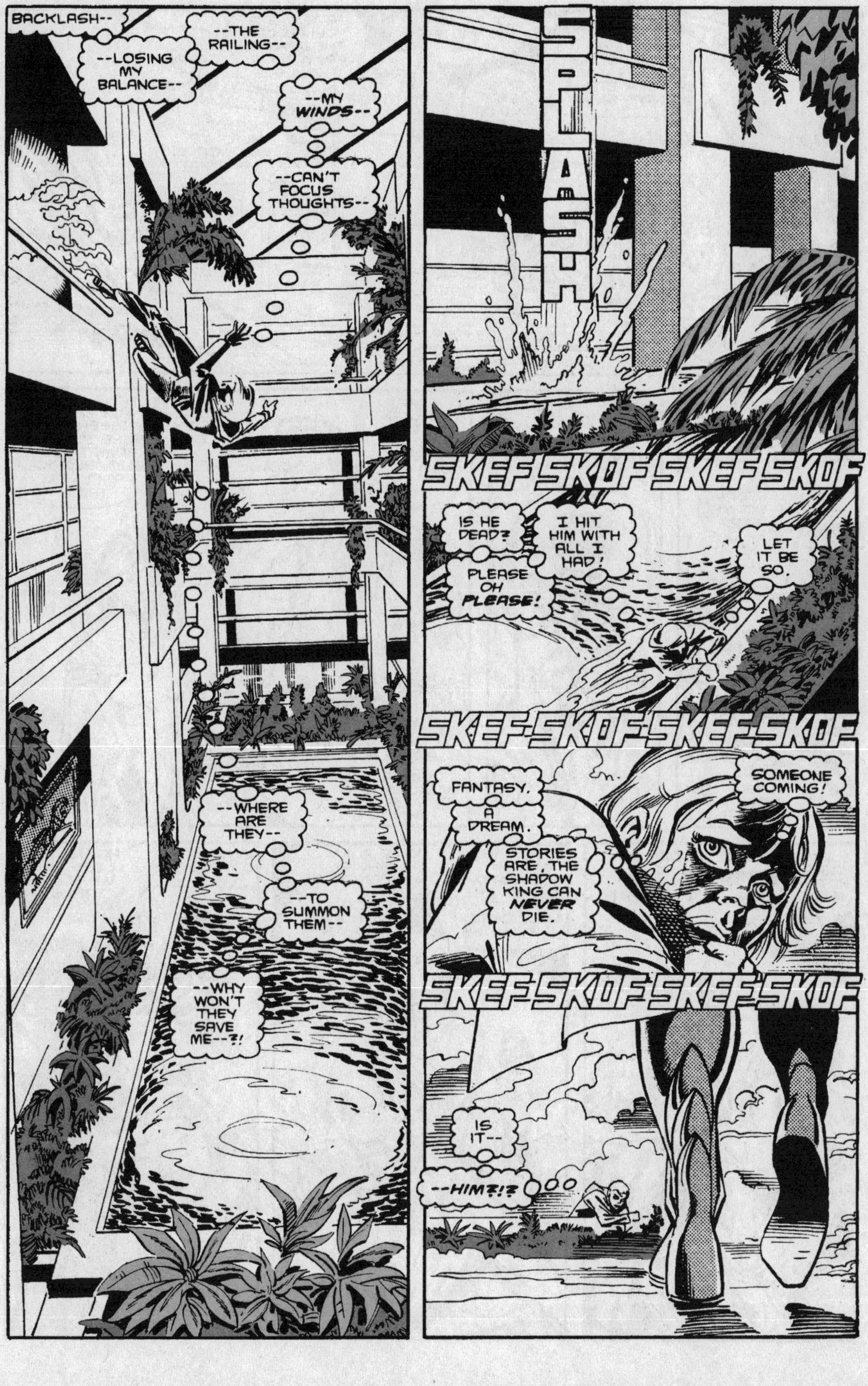
BACKLASH--
--LOSING MY BALANCE--
--THE RAILING--
--MY WINDS--
--CAN'T FOCUS THOUGHTS--
--WHERE ARE THEY--
--TO SUMMON THEM--
--WHY WON'T THEY SAVE ME--?!
SPLASH
SKEF SKOF SKEF SKOF
IS HE DEAD?
I HIT HIM WITH ALL I HAD!
PLEASE OH PLEASE!
LET IT BE SO.
SKEF SKOF SKEF SKOF
FANTASY. A DREAM.
STORIES ARE, THE SHADOW KING CAN NEVER DIE.
SOMEONE COMING!
SKEF SKOF SKEF SKOF
IS IT--
--HIM?!?

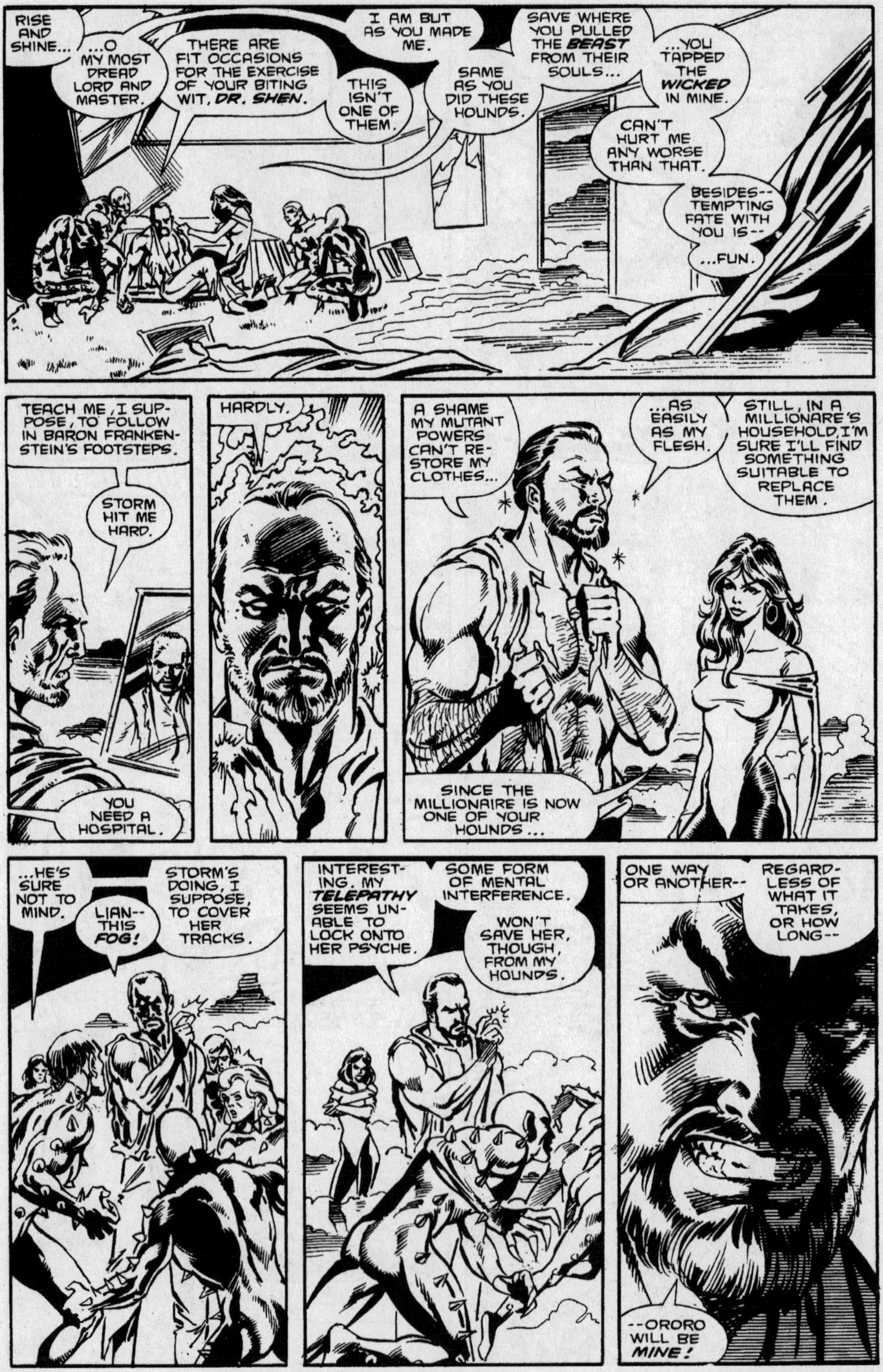
RISE AND SHINE...
...O MY MOST DREAD LORD AND MASTER.
THERE ARE FIT OCCASIONS FOR THE EXERCISE OF YOUR BITING WIT, DR. SHEN.
THIS ISN'T ONE OF THEM.
I AM BUT AS YOU MADE ME.
SAME AS YOU DID THESE HOUNDS.
SAVE WHERE YOU PULLED THE BEAST FROM THEIR SOULS...
...YOU TAPPED THE WICKED IN MINE.
CAN'T HURT ME ANY WORSE THAN THAT.
BESIDES-- TEMPTING FATE WITH YOU IS--
...FUN.
TEACH ME, I SUPPOSE, TO FOLLOW IN BARON FRANKENSTEIN'S FOOTSTEPS.
STORM HIT ME HARD.
YOU NEED A HOSPITAL.
HARDLY.
A SHAME MY MUTANT POWERS CAN'T RESTORE MY CLOTHES...
...AS EASILY AS MY FLESH.
STILL, IN A MILLIONARE'S HOUSEHOLD, I'M SURE I'LL FIND SOMETHING SUITABLE TO REPLACE THEM.
SINCE THE MILLIONAIRE IS NOW ONE OF YOUR HOUNDS...
...HE'S SURE NOT TO MIND.
LIAN-- THIS FOG!
STORM'S DOING, I SUPPOSE, TO COVER HER TRACKS.
INTERESTING. MY TELEPATHY SEEMS UNABLE TO LOCK ONTO HER PSYCHE.
SOME FORM OF MENTAL INTERFERENCE.
WON'T SAVE HER, THOUGH, FROM MY HOUNDS.
ONE WAY OR ANOTHER--
REGARDLESS OF WHAT IT TAKES, OR HOW LONG--
--ORORO WILL BE MINE!

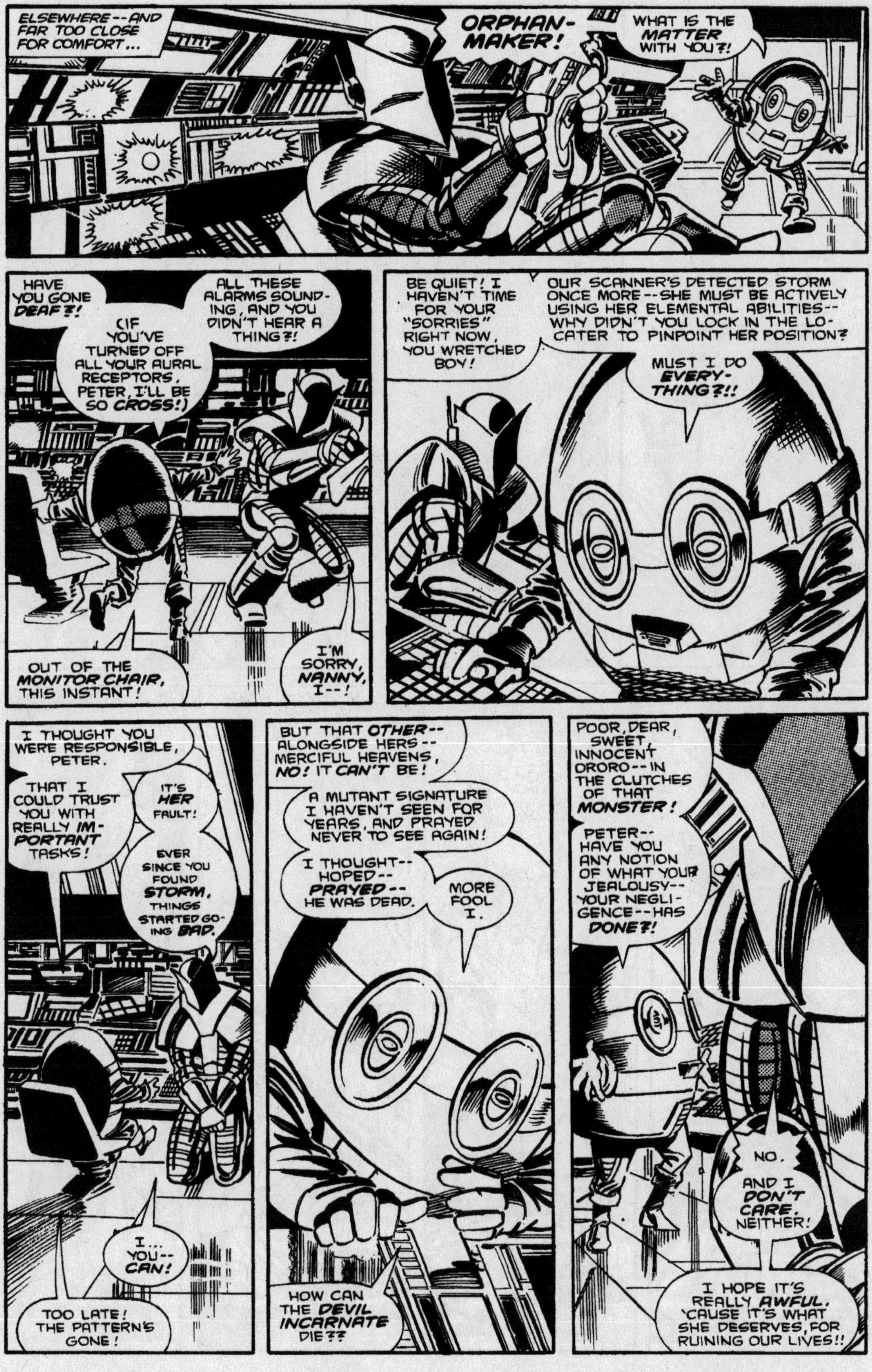
ELSEWHERE--AND FAR TOO CLOSE FOR COMFORT...
ORPHAN-MAKER!
WHAT IS THE MATTER WITH YOU?!
HAVE YOU GONE DEAF?!
ALL THESE ALARMS SOUNDING, AND YOU DIDN'T HEAR A THING?!
(IF YOU'VE TURNED OFF ALL YOUR AURAL RECEPTORS, PETER, I'LL BE SO CROSS!)
OUT OF THE MONITOR CHAIR, THIS INSTANT!
I'M SORRY, NANNY, I--!
BE QUIET! I HAVEN'T TIME FOR YOUR "SORRIES" RIGHT NOW, YOU WRETCHED BOY!
OUR SCANNER'S DETECTED STORM ONCE MORE--SHE MUST BE ACTIVELY USING HER ELEMENTAL ABILITIES--WHY DIDN'T YOU LOCK IN THE LOCATER TO PINPOINT HER POSITION?
MUST I DO EVERYTHING?!!
I THOUGHT YOU WERE RESPONSIBLE, PETER.
THAT I COULD TRUST YOU WITH REALLY IMPORTANT TASKS!
IT'S HER FAULT!
EVER SINCE YOU FOUND STORM, THINGS STARTED GOING BAD.
I... YOU--CAN!
TOO LATE! THE PATTERN'S GONE!
BUT THAT OTHER--ALONGSIDE HERS--MERCIFUL HEAVENS, NO! IT CAN'T BE!
A MUTANT SIGNATURE I HAVEN'T SEEN FOR YEARS, AND PRAYED NEVER TO SEE AGAIN!
I THOUGHT--HOPED--PRAYED--HE WAS DEAD.
MORE FOOL I.
HOW CAN THE DEVIL INCARNATE DIE??
POOR, DEAR, SWEET, INNOCENT ORORO--IN THE CLUTCHES OF THAT MONSTER!
PETER--HAVE YOU ANY NOTION OF WHAT YOUR JEALOUSY--YOUR NEGLIGENCE--HAS DONE?!
NO.
AND I DON'T CARE, NEITHER!
I HOPE IT'S REALLY AWFUL, 'CAUSE IT'S WHAT SHE DESERVES, FOR RUINING OUR LIVES!!

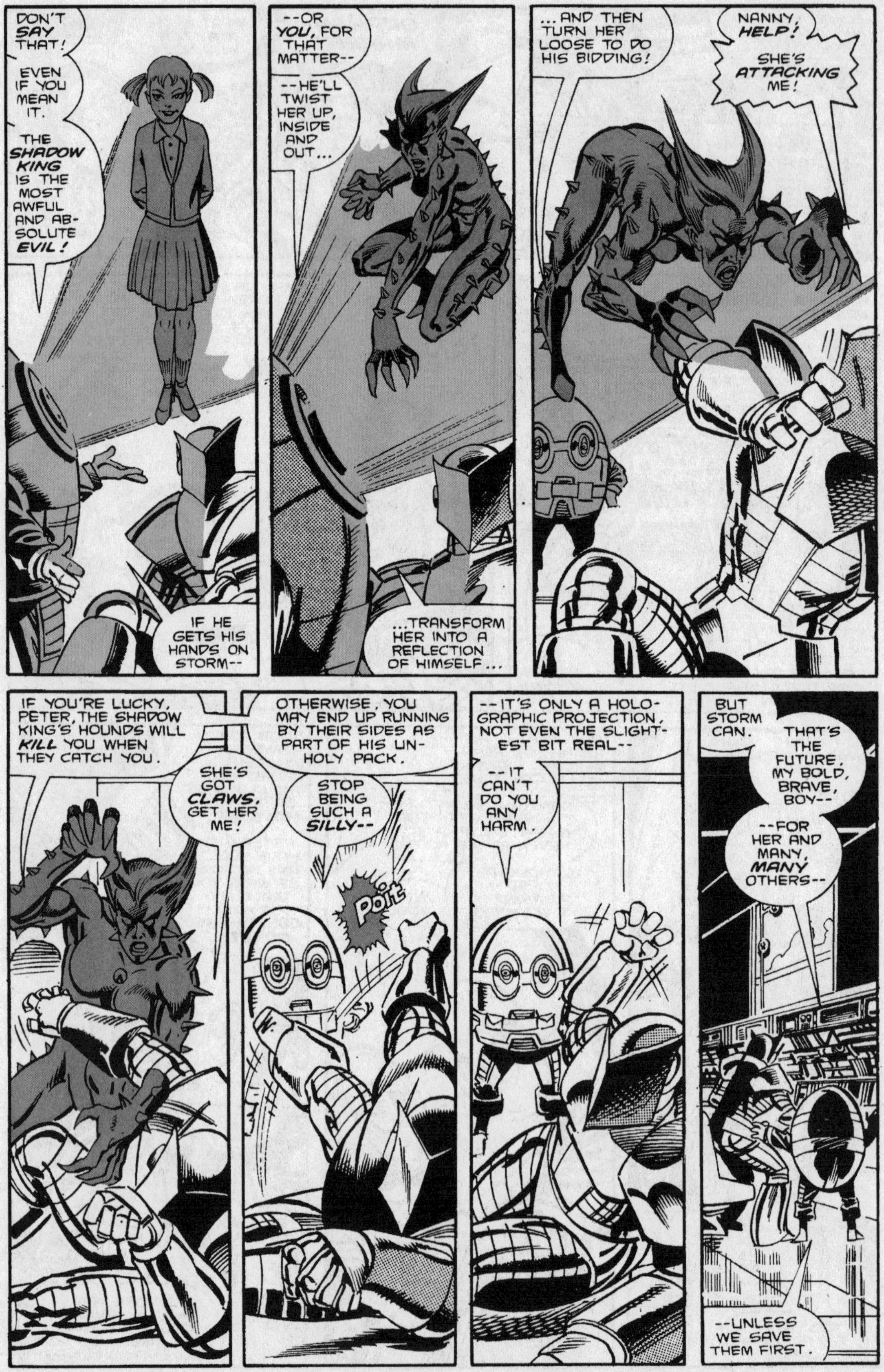
DON'T SAY THAT!
EVEN IF YOU MEAN IT.
THE SHADOW KING IS THE MOST AWFUL AND ABSOLUTE EVIL!
IF HE GETS HIS HANDS ON STORM--
--OR YOU, FOR THAT MATTER--
--HE'LL TWIST HER UP, INSIDE AND OUT...
...TRANSFORM HER INTO A REFLECTION OF HIMSELF...
...AND THEN TURN HER LOOSE TO DO HIS BIDDING!
NANNY, HELP!
SHE'S ATTACKING ME!
IF YOU'RE LUCKY, PETER, THE SHADOW KING'S HOUNDS WILL KILL YOU WHEN THEY CATCH YOU.
SHE'S GOT CLAWS. GET HER ME!
OTHERWISE, YOU MAY END UP RUNNING BY THEIR SIDES AS PART OF HIS UNHOLY PACK.
STOP BEING SUCH A SILLY--
POIT
--IT'S ONLY A HOLOGRAPHIC PROJECTION, NOT EVEN THE SLIGHTEST BIT REAL--
--IT CAN'T DO YOU ANY HARM.
BUT STORM CAN.
THAT'S THE FUTURE, MY BOLD, BRAVE, BOY--
--FOR HER AND MANY, MANY OTHERS--
--UNLESS WE SAVE THEM FIRST.

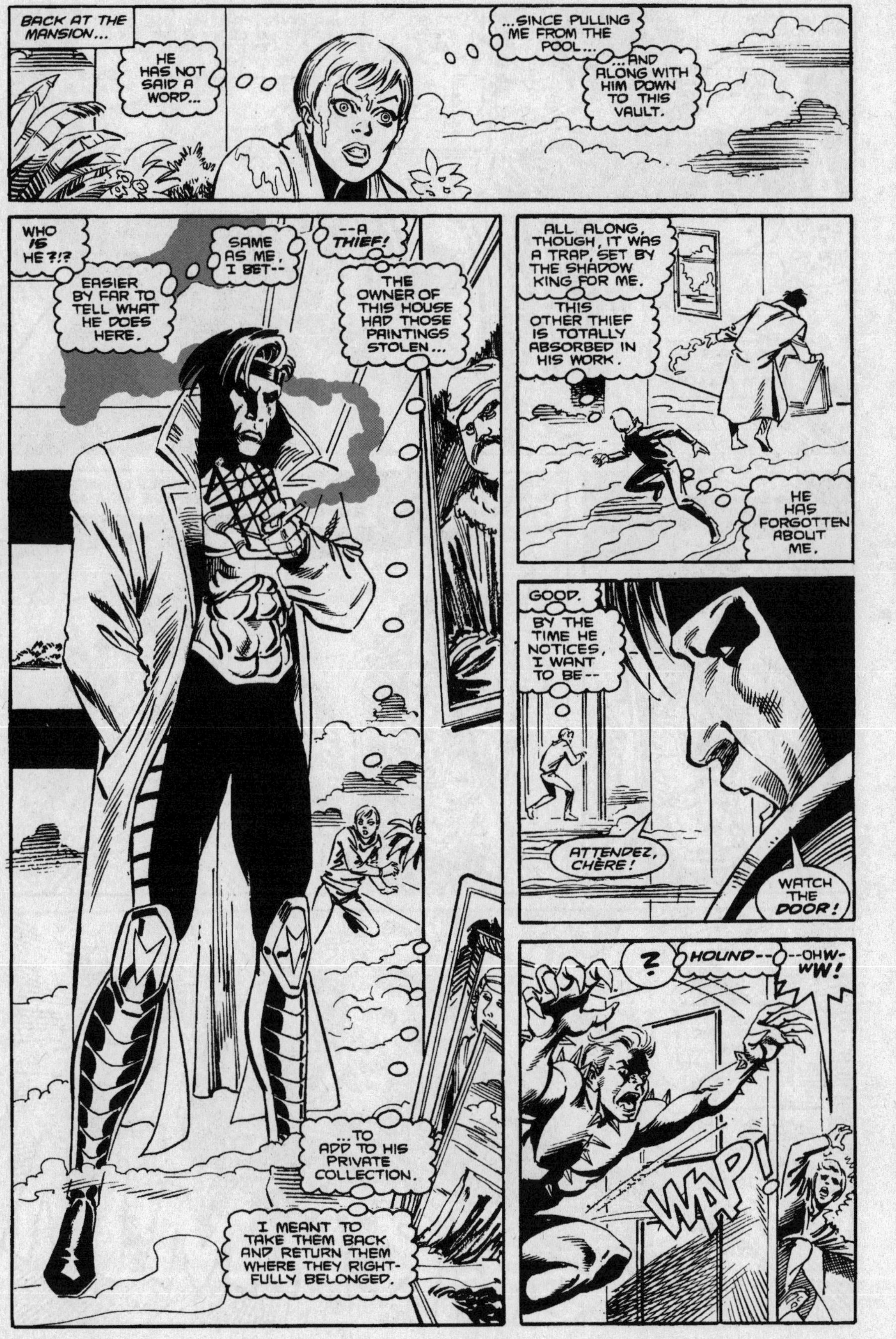
BACK AT THE MANSION...
HE HAS NOT SAID A WORD...
...SINCE PULLING ME FROM THE POOL...
...AND ALONG WITH HIM DOWN TO THIS VAULT.
WHO IS HE?!?
EASIER BY FAR TO TELL WHAT HE DOES HERE.
SAME AS ME, I BET--
--A THIEF!
THE OWNER OF THIS HOUSE HAD THOSE PAINTINGS STOLEN...
...TO ADD TO HIS PRIVATE COLLECTION.
I MEANT TO TAKE THEM BACK AND RETURN THEM WHERE THEY RIGHT-FULLY BELONGED.
ALL ALONG, THOUGH, IT WAS A TRAP, SET BY THE SHADOW KING FOR ME.
THIS OTHER THIEF IS TOTALLY ABSORBED IN HIS WORK.
HE HAS FORGOTTEN ABOUT ME.
GOOD.
BY THE TIME HE NOTICES, I WANT TO BE--
ATTENDEZ, CHÈRE!
WATCH THE DOOR!
?
HOUND--
--OHW-WW!
WAP!

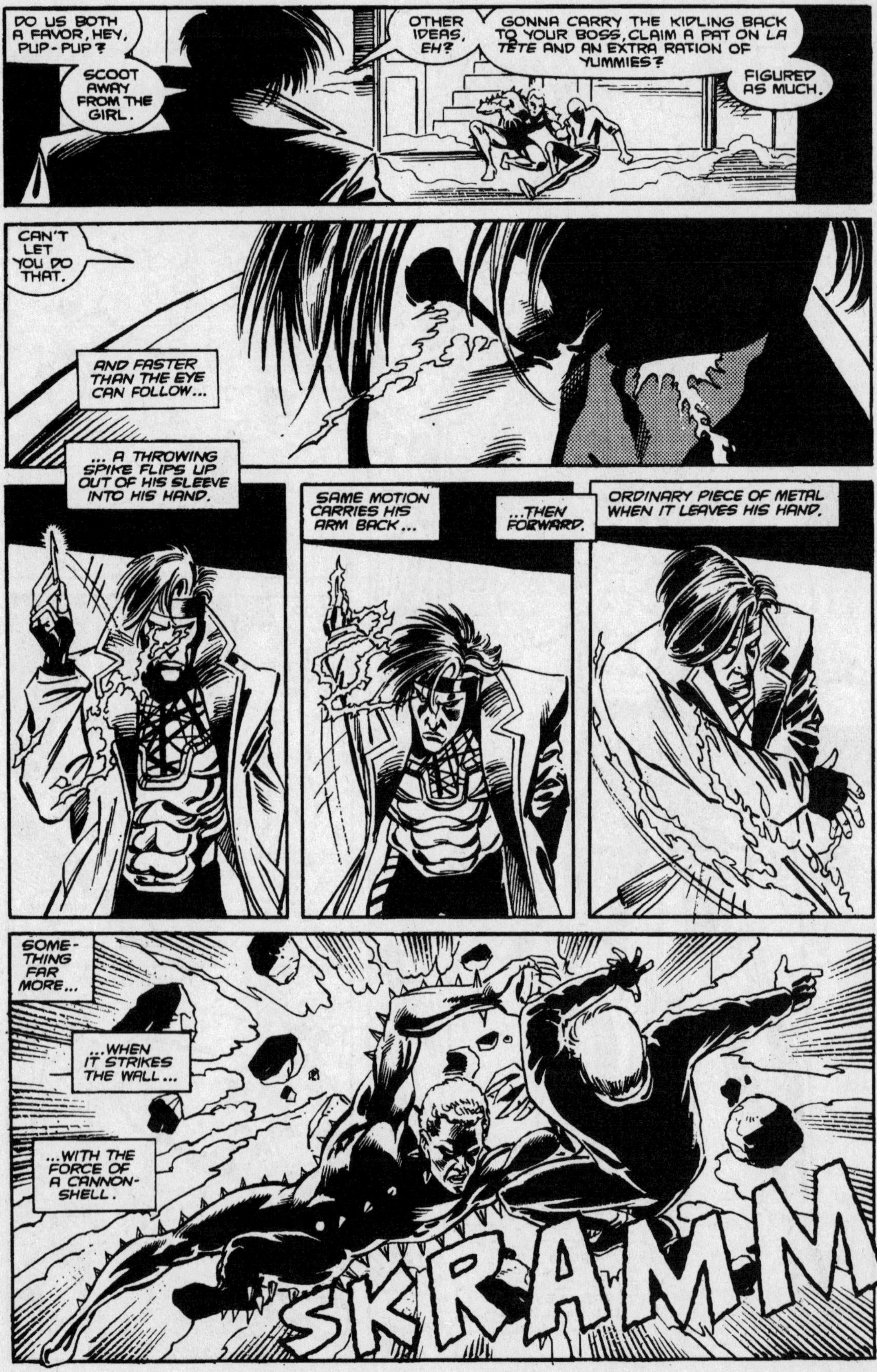
DO US BOTH A FAVOR, HEY, PUP-PUP?
SCOOT AWAY FROM THE GIRL.
OTHER IDEAS, EH?
GONNA CARRY THE KIDLING BACK TO YOUR BOSS, CLAIM A PAT ON LA TÊTE AND AN EXTRA RATION OF YUMMIES?
FIGURED AS MUCH.
CAN'T LET YOU DO THAT.
AND FASTER THAN THE EYE CAN FOLLOW...
... A THROWING SPIKE FLIPS UP OUT OF HIS SLEEVE INTO HIS HAND.
SAME MOTION CARRIES HIS ARM BACK...
...THEN FORWARD.
ORDINARY PIECE OF METAL WHEN IT LEAVES HIS HAND.
SOME-THING FAR MORE...
...WHEN IT STRIKES THE WALL...
...WITH THE FORCE OF A CANNON-SHELL.
SKRAMM

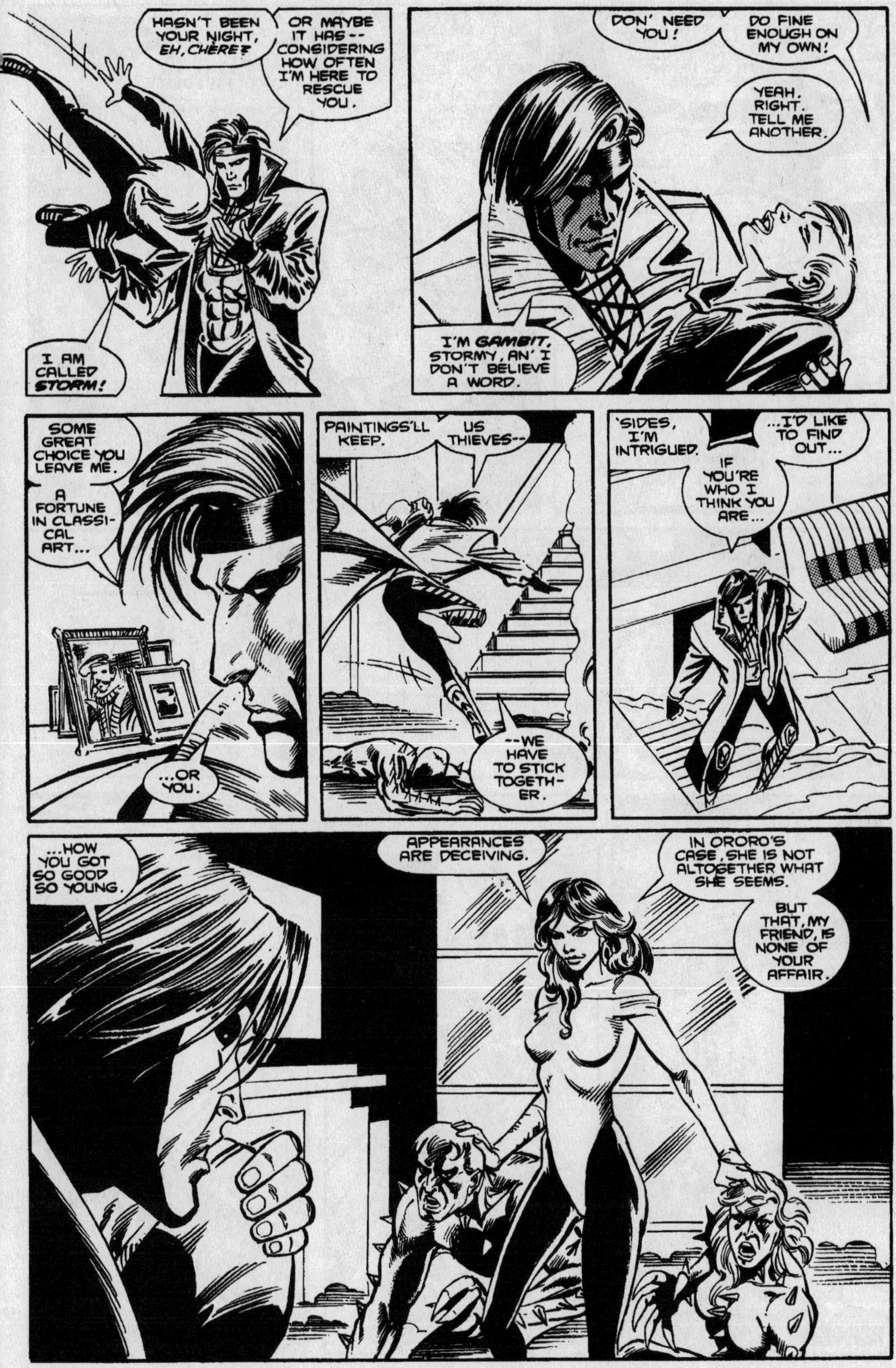
HASN'T BEEN YOUR NIGHT, EH, CHÈRE?
OR MAYBE IT HAS-- CONSIDERING HOW OFTEN I'M HERE TO RESCUE YOU.
I AM CALLED STORM!
DON' NEED YOU!
DO FINE ENOUGH ON MY OWN!
YEAH. RIGHT. TELL ME ANOTHER.
I'M GAMBIT, STORMY, AN' I DON'T BELIEVE A WORD.
SOME GREAT CHOICE YOU LEAVE ME.
A FORTUNE IN CLASSICAL ART...
...OR YOU.
PAINTINGS'LL KEEP.
US THIEVES--
--WE HAVE TO STICK TOGETHER.
'SIDES, I'M INTRIGUED.
...I'D LIKE TO FIND OUT...
IF YOU'RE WHO I THINK YOU ARE...
...HOW YOU GOT SO GOOD SO YOUNG.
APPEARANCES ARE DECEIVING.
IN ORORO'S CASE, SHE IS NOT ALTOGETHER WHAT SHE SEEMS.
BUT THAT, MY FRIEND, IS NONE OF YOUR AFFAIR.

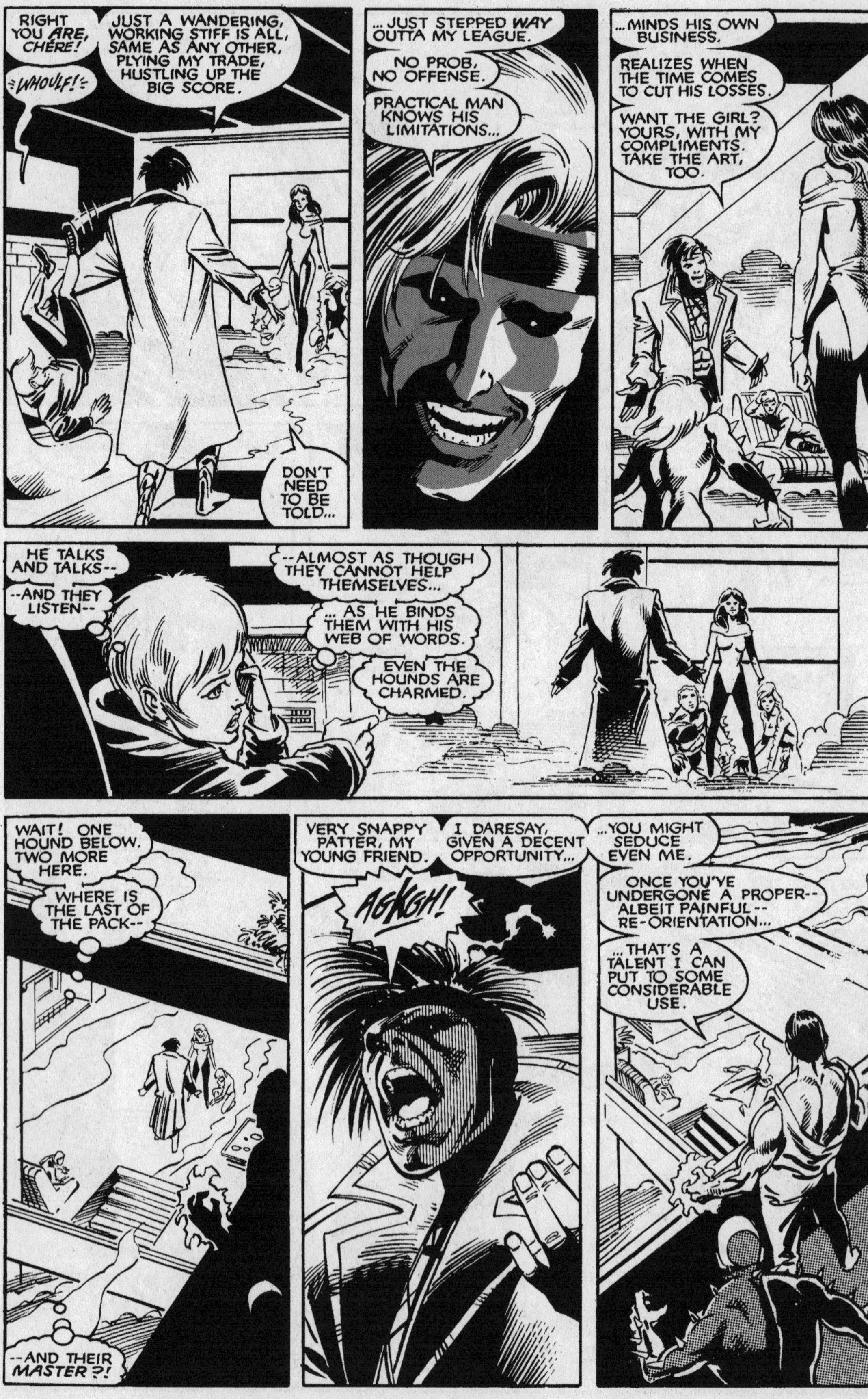
RIGHT YOU ARE, CHÉRE!
JUST A WANDERING, WORKING STIFF IS ALL, SAME AS ANY OTHER, PLYING MY TRADE, HUSTLING UP THE BIG SCORE.
WHOULF!
DON'T NEED TO BE TOLD...
...JUST STEPPED WAY OUTTA MY LEAGUE.
NO PROB, NO OFFENSE.
PRACTICAL MAN KNOWS HIS LIMITATIONS...
...MINDS HIS OWN BUSINESS.
REALIZES WHEN THE TIME COMES TO CUT HIS LOSSES.
WANT THE GIRL? YOURS, WITH MY COMPLIMENTS. TAKE THE ART, TOO.
HE TALKS AND TALKS--
--AND THEY LISTEN--
--ALMOST AS THOUGH THEY CANNOT HELP THEMSELVES...
...AS HE BINDS THEM WITH HIS WEB OF WORDS.
EVEN THE HOUNDS ARE CHARMED.
WAIT! ONE HOUND BELOW. TWO MORE HERE.
WHERE IS THE LAST OF THE PACK--
--AND THEIR MASTER?!
VERY SNAPPY PATTER, MY YOUNG FRIEND.
I DARESAY, GIVEN A DECENT OPPORTUNITY...
AGKGH!
...YOU MIGHT SEDUCE EVEN ME.
ONCE YOU'VE UNDERGONE A PROPER--ALBEIT PAINFUL--RE-ORIENTATION...
...THAT'S A TALENT I CAN PUT TO SOME CONSIDERABLE USE.

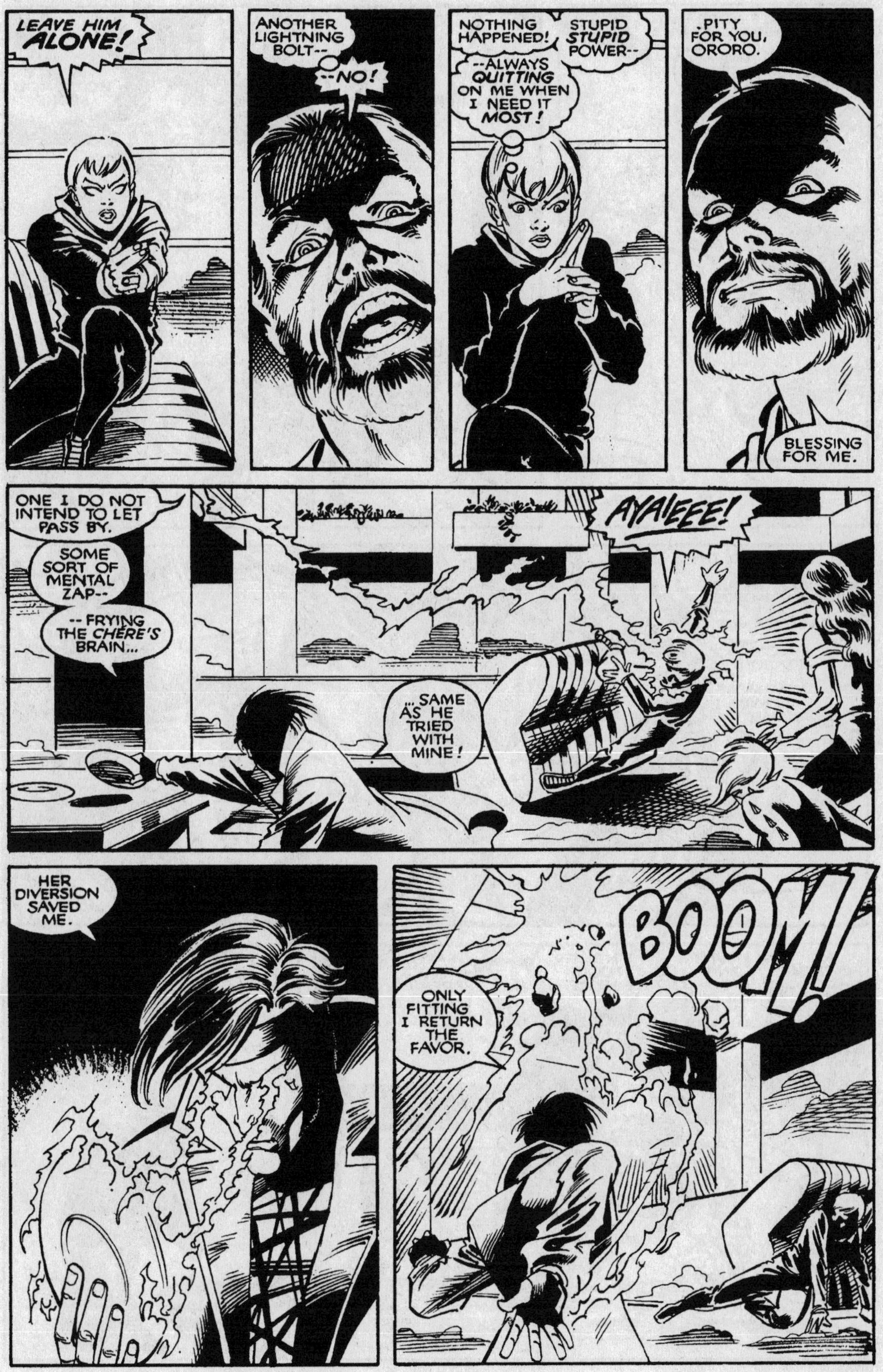
LEAVE HIM ALONE!
ANOTHER LIGHTNING BOLT--
--NO!
NOTHING HAPPENED!
STUPID STUPID POWER--
--ALWAYS QUITTING ON ME WHEN I NEED IT MOST!
...PITY FOR YOU, ORORO.
BLESSING FOR ME.
ONE I DO NOT INTEND TO LET PASS BY.
SOME SORT OF MENTAL ZAP--
--FRYING THE CHÈRE'S BRAIN...
AYAIEEE!
...SAME AS HE TRIED WITH MINE!
HER DIVERSION SAVED ME.
BOOM!
ONLY FITTING I RETURN THE FAVOR.

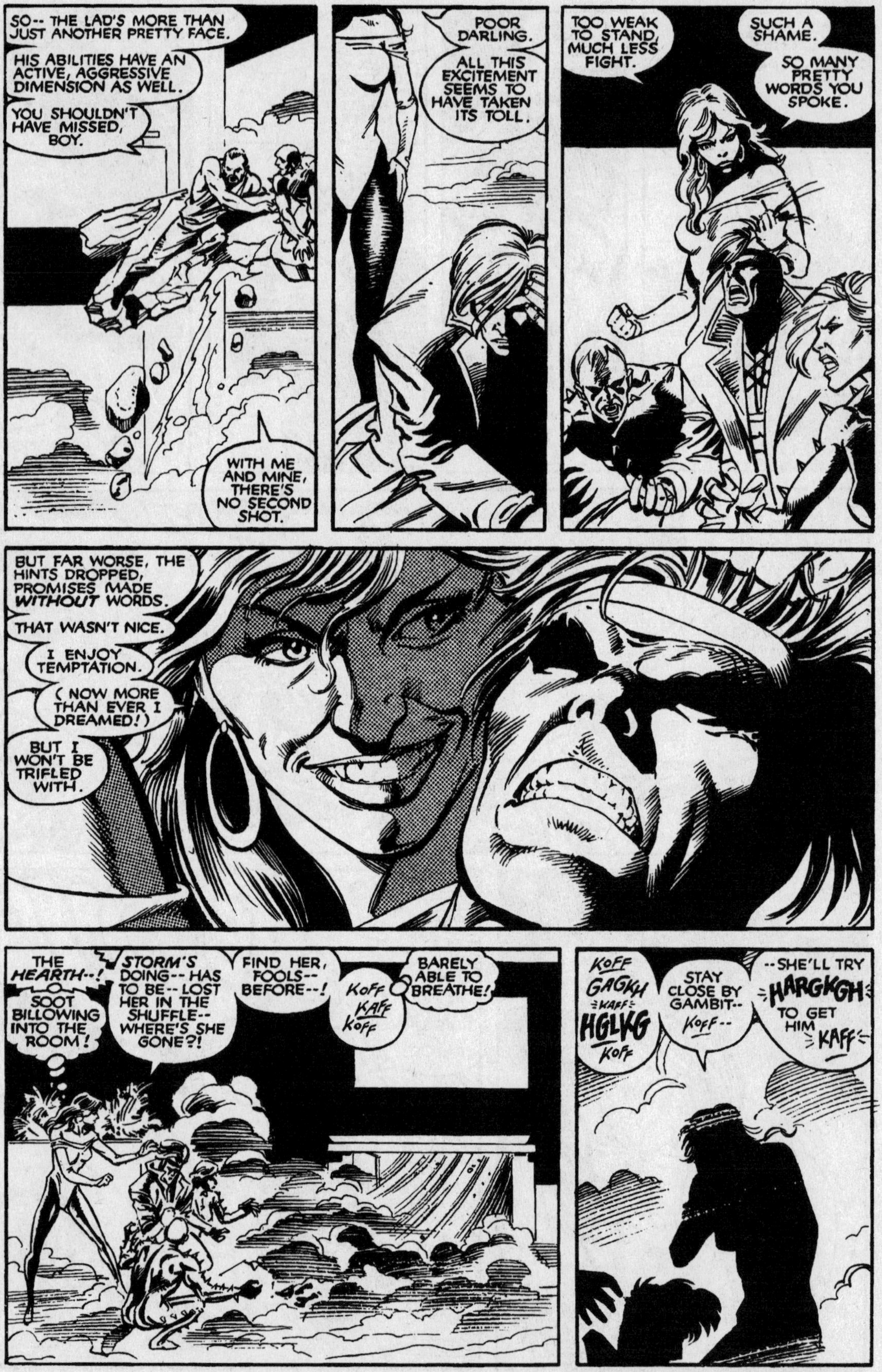
SO-- THE LAD'S MORE THAN JUST ANOTHER PRETTY FACE.
HIS ABILITIES HAVE AN ACTIVE, AGGRESSIVE DIMENSION AS WELL.
YOU SHOULDN'T HAVE MISSED, BOY.
WITH ME AND MINE, THERE'S NO SECOND SHOT.
POOR DARLING.
ALL THIS EXCITEMENT SEEMS TO HAVE TAKEN ITS TOLL.
TOO WEAK TO STAND, MUCH LESS FIGHT.
SUCH A SHAME.
SO MANY PRETTY WORDS YOU SPOKE.
BUT FAR WORSE, THE HINTS DROPPED, PROMISES MADE WITHOUT WORDS.
THAT WASN'T NICE.
I ENJOY TEMPTATION.
(NOW MORE THAN EVER I DREAMED!)
BUT I WON'T BE TRIFLED WITH.
THE HEARTH--!
SOOT BILLOWING INTO THE ROOM!
STORM'S DOING-- HAS TO BE-- LOST HER IN THE SHUFFLE-- WHERE'S SHE GONE?!
FIND HER, FOOLS-- BEFORE--!
KOFF KAFF KOFF
BARELY ABLE TO BREATHE!
KOFF GAGKH KAFF HGLKG KOFF
STAY CLOSE BY GAMBIT-- KOFF--
--SHE'LL TRY HARGKGH TO GET HIM KAFF

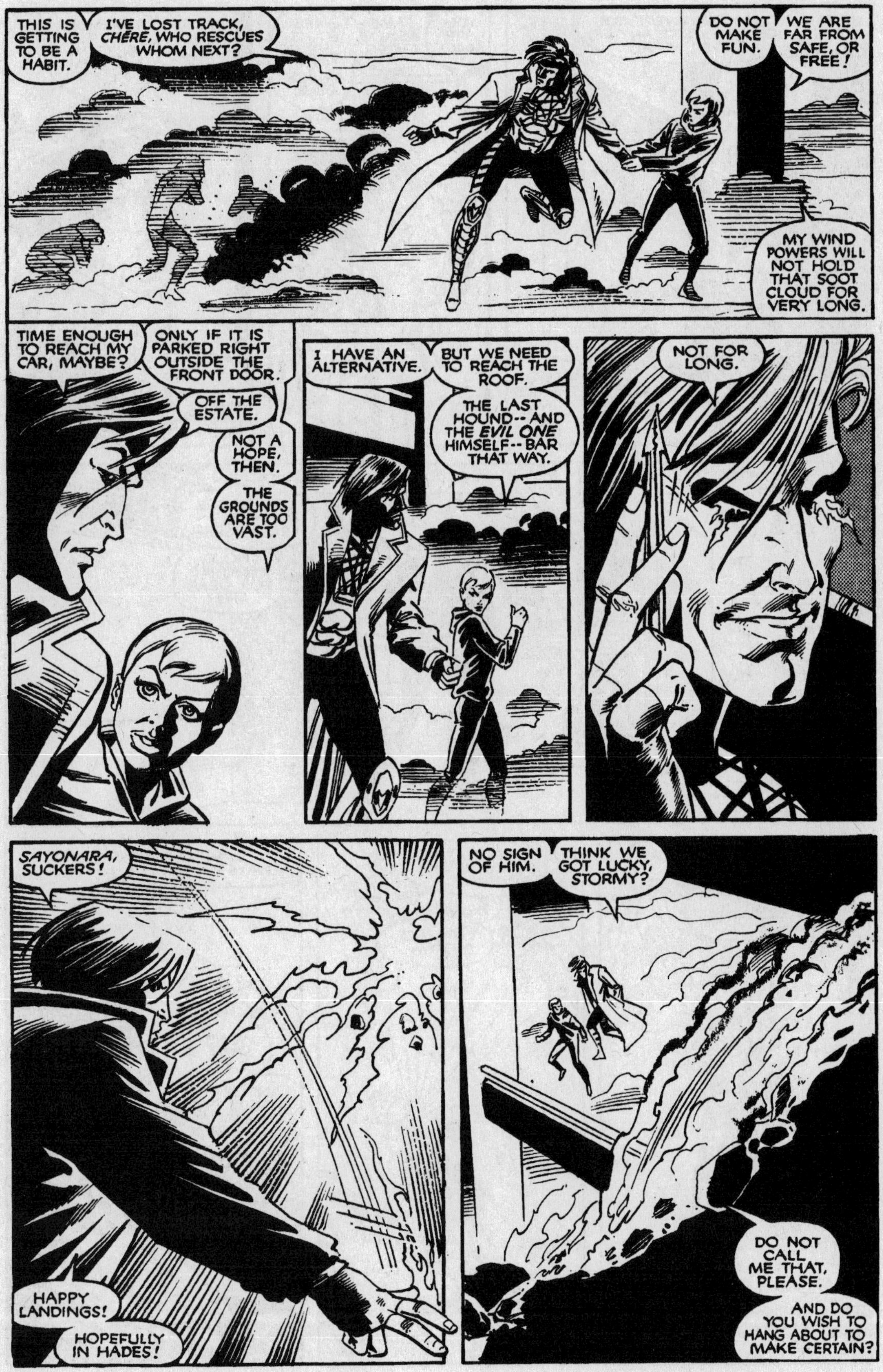
THIS IS GETTING TO BE A HABIT.
I'VE LOST TRACK, CHÈRE, WHO RESCUES WHOM NEXT?
DO NOT MAKE FUN.
WE ARE FAR FROM SAFE, OR FREE!
MY WIND POWERS WILL NOT HOLD THAT SOOT CLOUD FOR VERY LONG.
TIME ENOUGH TO REACH MY CAR, MAYBE?
ONLY IF IT IS PARKED RIGHT OUTSIDE THE FRONT DOOR.
OFF THE ESTATE.
NOT A HOPE, THEN.
THE GROUNDS ARE TOO VAST.
I HAVE AN ALTERNATIVE.
BUT WE NEED TO REACH THE ROOF.
THE LAST HOUND-- AND THE EVIL ONE HIMSELF-- BAR THAT WAY.
NOT FOR LONG.
SAYONARA, SUCKERS!
HAPPY LANDINGS!
HOPEFULLY IN HADES!
NO SIGN OF HIM.
THINK WE GOT LUCKY, STORMY?
DO NOT CALL ME THAT, PLEASE.
AND DO YOU WISH TO HANG ABOUT TO MAKE CERTAIN?

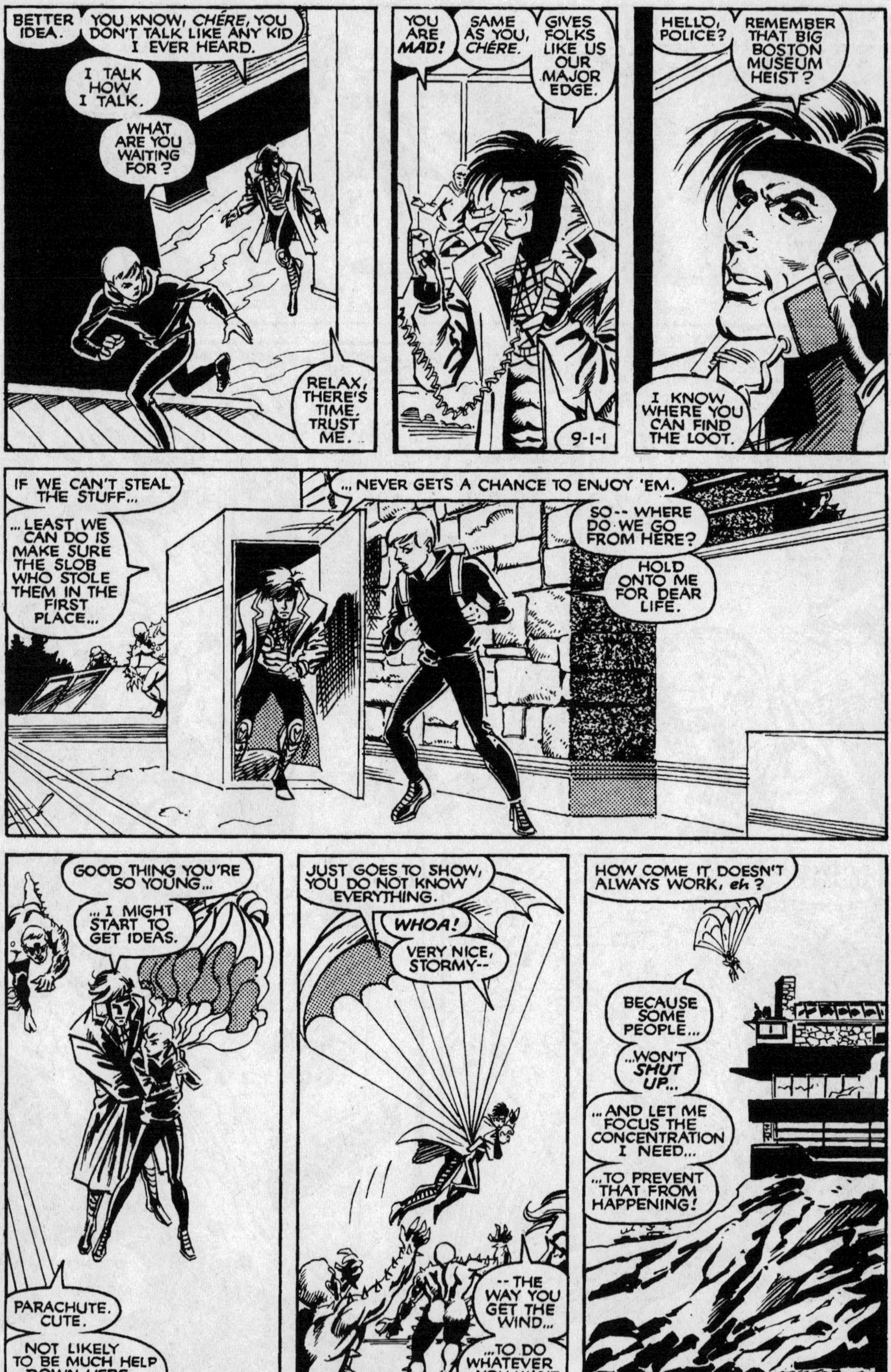

BETTER IDEA.
YOU KNOW, *CHÉRE*, YOU DON'T TALK LIKE ANY KID I EVER HEARD.
I TALK HOW I TALK.
WHAT ARE YOU WAITING FOR?
RELAX, THERE'S TIME. TRUST ME...
YOU ARE *MAD!*
SAME AS YOU, *CHÉRE*.
GIVES FOLKS LIKE US OUR MAJOR EDGE.
9-1-1
HELLO, POLICE?
REMEMBER THAT BIG BOSTON MUSEUM HEIST?
I KNOW WHERE YOU CAN FIND THE LOOT.
IF WE CAN'T STEAL THE STUFF...
...LEAST WE CAN DO IS MAKE SURE THE SLOB WHO STOLE THEM IN THE FIRST PLACE...
...NEVER GETS A CHANCE TO ENJOY 'EM.
SO-- WHERE DO WE GO FROM HERE?
HOLD ONTO ME FOR DEAR LIFE.
GOOD THING YOU'RE SO YOUNG...
...I MIGHT START TO GET IDEAS.
PARACHUTE. CUTE.
NOT LIKELY TO BE MUCH HELP DOWN HERE.
JUST GOES TO SHOW, YOU DO NOT KNOW EVERYTHING.
WHOA!
VERY NICE, STORMY--
-- THE WAY YOU GET THE WIND...
...TO DO WHATEVER YOU WANT.
HOW COME IT DOESN'T ALWAYS WORK, *eh*?
BECAUSE SOME PEOPLE...
...WON'T *SHUT UP*...
...AND LET ME FOCUS THE CONCENTRATION I NEED...
...TO PREVENT THAT FROM HAPPENING!

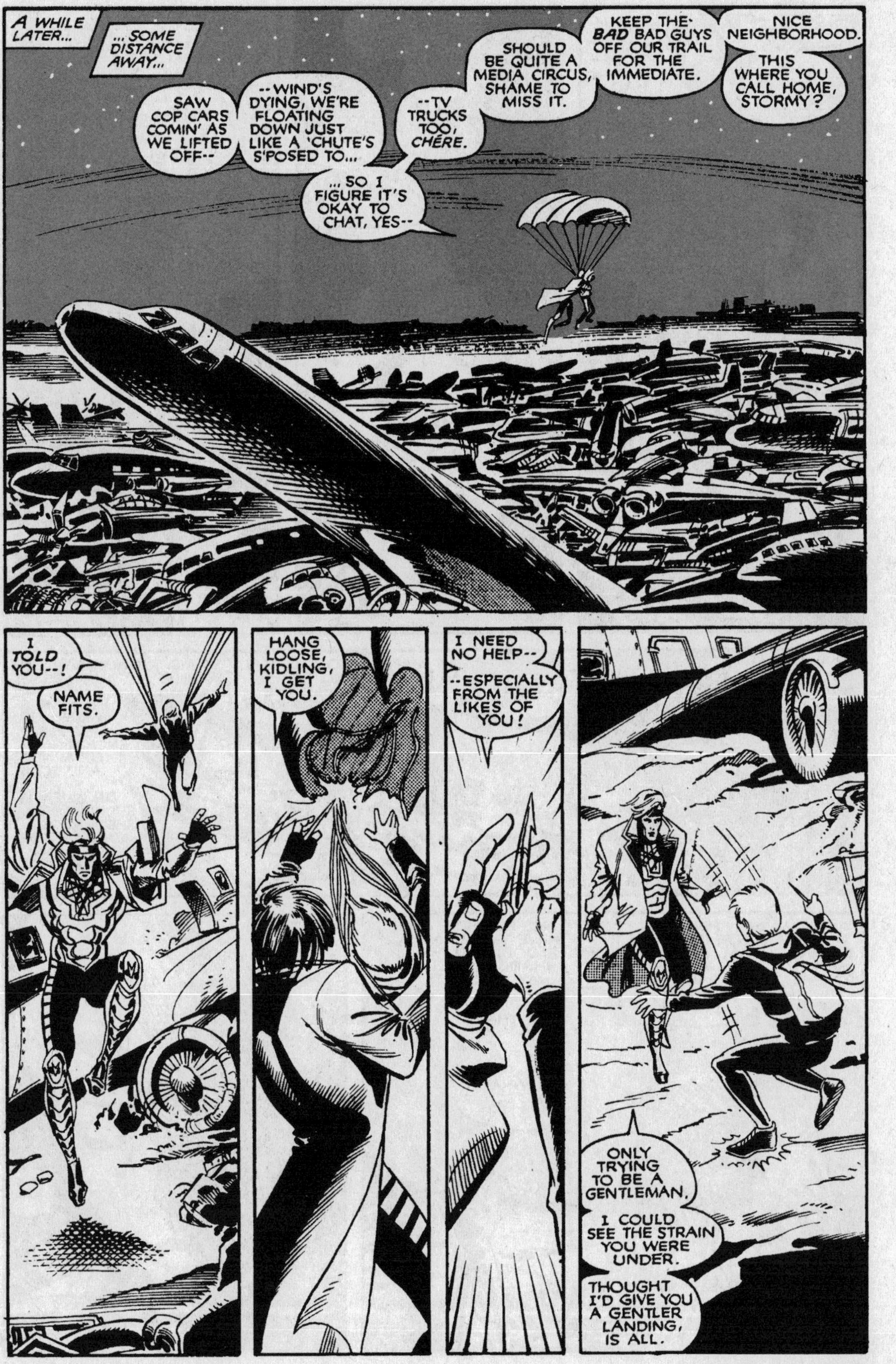
A WHILE LATER...
... SOME DISTANCE AWAY...
SAW COP CARS COMIN' AS WE LIFTED OFF--
--WIND'S DYING, WE'RE FLOATING DOWN JUST LIKE A 'CHUTE'S S'POSED TO...
... SO I FIGURE IT'S OKAY TO CHAT, YES--
--TV TRUCKS TOO, CHÉRE.
SHOULD BE QUITE A MEDIA CIRCUS, SHAME TO MISS IT.
KEEP THE BAD BAD GUYS OFF OUR TRAIL FOR THE IMMEDIATE.
NICE NEIGHBORHOOD.
THIS WHERE YOU CALL HOME, STORMY?
I TOLD YOU--!
NAME FITS.
HANG LOOSE, KIDLING, I GET YOU.
I NEED NO HELP--
--ESPECIALLY FROM THE LIKES OF YOU!
ONLY TRYING TO BE A GENTLEMAN.
I COULD SEE THE STRAIN YOU WERE UNDER.
THOUGHT I'D GIVE YOU A GENTLER LANDING, IS ALL.

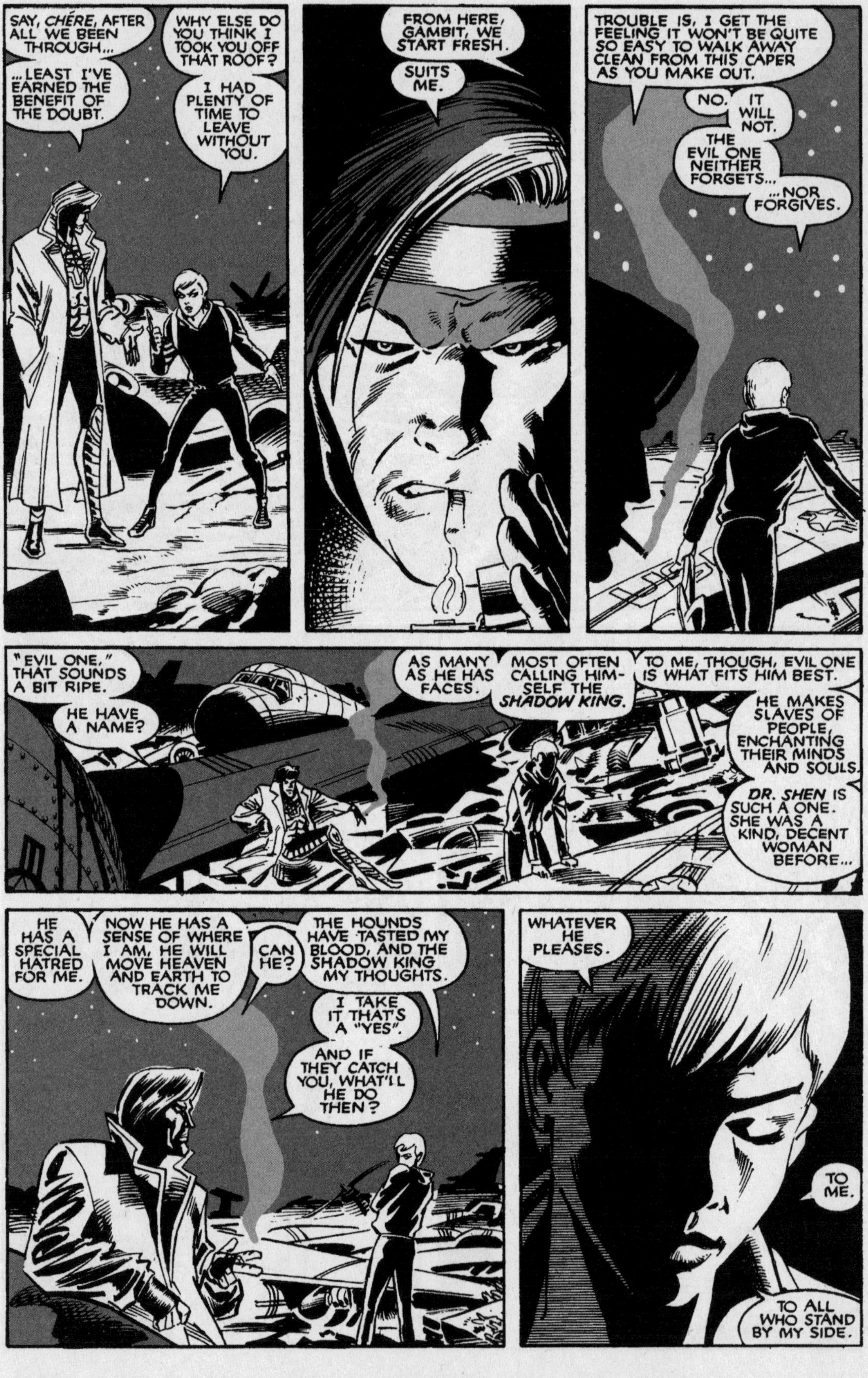
SAY, CHÉRE, AFTER ALL WE BEEN THROUGH...
...LEAST I'VE EARNED THE BENEFIT OF THE DOUBT.
WHY ELSE DO YOU THINK I TOOK YOU OFF THAT ROOF?
I HAD PLENTY OF TIME TO LEAVE WITHOUT YOU.
FROM HERE, GAMBIT, WE START FRESH.
SUITS ME.
TROUBLE IS, I GET THE FEELING IT WON'T BE QUITE SO EASY TO WALK AWAY CLEAN FROM THIS CAPER AS YOU MAKE OUT.
NO. IT WILL NOT.
THE EVIL ONE NEITHER FORGETS...
...NOR FORGIVES.
"EVIL ONE," THAT SOUNDS A BIT RIPE.
HE HAVE A NAME?
AS MANY AS HE HAS FACES.
MOST OFTEN CALLING HIMSELF THE SHADOW KING.
TO ME, THOUGH, EVIL ONE IS WHAT FITS HIM BEST.
HE MAKES SLAVES OF PEOPLE, ENCHANTING THEIR MINDS AND SOULS.
DR. SHEN IS SUCH A ONE. SHE WAS A KIND, DECENT WOMAN BEFORE...
HE HAS A SPECIAL HATRED FOR ME.
NOW HE HAS A SENSE OF WHERE I AM, HE WILL MOVE HEAVEN AND EARTH TO TRACK ME DOWN.
CAN HE?
THE HOUNDS HAVE TASTED MY BLOOD, AND THE SHADOW KING MY THOUGHTS.
I TAKE IT THAT'S A "YES".
AND IF THEY CATCH YOU, WHAT'LL HE DO THEN?
WHATEVER HE PLEASES.
TO ME.
TO ALL WHO STAND BY MY SIDE.

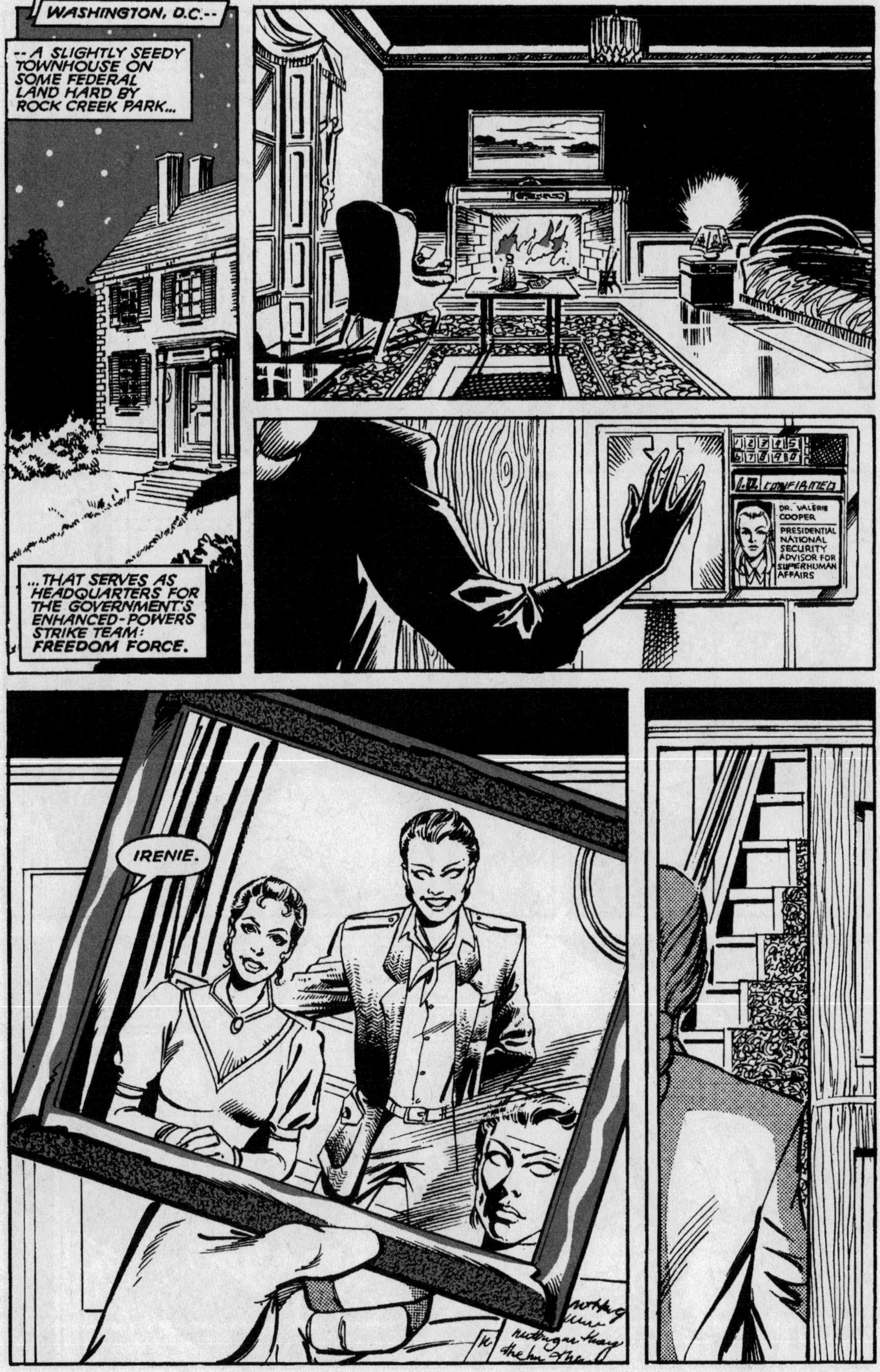
WASHINGTON, D.C.--
--A SLIGHTLY SEEDY TOWNHOUSE ON SOME FEDERAL LAND HARD BY ROCK CREEK PARK...
...THAT SERVES AS HEADQUARTERS FOR THE GOVERNMENT'S ENHANCED-POWERS STRIKE TEAM: FREEDOM FORCE.
I.D. CONFIRMED
DR. VALÉRIE COOPER
PRESIDENTIAL NATIONAL SECURITY ADVISOR FOR SUPERHUMAN AFFAIRS
IRENIE.

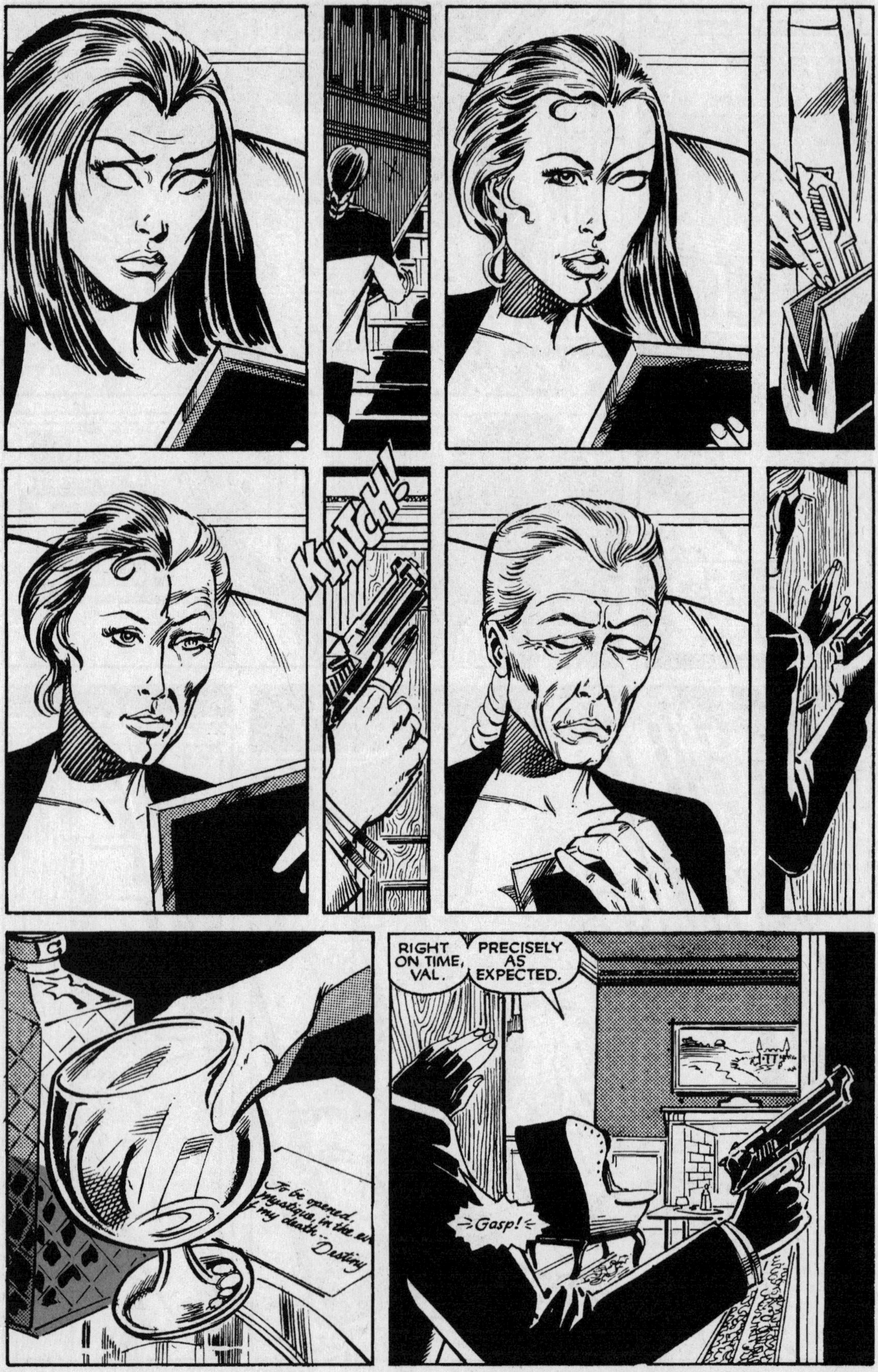
KLATCH!
To be opened,
mystique, in the ev
f my death.
Destiny
RIGHT ON TIME, VAL.
PRECISELY AS EXPECTED.
Gasp!

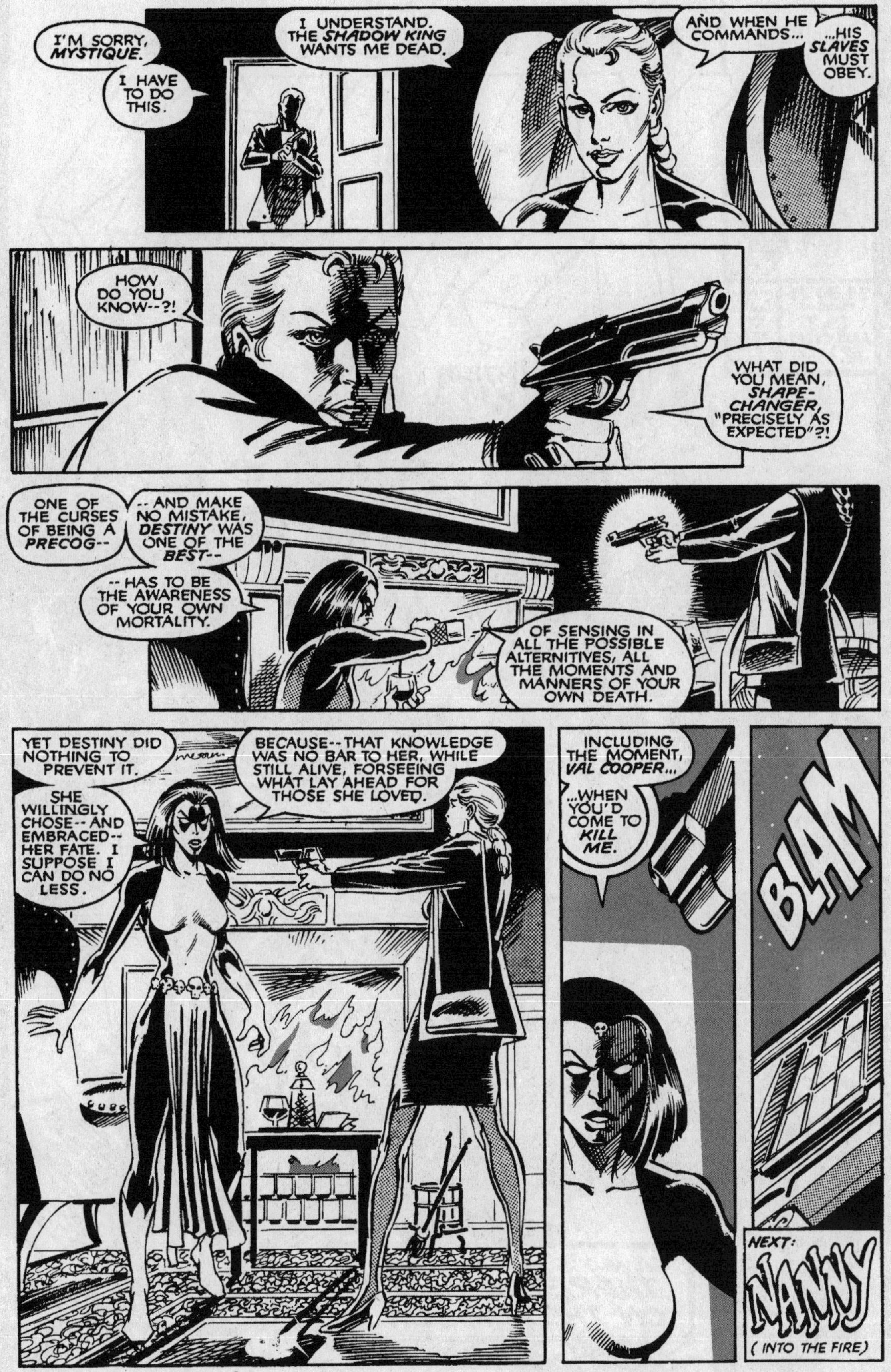
I'M SORRY, MYSTIQUE.
I HAVE TO DO THIS.
I UNDERSTAND. THE SHADOW KING WANTS ME DEAD.
AND WHEN HE COMMANDS...
...HIS SLAVES MUST OBEY.
HOW DO YOU KNOW--?!
WHAT DID YOU MEAN, SHAPE-CHANGER, "PRECISELY AS EXPECTED"?!
ONE OF THE CURSES OF BEING A PRECOG--
--AND MAKE NO MISTAKE, DESTINY WAS ONE OF THE BEST--
--HAS TO BE THE AWARENESS OF YOUR OWN MORTALITY.
OF SENSING IN ALL THE POSSIBLE ALTERNITIVES, ALL THE MOMENTS AND MANNERS OF YOUR OWN DEATH.
YET DESTINY DID NOTHING TO PREVENT IT.
SHE WILLINGLY CHOSE-- AND EMBRACED-- HER FATE. I SUPPOSE I CAN DO NO LESS.
BECAUSE-- THAT KNOWLEDGE WAS NO BAR TO HER, WHILE STILL ALIVE, FORSEEING WHAT LAY AHEAD FOR THOSE SHE LOVED.
INCLUDING THE MOMENT, VAL COOPER...
...WHEN YOU'D COME TO KILL ME.
BLAM
NEXT:
NANNY
(INTO THE FIRE)

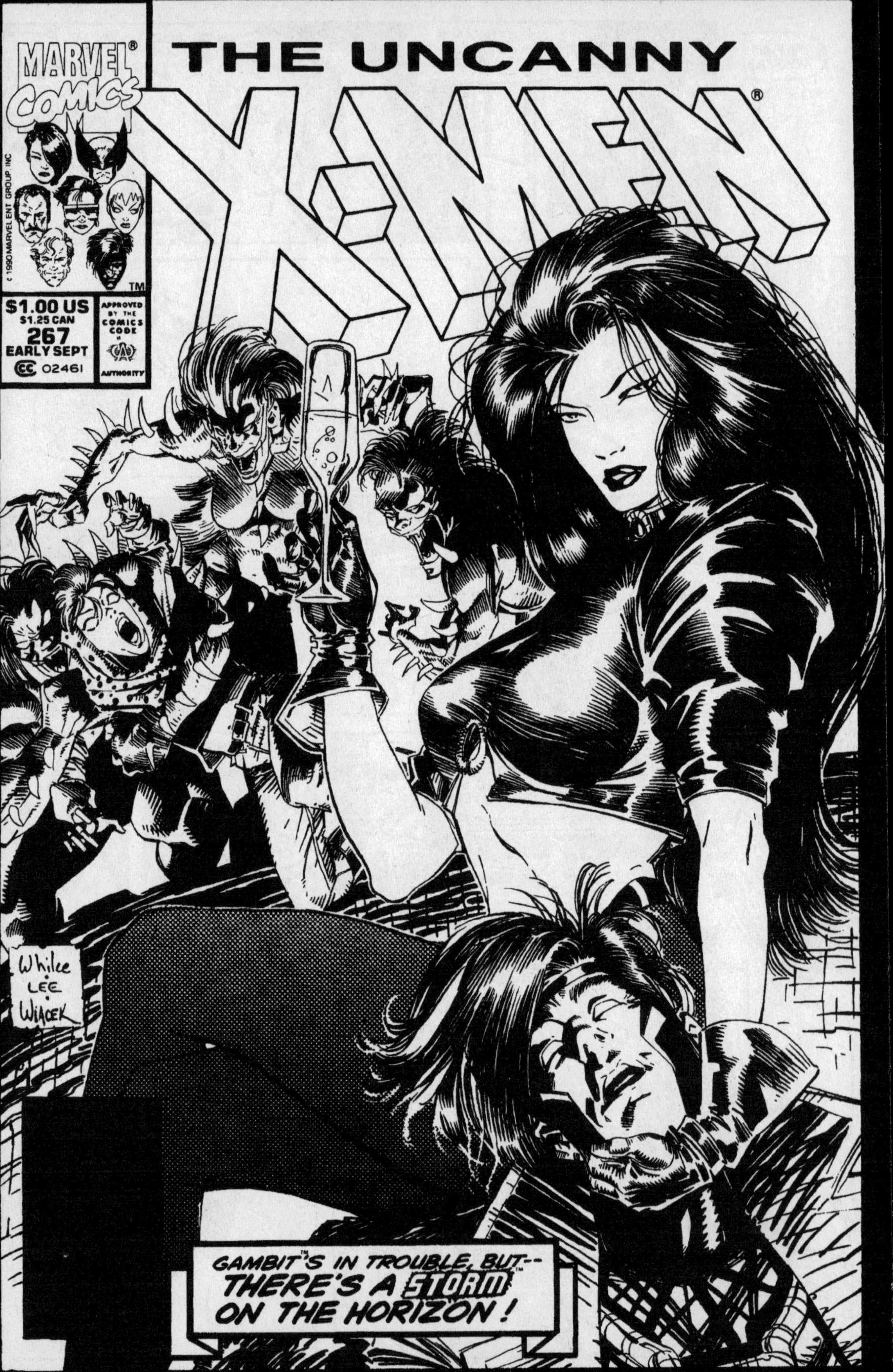
MARVEL® COMICS
THE UNCANNY
X-MEN®
© 1990 MARVEL ENT. GROUP, INC
$1.00 US
$1.25 CAN
267
EARLY SEPT
02461
APPROVED BY THE COMICS CODE AUTHORITY
Whilce LEE WIACEK
GAMBIT™'S IN TROUBLE, BUT--
THERE'S A STORM™
ON THE HORIZON!

STAN LEE *PRESENTS*

INTO THE FIRE

STARRING
STORM,
LEADER
OF THE
UNCANNY
X-MEN

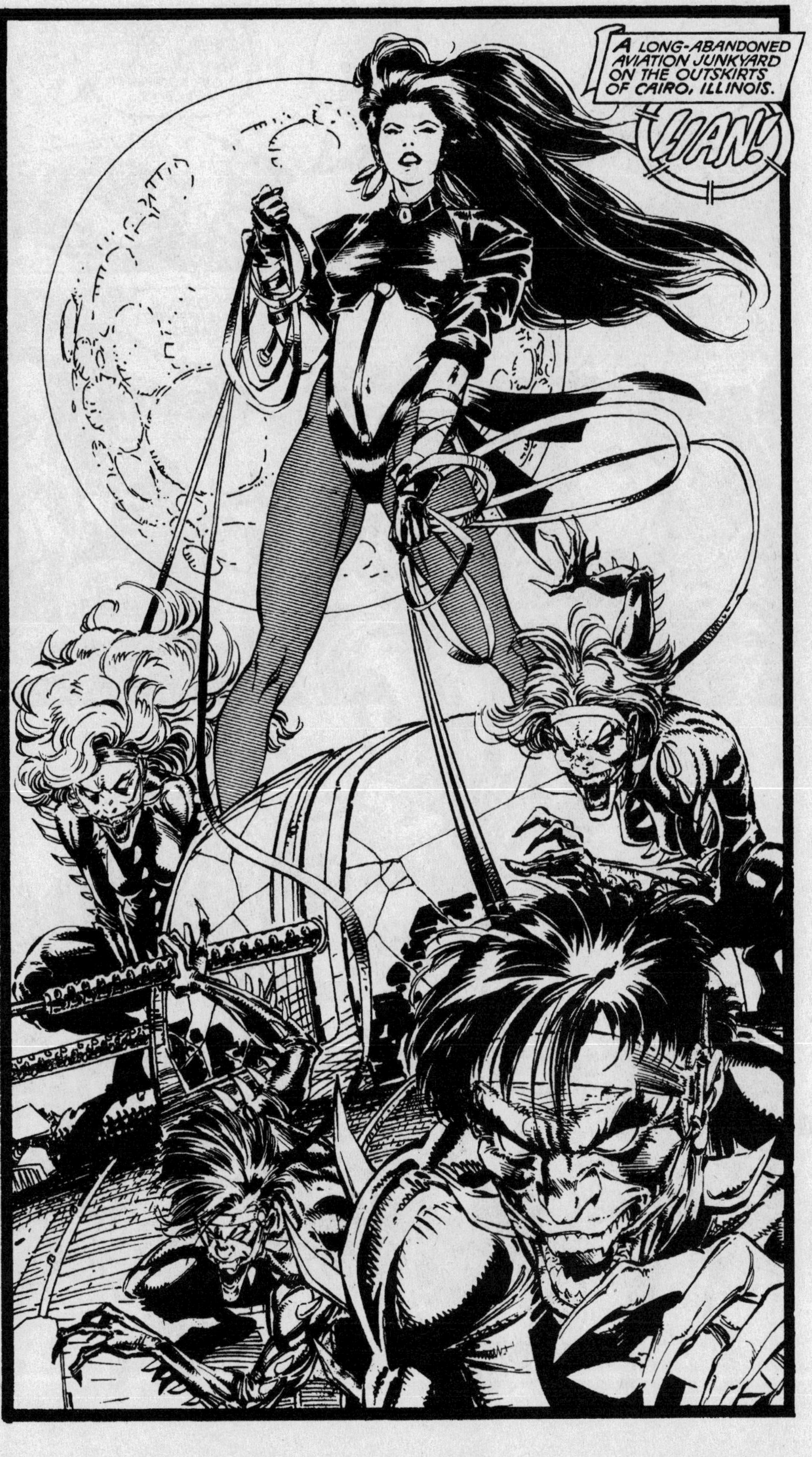
A LONG-ABANDONED AVIATION JUNKYARD ON THE OUTSKIRTS OF CAIRO, ILLINOIS.
LIAN!

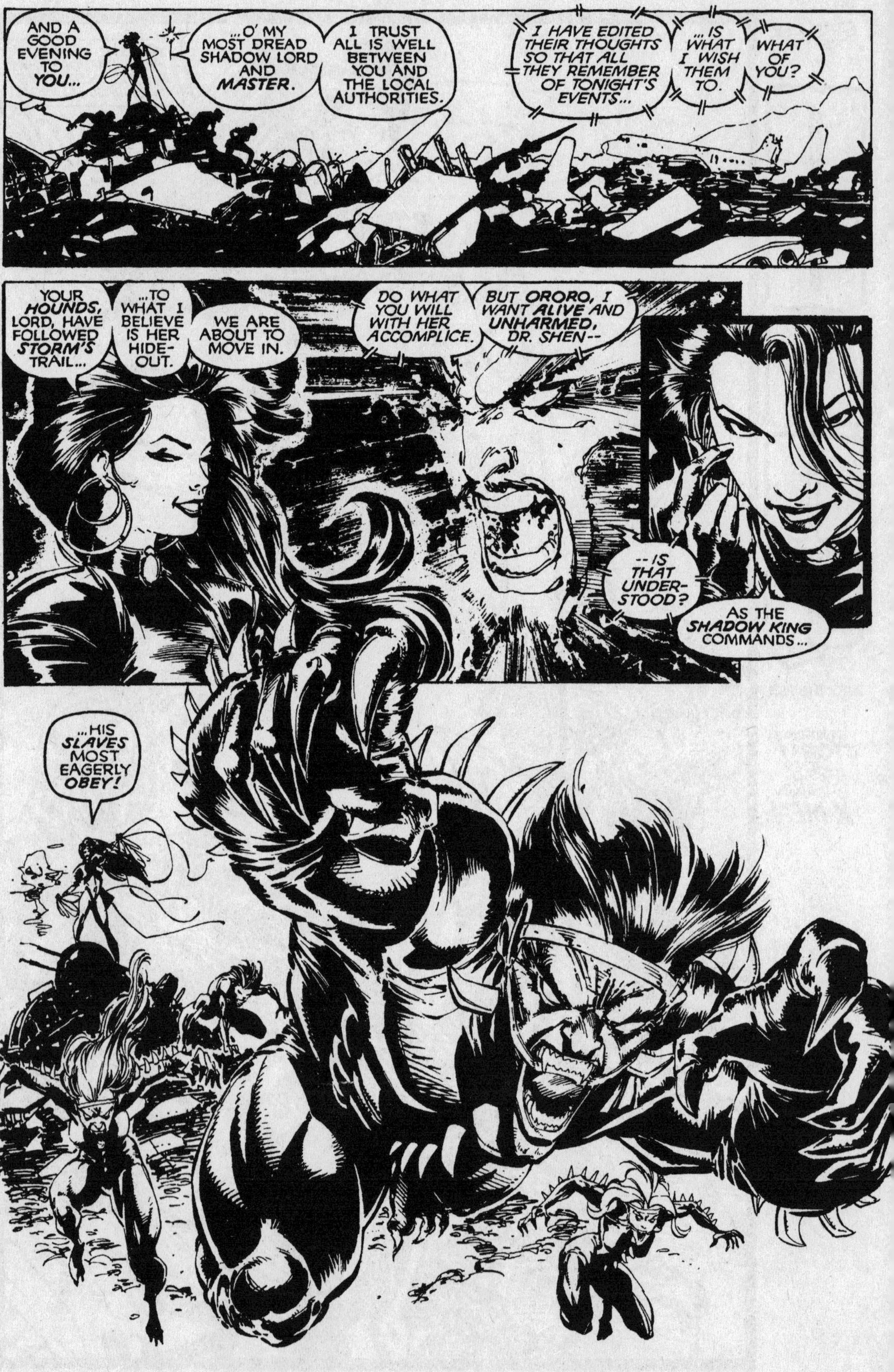
AND A GOOD EVENING TO YOU...
...O' MY MOST DREAD SHADOW LORD AND MASTER.
I TRUST ALL IS WELL BETWEEN YOU AND THE LOCAL AUTHORITIES.
I HAVE EDITED THEIR THOUGHTS SO THAT ALL THEY REMEMBER OF TONIGHT'S EVENTS...
...IS WHAT I WISH THEM TO.
WHAT OF YOU?
YOUR HOUNDS, LORD, HAVE FOLLOWED STORM'S TRAIL...
...TO WHAT I BELIEVE IS HER HIDE-OUT.
WE ARE ABOUT TO MOVE IN.
DO WHAT YOU WILL WITH HER ACCOMPLICE.
BUT ORORO, I WANT ALIVE AND UNHARMED, DR. SHEN--
--IS THAT UNDER-STOOD?
AS THE SHADOW KING COMMANDS...
...HIS SLAVES MOST EAGERLY OBEY!

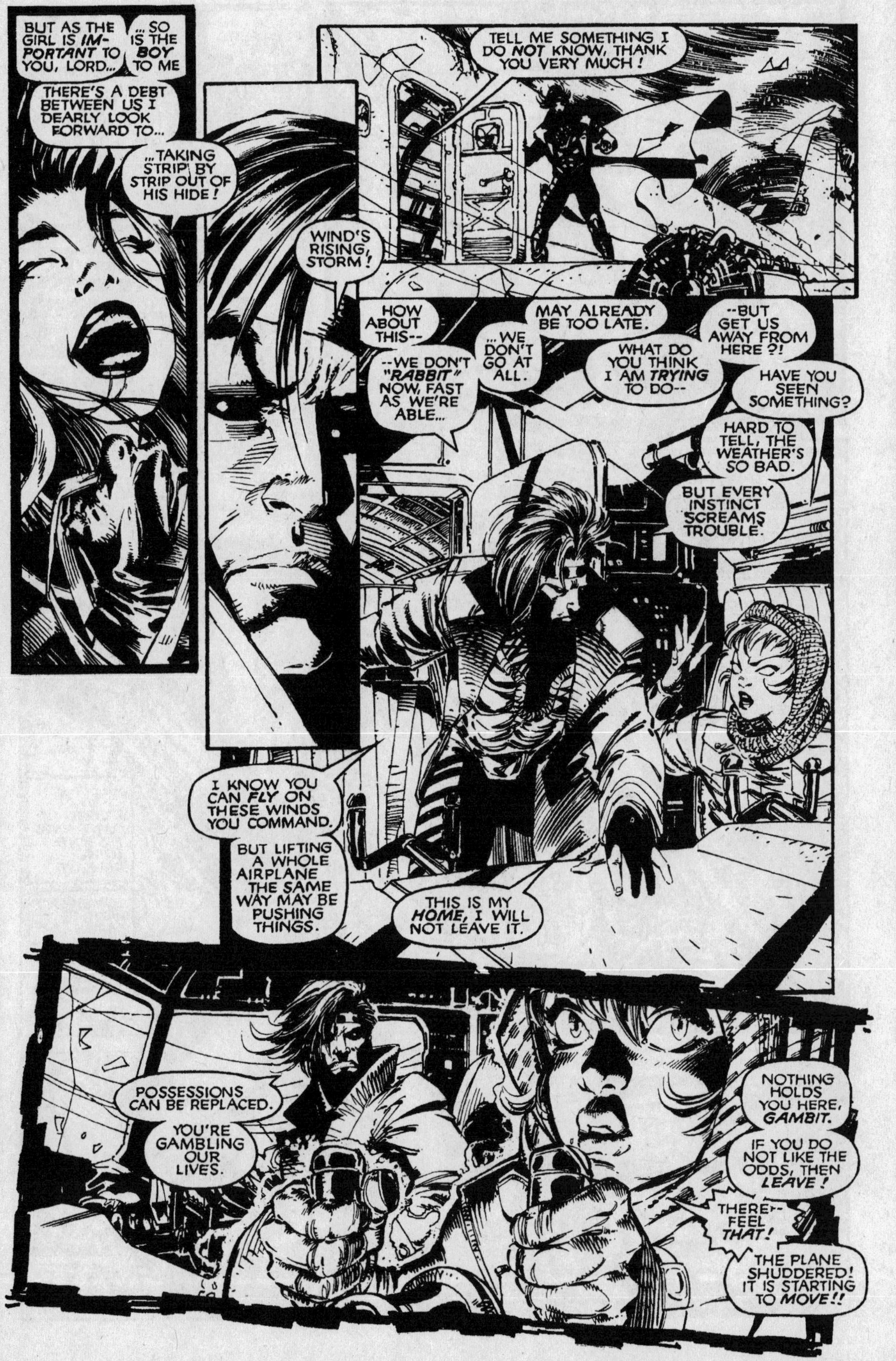
BUT AS THE GIRL IS IMPORTANT TO YOU, LORD...
...SO IS THE BOY TO ME
THERE'S A DEBT BETWEEN US I DEARLY LOOK FORWARD TO...
...TAKING STRIP BY STRIP OUT OF HIS HIDE!
TELL ME SOMETHING I DO NOT KNOW, THANK YOU VERY MUCH!
WIND'S RISING, STORM!
HOW ABOUT THIS--
--WE DON'T "RABBIT" NOW, FAST AS WE'RE ABLE...
...WE DON'T GO AT ALL.
MAY ALREADY BE TOO LATE.
WHAT DO YOU THINK I AM TRYING TO DO--
--BUT GET US AWAY FROM HERE?!
HAVE YOU SEEN SOMETHING?
HARD TO TELL, THE WEATHER'S SO BAD.
BUT EVERY INSTINCT SCREAMS TROUBLE.
I KNOW YOU CAN FLY ON THESE WINDS YOU COMMAND.
BUT LIFTING A WHOLE AIRPLANE THE SAME WAY MAY BE PUSHING THINGS.
THIS IS MY HOME, I WILL NOT LEAVE IT.
POSSESSIONS CAN BE REPLACED.
YOU'RE GAMBLING OUR LIVES.
NOTHING HOLDS YOU HERE, GAMBIT.
IF YOU DO NOT LIKE THE ODDS, THEN LEAVE!
THERE-- FEEL THAT!
THE PLANE SHUDDERED! IT IS STARTING TO MOVE!!

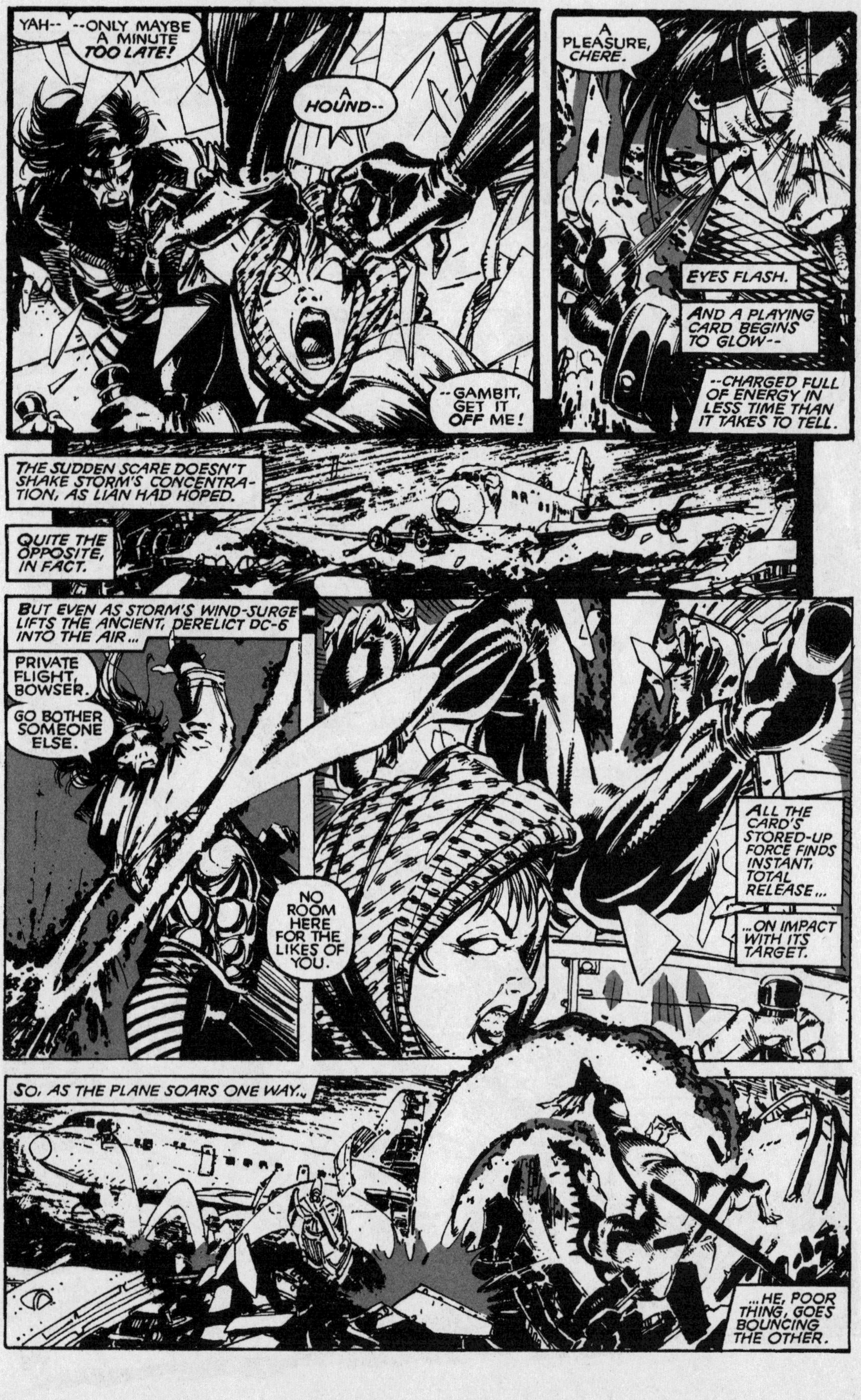
YAH--
--ONLY MAYBE A MINUTE TOO LATE!
A HOUND--
--GAMBIT, GET IT OFF ME!
A PLEASURE, CHERE.
EYES FLASH.
AND A PLAYING CARD BEGINS TO GLOW--
--CHARGED FULL OF ENERGY IN LESS TIME THAN IT TAKES TO TELL.
THE SUDDEN SCARE DOESN'T SHAKE STORM'S CONCENTRATION, AS LIAN HAD HOPED.
QUITE THE OPPOSITE, IN FACT.
BUT EVEN AS STORM'S WIND-SURGE LIFTS THE ANCIENT, DERELICT DC-6 INTO THE AIR...
PRIVATE FLIGHT, BOWSER.
GO BOTHER SOMEONE ELSE.
NO ROOM HERE FOR THE LIKES OF YOU.
ALL THE CARD'S STORED-UP FORCE FINDS INSTANT, TOTAL RELEASE...
...ON IMPACT WITH ITS TARGET.
SO, AS THE PLANE SOARS ONE WAY...
...HE, POOR THING, GOES BOUNCING THE OTHER.

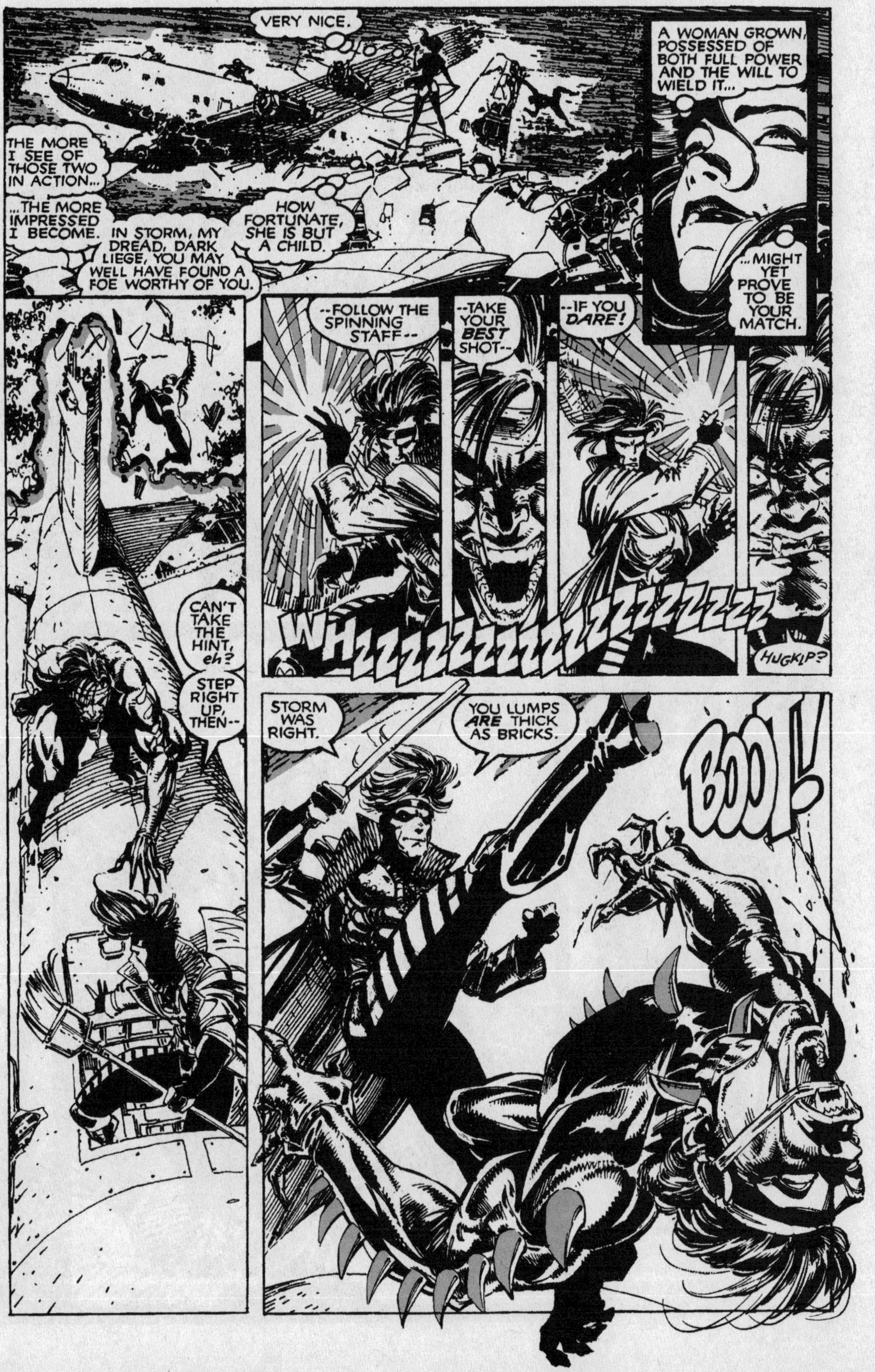
VERY NICE.
THE MORE I SEE OF THOSE TWO IN ACTION...
...THE MORE IMPRESSED I BECOME.
IN STORM, MY DREAD, DARK LIEGE, YOU MAY WELL HAVE FOUND A FOE WORTHY OF YOU.
HOW FORTUNATE, SHE IS BUT A CHILD.
A WOMAN GROWN, POSSESSED OF BOTH FULL POWER AND THE WILL TO WIELD IT...
...MIGHT YET PROVE TO BE YOUR MATCH.
CAN'T TAKE THE HINT, eh?
STEP RIGHT UP, THEN--
--FOLLOW THE SPINNING STAFF--
--TAKE YOUR BEST SHOT--
--IF YOU DARE!
WHZZZZZZZZZZZZZZZZZZZZZ
HUGKLP?
STORM WAS RIGHT.
YOU LUMPS ARE THICK AS BRICKS.
BOOT!

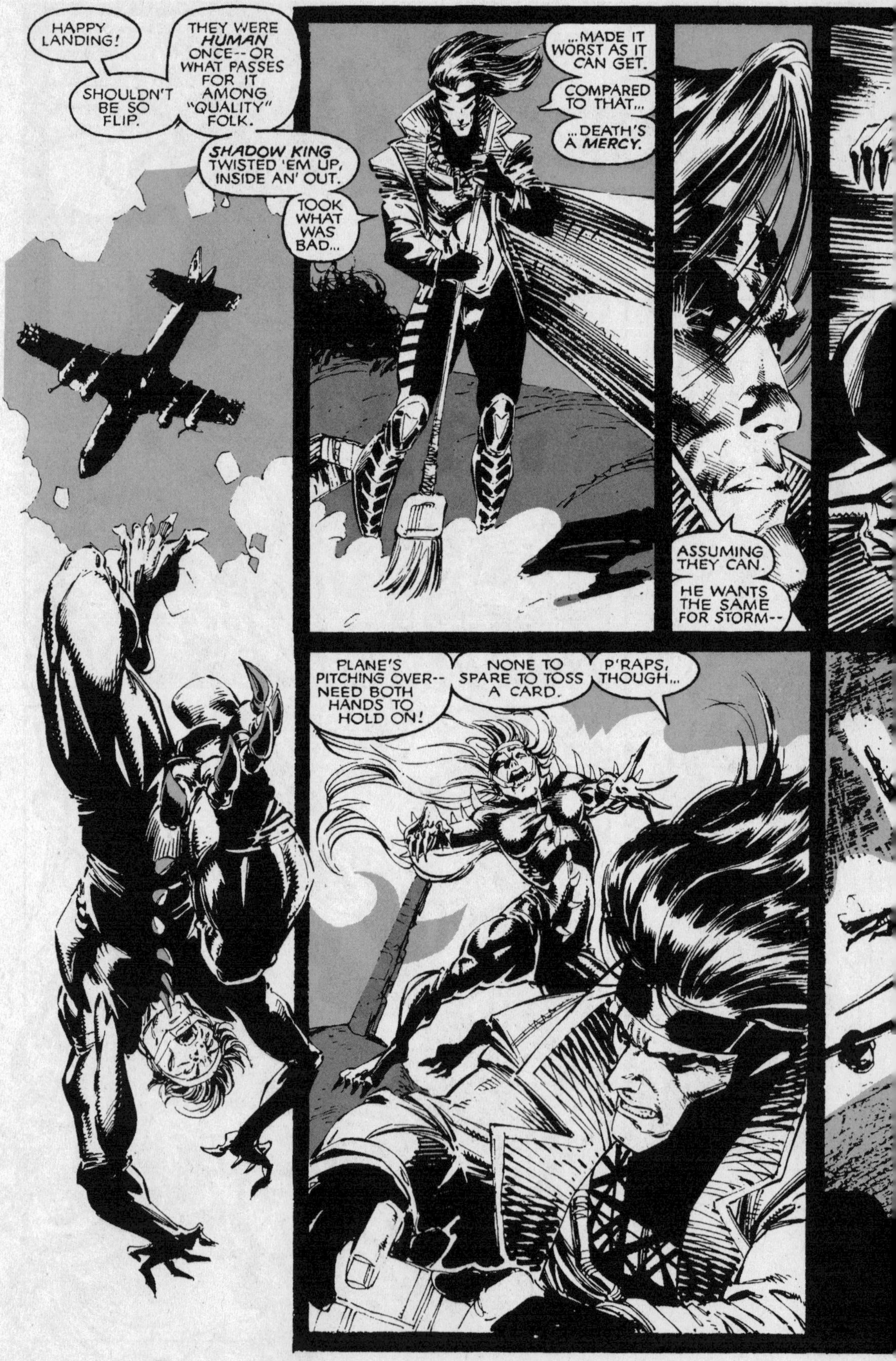
HAPPY LANDING!
SHOULDN'T BE SO FLIP.
THEY WERE HUMAN ONCE--OR WHAT PASSES FOR IT AMONG "QUALITY" FOLK.
SHADOW KING TWISTED 'EM UP, INSIDE AN' OUT.
TOOK WHAT WAS BAD...
...MADE IT WORST AS IT CAN GET.
COMPARED TO THAT...
...DEATH'S A MERCY.
ASSUMING THEY CAN.
HE WANTS THE SAME FOR STORM--
PLANE'S PITCHING OVER--NEED BOTH HANDS TO HOLD ON!
NONE TO SPARE TO TOSS A CARD.
P'RAPS, THOUGH...

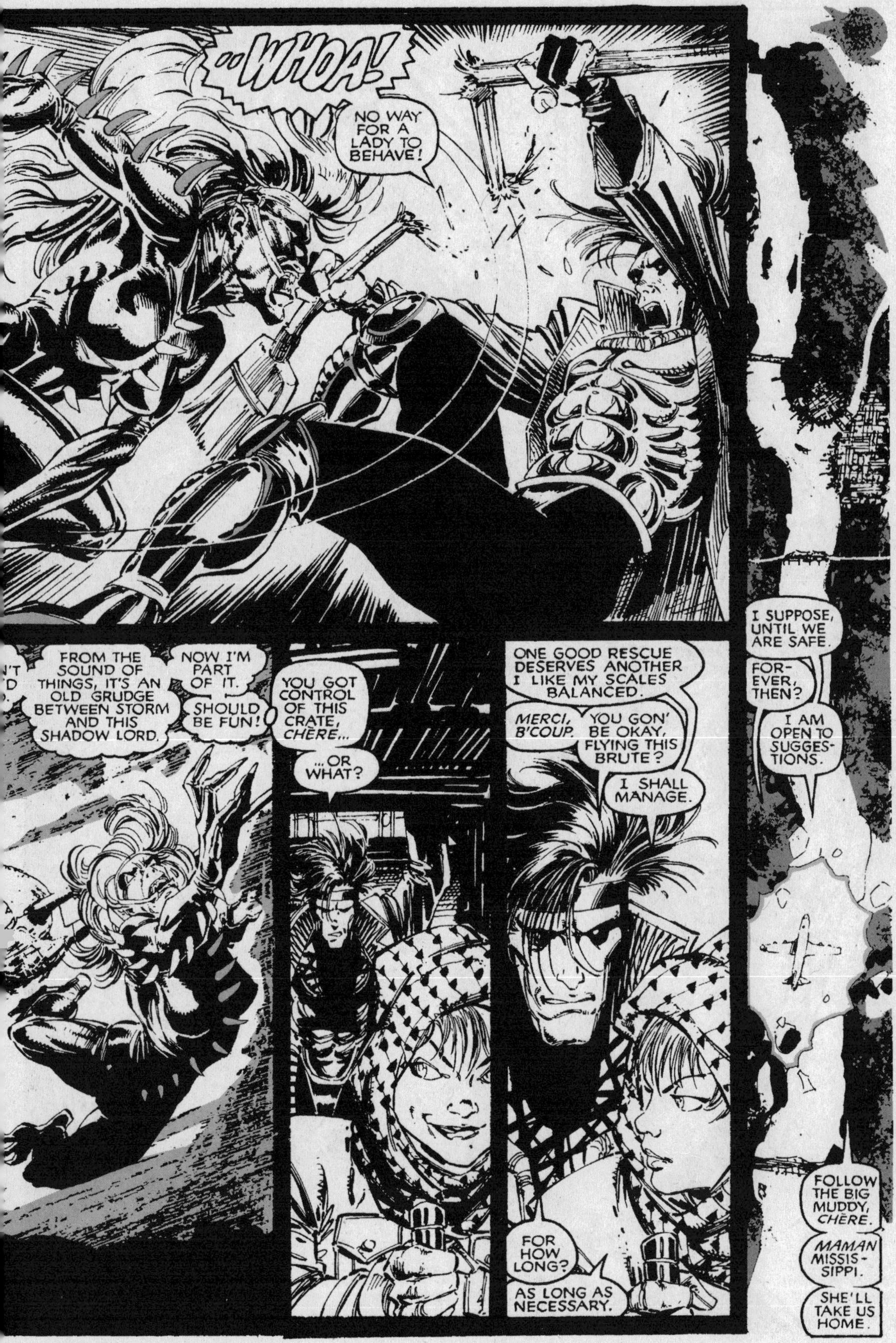
..WHOA!
NO WAY FOR A LADY TO BEHAVE!
FROM THE SOUND OF THINGS, IT'S AN OLD GRUDGE BETWEEN STORM AND THIS SHADOW LORD.
NOW I'M PART OF IT.
SHOULD BE FUN!
YOU GOT CONTROL OF THIS CRATE, CHÈRE...
...OR WHAT?
ONE GOOD RESCUE DESERVES ANOTHER I LIKE MY SCALES BALANCED.
MERCI, B'COUP.
YOU GON' BE OKAY, FLYING THIS BRUTE?
I SHALL MANAGE.
FOR HOW LONG?
AS LONG AS NECESSARY.
I SUPPOSE, UNTIL WE ARE SAFE.
FOR-EVER, THEN?
I AM OPEN TO SUGGES-TIONS.
FOLLOW THE BIG MUDDY, CHÈRE.
MAMAN MISSIS-SIPPI.
SHE'LL TAKE US HOME.

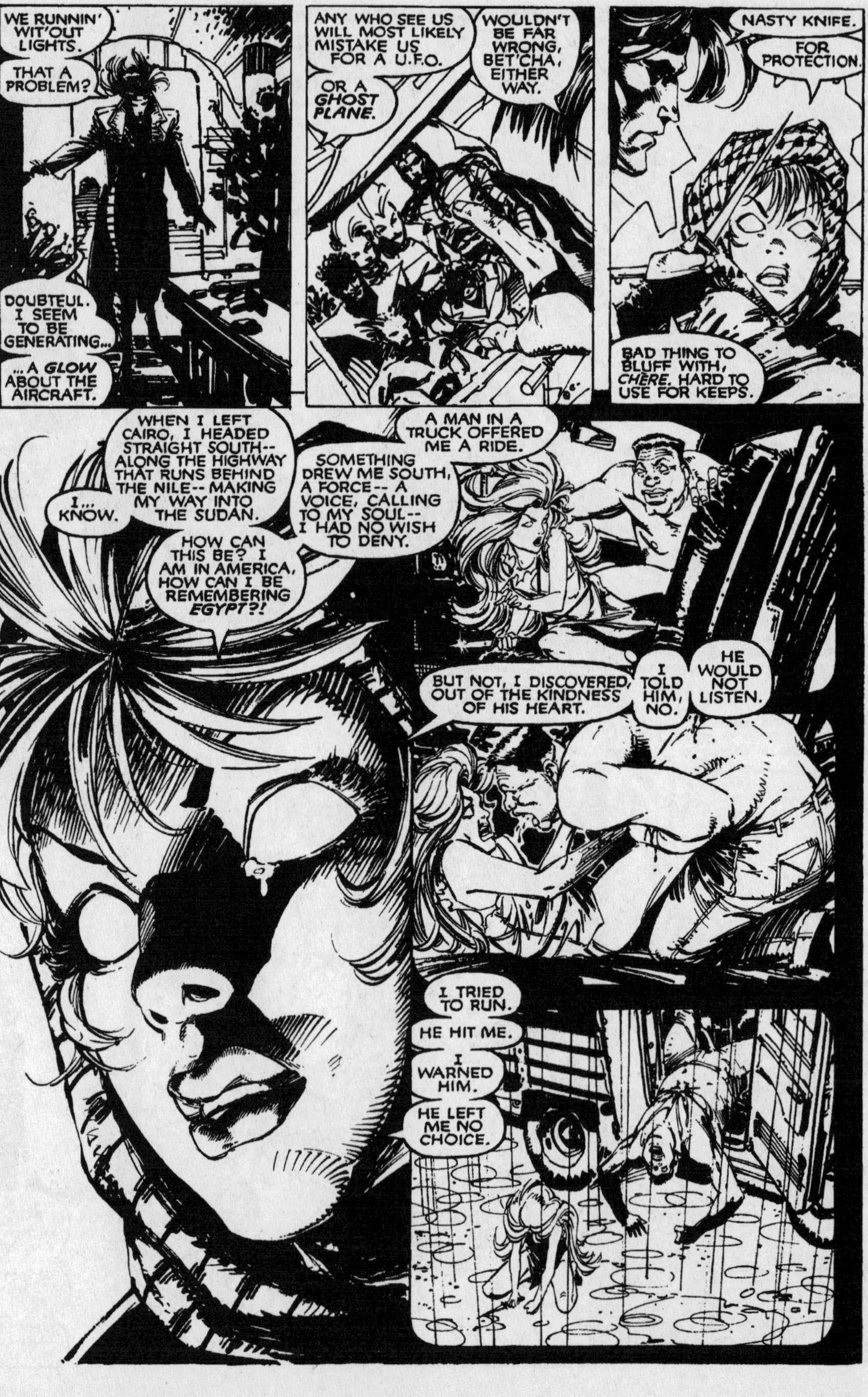
WE RUNNIN' WIT'OUT LIGHTS.
THAT A PROBLEM?
DOUBTFUL. I SEEM TO BE GENERATING...
...A GLOW ABOUT THE AIRCRAFT.
ANY WHO SEE US WILL MOST LIKELY MISTAKE US FOR A U.F.O.
OR A GHOST PLANE.
WOULDN'T BE FAR WRONG, BET'CHA, EITHER WAY.
NASTY KNIFE.
FOR PROTECTION.
BAD THING TO BLUFF WITH, CHÈRE. HARD TO USE FOR KEEPS.
I... KNOW.
WHEN I LEFT CAIRO, I HEADED STRAIGHT SOUTH-- ALONG THE HIGHWAY THAT RUNS BEHIND THE NILE-- MAKING MY WAY INTO THE SUDAN.
HOW CAN THIS BE? I AM IN AMERICA, HOW CAN I BE REMEMBERING EGYPT?!
SOMETHING DREW ME SOUTH, A FORCE-- A VOICE, CALLING TO MY SOUL-- I HAD NO WISH TO DENY.
A MAN IN A TRUCK OFFERED ME A RIDE.
BUT NOT, I DISCOVERED, OUT OF THE KINDNESS OF HIS HEART.
I TOLD HIM, NO.
HE WOULD NOT LISTEN.
I TRIED TO RUN.
HE HIT ME.
I WARNED HIM.
HE LEFT ME NO CHOICE.

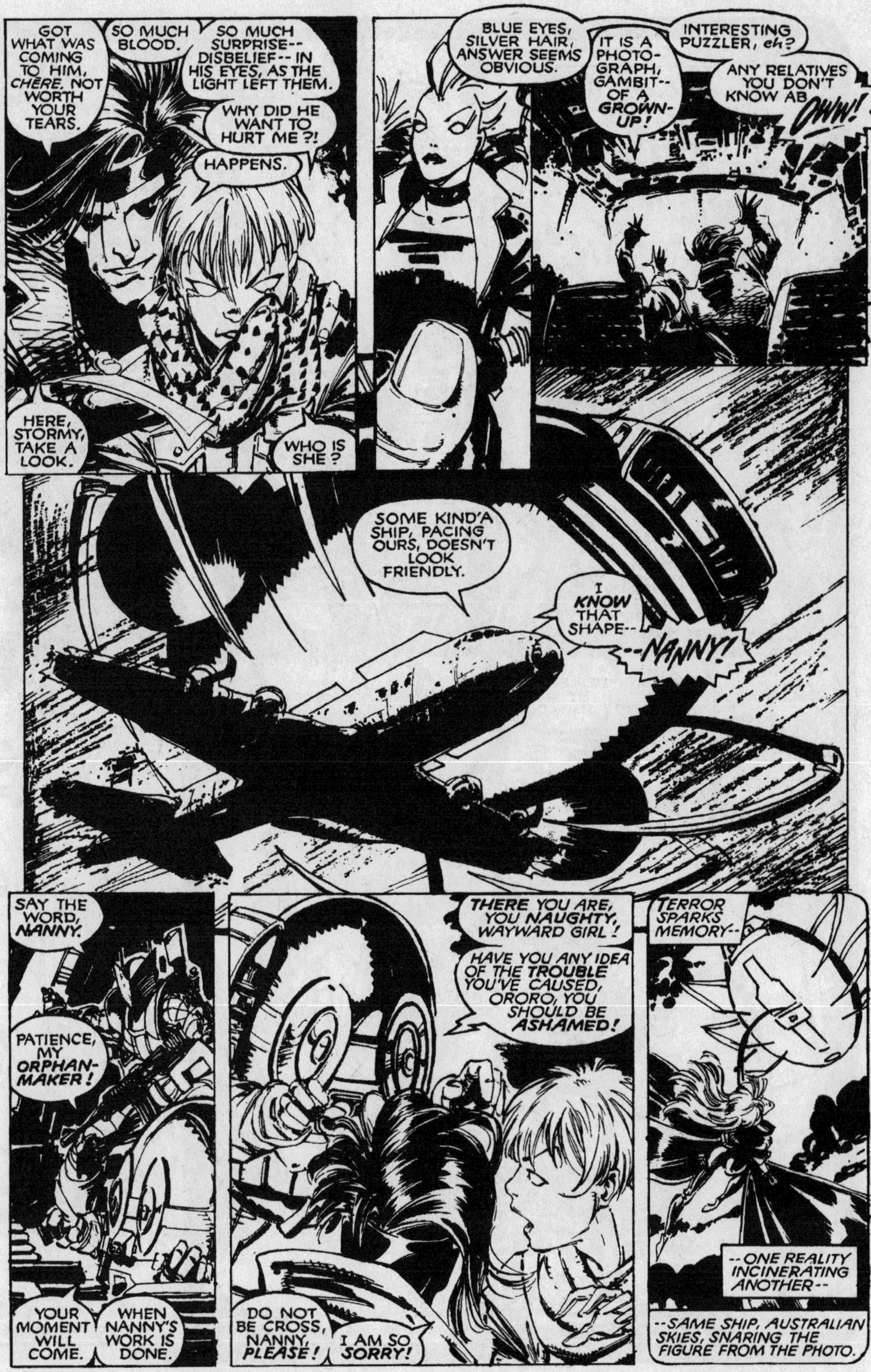
GOT WHAT WAS COMING TO HIM, CHÈRE. NOT WORTH YOUR TEARS.
SO MUCH BLOOD.
SO MUCH SURPRISE-- DISBELIEF-- IN HIS EYES, AS THE LIGHT LEFT THEM.
WHY DID HE WANT TO HURT ME ?!
HAPPENS.
HERE, STORMY, TAKE A LOOK.
WHO IS SHE ?
BLUE EYES, SILVER HAIR, ANSWER SEEMS OBVIOUS.
IT IS A PHOTO-GRAPH, GAMBIT-- OF A GROWN-UP!
INTERESTING PUZZLER, eh?
ANY RELATIVES YOU DON'T KNOW AB
OWW!
SOME KIND'A SHIP, PACING OURS, DOESN'T LOOK FRIENDLY.
I KNOW THAT SHAPE--
--NANNY!
SAY THE WORD, NANNY.
PATIENCE, MY ORPHAN-MAKER!
YOUR MOMENT WILL COME.
WHEN NANNY'S WORK IS DONE.
THERE YOU ARE, YOU NAUGHTY, WAYWARD GIRL!
HAVE YOU ANY IDEA OF THE TROUBLE YOU'VE CAUSED, ORORO, YOU SHOULD BE ASHAMED!
DO NOT BE CROSS, NANNY, PLEASE!
I AM SO SORRY!
TERROR SPARKS MEMORY--
--ONE REALITY INCINERATING ANOTHER--
--SAME SHIP, AUSTRALIAN SKIES, SNARING THE FIGURE FROM THE PHOTO.

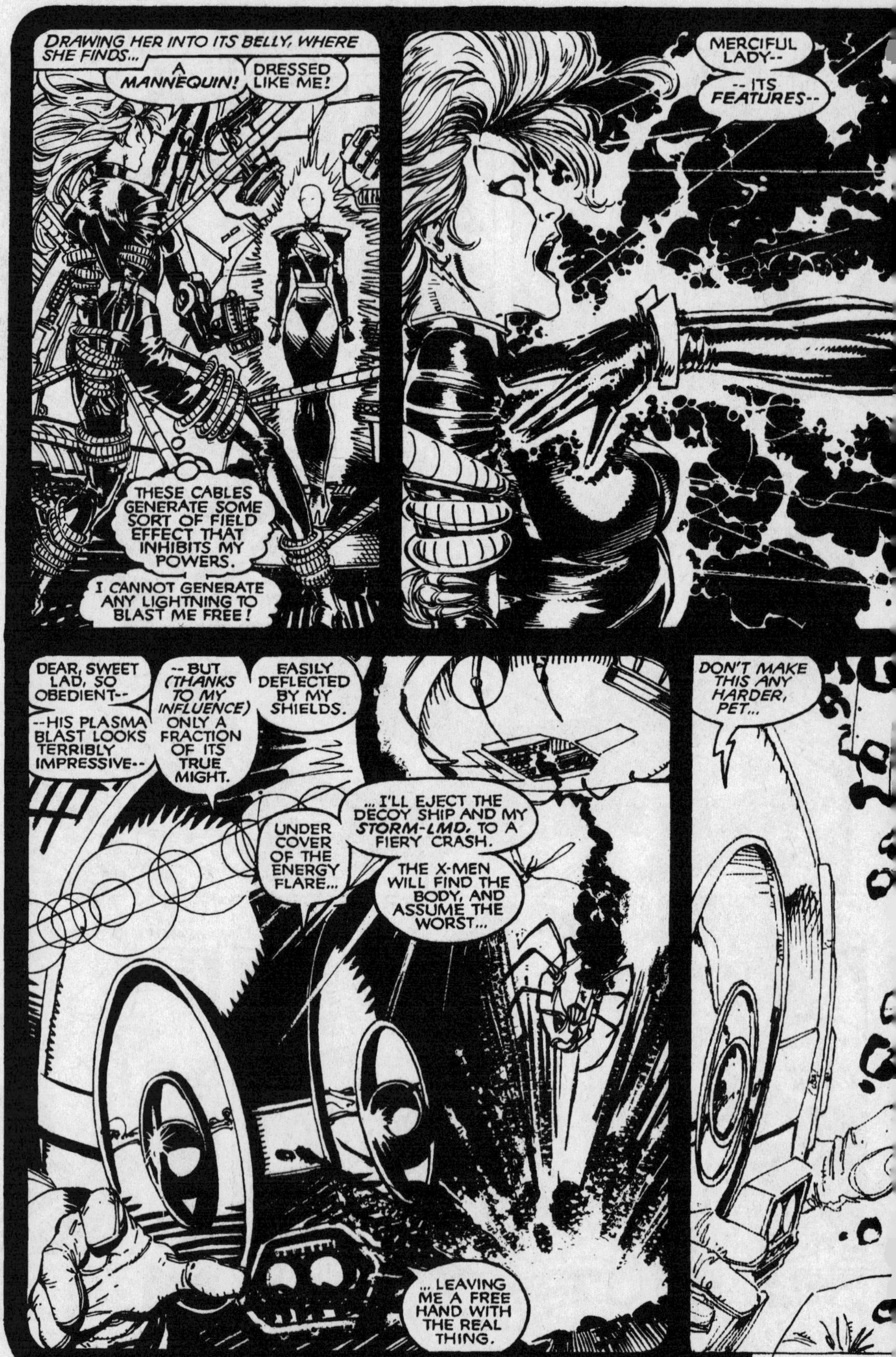
DRAWING HER INTO ITS BELLY, WHERE SHE FINDS...
A MANNEQUIN!
DRESSED LIKE ME!
THESE CABLES GENERATE SOME SORT OF FIELD EFFECT THAT INHIBITS MY POWERS.
I CANNOT GENERATE ANY LIGHTNING TO BLAST ME FREE!
MERCIFUL LADY--
-- ITS FEATURES--
DEAR, SWEET LAD, SO OBEDIENT--
--HIS PLASMA BLAST LOOKS TERRIBLY IMPRESSIVE--
-- BUT (THANKS TO MY INFLUENCE) ONLY A FRACTION OF ITS TRUE MIGHT.
EASILY DEFLECTED BY MY SHIELDS.
UNDER COVER OF THE ENERGY FLARE...
...I'LL EJECT THE DECOY SHIP AND MY STORM-LMD, TO A FIERY CRASH.
THE X-MEN WILL FIND THE BODY, AND ASSUME THE WORST...
...LEAVING ME A FREE HAND WITH THE REAL THING.
DON'T MAKE THIS ANY HARDER, PET...

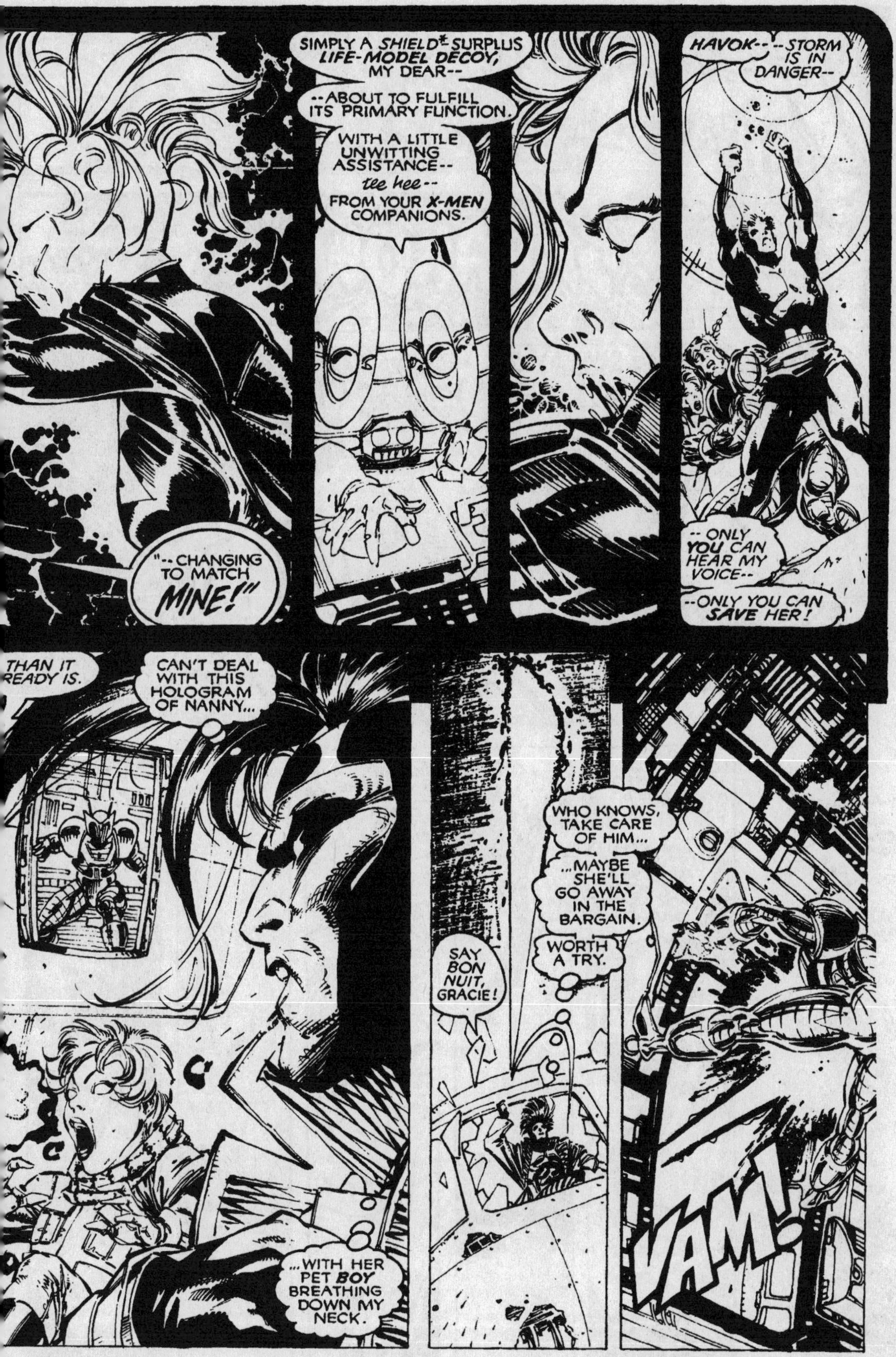
"--CHANGING TO MATCH MINE!"
SIMPLY A SHIELD® SURPLUS LIFE-MODEL DECOY, MY DEAR--
--ABOUT TO FULFILL ITS PRIMARY FUNCTION.
WITH A LITTLE UNWITTING ASSISTANCE-- tee hee-- FROM YOUR X-MEN COMPANIONS.
HAVOK-- --STORM IS IN DANGER--
--ONLY YOU CAN HEAR MY VOICE--
--ONLY YOU CAN SAVE HER!
THAN IT READY IS.
CAN'T DEAL WITH THIS HOLOGRAM OF NANNY...
...WITH HER PET BOY BREATHING DOWN MY NECK.
SAY BON NUIT, GRACIE!
WHO KNOWS, TAKE CARE OF HIM...
...MAYBE SHE'LL GO AWAY IN THE BARGAIN.
WORTH A TRY.
VAM!

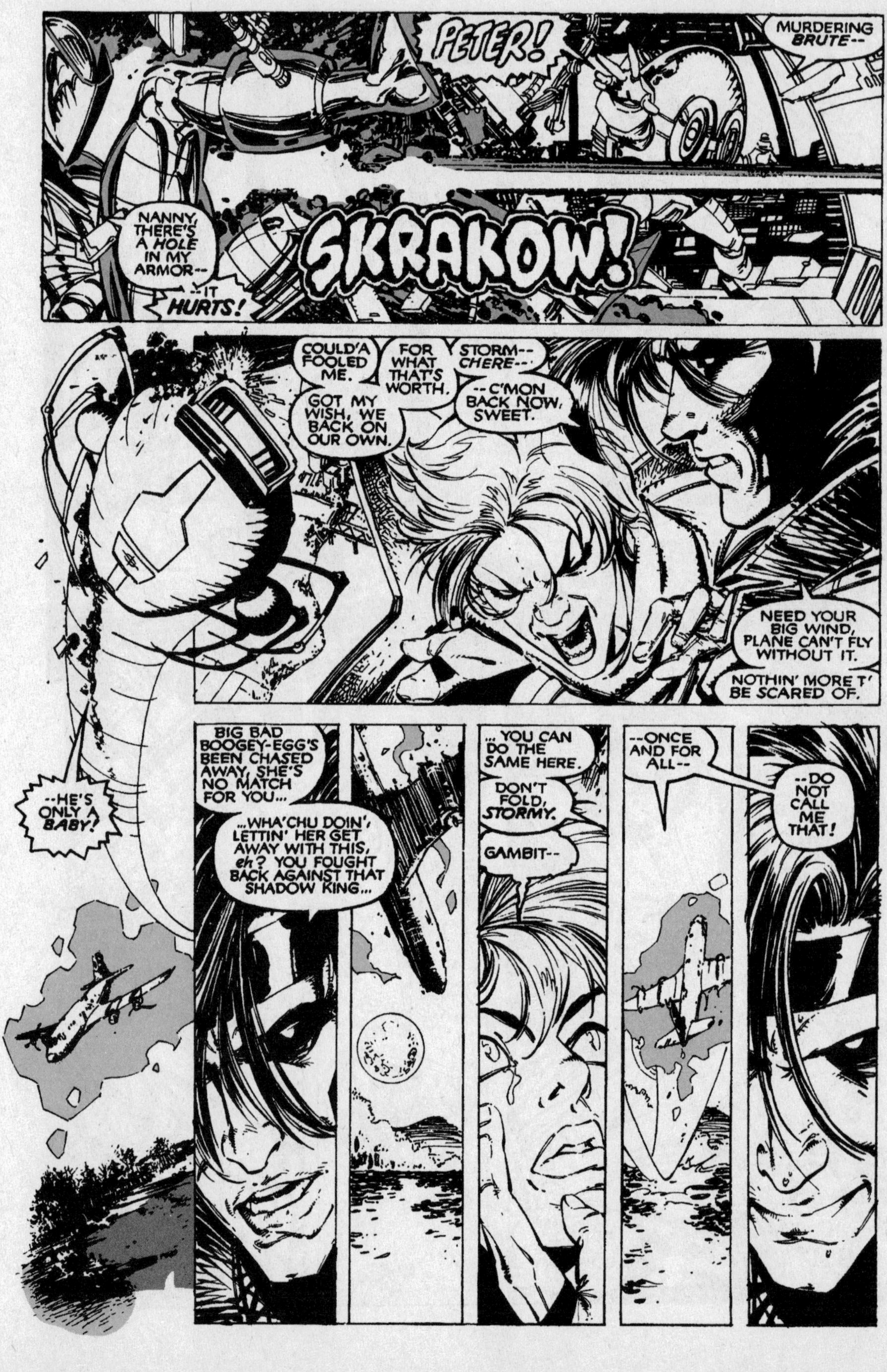
PETER!
MURDERING BRUTE--
NANNY, THERE'S A HOLE IN MY ARMOR--
--IT HURTS!
SKRAKOW!
COULD'A FOOLED ME.
GOT MY WISH, WE BACK ON OUR OWN.
FOR WHAT THAT'S WORTH.
STORM-- CHERE--
--C'MON BACK NOW, SWEET.
NEED YOUR BIG WIND, PLANE CAN'T FLY WITHOUT IT.
NOTHIN' MORE T' BE SCARED OF.
--HE'S ONLY A BABY!
BIG BAD BOOGEY-EGG'S BEEN CHASED AWAY, SHE'S NO MATCH FOR YOU...
...WHA'CHU DOIN', LETTIN' HER GET AWAY WITH THIS, eh? YOU FOUGHT BACK AGAINST THAT SHADOW KING...
...YOU CAN DO THE SAME HERE.
DON'T FOLD, STORMY.
GAMBIT--
--ONCE AND FOR ALL--
--DO NOT CALL ME THAT!

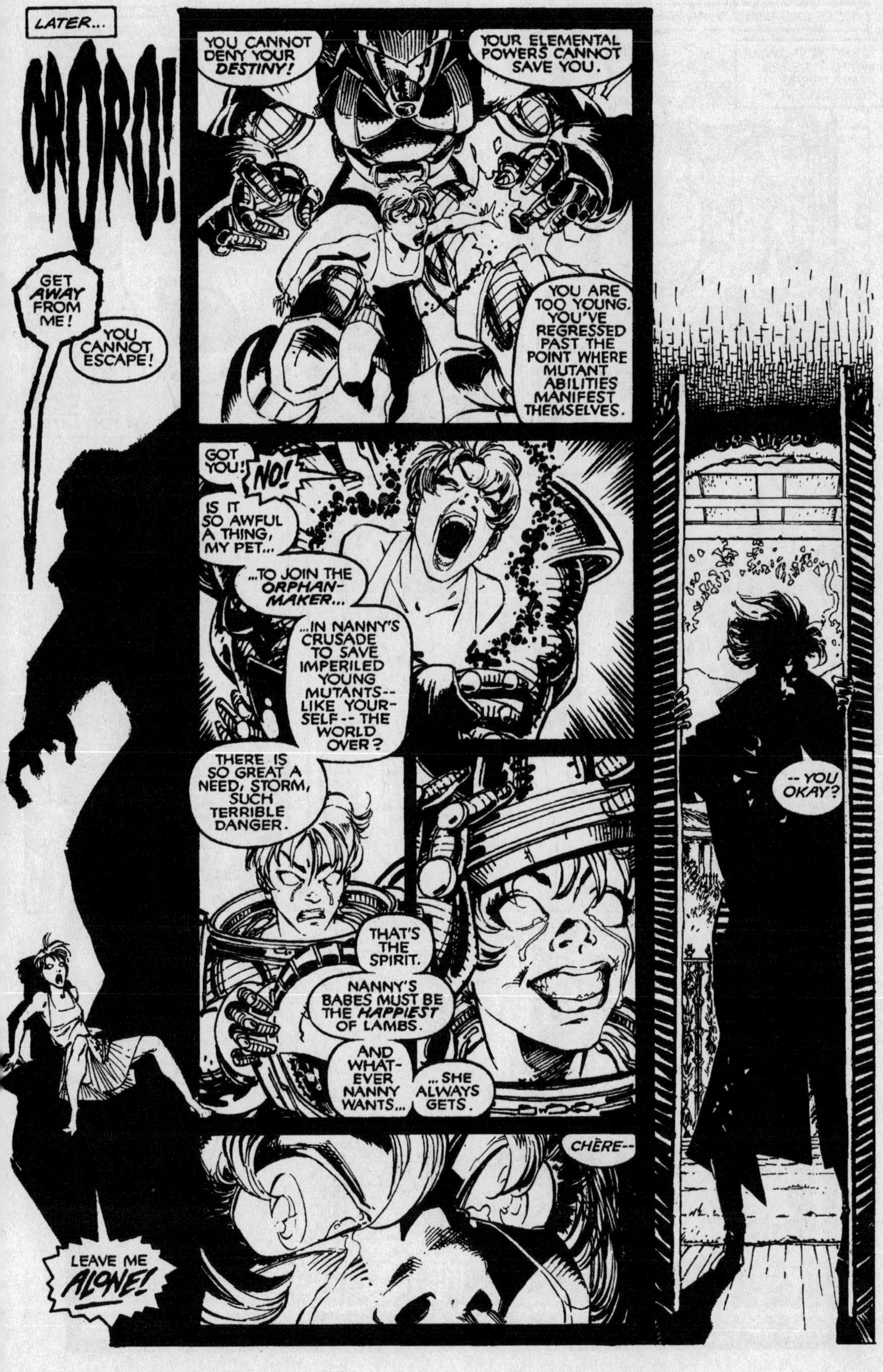
LATER...
ORORO!
YOU CANNOT DENY YOUR DESTINY!
YOUR ELEMENTAL POWERS CANNOT SAVE YOU.
GET AWAY FROM ME!
YOU CANNOT ESCAPE!
YOU ARE TOO YOUNG. YOU'VE REGRESSED PAST THE POINT WHERE MUTANT ABILITIES MANIFEST THEMSELVES.
GOT YOU!
NO!
IS IT SO AWFUL A THING, MY PET...
...TO JOIN THE ORPHAN-MAKER...
...IN NANNY'S CRUSADE TO SAVE IMPERILED YOUNG MUTANTS-- LIKE YOURSELF -- THE WORLD OVER?
THERE IS SO GREAT A NEED, STORM, SUCH TERRIBLE DANGER.
THAT'S THE SPIRIT.
NANNY'S BABES MUST BE THE HAPPIEST OF LAMBS.
AND WHATEVER NANNY WANTS...
...SHE ALWAYS GETS.
CHÈRE--
--YOU OKAY?
LEAVE ME ALONE!

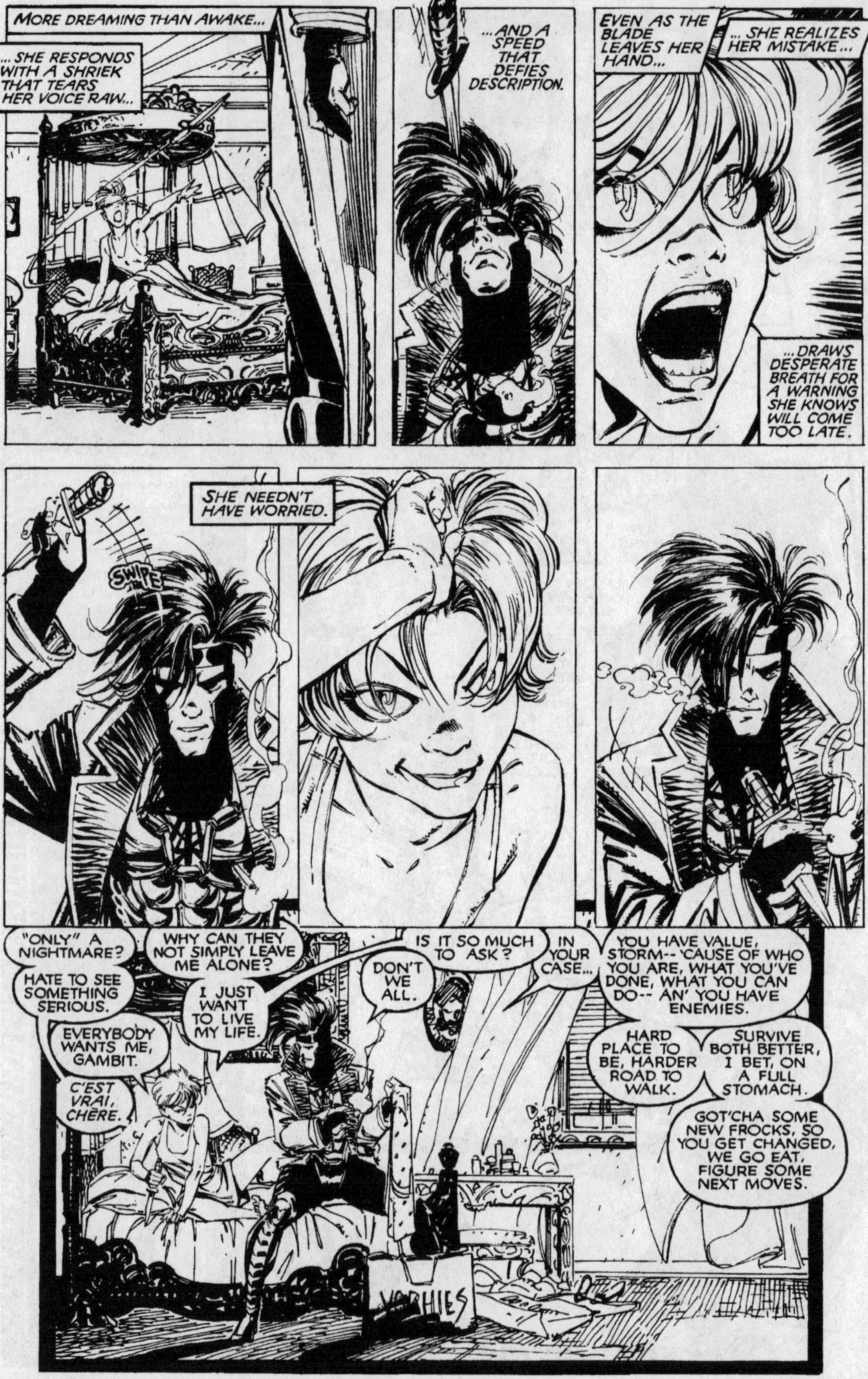
MORE DREAMING THAN AWAKE...
...SHE RESPONDS WITH A SHRIEK THAT TEARS HER VOICE RAW...
...AND A SPEED THAT DEFIES DESCRIPTION.
EVEN AS THE BLADE LEAVES HER HAND...
...SHE REALIZES HER MISTAKE...
...DRAWS DESPERATE BREATH FOR A WARNING SHE KNOWS WILL COME TOO LATE.
SHE NEEDN'T HAVE WORRIED.
SWIPE
"ONLY" A NIGHTMARE?
HATE TO SEE SOMETHING SERIOUS.
WHY CAN THEY NOT SIMPLY LEAVE ME ALONE?
I JUST WANT TO LIVE MY LIFE.
EVERYBODY WANTS ME, GAMBIT.
C'EST VRAI, CHÈRE.
IS IT SO MUCH TO ASK?
DON'T WE ALL.
IN YOUR CASE...
YOU HAVE VALUE, STORM-- 'CAUSE OF WHO YOU ARE, WHAT YOU'VE DONE, WHAT YOU CAN DO-- AN' YOU HAVE ENEMIES.
HARD PLACE TO BE, HARDER ROAD TO WALK.
SURVIVE BOTH BETTER, I BET, ON A FULL STOMACH.
GOT'CHA SOME NEW FROCKS, SO YOU GET CHANGED, WE GO EAT, FIGURE SOME NEXT MOVES.
VORHIES

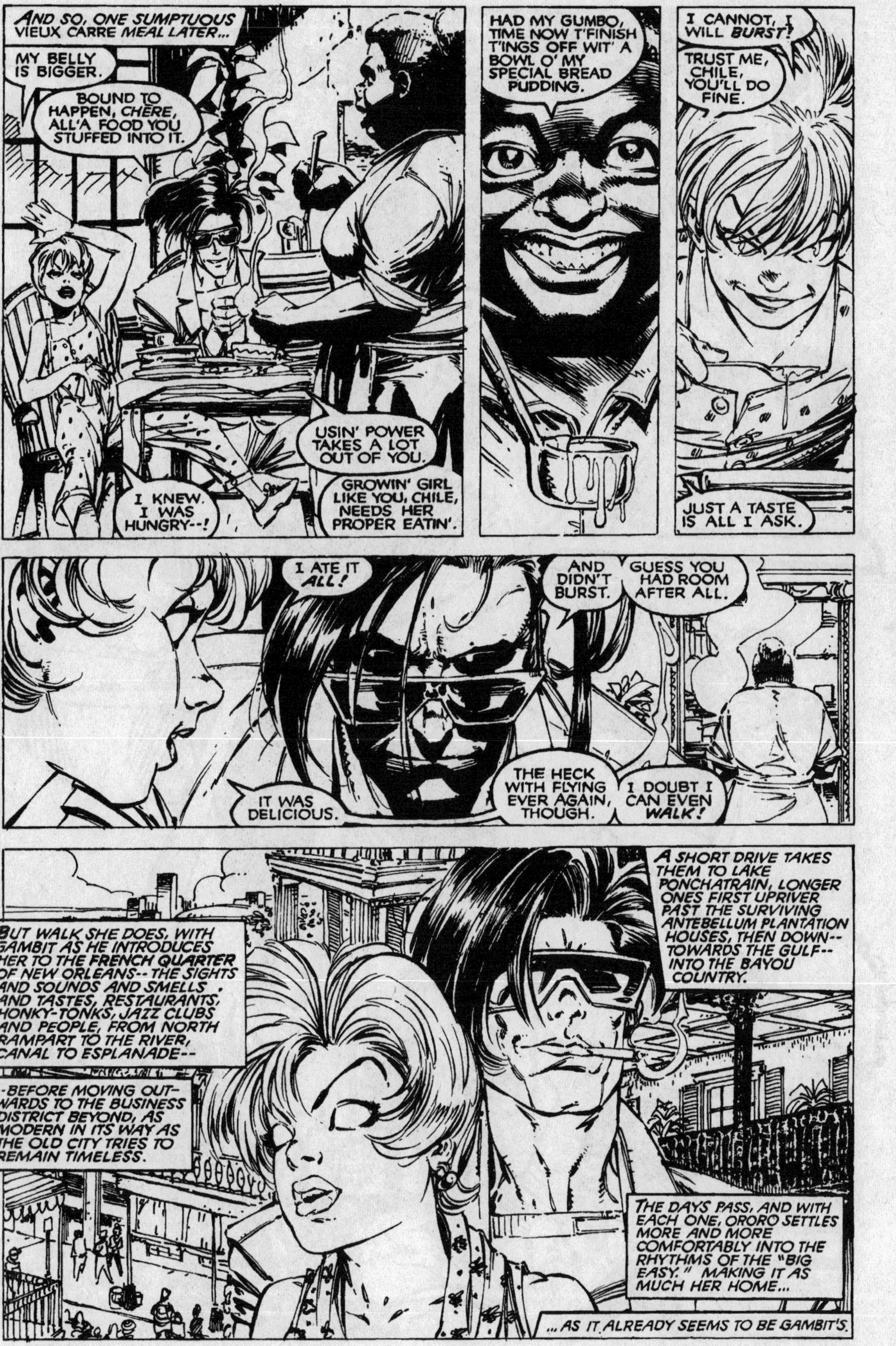
AND SO, ONE SUMPTUOUS VIEUX CARRE MEAL LATER...
MY BELLY IS BIGGER.
BOUND TO HAPPEN, CHÈRE, ALL'A FOOD YOU STUFFED INTO IT.
I KNEW. I WAS HUNGRY--!
USIN' POWER TAKES A LOT OUT OF YOU.
GROWIN' GIRL LIKE YOU, CHILE, NEEDS HER PROPER EATIN'.
HAD MY GUMBO, TIME NOW T'FINISH T'INGS OFF WIT' A BOWL O' MY SPECIAL BREAD PUDDING.
I CANNOT, I WILL BURST!
TRUST ME, CHILE, YOU'LL DO FINE.
JUST A TASTE IS ALL I ASK.
I ATE IT ALL!
IT WAS DELICIOUS.
AND DIDN'T BURST.
GUESS YOU HAD ROOM AFTER ALL.
THE HECK WITH FLYING EVER AGAIN, THOUGH.
I DOUBT I CAN EVEN WALK!
BUT WALK SHE DOES, WITH GAMBIT AS HE INTRODUCES HER TO THE FRENCH QUARTER OF NEW ORLEANS-- THE SIGHTS AND SOUNDS AND SMELLS AND TASTES, RESTAURANTS, HONKY-TONKS, JAZZ CLUBS AND PEOPLE, FROM NORTH RAMPART TO THE RIVER, CANAL TO ESPLANADE--
--BEFORE MOVING OUTWARDS TO THE BUSINESS DISTRICT BEYOND, AS MODERN IN ITS WAY AS THE OLD CITY TRIES TO REMAIN TIMELESS.
A SHORT DRIVE TAKES THEM TO LAKE PONCHATRAIN, LONGER ONES FIRST UPRIVER PAST THE SURVIVING ANTEBELLUM PLANTATION HOUSES, THEN DOWN-- TOWARDS THE GULF-- INTO THE BAYOU COUNTRY.
THE DAYS PASS, AND WITH EACH ONE, ORORO SETTLES MORE AND MORE COMFORTABLY INTO THE RHYTHMS OF THE "BIG EASY," MAKING IT AS MUCH HER HOME...
...AS IT ALREADY SEEMS TO BE GAMBIT'S.

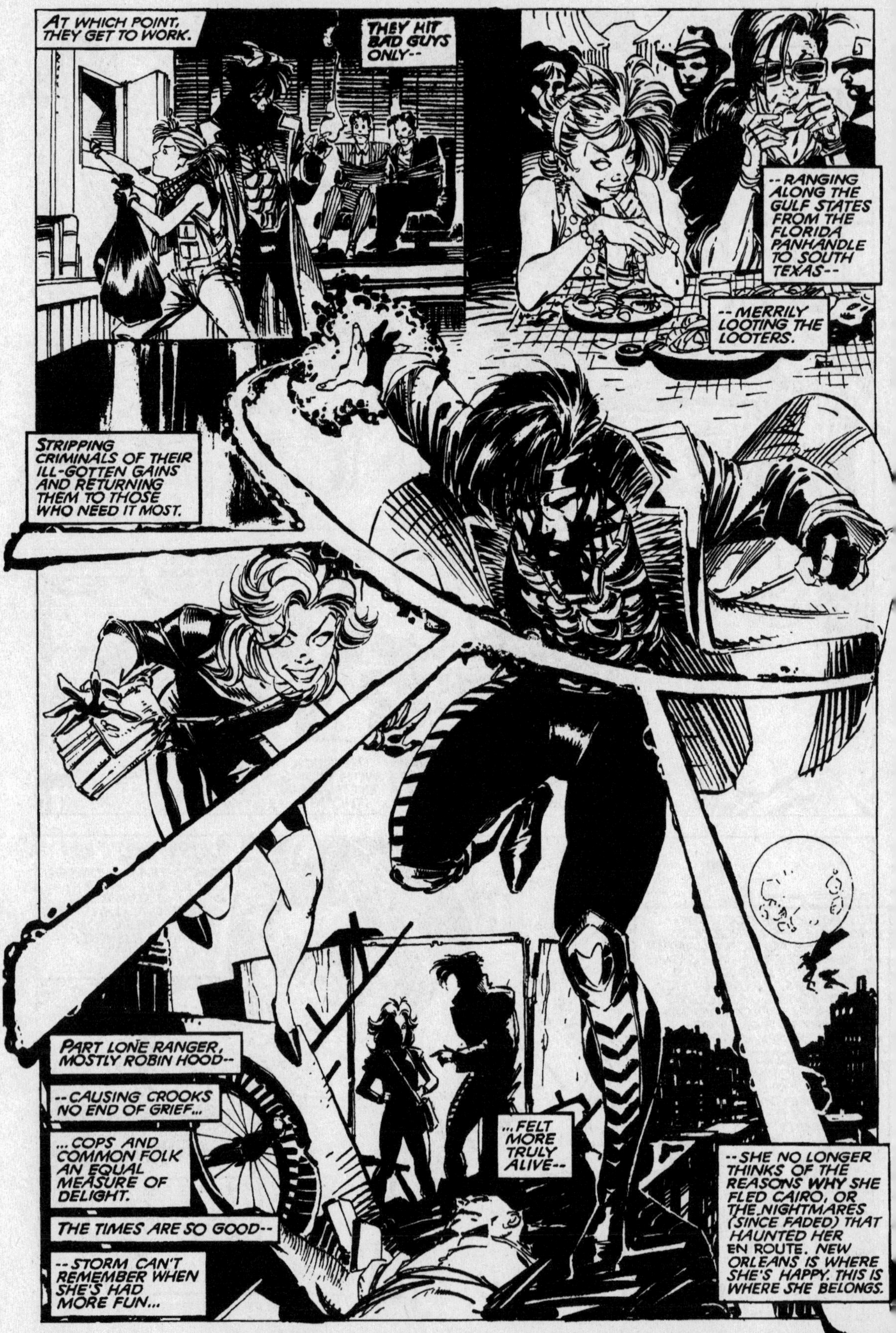
AT WHICH POINT, THEY GET TO WORK.
THEY HIT BAD GUYS ONLY--
--RANGING ALONG THE GULF STATES FROM THE FLORIDA PANHANDLE TO SOUTH TEXAS--
--MERRILY LOOTING THE LOOTERS.
STRIPPING CRIMINALS OF THEIR ILL-GOTTEN GAINS AND RETURNING THEM TO THOSE WHO NEED IT MOST.
PART LONE RANGER, MOSTLY ROBIN HOOD--
--CAUSING CROOKS NO END OF GRIEF...
...COPS AND COMMON FOLK AN EQUAL MEASURE OF DELIGHT.
THE TIMES ARE SO GOOD--
--STORM CAN'T REMEMBER WHEN SHE'S HAD MORE FUN...
...FELT MORE TRULY ALIVE--
--SHE NO LONGER THINKS OF THE REASONS WHY SHE FLED CAIRO, OR THE NIGHTMARES (SINCE FADED) THAT HAUNTED HER EN ROUTE. NEW ORLEANS IS WHERE SHE'S HAPPY. THIS IS WHERE SHE BELONGS.

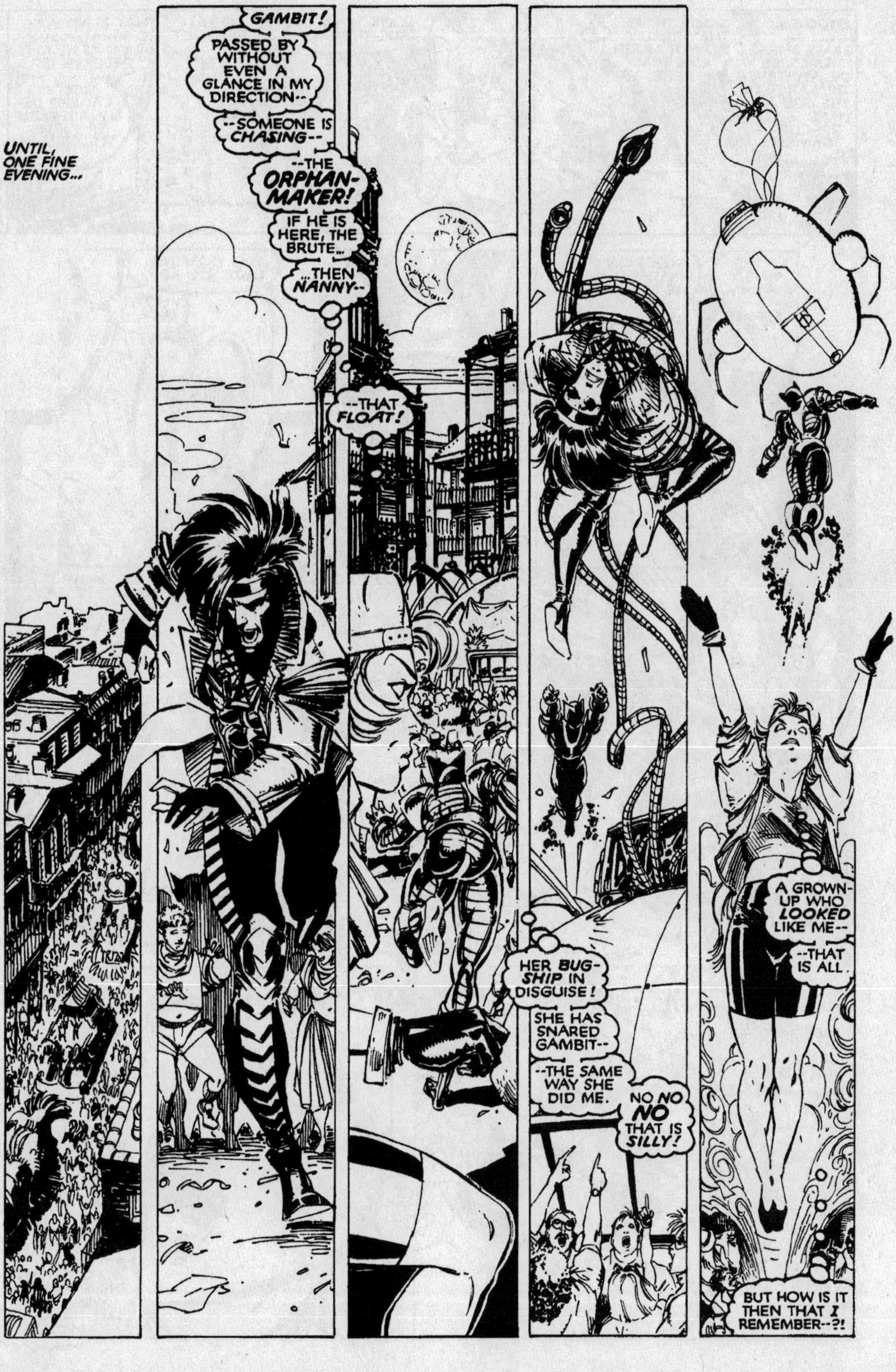
UNTIL, ONE FINE EVENING...
GAMBIT!
PASSED BY WITHOUT EVEN A GLANCE IN MY DIRECTION--
--SOMEONE IS CHASING--
--THE ORPHAN-MAKER!
IF HE IS HERE, THE BRUTE...
...THEN NANNY--
--THAT FLOAT!
HER BUG-SHIP IN DISGUISE!
SHE HAS SNARED GAMBIT--
--THE SAME WAY SHE DID ME.
NO NO NO THAT IS SILLY!
A GROWN-UP WHO LOOKED LIKE ME--
--THAT IS ALL.
BUT HOW IS IT THEN THAT I REMEMBER--?!

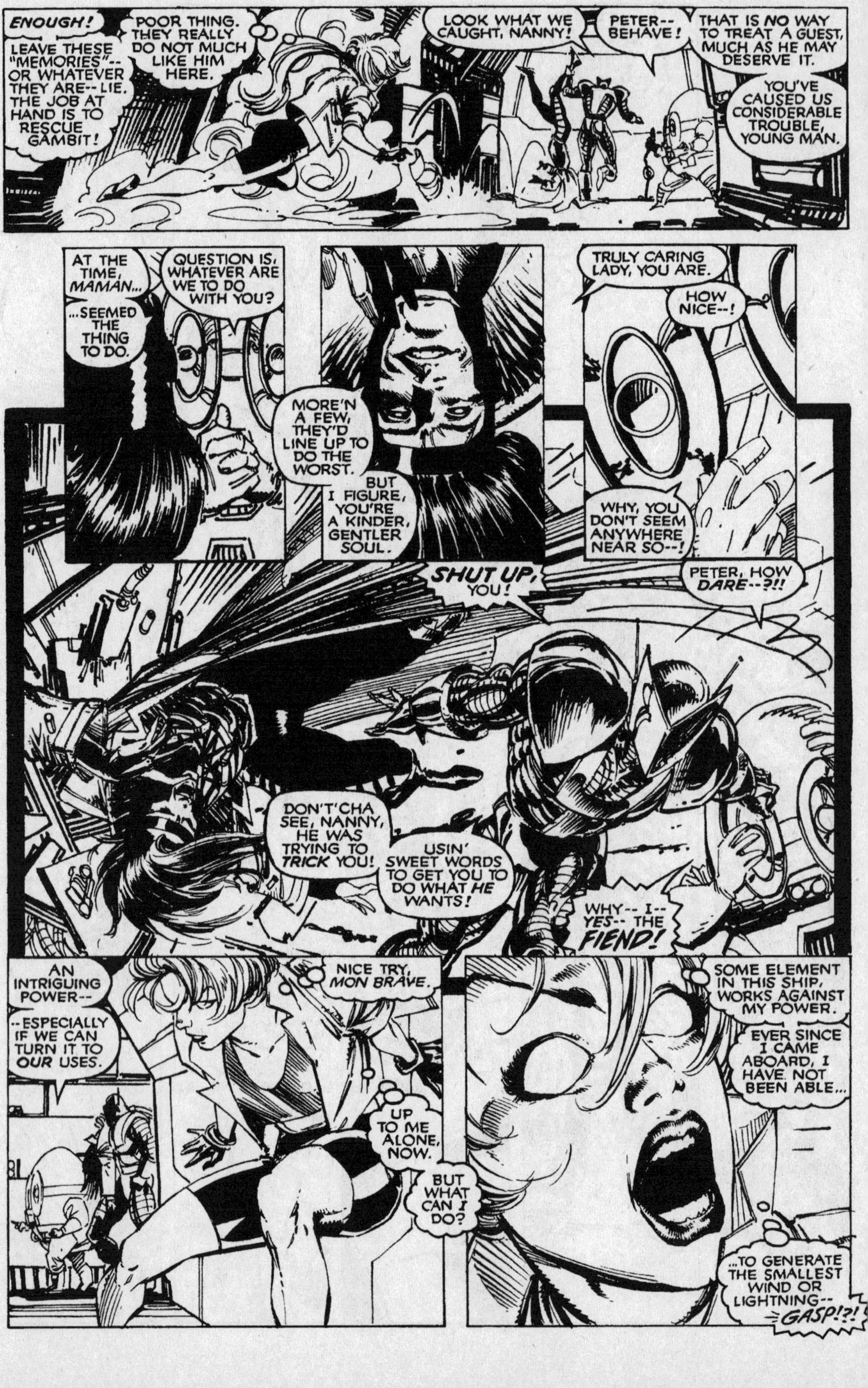
ENOUGH!
LEAVE THESE "MEMORIES"-- OR WHATEVER THEY ARE-- LIE. THE JOB AT HAND IS TO RESCUE GAMBIT!
POOR THING. THEY REALLY DO NOT MUCH LIKE HIM HERE.
LOOK WHAT WE CAUGHT, NANNY!
PETER-- BEHAVE!
THAT IS NO WAY TO TREAT A GUEST, MUCH AS HE MAY DESERVE IT.
YOU'VE CAUSED US CONSIDERABLE TROUBLE, YOUNG MAN.
AT THE TIME, MAMAN...
...SEEMED THE THING TO DO.
QUESTION IS, WHATEVER ARE WE TO DO WITH YOU?
MORE'N A FEW, THEY'D LINE UP TO DO THE WORST.
BUT I FIGURE, YOU'RE A KINDER, GENTLER SOUL.
TRULY CARING LADY, YOU ARE.
HOW NICE--!
WHY, YOU DON'T SEEM ANYWHERE NEAR SO--!
SHUT UP, YOU!
PETER, HOW DARE--?!!
DON'T'CHA SEE, NANNY, HE WAS TRYING TO TRICK YOU!
USIN' SWEET WORDS TO GET YOU TO DO WHAT HE WANTS!
WHY-- I-- YES-- THE FIEND!
AN INTRIGUING POWER--
--ESPECIALLY IF WE CAN TURN IT TO OUR USES.
NICE TRY, MON BRAVE.
UP TO ME ALONE, NOW.
BUT WHAT CAN I DO?
SOME ELEMENT IN THIS SHIP, WORKS AGAINST MY POWER.
EVER SINCE I CAME ABOARD, I HAVE NOT BEEN ABLE...
...TO GENERATE THE SMALLEST WIND OR LIGHTNING--
GASP!?!

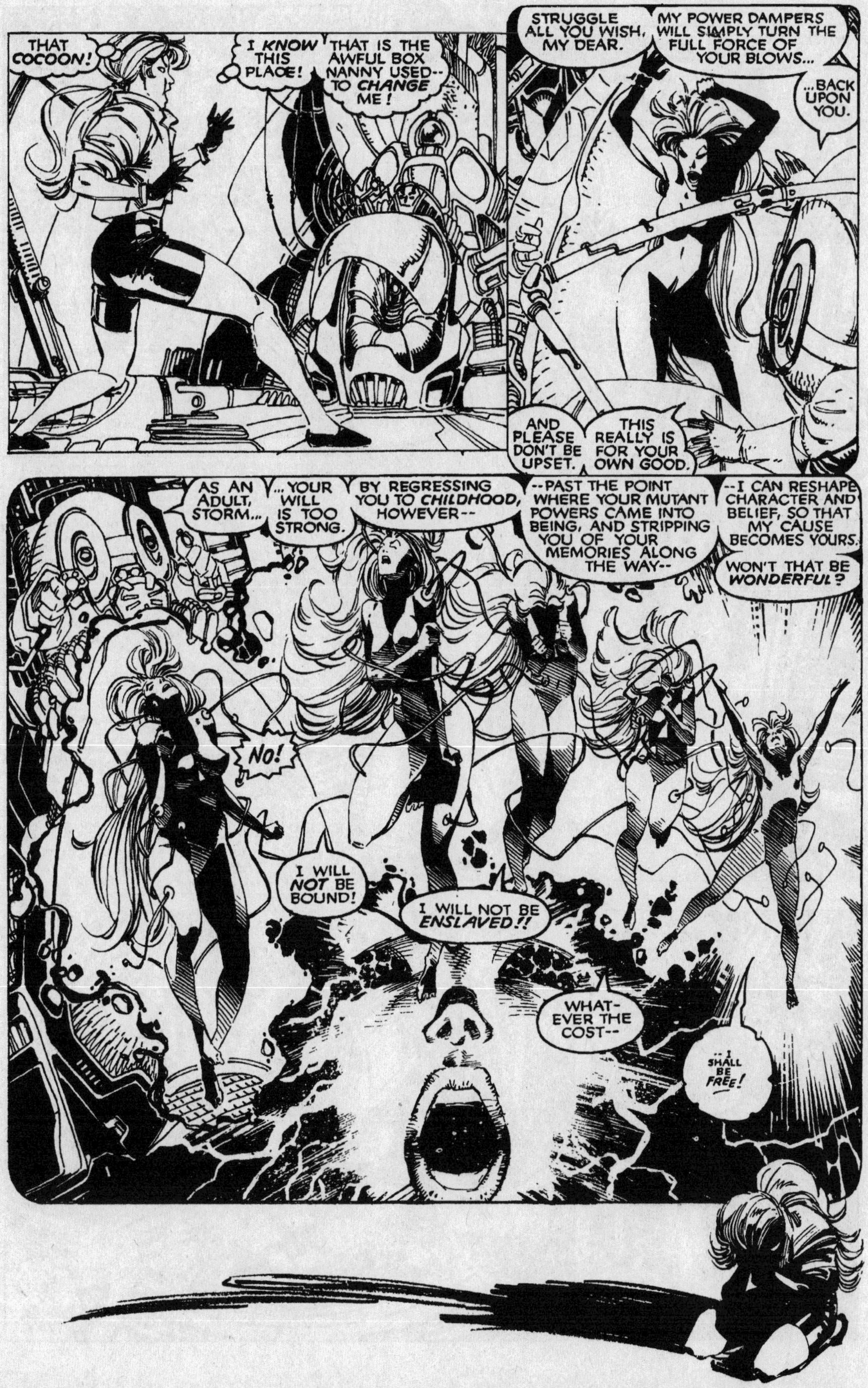
THAT COCOON!
I KNOW THIS PLACE!
THAT IS THE AWFUL BOX NANNY USED-- TO CHANGE ME!
STRUGGLE ALL YOU WISH, MY DEAR.
MY POWER DAMPERS WILL SIMPLY TURN THE FULL FORCE OF YOUR BLOWS...
...BACK UPON YOU.
AND PLEASE DON'T BE UPSET.
THIS REALLY IS FOR YOUR OWN GOOD.
AS AN ADULT, STORM...
...YOUR WILL IS TOO STRONG.
BY REGRESSING YOU TO CHILDHOOD, HOWEVER--
--PAST THE POINT WHERE YOUR MUTANT POWERS CAME INTO BEING, AND STRIPPING YOU OF YOUR MEMORIES ALONG THE WAY--
--I CAN RESHAPE CHARACTER AND BELIEF, SO THAT MY CAUSE BECOMES YOURS.
WON'T THAT BE WONDERFUL?
NO!
I WILL NOT BE BOUND!
I WILL NOT BE ENSLAVED!!
WHAT-EVER THE COST--
--I SHALL BE FREE!

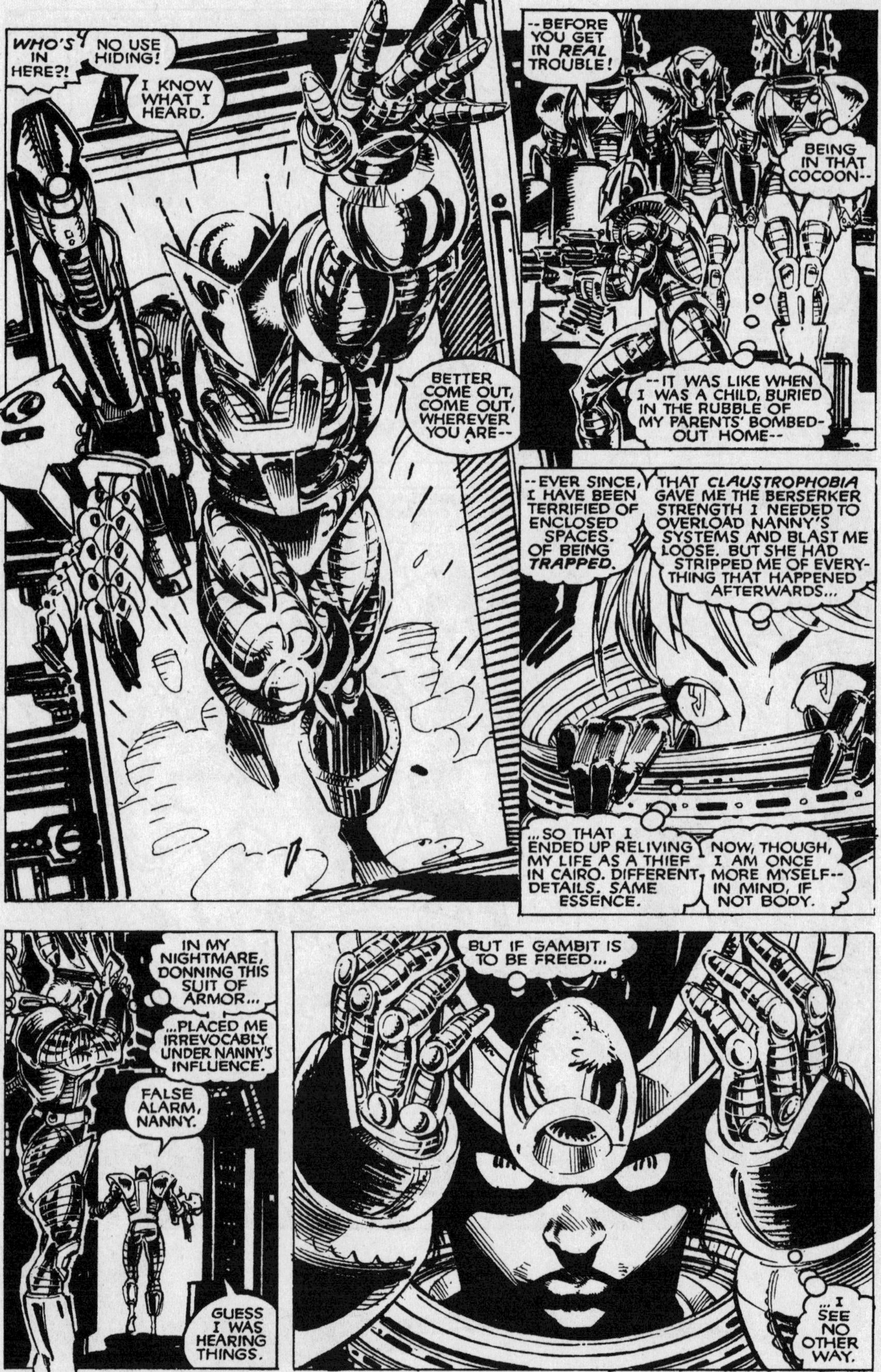
WHO'S IN HERE?!
NO USE HIDING!
I KNOW WHAT I HEARD.
BETTER COME OUT, COME OUT, WHEREVER YOU ARE--
--BEFORE YOU GET IN REAL TROUBLE!
BEING IN THAT COCOON--
--IT WAS LIKE WHEN I WAS A CHILD, BURIED IN THE RUBBLE OF MY PARENTS' BOMBED-OUT HOME--
--EVER SINCE, I HAVE BEEN TERRIFIED OF ENCLOSED SPACES. OF BEING TRAPPED.
THAT CLAUSTROPHOBIA GAVE ME THE BERSERKER STRENGTH I NEEDED TO OVERLOAD NANNY'S SYSTEMS AND BLAST ME LOOSE. BUT SHE HAD STRIPPED ME OF EVERYTHING THAT HAPPENED AFTERWARDS...
...SO THAT I ENDED UP RELIVING MY LIFE AS A THIEF IN CAIRO. DIFFERENT DETAILS. SAME ESSENCE.
NOW, THOUGH, I AM ONCE MORE MYSELF-- IN MIND, IF NOT BODY.
IN MY NIGHTMARE, DONNING THIS SUIT OF ARMOR...
...PLACED ME IRREVOCABLY UNDER NANNY'S INFLUENCE.
FALSE ALARM, NANNY.
GUESS I WAS HEARING THINGS.
BUT IF GAMBIT IS TO BE FREED...
...I SEE NO OTHER WAY.

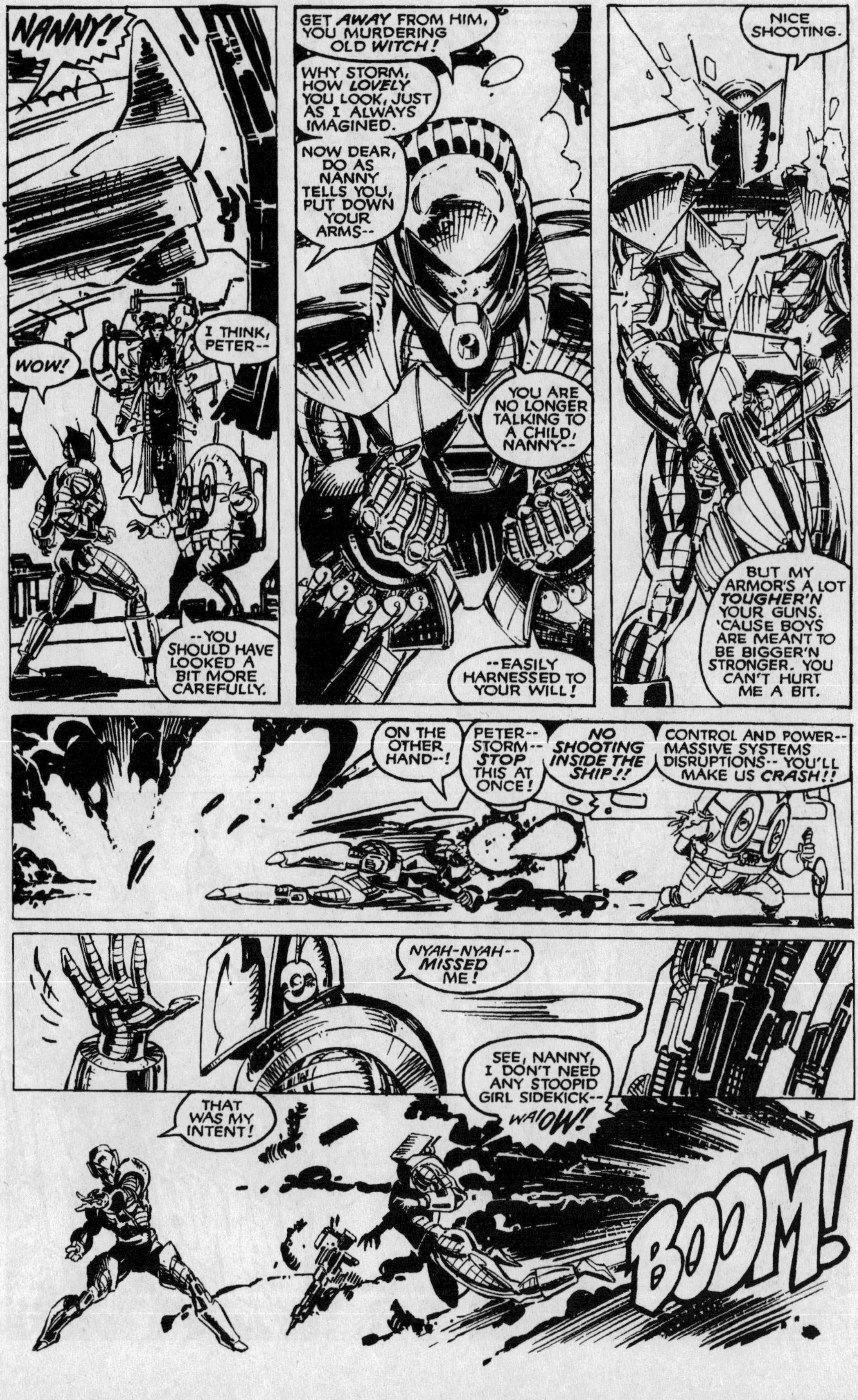
NANNY!
WOW!
I THINK, PETER--
--YOU SHOULD HAVE LOOKED A BIT MORE CAREFULLY.
GET AWAY FROM HIM, YOU MURDERING OLD WITCH!
WHY STORM, HOW LOVELY YOU LOOK, JUST AS I ALWAYS IMAGINED.
NOW DEAR, DO AS NANNY TELLS YOU, PUT DOWN YOUR ARMS--
YOU ARE NO LONGER TALKING TO A CHILD, NANNY--
--EASILY HARNESSED TO YOUR WILL!
NICE SHOOTING.
BUT MY ARMOR'S A LOT TOUGHER'N YOUR GUNS. 'CAUSE BOYS ARE MEANT TO BE BIGGER'N STRONGER. YOU CAN'T HURT ME A BIT.
ON THE OTHER HAND--!
PETER-- STORM-- STOP THIS AT ONCE!
NO SHOOTING INSIDE THE SHIP!!
CONTROL AND POWER-- MASSIVE SYSTEMS DISRUPTIONS-- YOU'LL MAKE US CRASH!!
NYAH-NYAH-- MISSED ME!
SEE, NANNY, I DON'T NEED ANY STOOPID GIRL SIDEKICK--
WAIOW!!
THAT WAS MY INTENT!
BOOM!

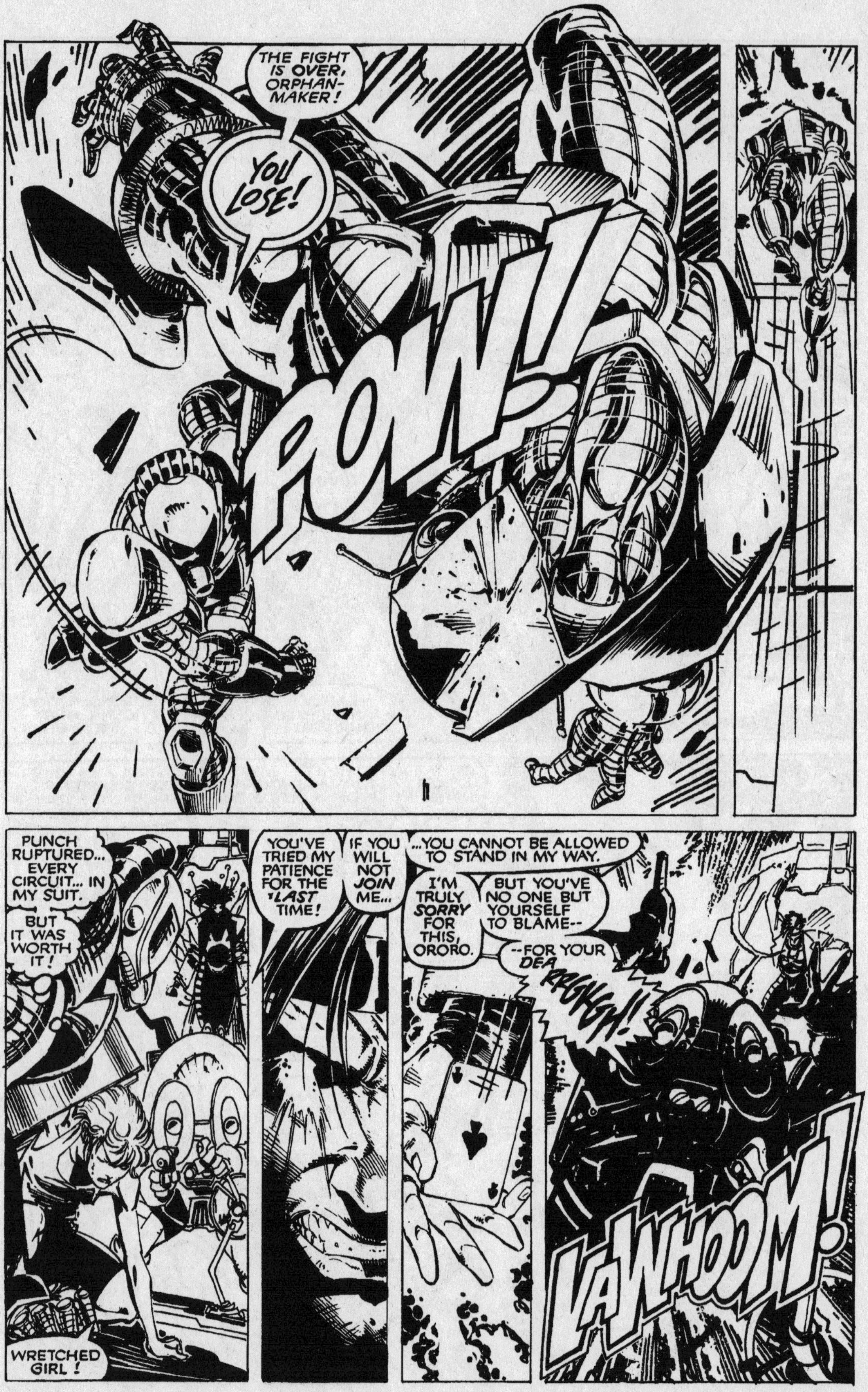
THE FIGHT IS OVER, ORPHAN-MAKER!
YOU LOSE!
POW!
PUNCH RUPTURED... EVERY CIRCUIT... IN MY SUIT.
BUT IT WAS WORTH IT!
WRETCHED GIRL!
YOU'VE TRIED MY PATIENCE FOR THE LAST TIME!
IF YOU WILL NOT JOIN ME...
...YOU CANNOT BE ALLOWED TO STAND IN MY WAY.
I'M TRULY SORRY FOR THIS, ORORO.
BUT YOU'VE NO ONE BUT YOURSELF TO BLAME--
--FOR YOUR DEA
RRGHGH!
VAWHOOM!

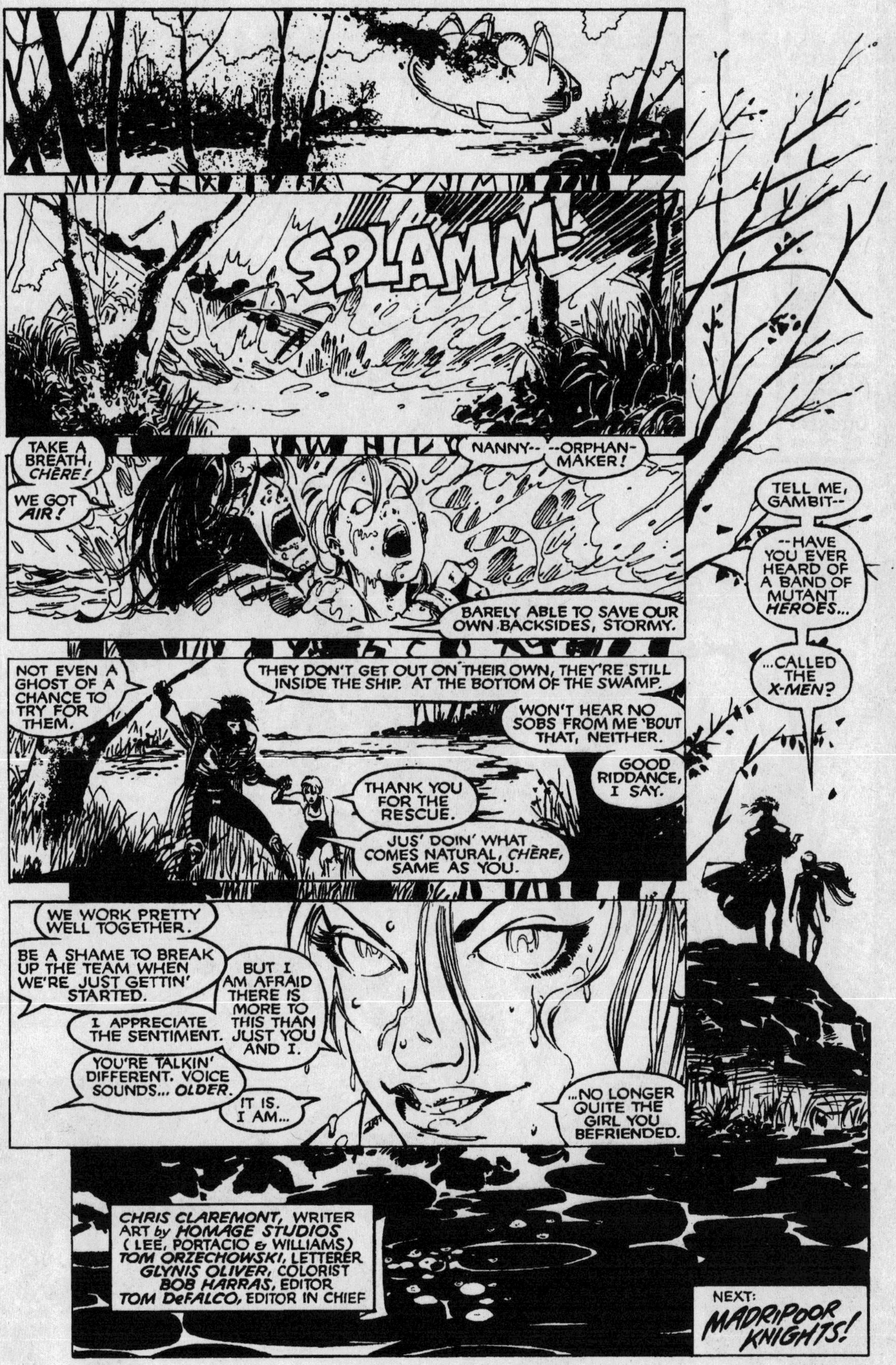
SPLAMM!
TAKE A BREATH, CHÈRE!
WE GOT AIR!
NANNY--
--ORPHAN-MAKER!
BARELY ABLE TO SAVE OUR OWN BACKSIDES, STORMY.
NOT EVEN A GHOST OF A CHANCE TO TRY FOR THEM.
THEY DON'T GET OUT ON THEIR OWN, THEY'RE STILL INSIDE THE SHIP. AT THE BOTTOM OF THE SWAMP.
WON'T HEAR NO SOBS FROM ME 'BOUT THAT, NEITHER.
GOOD RIDDANCE, I SAY.
THANK YOU FOR THE RESCUE.
JUS' DOIN' WHAT COMES NATURAL, CHÈRE, SAME AS YOU.
WE WORK PRETTY WELL TOGETHER.
BE A SHAME TO BREAK UP THE TEAM WHEN WE'RE JUST GETTIN' STARTED.
BUT I AM AFRAID THERE IS MORE TO THIS THAN JUST YOU AND I.
I APPRECIATE THE SENTIMENT.
YOU'RE TALKIN' DIFFERENT. VOICE SOUNDS... OLDER.
IT IS. I AM...
...NO LONGER QUITE THE GIRL YOU BEFRIENDED.
TELL ME, GAMBIT--
--HAVE YOU EVER HEARD OF A BAND OF MUTANT HEROES...
...CALLED THE X-MEN?
CHRIS CLAREMONT, WRITER
ART by HOMAGE STUDIOS
(LEE, PORTACIO & WILLIAMS)
TOM ORZECHOWSKI, LETTERER
GLYNIS OLIVER, COLORIST
BOB HARRAS, EDITOR
TOM DeFALCO, EDITOR IN CHIEF
NEXT:
MADRIPOOR KNIGHTS!

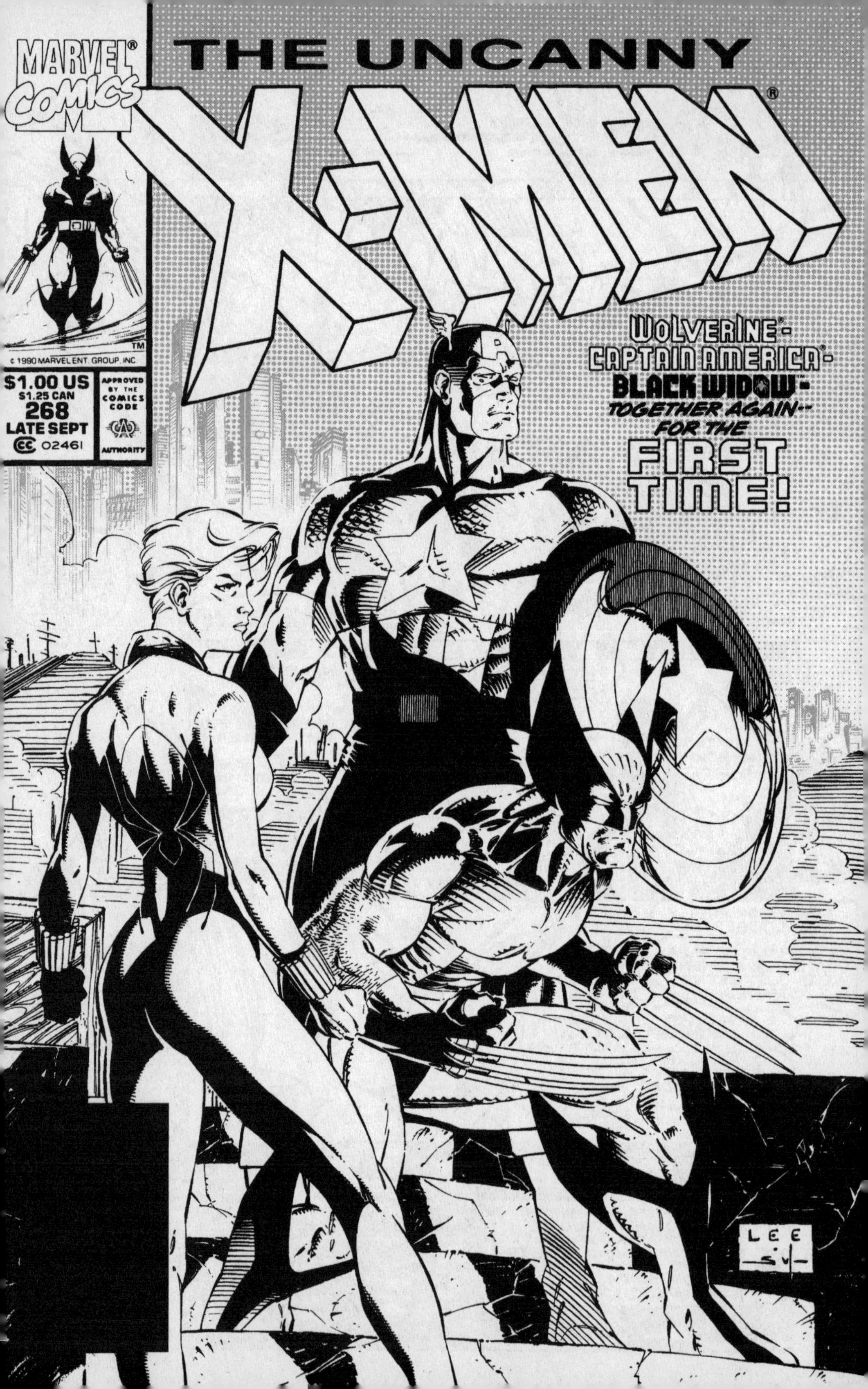

MARVEL® COMICS
THE UNCANNY
X-MEN®
WOLVERINE- CAPTAIN AMERICA®- BLACK WIDOW- TOGETHER AGAIN-- FOR THE FIRST TIME!
© 1990 MARVEL ENT. GROUP, INC.
$1.00 US
$1.25 CAN
268
LATE SEPT
02461
APPROVED BY THE COMICS CODE AUTHORITY
LEE

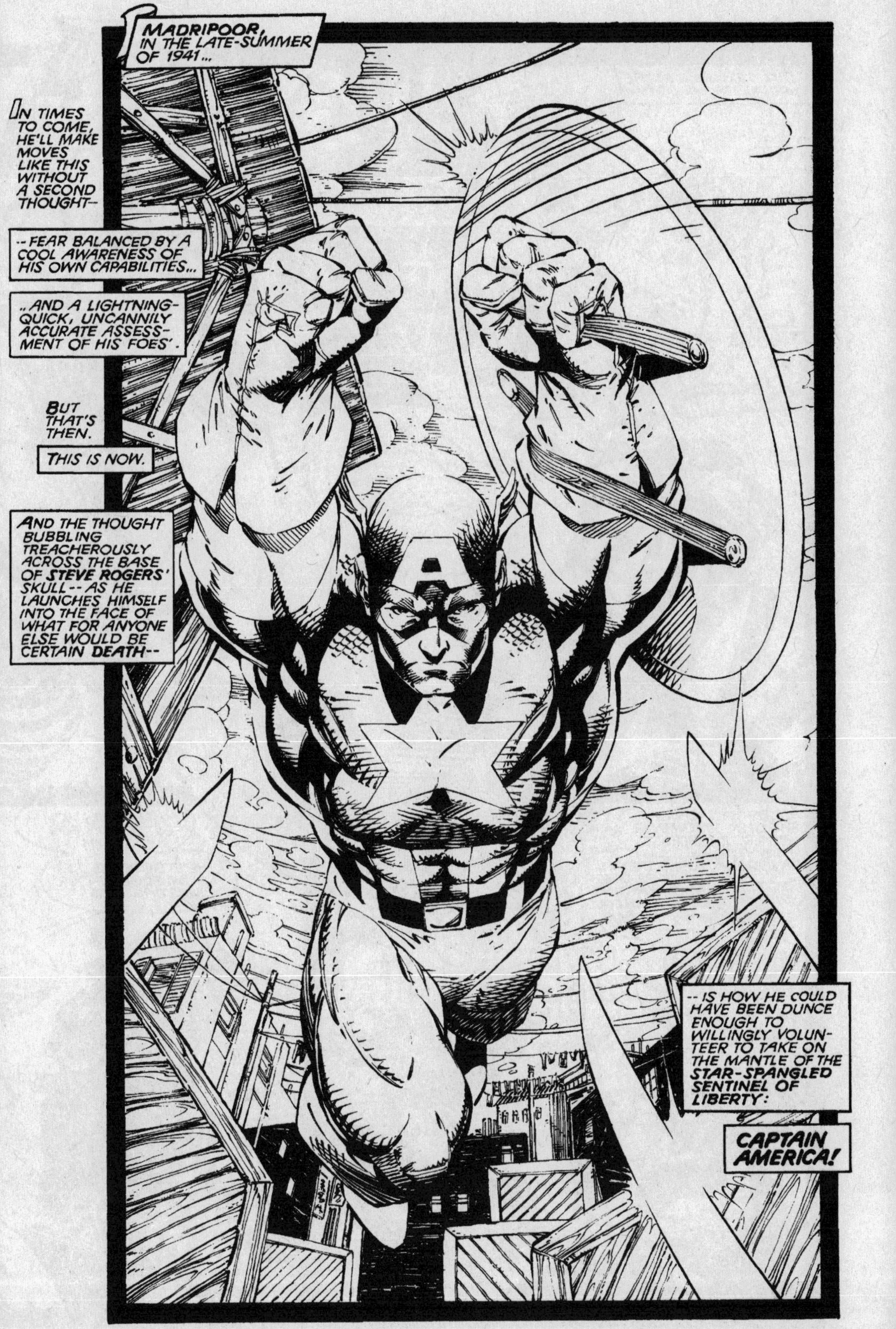
MADRIPOOR, IN THE LATE-SUMMER OF 1941...
IN TIMES TO COME, HE'LL MAKE MOVES LIKE THIS WITHOUT A SECOND THOUGHT--
--FEAR BALANCED BY A COOL AWARENESS OF HIS OWN CAPABILITIES...
..AND A LIGHTNING-QUICK, UNCANNILY ACCURATE ASSESSMENT OF HIS FOES'.
BUT THAT'S THEN.
THIS IS NOW.
AND THE THOUGHT BUBBLING TREACHEROUSLY ACROSS THE BASE OF STEVE ROGERS' SKULL--AS HE LAUNCHES HIMSELF INTO THE FACE OF WHAT FOR ANYONE ELSE WOULD BE CERTAIN DEATH--
--IS HOW HE COULD HAVE BEEN DUNCE ENOUGH TO WILLINGLY VOLUNTEER TO TAKE ON THE MANTLE OF THE STAR-SPANGLED SENTINEL OF LIBERTY:
CAPTAIN AMERICA!

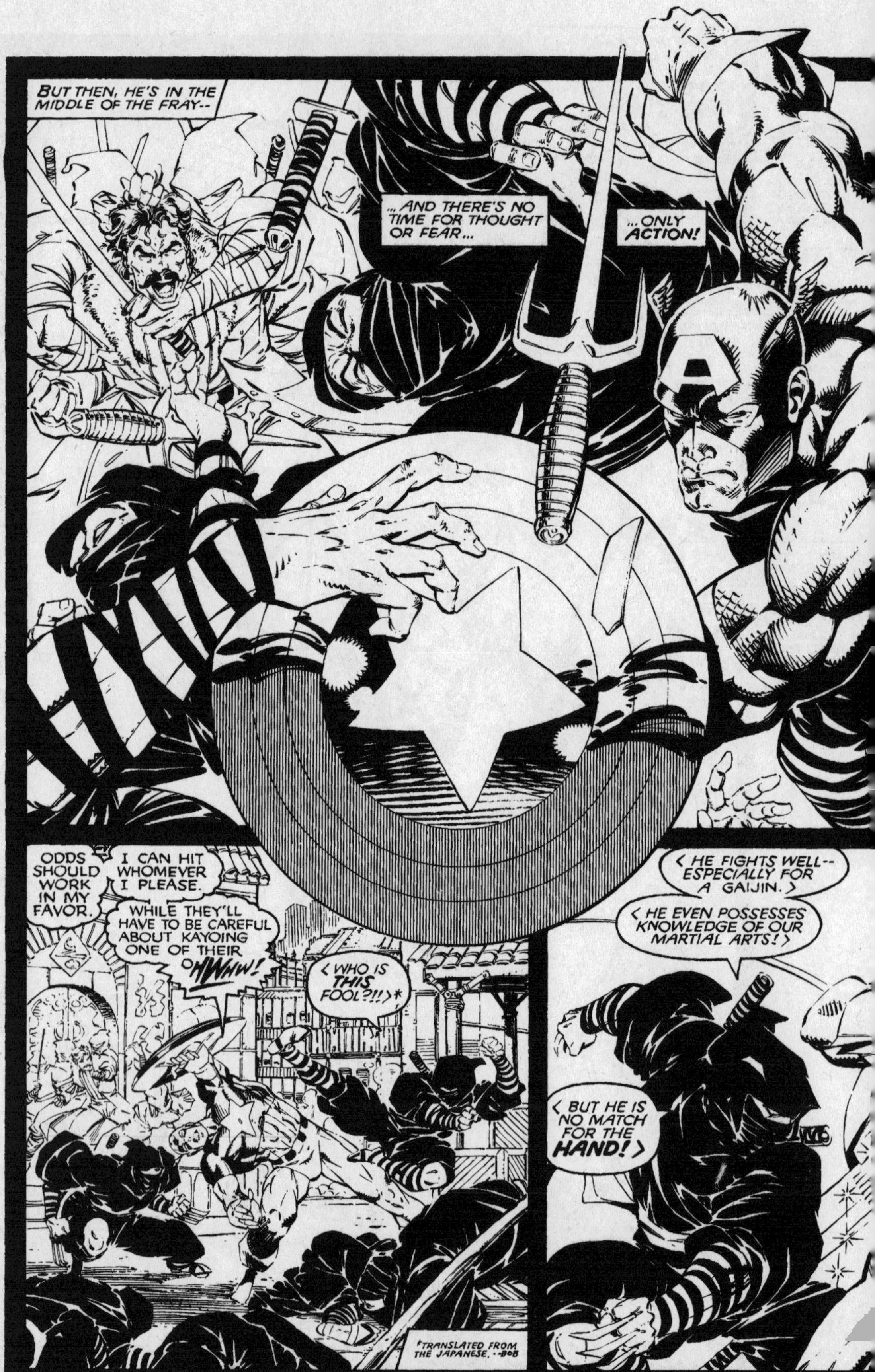
BUT THEN, HE'S IN THE MIDDLE OF THE FRAY--
...AND THERE'S NO TIME FOR THOUGHT OR FEAR...
...ONLY ACTION!
ODDS SHOULD WORK IN MY FAVOR.
I CAN HIT WHOMEVER I PLEASE.
WHILE THEY'LL HAVE TO BE CAREFUL ABOUT KAYOING ONE OF THEIR
OHWWW!
< WHO IS THIS FOOL?!! >*
*TRANSLATED FROM THE JAPANESE. --BOB
< HE FIGHTS WELL-- ESPECIALLY FOR A GAIJIN. >
< HE EVEN POSSESSES KNOWLEDGE OF OUR MARTIAL ARTS! >
< BUT HE IS NO MATCH FOR THE HAND! >

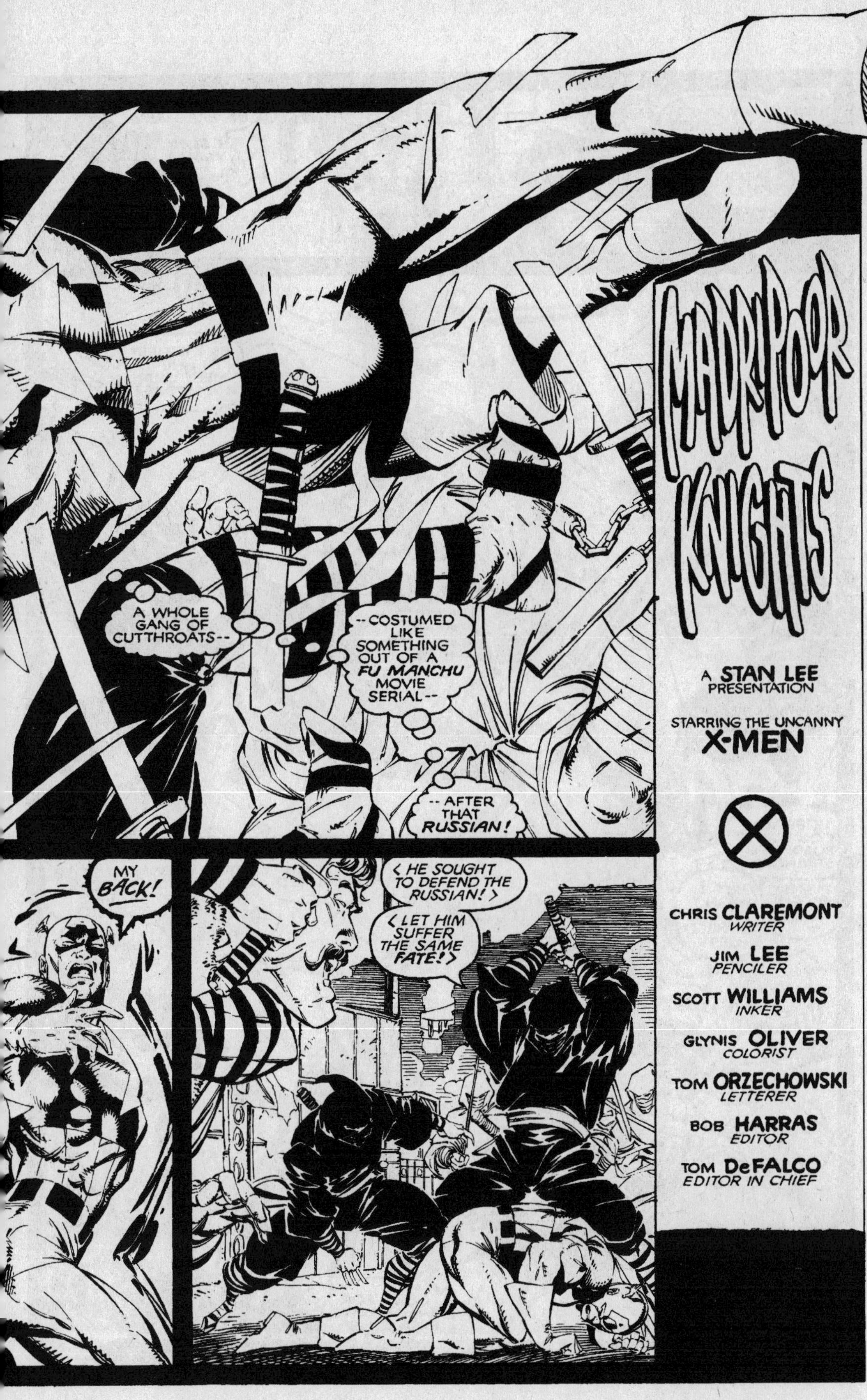
A WHOLE GANG OF CUTTHROATS--
--COSTUMED LIKE SOMETHING OUT OF A *FU MANCHU* MOVIE SERIAL--
--AFTER THAT *RUSSIAN!*
MADRIPOOR KNIGHTS
A STAN LEE PRESENTATION
STARRING THE UNCANNY X-MEN
CHRIS CLAREMONT WRITER
JIM LEE PENCILER
SCOTT WILLIAMS INKER
GLYNIS OLIVER COLORIST
TOM ORZECHOWSKI LETTERER
BOB HARRAS EDITOR
TOM DeFALCO EDITOR IN CHIEF
MY *BACK!*
‹ HE SOUGHT TO DEFEND THE RUSSIAN! ›
‹ LET HIM SUFFER THE SAME *FATE!* ›

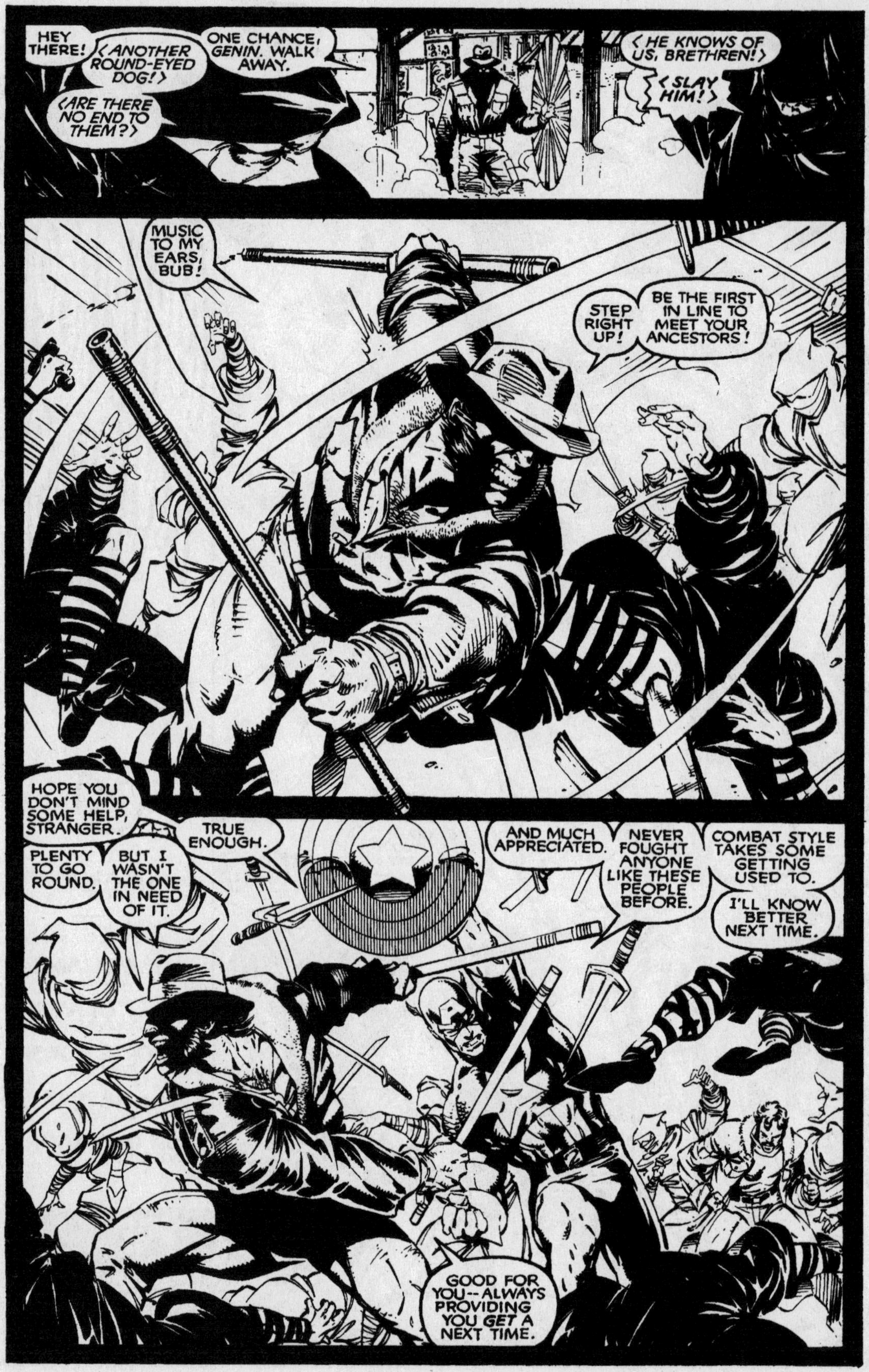
HEY THERE!
<ANOTHER ROUND-EYED DOG!>
<ARE THERE NO END TO THEM?>
ONE CHANCE, GENIN. WALK AWAY.
<HE KNOWS OF US, BRETHREN!>
<SLAY HIM!>
MUSIC TO MY EARS, BUB!
STEP RIGHT UP!
BE THE FIRST IN LINE TO MEET YOUR ANCESTORS!
HOPE YOU DON'T MIND SOME HELP, STRANGER.
PLENTY TO GO ROUND.
BUT I WASN'T THE ONE IN NEED OF IT.
TRUE ENOUGH.
AND MUCH APPRECIATED.
NEVER FOUGHT ANYONE LIKE THESE PEOPLE BEFORE.
COMBAT STYLE TAKES SOME GETTING USED TO.
I'LL KNOW BETTER NEXT TIME.
GOOD FOR YOU--ALWAYS PROVIDING YOU GET A NEXT TIME.

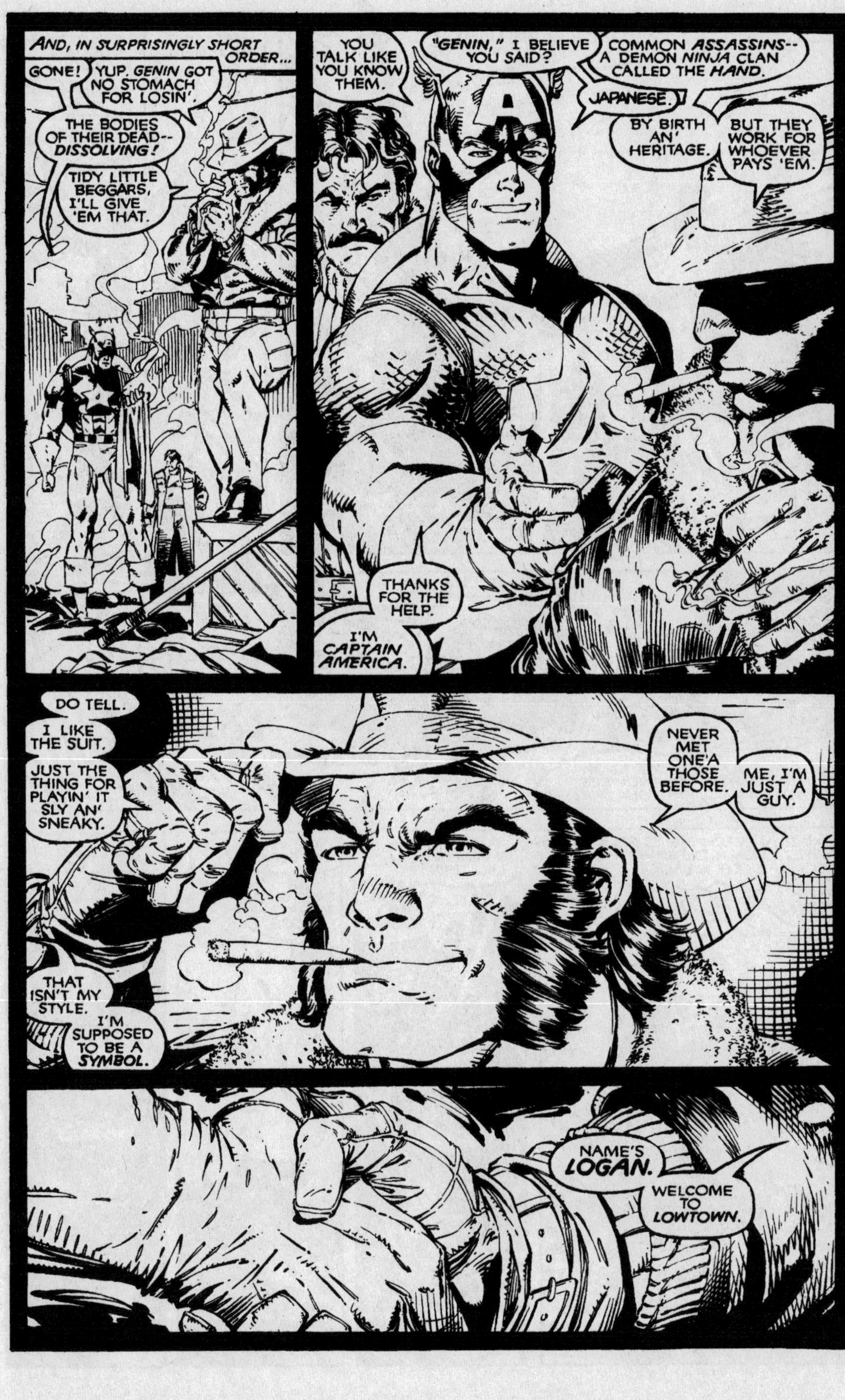
AND, IN SURPRISINGLY SHORT ORDER...
GONE!
YUP. GENIN GOT NO STOMACH FOR LOSIN'.
THE BODIES OF THEIR DEAD-- DISSOLVING!
TIDY LITTLE BEGGARS, I'LL GIVE 'EM THAT.
YOU TALK LIKE YOU KNOW THEM.
"GENIN," I BELIEVE YOU SAID?
COMMON ASSASSINS-- A DEMON NINJA CLAN CALLED THE HAND.
JAPANESE.
BY BIRTH AN' HERITAGE.
BUT THEY WORK FOR WHOEVER PAYS 'EM.
THANKS FOR THE HELP.
I'M CAPTAIN AMERICA.
DO TELL.
I LIKE THE SUIT.
JUST THE THING FOR PLAYIN' IT SLY AN' SNEAKY.
NEVER MET ONE'A THOSE BEFORE.
ME, I'M JUST A GUY.
THAT ISN'T MY STYLE.
I'M SUPPOSED TO BE A SYMBOL.
NAME'S LOGAN.
WELCOME TO LOWTOWN.

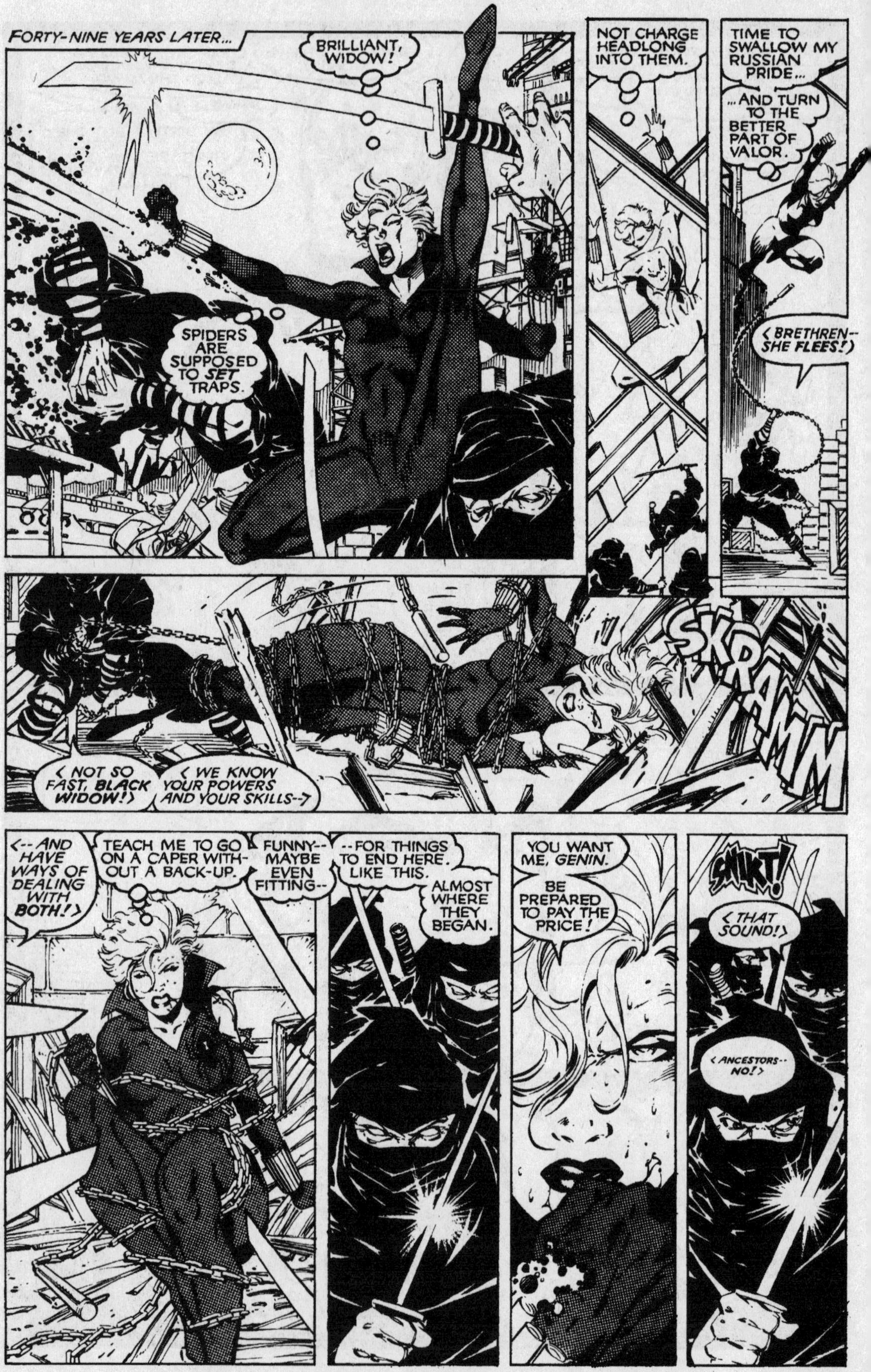
FORTY-NINE YEARS LATER...
BRILLIANT, WIDOW!
SPIDERS ARE SUPPOSED TO SET TRAPS.
NOT CHARGE HEADLONG INTO THEM.
TIME TO SWALLOW MY RUSSIAN PRIDE...
...AND TURN TO THE BETTER PART OF VALOR.
‹ BRETHREN-- SHE FLEES! ›
SKRAMM
‹ NOT SO FAST, BLACK WIDOW! ›
‹ WE KNOW YOUR POWERS AND YOUR SKILLS-- ›
‹ --AND HAVE WAYS OF DEALING WITH BOTH! ›
TEACH ME TO GO ON A CAPER WITHOUT A BACK-UP.
FUNNY-- MAYBE EVEN FITTING--
--FOR THINGS TO END HERE. LIKE THIS.
ALMOST WHERE THEY BEGAN.
YOU WANT ME, GENIN.
BE PREPARED TO PAY THE PRICE!
SNIKT!
‹ THAT SOUND! ›
‹ ANCESTORS-- NO! ›

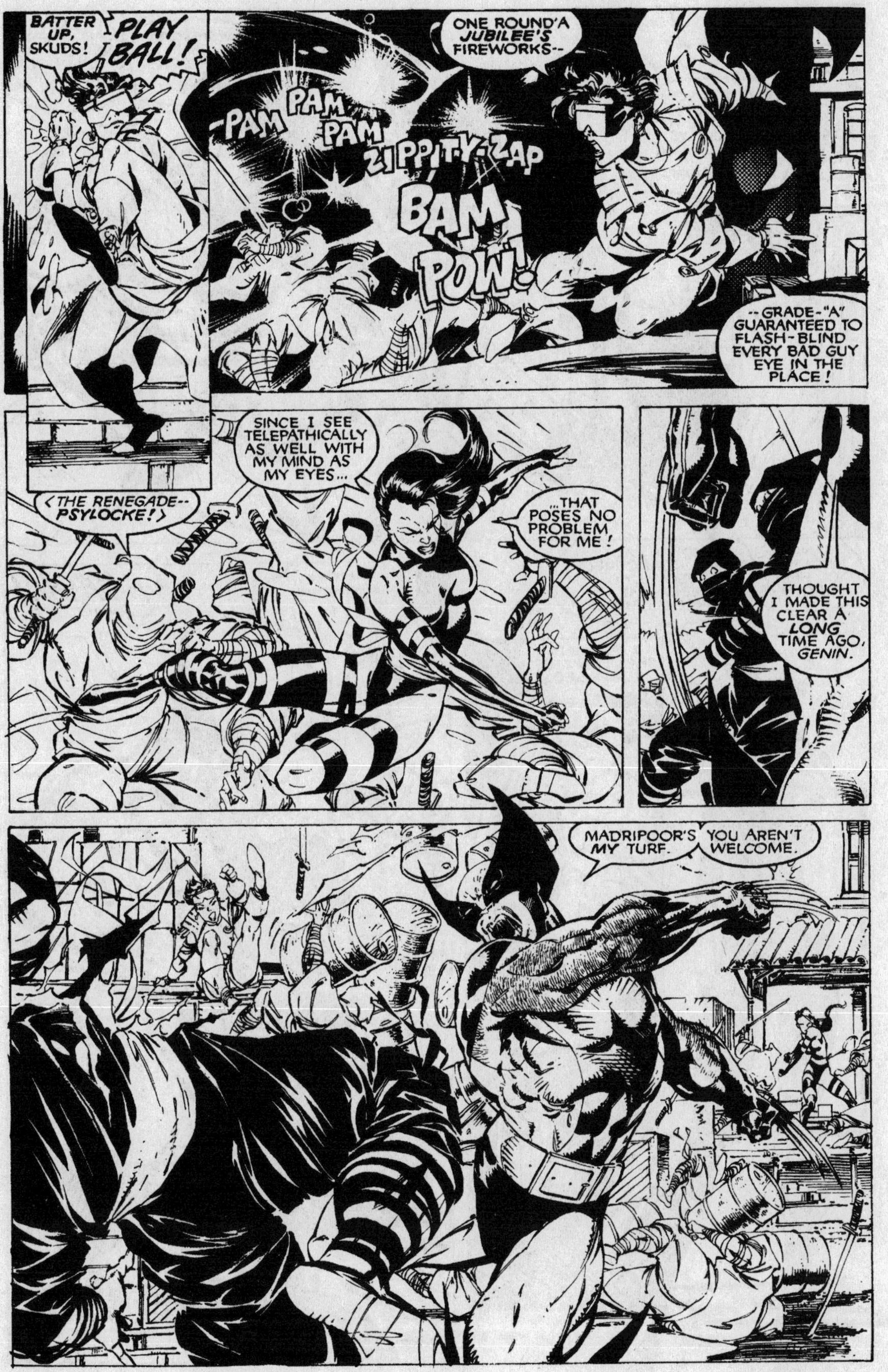
BATTER UP, SKUDS!
PLAY BALL!
ONE ROUND'A JUBILEE'S FIREWORKS--
PAM PAM PAM
ZIPPITY-ZAP
BAM
POW!
--GRADE-"A" GUARANTEED TO FLASH-BLIND EVERY BAD GUY EYE IN THE PLACE!
SINCE I SEE TELEPATHICALLY AS WELL WITH MY MIND AS MY EYES...
<THE RENEGADE--PSYLOCKE!>
...THAT POSES NO PROBLEM FOR ME!
THOUGHT I MADE THIS CLEAR A LONG TIME AGO, GENIN.
MADRIPOOR'S MY TURF.
YOU AREN'T WELCOME.

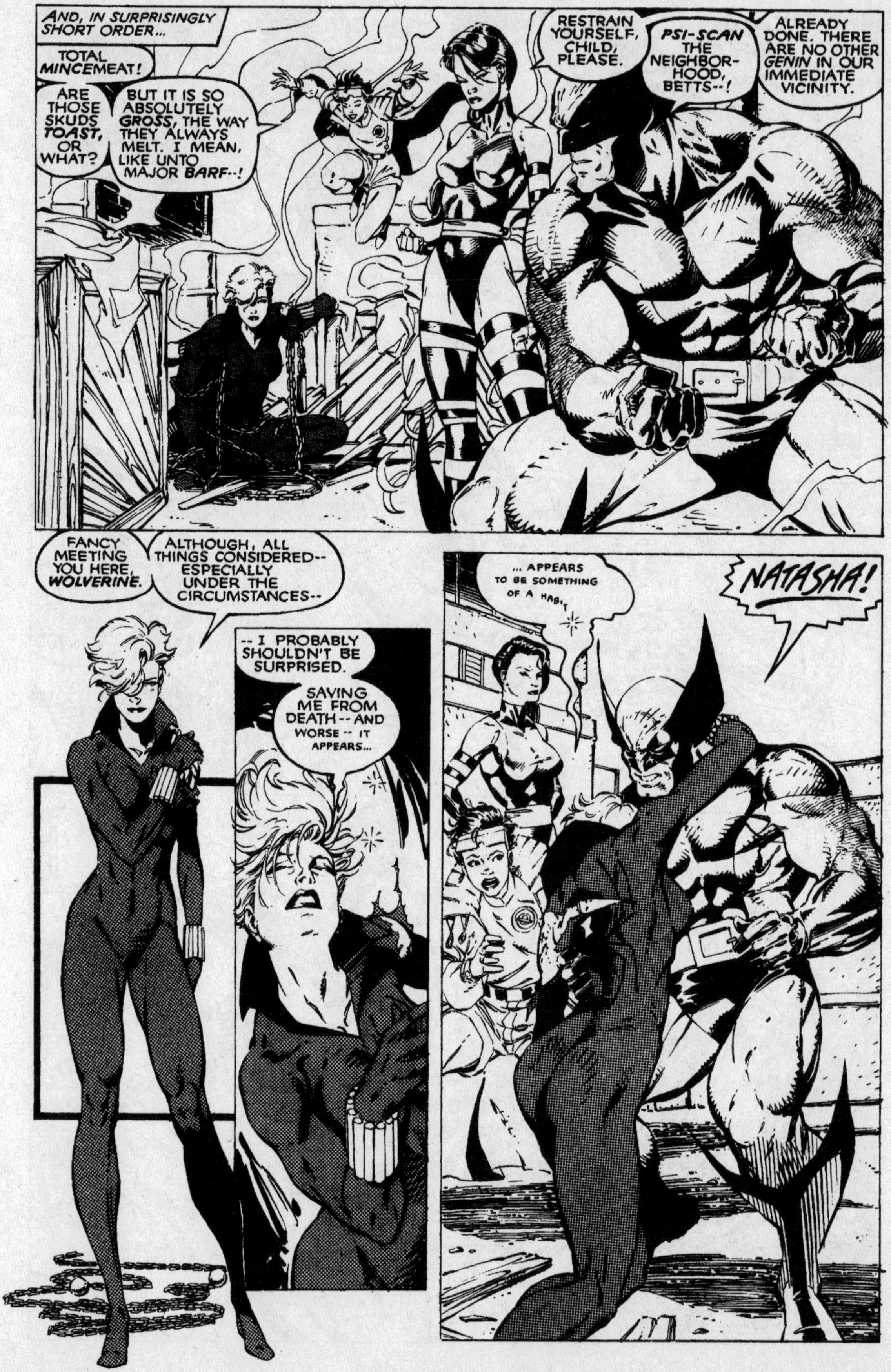
AND, IN SURPRISINGLY SHORT ORDER...
TOTAL MINCEMEAT!
ARE THOSE SKUDS TOAST, OR WHAT?
BUT IT IS SO ABSOLUTELY GROSS, THE WAY THEY ALWAYS MELT. I MEAN, LIKE UNTO MAJOR BARF--!
RESTRAIN YOURSELF, CHILD, PLEASE.
PSI-SCAN THE NEIGHBORHOOD, BETTS--!
ALREADY DONE. THERE ARE NO OTHER GENIN IN OUR IMMEDIATE VICINITY.
FANCY MEETING YOU HERE, WOLVERINE.
ALTHOUGH, ALL THINGS CONSIDERED-- ESPECIALLY UNDER THE CIRCUMSTANCES--
-- I PROBABLY SHOULDN'T BE SURPRISED.
SAVING ME FROM DEATH -- AND WORSE -- IT APPEARS...
... APPEARS TO BE SOMETHING OF A HABIT
NATASHA!

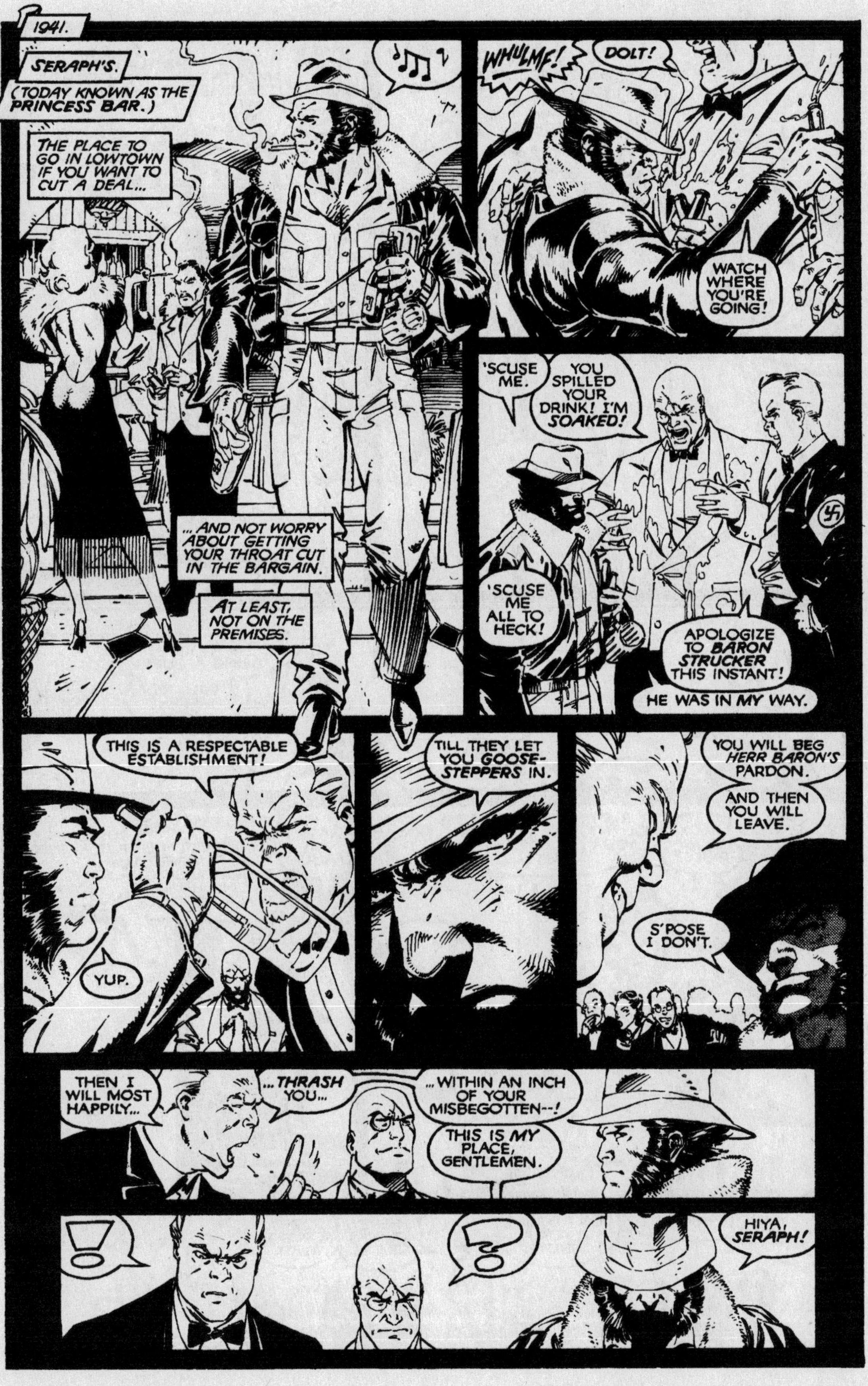
1941.
SERAPH'S.
(TODAY KNOWN AS THE PRINCESS BAR.)
THE PLACE TO GO IN LOWTOWN IF YOU WANT TO CUT A DEAL...
...AND NOT WORRY ABOUT GETTING YOUR THROAT CUT IN THE BARGAIN.
AT LEAST, NOT ON THE PREMISES.
WHULMF!
DOLT!
WATCH WHERE YOU'RE GOING!
'SCUSE ME.
YOU SPILLED YOUR DRINK! I'M SOAKED!
'SCUSE ME ALL TO HECK!
APOLOGIZE TO BARON STRUCKER THIS INSTANT!
HE WAS IN MY WAY.
THIS IS A RESPECTABLE ESTABLISHMENT!
YUP.
TILL THEY LET YOU GOOSE-STEPPERS IN.
YOU WILL BEG HERR BARON'S PARDON.
AND THEN YOU WILL LEAVE.
S'POSE I DON'T.
THEN I WILL MOST HAPPILY...
...THRASH YOU...
...WITHIN AN INCH OF YOUR MISBEGOTTEN--!
THIS IS MY PLACE, GENTLEMEN.
HIYA, SERAPH!

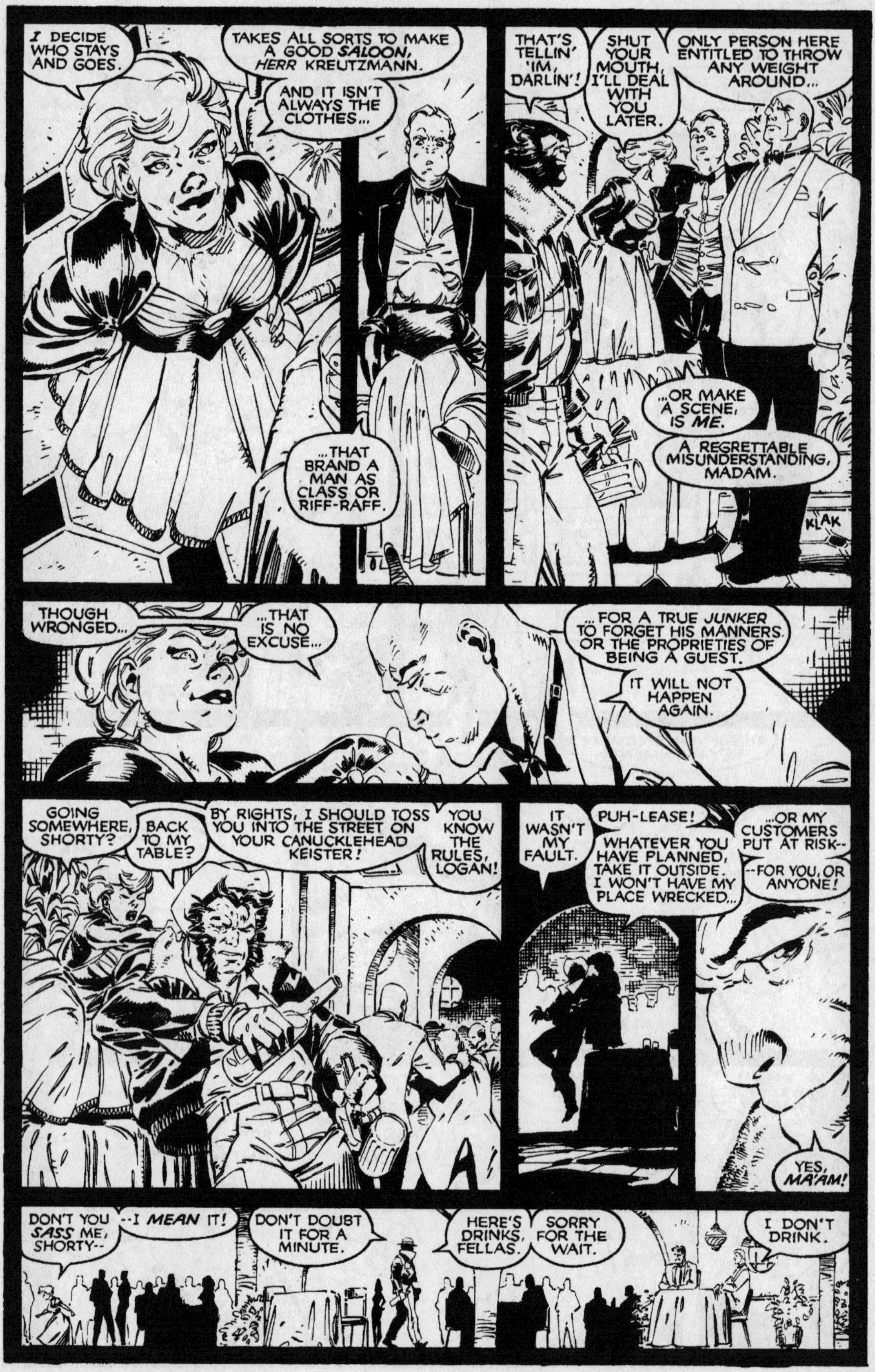

I DECIDE WHO STAYS AND GOES.
TAKES ALL SORTS TO MAKE A GOOD SALOON, HERR KREUTZMANN.
AND IT ISN'T ALWAYS THE CLOTHES...
...THAT BRAND A MAN AS CLASS OR RIFF-RAFF.
THAT'S TELLIN' 'IM, DARLIN'!
SHUT YOUR MOUTH, I'LL DEAL WITH YOU LATER.
ONLY PERSON HERE ENTITLED TO THROW ANY WEIGHT AROUND...
...OR MAKE A SCENE, IS ME.
A REGRETTABLE MISUNDERSTANDING, MADAM.
KLAK
THOUGH WRONGED...
...THAT IS NO EXCUSE...
...FOR A TRUE JUNKER TO FORGET HIS MANNERS. OR THE PROPRIETIES OF BEING A GUEST.
IT WILL NOT HAPPEN AGAIN.
GOING SOMEWHERE, SHORTY?
BACK TO MY TABLE?
BY RIGHTS, I SHOULD TOSS YOU INTO THE STREET ON YOUR CANUCKLEHEAD KEISTER!
YOU KNOW THE RULES, LOGAN!
IT WASN'T MY FAULT.
PUH-LEASE!
WHATEVER YOU HAVE PLANNED, TAKE IT OUTSIDE. I WON'T HAVE MY PLACE WRECKED...
...OR MY CUSTOMERS PUT AT RISK--
--FOR YOU, OR ANYONE!
YES, MA'AM!
DON'T YOU SASS ME, SHORTY--
--I MEAN IT!
DON'T DOUBT IT FOR A MINUTE.
HERE'S DRINKS, FELLAS.
SORRY FOR THE WAIT.
I DON'T DRINK.

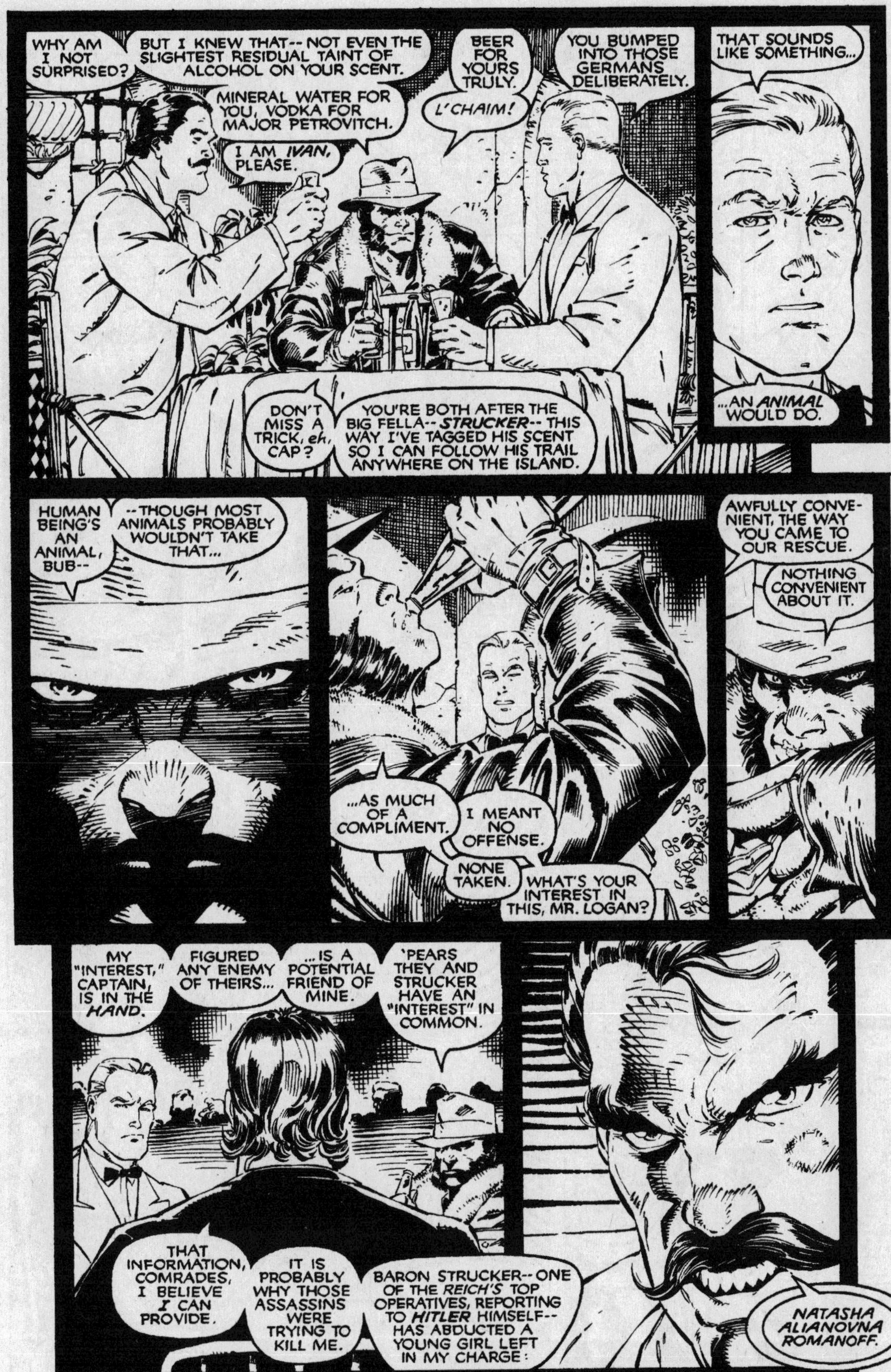
WHY AM I NOT SURPRISED?
BUT I KNEW THAT-- NOT EVEN THE SLIGHTEST RESIDUAL TAINT OF ALCOHOL ON YOUR SCENT.
MINERAL WATER FOR YOU, VODKA FOR MAJOR PETROVITCH.
I AM IVAN, PLEASE.
BEER FOR YOURS TRULY.
L'CHAIM!
YOU BUMPED INTO THOSE GERMANS DELIBERATELY.
DON'T MISS A TRICK, eh, CAP?
YOU'RE BOTH AFTER THE BIG FELLA-- STRUCKER-- THIS WAY I'VE TAGGED HIS SCENT SO I CAN FOLLOW HIS TRAIL ANYWHERE ON THE ISLAND.
THAT SOUNDS LIKE SOMETHING...
...AN ANIMAL WOULD DO.
HUMAN BEING'S AN ANIMAL, BUB--
--THOUGH MOST ANIMALS PROBABLY WOULDN'T TAKE THAT...
...AS MUCH OF A COMPLIMENT.
I MEANT NO OFFENSE.
NONE TAKEN.
WHAT'S YOUR INTEREST IN THIS, MR. LOGAN?
AWFULLY CONVENIENT, THE WAY YOU CAME TO OUR RESCUE.
NOTHING CONVENIENT ABOUT IT.
MY "INTEREST," CAPTAIN, IS IN THE HAND.
FIGURED ANY ENEMY OF THEIRS...
...IS A POTENTIAL FRIEND OF MINE.
'PEARS THEY AND STRUCKER HAVE AN "INTEREST" IN COMMON.
THAT INFORMATION, COMRADES, I BELIEVE I CAN PROVIDE.
IT IS PROBABLY WHY THOSE ASSASSINS WERE TRYING TO KILL ME.
BARON STRUCKER-- ONE OF THE REICH'S TOP OPERATIVES, REPORTING TO HITLER HIMSELF-- HAS ABDUCTED A YOUNG GIRL LEFT IN MY CHARGE:
NATASHA ALIANOVNA ROMANOFF.

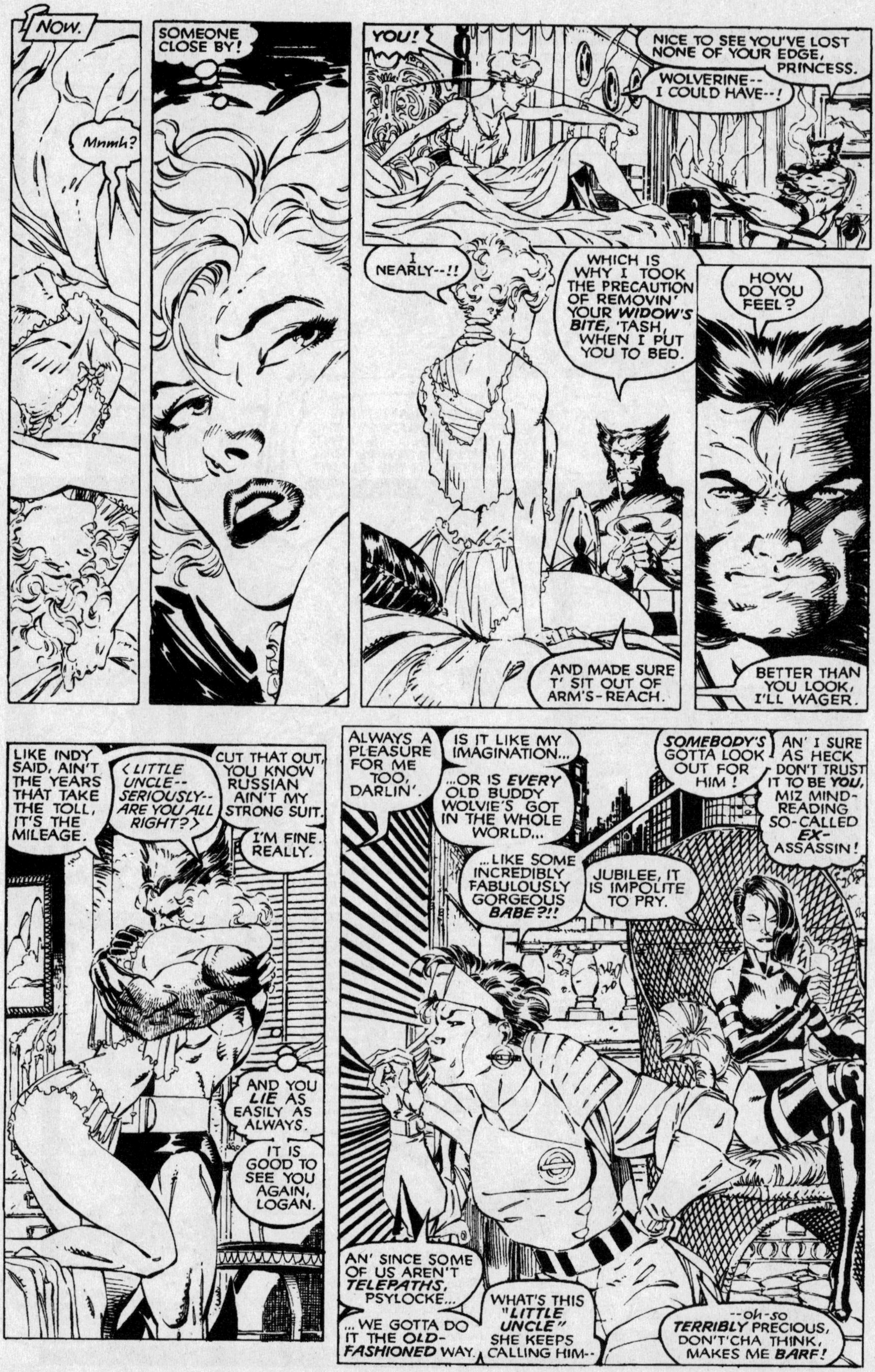

NOW.
Mnmh?
SOMEONE CLOSE BY!
YOU!
NICE TO SEE YOU'VE LOST NONE OF YOUR EDGE, PRINCESS.
WOLVERINE-- I COULD HAVE--!
I NEARLY--!!
WHICH IS WHY I TOOK THE PRECAUTION OF REMOVIN' YOUR WIDOW'S BITE, 'TASH, WHEN I PUT YOU TO BED.
AND MADE SURE T' SIT OUT OF ARM'S-REACH.
HOW DO YOU FEEL?
BETTER THAN YOU LOOK, I'LL WAGER.
LIKE INDY SAID, AIN'T THE YEARS THAT TAKE THE TOLL, IT'S THE MILEAGE.
<LITTLE UNCLE-- SERIOUSLY-- ARE YOU ALL RIGHT?>
CUT THAT OUT, YOU KNOW RUSSIAN AIN'T MY STRONG SUIT.
I'M FINE. REALLY.
AND YOU LIE AS EASILY AS ALWAYS.
IT IS GOOD TO SEE YOU AGAIN, LOGAN.
ALWAYS A PLEASURE FOR ME TOO, DARLIN'.
IS IT LIKE MY IMAGINATION...
...OR IS EVERY OLD BUDDY WOLVIE'S GOT IN THE WHOLE WORLD...
...LIKE SOME INCREDIBLY FABULOUSLY GORGEOUS BABE?!!
JUBILEE, IT IS IMPOLITE TO PRY.
SOMEBODY'S GOTTA LOOK OUT FOR HIM!
AN' I SURE AS HECK DON'T TRUST IT TO BE YOU, MIZ MIND-READING SO-CALLED EX-ASSASSIN!
AN' SINCE SOME OF US AREN'T TELEPATHS, PSYLOCKE...
...WE GOTTA DO IT THE OLD-FASHIONED WAY.
WHAT'S THIS "LITTLE UNCLE" SHE KEEPS CALLING HIM--
--oh-so TERRIBLY PRECIOUS, DON'T'CHA THINK, MAKES ME BARF!

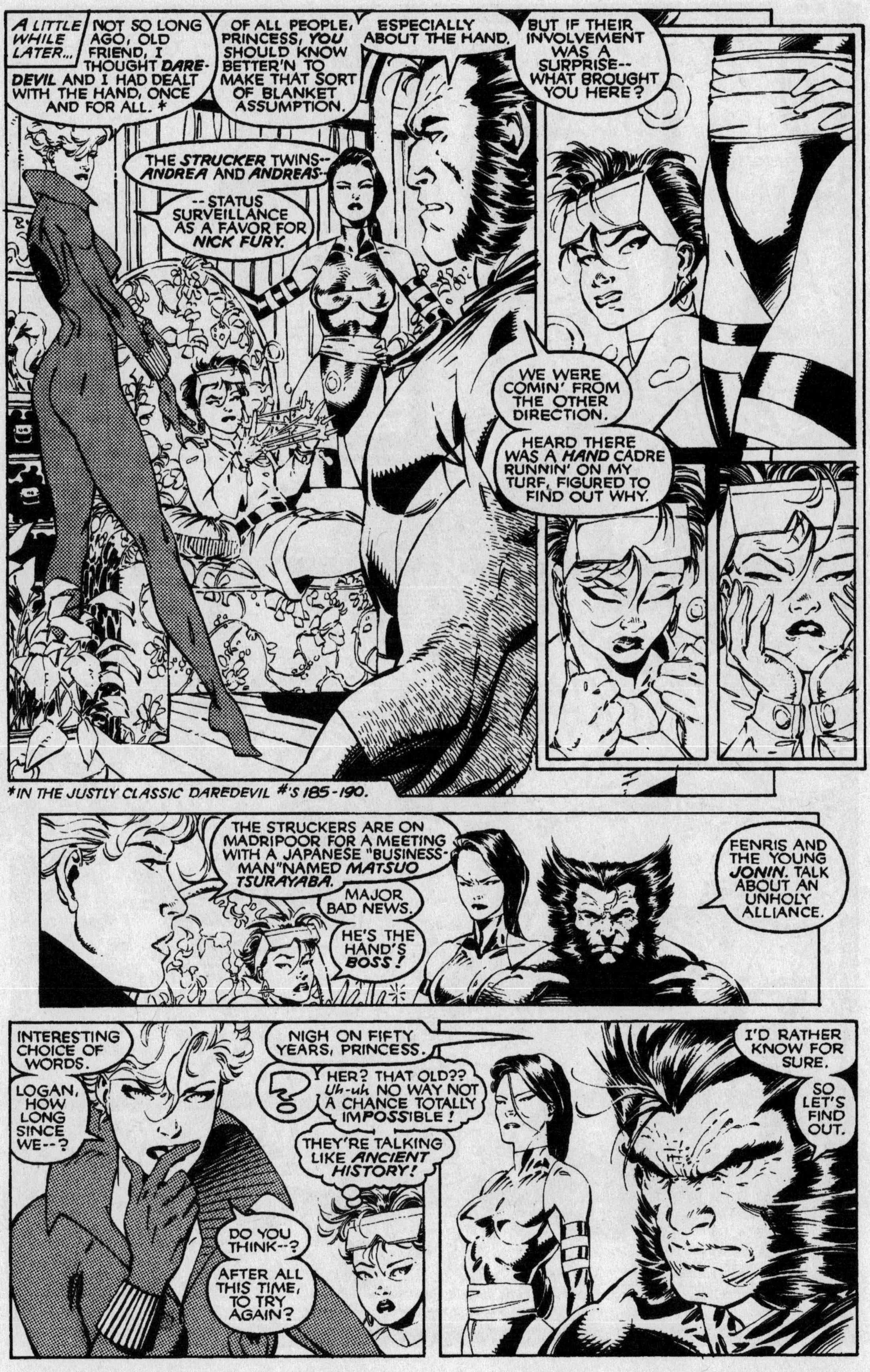
A LITTLE WHILE LATER...
NOT SO LONG AGO, OLD FRIEND, I THOUGHT DAREDEVIL AND I HAD DEALT WITH THE HAND, ONCE AND FOR ALL. *
-- OF ALL PEOPLE, PRINCESS, YOU SHOULD KNOW BETTER'N TO MAKE THAT SORT OF BLANKET ASSUMPTION.
ESPECIALLY ABOUT THE HAND.
BUT IF THEIR INVOLVEMENT WAS A SURPRISE-- WHAT BROUGHT YOU HERE?
THE STRUCKER TWINS-- ANDREA AND ANDREAS--
-- STATUS SURVEILLANCE AS A FAVOR FOR NICK FURY.
WE WERE COMIN' FROM THE OTHER DIRECTION.
HEARD THERE WAS A HAND CADRE RUNNIN' ON MY TURF, FIGURED TO FIND OUT WHY.
*IN THE JUSTLY CLASSIC DAREDEVIL #'S 185-190.
THE STRUCKERS ARE ON MADRIPOOR FOR A MEETING WITH A JAPANESE "BUSINESSMAN" NAMED MATSUO TSURAYABA.
MAJOR BAD NEWS.
HE'S THE HAND'S BOSS!
FENRIS AND THE YOUNG JONIN. TALK ABOUT AN UNHOLY ALLIANCE.
INTERESTING CHOICE OF WORDS.
LOGAN, HOW LONG SINCE WE--?
NIGH ON FIFTY YEARS, PRINCESS.
HER? THAT OLD?? Uh-uh NO WAY NOT A CHANCE TOTALLY IMPOSSIBLE!
THEY'RE TALKING LIKE ANCIENT HISTORY!
DO YOU THINK--?
AFTER ALL THIS TIME, TO TRY AGAIN?
I'D RATHER KNOW FOR SURE.
SO LET'S FIND OUT.

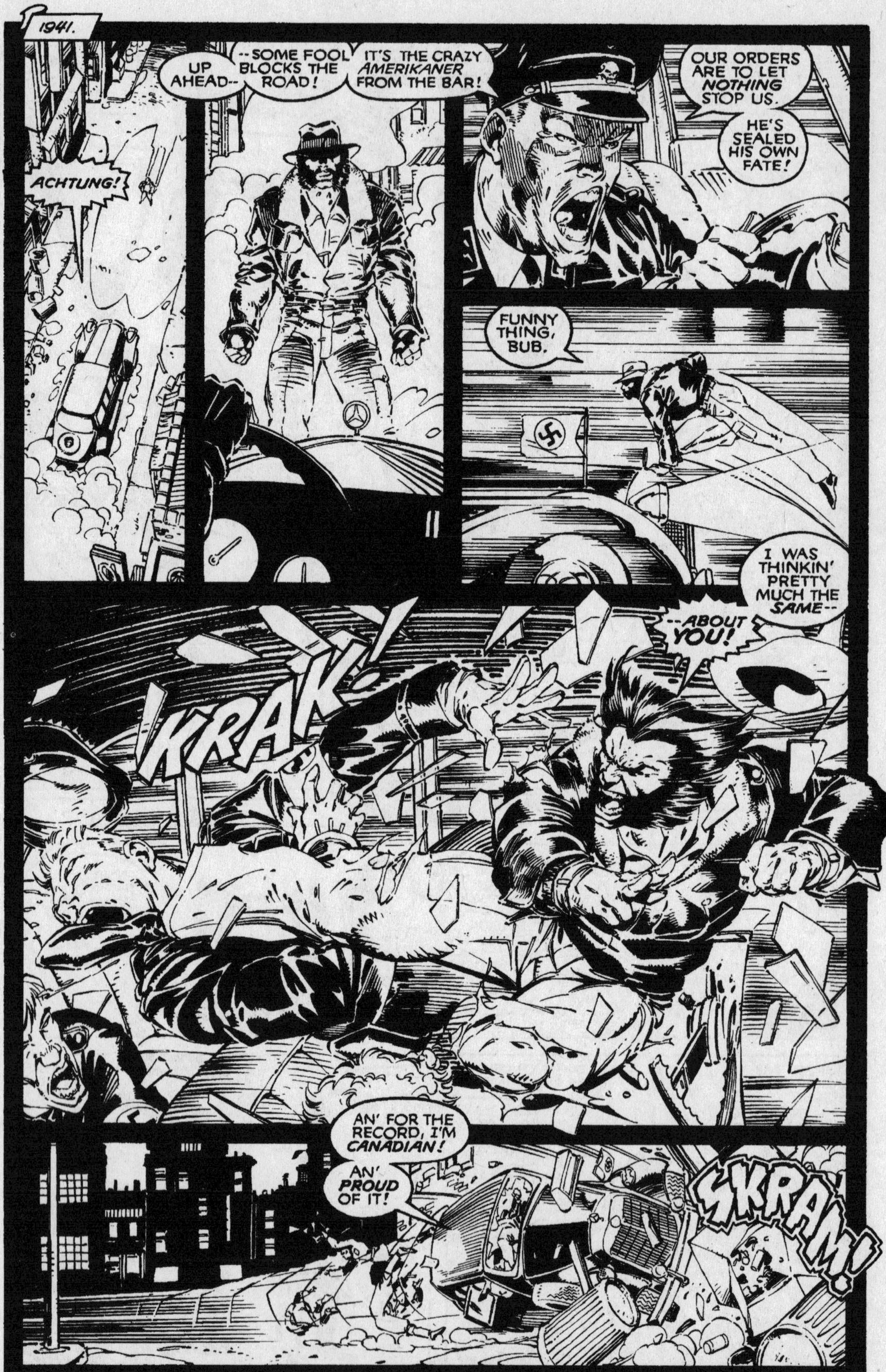
1941.
ACHTUNG!
UP AHEAD--
--SOME FOOL BLOCKS THE ROAD!
IT'S THE CRAZY AMERIKANER FROM THE BAR!
OUR ORDERS ARE TO LET NOTHING STOP US.
HE'S SEALED HIS OWN FATE!
FUNNY THING, BUB.
I WAS THINKIN' PRETTY MUCH THE SAME--
--ABOUT YOU!
KRAK!
AN' FOR THE RECORD, I'M CANADIAN!
AN' PROUD OF IT!
SKRAM!

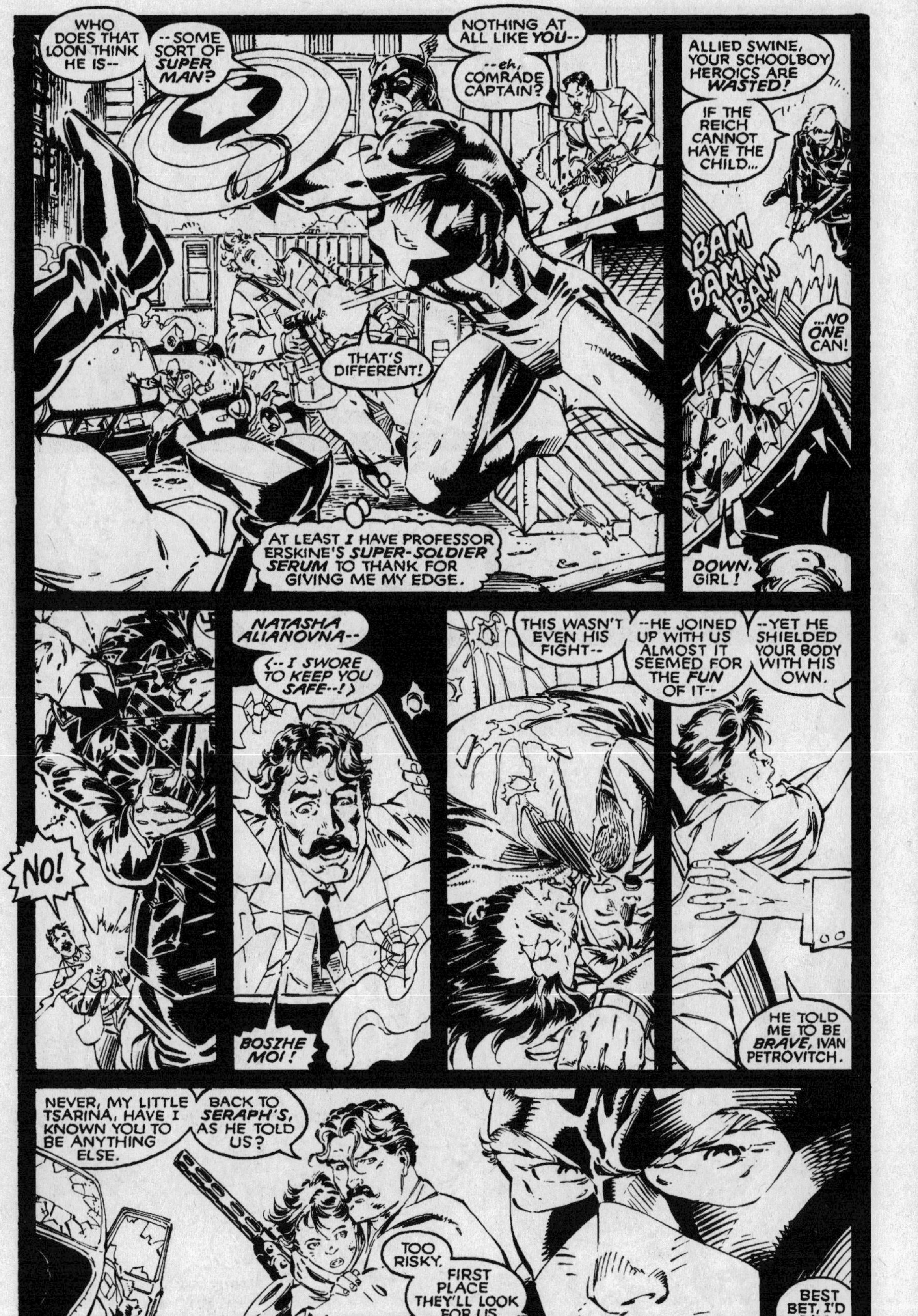
WHO DOES THAT LOON THINK HE IS--
--SOME SORT OF SUPER MAN?
NOTHING AT ALL LIKE YOU--
--eh, COMRADE CAPTAIN?
THAT'S DIFFERENT!
AT LEAST I HAVE PROFESSOR ERSKINE'S SUPER-SOLDIER SERUM TO THANK FOR GIVING ME MY EDGE.
ALLIED SWINE, YOUR SCHOOLBOY HEROICS ARE WASTED!
IF THE REICH CANNOT HAVE THE CHILD...
BAM BAM BAM
...NO ONE CAN!
DOWN, GIRL!
NO!
NATASHA ALIANOVNA--
<--I SWORE TO KEEP YOU SAFE--!>
BOSZHE MOI!
THIS WASN'T EVEN HIS FIGHT--
--HE JOINED UP WITH US ALMOST IT SEEMED FOR THE FUN OF IT--
--YET HE SHIELDED YOUR BODY WITH HIS OWN.
HE TOLD ME TO BE BRAVE, IVAN PETROVITCH.
NEVER, MY LITTLE TSARINA, HAVE I KNOWN YOU TO BE ANYTHING ELSE.
BACK TO SERAPH'S, AS HE TOLD US?
TOO RISKY. FIRST PLACE THEY'LL LOOK FOR US.
BEST BET, I'D SAY...

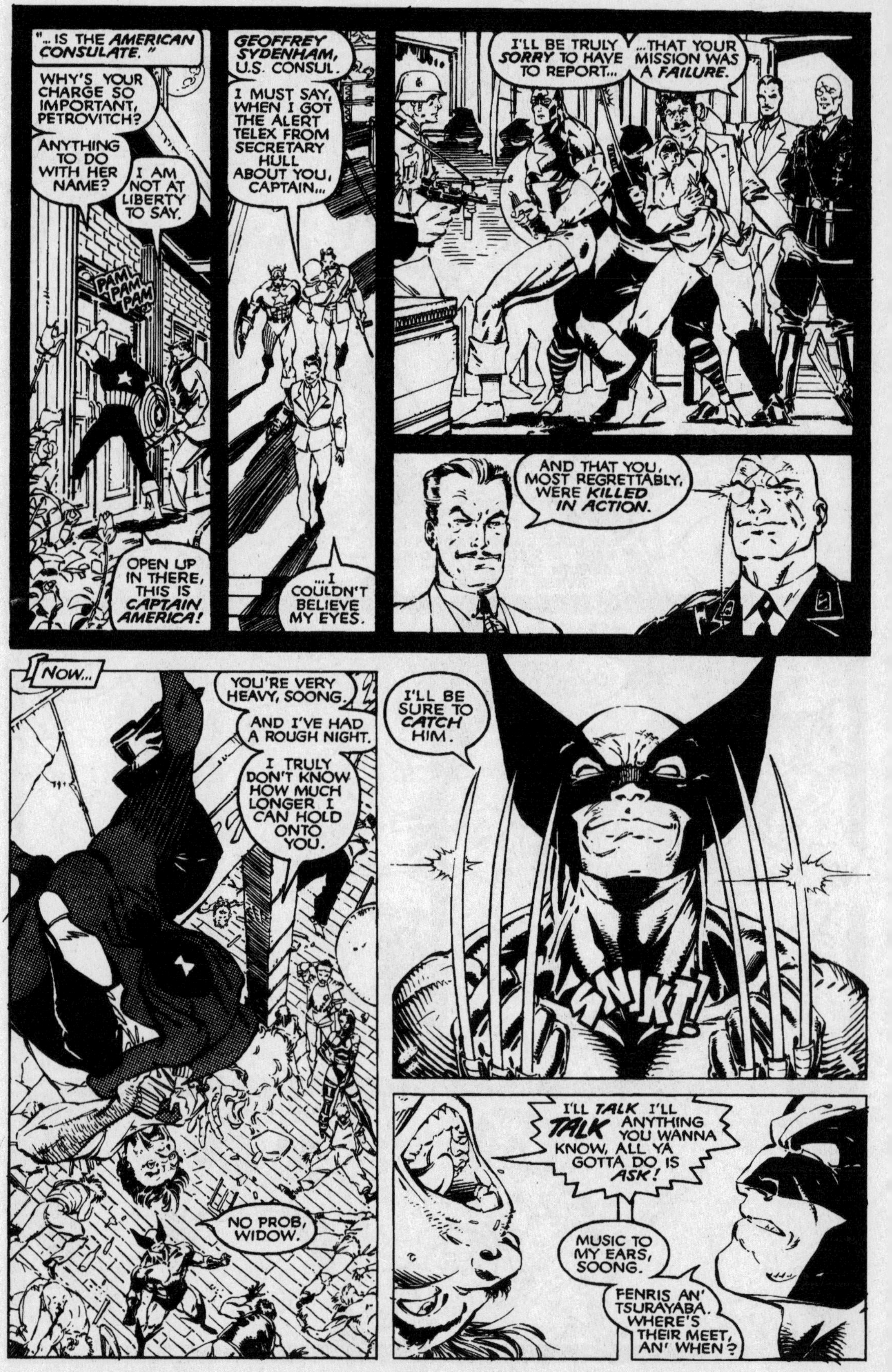
"...IS THE AMERICAN CONSULATE."
WHY'S YOUR CHARGE SO IMPORTANT, PETROVITCH?
ANYTHING TO DO WITH HER NAME?
I AM NOT AT LIBERTY TO SAY.
PAM PAM PAM
OPEN UP IN THERE, THIS IS CAPTAIN AMERICA!
GEOFFREY SYDENHAM, U.S. CONSUL.
I MUST SAY, WHEN I GOT THE ALERT TELEX FROM SECRETARY HULL ABOUT YOU, CAPTAIN...
...I COULDN'T BELIEVE MY EYES.
I'LL BE TRULY SORRY TO HAVE TO REPORT...
...THAT YOUR MISSION WAS A FAILURE.
AND THAT YOU, MOST REGRETTABLY, WERE KILLED IN ACTION.
NOW...
YOU'RE VERY HEAVY, SOONG.
AND I'VE HAD A ROUGH NIGHT.
I TRULY DON'T KNOW HOW MUCH LONGER I CAN HOLD ONTO YOU.
I'LL BE SURE TO CATCH HIM.
NO PROB, WIDOW.
SNIKT!
I'LL TALK I'LL TALK ANYTHING YOU WANNA KNOW, ALL YA GOTTA DO IS ASK!
MUSIC TO MY EARS, SOONG.
FENRIS AN' TSURAYABA. WHERE'S THEIR MEET, AN' WHEN?

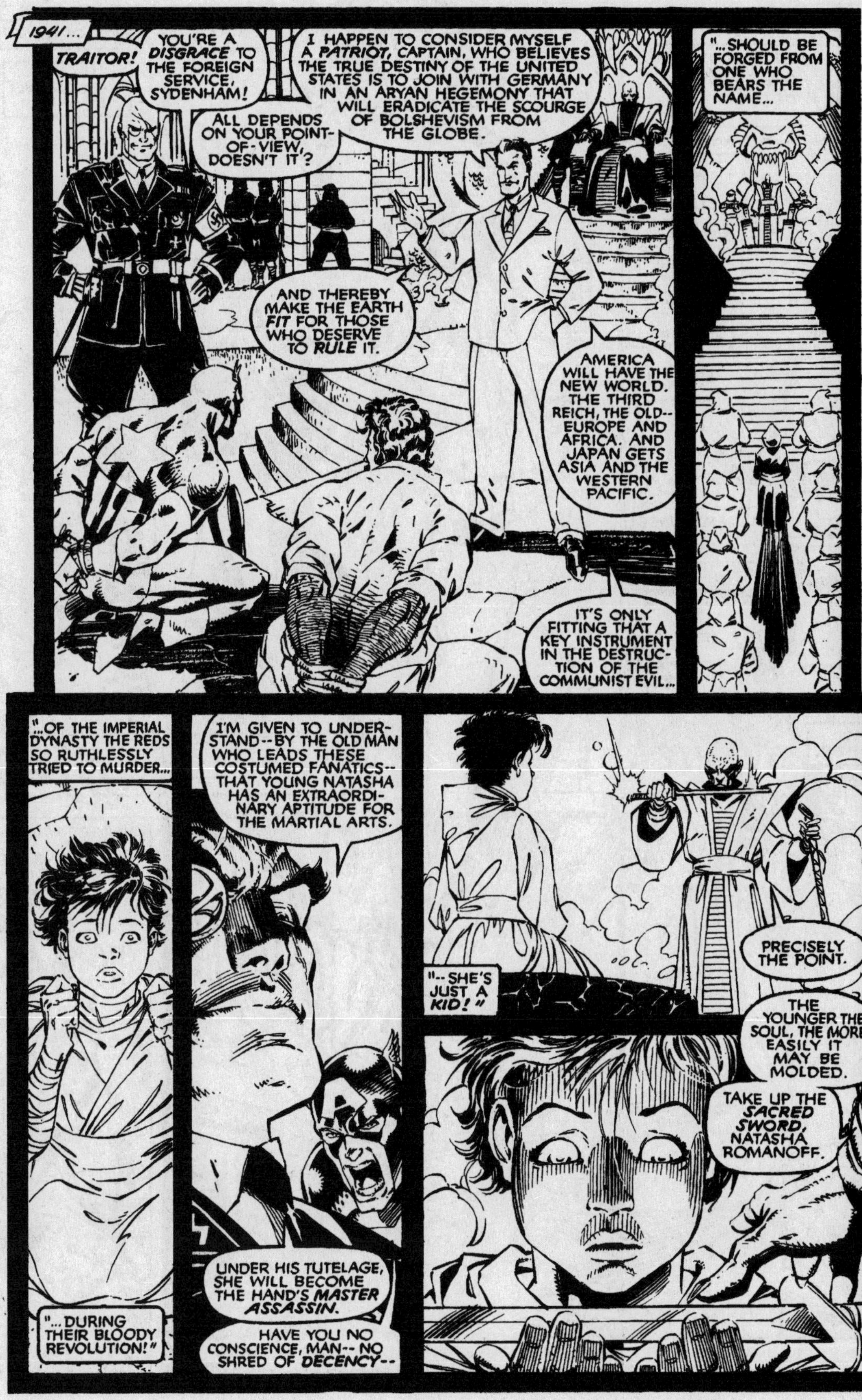
1941...
TRAITOR!
YOU'RE A DISGRACE TO THE FOREIGN SERVICE, SYDENHAM!
ALL DEPENDS ON YOUR POINT-OF-VIEW, DOESN'T IT?
I HAPPEN TO CONSIDER MYSELF A PATRIOT, CAPTAIN, WHO BELIEVES THE TRUE DESTINY OF THE UNITED STATES IS TO JOIN WITH GERMANY IN AN ARYAN HEGEMONY THAT WILL ERADICATE THE SCOURGE OF BOLSHEVISM FROM THE GLOBE.
AND THEREBY MAKE THE EARTH FIT FOR THOSE WHO DESERVE TO RULE IT.
AMERICA WILL HAVE THE NEW WORLD. THE THIRD REICH, THE OLD-- EUROPE AND AFRICA. AND JAPAN GETS ASIA AND THE WESTERN PACIFIC.
IT'S ONLY FITTING THAT A KEY INSTRUMENT IN THE DESTRUCTION OF THE COMMUNIST EVIL...
"...SHOULD BE FORGED FROM ONE WHO BEARS THE NAME...
"...OF THE IMPERIAL DYNASTY THE REDS SO RUTHLESSLY TRIED TO MURDER...
"...DURING THEIR BLOODY REVOLUTION!"
I'M GIVEN TO UNDERSTAND--BY THE OLD MAN WHO LEADS THESE COSTUMED FANATICS--THAT YOUNG NATASHA HAS AN EXTRAORDINARY APTITUDE FOR THE MARTIAL ARTS.
UNDER HIS TUTELAGE, SHE WILL BECOME THE HAND'S MASTER ASSASSIN.
HAVE YOU NO CONSCIENCE, MAN-- NO SHRED OF DECENCY--
"--SHE'S JUST A KID!"
PRECISELY THE POINT.
THE YOUNGER THE SOUL, THE MORE EASILY IT MAY BE MOLDED.
TAKE UP THE SACRED SWORD, NATASHA ROMANOFF.

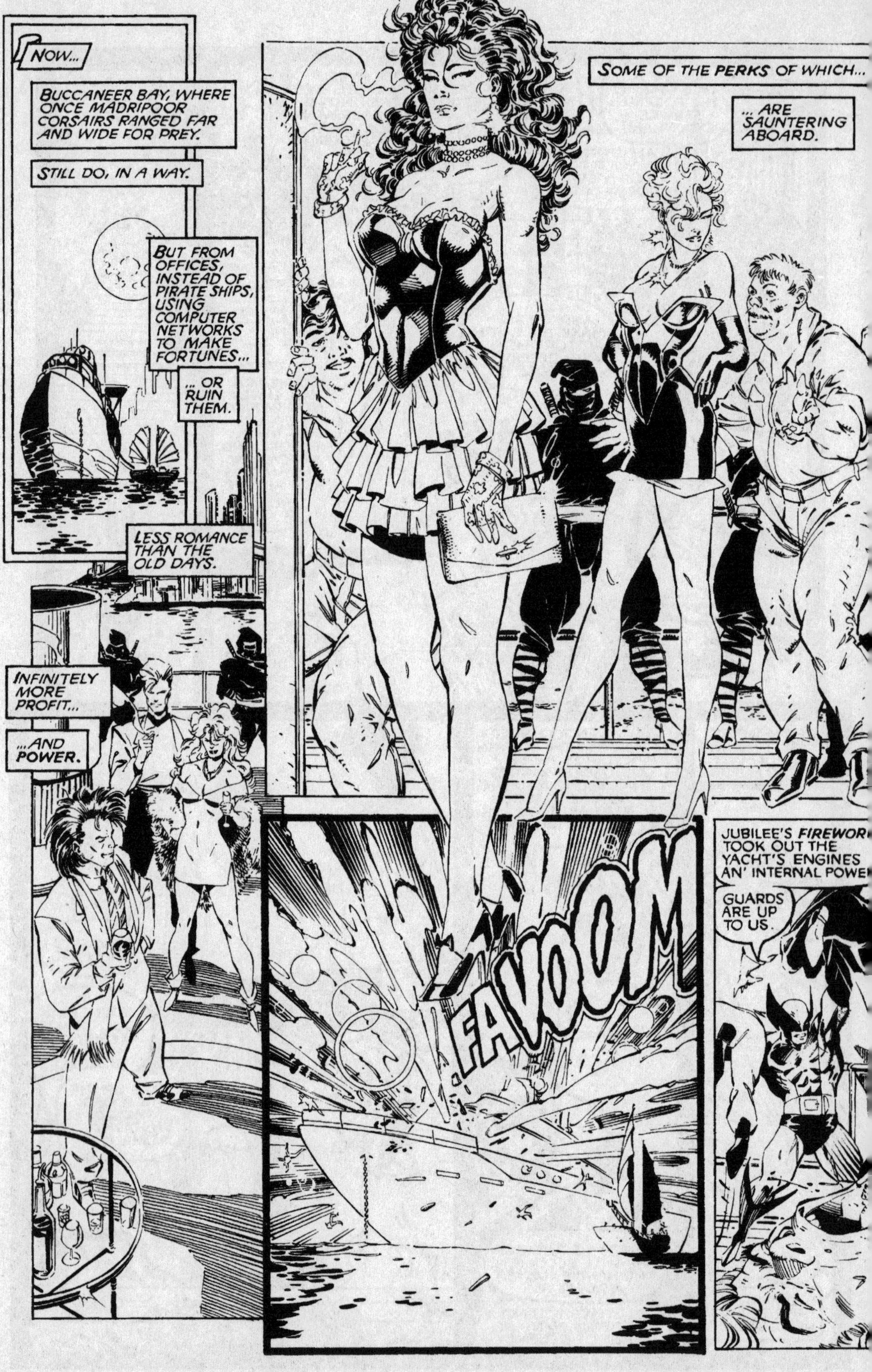
NOW...
BUCCANEER BAY, WHERE ONCE MADRIPOOR CORSAIRS RANGED FAR AND WIDE FOR PREY.
STILL DO, IN A WAY.
BUT FROM OFFICES, INSTEAD OF PIRATE SHIPS, USING COMPUTER NETWORKS TO MAKE FORTUNES...
...OR RUIN THEM.
LESS ROMANCE THAN THE OLD DAYS.
INFINITELY MORE PROFIT...
...AND POWER.
SOME OF THE PERKS OF WHICH...
...ARE SAUNTERING ABOARD.
FAVOOM
JUBILEE'S FIREWOR
TOOK OUT THE YACHT'S ENGINES AN' INTERNAL POWE
GUARDS ARE UP TO US.

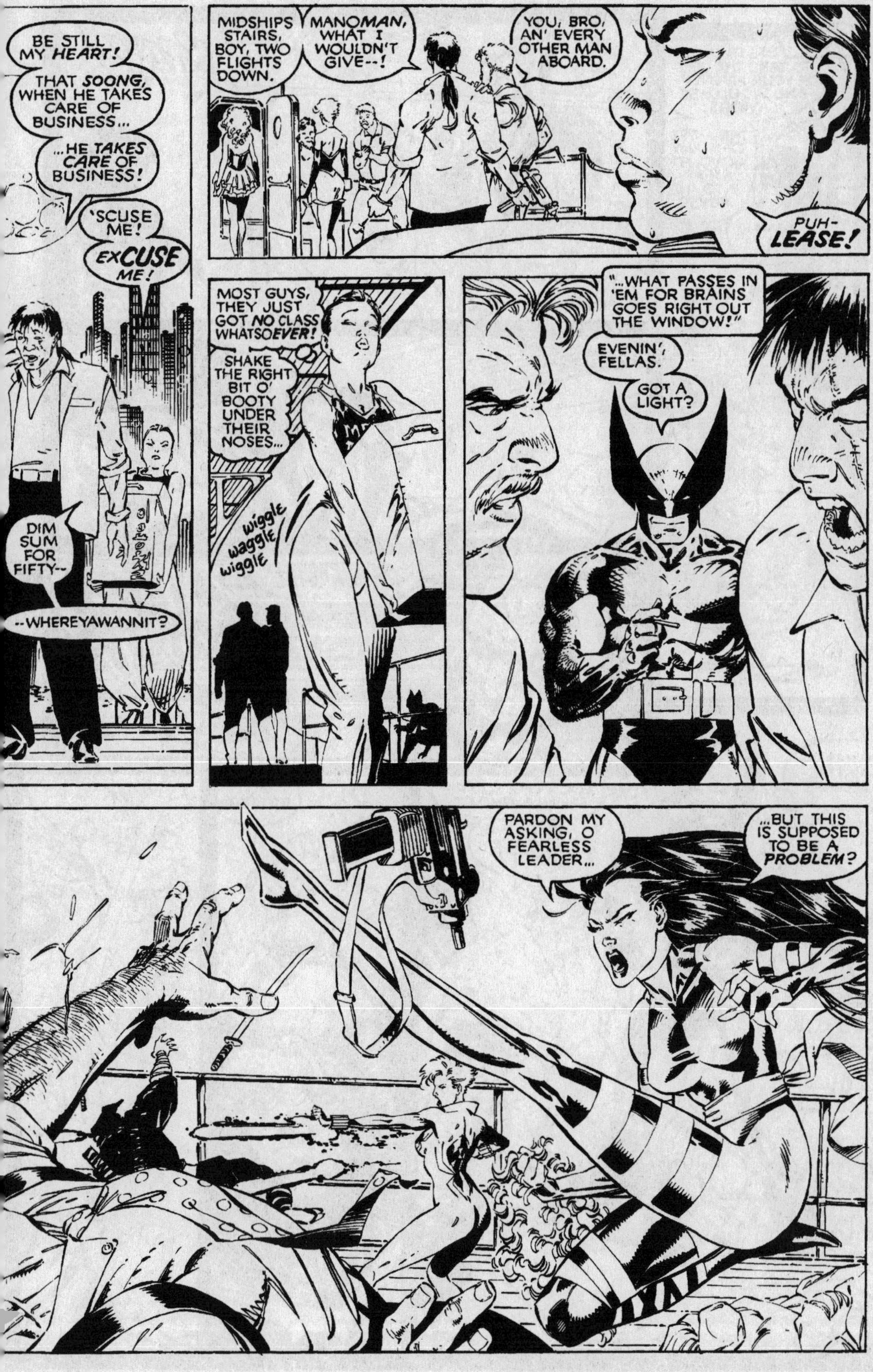
BE STILL MY HEART!
THAT SOONG, WHEN HE TAKES CARE OF BUSINESS...
...HE TAKES CARE OF BUSINESS!
'SCUSE ME!
EXCUSE ME!
DIM SUM FOR FIFTY--
--WHEREYAWANNIT?
MIDSHIPS STAIRS, BOY, TWO FLIGHTS DOWN.
MANOMAN, WHAT I WOULDN'T GIVE--!
YOU, BRO, AN' EVERY OTHER MAN ABOARD.
PUH-LEASE!
MOST GUYS, THEY JUST GOT NO CLASS WHATSOEVER!
SHAKE THE RIGHT BIT O' BOOTY UNDER THEIR NOSES...
wiggle waggle wiggle
"...WHAT PASSES IN 'EM FOR BRAINS GOES RIGHT OUT THE WINDOW!"
EVENIN', FELLAS.
GOT A LIGHT?
PARDON MY ASKING, O FEARLESS LEADER...
...BUT THIS IS SUPPOSED TO BE A PROBLEM?

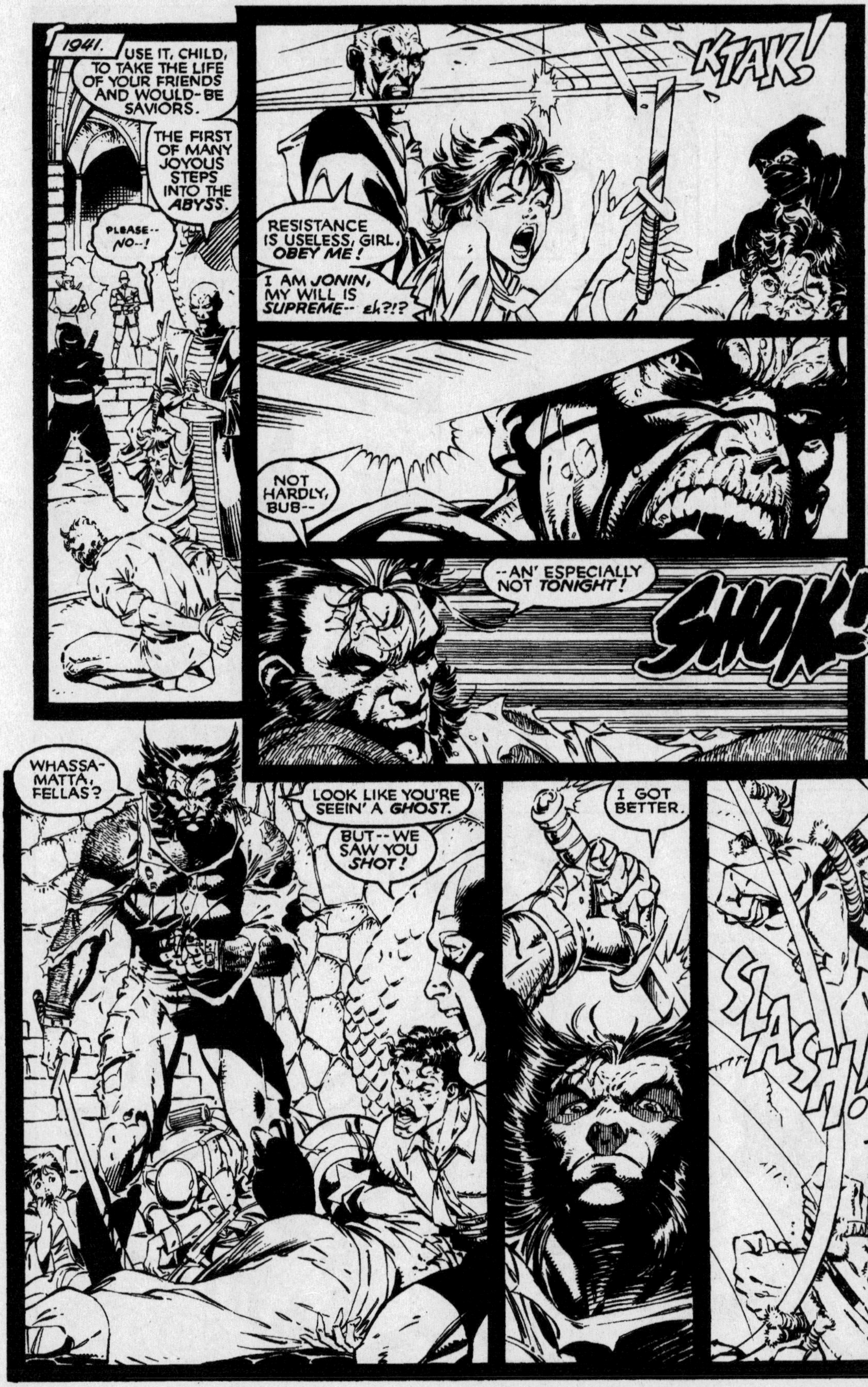
1941.
USE IT, CHILD, TO TAKE THE LIFE OF YOUR FRIENDS AND WOULD-BE SAVIORS.
THE FIRST OF MANY JOYOUS STEPS INTO THE ABYSS.
PLEASE-- NO--!
KTAK!
RESISTANCE IS USELESS, GIRL. OBEY ME!
I AM JONIN, MY WILL IS SUPREME-- eh?!?
NOT HARDLY, BUB--
--AN' ESPECIALLY NOT TONIGHT!
SHOK!
WHASSA-MATTA, FELLAS?
LOOK LIKE YOU'RE SEEIN' A GHOST.
BUT--WE SAW YOU SHOT!
I GOT BETTER.
SLASH!

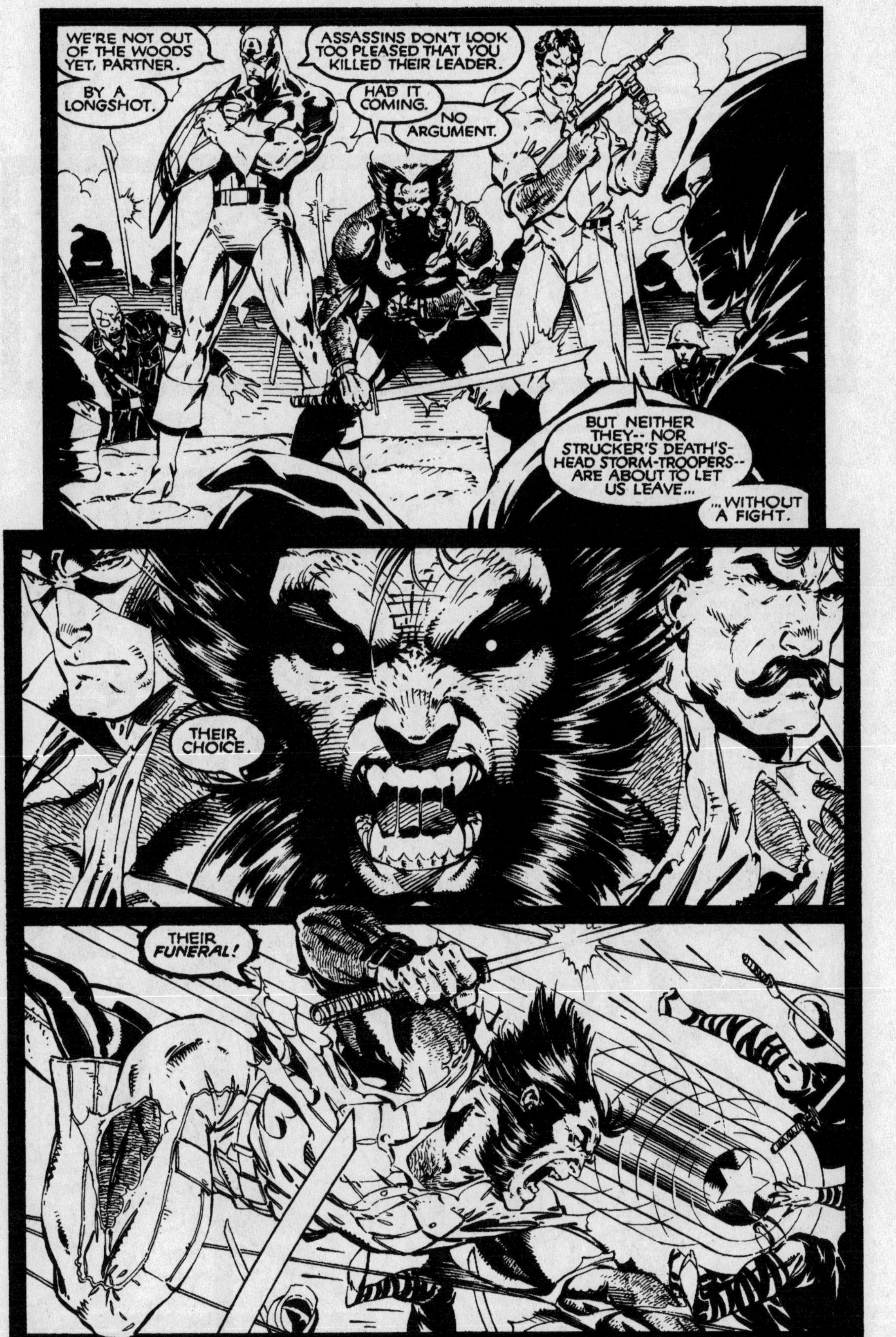
WE'RE NOT OUT OF THE WOODS YET, PARTNER.
BY A LONGSHOT.
ASSASSINS DON'T LOOK TOO PLEASED THAT YOU KILLED THEIR LEADER.
HAD IT COMING.
NO ARGUMENT.
BUT NEITHER THEY-- NOR STRUCKER'S DEATH'S-HEAD STORM-TROOPERS-- ARE ABOUT TO LET US LEAVE...
...WITHOUT A FIGHT.
THEIR CHOICE.
THEIR FUNERAL!

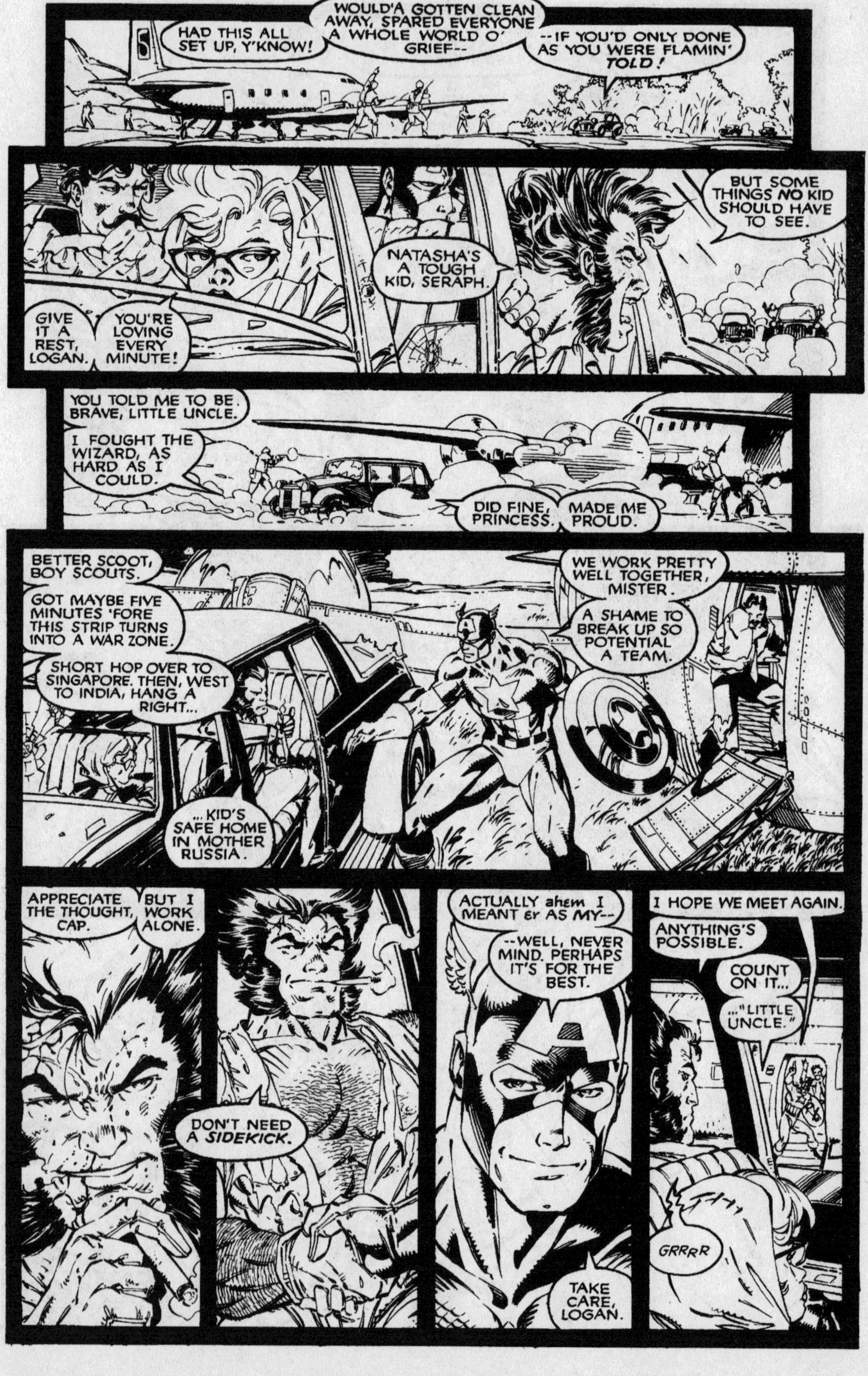
HAD THIS ALL SET UP, Y'KNOW!
WOULD'A GOTTEN CLEAN AWAY, SPARED EVERYONE A WHOLE WORLD O' GRIEF--
--IF YOU'D ONLY DONE AS YOU WERE FLAMIN' TOLD!
NATASHA'S A TOUGH KID, SERAPH.
BUT SOME THINGS NO KID SHOULD HAVE TO SEE.
GIVE IT A REST, LOGAN.
YOU'RE LOVING EVERY MINUTE!
YOU TOLD ME TO BE BRAVE, LITTLE UNCLE.
I FOUGHT THE WIZARD, AS HARD AS I COULD.
DID FINE, PRINCESS.
MADE ME PROUD.
BETTER SCOOT, BOY SCOUTS.
GOT MAYBE FIVE MINUTES 'FORE THIS STRIP TURNS INTO A WAR ZONE.
SHORT HOP OVER TO SINGAPORE. THEN, WEST TO INDIA, HANG A RIGHT...
...KID'S SAFE HOME IN MOTHER RUSSIA.
WE WORK PRETTY WELL TOGETHER, MISTER.
A SHAME TO BREAK UP SO POTENTIAL A TEAM.
APPRECIATE THE THOUGHT, CAP.
BUT I WORK ALONE.
DON'T NEED A SIDEKICK.
ACTUALLY ahem I MEANT er AS MY--
--WELL, NEVER MIND. PERHAPS IT'S FOR THE BEST.
TAKE CARE, LOGAN.
I HOPE WE MEET AGAIN.
ANYTHING'S POSSIBLE.
COUNT ON IT...
..."LITTLE UNCLE."
GRRRR

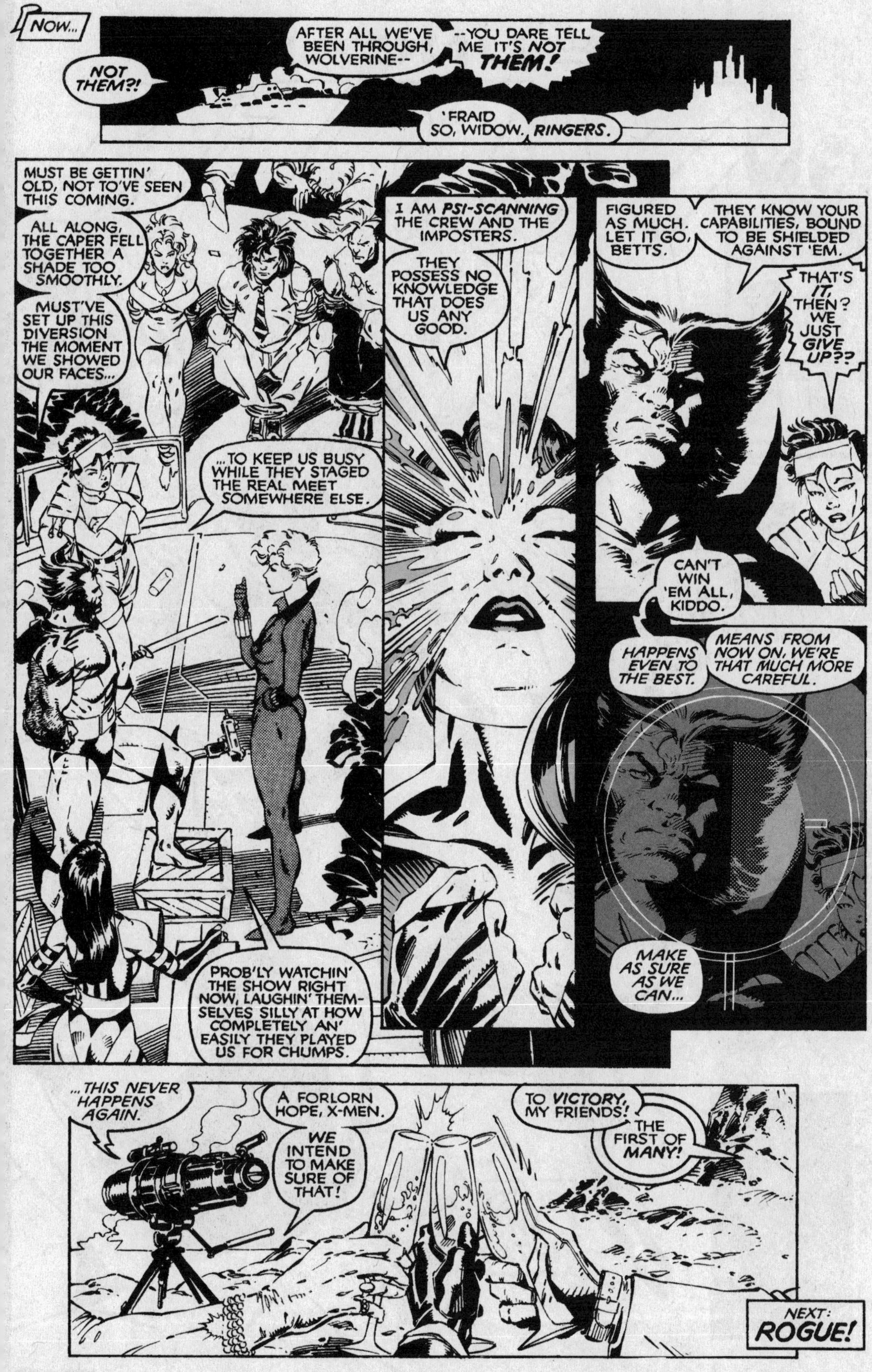
NOW...
NOT THEM?!
AFTER ALL WE'VE BEEN THROUGH, WOLVERINE--
--YOU DARE TELL ME IT'S NOT THEM!
'FRAID SO, WIDOW. RINGERS.
MUST BE GETTIN' OLD, NOT TO'VE SEEN THIS COMING.
ALL ALONG, THE CAPER FELL TOGETHER A SHADE TOO SMOOTHLY.
MUST'VE SET UP THIS DIVERSION THE MOMENT WE SHOWED OUR FACES...
...TO KEEP US BUSY WHILE THEY STAGED THE REAL MEET SOMEWHERE ELSE.
PROB'LY WATCHIN' THE SHOW RIGHT NOW, LAUGHIN' THEMSELVES SILLY AT HOW COMPLETELY AN' EASILY THEY PLAYED US FOR CHUMPS.
I AM PSI-SCANNING THE CREW AND THE IMPOSTERS.
THEY POSSESS NO KNOWLEDGE THAT DOES US ANY GOOD.
FIGURED AS MUCH. LET IT GO, BETTS.
THEY KNOW YOUR CAPABILITIES, BOUND TO BE SHIELDED AGAINST 'EM.
THAT'S IT, THEN? WE JUST GIVE UP??
CAN'T WIN 'EM ALL, KIDDO.
HAPPENS EVEN TO THE BEST.
MEANS FROM NOW ON, WE'RE THAT MUCH MORE CAREFUL.
MAKE AS SURE AS WE CAN...
...THIS NEVER HAPPENS AGAIN.
A FORLORN HOPE, X-MEN.
WE INTEND TO MAKE SURE OF THAT!
TO VICTORY, MY FRIENDS!
THE FIRST OF MANY!
NEXT: ROGUE!

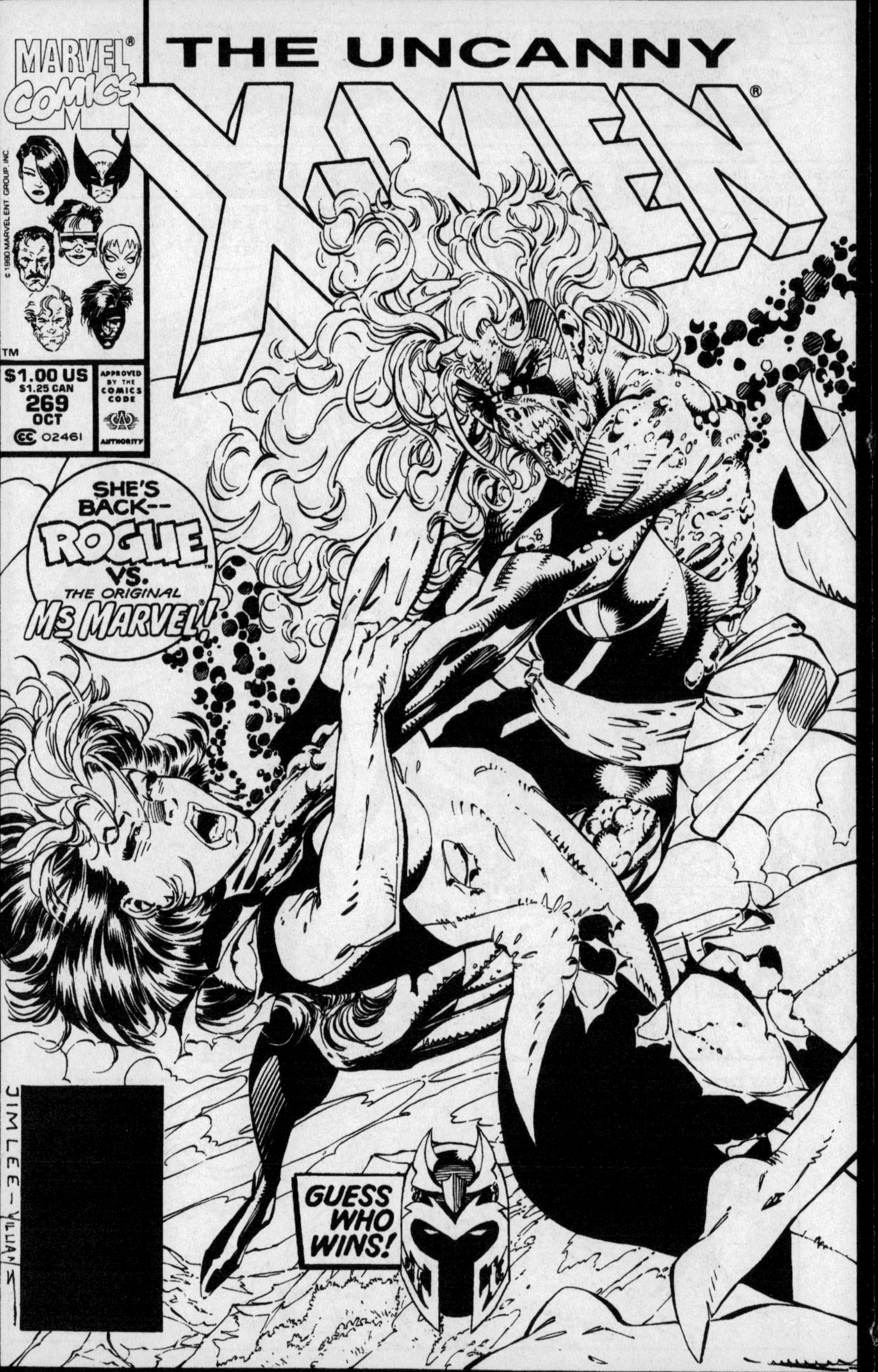
MARVEL® COMICS
THE UNCANNY
X-MEN®
© 1990 MARVEL ENT GROUP, INC.
TM
$1.00 US
$1.25 CAN
269
OCT
02461
APPROVED BY THE COMICS CODE AUTHORITY
SHE'S BACK--
ROGUE
VS.
THE ORIGINAL
Ms MARVEL!
GUESS WHO WINS!
JIM LEE - WILLIAMS

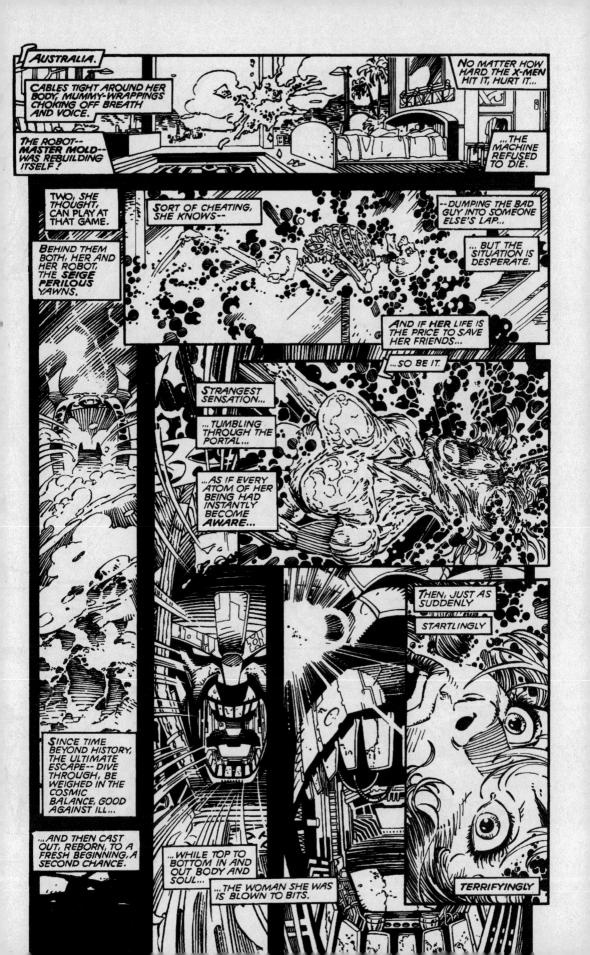

AUSTRALIA.

CABLES TIGHT AROUND HER BODY, MUMMY-WRAPPINGS CHOKING OFF BREATH AND VOICE.

THE ROBOT-- MASTER MOLD-- WAS REBUILDING ITSELF!

NO MATTER HOW HARD THE X-MEN HIT IT, HURT IT...

...THE MACHINE REFUSED TO DIE.

TWO, SHE THOUGHT, CAN PLAY AT THAT GAME.

SORT OF CHEATING, SHE KNOWS--

--DUMPING THE BAD GUY INTO SOMEONE ELSE'S LAP...

BEHIND THEM BOTH, HER AND HER ROBOT, THE SEIGE PERILOUS YAWNS.

...BUT THE SITUATION IS DESPERATE.

AND IF HER LIFE IS THE PRICE TO SAVE HER FRIENDS...

...SO BE IT.

STRANGEST SENSATION...

...TUMBLING THROUGH THE PORTAL...

...AS IF EVERY ATOM OF HER BEING HAD INSTANTLY BECOME AWARE...

THEN, JUST AS SUDDENLY

STARTLINGLY

SINCE TIME BEYOND HISTORY, THE ULTIMATE ESCAPE-- DIVE THROUGH, BE WEIGHED IN THE COSMIC BALANCE, GOOD AGAINST ILL...

...AND THEN CAST OUT, REBORN, TO A FRESH BEGINNING, A SECOND CHANCE.

...WHILE TOP TO BOTTOM IN AND OUT BODY AND SOUL...

...THE WOMAN SHE WAS IS BLOWN TO BITS.

TERRIFYINGLY

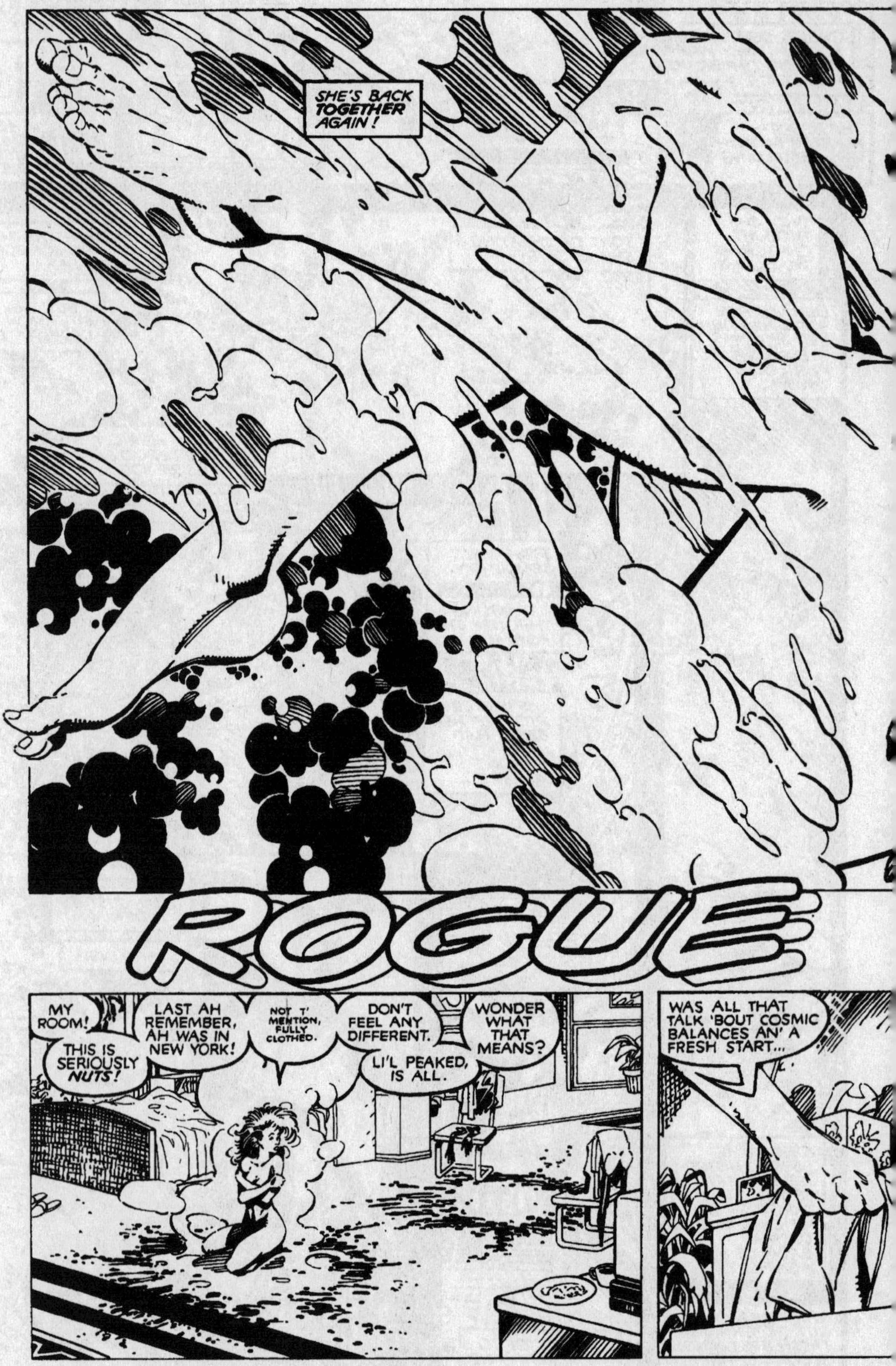
SHE'S BACK TOGETHER AGAIN!
ROGUE
MY ROOM!
THIS IS SERIOUSLY NUTS!
LAST AH REMEMBER, AH WAS IN NEW YORK!
NOT T' MENTION, FULLY CLOTHED.
DON'T FEEL ANY DIFFERENT.
LI'L PEAKED, IS ALL.
WONDER WHAT THAT MEANS?
WAS ALL THAT TALK 'BOUT COSMIC BALANCES AN' A FRESH START...

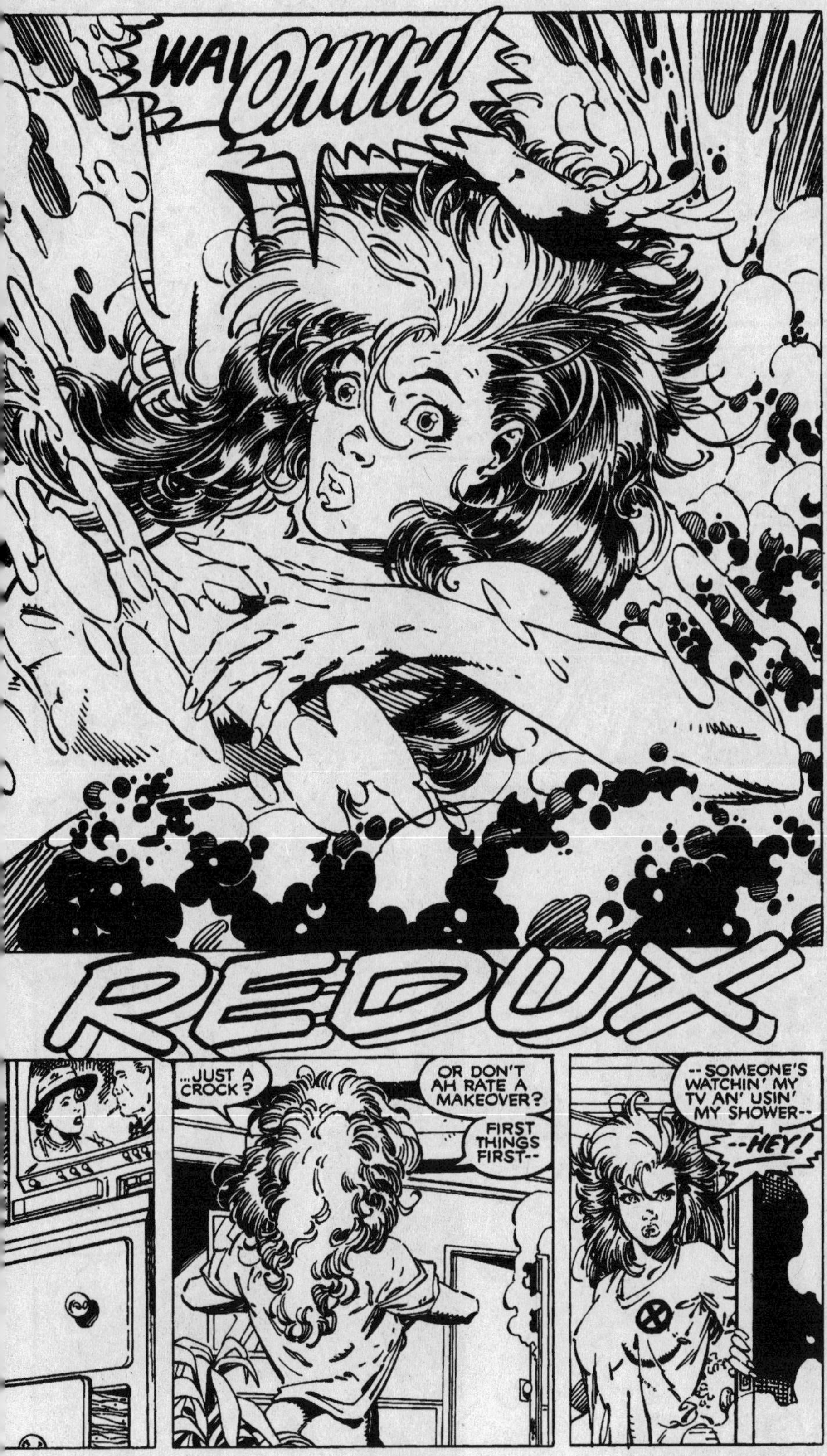

WAI
OHWW!
REDUX
...JUST A CROCK?
OR DON'T AH RATE A MAKEOVER?
FIRST THINGS FIRST--
--SOMEONE'S WATCHIN' MY TV AN' USIN' MY SHOWER--
--HEY!

CHRIS CLAREMONT
WRITER

JIM LEE
PENCILER

ART THIBERT
GUEST INKER

TASK FORCE "X"
LETTERER

STEVE BUCCELLATO
COLORIST

BOB HARRAS
EDITOR

TOM DeFALCO
EDITOR IN CHIEF

A STAN LEE PRESENTATION

STARRING THE UNCANNY X-MEN

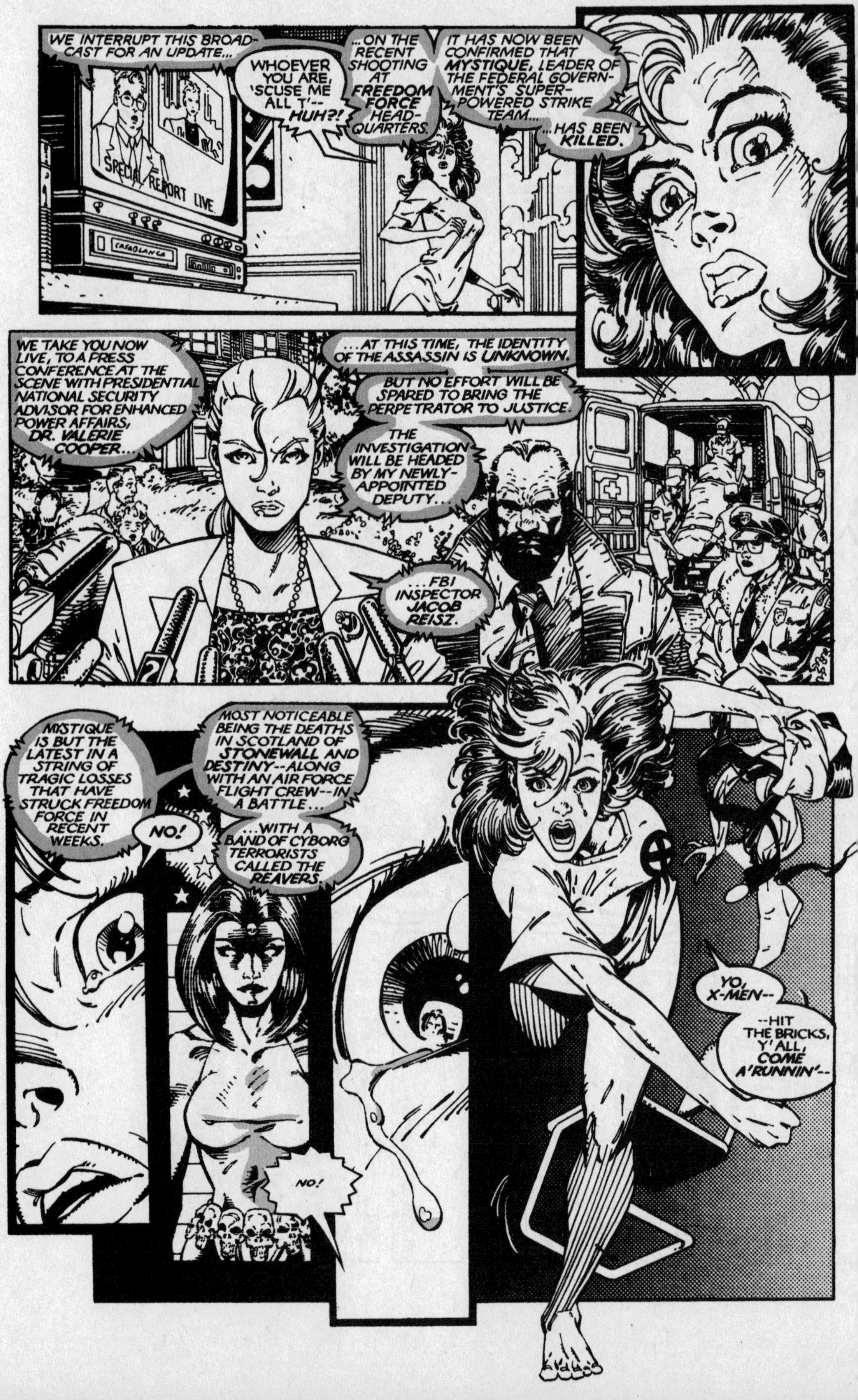

WE INTERRUPT THIS BROADCAST FOR AN UPDATE...
WHOEVER YOU ARE, 'SCUSE ME ALL T'-- HUH?!
...ON THE RECENT SHOOTING AT FREEDOM FORCE HEADQUARTERS.
IT HAS NOW BEEN CONFIRMED THAT MYSTIQUE, LEADER OF THE FEDERAL GOVERNMENT'S SUPER-POWERED STRIKE TEAM...
...HAS BEEN KILLED.
SPECIAL REPORT LIVE
CASABLANCA
WE TAKE YOU NOW LIVE, TO A PRESS CONFERENCE AT THE SCENE WITH PRESIDENTIAL NATIONAL SECURITY ADVISOR FOR ENHANCED POWER AFFAIRS, DR. VALERIE COOPER...
...AT THIS TIME, THE IDENTITY OF THE ASSASSIN IS UNKNOWN.
BUT NO EFFORT WILL BE SPARED TO BRING THE PERPETRATOR TO JUSTICE.
THE INVESTIGATION WILL BE HEADED BY MY NEWLY-APPOINTED DEPUTY...
...FBI INSPECTOR JACOB REISZ.
MYSTIQUE IS BUT THE LATEST IN A STRING OF TRAGIC LOSSES THAT HAVE STRUCK FREEDOM FORCE IN RECENT WEEKS.
MOST NOTICEABLE BEING THE DEATHS IN SCOTLAND OF STONEWALL AND DESTINY--ALONG WITH AN AIR FORCE FLIGHT CREW--IN A BATTLE...
...WITH A BAND OF CYBORG TERRORISTS CALLED THE REAVERS.
NO!
NO!
YO, X-MEN--
--HIT THE BRICKS, Y'ALL, COME A'RUNNIN'--

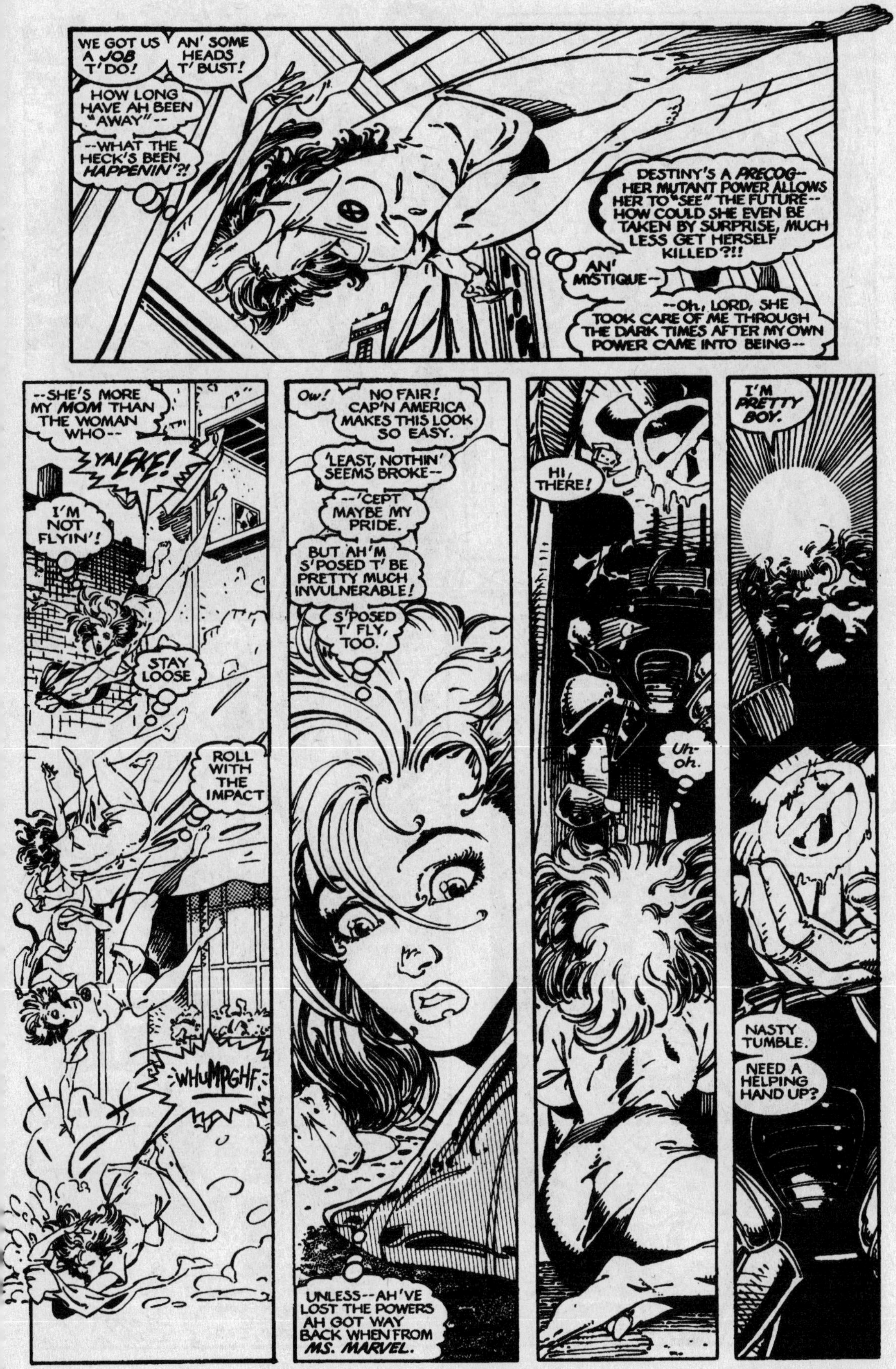
WE GOT US A JOB T'DO!
AN' SOME HEADS T' BUST!
HOW LONG HAVE AH BEEN "AWAY"--
--WHAT THE HECK'S BEEN HAPPENIN'?!
DESTINY'S A PRECOG-- HER MUTANT POWER ALLOWS HER TO "SEE" THE FUTURE-- HOW COULD SHE EVEN BE TAKEN BY SURPRISE, MUCH LESS GET HERSELF KILLED?!!
AN' MYSTIQUE--
--OH, LORD, SHE TOOK CARE OF ME THROUGH THE DARK TIMES AFTER MY OWN POWER CAME INTO BEING--
--SHE'S MORE MY MOM THAN THE WOMAN WHO--
YAIEEE!
I'M NOT FLYIN'!
STAY LOOSE
ROLL WITH THE IMPACT
WHUMPGHF
OW!
NO FAIR! CAP'N AMERICA MAKES THIS LOOK SO EASY.
'LEAST, NOTHIN' SEEMS BROKE--
--'CEPT MAYBE MY PRIDE.
BUT AH'M S'POSED T' BE PRETTY MUCH INVULNERABLE!
S'POSED T' FLY, TOO.
UNLESS--AH'VE LOST THE POWERS AH GOT WAY BACK WHEN FROM MS. MARVEL.
HI, THERE!
UH-OH.
I'M PRETTY BOY.
NASTY TUMBLE.
NEED A HELPING HAND UP?

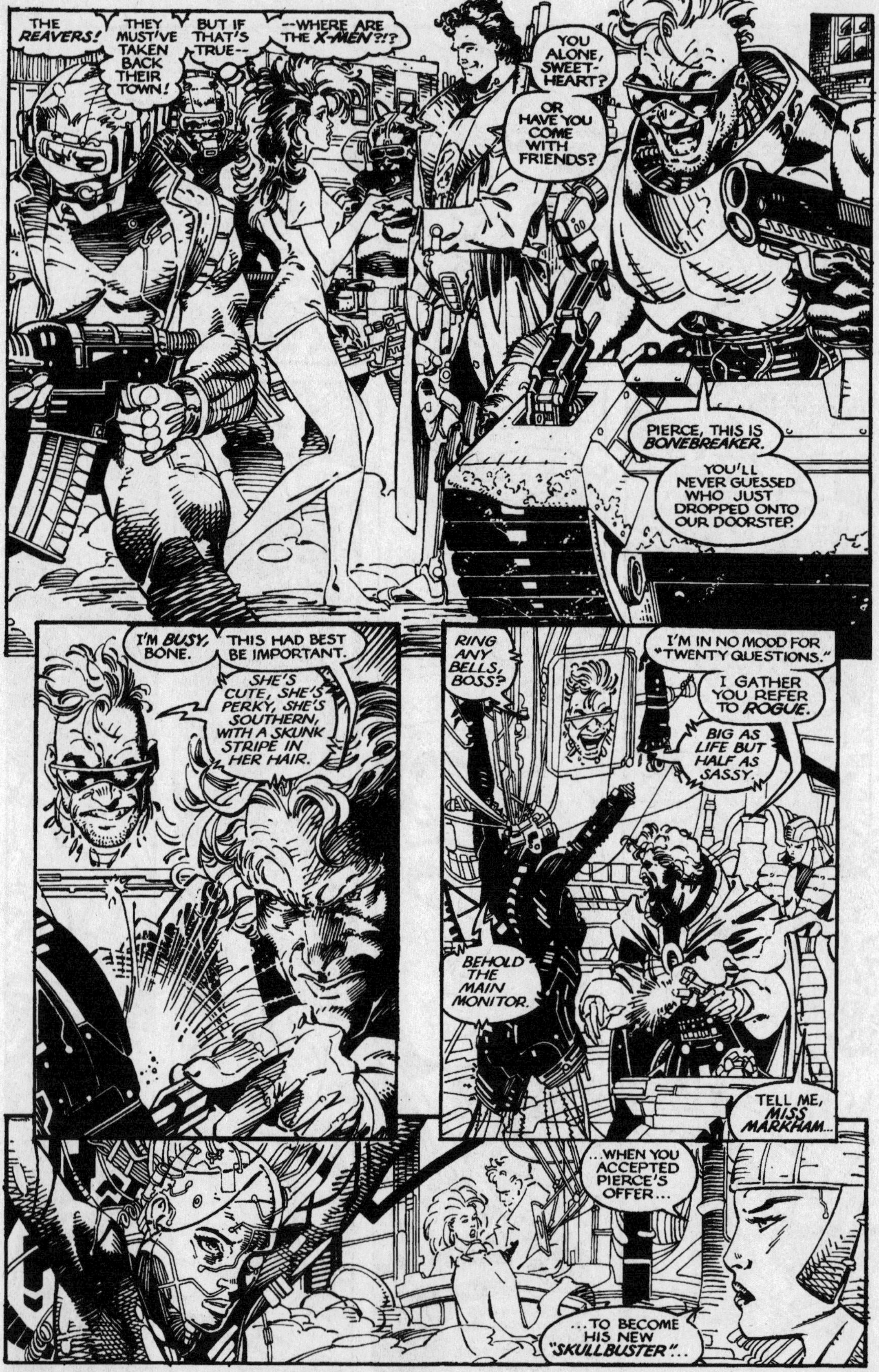
THE REAVERS!
THEY MUST'VE TAKEN BACK THEIR TOWN!
BUT IF THAT'S TRUE--
--WHERE ARE THE X-MEN?!?
YOU ALONE, SWEET-HEART?
OR HAVE YOU COME WITH FRIENDS?
PIERCE, THIS IS BONEBREAKER.
YOU'LL NEVER GUESSED WHO JUST DROPPED ONTO OUR DOORSTEP.
I'M BUSY, BONE.
THIS HAD BEST BE IMPORTANT.
SHE'S CUTE, SHE'S PERKY, SHE'S SOUTHERN, WITH A SKUNK STRIPE IN HER HAIR.
RING ANY BELLS, BOSS?
I'M IN NO MOOD FOR "TWENTY QUESTIONS."
I GATHER YOU REFER TO ROGUE.
BIG AS LIFE BUT HALF AS SASSY.
BEHOLD THE MAIN MONITOR.
TELL ME, MISS MARKHAM...
...WHEN YOU ACCEPTED PIERCE'S OFFER...
...TO BECOME HIS NEW "SKULLBUSTER"...

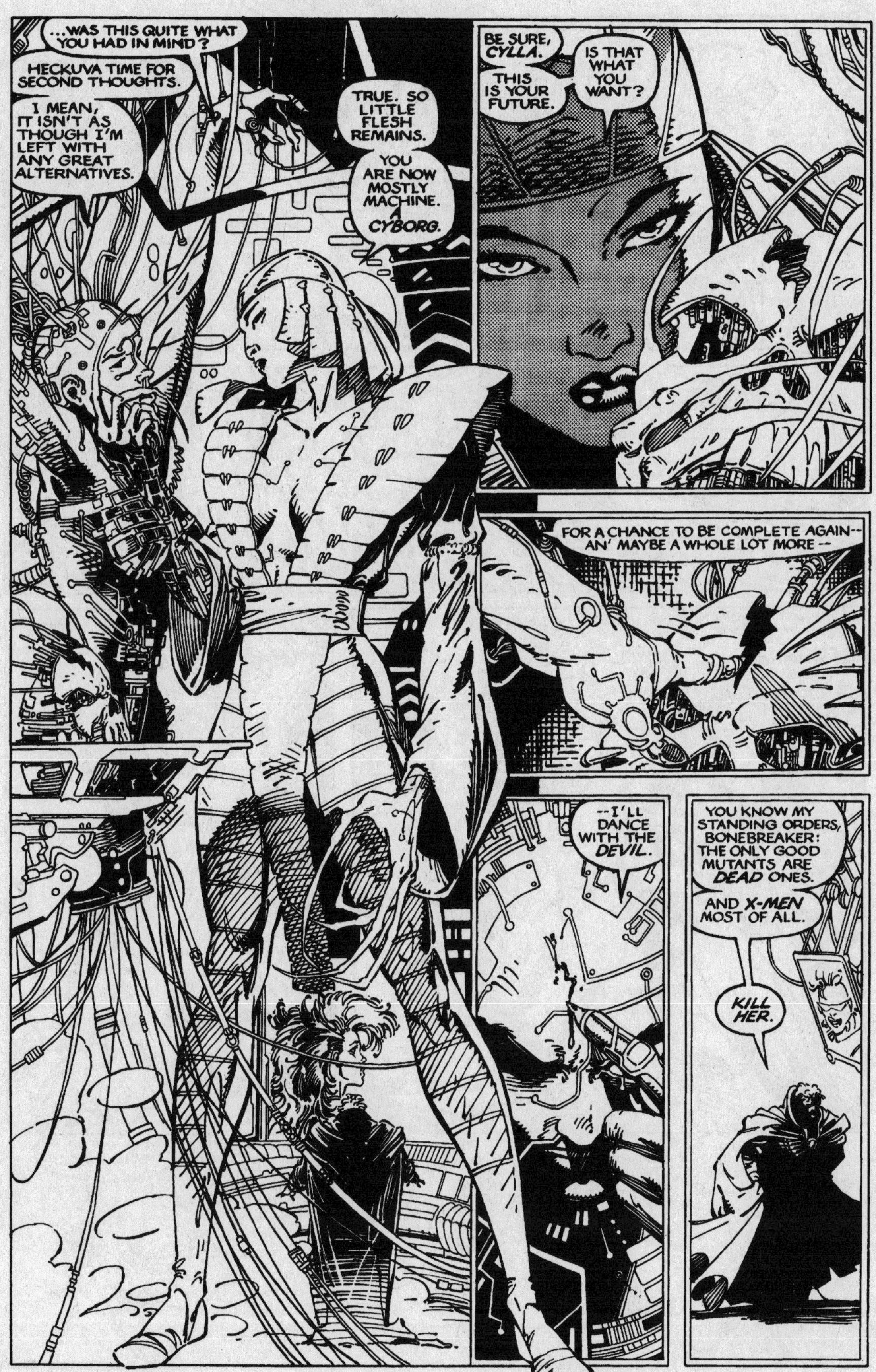

...WAS THIS QUITE WHAT YOU HAD IN MIND?
HECKUVA TIME FOR SECOND THOUGHTS.
I MEAN, IT ISN'T AS THOUGH I'M LEFT WITH ANY GREAT ALTERNATIVES.
TRUE. SO LITTLE FLESH REMAINS.
YOU ARE NOW MOSTLY MACHINE. A CYBORG.
BE SURE, CYLLA.
THIS IS YOUR FUTURE.
IS THAT WHAT YOU WANT?
FOR A CHANCE TO BE COMPLETE AGAIN-- AN' MAYBE A WHOLE LOT MORE --
--I'LL DANCE WITH THE DEVIL.
YOU KNOW MY STANDING ORDERS, BONEBREAKER: THE ONLY GOOD MUTANTS ARE DEAD ONES.
AND X-MEN MOST OF ALL.
KILL HER.

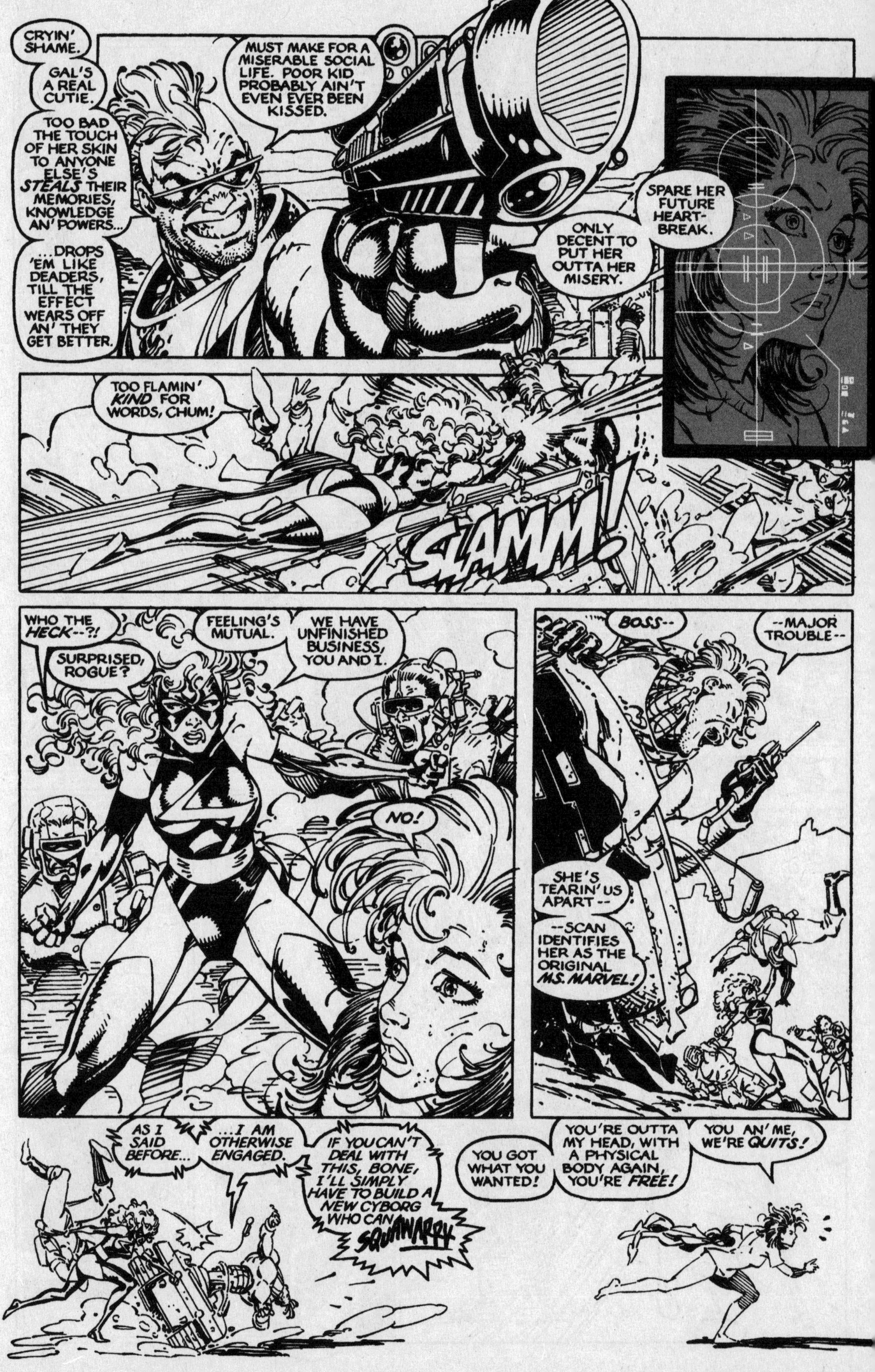
CRYIN' SHAME.
GAL'S A REAL CUTIE.
TOO BAD THE TOUCH OF HER SKIN TO ANYONE ELSE'S STEALS THEIR MEMORIES, KNOWLEDGE AN' POWERS...
...DROPS 'EM LIKE DEADERS, TILL THE EFFECT WEARS OFF AN' THEY GET BETTER.
MUST MAKE FOR A MISERABLE SOCIAL LIFE. POOR KID PROBABLY AIN'T EVEN EVER BEEN KISSED.
ONLY DECENT TO PUT HER OUTTA HER MISERY.
SPARE HER FUTURE HEART-BREAK.
TOO FLAMIN' KIND FOR WORDS, CHUM!
SLAMM!
WHO THE HECK--?!
SURPRISED, ROGUE?
FEELING'S MUTUAL.
WE HAVE UNFINISHED BUSINESS, YOU AND I.
NO!
BOSS--
--MAJOR TROUBLE--
SHE'S TEARIN' US APART--
--SCAN IDENTIFIES HER AS THE ORIGINAL MS. MARVEL!
AS I SAID BEFORE...
...I AM OTHERWISE ENGAGED.
IF YOU CAN'T DEAL WITH THIS, BONE, I'LL SIMPLY HAVE TO BUILD A NEW CYBORG WHO CAN
SQUAWWKK
YOU GOT WHAT YOU WANTED!
YOU'RE OUTTA MY HEAD, WITH A PHYSICAL BODY AGAIN, YOU'RE FREE!
YOU AN' ME, WE'RE QUITS!

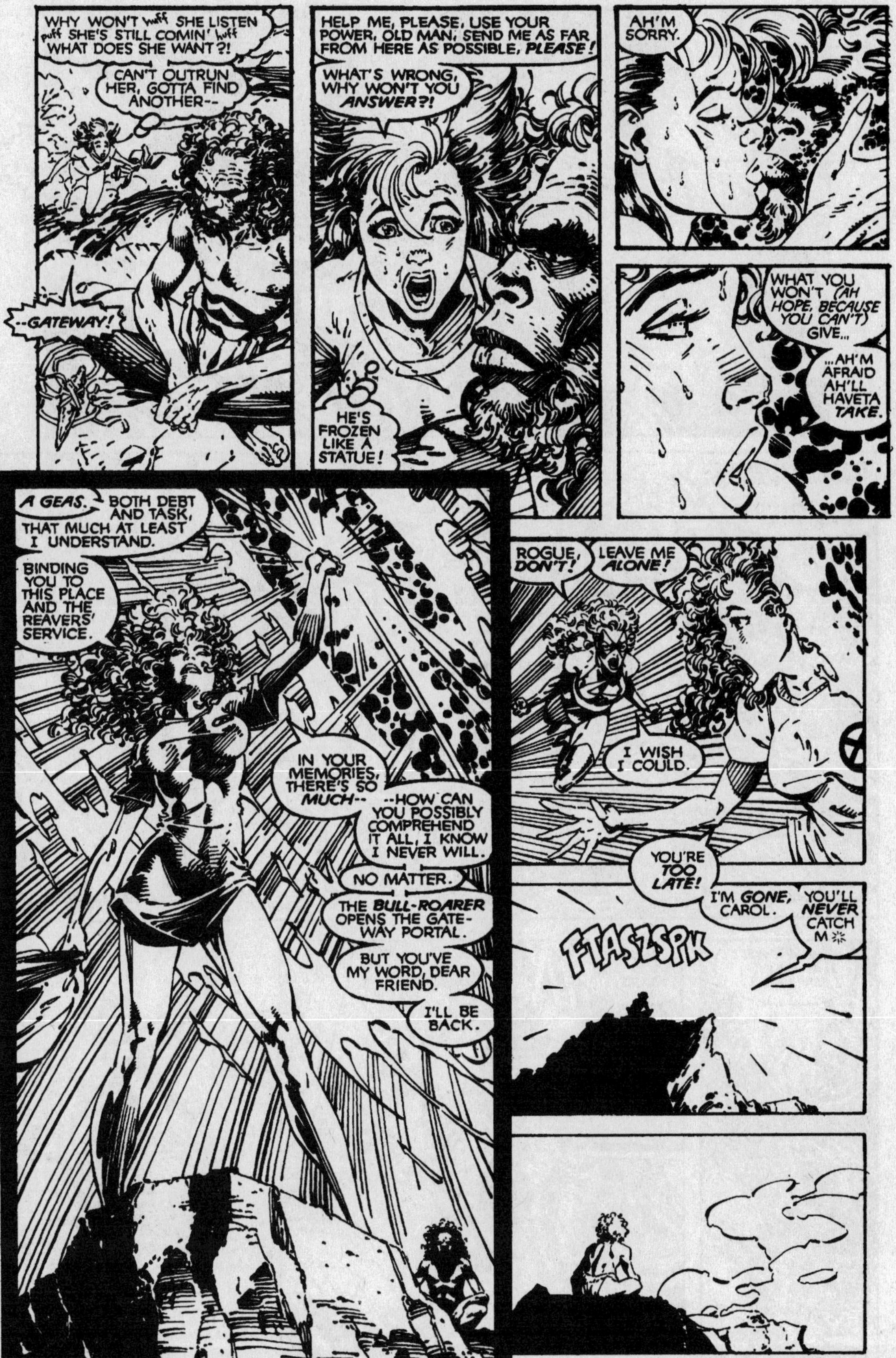

WHY WON'T huff SHE LISTEN puff SHE'S STILL COMIN' huff WHAT DOES SHE WANT?!
CAN'T OUTRUN HER, GOTTA FIND ANOTHER--
--GATEWAY!
HELP ME, PLEASE, USE YOUR POWER, OLD MAN, SEND ME AS FAR FROM HERE AS POSSIBLE, PLEASE!
WHAT'S WRONG, WHY WON'T YOU ANSWER?!
HE'S FROZEN LIKE A STATUE!
AH'M SORRY.
WHAT YOU WON'T (AH HOPE, BECAUSE YOU CAN'T) GIVE...
...AH'M AFRAID AH'LL HAVETA TAKE.
A GEAS.
BOTH DEBT AND TASK, THAT MUCH AT LEAST I UNDERSTAND.
BINDING YOU TO THIS PLACE AND THE REAVERS' SERVICE.
IN YOUR MEMORIES, THERE'S SO MUCH--
--HOW CAN YOU POSSIBLY COMPREHEND IT ALL, I KNOW I NEVER WILL.
NO MATTER.
THE BULL-ROARER OPENS THE GATEWAY PORTAL.
BUT YOU'VE MY WORD, DEAR FRIEND.
I'LL BE BACK.
ROGUE, DON'T!
LEAVE ME ALONE!
I WISH I COULD.
YOU'RE TOO LATE!
I'M GONE, CAROL.
YOU'LL NEVER CATCH M
FTASZSPK

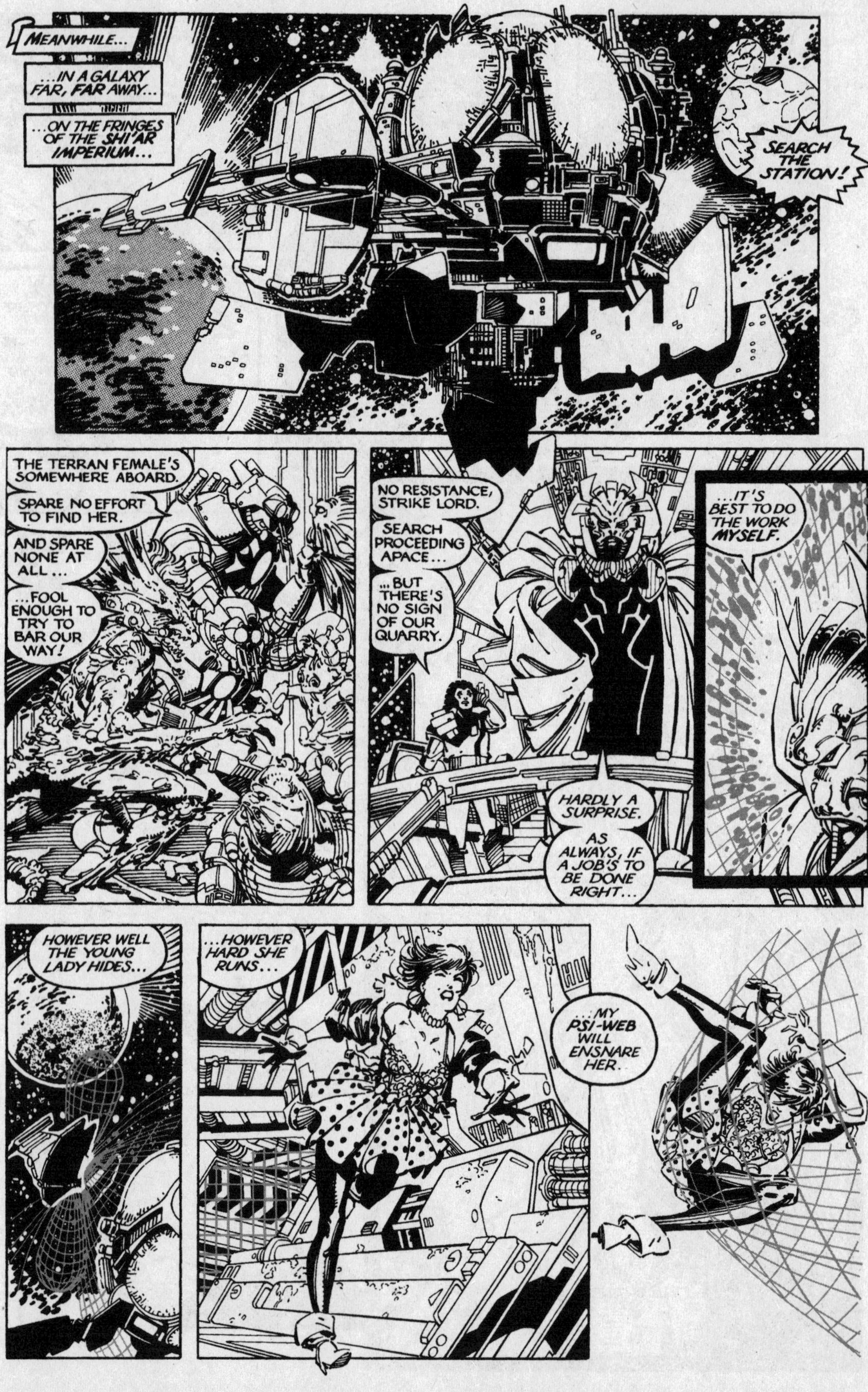
MEANWHILE...
...IN A GALAXY FAR, FAR AWAY...
...ON THE FRINGES OF THE SHI'AR IMPERIUM...
SEARCH THE STATION!
THE TERRAN FEMALE'S SOMEWHERE ABOARD.
SPARE NO EFFORT TO FIND HER.
AND SPARE NONE AT ALL...
...FOOL ENOUGH TO TRY TO BAR OUR WAY!
NO RESISTANCE, STRIKE LORD.
SEARCH PROCEEDING APACE...
...BUT THERE'S NO SIGN OF OUR QUARRY.
HARDLY A SURPRISE.
AS ALWAYS, IF A JOB'S TO BE DONE RIGHT...
...IT'S BEST TO DO THE WORK MYSELF.
HOWEVER WELL THE YOUNG LADY HIDES...
...HOWEVER HARD SHE RUNS...
...MY PSI-WEB WILL ENSNARE HER.

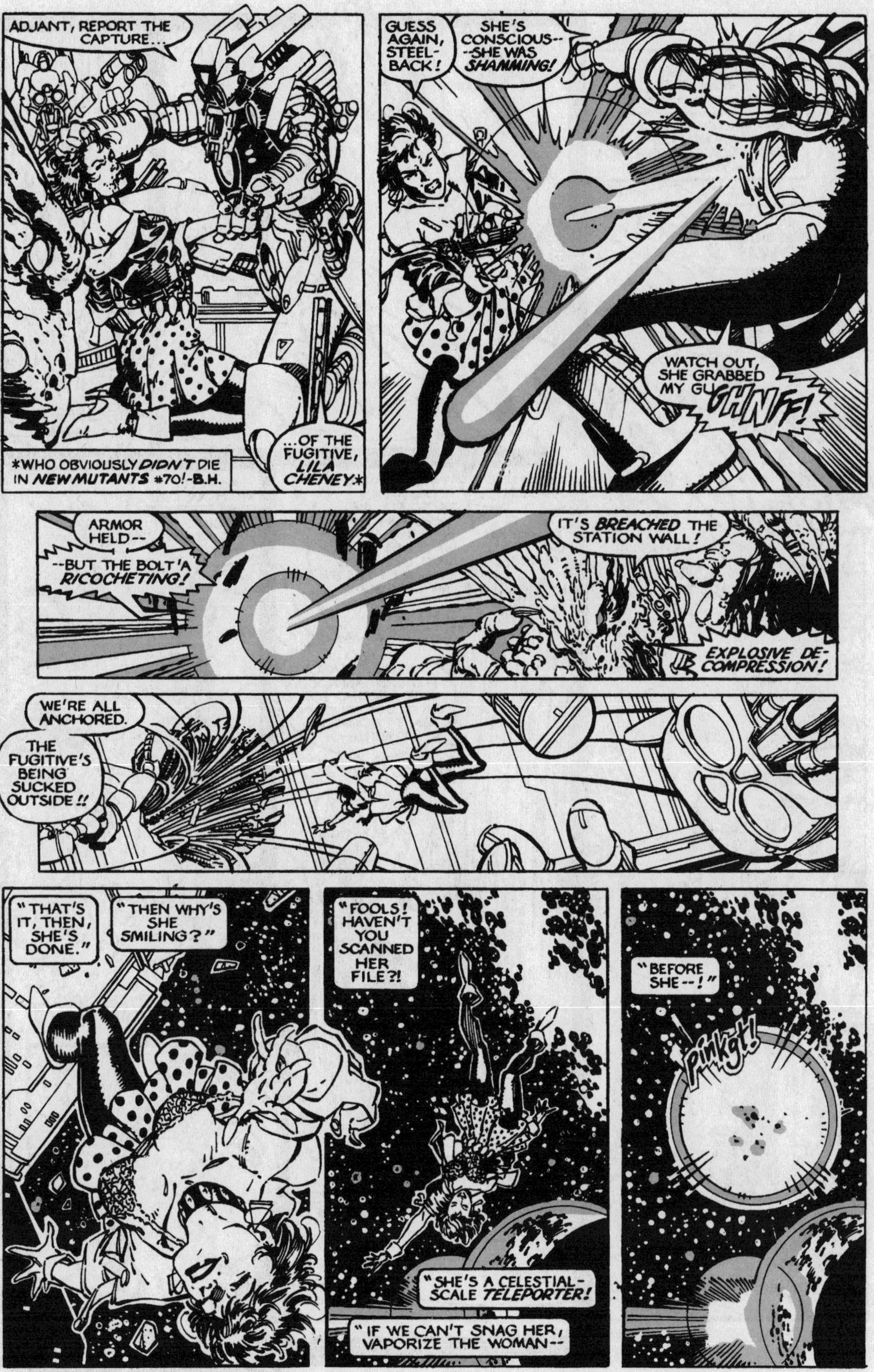
ADJANT, REPORT THE CAPTURE...
...OF THE FUGITIVE, LILA CHENEY.*
*WHO OBVIOUSLY DIDN'T DIE IN NEW MUTANTS #70!-B.H.
GUESS AGAIN, STEEL-BACK!
SHE'S CONSCIOUS-- --SHE WAS SHAMMING!
WATCH OUT, SHE GRABBED MY GU
GHNF!
ARMOR HELD--
--BUT THE BOLT'A RICOCHETING!
IT'S BREACHED THE STATION WALL!
EXPLOSIVE DE-COMPRESSION!
WE'RE ALL ANCHORED.
THE FUGITIVE'S BEING SUCKED OUTSIDE!!
"THAT'S IT, THEN, SHE'S DONE."
"THEN WHY'S SHE SMILING?"
"FOOLS! HAVEN'T YOU SCANNED HER FILE?!
"SHE'S A CELESTIAL-SCALE TELEPORTER!
"IF WE CAN'T SNAG HER, VAPORIZE THE WOMAN--
"BEFORE SHE--!"
pinkgt!

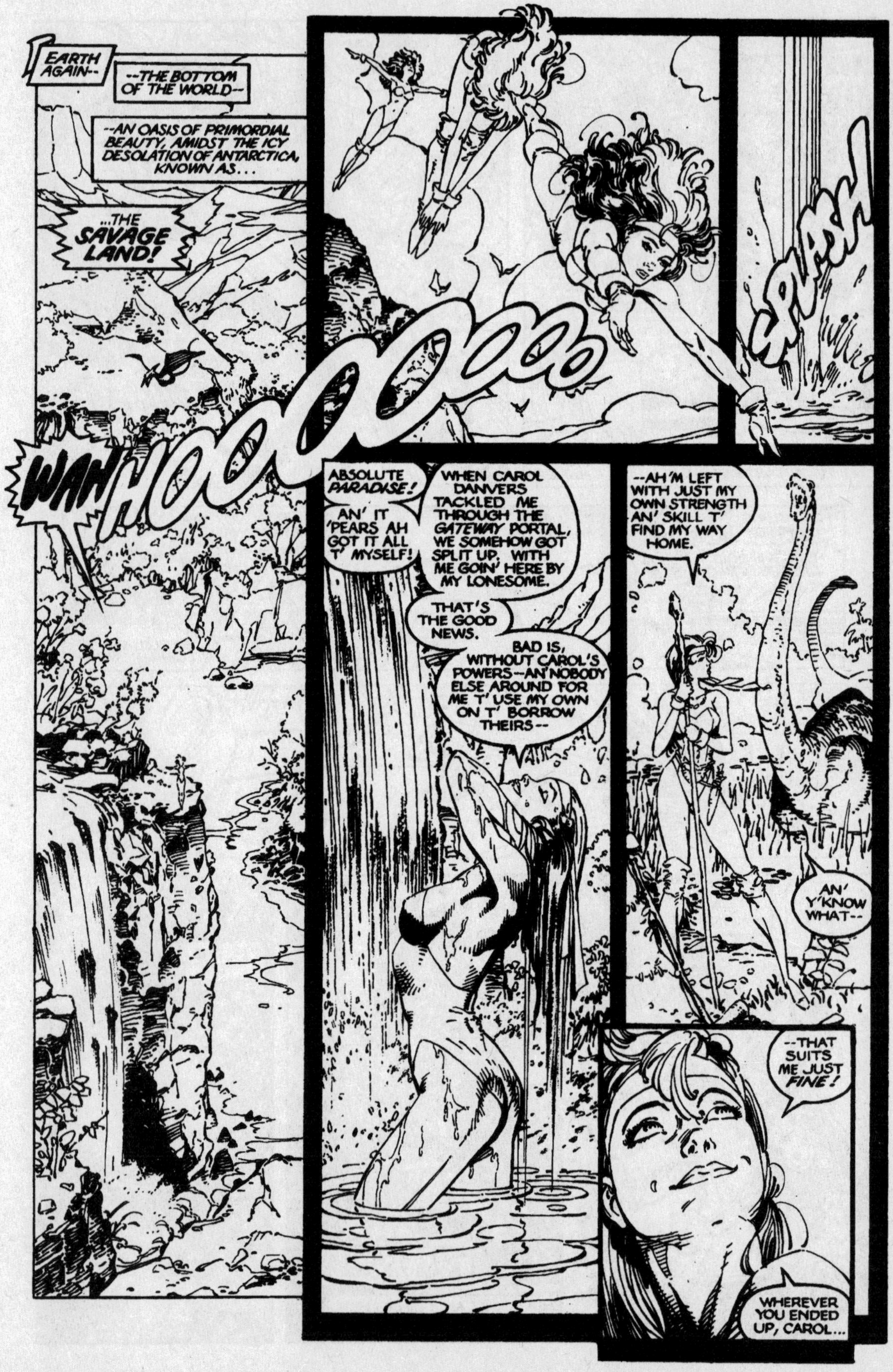
EARTH AGAIN--
--THE BOTTOM OF THE WORLD--
--AN OASIS OF PRIMORDIAL BEAUTY, AMIDST THE ICY DESOLATION OF ANTARCTICA, KNOWN AS...
...THE SAVAGE LAND!
WAHHOOOOOooo
SPLASH
ABSOLUTE PARADISE!
AN' IT 'PEARS AH GOT IT ALL T' MYSELF!
WHEN CAROL DANVERS TACKLED ME THROUGH THE GATEWAY PORTAL, WE SOMEHOW GOT SPLIT UP, WITH ME GOIN' HERE BY MY LONESOME.
THAT'S THE GOOD NEWS.
BAD IS, WITHOUT CAROL'S POWERS--AN' NOBODY ELSE AROUND FOR ME T' USE MY OWN ON T' BORROW THEIRS--
--AH'M LEFT WITH JUST MY OWN STRENGTH AN' SKILL T' FIND MY WAY HOME.
AN' Y'KNOW WHAT--
--THAT SUITS ME JUST FINE!
WHEREVER YOU ENDED UP, CAROL...

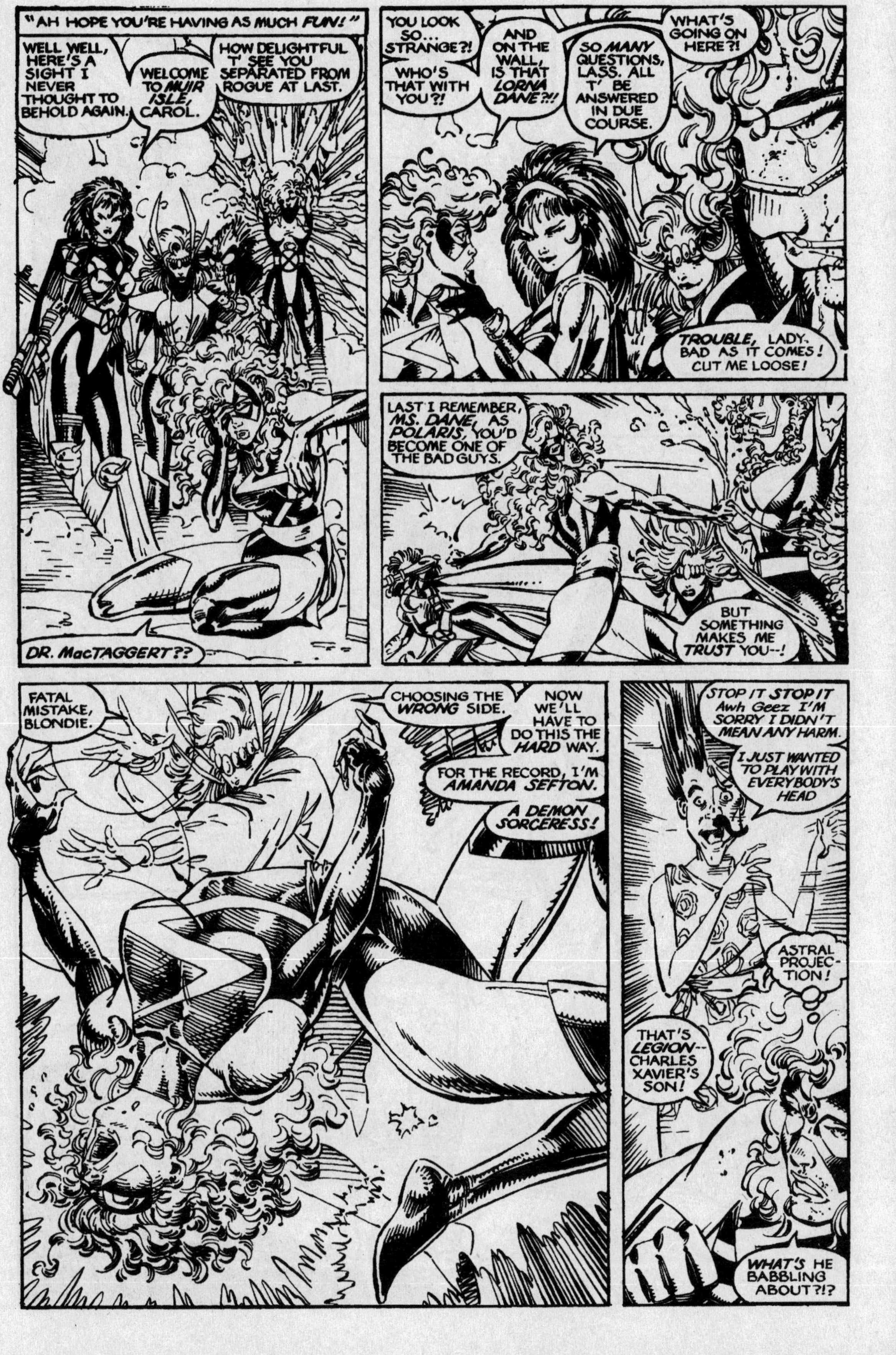
"AH HOPE YOU'RE HAVING AS MUCH FUN!"
WELL WELL, HERE'S A SIGHT I NEVER THOUGHT TO BEHOLD AGAIN.
WELCOME TO MUIR ISLE, CAROL.
HOW DELIGHTFUL T' SEE YOU SEPARATED FROM ROGUE AT LAST.
DR. MacTAGGERT??
YOU LOOK SO... STRANGE?!
WHO'S THAT WITH YOU?!
AND ON THE WALL, IS THAT LORNA DANE?!!
SO MANY QUESTIONS, LASS. ALL T' BE ANSWERED IN DUE COURSE.
WHAT'S GOING ON HERE?!
TROUBLE, LADY. BAD AS IT COMES! CUT ME LOOSE!
LAST I REMEMBER, MS. DANE, AS POLARIS, YOU'D BECOME ONE OF THE BAD GUYS.
BUT SOMETHING MAKES ME TRUST YOU--!
FATAL MISTAKE, BLONDIE.
CHOOSING THE WRONG SIDE.
NOW WE'LL HAVE TO DO THIS THE HARD WAY.
FOR THE RECORD, I'M AMANDA SEFTON.
A DEMON SORCERESS!
STOP IT STOP IT Awh Geez I'M SORRY I DIDN'T MEAN ANY HARM.
I JUST WANTED TO PLAY WITH EVERYBODY'S HEAD
ASTRAL PROJECTION!
THAT'S LEGION-- CHARLES XAVIER'S SON!
WHAT'S HE BABBLING ABOUT?!?

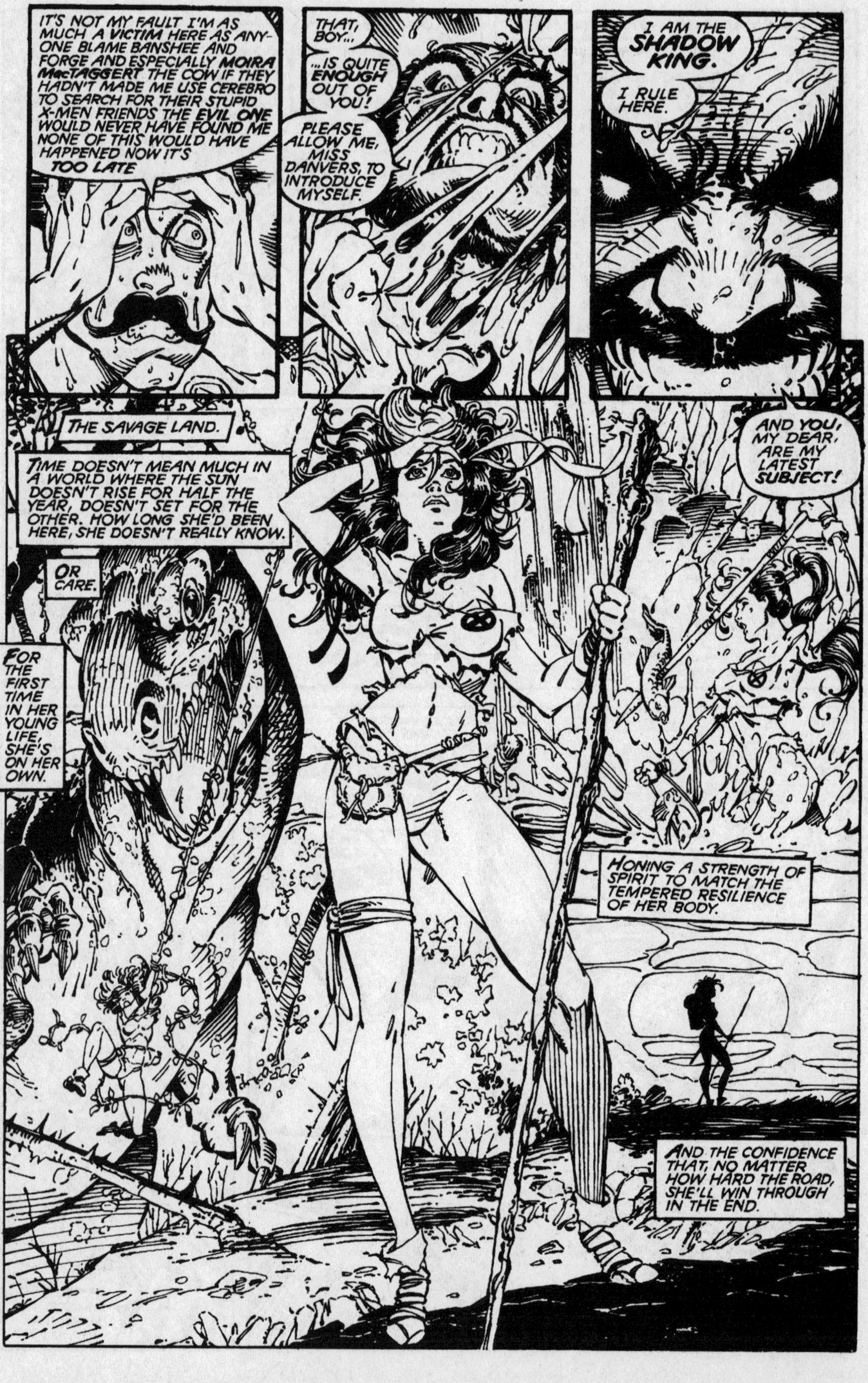
IT'S NOT MY FAULT I'M AS MUCH A VICTIM HERE AS ANYONE BLAME BANSHEE AND FORGE AND ESPECIALLY MOIRA MacTAGGERT THE COW IF THEY HADN'T MADE ME USE CEREBRO TO SEARCH FOR THEIR STUPID X-MEN FRIENDS THE EVIL ONE WOULD NEVER HAVE FOUND ME NONE OF THIS WOULD HAVE HAPPENED NOW IT'S TOO LATE
THAT, BOY...
...IS QUITE ENOUGH OUT OF YOU!
PLEASE ALLOW ME, MISS DANVERS, TO INTRODUCE MYSELF.
I AM THE SHADOW KING.
I RULE HERE.
THE SAVAGE LAND.
TIME DOESN'T MEAN MUCH IN A WORLD WHERE THE SUN DOESN'T RISE FOR HALF THE YEAR, DOESN'T SET FOR THE OTHER. HOW LONG SHE'D BEEN HERE, SHE DOESN'T REALLY KNOW.
OR CARE.
AND YOU, MY DEAR, ARE MY LATEST SUBJECT!
FOR THE FIRST TIME IN HER YOUNG LIFE, SHE'S ON HER OWN.
HONING A STRENGTH OF SPIRIT TO MATCH THE TEMPERED RESILIENCE OF HER BODY.
AND THE CONFIDENCE THAT, NO MATTER HOW HARD THE ROAD, SHE'LL WIN THROUGH IN THE END.

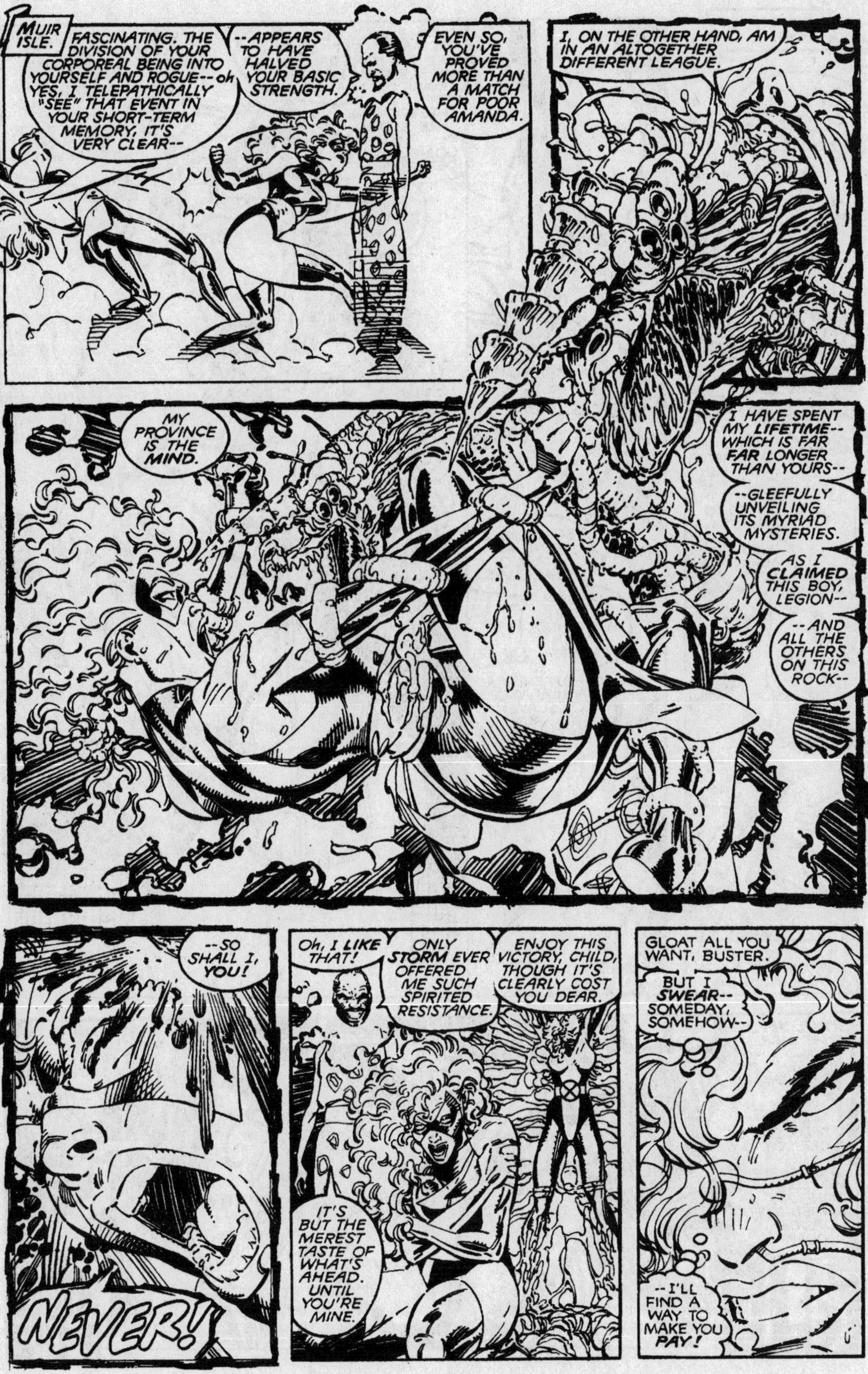
MUIR ISLE.
FASCINATING. THE DIVISION OF YOUR CORPOREAL BEING INTO YOURSELF AND ROGUE-- oh YES, I TELEPATHICALLY "SEE" THAT EVENT IN YOUR SHORT-TERM MEMORY, IT'S VERY CLEAR--
--APPEARS TO HAVE HALVED YOUR BASIC STRENGTH.
EVEN SO, YOU'VE PROVED MORE THAN A MATCH FOR POOR AMANDA.
I, ON THE OTHER HAND, AM IN AN ALTOGETHER DIFFERENT LEAGUE.
MY PROVINCE IS THE MIND.
I HAVE SPENT MY LIFETIME-- WHICH IS FAR FAR LONGER THAN YOURS--
--GLEEFULLY UNVEILING ITS MYRIAD MYSTERIES.
AS I CLAIMED THIS BOY, LEGION--
--AND ALL THE OTHERS ON THIS ROCK--
--SO SHALL I, YOU!
NEVER!
Oh, I LIKE THAT!
ONLY STORM EVER OFFERED ME SUCH SPIRITED RESISTANCE.
ENJOY THIS VICTORY, CHILD, THOUGH IT'S CLEARLY COST YOU DEAR.
IT'S BUT THE MEREST TASTE OF WHAT'S AHEAD. UNTIL YOU'RE MINE.
GLOAT ALL YOU WANT, BUSTER.
BUT I SWEAR-- SOMEDAY, SOMEHOW--
--I'LL FIND A WAY TO MAKE YOU PAY!

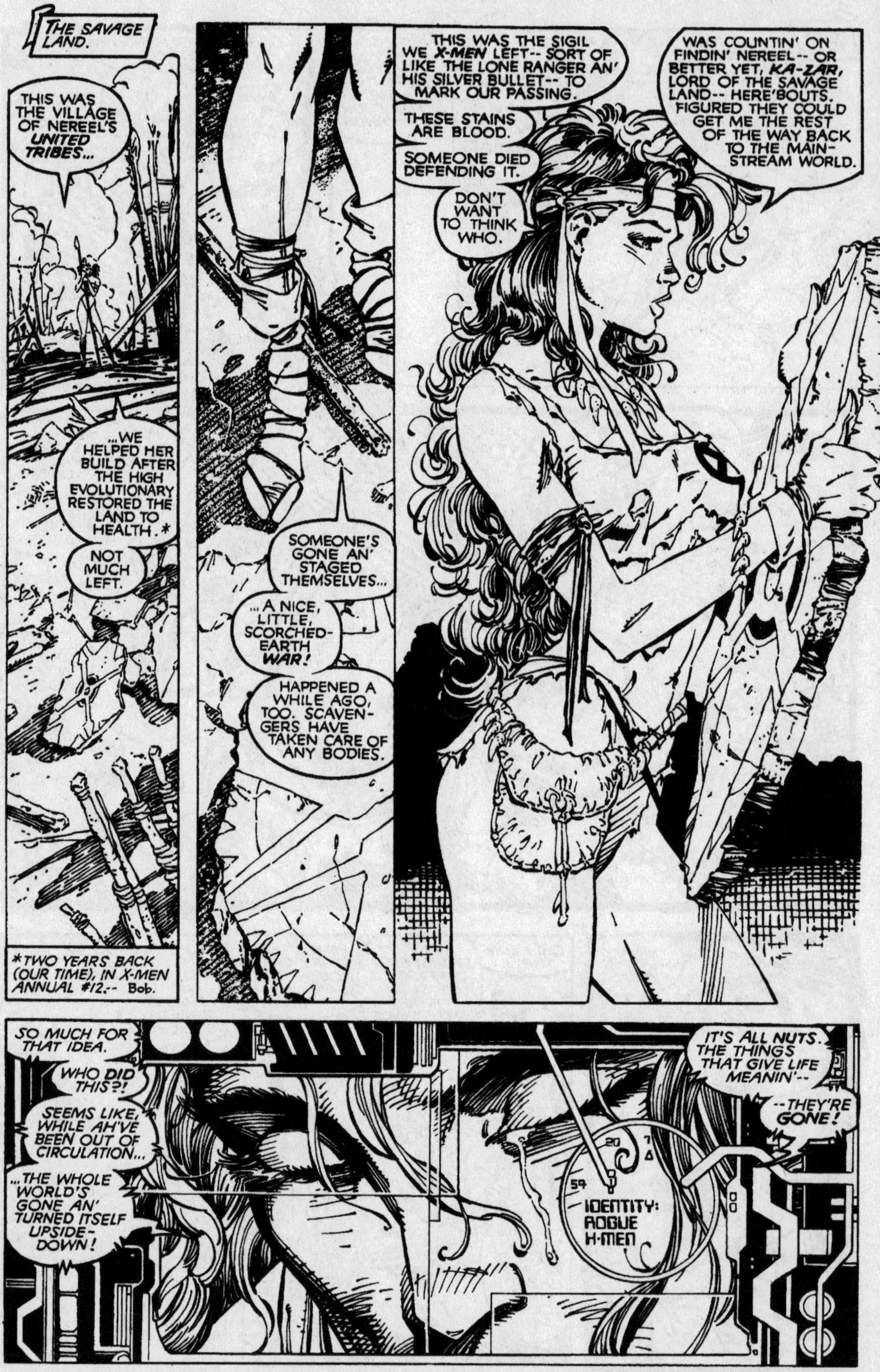

THE SAVAGE LAND.
THIS WAS THE VILLAGE OF NEREEL'S UNITED TRIBES...
...WE HELPED HER BUILD AFTER THE HIGH EVOLUTIONARY RESTORED THE LAND TO HEALTH.*
NOT MUCH LEFT.
*TWO YEARS BACK (OUR TIME), IN X-MEN ANNUAL #12.-- Bob.
SOMEONE'S GONE AN' STAGED THEMSELVES...
...A NICE, LITTLE, SCORCHED-EARTH WAR!
HAPPENED A WHILE AGO, TOO. SCAVENGERS HAVE TAKEN CARE OF ANY BODIES.
THIS WAS THE SIGIL WE X-MEN LEFT-- SORT OF LIKE THE LONE RANGER AN' HIS SILVER BULLET-- TO MARK OUR PASSING.
THESE STAINS ARE BLOOD.
SOMEONE DIED DEFENDING IT.
DON'T WANT TO THINK WHO.
WAS COUNTIN' ON FINDIN' NEREEL-- OR BETTER YET, KA-ZAR, LORD OF THE SAVAGE LAND-- HERE'BOUTS. FIGURED THEY COULD GET ME THE REST OF THE WAY BACK TO THE MAIN-STREAM WORLD.
SO MUCH FOR THAT IDEA.
WHO DID THIS?!
SEEMS LIKE, WHILE AH'VE BEEN OUT OF CIRCULATION...
...THE WHOLE WORLD'S GONE AN' TURNED ITSELF UPSIDE-DOWN!
IDENTITY: ROGUE X-MEN
IT'S ALL NUTS. THE THINGS THAT GIVE LIFE MEANIN'--
--THEY'RE GONE!

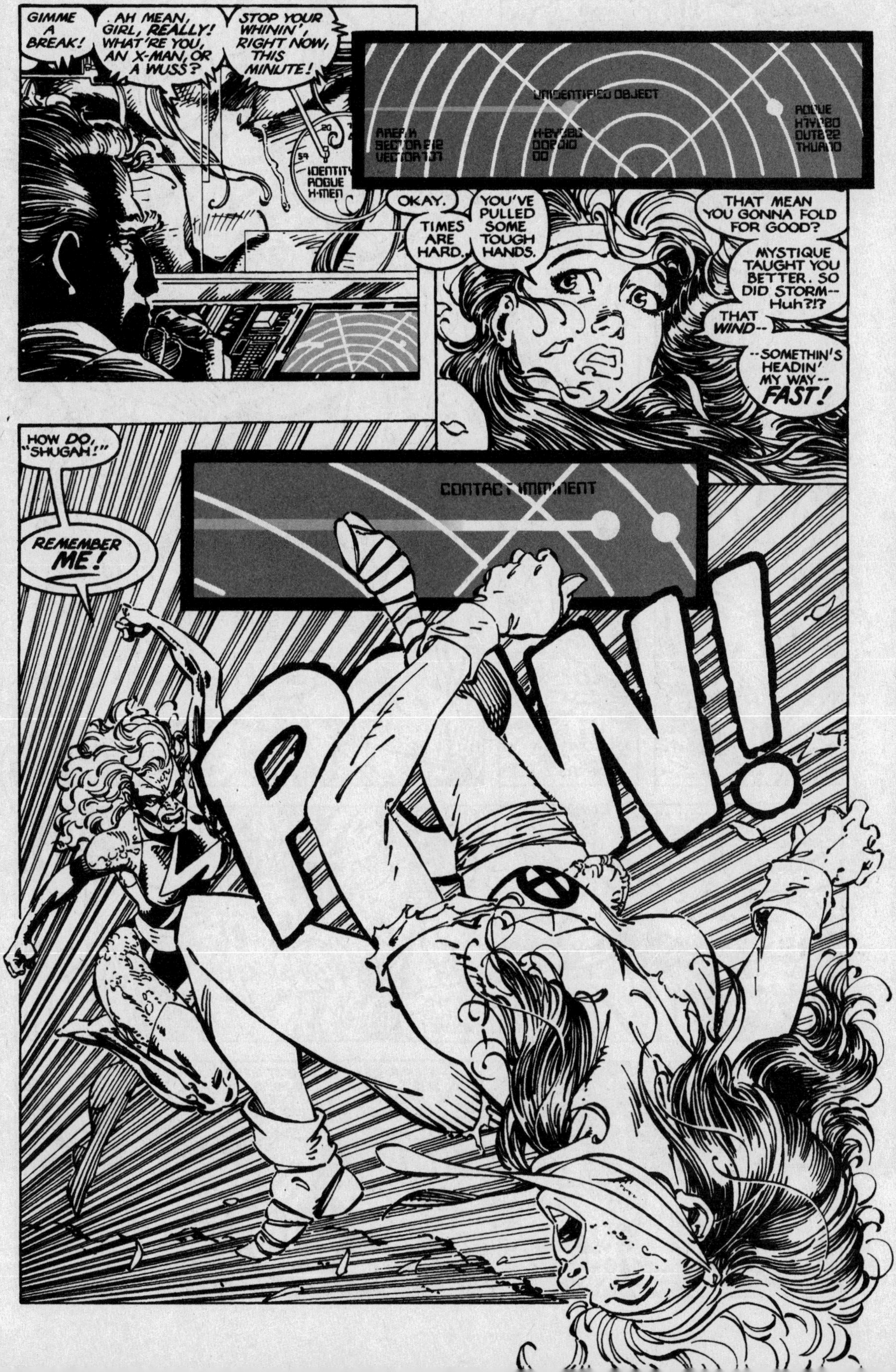
GIMME A BREAK!
AH MEAN, GIRL, REALLY! WHAT'RE YOU, AN X-MAN, OR A WUSS?
STOP YOUR WHININ', RIGHT NOW, THIS MINUTE!
UNIDENTIFIED OBJECT
IDENTITY ROGUE X-MEN
OKAY. TIMES ARE HARD.
YOU'VE PULLED SOME TOUGH HANDS.
THAT MEAN YOU GONNA FOLD FOR GOOD?
MYSTIQUE TAUGHT YOU BETTER. SO DID STORM-- Huh?!?
THAT WIND--
--SOMETHIN'S HEADIN' MY WAY-- FAST!
HOW DO, "SHUGAH!"
REMEMBER ME!
CONTACT IMMINENT
POW!

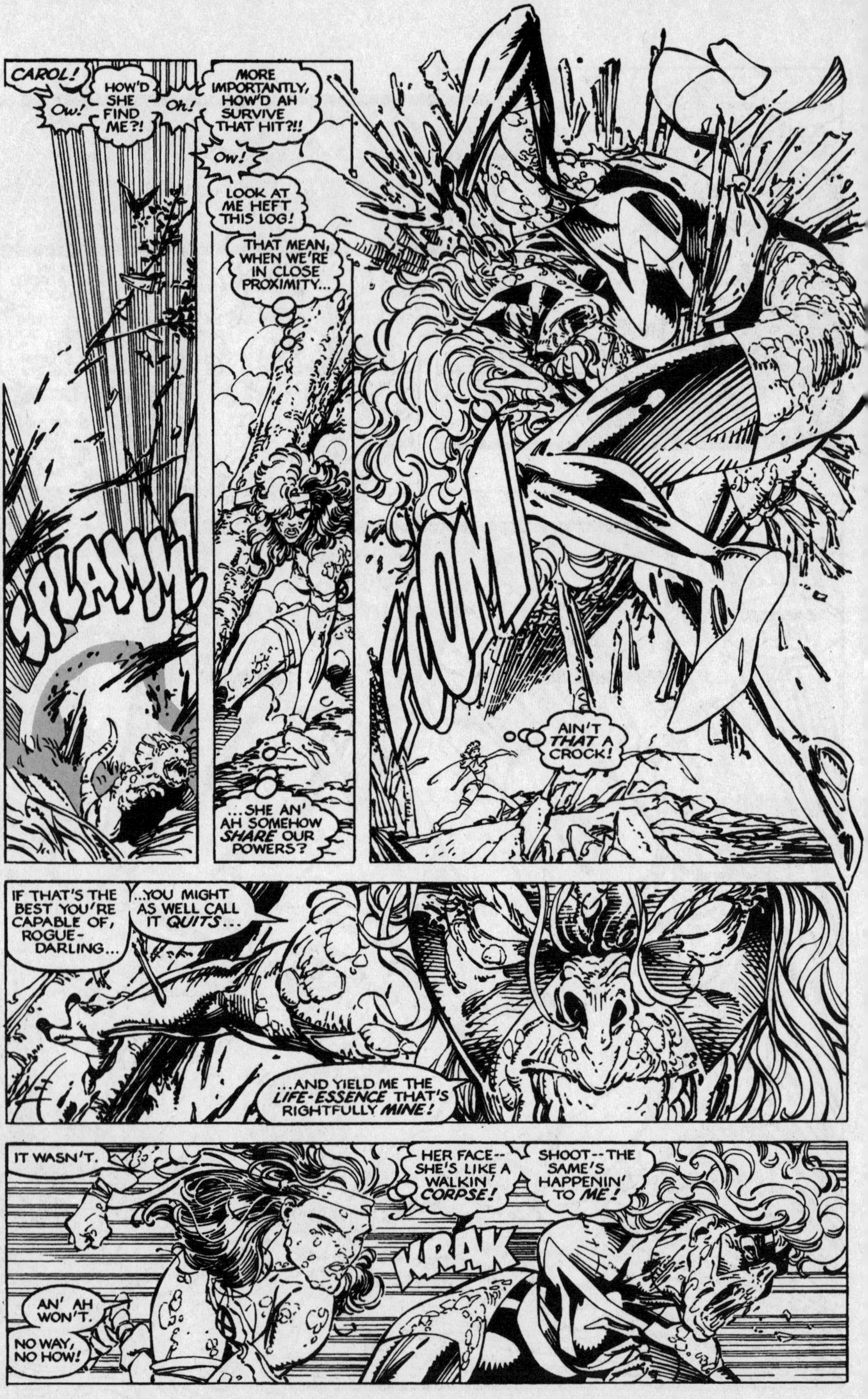
CAROL!
Ow!
HOW'D SHE FIND ME?!
Oh!
SPLAMM!
MORE IMPORTANTLY, HOW'D AH SURVIVE THAT HIT?!!
Ow!
LOOK AT ME HEFT THIS LOG!
THAT MEAN, WHEN WE'RE IN CLOSE PROXIMITY...
...SHE AN' AH SOMEHOW SHARE OUR POWERS?
FOOOM
AIN'T THAT A CROCK!
IF THAT'S THE BEST YOU'RE CAPABLE OF, ROGUE-DARLING...
...YOU MIGHT AS WELL CALL IT QUITS...
...AND YIELD ME THE LIFE-ESSENCE THAT'S RIGHTFULLY MINE!
IT WASN'T.
HER FACE--SHE'S LIKE A WALKIN' CORPSE!
SHOOT--THE SAME'S HAPPENIN' TO ME!
KRAK
AN' AH WON'T.
NO WAY, NO HOW!

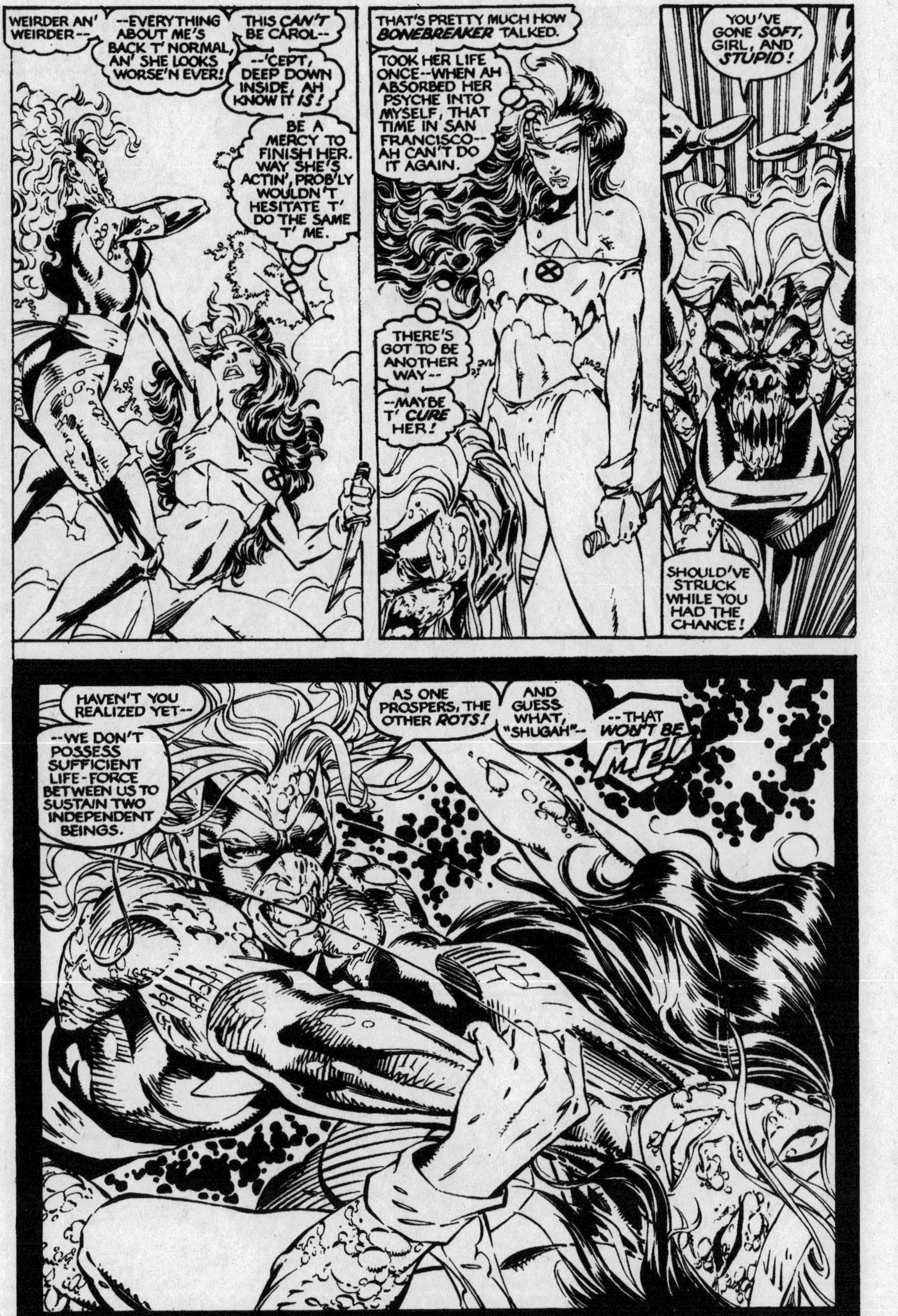
WEIRDER AN' WEIRDER--
--EVERYTHING ABOUT ME'S BACK T' NORMAL, AN' SHE LOOKS WORSE'N EVER!
THIS CAN'T BE CAROL--
--'CEPT, DEEP DOWN INSIDE, AH KNOW IT IS!
BE A MERCY TO FINISH HER. WAY SHE'S ACTIN', PROB'LY WOULDN'T HESITATE T' DO THE SAME T' ME.
THAT'S PRETTY MUCH HOW BONEBREAKER TALKED.
TOOK HER LIFE ONCE--WHEN AH ABSORBED HER PSYCHE INTO MYSELF, THAT TIME IN SAN FRANCISCO--AH CAN'T DO IT AGAIN.
THERE'S GOT TO BE ANOTHER WAY--
--MAYBE T' CURE HER!
YOU'VE GONE SOFT, GIRL, AND STUPID!
SHOULD'VE STRUCK WHILE YOU HAD THE CHANCE!
HAVEN'T YOU REALIZED YET--
--WE DON'T POSSESS SUFFICIENT LIFE-FORCE BETWEEN US TO SUSTAIN TWO INDEPENDENT BEINGS.
AS ONE PROSPERS, THE OTHER ROTS!
AND GUESS WHAT, "SHUGAH"--
--THAT WON'T BE ME!

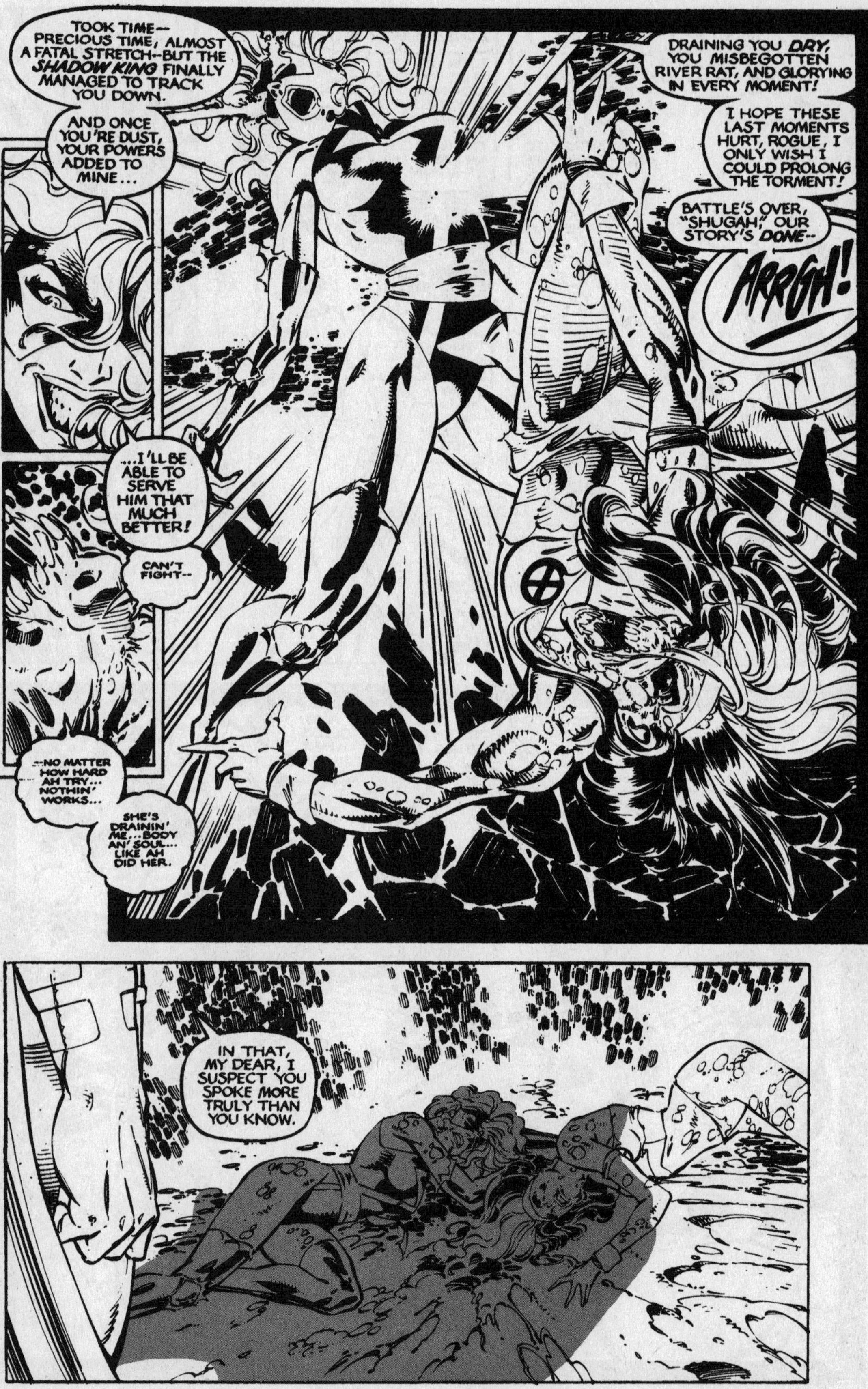
TOOK TIME-- PRECIOUS TIME, ALMOST A FATAL STRETCH--BUT THE SHADOW KING FINALLY MANAGED TO TRACK YOU DOWN.
AND ONCE YOU'RE DUST, YOUR POWERS ADDED TO MINE...
...I'LL BE ABLE TO SERVE HIM THAT MUCH BETTER!
DRAINING YOU DRY, YOU MISBEGOTTEN RIVER RAT, AND GLORYING IN EVERY MOMENT!
I HOPE THESE LAST MOMENTS HURT, ROGUE, I ONLY WISH I COULD PROLONG THE TORMENT!
CAN'T FIGHT--
--NO MATTER HOW HARD AH TRY... NOTHIN' WORKS...
SHE'S DRAININ' ME... BODY AN' SOUL... LIKE AH DID HER.
BATTLE'S OVER, "SHUGAH," OUR STORY'S DONE--
ARRGH!
IN THAT, MY DEAR, I SUSPECT YOU SPOKE MORE TRULY THAN YOU KNOW.

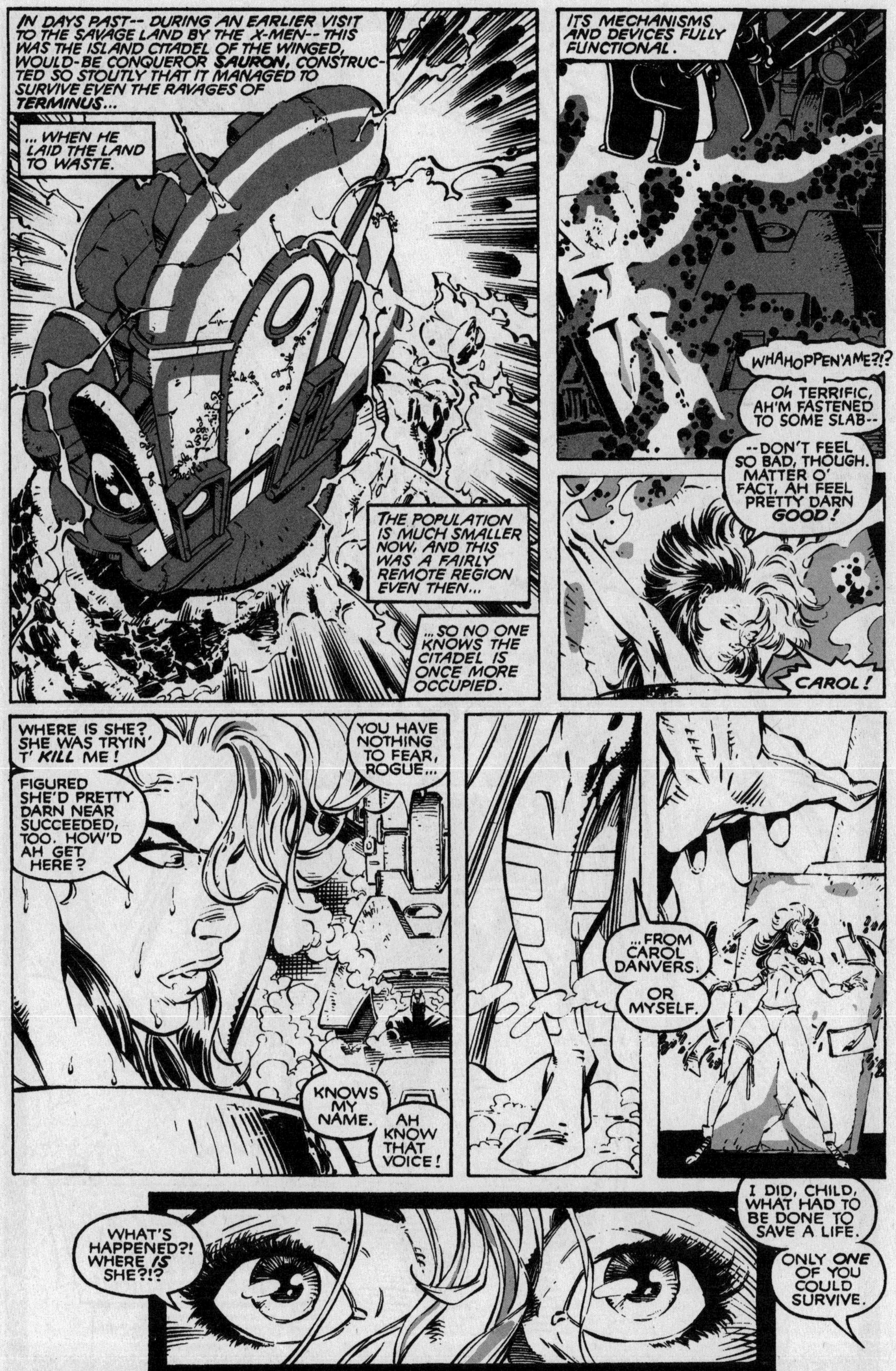
IN DAYS PAST-- DURING AN EARLIER VISIT TO THE SAVAGE LAND BY THE X-MEN-- THIS WAS THE ISLAND CITADEL OF THE WINGED, WOULD-BE CONQUEROR SAURON, CONSTRUCTED SO STOUTLY THAT IT MANAGED TO SURVIVE EVEN THE RAVAGES OF TERMINUS...
...WHEN HE LAID THE LAND TO WASTE.
THE POPULATION IS MUCH SMALLER NOW, AND THIS WAS A FAIRLY REMOTE REGION EVEN THEN...
...SO NO ONE KNOWS THE CITADEL IS ONCE MORE OCCUPIED.
ITS MECHANISMS AND DEVICES FULLY FUNCTIONAL.
WHAHOPPEN'AME?!?
Oh TERRIFIC, AH'M FASTENED TO SOME SLAB--
--DON'T FEEL SO BAD, THOUGH. MATTER O' FACT, AH FEEL PRETTY DARN GOOD!
CAROL!
WHERE IS SHE? SHE WAS TRYIN' T' KILL ME!
FIGURED SHE'D PRETTY DARN NEAR SUCCEEDED, TOO. HOW'D AH GET HERE?
YOU HAVE NOTHING TO FEAR, ROGUE...
KNOWS MY NAME.
AH KNOW THAT VOICE!
...FROM CAROL DANVERS.
OR MYSELF.
WHAT'S HAPPENED?! WHERE IS SHE?!?
I DID, CHILD, WHAT HAD TO BE DONE TO SAVE A LIFE.
ONLY ONE OF YOU COULD SURVIVE.

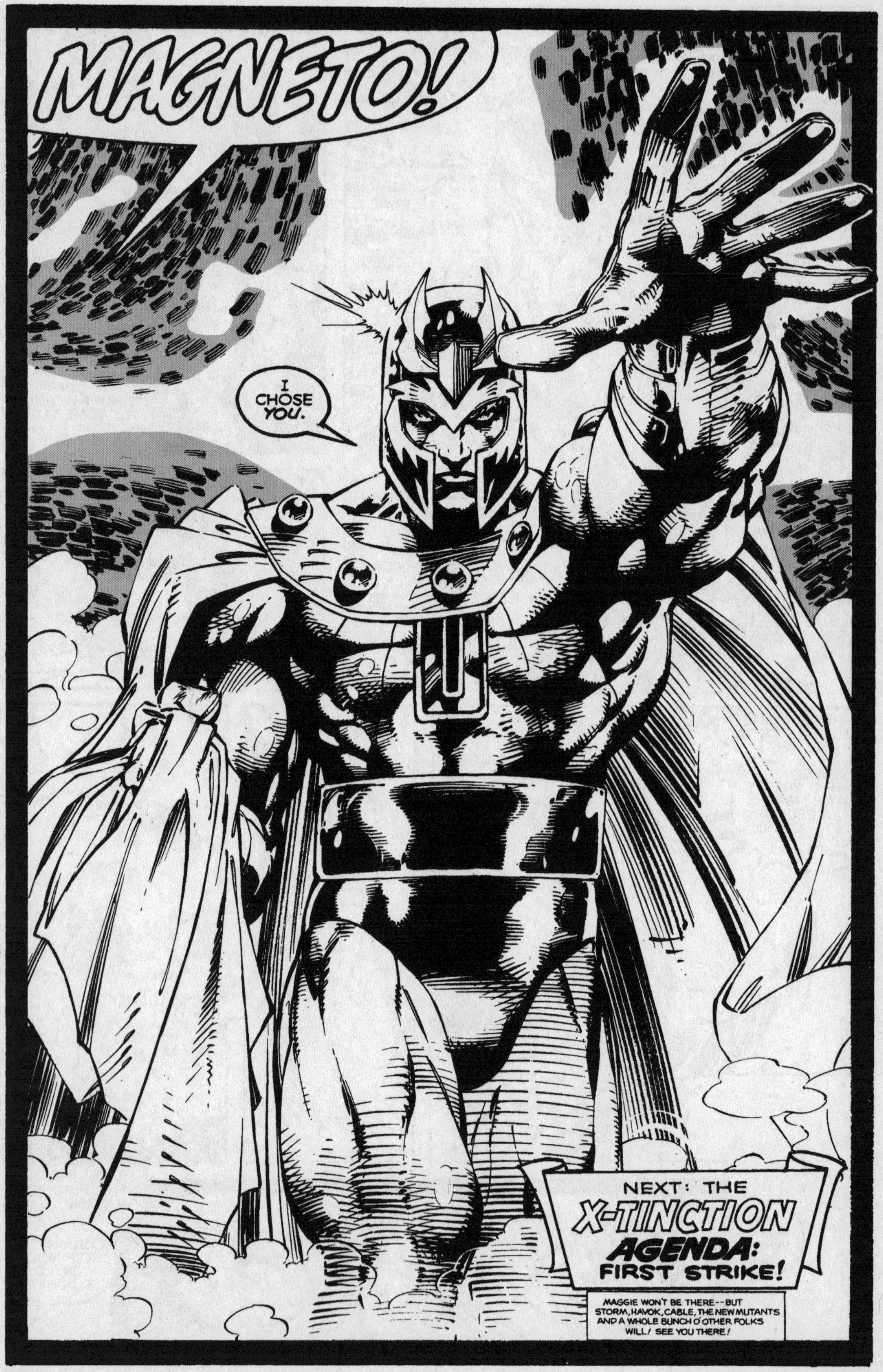
MAGNETO!
I CHOSE YOU.
NEXT: THE X-TINCTION AGENDA: FIRST STRIKE!
MAGGIE WON'T BE THERE--BUT STORM, HAVOK, CABLE, THE NEW MUTANTS AND A WHOLE BUNCH O' OTHER FOLKS WILL! SEE YOU THERE!

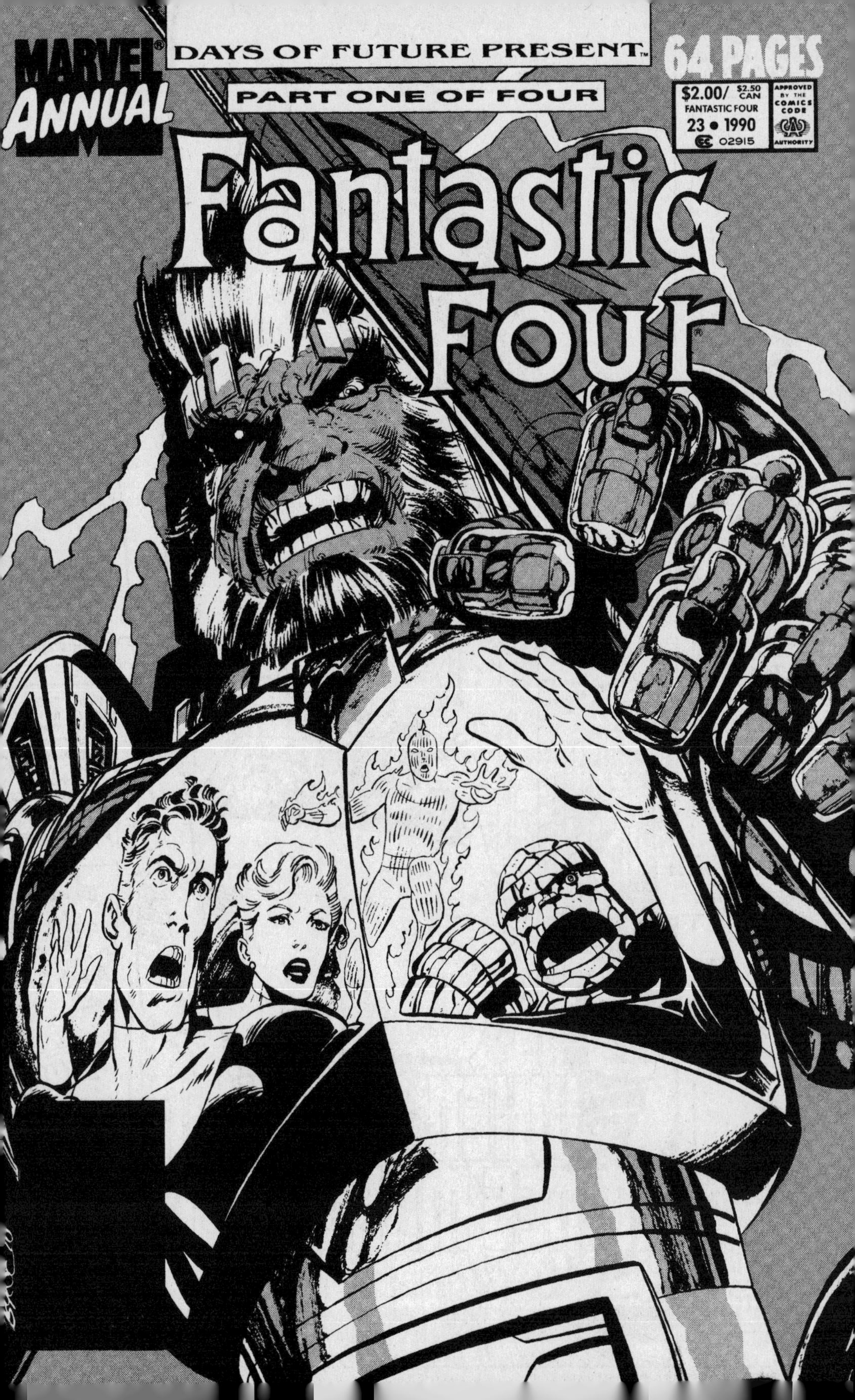
MARVEL ANNUAL
DAYS OF FUTURE PRESENT
PART ONE OF FOUR
64 PAGES
$2.00/ $2.50 CAN
FANTASTIC FOUR
23 • 1990
02915
APPROVED BY THE COMICS CODE AUTHORITY
Fantastic Four

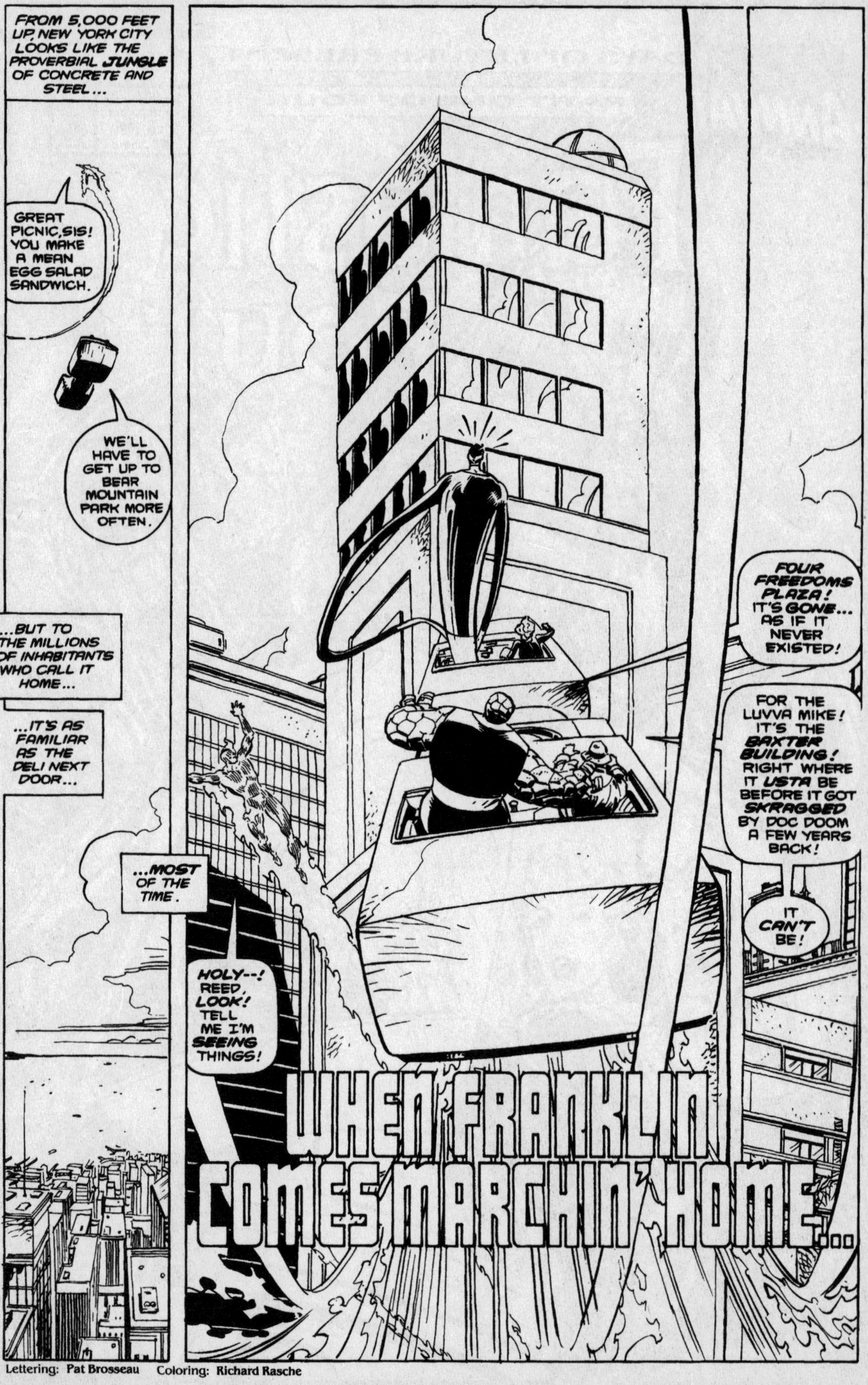
FROM 5,000 FEET UP, NEW YORK CITY LOOKS LIKE THE PROVERBIAL JUNGLE OF CONCRETE AND STEEL...
GREAT PICNIC, SIS! YOU MAKE A MEAN EGG SALAD SANDWICH.
WE'LL HAVE TO GET UP TO BEAR MOUNTAIN PARK MORE OFTEN.
...BUT TO THE MILLIONS OF INHABITANTS WHO CALL IT HOME...
...IT'S AS FAMILIAR AS THE DELI NEXT DOOR...
...MOST OF THE TIME.
HOLY--! REED, LOOK! TELL ME I'M SEEING THINGS!
FOUR FREEDOMS PLAZA! IT'S GONE... AS IF IT NEVER EXISTED!
FOR THE LUVVA MIKE! IT'S THE BAXTER BUILDING! RIGHT WHERE IT USTA BE BEFORE IT GOT SKRAGGED BY DOC DOOM A FEW YEARS BACK!
IT CAN'T BE!
WHEN FRANKLIN COMES MARCHIN' HOME...

Lettering: Pat Brosseau Coloring: Richard Rasche

BUT IT *IS*, BEN!

A QUICK SPECTRUM SCAN SHOWS NO UNUSUAL ENERGY CONFIGURATIONS... NO CHRONO-DISPLACEMENT PATTERNS! EVERYTHING APPEARS COMPLETELY NORMAL.

EXCEPT THAT IT'S *THERE!* AND IT'S NO MIRAGE.

WE'D BETTER BE CAUTIOUS.

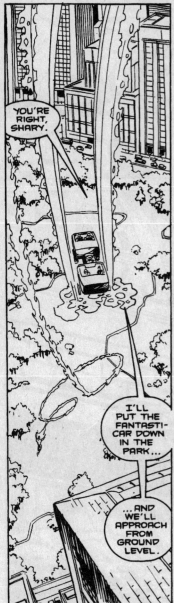

YOU'RE RIGHT, SHARY.

I'LL PUT THE FANTASTI-CAR DOWN IN THE PARK...

...AND WE'LL APPROACH FROM GROUND LEVEL.

COULD THIS BE SOME PLOY BY ONE OF OUR OLD ENEMIES, REED? DR. DOOM? THE MAD THINKER?

I DOUBT THAT ANY OF THEM WOULD BE CAPABLE OF CREATING THIS SORT OF THING, DARLING.

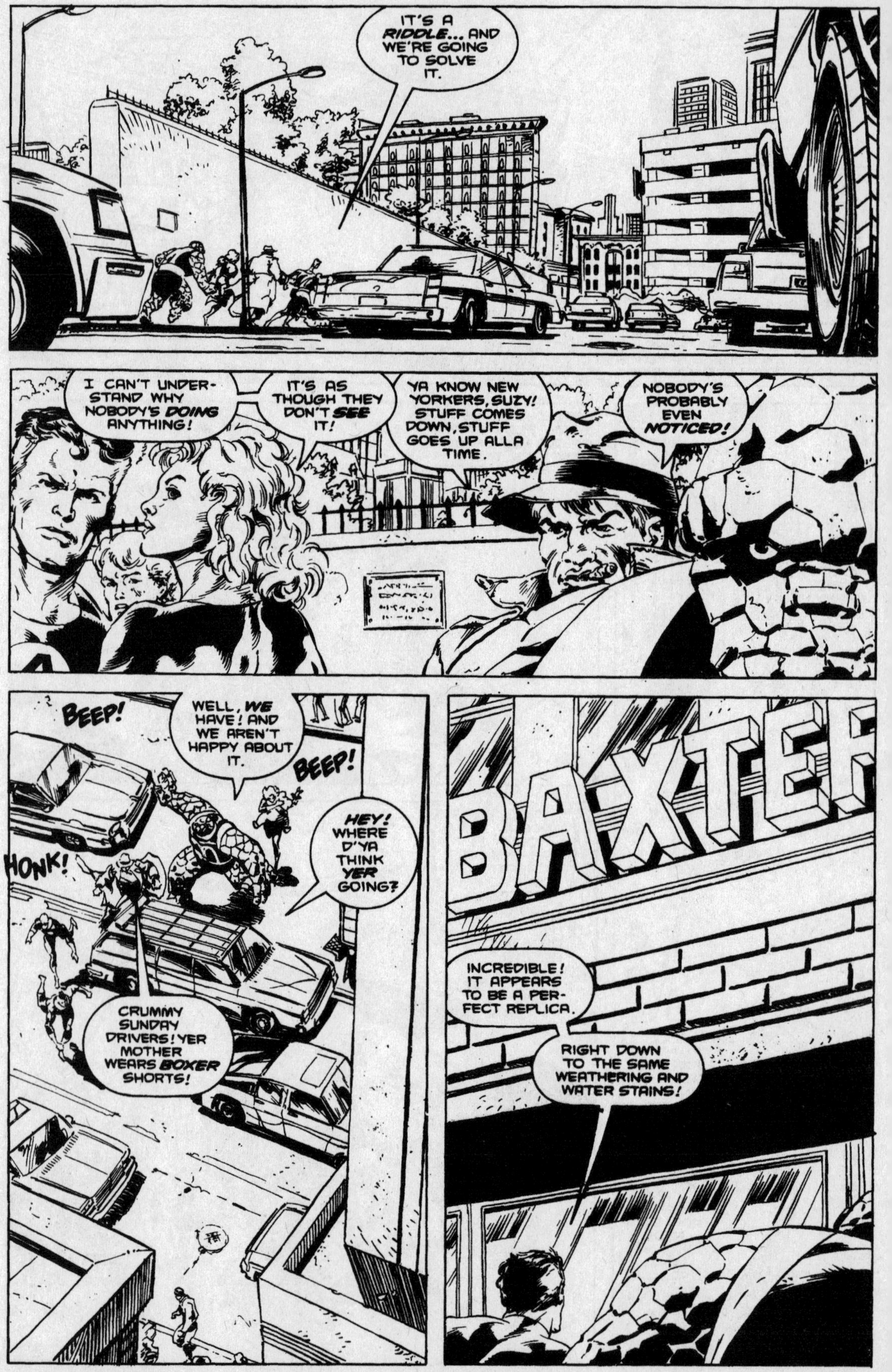
IT'S A RIDDLE... AND WE'RE GOING TO SOLVE IT.
I CAN'T UNDERSTAND WHY NOBODY'S DOING ANYTHING!
IT'S AS THOUGH THEY DON'T SEE IT!
YA KNOW NEW YORKERS, SUZY! STUFF COMES DOWN, STUFF GOES UP ALLA TIME.
NOBODY'S PROBABLY EVEN NOTICED!
BEEP!
WELL, WE HAVE! AND WE AREN'T HAPPY ABOUT IT.
BEEP!
HONK!
HEY! WHERE D'YA THINK YER GOING?
CRUMMY SUNDAY DRIVERS! YER MOTHER WEARS BOXER SHORTS!
BAXTER
INCREDIBLE! IT APPEARS TO BE A PERFECT REPLICA.
RIGHT DOWN TO THE SAME WEATHERING AND WATER STAINS!

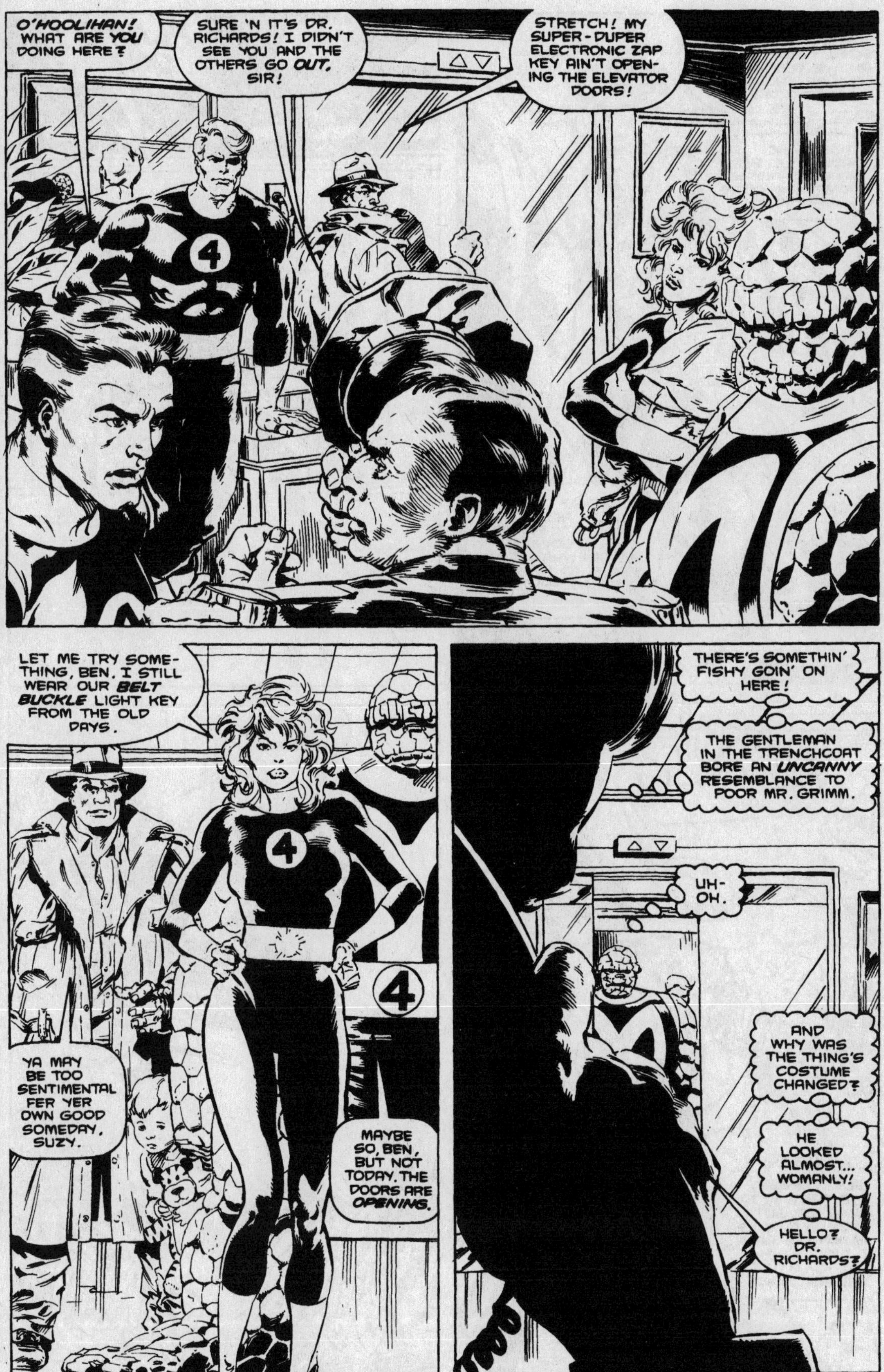
O'HOOLIHAN! WHAT ARE YOU DOING HERE?
SURE 'N IT'S DR. RICHARDS! I DIDN'T SEE YOU AND THE OTHERS GO OUT, SIR!
STRETCH! MY SUPER-DUPER ELECTRONIC ZAP KEY AIN'T OPENING THE ELEVATOR DOORS!
LET ME TRY SOMETHING, BEN. I STILL WEAR OUR BELT BUCKLE LIGHT KEY FROM THE OLD DAYS.
YA MAY BE TOO SENTIMENTAL FER YER OWN GOOD SOMEDAY, SUZY.
MAYBE SO, BEN, BUT NOT TODAY. THE DOORS ARE OPENING.
THERE'S SOMETHIN' FISHY GOIN' ON HERE!
THE GENTLEMAN IN THE TRENCHCOAT BORE AN UNCANNY RESEMBLANCE TO POOR MR. GRIMM.
UH-OH.
AND WHY WAS THE THING'S COSTUME CHANGED?
HE LOOKED ALMOST... WOMANLY!
HELLO? DR. RICHARDS?

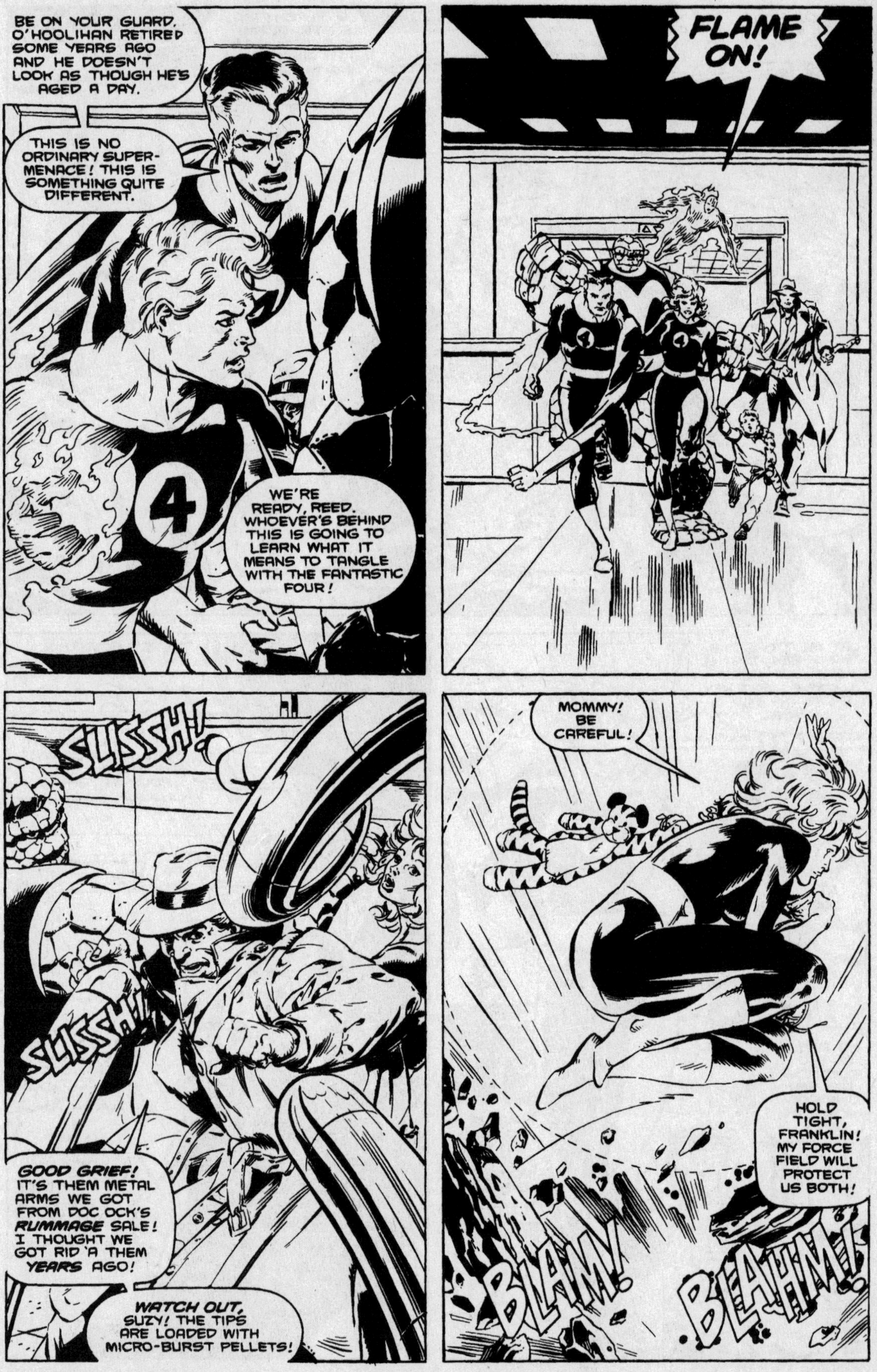
BE ON YOUR GUARD. O'HOOLIHAN RETIRED SOME YEARS AGO AND HE DOESN'T LOOK AS THOUGH HE'S AGED A DAY.
THIS IS NO ORDINARY SUPER-MENACE! THIS IS SOMETHING QUITE DIFFERENT.
WE'RE READY, REED. WHOEVER'S BEHIND THIS IS GOING TO LEARN WHAT IT MEANS TO TANGLE WITH THE FANTASTIC FOUR!
FLAME ON!
SLISSH!
SLISSH!
GOOD GRIEF! IT'S THEM METAL ARMS WE GOT FROM DOC OCK'S RUMMAGE SALE! I THOUGHT WE GOT RID 'A THEM YEARS AGO!
WATCH OUT, SUZY! THE TIPS ARE LOADED WITH MICRO-BURST PELLETS!
MOMMY! BE CAREFUL!
HOLD TIGHT, FRANKLIN! MY FORCE FIELD WILL PROTECT US BOTH!
BLAM!
BLAHM!

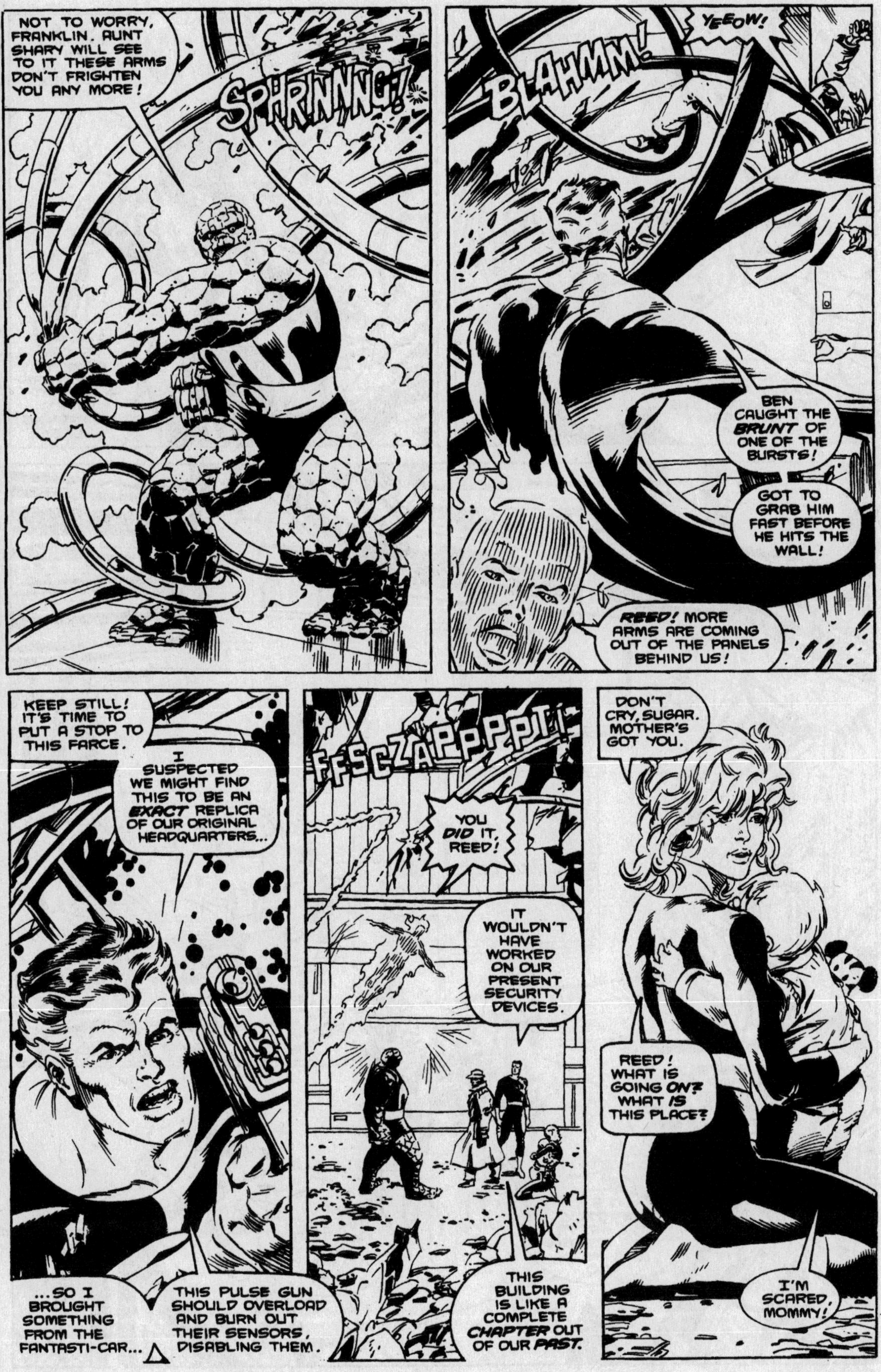
NOT TO WORRY, FRANKLIN. AUNT SHARY WILL SEE TO IT THESE ARMS DON'T FRIGHTEN YOU ANY MORE!
SPHRINNNG!
YEEOW!
BLAHMM!
BEN CAUGHT THE BRUNT OF ONE OF THE BURSTS!
GOT TO GRAB HIM FAST BEFORE HE HITS THE WALL!
REED! MORE ARMS ARE COMING OUT OF THE PANELS BEHIND US!
KEEP STILL! IT'S TIME TO PUT A STOP TO THIS FARCE.
I SUSPECTED WE MIGHT FIND THIS TO BE AN EXACT REPLICA OF OUR ORIGINAL HEADQUARTERS...
...SO I BROUGHT SOMETHING FROM THE FANTASTI-CAR...
THIS PULSE GUN SHOULD OVERLOAD AND BURN OUT THEIR SENSORS, DISABLING THEM.
FFSCZAPPPPT!
YOU DID IT, REED!
IT WOULDN'T HAVE WORKED ON OUR PRESENT SECURITY DEVICES.
THIS BUILDING IS LIKE A COMPLETE CHAPTER OUT OF OUR PAST.
DON'T CRY, SUGAR. MOTHER'S GOT YOU.
REED! WHAT IS GOING ON? WHAT IS THIS PLACE?
I'M SCARED, MOMMY!

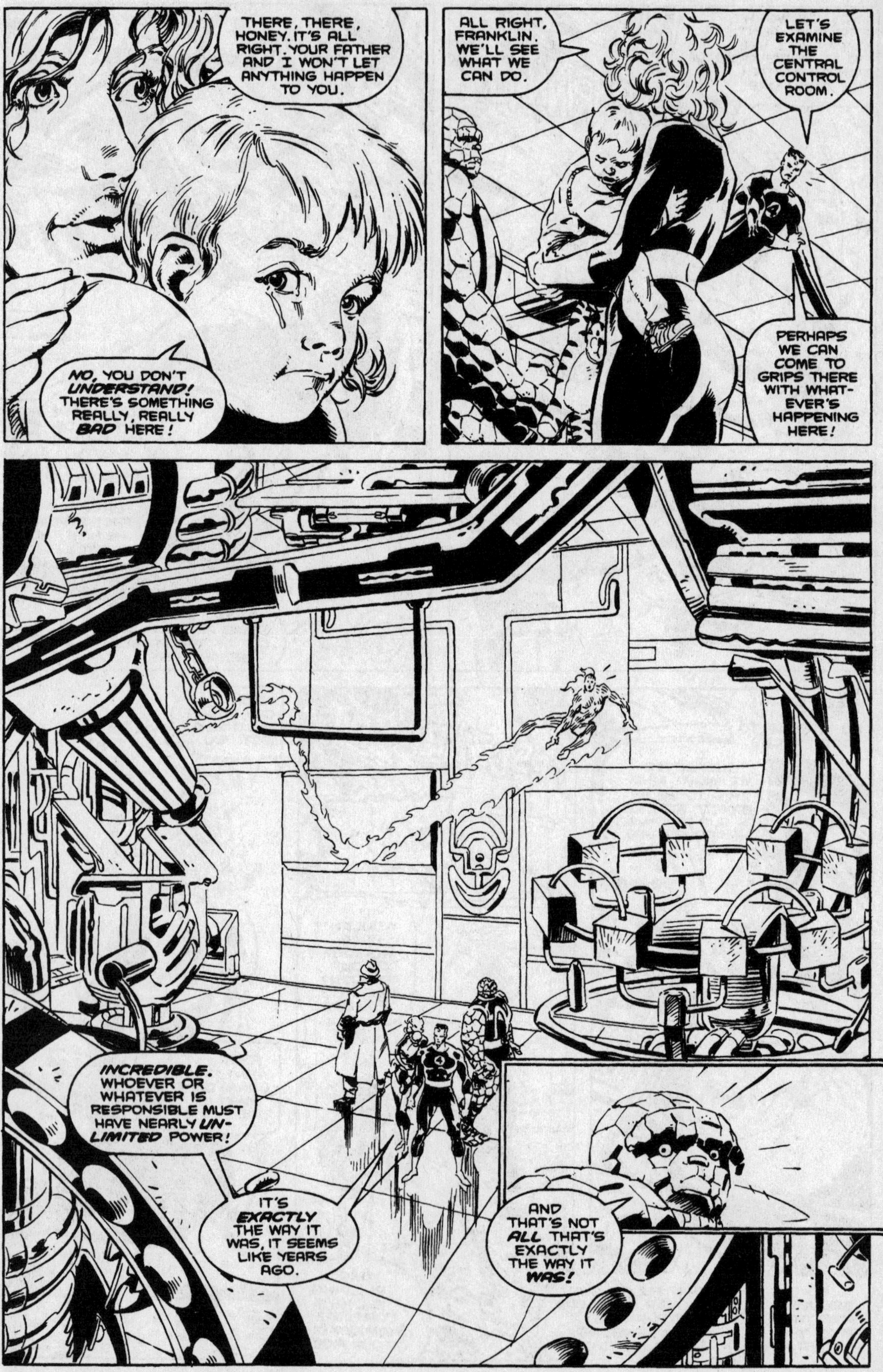
THERE, THERE, HONEY. IT'S ALL RIGHT. YOUR FATHER AND I WON'T LET ANYTHING HAPPEN TO YOU.
NO, YOU DON'T UNDERSTAND! THERE'S SOMETHING REALLY, REALLY BAD HERE!
ALL RIGHT, FRANKLIN. WE'LL SEE WHAT WE CAN DO.
LET'S EXAMINE THE CENTRAL CONTROL ROOM.
PERHAPS WE CAN COME TO GRIPS THERE WITH WHAT-EVER'S HAPPENING HERE!
INCREDIBLE. WHOEVER OR WHATEVER IS RESPONSIBLE MUST HAVE NEARLY UN-LIMITED POWER!
IT'S EXACTLY THE WAY IT WAS, IT SEEMS LIKE YEARS AGO.
AND THAT'S NOT ALL THAT'S EXACTLY THE WAY IT WAS!

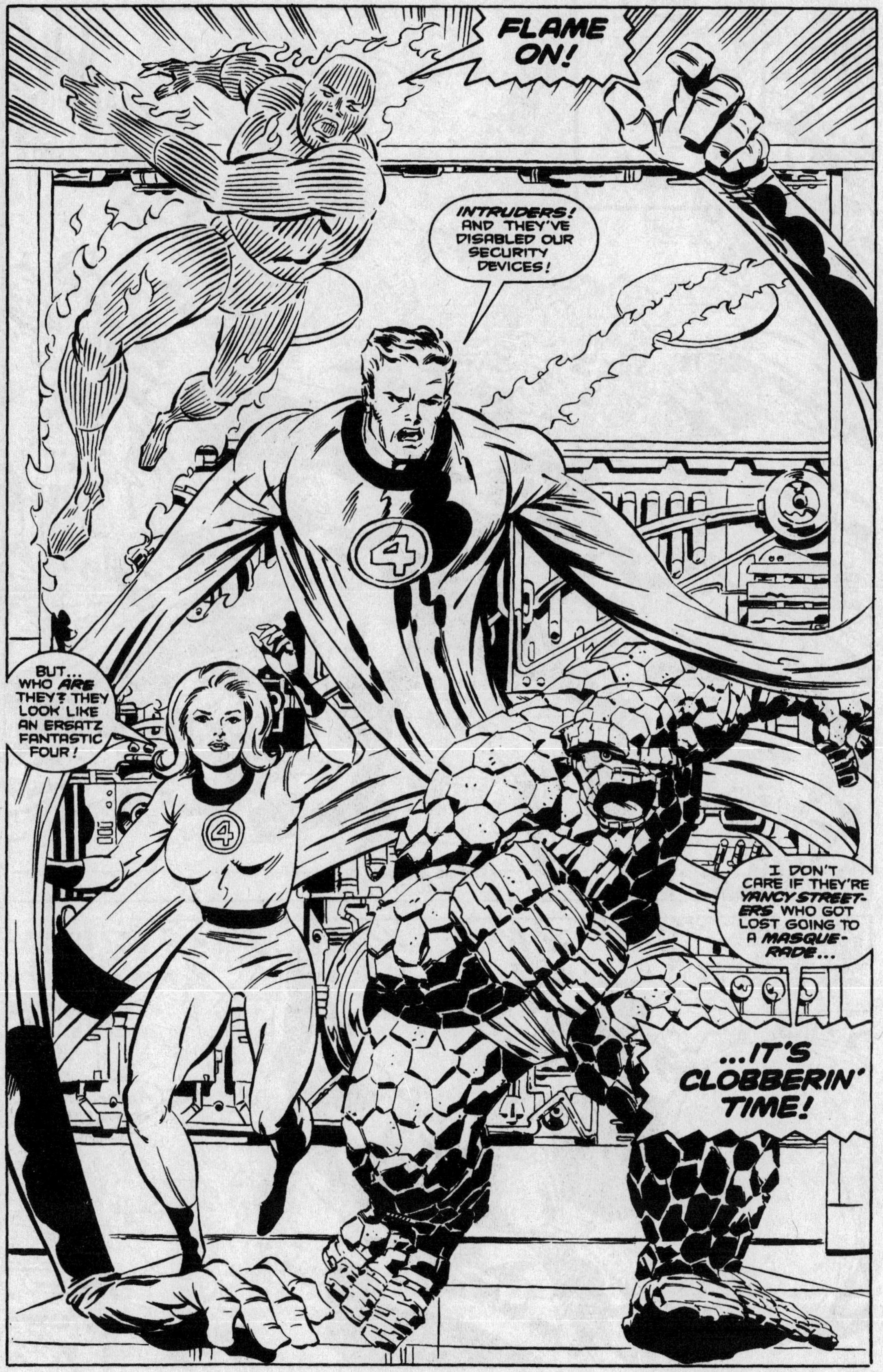
FLAME ON!
INTRUDERS! AND THEY'VE DISABLED OUR SECURITY DEVICES!
BUT... WHO ARE THEY? THEY LOOK LIKE AN ERSATZ FANTASTIC FOUR!
I DON'T CARE IF THEY'RE YANCY STREET-ERS WHO GOT LOST GOING TO A MASQUE-RADE...
...IT'S CLOBBERIN' TIME!

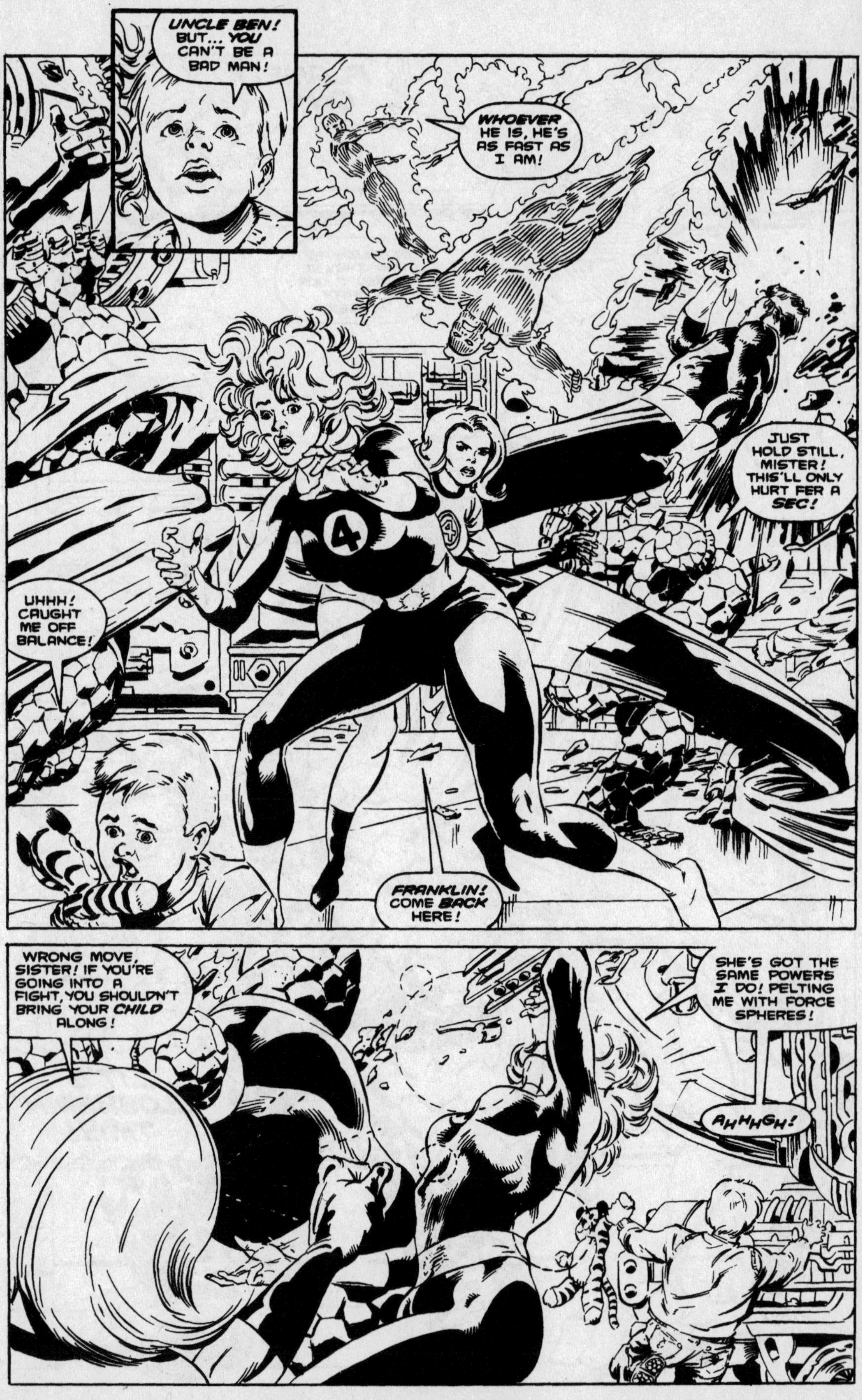
UNCLE BEN! BUT... YOU CAN'T BE A BAD MAN!
WHOEVER HE IS, HE'S AS FAST AS I AM!
JUST HOLD STILL, MISTER! THIS'LL ONLY HURT FER A SEC!
UHHH! CAUGHT ME OFF BALANCE!
FRANKLIN! COME BACK HERE!
WRONG MOVE, SISTER! IF YOU'RE GOING INTO A FIGHT, YOU SHOULDN'T BRING YOUR CHILD ALONG!
SHE'S GOT THE SAME POWERS I DO! PELTING ME WITH FORCE SPHERES!
AHHHGH!

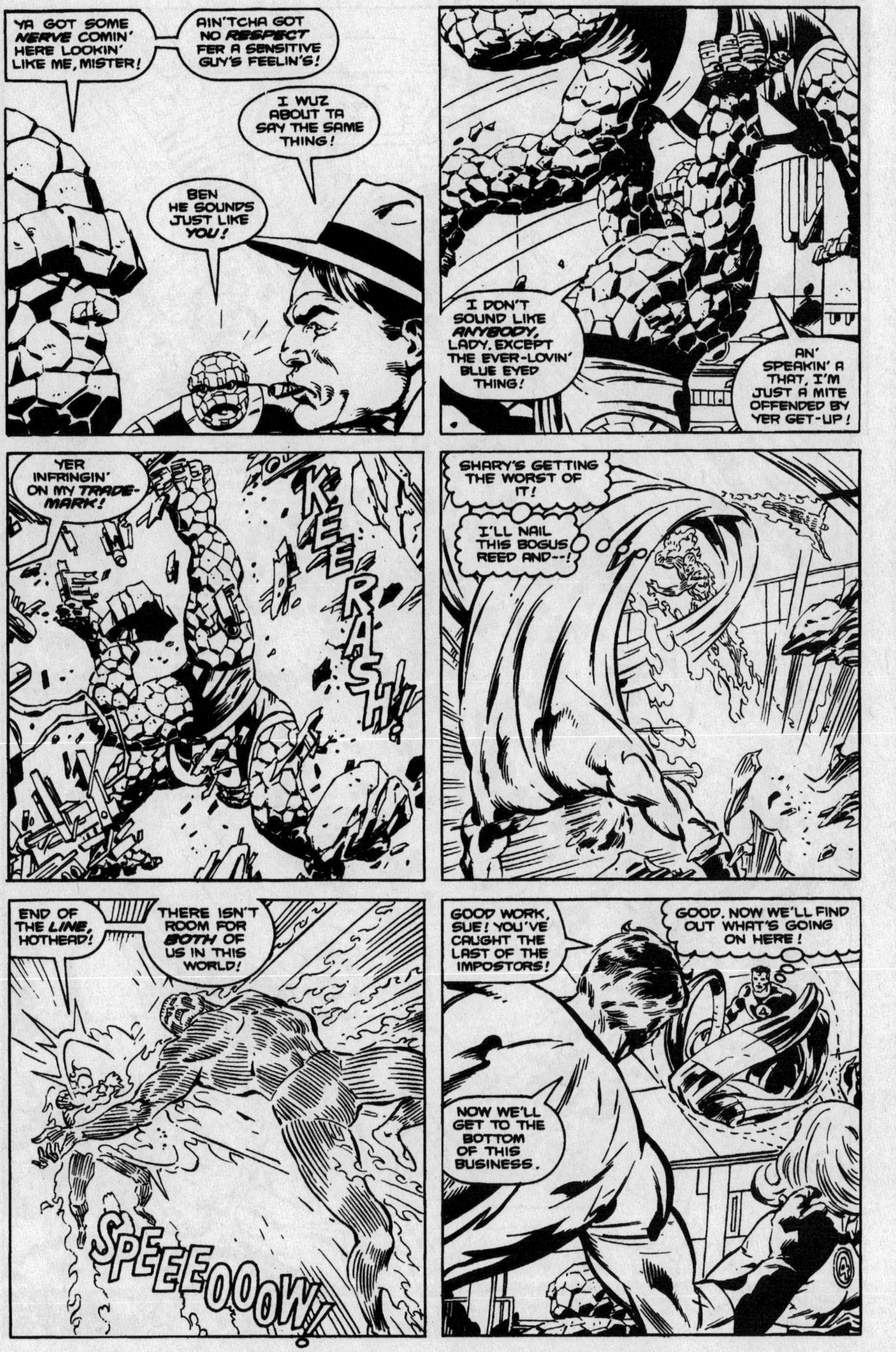
YA GOT SOME NERVE COMIN' HERE LOOKIN' LIKE ME, MISTER!
AIN'TCHA GOT NO RESPECT FER A SENSITIVE GUY'S FEELIN'S!
I WUZ ABOUT TA SAY THE SAME THING!
BEN HE SOUNDS JUST LIKE YOU!
I DON'T SOUND LIKE ANYBODY, LADY. EXCEPT THE EVER-LOVIN' BLUE EYED THING!
AN' SPEAKIN' A THAT, I'M JUST A MITE OFFENDED BY YER GET-UP!
YER INFRINGIN' ON MY TRADE-MARK!
KEERASH!
SHARY'S GETTING THE WORST OF IT!
I'LL NAIL THIS BOGUS REED AND--!
END OF THE LINE, HOTHEAD!
THERE ISN'T ROOM FOR BOTH OF US IN THIS WORLD!
SPEEEOOOW!
GOOD WORK, SUE! YOU'VE CAUGHT THE LAST OF THE IMPOSTORS!
GOOD. NOW WE'LL FIND OUT WHAT'S GOING ON HERE!
NOW WE'LL GET TO THE BOTTOM OF THIS BUSINESS.

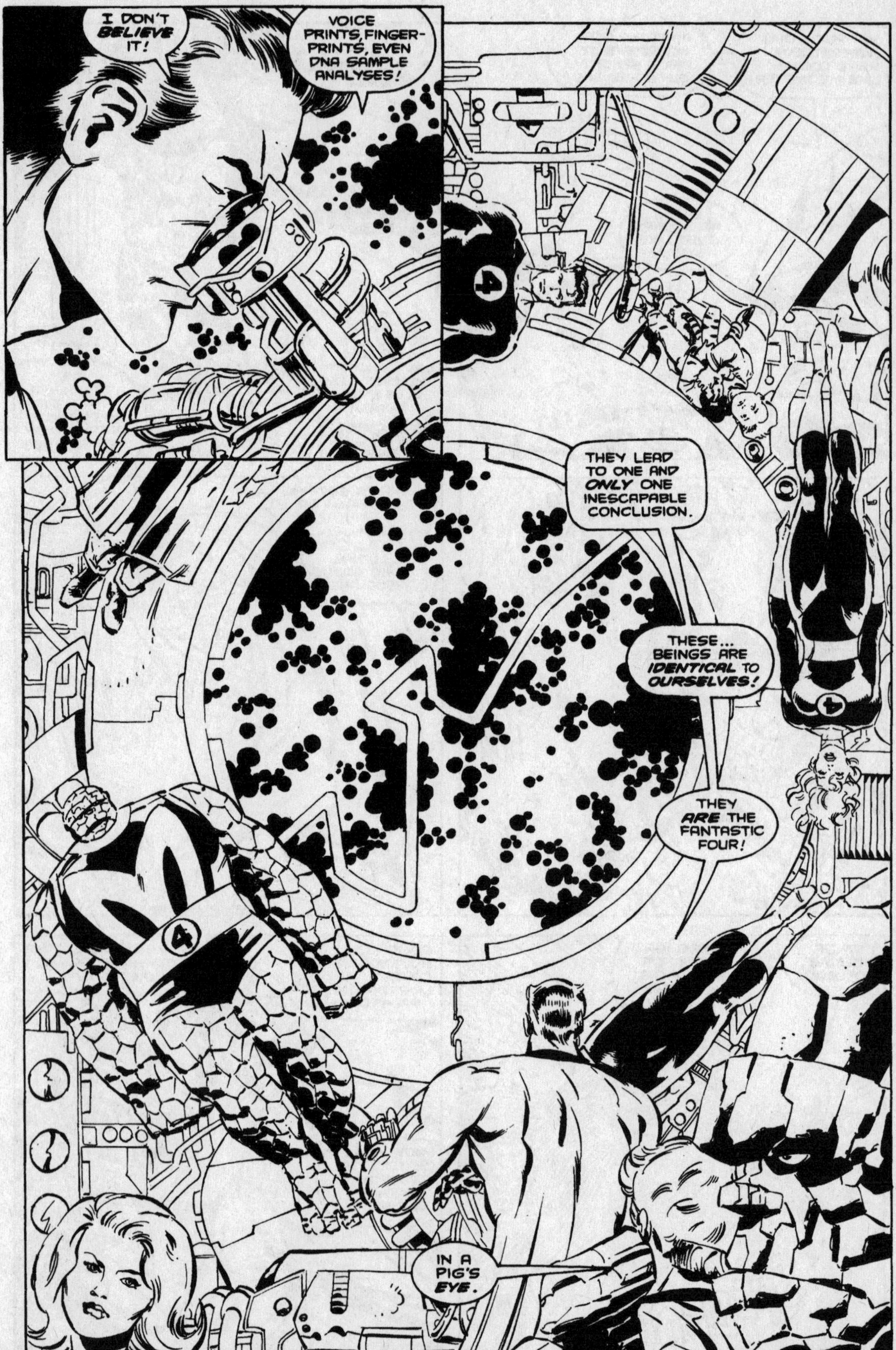
I DON'T BELIEVE IT!
VOICE PRINTS, FINGER-PRINTS, EVEN DNA SAMPLE ANALYSES!
THEY LEAD TO ONE AND ONLY ONE INESCAPABLE CONCLUSION.
THESE... BEINGS ARE IDENTICAL TO OURSELVES!
THEY ARE THE FANTASTIC FOUR!
IN A PIG'S EYE.

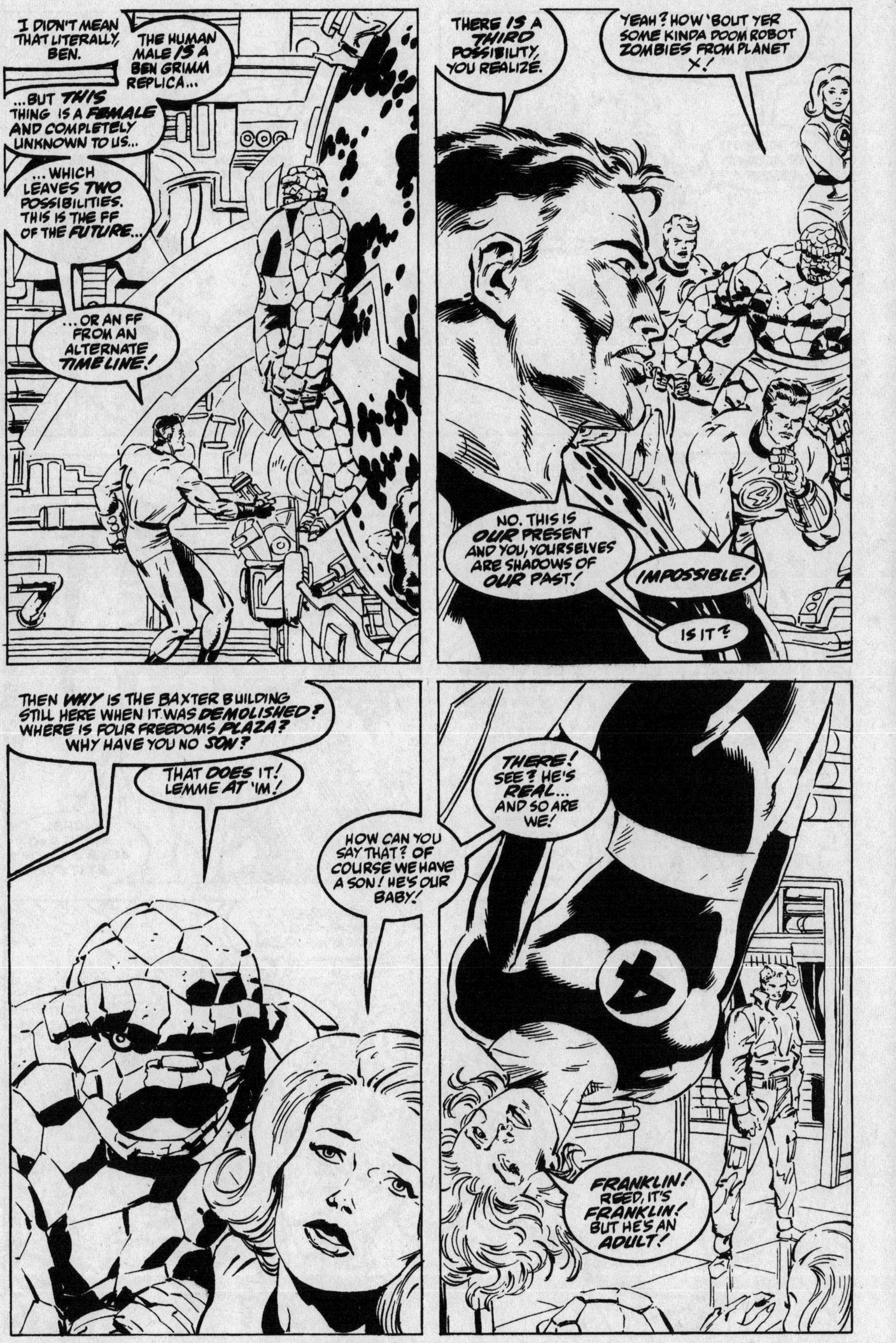
I DIDN'T MEAN THAT LITERALLY, BEN.
THE HUMAN MALE IS A BEN GRIMM REPLICA...
...BUT THIS THING IS A FEMALE AND COMPLETELY UNKNOWN TO US...
...WHICH LEAVES TWO POSSIBILITIES. THIS IS THE FF OF THE FUTURE...
...OR AN FF FROM AN ALTERNATE TIMELINE!
THERE IS A THIRD POSSIBILITY, YOU REALIZE.
YEAH? HOW 'BOUT YER SOME KINDA DOOM ROBOT ZOMBIES FROM PLANET X!
NO. THIS IS OUR PRESENT AND YOU, YOURSELVES ARE SHADOWS OF OUR PAST!
IMPOSSIBLE!
IS IT?
THEN WHY IS THE BAXTER BUILDING STILL HERE WHEN IT WAS DEMOLISHED? WHERE IS FOUR FREEDOMS PLAZA? WHY HAVE YOU NO SON?
THAT DOES IT! LEMME AT 'IM!
HOW CAN YOU SAY THAT? OF COURSE WE HAVE A SON! HE'S OUR BABY!
THERE! SEE? HE'S REAL... AND SO ARE WE!
FRANKLIN! REED, IT'S FRANKLIN! BUT HE'S AN ADULT!

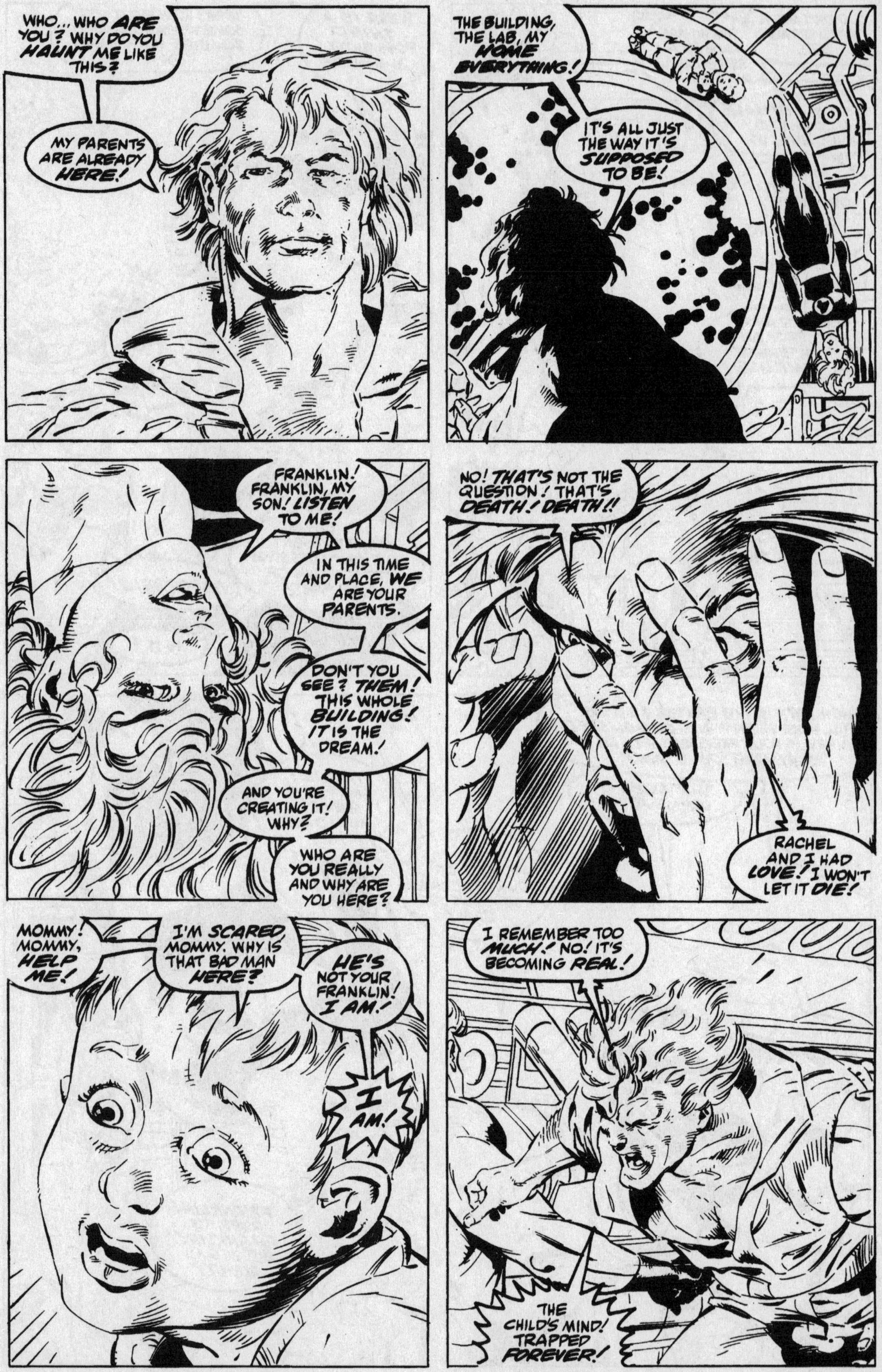
WHO... WHO ARE YOU? WHY DO YOU HAUNT ME LIKE THIS?
MY PARENTS ARE ALREADY HERE!
THE BUILDING, THE LAB, MY HOME EVERYTHING!
IT'S ALL JUST THE WAY IT'S SUPPOSED TO BE!
FRANKLIN! FRANKLIN, MY SON! LISTEN TO ME!
IN THIS TIME AND PLACE, WE ARE YOUR PARENTS.
DON'T YOU SEE? THEM! THIS WHOLE BUILDING! IT IS THE DREAM!
AND YOU'RE CREATING IT! WHY?
WHO ARE YOU REALLY AND WHY ARE YOU HERE?
NO! THAT'S NOT THE QUESTION! THAT'S DEATH! DEATH!!
RACHEL AND I HAD LOVE! I WON'T LET IT DIE!
MOMMY! MOMMY, HELP ME!
I'M SCARED, MOMMY. WHY IS THAT BAD MAN HERE?
HE'S NOT YOUR FRANKLIN! I AM!
I AM!
I REMEMBER TOO MUCH! NO! IT'S BECOMING REAL!
THE CHILD'S MIND! TRAPPED FOREVER!

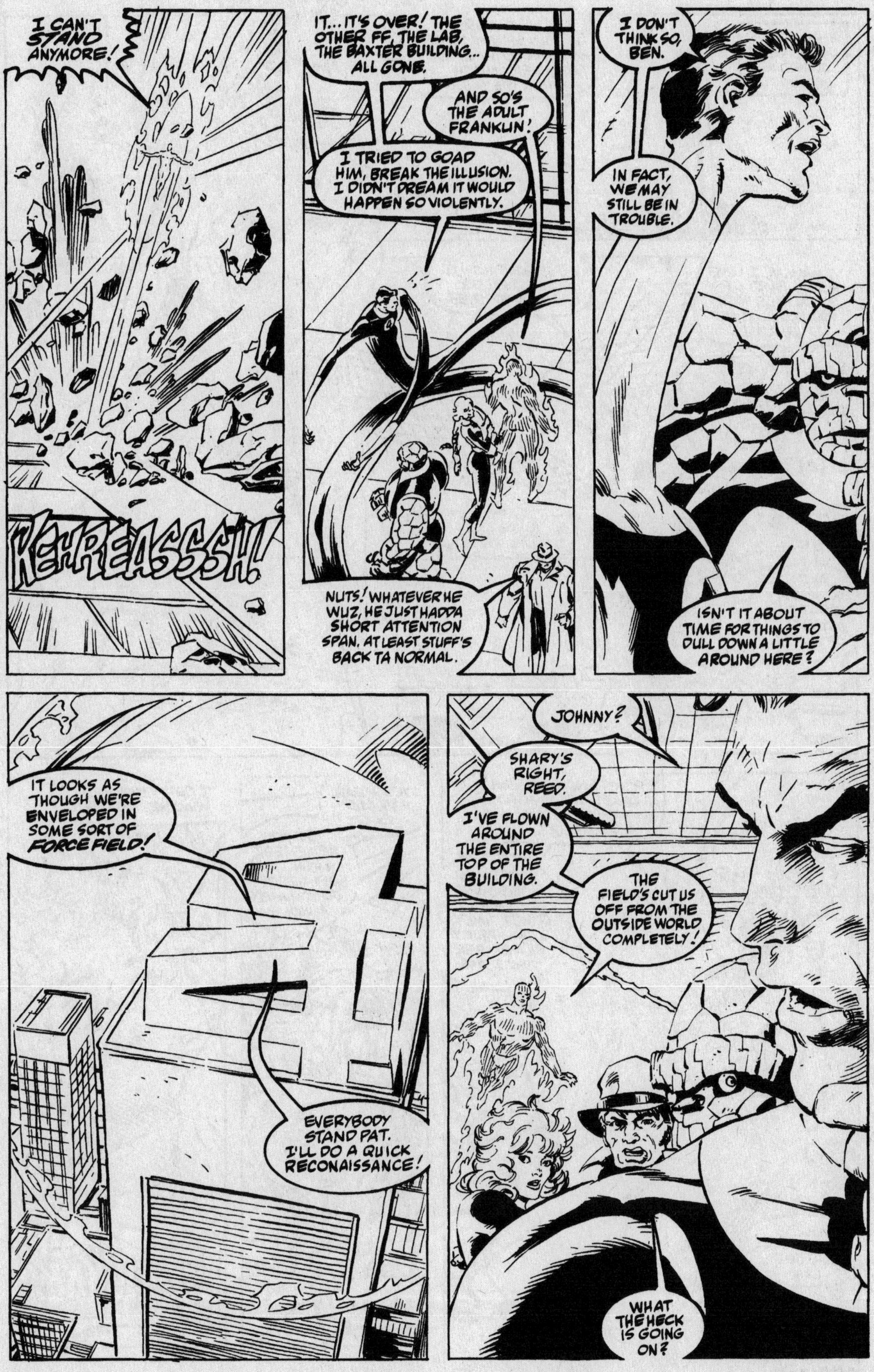
I CAN'T STAND ANYMORE!
KE-HREASSSH!
IT... IT'S OVER! THE OTHER FF, THE LAB, THE BAXTER BUILDING... ALL GONE.
AND SO'S THE ADULT FRANKLIN!
I TRIED TO GOAD HIM, BREAK THE ILLUSION. I DIDN'T DREAM IT WOULD HAPPEN SO VIOLENTLY.
NUTS! WHATEVER HE WUZ, HE JUST HADDA SHORT ATTENTION SPAN. AT LEAST STUFF'S BACK TA NORMAL.
I DON'T THINK SO, BEN.
IN FACT, WE MAY STILL BE IN TROUBLE.
ISN'T IT ABOUT TIME FOR THINGS TO DULL DOWN A LITTLE AROUND HERE?
IT LOOKS AS THOUGH WE'RE ENVELOPED IN SOME SORT OF FORCE FIELD!
EVERYBODY STAND PAT. I'LL DO A QUICK RECONAISSANCE!
JOHNNY?
SHARY'S RIGHT, REED.
I'VE FLOWN AROUND THE ENTIRE TOP OF THE BUILDING.
THE FIELD'S CUT US OFF FROM THE OUTSIDE WORLD COMPLETELY!
WHAT THE HECK IS GOING ON?

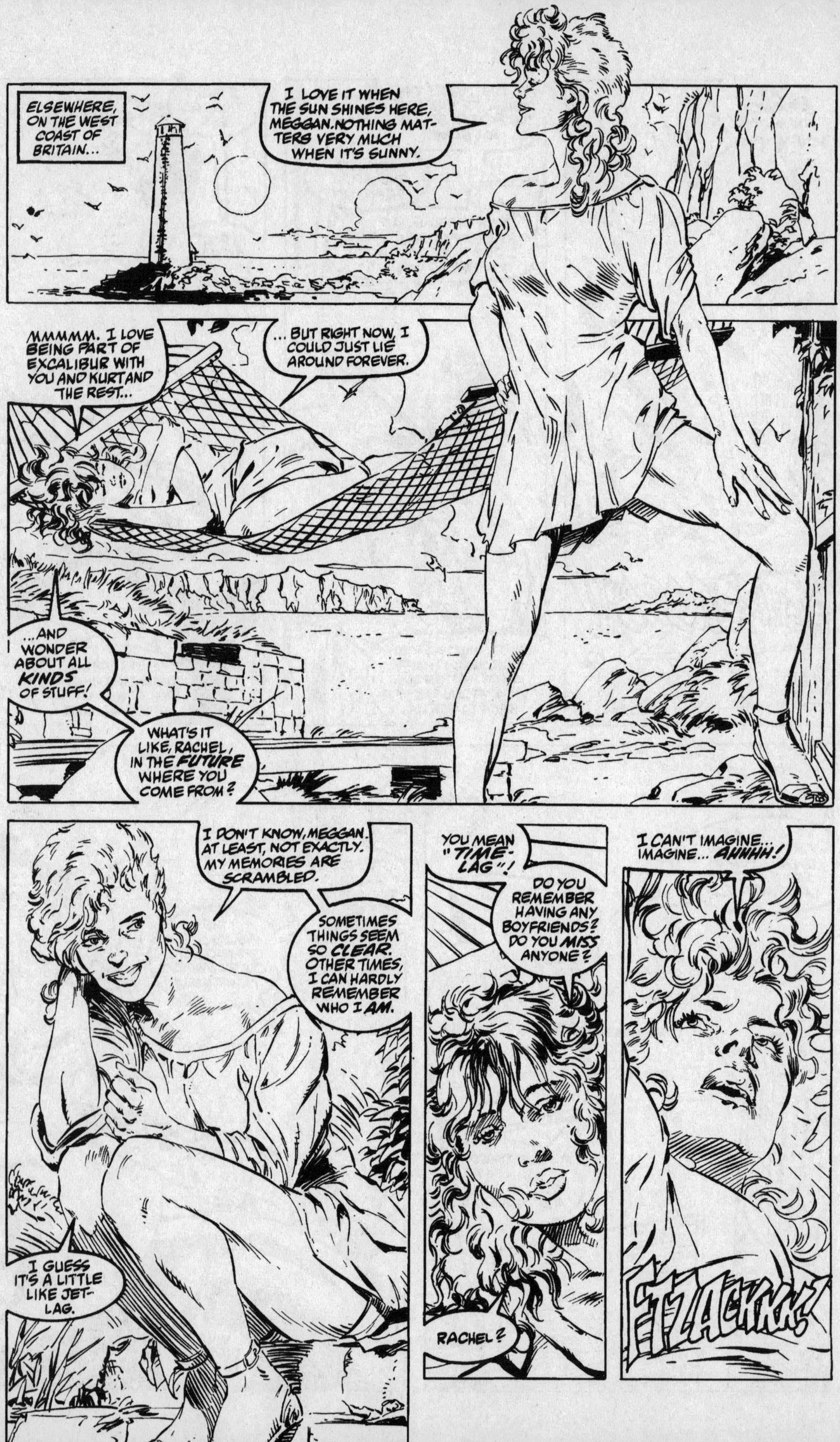
ELSEWHERE, ON THE WEST COAST OF BRITAIN...
I LOVE IT WHEN THE SUN SHINES HERE, MEGGAN. NOTHING MATTERS VERY MUCH WHEN IT'S SUNNY.
MMMMM. I LOVE BEING PART OF EXCALIBUR WITH YOU AND KURT AND THE REST...
... BUT RIGHT NOW, I COULD JUST LIE AROUND FOREVER.
...AND WONDER ABOUT ALL KINDS OF STUFF!
WHAT'S IT LIKE, RACHEL, IN THE FUTURE WHERE YOU COME FROM?
I DON'T KNOW, MEGGAN. AT LEAST, NOT EXACTLY. MY MEMORIES ARE SCRAMBLED.
SOMETIMES THINGS SEEM SO CLEAR. OTHER TIMES, I CAN HARDLY REMEMBER WHO I AM.
I GUESS IT'S A LITTLE LIKE JET-LAG.
YOU MEAN "TIME-LAG"!
DO YOU REMEMBER HAVING ANY BOYFRIENDS? DO YOU MISS ANYONE?
RACHEL?
I CAN'T IMAGINE... IMAGINE... AHHHH!
FTZACKKK!

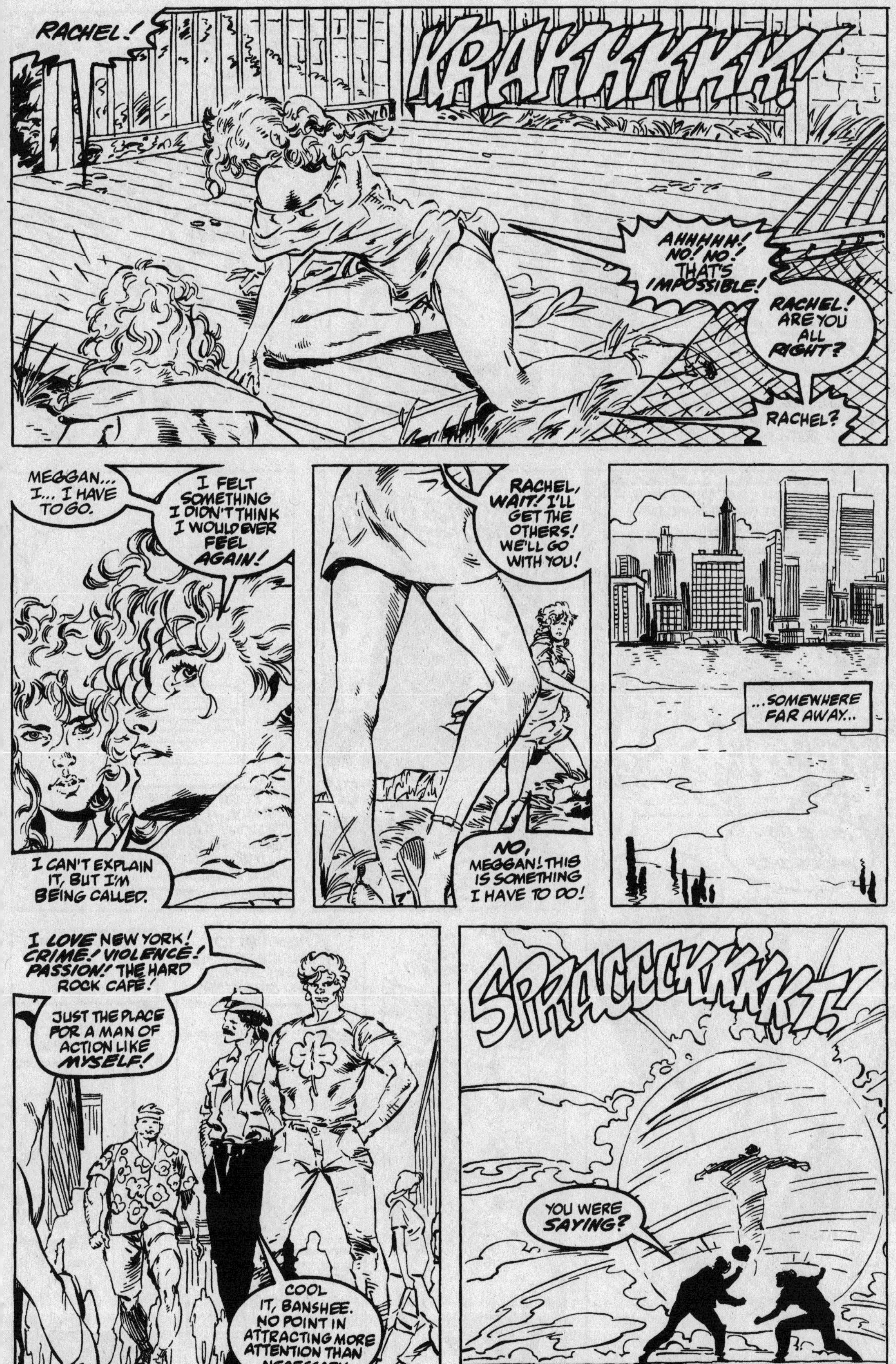
RACHEL!
KRAKKKKKK!
AHHHHH! NO! NO! THAT'S IMPOSSIBLE!
RACHEL! ARE YOU ALL RIGHT?
RACHEL?
MEGGAN... I... I HAVE TO GO.
I FELT SOMETHING I DIDN'T THINK I WOULD EVER FEEL AGAIN!
I CAN'T EXPLAIN IT, BUT I'M BEING CALLED.
RACHEL, WAIT! I'LL GET THE OTHERS! WE'LL GO WITH YOU!
NO, MEGGAN! THIS IS SOMETHING I HAVE TO DO!
...SOMEWHERE FAR AWAY...
I LOVE NEW YORK! CRIME! VIOLENCE! PASSION! THE HARD ROCK CAFÉ!
JUST THE PLACE FOR A MAN OF ACTION LIKE MYSELF!
COOL IT, BANSHEE. NO POINT IN ATTRACTING MORE ATTENTION THAN NECESSARY.
SPRACCCKKKKT!
YOU WERE SAYING?

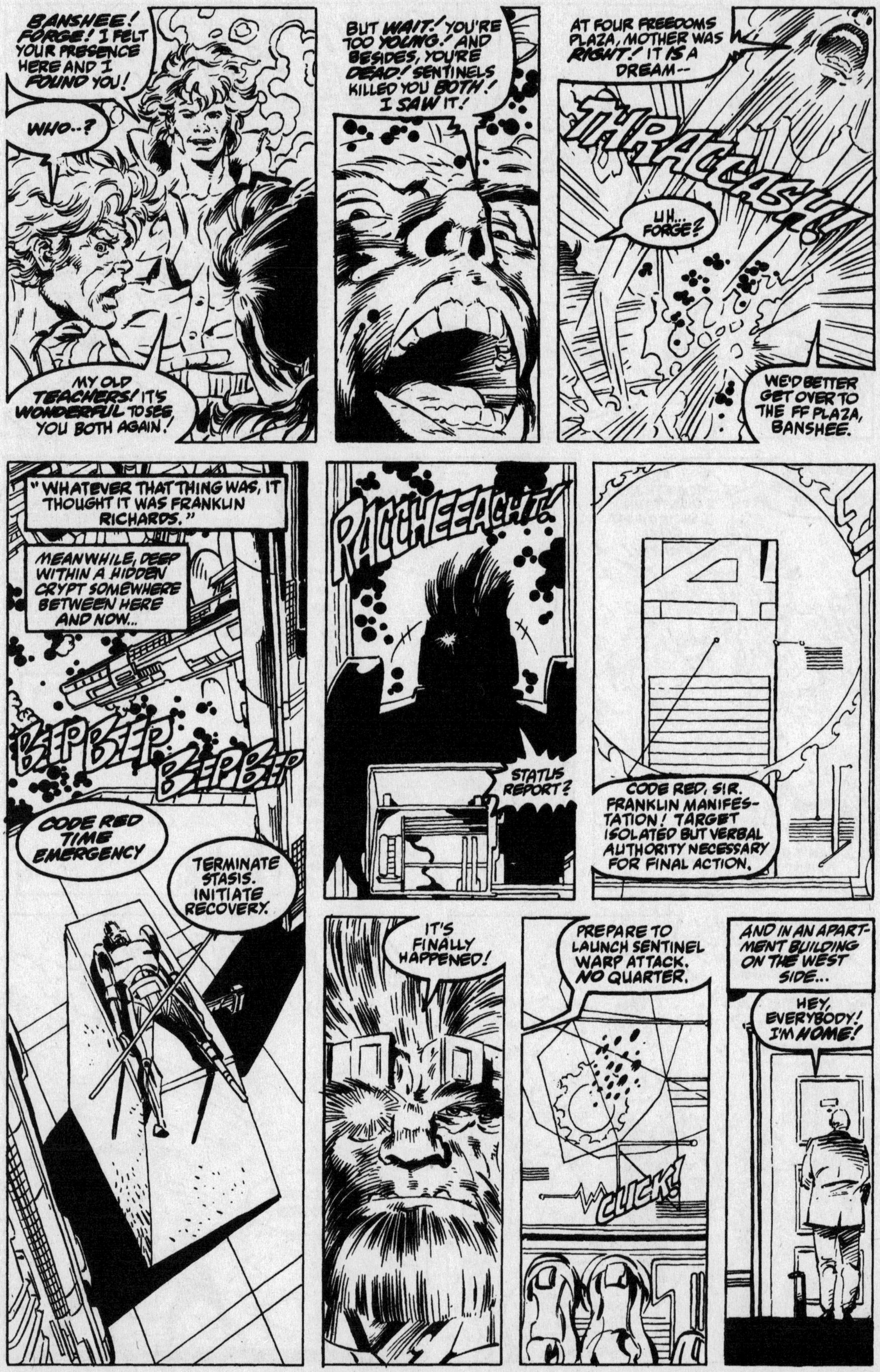
BANSHEE! FORGE! I FELT YOUR PRESENCE HERE AND I FOUND YOU!
WHO..?
MY OLD TEACHERS! IT'S WONDERFUL TO SEE YOU BOTH AGAIN!
BUT WAIT! YOU'RE TOO YOUNG! AND BESIDES, YOU'RE DEAD! SENTINELS KILLED YOU BOTH! I SAW IT!
AT FOUR FREEDOMS PLAZA, MOTHER WAS RIGHT! IT IS A DREAM--
THRACCASH!
UH... FORGE?
WE'D BETTER GET OVER TO THE FF PLAZA, BANSHEE.
"WHATEVER THAT THING WAS, IT THOUGHT IT WAS FRANKLIN RICHARDS."
MEANWHILE, DEEP WITHIN A HIDDEN CRYPT SOMEWHERE BETWEEN HERE AND NOW...
BEEP BEEP BEEP BEEP
CODE RED TIME EMERGENCY
TERMINATE STASIS. INITIATE RECOVERY.
RACCHEEACHT!
STATUS REPORT?
CODE RED, SIR. FRANKLIN MANIFESTATION! TARGET ISOLATED BUT VERBAL AUTHORITY NECESSARY FOR FINAL ACTION.
IT'S FINALLY HAPPENED!
PREPARE TO LAUNCH SENTINEL WARP ATTACK. NO QUARTER.
CLICK!
AND IN AN APARTMENT BUILDING ON THE WEST SIDE...
HEY, EVERYBODY! I'M HOME!

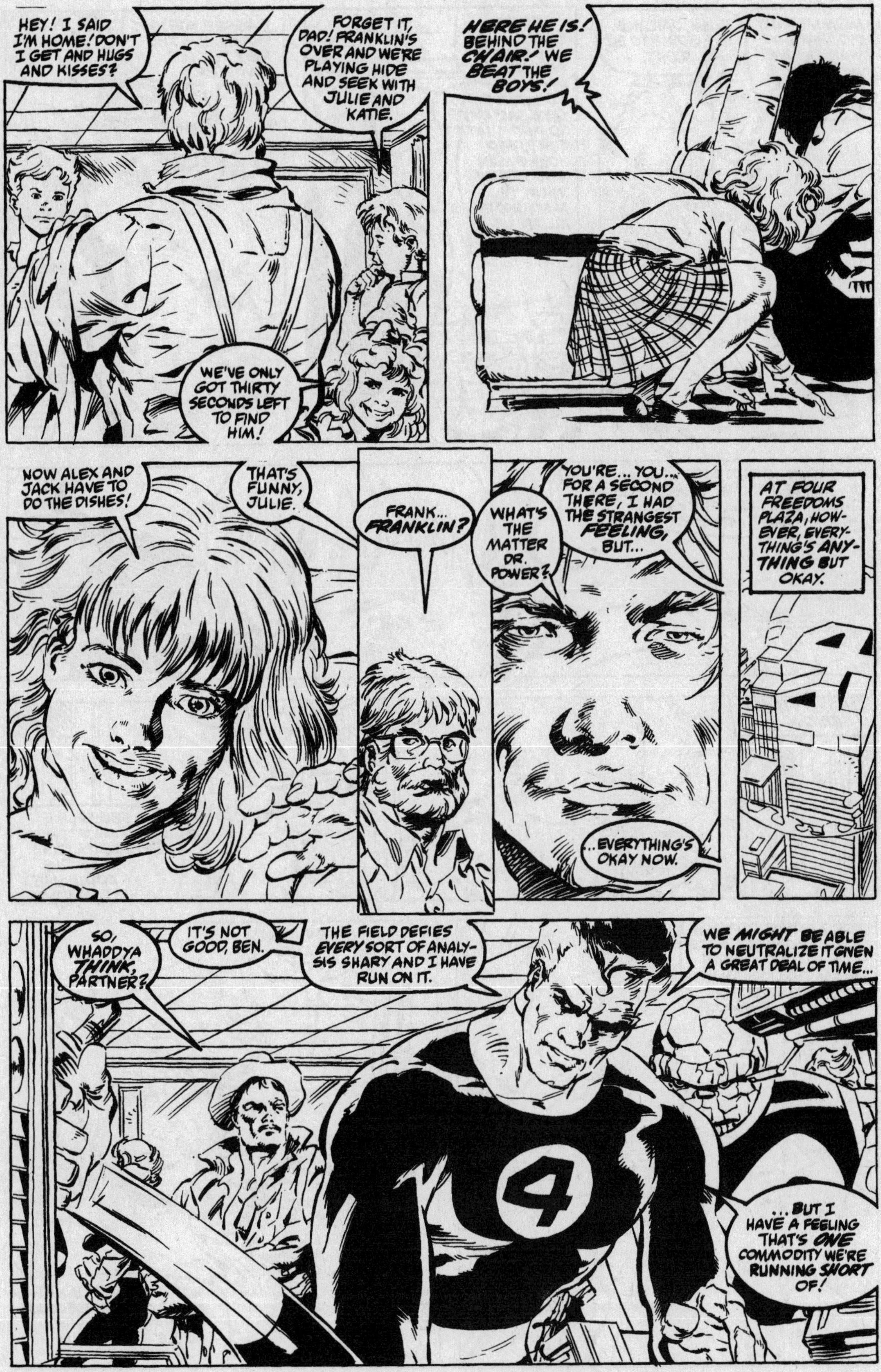
HEY! I SAID I'M HOME! DON'T I GET AND HUGS AND KISSES?
FORGET IT, DAD! FRANKLIN'S OVER AND WE'RE PLAYING HIDE AND SEEK WITH JULIE AND KATIE.
WE'VE ONLY GOT THIRTY SECONDS LEFT TO FIND HIM!
HERE HE IS! BEHIND THE CHAIR! WE BEAT THE BOYS!
NOW ALEX AND JACK HAVE TO DO THE DISHES!
THAT'S FUNNY, JULIE.
FRANK... FRANKLIN?
WHAT'S THE MATTER DR. POWER?
YOU'RE... YOU... FOR A SECOND THERE, I HAD THE STRANGEST FEELING, BUT...
...EVERYTHING'S OKAY NOW.
AT FOUR FREEDOMS PLAZA, HOWEVER, EVERYTHING'S ANYTHING BUT OKAY.
SO, WHADDYA THINK, PARTNER?
IT'S NOT GOOD, BEN.
THE FIELD DEFIES EVERY SORT OF ANALYSIS SHARY AND I HAVE RUN ON IT.
WE MIGHT BE ABLE TO NEUTRALIZE IT GIVEN A GREAT DEAL OF TIME...
...BUT I HAVE A FEELING THAT'S ONE COMMODITY WE'RE RUNNING SHORT OF!

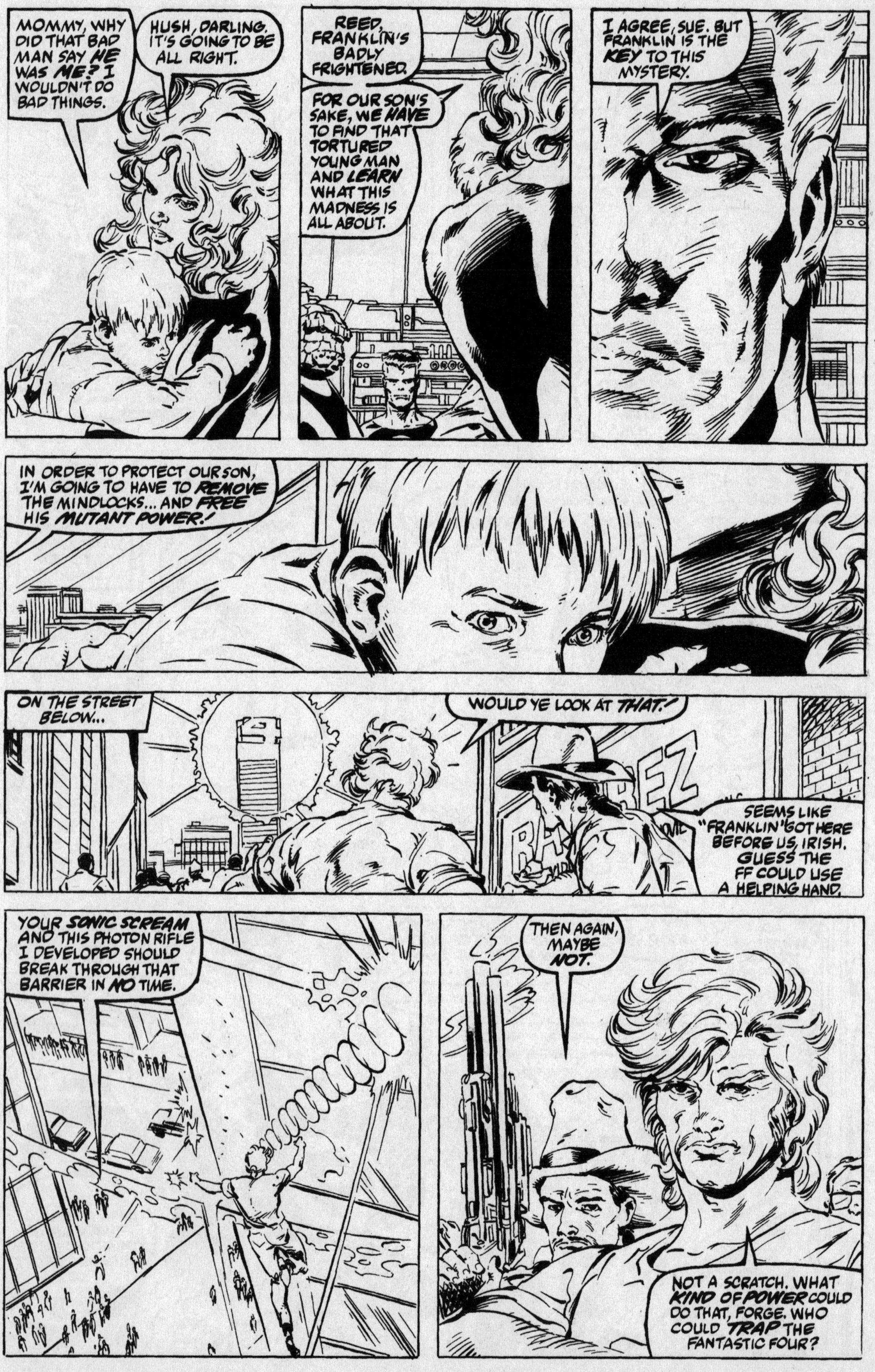
MOMMY, WHY DID THAT BAD MAN SAY HE WAS ME? I WOULDN'T DO BAD THINGS.
HUSH, DARLING. IT'S GOING TO BE ALL RIGHT.
REED, FRANKLIN'S BADLY FRIGHTENED.
FOR OUR SON'S SAKE, WE HAVE TO FIND THAT TORTURED YOUNG MAN AND LEARN WHAT THIS MADNESS IS ALL ABOUT.
I AGREE, SUE. BUT FRANKLIN IS THE KEY TO THIS MYSTERY.
IN ORDER TO PROTECT OUR SON, I'M GOING TO HAVE TO REMOVE THE MINDLOCKS... AND FREE HIS MUTANT POWER!
ON THE STREET BELOW...
WOULD YE LOOK AT THAT!
SEEMS LIKE "FRANKLIN" GOT HERE BEFORE US, IRISH. GUESS THE FF COULD USE A HELPING HAND.
YOUR SONIC SCREAM AND THIS PHOTON RIFLE I DEVELOPED SHOULD BREAK THROUGH THAT BARRIER IN NO TIME.
THEN AGAIN, MAYBE NOT.
NOT A SCRATCH. WHAT KIND OF POWER COULD DO THAT, FORGE. WHO COULD TRAP THE FANTASTIC FOUR?

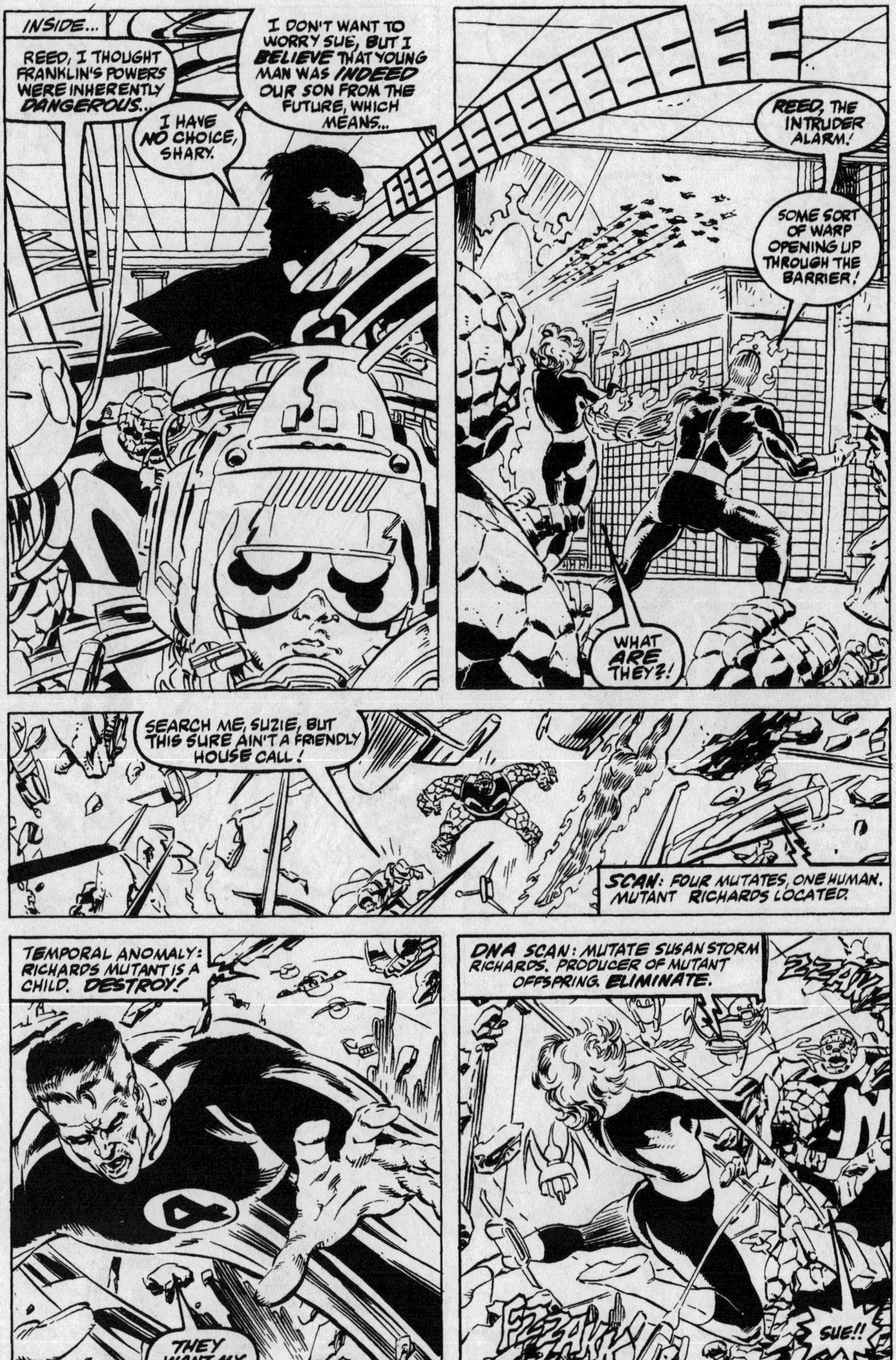
INSIDE...
REED, I THOUGHT FRANKLIN'S POWERS WERE INHERENTLY DANGEROUS...
I HAVE NO CHOICE, SHARY.
I DON'T WANT TO WORRY SUE, BUT I BELIEVE THAT YOUNG MAN WAS INDEED OUR SON FROM THE FUTURE, WHICH MEANS...
EEEEEEEEEEEEEEEE
REED, THE INTRUDER ALARM!
SOME SORT OF WARP OPENING UP THROUGH THE BARRIER!
WHAT ARE THEY?!
SEARCH ME, SUZIE, BUT THIS SURE AIN'T A FRIENDLY HOUSE CALL!
SCAN: FOUR MUTATES, ONE HUMAN. MUTANT RICHARDS LOCATED.
TEMPORAL ANOMALY: RICHARDS MUTANT IS A CHILD. DESTROY!
THEY WANT MY SON!
DNA SCAN: MUTATE SUSAN STORM RICHARDS. PRODUCER OF MUTANT OFFSPRING. ELIMINATE.
FZAAKK
SUE!!

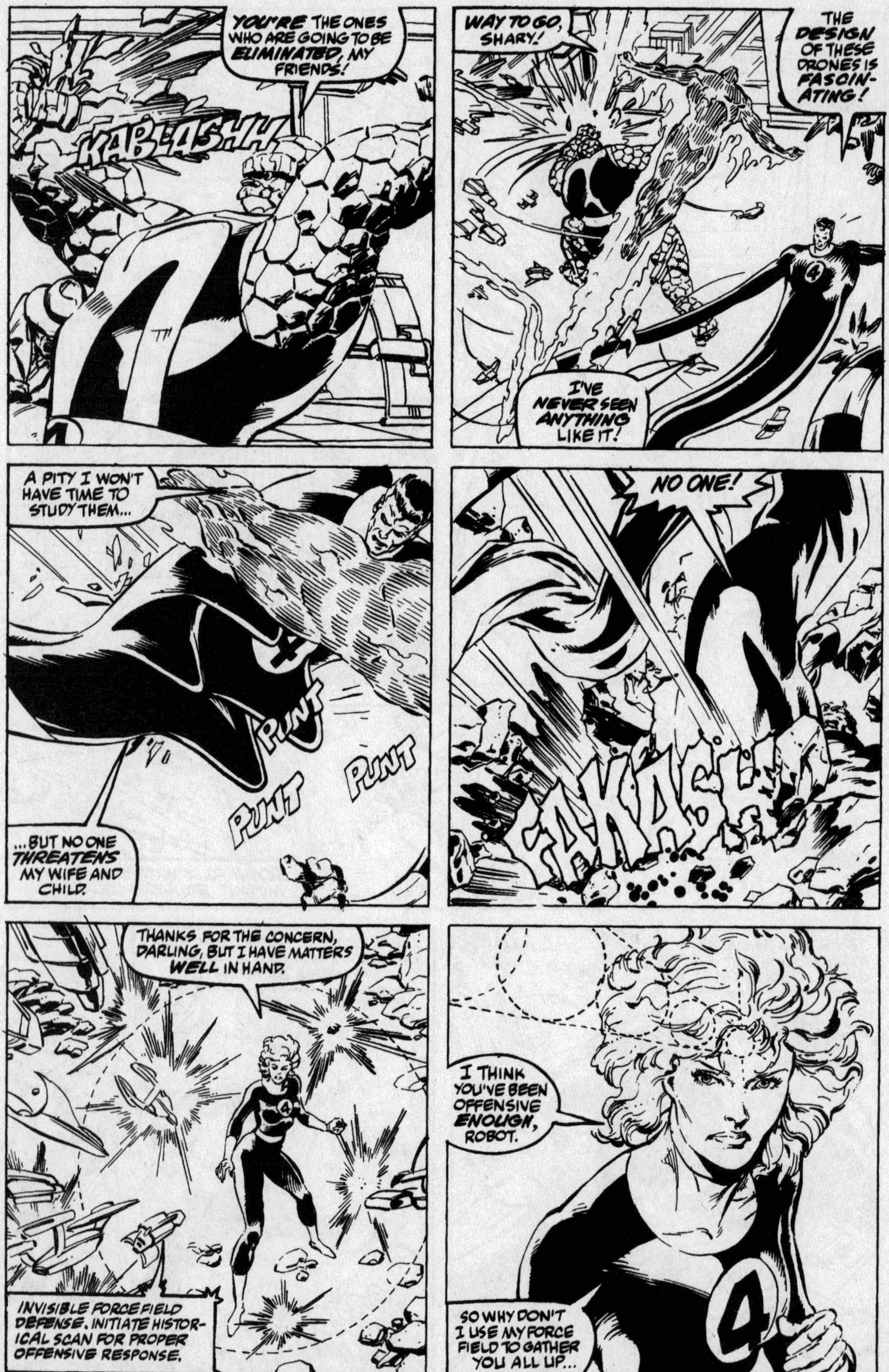

YOU'RE THE ONES WHO ARE GOING TO BE ELIMINATED, MY FRIENDS!
KABLASHH
WAY TO GO, SHARY!
THE DESIGN OF THESE DRONES IS FASCIN-ATING!
I'VE NEVER SEEN ANYTHING LIKE IT!
A PITY I WON'T HAVE TIME TO STUDY THEM...
PUNT
PUNT
PUNT
...BUT NO ONE THREATENS MY WIFE AND CHILD.
NO ONE!
THANKS FOR THE CONCERN, DARLING, BUT I HAVE MATTERS WELL IN HAND.
INVISIBLE FORCE FIELD DEFENSE. INITIATE HISTOR-ICAL SCAN FOR PROPER OFFENSIVE RESPONSE.
I THINK YOU'VE BEEN OFFENSIVE ENOUGH, ROBOT.
SO WHY DON'T I USE MY FORCE FIELD TO GATHER YOU ALL UP...

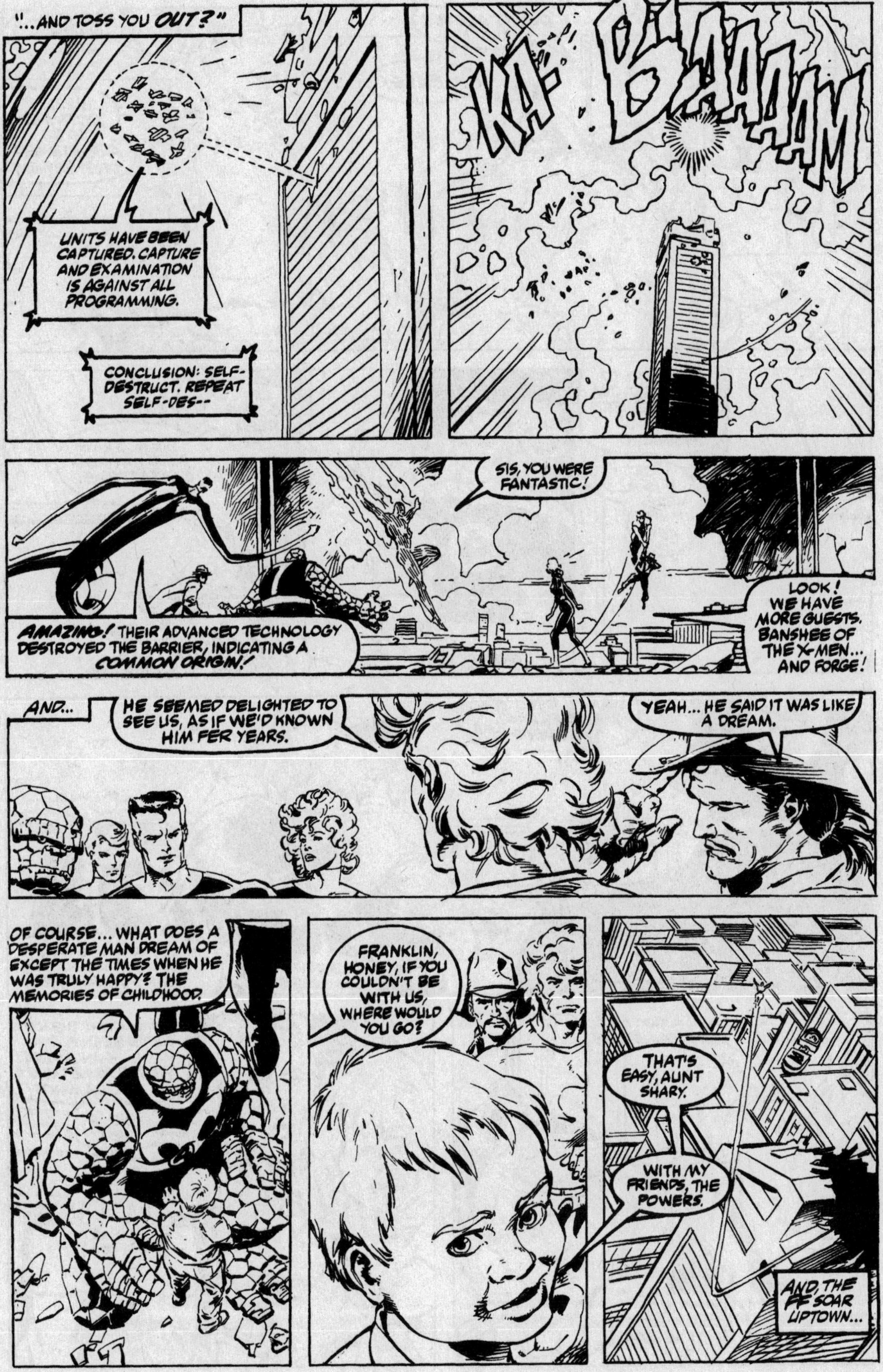
"...AND TOSS YOU OUT?"
UNITS HAVE BEEN CAPTURED. CAPTURE AND EXAMINATION IS AGAINST ALL PROGRAMMING.
CONCLUSION: SELF-DESTRUCT. REPEAT SELF-DES--
KA-BLAAAAM
SIS, YOU WERE FANTASTIC!
AMAZING! THEIR ADVANCED TECHNOLOGY DESTROYED THE BARRIER, INDICATING A COMMON ORIGIN!
LOOK! WE HAVE MORE GUESTS. BANSHEE OF THE X-MEN... AND FORGE!
AND...
HE SEEMED DELIGHTED TO SEE US, AS IF WE'D KNOWN HIM FER YEARS.
YEAH... HE SAID IT WAS LIKE A DREAM.
OF COURSE... WHAT DOES A DESPERATE MAN DREAM OF EXCEPT THE TIMES WHEN HE WAS TRULY HAPPY? THE MEMORIES OF CHILDHOOD.
FRANKLIN, HONEY, IF YOU COULDN'T BE WITH US, WHERE WOULD YOU GO?
THAT'S EASY, AUNT SHARY.
WITH MY FRIENDS, THE POWERS.
AND, THE FF SOAR UPTOWN...

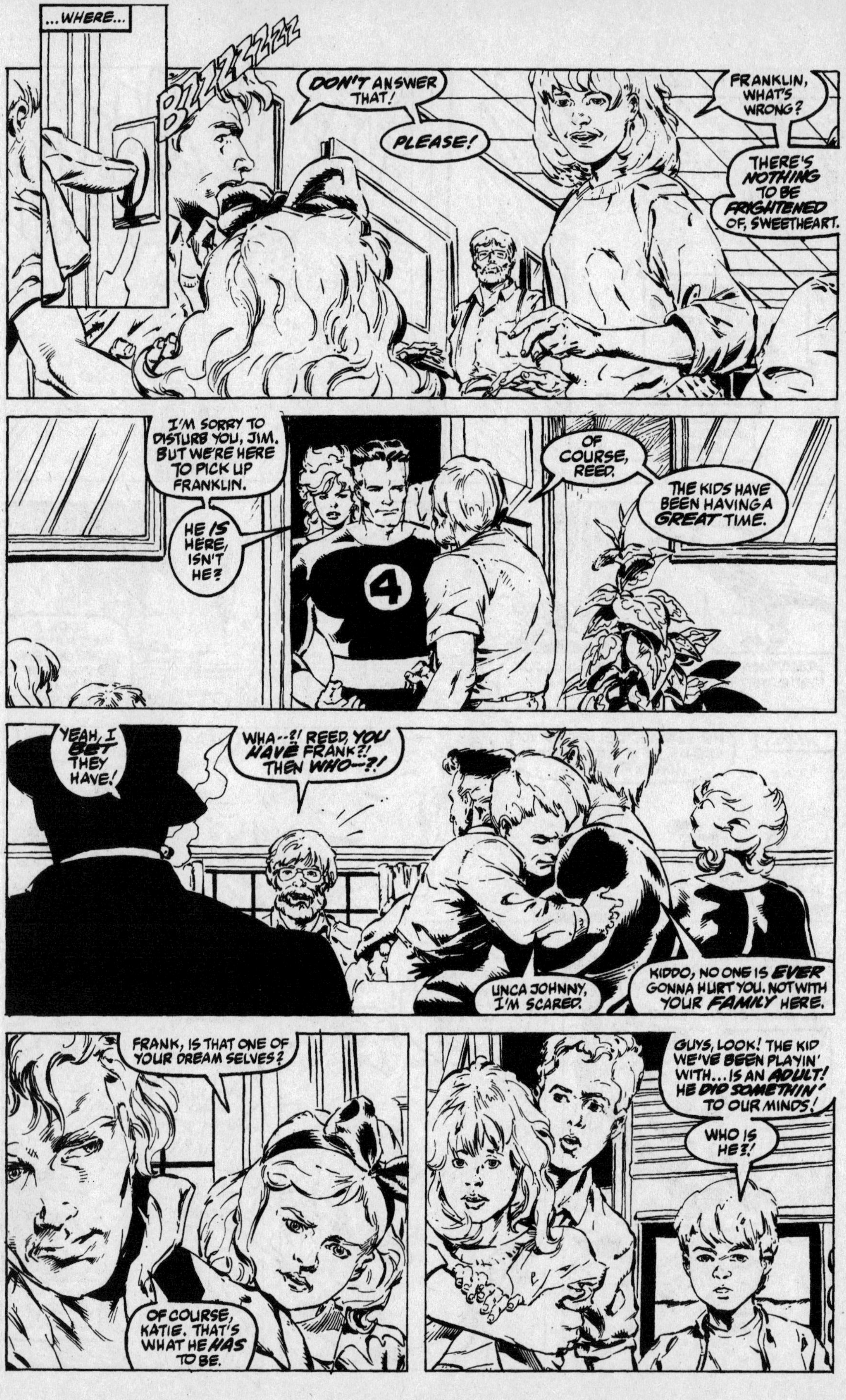
...WHERE...
BZZZZZZZ
DON'T ANSWER THAT!
PLEASE!
FRANKLIN, WHAT'S WRONG?
THERE'S NOTHING TO BE FRIGHTENED OF, SWEETHEART.
I'M SORRY TO DISTURB YOU, JIM. BUT WE'RE HERE TO PICK UP FRANKLIN.
HE IS HERE, ISN'T HE?
OF COURSE, REED.
THE KIDS HAVE BEEN HAVING A GREAT TIME.
YEAH, I BET THEY HAVE!
WHA--?! REED, YOU HAVE FRANK?! THEN WHO--?!
UNCA JOHNNY, I'M SCARED.
KIDDO, NO ONE IS EVER GONNA HURT YOU. NOT WITH YOUR FAMILY HERE.
FRANK, IS THAT ONE OF YOUR DREAM SELVES?
OF COURSE, KATIE. THAT'S WHAT HE HAS TO BE.
GUYS, LOOK! THE KID WE'VE BEEN PLAYIN' WITH...IS AN ADULT! HE DID SOMETHIN' TO OUR MINDS!
WHO IS HE?!

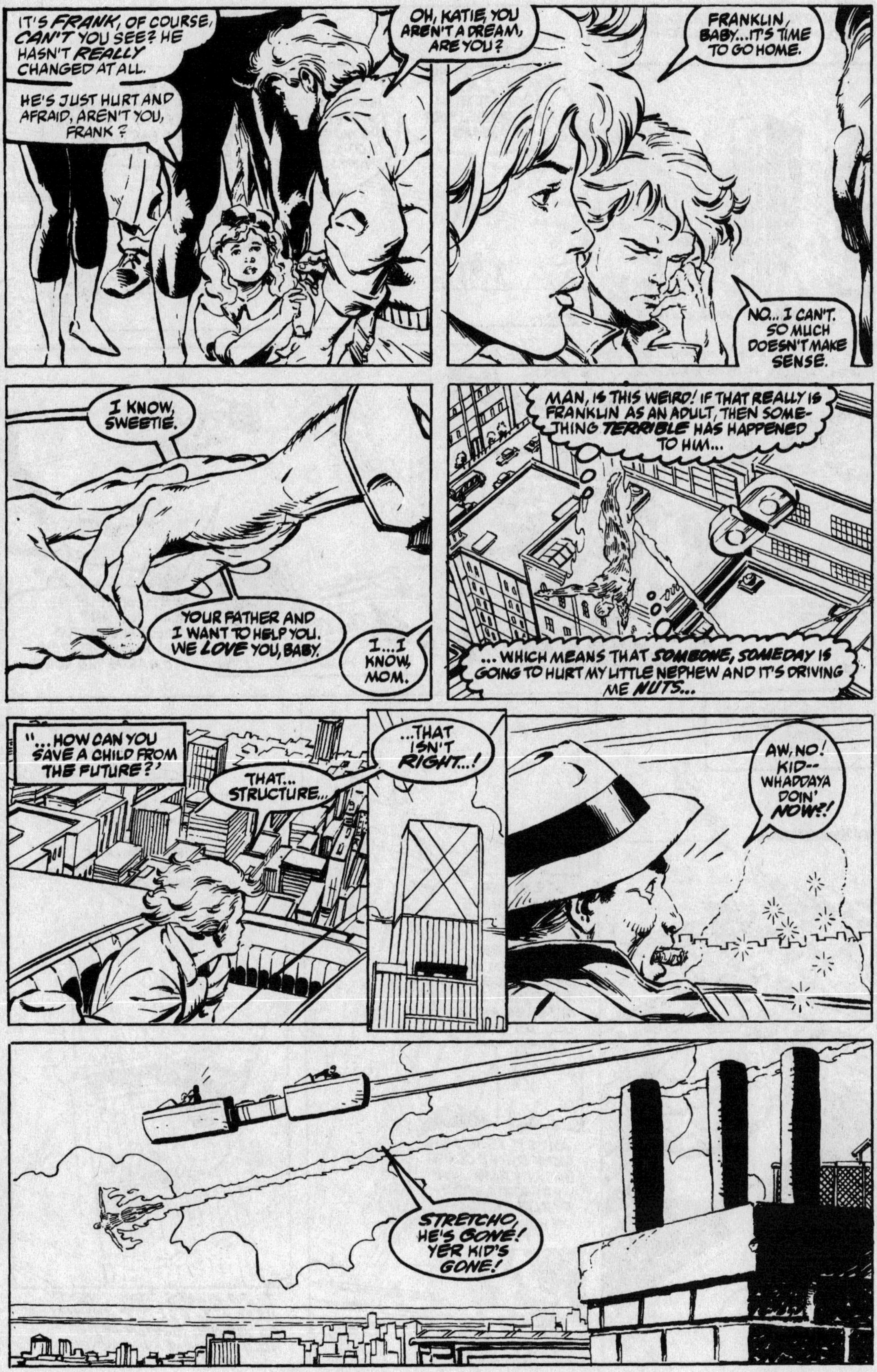
IT'S FRANK, OF COURSE, CAN'T YOU SEE? HE HASN'T REALLY CHANGED AT ALL.
HE'S JUST HURT AND AFRAID, AREN'T YOU, FRANK?
OH, KATIE, YOU AREN'T A DREAM, ARE YOU?
FRANKLIN, BABY...IT'S TIME TO GO HOME.
NO... I CAN'T. SO MUCH DOESN'T MAKE SENSE.
I KNOW, SWEETIE.
YOUR FATHER AND I WANT TO HELP YOU. WE LOVE YOU, BABY.
I...I KNOW, MOM.
MAN, IS THIS WEIRD! IF THAT REALLY IS FRANKLIN AS AN ADULT, THEN SOMETHING TERRIBLE HAS HAPPENED TO HIM...
... WHICH MEANS THAT SOMEONE, SOMEDAY IS GOING TO HURT MY LITTLE NEPHEW AND IT'S DRIVING ME NUTS...
"...HOW CAN YOU SAVE A CHILD FROM THE FUTURE?'
THAT... STRUCTURE...
...THAT ISN'T RIGHT...!
AW, NO! KID-- WHADDAYA DOIN' NOW?!
STRETCHO, HE'S GONE! YER KID'S GONE!

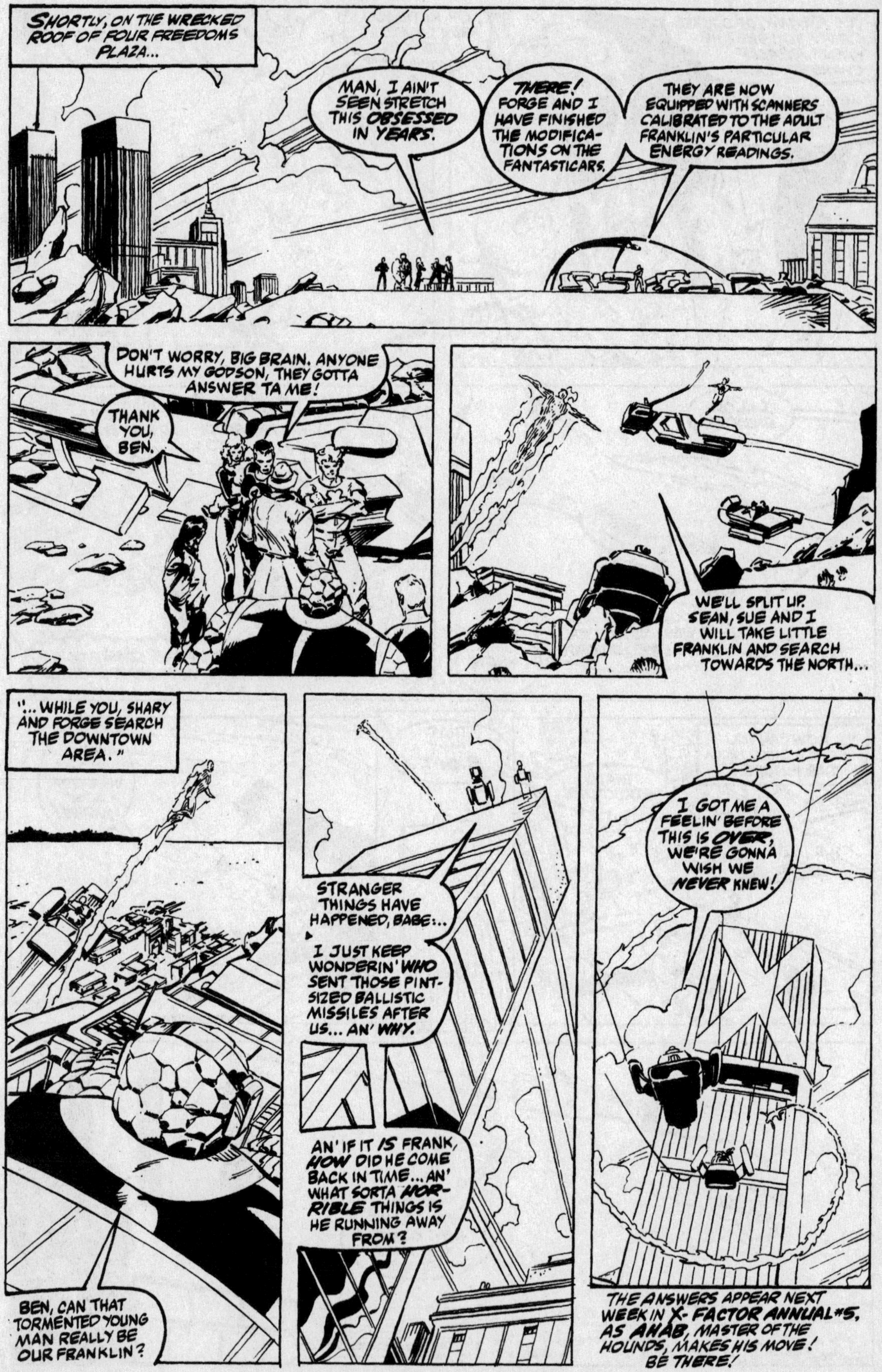

SHORTLY, ON THE WRECKED ROOF OF FOUR FREEDOMS PLAZA...
MAN, I AIN'T SEEN STRETCH THIS OBSESSED IN YEARS.
THERE! FORGE AND I HAVE FINISHED THE MODIFICATIONS ON THE FANTASTICARS.
THEY ARE NOW EQUIPPED WITH SCANNERS CALIBRATED TO THE ADULT FRANKLIN'S PARTICULAR ENERGY READINGS.
DON'T WORRY, BIG BRAIN. ANYONE HURTS MY GODSON, THEY GOTTA ANSWER TA ME!
THANK YOU, BEN.
WE'LL SPLIT UP. SEAN, SUE AND I WILL TAKE LITTLE FRANKLIN AND SEARCH TOWARDS THE NORTH...
"...WHILE YOU, SHARY AND FORGE SEARCH THE DOWNTOWN AREA."
BEN, CAN THAT TORMENTED YOUNG MAN REALLY BE OUR FRANKLIN?
STRANGER THINGS HAVE HAPPENED, BABE...
I JUST KEEP WONDERIN' WHO SENT THOSE PINT-SIZED BALLISTIC MISSILES AFTER US... AN' WHY.
AN' IF IT IS FRANK, HOW DID HE COME BACK IN TIME... AN' WHAT SORTA HORRIBLE THINGS IS HE RUNNING AWAY FROM?
I GOT ME A FEELIN' BEFORE THIS IS OVER, WE'RE GONNA WISH WE NEVER KNEW!
THE ANSWERS APPEAR NEXT WEEK IN X-FACTOR ANNUAL #5, AS AHAB, MASTER OF THE HOUNDS, MAKES HIS MOVE! BE THERE!

X-MEN

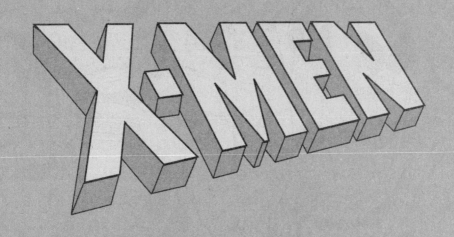

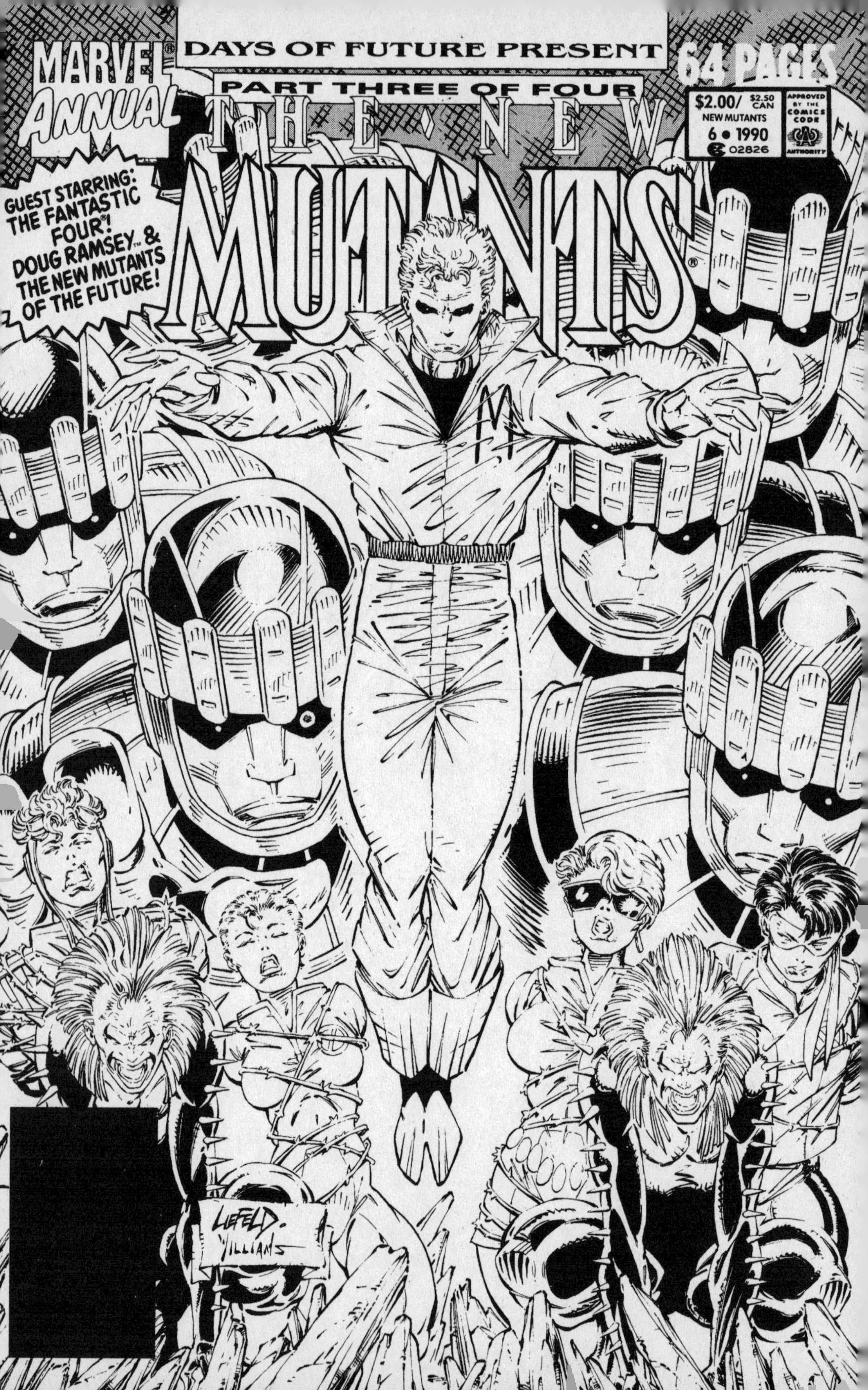
MARVEL® ANNUAL
DAYS OF FUTURE PRESENT
PART THREE OF FOUR
THE NEW MUTANTS®
64 PAGES
$2.00/ $2.50 CAN
NEW MUTANTS
6 • 1990
02826
APPROVED BY THE COMICS CODE AUTHORITY
GUEST STARRING: THE FANTASTIC FOUR®! DOUG RAMSEY™ & THE NEW MUTANTS OF THE FUTURE!
LIEFELD. WILLIAMS

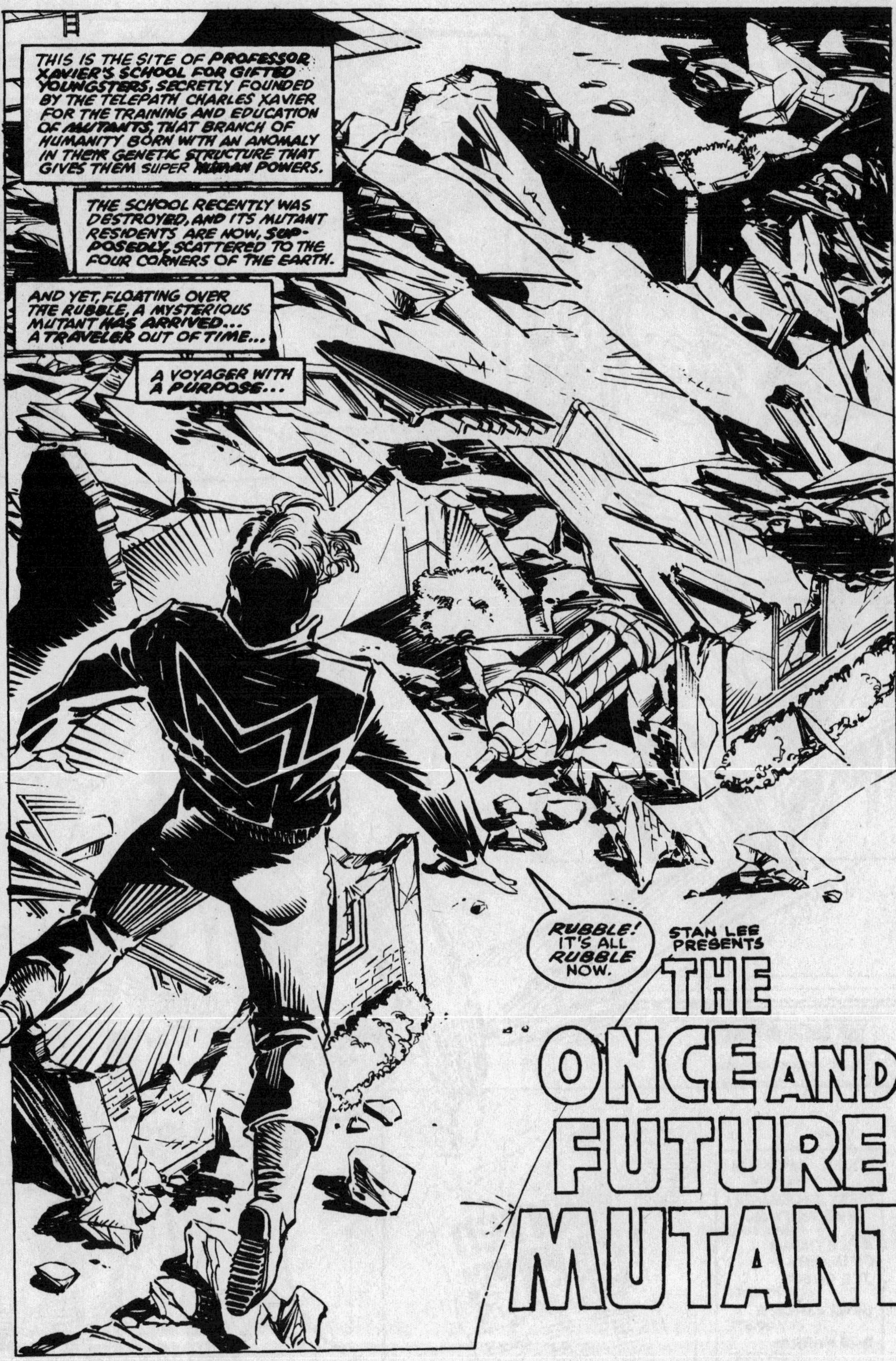
THIS IS THE SITE OF PROFESSOR XAVIER'S SCHOOL FOR GIFTED YOUNGSTERS, SECRETLY FOUNDED BY THE TELEPATH CHARLES XAVIER FOR THE TRAINING AND EDUCATION OF MUTANTS, THAT BRANCH OF HUMANITY BORN WITH AN ANOMALY IN THEIR GENETIC STRUCTURE THAT GIVES THEM SUPER HUMAN POWERS.
THE SCHOOL RECENTLY WAS DESTROYED, AND ITS MUTANT RESIDENTS ARE NOW, SUPPOSEDLY, SCATTERED TO THE FOUR CORNERS OF THE EARTH.
AND YET, FLOATING OVER THE RUBBLE, A MYSTERIOUS MUTANT HAS ARRIVED... A TRAVELER OUT OF TIME...
A VOYAGER WITH A PURPOSE...
RUBBLE! IT'S ALL RUBBLE NOW.
STAN LEE PRESENTS
THE ONCE AND FUTURE MUTANT

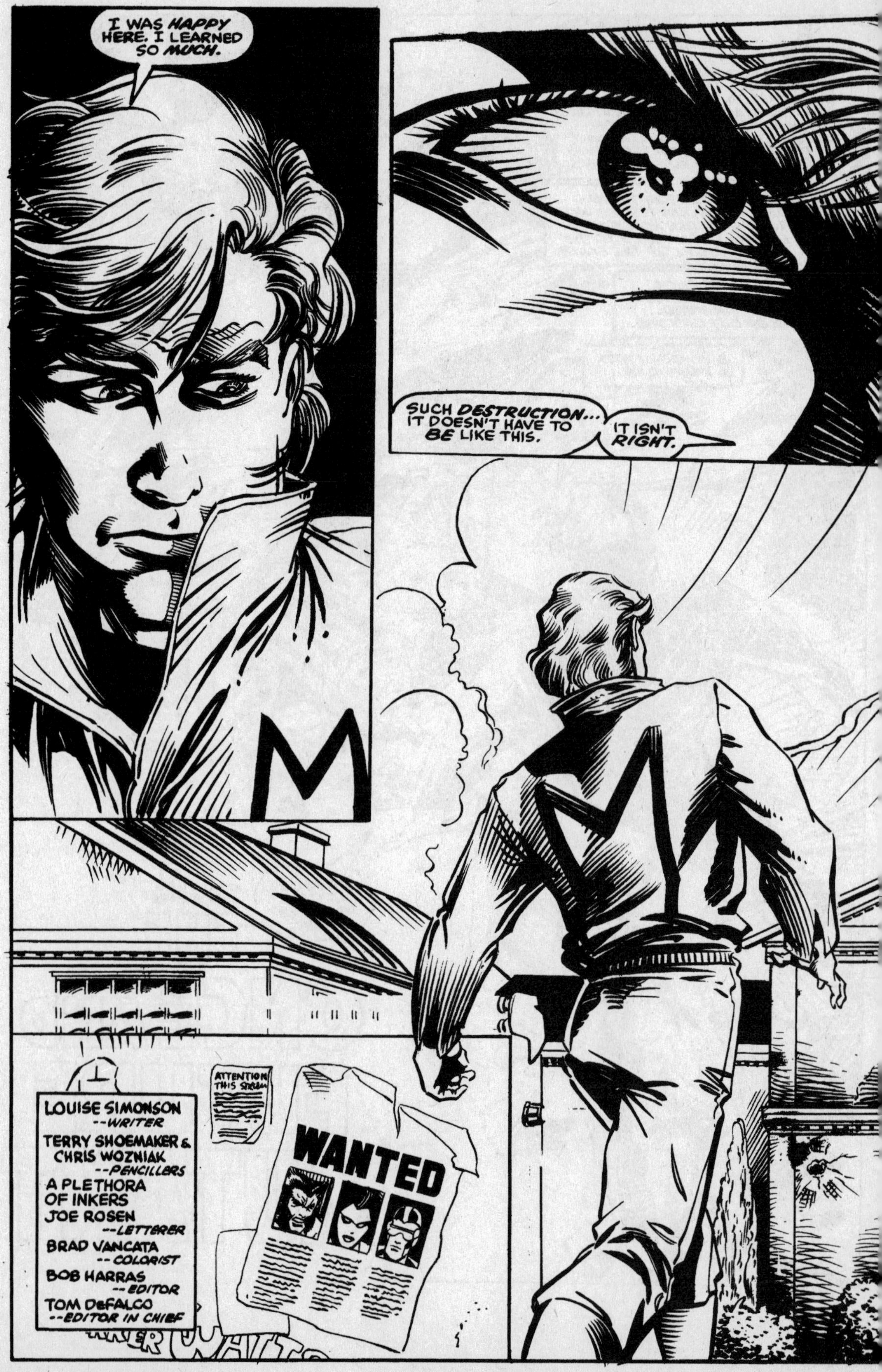
I WAS HAPPY HERE. I LEARNED SO MUCH.
SUCH DESTRUCTION... IT DOESN'T HAVE TO BE LIKE THIS.
IT ISN'T RIGHT.
ATTENTION THIS SIGN...
WANTED
LOUISE SIMONSON --WRITER
TERRY SHOEMAKER & CHRIS WOZNIAK --PENCILLERS
A PLETHORA OF INKERS
JOE ROSEN --LETTERER
BRAD VANCATA --COLORIST
BOB HARRAS --EDITOR
TOM DeFALCO --EDITOR IN CHIEF

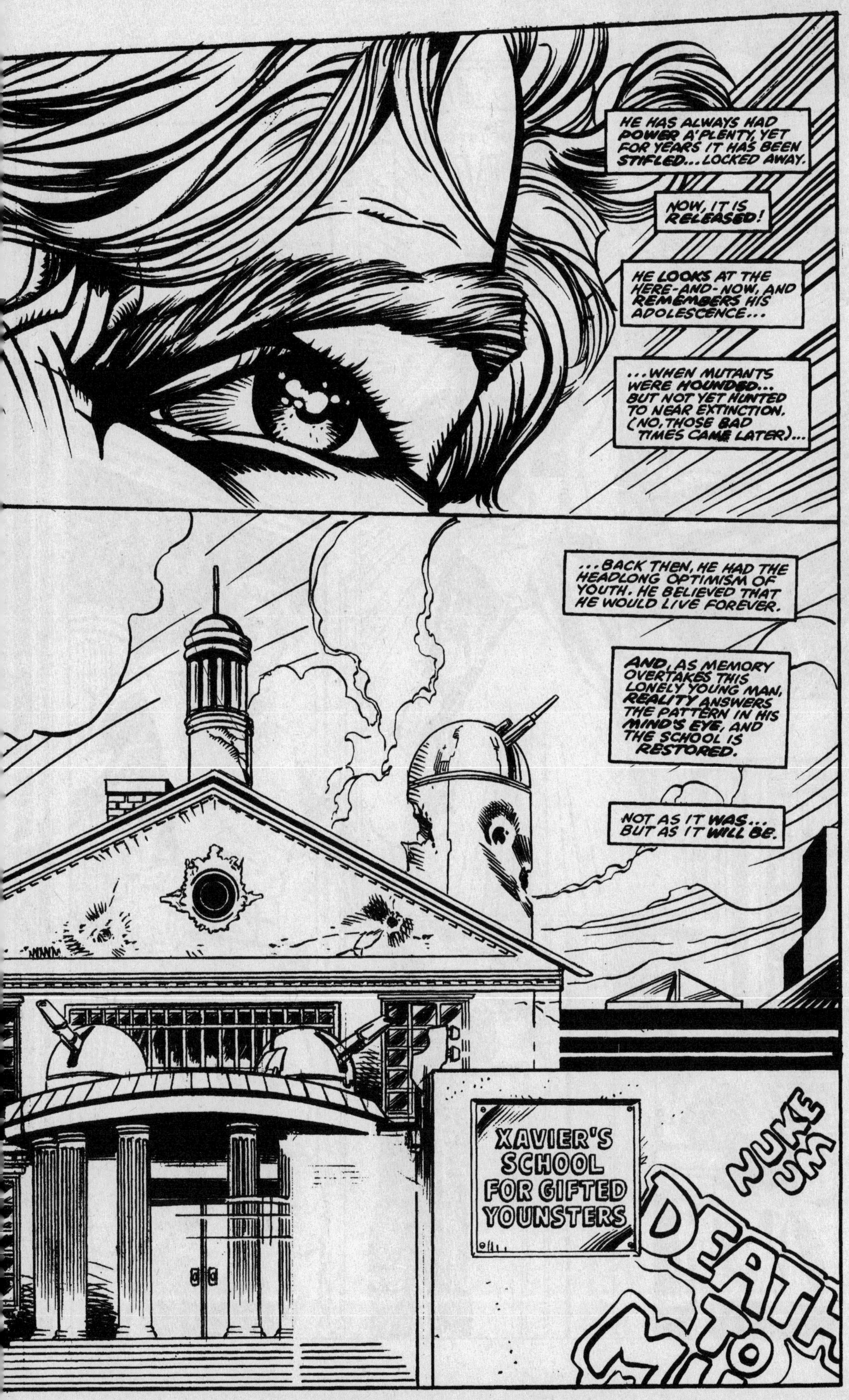
HE HAS ALWAYS HAD POWER A'PLENTY, YET FOR YEARS IT HAS BEEN STIFLED... LOCKED AWAY.
NOW, IT IS RELEASED!
HE LOOKS AT THE HERE-AND-NOW, AND REMEMBERS HIS ADOLESCENCE...
...WHEN MUTANTS WERE HOUNDED... BUT NOT YET HUNTED TO NEAR EXTINCTION. (NO, THOSE BAD TIMES CAME LATER)...
...BACK THEN, HE HAD THE HEADLONG OPTIMISM OF YOUTH. HE BELIEVED THAT HE WOULD LIVE FOREVER.
AND, AS MEMORY OVERTAKES THIS LONELY YOUNG MAN, REALITY ANSWERS THE PATTERN IN HIS MIND'S EYE, AND THE SCHOOL IS RESTORED.
NOT AS IT WAS... BUT AS IT WILL BE.
XAVIER'S SCHOOL FOR GIFTED YOUNSTERS
NUKE UM
DEATH TO

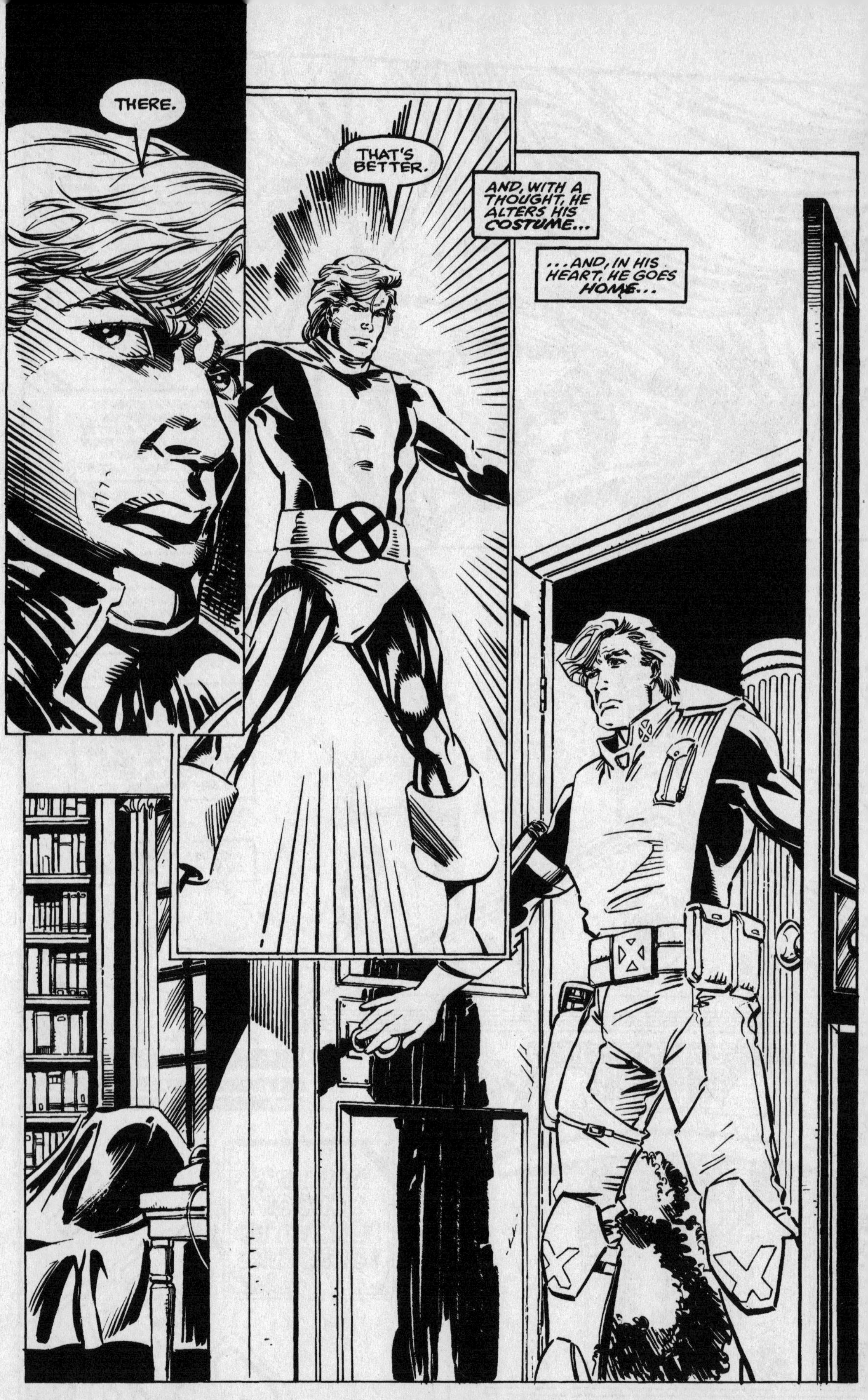
THERE.
THAT'S BETTER.
AND, WITH A THOUGHT, HE ALTERS HIS COSTUME...
...AND, IN HIS HEART, HE GOES HOME...

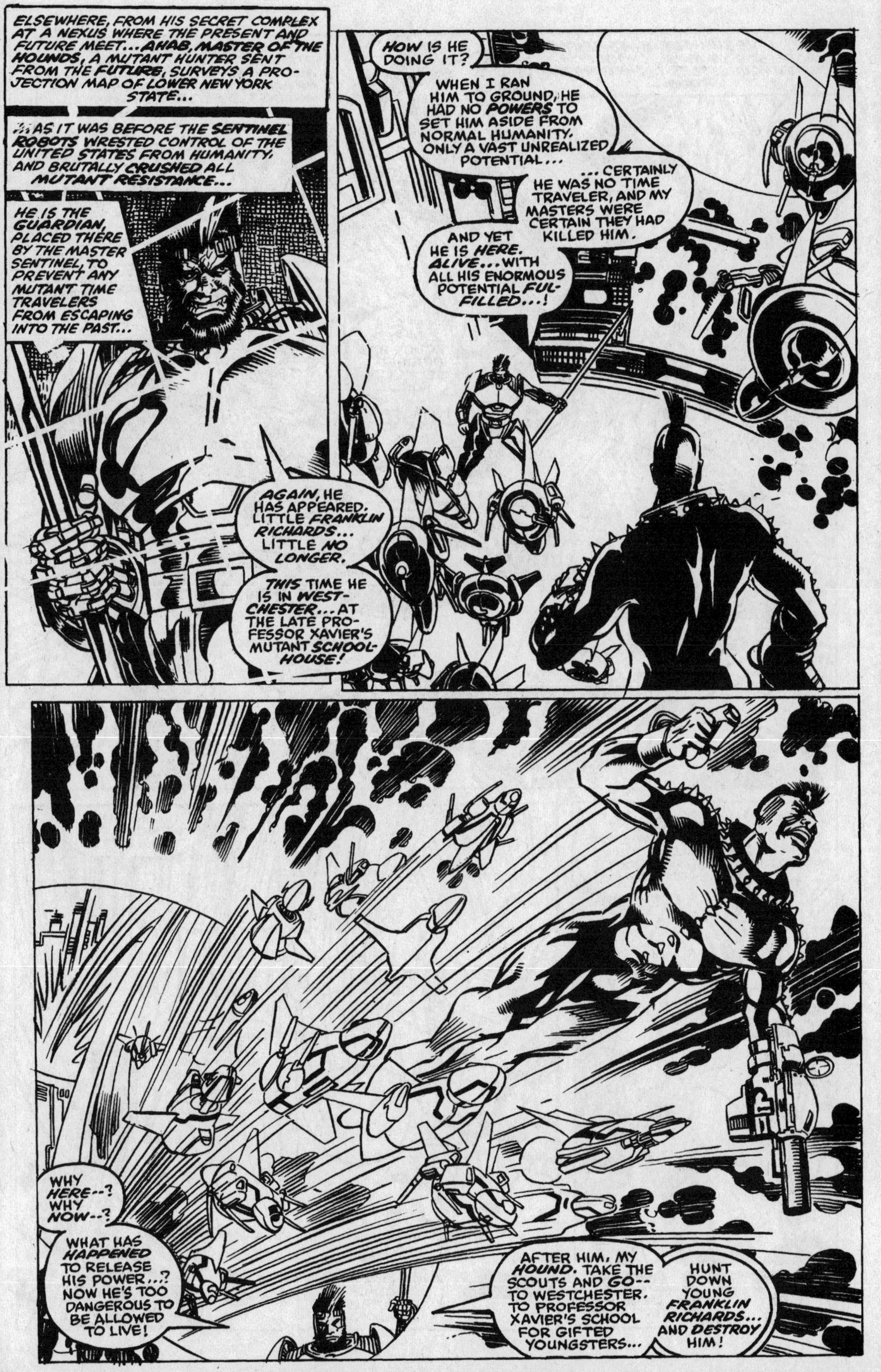
ELSEWHERE, FROM HIS SECRET COMPLEX AT A NEXUS WHERE THE PRESENT AND FUTURE MEET... AHAB, MASTER OF THE HOUNDS, A MUTANT HUNTER SENT FROM THE FUTURE, SURVEYS A PROJECTION MAP OF LOWER NEW YORK STATE...
...AS IT WAS BEFORE THE SENTINEL ROBOTS WRESTED CONTROL OF THE UNITED STATES FROM HUMANITY, AND BRUTALLY CRUSHED ALL MUTANT RESISTANCE...
HE IS THE GUARDIAN, PLACED THERE BY THE MASTER SENTINEL, TO PREVENT ANY MUTANT TIME TRAVELERS FROM ESCAPING INTO THE PAST...
HOW IS HE DOING IT?
WHEN I RAN HIM TO GROUND, HE HAD NO POWERS TO SET HIM ASIDE FROM NORMAL HUMANITY. ONLY A VAST UNREALIZED POTENTIAL...
...CERTAINLY HE WAS NO TIME TRAVELER, AND MY MASTERS WERE CERTAIN THEY HAD KILLED HIM.
AND YET HE IS HERE. ALIVE... WITH ALL HIS ENORMOUS POTENTIAL FULFILLED...!
AGAIN, HE HAS APPEARED. LITTLE FRANKLIN RICHARDS... LITTLE NO LONGER.
THIS TIME HE IS IN WESTCHESTER... AT THE LATE PROFESSOR XAVIER'S MUTANT SCHOOLHOUSE!
WHY HERE--? WHY NOW--?
WHAT HAS HAPPENED TO RELEASE HIS POWER...? NOW HE'S TOO DANGEROUS TO BE ALLOWED TO LIVE!
AFTER HIM, MY HOUND. TAKE THE SCOUTS AND GO--TO WESTCHESTER. TO PROFESSOR XAVIER'S SCHOOL FOR GIFTED YOUNGSTERS...
HUNT DOWN YOUNG FRANKLIN RICHARDS... AND DESTROY HIM!

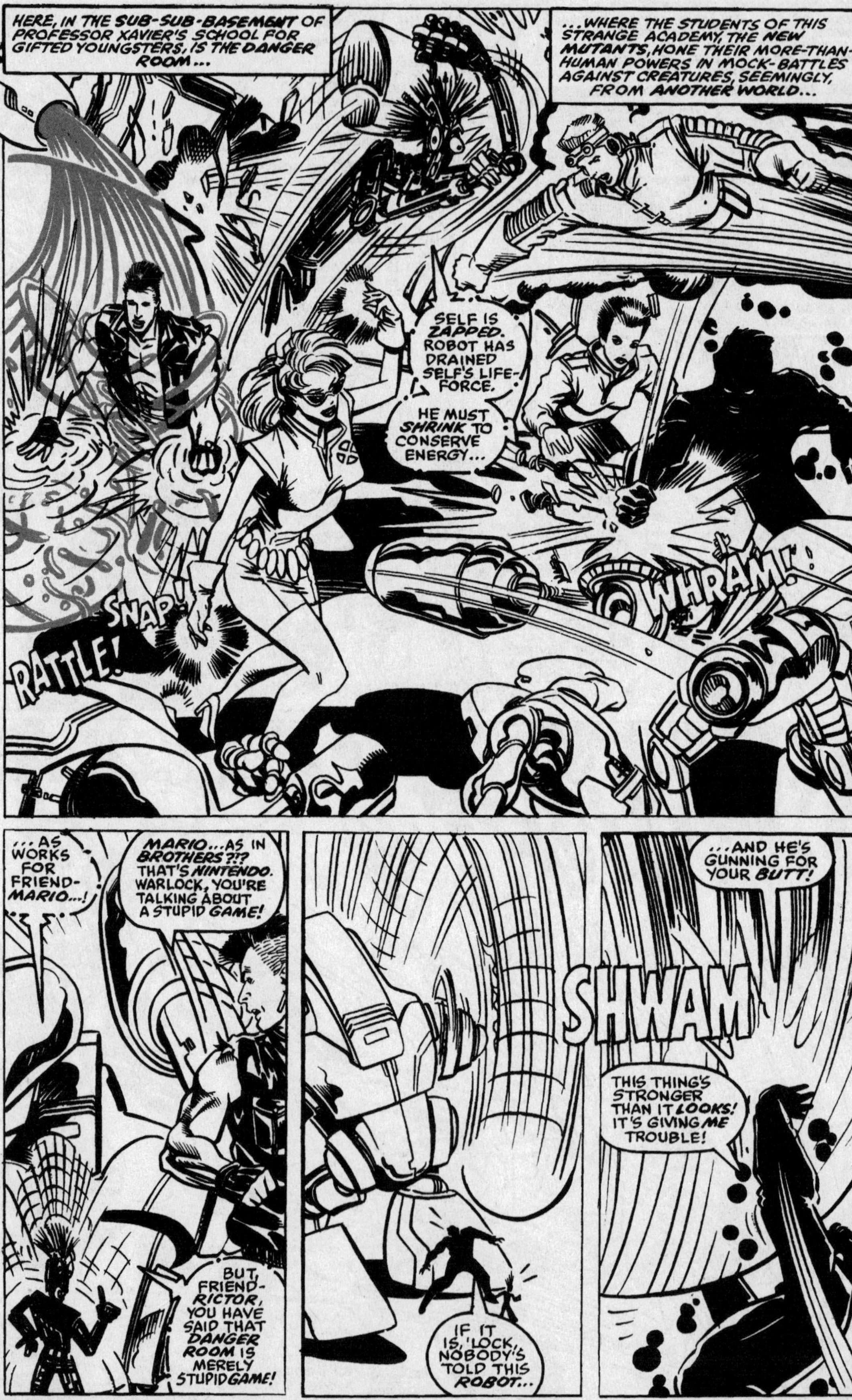
HERE, IN THE SUB-SUB-BASEMENT OF PROFESSOR XAVIER'S SCHOOL FOR GIFTED YOUNGSTERS, IS THE DANGER ROOM...
...WHERE THE STUDENTS OF THIS STRANGE ACADEMY, THE NEW MUTANTS, HONE THEIR MORE-THAN-HUMAN POWERS IN MOCK-BATTLES AGAINST CREATURES, SEEMINGLY, FROM ANOTHER WORLD...
SELF IS ZAPPED. ROBOT HAS DRAINED SELF'S LIFE-FORCE.
HE MUST SHRINK TO CONSERVE ENERGY...
WHRAM!
SNAP!
RATTLE!
...AS WORKS FOR FRIEND-MARIO...!
MARIO...AS IN BROTHERS?!? THAT'S NINTENDO. WARLOCK, YOU'RE TALKING ABOUT A STUPID GAME!
BUT, FRIEND-RICTOR, YOU HAVE SAID THAT DANGER ROOM IS MERELY STUPID GAME!
IF IT IS, 'LOCK, NOBODY'S TOLD THIS ROBOT...
...AND HE'S GUNNING FOR YOUR BUTT!
SHWAM
THIS THING'S STRONGER THAN IT LOOKS! IT'S GIVING ME TROUBLE!

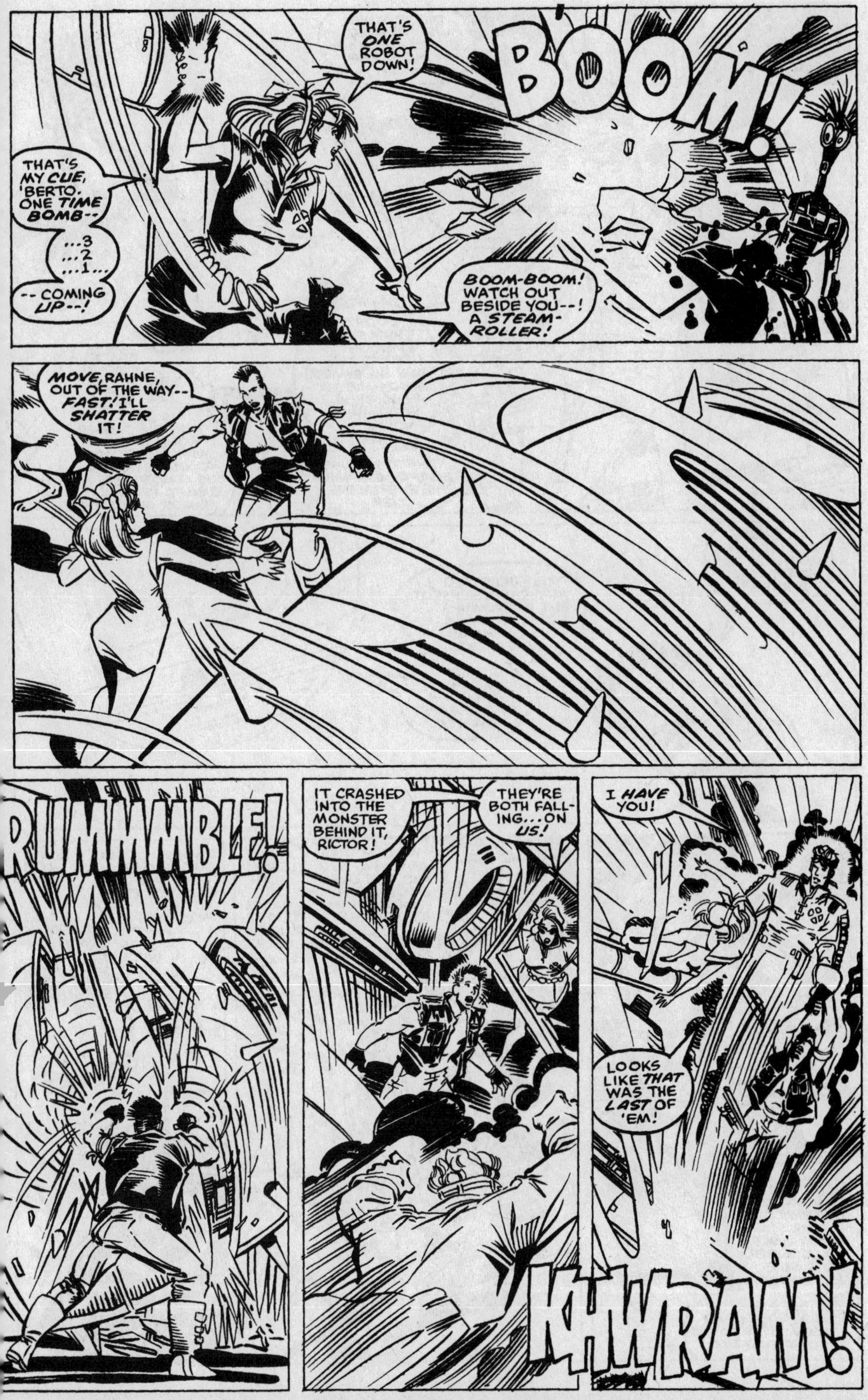
THAT'S ONE ROBOT DOWN!
BOOM!
THAT'S MY CUE, 'BERTO. ONE TIME BOMB-- ...3 ...2 ...1... --COMING UP--!
BOOM-BOOM! WATCH OUT BESIDE YOU--! A STEAM-ROLLER!
MOVE, RAHNE, OUT OF THE WAY-- FAST! I'LL SHATTER IT!
RUMMMBLE!
IT CRASHED INTO THE MONSTER BEHIND IT, RICTOR!
THEY'RE BOTH FALLING... ON US!
I HAVE YOU!
LOOKS LIKE THAT WAS THE LAST OF 'EM!
KHWRAM!

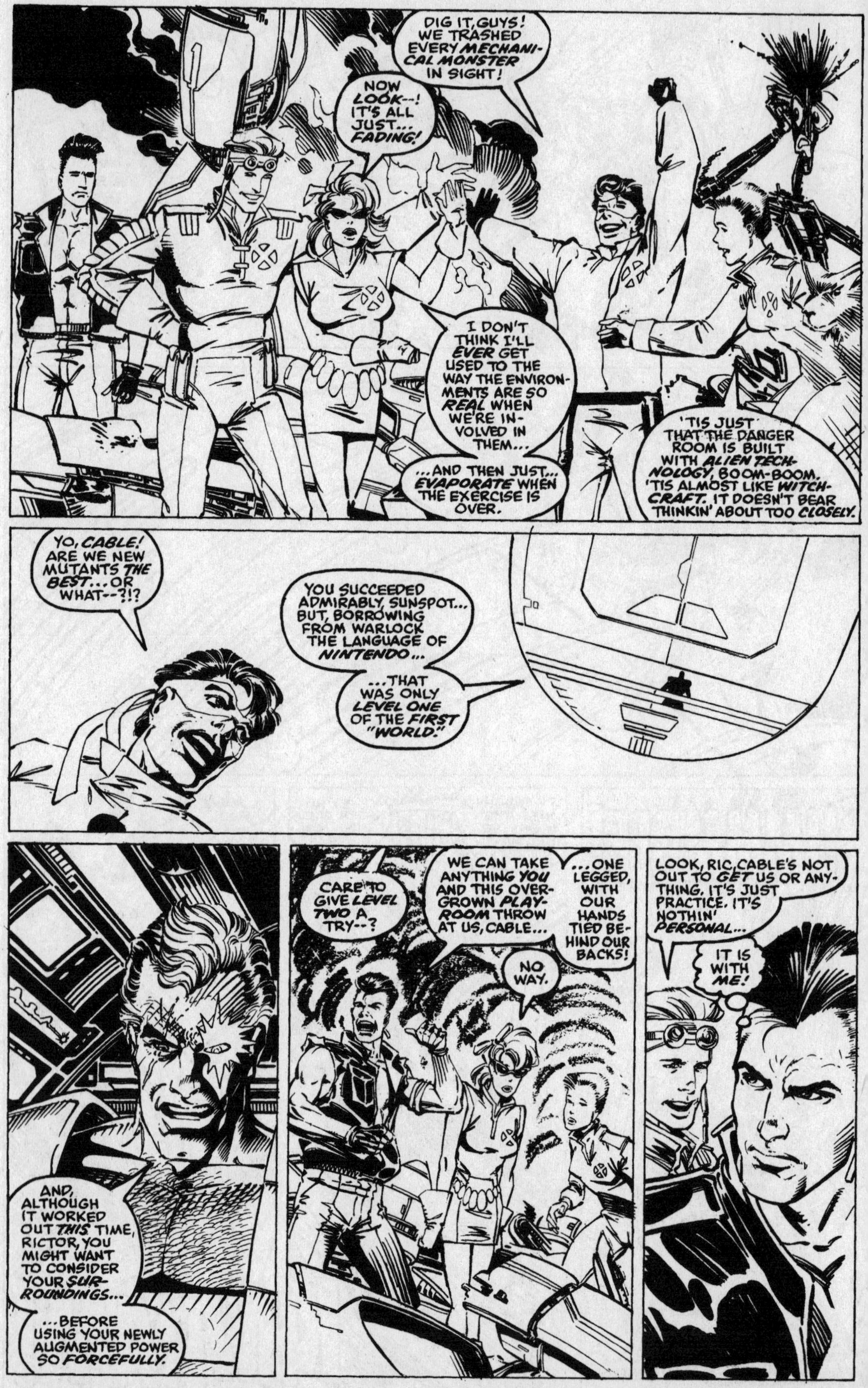
DIG IT, GUYS! WE TRASHED EVERY MECHANICAL MONSTER IN SIGHT!
NOW LOOK--! IT'S ALL JUST... FADING!
I DON'T THINK I'LL EVER GET USED TO THE WAY THE ENVIRONMENTS ARE SO REAL WHEN WE'RE INVOLVED IN THEM...
...AND THEN JUST... EVAPORATE WHEN THE EXERCISE IS OVER.
'TIS JUST THAT THE DANGER ROOM IS BUILT WITH ALIEN TECHNOLOGY, BOOM-BOOM. 'TIS ALMOST LIKE WITCHCRAFT. IT DOESN'T BEAR THINKIN' ABOUT TOO CLOSELY.
YO, CABLE! ARE WE NEW MUTANTS THE BEST... OR WHAT--?!?
YOU SUCCEEDED ADMIRABLY, SUNSPOT... BUT, BORROWING FROM WARLOCK THE LANGUAGE OF NINTENDO...
...THAT WAS ONLY LEVEL ONE OF THE FIRST "WORLD."
AND, ALTHOUGH IT WORKED OUT THIS TIME, RICTOR, YOU MIGHT WANT TO CONSIDER YOUR SURROUNDINGS...
...BEFORE USING YOUR NEWLY AUGMENTED POWER SO FORCEFULLY.
CARE TO GIVE LEVEL TWO A TRY--?
WE CAN TAKE ANYTHING YOU AND THIS OVERGROWN PLAYROOM THROW AT US, CABLE...
...ONE LEGGED, WITH OUR HANDS TIED BEHIND OUR BACKS!
NO WAY.
LOOK, RIC, CABLE'S NOT OUT TO GET US OR ANYTHING. IT'S JUST PRACTICE. IT'S NOTHIN' PERSONAL...
IT IS WITH ME!

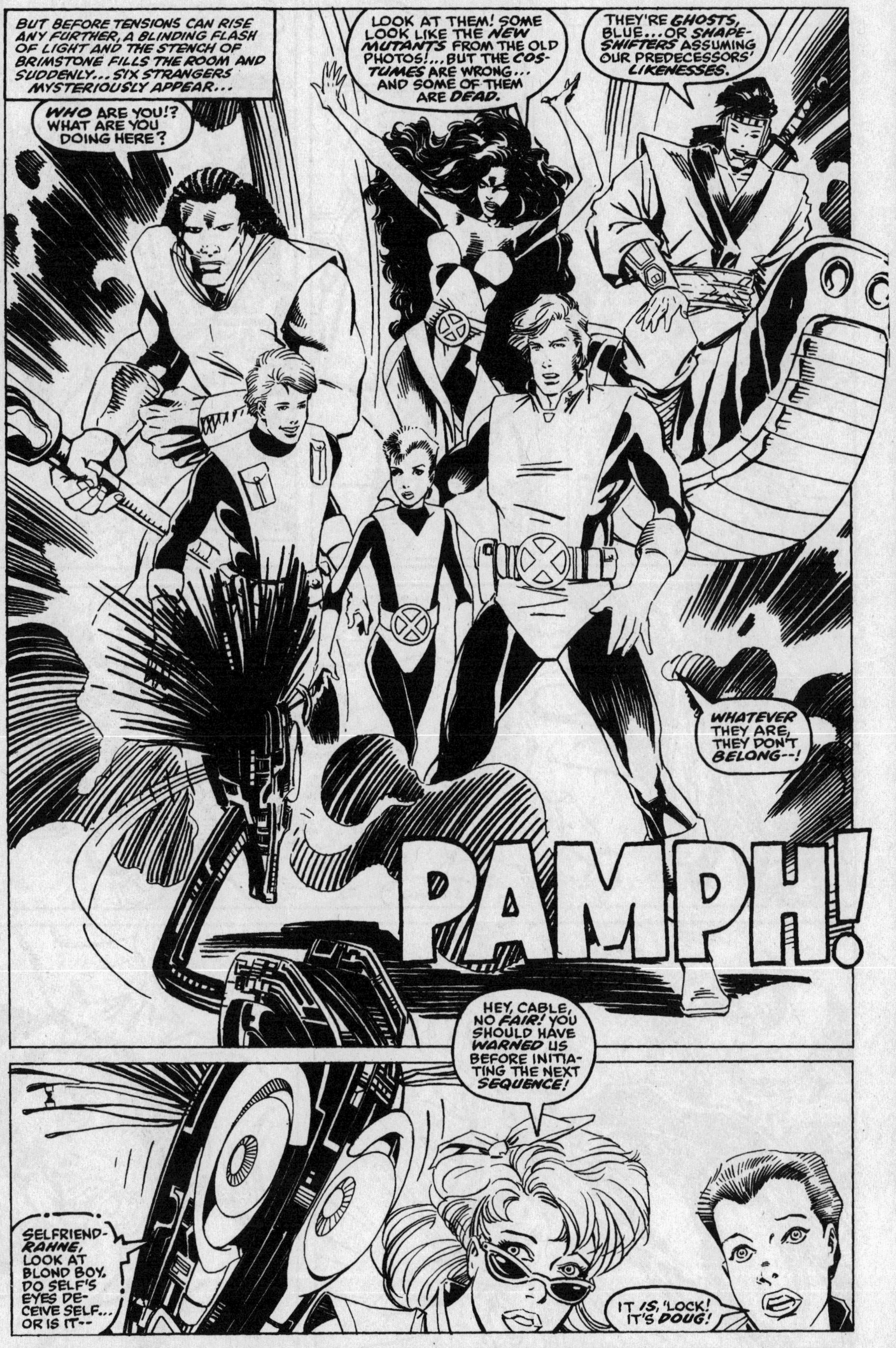
BUT BEFORE TENSIONS CAN RISE ANY FURTHER, A BLINDING FLASH OF LIGHT AND THE STENCH OF BRIMSTONE FILLS THE ROOM AND SUDDENLY... SIX STRANGERS MYSTERIOUSLY APPEAR...
WHO ARE YOU!? WHAT ARE YOU DOING HERE?
LOOK AT THEM! SOME LOOK LIKE THE NEW MUTANTS FROM THE OLD PHOTOS!... BUT THE COSTUMES ARE WRONG... AND SOME OF THEM ARE DEAD.
THEY'RE GHOSTS, BLUE... OR SHAPE-SHIFTERS ASSUMING OUR PREDECESSORS' LIKENESSES.
WHATEVER THEY ARE, THEY DON'T BELONG--!
PAMPH!
HEY, CABLE, NO FAIR! YOU SHOULD HAVE WARNED US BEFORE INITIATING THE NEXT SEQUENCE!
SELFRIEND-RAHNE, LOOK AT BLOND BOY. DO SELF'S EYES DECEIVE SELF... OR IS IT--
IT IS, 'LOCK! IT'S DOUG!

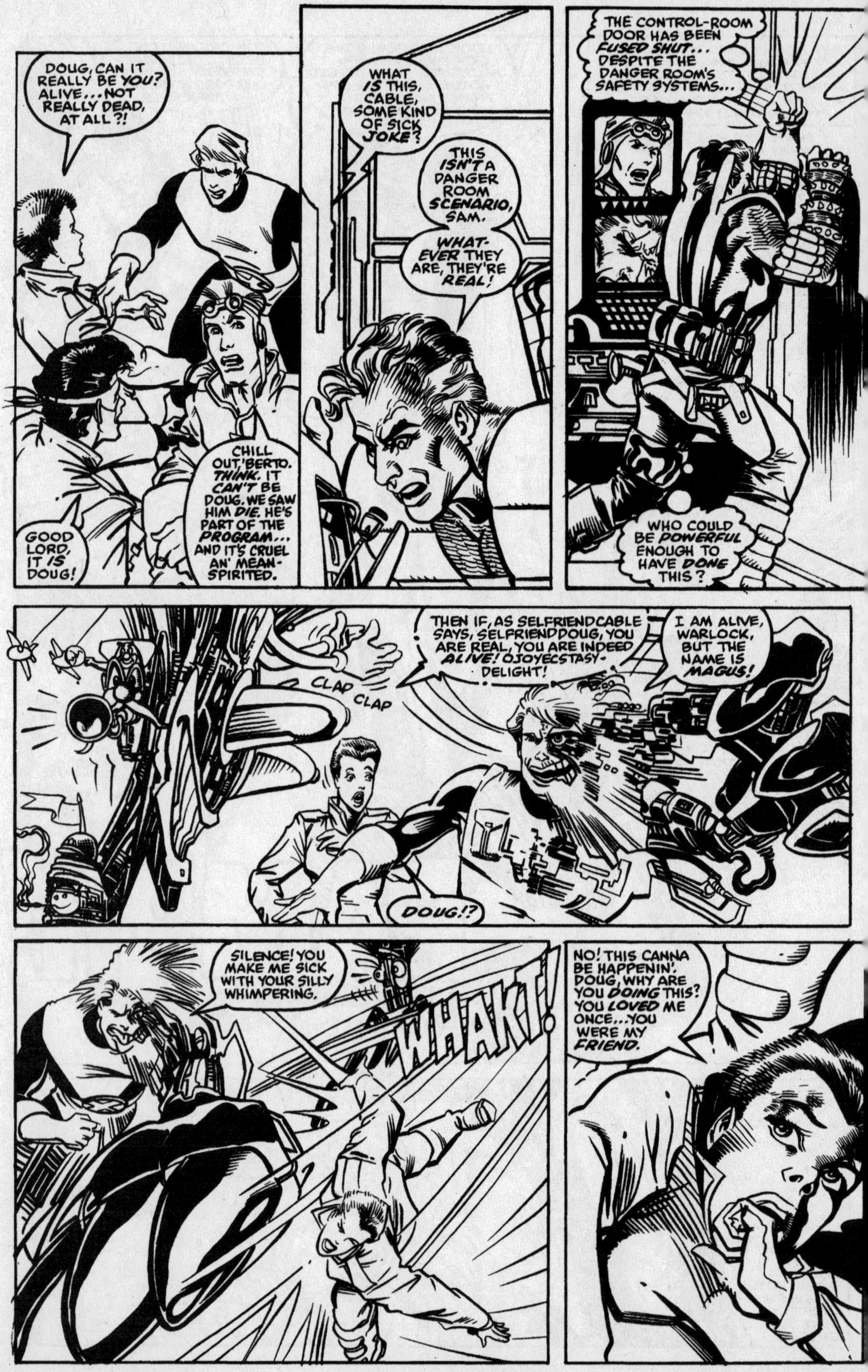
DOUG, CAN IT REALLY BE YOU? ALIVE... NOT REALLY DEAD, AT ALL?!
GOOD LORD, IT IS DOUG!
CHILL OUT, 'BERTO. THINK. IT CAN'T BE DOUG. WE SAW HIM DIE. HE'S PART OF THE PROGRAM... AND IT'S CRUEL AN' MEAN-SPIRITED.
WHAT IS THIS, CABLE, SOME KIND OF SICK JOKE?
THIS ISN'T A DANGER ROOM SCENARIO, SAM.
WHAT-EVER THEY ARE, THEY'RE REAL!
THE CONTROL-ROOM DOOR HAS BEEN FUSED SHUT... DESPITE THE DANGER ROOM'S SAFETY SYSTEMS...
WHO COULD BE POWERFUL ENOUGH TO HAVE DONE THIS?
CLAP CLAP
THEN IF, AS SELFRIENDCABLE SAYS, SELFRIENDDOUG, YOU ARE REAL, YOU ARE INDEED ALIVE! OJOYECSTASY-DELIGHT!
I AM ALIVE, WARLOCK, BUT THE NAME IS MAGUS!
DOUG!?
SILENCE! YOU MAKE ME SICK WITH YOUR SILLY WHIMPERING.
WHAKT!
NO! THIS CANNA BE HAPPENIN'. DOUG, WHY ARE YOU DOING THIS? YOU LOVED ME ONCE... YOU WERE MY FRIEND.

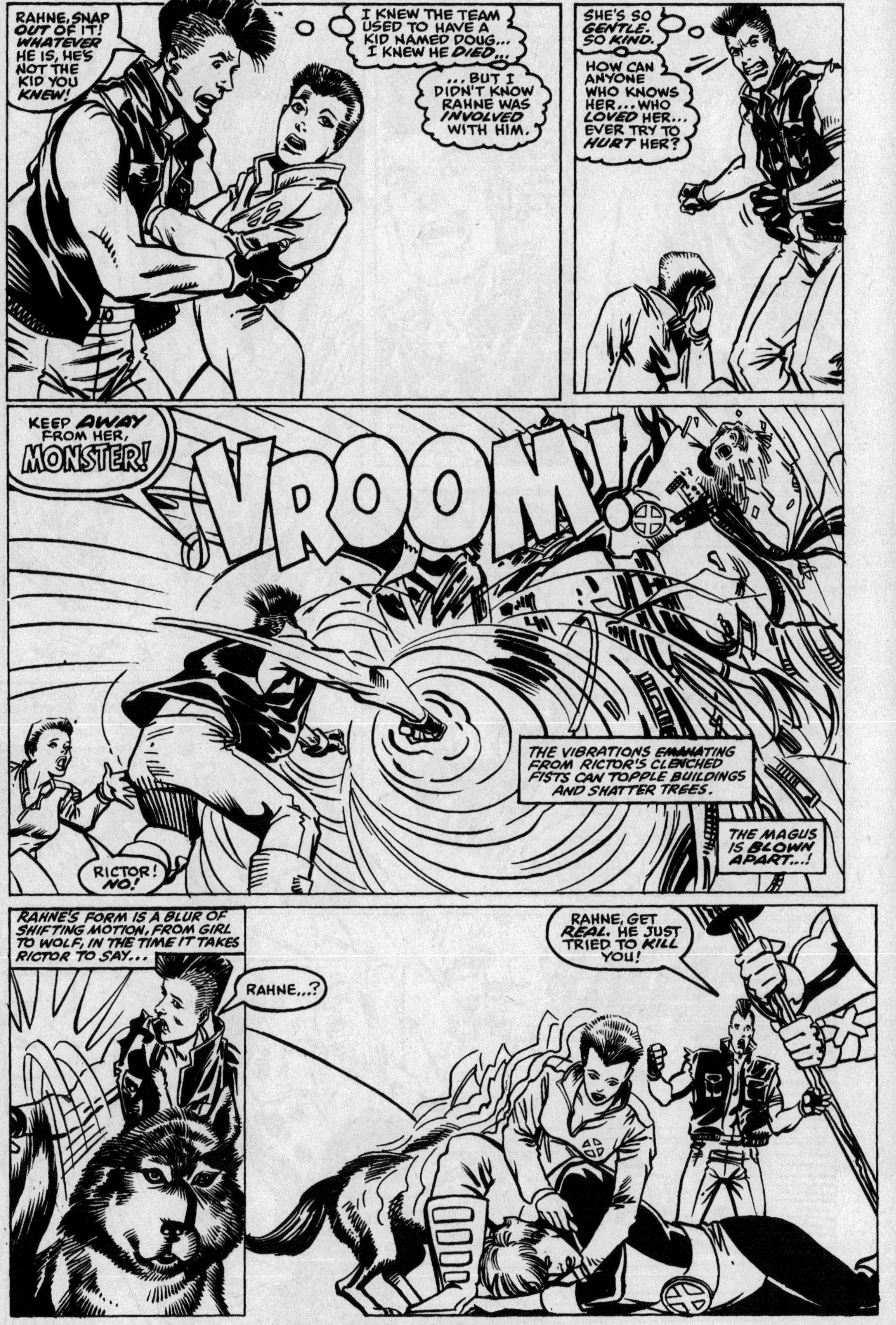
RAHNE, SNAP OUT OF IT! WHATEVER HE IS, HE'S NOT THE KID YOU KNEW!
I KNEW THE TEAM USED TO HAVE A KID NAMED DOUG... I KNEW HE DIED...
...BUT I DIDN'T KNOW RAHNE WAS INVOLVED WITH HIM.
SHE'S SO GENTLE. SO KIND.
HOW CAN ANYONE WHO KNOWS HER... WHO LOVED HER... EVER TRY TO HURT HER?
KEEP AWAY FROM HER, MONSTER!
VROOM!
THE VIBRATIONS EMANATING FROM RICTOR'S CLENCHED FISTS CAN TOPPLE BUILDINGS AND SHATTER TREES.
RICTOR! NO!
THE MAGUS IS BLOWN APART...!
RAHNE'S FORM IS A BLUR OF SHIFTING MOTION, FROM GIRL TO WOLF, IN THE TIME IT TAKES RICTOR TO SAY...
RAHNE...?
RAHNE, GET REAL. HE JUST TRIED TO KILL YOU!

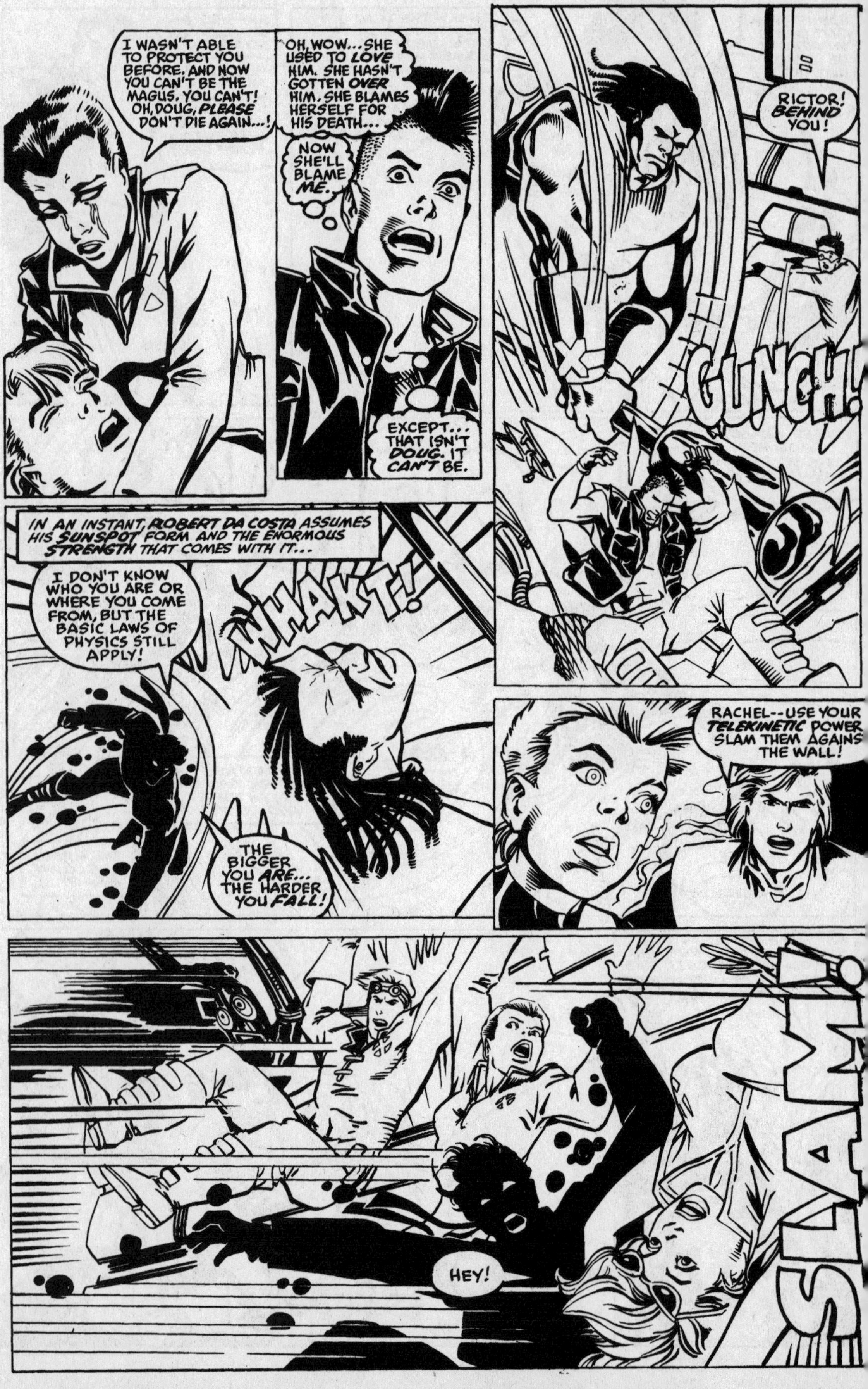
I WASN'T ABLE TO PROTECT YOU BEFORE. AND NOW YOU CAN'T BE THE MAGUS. YOU CAN'T! OH, DOUG, PLEASE DON'T DIE AGAIN...!
OH, WOW... SHE USED TO LOVE HIM. SHE HASN'T GOTTEN OVER HIM. SHE BLAMES HERSELF FOR HIS DEATH...
NOW SHE'LL BLAME ME.
EXCEPT... THAT ISN'T DOUG. IT CAN'T BE.
RICTOR! BEHIND YOU!
GUNCH!
IN AN INSTANT, ROBERT DA COSTA ASSUMES HIS SUNSPOT FORM AND THE ENORMOUS STRENGTH THAT COMES WITH IT...
I DON'T KNOW WHO YOU ARE OR WHERE YOU COME FROM, BUT THE BASIC LAWS OF PHYSICS STILL APPLY!
WHAKT!
THE BIGGER YOU ARE... THE HARDER YOU FALL!
RACHEL--USE YOUR TELEKINETIC POWER SLAM THEM AGAINS THE WALL!
HEY!
SLAM!

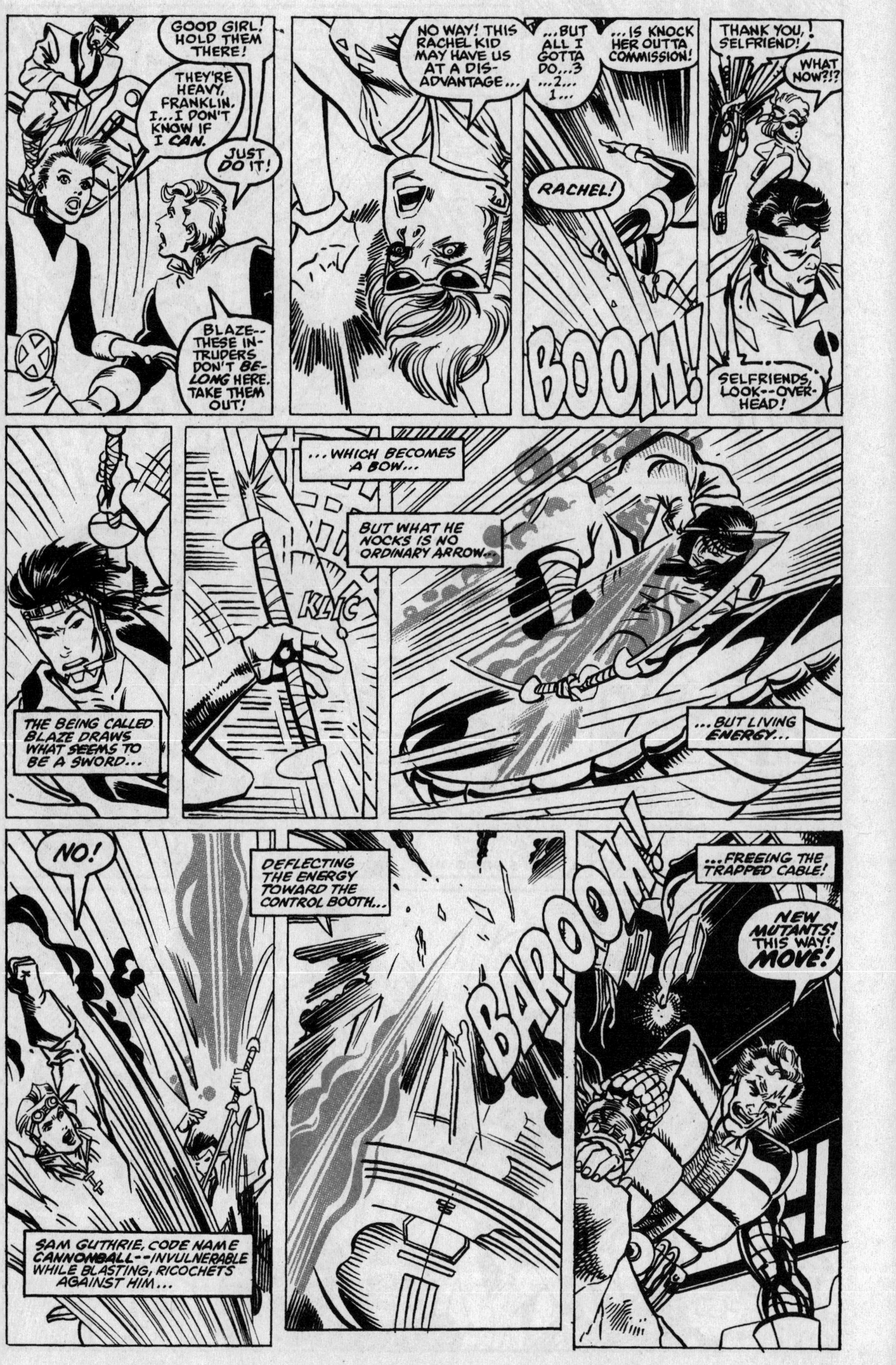
GOOD GIRL! HOLD THEM THERE!
THEY'RE HEAVY, FRANKLIN. I...I DON'T KNOW IF I CAN.
JUST DO IT!
BLAZE--THESE INTRUDERS DON'T BELONG HERE. TAKE THEM OUT!
NO WAY! THIS RACHEL KID MAY HAVE US AT A DISADVANTAGE...
...BUT ALL I GOTTA DO...3 ...2... 1...
...IS KNOCK HER OUTTA COMMISSION!
RACHEL!
BOOM!
THANK YOU, SELFRIEND!
WHAT NOW?!?
SELFRIENDS, LOOK--OVERHEAD!
THE BEING CALLED BLAZE DRAWS WHAT SEEMS TO BE A SWORD...
...WHICH BECOMES A BOW...
KLIC
BUT WHAT HE NOCKS IS NO ORDINARY ARROW...
...BUT LIVING ENERGY...
NO!
SAM GUTHRIE, CODE NAME CANNONBALL--INVULNERABLE WHILE BLASTING, RICOCHETS AGAINST HIM...
DEFLECTING THE ENERGY TOWARD THE CONTROL BOOTH...
BAROOM!
...FREEING THE TRAPPED CABLE!
NEW MUTANTS! THIS WAY! MOVE!

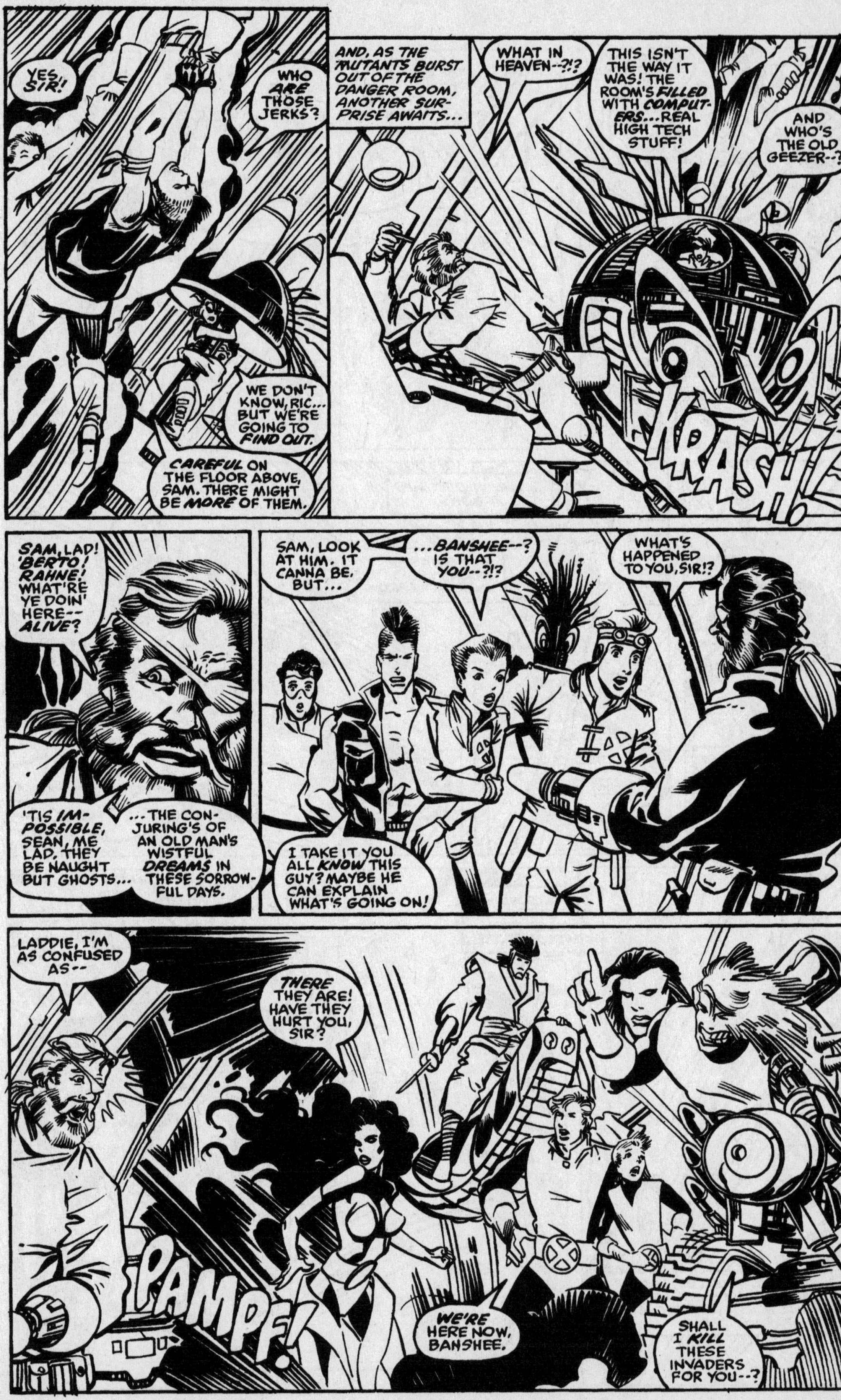
YES, SIR!
WHO ARE THOSE JERKS?
WE DON'T KNOW, RIC... BUT WE'RE GOING TO FIND OUT.
CAREFUL ON THE FLOOR ABOVE, SAM. THERE MIGHT BE MORE OF THEM.
AND, AS THE MUTANTS BURST OUT OF THE DANGER ROOM, ANOTHER SURPRISE AWAITS...
WHAT IN HEAVEN--?!?
THIS ISN'T THE WAY IT WAS! THE ROOM'S FILLED WITH COMPUTERS... REAL HIGH TECH STUFF!
AND WHO'S THE OLD GEEZER--?
KRASH!
SAM, LAD! 'BERTO! RAHNE! WHAT'RE YE DOIN' HERE--ALIVE?
'TIS IMPOSSIBLE, SEAN, ME LAD, THEY BE NAUGHT BUT GHOSTS...
...THE CONJURING'S OF AN OLD MAN'S WISTFUL DREAMS IN THESE SORROWFUL DAYS.
SAM, LOOK AT HIM. IT CANNA BE. BUT...
...BANSHEE--? IS THAT YOU--?!?
WHAT'S HAPPENED TO YOU, SIR!?
I TAKE IT YOU ALL KNOW THIS GUY? MAYBE HE CAN EXPLAIN WHAT'S GOING ON!
LADDIE, I'M AS CONFUSED AS--
THERE THEY ARE! HAVE THEY HURT YOU, SIR?
PAMPF!
WE'RE HERE NOW, BANSHEE.
SHALL I KILL THESE INVADERS FOR YOU--?

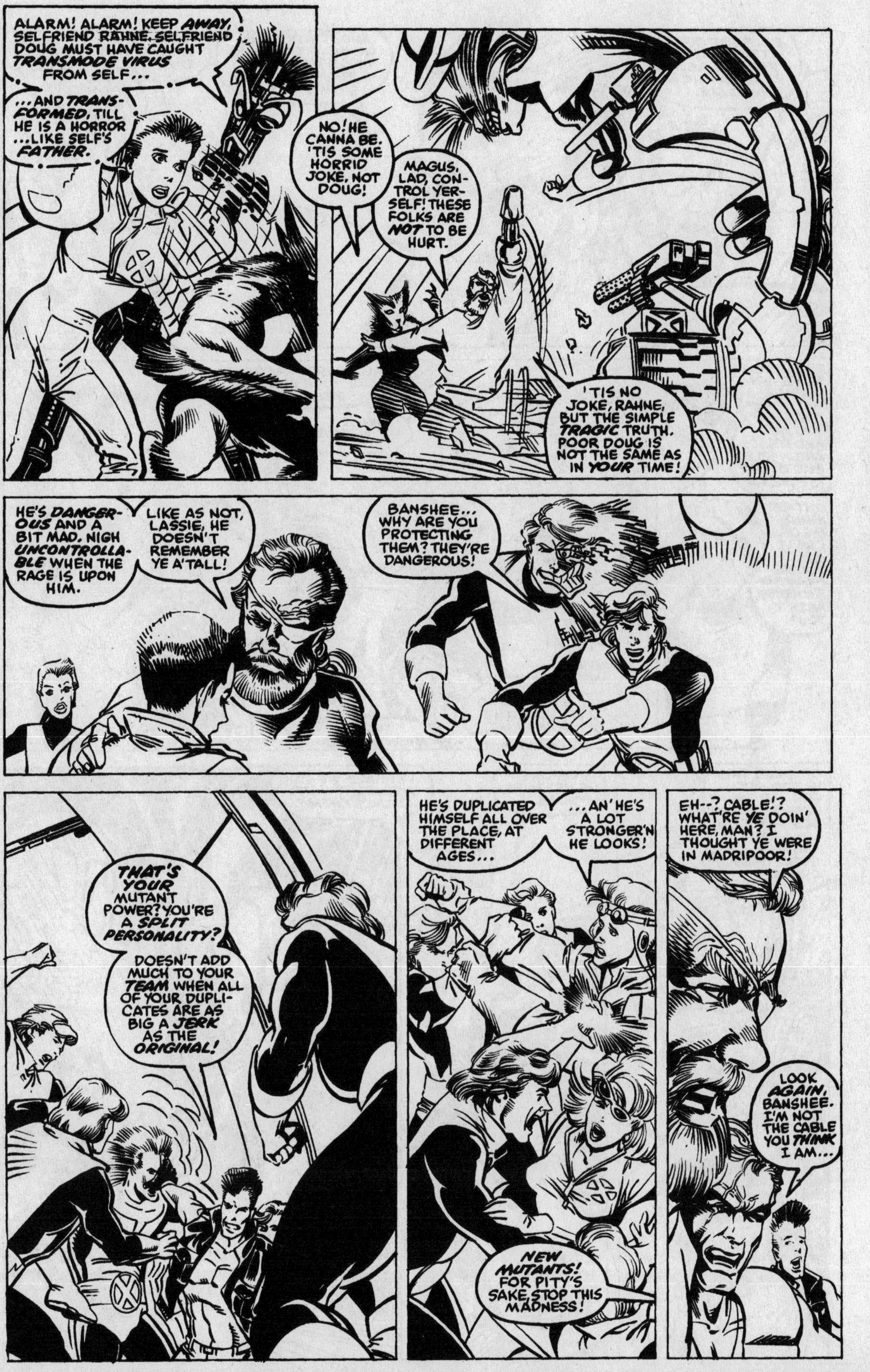

ALARM! ALARM! KEEP AWAY, SELFRIEND RAHNE. SELFRIEND DOUG MUST HAVE CAUGHT TRANSMODE VIRUS FROM SELF...
...AND TRANSFORMED, TILL HE IS A HORROR ...LIKE SELF'S FATHER.
NO! HE CANNA BE. 'TIS SOME HORRID JOKE, NOT DOUG!
MAGUS, LAD, CONTROL YERSELF! THESE FOLKS ARE NOT TO BE HURT.
'TIS NO JOKE, RAHNE, BUT THE SIMPLE TRAGIC TRUTH. POOR DOUG IS NOT THE SAME AS IN YOUR TIME!
HE'S DANGEROUS AND A BIT MAD, NIGH UNCONTROLLABLE WHEN THE RAGE IS UPON HIM.
LIKE AS NOT, LASSIE, HE DOESN'T REMEMBER YE A'TALL!
BANSHEE... WHY ARE YOU PROTECTING THEM? THEY'RE DANGEROUS!
THAT'S YOUR MUTANT POWER? YOU'RE A SPLIT PERSONALITY?
DOESN'T ADD MUCH TO YOUR TEAM WHEN ALL OF YOUR DUPLICATES ARE AS BIG A JERK AS THE ORIGINAL!
HE'S DUPLICATED HIMSELF ALL OVER THE PLACE, AT DIFFERENT AGES...
...AN' HE'S A LOT STRONGER'N HE LOOKS!
NEW MUTANTS! FOR PITY'S SAKE, STOP THIS MADNESS!
EH--? CABLE!? WHAT'RE YE DOIN' HERE, MAN? I THOUGHT YE WERE IN MADRIPOOR!
LOOK AGAIN, BANSHEE. I'M NOT THE CABLE YOU THINK I AM...

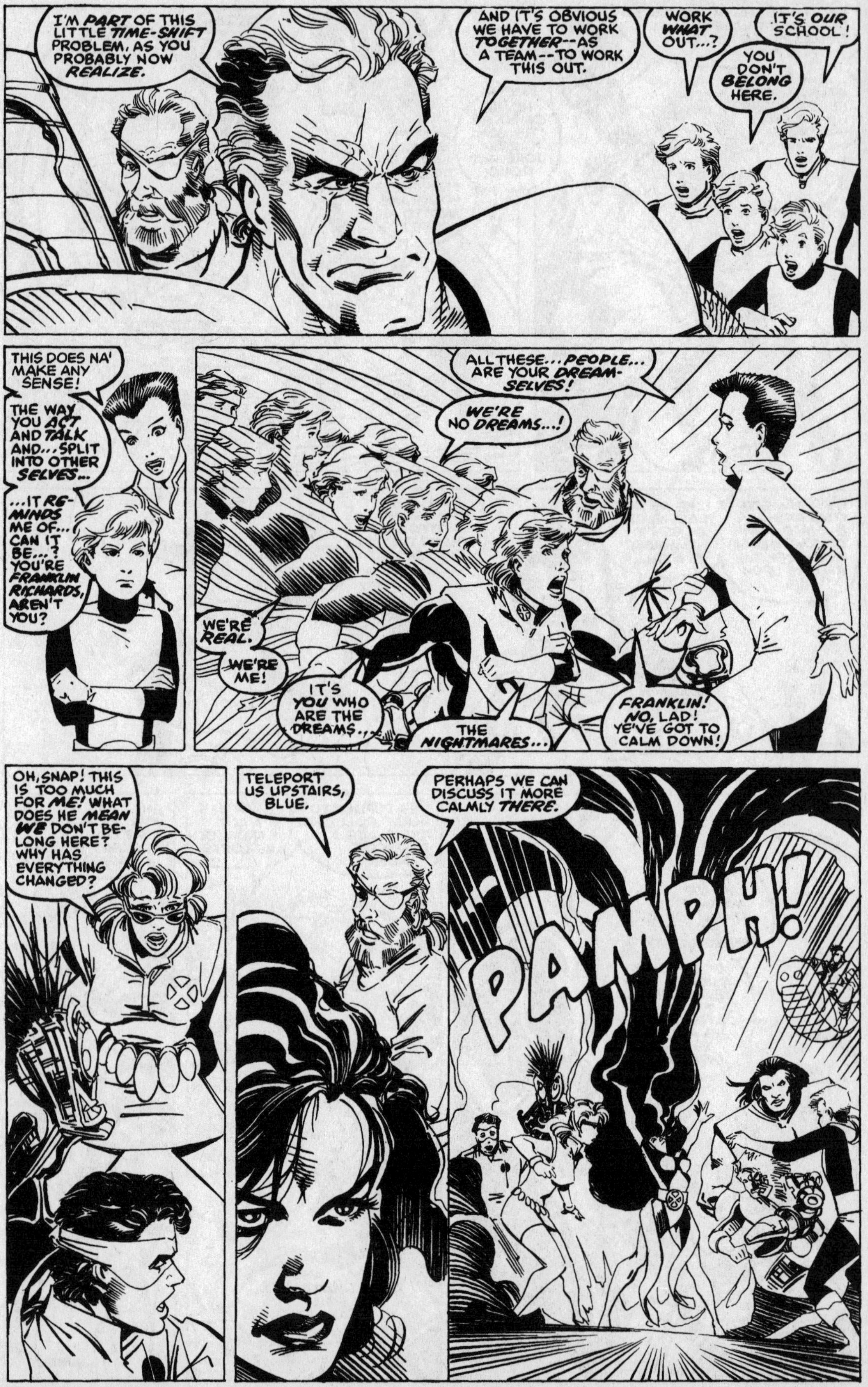
I'M PART OF THIS LITTLE TIME-SHIFT PROBLEM, AS YOU PROBABLY NOW REALIZE.
AND IT'S OBVIOUS WE HAVE TO WORK TOGETHER--AS A TEAM--TO WORK THIS OUT.
WORK WHAT OUT...?
IT'S OUR SCHOOL!
YOU DON'T BELONG HERE.
THIS DOES NA' MAKE ANY SENSE!
THE WAY YOU ACT AND TALK AND... SPLIT INTO OTHER SELVES...
...IT RE-MINDS ME OF... CAN IT BE...? YOU'RE FRANKLIN RICHARDS, AREN'T YOU?
ALL THESE... PEOPLE... ARE YOUR DREAM-SELVES!
WE'RE NO DREAMS...!
WE'RE REAL.
WE'RE ME!
IT'S YOU WHO ARE THE DREAMS...
THE NIGHTMARES...
FRANKLIN! NO, LAD! YE'VE GOT TO CALM DOWN!
OH, SNAP! THIS IS TOO MUCH FOR ME! WHAT DOES HE MEAN WE DON'T BE-LONG HERE? WHY HAS EVERYTHING CHANGED?
TELEPORT US UPSTAIRS, BLUE.
PERHAPS WE CAN DISCUSS IT MORE CALMLY THERE.
PAMPH!

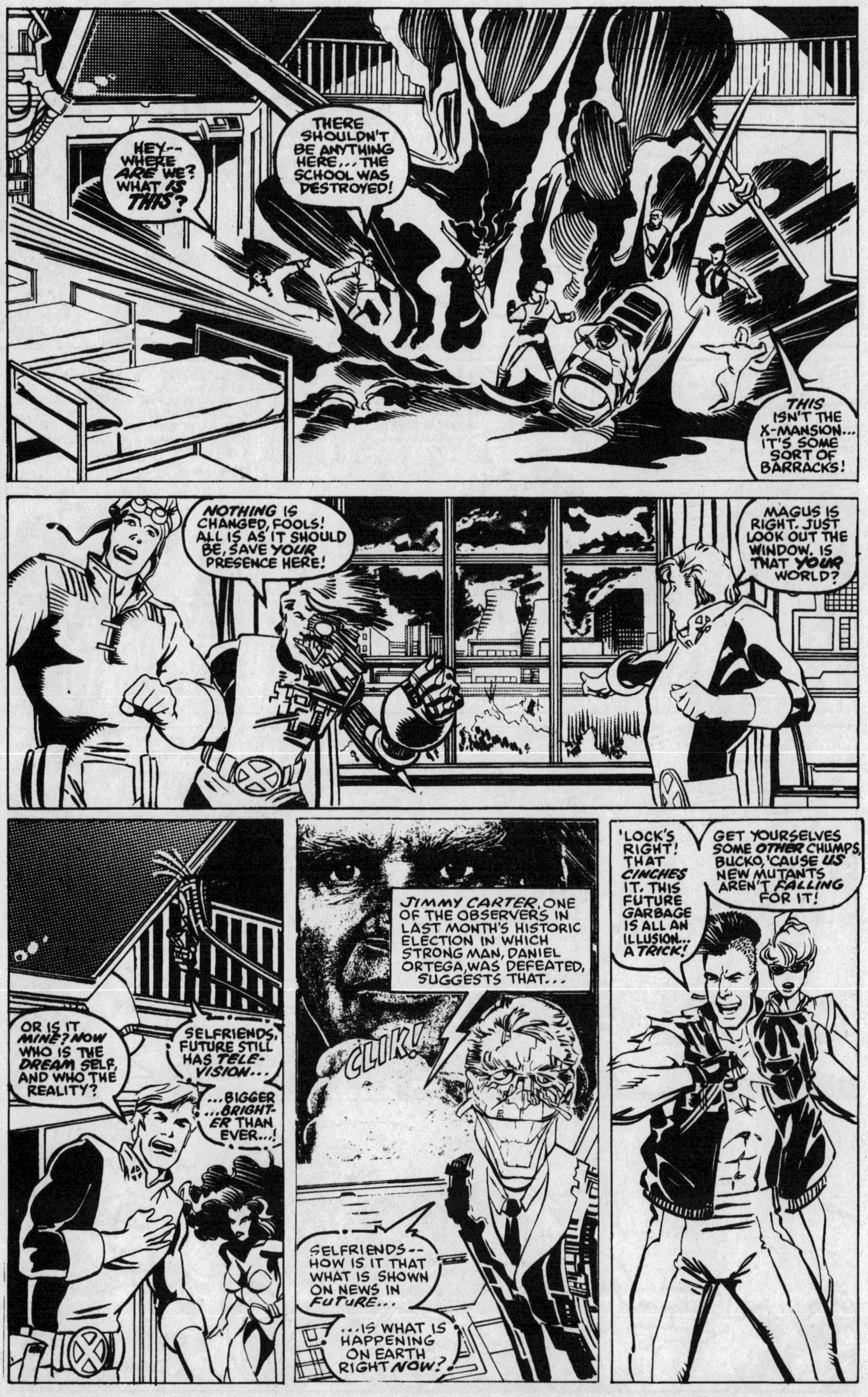
HEY-- WHERE ARE WE? WHAT IS THIS?
THERE SHOULDN'T BE ANYTHING HERE... THE SCHOOL WAS DESTROYED!
THIS ISN'T THE X-MANSION... IT'S SOME SORT OF BARRACKS!
NOTHING IS CHANGED, FOOLS! ALL IS AS IT SHOULD BE, SAVE YOUR PRESENCE HERE!
MAGUS IS RIGHT. JUST LOOK OUT THE WINDOW. IS THAT YOUR WORLD?
OR IS IT MINE? NOW WHO IS THE DREAM SELF, AND WHO THE REALITY?
SELFRIENDS, FUTURE STILL HAS TELE-VISION...
...BIGGER ...BRIGHT-ER THAN EVER...!
JIMMY CARTER, ONE OF THE OBSERVERS IN LAST MONTH'S HISTORIC ELECTION IN WHICH STRONG MAN, DANIEL ORTEGA, WAS DEFEATED, SUGGESTS THAT...
CLIK!
SELFRIENDS-- HOW IS IT THAT WHAT IS SHOWN ON NEWS IN FUTURE...
...IS WHAT IS HAPPENING ON EARTH RIGHT NOW?
'LOCK'S RIGHT! THAT CINCHES IT. THIS FUTURE GARBAGE IS ALL AN ILLUSION... A TRICK!
GET YOURSELVES SOME OTHER CHUMPS, BUCKO, 'CAUSE US NEW MUTANTS AREN'T FALLING FOR IT!

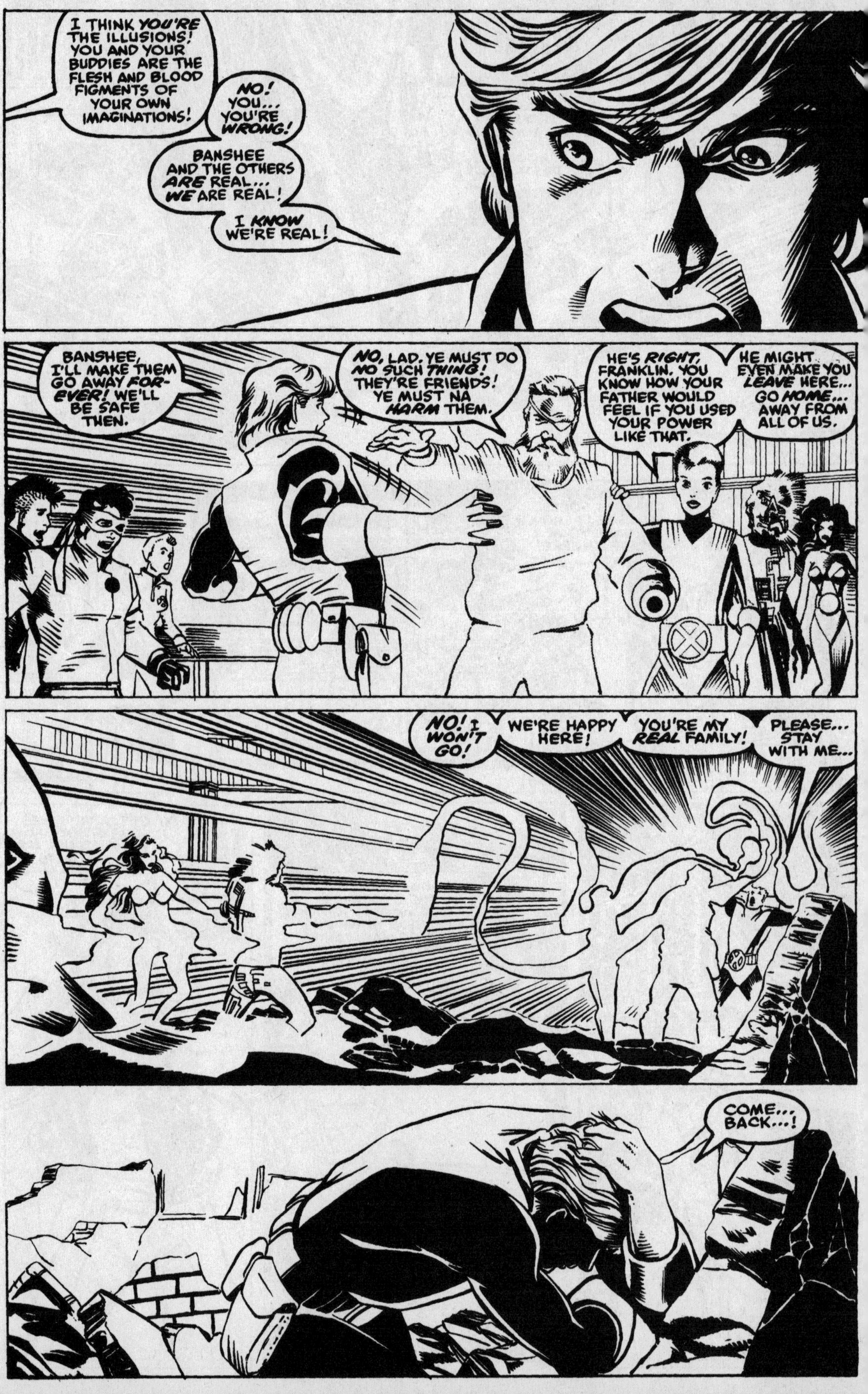
I THINK YOU'RE THE ILLUSIONS! YOU AND YOUR BUDDIES ARE THE FLESH AND BLOOD FIGMENTS OF YOUR OWN IMAGINATIONS!
NO! YOU... YOU'RE WRONG!
BANSHEE AND THE OTHERS ARE REAL... WE ARE REAL!
I KNOW WE'RE REAL!
BANSHEE, I'LL MAKE THEM GO AWAY FOREVER! WE'LL BE SAFE THEN.
NO, LAD. YE MUST DO NO SUCH THING! THEY'RE FRIENDS! YE MUST NA HARM THEM.
HE'S RIGHT, FRANKLIN. YOU KNOW HOW YOUR FATHER WOULD FEEL IF YOU USED YOUR POWER LIKE THAT.
HE MIGHT EVEN MAKE YOU LEAVE HERE... GO HOME... AWAY FROM ALL OF US.
NO! I WON'T GO!
WE'RE HAPPY HERE!
YOU'RE MY REAL FAMILY!
PLEASE... STAY WITH ME...
COME... BACK...!

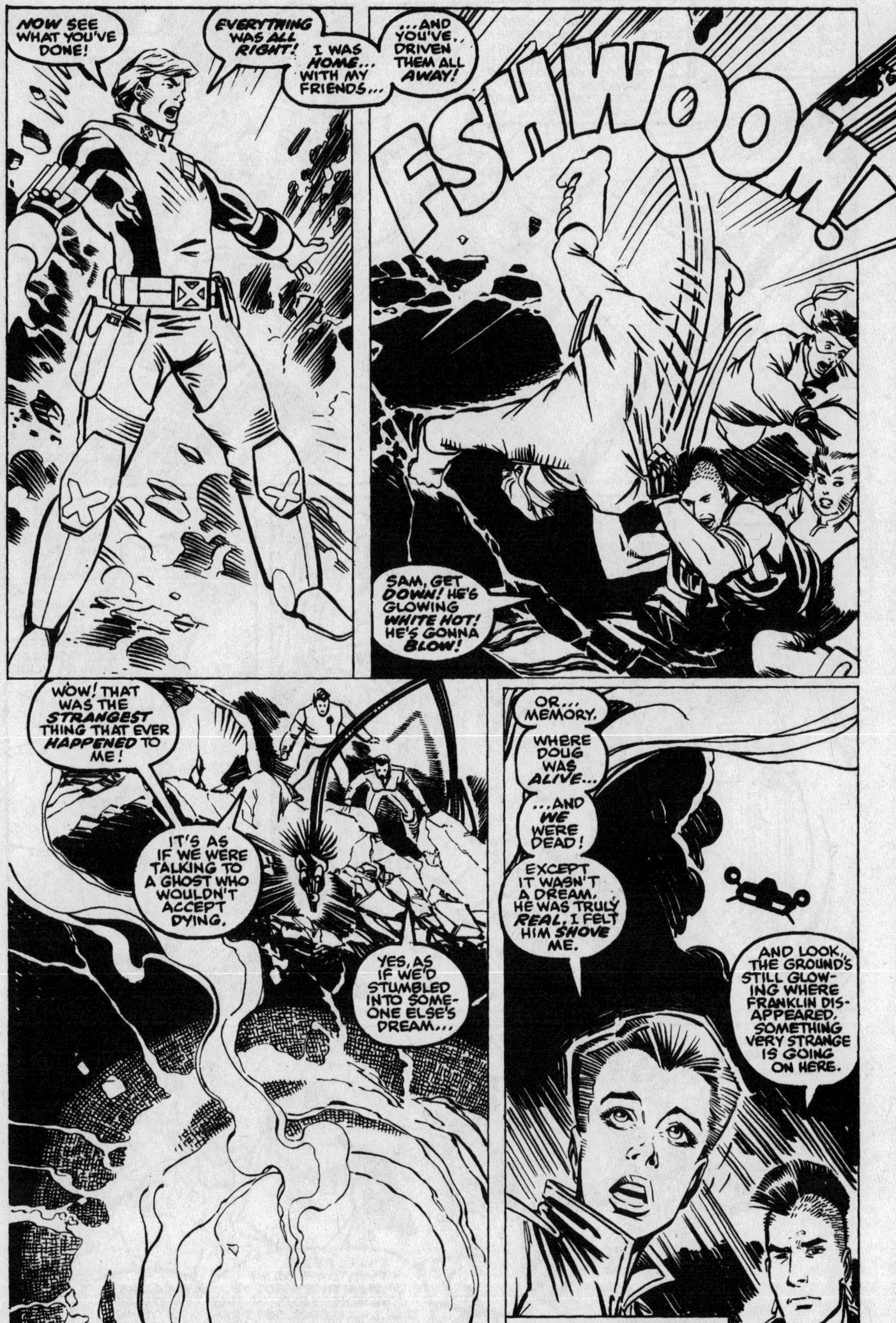
NOW SEE WHAT YOU'VE DONE!
EVERYTHING WAS ALL RIGHT! I WAS HOME... WITH MY FRIENDS...
...AND YOU'VE DRIVEN THEM ALL AWAY!
FSHWOOM!
SAM, GET DOWN! HE'S GLOWING WHITE HOT! HE'S GONNA BLOW!
WOW! THAT WAS THE STRANGEST THING THAT EVER HAPPENED TO ME!
IT'S AS IF WE WERE TALKING TO A GHOST WHO WOULDN'T ACCEPT DYING.
YES, AS IF WE'D STUMBLED INTO SOMEONE ELSE'S DREAM...
OR... MEMORY.
WHERE DOUG WAS ALIVE...
...AND WE WERE DEAD!
EXCEPT IT WASN'T A DREAM. HE WAS TRULY REAL. I FELT HIM SHOVE ME.
AND LOOK... THE GROUND'S STILL GLOWING WHERE FRANKLIN DISAPPEARED. SOMETHING VERY STRANGE IS GOING ON HERE.
FROM OUT OF THE SKY A HOVERCRAFT APPEARS...

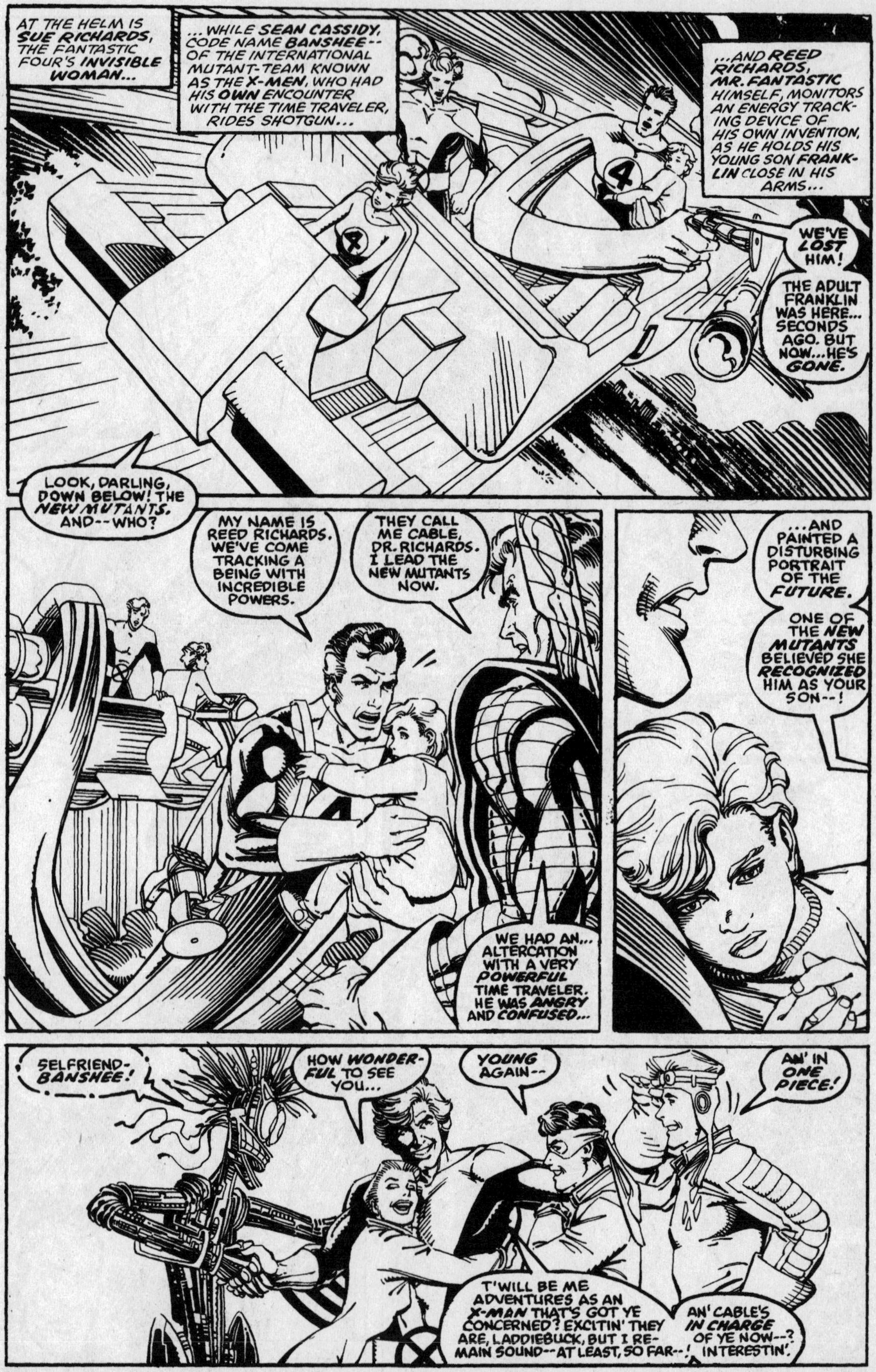

AT THE HELM IS SUE RICHARDS, THE FANTASTIC FOUR'S INVISIBLE WOMAN...
...WHILE SEAN CASSIDY, CODE NAME BANSHEE--OF THE INTERNATIONAL MUTANT-TEAM KNOWN AS THE X-MEN, WHO HAD HIS OWN ENCOUNTER WITH THE TIME TRAVELER, RIDES SHOTGUN...
...AND REED RICHARDS, MR. FANTASTIC HIMSELF, MONITORS AN ENERGY TRACKING DEVICE OF HIS OWN INVENTION, AS HE HOLDS HIS YOUNG SON FRANKLIN CLOSE IN HIS ARMS...
WE'VE LOST HIM!
THE ADULT FRANKLIN WAS HERE... SECONDS AGO. BUT NOW... HE'S GONE.
LOOK, DARLING, DOWN BELOW! THE NEW MUTANTS. AND--WHO?
MY NAME IS REED RICHARDS. WE'VE COME TRACKING A BEING WITH INCREDIBLE POWERS.
THEY CALL ME CABLE, DR. RICHARDS. I LEAD THE NEW MUTANTS NOW.
WE HAD AN... ALTERCATION WITH A VERY POWERFUL TIME TRAVELER. HE WAS ANGRY AND CONFUSED...
...AND PAINTED A DISTURBING PORTRAIT OF THE FUTURE.
ONE OF THE NEW MUTANTS BELIEVED SHE RECOGNIZED HIM AS YOUR SON--!
SELFRIEND-BANSHEE!
HOW WONDERFUL TO SEE YOU...
YOUNG AGAIN--
AN' IN ONE PIECE!
T'WILL BE ME ADVENTURES AS AN X-MAN THAT'S GOT YE CONCERNED? EXCITIN' THEY ARE, LADDIEBUCK, BUT I REMAIN SOUND--AT LEAST, SO FAR--!
AN' CABLE'S IN CHARGE OF YE NOW--? INTERESTIN'.

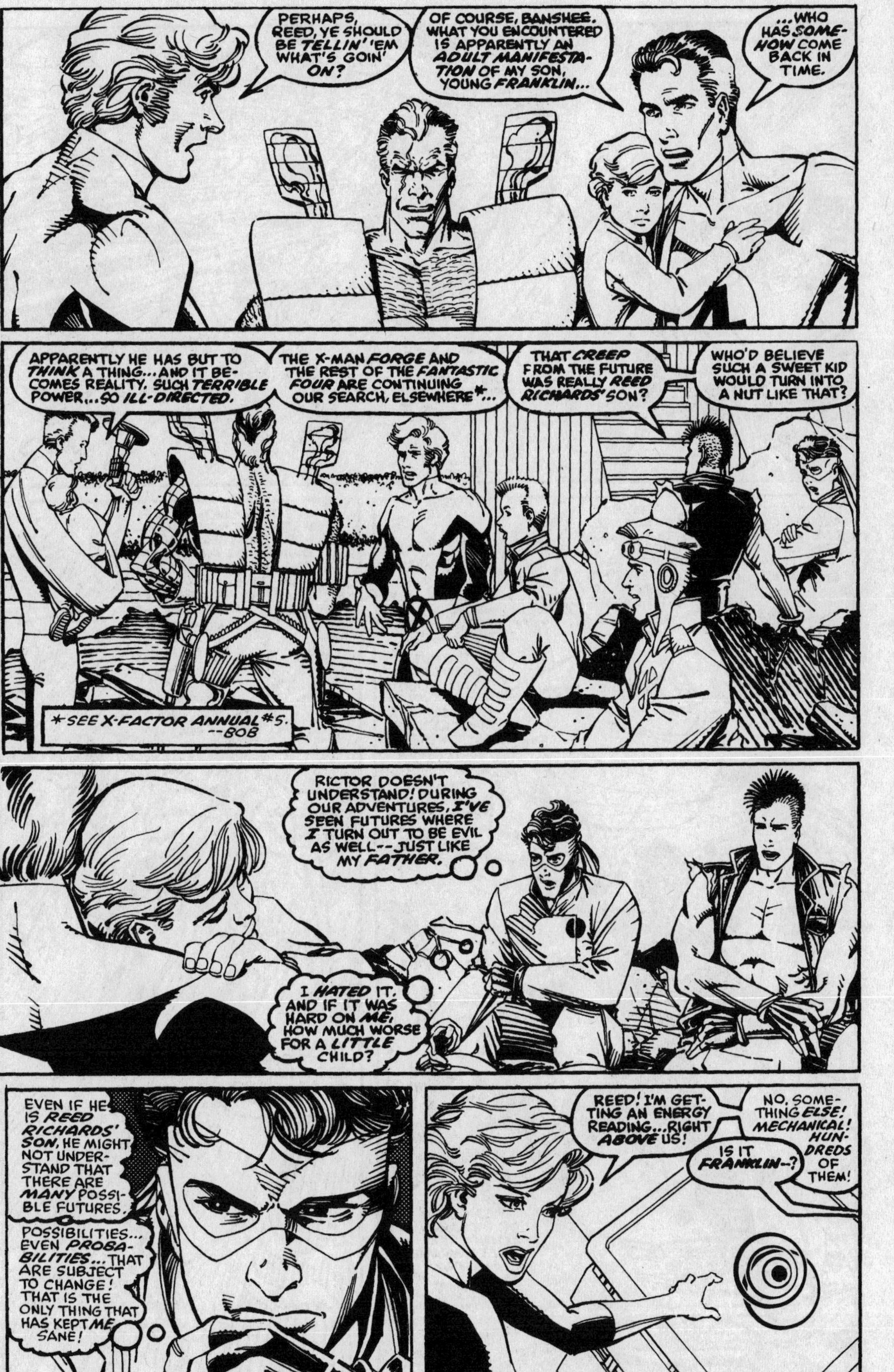
PERHAPS, REED, YE SHOULD BE TELLIN' 'EM WHAT'S GOIN' ON?
OF COURSE, BANSHEE. WHAT YOU ENCOUNTERED IS APPARENTLY AN ADULT MANIFESTATION OF MY SON, YOUNG FRANKLIN...
...WHO HAS SOMEHOW COME BACK IN TIME.
APPARENTLY HE HAS BUT TO THINK A THING... AND IT BECOMES REALITY. SUCH TERRIBLE POWER... SO ILL-DIRECTED.
THE X-MAN FORGE AND THE REST OF THE FANTASTIC FOUR ARE CONTINUING OUR SEARCH, ELSEWHERE*...
THAT CREEP FROM THE FUTURE WAS REALLY REED RICHARDS' SON?
WHO'D BELIEVE SUCH A SWEET KID WOULD TURN INTO A NUT LIKE THAT?
*SEE X-FACTOR ANNUAL #5. --BOB
RICTOR DOESN'T UNDERSTAND! DURING OUR ADVENTURES, I'VE SEEN FUTURES WHERE I TURN OUT TO BE EVIL AS WELL--JUST LIKE MY FATHER.
I HATED IT. AND IF IT WAS HARD ON ME, HOW MUCH WORSE FOR A LITTLE CHILD?
EVEN IF HE IS REED RICHARDS' SON, HE MIGHT NOT UNDERSTAND THAT THERE ARE MANY POSSIBLE FUTURES.
POSSIBILITIES... EVEN PROBABILITIES... THAT ARE SUBJECT TO CHANGE! THAT IS THE ONLY THING THAT HAS KEPT ME SANE!
REED! I'M GETTING AN ENERGY READING... RIGHT ABOVE US!
IS IT FRANKLIN--?
NO, SOMETHING ELSE! MECHANICAL! HUNDREDS OF THEM!

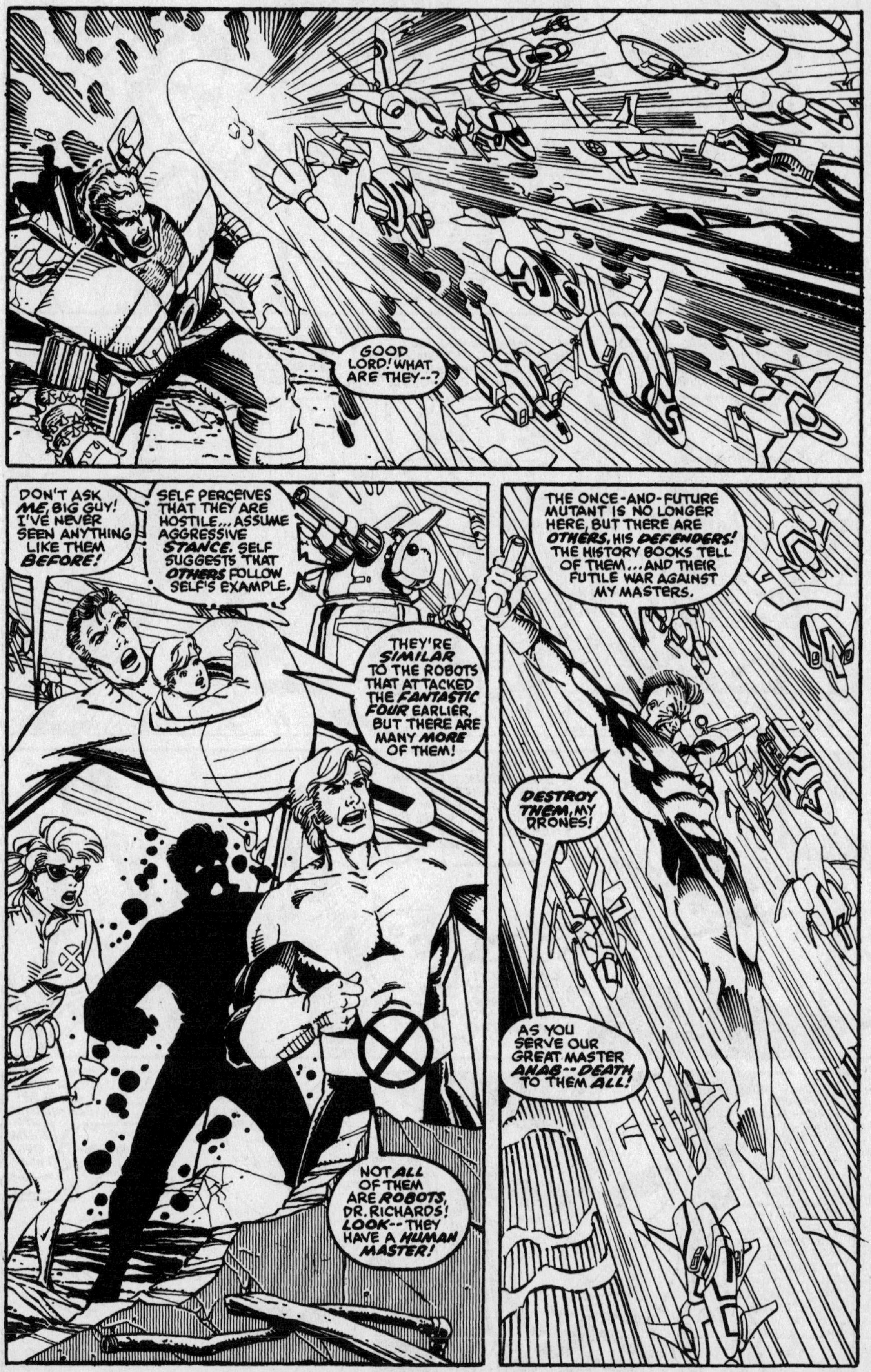
GOOD LORD! WHAT ARE THEY--?
DON'T ASK ME, BIG GUY! I'VE NEVER SEEN ANYTHING LIKE THEM BEFORE!
SELF PERCEIVES THAT THEY ARE HOSTILE... ASSUME AGGRESSIVE STANCE. SELF SUGGESTS THAT OTHERS FOLLOW SELF'S EXAMPLE.
THEY'RE SIMILAR TO THE ROBOTS THAT ATTACKED THE FANTASTIC FOUR EARLIER, BUT THERE ARE MANY MORE OF THEM!
NOT ALL OF THEM ARE ROBOTS, DR. RICHARDS! LOOK-- THEY HAVE A HUMAN MASTER!
THE ONCE-AND-FUTURE MUTANT IS NO LONGER HERE, BUT THERE ARE OTHERS, HIS DEFENDERS! THE HISTORY BOOKS TELL OF THEM... AND THEIR FUTILE WAR AGAINST MY MASTERS.
DESTROY THEM, MY DRONES!
AS YOU SERVE OUR GREAT MASTER ANAB--DEATH TO THEM ALL!

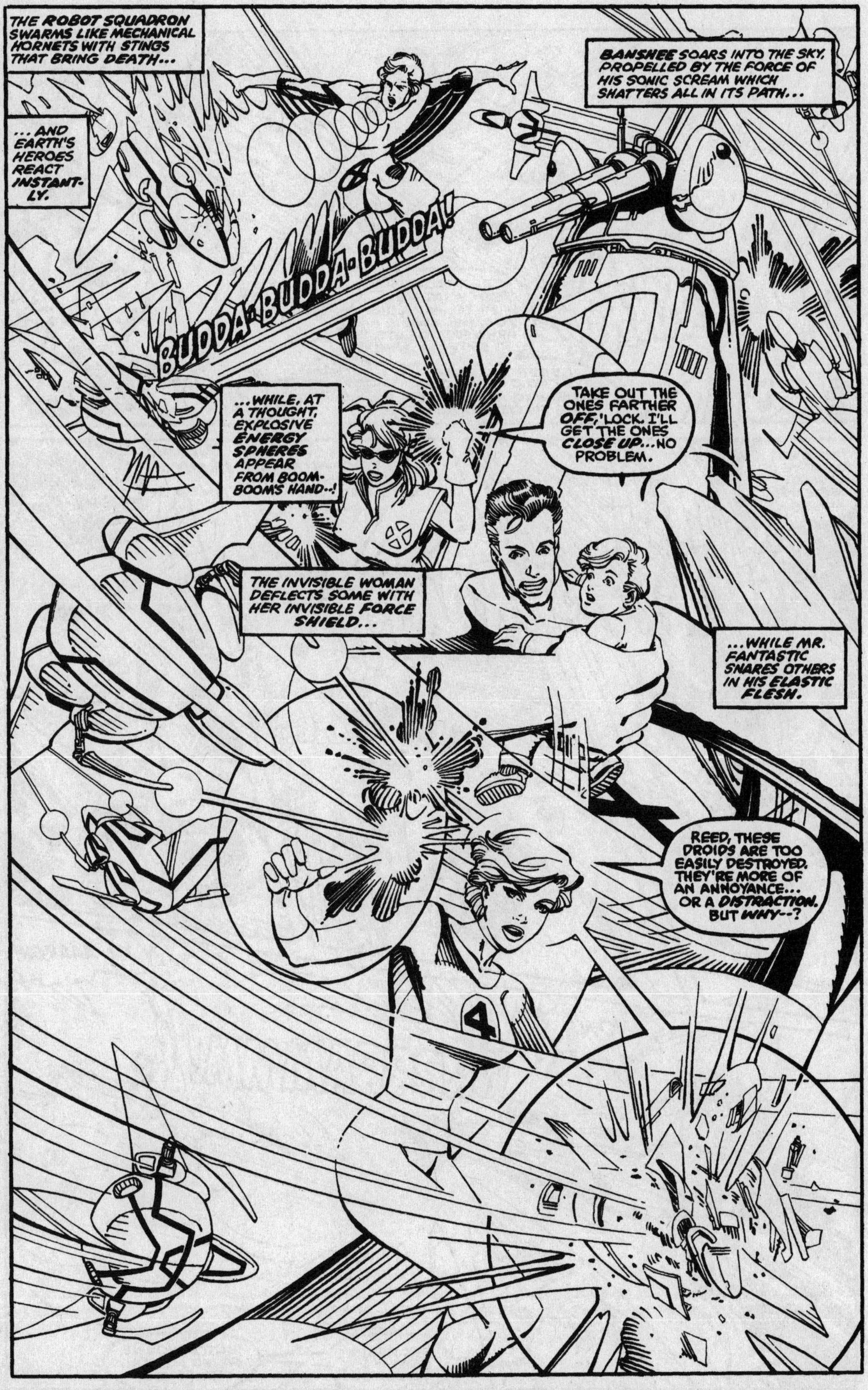
THE ROBOT SQUADRON SWARMS LIKE MECHANICAL HORNETS WITH STINGS THAT BRING DEATH...
...AND EARTH'S HEROES REACT INSTANT-LY.
BANSHEE SOARS INTO THE SKY, PROPELLED BY THE FORCE OF HIS SONIC SCREAM WHICH SHATTERS ALL IN ITS PATH...
BUDDA-BUDDA-BUDDA-BUDDA!
...WHILE, AT A THOUGHT, EXPLOSIVE ENERGY SPHERES APPEAR FROM BOOM-BOOM'S HAND--!
TAKE OUT THE ONES FARTHER OFF, 'LOCK. I'LL GET THE ONES CLOSE UP... NO PROBLEM.
THE INVISIBLE WOMAN DEFLECTS SOME WITH HER INVISIBLE FORCE SHIELD...
...WHILE MR. FANTASTIC SNARES OTHERS IN HIS ELASTIC FLESH.
REED, THESE DROIDS ARE TOO EASILY DESTROYED. THEY'RE MORE OF AN ANNOYANCE... OR A DISTRACTION. BUT WHY--?

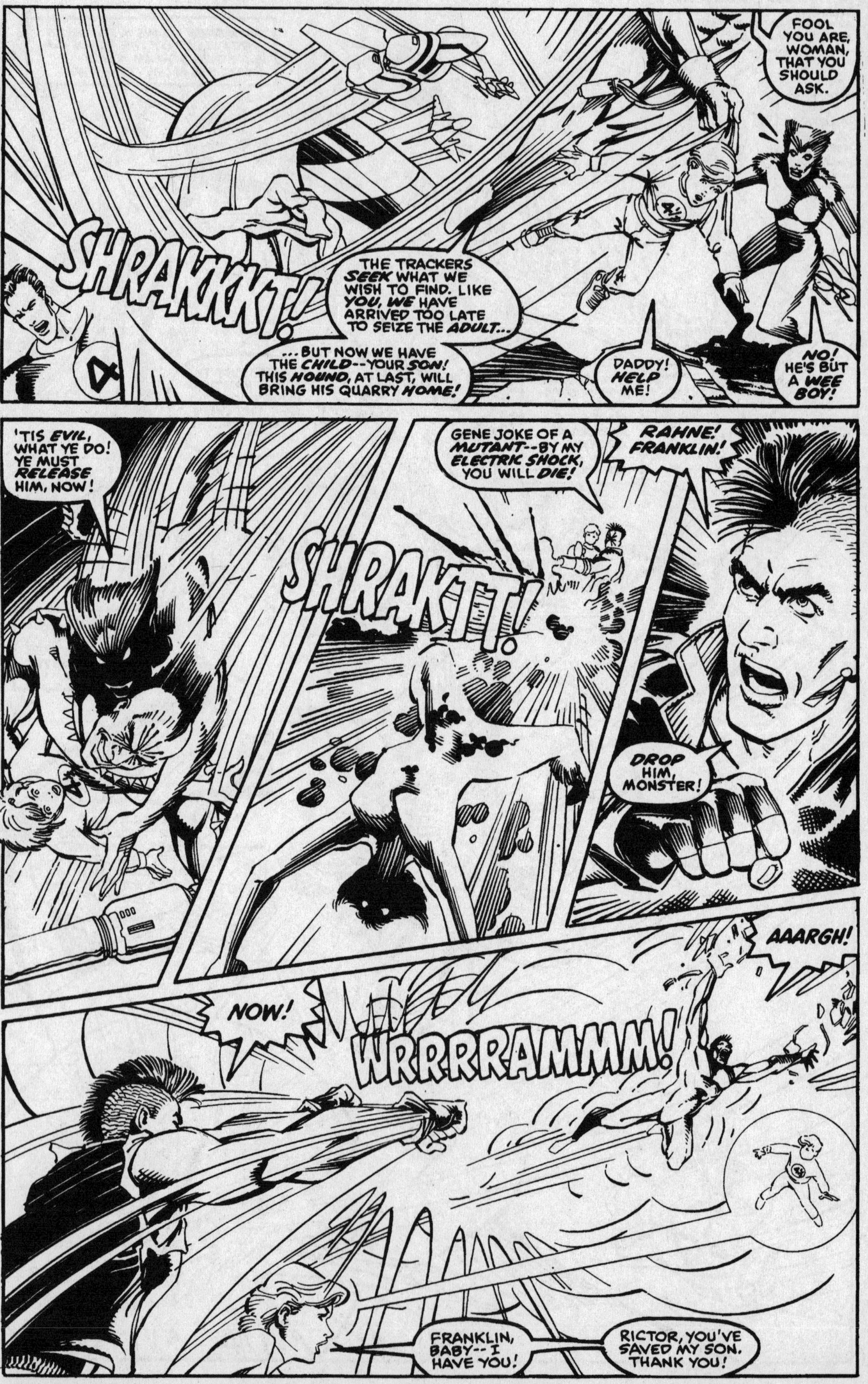
FOOL YOU ARE, WOMAN, THAT YOU SHOULD ASK.
SHRAKKKKT!
THE TRACKERS SEEK WHAT WE WISH TO FIND. LIKE YOU, WE HAVE ARRIVED TOO LATE TO SEIZE THE ADULT...
...BUT NOW WE HAVE THE CHILD--YOUR SON! THIS HOUND, AT LAST, WILL BRING HIS QUARRY HOME!
DADDY! HELP ME!
NO! HE'S BUT A WEE BOY!
'TIS EVIL, WHAT YE DO! YE MUST RELEASE HIM, NOW!
GENE JOKE OF A MUTANT--BY MY ELECTRIC SHOCK, YOU WILL DIE!
SHRAKTT!
RAHNE! FRANKLIN!
DROP HIM, MONSTER!
AAARGH!
NOW!
WRRRRAMMMM!
FRANKLIN, BABY--I HAVE YOU!
RICTOR, YOU'VE SAVED MY SON. THANK YOU!

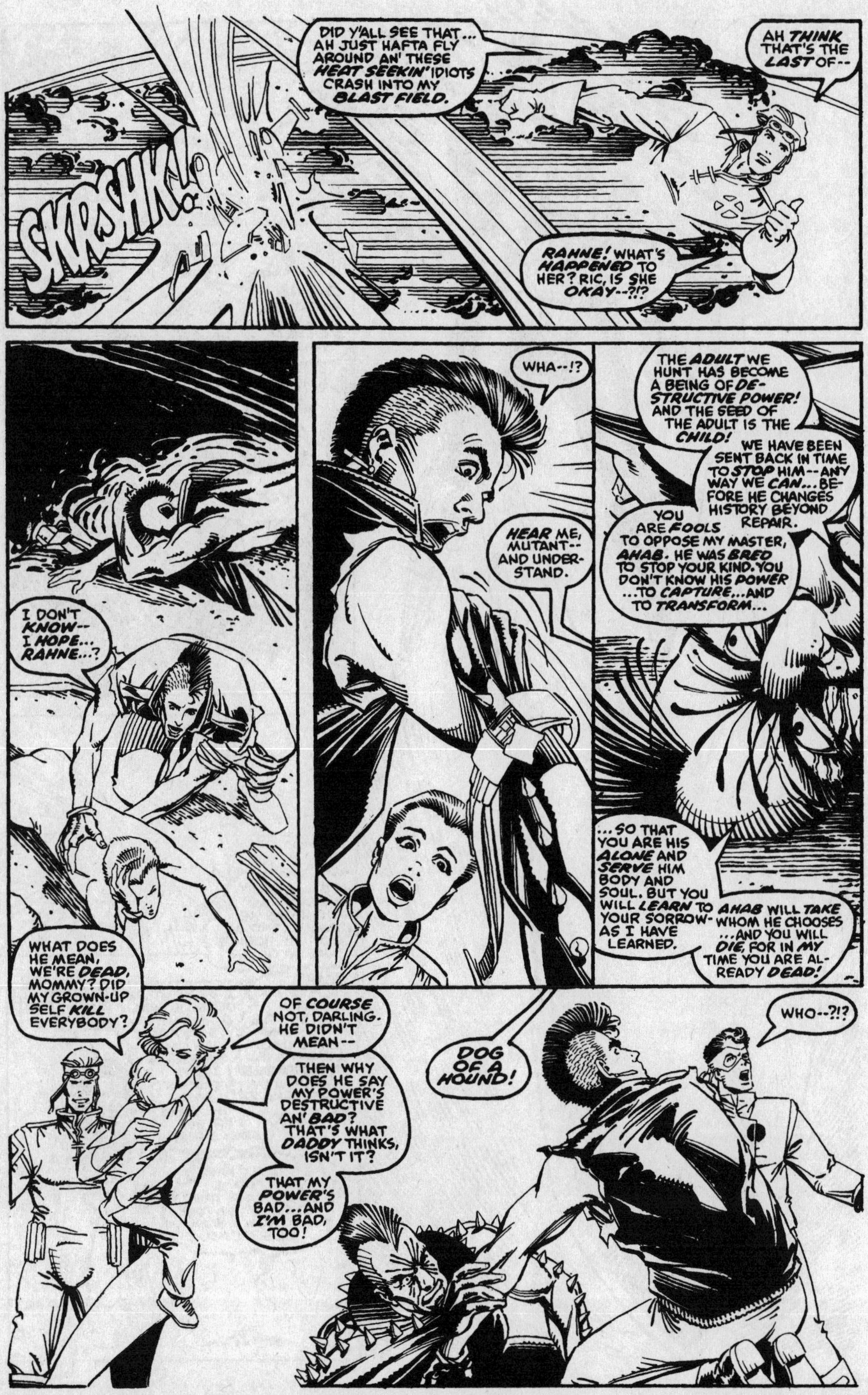
DID Y'ALL SEE THAT... AH JUST HAFTA FLY AROUND AN' THESE HEAT SEEKIN' IDIOTS CRASH INTO MY BLAST FIELD.
AH THINK THAT'S THE LAST OF--
SKRSHK!
RAHNE! WHAT'S HAPPENED TO HER? RIC, IS SHE OKAY--?!?
I DON'T KNOW-- I HOPE... RAHNE...?
WHA--!?
HEAR ME, MUTANT-- AND UNDERSTAND.
THE ADULT WE HUNT HAS BECOME A BEING OF DESTRUCTIVE POWER! AND THE SEED OF THE ADULT IS THE CHILD!
WE HAVE BEEN SENT BACK IN TIME TO STOP HIM--ANY WAY WE CAN... BEFORE HE CHANGES HISTORY BEYOND REPAIR.
YOU ARE FOOLS TO OPPOSE MY MASTER, AHAB. HE WAS BRED TO STOP YOUR KIND. YOU DON'T KNOW HIS POWER ...TO CAPTURE...AND TO TRANSFORM...
...SO THAT YOU ARE HIS ALONE AND SERVE HIM BODY AND SOUL. BUT YOU WILL LEARN TO YOUR SORROW-AS I HAVE LEARNED.
AHAB WILL TAKE WHOM HE CHOOSES ...AND YOU WILL DIE, FOR IN MY TIME YOU ARE ALREADY DEAD!
WHAT DOES HE MEAN, WE'RE DEAD, MOMMY? DID MY GROWN-UP SELF KILL EVERYBODY?
OF COURSE NOT, DARLING. HE DIDN'T MEAN--
THEN WHY DOES HE SAY MY POWER'S DESTRUCTIVE AN' BAD? THAT'S WHAT DADDY THINKS, ISN'T IT?
THAT MY POWER'S BAD... AND I'M BAD, TOO!
DOG OF A HOUND!
WHO--?!?

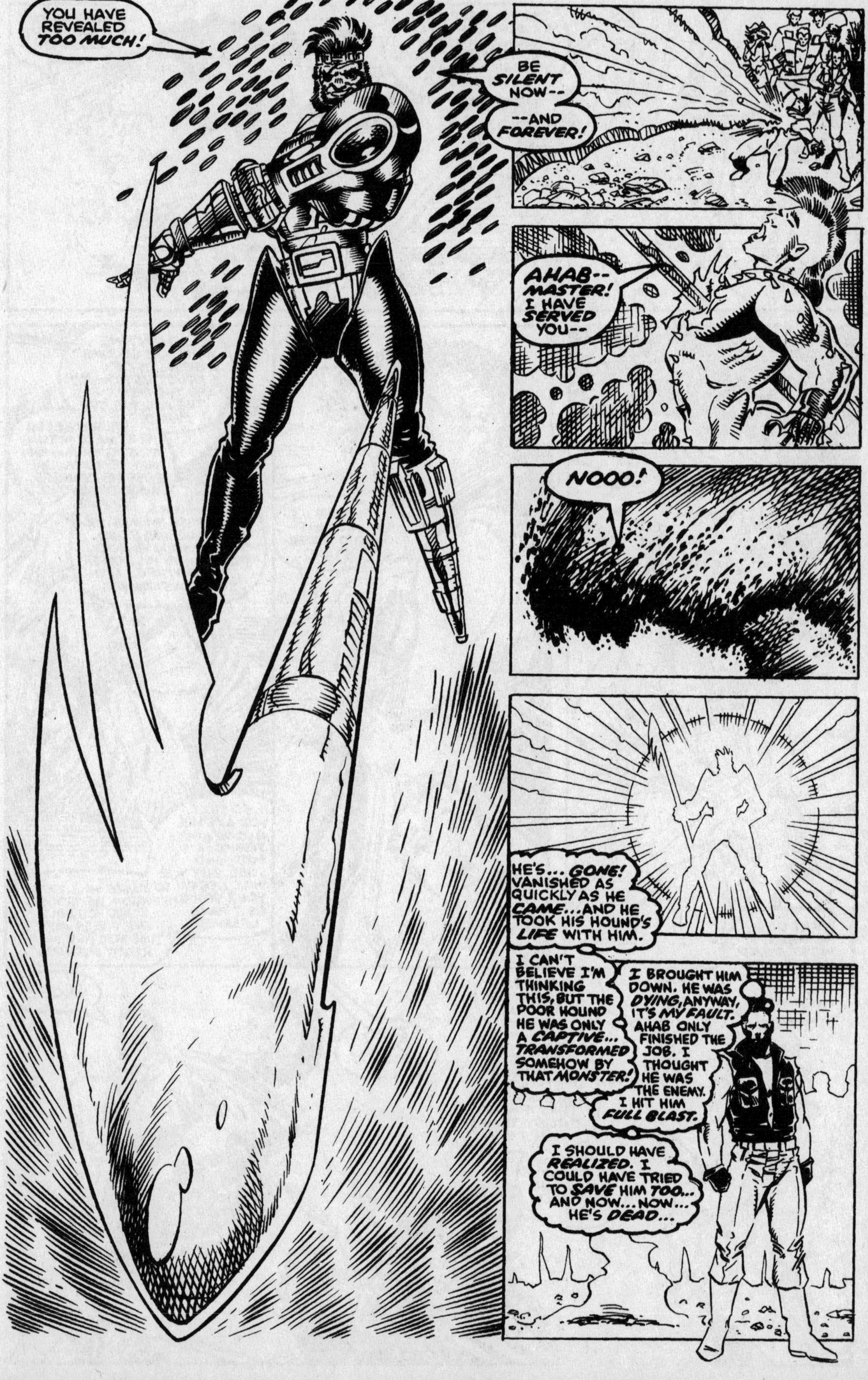
YOU HAVE REVEALED TOO MUCH!
BE SILENT NOW--
--AND FOREVER!
AHAB--MASTER! I HAVE SERVED YOU--
NOOO!
HE'S... GONE! VANISHED AS QUICKLY AS HE CAME...AND HE TOOK HIS HOUND'S LIFE WITH HIM.
I CAN'T BELIEVE I'M THINKING THIS, BUT THE POOR HOUND HE WAS ONLY A CAPTIVE... TRANSFORMED SOMEHOW BY THAT MONSTER!
I BROUGHT HIM DOWN. HE WAS DYING, ANYWAY, IT'S MY FAULT. AHAB ONLY FINISHED THE JOB. I THOUGHT HE WAS THE ENEMY. I HIT HIM FULL BLAST.
I SHOULD HAVE REALIZED. I COULD HAVE TRIED TO SAVE HIM TOO... AND NOW... NOW... HE'S DEAD...

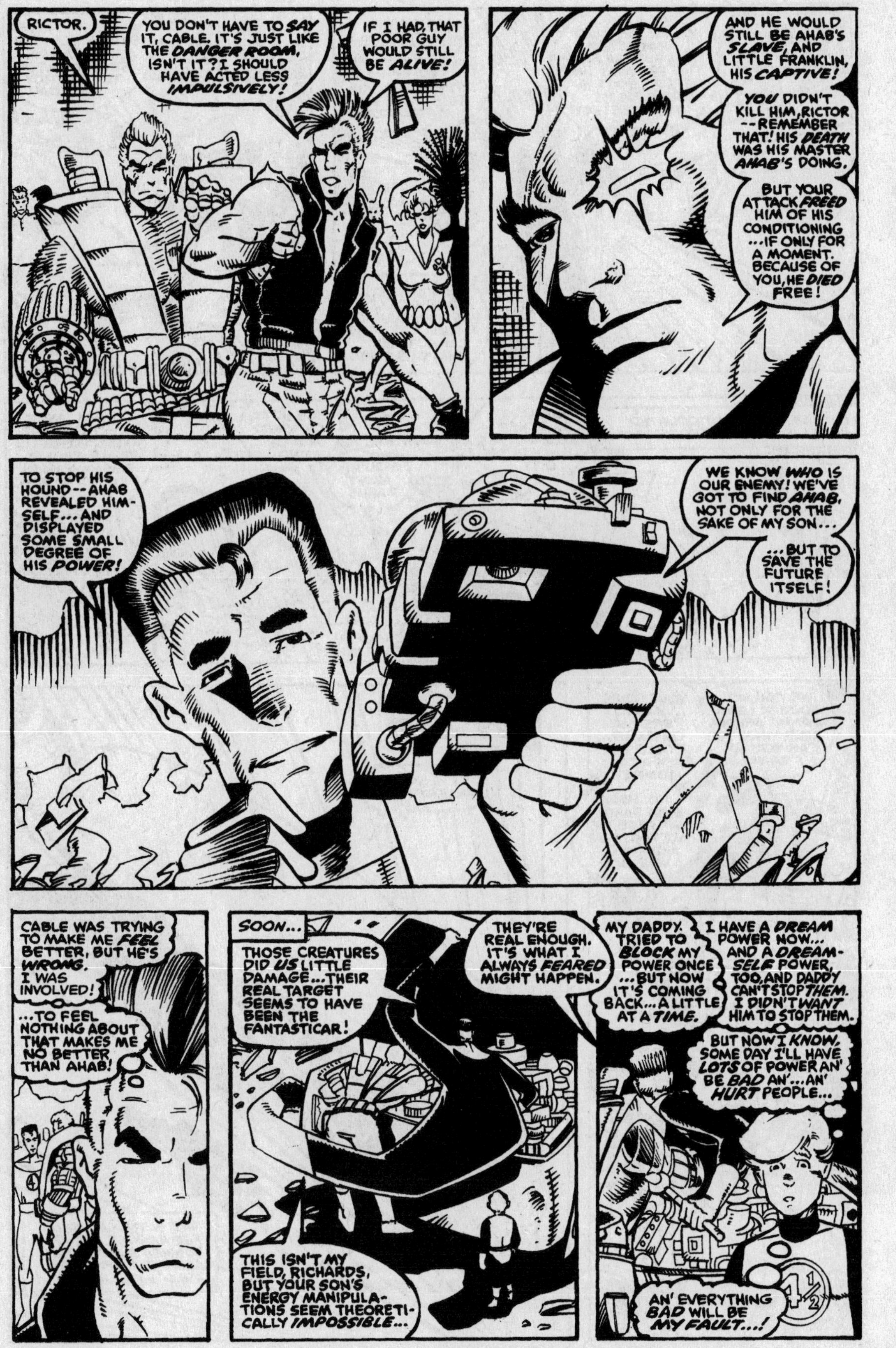
RICTOR.
YOU DON'T HAVE TO SAY IT, CABLE. IT'S JUST LIKE THE DANGER ROOM, ISN'T IT? I SHOULD HAVE ACTED LESS IMPULSIVELY!
IF I HAD, THAT POOR GUY WOULD STILL BE ALIVE!
AND HE WOULD STILL BE AHAB'S SLAVE, AND LITTLE FRANKLIN, HIS CAPTIVE!
YOU DIDN'T KILL HIM, RICTOR -- REMEMBER THAT! HIS DEATH WAS HIS MASTER AHAB'S DOING.
BUT YOUR ATTACK FREED HIM OF HIS CONDITIONING ...IF ONLY FOR A MOMENT. BECAUSE OF YOU, HE DIED FREE!
TO STOP HIS HOUND -- AHAB REVEALED HIMSELF... AND DISPLAYED SOME SMALL DEGREE OF HIS POWER!
WE KNOW WHO IS OUR ENEMY! WE'VE GOT TO FIND AHAB, NOT ONLY FOR THE SAKE OF MY SON...
...BUT TO SAVE THE FUTURE ITSELF!
CABLE WAS TRYING TO MAKE ME FEEL BETTER, BUT HE'S WRONG. I WAS INVOLVED!
...TO FEEL NOTHING ABOUT THAT MAKES ME NO BETTER THAN AHAB!
SOON...
THOSE CREATURES DID US LITTLE DAMAGE... THEIR REAL TARGET SEEMS TO HAVE BEEN THE FANTASTICAR!
THIS ISN'T MY FIELD, RICHARDS, BUT YOUR SON'S ENERGY MANIPULATIONS SEEM THEORETICALLY IMPOSSIBLE...
THEY'RE REAL ENOUGH. IT'S WHAT I ALWAYS FEARED MIGHT HAPPEN.
MY DADDY. TRIED TO BLOCK MY POWER ONCE ...BUT NOW IT'S COMING BACK... A LITTLE AT A TIME.
I HAVE A DREAM POWER NOW... AND A DREAM-SELF POWER, TOO, AND DADDY CAN'T STOP THEM. I DIDN'T WANT HIM TO STOP THEM.
BUT NOW I KNOW. SOME DAY I'LL HAVE LOTS OF POWER AN' BE BAD AN'... AN' HURT PEOPLE...
AN' EVERYTHING BAD WILL BE MY FAULT...!

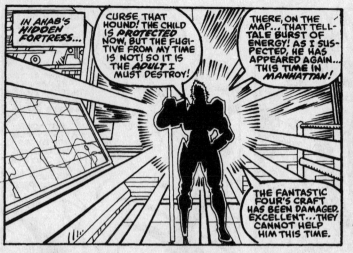

IN AHAB'S *HIDDEN FORTRESS*...

CURSE THAT *HOUND!* THE CHILD IS *PROTECTED* NOW, BUT THE FUGITIVE FROM MY TIME IS *NOT!* SO IT IS THE *ADULT* I MUST DESTROY!

THERE, ON THE *MAP*... THAT *TELL-TALE BURST* OF ENERGY! AS I SUSPECTED, HE HAS APPEARED AGAIN... THIS TIME IN *MANHATTAN!*

THE FANTASTIC FOUR'S CRAFT HAS BEEN DAMAGED. EXCELLENT...THEY CANNOT HELP HIM THIS TIME.

WHILE HIS FATHER STRUGGLES WITH *REPAIRS*, I WILL SEND MY *ARMY* TO DESTROY HIS *SON!*

BUT AHAB HAS NOT COUNTED ON *THE GENIUS REED RICHARDS*...

WE HAVE ANOTHER READING, HE'S BACK IN THE CITY.

I... I'M COMING WITH YOU!

YOU'RE *HURT*, RAHNE.

'TIS BUT A *CRACKED RIB* OR TWO...

CABLE, IS THAT WISE?

YOU WILL AVOID *DIRECT COMBAT* WHERE POSSIBLE, RAHNE. BROKEN RIBS HAVE BEEN KNOWN TO PUNCTURE LUNGS...!

WE CAN NO SOONER LEAVE RAHNE BEHIND, REED, THAN YOU CAN YOUNG *FRANKLIN*.

YOUR SON'S ...*ADULT* PERSONA... OR *AHAB*... COULD BE BACK AT ANY MOMENT.

NO. *WHATEVER* DANGER WE FACE, WE FACE *TOGETHER*. AND NOW, WARLOCK...

"...IF YOU WILL BECOME ANOTHER *HOVERCRAFT?*"

IT IS SELF'S *PLEASURE!*

AND WITH A RUMBLE, THE HEROES SPEED TOWARD MANHATTAN... AND THEIR APPOINTMENT WITH DESTINY...!

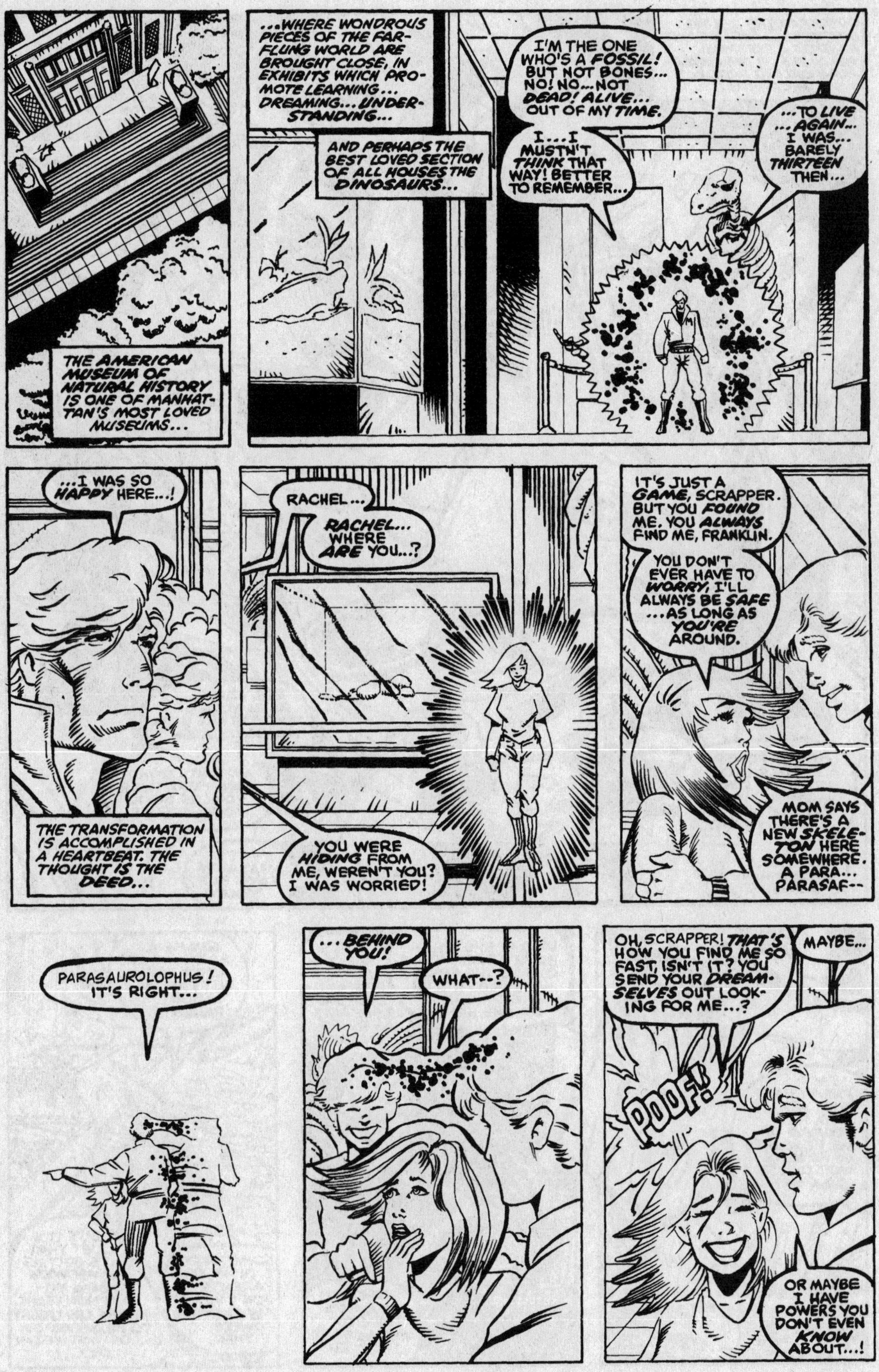
THE AMERICAN MUSEUM OF NATURAL HISTORY IS ONE OF MANHATTAN'S MOST LOVED MUSEUMS...
...WHERE WONDROUS PIECES OF THE FAR-FLUNG WORLD ARE BROUGHT CLOSE, IN EXHIBITS WHICH PROMOTE LEARNING... DREAMING... UNDERSTANDING...
AND PERHAPS THE BEST LOVED SECTION OF ALL HOUSES THE DINOSAURS...
I'M THE ONE WHO'S A FOSSIL! BUT NOT BONES... NO! NO... NOT DEAD! ALIVE... OUT OF MY TIME.
I... I MUSTN'T THINK THAT WAY! BETTER TO REMEMBER...
...TO LIVE ...AGAIN... I WAS... BARELY THIRTEEN THEN...
...I WAS SO HAPPY HERE...!
THE TRANSFORMATION IS ACCOMPLISHED IN A HEARTBEAT. THE THOUGHT IS THE DEED...
RACHEL...
RACHEL... WHERE ARE YOU...?
YOU WERE HIDING FROM ME, WEREN'T YOU? I WAS WORRIED!
IT'S JUST A GAME, SCRAPPER. BUT YOU FOUND ME. YOU ALWAYS FIND ME, FRANKLIN.
YOU DON'T EVER HAVE TO WORRY, I'LL ALWAYS BE SAFE ...AS LONG AS YOU'RE AROUND.
MOM SAYS THERE'S A NEW SKELETON HERE SOMEWHERE. A PARA... PARASAF--
PARASAUROLOPHUS! IT'S RIGHT...
...BEHIND YOU!
WHAT--?
OH, SCRAPPER! THAT'S HOW YOU FIND ME SO FAST, ISN'T IT? YOU SEND YOUR DREAM-SELVES OUT LOOKING FOR ME...?
MAYBE...
POOF!
OR MAYBE I HAVE POWERS YOU DON'T EVEN KNOW ABOUT...!

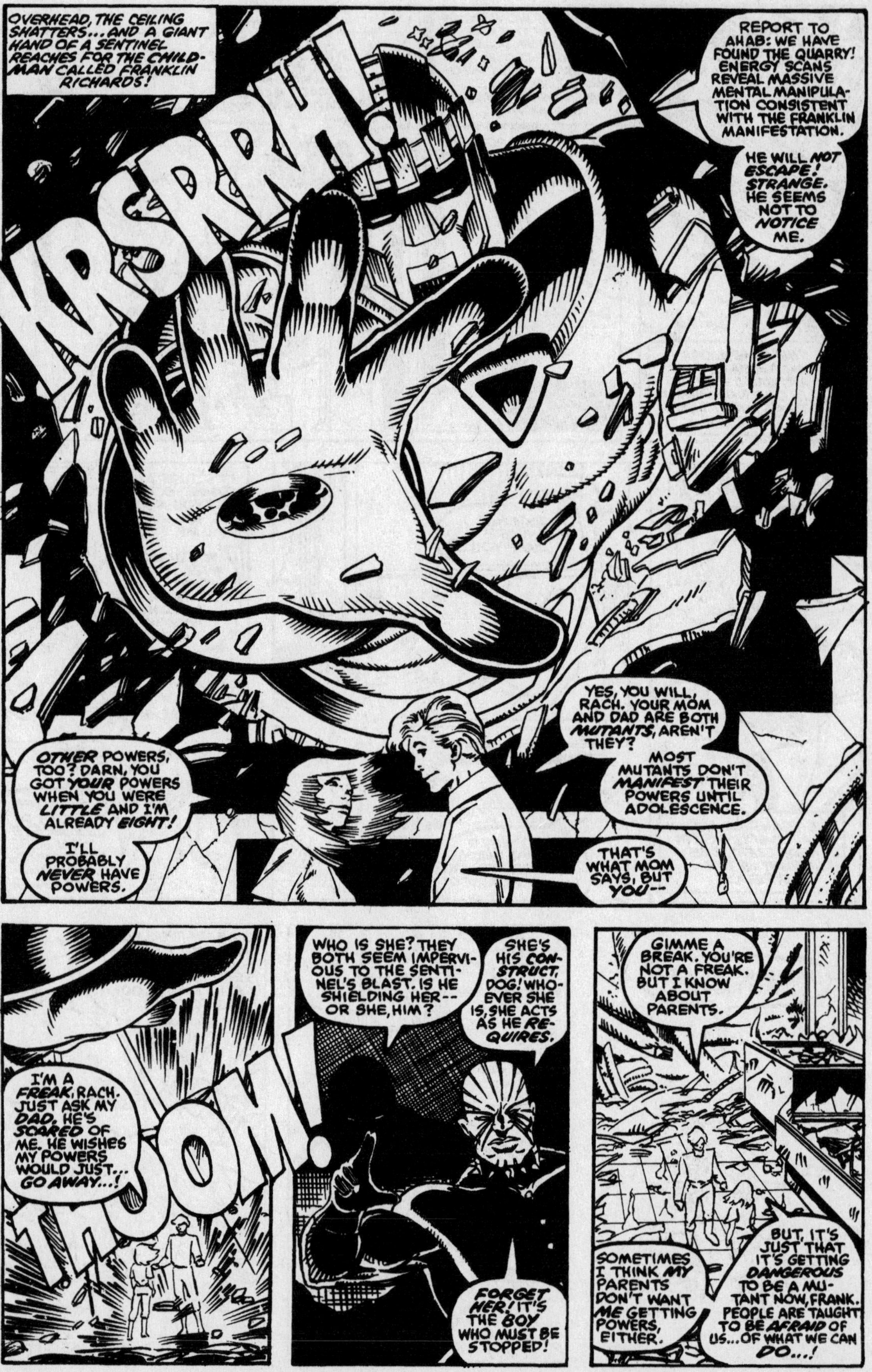

OVERHEAD, THE CEILING SHATTERS... AND A GIANT HAND OF A SENTINEL REACHES FOR THE CHILD-MAN CALLED FRANKLIN RICHARDS!
KRSRRH!
REPORT TO AHAB: WE HAVE FOUND THE QUARRY! ENERGY SCANS REVEAL MASSIVE MENTAL MANIPULATION CONSISTENT WITH THE FRANKLIN MANIFESTATION.
HE WILL NOT ESCAPE! STRANGE. HE SEEMS NOT TO NOTICE ME.
OTHER POWERS, TOO? DARN, YOU GOT YOUR POWERS WHEN YOU WERE LITTLE AND I'M ALREADY EIGHT!
I'LL PROBABLY NEVER HAVE POWERS.
YES, YOU WILL, RACH. YOUR MOM AND DAD ARE BOTH MUTANTS, AREN'T THEY?
MOST MUTANTS DON'T MANIFEST THEIR POWERS UNTIL ADOLESCENCE.
THAT'S WHAT MOM SAYS, BUT YOU--
I'M A FREAK, RACH. JUST ASK MY DAD. HE'S SCARED OF ME. HE WISHES MY POWERS WOULD JUST... GO AWAY...!
THOOM!
WHO IS SHE? THEY BOTH SEEM IMPERVIOUS TO THE SENTINEL'S BLAST. IS HE SHIELDING HER-- OR SHE, HIM?
SHE'S HIS CONSTRUCT, DOG! WHOEVER SHE IS, SHE ACTS AS HE REQUIRES.
FORGET HER! IT'S THE BOY WHO MUST BE STOPPED!
GIMME A BREAK. YOU'RE NOT A FREAK. BUT I KNOW ABOUT PARENTS.
SOMETIMES I THINK MY PARENTS DON'T WANT ME GETTING POWERS, EITHER.
BUT, IT'S JUST THAT IT'S GETTING DANGEROUS TO BE A MUTANT NOW, FRANK. PEOPLE ARE TAUGHT TO BE AFRAID OF US... OF WHAT WE CAN DO...!

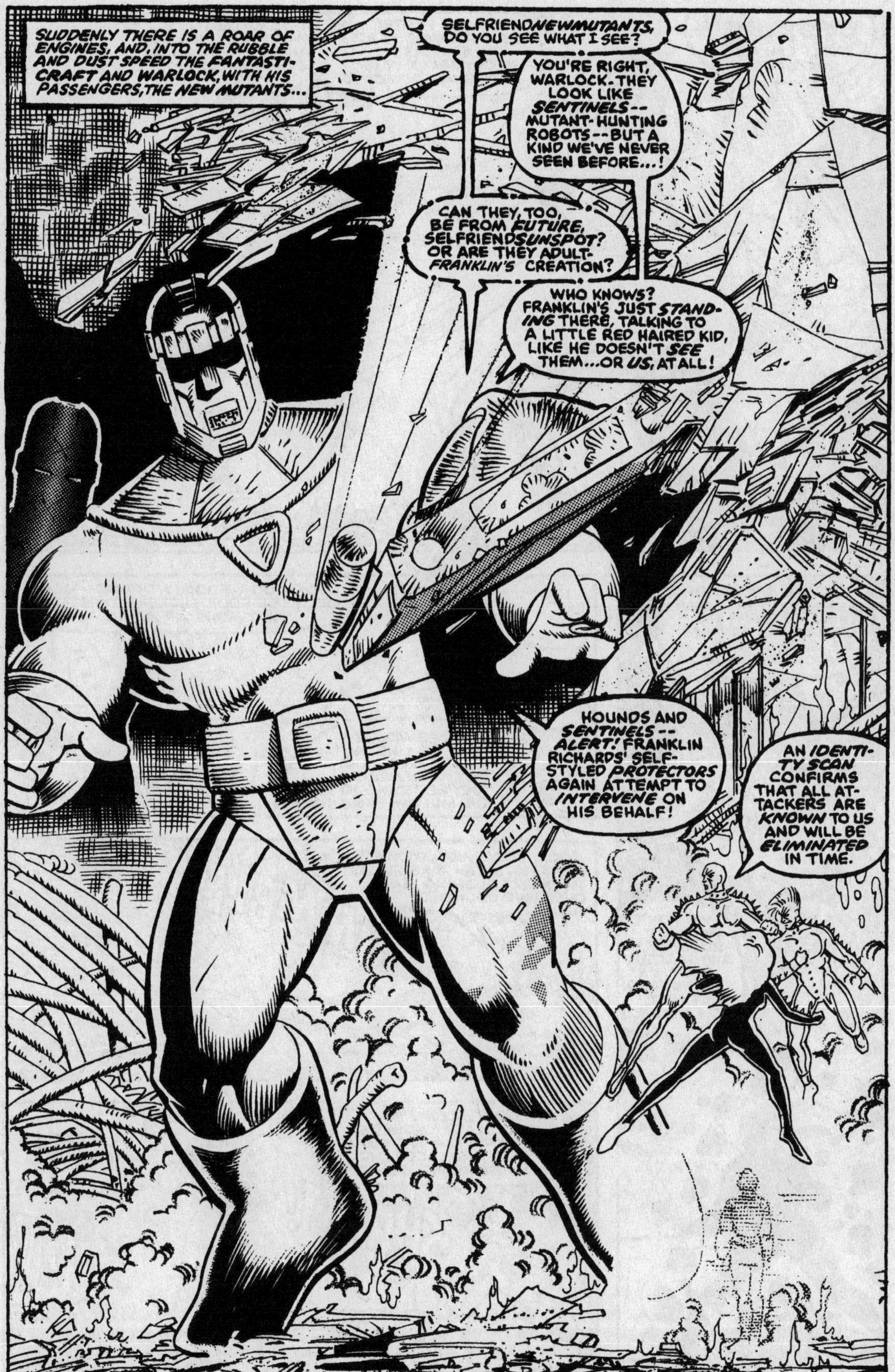
SUDDENLY THERE IS A ROAR OF ENGINES, AND, INTO THE RUBBLE AND DUST SPEED THE FANTASTI-CRAFT AND WARLOCK, WITH HIS PASSENGERS, THE NEW MUTANTS...
SELFRIENDNEWMUTANTS, DO YOU SEE WHAT I SEE?
YOU'RE RIGHT, WARLOCK. THEY LOOK LIKE SENTINELS-- MUTANT-HUNTING ROBOTS--BUT A KIND WE'VE NEVER SEEN BEFORE...!
CAN THEY, TOO, BE FROM FUTURE, SELFRIENDSUNSPOT? OR ARE THEY ADULT-FRANKLIN'S CREATION?
WHO KNOWS? FRANKLIN'S JUST STANDING THERE, TALKING TO A LITTLE RED HAIRED KID, LIKE HE DOESN'T SEE THEM...OR US, AT ALL!
HOUNDS AND SENTINELS-- ALERT! FRANKLIN RICHARDS' SELF-STYLED PROTECTORS AGAIN ATTEMPT TO INTERVENE ON HIS BEHALF!
AN IDENTITY SCAN CONFIRMS THAT ALL ATTACKERS ARE KNOWN TO US AND WILL BE ELIMINATED IN TIME.

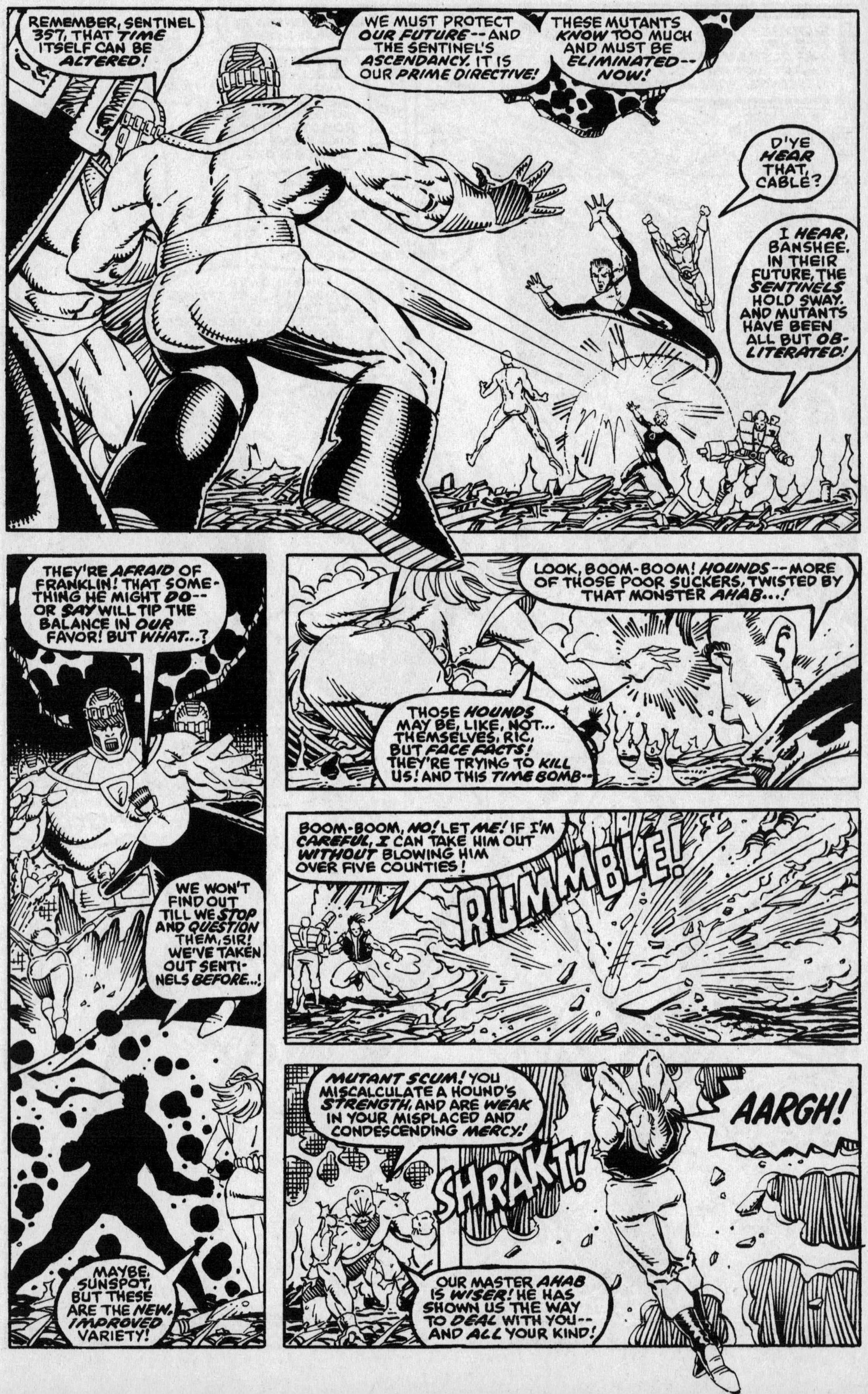
REMEMBER, SENTINEL 357, THAT TIME ITSELF CAN BE ALTERED!
WE MUST PROTECT OUR FUTURE--AND THE SENTINEL'S ASCENDANCY. IT IS OUR PRIME DIRECTIVE!
THESE MUTANTS KNOW TOO MUCH AND MUST BE ELIMINATED--NOW!
D'YE HEAR THAT, CABLE?
I HEAR, BANSHEE. IN THEIR FUTURE, THE SENTINELS HOLD SWAY. AND MUTANTS HAVE BEEN ALL BUT OBLITERATED!
THEY'RE AFRAID OF FRANKLIN! THAT SOMETHING HE MIGHT DO--OR SAY WILL TIP THE BALANCE IN OUR FAVOR! BUT WHAT...?
WE WON'T FIND OUT TILL WE STOP AND QUESTION THEM, SIR! WE'VE TAKEN OUT SENTINELS BEFORE...!
MAYBE, SUNSPOT, BUT THESE ARE THE NEW, IMPROVED VARIETY!
LOOK, BOOM-BOOM! HOUNDS--MORE OF THOSE POOR SUCKERS, TWISTED BY THAT MONSTER AHAB...!
THOSE HOUNDS MAY BE, LIKE, NOT... THEMSELVES, RIC, BUT FACE FACTS! THEY'RE TRYING TO KILL US! AND THIS TIME BOMB--
BOOM-BOOM, NO! LET ME! IF I'M CAREFUL, I CAN TAKE HIM OUT WITHOUT BLOWING HIM OVER FIVE COUNTIES!
RUMMBLE!
MUTANT SCUM! YOU MISCALCULATE A HOUND'S STRENGTH, AND ARE WEAK IN YOUR MISPLACED AND CONDESCENDING MERCY!
AARGH!
SHRAKT!
OUR MASTER AHAB IS WISER! HE HAS SHOWN US THE WAY TO DEAL WITH YOU--AND ALL YOUR KIND!

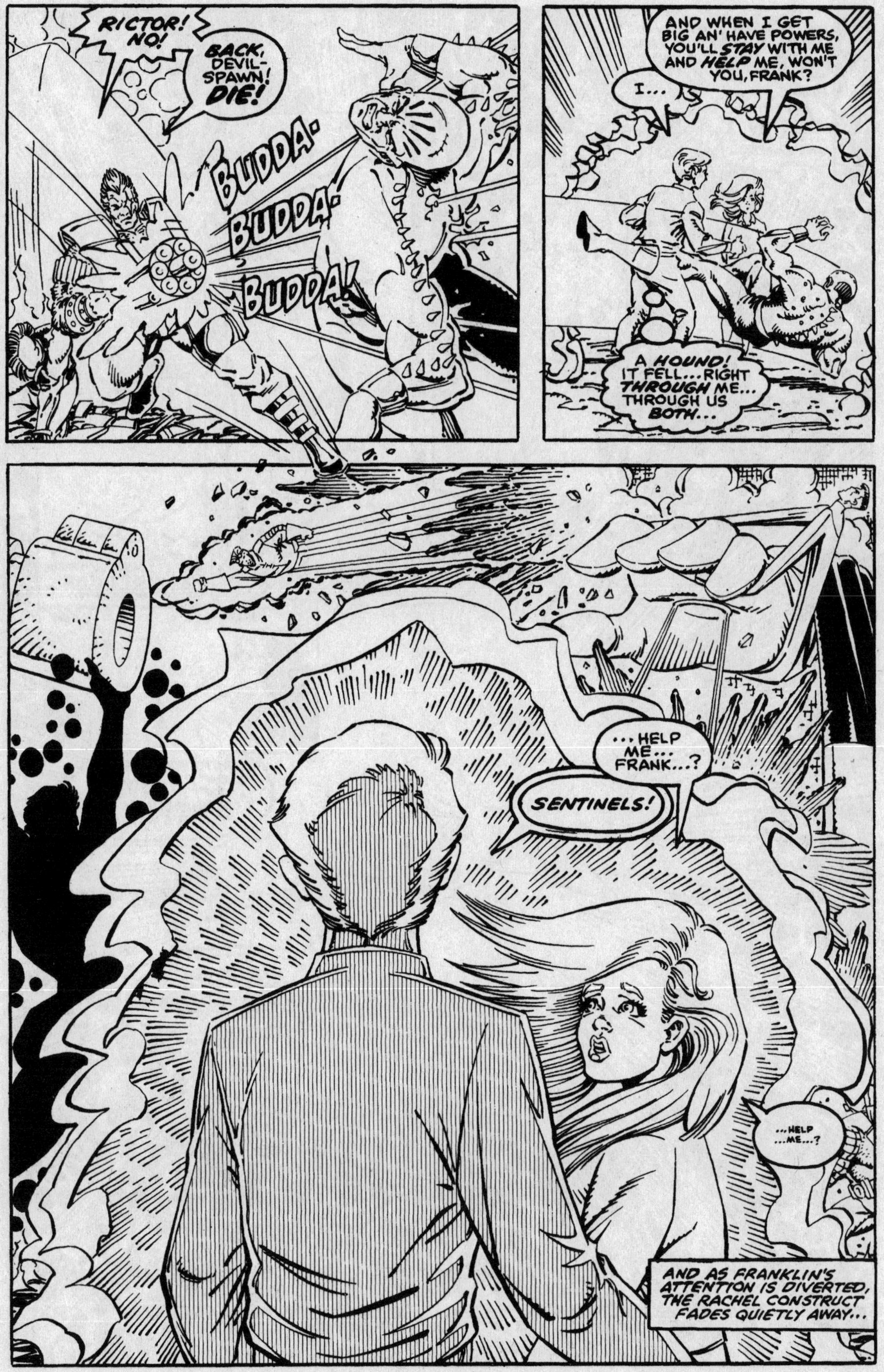
RICTOR! NO!
BACK, DEVIL-SPAWN! DIE!
BUDDA-
BUDDA-
BUDDA!
AND WHEN I GET BIG AN' HAVE POWERS, YOU'LL STAY WITH ME AND HELP ME, WON'T YOU, FRANK?
I...
A HOUND! IT FELL... RIGHT THROUGH ME... THROUGH US BOTH...
...HELP ME... FRANK...?
SENTINELS!
...HELP ...ME...?
AND AS FRANKLIN'S ATTENTION IS DIVERTED, THE RACHEL CONSTRUCT FADES QUIETLY AWAY...

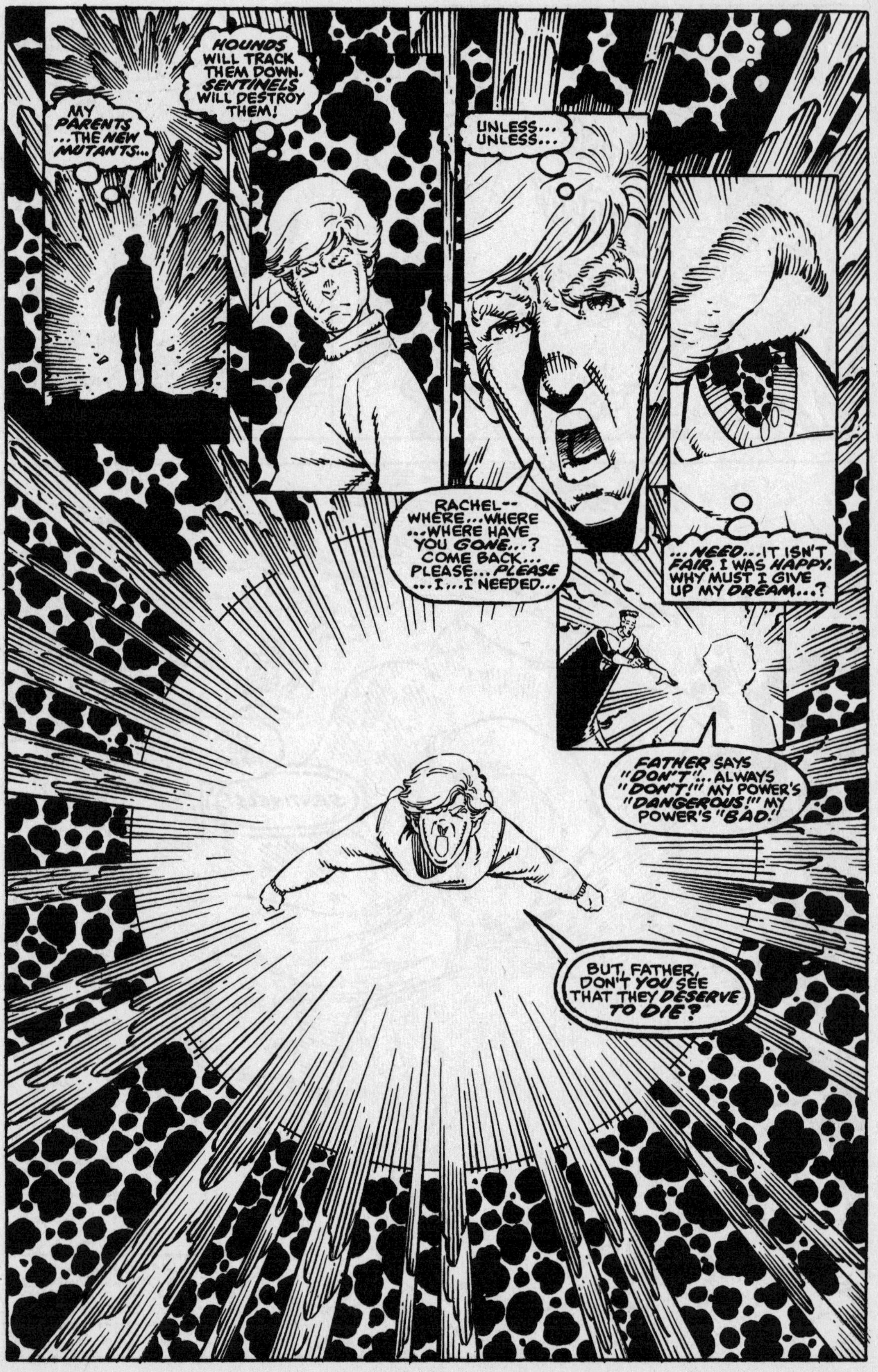
MY PARENTS ...THE NEW MUTANTS...
HOUNDS WILL TRACK THEM DOWN. SENTINELS WILL DESTROY THEM!
UNLESS... UNLESS...
RACHEL-- WHERE...WHERE ...WHERE HAVE YOU GONE...? COME BACK... PLEASE...PLEASE ...I...I NEEDED...
...NEED...IT ISN'T FAIR. I WAS HAPPY. WHY MUST I GIVE UP MY DREAM...?
FATHER SAYS "DON'T"...ALWAYS "DON'T!" MY POWER'S "DANGEROUS!" MY POWER'S "BAD."
BUT, FATHER, DON'T YOU SEE THAT THEY DESERVE TO DIE?

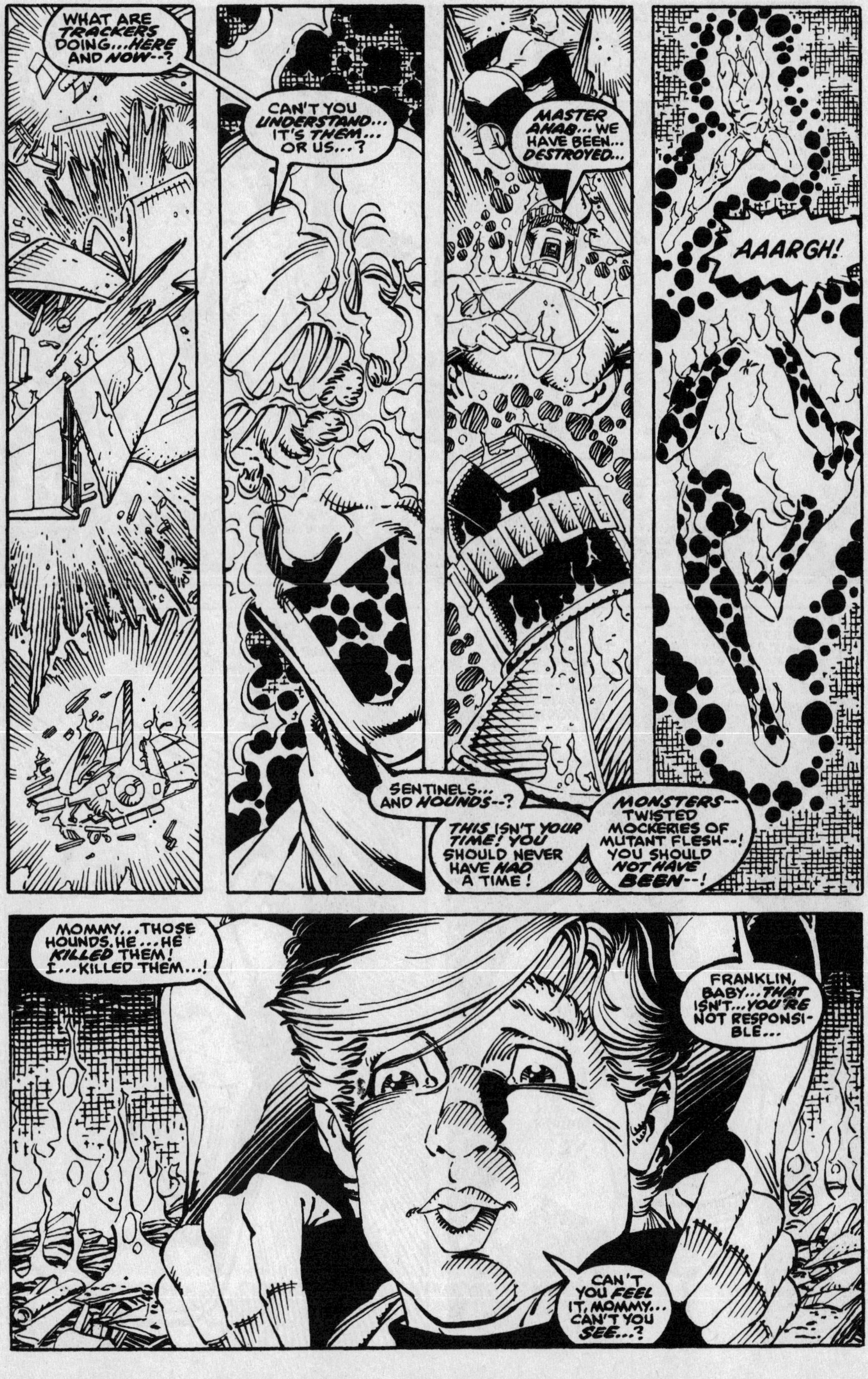
WHAT ARE TRACKERS DOING...HERE AND NOW--?
CAN'T YOU UNDERSTAND... IT'S THEM... OR US...?
MASTER AHAB... WE HAVE BEEN... DESTROYED...
AAARGH!
SENTINELS... AND HOUNDS--?
THIS ISN'T YOUR TIME! YOU SHOULD NEVER HAVE HAD A TIME!
MONSTERS-- TWISTED MOCKERIES OF MUTANT FLESH--! YOU SHOULD NOT HAVE BEEN--!
MOMMY...THOSE HOUNDS. HE...HE KILLED THEM! I...KILLED THEM...!
FRANKLIN, BABY...THAT ISN'T...YOU'RE NOT RESPONSIBLE...
CAN'T YOU FEEL IT, MOMMY... CAN'T YOU SEE...?

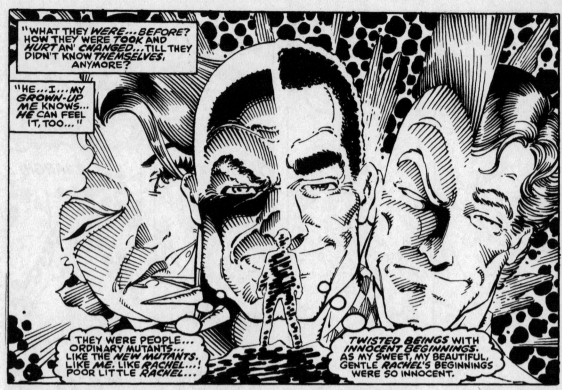

"WHAT THEY *WERE*...BEFORE? HOW THEY WERE *TOOK* AND *HURT* AN' *CHANGED*...TILL THEY DIDN'T KNOW *THEMSELVES*, ANYMORE?

"HE...I...MY *GROWN-UP* ME KNOWS... *HE* CAN FEEL IT, TOO..."

THEY WERE PEOPLE... ORDINARY MUTANTS... LIKE THE *NEW MUTANTS*. LIKE *ME*. LIKE *RACHEL*...! POOR LITTLE *RACHEL*...

TWISTED BEINGS WITH *INNOCENT BEGINNINGS.* AS MY SWEET, MY BEAUTIFUL, *GENTLE RACHEL'S* BEGINNINGS WERE SO INNOCENT.

AHAB STOLE THEIR SOULS, LIKE HE STOLE *HERS*... BUT AM *I* ANY BETTER... *I*, WHO *KNOW* WHAT THEY HAVE BEEN...WHAT THEY *COULD* BE...?

I CAME HERE SEARCHING FOR THE *INNOCENCE* IN MYSELF. AND INSTEAD, I HAVE COMMITTED THE *ULTIMATE BETRAYAL*...

...THE *DESTRUCTION*... OF THE *INNOCENCE* I CAME SO *FAR* TO FIND.

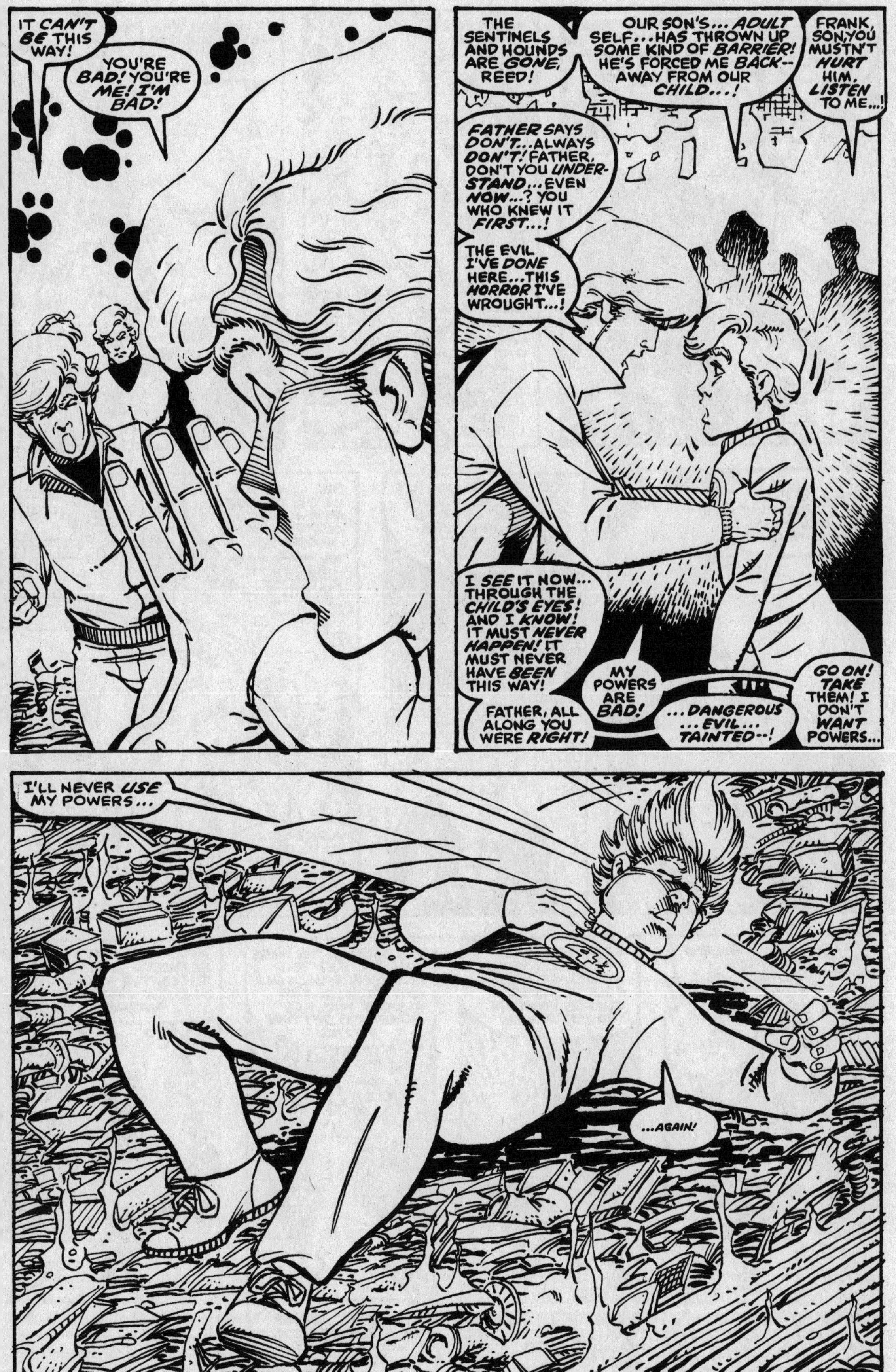
IT CAN'T BE THIS WAY!
YOU'RE BAD! YOU'RE ME! I'M BAD!
THE SENTINELS AND HOUNDS ARE GONE, REED!
OUR SON'S... ADULT SELF... HAS THROWN UP SOME KIND OF BARRIER! HE'S FORCED ME BACK-- AWAY FROM OUR CHILD...!
FRANK, SON, YOU MUSTN'T HURT HIM. LISTEN TO ME...!
FATHER SAYS DON'T... ALWAYS DON'T! FATHER, DON'T YOU UNDERSTAND... EVEN NOW...? YOU WHO KNEW IT FIRST...!
THE EVIL I'VE DONE HERE... THIS HORROR I'VE WROUGHT...!
I SEE IT NOW... THROUGH THE CHILD'S EYES! AND I KNOW! IT MUST NEVER HAPPEN! IT MUST NEVER HAVE BEEN THIS WAY!
FATHER, ALL ALONG YOU WERE RIGHT!
MY POWERS ARE BAD!
...DANGEROUS ...EVIL... TAINTED--!
GO ON! TAKE THEM! I DON'T WANT POWERS...
I'LL NEVER USE MY POWERS...
...AGAIN!

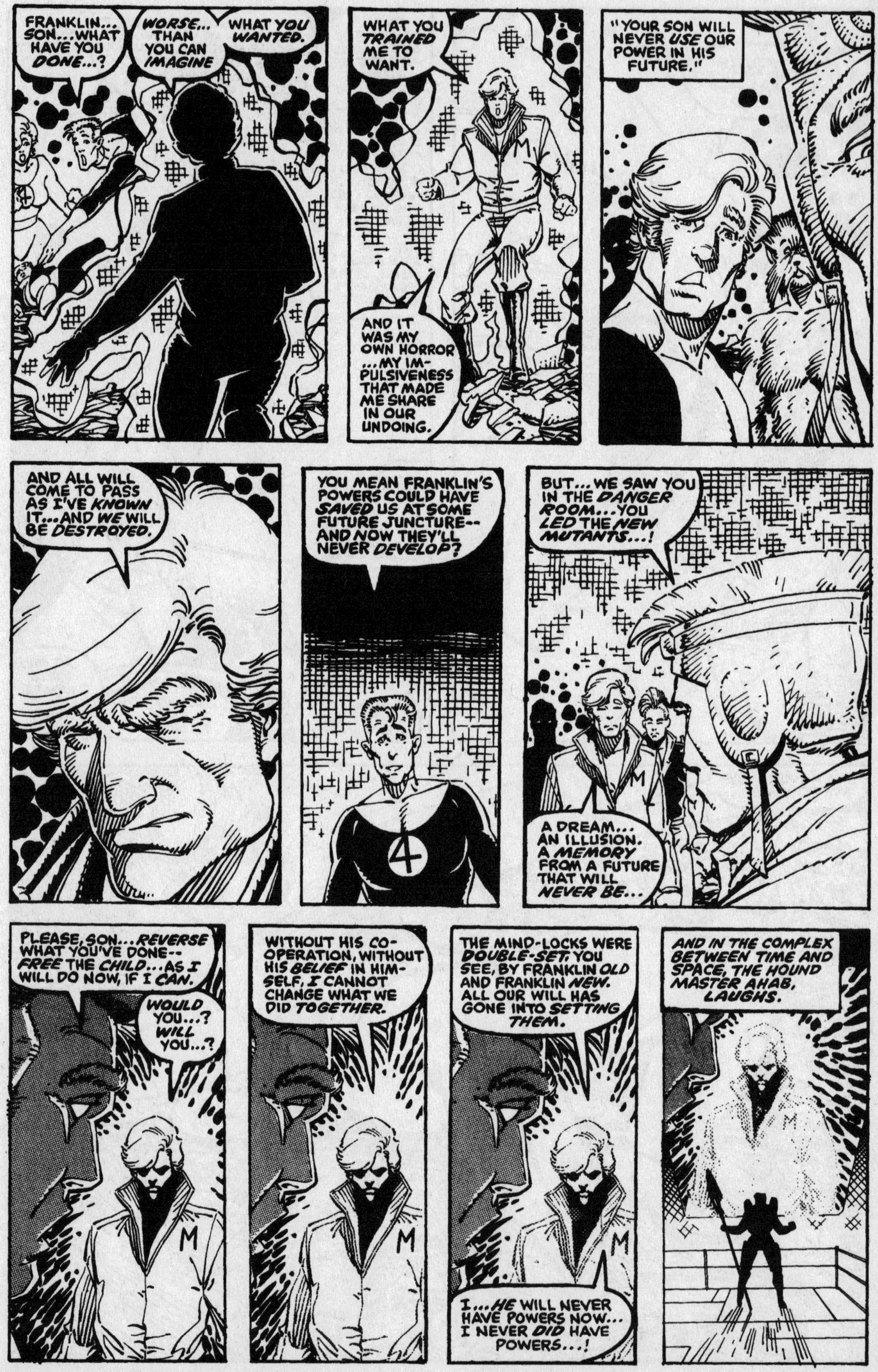
FRANKLIN... SON... WHAT HAVE YOU DONE...?
WORSE... THAN YOU CAN IMAGINE
WHAT YOU WANTED.
WHAT YOU TRAINED ME TO WANT.
AND IT WAS MY OWN HORROR ...MY IMPULSIVENESS THAT MADE ME SHARE IN OUR UNDOING.
"YOUR SON WILL NEVER USE OUR POWER IN HIS FUTURE."
AND ALL WILL COME TO PASS AS I'VE KNOWN IT...AND WE WILL BE DESTROYED.
YOU MEAN FRANKLIN'S POWERS COULD HAVE SAVED US AT SOME FUTURE JUNCTURE-- AND NOW THEY'LL NEVER DEVELOP?
BUT... WE SAW YOU IN THE DANGER ROOM... YOU LED THE NEW MUTANTS...!
A DREAM... AN ILLUSION. A MEMORY FROM A FUTURE THAT WILL NEVER BE...
PLEASE, SON... REVERSE WHAT YOU'VE DONE-- FREE THE CHILD... AS I WILL DO NOW, IF I CAN.
WOULD YOU...? WILL YOU...?
WITHOUT HIS CO-OPERATION, WITHOUT HIS BELIEF IN HIMSELF, I CANNOT CHANGE WHAT WE DID TOGETHER.
THE MIND-LOCKS WERE DOUBLE-SET, YOU SEE, BY FRANKLIN OLD AND FRANKLIN NEW. ALL OUR WILL HAS GONE INTO SETTING THEM.
I...HE WILL NEVER HAVE POWERS NOW... I NEVER DID HAVE POWERS...!
AND IN THE COMPLEX BETWEEN TIME AND SPACE, THE HOUND MASTER AHAB, LAUGHS.

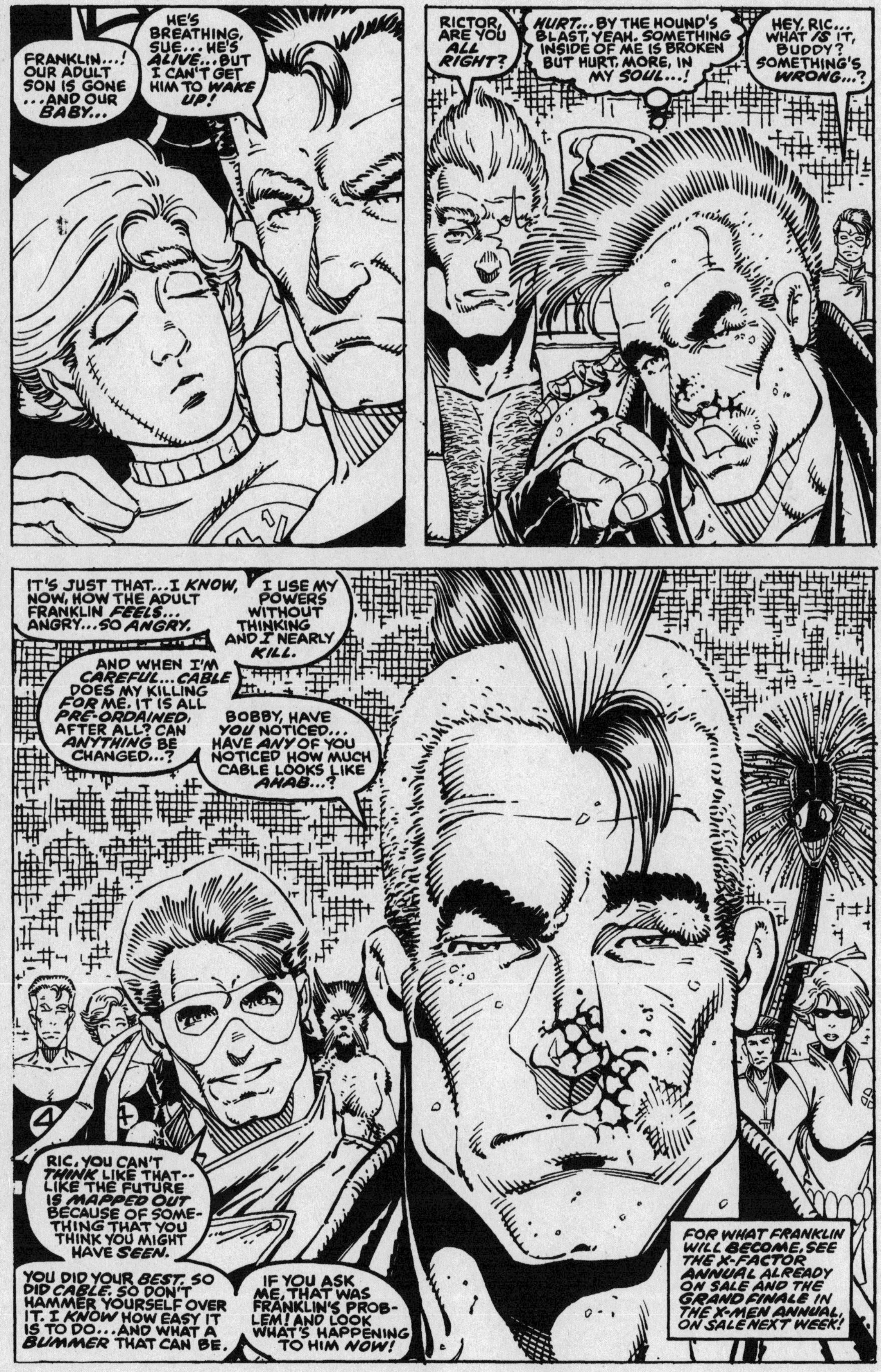
FRANKLIN...! OUR ADULT SON IS GONE ...AND OUR BABY...
HE'S BREATHING, SUE... HE'S ALIVE...BUT I CAN'T GET HIM TO WAKE UP!
RICTOR, ARE YOU ALL RIGHT?
HURT...BY THE HOUND'S BLAST, YEAH. SOMETHING INSIDE OF ME IS BROKEN BUT HURT, MORE, IN MY SOUL...!
HEY, RIC... WHAT IS IT, BUDDY? SOMETHING'S WRONG...?
IT'S JUST THAT...I KNOW, NOW, HOW THE ADULT FRANKLIN FEELS... ANGRY...SO ANGRY.
I USE MY POWERS WITHOUT THINKING AND I NEARLY KILL.
AND WHEN I'M CAREFUL...CABLE DOES MY KILLING FOR ME. IT IS ALL PRE-ORDAINED, AFTER ALL? CAN ANYTHING BE CHANGED...?
BOBBY, HAVE YOU NOTICED... HAVE ANY OF YOU NOTICED HOW MUCH CABLE LOOKS LIKE AHAB...?
RIC, YOU CAN'T THINK LIKE THAT-- LIKE THE FUTURE IS MAPPED OUT BECAUSE OF SOMETHING THAT YOU THINK YOU MIGHT HAVE SEEN.
YOU DID YOUR BEST. SO DID CABLE. SO DON'T HAMMER YOURSELF OVER IT. I KNOW HOW EASY IT IS TO DO...AND WHAT A BUMMER THAT CAN BE.
IF YOU ASK ME, THAT WAS FRANKLIN'S PROBLEM! AND LOOK WHAT'S HAPPENING TO HIM NOW!
FOR WHAT FRANKLIN WILL BECOME, SEE THE X-FACTOR ANNUAL ALREADY ON SALE AND THE GRAND FINALE IN THE X-MEN ANNUAL, ON SALE NEXT WEEK!

X-MEN

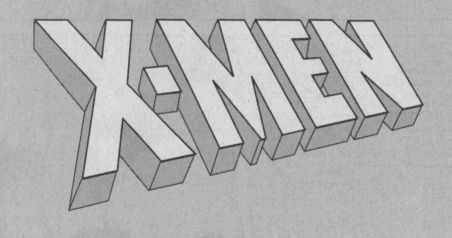

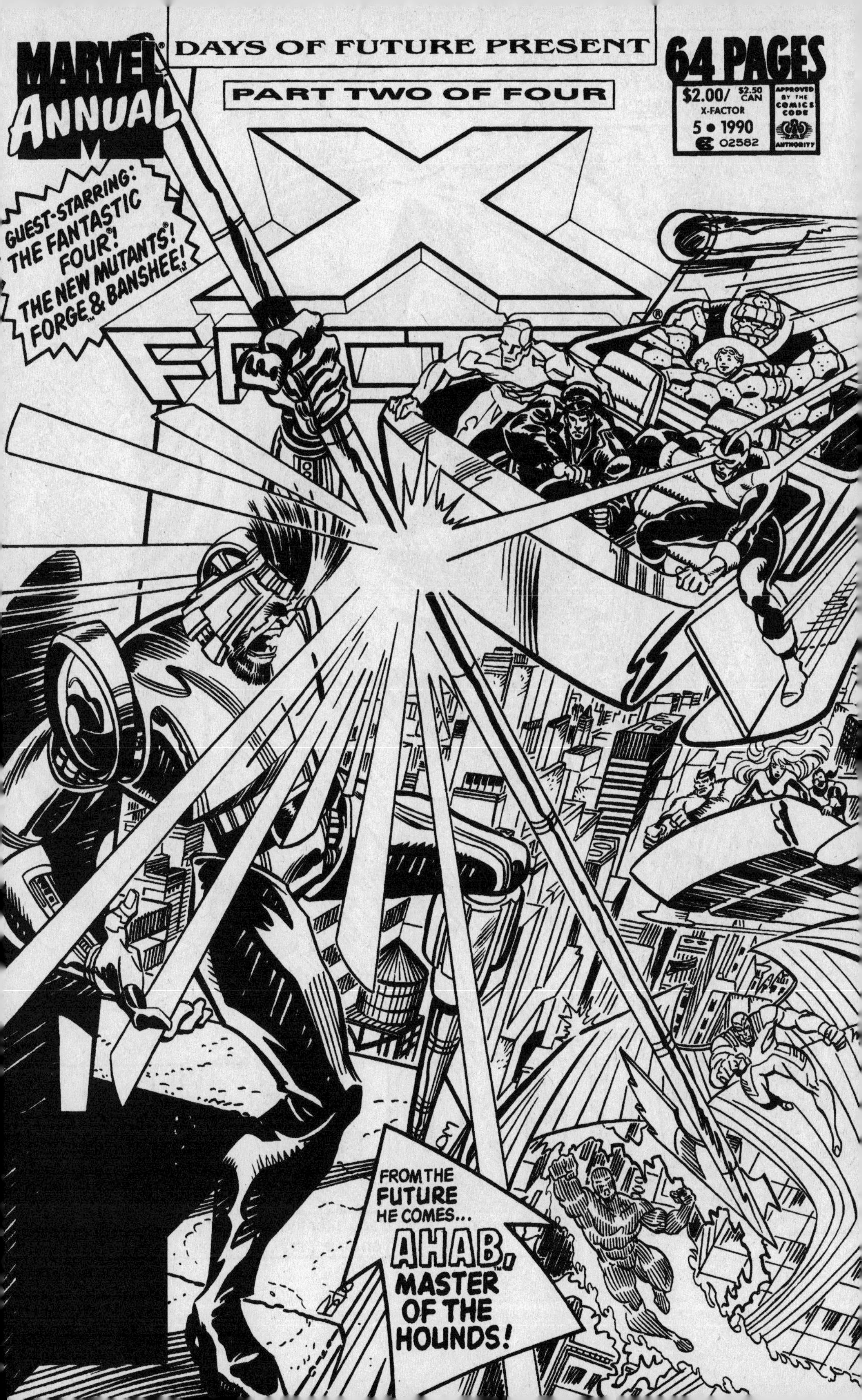
MARVEL ANNUAL
DAYS OF FUTURE PRESENT
PART TWO OF FOUR
64 PAGES
$2.00/ $2.50 CAN
X-FACTOR
5 • 1990
02582
APPROVED BY THE COMICS CODE AUTHORITY
X-FACTOR
GUEST-STARRING: THE FANTASTIC FOUR! THE NEW MUTANTS! FORGE & BANSHEE!
FROM THE FUTURE HE COMES...
AHAB, MASTER OF THE HOUNDS!

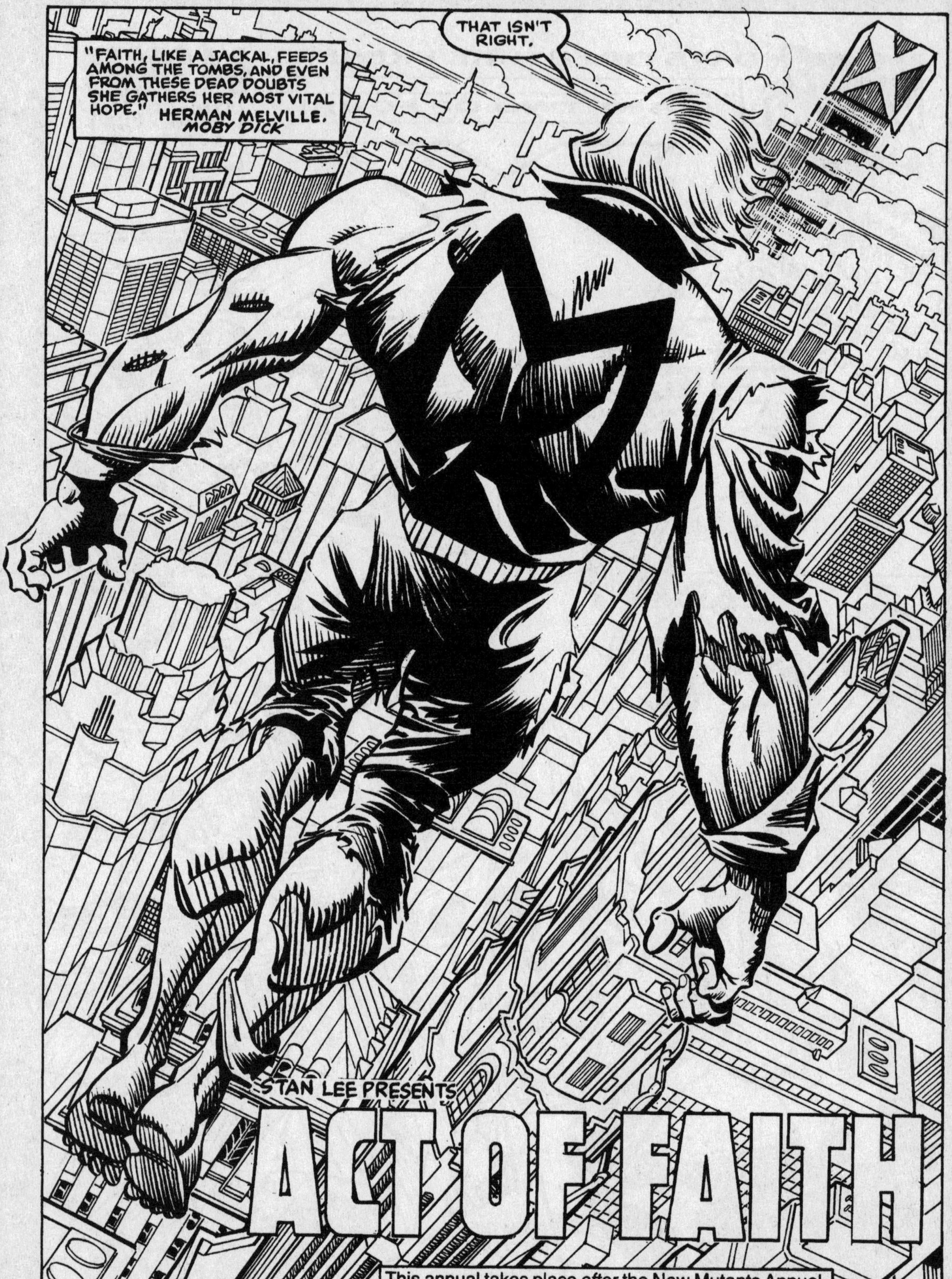
"FAITH, LIKE A JACKAL, FEEDS AMONG THE TOMBS, AND EVEN FROM THESE DEAD DOUBTS SHE GATHERS HER MOST VITAL HOPE." HERMAN MELVILLE. MOBY DICK
THAT ISN'T RIGHT.
STAN LEE PRESENTS
ACT OF FAITH
This annual takes place *after* the New Mutants Annual. Why is it on sale first? Go Figure!

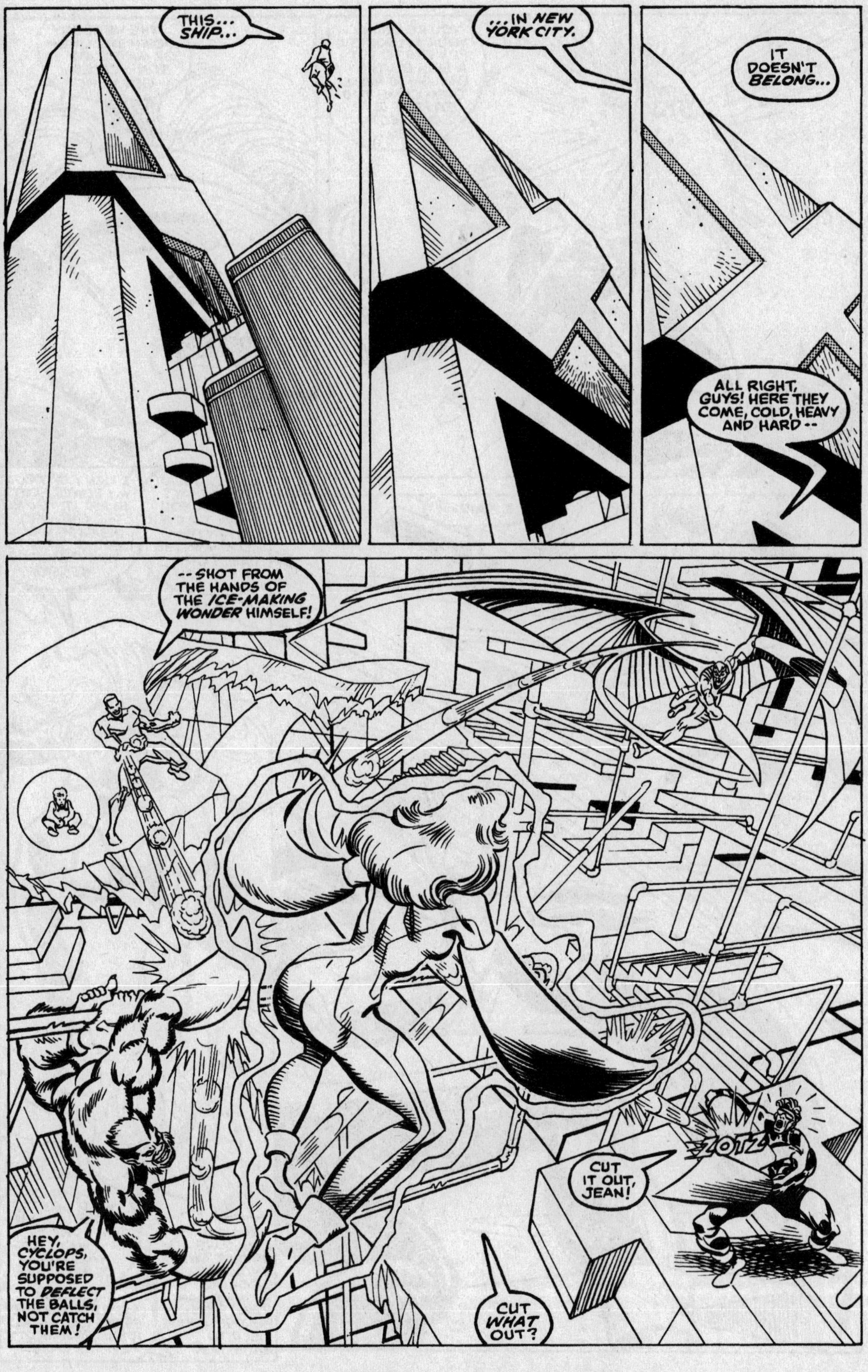
THIS... SHIP...
...IN NEW YORK CITY.
IT DOESN'T BELONG...
ALL RIGHT, GUYS! HERE THEY COME, COLD, HEAVY AND HARD --
-- SHOT FROM THE HANDS OF THE ICE-MAKING WONDER HIMSELF!
ZOTZ
CUT IT OUT, JEAN!
HEY, CYCLOPS, YOU'RE SUPPOSED TO DEFLECT THE BALLS, NOT CATCH THEM!
CUT WHAT OUT?

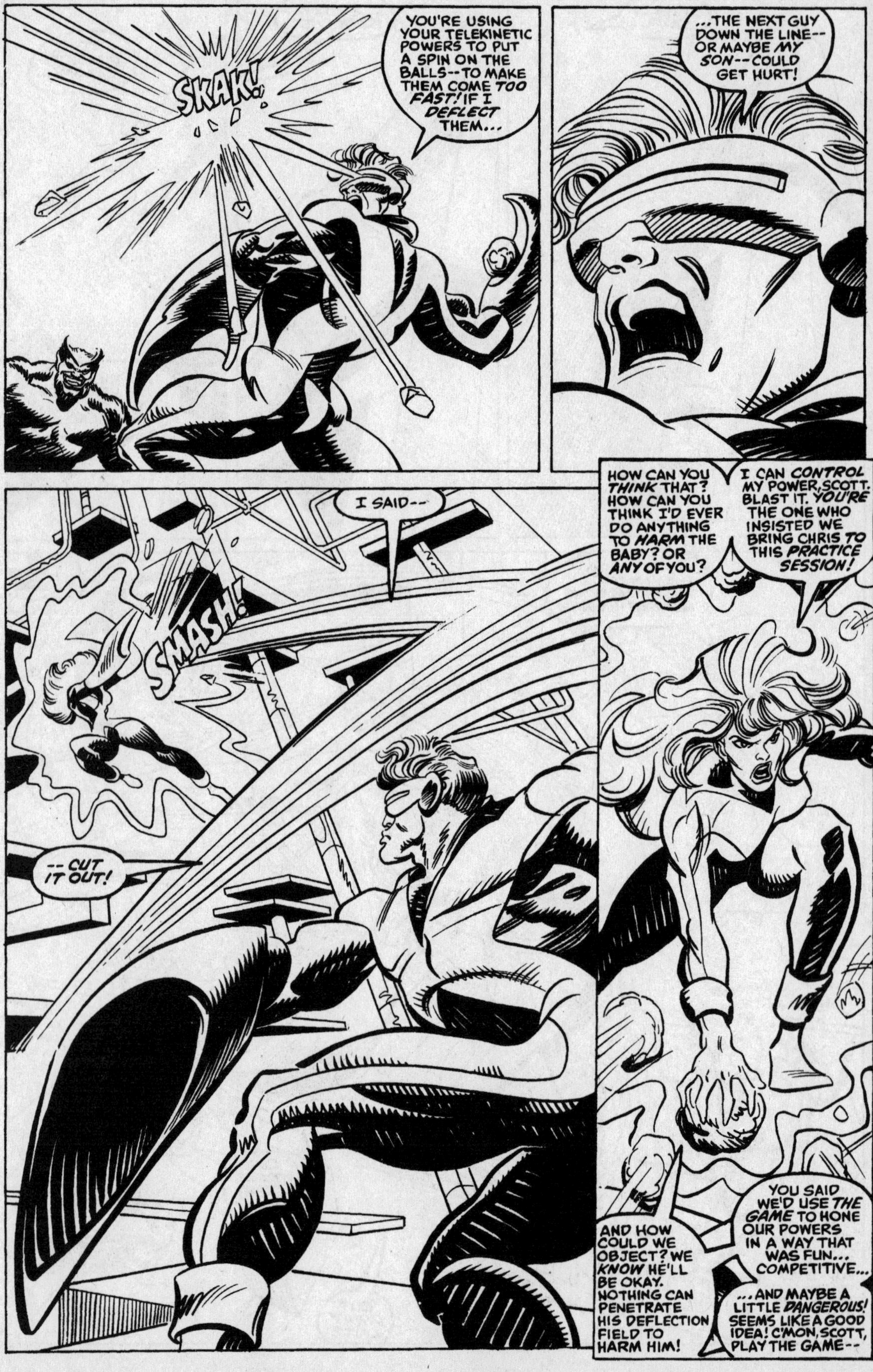

SKAK!
YOU'RE USING YOUR TELEKINETIC POWERS TO PUT A SPIN ON THE BALLS--TO MAKE THEM COME TOO FAST! IF I DEFLECT THEM...
...THE NEXT GUY DOWN THE LINE--OR MAYBE MY SON--COULD GET HURT!
I SAID--
SMASH!
--CUT IT OUT!
HOW CAN YOU THINK THAT? HOW CAN YOU THINK I'D EVER DO ANYTHING TO HARM THE BABY? OR ANY OF YOU?
I CAN CONTROL MY POWER, SCOTT. BLAST IT. YOU'RE THE ONE WHO INSISTED WE BRING CHRIS TO THIS PRACTICE SESSION!
AND HOW COULD WE OBJECT? WE KNOW HE'LL BE OKAY. NOTHING CAN PENETRATE HIS DEFLECTION FIELD TO HARM HIM!
YOU SAID WE'D USE THE GAME TO HONE OUR POWERS IN A WAY THAT WAS FUN... COMPETITIVE...
...AND MAYBE A LITTLE DANGEROUS! SEEMS LIKE A GOOD IDEA! C'MON, SCOTT, PLAY THE GAME--

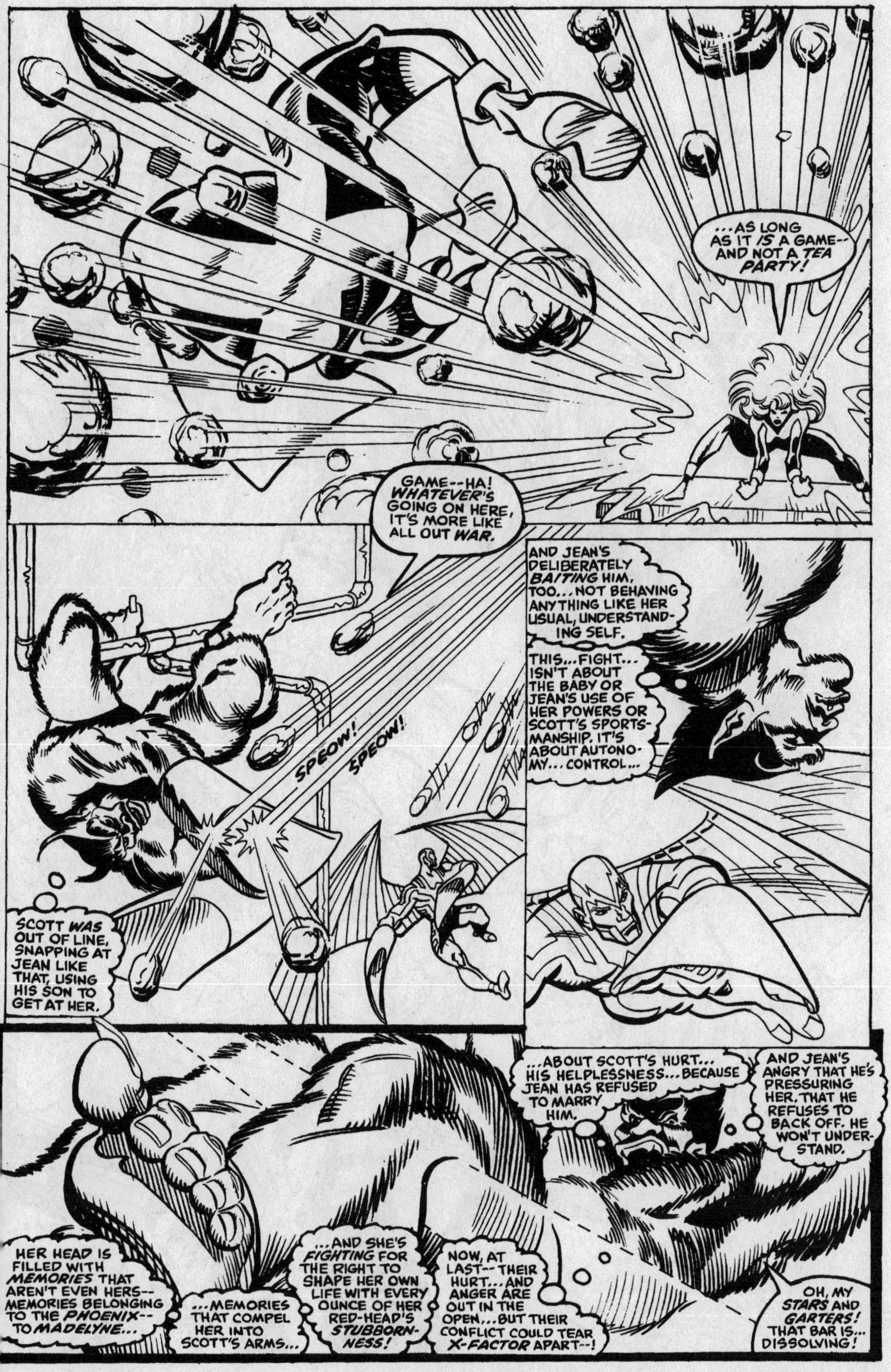
...AS LONG AS IT IS A GAME--AND NOT A TEA PARTY!
GAME--HA! WHATEVER'S GOING ON HERE, IT'S MORE LIKE ALL OUT WAR.
AND JEAN'S DELIBERATELY BAITING HIM, TOO... NOT BEHAVING ANYTHING LIKE HER USUAL, UNDERSTANDING SELF.
THIS... FIGHT... ISN'T ABOUT THE BABY OR JEAN'S USE OF HER POWERS OR SCOTT'S SPORTSMANSHIP. IT'S ABOUT AUTONOMY... CONTROL...
SPEOW! SPEOW!
SCOTT WAS OUT OF LINE, SNAPPING AT JEAN LIKE THAT, USING HIS SON TO GET AT HER.
...ABOUT SCOTT'S HURT... HIS HELPLESSNESS... BECAUSE JEAN HAS REFUSED TO MARRY HIM.
AND JEAN'S ANGRY THAT HE'S PRESSURING HER. THAT HE REFUSES TO BACK OFF. HE WON'T UNDERSTAND.
HER HEAD IS FILLED WITH MEMORIES THAT AREN'T EVEN HERS--MEMORIES BELONGING TO THE PHOENIX--TO MADELYNE...
...MEMORIES THAT COMPEL HER INTO SCOTT'S ARMS...
...AND SHE'S FIGHTING FOR THE RIGHT TO SHAPE HER OWN LIFE WITH EVERY OUNCE OF HER RED-HEAD'S STUBBORNNESS!
NOW, AT LAST--THEIR HURT... AND ANGER ARE OUT IN THE OPEN... BUT THEIR CONFLICT COULD TEAR X-FACTOR APART--!
OH, MY STARS AND GARTERS! THAT BAR IS... DISSOLVING!

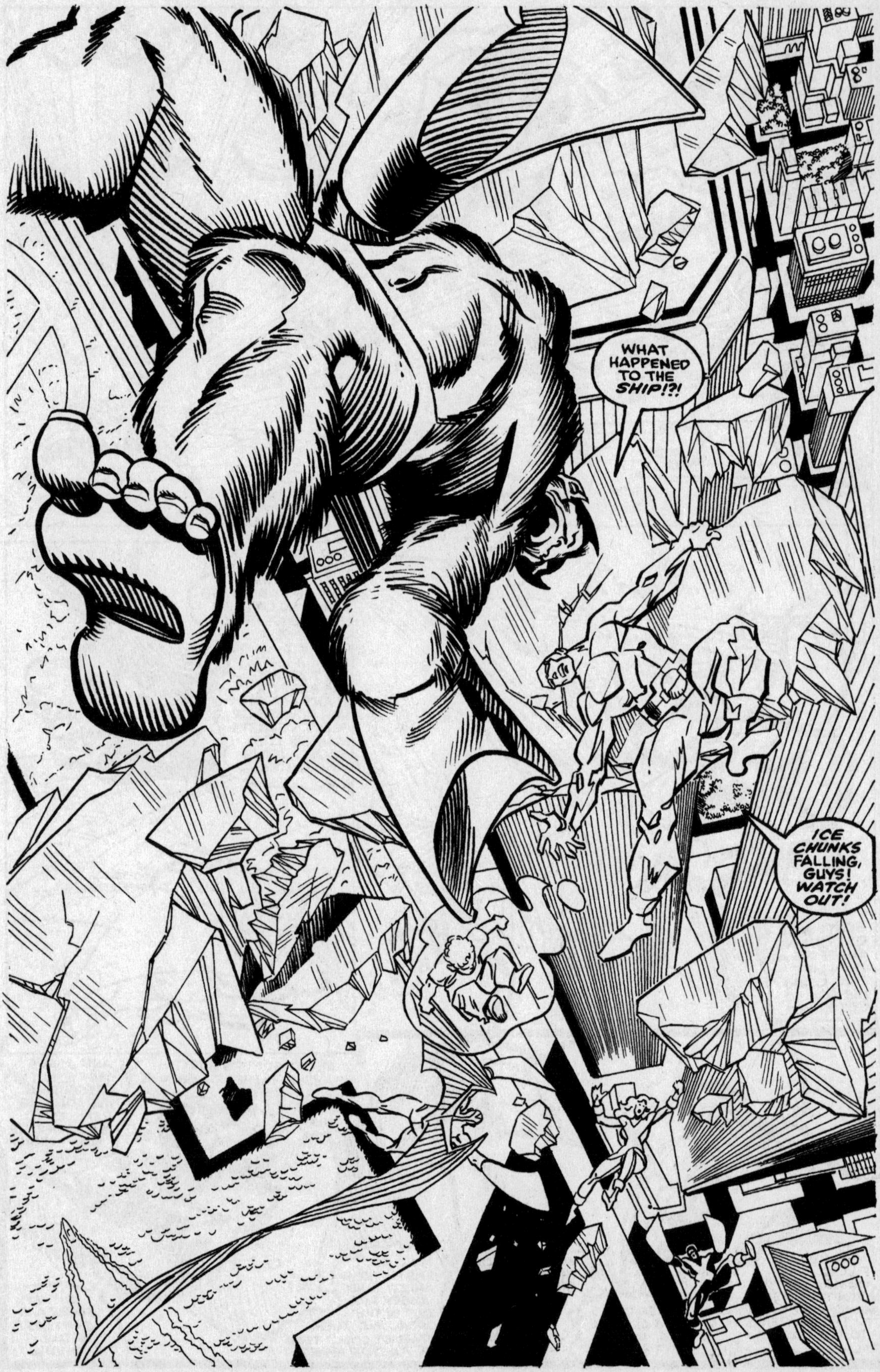
WHAT HAPPENED TO THE SHIP!?!
ICE CHUNKS FALLING, GUYS! WATCH OUT!

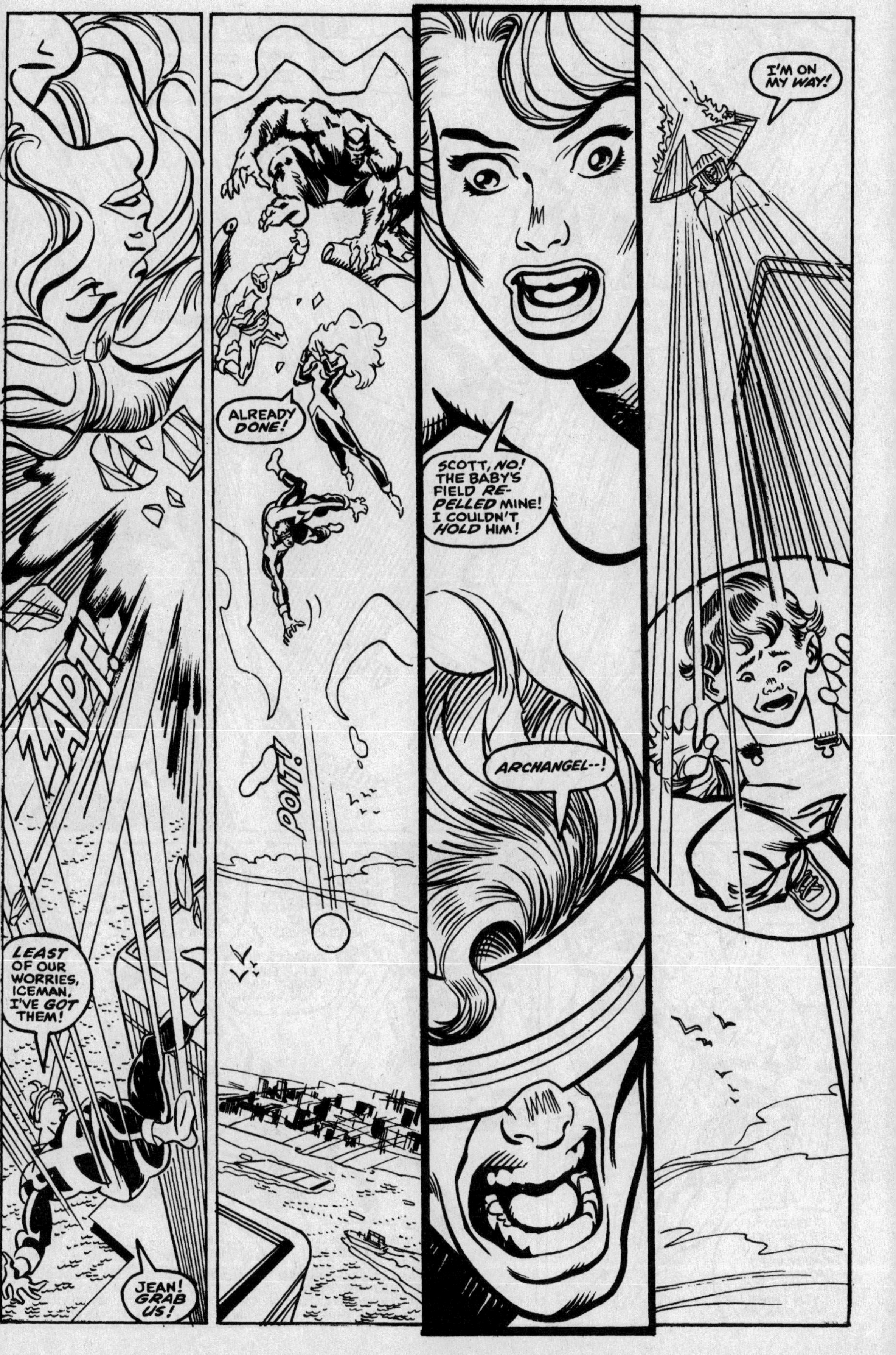
ZAPT!
LEAST OF OUR WORRIES, ICEMAN. I'VE GOT THEM!
JEAN! GRAB US!
ALREADY DONE!
POIT!
SCOTT, NO! THE BABY'S FIELD RE-PELLED MINE! I COULDN'T HOLD HIM!
ARCHANGEL--!
I'M ON MY WAY!

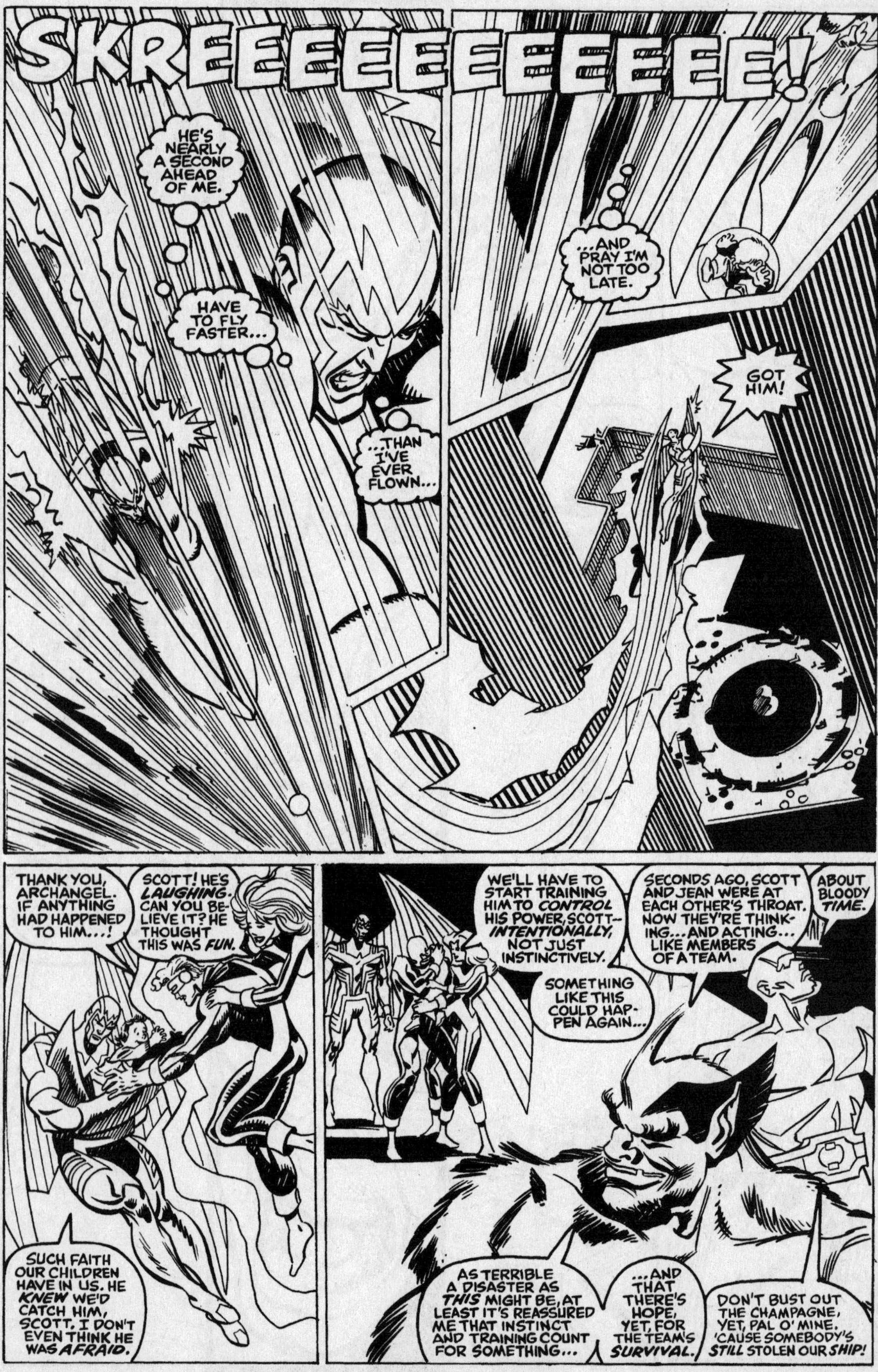
SKREEEEEEEEEEEE!
HE'S NEARLY A SECOND AHEAD OF ME.
HAVE TO FLY FASTER...
...THAN I'VE EVER FLOWN...
...AND PRAY I'M NOT TOO LATE.
GOT HIM!
THANK YOU, ARCHANGEL. IF ANYTHING HAD HAPPENED TO HIM...!
SCOTT! HE'S LAUGHING. CAN YOU BELIEVE IT? HE THOUGHT THIS WAS FUN.
SUCH FAITH OUR CHILDREN HAVE IN US. HE KNEW WE'D CATCH HIM, SCOTT. I DON'T EVEN THINK HE WAS AFRAID.
WE'LL HAVE TO START TRAINING HIM TO CONTROL HIS POWER, SCOTT-- INTENTIONALLY, NOT JUST INSTINCTIVELY.
SOMETHING LIKE THIS COULD HAPPEN AGAIN...
SECONDS AGO, SCOTT AND JEAN WERE AT EACH OTHER'S THROAT. NOW THEY'RE THINKING... AND ACTING... LIKE MEMBERS OF A TEAM.
ABOUT BLOODY TIME.
AS TERRIBLE A DISASTER AS THIS MIGHT BE, AT LEAST IT'S REASSURED ME THAT INSTINCT AND TRAINING COUNT FOR SOMETHING...
...AND THAT THERE'S HOPE, YET, FOR THE TEAM'S SURVIVAL.
DON'T BUST OUT THE CHAMPAGNE, YET, PAL O' MINE. 'CAUSE SOMEBODY'S STILL STOLEN OUR SHIP!

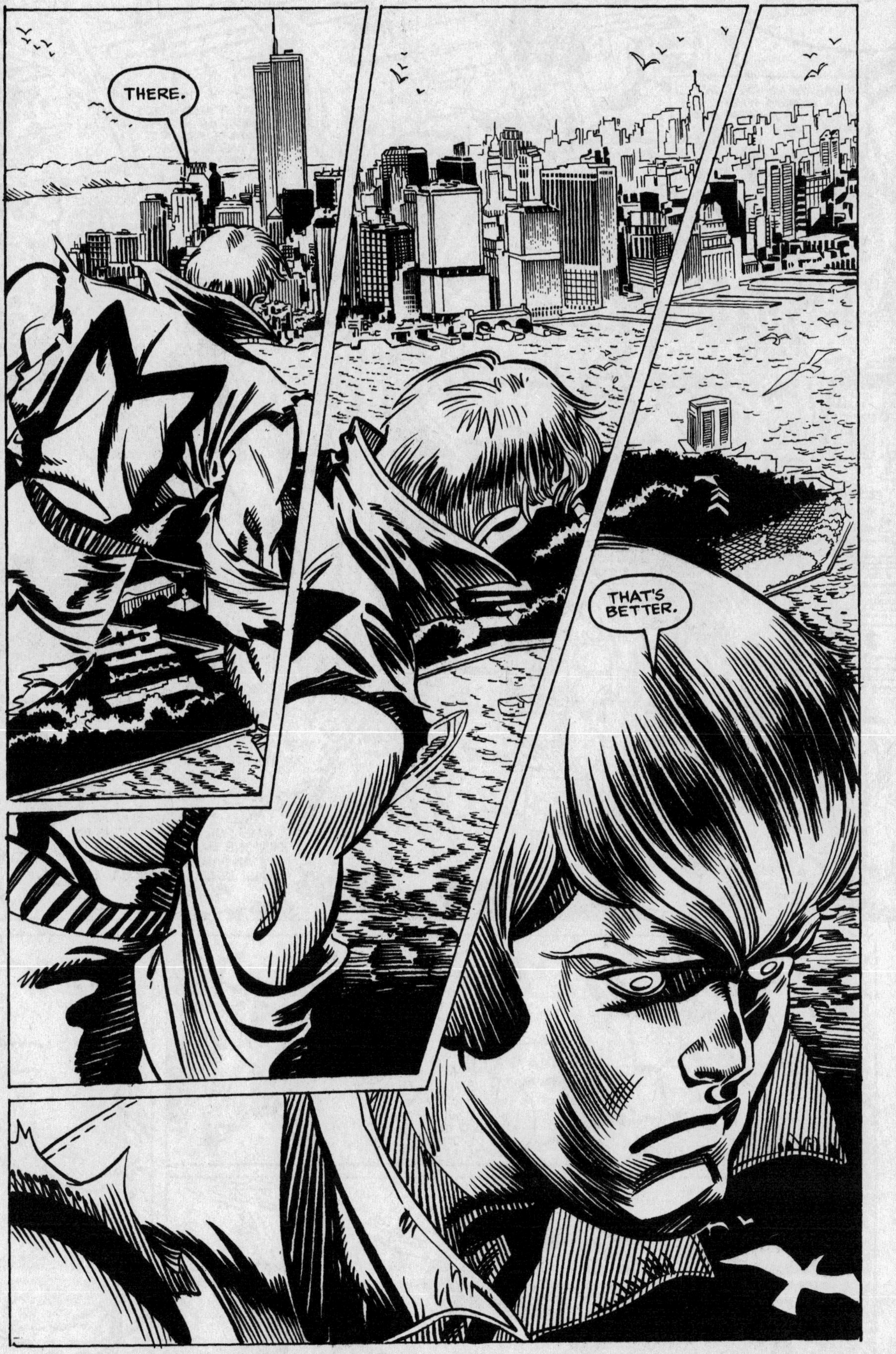
THERE.
THAT'S BETTER.

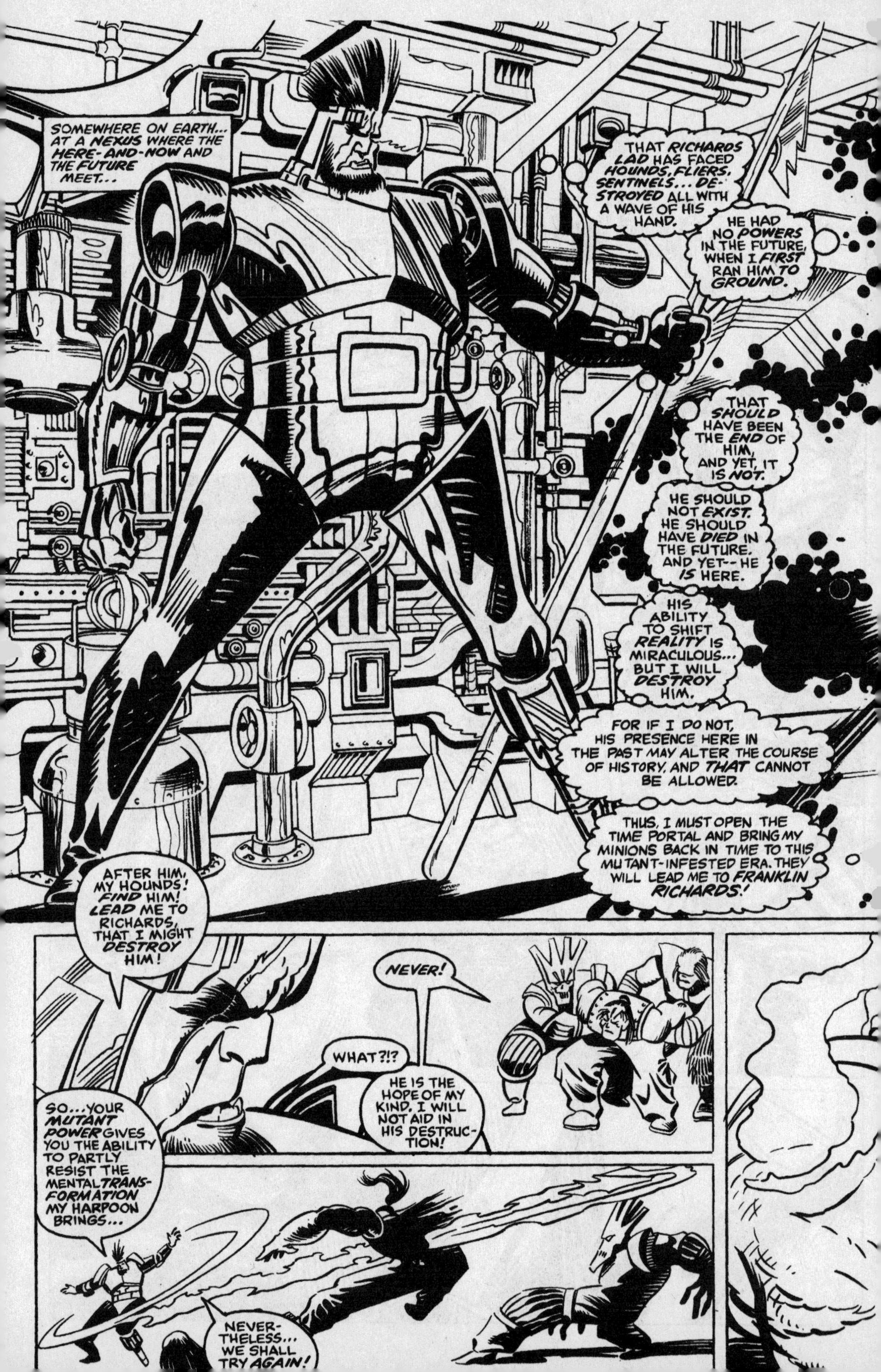
SOMEWHERE ON EARTH... AT A NEXUS WHERE THE HERE-AND-NOW AND THE FUTURE MEET...
THAT RICHARDS LAD HAS FACED HOUNDS, FLIERS, SENTINELS... DESTROYED ALL WITH A WAVE OF HIS HAND.
HE HAD NO POWERS IN THE FUTURE, WHEN I FIRST RAN HIM TO GROUND.
THAT SHOULD HAVE BEEN THE END OF HIM, AND YET, IT IS NOT.
HE SHOULD NOT EXIST. HE SHOULD HAVE DIED IN THE FUTURE. AND YET-- HE IS HERE.
HIS ABILITY TO SHIFT REALITY IS MIRACULOUS... BUT I WILL DESTROY HIM.
FOR IF I DO NOT, HIS PRESENCE HERE IN THE PAST MAY ALTER THE COURSE OF HISTORY, AND THAT CANNOT BE ALLOWED.
THUS, I MUST OPEN THE TIME PORTAL AND BRING MY MINIONS BACK IN TIME TO THIS MUTANT-INFESTED ERA. THEY WILL LEAD ME TO FRANKLIN RICHARDS!
AFTER HIM, MY HOUNDS! FIND HIM! LEAD ME TO RICHARDS, THAT I MIGHT DESTROY HIM!
NEVER!
WHAT?!?
HE IS THE HOPE OF MY KIND. I WILL NOT AID IN HIS DESTRUCTION!
SO... YOUR MUTANT POWER GIVES YOU THE ABILITY TO PARTLY RESIST THE MENTAL TRANSFORMATION MY HARPOON BRINGS...
NEVERTHELESS... WE SHALL TRY AGAIN!

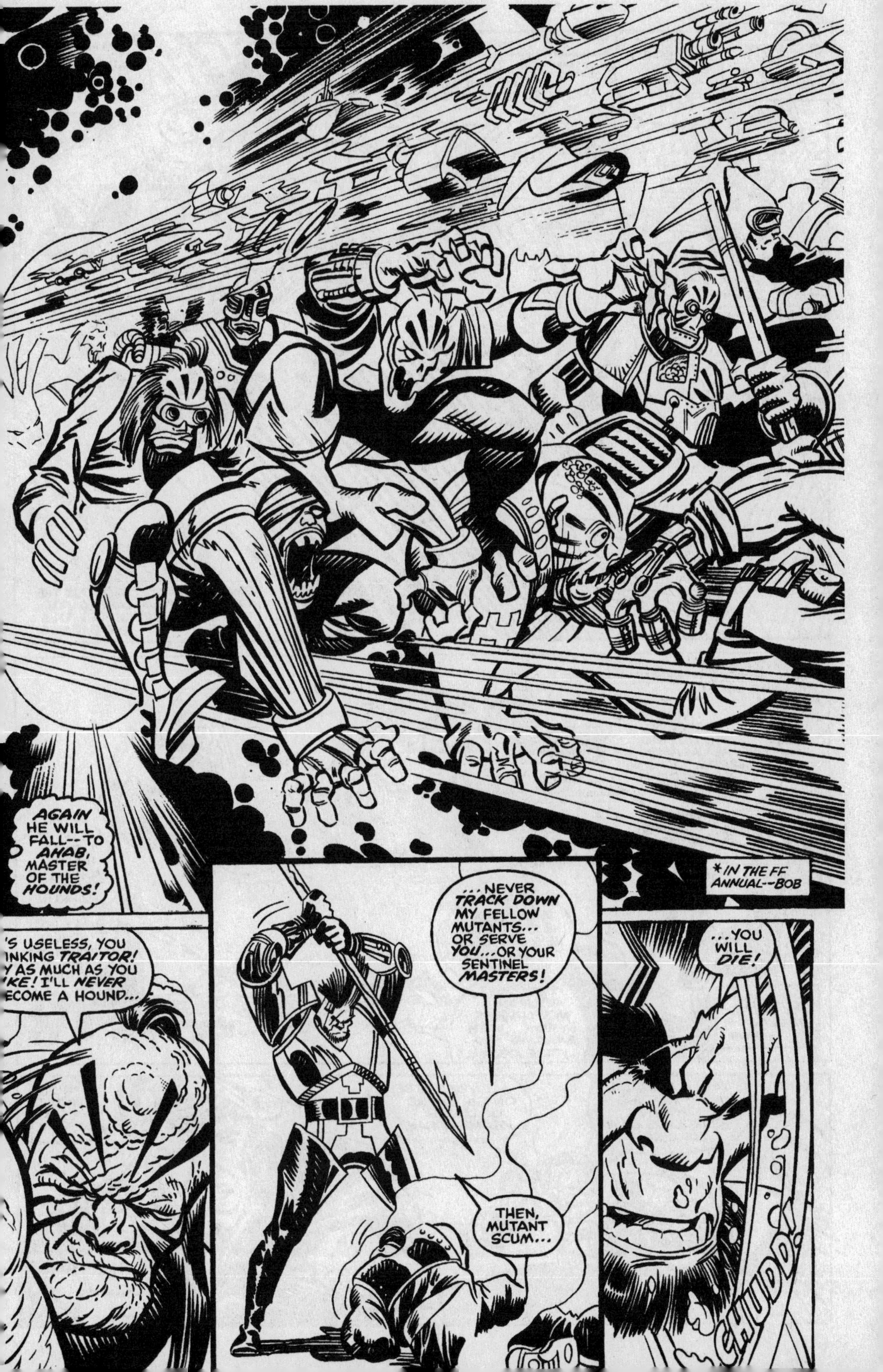
AGAIN HE WILL FALL--TO AHAB, MASTER OF THE HOUNDS!
*IN THE FF ANNUAL--BOB
'S USELESS, YOU INKING TRAITOR! Y AS MUCH AS YOU KE! I'LL NEVER ECOME A HOUND...
...NEVER TRACK DOWN MY FELLOW MUTANTS... OR SERVE YOU...OR YOUR SENTINEL MASTERS!
THEN, MUTANT SCUM...
...YOU WILL DIE!
CHUDD!

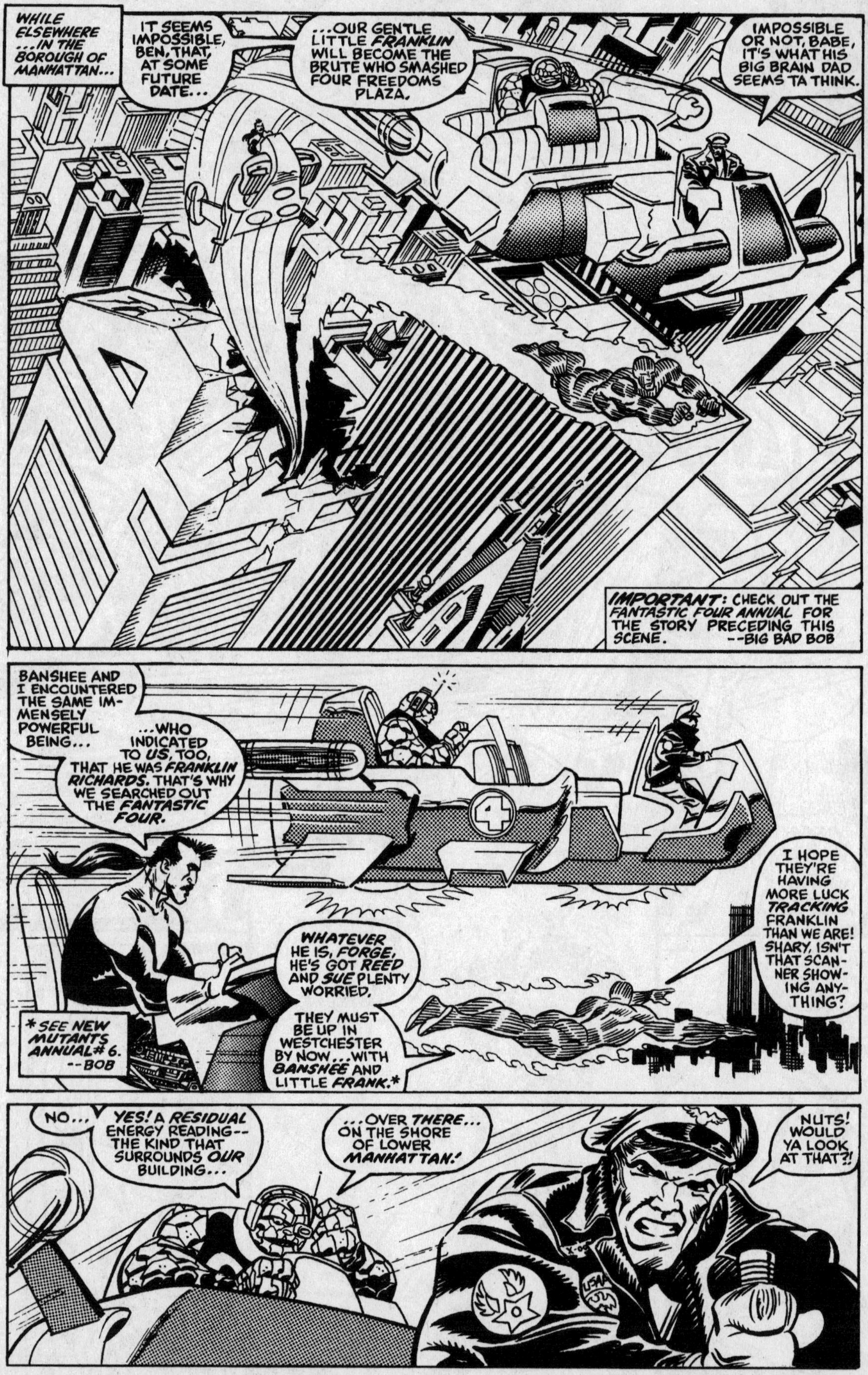
WHILE ELSEWHERE ...IN THE BOROUGH OF MANHATTAN...
IT SEEMS IMPOSSIBLE, BEN, THAT, AT SOME FUTURE DATE...
...OUR GENTLE LITTLE FRANKLIN WILL BECOME THE BRUTE WHO SMASHED FOUR FREEDOMS PLAZA.
IMPOSSIBLE OR NOT, BABE, IT'S WHAT HIS BIG BRAIN DAD SEEMS TA THINK.
IMPORTANT: CHECK OUT THE FANTASTIC FOUR ANNUAL FOR THE STORY PRECEDING THIS SCENE. --BIG BAD BOB
BANSHEE AND I ENCOUNTERED THE SAME IMMENSELY POWERFUL BEING...
...WHO INDICATED TO US, TOO, THAT HE WAS FRANKLIN RICHARDS. THAT'S WHY WE SEARCHED OUT THE FANTASTIC FOUR.
WHATEVER HE IS, FORGE, HE'S GOT REED AND SUE PLENTY WORRIED.
THEY MUST BE UP IN WESTCHESTER BY NOW...WITH BANSHEE AND LITTLE FRANK.*
I HOPE THEY'RE HAVING MORE LUCK TRACKING FRANKLIN THAN WE ARE! SHARY, ISN'T THAT SCANNER SHOWING ANYTHING?
*SEE NEW MUTANTS ANNUAL #6. --BOB
NO...
YES! A RESIDUAL ENERGY READING--THE KIND THAT SURROUNDS OUR BUILDING...
...OVER THERE... ON THE SHORE OF LOWER MANHATTAN!
NUTS! WOULD YA LOOK AT THAT?!

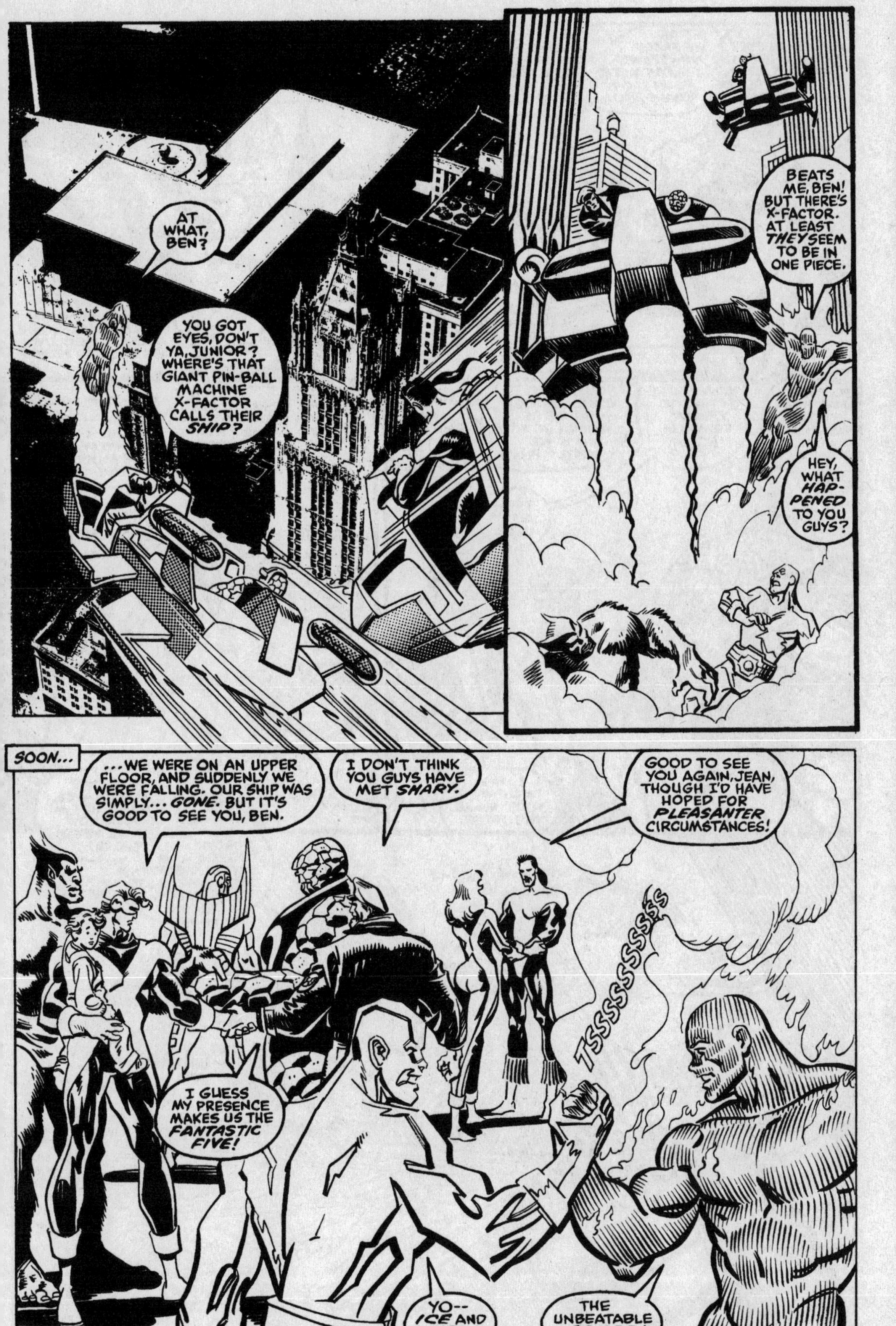
AT WHAT, BEN?
YOU GOT EYES, DON'T YA, JUNIOR? WHERE'S THAT GIANT PIN-BALL MACHINE X-FACTOR CALLS THEIR SHIP?
BEATS ME, BEN! BUT THERE'S X-FACTOR. AT LEAST THEY SEEM TO BE IN ONE PIECE.
HEY, WHAT HAP-PENED TO YOU GUYS?
SOON...
...WE WERE ON AN UPPER FLOOR, AND SUDDENLY WE WERE FALLING. OUR SHIP WAS SIMPLY... GONE. BUT IT'S GOOD TO SEE YOU, BEN.
I DON'T THINK YOU GUYS HAVE MET SHARY.
GOOD TO SEE YOU AGAIN, JEAN, THOUGH I'D HAVE HOPED FOR PLEASANTER CIRCUMSTANCES!
TSSSSSSSSSS
I GUESS MY PRESENCE MAKES US THE FANTASTIC FIVE!
YO-- ICE AND FIRE!
THE UNBEATABLE COMBO!

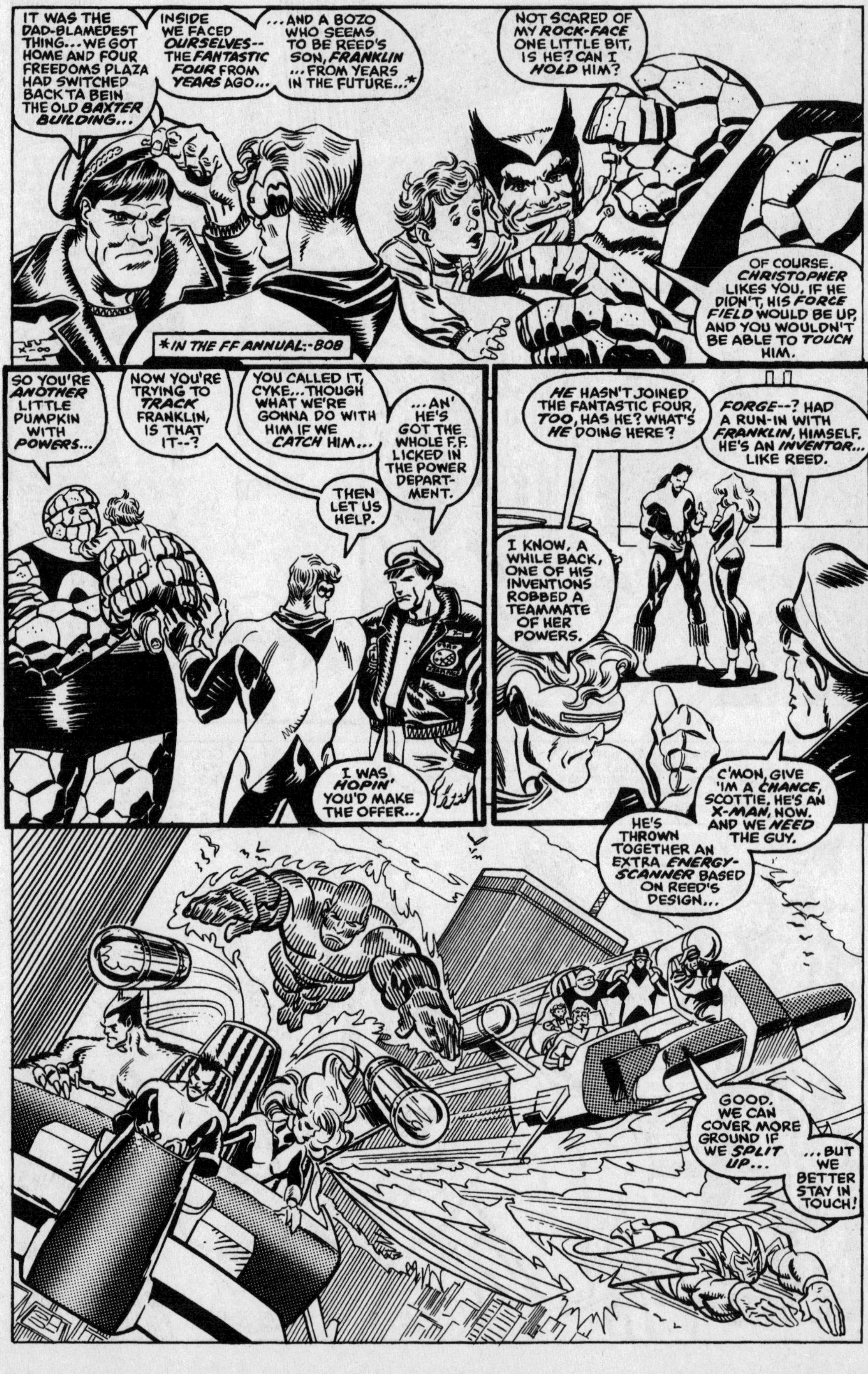
IT WAS THE DAD-BLAMEDEST THING... WE GOT HOME AND FOUR FREEDOMS PLAZA HAD SWITCHED BACK TA BEIN THE OLD BAXTER BUILDING...
INSIDE WE FACED OURSELVES-- THE FANTASTIC FOUR FROM YEARS AGO...
...AND A BOZO WHO SEEMS TO BE REED'S SON, FRANKLIN ...FROM YEARS IN THE FUTURE...*
NOT SCARED OF MY ROCK-FACE ONE LITTLE BIT, IS HE? CAN I HOLD HIM?
OF COURSE. CHRISTOPHER LIKES YOU. IF HE DIDN'T, HIS FORCE FIELD WOULD BE UP, AND YOU WOULDN'T BE ABLE TO TOUCH HIM.
*IN THE FF ANNUAL:-BOB
SO YOU'RE ANOTHER LITTLE PUMPKIN WITH POWERS...
NOW YOU'RE TRYING TO TRACK FRANKLIN, IS THAT IT--?
YOU CALLED IT, CYKE...THOUGH WHAT WE'RE GONNA DO WITH HIM IF WE CATCH HIM...
...AN' HE'S GOT THE WHOLE F.F. LICKED IN THE POWER DEPARTMENT.
THEN LET US HELP.
I WAS HOPIN' YOU'D MAKE THE OFFER...
HE HASN'T JOINED THE FANTASTIC FOUR, TOO, HAS HE? WHAT'S HE DOING HERE?
FORGE--? HAD A RUN-IN WITH FRANKLIN, HIMSELF. HE'S AN INVENTOR... LIKE REED.
I KNOW. A WHILE BACK, ONE OF HIS INVENTIONS ROBBED A TEAMMATE OF HER POWERS.
C'MON, GIVE 'IM A CHANCE, SCOTTIE. HE'S AN X-MAN, NOW. AND WE NEED THE GUY.
HE'S THROWN TOGETHER AN EXTRA ENERGY-SCANNER BASED ON REED'S DESIGN...
GOOD. WE CAN COVER MORE GROUND IF WE SPLIT UP...
...BUT WE BETTER STAY IN TOUCH!

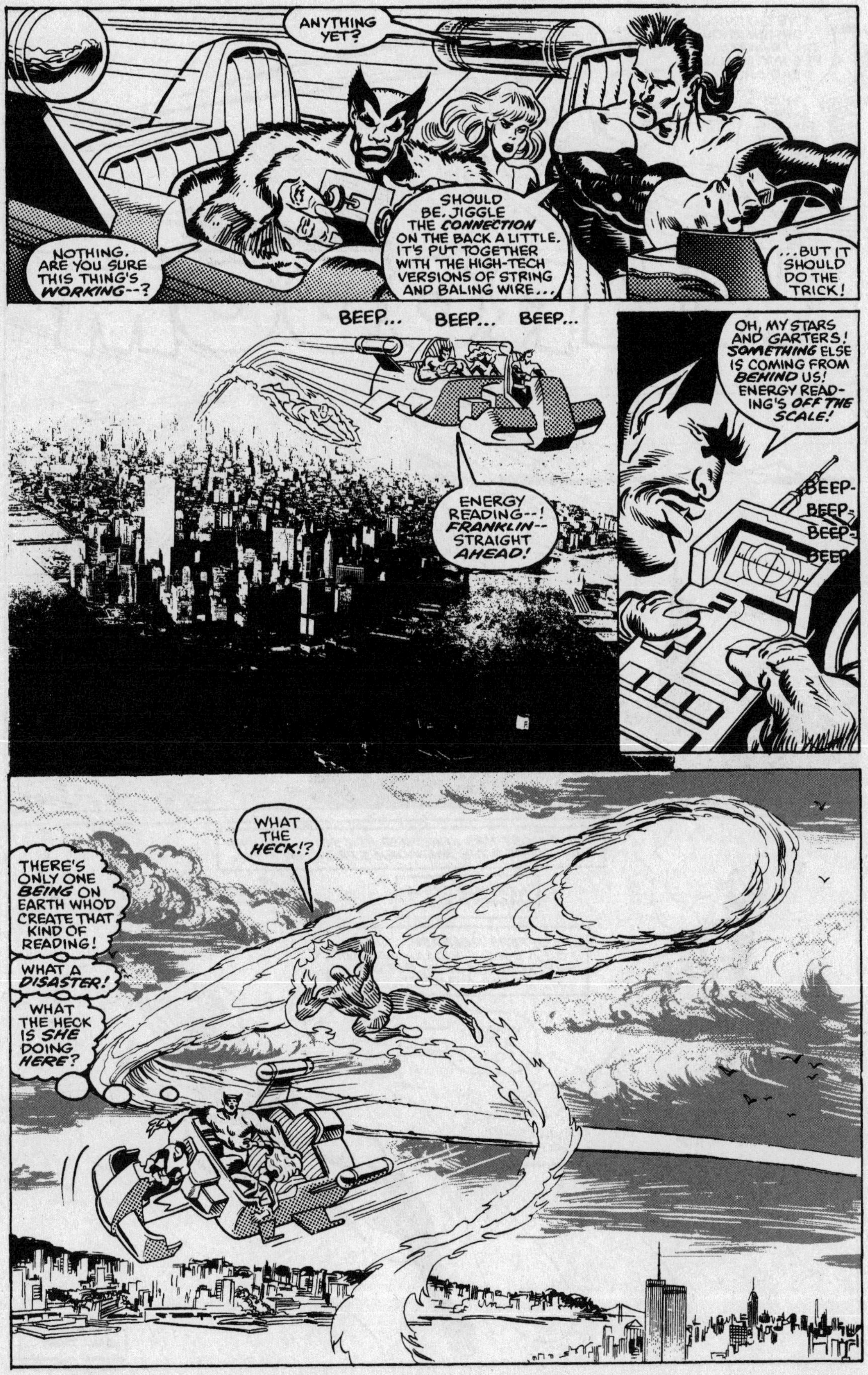
ANYTHING YET?
NOTHING. ARE YOU SURE THIS THING'S WORKING--?
SHOULD BE. JIGGLE THE CONNECTION ON THE BACK A LITTLE. IT'S PUT TOGETHER WITH THE HIGH-TECH VERSIONS OF STRING AND BALING WIRE...
...BUT IT SHOULD DO THE TRICK!
BEEP... BEEP... BEEP...
ENERGY READING--! FRANKLIN-- STRAIGHT AHEAD!
OH, MY STARS AND GARTERS! SOMETHING ELSE IS COMING FROM BEHIND US! ENERGY READING'S OFF THE SCALE!
BEEP- BEEP- BEEP-
WHAT THE HECK!?
THERE'S ONLY ONE BEING ON EARTH WHO'D CREATE THAT KIND OF READING!
WHAT A DISASTER!
WHAT THE HECK IS SHE DOING HERE?

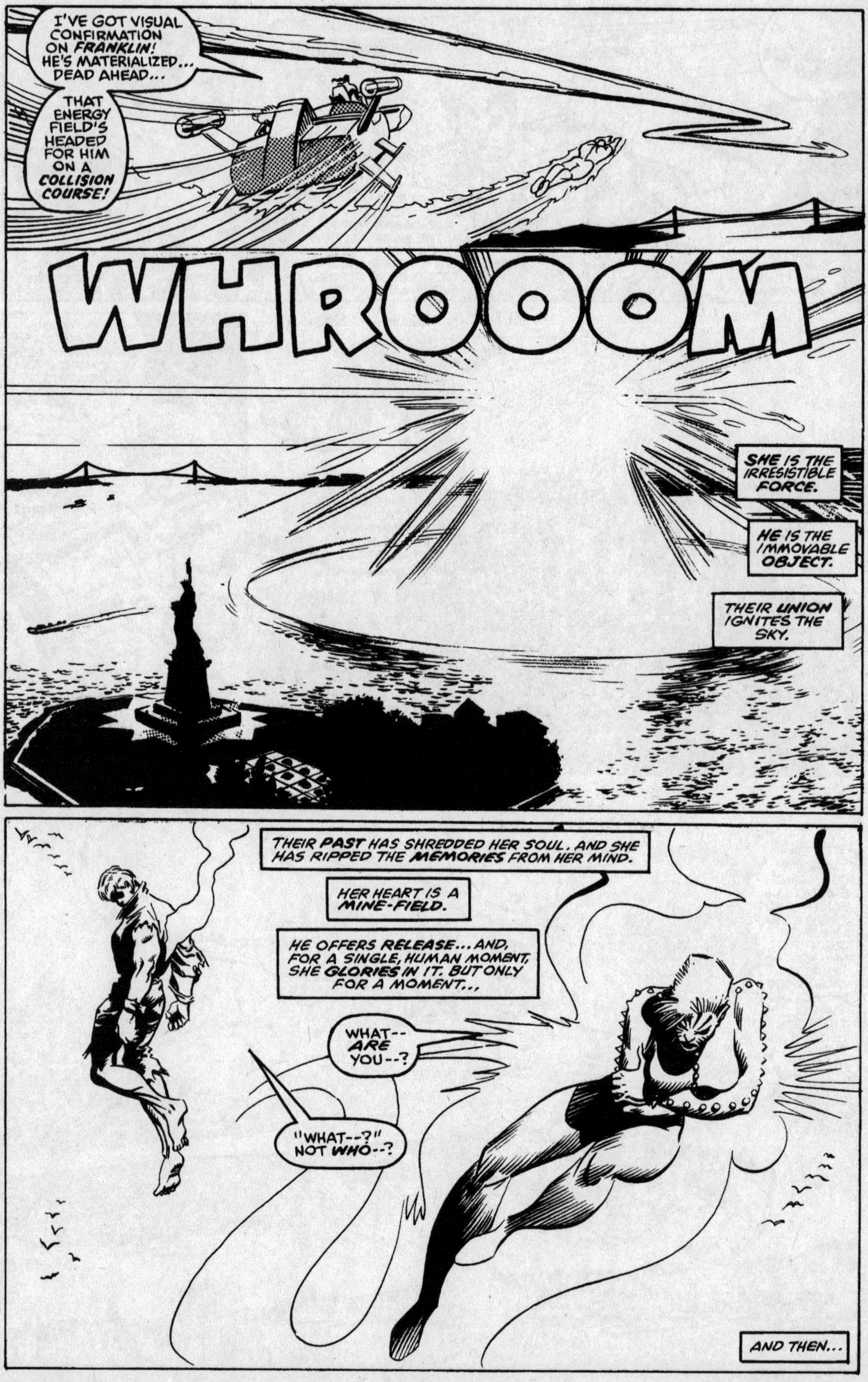

I'VE GOT VISUAL CONFIRMATION ON FRANKLIN! HE'S MATERIALIZED... DEAD AHEAD...
THAT ENERGY FIELD'S HEADED FOR HIM ON A COLLISION COURSE!
WHROOOM
SHE IS THE IRRESISTIBLE FORCE.
HE IS THE IMMOVABLE OBJECT.
THEIR UNION IGNITES THE SKY.
THEIR PAST HAS SHREDDED HER SOUL. AND SHE HAS RIPPED THE MEMORIES FROM HER MIND.
HER HEART IS A MINE-FIELD.
HE OFFERS RELEASE... AND, FOR A SINGLE, HUMAN MOMENT, SHE GLORIES IN IT. BUT ONLY FOR A MOMENT...
WHAT-- ARE YOU--?
"WHAT--?" NOT WHO--?
AND THEN...

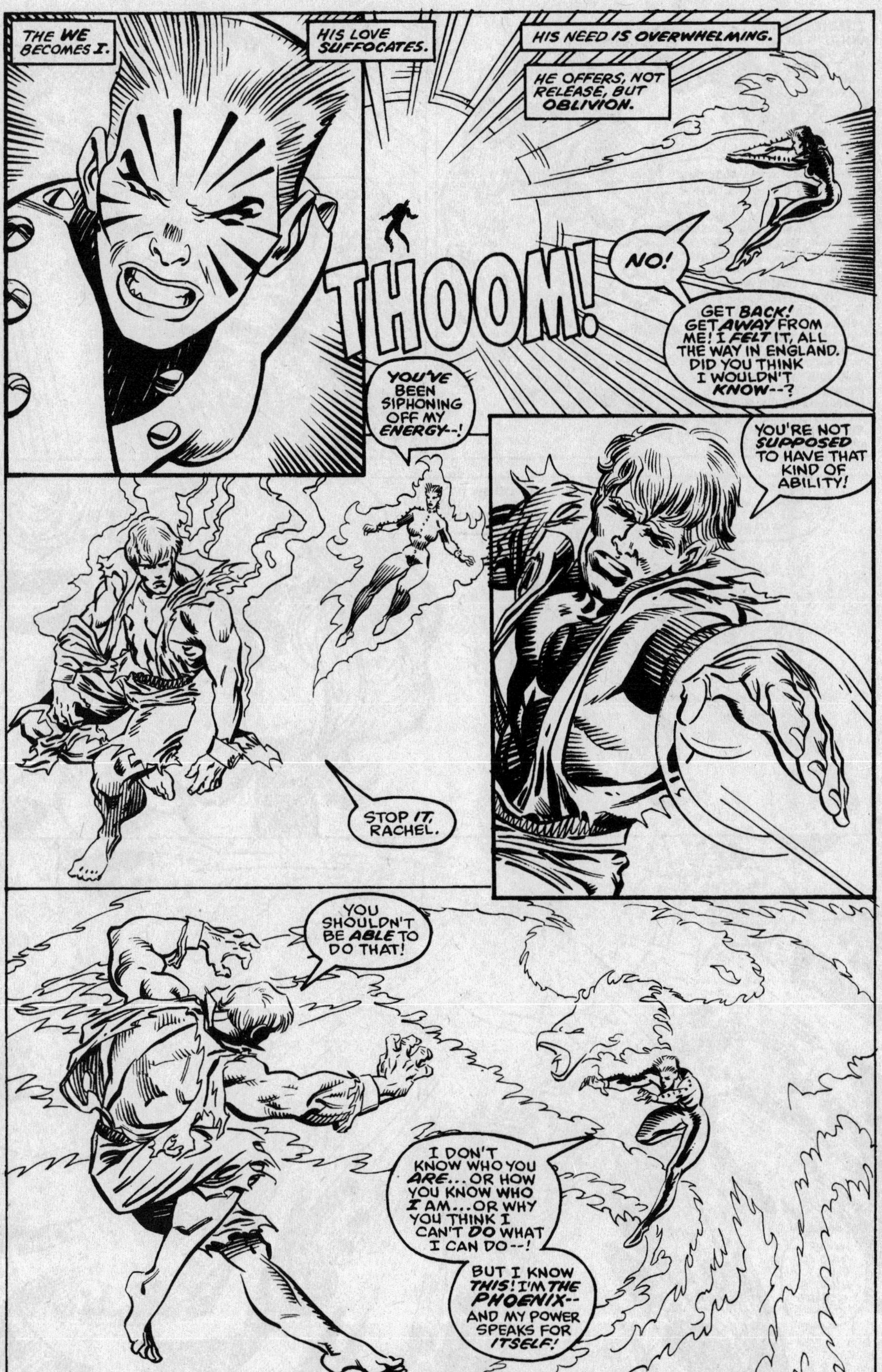
THE WE BECOMES I.
HIS LOVE SUFFOCATES.
HIS NEED IS OVERWHELMING.
HE OFFERS, NOT RELEASE, BUT OBLIVION.
THOOM!
NO!
GET BACK! GET AWAY FROM ME! I FELT IT, ALL THE WAY IN ENGLAND. DID YOU THINK I WOULDN'T KNOW--?
YOU'VE BEEN SIPHONING OFF MY ENERGY--!
YOU'RE NOT SUPPOSED TO HAVE THAT KIND OF ABILITY!
STOP IT, RACHEL.
YOU SHOULDN'T BE ABLE TO DO THAT!
I DON'T KNOW WHO YOU ARE... OR HOW YOU KNOW WHO I AM... OR WHY YOU THINK I CAN'T DO WHAT I CAN DO--!
BUT I KNOW THIS! I'M THE PHOENIX-- AND MY POWER SPEAKS FOR ITSELF!

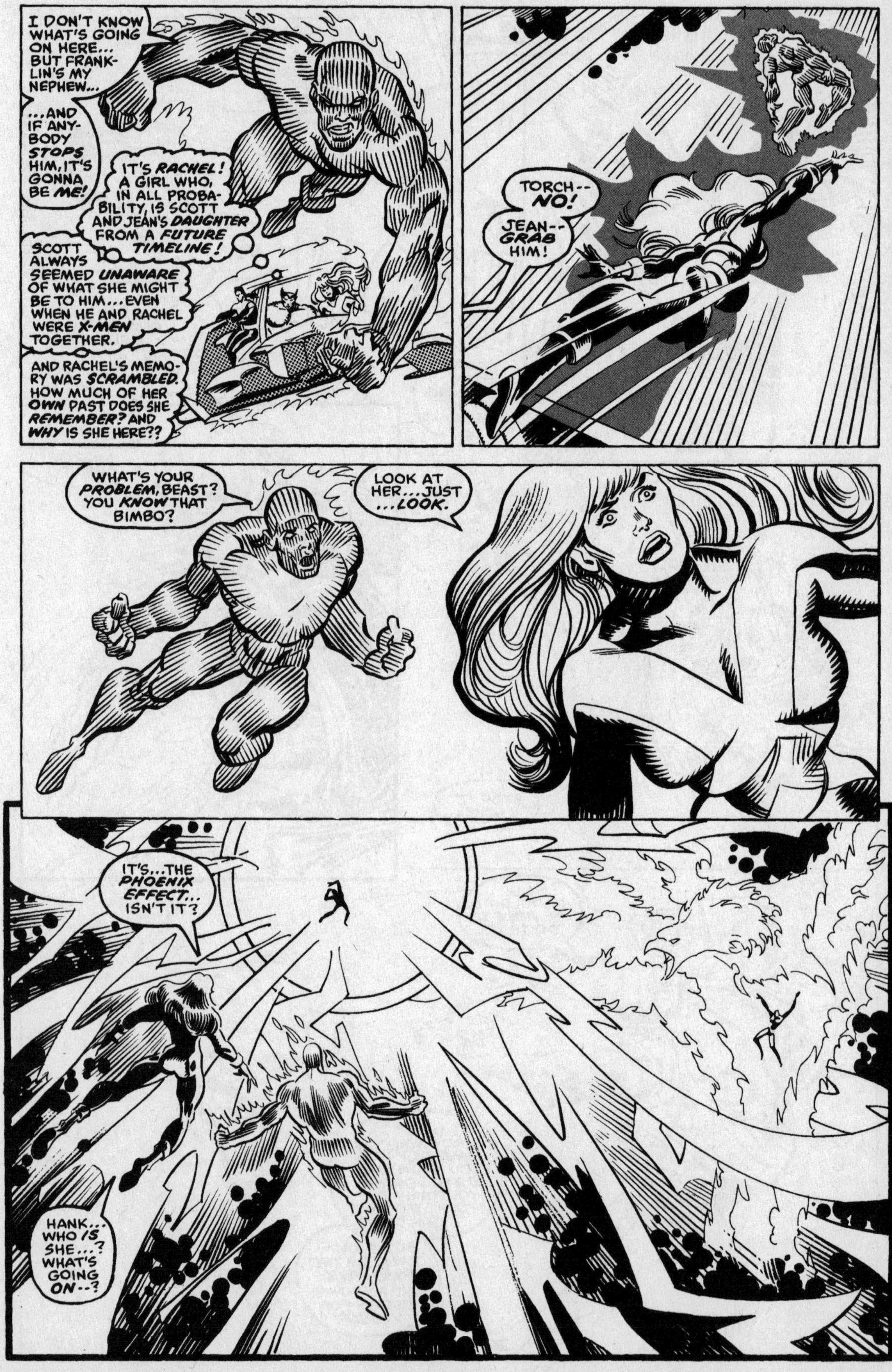
I DON'T KNOW WHAT'S GOING ON HERE... BUT FRANKLIN'S MY NEPHEW...
...AND IF ANYBODY STOPS HIM, IT'S GONNA BE ME!
IT'S RACHEL! A GIRL WHO, IN ALL PROBABILITY, IS SCOTT AND JEAN'S DAUGHTER FROM A FUTURE TIMELINE!
SCOTT ALWAYS SEEMED UNAWARE OF WHAT SHE MIGHT BE TO HIM... EVEN WHEN HE AND RACHEL WERE X-MEN TOGETHER.
AND RACHEL'S MEMORY WAS SCRAMBLED. HOW MUCH OF HER OWN PAST DOES SHE REMEMBER? AND WHY IS SHE HERE??
TORCH-- NO!
JEAN-- GRAB HIM!
WHAT'S YOUR PROBLEM, BEAST? YOU KNOW THAT BIMBO?
LOOK AT HER... JUST ...LOOK.
IT'S...THE PHOENIX EFFECT... ISN'T IT?
HANK... WHO IS SHE...? WHAT'S GOING ON--?

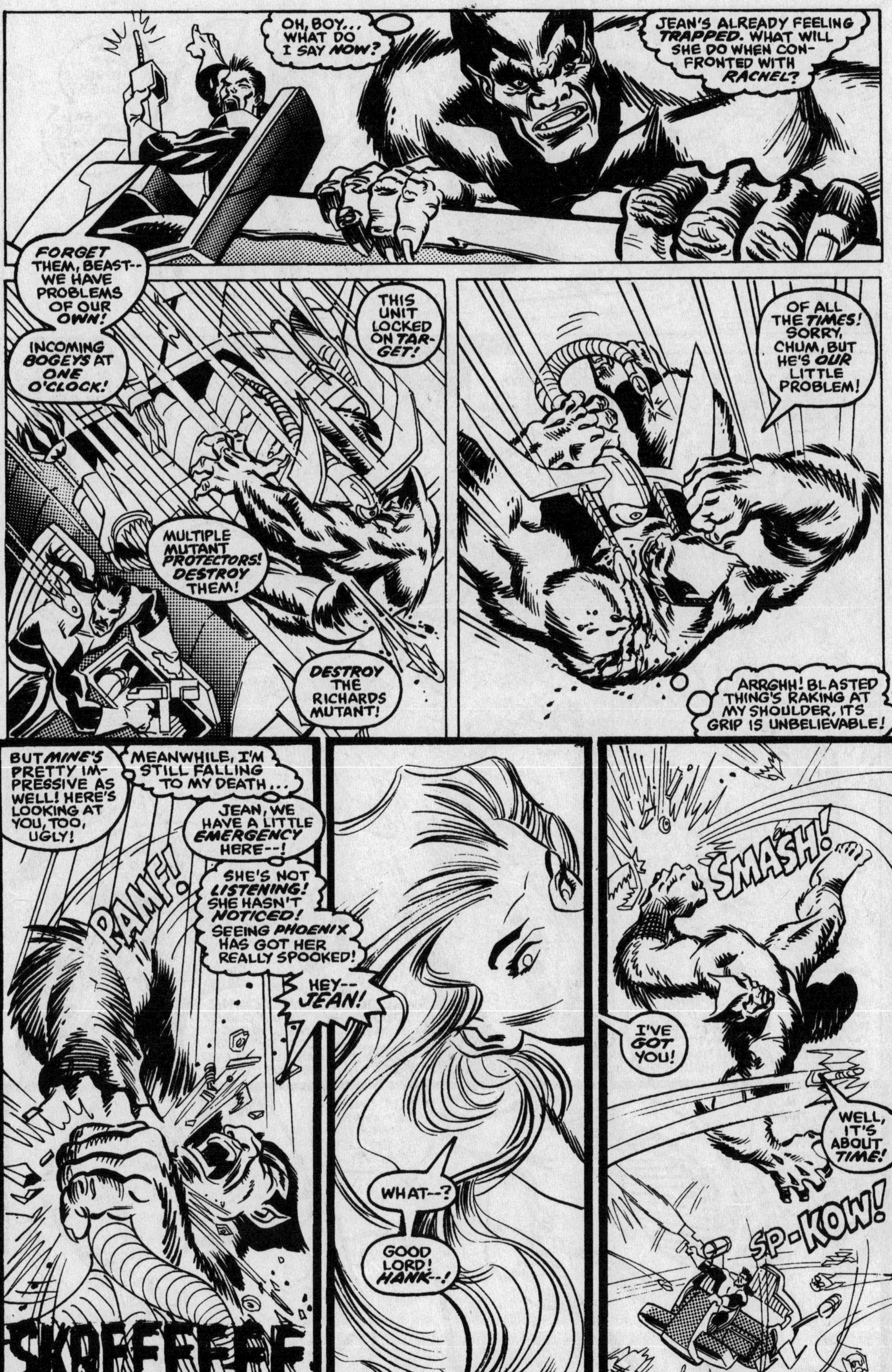
OH, BOY... WHAT DO I SAY NOW?
JEAN'S ALREADY FEELING TRAPPED. WHAT WILL SHE DO WHEN CONFRONTED WITH RACHEL?
FORGET THEM, BEAST--WE HAVE PROBLEMS OF OUR OWN!
INCOMING BOGEYS AT ONE O'CLOCK!
THIS UNIT LOCKED ON TARGET!
MULTIPLE MUTANT PROTECTORS! DESTROY THEM!
DESTROY THE RICHARDS MUTANT!
OF ALL THE TIMES! SORRY, CHUM, BUT HE'S OUR LITTLE PROBLEM!
ARRGHH! BLASTED THING'S RAKING AT MY SHOULDER, ITS GRIP IS UNBELIEVABLE!
BUT MINE'S PRETTY IMPRESSIVE AS WELL! HERE'S LOOKING AT YOU, TOO, UGLY!
MEANWHILE, I'M STILL FALLING TO MY DEATH...
JEAN, WE HAVE A LITTLE EMERGENCY HERE--!
SHE'S NOT LISTENING! SHE HASN'T NOTICED! SEEING PHOENIX HAS GOT HER REALLY SPOOKED!
PAMF!
HEY--JEAN!
SKREEEEEE
WHAT--?
GOOD LORD! HANK--!
SMASH!
I'VE GOT YOU!
WELL, IT'S ABOUT TIME!
SP-KOW!

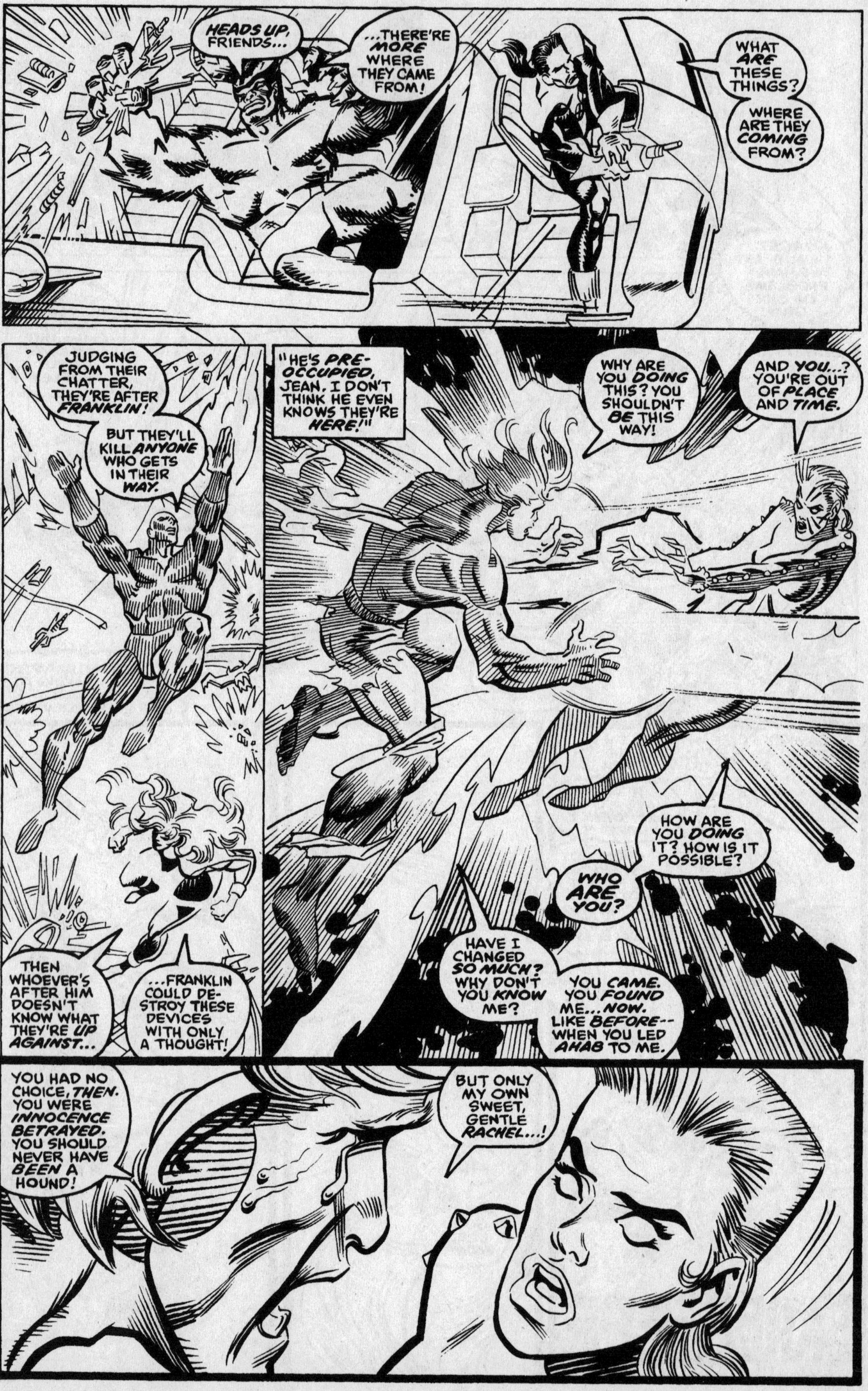

HEADS UP, FRIENDS...
...THERE'RE MORE WHERE THEY CAME FROM!
WHAT ARE THESE THINGS?
WHERE ARE THEY COMING FROM?
JUDGING FROM THEIR CHATTER, THEY'RE AFTER FRANKLIN!
BUT THEY'LL KILL ANYONE WHO GETS IN THEIR WAY.
THEN WHOEVER'S AFTER HIM DOESN'T KNOW WHAT THEY'RE UP AGAINST...
...FRANKLIN COULD DE-STROY THESE DEVICES WITH ONLY A THOUGHT!
"HE'S PRE-OCCUPIED, JEAN. I DON'T THINK HE EVEN KNOWS THEY'RE HERE!"
WHY ARE YOU DOING THIS? YOU SHOULDN'T BE THIS WAY!
AND YOU...? YOU'RE OUT OF PLACE AND TIME.
HOW ARE YOU DOING IT? HOW IS IT POSSIBLE?
WHO ARE YOU?
HAVE I CHANGED SO MUCH? WHY DON'T YOU KNOW ME?
YOU CAME. YOU FOUND ME... NOW. LIKE BEFORE-- WHEN YOU LED AHAB TO ME.
YOU HAD NO CHOICE, THEN. YOU WERE INNOCENCE BETRAYED. YOU SHOULD NEVER HAVE BEEN A HOUND!
BUT ONLY MY OWN SWEET, GENTLE RACHEL...!

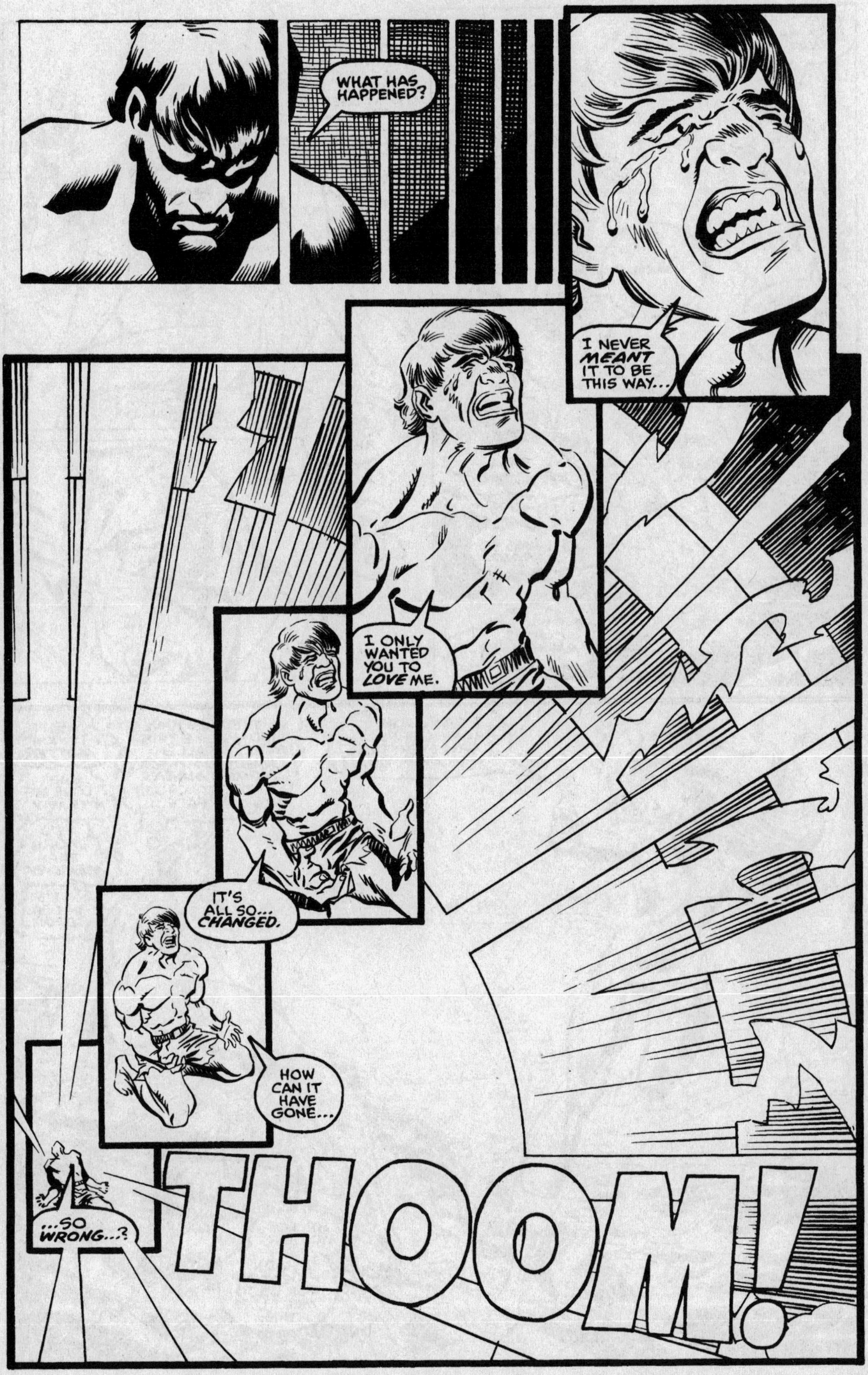
WHAT HAS HAPPENED?
I NEVER MEANT IT TO BE THIS WAY...
I ONLY WANTED YOU TO LOVE ME.
IT'S ALL SO... CHANGED.
HOW CAN IT HAVE GONE...
...SO WRONG...?
THOOM!

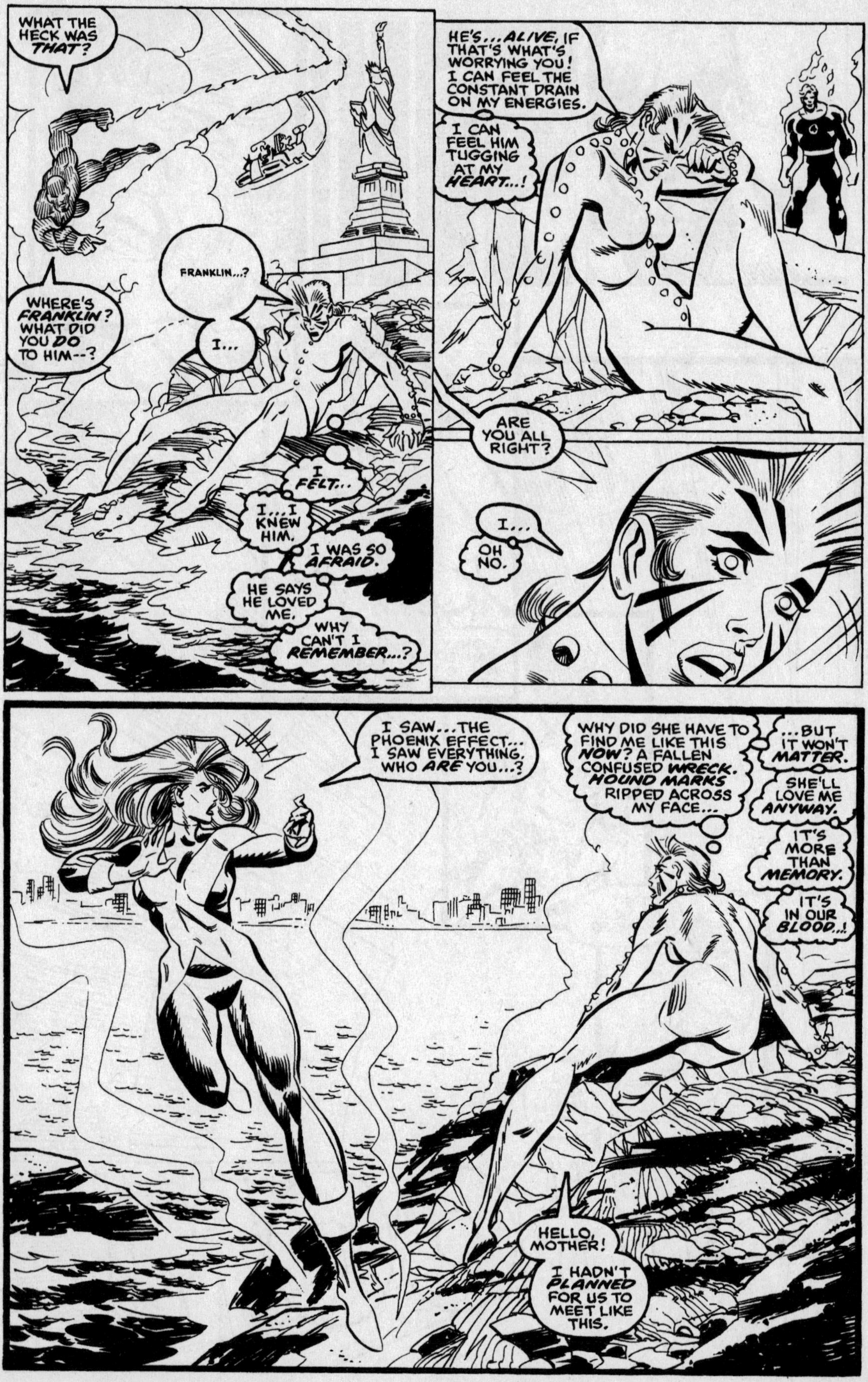
WHAT THE HECK WAS THAT?
WHERE'S FRANKLIN? WHAT DID YOU DO TO HIM--?
FRANKLIN...?
I...
I FELT...
I... I KNEW HIM.
I WAS SO AFRAID.
HE SAYS HE LOVED ME.
WHY CAN'T I REMEMBER...?
HE'S... ALIVE, IF THAT'S WORRYING YOU! I CAN FEEL THE CONSTANT DRAIN ON MY ENERGIES.
I CAN FEEL HIM TUGGING AT MY HEART...!
ARE YOU ALL RIGHT?
I...
OH NO.
I SAW... THE PHOENIX EFFECT... I SAW EVERYTHING. WHO ARE YOU...?
WHY DID SHE HAVE TO FIND ME LIKE THIS NOW? A FALLEN CONFUSED WRECK. HOUND MARKS RIPPED ACROSS MY FACE...
...BUT IT WON'T MATTER.
SHE'LL LOVE ME ANYWAY.
IT'S MORE THAN MEMORY.
IT'S IN OUR BLOOD...!
HELLO, MOTHER!
I HADN'T PLANNED FOR US TO MEET LIKE THIS.

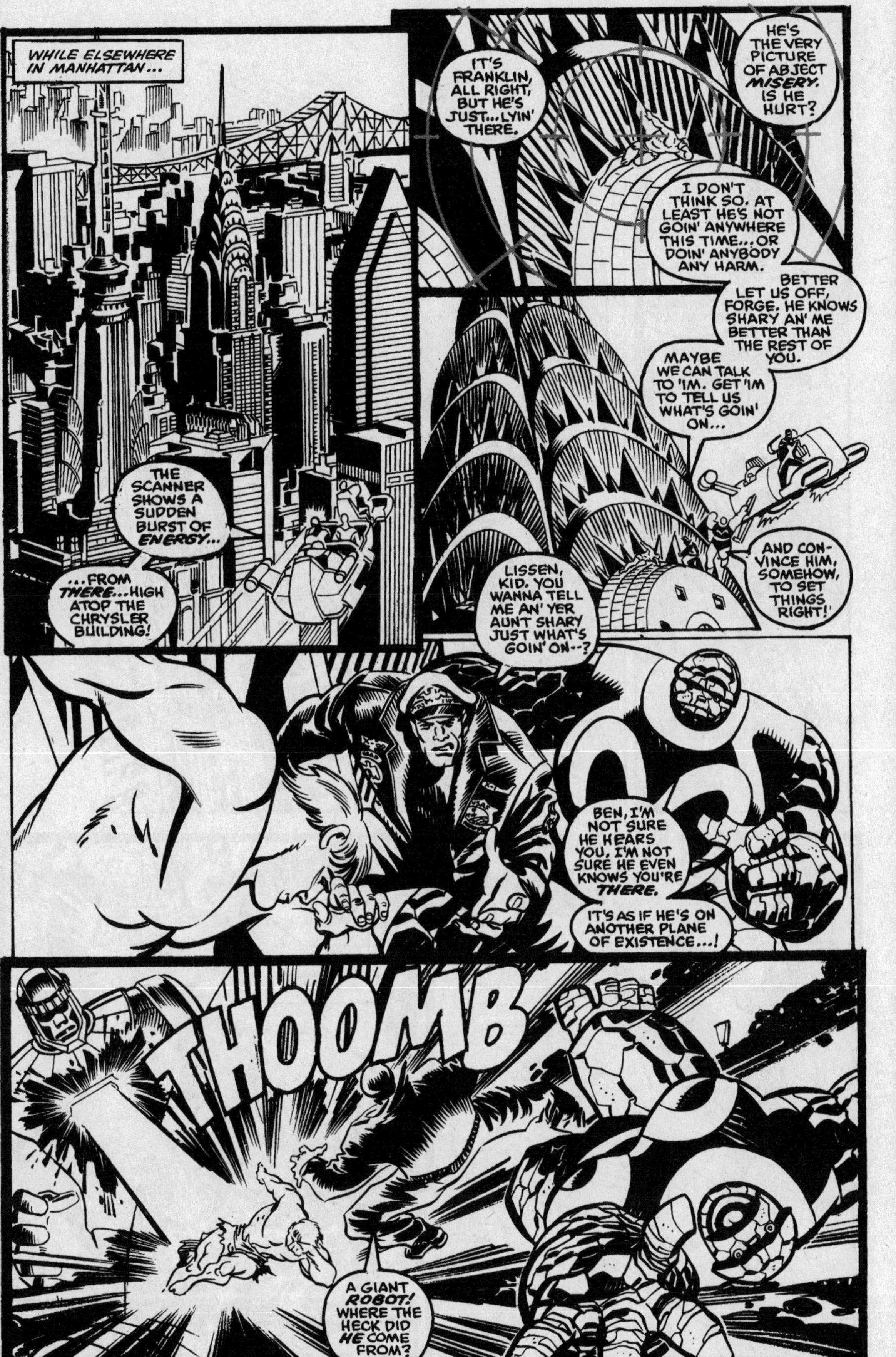
WHILE ELSEWHERE IN MANHATTAN...
THE SCANNER SHOWS A SUDDEN BURST OF ENERGY...
...FROM THERE...HIGH ATOP THE CHRYSLER BUILDING!
IT'S FRANKLIN, ALL RIGHT, BUT HE'S JUST...LYIN' THERE.
HE'S THE VERY PICTURE OF ABJECT MISERY. IS HE HURT?
I DON'T THINK SO. AT LEAST HE'S NOT GOIN' ANYWHERE THIS TIME...OR DOIN' ANYBODY ANY HARM.
BETTER LET US OFF, FORGE. HE KNOWS SHARY AN' ME BETTER THAN THE REST OF YOU.
MAYBE WE CAN TALK TO 'IM. GET 'IM TO TELL US WHAT'S GOIN' ON...
AND CONVINCE HIM, SOMEHOW, TO SET THINGS RIGHT!
LISSEN, KID. YOU WANNA TELL ME AN' YER AUNT SHARY JUST WHAT'S GOIN' ON--?
BEN, I'M NOT SURE HE HEARS YOU. I'M NOT SURE HE EVEN KNOWS YOU'RE THERE.
IT'S AS IF HE'S ON ANOTHER PLANE OF EXISTENCE...!
THOOMB
A GIANT ROBOT! WHERE THE HECK DID HE COME FROM?

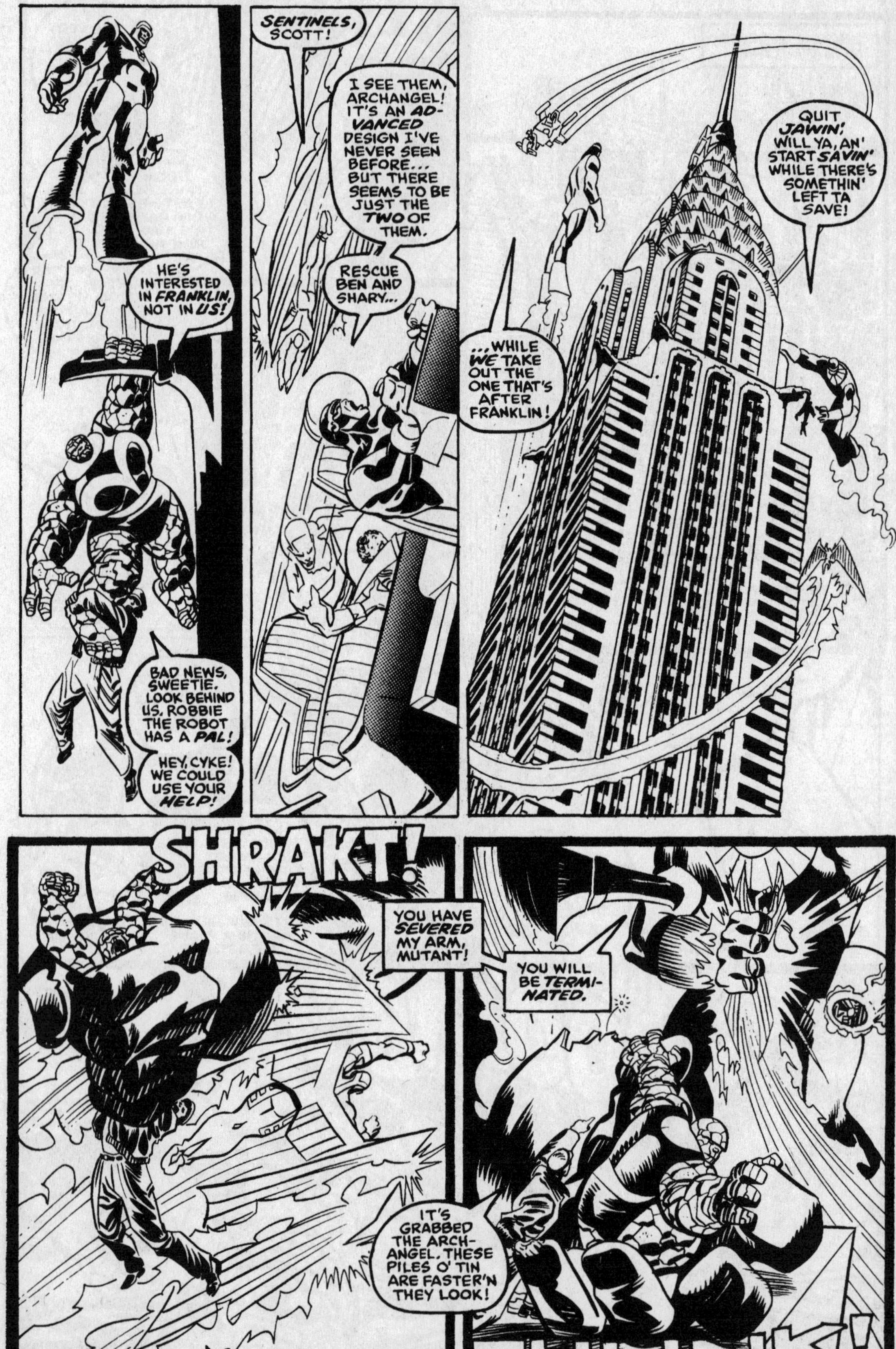
HE'S INTERESTED IN FRANKLIN, NOT IN US!
BAD NEWS, SWEETIE. LOOK BEHIND US. ROBBIE THE ROBOT HAS A PAL!
HEY, CYKE! WE COULD USE YOUR HELP!
SENTINELS, SCOTT!
I SEE THEM, ARCHANGEL! IT'S AN ADVANCED DESIGN I'VE NEVER SEEN BEFORE... BUT THERE SEEMS TO BE JUST THE TWO OF THEM.
RESCUE BEN AND SHARY...
...WHILE WE TAKE OUT THE ONE THAT'S AFTER FRANKLIN!
QUIT JAWIN', WILL YA, AN' START SAVIN' WHILE THERE'S SOMETHIN' LEFT TA SAVE!
SHRAKT!
YOU HAVE SEVERED MY ARM, MUTANT!
YOU WILL BE TERMINATED.
IT'S GRABBED THE ARCHANGEL. THESE PILES O' TIN ARE FASTER'N THEY LOOK!
THUNK!

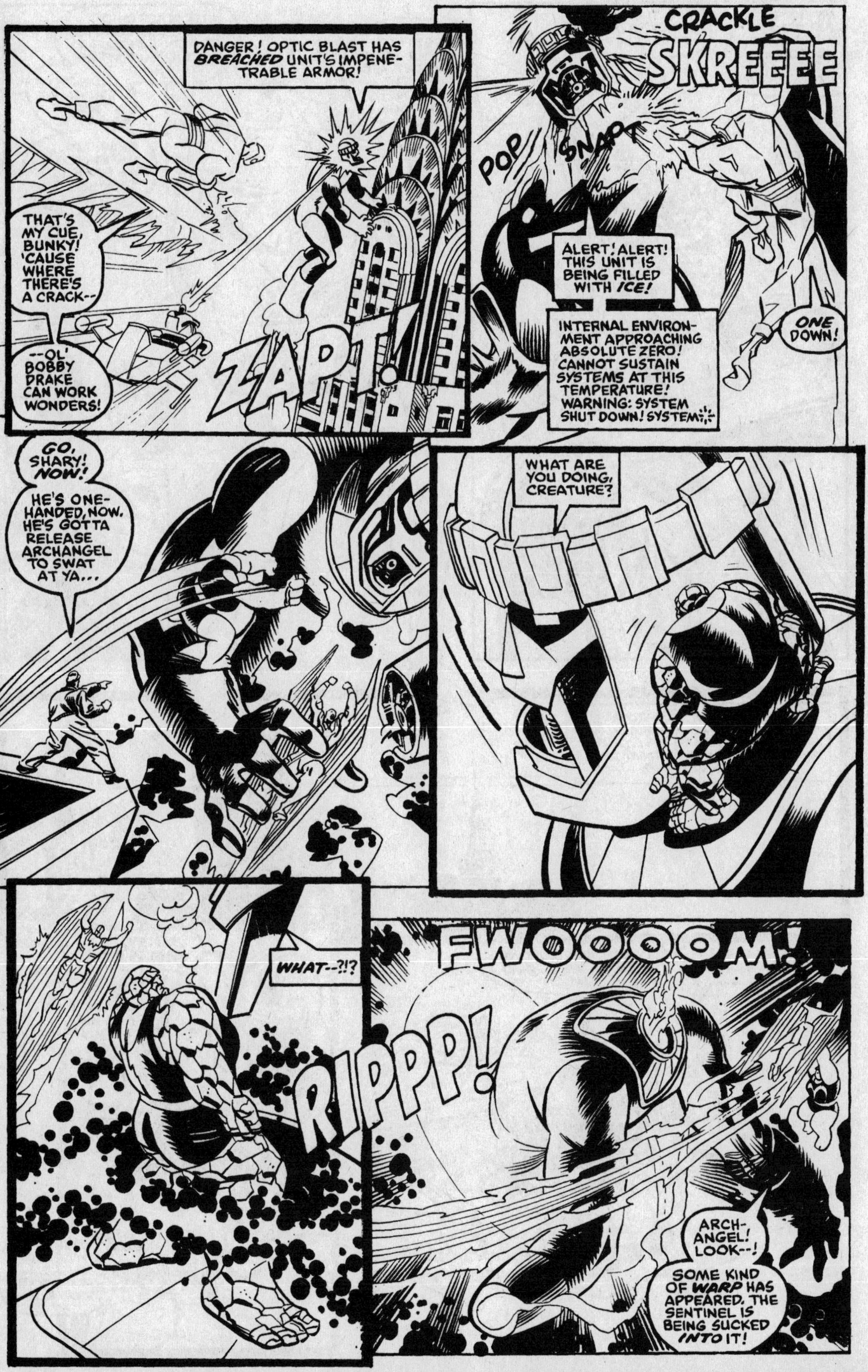
DANGER! OPTIC BLAST HAS BREACHED UNIT'S IMPENETRABLE ARMOR!
THAT'S MY CUE, BUNKY! 'CAUSE WHERE THERE'S A CRACK--
--OL' BOBBY DRAKE CAN WORK WONDERS!
ZAPT!
CRACKLE
SKREEEE
POP
SNAP
ALERT! ALERT! THIS UNIT IS BEING FILLED WITH ICE!
INTERNAL ENVIRONMENT APPROACHING ABSOLUTE ZERO! CANNOT SUSTAIN SYSTEMS AT THIS TEMPERATURE! WARNING: SYSTEM SHUT DOWN! SYSTEM
ONE DOWN!
GO, SHARY! NOW!
HE'S ONE-HANDED, NOW. HE'S GOTTA RELEASE ARCHANGEL TO SWAT AT YA...
WHAT ARE YOU DOING, CREATURE?
WHAT--?!?
RIPPP!
FWOOOOM!
ARCH-ANGEL! LOOK--!
SOME KIND OF WARP HAS APPEARED. THE SENTINEL IS BEING SUCKED INTO IT!

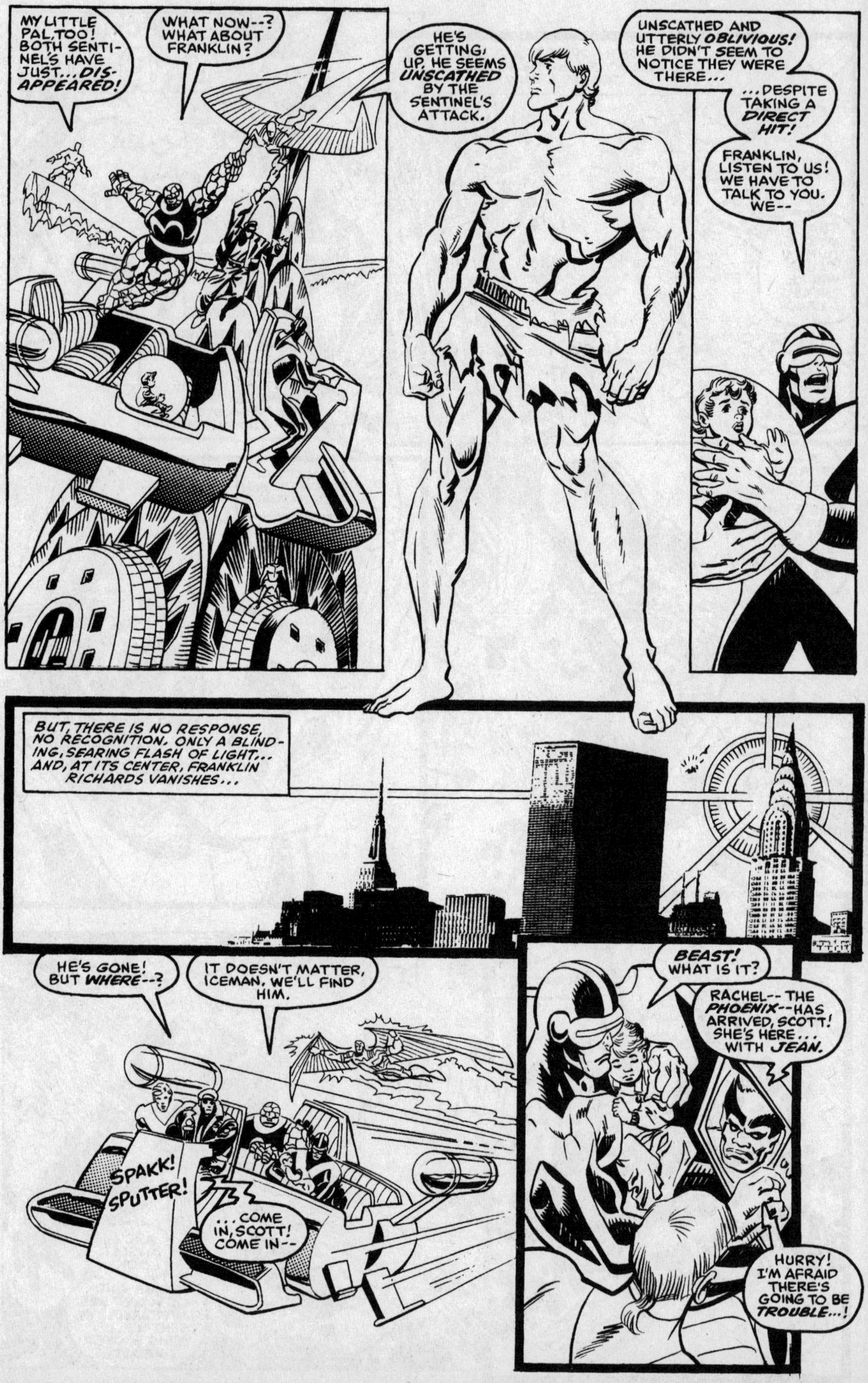
MY LITTLE PAL, TOO! BOTH SENTINEL'S HAVE JUST... DISAPPEARED!
WHAT NOW--? WHAT ABOUT FRANKLIN?
HE'S GETTING UP. HE SEEMS UNSCATHED BY THE SENTINEL'S ATTACK.
UNSCATHED AND UTTERLY OBLIVIOUS! HE DIDN'T SEEM TO NOTICE THEY WERE THERE...
...DESPITE TAKING A DIRECT HIT!
FRANKLIN, LISTEN TO US! WE HAVE TO TALK TO YOU. WE--
BUT, THERE IS NO RESPONSE, NO RECOGNITION, ONLY A BLINDING, SEARING FLASH OF LIGHT... AND, AT ITS CENTER, FRANKLIN RICHARDS VANISHES...
HE'S GONE! BUT WHERE--?
IT DOESN'T MATTER, ICEMAN. WE'LL FIND HIM.
SPAKK! SPUTTER!
...COME IN, SCOTT! COME IN--
BEAST! WHAT IS IT?
RACHEL-- THE PHOENIX--HAS ARRIVED, SCOTT! SHE'S HERE... WITH JEAN.
HURRY! I'M AFRAID THERE'S GOING TO BE TROUBLE...!

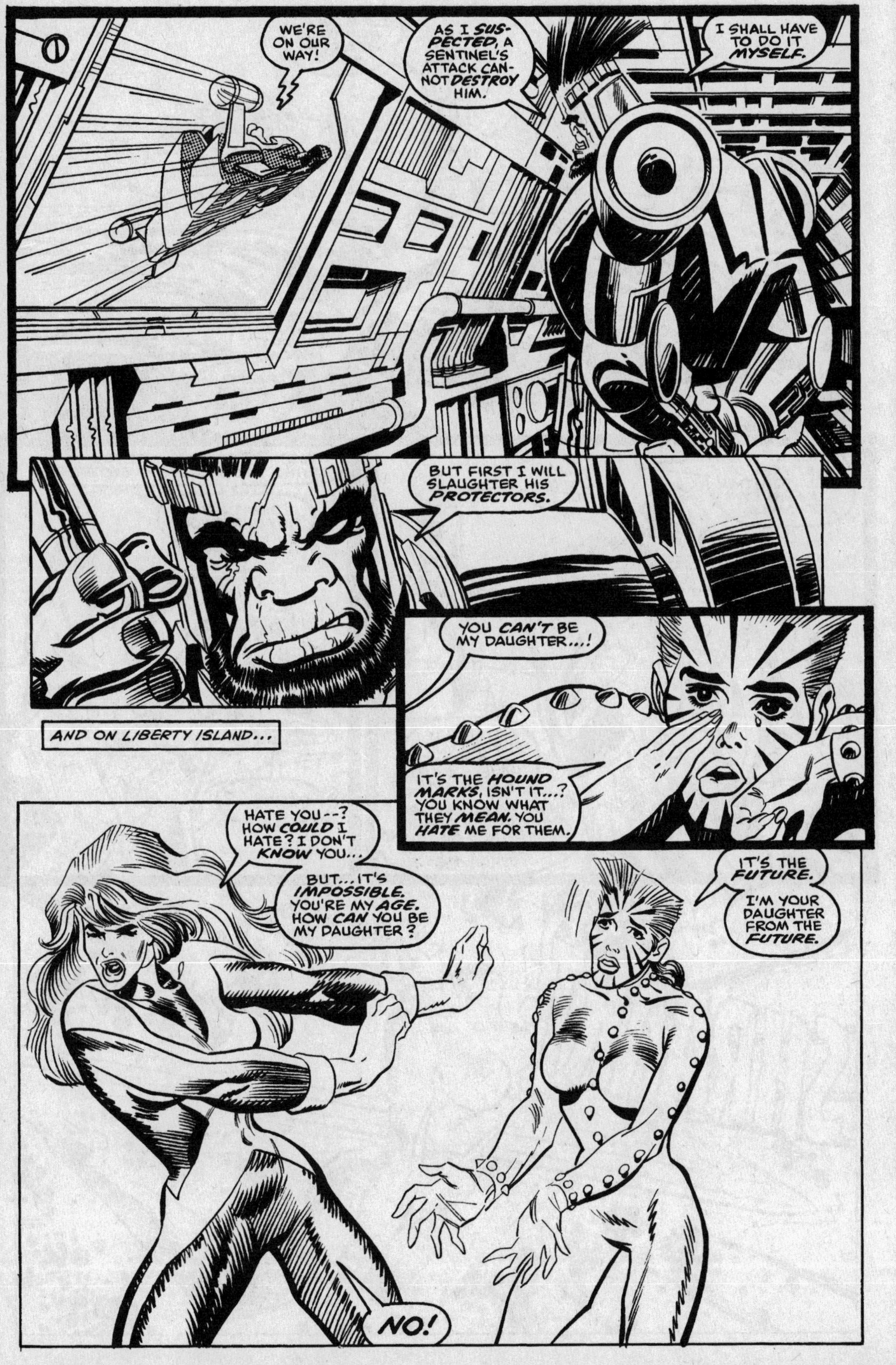
WE'RE ON OUR WAY!
AS I SUSPECTED, A SENTINEL'S ATTACK CANNOT DESTROY HIM.
I SHALL HAVE TO DO IT MYSELF.
BUT FIRST I WILL SLAUGHTER HIS PROTECTORS.
YOU CAN'T BE MY DAUGHTER...!
IT'S THE HOUND MARKS, ISN'T IT...? YOU KNOW WHAT THEY MEAN. YOU HATE ME FOR THEM.
AND ON LIBERTY ISLAND...
HATE YOU--? HOW COULD I HATE? I DON'T KNOW YOU...
BUT...IT'S IMPOSSIBLE. YOU'RE MY AGE. HOW CAN YOU BE MY DAUGHTER?
IT'S THE FUTURE.
I'M YOUR DAUGHTER FROM THE FUTURE.
NO!

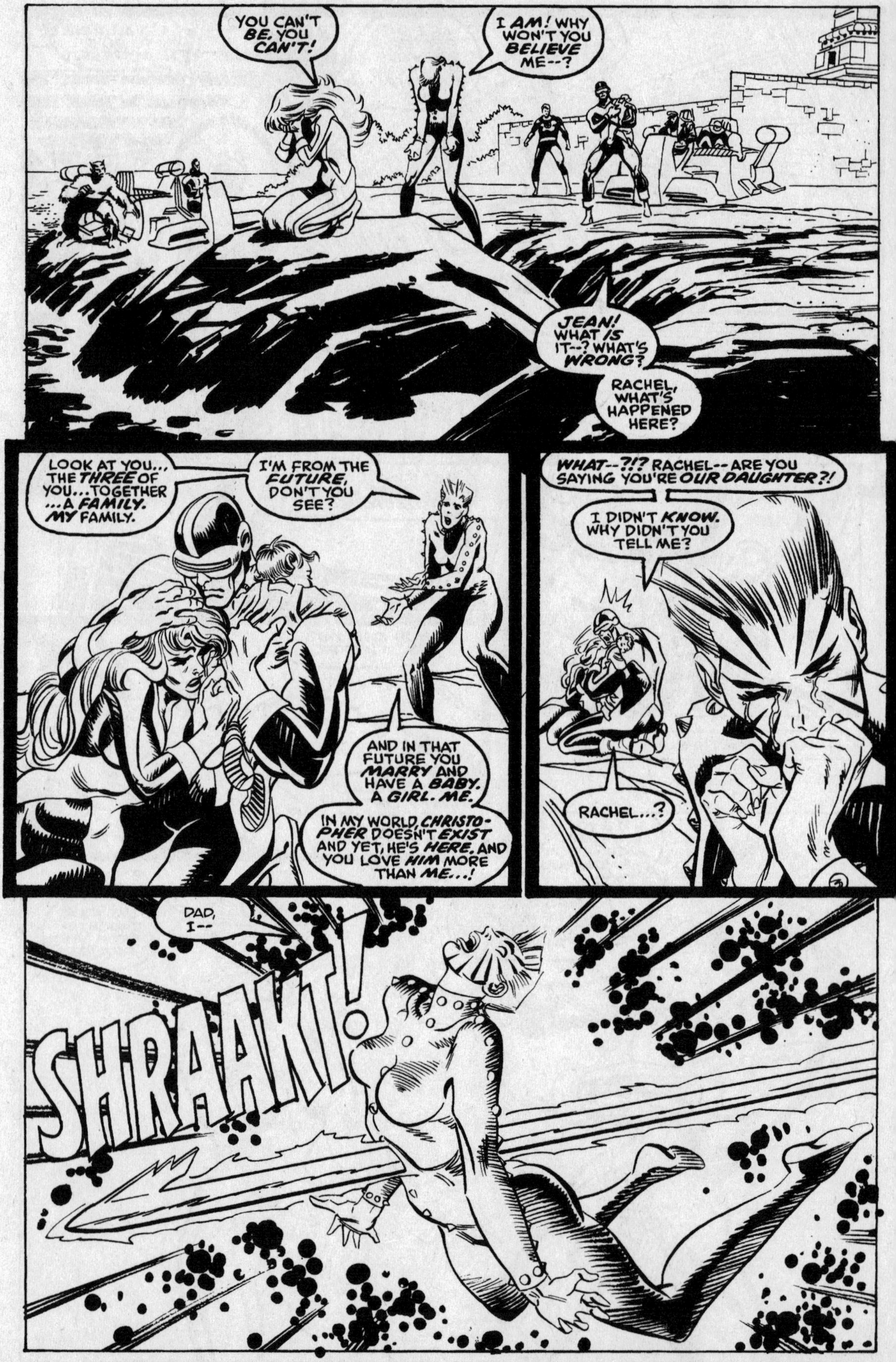
YOU CAN'T BE, YOU CAN'T!
I AM! WHY WON'T YOU BELIEVE ME--?
JEAN! WHAT IS IT--? WHAT'S WRONG?
RACHEL, WHAT'S HAPPENED HERE?
LOOK AT YOU... THE THREE OF YOU... TOGETHER ...A FAMILY. MY FAMILY.
I'M FROM THE FUTURE, DON'T YOU SEE?
AND IN THAT FUTURE YOU MARRY AND HAVE A BABY. A GIRL. ME.
IN MY WORLD, CHRISTOPHER DOESN'T EXIST AND YET, HE'S HERE. AND YOU LOVE HIM MORE THAN ME...!
WHAT--?!? RACHEL--ARE YOU SAYING YOU'RE OUR DAUGHTER?!
I DIDN'T KNOW. WHY DIDN'T YOU TELL ME?
RACHEL...?
DAD, I--
SHRAAKT!

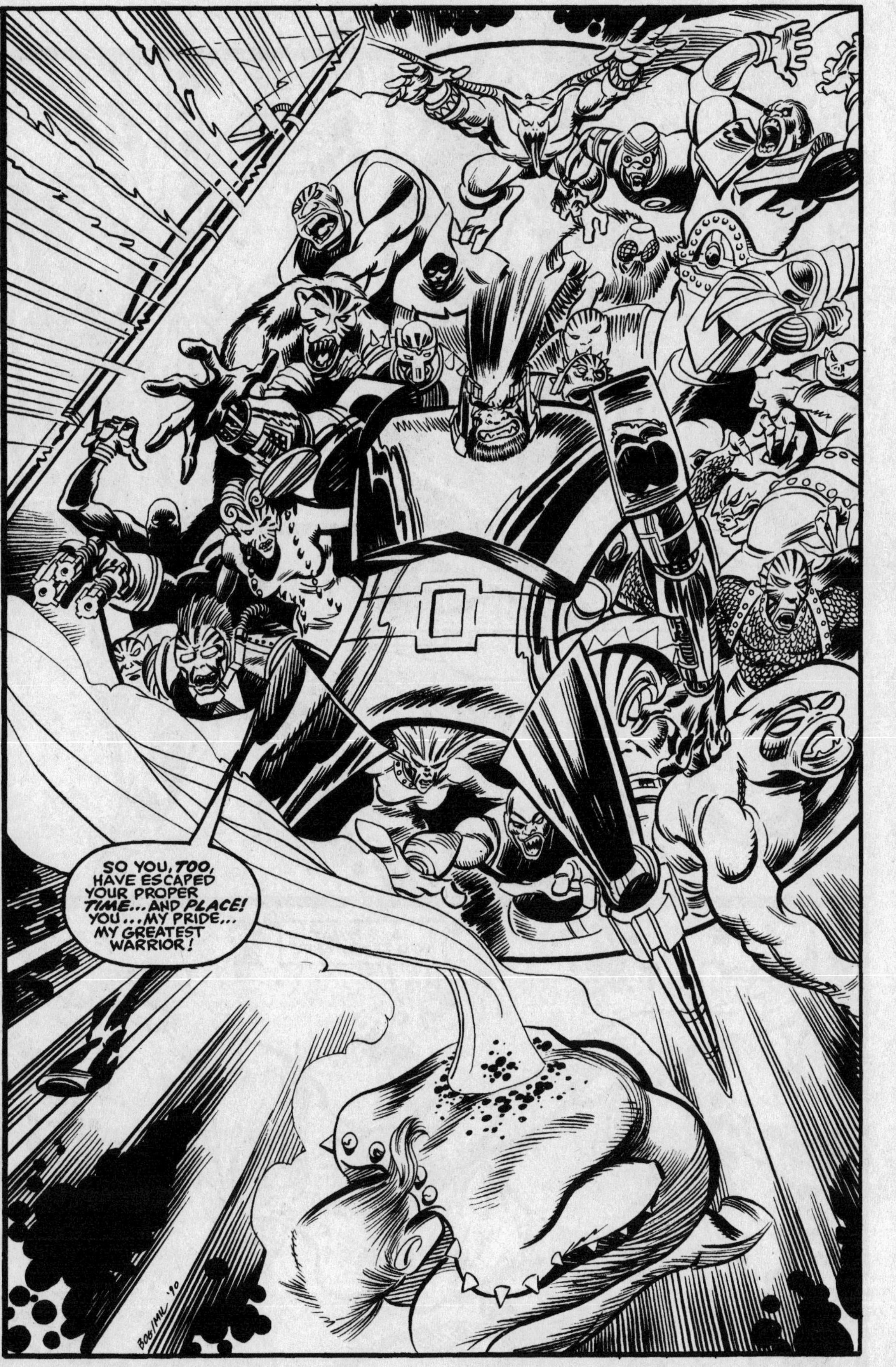
SO YOU, *TOO*, HAVE ESCAPED YOUR PROPER *TIME*... AND *PLACE!* YOU... MY PRIDE... MY GREATEST WARRIOR!
BOG/MIL '90

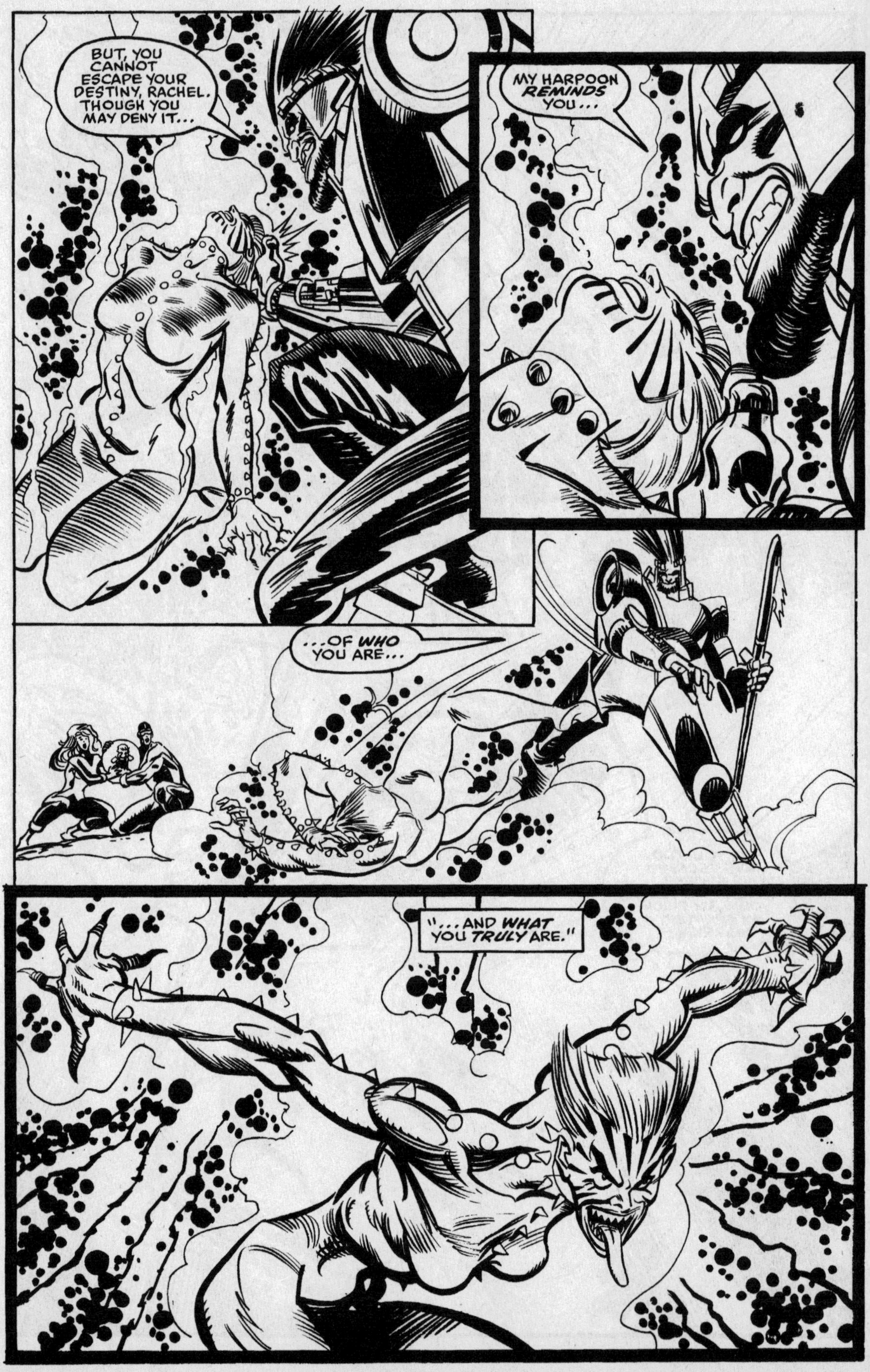
BUT, YOU CANNOT ESCAPE YOUR DESTINY, RACHEL. THOUGH YOU MAY DENY IT...
MY HARPOON *REMINDS* YOU...
...OF *WHO* YOU ARE...
"...AND *WHAT* YOU *TRULY* ARE."

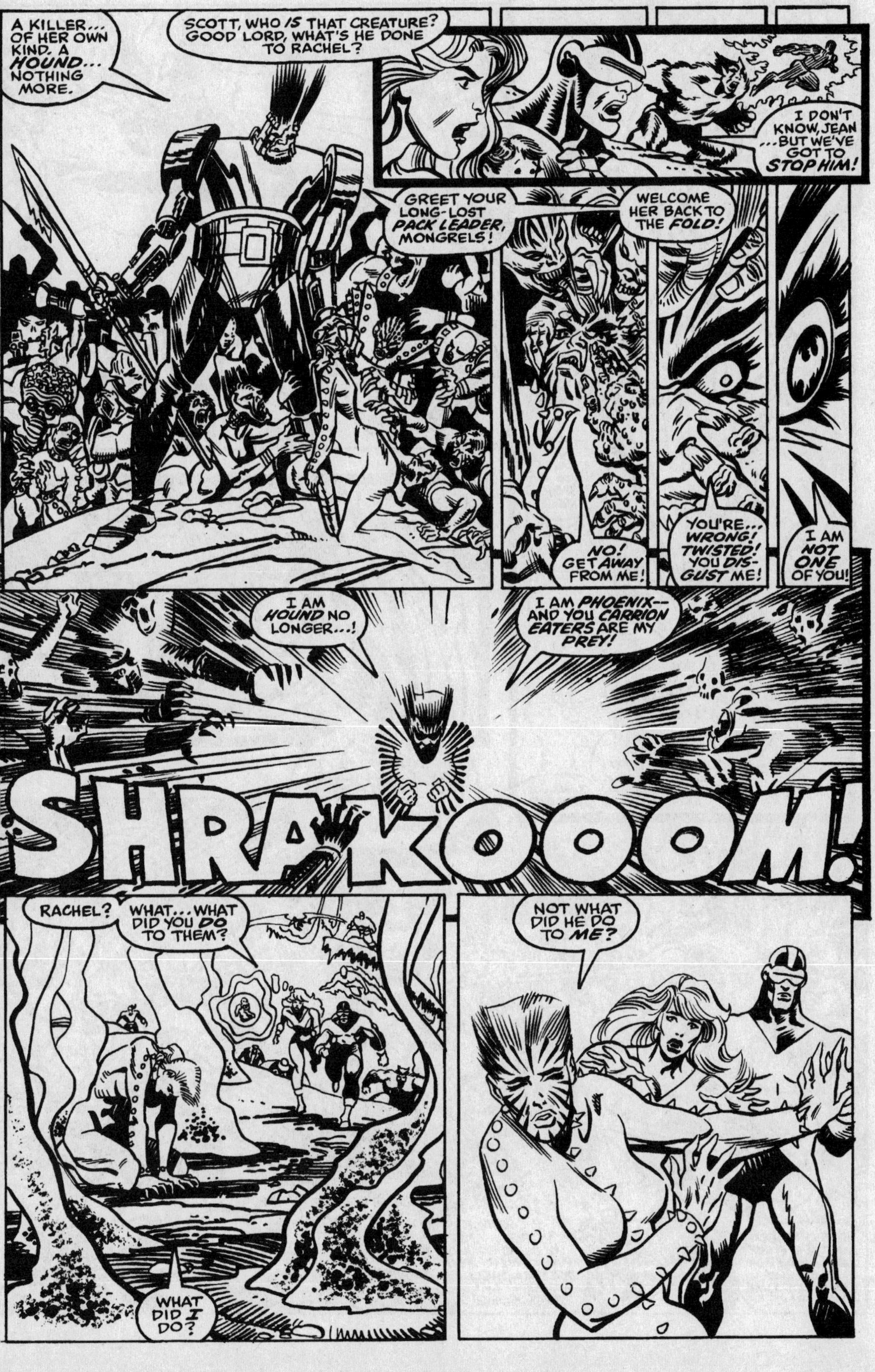
A KILLER... OF HER OWN KIND. A HOUND... NOTHING MORE.
SCOTT, WHO IS THAT CREATURE? GOOD LORD, WHAT'S HE DONE TO RACHEL?
I DON'T KNOW, JEAN ...BUT WE'VE GOT TO STOP HIM!
GREET YOUR LONG-LOST PACK LEADER, MONGRELS!
WELCOME HER BACK TO THE FOLD!
NO! GET AWAY FROM ME!
YOU'RE... WRONG! TWISTED! YOU DISGUST ME!
I AM NOT ONE OF YOU!
I AM HOUND NO LONGER...!
I AM PHOENIX-- AND YOU CARRION EATERS ARE MY PREY!
SHRAKOOOM!
RACHEL?
WHAT... WHAT DID YOU DO TO THEM?
WHAT DID I DO?
NOT WHAT DID HE DO TO ME?

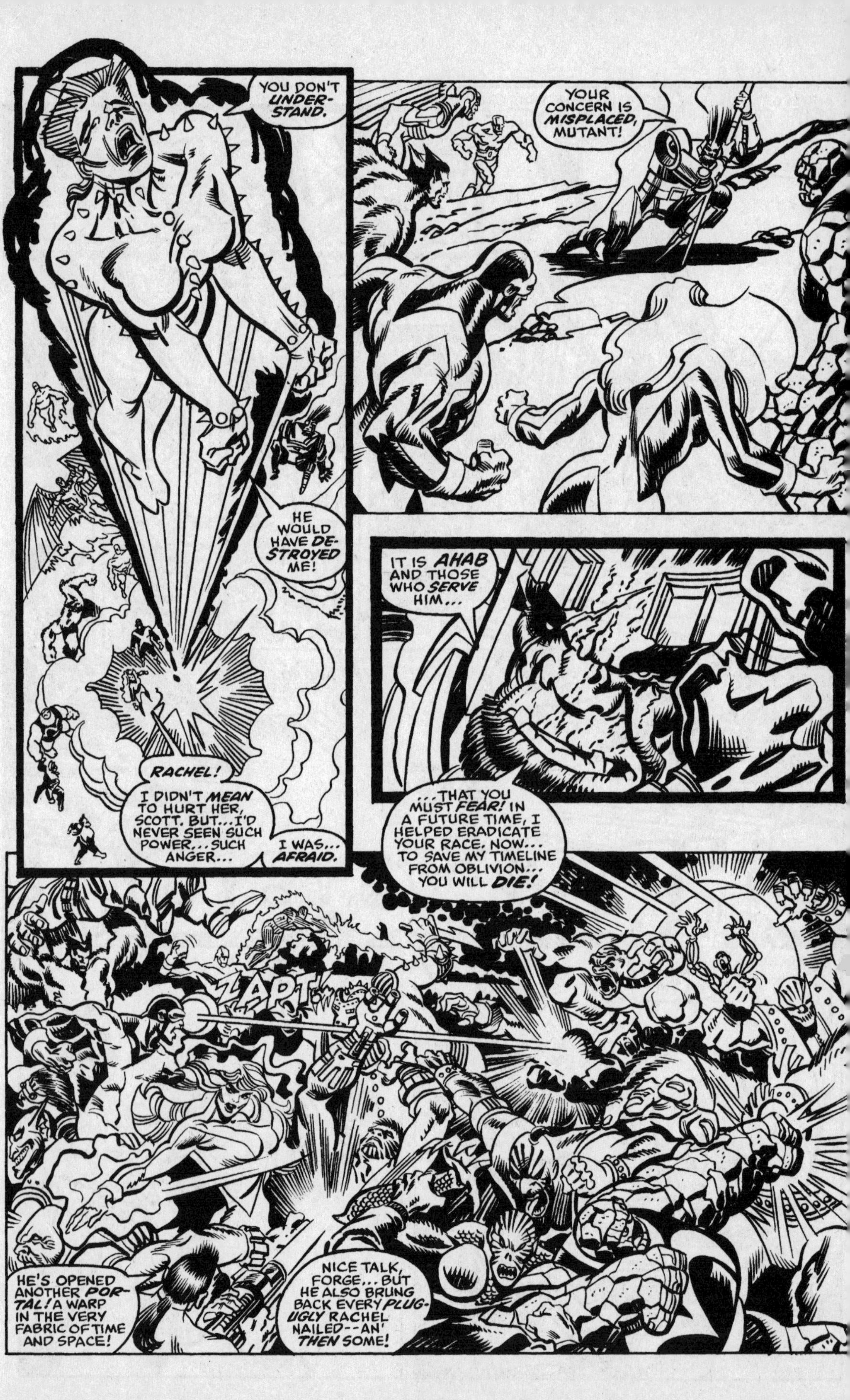
YOU DON'T UNDER-STAND.
YOUR CONCERN IS MISPLACED, MUTANT!
HE WOULD HAVE DE-STROYED ME!
IT IS AHAB AND THOSE WHO SERVE HIM...
RACHEL!
I DIDN'T MEAN TO HURT HER, SCOTT. BUT...I'D NEVER SEEN SUCH POWER...SUCH ANGER...
I WAS... AFRAID.
...THAT YOU MUST FEAR! IN A FUTURE TIME, I HELPED ERADICATE YOUR RACE. NOW... TO SAVE MY TIMELINE FROM OBLIVION... YOU WILL DIE!
ZAPT
HE'S OPENED ANOTHER PORTAL! A WARP IN THE VERY FABRIC OF TIME AND SPACE!
NICE TALK, FORGE... BUT HE ALSO BRUNG BACK EVERY PLUG-UGLY RACHEL NAILED--AN' THEN SOME!

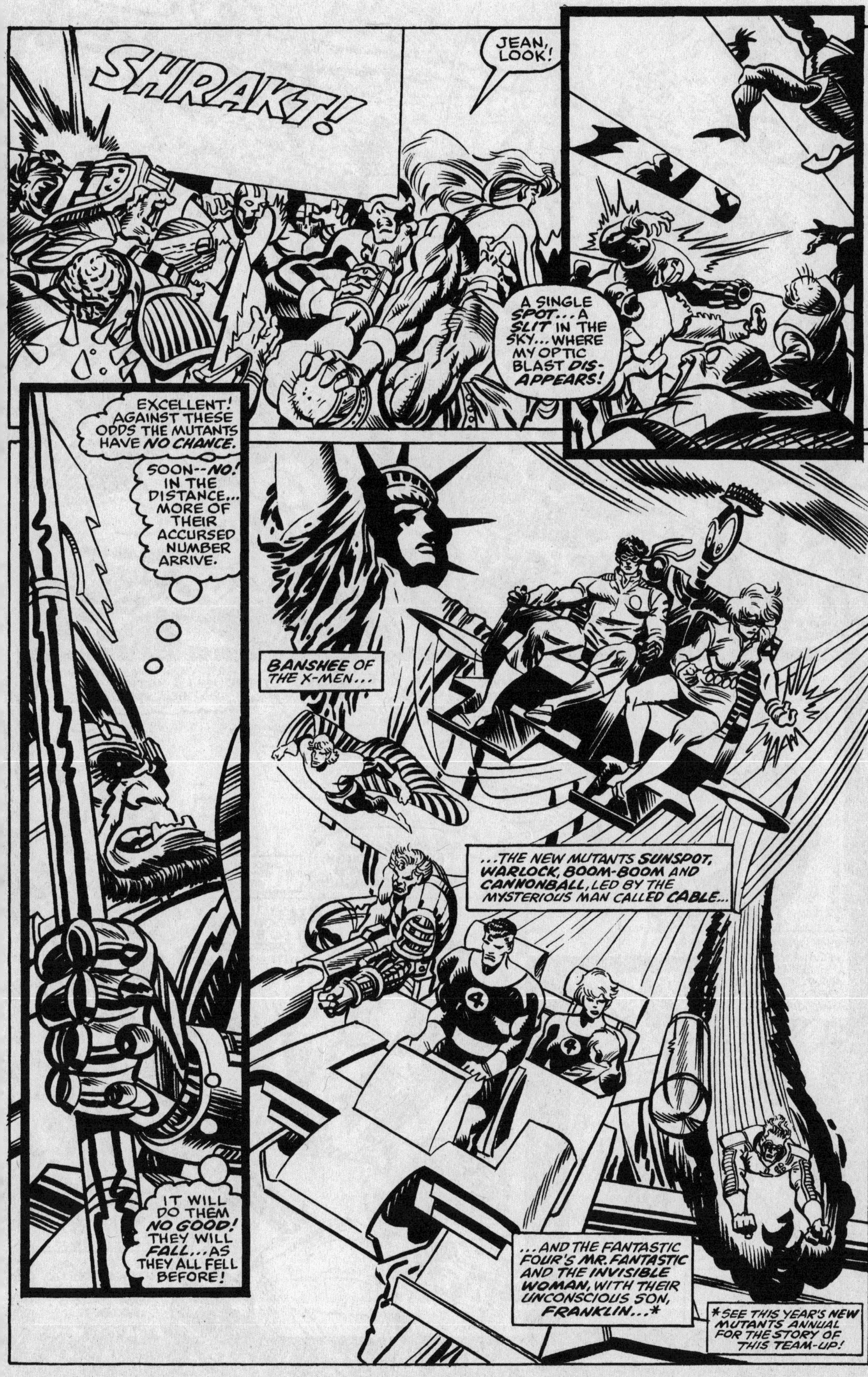
SHRAKT!
JEAN, LOOK!
A SINGLE SPOT... A SLIT IN THE SKY... WHERE MY OPTIC BLAST DIS-APPEARS!
EXCELLENT! AGAINST THESE ODDS THE MUTANTS HAVE NO CHANCE.
SOON--NO! IN THE DISTANCE... MORE OF THEIR ACCURSED NUMBER ARRIVE.
IT WILL DO THEM NO GOOD! THEY WILL FALL... AS THEY ALL FELL BEFORE!
BANSHEE OF THE X-MEN...
...THE NEW MUTANTS SUNSPOT, WARLOCK, BOOM-BOOM AND CANNONBALL, LED BY THE MYSTERIOUS MAN CALLED CABLE...
...AND THE FANTASTIC FOUR'S MR. FANTASTIC AND THE INVISIBLE WOMAN, WITH THEIR UNCONSCIOUS SON, FRANKLIN...*
*SEE THIS YEAR'S NEW MUTANTS ANNUAL FOR THE STORY OF THIS TEAM-UP!

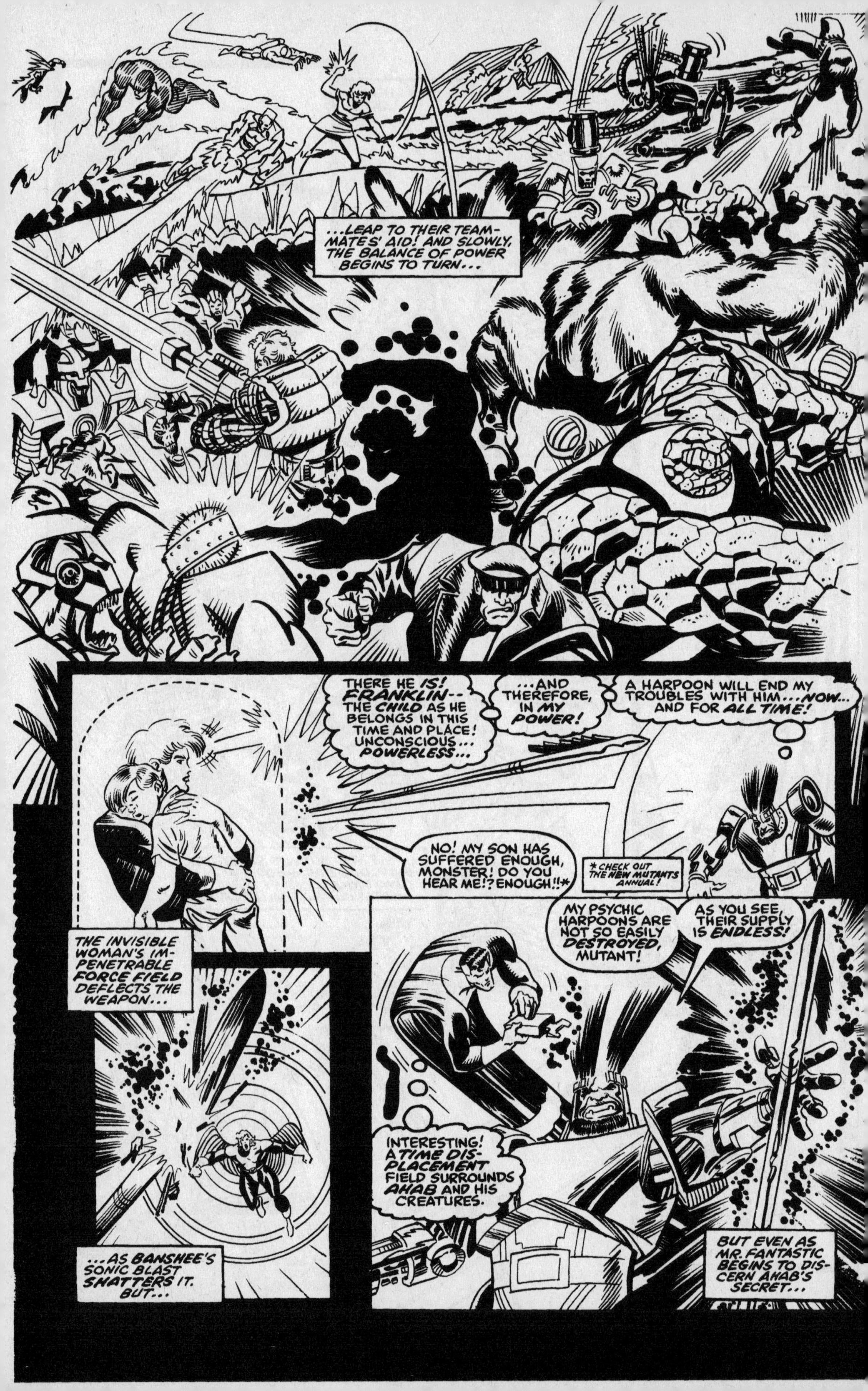
...LEAP TO THEIR TEAM-MATES' AID! AND SLOWLY, THE BALANCE OF POWER BEGINS TO TURN...
THERE HE IS! FRANKLIN--THE CHILD AS HE BELONGS IN THIS TIME AND PLACE! UNCONSCIOUS... POWERLESS...
...AND THEREFORE, IN MY POWER!
A HARPOON WILL END MY TROUBLES WITH HIM...NOW... AND FOR ALL TIME!
NO! MY SON HAS SUFFERED ENOUGH, MONSTER! DO YOU HEAR ME!? ENOUGH!!*
* CHECK OUT THE NEW MUTANTS ANNUAL!
THE INVISIBLE WOMAN'S IMPENETRABLE FORCE FIELD DEFLECTS THE WEAPON...
MY PSYCHIC HARPOONS ARE NOT SO EASILY DESTROYED, MUTANT!
AS YOU SEE, THEIR SUPPLY IS ENDLESS!
...AS BANSHEE'S SONIC BLAST SHATTERS IT. BUT...
INTERESTING! A TIME DISPLACEMENT FIELD SURROUNDS AHAB AND HIS CREATURES.
BUT EVEN AS MR. FANTASTIC BEGINS TO DISCERN AHAB'S SECRET...

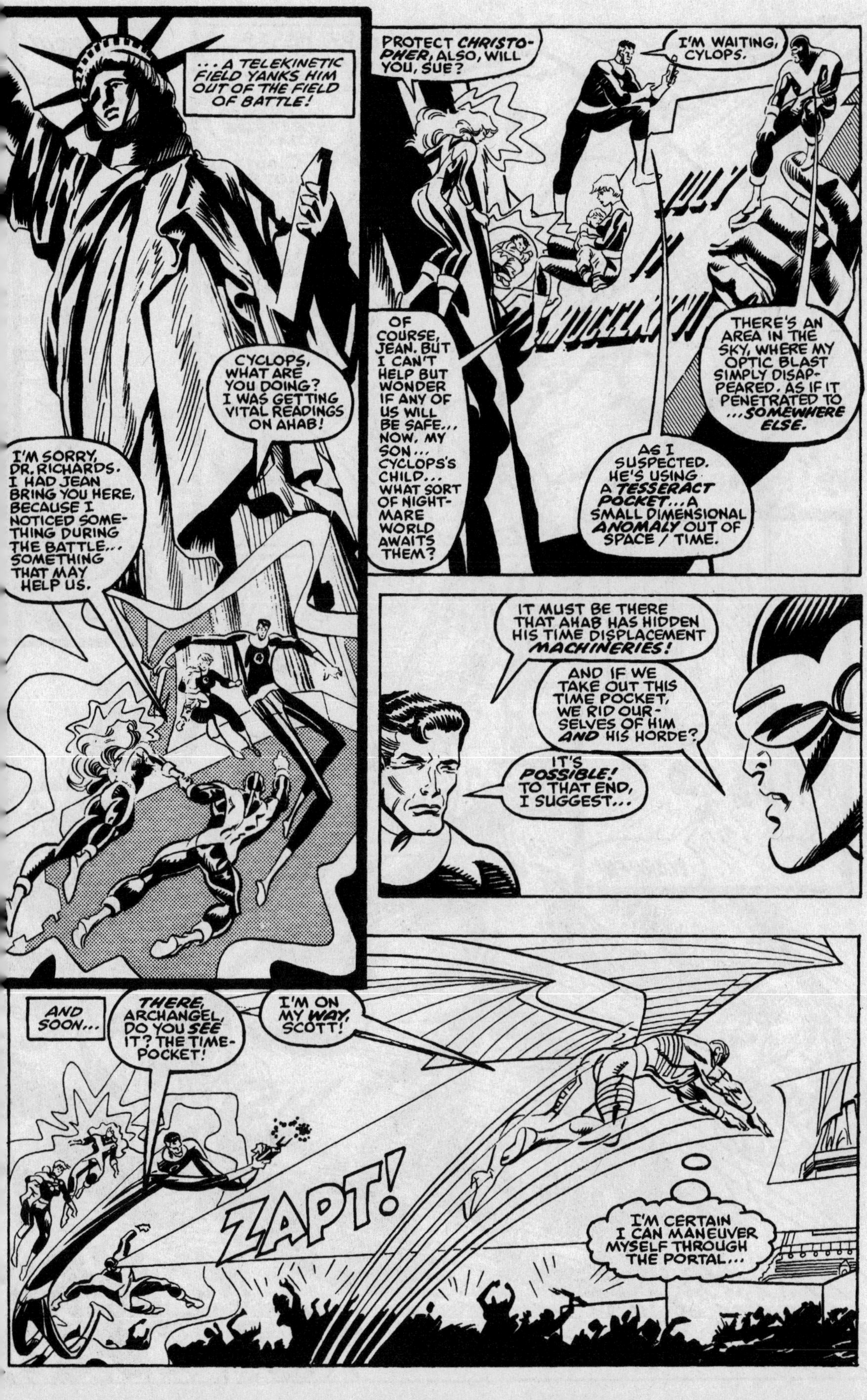
...A TELEKINETIC FIELD YANKS HIM OUT OF THE FIELD OF BATTLE!
CYCLOPS, WHAT ARE YOU DOING? I WAS GETTING VITAL READINGS ON AHAB!
I'M SORRY, DR. RICHARDS. I HAD JEAN BRING YOU HERE, BECAUSE I NOTICED SOMETHING DURING THE BATTLE... SOMETHING THAT MAY HELP US.
PROTECT CHRISTOPHER, ALSO, WILL YOU, SUE?
OF COURSE, JEAN. BUT I CAN'T HELP BUT WONDER IF ANY OF US WILL BE SAFE... NOW, MY SON... CYCLOPS'S CHILD... WHAT SORT OF NIGHTMARE WORLD AWAITS THEM?
I'M WAITING, CYLOPS.
THERE'S AN AREA IN THE SKY, WHERE MY OPTIC BLAST SIMPLY DISAPPEARED. AS IF IT PENETRATED TO ...SOMEWHERE ELSE.
AS I SUSPECTED. HE'S USING A TESSERACT POCKET... A SMALL DIMENSIONAL ANOMALY OUT OF SPACE / TIME.
IT MUST BE THERE THAT AHAB HAS HIDDEN HIS TIME DISPLACEMENT MACHINERIES!
AND IF WE TAKE OUT THIS TIME POCKET, WE RID OURSELVES OF HIM AND HIS HORDE?
IT'S POSSIBLE! TO THAT END, I SUGGEST...
AND SOON...
THERE, ARCHANGEL, DO YOU SEE IT? THE TIME-POCKET!
I'M ON MY WAY, SCOTT!
ZAPT!
I'M CERTAIN I CAN MANEUVER MYSELF THROUGH THE PORTAL...

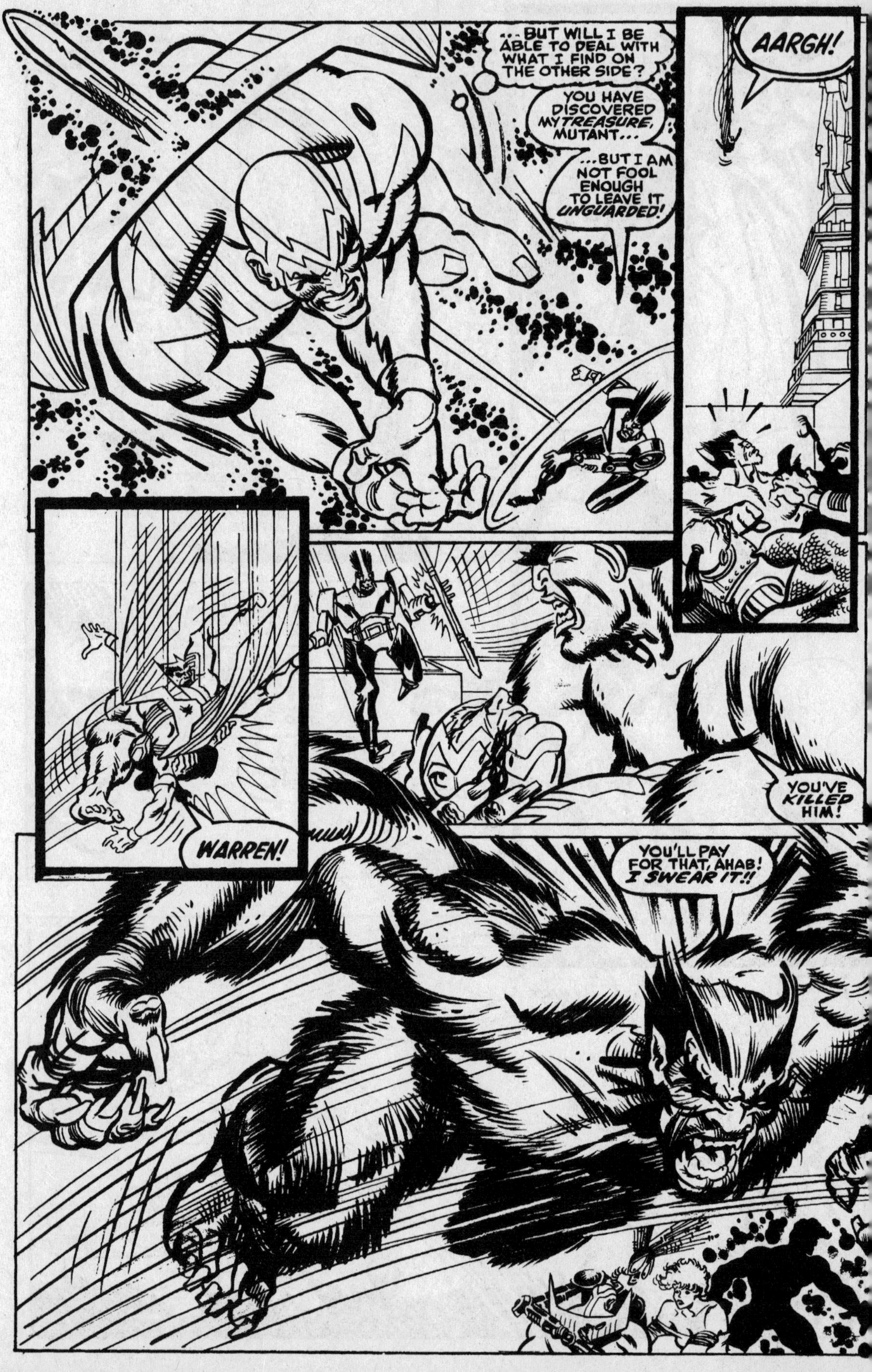
...BUT WILL I BE ABLE TO DEAL WITH WHAT I FIND ON THE OTHER SIDE?
YOU HAVE DISCOVERED MY TREASURE, MUTANT...
...BUT I AM NOT FOOL ENOUGH TO LEAVE IT UNGUARDED!
AARGH!
WARREN!
YOU'VE KILLED HIM!
YOU'LL PAY FOR THAT, AHAB! I SWEAR IT!!

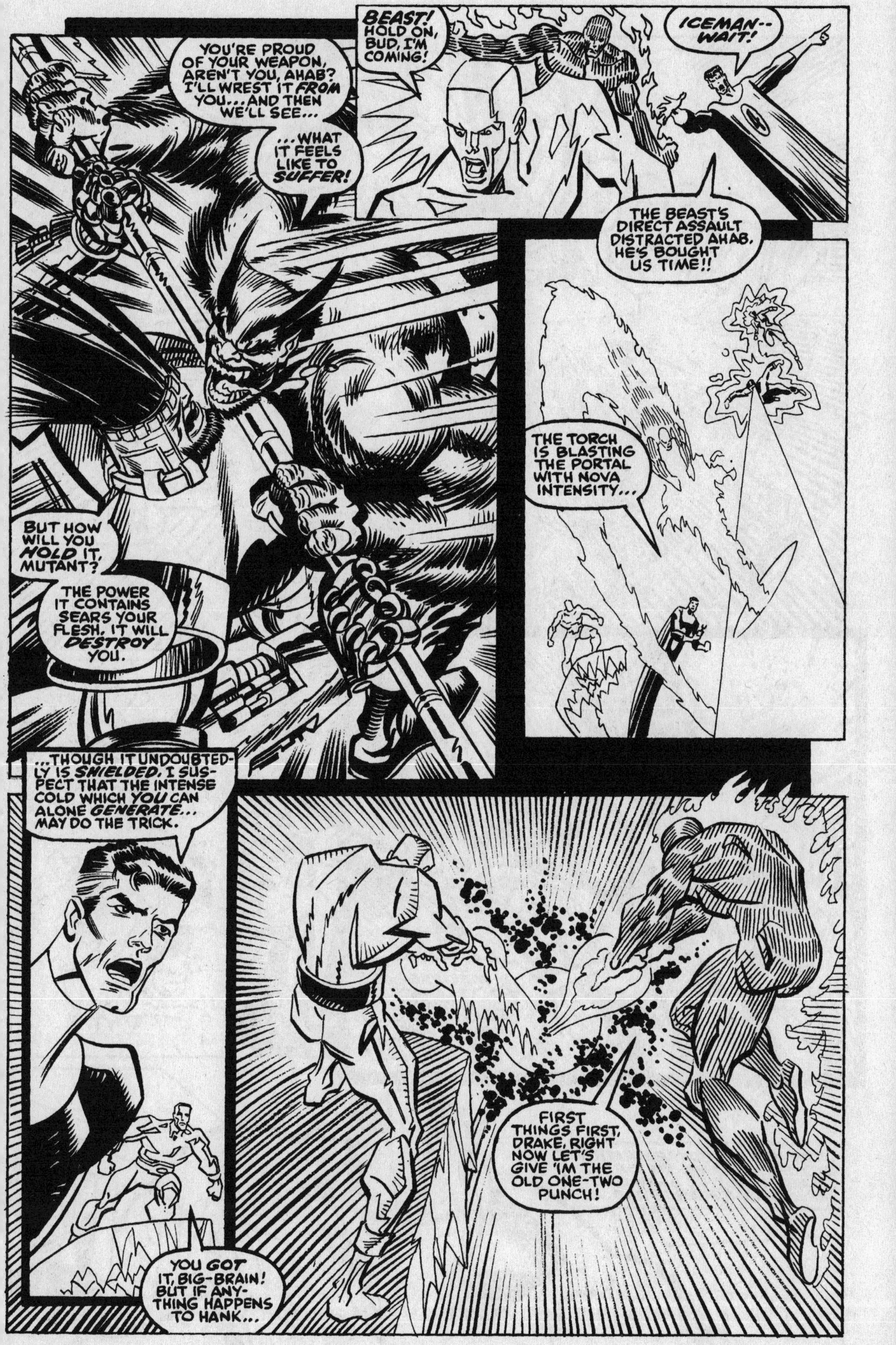

YOU'RE PROUD OF YOUR WEAPON, AREN'T YOU, AHAB? I'LL WREST IT FROM YOU... AND THEN WE'LL SEE...
...WHAT IT FEELS LIKE TO SUFFER!
BEAST! HOLD ON, BUD, I'M COMING!
ICEMAN-- WAIT!
THE BEAST'S DIRECT ASSAULT DISTRACTED AHAB. HE'S BOUGHT US TIME!!
THE TORCH IS BLASTING THE PORTAL WITH NOVA INTENSITY...
BUT HOW WILL YOU HOLD IT, MUTANT?
THE POWER IT CONTAINS SEARS YOUR FLESH. IT WILL DESTROY YOU.
...THOUGH IT UNDOUBTEDLY IS SHIELDED, I SUSPECT THAT THE INTENSE COLD WHICH YOU CAN ALONE GENERATE... MAY DO THE TRICK.
YOU GOT IT, BIG-BRAIN! BUT IF ANYTHING HAPPENS TO HANK...
FIRST THINGS FIRST, DRAKE, RIGHT NOW LET'S GIVE 'IM THE OLD ONE-TWO PUNCH!

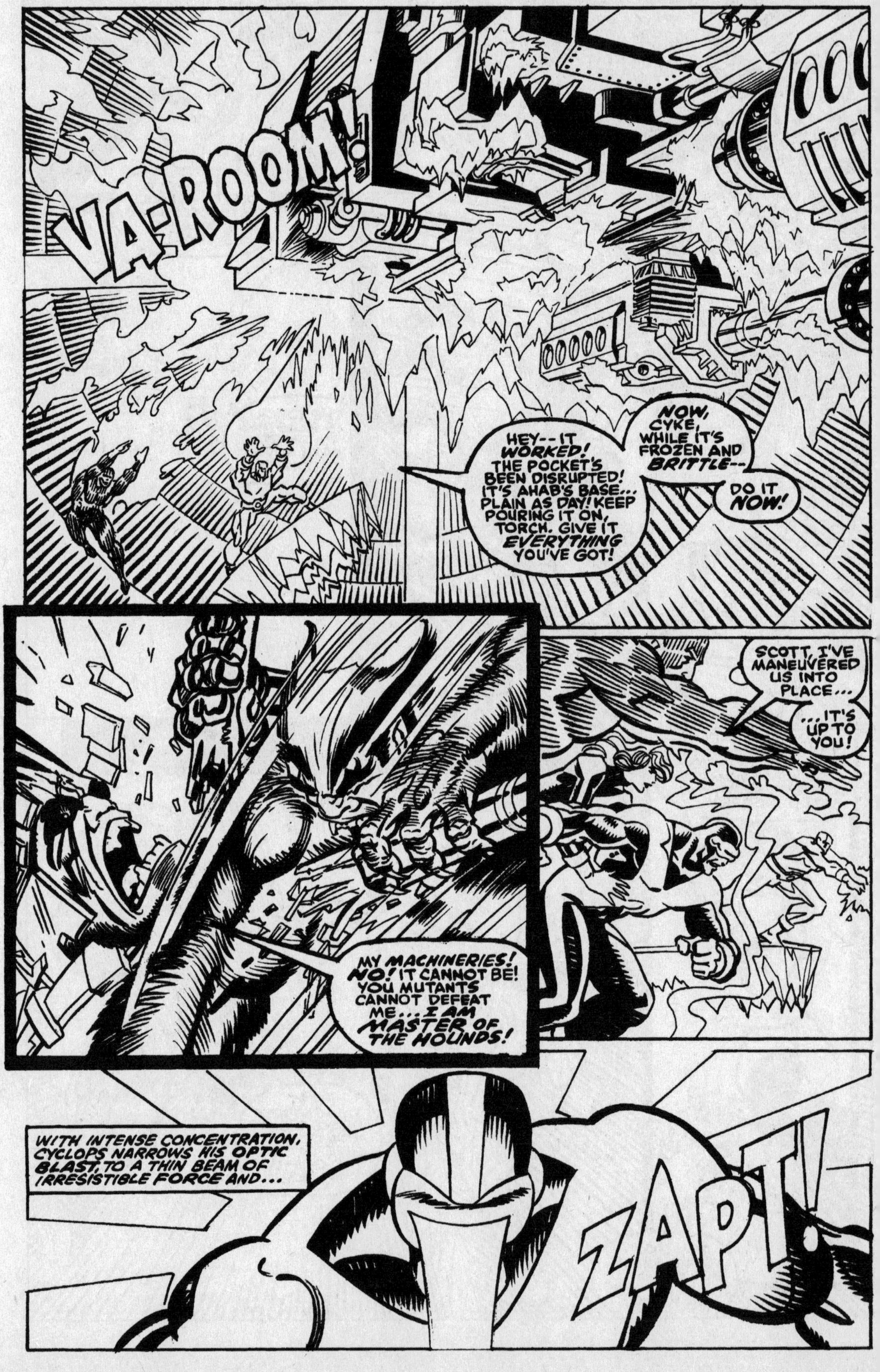
VA-ROOM!
HEY--IT WORKED! THE POCKET'S BEEN DISRUPTED! IT'S AHAB'S BASE... PLAIN AS DAY! KEEP POURING IT ON, TORCH. GIVE IT EVERYTHING YOU'VE GOT!
NOW, CYKE, WHILE IT'S FROZEN AND BRITTLE--
DO IT NOW!
MY MACHINERIES! NO! IT CANNOT BE! YOU MUTANTS CANNOT DEFEAT ME... I AM MASTER OF THE HOUNDS!
SCOTT, I'VE MANEUVERED US INTO PLACE...
...IT'S UP TO YOU!
WITH INTENSE CONCENTRATION, CYCLOPS NARROWS HIS OPTIC BLAST, TO A THIN BEAM OF IRRESISTIBLE FORCE AND...
ZAPT!

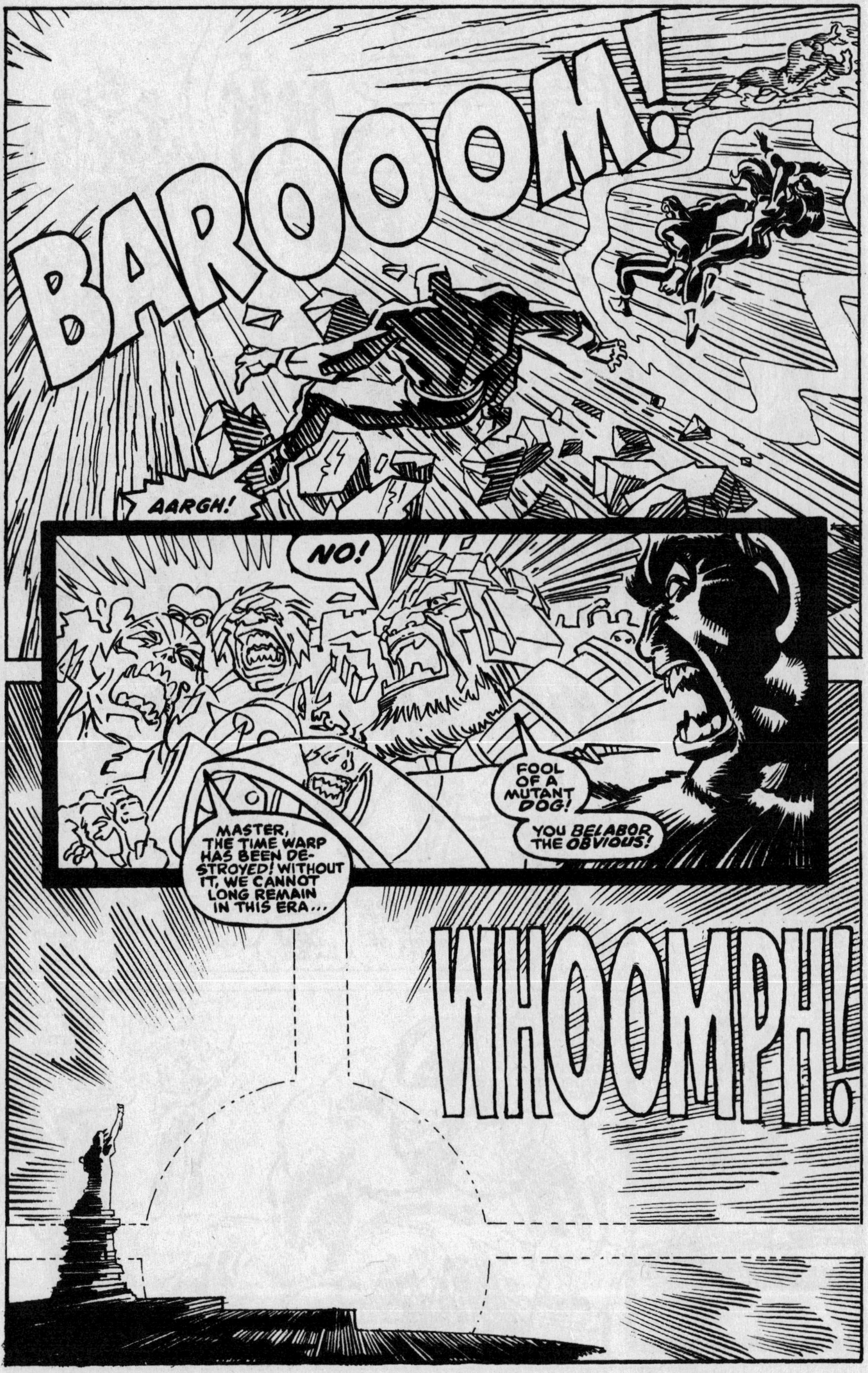
BAROOOM!
AARGH!
NO!
MASTER, THE TIME WARP HAS BEEN DE-STROYED! WITHOUT IT, WE CANNOT LONG REMAIN IN THIS ERA...
FOOL OF A MUTANT DOG!
YOU BELABOR THE OBVIOUS!
WHOOMPH!

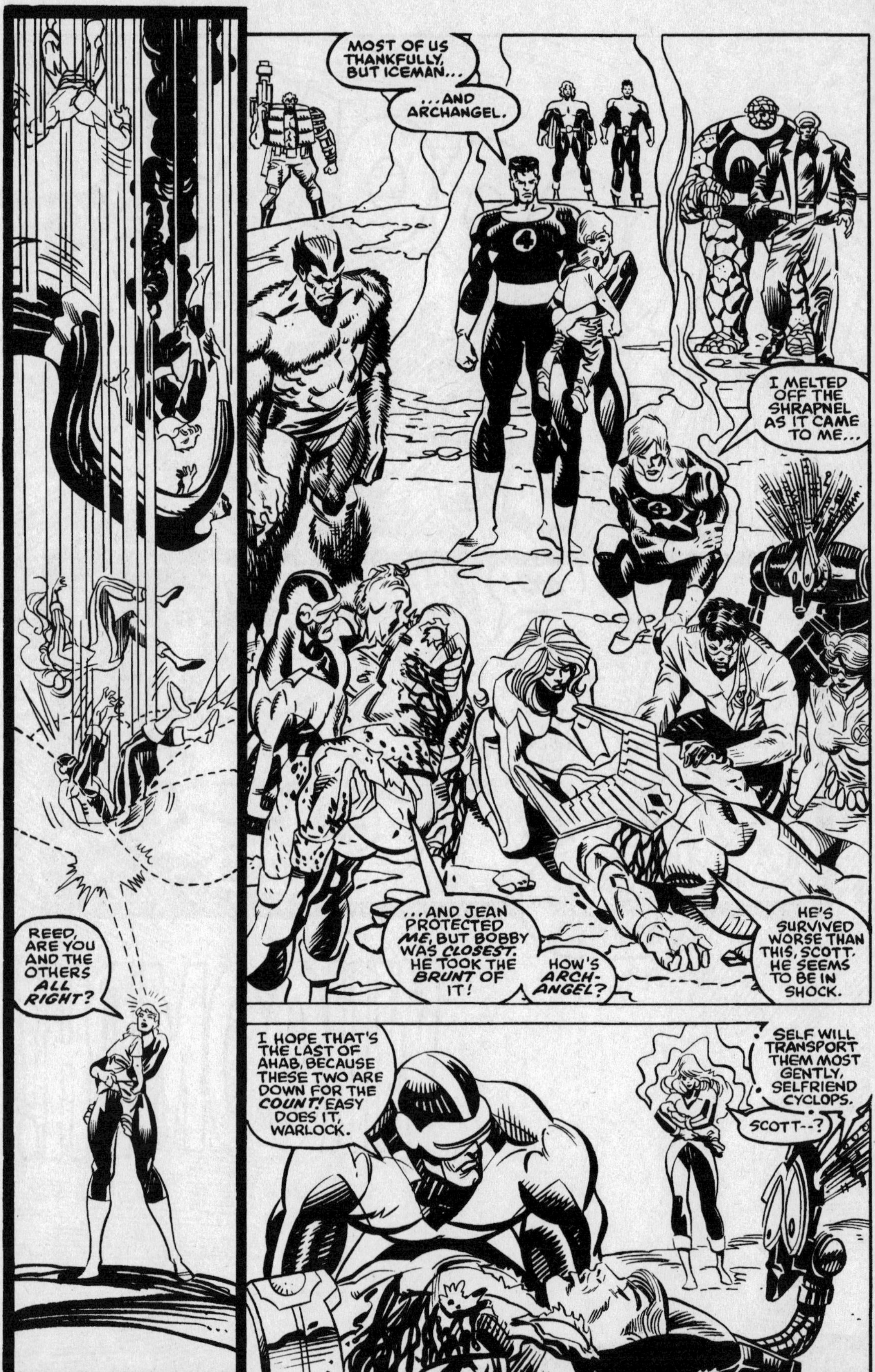
REED, ARE YOU AND THE OTHERS ALL RIGHT?
MOST OF US THANKFULLY, BUT ICEMAN...
...AND ARCHANGEL.
I MELTED OFF THE SHRAPNEL AS IT CAME TO ME...
...AND JEAN PROTECTED ME, BUT BOBBY WAS CLOSEST. HE TOOK THE BRUNT OF IT!
HOW'S ARCH-ANGEL?
HE'S SURVIVED WORSE THAN THIS, SCOTT. HE SEEMS TO BE IN SHOCK.
I HOPE THAT'S THE LAST OF AHAB, BECAUSE THESE TWO ARE DOWN FOR THE COUNT! EASY DOES IT, WARLOCK.
SELF WILL TRANSPORT THEM MOST GENTLY, SELFRIEND CYCLOPS.
SCOTT--?

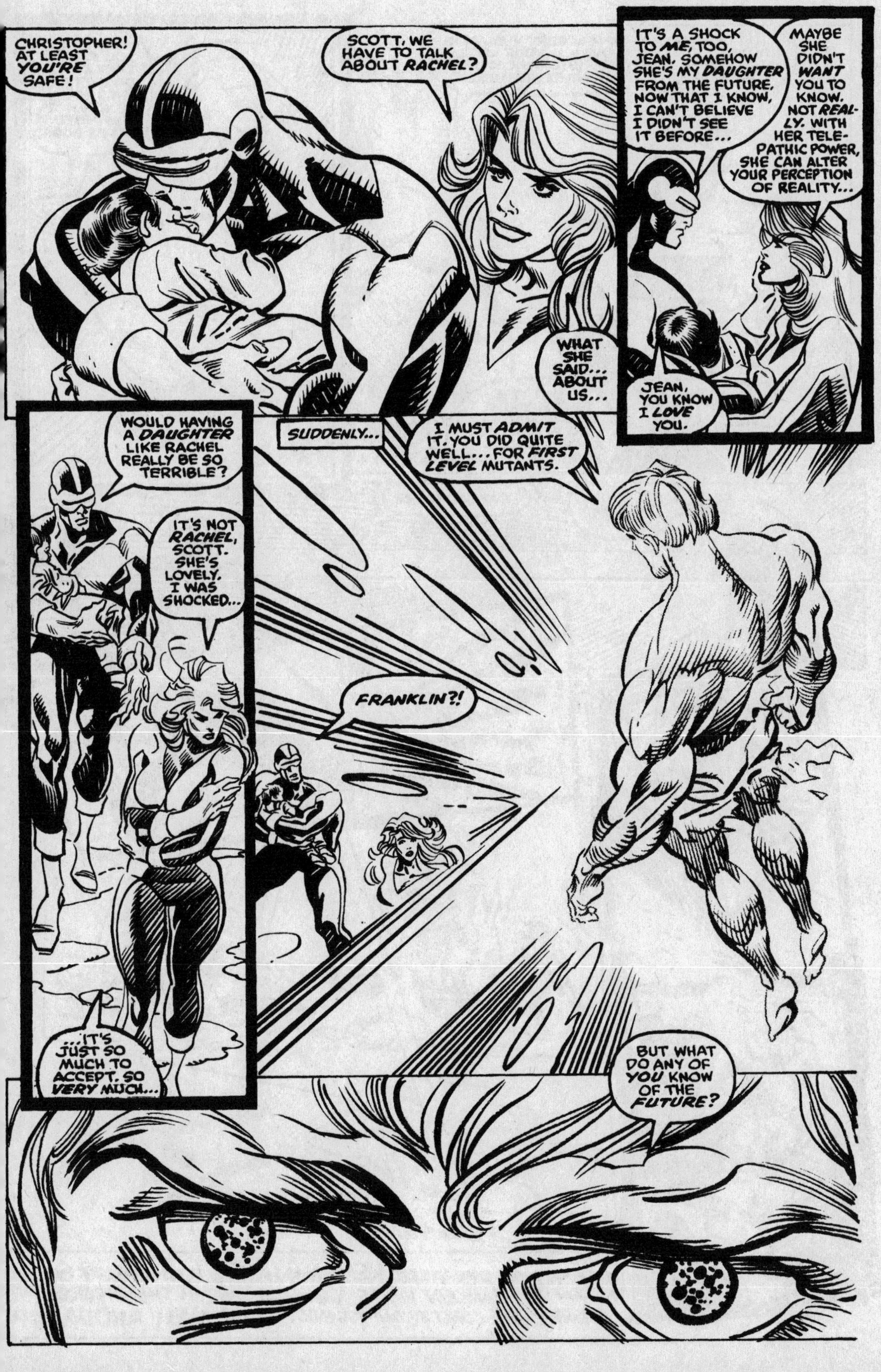
CHRISTOPHER! AT LEAST YOU'RE SAFE!
SCOTT, WE HAVE TO TALK ABOUT RACHEL?
WHAT SHE SAID... ABOUT US...
IT'S A SHOCK TO ME, TOO, JEAN. SOMEHOW SHE'S MY DAUGHTER FROM THE FUTURE. NOW THAT I KNOW, I CAN'T BELIEVE I DIDN'T SEE IT BEFORE...
MAYBE SHE DIDN'T WANT YOU TO KNOW. NOT REALLY. WITH HER TELEPATHIC POWER, SHE CAN ALTER YOUR PERCEPTION OF REALITY...
JEAN, YOU KNOW I LOVE YOU.
WOULD HAVING A DAUGHTER LIKE RACHEL REALLY BE SO TERRIBLE?
IT'S NOT RACHEL, SCOTT. SHE'S LOVELY. I WAS SHOCKED...
...IT'S JUST SO MUCH TO ACCEPT. SO VERY MUCH...
SUDDENLY...
I MUST ADMIT IT. YOU DID QUITE WELL... FOR FIRST LEVEL MUTANTS.
FRANKLIN?!
BUT WHAT DO ANY OF YOU KNOW OF THE FUTURE?

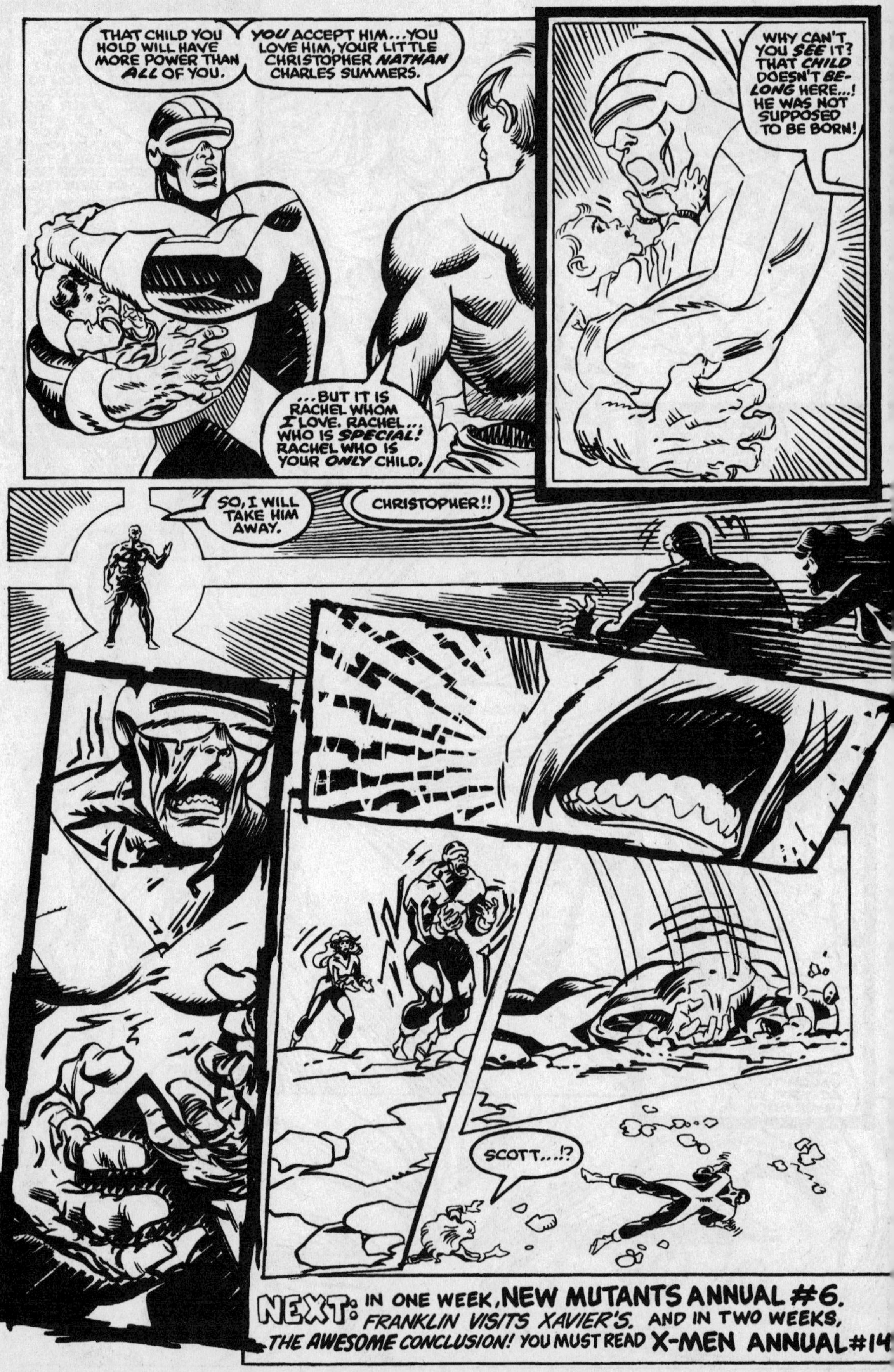
THAT CHILD YOU HOLD WILL HAVE MORE POWER THAN ALL OF YOU.
YOU ACCEPT HIM... YOU LOVE HIM, YOUR LITTLE CHRISTOPHER NATHAN CHARLES SUMMERS.
...BUT IT IS RACHEL WHOM I LOVE. RACHEL... WHO IS SPECIAL! RACHEL WHO IS YOUR ONLY CHILD.
WHY CAN'T YOU SEE IT? THAT CHILD DOESN'T BE-LONG HERE...! HE WAS NOT SUPPOSED TO BE BORN!
SO, I WILL TAKE HIM AWAY.
CHRISTOPHER!!
SCOTT...!?
NEXT: IN ONE WEEK, NEW MUTANTS ANNUAL #6. FRANKLIN VISITS XAVIER'S. AND IN TWO WEEKS, THE AWESOME CONCLUSION! YOU MUST READ X-MEN ANNUAL #14

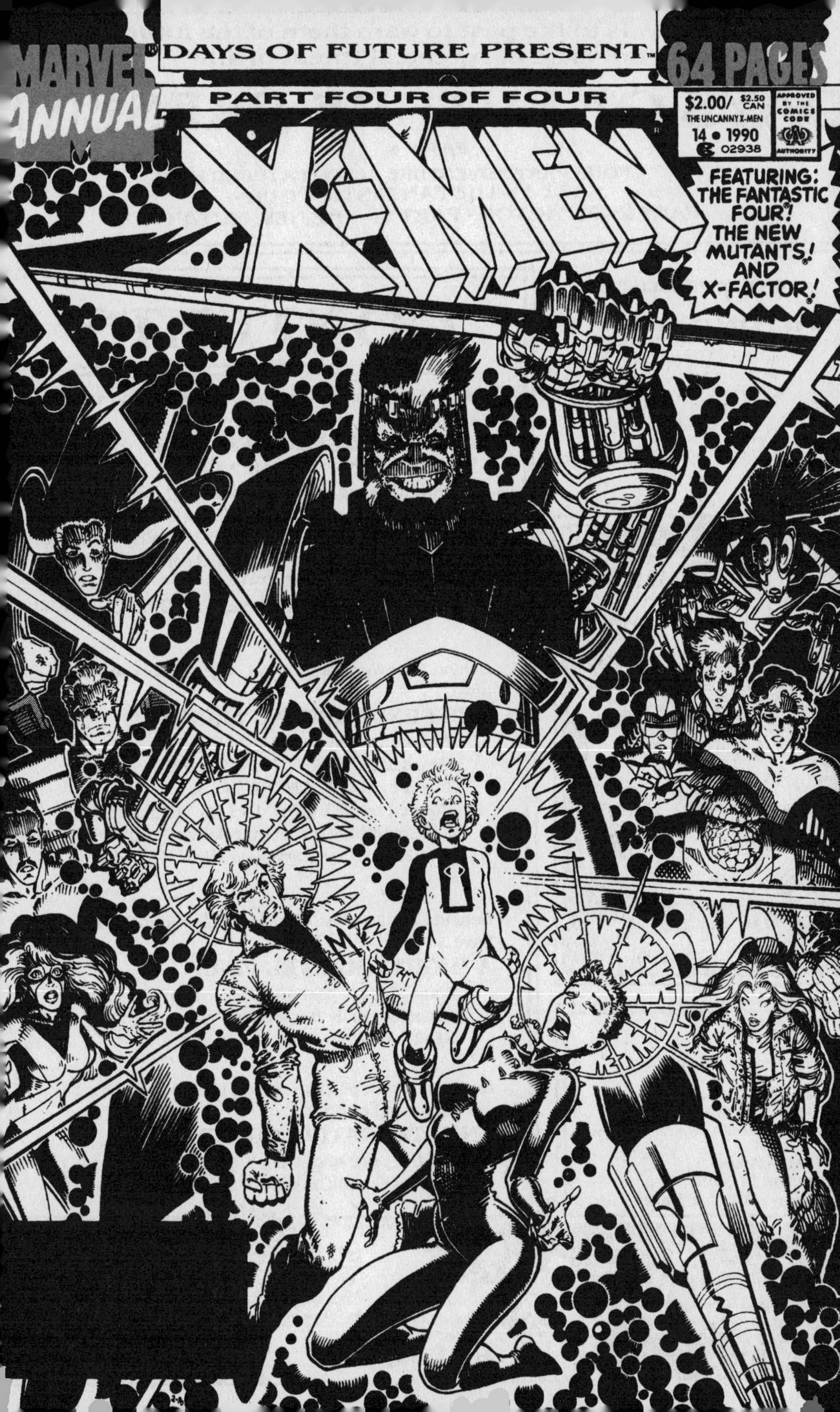

MARVEL ANNUAL
DAYS OF FUTURE PRESENT
64 PAGES
PART FOUR OF FOUR
$2.00/ $2.50 CAN
THE UNCANNY X-MEN
14 • 1990
02938
APPROVED BY THE COMICS CODE AUTHORITY
X-MEN
FEATURING: THE FANTASTIC FOUR! THE NEW MUTANTS! AND X-FACTOR!

He travels to the past to warn them of the future.
But is he the greatest threat of all?

DAYS OF FUTURE PRESENT

PART 4

A FOUR PART ADVENTURE ALSO FEATURED IN:
PART 1—THE FANTASTIC FOUR •
PART 2—X-FACTOR • PART 3—THE NEW MUTANTS

STAN LEE PRESENTS:

THE UNCANNY X-MEN

BOB HARRAS
EDITOR
--Our very own Monty Hall

SUZANNE GAFFNEY
ASSISTANT EDITOR
--Carol Merrill's favorite protegee

TOM DeFALCO
EDITOR IN CHIEF
--Today's Big Prize Winner

CONTENTS

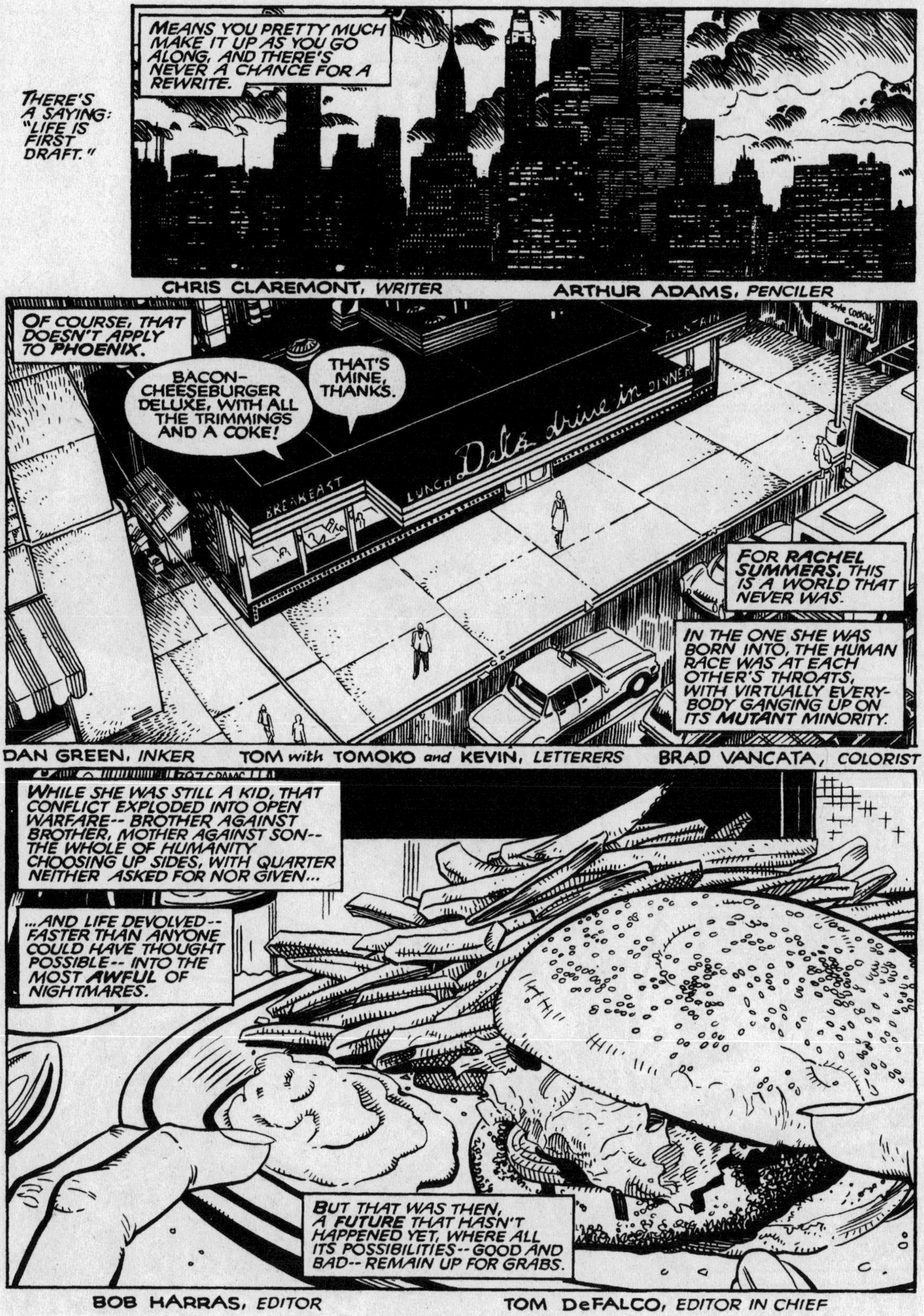

THERE'S A SAYING: "LIFE IS FIRST DRAFT."
MEANS YOU PRETTY MUCH MAKE IT UP AS YOU GO ALONG, AND THERE'S NEVER A CHANCE FOR A REWRITE.
CHRIS CLAREMONT, WRITER
ARTHUR ADAMS, PENCILER
OF COURSE, THAT DOESN'T APPLY TO PHOENIX.
BACON-CHEESEBURGER DELUXE, WITH ALL THE TRIMMINGS AND A COKE!
THAT'S MINE, THANKS.
Del's drive in DINNER
BREAKFAST
LUNCH
FOUNTAIN
FOR RACHEL SUMMERS, THIS IS A WORLD THAT NEVER WAS.
IN THE ONE SHE WAS BORN INTO, THE HUMAN RACE WAS AT EACH OTHER'S THROATS, WITH VIRTUALLY EVERYBODY GANGING UP ON ITS MUTANT MINORITY.
DAN GREEN, INKER
TOM with TOMOKO and KEVIN, LETTERERS
BRAD VANCATA, COLORIST
WHILE SHE WAS STILL A KID, THAT CONFLICT EXPLODED INTO OPEN WARFARE-- BROTHER AGAINST BROTHER, MOTHER AGAINST SON-- THE WHOLE OF HUMANITY CHOOSING UP SIDES, WITH QUARTER NEITHER ASKED FOR NOR GIVEN...
...AND LIFE DEVOLVED-- FASTER THAN ANYONE COULD HAVE THOUGHT POSSIBLE-- INTO THE MOST AWFUL OF NIGHTMARES.
BUT THAT WAS THEN, A FUTURE THAT HASN'T HAPPENED YET, WHERE ALL ITS POSSIBILITIES-- GOOD AND BAD-- REMAIN UP FOR GRABS.
BOB HARRAS, EDITOR
TOM DeFALCO, EDITOR IN CHIEF

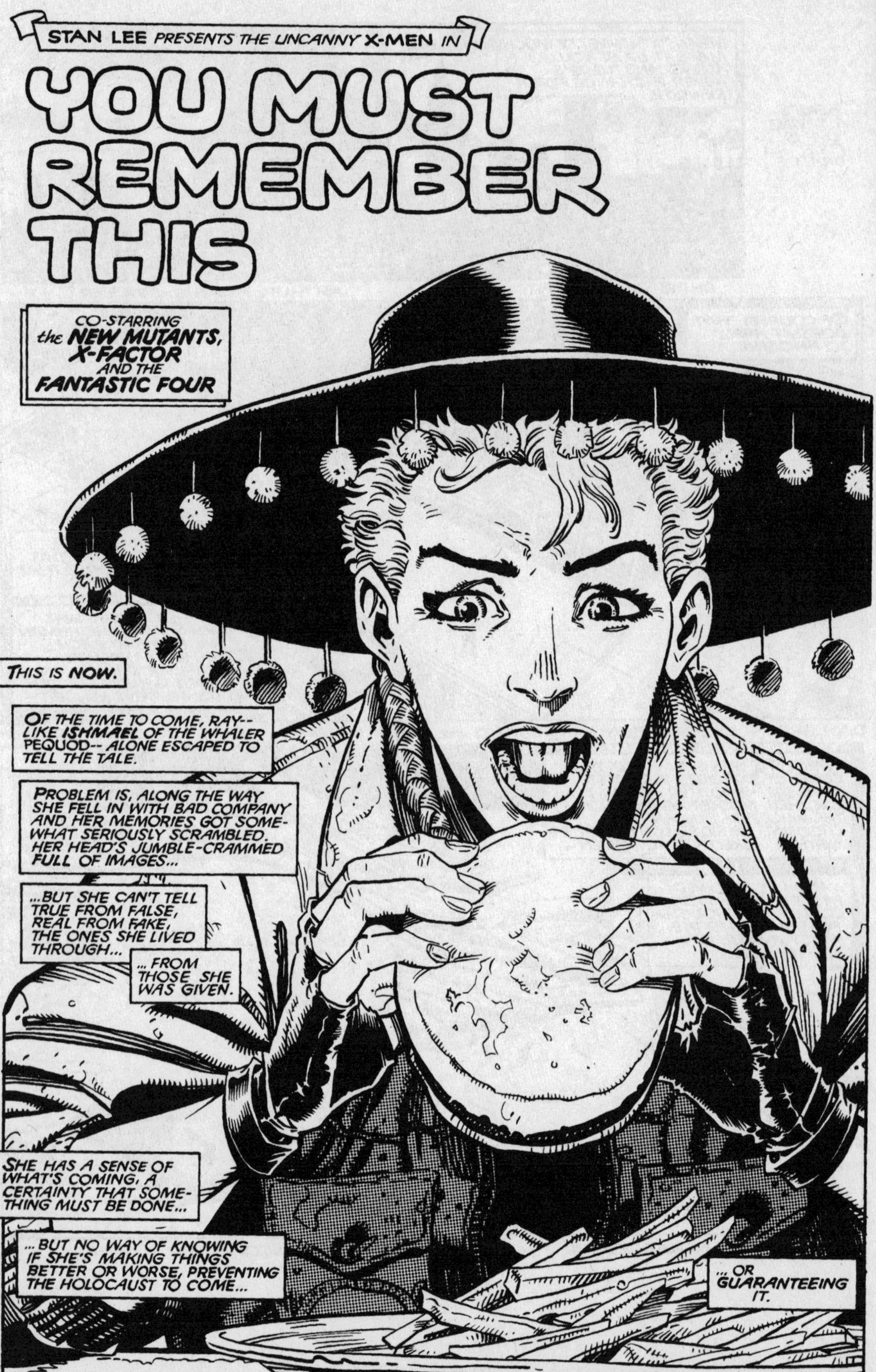

STAN LEE PRESENTS THE UNCANNY X-MEN IN
YOU MUST REMEMBER THIS
CO-STARRING the NEW MUTANTS, X-FACTOR AND THE FANTASTIC FOUR
THIS IS NOW.
OF THE TIME TO COME, RAY-- LIKE ISHMAEL OF THE WHALER PEQUOD-- ALONE ESCAPED TO TELL THE TALE.
PROBLEM IS, ALONG THE WAY SHE FELL IN WITH BAD COMPANY AND HER MEMORIES GOT SOMEWHAT SERIOUSLY SCRAMBLED. HER HEAD'S JUMBLE-CRAMMED FULL OF IMAGES...
...BUT SHE CAN'T TELL TRUE FROM FALSE, REAL FROM FAKE, THE ONES SHE LIVED THROUGH...
...FROM THOSE SHE WAS GIVEN.
SHE HAS A SENSE OF WHAT'S COMING, A CERTAINTY THAT SOMETHING MUST BE DONE...
...BUT NO WAY OF KNOWING IF SHE'S MAKING THINGS BETTER OR WORSE, PREVENTING THE HOLOCAUST TO COME...
...OR GUARANTEEING IT.

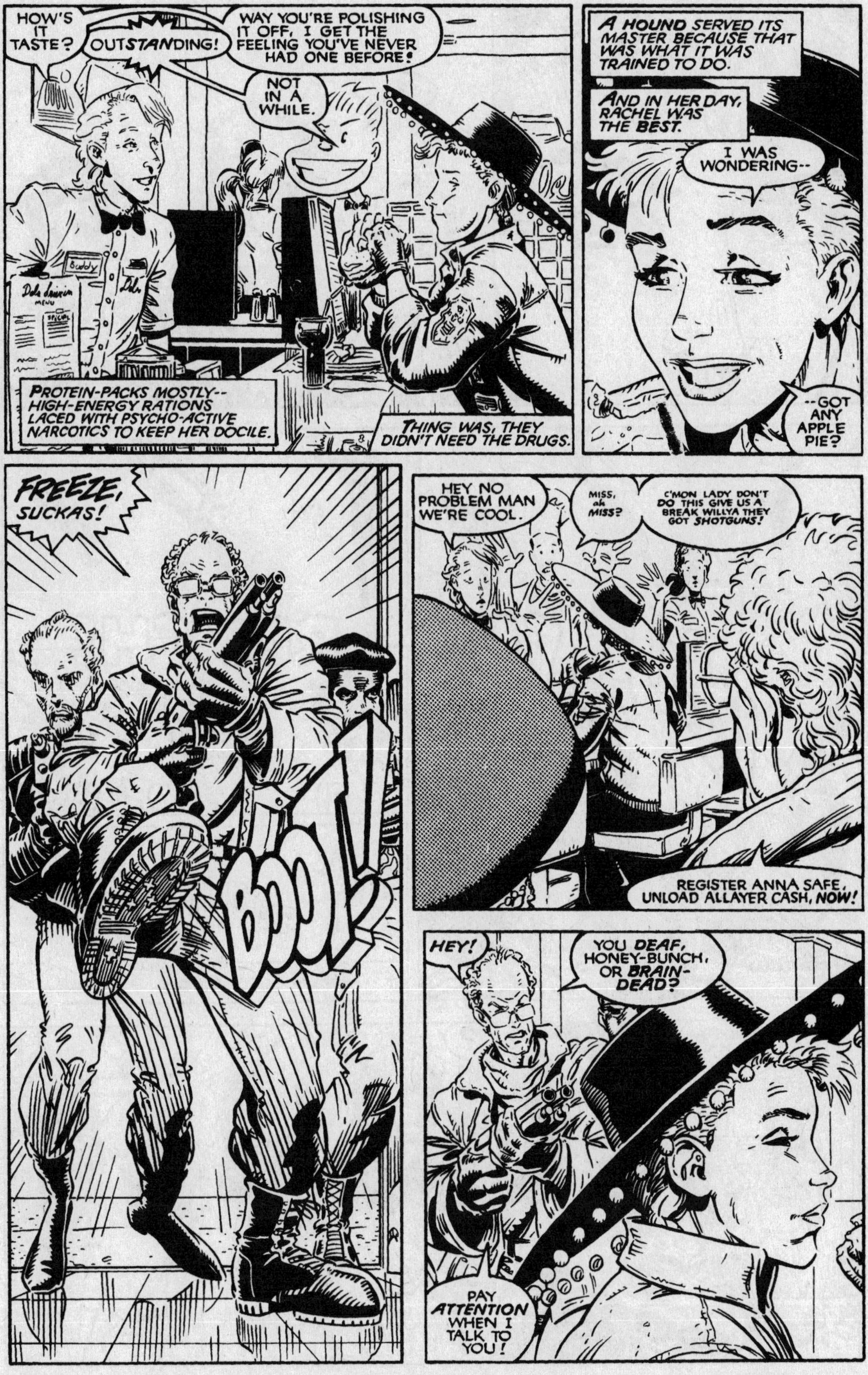
HOW'S IT TASTE?
OUTSTANDING!
WAY YOU'RE POLISHING IT OFF, I GET THE FEELING YOU'VE NEVER HAD ONE BEFORE!
NOT IN A WHILE.
PROTEIN-PACKS MOSTLY--HIGH-ENERGY RATIONS LACED WITH PSYCHO-ACTIVE NARCOTICS TO KEEP HER DOCILE.
THING WAS, THEY DIDN'T NEED THE DRUGS.
A HOUND SERVED ITS MASTER BECAUSE THAT WAS WHAT IT WAS TRAINED TO DO.
AND IN HER DAY, RACHEL WAS THE BEST.
I WAS WONDERING--
--GOT ANY APPLE PIE?
FREEZE, SUCKAS!
BOOT!
HEY NO PROBLEM MAN WE'RE COOL.
MISS, ah MISS?
C'MON LADY DON'T DO THIS GIVE US A BREAK WILLYA THEY GOT SHOTGUNS!
REGISTER ANNA SAFE, UNLOAD ALLAYER CASH, NOW!
HEY!
YOU DEAF, HONEY-BUNCH, OR BRAIN-DEAD?
PAY ATTENTION WHEN I TALK TO YOU!

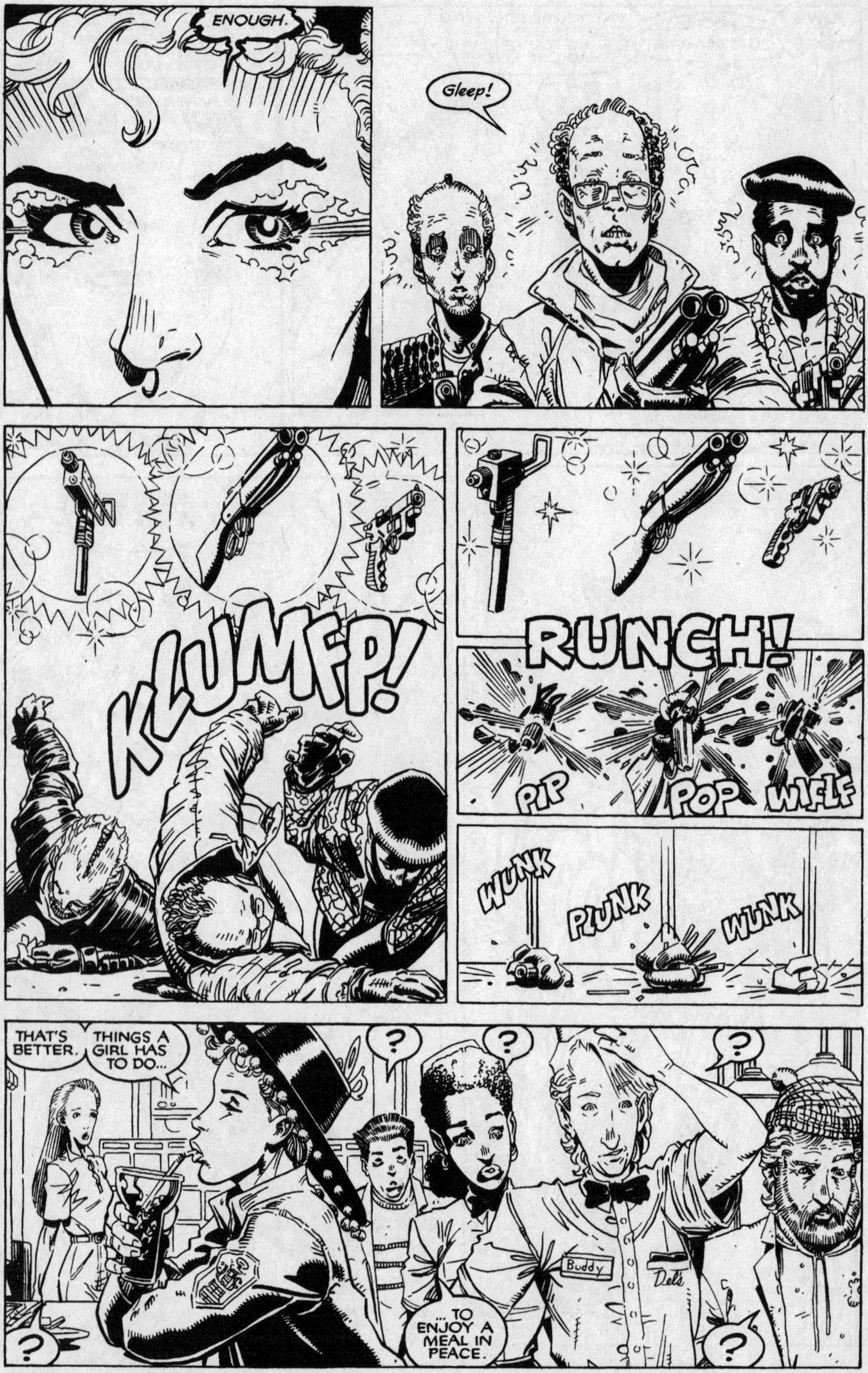
ENOUGH.
Gleep!
KLUMFP!
RUNCH!
PIP
POP
WIFLF
WUNK
PLUNK
WUNK
THAT'S BETTER.
THINGS A GIRL HAS TO DO...
?
?
?
?
... TO ENJOY A MEAL IN PEACE.
?
Buddy
Del's

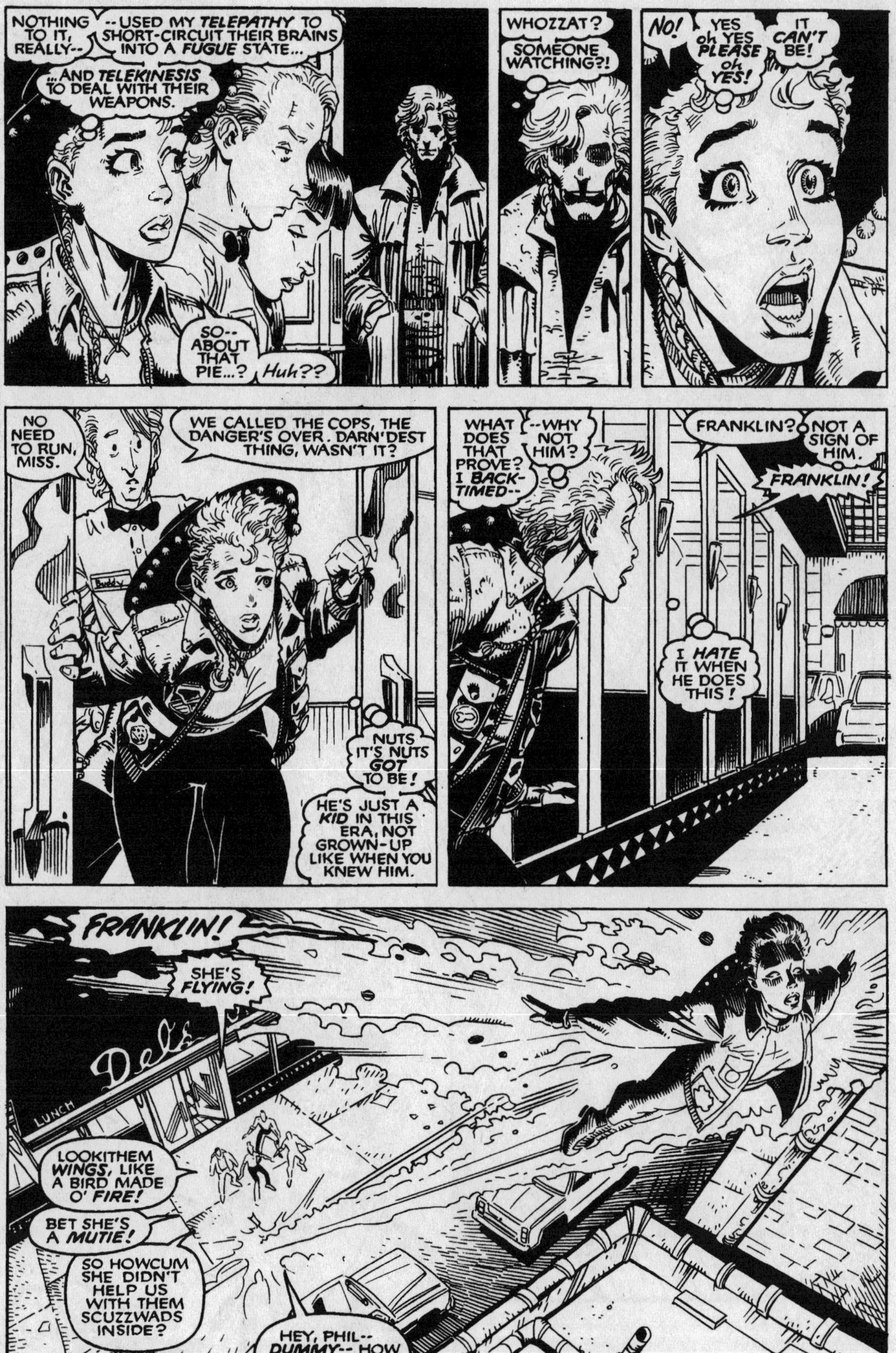

NOTHING TO IT, REALLY--
--USED MY TELEPATHY TO SHORT-CIRCUIT THEIR BRAINS INTO A FUGUE STATE...
...AND TELEKINESIS TO DEAL WITH THEIR WEAPONS.
SO--ABOUT THAT PIE...?
Huh??
WHOZZAT?
SOMEONE WATCHING?!
NO!
YES oh YES PLEASE oh YES!
IT CAN'T BE!
NO NEED TO RUN, MISS.
WE CALLED THE COPS, THE DANGER'S OVER. DARN'DEST THING, WASN'T IT?
NUTS IT'S NUTS GOT TO BE!
HE'S JUST A KID IN THIS ERA, NOT GROWN-UP LIKE WHEN YOU KNEW HIM.
WHAT DOES THAT PROVE? I BACK-TIMED--
--WHY NOT HIM?
FRANKLIN?
NOT A SIGN OF HIM.
FRANKLIN!
I HATE IT WHEN HE DOES THIS!
FRANKLIN!
SHE'S FLYING!
LUNCH
LOOKITHEM WINGS, LIKE A BIRD MADE O' FIRE!
BET SHE'S A MUTIE!
SO HOWCUM SHE DIDN'T HELP US WITH THEM SCUZZWADS INSIDE?
HEY, PHIL--DUMMY--HOW D'YOU KNOW SHE DIDN'T?

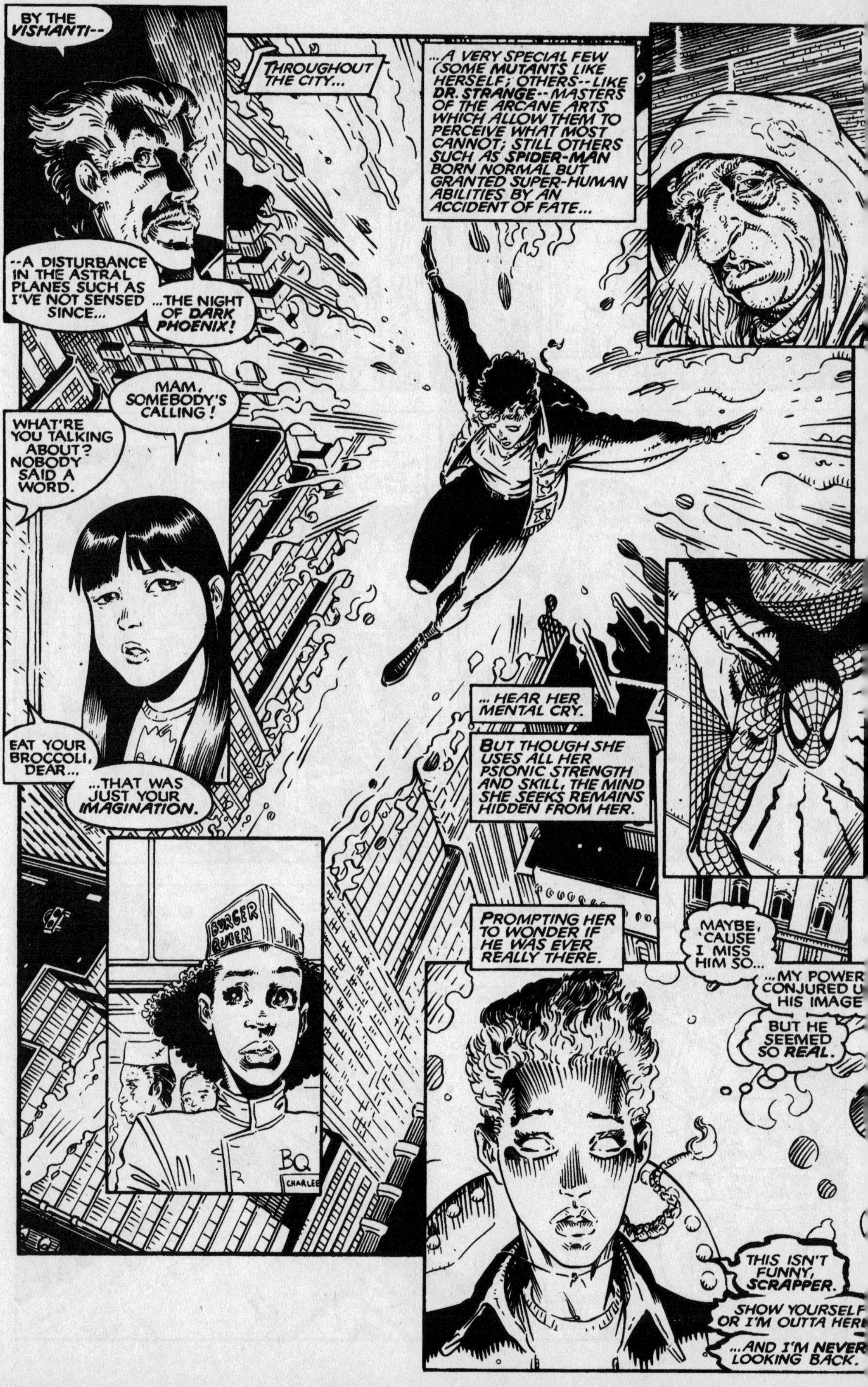
BY THE VISHANTI--
--A DISTURBANCE IN THE ASTRAL PLANES SUCH AS I'VE NOT SENSED SINCE...
...THE NIGHT OF DARK PHOENIX!
THROUGHOUT THE CITY...
...A VERY SPECIAL FEW (SOME MUTANTS LIKE HERSELF; OTHERS--LIKE DR. STRANGE--MASTERS OF THE ARCANE ARTS WHICH ALLOW THEM TO PERCEIVE WHAT MOST CANNOT; STILL OTHERS SUCH AS SPIDER-MAN BORN NORMAL BUT GRANTED SUPER-HUMAN ABILITIES BY AN ACCIDENT OF FATE...
MAM, SOMEBODY'S CALLING!
WHAT'RE YOU TALKING ABOUT? NOBODY SAID A WORD.
EAT YOUR BROCCOLI, DEAR...
...THAT WAS JUST YOUR IMAGINATION.
...HEAR HER MENTAL CRY.
BUT THOUGH SHE USES ALL HER PSIONIC STRENGTH AND SKILL, THE MIND SHE SEEKS REMAINS HIDDEN FROM HER.
BURGER QUEEN
BQ
PROMPTING HER TO WONDER IF HE WAS EVER REALLY THERE.
MAYBE, 'CAUSE I MISS HIM SO...
BUT HE SEEMED SO REAL.
THIS ISN'T FUNNY, SCRAPPER.
...AND I'M NEVER LOOKING BACK.

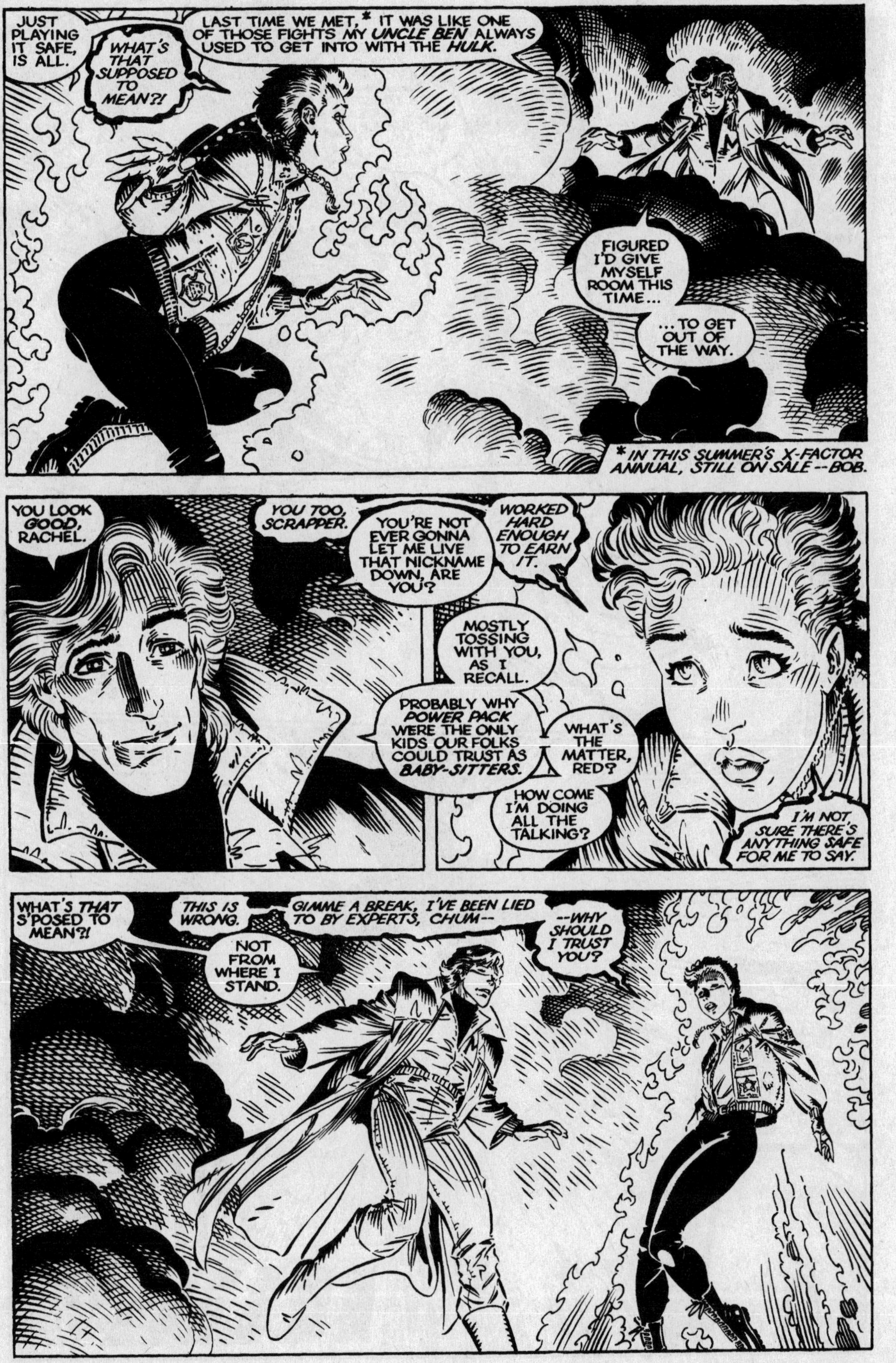
JUST PLAYING IT SAFE, IS ALL.
WHAT'S THAT SUPPOSED TO MEAN?!
LAST TIME WE MET,* IT WAS LIKE ONE OF THOSE FIGHTS MY UNCLE BEN ALWAYS USED TO GET INTO WITH THE HULK.
FIGURED I'D GIVE MYSELF ROOM THIS TIME...
...TO GET OUT OF THE WAY.
* IN THIS SUMMER'S X-FACTOR ANNUAL, STILL ON SALE --BOB.
YOU LOOK GOOD, RACHEL.
YOU TOO, SCRAPPER.
YOU'RE NOT EVER GONNA LET ME LIVE THAT NICKNAME DOWN, ARE YOU?
WORKED HARD ENOUGH TO EARN IT.
MOSTLY TOSSING WITH YOU, AS I RECALL.
PROBABLY WHY POWER PACK WERE THE ONLY KIDS OUR FOLKS COULD TRUST AS BABY-SITTERS.
WHAT'S THE MATTER, RED?
HOW COME I'M DOING ALL THE TALKING?
I'M NOT SURE THERE'S ANYTHING SAFE FOR ME TO SAY.
WHAT'S THAT S'POSED TO MEAN?!
THIS IS WRONG.
NOT FROM WHERE I STAND.
GIMME A BREAK, I'VE BEEN LIED TO BY EXPERTS, CHUM--
--WHY SHOULD I TRUST YOU?

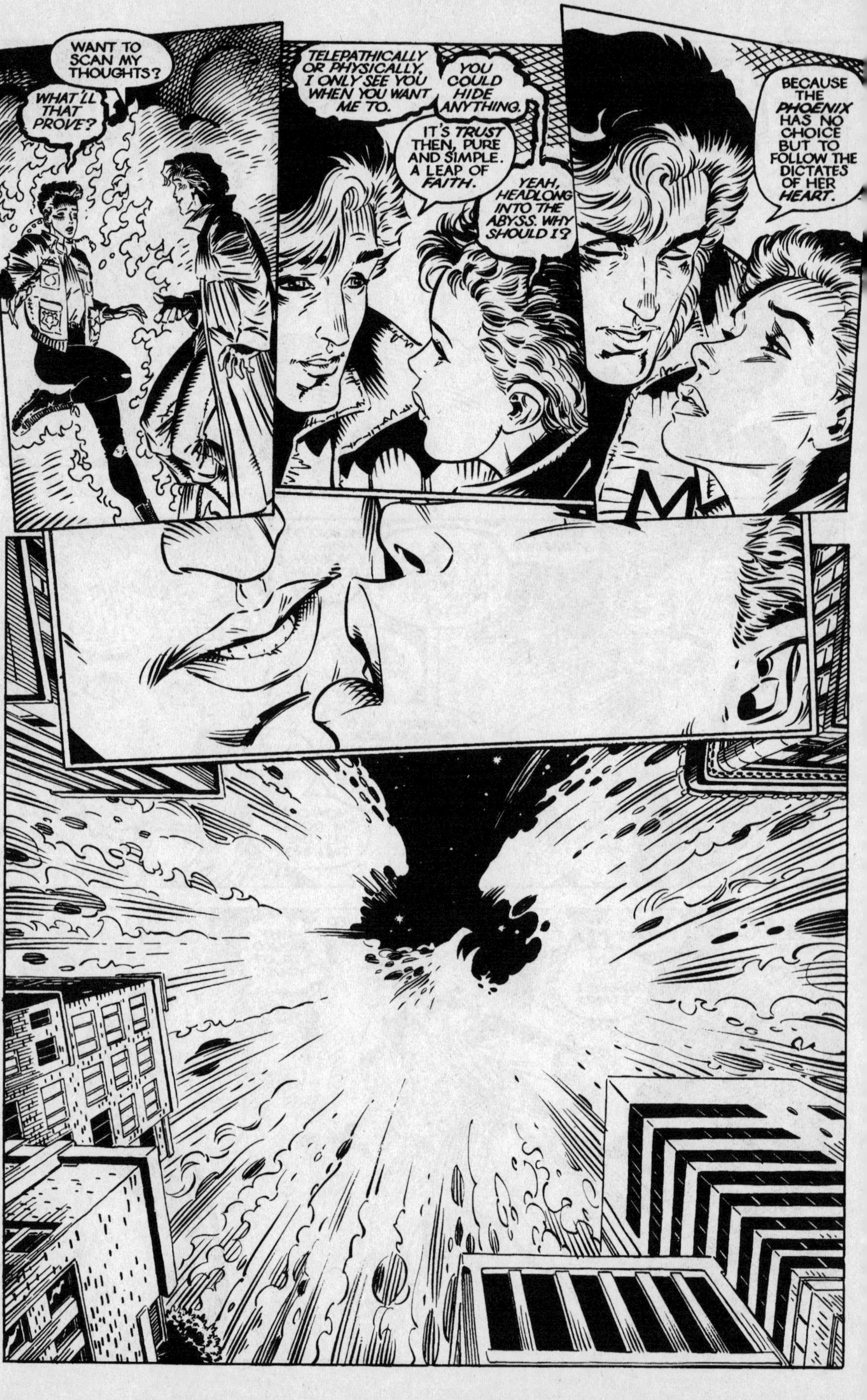

WANT TO SCAN MY THOUGHTS?
WHAT'LL THAT PROVE?
TELEPATHICALLY OR PHYSICALLY, I ONLY SEE YOU WHEN YOU WANT ME TO.
YOU COULD HIDE ANYTHING.
IT'S TRUST THEN, PURE AND SIMPLE. A LEAP OF FAITH.
YEAH, HEADLONG INTO THE ABYSS. WHY SHOULD I?
BECAUSE THE PHOENIX HAS NO CHOICE BUT TO FOLLOW THE DICTATES OF HER HEART.

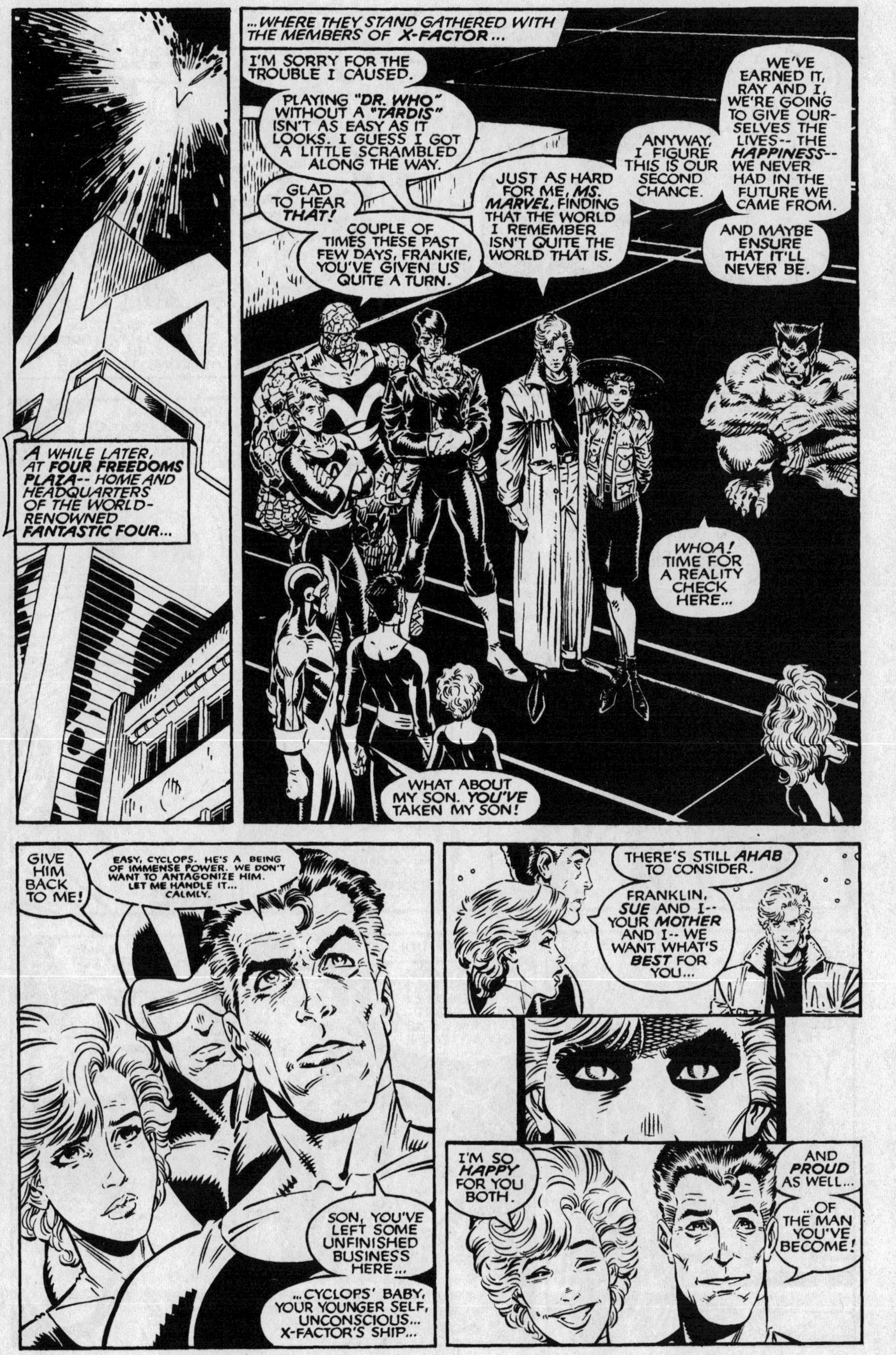
A WHILE LATER, AT FOUR FREEDOMS PLAZA-- HOME AND HEADQUARTERS OF THE WORLD-RENOWNED FANTASTIC FOUR...
...WHERE THEY STAND GATHERED WITH THE MEMBERS OF X-FACTOR...
I'M SORRY FOR THE TROUBLE I CAUSED.
PLAYING "DR. WHO" WITHOUT A "TARDIS" ISN'T AS EASY AS IT LOOKS. I GUESS I GOT A LITTLE SCRAMBLED ALONG THE WAY.
GLAD TO HEAR THAT!
COUPLE OF TIMES THESE PAST FEW DAYS, FRANKIE, YOU'VE GIVEN US QUITE A TURN.
JUST AS HARD FOR ME, MS. MARVEL, FINDING THAT THE WORLD I REMEMBER ISN'T QUITE THE WORLD THAT IS.
ANYWAY, I FIGURE THIS IS OUR SECOND CHANCE.
WE'VE EARNED IT, RAY AND I. WE'RE GOING TO GIVE OURSELVES THE LIVES-- THE HAPPINESS-- WE NEVER HAD IN THE FUTURE WE CAME FROM.
AND MAYBE ENSURE THAT IT'LL NEVER BE.
WHOA! TIME FOR A REALITY CHECK HERE...
WHAT ABOUT MY SON. YOU'VE TAKEN MY SON!
GIVE HIM BACK TO ME!
EASY, CYCLOPS. HE'S A BEING OF IMMENSE POWER. WE DON'T WANT TO ANTAGONIZE HIM. LET ME HANDLE IT... CALMLY.
SON, YOU'VE LEFT SOME UNFINISHED BUSINESS HERE...
...CYCLOPS' BABY, YOUR YOUNGER SELF, UNCONSCIOUS... X-FACTOR'S SHIP...
THERE'S STILL AHAB TO CONSIDER.
FRANKLIN, SUE AND I-- YOUR MOTHER AND I-- WE WANT WHAT'S BEST FOR YOU...
I'M SO HAPPY FOR YOU BOTH.
AND PROUD AS WELL...
...OF THE MAN YOU'VE BECOME!

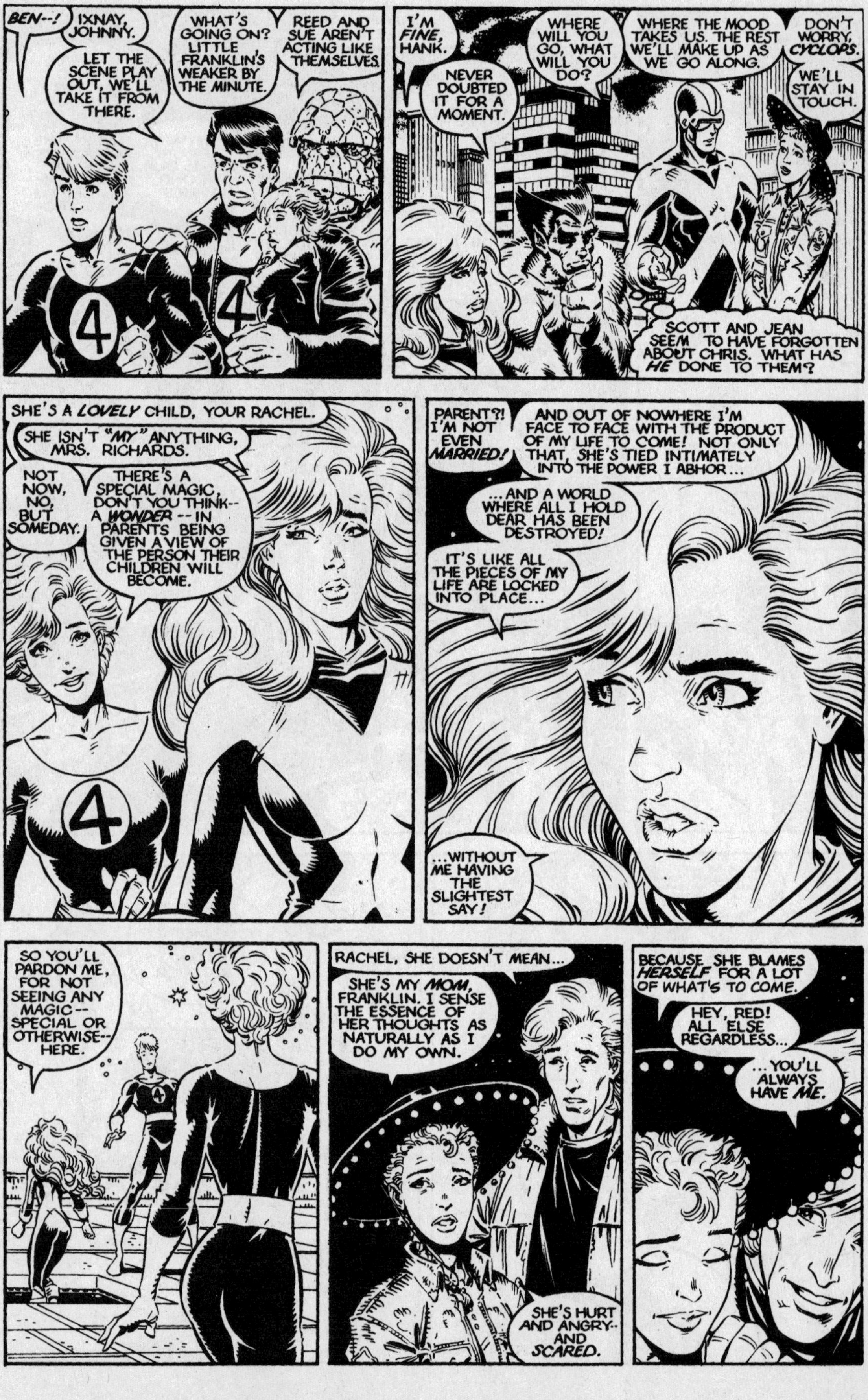
BEN--!
IXNAY, JOHNNY.
LET THE SCENE PLAY OUT, WE'LL TAKE IT FROM THERE.
WHAT'S GOING ON? LITTLE FRANKLIN'S WEAKER BY THE MINUTE.
REED AND SUE AREN'T ACTING LIKE THEMSELVES.
I'M FINE, HANK.
NEVER DOUBTED IT FOR A MOMENT.
WHERE WILL YOU GO, WHAT WILL YOU DO?
WHERE THE MOOD TAKES US. THE REST WE'LL MAKE UP AS WE GO ALONG.
DON'T WORRY, CYCLOPS.
WE'LL STAY IN TOUCH.
SCOTT AND JEAN SEEM TO HAVE FORGOTTEN ABOUT CHRIS. WHAT HAS HE DONE TO THEM?
SHE'S A LOVELY CHILD, YOUR RACHEL.
SHE ISN'T "MY" ANYTHING, MRS. RICHARDS.
NOT NOW, NO, BUT SOMEDAY.
THERE'S A SPECIAL MAGIC, DON'T YOU THINK-- A WONDER --IN PARENTS BEING GIVEN A VIEW OF THE PERSON THEIR CHILDREN WILL BECOME.
PARENT?! I'M NOT EVEN MARRIED!
AND OUT OF NOWHERE I'M FACE TO FACE WITH THE PRODUCT OF MY LIFE TO COME! NOT ONLY THAT, SHE'S TIED INTIMATELY INTO THE POWER I ABHOR...
...AND A WORLD WHERE ALL I HOLD DEAR HAS BEEN DESTROYED!
IT'S LIKE ALL THE PIECES OF MY LIFE ARE LOCKED INTO PLACE...
...WITHOUT ME HAVING THE SLIGHTEST SAY!
SO YOU'LL PARDON ME, FOR NOT SEEING ANY MAGIC-- SPECIAL OR OTHERWISE-- HERE.
RACHEL, SHE DOESN'T MEAN...
SHE'S MY MOM, FRANKLIN. I SENSE THE ESSENCE OF HER THOUGHTS AS NATURALLY AS I DO MY OWN.
SHE'S HURT AND ANGRY-- AND SCARED.
BECAUSE SHE BLAMES HERSELF FOR A LOT OF WHAT'S TO COME.
HEY, RED! ALL ELSE REGARDLESS...
...YOU'LL ALWAYS HAVE ME.

TAKE CARE, SON.

BE WELL.

YOU EVER NEED US, DAD, JUST GIVE A YELL.

WE'LL BE THERE.

I'M GLAD YOU FOUND EACH OTHER.

GIVE JEAN TIME, DEAR.

SHE'S SURE TO COME AROUND.

WHAT A GLORIOUS DAY, DON'T YOU THINK??

I BELIEVE A CELEBRATION IS IN ORDER.

HOW 'BOUT A RAIN CHECK, STRETCH--

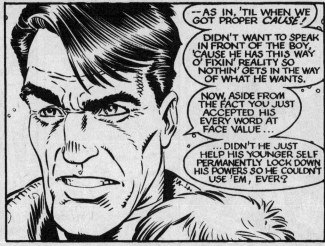

--AS IN, 'TIL WHEN WE GOT PROPER CAUSE!

DIDN'T WANT TO SPEAK IN FRONT OF THE BOY, 'CAUSE HE HAS THIS WAY O' FIXIN' REALITY SO NOTHIN' GETS IN THE WAY OF WHAT HE WANTS.

NOW, ASIDE FROM THE FACT YOU JUST ACCEPTED HIS EVERY WORD AT FACE VALUE...

...DIDN'T HE JUST HELP HIS YOUNGER SELF PERMANENTLY LOCK DOWN HIS POWERS SO HE COULDN'T USE 'EM, EVER?

MAYBE I'M MISSIN' SOMETHIN', REED, BUT IF YOUNG FRANKLIN --AS OF NOW-- DOESN'T HAVE ANY SUPER-POWERS--

...WHERE'D HIS OLDER SELF GAIN THE ABILITY TO TRAVEL IN TIME, NOT TO MENTION ALL THE OTHER STUNTS HE'S BEEN PUSHIN'?

REED... MY HEAD ...?

THE STRANGEST SENSATION... AS THOUGH MY VERY THOUGHTS WERE BEING TURNED INSIDE

OUT!

BEN-- FRANKLIN --!

ZAPPED YOU, I FIGURE, T' MAKE YOU SEE THINGS HIS WAY.

A TRANSITORY RECONFIGURATION OF REALITY--!

WHATEVER. LEAST HE DIDN'T NAIL US ALL.

HE ISN'T HOSTILE, BEN, SIMPLY DIRECTED-- I FEAR, TO THE POINT OF OBSESSION.

HE'S DESPERATELY AFRAID, THAT MUCH I SENSE. (BUT OF WHAT?) AND SEEKING SAFETY.

TO GET IT, HE'S PREPARED TO DO ANYTHING.

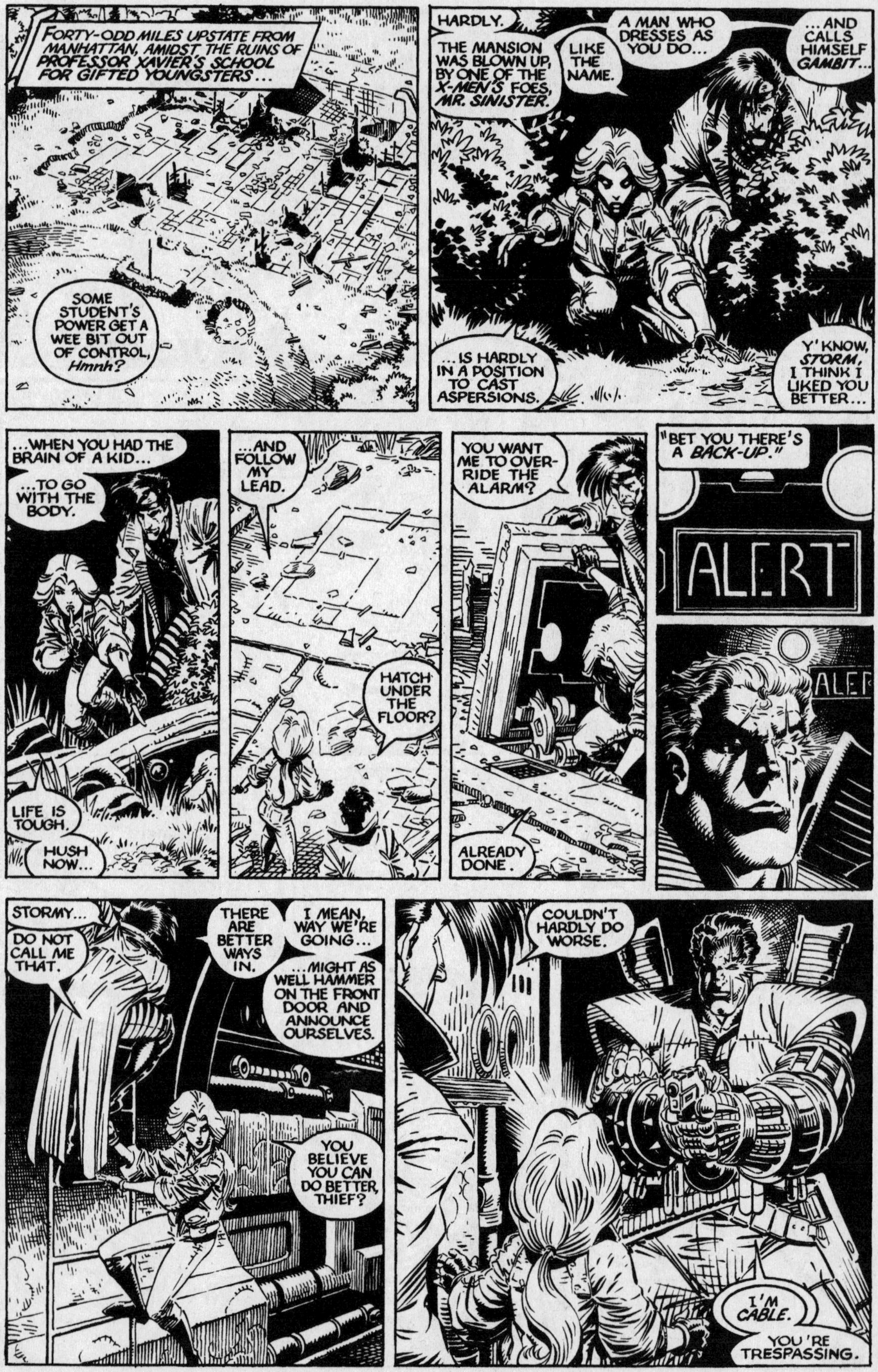
Forty-odd miles upstate from Manhattan, amidst the ruins of Professor Xavier's School for Gifted Youngsters...
SOME STUDENT'S POWER GET A WEE BIT OUT OF CONTROL, Hmnh?
HARDLY.
THE MANSION WAS BLOWN UP, BY ONE OF THE X-MEN'S FOES, MR. SINISTER.
LIKE THE NAME.
A MAN WHO DRESSES AS YOU DO...
...AND CALLS HIMSELF GAMBIT...
...IS HARDLY IN A POSITION TO CAST ASPERSIONS.
Y' KNOW, STORM, I THINK I LIKED YOU BETTER...
...WHEN YOU HAD THE BRAIN OF A KID...
...TO GO WITH THE BODY.
LIFE IS TOUGH.
HUSH NOW...
...AND FOLLOW MY LEAD.
HATCH UNDER THE FLOOR?
YOU WANT ME TO OVER-RIDE THE ALARM?
ALREADY DONE.
"BET YOU THERE'S A BACK-UP."
ALERT
STORMY...
DO NOT CALL ME THAT.
THERE ARE BETTER WAYS IN.
I MEAN, WAY WE'RE GOING...
...MIGHT AS WELL HAMMER ON THE FRONT DOOR AND ANNOUNCE OURSELVES.
YOU BELIEVE YOU CAN DO BETTER, THIEF?
COULDN'T HARDLY DO WORSE.
I'M CABLE.
YOU'RE TRESPASSING.

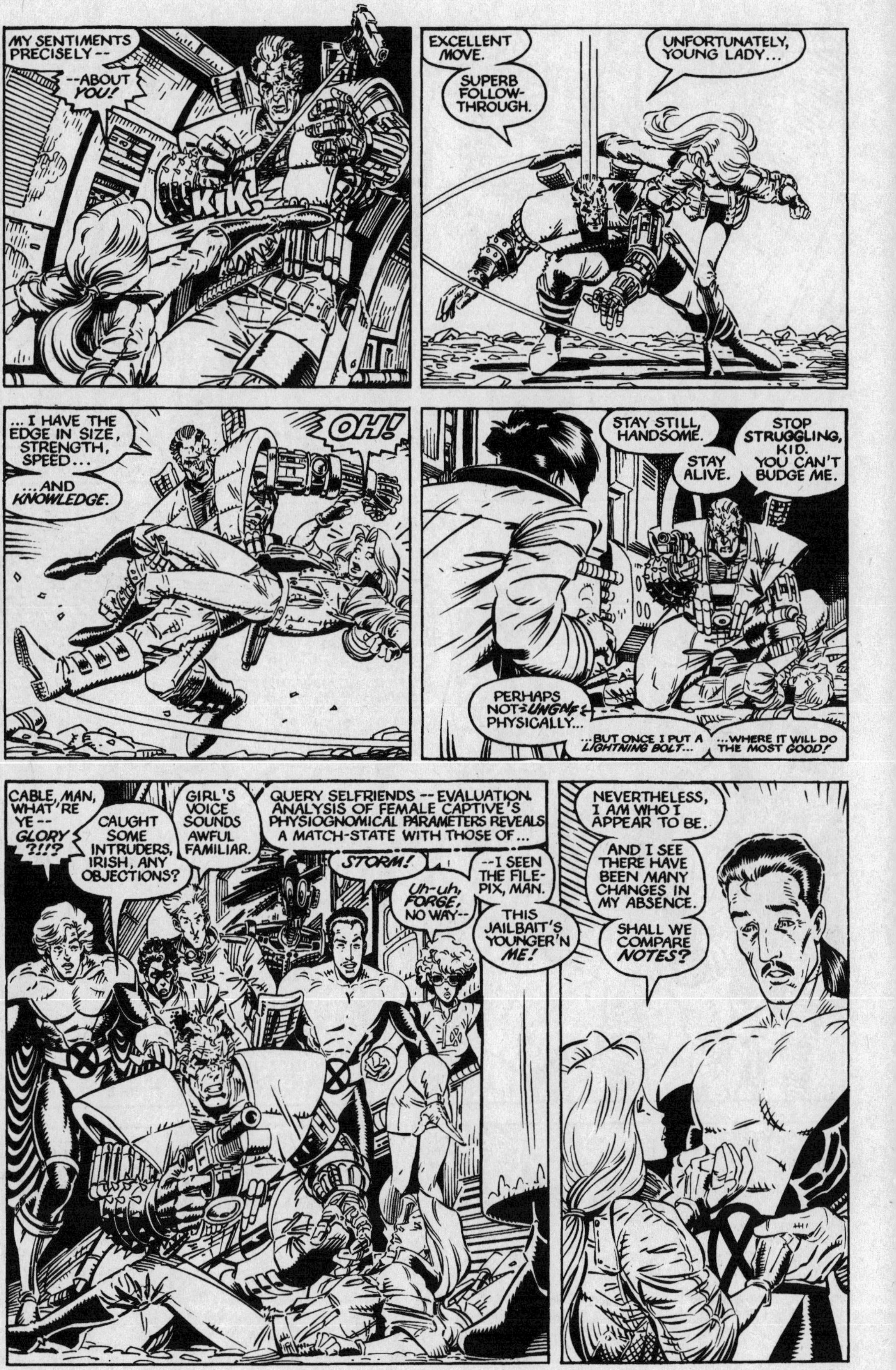
MY SENTIMENTS PRECISELY --
--ABOUT YOU!
KIK!
EXCELLENT MOVE.
SUPERB FOLLOW-THROUGH.
UNFORTUNATELY, YOUNG LADY...
... I HAVE THE EDGE IN SIZE, STRENGTH, SPEED...
...AND KNOWLEDGE.
OH!
STAY STILL, HANDSOME.
STAY ALIVE.
STOP STRUGGLING, KID. YOU CAN'T BUDGE ME.
PERHAPS NOT--UNGNF--PHYSICALLY...
...BUT ONCE I PUT A LIGHTNING BOLT...
...WHERE IT WILL DO THE MOST GOOD!
CABLE, MAN, WHAT'RE YE -- GLORY ?!!?
CAUGHT SOME INTRUDERS, IRISH, ANY OBJECTIONS?
GIRL'S VOICE SOUNDS AWFUL FAMILIAR.
QUERY SELFRIENDS -- EVALUATION. ANALYSIS OF FEMALE CAPTIVE'S PHYSIOGNOMICAL PARAMETERS REVEALS A MATCH-STATE WITH THOSE OF...
STORM!
Uh-uh, FORGE, NO WAY--
--I SEEN THE FILE-PIX, MAN.
THIS JAILBAIT'S YOUNGER'N ME!
NEVERTHELESS, I AM WHO I APPEAR TO BE.
AND I SEE THERE HAVE BEEN MANY CHANGES IN MY ABSENCE.
SHALL WE COMPARE NOTES?

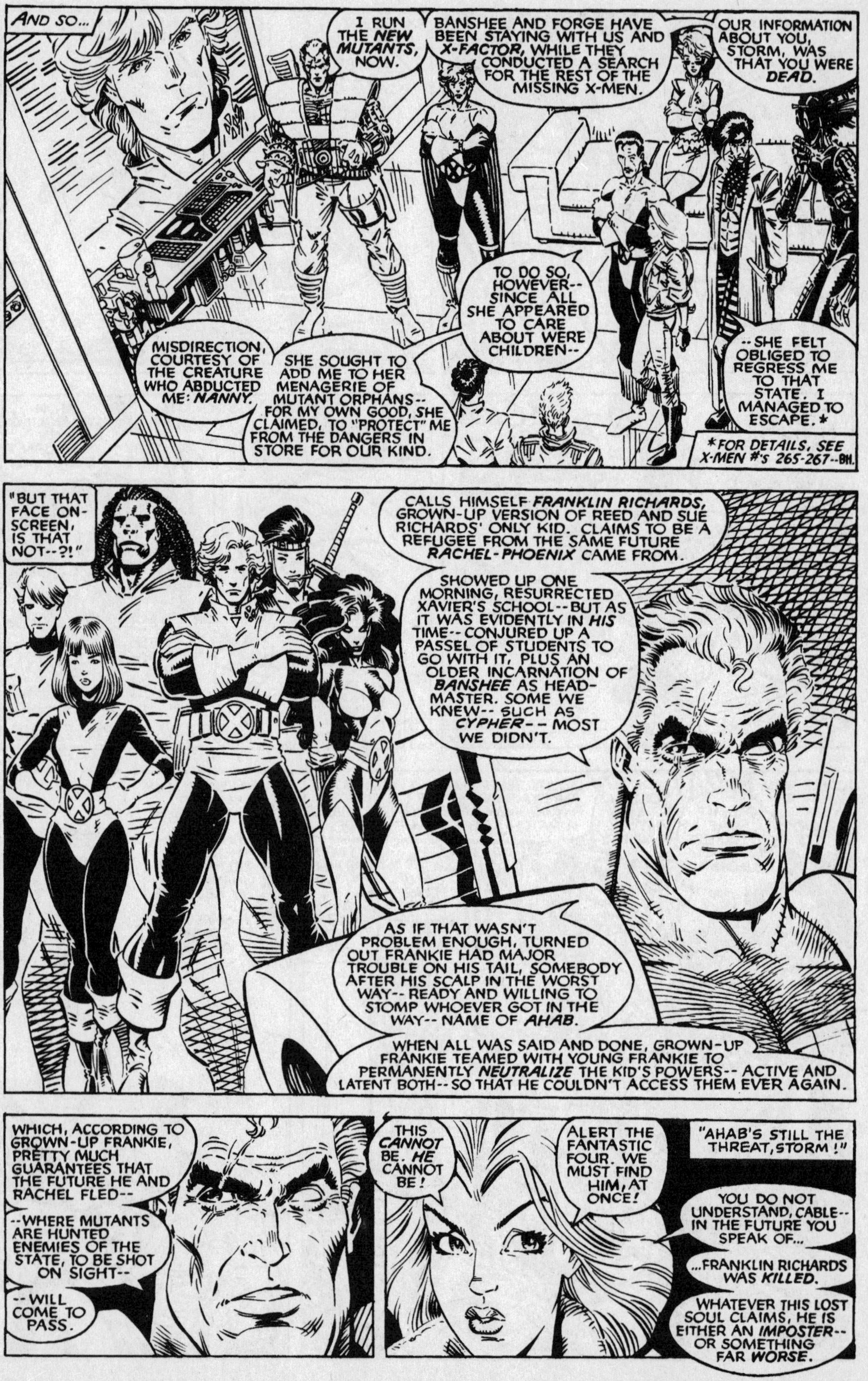
AND SO...
I RUN THE NEW MUTANTS, NOW.
BANSHEE AND FORGE HAVE BEEN STAYING WITH US AND X-FACTOR, WHILE THEY CONDUCTED A SEARCH FOR THE REST OF THE MISSING X-MEN.
OUR INFORMATION ABOUT YOU, STORM, WAS THAT YOU WERE DEAD.
MISDIRECTION, COURTESY OF THE CREATURE WHO ABDUCTED ME: NANNY.
SHE SOUGHT TO ADD ME TO HER MENAGERIE OF MUTANT ORPHANS--FOR MY OWN GOOD, SHE CLAIMED, TO "PROTECT" ME FROM THE DANGERS IN STORE FOR OUR KIND.
TO DO SO, HOWEVER--SINCE ALL SHE APPEARED TO CARE ABOUT WERE CHILDREN--
--SHE FELT OBLIGED TO REGRESS ME TO THAT STATE. I MANAGED TO ESCAPE.*
*FOR DETAILS, SEE X-MEN #'s 265-267--BH.
"BUT THAT FACE ON-SCREEN, IS THAT NOT--?!"
CALLS HIMSELF FRANKLIN RICHARDS, GROWN-UP VERSION OF REED AND SUE RICHARDS' ONLY KID. CLAIMS TO BE A REFUGEE FROM THE SAME FUTURE RACHEL-PHOENIX CAME FROM.
SHOWED UP ONE MORNING, RESURRECTED XAVIER'S SCHOOL--BUT AS IT WAS EVIDENTLY IN HIS TIME--CONJURED UP A PASSEL OF STUDENTS TO GO WITH IT, PLUS AN OLDER INCARNATION OF BANSHEE AS HEAD-MASTER. SOME WE KNEW--SUCH AS CYPHER--MOST WE DIDN'T.
AS IF THAT WASN'T PROBLEM ENOUGH, TURNED OUT FRANKIE HAD MAJOR TROUBLE ON HIS TAIL, SOMEBODY AFTER HIS SCALP IN THE WORST WAY--READY AND WILLING TO STOMP WHOEVER GOT IN THE WAY--NAME OF AHAB.
WHEN ALL WAS SAID AND DONE, GROWN-UP FRANKIE TEAMED WITH YOUNG FRANKIE TO PERMANENTLY NEUTRALIZE THE KID'S POWERS--ACTIVE AND LATENT BOTH--SO THAT HE COULDN'T ACCESS THEM EVER AGAIN.
WHICH, ACCORDING TO GROWN-UP FRANKIE, PRETTY MUCH GUARANTEES THAT THE FUTURE HE AND RACHEL FLED--
--WHERE MUTANTS ARE HUNTED ENEMIES OF THE STATE, TO BE SHOT ON SIGHT--
--WILL COME TO PASS.
THIS CANNOT BE. HE CANNOT BE!
ALERT THE FANTASTIC FOUR. WE MUST FIND HIM, AT ONCE!
"AHAB'S STILL THE THREAT, STORM!"
YOU DO NOT UNDERSTAND, CABLE--IN THE FUTURE YOU SPEAK OF...
...FRANKLIN RICHARDS WAS KILLED.
WHATEVER THIS LOST SOUL CLAIMS, HE IS EITHER AN IMPOSTER--OR SOMETHING FAR WORSE.

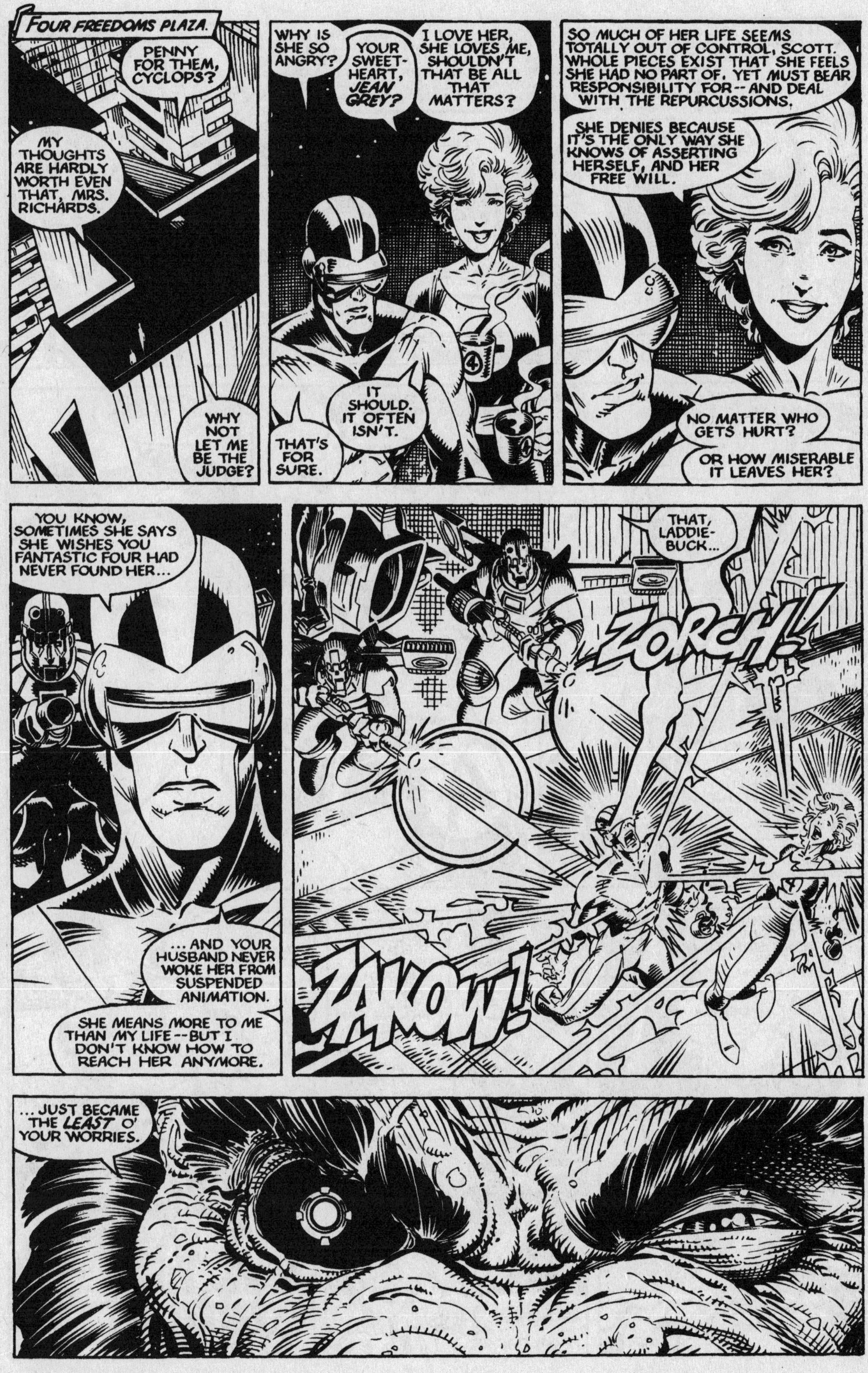
FOUR FREEDOMS PLAZA.
PENNY FOR THEM, CYCLOPS?
MY THOUGHTS ARE HARDLY WORTH EVEN THAT, MRS. RICHARDS.
WHY NOT LET ME BE THE JUDGE?
WHY IS SHE SO ANGRY?
YOUR SWEET-HEART, JEAN GREY?
I LOVE HER, SHE LOVES ME, SHOULDN'T THAT BE ALL THAT MATTERS?
IT SHOULD. IT OFTEN ISN'T.
THAT'S FOR SURE.
SO MUCH OF HER LIFE SEEMS TOTALLY OUT OF CONTROL, SCOTT. WHOLE PIECES EXIST THAT SHE FEELS SHE HAD NO PART OF. YET MUST BEAR RESPONSIBILITY FOR--AND DEAL WITH THE REPURCUSSIONS.
SHE DENIES BECAUSE IT'S THE ONLY WAY SHE KNOWS OF ASSERTING HERSELF, AND HER FREE WILL.
NO MATTER WHO GETS HURT?
OR HOW MISERABLE IT LEAVES HER?
YOU KNOW, SOMETIMES SHE SAYS SHE WISHES YOU FANTASTIC FOUR HAD NEVER FOUND HER...
...AND YOUR HUSBAND NEVER WOKE HER FROM SUSPENDED ANIMATION.
SHE MEANS MORE TO ME THAN MY LIFE--BUT I DON'T KNOW HOW TO REACH HER ANYMORE.
THAT, LADDIE-BUCK...
ZORCH!
ZAKOW!
...JUST BECAME THE LEAST O' YOUR WORRIES.

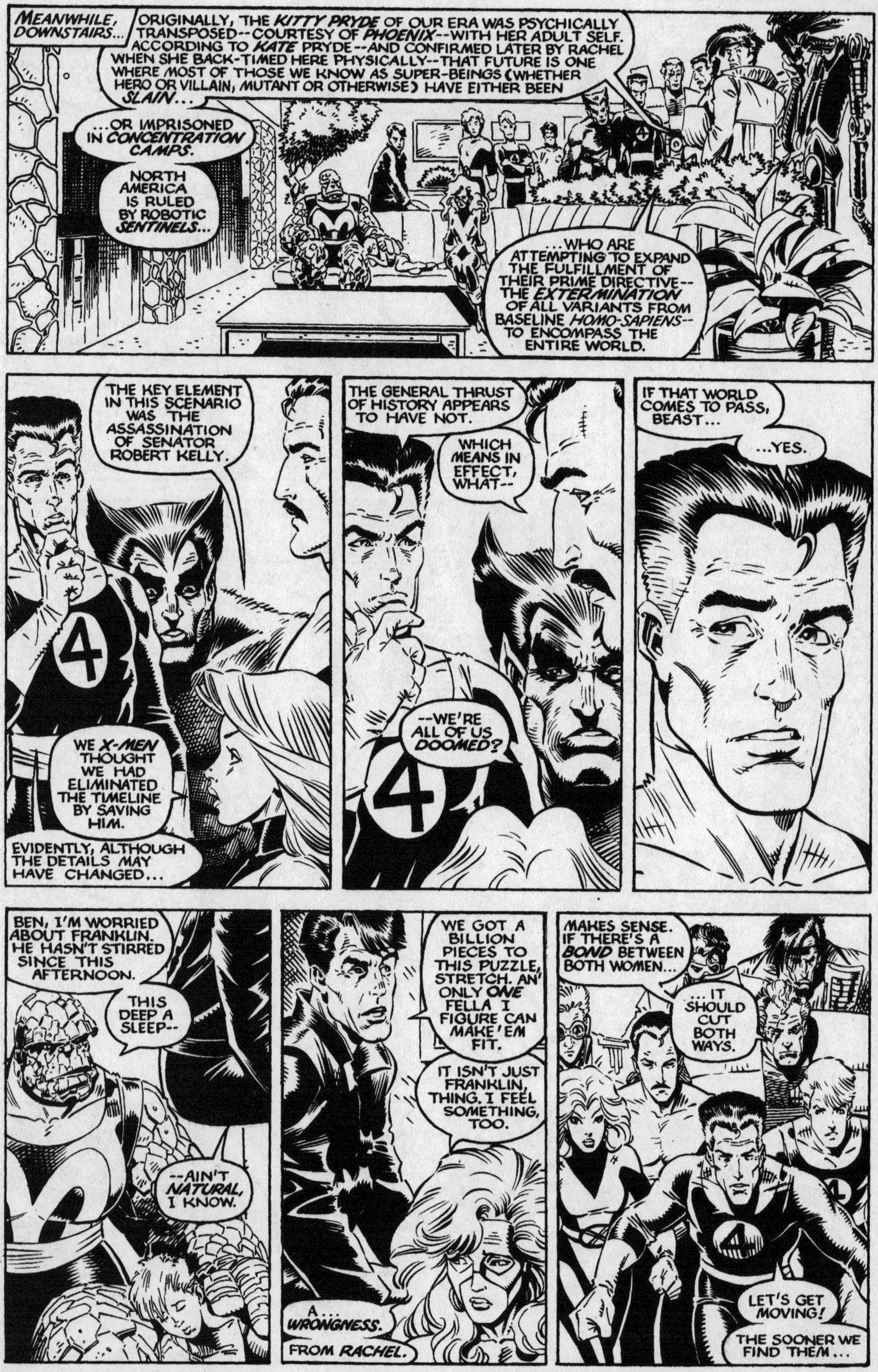
MEANWHILE, DOWNSTAIRS...
ORIGINALLY, THE KITTY PRYDE OF OUR ERA WAS PSYCHICALLY TRANSPOSED--COURTESY OF PHOENIX--WITH HER ADULT SELF. ACCORDING TO KATE PRYDE--AND CONFIRMED LATER BY RACHEL WHEN SHE BACK-TIMED HERE PHYSICALLY--THAT FUTURE IS ONE WHERE MOST OF THOSE WE KNOW AS SUPER-BEINGS (WHETHER HERO OR VILLAIN, MUTANT OR OTHERWISE) HAVE EITHER BEEN SLAIN...
...OR IMPRISONED IN CONCENTRATION CAMPS.
NORTH AMERICA IS RULED BY ROBOTIC SENTINELS...
...WHO ARE ATTEMPTING TO EXPAND THE FULFILLMENT OF THEIR PRIME DIRECTIVE--THE EXTERMINATION OF ALL VARIANTS FROM BASELINE HOMO-SAPIENS--TO ENCOMPASS THE ENTIRE WORLD.
THE KEY ELEMENT IN THIS SCENARIO WAS THE ASSASSINATION OF SENATOR ROBERT KELLY.
WE X-MEN THOUGHT WE HAD ELIMINATED THE TIMELINE BY SAVING HIM.
EVIDENTLY, ALTHOUGH THE DETAILS MAY HAVE CHANGED...
THE GENERAL THRUST OF HISTORY APPEARS TO HAVE NOT.
WHICH MEANS IN EFFECT, WHAT--
--WE'RE ALL OF US DOOMED?
IF THAT WORLD COMES TO PASS, BEAST...
...YES.
BEN, I'M WORRIED ABOUT FRANKLIN. HE HASN'T STIRRED SINCE THIS AFTERNOON.
THIS DEEP A SLEEP--
--AIN'T NATURAL, I KNOW.
WE GOT A BILLION PIECES TO THIS PUZZLE, STRETCH. AN' ONLY ONE FELLA I FIGURE CAN MAKE 'EM FIT.
IT ISN'T JUST FRANKLIN, THING. I FEEL SOMETHING, TOO.
A... WRONGNESS.
FROM RACHEL.
MAKES SENSE. IF THERE'S A BOND BETWEEN BOTH WOMEN...
...IT SHOULD CUT BOTH WAYS.
LET'S GET MOVING!
THE SOONER WE FIND THEM...

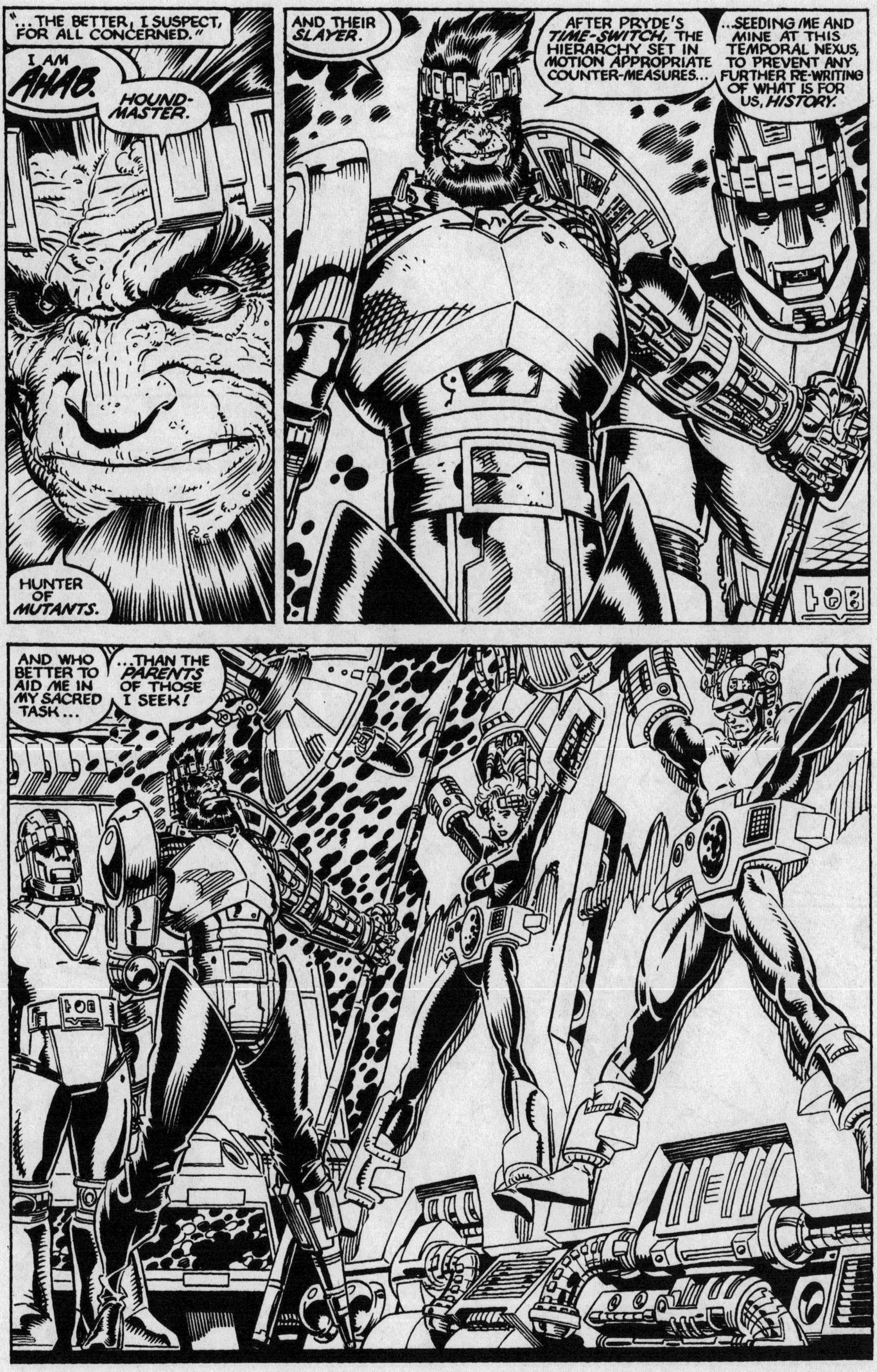
"...THE BETTER, I SUSPECT, FOR ALL CONCERNED."
I AM AHAB.
HOUND-MASTER.
HUNTER OF MUTANTS.
AND THEIR SLAYER.
AFTER PRYDE'S TIME-SWITCH, THE HIERARCHY SET IN MOTION APPROPRIATE COUNTER-MEASURES...
...SEEDING ME AND MINE AT THIS TEMPORAL NEXUS, TO PREVENT ANY FURTHER RE-WRITING OF WHAT IS FOR US, HISTORY.
AND WHO BETTER TO AID ME IN MY SACRED TASK...
...THAN THE PARENTS OF THOSE I SEEK!

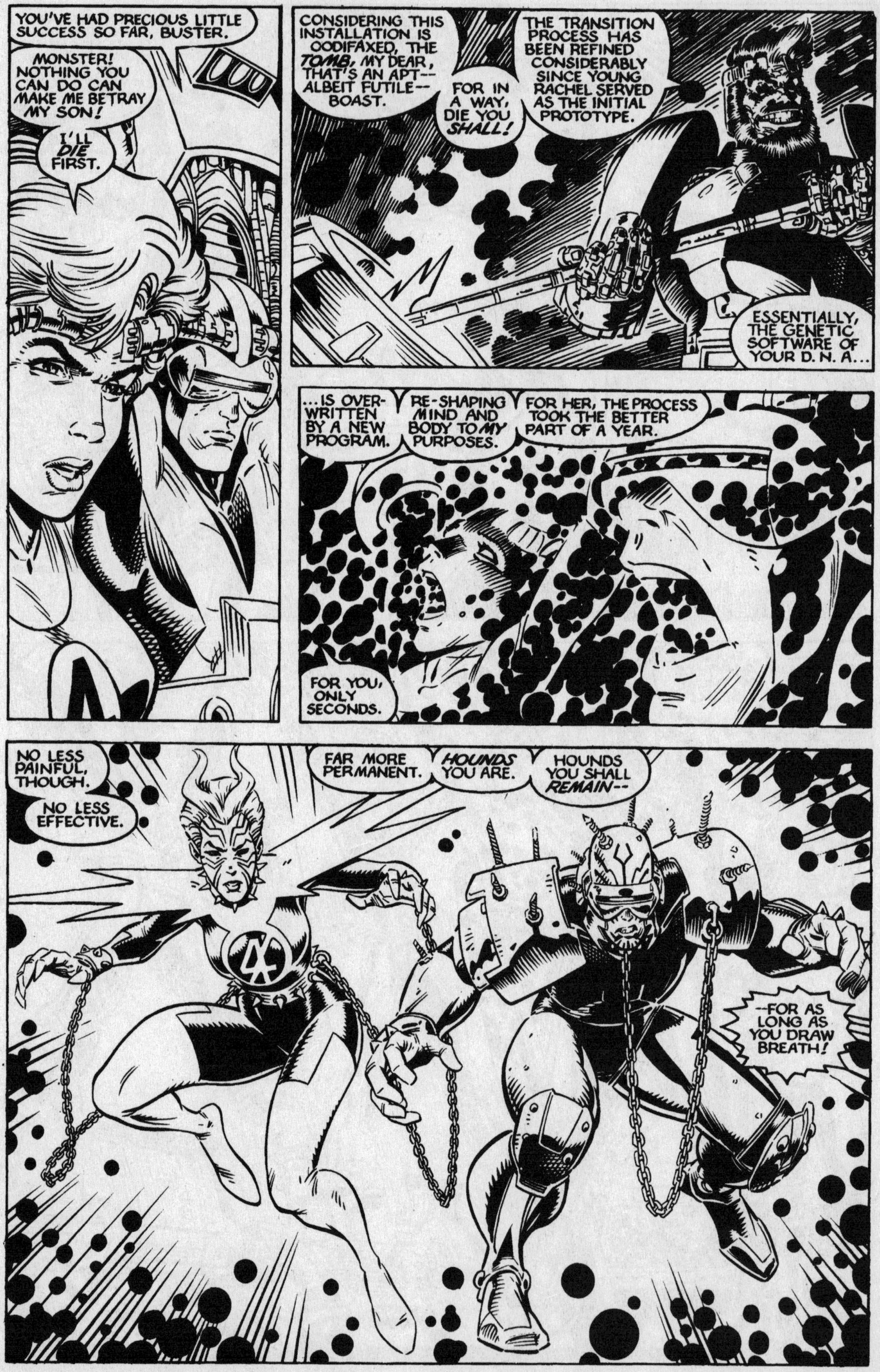
YOU'VE HAD PRECIOUS LITTLE SUCCESS SO FAR, BUSTER.
MONSTER! NOTHING YOU CAN DO CAN MAKE ME BETRAY MY SON!
I'LL DIE FIRST.
CONSIDERING THIS INSTALLATION IS OODIFAXED, THE TOMB, MY DEAR, THAT'S AN APT-- ALBEIT FUTILE-- BOAST.
FOR IN A WAY, DIE YOU SHALL!
THE TRANSITION PROCESS HAS BEEN REFINED CONSIDERABLY SINCE YOUNG RACHEL SERVED AS THE INITIAL PROTOTYPE.
ESSENTIALLY, THE GENETIC SOFTWARE OF YOUR D. N. A...
...IS OVER-WRITTEN BY A NEW PROGRAM.
RE-SHAPING MIND AND BODY TO MY PURPOSES.
FOR HER, THE PROCESS TOOK THE BETTER PART OF A YEAR.
FOR YOU, ONLY SECONDS.
NO LESS PAINFUL, THOUGH.
NO LESS EFFECTIVE.
FAR MORE PERMANENT.
HOUNDS YOU ARE.
HOUNDS YOU SHALL REMAIN--
--FOR AS LONG AS YOU DRAW BREATH!

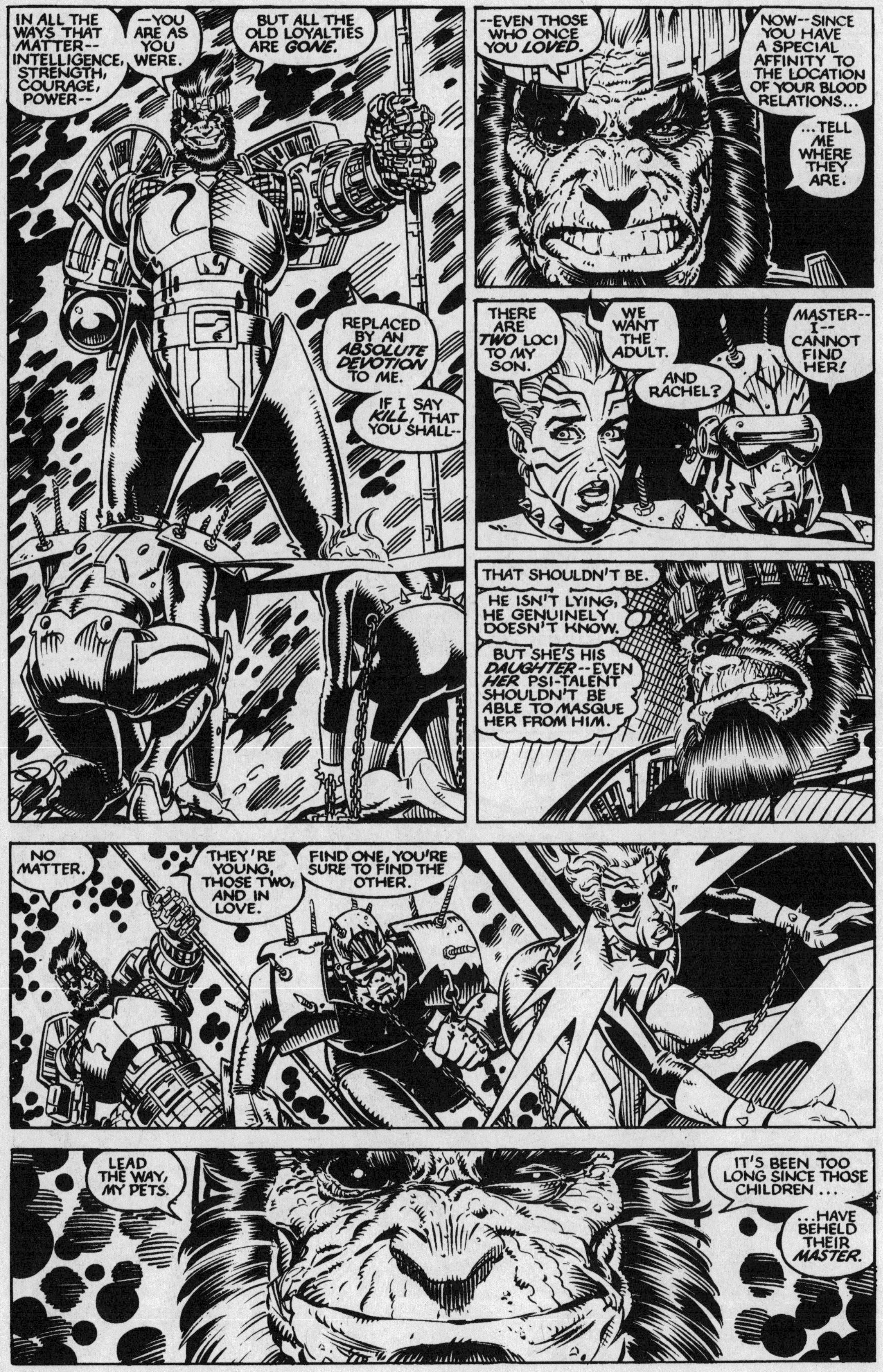
IN ALL THE WAYS THAT MATTER-- INTELLIGENCE, STRENGTH, COURAGE, POWER--
--YOU ARE AS YOU WERE.
BUT ALL THE OLD LOYALTIES ARE GONE.
REPLACED BY AN ABSOLUTE DEVOTION TO ME.
IF I SAY KILL, THAT YOU SHALL--
--EVEN THOSE WHO ONCE YOU LOVED.
NOW--SINCE YOU HAVE A SPECIAL AFFINITY TO THE LOCATION OF YOUR BLOOD RELATIONS...
...TELL ME WHERE THEY ARE.
THERE ARE TWO LOCI TO MY SON.
WE WANT THE ADULT.
AND RACHEL?
MASTER-- I-- CANNOT FIND HER!
THAT SHOULDN'T BE.
HE ISN'T LYING, HE GENUINELY DOESN'T KNOW.
BUT SHE'S HIS DAUGHTER--EVEN HER PSI-TALENT SHOULDN'T BE ABLE TO MASQUE HER FROM HIM.
NO MATTER.
THEY'RE YOUNG, THOSE TWO, AND IN LOVE.
FIND ONE, YOU'RE SURE TO FIND THE OTHER.
LEAD THE WAY, MY PETS.
IT'S BEEN TOO LONG SINCE THOSE CHILDREN ...
...HAVE BEHELD THEIR MASTER.

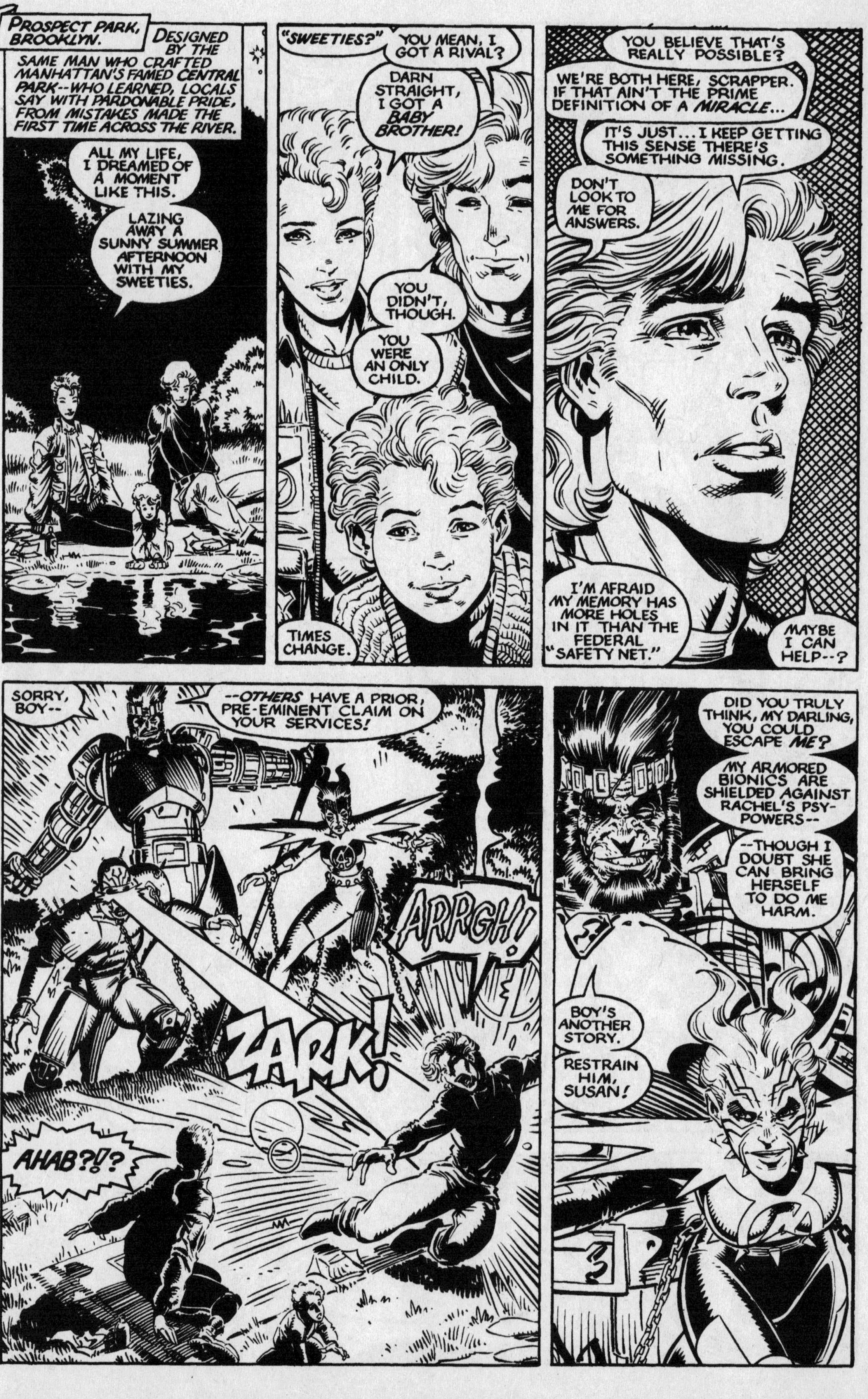
PROSPECT PARK, BROOKLYN.
DESIGNED BY THE SAME MAN WHO CRAFTED MANHATTAN'S FAMED CENTRAL PARK--WHO LEARNED, LOCALS SAY WITH PARDONABLE PRIDE, FROM MISTAKES MADE THE FIRST TIME ACROSS THE RIVER.
ALL MY LIFE, I DREAMED OF A MOMENT LIKE THIS.
LAZING AWAY A SUNNY SUMMER AFTERNOON WITH MY SWEETIES.
"SWEETIES?"
YOU MEAN, I GOT A RIVAL?
DARN STRAIGHT, I GOT A BABY BROTHER!
YOU DIDN'T, THOUGH.
YOU WERE AN ONLY CHILD.
TIMES CHANGE.
YOU BELIEVE THAT'S REALLY POSSIBLE?
WE'RE BOTH HERE, SCRAPPER. IF THAT AIN'T THE PRIME DEFINITION OF A MIRACLE...
IT'S JUST... I KEEP GETTING THIS SENSE THERE'S SOMETHING MISSING.
DON'T LOOK TO ME FOR ANSWERS.
I'M AFRAID MY MEMORY HAS MORE HOLES IN IT THAN THE FEDERAL "SAFETY NET."
MAYBE I CAN HELP--?
SORRY, BOY--
--OTHERS HAVE A PRIOR, PRE-EMINENT CLAIM ON YOUR SERVICES!
ARRGH!
ZARK!
AHAB?!!?
DID YOU TRULY THINK, MY DARLING, YOU COULD ESCAPE ME?
MY ARMORED BIONICS ARE SHIELDED AGAINST RACHEL'S PSY-POWERS--
--THOUGH I DOUBT SHE CAN BRING HERSELF TO DO ME HARM.
BOY'S ANOTHER STORY.
RESTRAIN HIM, SUSAN!

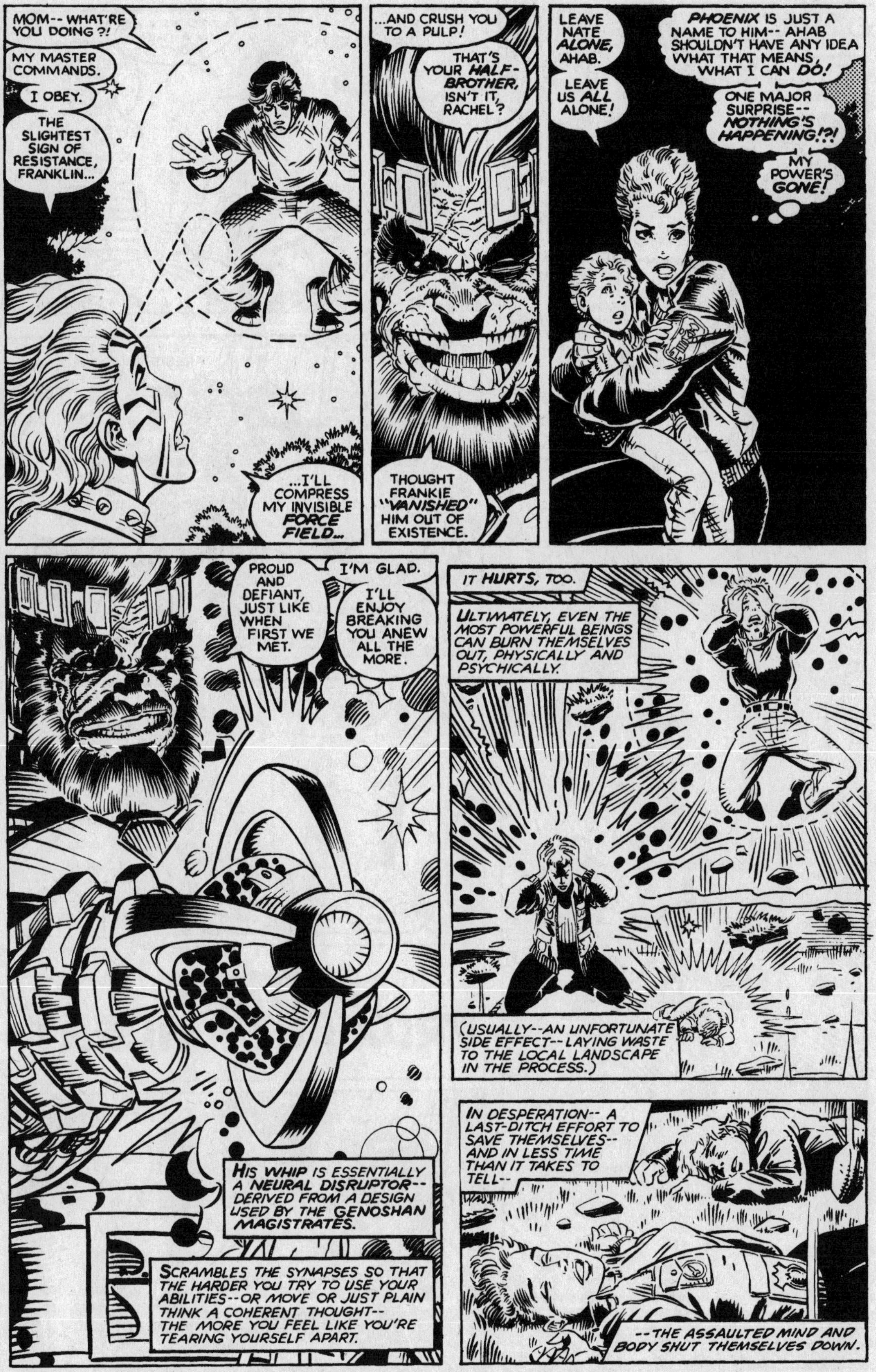
MOM-- WHAT'RE YOU DOING?!
MY MASTER COMMANDS.
I OBEY.
THE SLIGHTEST SIGN OF RESISTANCE, FRANKLIN...
...I'LL COMPRESS MY INVISIBLE FORCE FIELD...
...AND CRUSH YOU TO A PULP!
THAT'S YOUR HALF-BROTHER, ISN'T IT, RACHEL?
THOUGHT FRANKIE "VANISHED" HIM OUT OF EXISTENCE.
LEAVE NATE ALONE, AHAB.
LEAVE US ALL ALONE!
PHOENIX IS JUST A NAME TO HIM-- AHAB SHOULDN'T HAVE ANY IDEA WHAT THAT MEANS, WHAT I CAN DO!
ONE MAJOR SURPRISE-- NOTHING'S HAPPENING!?!
MY POWER'S GONE!
PROUD AND DEFIANT, JUST LIKE WHEN FIRST WE MET.
I'M GLAD.
I'LL ENJOY BREAKING YOU ANEW ALL THE MORE.
HIS WHIP IS ESSENTIALLY A NEURAL DISRUPTOR-- DERIVED FROM A DESIGN USED BY THE GENOSHAN MAGISTRATES.
SCRAMBLES THE SYNAPSES SO THAT THE HARDER YOU TRY TO USE YOUR ABILITIES--OR MOVE OR JUST PLAIN THINK A COHERENT THOUGHT-- THE MORE YOU FEEL LIKE YOU'RE TEARING YOURSELF APART.
IT HURTS, TOO.
ULTIMATELY, EVEN THE MOST POWERFUL BEINGS CAN BURN THEMSELVES OUT, PHYSICALLY AND PSYCHICALLY.
(USUALLY--AN UNFORTUNATE SIDE EFFECT--LAYING WASTE TO THE LOCAL LANDSCAPE IN THE PROCESS.)
IN DESPERATION-- A LAST-DITCH EFFORT TO SAVE THEMSELVES-- AND IN LESS TIME THAN IT TAKES TO TELL--
--THE ASSAULTED MIND AND BODY SHUT THEMSELVES DOWN.

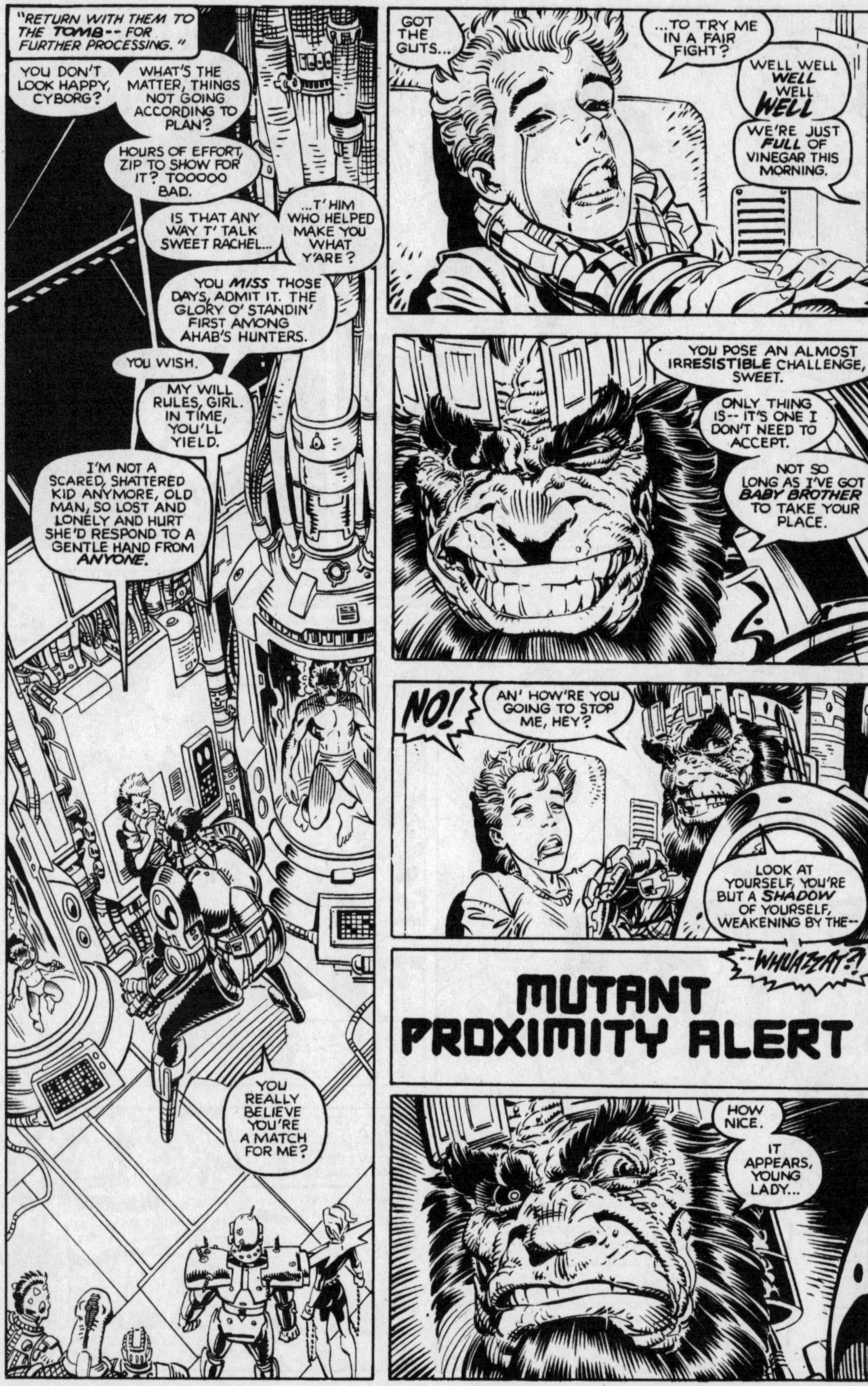
"RETURN WITH THEM TO THE TOMB-- FOR FURTHER PROCESSING."
YOU DON'T LOOK HAPPY, CYBORG?
WHAT'S THE MATTER, THINGS NOT GOING ACCORDING TO PLAN?
HOURS OF EFFORT, ZIP TO SHOW FOR IT? TOOOOO BAD.
IS THAT ANY WAY T' TALK SWEET RACHEL...
...T' HIM WHO HELPED MAKE YOU WHAT Y'ARE?
YOU MISS THOSE DAYS, ADMIT IT. THE GLORY O' STANDIN' FIRST AMONG AHAB'S HUNTERS.
YOU WISH.
MY WILL RULES, GIRL. IN TIME, YOU'LL YIELD.
I'M NOT A SCARED, SHATTERED KID ANYMORE, OLD MAN, SO LOST AND LONELY AND HURT SHE'D RESPOND TO A GENTLE HAND FROM ANYONE.
YOU REALLY BELIEVE YOU'RE A MATCH FOR ME?
GOT THE GUTS...
...TO TRY ME IN A FAIR FIGHT?
WELL WELL WELL WELL
WE'RE JUST FULL OF VINEGAR THIS MORNING.
YOU POSE AN ALMOST IRRESISTIBLE CHALLENGE, SWEET.
ONLY THING IS-- IT'S ONE I DON'T NEED TO ACCEPT.
NOT SO LONG AS I'VE GOT BABY BROTHER TO TAKE YOUR PLACE.
NO!
AN' HOW'RE YOU GOING TO STOP ME, HEY?
LOOK AT YOURSELF, YOU'RE BUT A SHADOW OF YOURSELF, WEAKENING BY THE--
--WHUAZZAT?!
MUTANT PROXIMITY ALERT
HOW NICE.
IT APPEARS, YOUNG LADY...

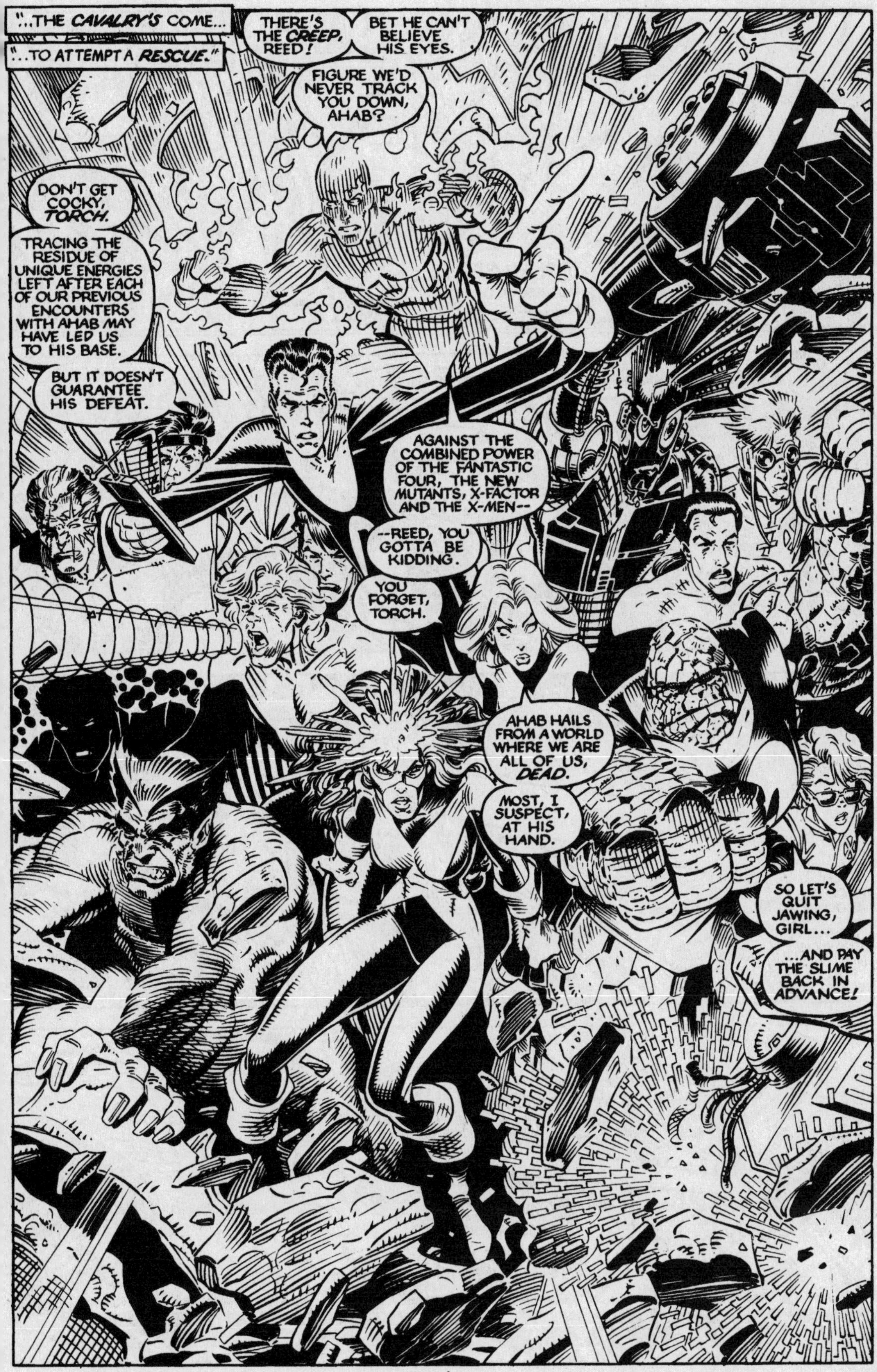
"...THE CAVALRY'S COME...
"...TO ATTEMPT A RESCUE."
THERE'S THE CREEP, REED!
BET HE CAN'T BELIEVE HIS EYES.
FIGURE WE'D NEVER TRACK YOU DOWN, AHAB?
DON'T GET COCKY, TORCH.
TRACING THE RESIDUE OF UNIQUE ENERGIES LEFT AFTER EACH OF OUR PREVIOUS ENCOUNTERS WITH AHAB MAY HAVE LED US TO HIS BASE.
BUT IT DOESN'T GUARANTEE HIS DEFEAT.
AGAINST THE COMBINED POWER OF THE FANTASTIC FOUR, THE NEW MUTANTS, X-FACTOR AND THE X-MEN--
--REED, YOU GOTTA BE KIDDING.
YOU FORGET, TORCH.
AHAB HAILS FROM A WORLD WHERE WE ARE ALL OF US, DEAD.
MOST, I SUSPECT, AT HIS HAND.
SO LET'S QUIT JAWING, GIRL...
...AND PAY THE SLIME BACK IN ADVANCE!

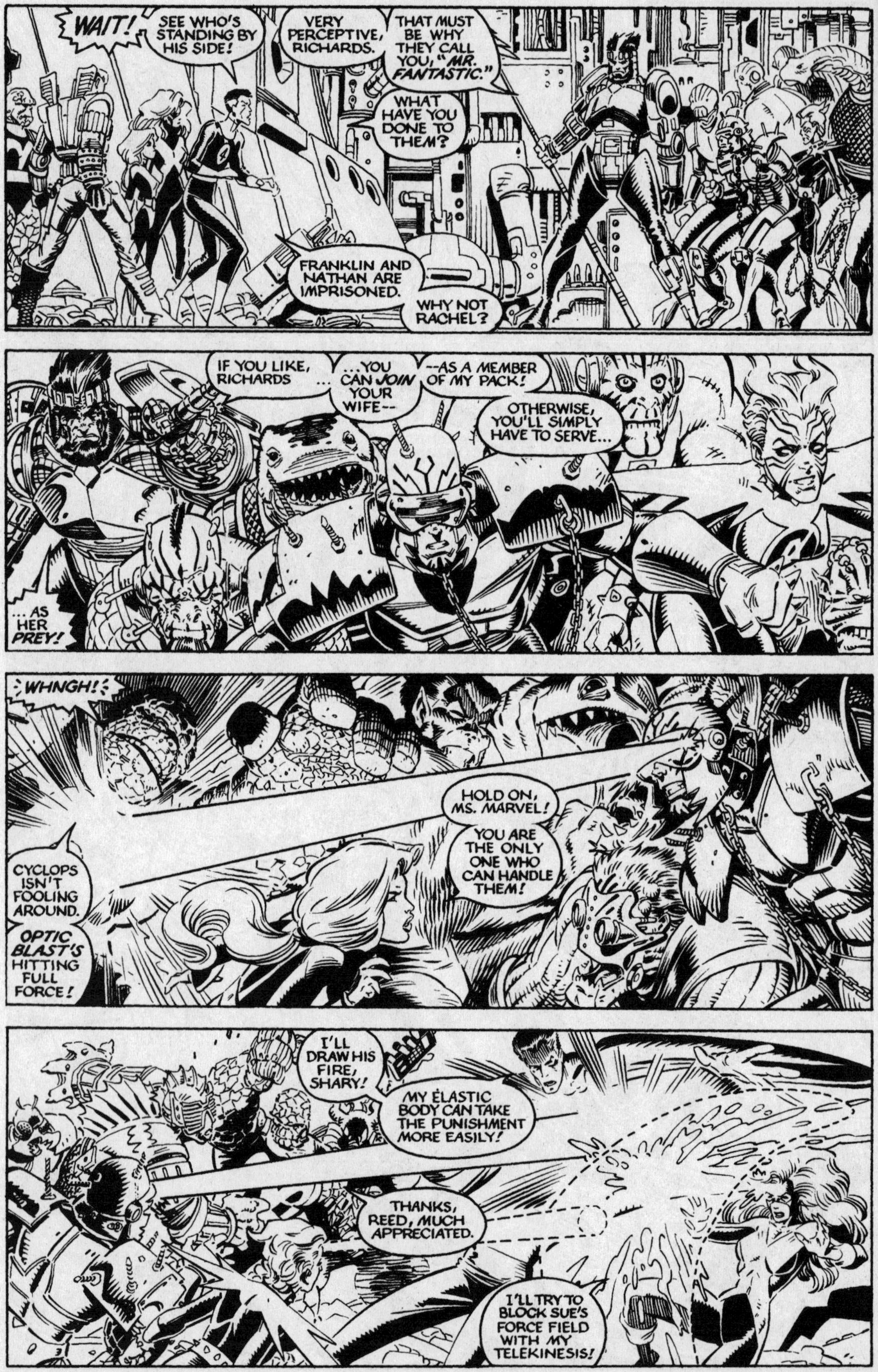
WAIT!
SEE WHO'S STANDING BY HIS SIDE!
VERY PERCEPTIVE, RICHARDS.
THAT MUST BE WHY THEY CALL YOU, "MR. FANTASTIC."
WHAT HAVE YOU DONE TO THEM?
FRANKLIN AND NATHAN ARE IMPRISONED.
WHY NOT RACHEL?
IF YOU LIKE, RICHARDS...
...YOU CAN JOIN YOUR WIFE--
--AS A MEMBER OF MY PACK!
OTHERWISE, YOU'LL SIMPLY HAVE TO SERVE...
...AS HER PREY!
WHNGH!
HOLD ON, MS. MARVEL!
YOU ARE THE ONLY ONE WHO CAN HANDLE THEM!
CYCLOPS ISN'T FOOLING AROUND.
OPTIC BLAST'S HITTING FULL FORCE!
I'LL DRAW HIS FIRE, SHARY!
MY ELASTIC BODY CAN TAKE THE PUNISHMENT MORE EASILY!
THANKS, REED, MUCH APPRECIATED.
I'LL TRY TO BLOCK SUE'S FORCE FIELD WITH MY TELEKINESIS!

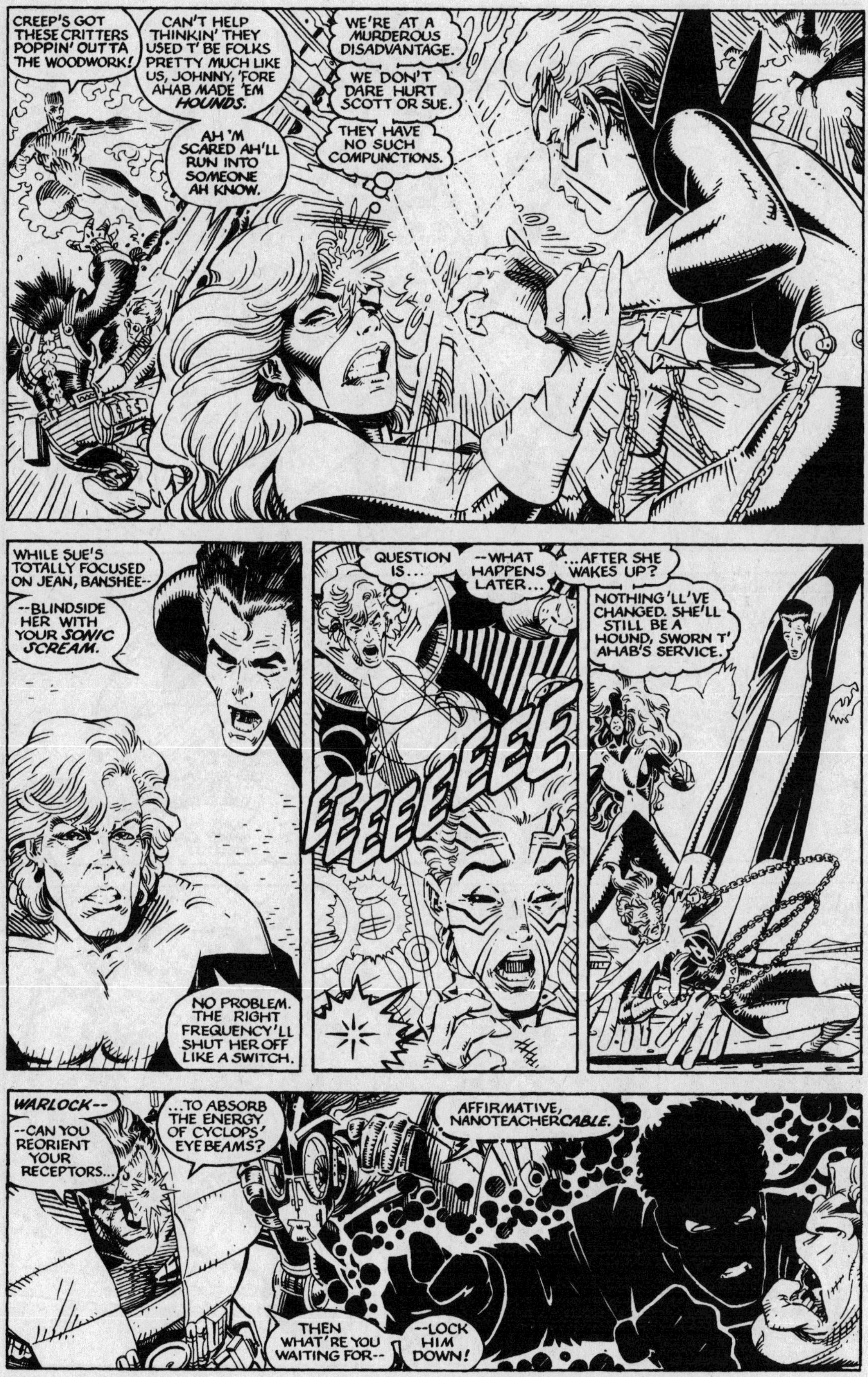
CREEP'S GOT THESE CRITTERS POPPIN' OUTTA THE WOODWORK!
CAN'T HELP THINKIN' THEY USED T' BE FOLKS PRETTY MUCH LIKE US, JOHNNY, 'FORE AHAB MADE 'EM HOUNDS.
AH 'M SCARED AH'LL RUN INTO SOMEONE AH KNOW.
WE'RE AT A MURDEROUS DISADVANTAGE.
WE DON'T DARE HURT SCOTT OR SUE.
THEY HAVE NO SUCH COMPUNCTIONS.
WHILE SUE'S TOTALLY FOCUSED ON JEAN, BANSHEE--
--BLINDSIDE HER WITH YOUR SONIC SCREAM.
NO PROBLEM. THE RIGHT FREQUENCY'LL SHUT HER OFF LIKE A SWITCH.
QUESTION IS...
--WHAT HAPPENS LATER...
...AFTER SHE WAKES UP?
EEEEEEEE
NOTHING'LL'VE CHANGED. SHE'LL STILL BE A HOUND, SWORN T' AHAB'S SERVICE.
WARLOCK--
--CAN YOU REORIENT YOUR RECEPTORS...
...TO ABSORB THE ENERGY OF CYCLOPS' EYE BEAMS?
AFFIRMATIVE, NANOTEACHER CABLE.
THEN WHAT'RE YOU WAITING FOR--
--LOCK HIM DOWN!

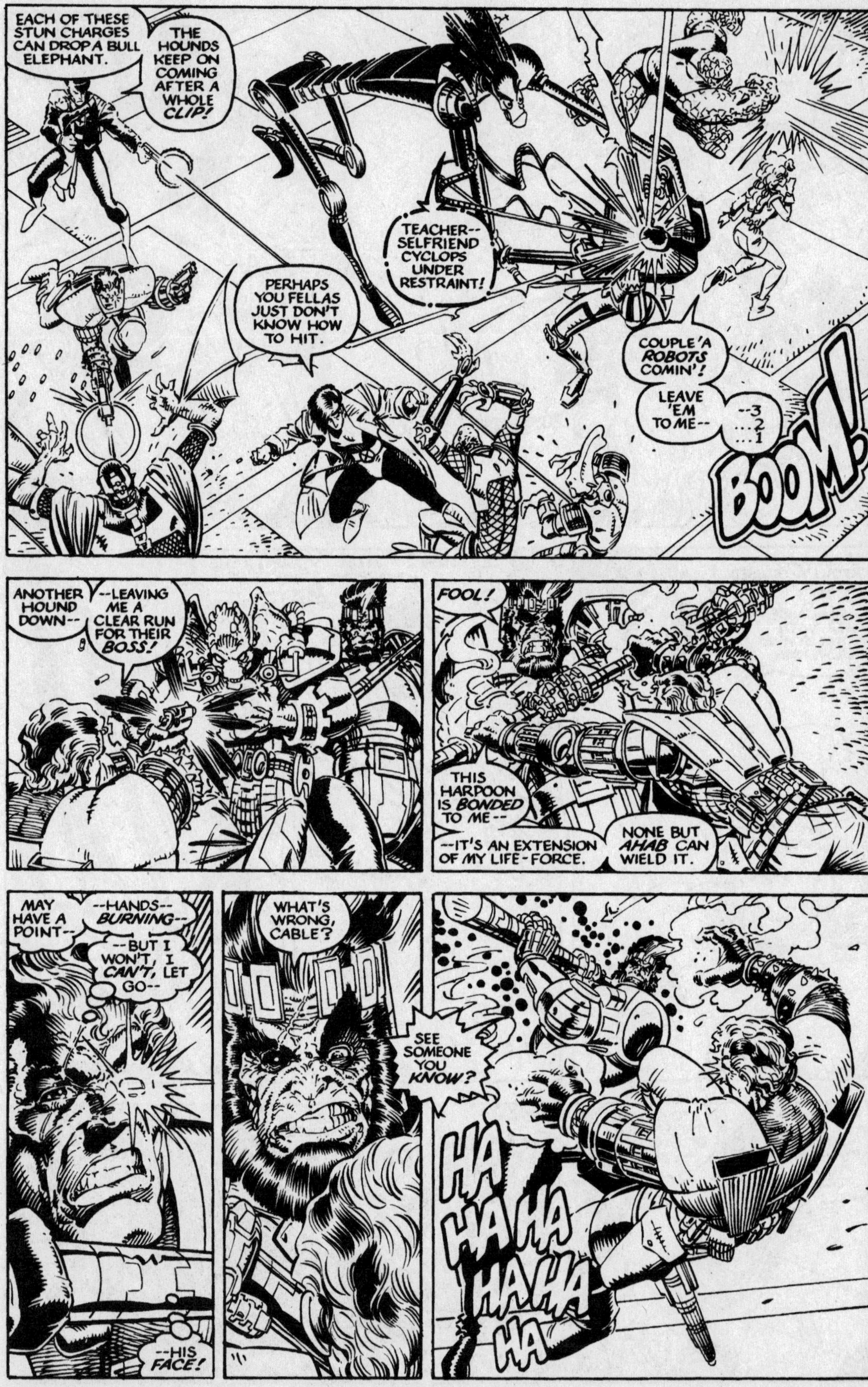
EACH OF THESE STUN CHARGES CAN DROP A BULL ELEPHANT.
THE HOUNDS KEEP ON COMING AFTER A WHOLE CLIP!
TEACHER--SELFRIEND CYCLOPS UNDER RESTRAINT!
PERHAPS YOU FELLAS JUST DON'T KNOW HOW TO HIT.
COUPLE'A ROBOTS COMIN'!
LEAVE 'EM TO ME--
--3 ...2 ...1
BOOM!
ANOTHER HOUND DOWN--
--LEAVING ME A CLEAR RUN FOR THEIR BOSS!
FOOL!
THIS HARPOON IS BONDED TO ME--
--IT'S AN EXTENSION OF MY LIFE-FORCE.
NONE BUT AHAB CAN WIELD IT.
MAY HAVE A POINT--
--HANDS--BURNING--
--BUT I WON'T, I CAN'T, LET GO--
--HIS FACE!
WHAT'S WRONG, CABLE?
SEE SOMEONE YOU KNOW?
HA HA HA HA HA HA

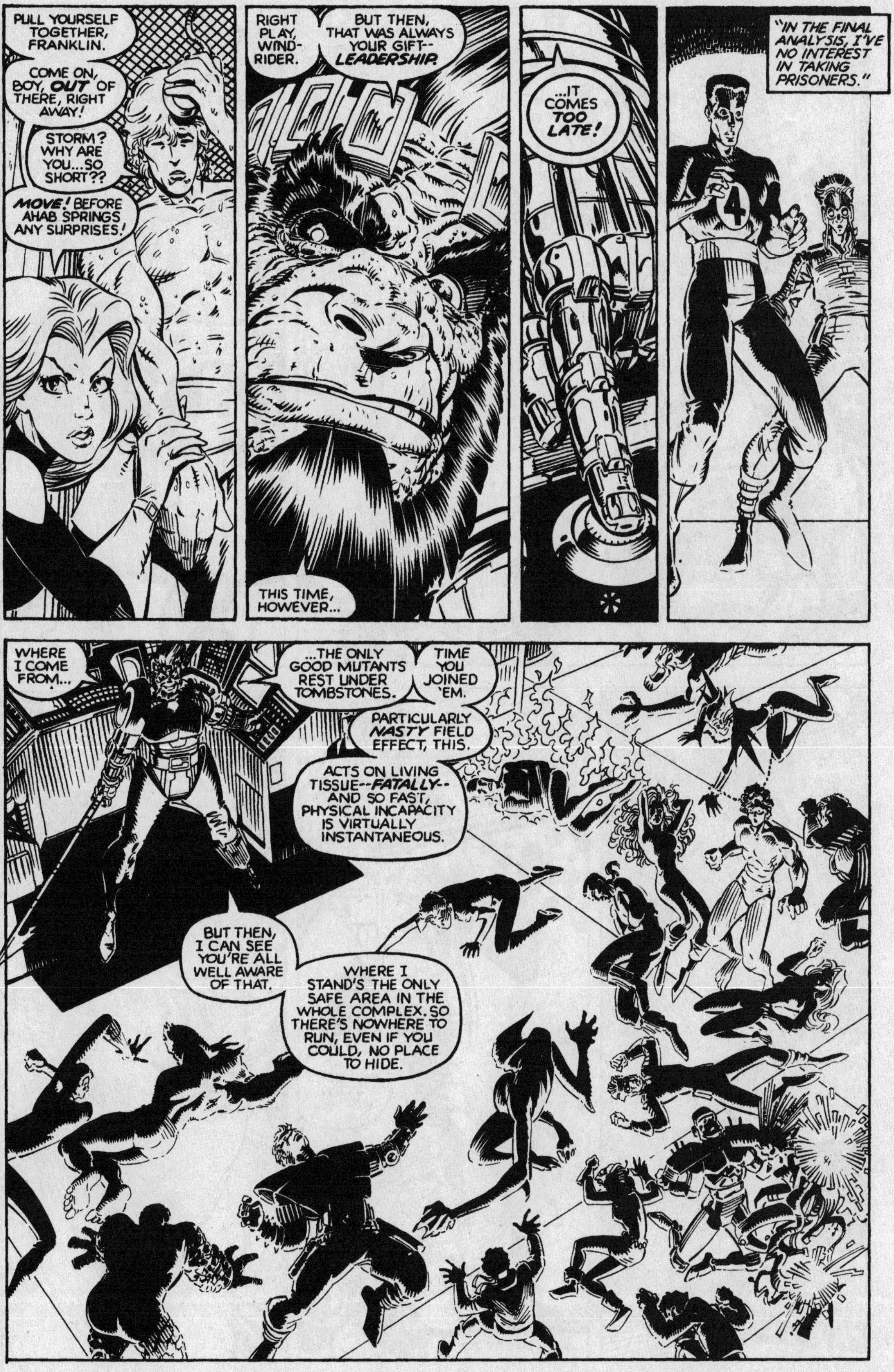
PULL YOURSELF TOGETHER, FRANKLIN.
COME ON, BOY, OUT OF THERE, RIGHT AWAY!
STORM? WHY ARE YOU...SO SHORT??
MOVE! BEFORE AHAB SPRINGS ANY SURPRISES!
RIGHT PLAY, WIND-RIDER.
BUT THEN, THAT WAS ALWAYS YOUR GIFT-- LEADERSHIP.
THIS TIME, HOWEVER...
...IT COMES TOO LATE!
"IN THE FINAL ANALYSIS, I'VE NO INTEREST IN TAKING PRISONERS."
WHERE I COME FROM...
...THE ONLY GOOD MUTANTS REST UNDER TOMBSTONES.
TIME YOU JOINED 'EM.
PARTICULARLY NASTY FIELD EFFECT, THIS.
ACTS ON LIVING TISSUE--FATALLY-- AND SO FAST, PHYSICAL INCAPACITY IS VIRTUALLY INSTANTANEOUS.
BUT THEN, I CAN SEE YOU'RE ALL WELL AWARE OF THAT.
WHERE I STAND'S THE ONLY SAFE AREA IN THE WHOLE COMPLEX. SO THERE'S NOWHERE TO RUN, EVEN IF YOU COULD, NO PLACE TO HIDE.

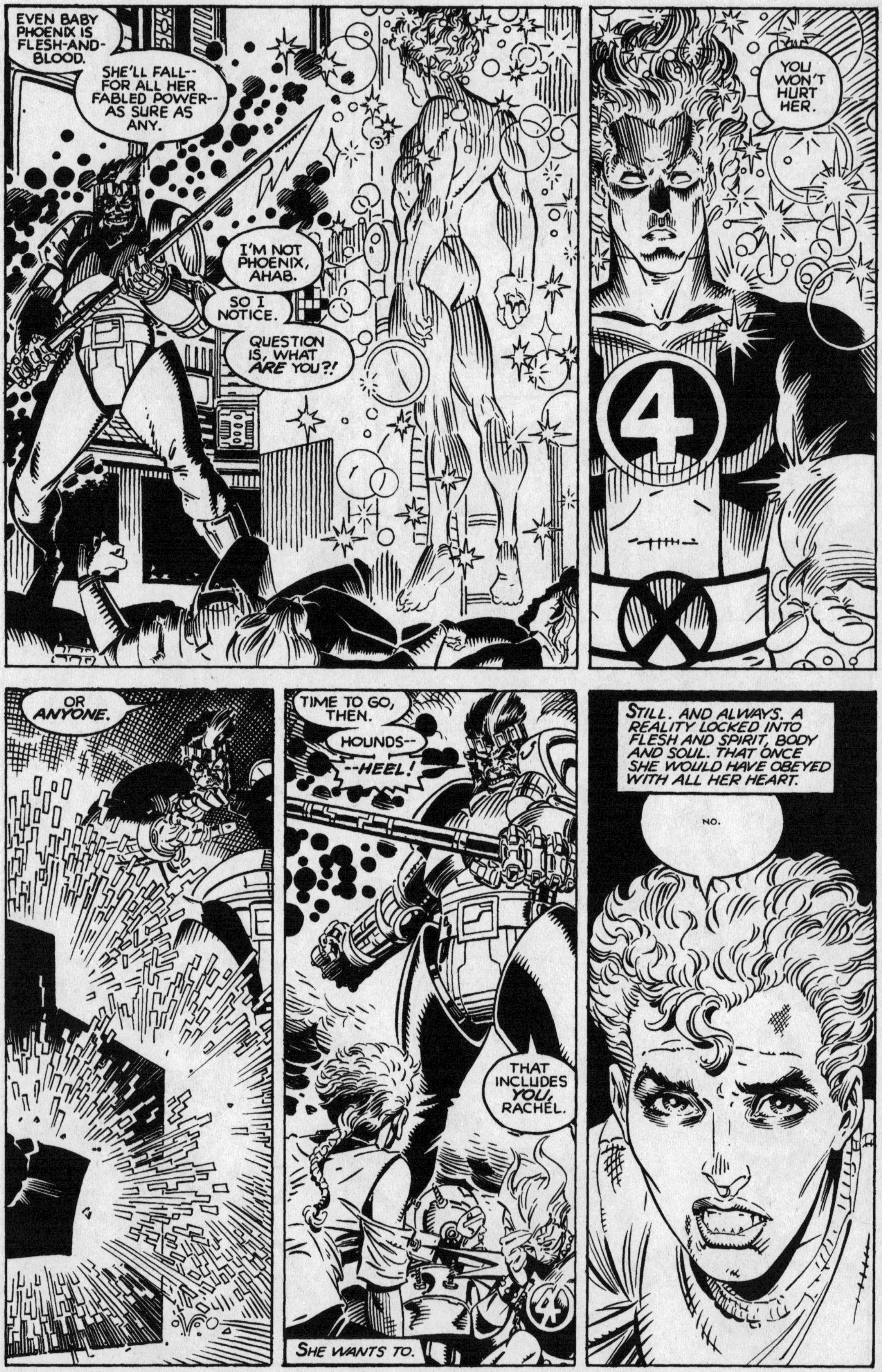
EVEN BABY PHOENIX IS FLESH-AND-BLOOD.
SHE'LL FALL-- FOR ALL HER FABLED POWER-- AS SURE AS ANY.
I'M NOT PHOENIX, AHAB.
SO I NOTICE.
QUESTION IS, WHAT *ARE* YOU?!
YOU WON'T HURT HER.
OR *ANYONE*.
TIME TO GO, THEN.
HOUNDS--
--*HEEL!*
THAT INCLUDES *YOU*, RACHEL.
SHE WANTS TO.
STILL. AND ALWAYS. A REALITY LOCKED INTO FLESH AND SPIRIT, BODY AND SOUL. THAT ONCE SHE WOULD HAVE OBEYED WITH ALL HER HEART.
NO.

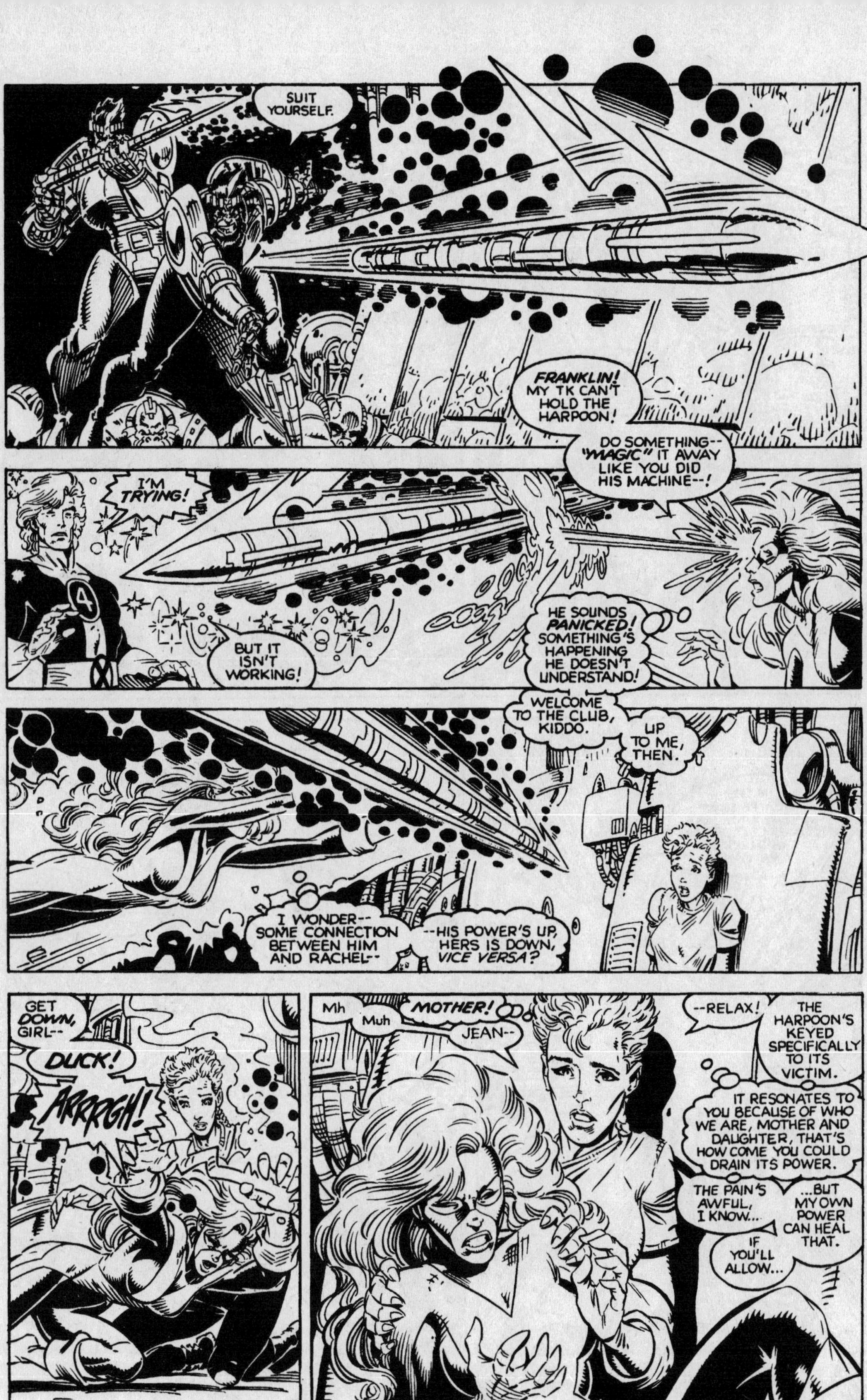

SUIT YOURSELF.
FRANKLIN! MY TK CAN'T HOLD THE HARPOON!
DO SOMETHING-- "MAGIC" IT AWAY LIKE YOU DID HIS MACHINE--!
I'M TRYING!
BUT IT ISN'T WORKING!
HE SOUNDS PANICKED! SOMETHING'S HAPPENING HE DOESN'T UNDERSTAND!
WELCOME TO THE CLUB, KIDDO.
UP TO ME, THEN.
I WONDER-- SOME CONNECTION BETWEEN HIM AND RACHEL--
--HIS POWER'S UP, HERS IS DOWN, VICE VERSA?
GET DOWN, GIRL--
DUCK!
ARRRGH!
Mh
Muh
MOTHER!
JEAN--
--RELAX!
THE HARPOON'S KEYED SPECIFICALLY TO ITS VICTIM.
IT RESONATES TO YOU BECAUSE OF WHO WE ARE, MOTHER AND DAUGHTER, THAT'S HOW COME YOU COULD DRAIN ITS POWER.
THE PAIN'S AWFUL, I KNOW...
...BUT MY OWN POWER CAN HEAL THAT.
IF YOU'LL ALLOW...

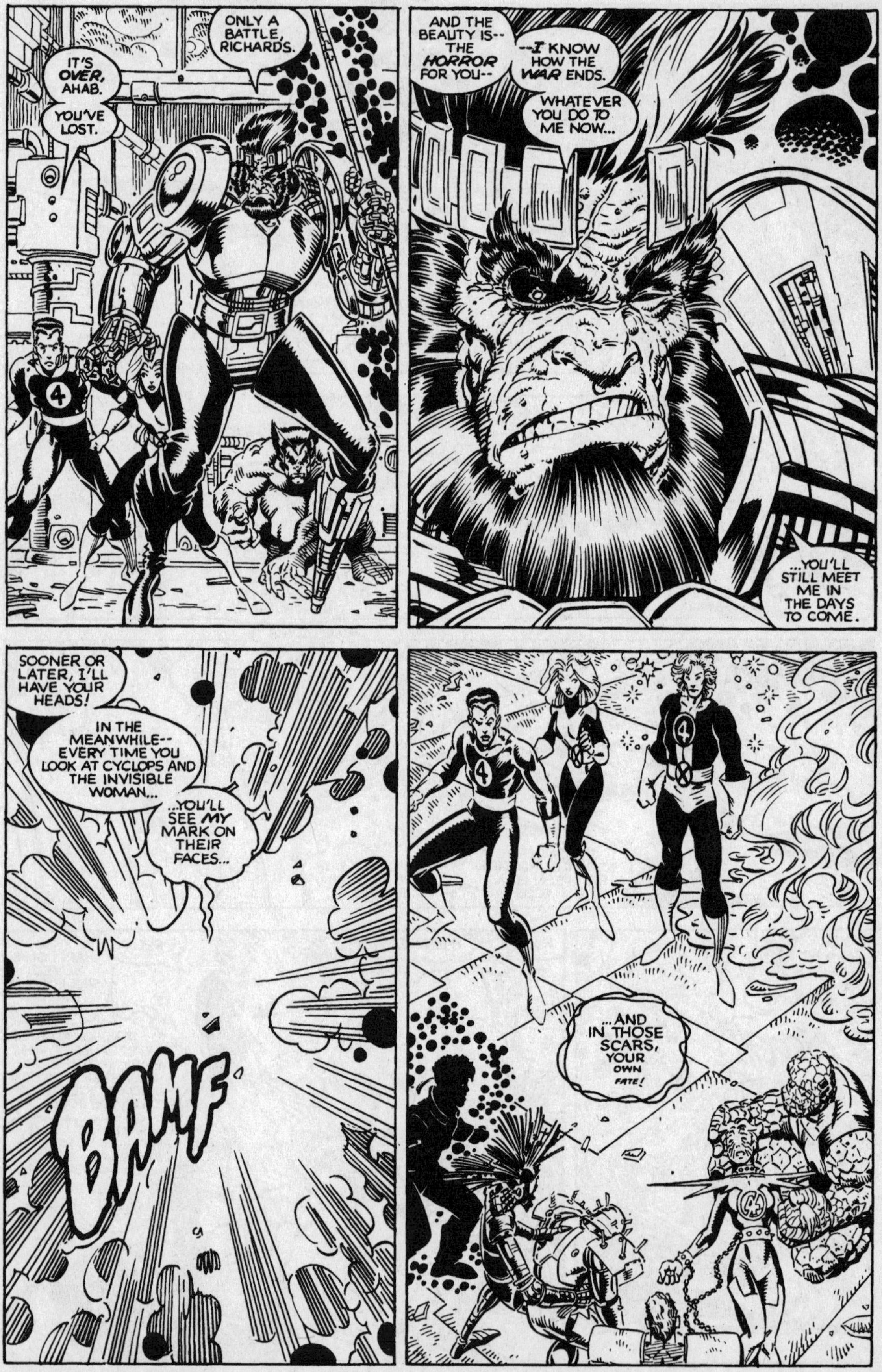
IT'S OVER, AHAB.
YOU'VE LOST.
ONLY A BATTLE, RICHARDS.
AND THE BEAUTY IS--THE HORROR FOR YOU--
--I KNOW HOW THE WAR ENDS.
WHATEVER YOU DO TO ME NOW...
...YOU'LL STILL MEET ME IN THE DAYS TO COME.
SOONER OR LATER, I'LL HAVE YOUR HEADS!
IN THE MEANWHILE--EVERY TIME YOU LOOK AT CYCLOPS AND THE INVISIBLE WOMAN...
...YOU'LL SEE MY MARK ON THEIR FACES...
BAMF
...AND IN THOSE SCARS, YOUR OWN FATE!

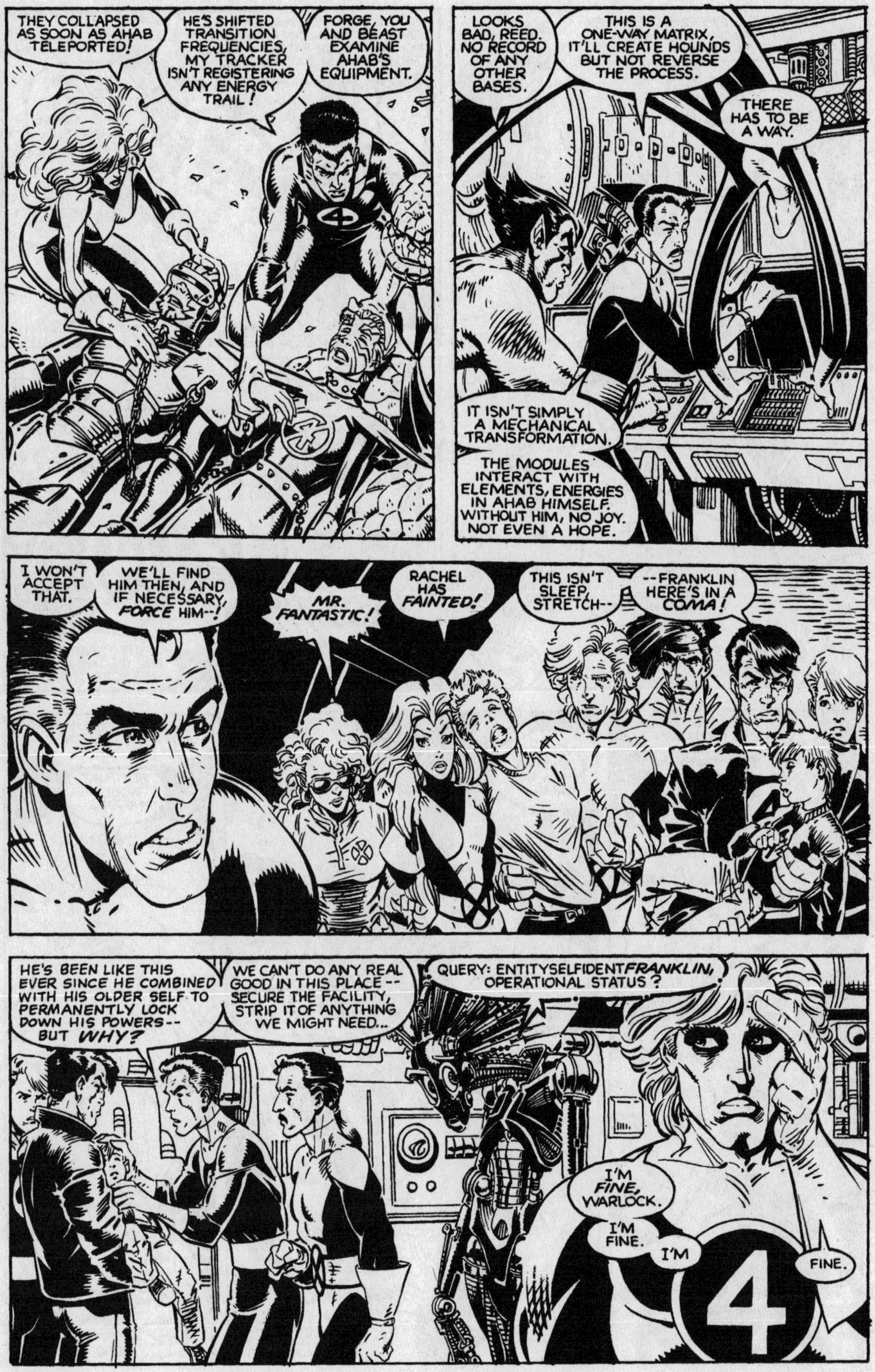

THEY COLLAPSED AS SOON AS AHAB TELEPORTED!
HE'S SHIFTED TRANSITION FREQUENCIES, MY TRACKER ISN'T REGISTERING ANY ENERGY TRAIL!
FORGE, YOU AND BEAST EXAMINE AHAB'S EQUIPMENT.
LOOKS BAD, REED. NO RECORD OF ANY OTHER BASES.
THIS IS A ONE-WAY MATRIX, IT'LL CREATE HOUNDS BUT NOT REVERSE THE PROCESS.
THERE HAS TO BE A WAY.
IT ISN'T SIMPLY A MECHANICAL TRANSFORMATION.
THE MODULES INTERACT WITH ELEMENTS, ENERGIES IN AHAB HIMSELF. WITHOUT HIM, NO JOY. NOT EVEN A HOPE.
I WON'T ACCEPT THAT.
WE'LL FIND HIM THEN, AND IF NECESSARY, FORCE HIM--!
MR. FANTASTIC!
RACHEL HAS FAINTED!
THIS ISN'T SLEEP, STRETCH--
--FRANKLIN HERE'S IN A COMA!
HE'S BEEN LIKE THIS EVER SINCE HE COMBINED WITH HIS OLDER SELF TO PERMANENTLY LOCK DOWN HIS POWERS-- BUT WHY?
WE CAN'T DO ANY REAL GOOD IN THIS PLACE -- SECURE THE FACILITY, STRIP IT OF ANYTHING WE MIGHT NEED...
QUERY: ENTITYSELFIDENTFRANKLIN, OPERATIONAL STATUS?
I'M FINE, WARLOCK.
I'M FINE.
I'M
FINE.

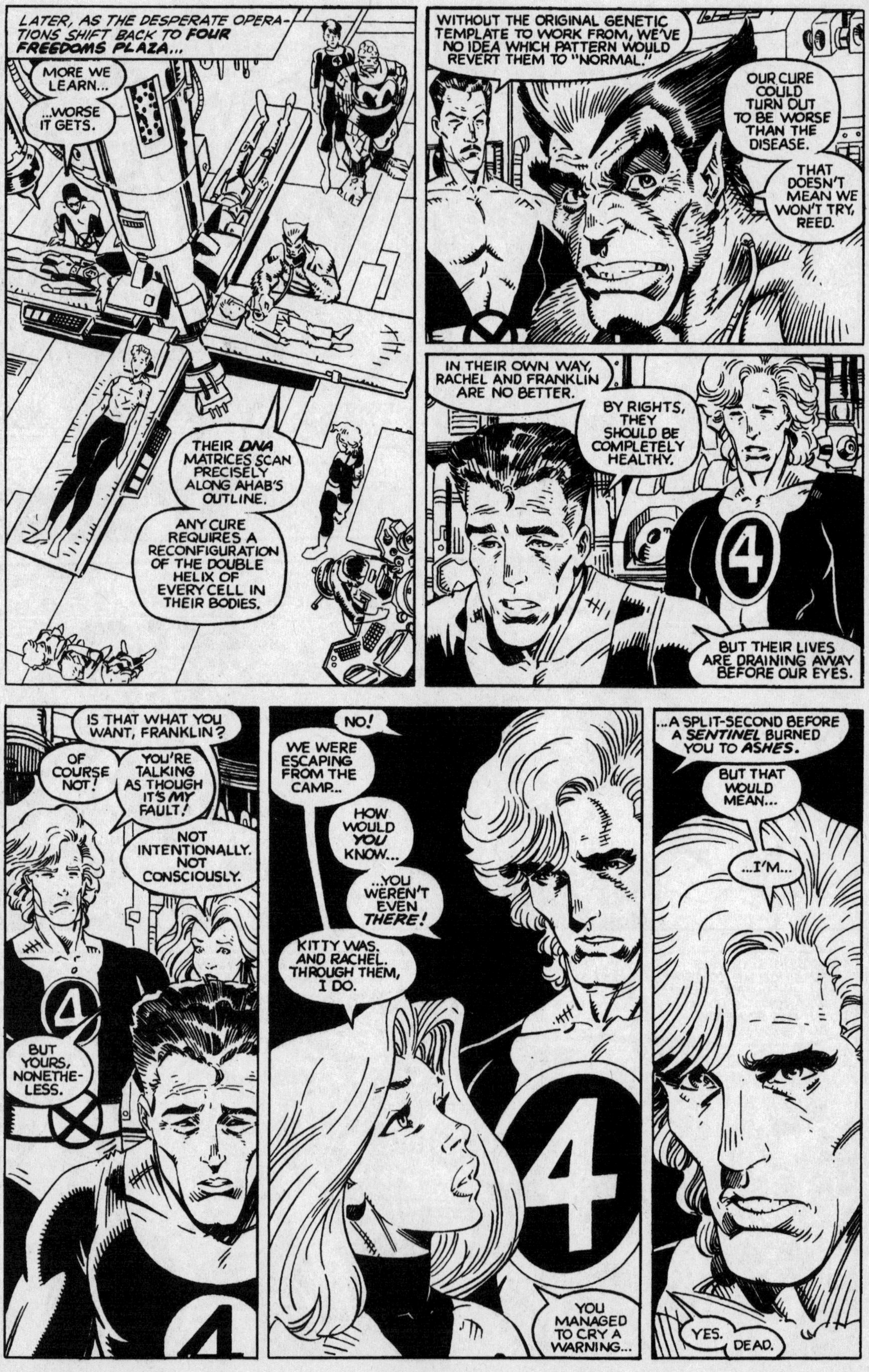

LATER, AS THE DESPERATE OPERATIONS SHIFT BACK TO FOUR FREEDOMS PLAZA...
MORE WE LEARN...
...WORSE IT GETS.
THEIR DNA MATRICES SCAN PRECISELY ALONG AHAB'S OUTLINE.
ANY CURE REQUIRES A RECONFIGURATION OF THE DOUBLE HELIX OF EVERY CELL IN THEIR BODIES.
WITHOUT THE ORIGINAL GENETIC TEMPLATE TO WORK FROM, WE'VE NO IDEA WHICH PATTERN WOULD REVERT THEM TO "NORMAL."
OUR CURE COULD TURN OUT TO BE WORSE THAN THE DISEASE.
THAT DOESN'T MEAN WE WON'T TRY, REED.
IN THEIR OWN WAY, RACHEL AND FRANKLIN ARE NO BETTER.
BY RIGHTS, THEY SHOULD BE COMPLETELY HEALTHY.
BUT THEIR LIVES ARE DRAINING AWAY BEFORE OUR EYES.
IS THAT WHAT YOU WANT, FRANKLIN?
OF COURSE NOT!
YOU'RE TALKING AS THOUGH IT'S MY FAULT!
NOT INTENTIONALLY. NOT CONSCIOUSLY.
BUT YOURS, NONETHELESS.
NO!
WE WERE ESCAPING FROM THE CAMP...
HOW WOULD YOU KNOW...
...YOU WEREN'T EVEN THERE!
KITTY WAS. AND RACHEL. THROUGH THEM, I DO.
YOU MANAGED TO CRY A WARNING...
...A SPLIT-SECOND BEFORE A SENTINEL BURNED YOU TO ASHES.
BUT THAT WOULD MEAN...
...I'M...
YES.
DEAD.

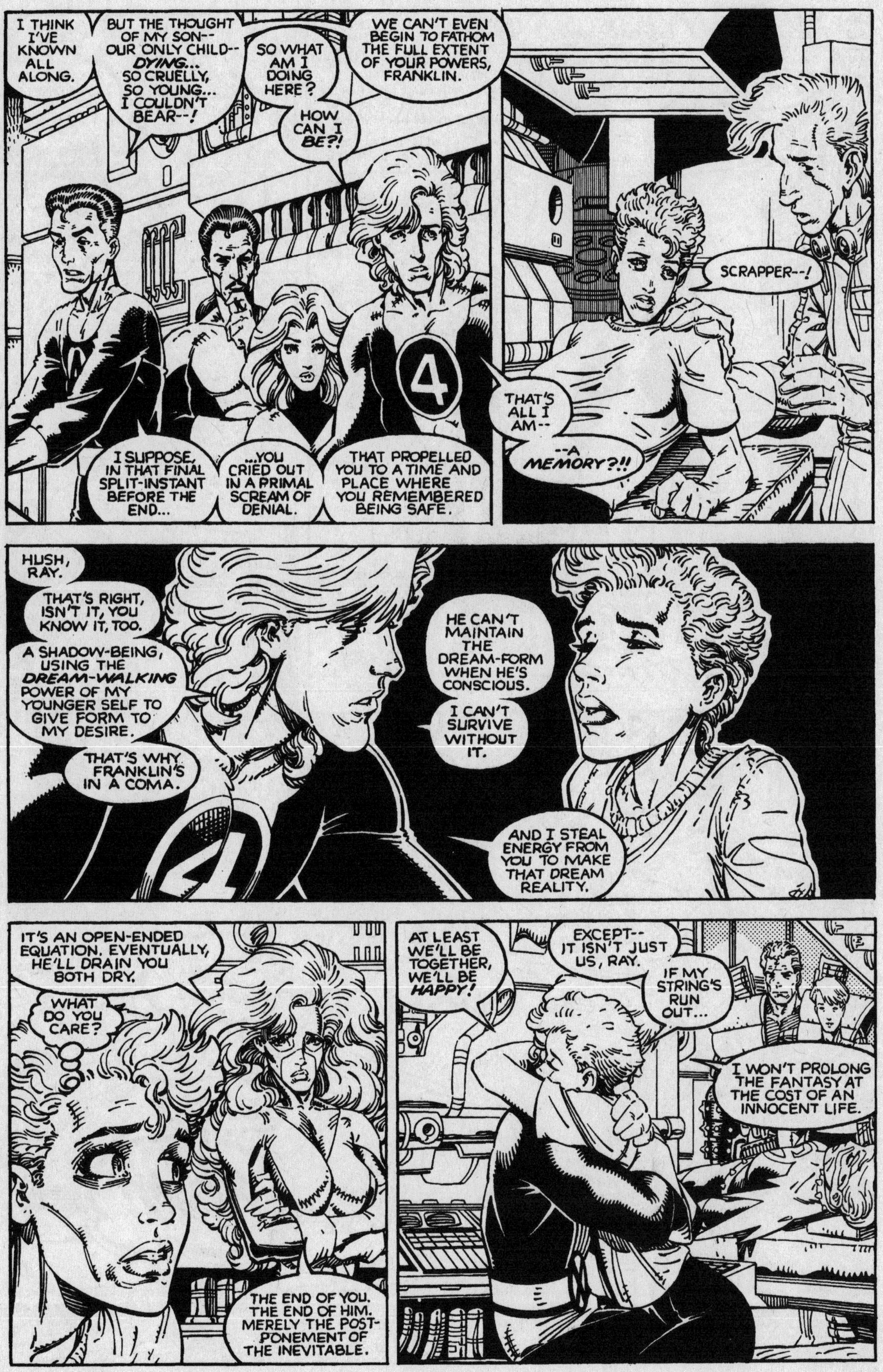
I THINK I'VE KNOWN ALL ALONG.
BUT THE THOUGHT OF MY SON-- OUR ONLY CHILD-- DYING... SO CRUELLY, SO YOUNG... I COULDN'T BEAR--!
SO WHAT AM I DOING HERE?
HOW CAN I BE?!
WE CAN'T EVEN BEGIN TO FATHOM THE FULL EXTENT OF YOUR POWERS, FRANKLIN.
I SUPPOSE, IN THAT FINAL SPLIT-INSTANT BEFORE THE END...
...YOU CRIED OUT IN A PRIMAL SCREAM OF DENIAL.
THAT PROPELLED YOU TO A TIME AND PLACE WHERE YOU REMEMBERED BEING SAFE.
THAT'S ALL I AM--
--A MEMORY?!!
SCRAPPER--!
HUSH, RAY.
THAT'S RIGHT, ISN'T IT, YOU KNOW IT, TOO.
A SHADOW-BEING, USING THE DREAM-WALKING POWER OF MY YOUNGER SELF TO GIVE FORM TO MY DESIRE.
THAT'S WHY FRANKLIN'S IN A COMA.
HE CAN'T MAINTAIN THE DREAM-FORM WHEN HE'S CONSCIOUS.
I CAN'T SURVIVE WITHOUT IT.
AND I STEAL ENERGY FROM YOU TO MAKE THAT DREAM REALITY.
IT'S AN OPEN-ENDED EQUATION. EVENTUALLY, HE'LL DRAIN YOU BOTH DRY.
WHAT DO YOU CARE?
THE END OF YOU. THE END OF HIM. MERELY THE POST-PONEMENT OF THE INEVITABLE.
AT LEAST WE'LL BE TOGETHER, WE'LL BE HAPPY!
EXCEPT-- IT ISN'T JUST US, RAY.
IF MY STRING'S RUN OUT...
I WON'T PROLONG THE FANTASY AT THE COST OF AN INNOCENT LIFE.

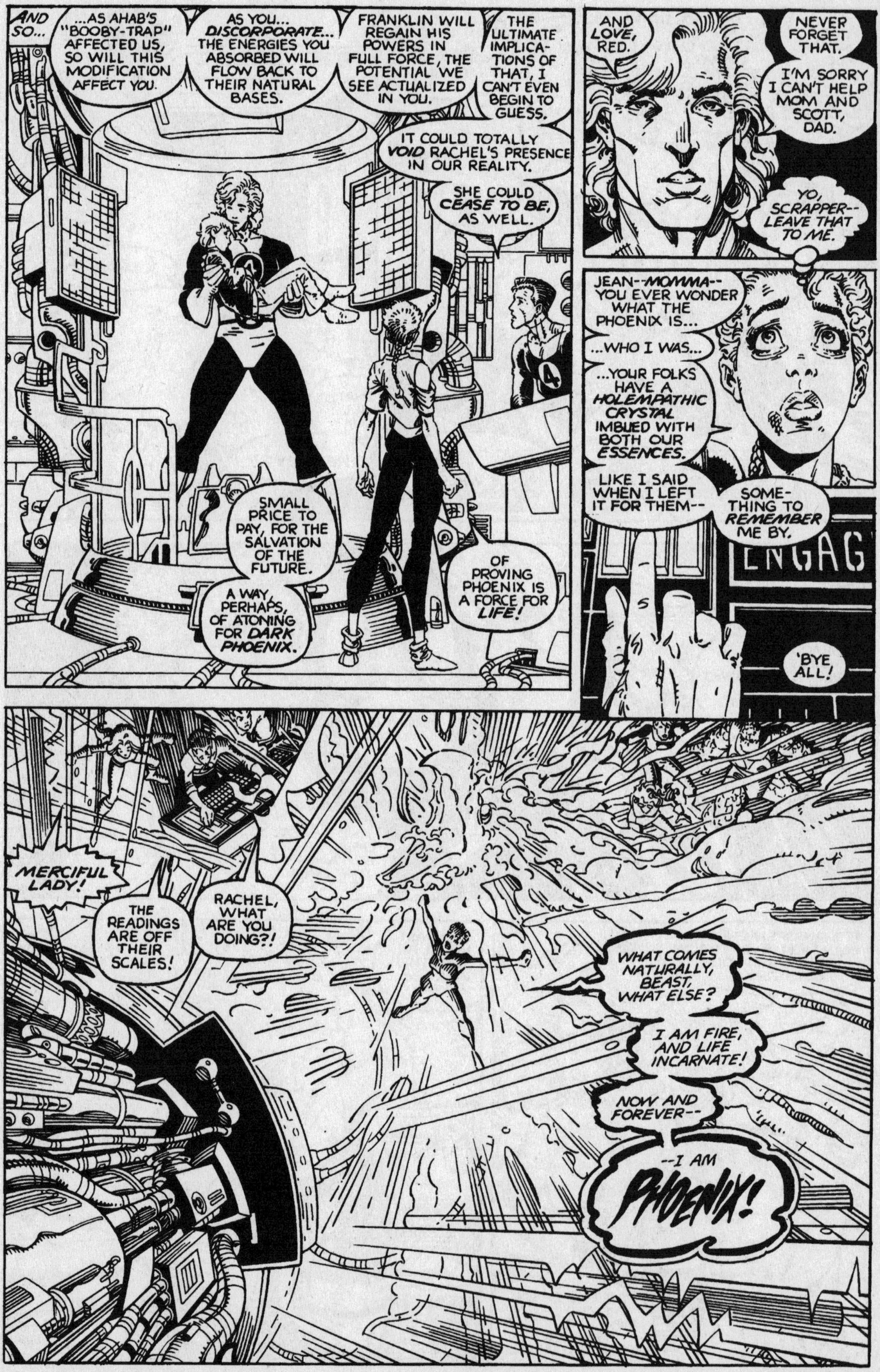
AND SO...
...AS AHAB'S "BOOBY-TRAP" AFFECTED US, SO WILL THIS MODIFICATION AFFECT YOU.
AS YOU... DISCORPORATE... THE ENERGIES YOU ABSORBED WILL FLOW BACK TO THEIR NATURAL BASES.
FRANKLIN WILL REGAIN HIS POWERS IN FULL FORCE, THE POTENTIAL WE SEE ACTUALIZED IN YOU.
THE ULTIMATE IMPLICATIONS OF THAT, I CAN'T EVEN BEGIN TO GUESS.
IT COULD TOTALLY VOID RACHEL'S PRESENCE IN OUR REALITY.
SHE COULD CEASE TO BE, AS WELL.
SMALL PRICE TO PAY, FOR THE SALVATION OF THE FUTURE.
A WAY, PERHAPS, OF ATONING FOR DARK PHOENIX.
OF PROVING PHOENIX IS A FORCE FOR LIFE!
AND LOVE, RED.
NEVER FORGET THAT.
I'M SORRY I CAN'T HELP MOM AND SCOTT, DAD.
YO, SCRAPPER-- LEAVE THAT TO ME.
JEAN--MOMMA-- YOU EVER WONDER WHAT THE PHOENIX IS...
...WHO I WAS...
...YOUR FOLKS HAVE A HOLEMPATHIC CRYSTAL IMBUED WITH BOTH OUR ESSENCES.
LIKE I SAID WHEN I LEFT IT FOR THEM--
SOMETHING TO REMEMBER ME BY.
ENGAG
'BYE ALL!
MERCIFUL LADY!
THE READINGS ARE OFF THEIR SCALES!
RACHEL, WHAT ARE YOU DOING?!
WHAT COMES NATURALLY, BEAST, WHAT ELSE?
I AM FIRE, AND LIFE INCARNATE!
NOW AND FOREVER--
--I AM
PHOENIX!

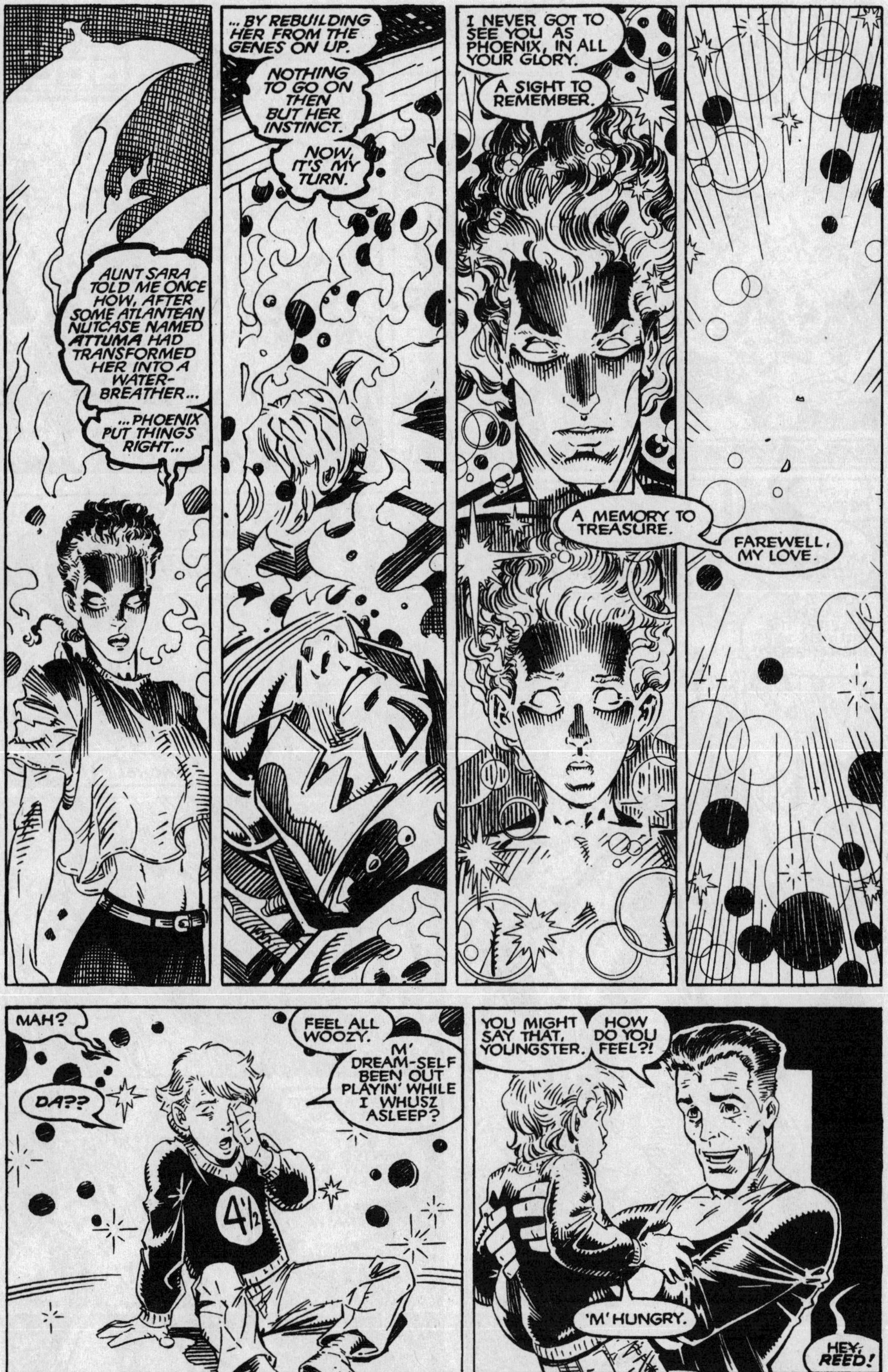
AUNT SARA TOLD ME ONCE HOW, AFTER SOME ATLANTEAN NUTCASE NAMED ATTUMA HAD TRANSFORMED HER INTO A WATER-BREATHER...
...PHOENIX PUT THINGS RIGHT...
...BY REBUILDING HER FROM THE GENES ON UP.
NOTHING TO GO ON THEN BUT HER INSTINCT.
NOW, IT'S MY TURN.
I NEVER GOT TO SEE YOU AS PHOENIX, IN ALL YOUR GLORY.
A SIGHT TO REMEMBER.
A MEMORY TO TREASURE.
FAREWELL, MY LOVE.
MAH?
DA??
FEEL ALL WOOZY.
M' DREAM-SELF BEEN OUT PLAYIN' WHILE I WHUSZ ASLEEP?
YOU MIGHT SAY THAT, YOUNGSTER.
HOW DO YOU FEEL?!
'M' HUNGRY.
HEY, REED!

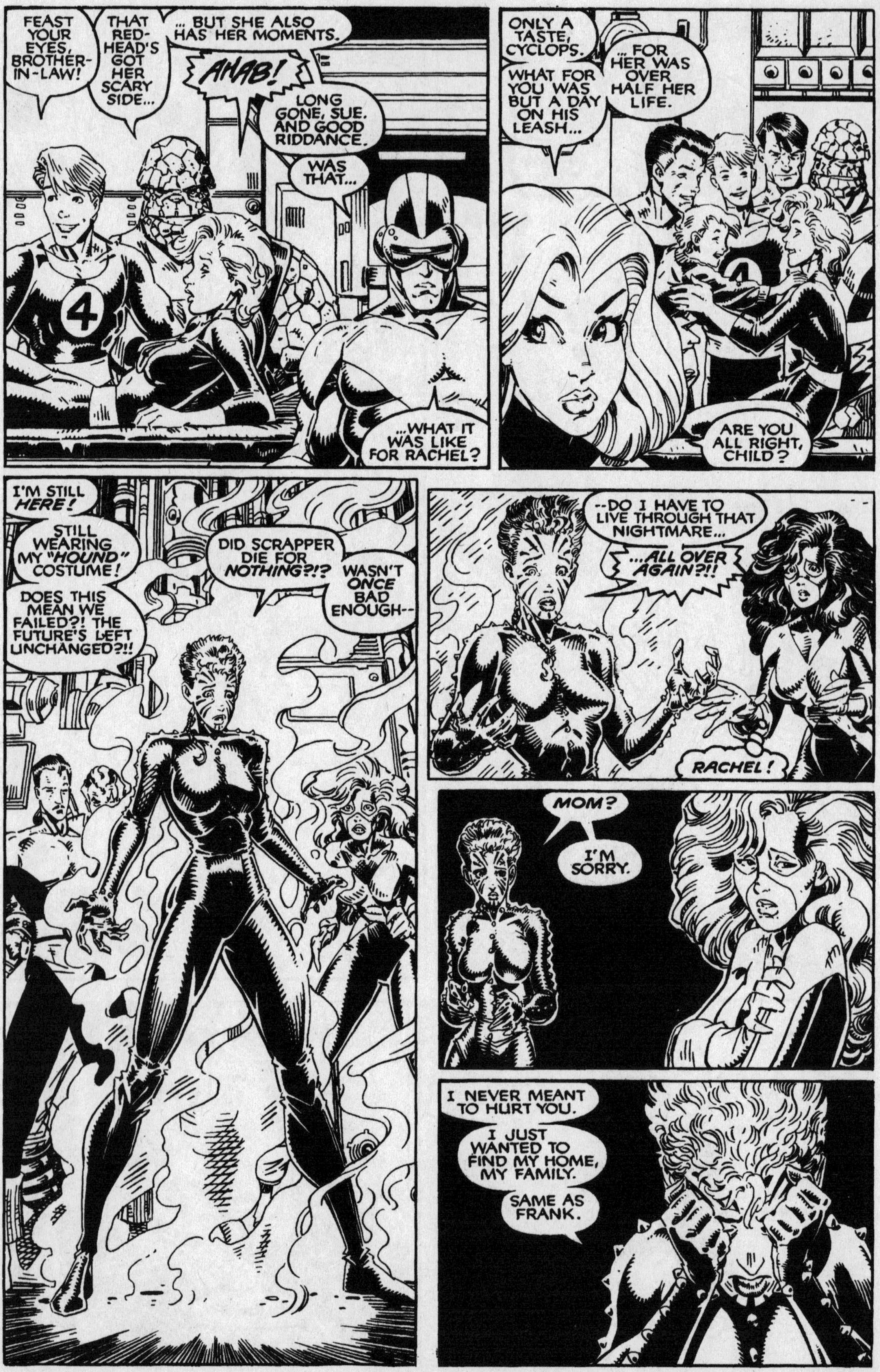
FEAST YOUR EYES, BROTHER-IN-LAW!
THAT RED-HEAD'S GOT HER SCARY SIDE...
... BUT SHE ALSO HAS HER MOMENTS.
AHAB!
LONG GONE, SUE. AND GOOD RIDDANCE.
WAS THAT...
...WHAT IT WAS LIKE FOR RACHEL?
ONLY A TASTE, CYCLOPS.
WHAT FOR YOU WAS BUT A DAY ON HIS LEASH...
... FOR HER WAS OVER HALF HER LIFE.
ARE YOU ALL RIGHT, CHILD?
I'M STILL HERE!
STILL WEARING MY "HOUND" COSTUME!
DOES THIS MEAN WE FAILED?! THE FUTURE'S LEFT UNCHANGED?!!
DID SCRAPPER DIE FOR NOTHING?!?
WASN'T ONCE BAD ENOUGH--
--DO I HAVE TO LIVE THROUGH THAT NIGHTMARE...
...ALL OVER AGAIN?!!
RACHEL!
MOM?
I'M SORRY.
I NEVER MEANT TO HURT YOU.
I JUST WANTED TO FIND MY HOME, MY FAMILY.
SAME AS FRANK.

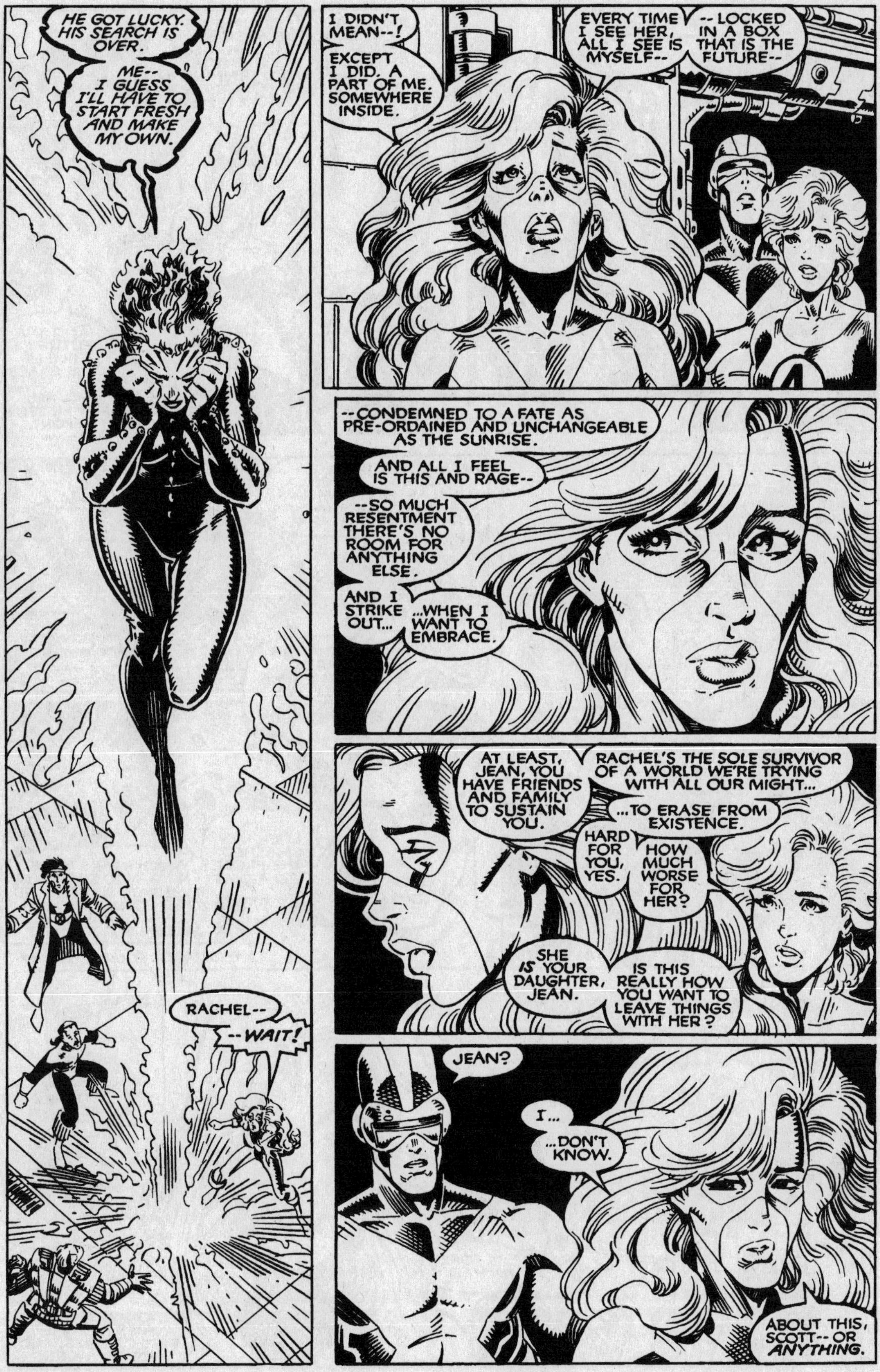
HE GOT LUCKY. HIS SEARCH IS OVER.
ME-- I GUESS I'LL HAVE TO START FRESH AND MAKE MY OWN.
RACHEL--
--WAIT!
I DIDN'T MEAN--!
EXCEPT I DID. A PART OF ME. SOMEWHERE INSIDE.
EVERY TIME I SEE HER, ALL I SEE IS MYSELF--
--LOCKED IN A BOX THAT IS THE FUTURE--
--CONDEMNED TO A FATE AS PRE-ORDAINED AND UNCHANGEABLE AS THE SUNRISE.
AND ALL I FEEL IS THIS AND RAGE--
--SO MUCH RESENTMENT THERE'S NO ROOM FOR ANYTHING ELSE.
AND I STRIKE OUT...
...WHEN I WANT TO EMBRACE.
AT LEAST, JEAN, YOU HAVE FRIENDS AND FAMILY TO SUSTAIN YOU.
RACHEL'S THE SOLE SURVIVOR OF A WORLD WE'RE TRYING WITH ALL OUR MIGHT...
...TO ERASE FROM EXISTENCE.
HARD FOR YOU, YES.
HOW MUCH WORSE FOR HER?
SHE IS YOUR DAUGHTER, JEAN.
IS THIS REALLY HOW YOU WANT TO LEAVE THINGS WITH HER?
JEAN?
I...
...DON'T KNOW.
ABOUT THIS, SCOTT--OR ANYTHING.

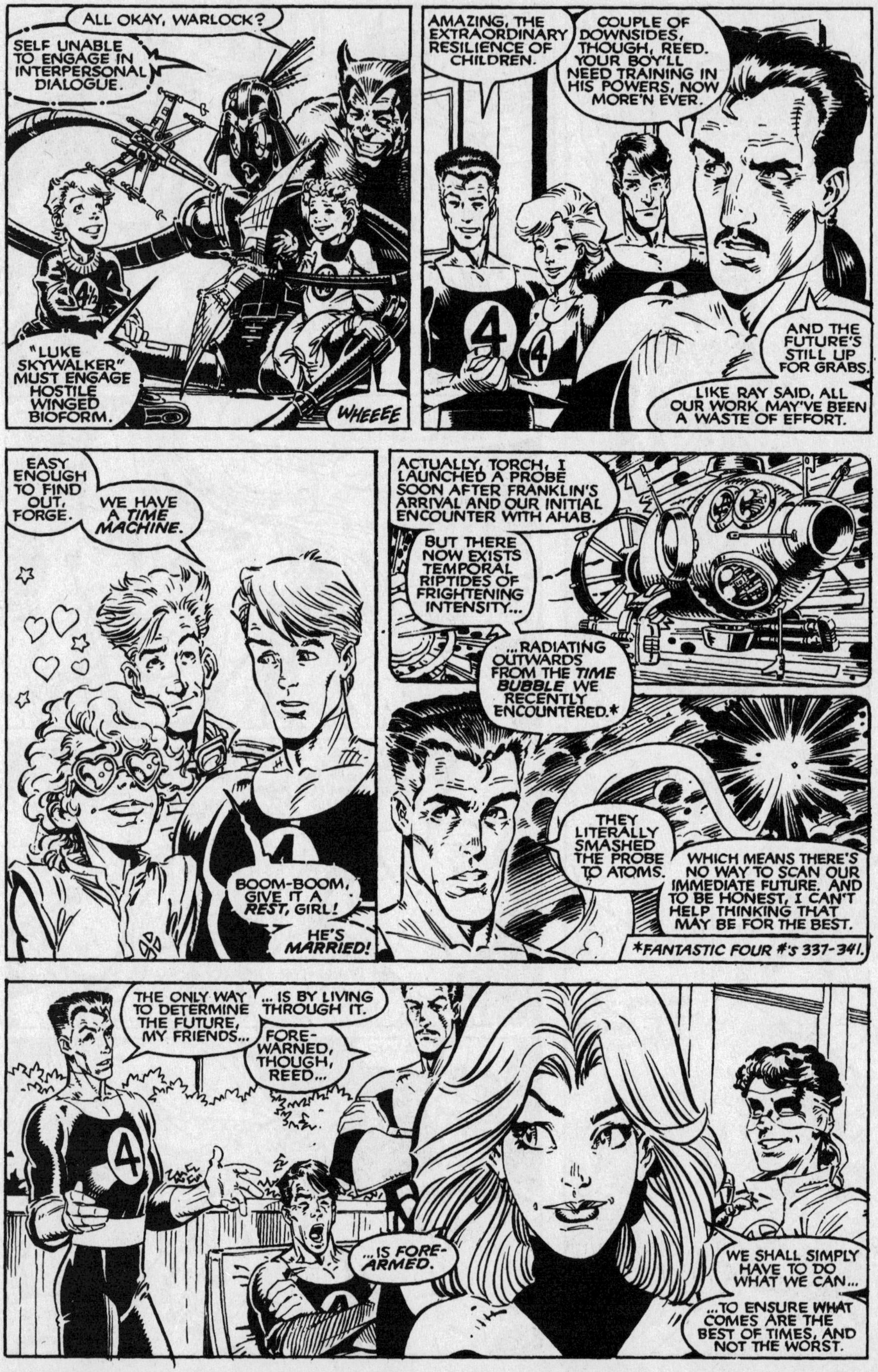

ALL OKAY, WARLOCK?
SELF UNABLE TO ENGAGE IN INTERPERSONAL DIALOGUE.
"LUKE SKYWALKER" MUST ENGAGE HOSTILE WINGED BIOFORM.
WHEEEE
AMAZING, THE EXTRAORDINARY RESILIENCE OF CHILDREN.
COUPLE OF DOWNSIDES, THOUGH, REED. YOUR BOY'LL NEED TRAINING IN HIS POWERS, NOW MORE'N EVER.
AND THE FUTURE'S STILL UP FOR GRABS.
LIKE RAY SAID, ALL OUR WORK MAY'VE BEEN A WASTE OF EFFORT.
EASY ENOUGH TO FIND OUT, FORGE.
WE HAVE A *TIME MACHINE*.
BOOM-BOOM, GIVE IT A **REST**, GIRL!
HE'S **MARRIED!**
ACTUALLY, TORCH, I LAUNCHED A PROBE SOON AFTER FRANKLIN'S ARRIVAL AND OUR INITIAL ENCOUNTER WITH AHAB.
BUT THERE NOW EXISTS TEMPORAL RIPTIDES OF FRIGHTENING INTENSITY...
...RADIATING OUTWARDS FROM THE *TIME BUBBLE* WE RECENTLY ENCOUNTERED.*
THEY LITERALLY SMASHED THE PROBE TO ATOMS.
WHICH MEANS THERE'S NO WAY TO SCAN OUR IMMEDIATE FUTURE. AND TO BE HONEST, I CAN'T HELP THINKING THAT MAY BE FOR THE BEST.
*FANTASTIC FOUR #'s 337-341.
THE ONLY WAY TO DETERMINE THE FUTURE, MY FRIENDS...
...IS BY LIVING THROUGH IT.
FORE-WARNED, THOUGH, REED...
...IS *FORE-ARMED*.
WE SHALL SIMPLY HAVE TO DO WHAT WE CAN...
...TO ENSURE WHAT COMES ARE THE BEST OF TIMES, AND NOT THE WORST.

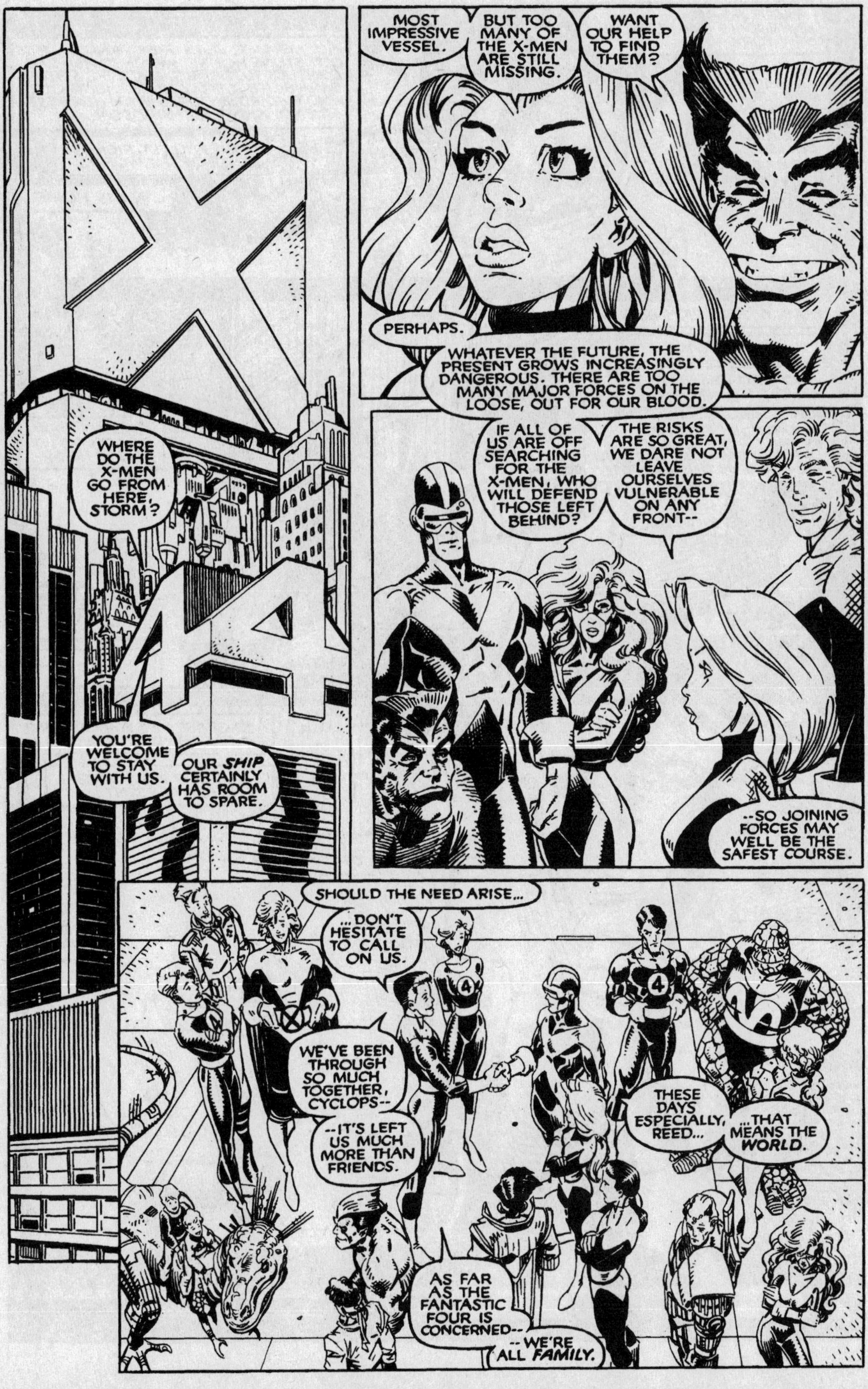
MOST IMPRESSIVE VESSEL.
BUT TOO MANY OF THE X-MEN ARE STILL MISSING.
WANT OUR HELP TO FIND THEM?
PERHAPS.
WHATEVER THE FUTURE, THE PRESENT GROWS INCREASINGLY DANGEROUS. THERE ARE TOO MANY MAJOR FORCES ON THE LOOSE, OUT FOR OUR BLOOD.
WHERE DO THE X-MEN GO FROM HERE, STORM?
YOU'RE WELCOME TO STAY WITH US.
OUR SHIP CERTAINLY HAS ROOM TO SPARE.
IF ALL OF US ARE OFF SEARCHING FOR THE X-MEN, WHO WILL DEFEND THOSE LEFT BEHIND?
THE RISKS ARE SO GREAT, WE DARE NOT LEAVE OURSELVES VULNERABLE ON ANY FRONT--
--SO JOINING FORCES MAY WELL BE THE SAFEST COURSE.
SHOULD THE NEED ARISE...
...DON'T HESITATE TO CALL ON US.
WE'VE BEEN THROUGH SO MUCH TOGETHER, CYCLOPS--
--IT'S LEFT US MUCH MORE THAN FRIENDS.
THESE DAYS ESPECIALLY, REED...
...THAT MEANS THE WORLD.
AS FAR AS THE FANTASTIC FOUR IS CONCERNED--
--WE'RE ALL FAMILY.

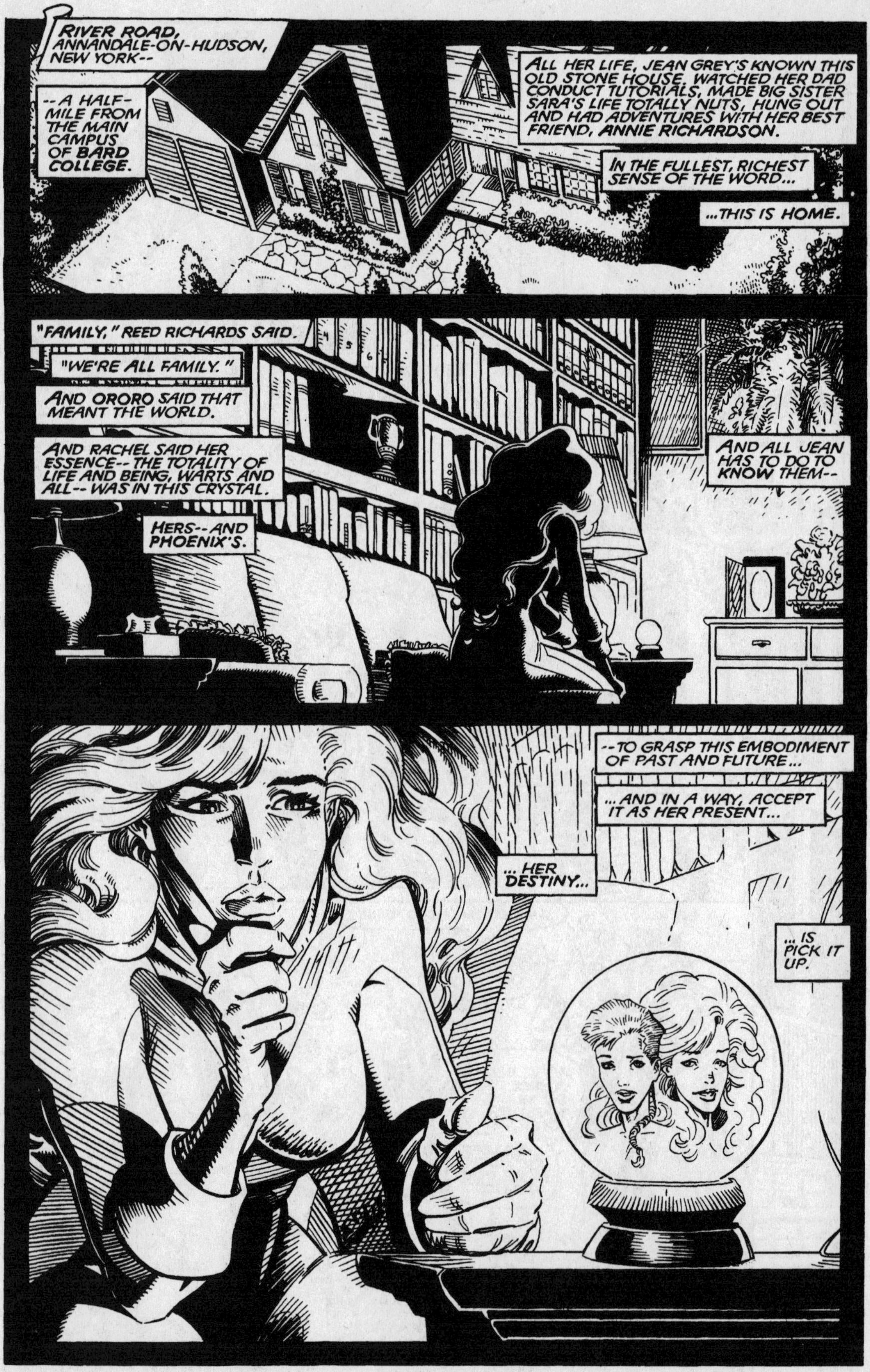
RIVER ROAD, ANNANDALE-ON-HUDSON, NEW YORK--
--A HALF-MILE FROM THE MAIN CAMPUS OF BARD COLLEGE.
ALL HER LIFE, JEAN GREY'S KNOWN THIS OLD STONE HOUSE. WATCHED HER DAD CONDUCT TUTORIALS, MADE BIG SISTER SARA'S LIFE TOTALLY NUTS, HUNG OUT AND HAD ADVENTURES WITH HER BEST FRIEND, ANNIE RICHARDSON.
IN THE FULLEST, RICHEST SENSE OF THE WORD...
...THIS IS HOME.
"FAMILY," REED RICHARDS SAID.
"WE'RE ALL FAMILY."
AND ORORO SAID THAT MEANT THE WORLD.
AND RACHEL SAID HER ESSENCE-- THE TOTALITY OF LIFE AND BEING, WARTS AND ALL-- WAS IN THIS CRYSTAL.
HERS--AND PHOENIX'S.
AND ALL JEAN HAS TO DO TO KNOW THEM--
--TO GRASP THIS EMBODIMENT OF PAST AND FUTURE...
...AND IN A WAY, ACCEPT IT AS HER PRESENT...
...HER DESTINY...
...IS PICK IT UP.

STAN LEE PRESENTS
THE FUNDAMENTAL THINGS
Starring WOLVERINE. JUBILEE. PSYLOCKE
SHE'S A FIRECRACKER, THIS ONE.
AND DEARLY LOVES TO SHOW IT OFF.
COME ONE, COME ALL--
--OPEN YOUR EYES AND UNCORK YOUR IMAGINATIONS--
--'CAUSE THE SHOW OF SHOWS IS ABOUT TO START!

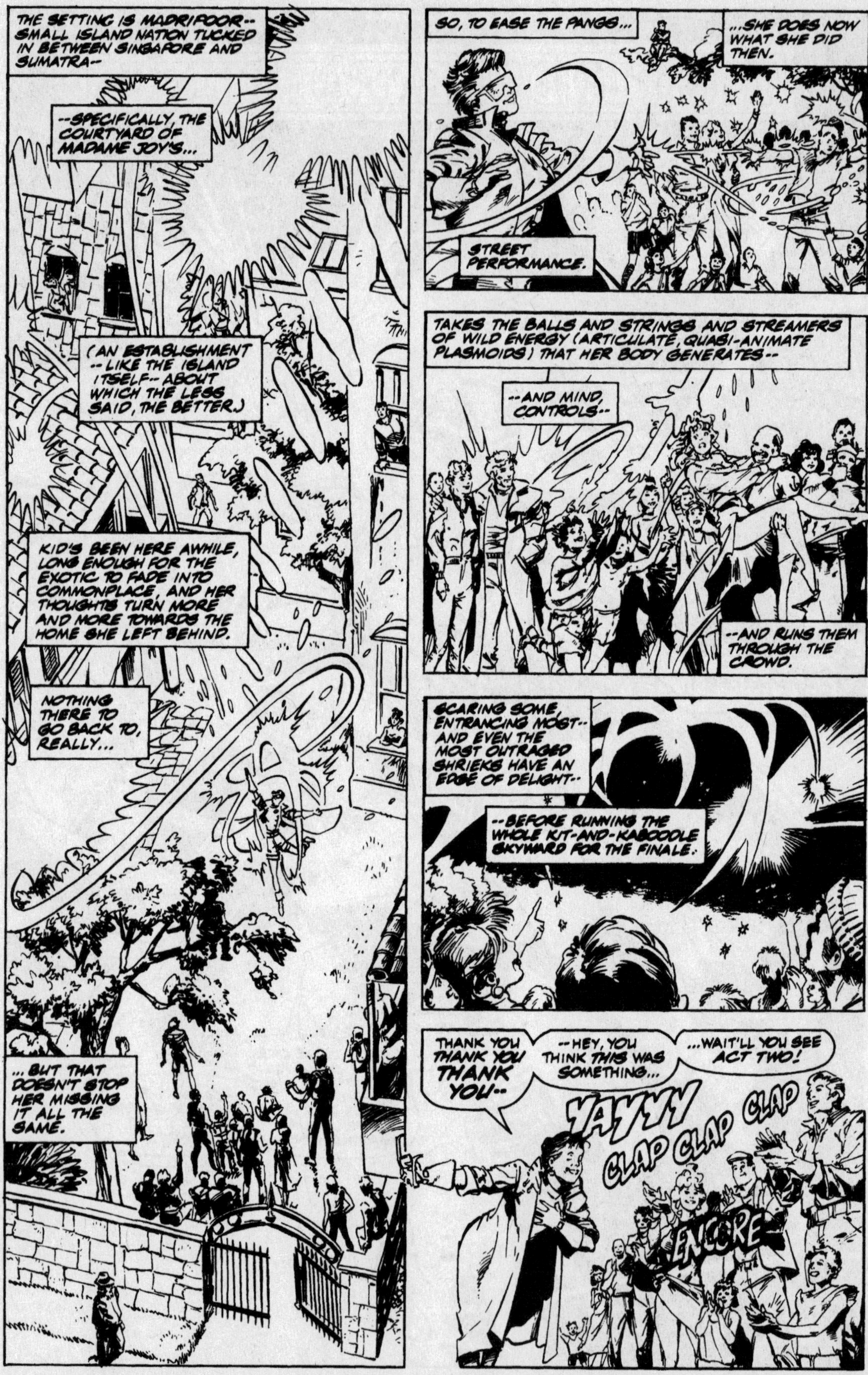
THE SETTING IS MADRIPOOR-- SMALL ISLAND NATION TUCKED IN BETWEEN SINGAPORE AND SUMATRA--
--SPECIFICALLY, THE COURTYARD OF MADAME JOY'S...
(AN ESTABLISHMENT --LIKE THE ISLAND ITSELF-- ABOUT WHICH THE LESS SAID, THE BETTER.)
KID'S BEEN HERE AWHILE, LONG ENOUGH FOR THE EXOTIC TO FADE INTO COMMONPLACE, AND HER THOUGHTS TURN MORE AND MORE TOWARDS THE HOME SHE LEFT BEHIND.
NOTHING THERE TO GO BACK TO, REALLY...
...BUT THAT DOESN'T STOP HER MISSING IT ALL THE SAME.
SO, TO EASE THE PANGS...
...SHE DOES NOW WHAT SHE DID THEN.
STREET PERFORMANCE.
TAKES THE BALLS AND STRINGS AND STREAMERS OF WILD ENERGY (ARTICULATE, QUASI-ANIMATE PLASMOIDS) THAT HER BODY GENERATES--
--AND MIND, CONTROLS--
--AND RUNS THEM THROUGH THE CROWD.
SCARING SOME, ENTRANCING MOST-- AND EVEN THE MOST OUTRAGED SHRIEKS HAVE AN EDGE OF DELIGHT--
--BEFORE RUNNING THE WHOLE KIT-AND-KABOODLE SKYWARD FOR THE FINALE.
THANK YOU THANK YOU THANK YOU--
--HEY, YOU THINK THIS WAS SOMETHING...
...WAIT'LL YOU SEE ACT TWO!
YAYYY
CLAP CLAP CLAP
ENCORE

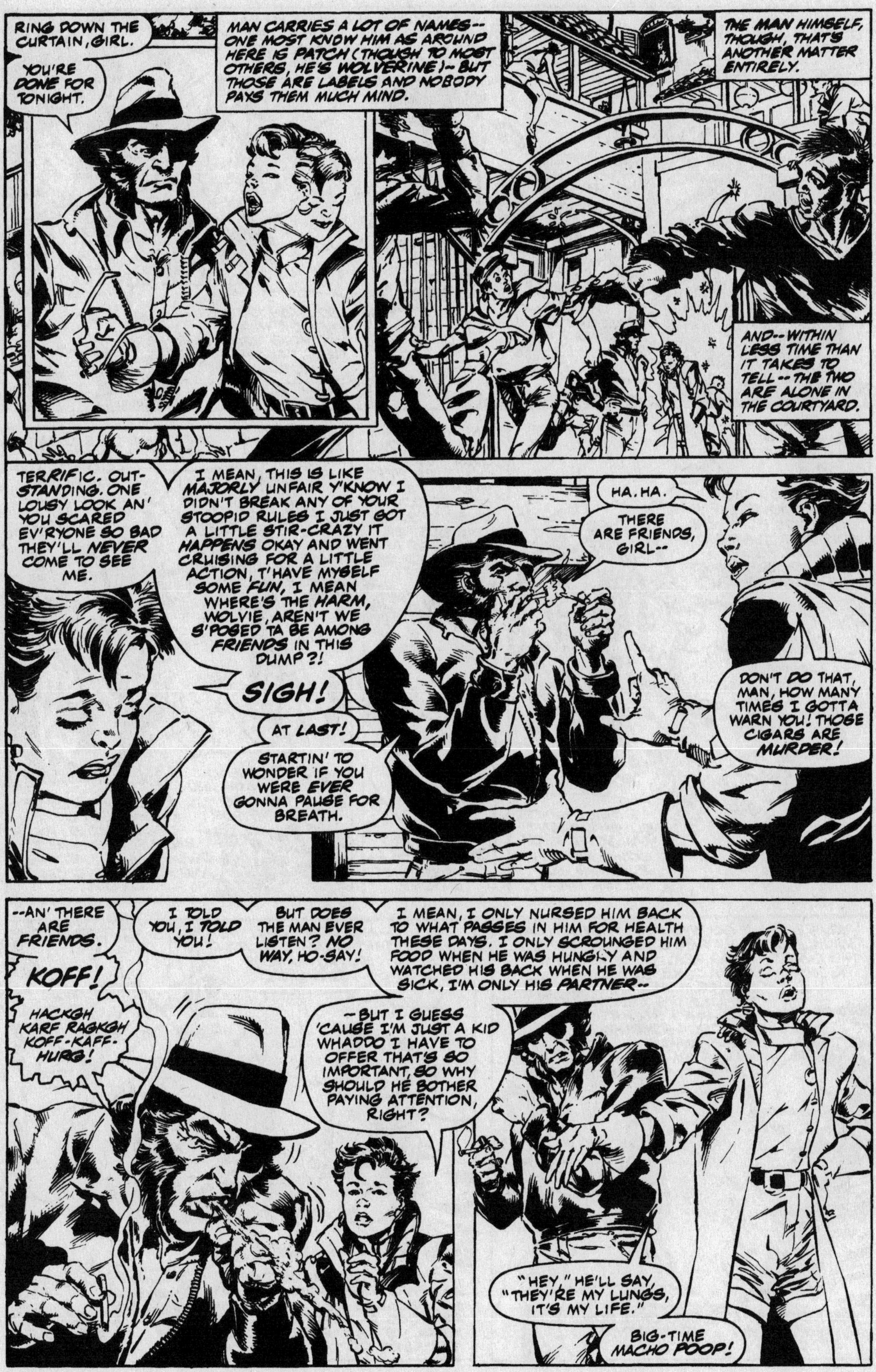
RING DOWN THE CURTAIN, GIRL.
YOU'RE DONE FOR TONIGHT.
MAN CARRIES A LOT OF NAMES-- ONE MOST KNOW HIM AS AROUND HERE IS PATCH (THOUGH TO MOST OTHERS, HE'S WOLVERINE)-- BUT THOSE ARE LABELS AND NOBODY PAYS THEM MUCH MIND.
THE MAN HIMSELF, THOUGH, THAT'S ANOTHER MATTER ENTIRELY.
AND-- WITHIN LESS TIME THAN IT TAKES TO TELL -- THE TWO ARE ALONE IN THE COURTYARD.
TERRIFIC. OUTSTANDING. ONE LOUSY LOOK AN' YOU SCARED EV'RYONE SO BAD THEY'LL NEVER COME TO SEE ME.
I MEAN, THIS IS LIKE MAJORLY UNFAIR Y'KNOW I DIDN'T BREAK ANY OF YOUR STOOPID RULES I JUST GOT A LITTLE STIR-CRAZY IT HAPPENS OKAY AND WENT CRUISING FOR A LITTLE ACTION, T'HAVE MYSELF SOME FUN, I MEAN WHERE'S THE HARM, WOLVIE, AREN'T WE S'POSED TA BE AMONG FRIENDS IN THIS DUMP?!
SIGH!
AT LAST!
STARTIN' TO WONDER IF YOU WERE EVER GONNA PAUSE FOR BREATH.
HA. HA.
THERE ARE FRIENDS, GIRL--
DON'T DO THAT, MAN, HOW MANY TIMES I GOTTA WARN YOU! THOSE CIGARS ARE MURDER!
--AN' THERE ARE FRIENDS.
KOFF!
HACKGH KARF RAGKGH KOFF-KAFF-HURG!
I TOLD YOU, I TOLD YOU!
BUT DOES THE MAN EVER LISTEN? NO WAY, HO-SAY!
I MEAN, I ONLY NURSED HIM BACK TO WHAT PASSES IN HIM FOR HEALTH THESE DAYS. I ONLY SCROUNGED HIM FOOD WHEN HE WAS HUNGRY AND WATCHED HIS BACK WHEN HE WAS SICK, I'M ONLY HIS PARTNER--
--BUT I GUESS 'CAUSE I'M JUST A KID WHADDO I HAVE TO OFFER THAT'S SO IMPORTANT, SO WHY SHOULD HE BOTHER PAYING ATTENTION, RIGHT?
"HEY," HE'LL SAY, "THEY'RE MY LUNGS, IT'S MY LIFE."
BIG-TIME MACHO POOP!

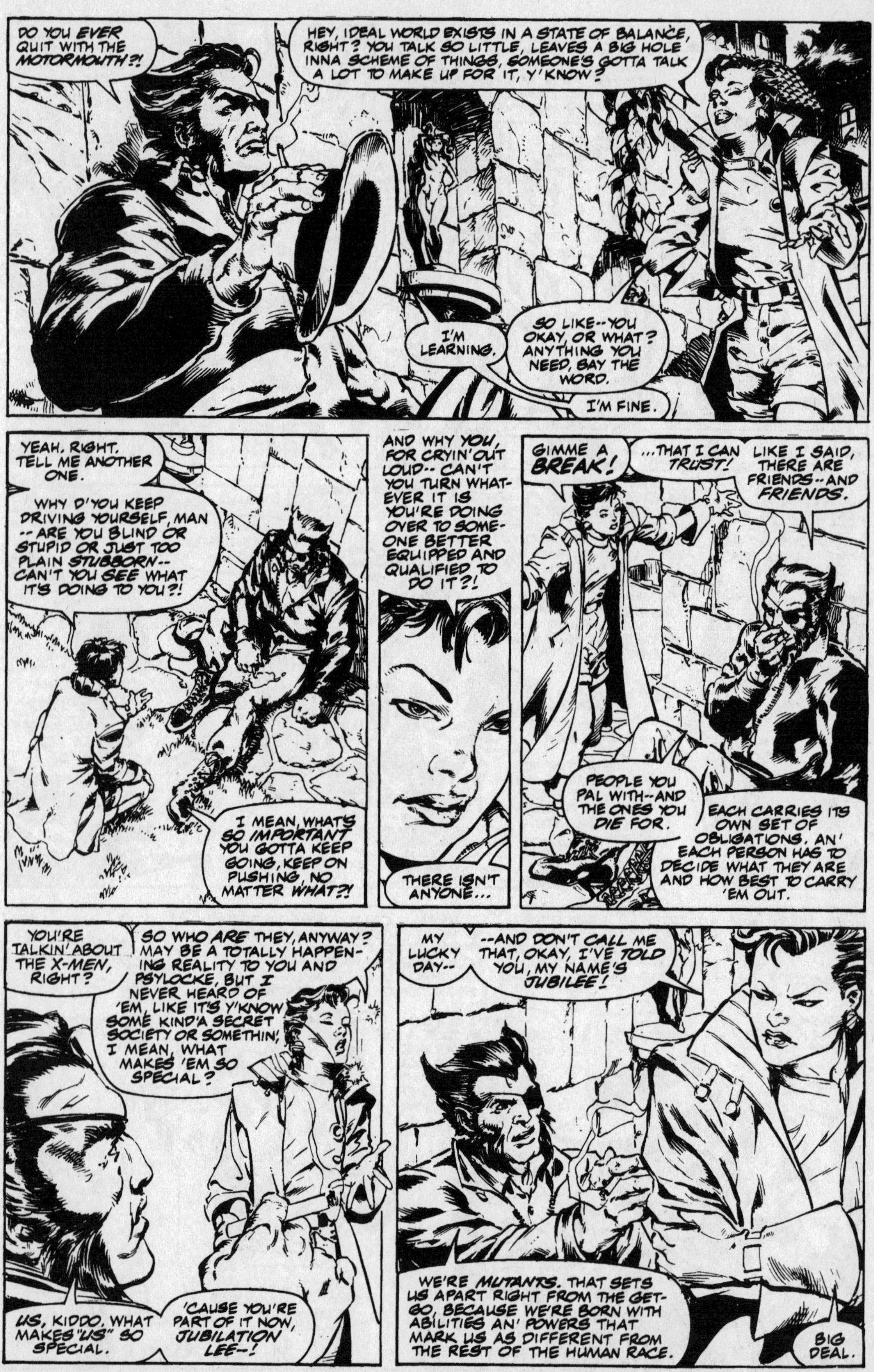
DO YOU EVER QUIT WITH THE MOTORMOUTH?!
HEY, IDEAL WORLD EXISTS IN A STATE OF BALANCE, RIGHT? YOU TALK SO LITTLE, LEAVES A BIG HOLE INNA SCHEME OF THINGS, SOMEONE'S GOTTA TALK A LOT TO MAKE UP FOR IT, Y'KNOW?
I'M LEARNING.
SO LIKE--YOU OKAY, OR WHAT? ANYTHING YOU NEED, SAY THE WORD.
I'M FINE.
YEAH. RIGHT. TELL ME ANOTHER ONE.
WHY D'YOU KEEP DRIVING YOURSELF, MAN --ARE YOU BLIND OR STUPID OR JUST TOO PLAIN STUBBORN--CAN'T YOU SEE WHAT IT'S DOING TO YOU?!
I MEAN, WHAT'S SO IMPORTANT YOU GOTTA KEEP GOING, KEEP ON PUSHING, NO MATTER WHAT?!
AND WHY YOU, FOR CRYIN' OUT LOUD--CAN'T YOU TURN WHATEVER IT IS YOU'RE DOING OVER TO SOMEONE BETTER EQUIPPED AND QUALIFIED TO DO IT?!
THERE ISN'T ANYONE...
GIMME A BREAK!
...THAT I CAN TRUST!
LIKE I SAID, THERE ARE FRIENDS--AND FRIENDS.
PEOPLE YOU PAL WITH--AND THE ONES YOU DIE FOR.
EACH CARRIES ITS OWN SET OF OBLIGATIONS. AN' EACH PERSON HAS TO DECIDE WHAT THEY ARE AND HOW BEST TO CARRY 'EM OUT.
YOU'RE TALKIN' ABOUT THE X-MEN, RIGHT?
SO WHO ARE THEY, ANYWAY? MAY BE A TOTALLY HAPPENING REALITY TO YOU AND PSYLOCKE, BUT I NEVER HEARD OF 'EM, LIKE IT'S Y'KNOW SOME KIND'A SECRET SOCIETY OR SOMETHIN', I MEAN, WHAT MAKES 'EM SO SPECIAL?
US, KIDDO. WHAT MAKES "US" SO SPECIAL.
'CAUSE YOU'RE PART OF IT NOW, JUBILATION LEE--!
MY LUCKY DAY--
--AND DON'T CALL ME THAT, OKAY, I'VE TOLD YOU, MY NAME'S JUBILEE!
WE'RE MUTANTS. THAT SETS US APART RIGHT FROM THE GET-GO, BECAUSE WE'RE BORN WITH ABILITIES AN' POWERS THAT MARK US AS DIFFERENT FROM THE REST OF THE HUMAN RACE.
BIG DEAL.

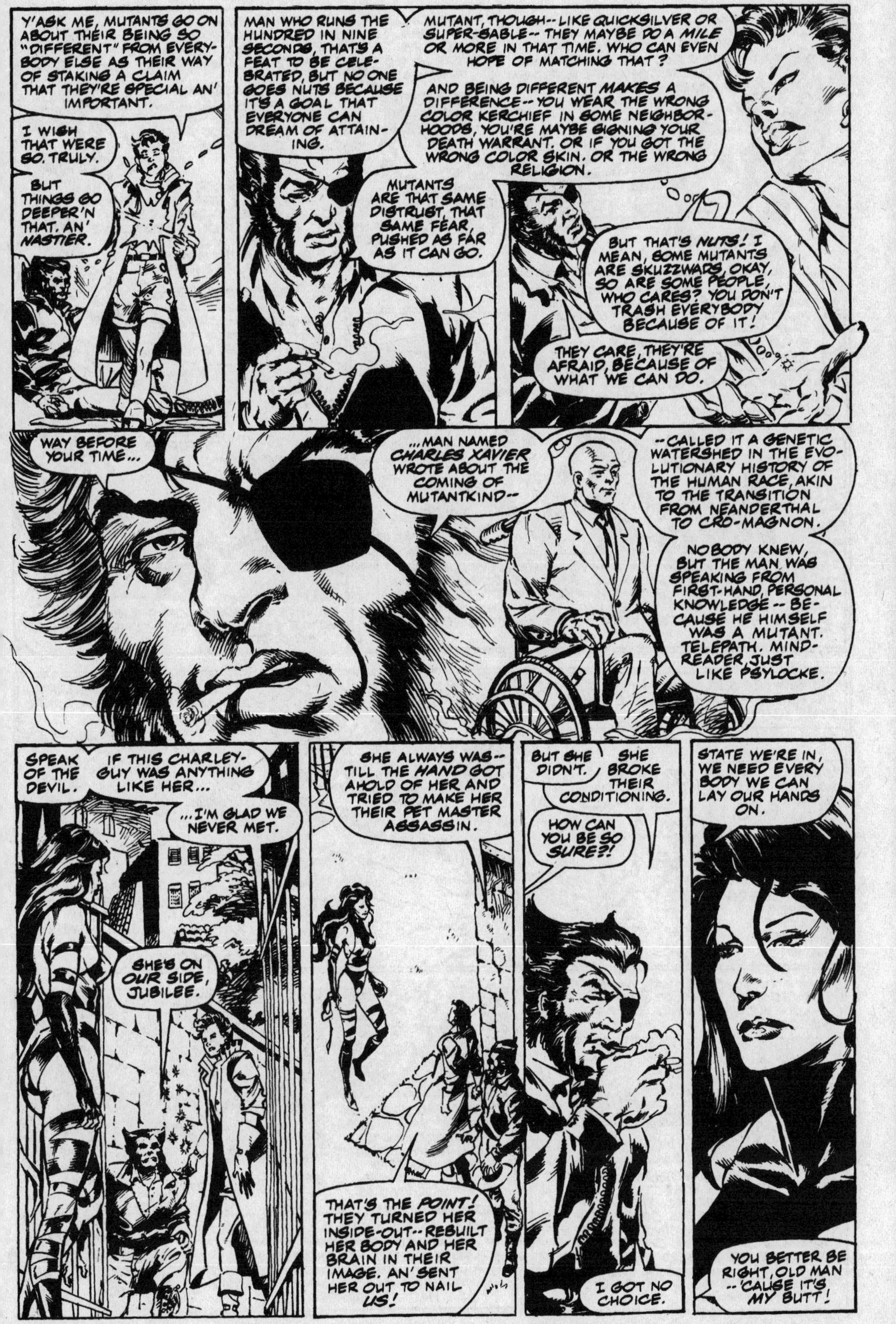
Y'ASK ME, MUTANTS GO ON ABOUT THEIR BEING SO "DIFFERENT" FROM EVERYBODY ELSE AS THEIR WAY OF STAKING A CLAIM THAT THEY'RE SPECIAL AN' IMPORTANT.
I WISH THAT WERE SO. TRULY.
BUT THINGS GO DEEPER'N THAT. AN' NASTIER.
MAN WHO RUNS THE HUNDRED IN NINE SECONDS, THAT'S A FEAT TO BE CELEBRATED, BUT NO ONE GOES NUTS BECAUSE IT'S A GOAL THAT EVERYONE CAN DREAM OF ATTAINING.
MUTANT, THOUGH-- LIKE QUICKSILVER OR SUPER-SABLE-- THEY MAYBE DO A MILE OR MORE IN THAT TIME. WHO CAN EVEN HOPE OF MATCHING THAT?
AND BEING DIFFERENT MAKES A DIFFERENCE-- YOU WEAR THE WRONG COLOR KERCHIEF IN SOME NEIGHBORHOODS, YOU'RE MAYBE SIGNING YOUR DEATH WARRANT. OR IF YOU GOT THE WRONG COLOR SKIN. OR THE WRONG RELIGION.
MUTANTS ARE THAT SAME DISTRUST, THAT SAME FEAR, PUSHED AS FAR AS IT CAN GO.
BUT THAT'S NUTS! I MEAN, SOME MUTANTS ARE SKUZZWARS, OKAY, SO ARE SOME PEOPLE, WHO CARES? YOU DON'T TRASH EVERYBODY BECAUSE OF IT!
THEY CARE, THEY'RE AFRAID, BECAUSE OF WHAT WE CAN DO.
WAY BEFORE YOUR TIME...
...MAN NAMED CHARLES XAVIER WROTE ABOUT THE COMING OF MUTANTKIND--
--CALLED IT A GENETIC WATERSHED IN THE EVOLUTIONARY HISTORY OF THE HUMAN RACE, AKIN TO THE TRANSITION FROM NEANDERTHAL TO CRO-MAGNON.
NOBODY KNEW, BUT THE MAN WAS SPEAKING FROM FIRST-HAND, PERSONAL KNOWLEDGE -- BECAUSE HE HIMSELF WAS A MUTANT. TELEPATH. MIND-READER, JUST LIKE PSYLOCKE.
SPEAK OF THE DEVIL.
IF THIS CHARLEY-GUY WAS ANYTHING LIKE HER...
...I'M GLAD WE NEVER MET.
SHE'S ON OUR SIDE, JUBILEE.
SHE ALWAYS WAS-- TILL THE HAND GOT AHOLD OF HER AND TRIED TO MAKE HER THEIR PET MASTER ASSASSIN.
THAT'S THE POINT! THEY TURNED HER INSIDE-OUT-- REBUILT HER BODY AND HER BRAIN IN THEIR IMAGE. AN' SENT HER OUT TO NAIL US!
BUT SHE DIDN'T.
SHE BROKE THEIR CONDITIONING.
HOW CAN YOU BE SO SURE?!
I GOT NO CHOICE.
STATE WE'RE IN, WE NEED EVERY BODY WE CAN LAY OUR HANDS ON.
YOU BETTER BE RIGHT, OLD MAN --'CAUSE IT'S MY BUTT!

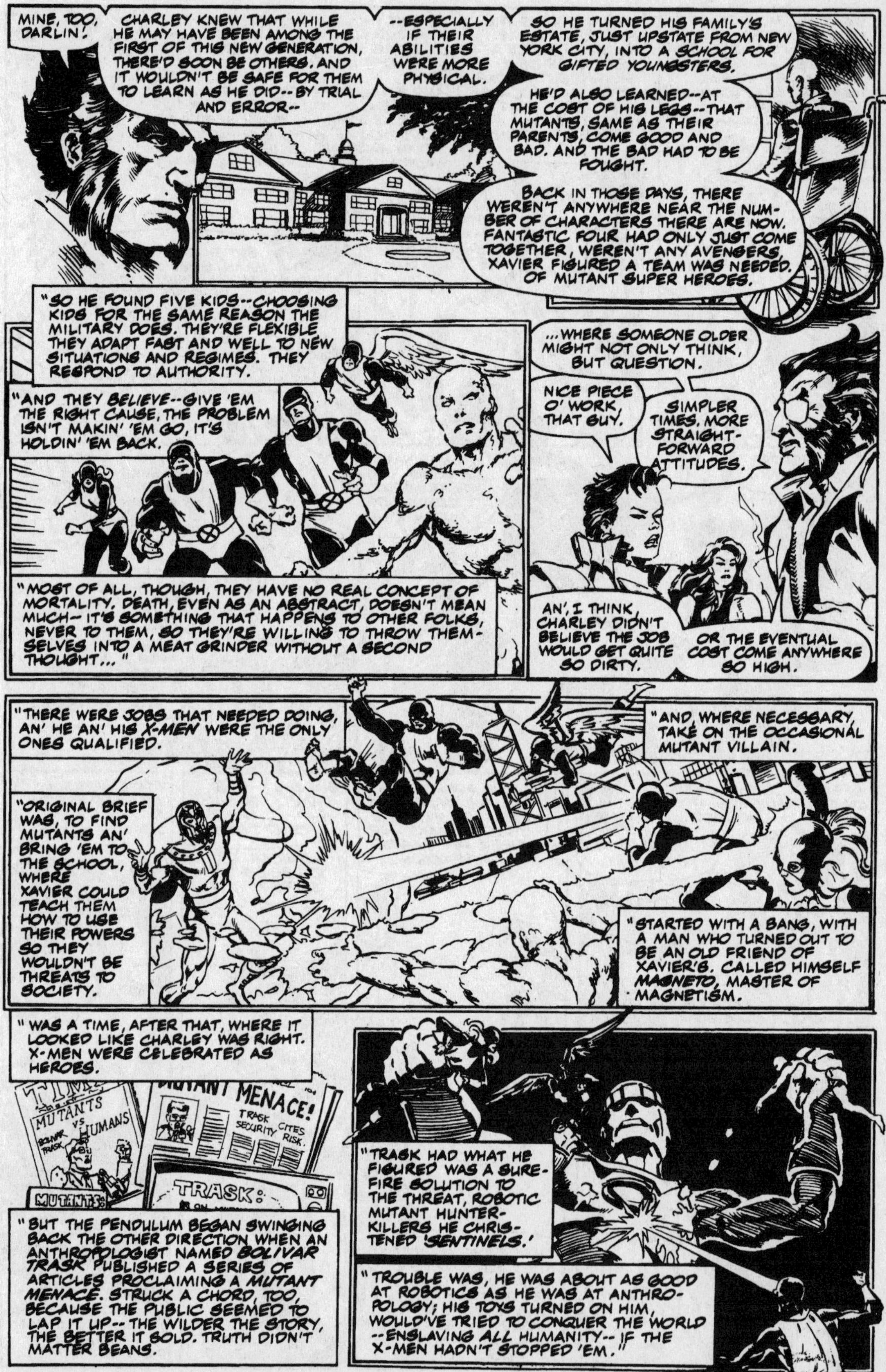
MINE, TOO, DARLIN'.
CHARLEY KNEW THAT WHILE HE MAY HAVE BEEN AMONG THE FIRST OF THIS NEW GENERATION, THERE'D SOON BE OTHERS. AND IT WOULDN'T BE SAFE FOR THEM TO LEARN AS HE DID-- BY TRIAL AND ERROR--
--ESPECIALLY IF THEIR ABILITIES WERE MORE PHYSICAL.
SO HE TURNED HIS FAMILY'S ESTATE, JUST UPSTATE FROM NEW YORK CITY, INTO A SCHOOL FOR GIFTED YOUNGSTERS.
HE'D ALSO LEARNED--AT THE COST OF HIS LEGS--THAT MUTANTS, SAME AS THEIR PARENTS, COME GOOD AND BAD. AND THE BAD HAD TO BE FOUGHT.
BACK IN THOSE DAYS, THERE WEREN'T ANYWHERE NEAR THE NUMBER OF CHARACTERS THERE ARE NOW. FANTASTIC FOUR HAD ONLY JUST COME TOGETHER, WEREN'T ANY AVENGERS. XAVIER FIGURED A TEAM WAS NEEDED, OF MUTANT SUPER HEROES.
"SO HE FOUND FIVE KIDS--CHOOSING KIDS FOR THE SAME REASON THE MILITARY DOES. THEY'RE FLEXIBLE THEY ADAPT FAST AND WELL TO NEW SITUATIONS AND REGIMES. THEY RESPOND TO AUTHORITY.
"AND THEY BELIEVE--GIVE 'EM THE RIGHT CAUSE, THE PROBLEM ISN'T MAKIN' 'EM GO, IT'S HOLDIN' 'EM BACK.
"MOST OF ALL, THOUGH, THEY HAVE NO REAL CONCEPT OF MORTALITY. DEATH, EVEN AS AN ABSTRACT, DOESN'T MEAN MUCH-- IT'S SOMETHING THAT HAPPENS TO OTHER FOLKS, NEVER TO THEM, SO THEY'RE WILLING TO THROW THEMSELVES INTO A MEAT GRINDER WITHOUT A SECOND THOUGHT..."
...WHERE SOMEONE OLDER MIGHT NOT ONLY THINK, BUT QUESTION.
NICE PIECE O' WORK, THAT GUY.
SIMPLER TIMES. MORE STRAIGHT-FORWARD ATTITUDES.
AN', I THINK, CHARLEY DIDN'T BELIEVE THE JOB WOULD GET QUITE SO DIRTY.
OR THE EVENTUAL COST COME ANYWHERE SO HIGH.
"THERE WERE JOBS THAT NEEDED DOING, AN' HE AN' HIS X-MEN WERE THE ONLY ONES QUALIFIED.
"AND, WHERE NECESSARY, TAKE ON THE OCCASIONAL MUTANT VILLAIN.
"ORIGINAL BRIEF WAS, TO FIND MUTANTS AN' BRING 'EM TO THE SCHOOL, WHERE XAVIER COULD TEACH THEM HOW TO USE THEIR POWERS SO THEY WOULDN'T BE THREATS TO SOCIETY.
"STARTED WITH A BANG, WITH A MAN WHO TURNED OUT TO BE AN OLD FRIEND OF XAVIER'S. CALLED HIMSELF MAGNETO, MASTER OF MAGNETISM.
"WAS A TIME, AFTER THAT, WHERE IT LOOKED LIKE CHARLEY WAS RIGHT. X-MEN WERE CELEBRATED AS HEROES.
MUTANTS VS HUMANS
BOLIVAR TRASK
MUTANT MENACE!
TRASK SECURITY CITES RISK.
TRASK:
MUTANTS
"BUT THE PENDULUM BEGAN SWINGING BACK THE OTHER DIRECTION WHEN AN ANTHROPOLOGIST NAMED BOLIVAR TRASK PUBLISHED A SERIES OF ARTICLES PROCLAIMING A MUTANT MENACE. STRUCK A CHORD, TOO, BECAUSE THE PUBLIC SEEMED TO LAP IT UP-- THE WILDER THE STORY, THE BETTER IT SOLD. TRUTH DIDN'T MATTER BEANS.
"TRASK HAD WHAT HE FIGURED WAS A SURE-FIRE SOLUTION TO THE THREAT, ROBOTIC MUTANT HUNTER-KILLERS HE CHRISTENED 'SENTINELS.'
"TROUBLE WAS, HE WAS ABOUT AS GOOD AT ROBOTICS AS HE WAS AT ANTHROPOLOGY; HIS TOYS TURNED ON HIM, WOULD'VE TRIED TO CONQUER THE WORLD --ENSLAVING ALL HUMANITY-- IF THE X-MEN HADN'T STOPPED 'EM."

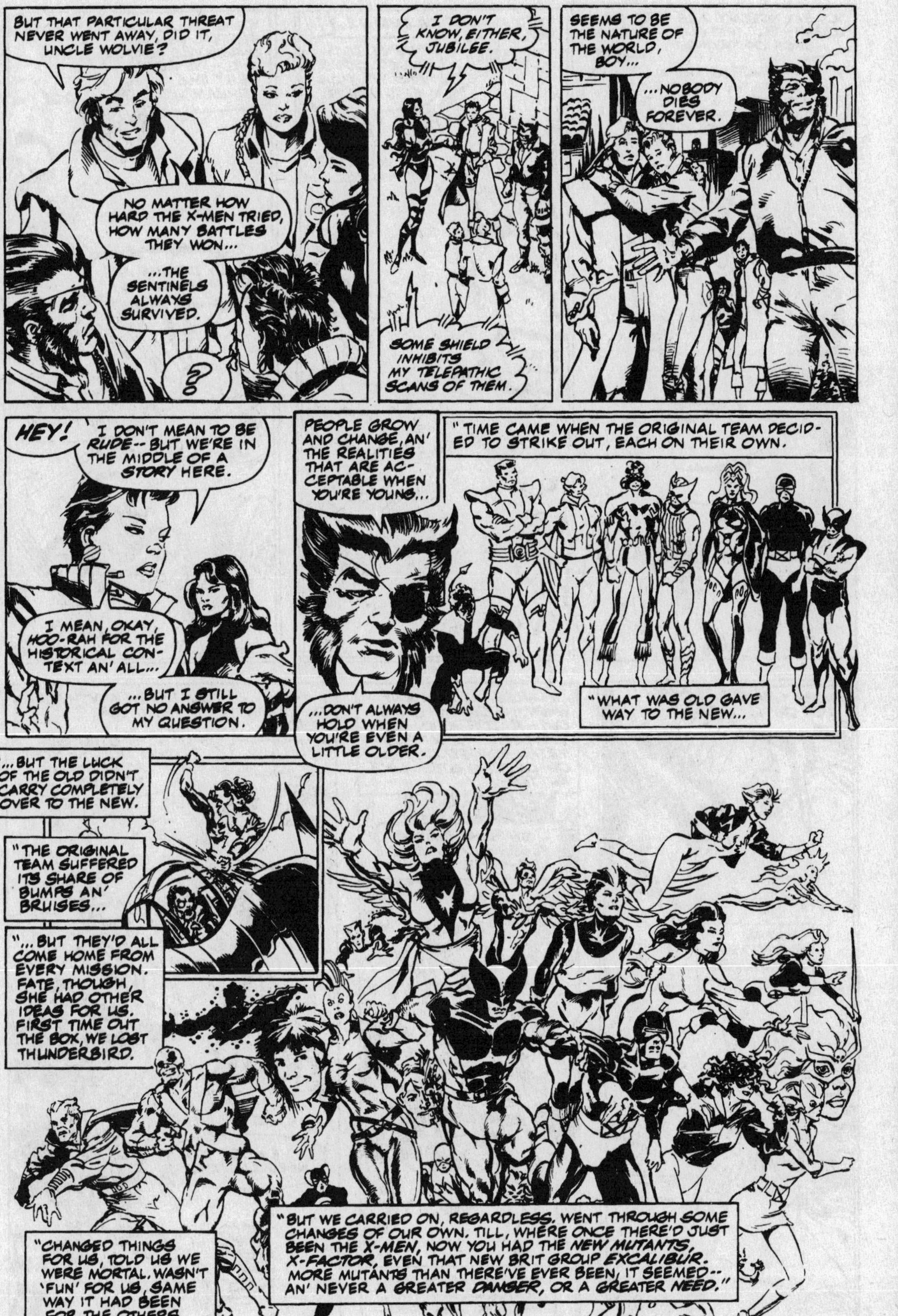
BUT THAT PARTICULAR THREAT NEVER WENT AWAY, DID IT, UNCLE WOLVIE?
NO MATTER HOW HARD THE X-MEN TRIED, HOW MANY BATTLES THEY WON...
...THE SENTINELS ALWAYS SURVIVED.
?
I DON'T KNOW, EITHER, JUBILEE.
SOME SHIELD INHIBITS MY TELEPATHIC SCANS OF THEM.
SEEMS TO BE THE NATURE OF THE WORLD, BOY...
...NOBODY DIES FOREVER.
HEY!
I DON'T MEAN TO BE RUDE-- BUT WE'RE IN THE MIDDLE OF A STORY HERE.
I MEAN, OKAY, HOO-RAH FOR THE HISTORICAL CONTEXT AN' ALL...
...BUT I STILL GOT NO ANSWER TO MY QUESTION.
PEOPLE GROW AND CHANGE, AN' THE REALITIES THAT ARE ACCEPTABLE WHEN YOU'RE YOUNG...
...DON'T ALWAYS HOLD WHEN YOU'RE EVEN A LITTLE OLDER.
"TIME CAME WHEN THE ORIGINAL TEAM DECIDED TO STRIKE OUT, EACH ON THEIR OWN.
"WHAT WAS OLD GAVE WAY TO THE NEW...
"...BUT THE LUCK OF THE OLD DIDN'T CARRY COMPLETELY OVER TO THE NEW.
"THE ORIGINAL TEAM SUFFERED ITS SHARE OF BUMPS AN' BRUISES...
"...BUT THEY'D ALL COME HOME FROM EVERY MISSION. FATE, THOUGH, SHE HAD OTHER IDEAS FOR US. FIRST TIME OUT THE BOX, WE LOST THUNDERBIRD.
"CHANGED THINGS FOR US, TOLD US WE WERE MORTAL. WASN'T 'FUN' FOR US, SAME WAY IT HAD BEEN FOR THE OTHERS.
"BUT WE CARRIED ON, REGARDLESS. WENT THROUGH SOME CHANGES OF OUR OWN. TILL, WHERE ONCE THERE'D JUST BEEN THE X-MEN, NOW YOU HAD THE NEW MUTANTS, X-FACTOR, EVEN THAT NEW BRIT GROUP EXCALIBUR. MORE MUTANTS THAN THERE'VE EVER BEEN, IT SEEMED-- AN' NEVER A GREATER DANGER, OR A GREATER NEED."

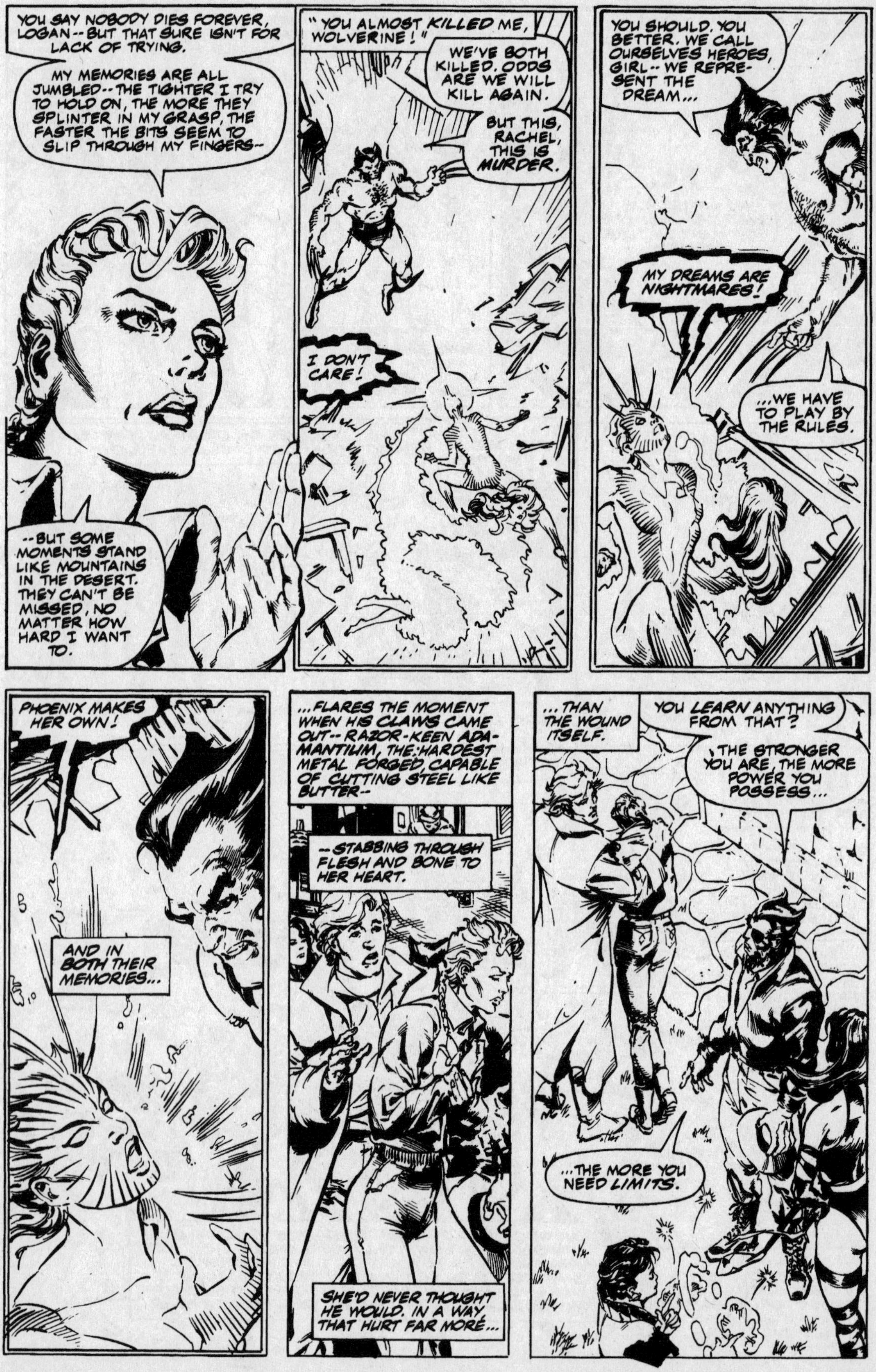

YOU SAY NOBODY DIES FOREVER, LOGAN -- BUT THAT SURE ISN'T FOR LACK OF TRYING.
MY MEMORIES ARE ALL JUMBLED -- THE TIGHTER I TRY TO HOLD ON, THE MORE THEY SPLINTER IN MY GRASP, THE FASTER THE BITS SEEM TO SLIP THROUGH MY FINGERS --
-- BUT SOME MOMENTS STAND LIKE MOUNTAINS IN THE DESERT. THEY CAN'T BE MISSED, NO MATTER HOW HARD I WANT TO.
"YOU ALMOST KILLED ME, WOLVERINE!"
WE'VE BOTH KILLED. ODDS ARE WE WILL KILL AGAIN.
BUT THIS, RACHEL, THIS IS MURDER.
I DON'T CARE!
YOU SHOULD. YOU BETTER. WE CALL OURSELVES HEROES, GIRL -- WE REPRESENT THE DREAM...
MY DREAMS ARE NIGHTMARES!
...WE HAVE TO PLAY BY THE RULES.
PHOENIX MAKES HER OWN!
AND IN BOTH THEIR MEMORIES...
...FLARES THE MOMENT WHEN HIS CLAWS CAME OUT -- RAZOR-KEEN ADAMANTIUM, THE HARDEST METAL FORGED, CAPABLE OF CUTTING STEEL LIKE BUTTER --
-- STABBING THROUGH FLESH AND BONE TO HER HEART.
SHE'D NEVER THOUGHT HE WOULD. IN A WAY, THAT HURT FAR MORE...
...THAN THE WOUND ITSELF.
YOU LEARN ANYTHING FROM THAT?
THE STRONGER YOU ARE, THE MORE POWER YOU POSSESS...
...THE MORE YOU NEED LIMITS.

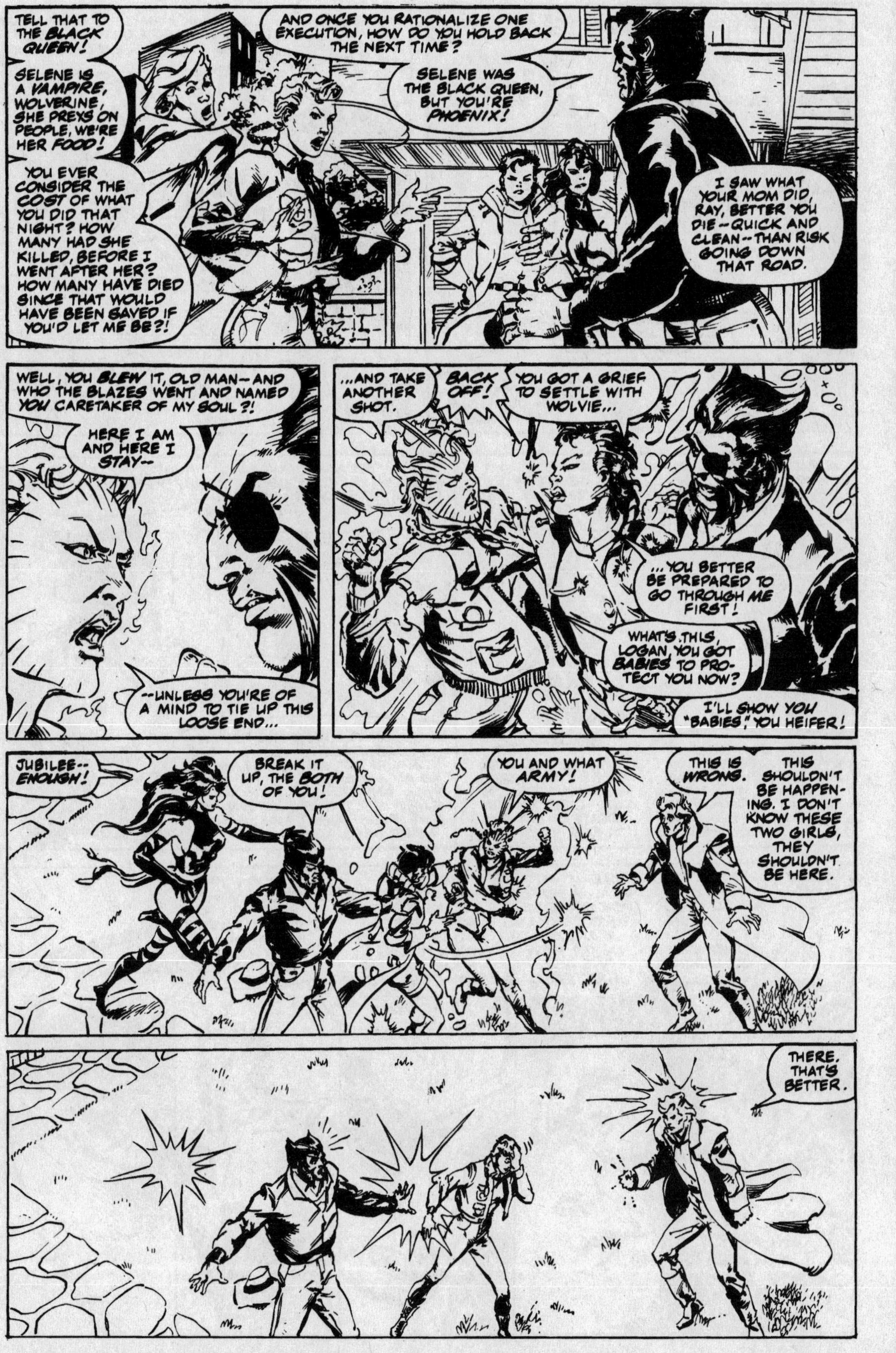
TELL THAT TO THE BLACK QUEEN!
AND ONCE YOU RATIONALIZE ONE EXECUTION, HOW DO YOU HOLD BACK THE NEXT TIME?
SELENE IS A VAMPIRE, WOLVERINE, SHE PREYS ON PEOPLE, WE'RE HER FOOD!
SELENE WAS THE BLACK QUEEN, BUT YOU'RE PHOENIX!
YOU EVER CONSIDER THE COST OF WHAT YOU DID THAT NIGHT? HOW MANY HAD SHE KILLED, BEFORE I WENT AFTER HER? HOW MANY HAVE DIED SINCE THAT WOULD HAVE BEEN SAVED IF YOU'D LET ME BE?!
I SAW WHAT YOUR MOM DID, RAY, BETTER YOU DIE--QUICK AND CLEAN--THAN RISK GOING DOWN THAT ROAD.
WELL, YOU BLEW IT, OLD MAN--AND WHO THE BLAZES WENT AND NAMED YOU CARETAKER OF MY SOUL?!
HERE I AM AND HERE I STAY--
--UNLESS YOU'RE OF A MIND TO TIE UP THIS LOOSE END...
...AND TAKE ANOTHER SHOT.
BACK OFF!
YOU GOT A GRIEF TO SETTLE WITH WOLVIE...
...YOU BETTER BE PREPARED TO GO THROUGH ME FIRST!
WHAT'S THIS, LOGAN, YOU GOT BABIES TO PROTECT YOU NOW?
I'LL SHOW YOU "BABIES," YOU HEIFER!
JUBILEE--ENOUGH!
BREAK IT UP, THE BOTH OF YOU!
YOU AND WHAT ARMY!
THIS IS WRONG.
THIS SHOULDN'T BE HAPPENING. I DON'T KNOW THESE TWO GIRLS, THEY SHOULDN'T BE HERE.
THERE. THAT'S BETTER.

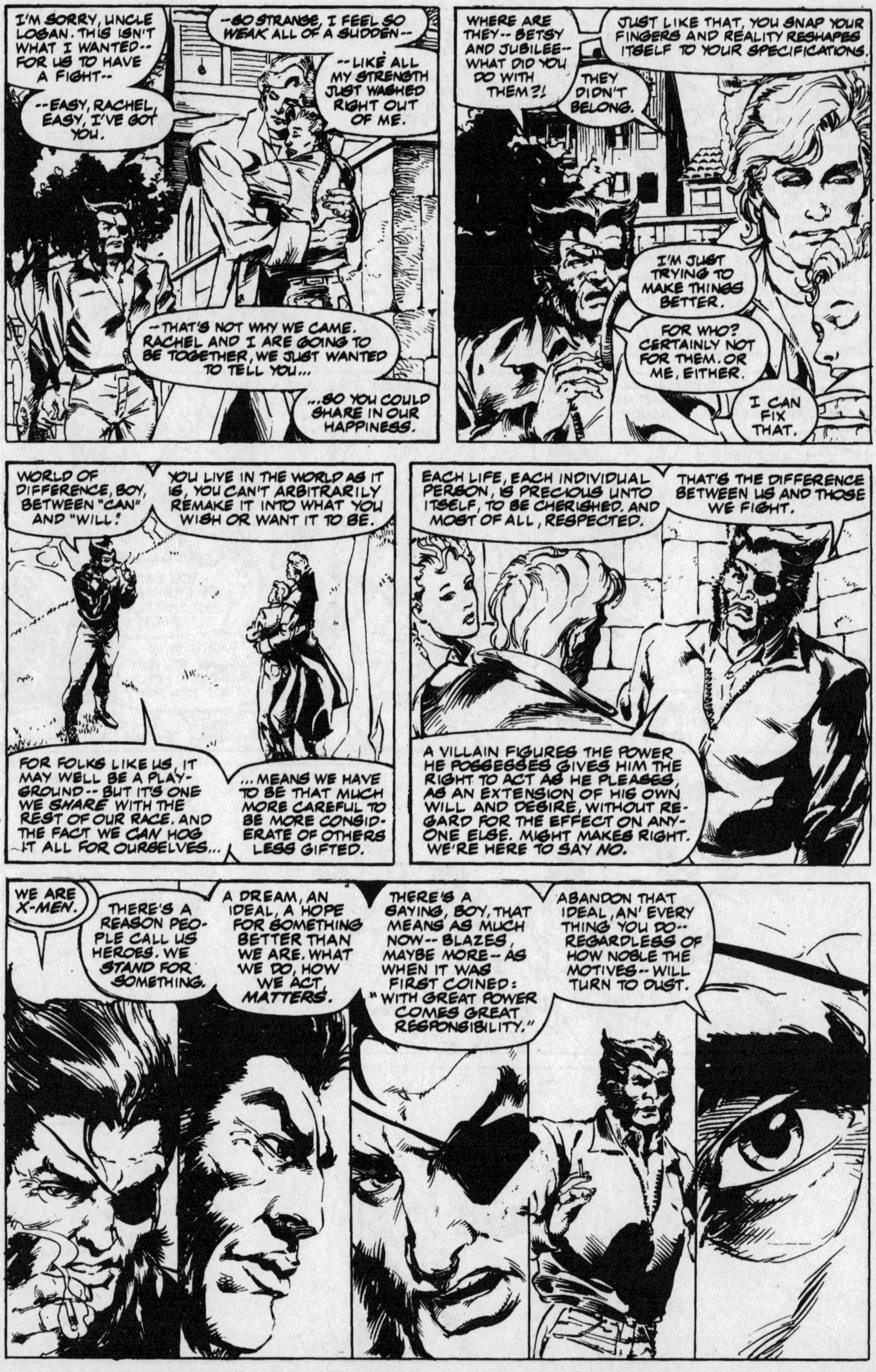

I'M SORRY, UNCLE LOGAN. THIS ISN'T WHAT I WANTED-- FOR US TO HAVE A FIGHT--
--SO STRANGE, I FEEL SO WEAK ALL OF A SUDDEN--
--LIKE ALL MY STRENGTH JUST WASHED RIGHT OUT OF ME.
--EASY, RACHEL, EASY, I'VE GOT YOU.
--THAT'S NOT WHY WE CAME. RACHEL AND I ARE GOING TO BE TOGETHER, WE JUST WANTED TO TELL YOU...
...SO YOU COULD SHARE IN OUR HAPPINESS.
WHERE ARE THEY-- BETSY AND JUBILEE-- WHAT DID YOU DO WITH THEM?!
THEY DIDN'T BELONG.
JUST LIKE THAT, YOU SNAP YOUR FINGERS AND REALITY RESHAPES ITSELF TO YOUR SPECIFICATIONS.
I'M JUST TRYING TO MAKE THINGS BETTER.
FOR WHO? CERTAINLY NOT FOR THEM. OR ME, EITHER.
I CAN FIX THAT.
WORLD OF DIFFERENCE, BOY, BETWEEN "CAN" AND "WILL."
YOU LIVE IN THE WORLD AS IT IS, YOU CAN'T ARBITRARILY REMAKE IT INTO WHAT YOU WISH OR WANT IT TO BE.
FOR FOLKS LIKE US, IT MAY WELL BE A PLAYGROUND-- BUT IT'S ONE WE SHARE WITH THE REST OF OUR RACE. AND THE FACT WE CAN HOG IT ALL FOR OURSELVES...
...MEANS WE HAVE TO BE THAT MUCH MORE CAREFUL TO BE MORE CONSIDERATE OF OTHERS LESS GIFTED.
EACH LIFE, EACH INDIVIDUAL PERSON, IS PRECIOUS UNTO ITSELF, TO BE CHERISHED. AND MOST OF ALL, RESPECTED.
THAT'S THE DIFFERENCE BETWEEN US AND THOSE WE FIGHT.
A VILLAIN FIGURES THE POWER HE POSSESSES GIVES HIM THE RIGHT TO ACT AS HE PLEASES, AS AN EXTENSION OF HIS OWN WILL AND DESIRE, WITHOUT REGARD FOR THE EFFECT ON ANYONE ELSE. MIGHT MAKES RIGHT. WE'RE HERE TO SAY NO.
WE ARE X-MEN.
THERE'S A REASON PEOPLE CALL US HEROES. WE STAND FOR SOMETHING.
A DREAM, AN IDEAL, A HOPE FOR SOMETHING BETTER THAN WE ARE. WHAT WE DO, HOW WE ACT, MATTERS.
THERE'S A SAYING, BOY, THAT MEANS AS MUCH NOW-- BLAZES, MAYBE MORE-- AS WHEN IT WAS FIRST COINED: "WITH GREAT POWER COMES GREAT RESPONSIBILITY."
ABANDON THAT IDEAL, AN' EVERY THING YOU DO-- REGARDLESS OF HOW NOBLE THE MOTIVES-- WILL TURN TO DUST.

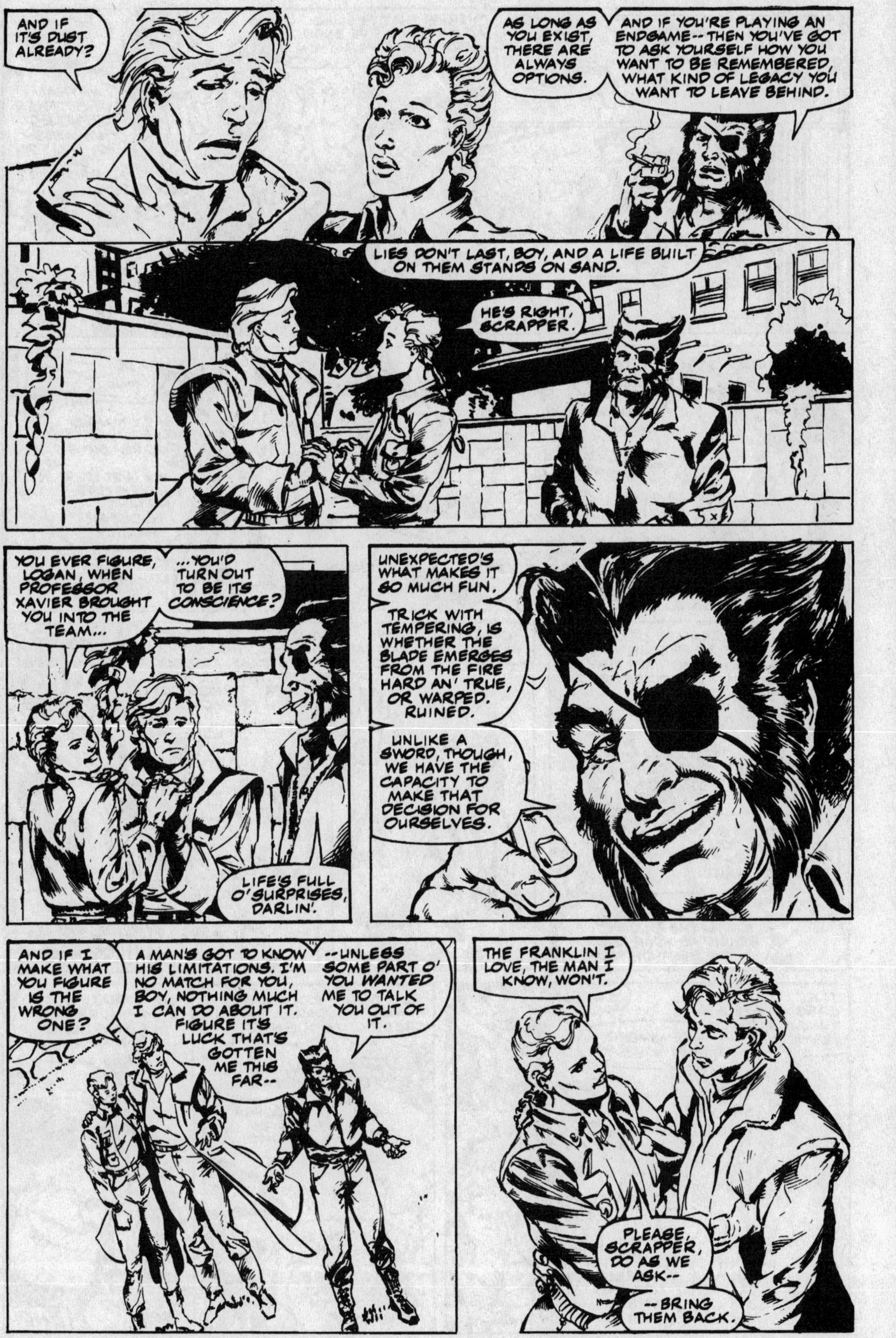
AND IF IT'S DUST ALREADY?
AS LONG AS YOU EXIST, THERE ARE ALWAYS OPTIONS.
AND IF YOU'RE PLAYING AN ENDGAME-- THEN YOU'VE GOT TO ASK YOURSELF HOW YOU WANT TO BE REMEMBERED, WHAT KIND OF LEGACY YOU WANT TO LEAVE BEHIND.
LIES DON'T LAST, BOY, AND A LIFE BUILT ON THEM STANDS ON SAND.
HE'S RIGHT, SCRAPPER.
YOU EVER FIGURE, LOGAN, WHEN PROFESSOR XAVIER BROUGHT YOU INTO THE TEAM...
...YOU'D TURN OUT TO BE ITS CONSCIENCE?
LIFE'S FULL O' SURPRISES, DARLIN'.
UNEXPECTED'S WHAT MAKES IT SO MUCH FUN.
TRICK WITH TEMPERING, IS WHETHER THE BLADE EMERGES FROM THE FIRE HARD AN' TRUE, OR WARPED. RUINED.
UNLIKE A SWORD, THOUGH, WE HAVE THE CAPACITY TO MAKE THAT DECISION FOR OURSELVES.
AND IF I MAKE WHAT YOU FIGURE IS THE WRONG ONE?
A MAN'S GOT TO KNOW HIS LIMITATIONS. I'M NO MATCH FOR YOU, BOY, NOTHING MUCH I CAN DO ABOUT IT. FIGURE IT'S LUCK THAT'S GOTTEN ME THIS FAR--
--UNLESS SOME PART O' YOU WANTED ME TO TALK YOU OUT OF IT.
THE FRANKLIN I LOVE, THE MAN I KNOW, WON'T.
PLEASE, SCRAPPER, DO AS WE ASK--
--BRING THEM BACK.

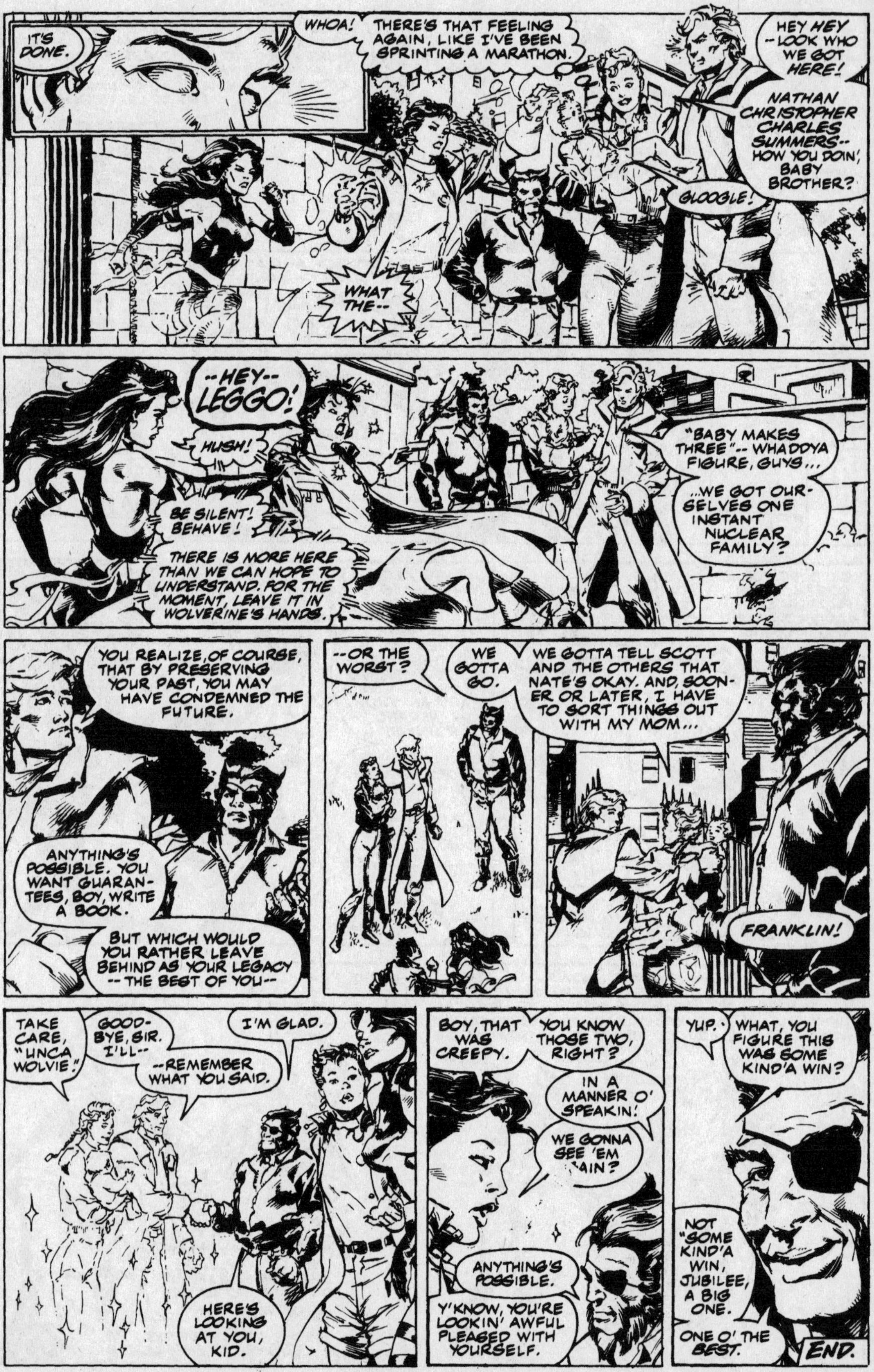
IT'S DONE.
WHOA!
THERE'S THAT FEELING AGAIN, LIKE I'VE BEEN SPRINTING A MARATHON.
HEY HEY --LOOK WHO WE GOT HERE!
NATHAN CHRISTOPHER CHARLES SUMMERS-- HOW YOU DOIN', BABY BROTHER?
GLOOGLE!
WHAT THE--
--HEY-- LEGGO!
HUSH!
BE SILENT! BEHAVE!
THERE IS MORE HERE THAN WE CAN HOPE TO UNDERSTAND. FOR THE MOMENT, LEAVE IT IN WOLVERINE'S HANDS.
"BABY MAKES THREE"-- WHADDYA FIGURE, GUYS...
...WE GOT OURSELVES ONE INSTANT NUCLEAR FAMILY?
YOU REALIZE, OF COURSE, THAT BY PRESERVING YOUR PAST, YOU MAY HAVE CONDEMNED THE FUTURE.
ANYTHING'S POSSIBLE. YOU WANT GUARANTEES, BOY, WRITE A BOOK.
BUT WHICH WOULD YOU RATHER LEAVE BEHIND AS YOUR LEGACY -- THE BEST OF YOU--
--OR THE WORST?
WE GOTTA GO.
WE GOTTA TELL SCOTT AND THE OTHERS THAT NATE'S OKAY. AND, SOONER OR LATER, I HAVE TO SORT THINGS OUT WITH MY MOM...
FRANKLIN!
TAKE CARE, "UNCA WOLVIE."
GOOD-BYE, SIR. I'LL--
--REMEMBER WHAT YOU SAID.
I'M GLAD.
HERE'S LOOKING AT YOU, KID.
BOY, THAT WAS CREEPY.
YOU KNOW THOSE TWO, RIGHT?
IN A MANNER O' SPEAKIN'.
WE GONNA SEE 'EM AGAIN?
ANYTHING'S POSSIBLE.
Y'KNOW, YOU'RE LOOKIN' AWFUL PLEASED WITH YOURSELF.
YUP.
WHAT, YOU FIGURE THIS WAS SOME KIND'A WIN?
NOT "SOME KIND'A WIN, JUBILEE, A BIG ONE.
ONE O' THE BEST.
END.

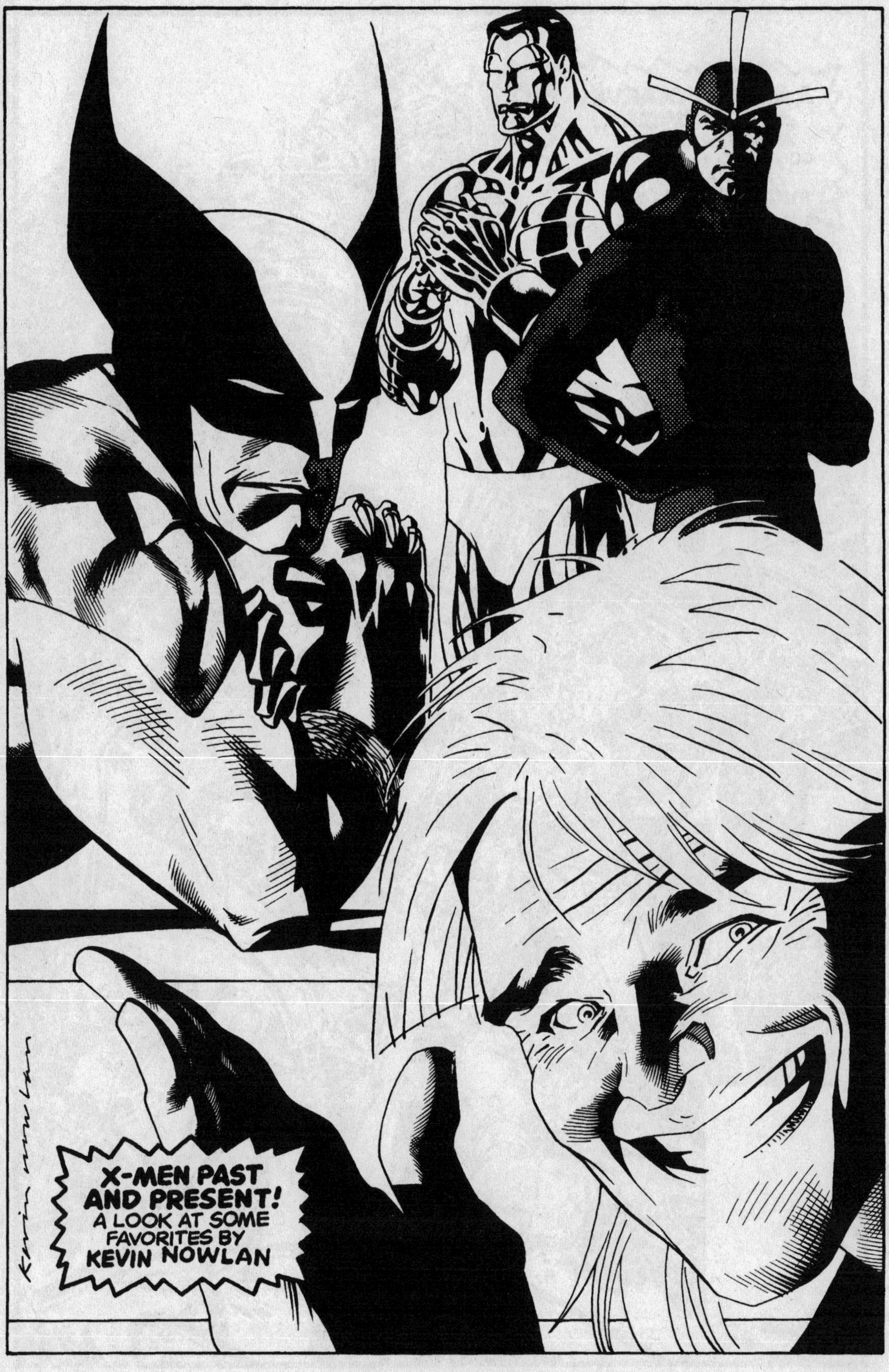
X-MEN PAST AND PRESENT!
A LOOK AT SOME FAVORITES BY
KEVIN NOWLAN

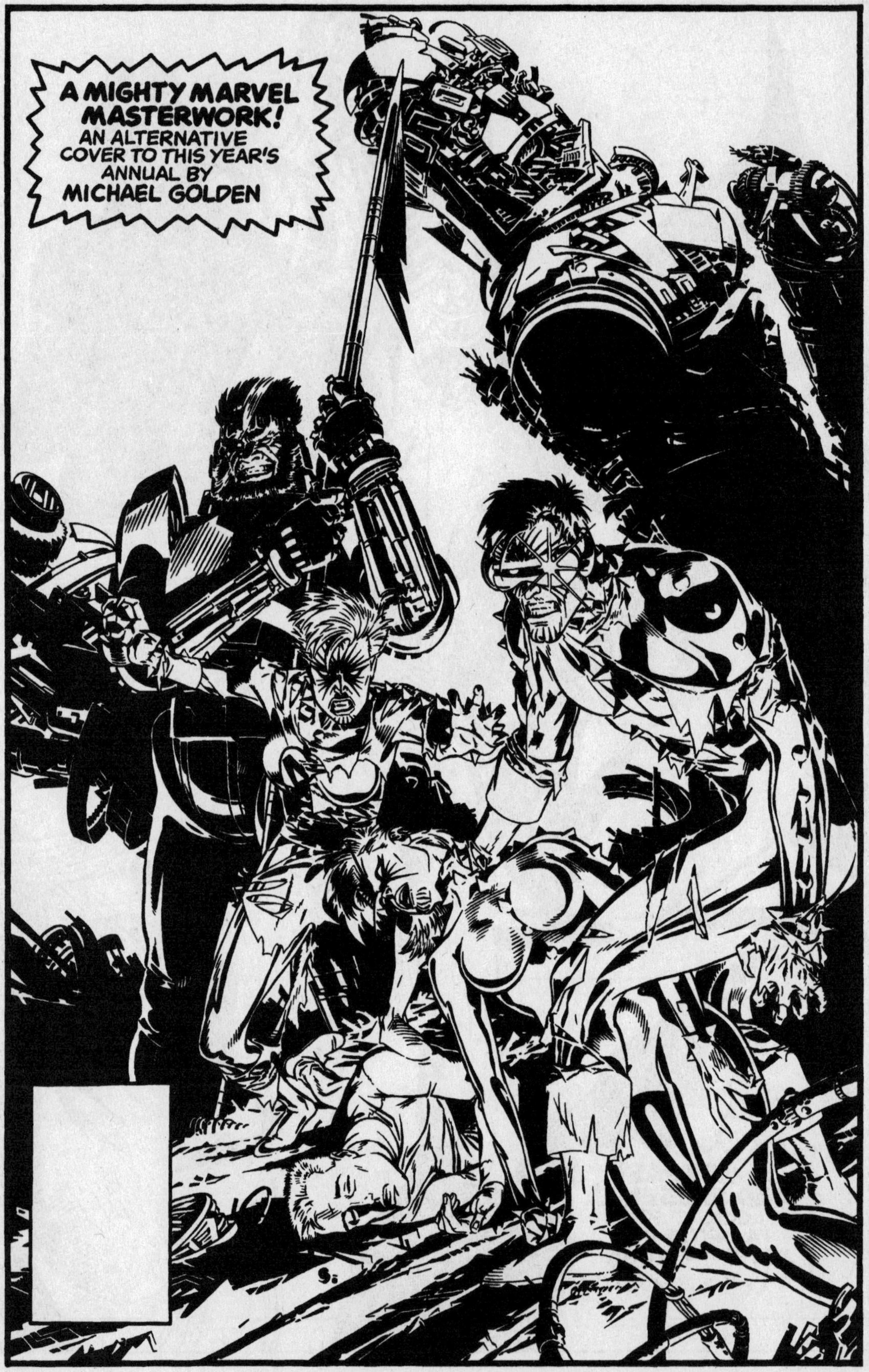
A MIGHTY MARVEL MASTERWORK!
AN ALTERNATIVE COVER TO THIS YEAR'S ANNUAL BY MICHAEL GOLDEN

X-MEN

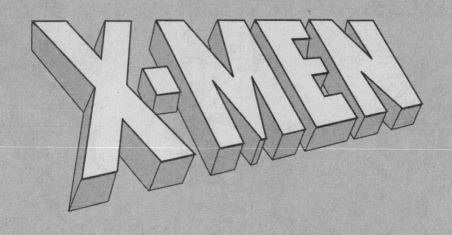

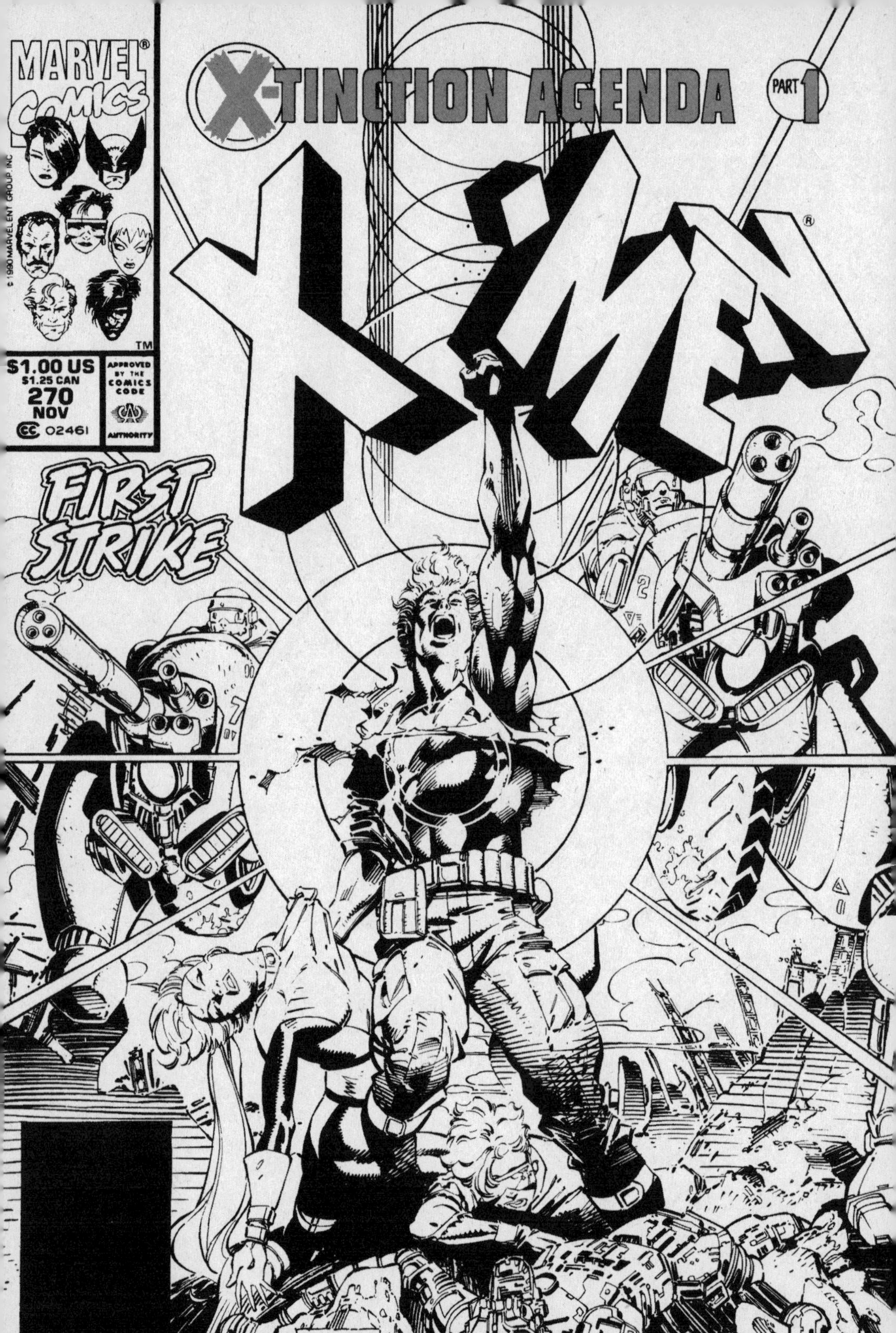
MARVEL COMICS
X-TINCTION AGENDA
PART 1
X-MEN
TM
$1.00 US
$1.25 CAN
270
NOV
02461
APPROVED BY THE COMICS CODE AUTHORITY
FIRST STRIKE
JIM LEE

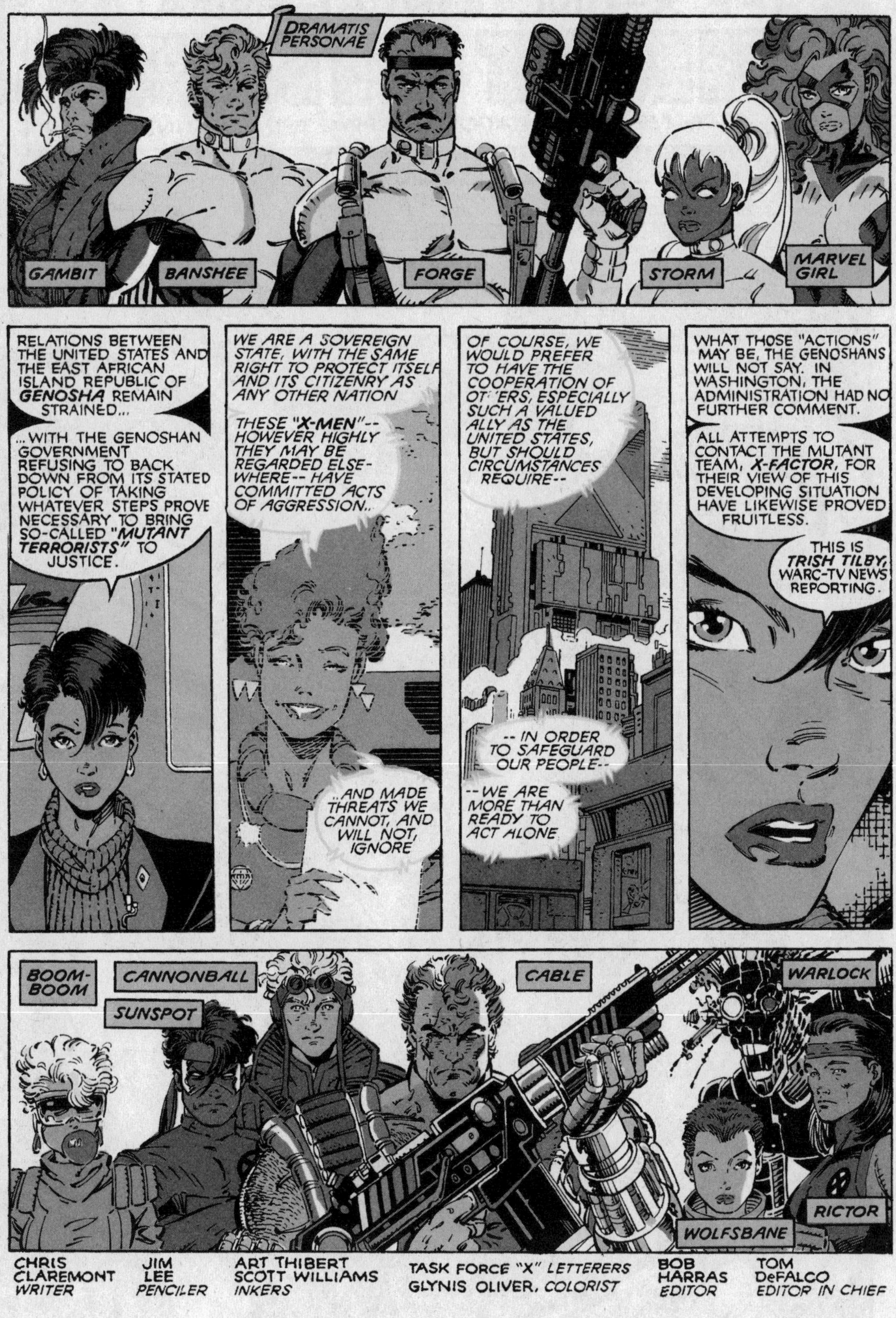
DRAMATIS PERSONAE
GAMBIT
BANSHEE
FORGE
STORM
MARVEL GIRL
RELATIONS BETWEEN THE UNITED STATES AND THE EAST AFRICAN ISLAND REPUBLIC OF GENOSHA REMAIN STRAINED...
...WITH THE GENOSHAN GOVERNMENT REFUSING TO BACK DOWN FROM ITS STATED POLICY OF TAKING WHATEVER STEPS PROVE NECESSARY TO BRING SO-CALLED "MUTANT TERRORISTS" TO JUSTICE.
WE ARE A SOVEREIGN STATE, WITH THE SAME RIGHT TO PROTECT ITSELF AND ITS CITIZENRY AS ANY OTHER NATION
THESE "X-MEN"-- HOWEVER HIGHLY THEY MAY BE REGARDED ELSE-WHERE-- HAVE COMMITTED ACTS OF AGGRESSION...
...AND MADE THREATS WE CANNOT, AND WILL NOT, IGNORE
OF COURSE, WE WOULD PREFER TO HAVE THE COOPERATION OF OTHERS, ESPECIALLY SUCH A VALUED ALLY AS THE UNITED STATES, BUT SHOULD CIRCUMSTANCES REQUIRE--
-- IN ORDER TO SAFEGUARD OUR PEOPLE--
--WE ARE MORE THAN READY TO ACT ALONE
WHAT THOSE "ACTIONS" MAY BE, THE GENOSHANS WILL NOT SAY. IN WASHINGTON, THE ADMINISTRATION HAD NO FURTHER COMMENT.
ALL ATTEMPTS TO CONTACT THE MUTANT TEAM, X-FACTOR, FOR THEIR VIEW OF THIS DEVELOPING SITUATION HAVE LIKEWISE PROVED FRUITLESS.
THIS IS TRISH TILBY, WARC-TV NEWS REPORTING.
BOOM-BOOM
CANNONBALL
SUNSPOT
CABLE
WARLOCK
RICTOR
WOLFSBANE

CHRIS CLAREMONT *WRITER* · JIM LEE *PENCILER* · ART THIBERT, SCOTT WILLIAMS *INKERS* · TASK FORCE "X" *LETTERERS* · GLYNIS OLIVER, *COLORIST* · BOB HARRAS *EDITOR* · TOM DeFALCO *EDITOR IN CHIEF*

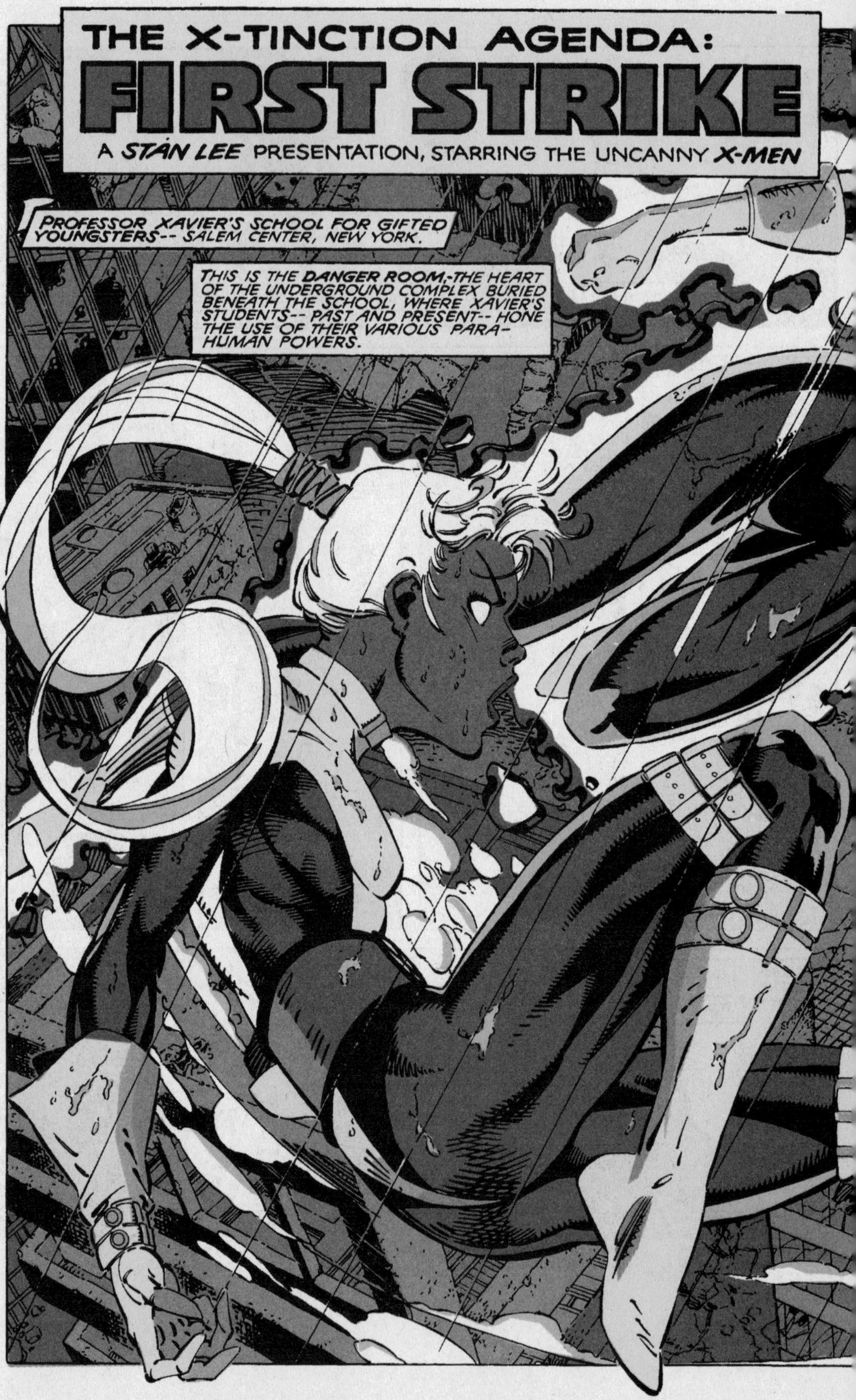
THE X-TINCTION AGENDA:
FIRST STRIKE
A STAN LEE PRESENTATION, STARRING THE UNCANNY X-MEN
PROFESSOR XAVIER'S SCHOOL FOR GIFTED YOUNGSTERS-- SALEM CENTER, NEW YORK.
THIS IS THE DANGER ROOM,-THE HEART OF THE UNDERGROUND COMPLEX BURIED BENEATH THE SCHOOL, WHERE XAVIER'S STUDENTS-- PAST AND PRESENT-- HONE THE USE OF THEIR VARIOUS PARA-HUMAN POWERS.

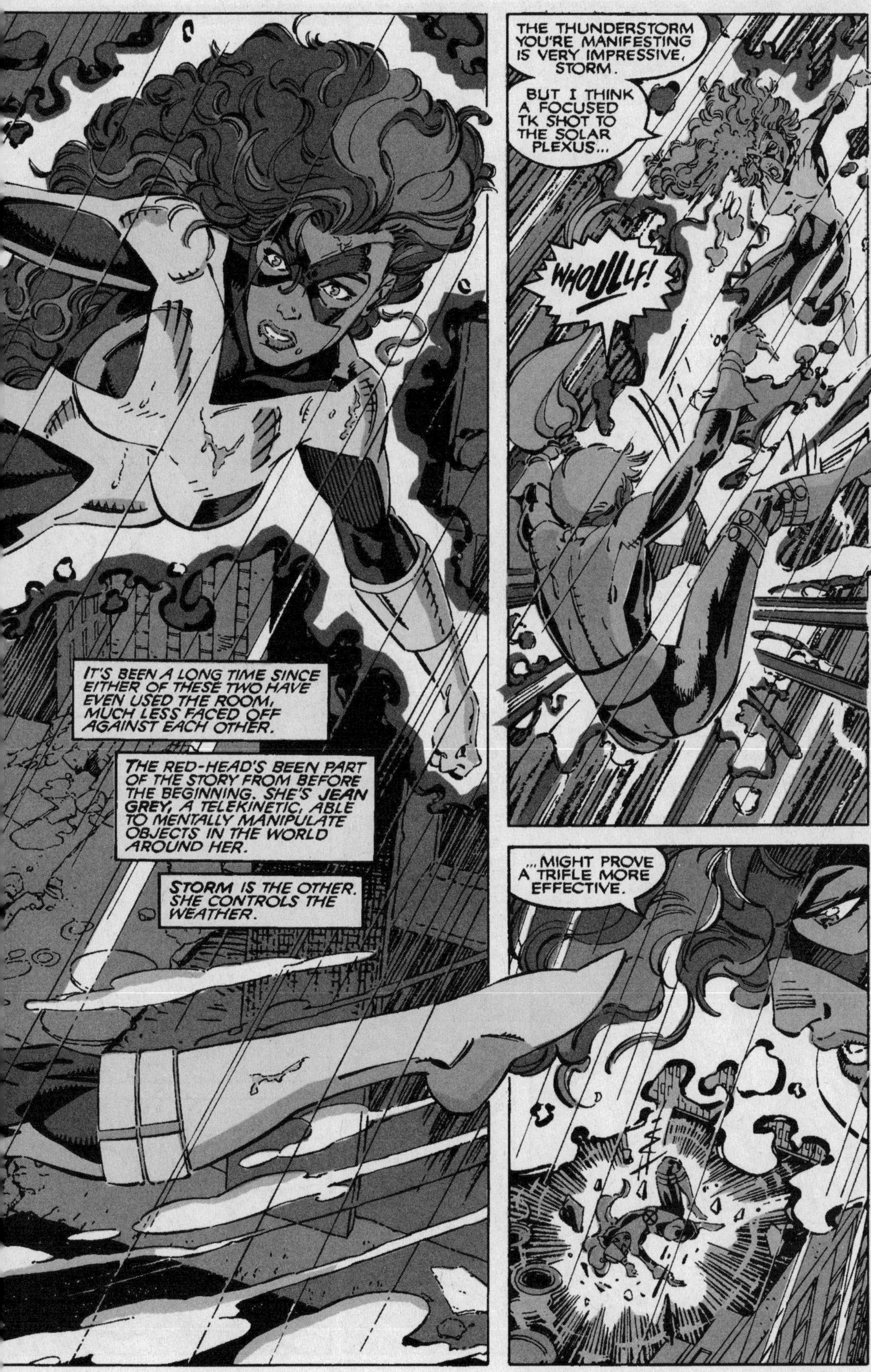
IT'S BEEN A LONG TIME SINCE EITHER OF THESE TWO HAVE EVEN USED THE ROOM, MUCH LESS FACED OFF AGAINST EACH OTHER.
THE RED-HEAD'S BEEN PART OF THE STORY FROM BEFORE THE BEGINNING. SHE'S JEAN GREY, A TELEKINETIC, ABLE TO MENTALLY MANIPULATE OBJECTS IN THE WORLD AROUND HER.
STORM IS THE OTHER. SHE CONTROLS THE WEATHER.
THE THUNDERSTORM YOU'RE MANIFESTING IS VERY IMPRESSIVE, STORM.
BUT I THINK A FOCUSED TK SHOT TO THE SOLAR PLEXUS...
WHOULLF!
...MIGHT PROVE A TRIFLE MORE EFFECTIVE.

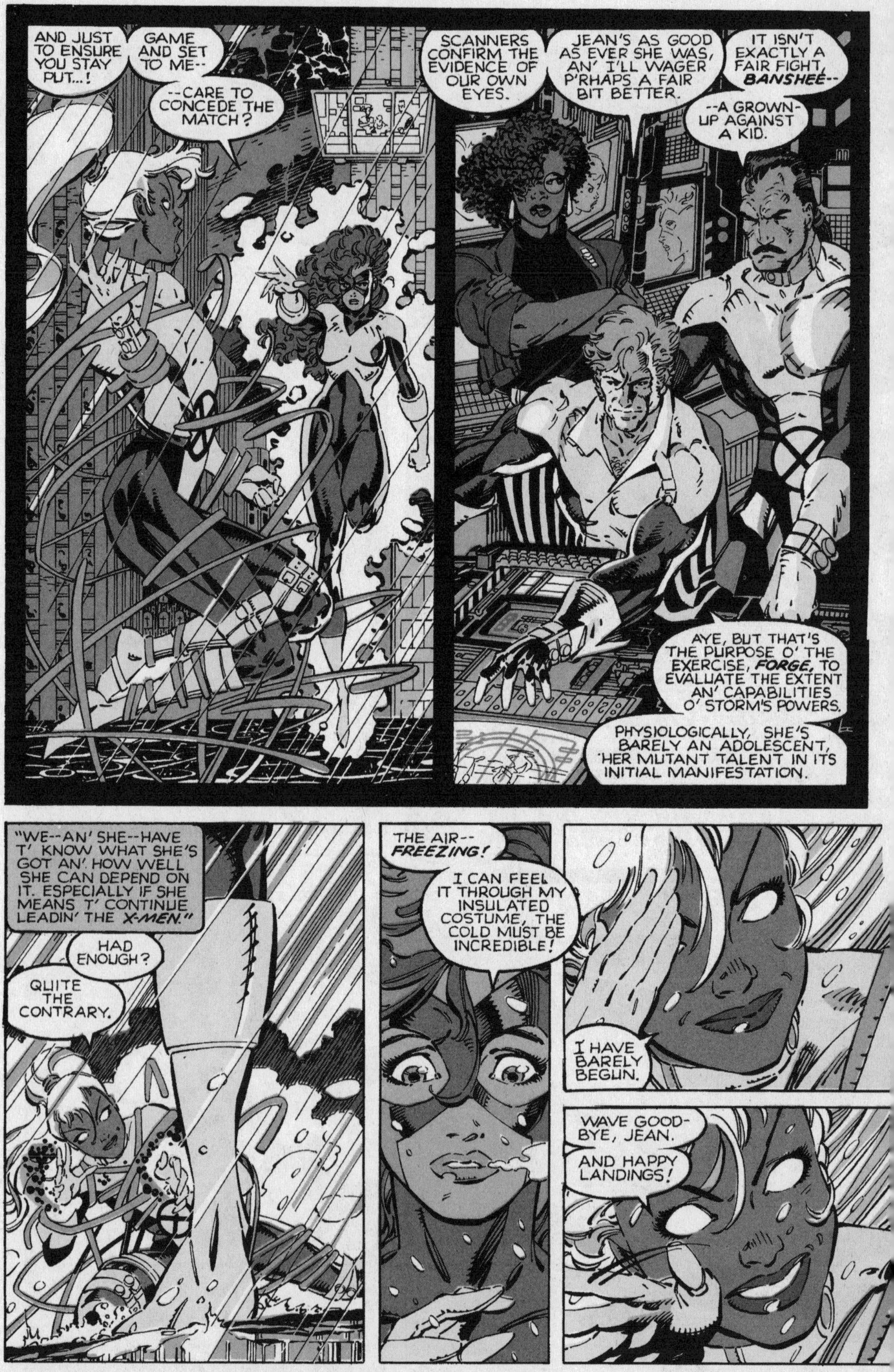
AND JUST TO ENSURE YOU STAY PUT...!
GAME AND SET TO ME--
--CARE TO CONCEDE THE MATCH?
SCANNERS CONFIRM THE EVIDENCE OF OUR OWN EYES.
JEAN'S AS GOOD AS EVER SHE WAS, AN' I'LL WAGER P'RHAPS A FAIR BIT BETTER.
IT ISN'T EXACTLY A FAIR FIGHT, BANSHEE--
--A GROWN-UP AGAINST A KID.
AYE, BUT THAT'S THE PURPOSE O' THE EXERCISE, FORGE, TO EVALUATE THE EXTENT AN' CAPABILITIES O' STORM'S POWERS.
PHYSIOLOGICALLY, SHE'S BARELY AN ADOLESCENT, HER MUTANT TALENT IN ITS INITIAL MANIFESTATION.
"WE--AN' SHE--HAVE T' KNOW WHAT SHE'S GOT AN' HOW WELL SHE CAN DEPEND ON IT. ESPECIALLY IF SHE MEANS T' CONTINUE LEADIN' THE X-MEN."
HAD ENOUGH?
QUITE THE CONTRARY.
THE AIR--FREEZING!
I CAN FEEL IT THROUGH MY INSULATED COSTUME, THE COLD MUST BE INCREDIBLE!
I HAVE BARELY BEGUN.
WAVE GOOD-BYE, JEAN.
AND HAPPY LANDINGS!

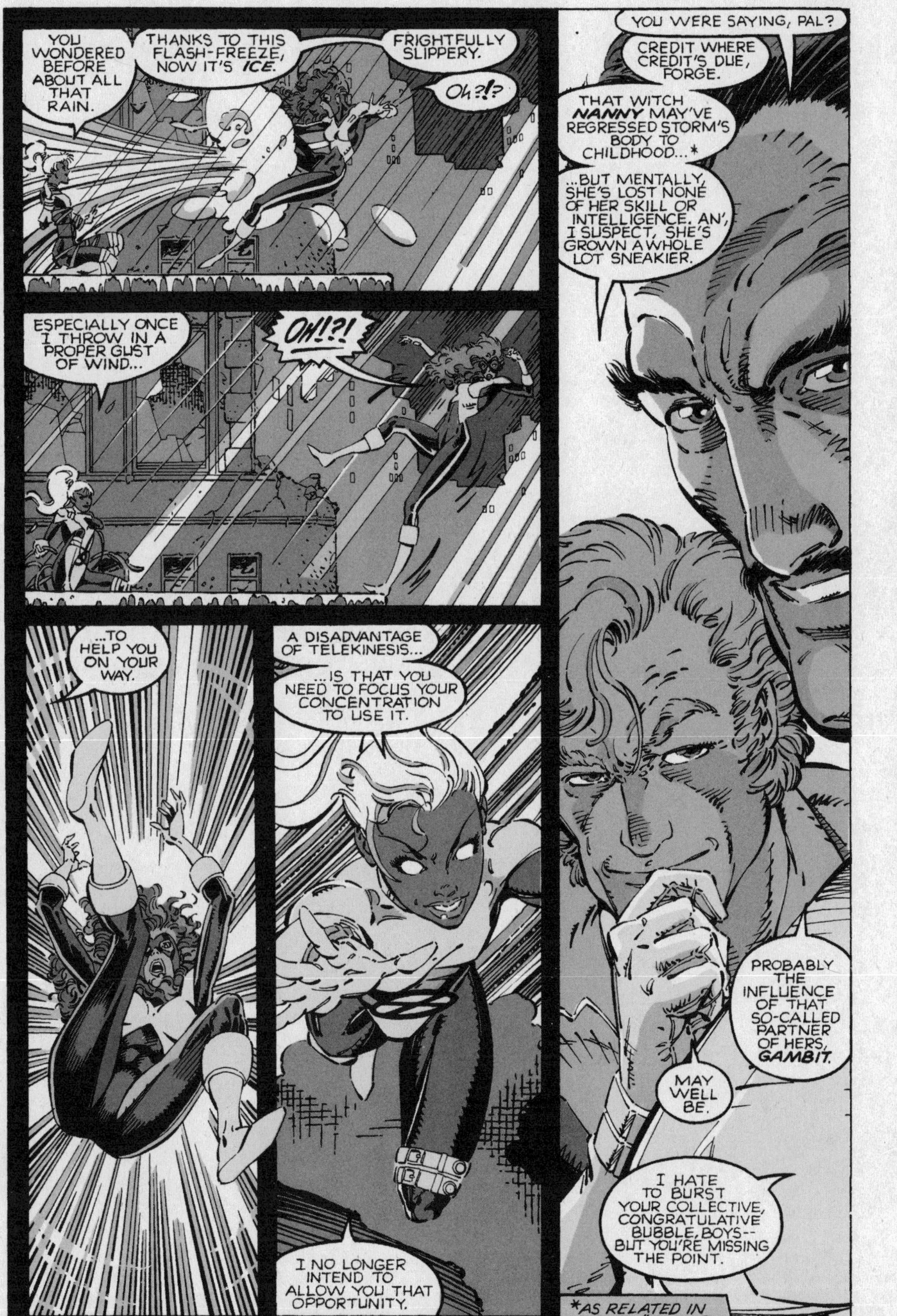
YOU WONDERED BEFORE ABOUT ALL THAT RAIN.
THANKS TO THIS FLASH-FREEZE, NOW IT'S ICE.
FRIGHTFULLY SLIPPERY.
Oh?!?
ESPECIALLY ONCE I THROW IN A PROPER GUST OF WIND...
OH!?!
...TO HELP YOU ON YOUR WAY.
A DISADVANTAGE OF TELEKINESIS...
...IS THAT YOU NEED TO FOCUS YOUR CONCENTRATION TO USE IT.
I NO LONGER INTEND TO ALLOW YOU THAT OPPORTUNITY.
YOU WERE SAYING, PAL?
CREDIT WHERE CREDIT'S DUE, FORGE.
THAT WITCH NANNY MAY'VE REGRESSED STORM'S BODY TO CHILDHOOD...*
...BUT MENTALLY, SHE'S LOST NONE OF HER SKILL OR INTELLIGENCE. AN', I SUSPECT, SHE'S GROWN A WHOLE LOT SNEAKIER.
PROBABLY THE INFLUENCE OF THAT SO-CALLED PARTNER OF HERS, GAMBIT.
MAY WELL BE.
I HATE TO BURST YOUR COLLECTIVE, CONGRATULATIVE BUBBLE, BOYS-- BUT YOU'RE MISSING THE POINT.
*AS RELATED IN X-MEN #267--BH

X-MEN

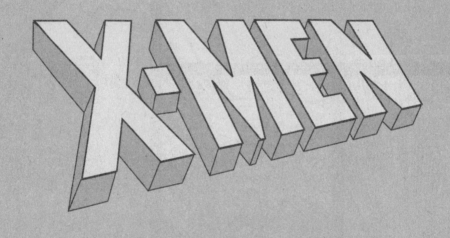

AS YOU YOURSELF SAID, BANSHEE, PHYSICALLY SHE'S A YOUNGSTER. HER BODY'S STILL GROWING.

TOO MUCH OF THE WRONG KIND OF STRESS-- LIKE PUSHING HER ELEMENTAL POWERS BEYOND THEIR LIMIT--

--COULD CAUSE PERMANENT INJURY.

I THINK, *MS. HUNTER,* STORM'S WELL AWARE OF HER LIMITATIONS.

THIS IS *RICTOR,* REQUESTING ACCESS TO THE DANGER ROOM.

ADULT KNOWLEDGE, FORGE, OF AN *ADULT* INSTRUMENT.

BUT HER CURRENT REALITY IS THAT OF A CHILD!

*"LAST SEEN IN--UM, EVEN *WE* CAN'T REMEMBER!"

WE'RE RUNNING AN EVALUATION SEQUENCE, LAD.

I'M SORRY, BUT YE'LL HAVE T' WAIT.

DANGER ROOM SEQUENCE ACTIVATE RUNNING ENTRY PR

HEY SURE WHY NOT NO PROBLEM.

I MEAN, IT'S ONLY *OUR* HOUSE.

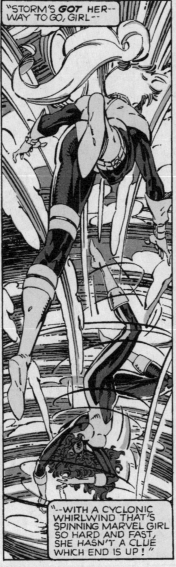

"STORM'S *GOT* HER-- WAY TO GO, GIRL--

"--WITH A CYCLONIC WHIRLWIND THAT'S SPINNING MARVEL GIRL SO HARD AND FAST, SHE HASN'T A CLUE WHICH END IS UP!"

ENOUGH!

SHE'S USING TOO MUCH POWER, SPINNING JEAN TOO FAST!

DANGER ROUTINE SCENARIO 707 DISENG

HER BODY HASN'T THE RESOURCES TO HANDLE THAT KIND OF LOAD--

--SHE'S LOSING CONTROL!

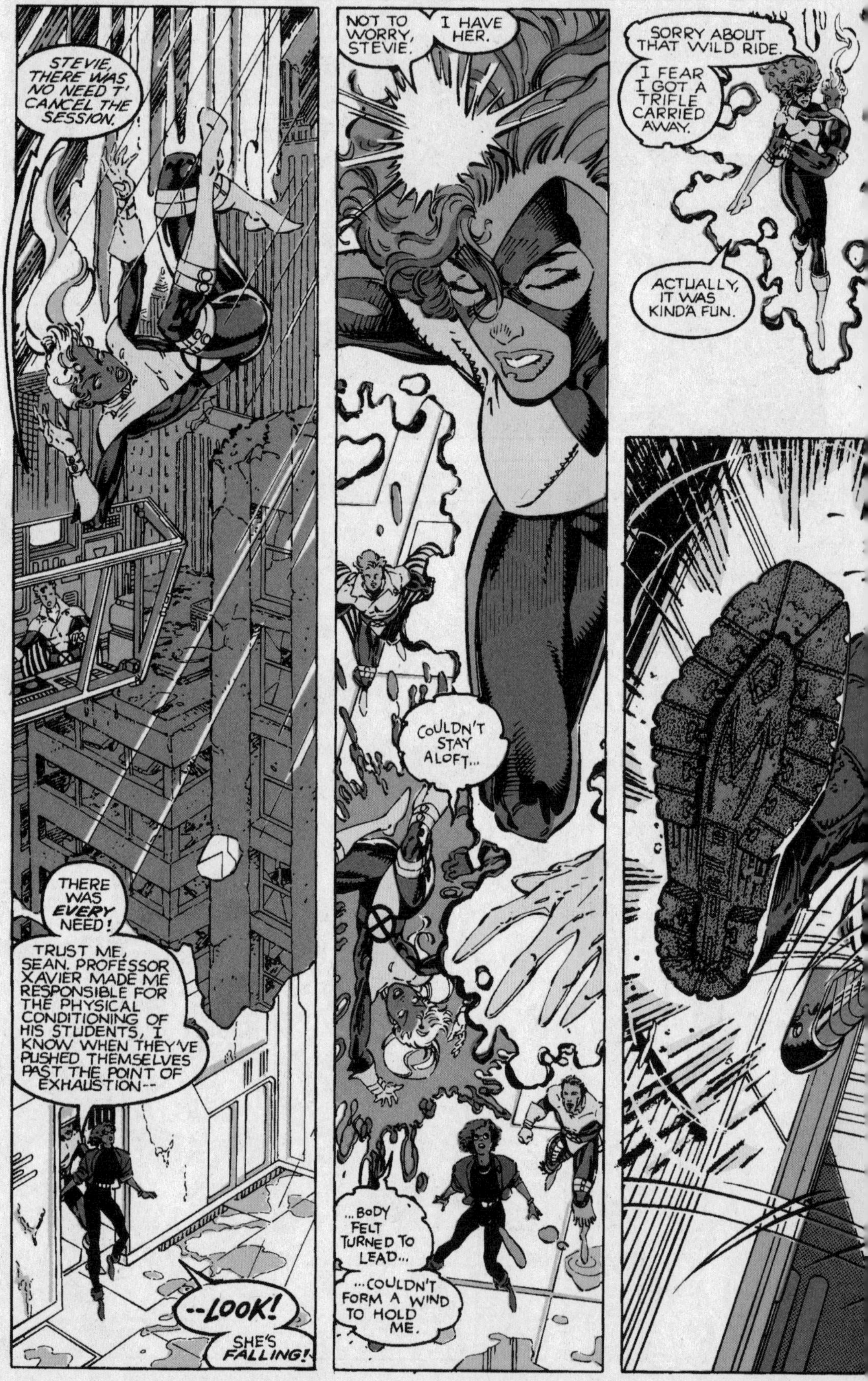
STEVIE, THERE WAS NO NEED T' CANCEL THE SESSION.
THERE WAS EVERY NEED!
TRUST ME, SEAN. PROFESSOR XAVIER MADE ME RESPONSIBLE FOR THE PHYSICAL CONDITIONING OF HIS STUDENTS, I KNOW WHEN THEY'VE PUSHED THEMSELVES PAST THE POINT OF EXHAUSTION--
--LOOK!
SHE'S FALLING!
...BODY FELT TURNED TO LEAD...
...COULDN'T FORM A WIND TO HOLD ME.
COULDN'T STAY ALOFT...
NOT TO WORRY, STEVIE.
I HAVE HER.
SORRY ABOUT THAT WILD RIDE.
I FEAR I GOT A TRIFLE CARRIED AWAY.
ACTUALLY, IT WAS KIND'A FUN.

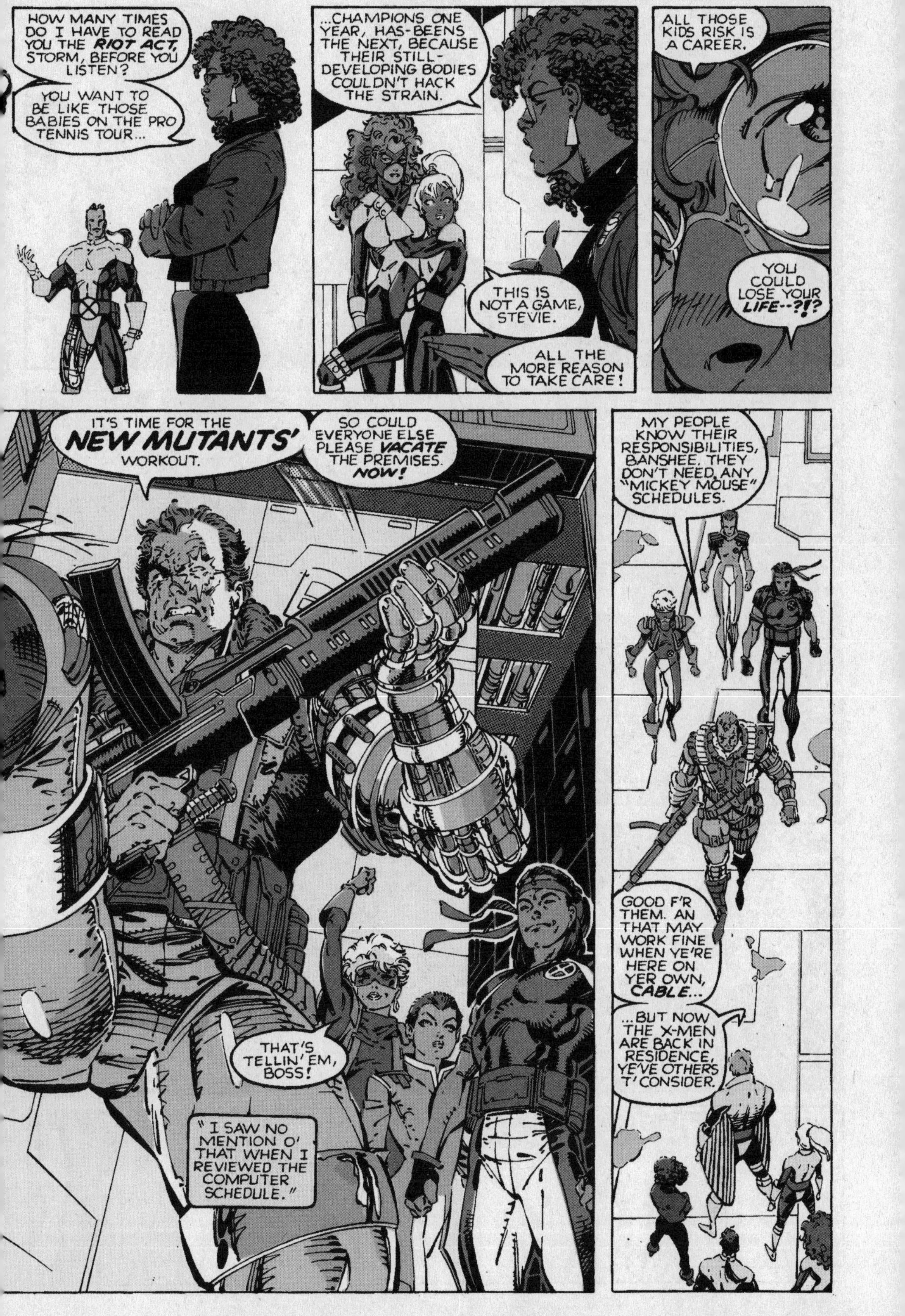
HOW MANY TIMES DO I HAVE TO READ YOU THE RIOT ACT, STORM, BEFORE YOU LISTEN?
YOU WANT TO BE LIKE THOSE BABIES ON THE PRO TENNIS TOUR...
...CHAMPIONS ONE YEAR, HAS-BEENS THE NEXT, BECAUSE THEIR STILL-DEVELOPING BODIES COULDN'T HACK THE STRAIN.
THIS IS NOT A GAME, STEVIE.
ALL THE MORE REASON TO TAKE CARE!
ALL THOSE KIDS RISK IS A CAREER.
YOU COULD LOSE YOUR LIFE--?!?
IT'S TIME FOR THE NEW MUTANTS' WORKOUT.
SO COULD EVERYONE ELSE PLEASE VACATE THE PREMISES. NOW!
THAT'S TELLIN' EM, BOSS!
"I SAW NO MENTION O' THAT WHEN I REVIEWED THE COMPUTER SCHEDULE."
MY PEOPLE KNOW THEIR RESPONSIBILITIES, BANSHEE. THEY DON'T NEED ANY "MICKEY MOUSE" SCHEDULES.
GOOD F'R THEM. AN THAT MAY WORK FINE WHEN YE'RE HERE ON YER OWN, CABLE...
...BUT NOW THE X-MEN ARE BACK IN RESIDENCE, YE'VE OTHERS T'CONSIDER.

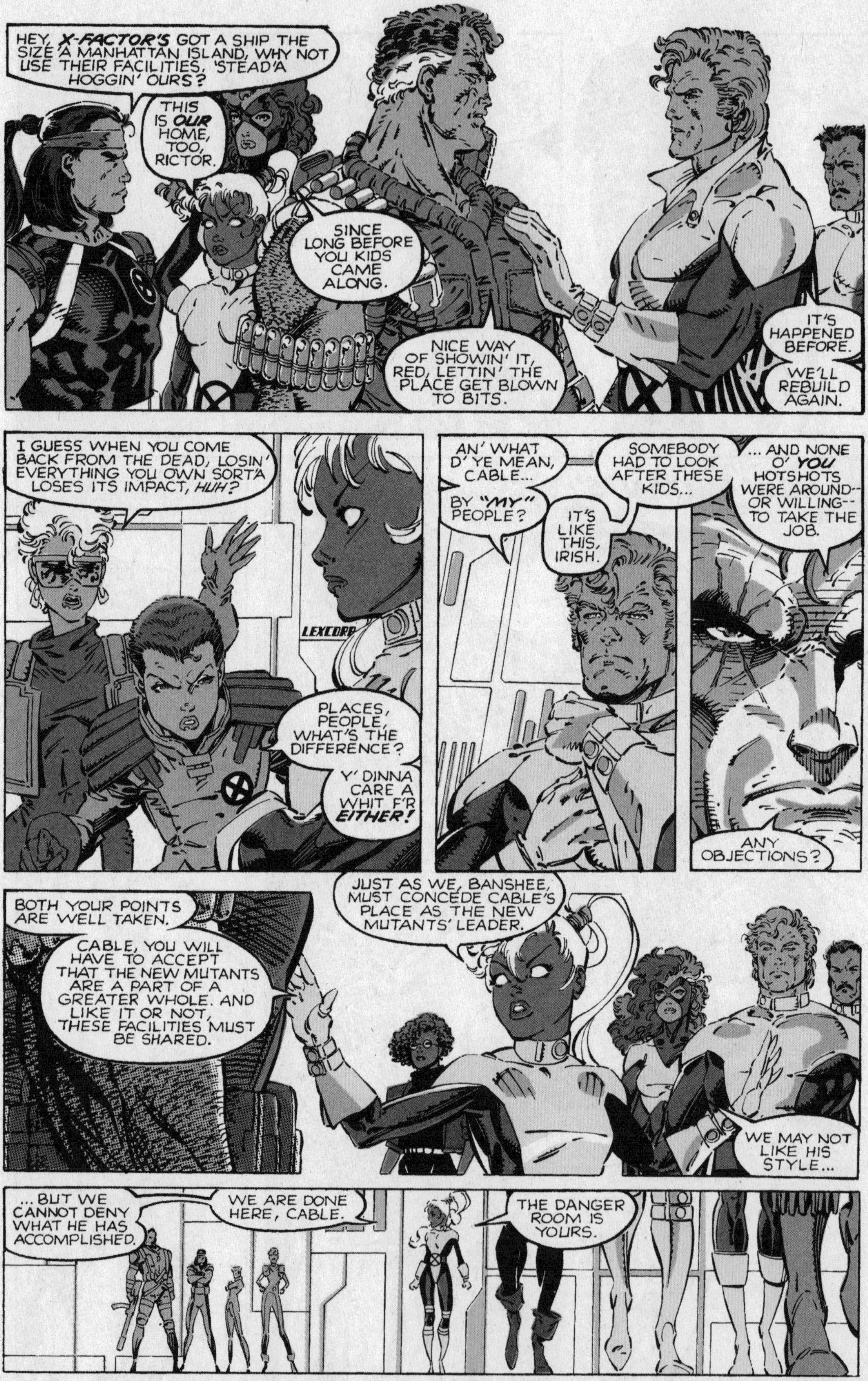
HEY, X-FACTOR'S GOT A SHIP THE SIZE 'A MANHATTAN ISLAND, WHY NOT USE THEIR FACILITIES, 'STEAD'A HOGGIN' OURS?
THIS IS OUR HOME, TOO, RICTOR.
SINCE LONG BEFORE YOU KIDS CAME ALONG.
NICE WAY OF SHOWIN' IT, RED, LETTIN' THE PLACE GET BLOWN TO BITS.
IT'S HAPPENED BEFORE.
WE'LL REBUILD AGAIN.
I GUESS WHEN YOU COME BACK FROM THE DEAD, LOSIN' EVERYTHING YOU OWN SORTA LOSES ITS IMPACT, HUH?
LEXCORP
PLACES, PEOPLE, WHAT'S THE DIFFERENCE?
Y' DINNA CARE A WHIT F'R EITHER!
AN' WHAT D' YE MEAN, CABLE...
BY "MY" PEOPLE?
IT'S LIKE THIS, IRISH.
SOMEBODY HAD TO LOOK AFTER THESE KIDS...
... AND NONE O' YOU HOTSHOTS WERE AROUND-- OR WILLING-- TO TAKE THE JOB.
ANY OBJECTIONS?
BOTH YOUR POINTS ARE WELL TAKEN.
CABLE, YOU WILL HAVE TO ACCEPT THAT THE NEW MUTANTS ARE A PART OF A GREATER WHOLE. AND LIKE IT OR NOT, THESE FACILITIES MUST BE SHARED.
JUST AS WE, BANSHEE, MUST CONCEDE CABLE'S PLACE AS THE NEW MUTANTS' LEADER.
WE MAY NOT LIKE HIS STYLE...
... BUT WE CANNOT DENY WHAT HE HAS ACCOMPLISHED.
WE ARE DONE HERE, CABLE.
THE DANGER ROOM IS YOURS.

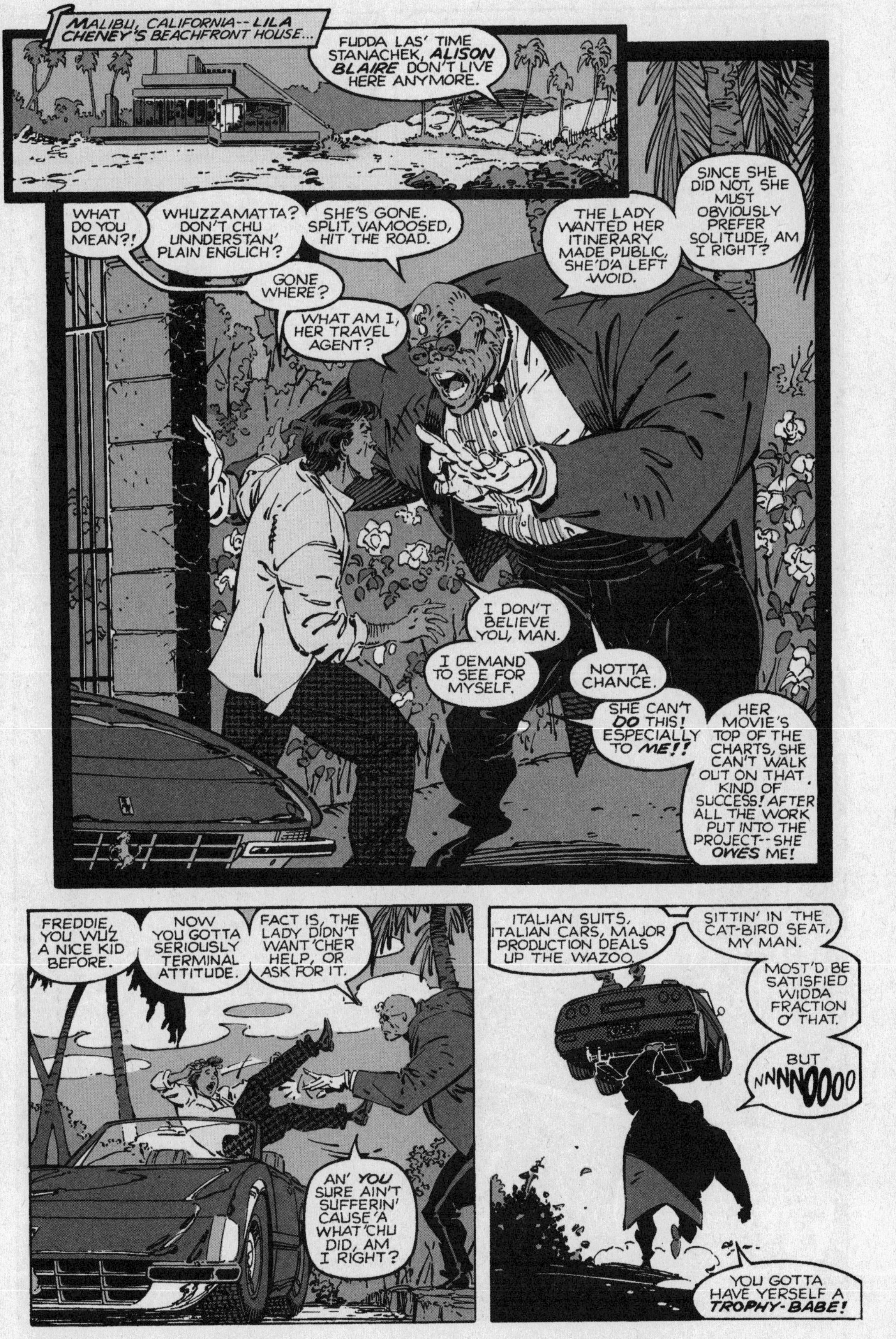
MALIBU, CALIFORNIA-- LILA CHENEY'S BEACHFRONT HOUSE...
FUDDA LAS' TIME STANACHEK, ALISON BLAIRE DON'T LIVE HERE ANYMORE.
WHAT DO YOU MEAN?!
WHUZZAMATTA? DON'T CHU UNNDERSTAN' PLAIN ENGLICH?
SHE'S GONE. SPLIT, VAMOOSED, HIT THE ROAD.
THE LADY WANTED HER ITINERARY MADE PUBLIC, SHE'D'A LEFT -WOID.
SINCE SHE DID NOT, SHE MUST OBVIOUSLY PREFER SOLITUDE, AM I RIGHT?
GONE WHERE?
WHAT AM I, HER TRAVEL AGENT?
I DON'T BELIEVE YOU, MAN.
I DEMAND TO SEE FOR MYSELF.
NOTTA CHANCE.
SHE CAN'T DO THIS! ESPECIALLY TO ME!!
HER MOVIE'S TOP OF THE CHARTS, SHE CAN'T WALK OUT ON THAT KIND OF SUCCESS! AFTER ALL THE WORK I PUT INTO THE PROJECT--SHE OWES ME!
FREDDIE, YOU WUZ A NICE KID BEFORE.
NOW YOU GOTTA SERIOUSLY TERMINAL ATTITUDE.
FACT IS, THE LADY DIDN'T WANT 'CHER HELP, OR ASK FOR IT.
AN' YOU SURE AIN'T SUFFERIN' CAUSE 'A WHAT 'CHU DID, AM I RIGHT?
ITALIAN SUITS, ITALIAN CARS, MAJOR PRODUCTION DEALS UP THE WAZOO.
SITTIN' IN THE CAT-BIRD SEAT, MY MAN.
MOST'D BE SATISFIED WIDDA FRACTION O' THAT.
BUT NNNNOOOO
YOU GOTTA HAVE YERSELF A TROPHY-BABE!

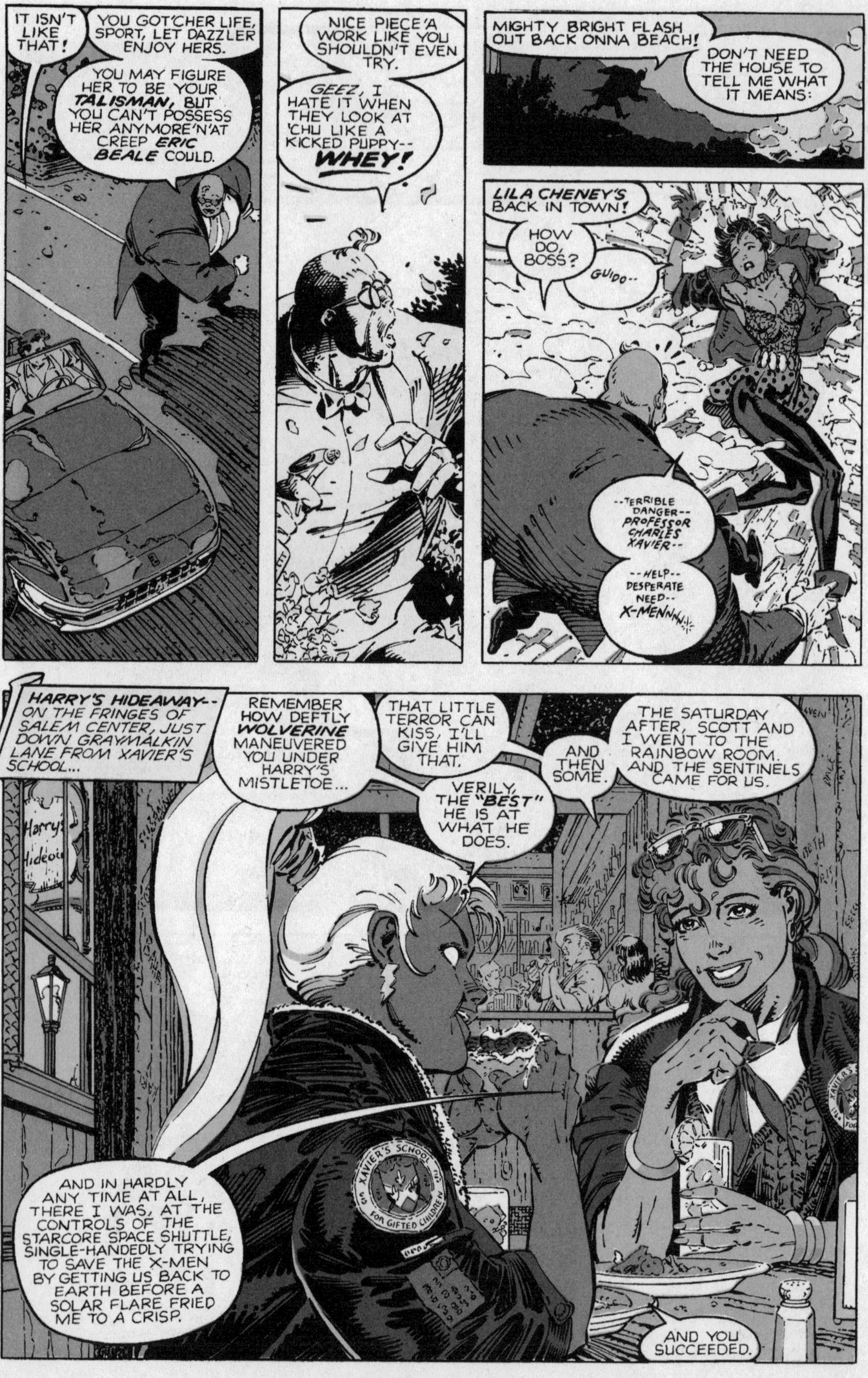
IT ISN'T LIKE THAT!
YOU GOT'CHER LIFE, SPORT, LET DAZZLER ENJOY HERS.
YOU MAY FIGURE HER TO BE YOUR TALISMAN, BUT YOU CAN'T POSSESS HER ANYMORE'N'AT CREEP ERIC BEALE COULD.
NICE PIECE'A WORK LIKE YOU SHOULDN'T EVEN TRY.
GEEZ, I HATE IT WHEN THEY LOOK AT 'CHU LIKE A KICKED PUPPY-- WHEY!
MIGHTY BRIGHT FLASH OUT BACK ONNA BEACH!
DON'T NEED THE HOUSE TO TELL ME WHAT IT MEANS:
LILA CHENEY'S BACK IN TOWN!
HOW DO, BOSS?
GUIDO--
--TERRIBLE DANGER-- PROFESSOR CHARLES XAVIER--
--HELP-- DESPERATE NEED-- X-MENNN
HARRY'S HIDEAWAY-- ON THE FRINGES OF SALEM CENTER, JUST DOWN GRAYMALKIN LANE FROM XAVIER'S SCHOOL...
REMEMBER HOW DEFTLY WOLVERINE MANEUVERED YOU UNDER HARRY'S MISTLETOE...
THAT LITTLE TERROR CAN KISS, I'LL GIVE HIM THAT.
VERILY, THE "BEST" HE IS AT WHAT HE DOES.
AND THEN SOME.
THE SATURDAY AFTER, SCOTT AND I WENT TO THE RAINBOW ROOM. AND THE SENTINELS CAME FOR US.
AND IN HARDLY ANY TIME AT ALL, THERE I WAS, AT THE CONTROLS OF THE STARCORE SPACE SHUTTLE, SINGLE-HANDEDLY TRYING TO SAVE THE X-MEN BY GETTING US BACK TO EARTH BEFORE A SOLAR FLARE FRIED ME TO A CRISP.
AND YOU SUCCEEDED.

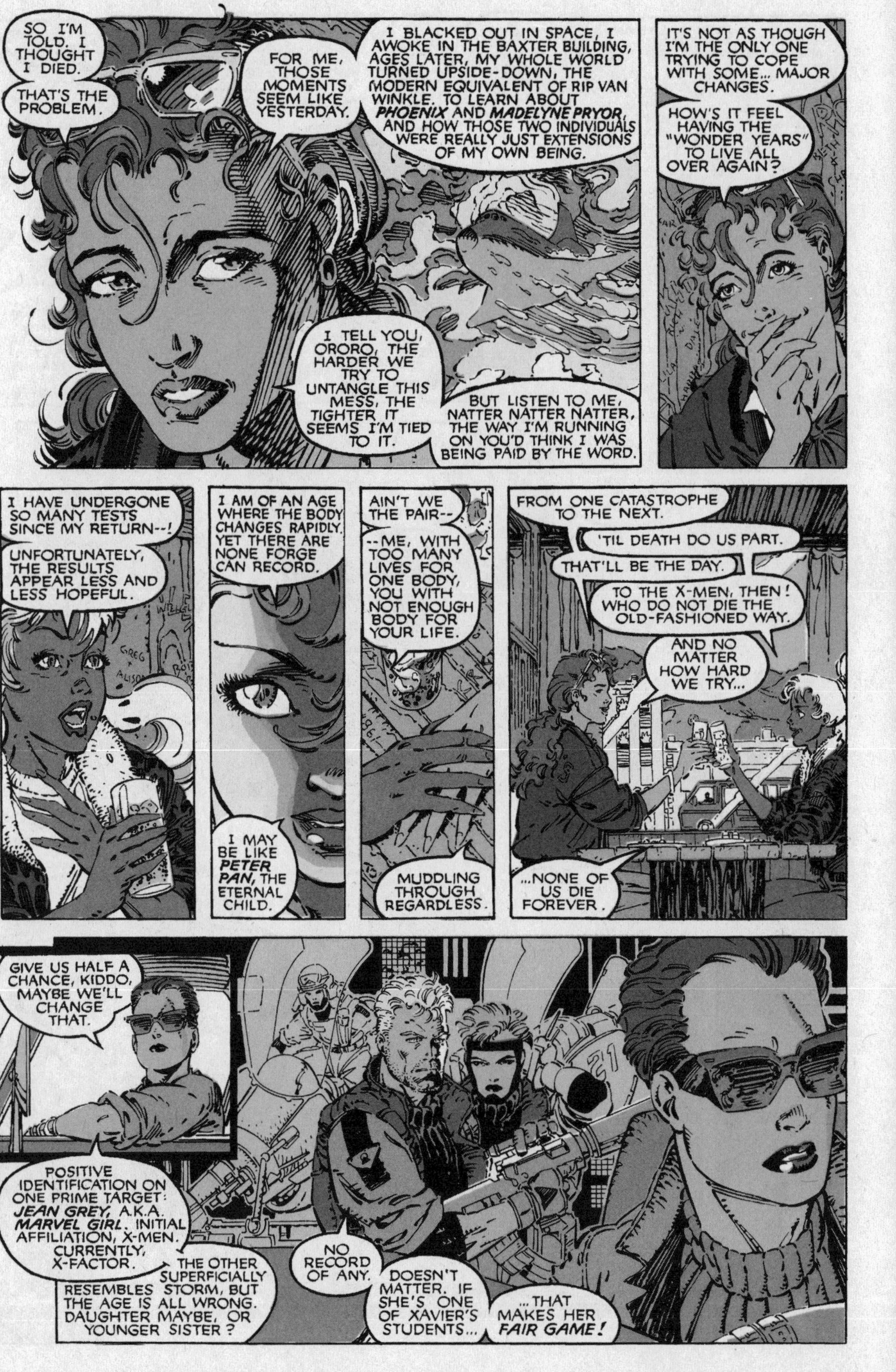
SO I'M TOLD. I THOUGHT I DIED.
THAT'S THE PROBLEM.
FOR ME, THOSE MOMENTS SEEM LIKE YESTERDAY.
I BLACKED OUT IN SPACE, I AWOKE IN THE BAXTER BUILDING, AGES LATER, MY WHOLE WORLD TURNED UPSIDE-DOWN, THE MODERN EQUIVALENT OF RIP VAN WINKLE. TO LEARN ABOUT PHOENIX AND MADELYNE PRYOR, AND HOW THOSE TWO INDIVIDUALS WERE REALLY JUST EXTENSIONS OF MY OWN BEING.
I TELL YOU, ORORO, THE HARDER WE TRY TO UNTANGLE THIS MESS, THE TIGHTER IT SEEMS I'M TIED TO IT.
BUT LISTEN TO ME, NATTER NATTER NATTER, THE WAY I'M RUNNING ON YOU'D THINK I WAS BEING PAID BY THE WORD.
IT'S NOT AS THOUGH I'M THE ONLY ONE TRYING TO COPE WITH SOME... MAJOR CHANGES.
HOW'S IT FEEL HAVING THE "WONDER YEARS" TO LIVE ALL OVER AGAIN?
I HAVE UNDERGONE SO MANY TESTS SINCE MY RETURN--!
UNFORTUNATELY, THE RESULTS APPEAR LESS AND LESS HOPEFUL.
I AM OF AN AGE WHERE THE BODY CHANGES RAPIDLY, YET THERE ARE NONE FORGE CAN RECORD.
I MAY BE LIKE PETER PAN, THE ETERNAL CHILD.
AIN'T WE THE PAIR--
--ME, WITH TOO MANY LIVES FOR ONE BODY, YOU WITH NOT ENOUGH BODY FOR YOUR LIFE.
MUDDLING THROUGH REGARDLESS.
FROM ONE CATASTROPHE TO THE NEXT.
'TIL DEATH DO US PART.
THAT'LL BE THE DAY.
TO THE X-MEN, THEN! WHO DO NOT DIE THE OLD-FASHIONED WAY.
AND NO MATTER HOW HARD WE TRY...
...NONE OF US DIE FOREVER.
GIVE US HALF A CHANCE, KIDDO, MAYBE WE'LL CHANGE THAT.
POSITIVE IDENTIFICATION ON ONE PRIME TARGET: JEAN GREY, A.K.A. MARVEL GIRL. INITIAL AFFILIATION, X-MEN. CURRENTLY, X-FACTOR.
THE OTHER SUPERFICIALLY RESEMBLES STORM, BUT THE AGE IS ALL WRONG. DAUGHTER MAYBE, OR YOUNGER SISTER?
NO RECORD OF ANY.
DOESN'T MATTER. IF SHE'S ONE OF XAVIER'S STUDENTS...
...THAT MAKES HER FAIR GAME!

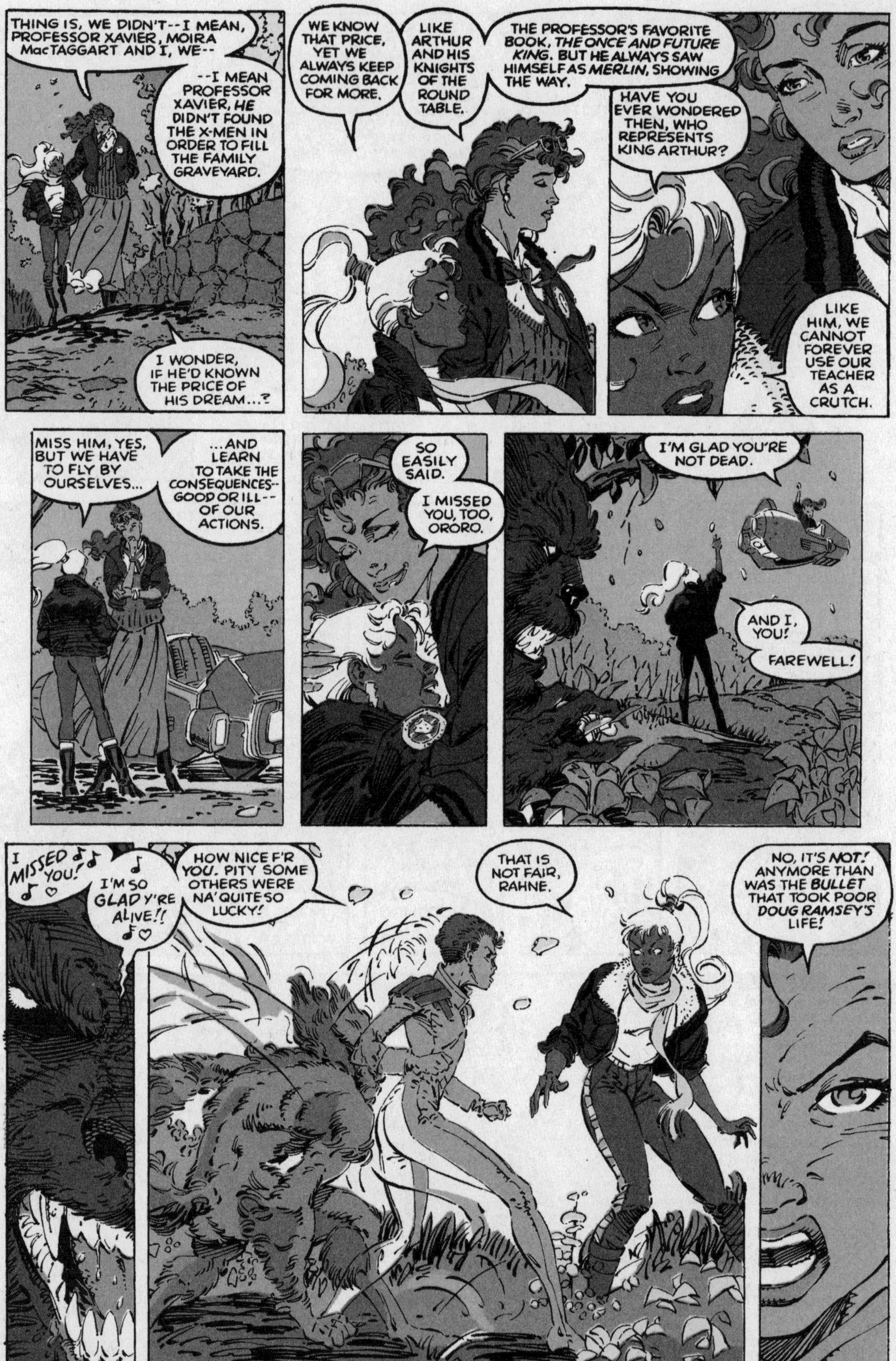
THING IS, WE DIDN'T--I MEAN, PROFESSOR XAVIER, MOIRA MacTAGGART AND I, WE--
--I MEAN PROFESSOR XAVIER, HE DIDN'T FOUND THE X-MEN IN ORDER TO FILL THE FAMILY GRAVEYARD.
I WONDER, IF HE'D KNOWN THE PRICE OF HIS DREAM...?
WE KNOW THAT PRICE, YET WE ALWAYS KEEP COMING BACK FOR MORE.
LIKE ARTHUR AND HIS KNIGHTS OF THE ROUND TABLE.
THE PROFESSOR'S FAVORITE BOOK, THE ONCE AND FUTURE KING. BUT HE ALWAYS SAW HIMSELF AS MERLIN, SHOWING THE WAY.
HAVE YOU EVER WONDERED THEN, WHO REPRESENTS KING ARTHUR?
LIKE HIM, WE CANNOT FOREVER USE OUR TEACHER AS A CRUTCH.
MISS HIM, YES, BUT WE HAVE TO FLY BY OURSELVES...
...AND LEARN TO TAKE THE CONSEQUENCES--GOOD OR ILL--OF OUR ACTIONS.
SO EASILY SAID.
I MISSED YOU, TOO, ORORO.
I'M GLAD YOU'RE NOT DEAD.
AND I, YOU!
FAREWELL!
I MISSED YOU!
I'M SO GLAD Y'RE ALIVE!!
HOW NICE F'R YOU. PITY SOME OTHERS WERE NA' QUITE SO LUCKY!
THAT IS NOT FAIR, RAHNE.
NO, IT'S NOT! ANYMORE THAN WAS THE BULLET THAT TOOK POOR DOUG RAMSEY'S LIFE!

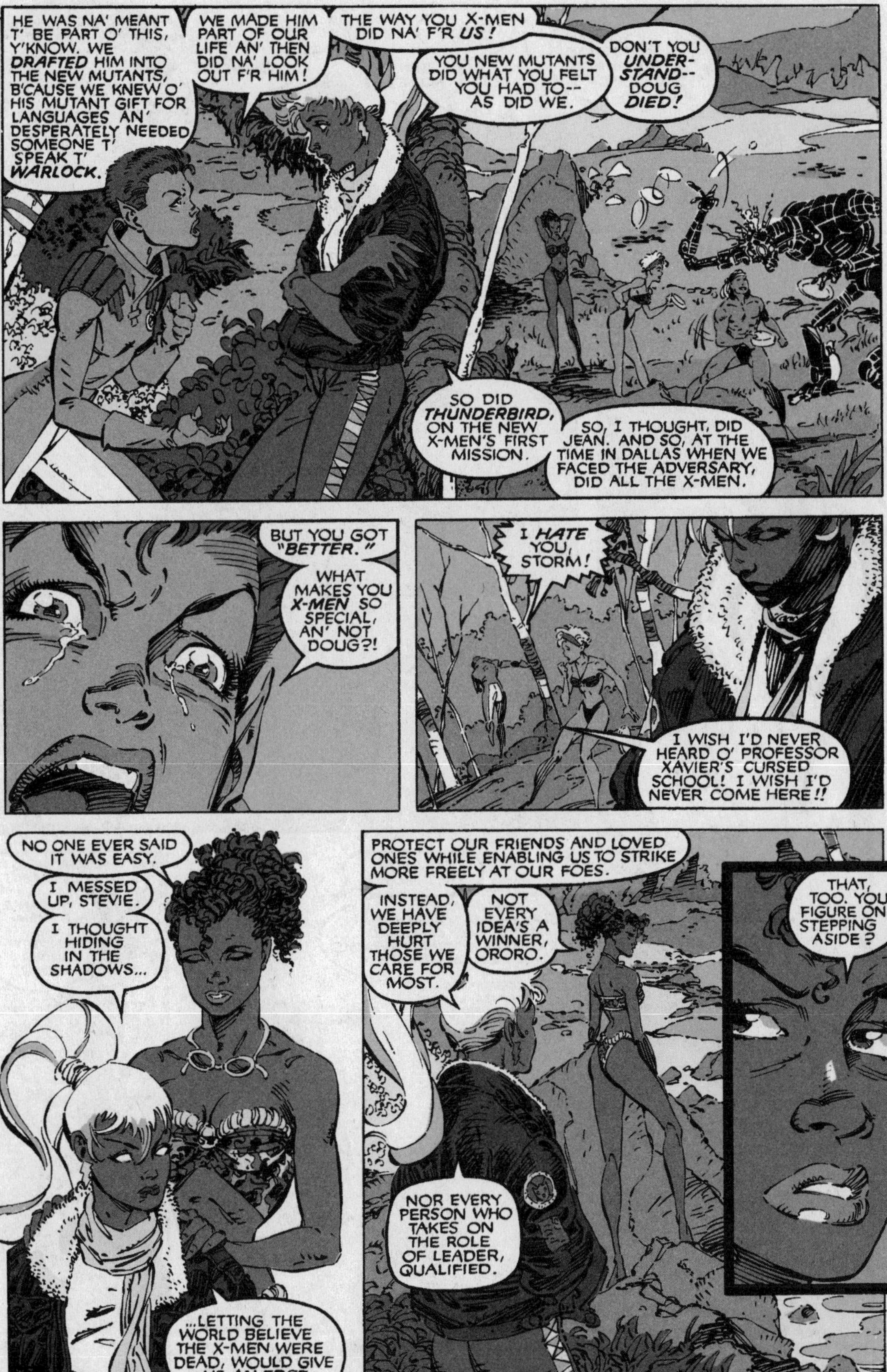
HE WAS NA' MEANT T' BE PART O' THIS, Y'KNOW. WE DRAFTED HIM INTO THE NEW MUTANTS, B'CAUSE WE KNEW O' HIS MUTANT GIFT FOR LANGUAGES AN' DESPERATELY NEEDED SOMEONE T' SPEAK T' WARLOCK.
WE MADE HIM PART OF OUR LIFE AN' THEN DID NA' LOOK OUT F'R HIM!
THE WAY YOU X-MEN DID NA' F'R US!
YOU NEW MUTANTS DID WHAT YOU FELT YOU HAD TO-- AS DID WE.
DON'T YOU UNDER-STAND--DOUG DIED!
SO DID THUNDERBIRD, ON THE NEW X-MEN'S FIRST MISSION.
SO, I THOUGHT, DID JEAN. AND SO, AT THE TIME IN DALLAS WHEN WE FACED THE ADVERSARY, DID ALL THE X-MEN.
BUT YOU GOT "BETTER."
WHAT MAKES YOU X-MEN SO SPECIAL, AN' NOT DOUG?!
I HATE YOU, STORM!
I WISH I'D NEVER HEARD O' PROFESSOR XAVIER'S CURSED SCHOOL! I WISH I'D NEVER COME HERE!!
NO ONE EVER SAID IT WAS EASY.
I MESSED UP, STEVIE.
I THOUGHT HIDING IN THE SHADOWS...
...LETTING THE WORLD BELIEVE THE X-MEN WERE DEAD, WOULD GIVE US AN EDGE.
PROTECT OUR FRIENDS AND LOVED ONES WHILE ENABLING US TO STRIKE MORE FREELY AT OUR FOES.
INSTEAD, WE HAVE DEEPLY HURT THOSE WE CARE FOR MOST.
NOT EVERY IDEA'S A WINNER, ORORO.
NOR EVERY PERSON WHO TAKES ON THE ROLE OF LEADER, QUALIFIED.
THAT, TOO. YOU FIGURE ON STEPPING ASIDE?

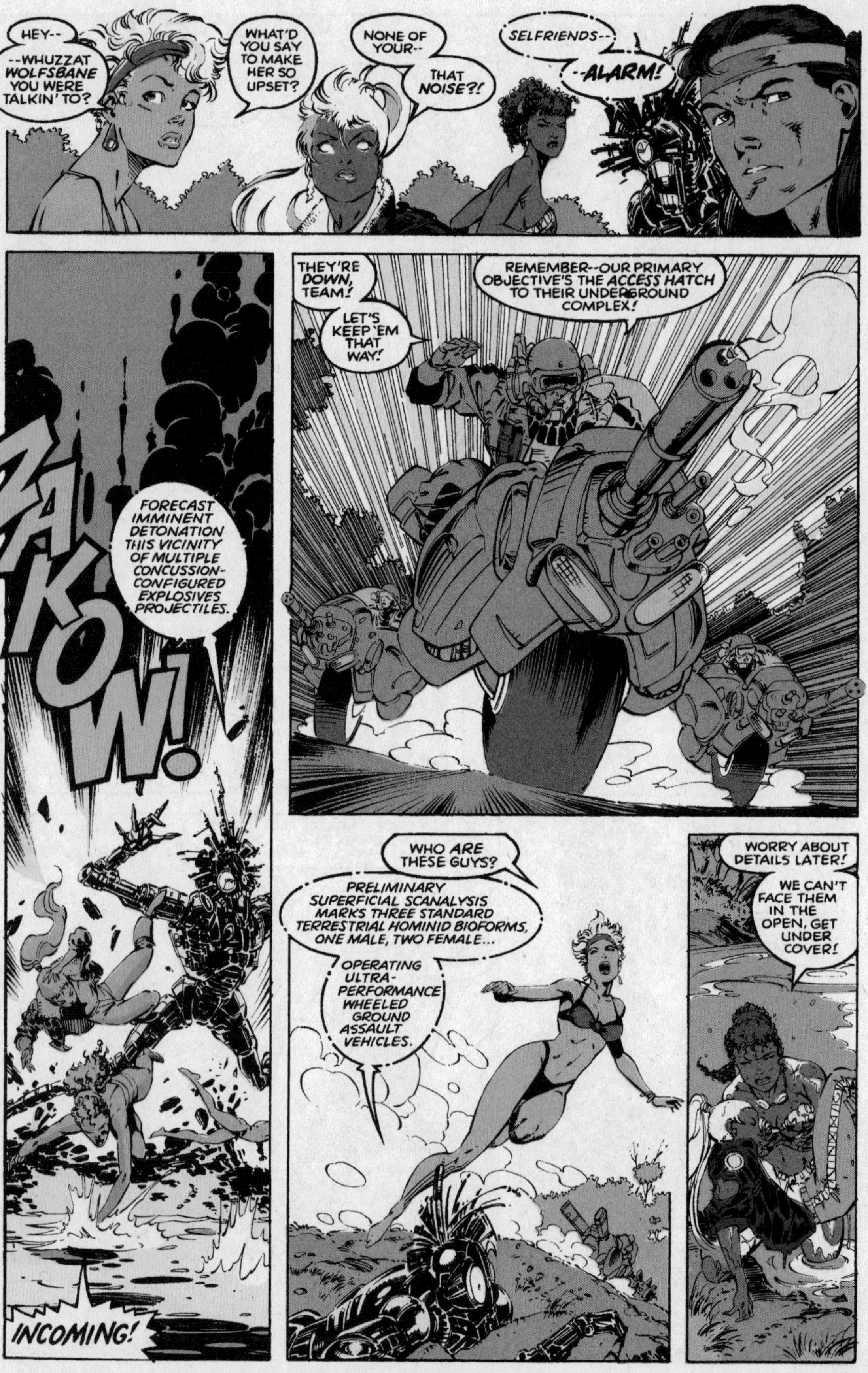
HEY--
--WHUZZAT WOLFSBANE YOU WERE TALKIN' TO?
WHAT'D YOU SAY TO MAKE HER SO UPSET?
NONE OF YOUR--
THAT NOISE?!
SELFRIENDS--
--ALARM!
ZAKOW!
FORECAST IMMINENT DETONATION THIS VICINITY OF MULTIPLE CONCUSSION-CONFIGURED EXPLOSIVES PROJECTILES.
INCOMING!
THEY'RE DOWN, TEAM!
LET'S KEEP 'EM THAT WAY!
REMEMBER--OUR PRIMARY OBJECTIVE'S THE ACCESS HATCH TO THEIR UNDERGROUND COMPLEX!
WHO ARE THESE GUYS?
PRELIMINARY SUPERFICIAL SCANALYSIS MARKS THREE STANDARD TERRESTRIAL HOMINID BIOFORMS, ONE MALE, TWO FEMALE...
OPERATING ULTRA-PERFORMANCE WHEELED GROUND ASSAULT VEHICLES.
WORRY ABOUT DETAILS LATER!
WE CAN'T FACE THEM IN THE OPEN, GET UNDER COVER!

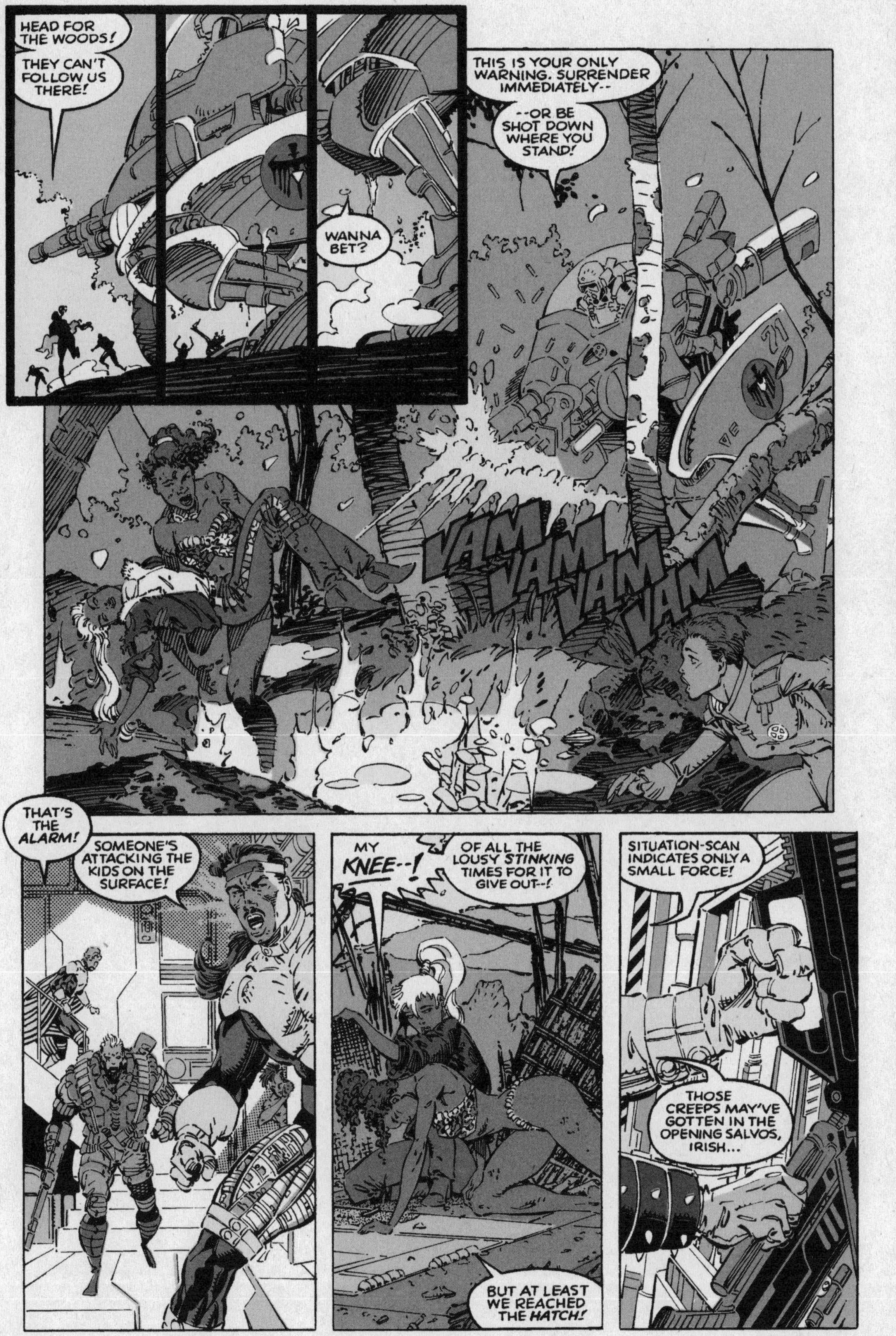

HEAD FOR THE WOODS!
THEY CAN'T FOLLOW US THERE!
WANNA BET?
THIS IS YOUR ONLY WARNING. SURRENDER IMMEDIATELY--
--OR BE SHOT DOWN WHERE YOU STAND!
VAM VAM VAM VAM
THAT'S THE ALARM!
SOMEONE'S ATTACKING THE KIDS ON THE SURFACE!
MY KNEE--!
OF ALL THE LOUSY STINKING TIMES FOR IT TO GIVE OUT--!
BUT AT LEAST WE REACHED THE HATCH!
SITUATION-SCAN INDICATES ONLY A SMALL FORCE!
THOSE CREEPS MAY'VE GOTTEN IN THE OPENING SALVOS, IRISH...

X-MEN

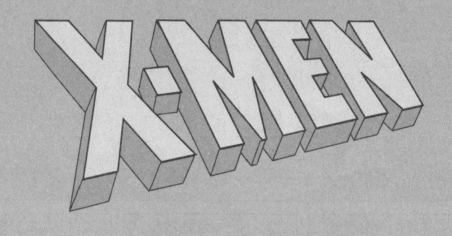

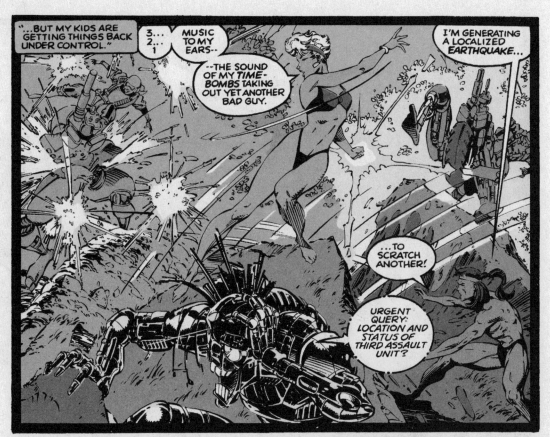

"...BUT MY KIDS ARE GETTING THINGS BACK UNDER CONTROL."

3... 2... 1

MUSIC TO MY EARS--

--THE SOUND OF MY *TIME-BOMBS* TAKING OUT YET ANOTHER BAD GUY.

I'M GENERATING A LOCALIZED *EARTHQUAKE*...

...TO SCRATCH ANOTHER!

URGENT QUERY: LOCATION AND STATUS OF THIRD ASSAULT UNIT?

COMING OUR WAY, FAST!

THE UNIFORMS AND EQUIPMENT--

--THESE ARE *GENOSHAN MAGISTRATES!*

OPERATING ON UNITED STATES SOIL? THEY WOULDN'T DARE!

THEY HAVE DONE IT BEFORE.

NEW MUTANTS! WE MUST WITHDRAW BELOW GROUND-- AT ONCE!

WHY BOTHER?

WE'VE PRETTY MUCH WON!

B'SIDES, WE DON'T TAKE ORDERS FROM THE X-MEN!

FATAL MISTAKE, GENEJOKE.

SHOULD'VE SCAMPERED WHILE YOU HAD THE CHANCE.

BZEEP!

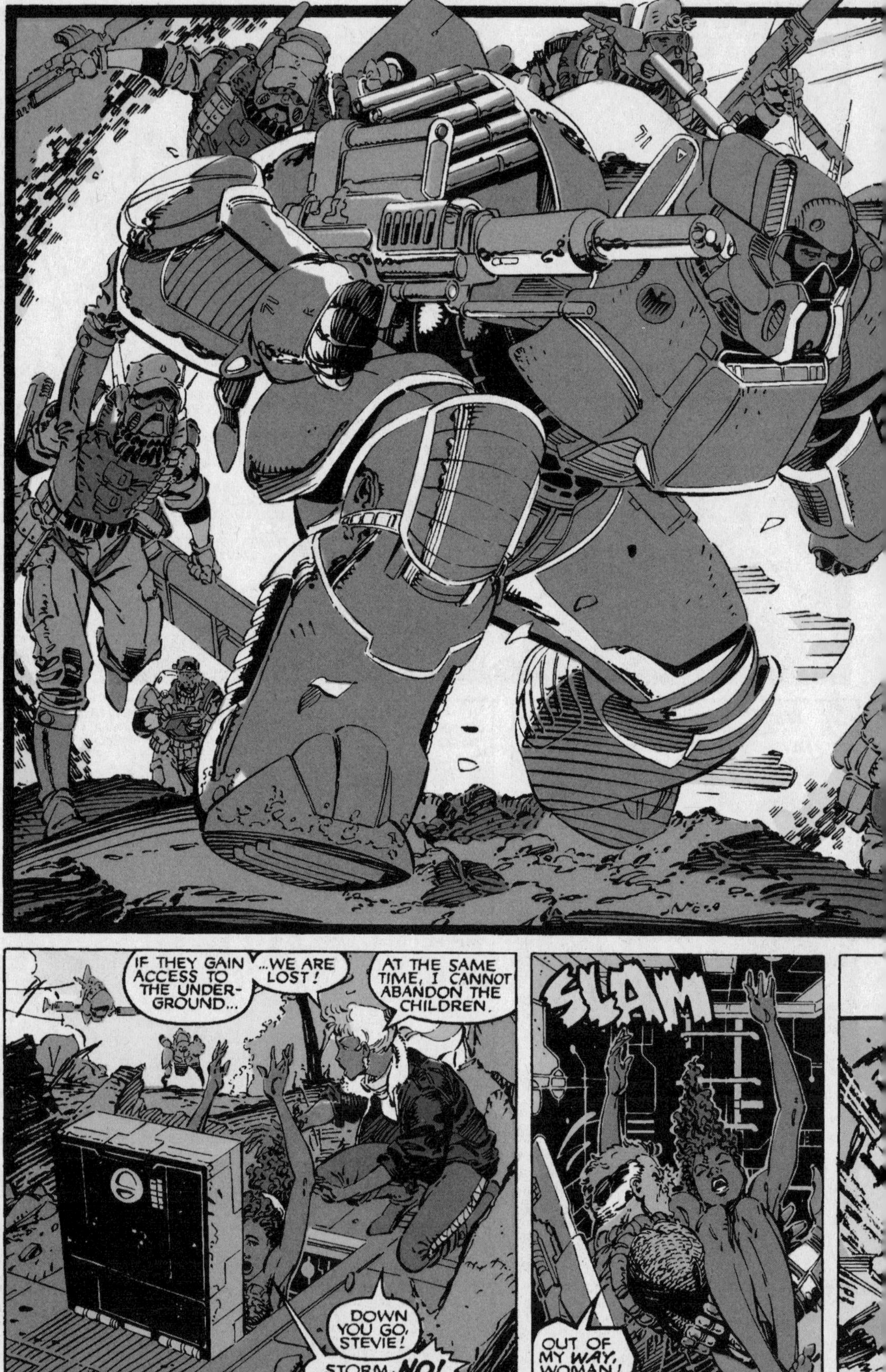
IF THEY GAIN ACCESS TO THE UNDER-GROUND...
...WE ARE LOST!
AT THE SAME TIME, I CANNOT ABANDON THE CHILDREN.
DOWN YOU GO, STEVIE!
STORM, NO!
SLAM
OUT OF MY WAY, WOMAN!

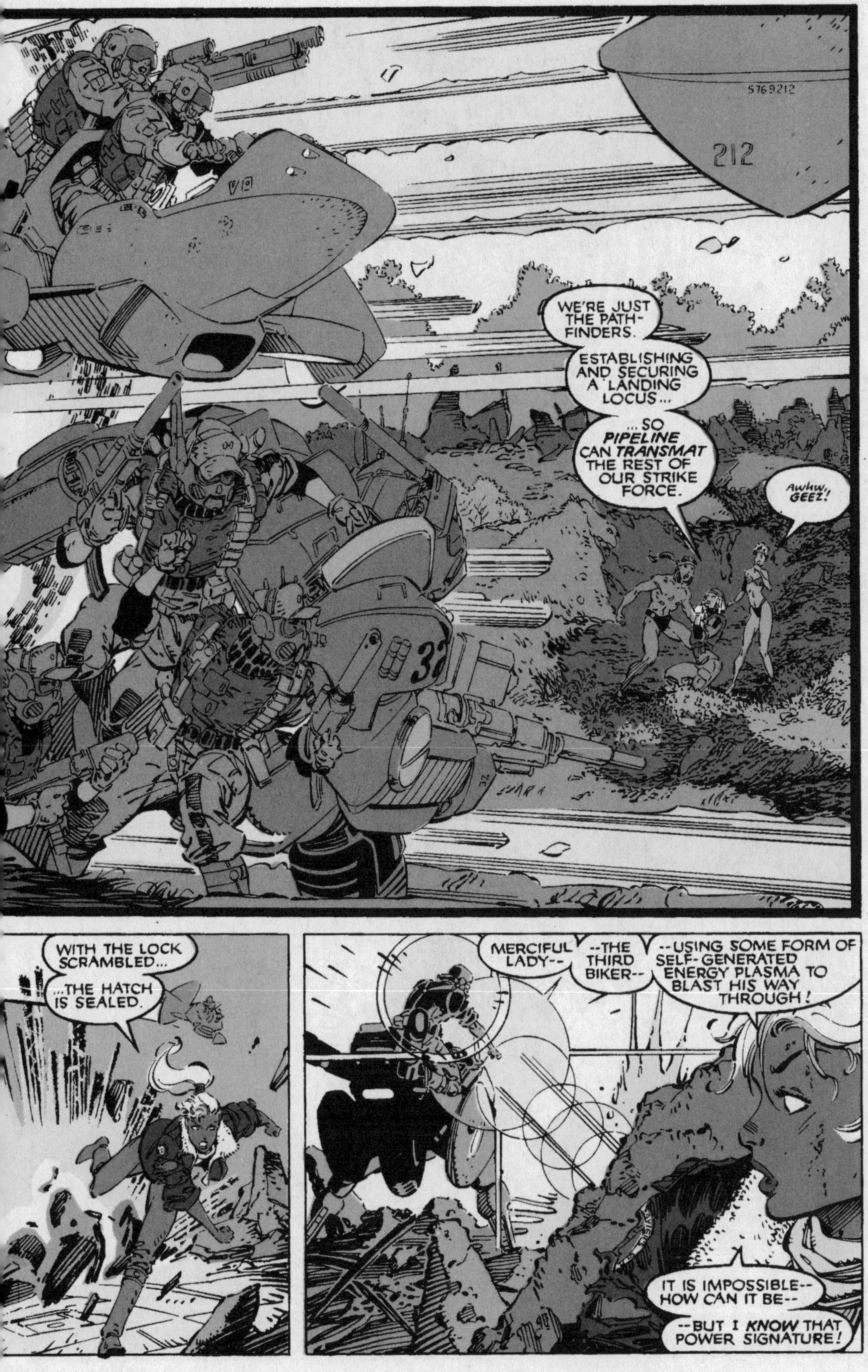

5769212
212
WE'RE JUST THE PATH-FINDERS.
ESTABLISHING AND SECURING A LANDING LOCUS...
...SO PIPELINE CAN TRANSMAT THE REST OF OUR STRIKE FORCE.
Awhw, GEEZ!
WITH THE LOCK SCRAMBLED...
...THE HATCH IS SEALED.
MERCIFUL LADY--
--THE THIRD BIKER--
--USING SOME FORM OF SELF-GENERATED ENERGY PLASMA TO BLAST HIS WAY THROUGH!
IT IS IMPOSSIBLE-- HOW CAN IT BE--
--BUT I KNOW THAT POWER SIGNATURE!

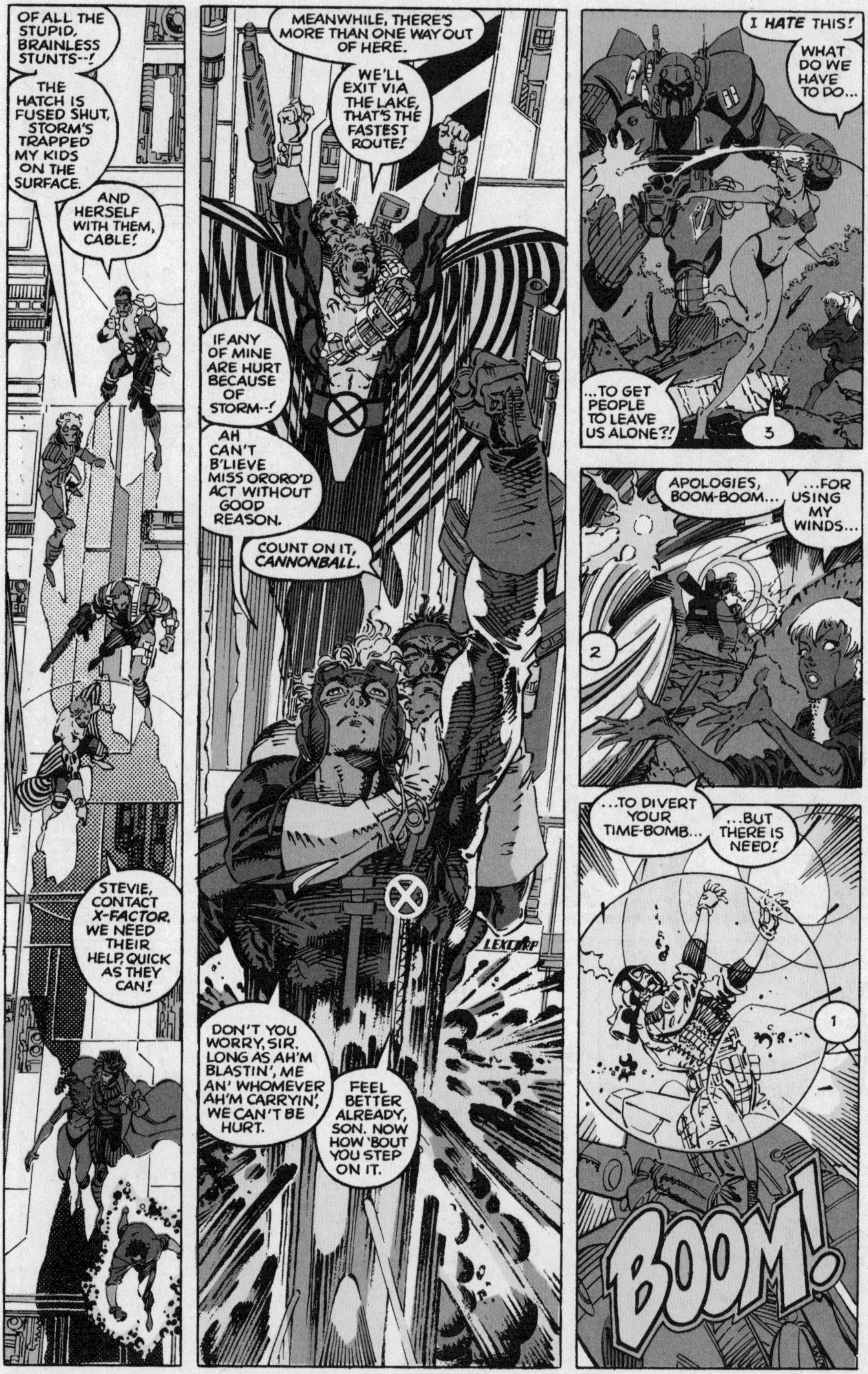
OF ALL THE STUPID, BRAINLESS STUNTS--!
THE HATCH IS FUSED SHUT, STORM'S TRAPPED MY KIDS ON THE SURFACE.
AND HERSELF WITH THEM, CABLE!
STEVIE, CONTACT X-FACTOR. WE NEED THEIR HELP, QUICK AS THEY CAN!
MEANWHILE, THERE'S MORE THAN ONE WAY OUT OF HERE.
WE'LL EXIT VIA THE LAKE, THAT'S THE FASTEST ROUTE!
IF ANY OF MINE ARE HURT BECAUSE OF STORM--!
AH CAN'T B'LIEVE MISS ORORO'D ACT WITHOUT GOOD REASON.
COUNT ON IT, CANNONBALL.
LEXCARP
DON'T YOU WORRY, SIR. LONG AS AH'M BLASTIN', ME AN' WHOMEVER AH'M CARRYIN', WE CAN'T BE HURT.
FEEL BETTER ALREADY, SON. NOW HOW 'BOUT YOU STEP ON IT.
I HATE THIS!
WHAT DO WE HAVE TO DO...
...TO GET PEOPLE TO LEAVE US ALONE?!
3
APOLOGIES, BOOM-BOOM...
...FOR USING MY WINDS...
2
...TO DIVERT YOUR TIME-BOMB...
...BUT THERE IS NEED!
1
BOOM!

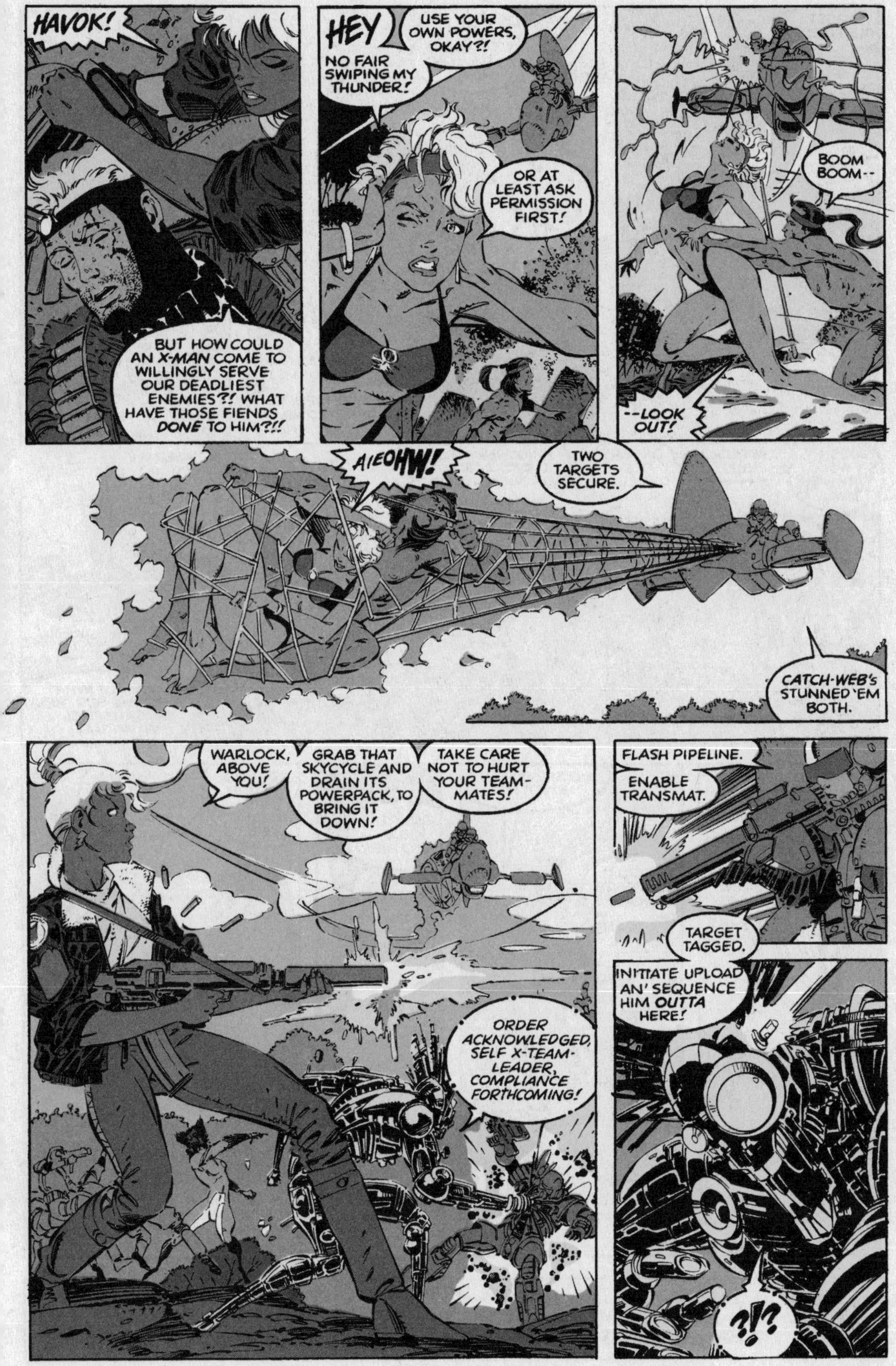
HAVOK!
BUT HOW COULD AN X-MAN COME TO WILLINGLY SERVE OUR DEADLIEST ENEMIES?! WHAT HAVE THOSE FIENDS DONE TO HIM?!!
HEY
NO FAIR SWIPING MY THUNDER!
USE YOUR OWN POWERS, OKAY?!
OR AT LEAST ASK PERMISSION FIRST!
BOOM BOOM--
--LOOK OUT!
AIEOHW!
TWO TARGETS SECURE.
CATCH-WEB'S STUNNED 'EM BOTH.
WARLOCK, ABOVE YOU!
GRAB THAT SKYCYCLE AND DRAIN ITS POWERPACK, TO BRING IT DOWN!
TAKE CARE NOT TO HURT YOUR TEAM-MATES!
ORDER ACKNOWLEDGED, SELF X-TEAM-LEADER, COMPLIANCE FORTHCOMING!
FLASH PIPELINE.
ENABLE TRANSMAT.
TARGET TAGGED.
INITIATE UPLOAD AN' SEQUENCE HIM OUTTA HERE!
?!?

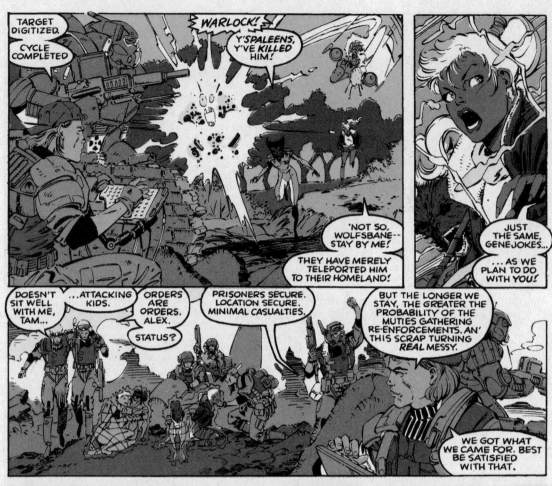

TARGET DIGITIZED.

CYCLE COMPLETED

WARLOCK!

Y'SPALEENS, Y'VE KILLED HIM!

'NOT SO, WOLFSBANE-- STAY BY ME!

THEY HAVE MERELY TELEPORTED HIM TO THEIR HOMELAND!

JUST THE SAME, GENEJOKES...

...AS WE PLAN TO DO WITH YOU!

DOESN'T SIT WELL WITH ME, TAM...

...ATTACKING KIDS.

ORDERS ARE ORDERS, ALEX.

STATUS?

PRISONERS SECURE. LOCATION SECURE. MINIMAL CASUALTIES.

BUT THE LONGER WE STAY, THE GREATER THE PROBABILITY OF THE MUTIES GATHERING RE-ENFORCEMENTS. AN' THIS SCRAP TURNING REAL MESSY.

WE GOT WHAT WE CAME FOR. BEST BE SATISFIED WITH THAT.

SCANT SECONDS LATER...

SENSORS MARK...

...A PULSED ENERGY SURGE ASHORE!

NO SIGN OF ANY HOSTILES!

RESIDUAL ELEMENTS INDICATE...

...A TRANSPORTER EFFECT.

NO BLOOD, NO BODIES, THEIRS OR OURS.

ONLY THE KID'S CLOTHES.

XAVIERS FOR...

I DUNNO WHO DID THIS, INDIAN-- YET!

BUT WHEN I FIND OUT, YOU GOT MY WORD...

...THE PEOPLE RESPONSIBLE ARE GONNA WISH THEY'D NEVER BEEN BORN!

NEXT: PART 2 OF THE X-TINCTION AGENDA FOLLOWS IN NEW MUTANTS #95 AND, IN 30 DAYS, IN THE X-MEN-- IT'S WOLVIE'S TURN!

X-MEN

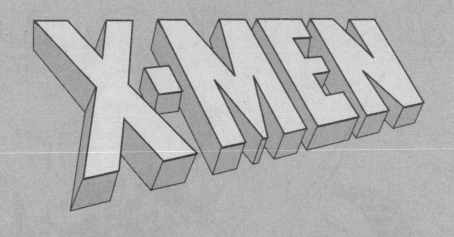

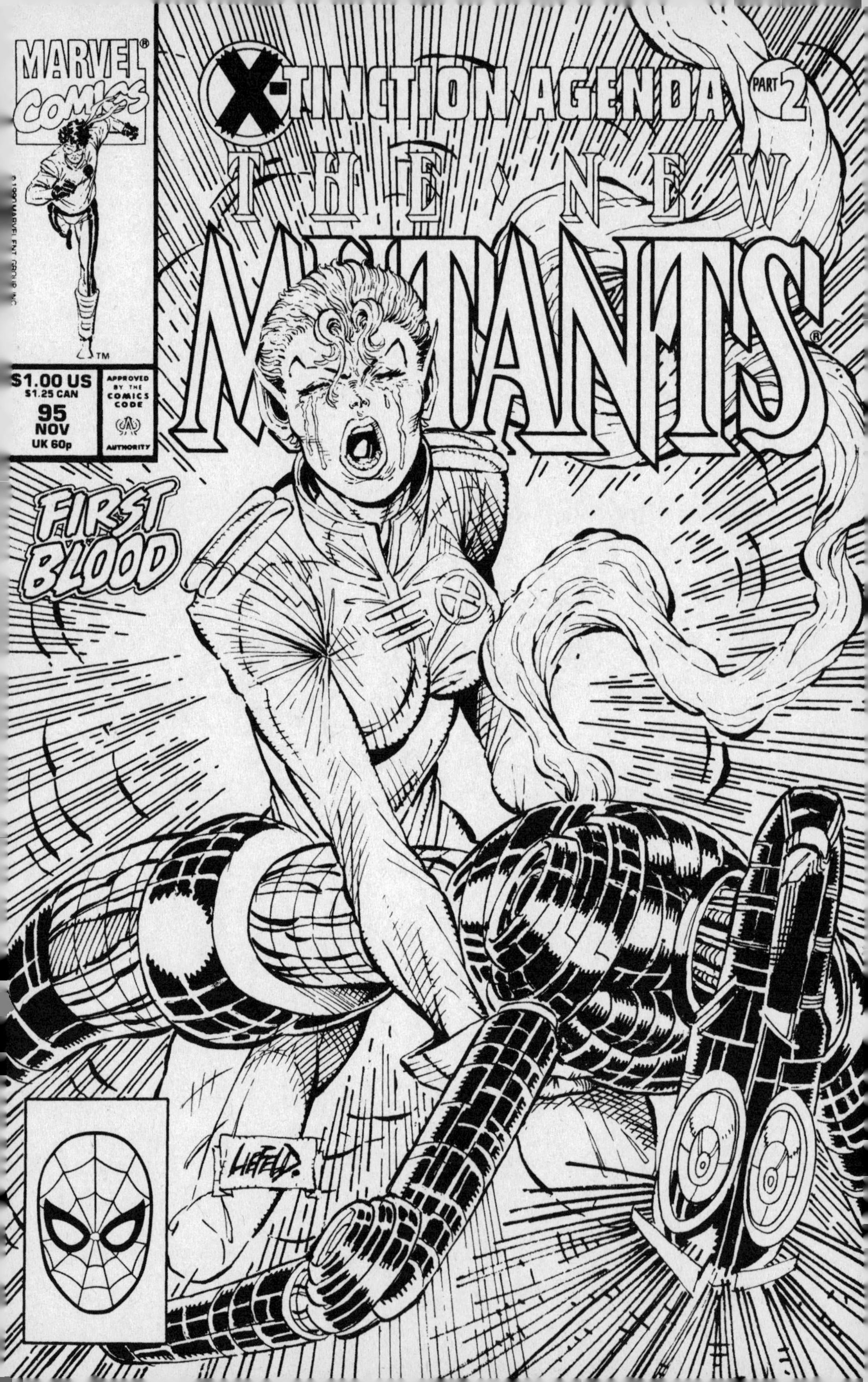
MARVEL® COMICS
X-TINCTION AGENDA PART 2
THE NEW MUTANTS®
$1.00 US
$1.25 CAN
95
NOV
UK 60p
APPROVED BY THE COMICS CODE AUTHORITY
FIRST BLOOD
LIEFELD.

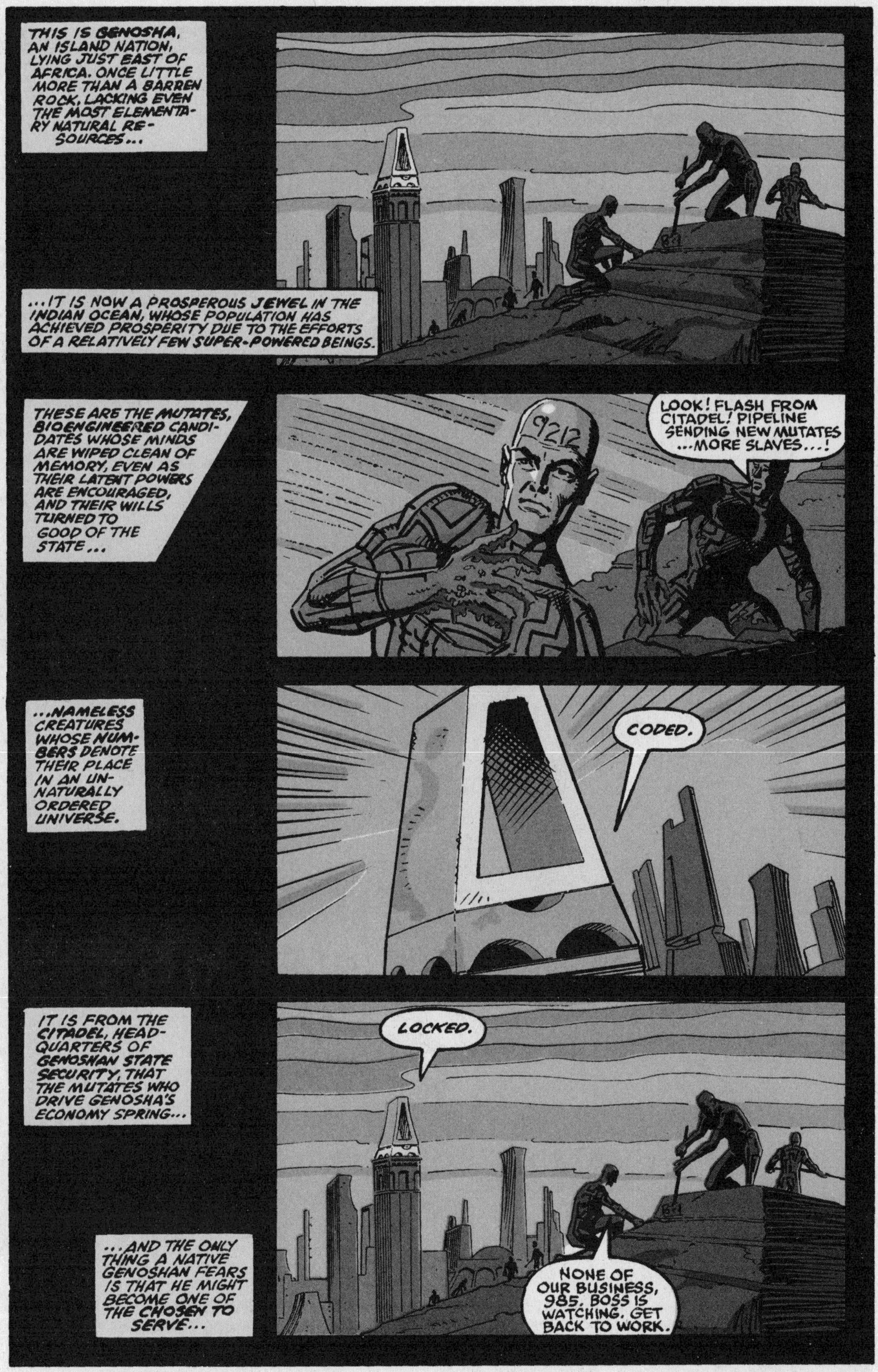
THIS IS GENOSHA, AN ISLAND NATION, LYING JUST EAST OF AFRICA. ONCE LITTLE MORE THAN A BARREN ROCK, LACKING EVEN THE MOST ELEMENTARY NATURAL RESOURCES...
...IT IS NOW A PROSPEROUS JEWEL IN THE INDIAN OCEAN, WHOSE POPULATION HAS ACHIEVED PROSPERITY DUE TO THE EFFORTS OF A RELATIVELY FEW SUPER-POWERED BEINGS.
THESE ARE THE MUTATES, BIOENGINEERED CANDIDATES WHOSE MINDS ARE WIPED CLEAN OF MEMORY, EVEN AS THEIR LATENT POWERS ARE ENCOURAGED, AND THEIR WILLS TURNED TO GOOD OF THE STATE...
9212
LOOK! FLASH FROM CITADEL! PIPELINE SENDING NEW MUTATES ...MORE SLAVES...!
...NAMELESS CREATURES WHOSE NUMBERS DENOTE THEIR PLACE IN AN UNNATURALLY ORDERED UNIVERSE.
CODED.
IT IS FROM THE CITADEL, HEADQUARTERS OF GENOSHAN STATE SECURITY, THAT THE MUTATES WHO DRIVE GENOSHA'S ECONOMY SPRING...
LOCKED.
...AND THE ONLY THING A NATIVE GENOSHAN FEARS IS THAT HE MIGHT BECOME ONE OF THE CHOSEN TO SERVE...
NONE OF OUR BUSINESS, 985. BOSS IS WATCHING. GET BACK TO WORK.

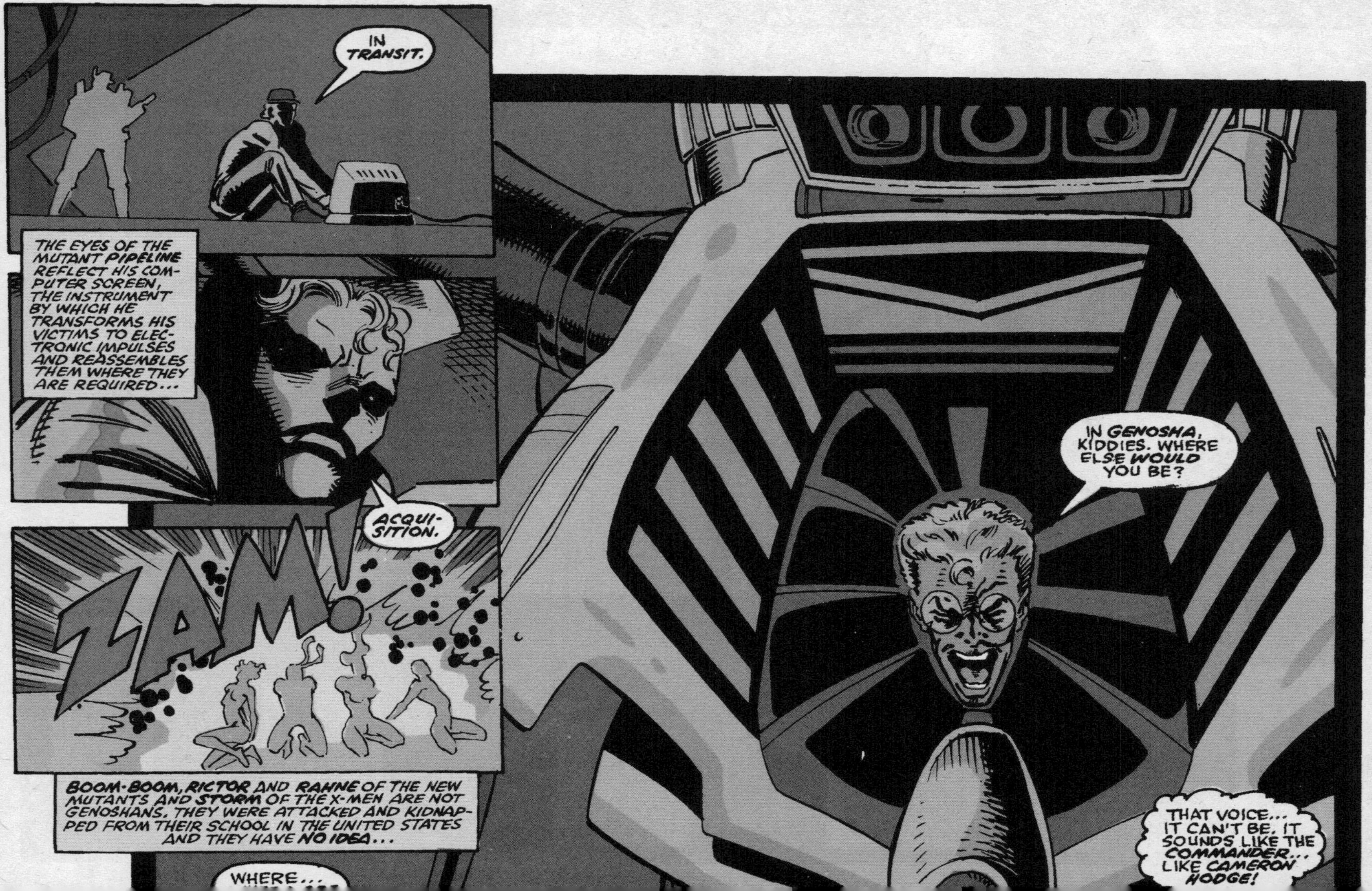
IN TRANSIT.
THE EYES OF THE MUTANT PIPELINE REFLECT HIS COMPUTER SCREEN, THE INSTRUMENT BY WHICH HE TRANSFORMS HIS VICTIMS TO ELECTRONIC IMPULSES AND REASSEMBLES THEM WHERE THEY ARE REQUIRED...
ACQUISITION.
ZAM!
BOOM-BOOM, RICTOR AND RAHNE OF THE NEW MUTANTS AND STORM OF THE X-MEN ARE NOT GENOSHANS. THEY WERE ATTACKED AND KIDNAPPED FROM THEIR SCHOOL IN THE UNITED STATES AND THEY HAVE NO IDEA...
WHERE...
IN GENOSHA, KIDDIES. WHERE ELSE WOULD YOU BE?
THAT VOICE... IT CAN'T BE. IT SOUNDS LIKE THE COMMANDER... LIKE CAMERON HODGE!

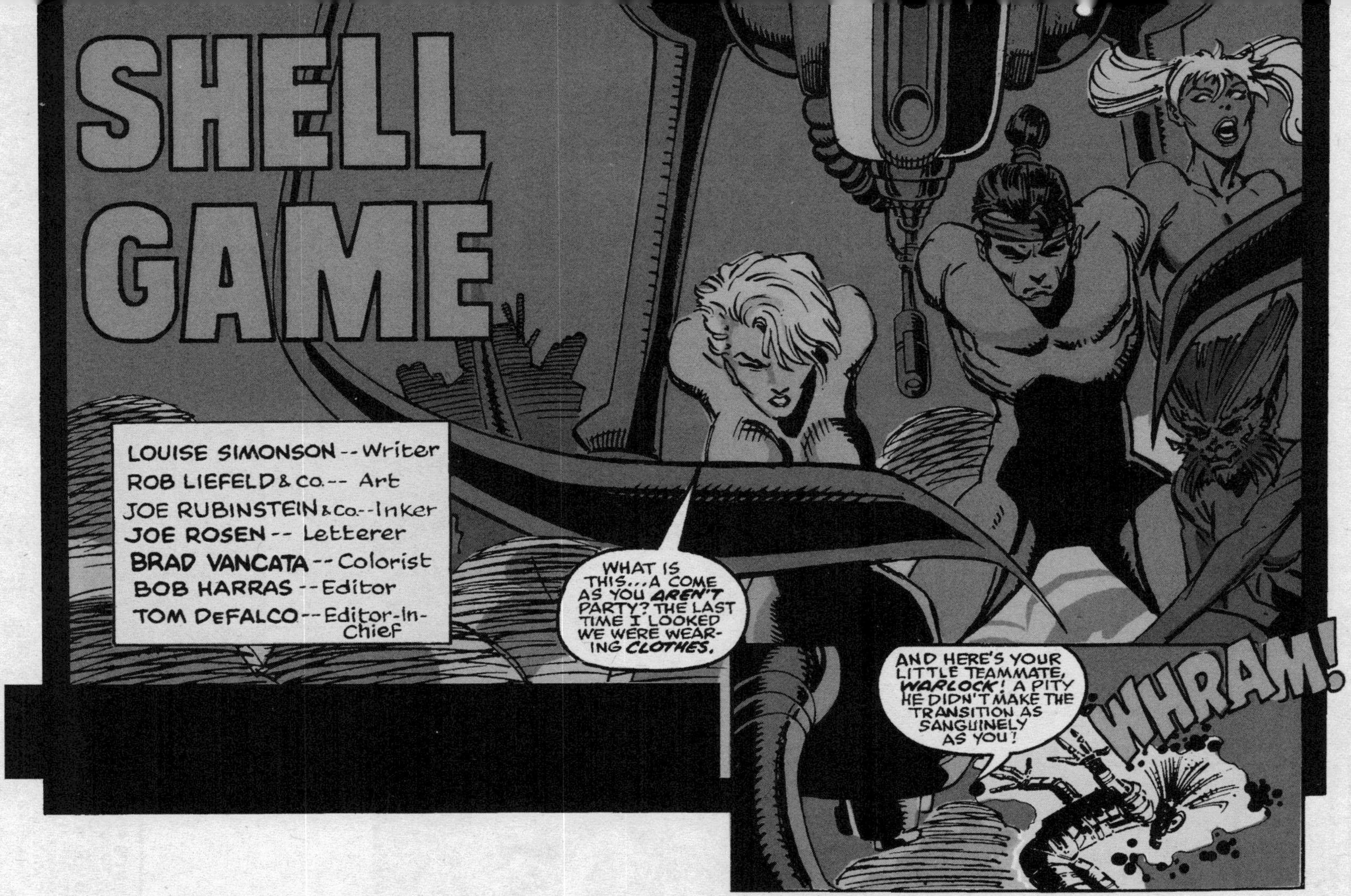
SHELL GAME
LOUISE SIMONSON -- Writer
ROB LIEFELD & CO. -- Art
JOE RUBINSTEIN & CO. -- Inker
JOE ROSEN -- Letterer
BRAD VANCATA -- Colorist
BOB HARRAS -- Editor
TOM DeFALCO -- Editor-in-Chief
WHAT IS THIS...A COME AS YOU AREN'T PARTY? THE LAST TIME I LOOKED WE WERE WEARING CLOTHES.
AND HERE'S YOUR LITTLE TEAMMATE, WARLOCK! A PITY HE DIDN'T MAKE THE TRANSITION AS SANGUINELY AS YOU!
WHRAM!

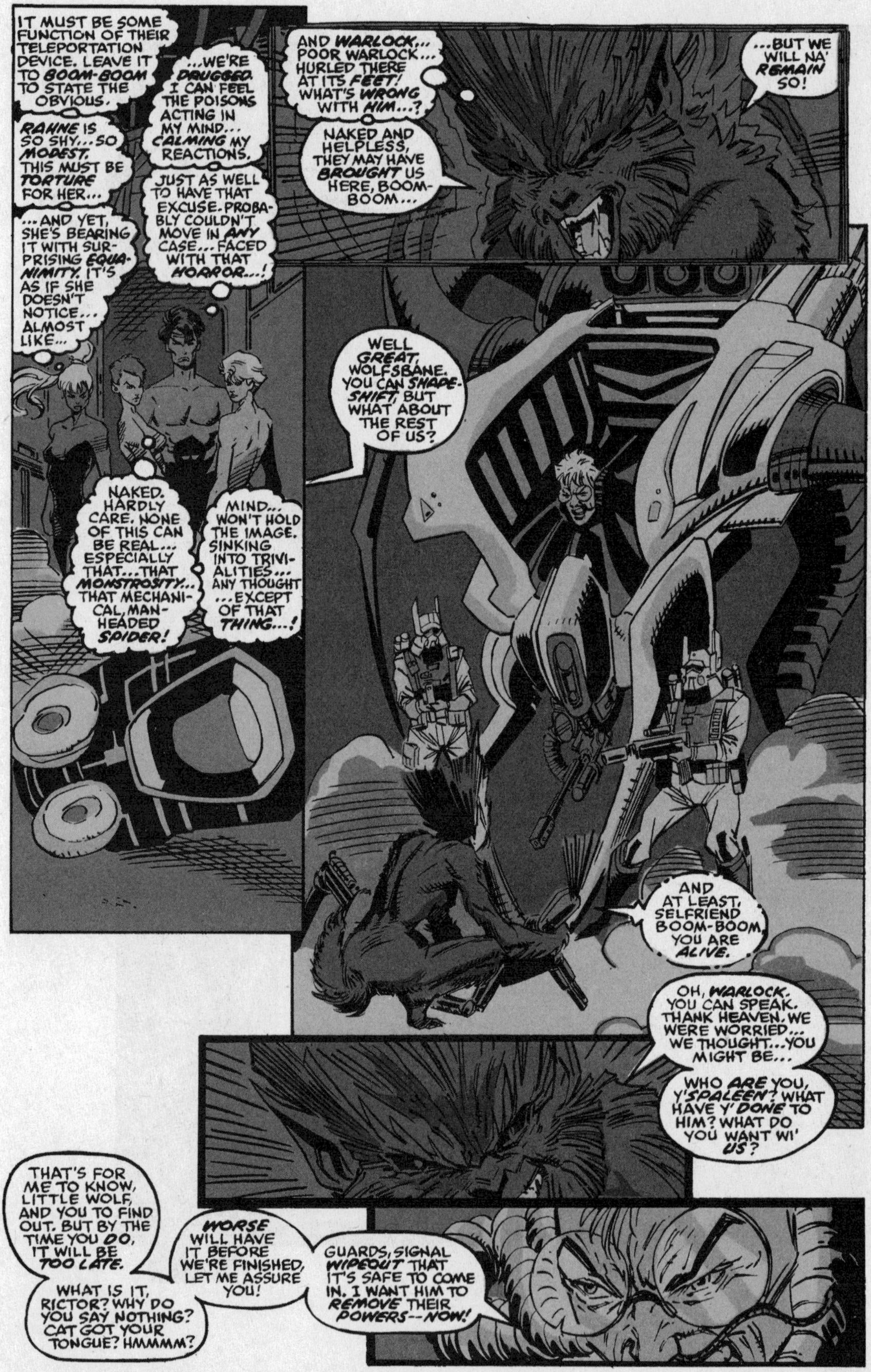

IT MUST BE SOME FUNCTION OF THEIR TELEPORTATION DEVICE. LEAVE IT TO BOOM-BOOM TO STATE THE OBVIOUS.
RAHNE IS SO SHY... SO MODEST. THIS MUST BE TORTURE FOR HER...
...AND YET, SHE'S BEARING IT WITH SURPRISING EQUANIMITY. IT'S AS IF SHE DOESN'T NOTICE... ALMOST LIKE...
...WE'RE DRUGGED. I CAN FEEL THE POISONS ACTING IN MY MIND... CALMING MY REACTIONS.
JUST AS WELL TO HAVE THAT EXCUSE. PROBABLY COULDN'T MOVE IN ANY CASE... FACED WITH THAT HORROR...!
NAKED. HARDLY CARE. NONE OF THIS CAN BE REAL... ESPECIALLY THAT... THAT MONSTROSITY... THAT MECHANICAL, MAN-HEADED SPIDER!
MIND... WON'T HOLD THE IMAGE. SINKING INTO TRIVIALITIES... ANY THOUGHT ...EXCEPT OF THAT THING...!
AND WARLOCK... POOR WARLOCK... HURLED THERE AT ITS FEET! WHAT'S WRONG WITH HIM...?
NAKED AND HELPLESS, THEY MAY HAVE BROUGHT US HERE, BOOM-BOOM...
...BUT WE WILL NA' REMAIN SO!
WELL GREAT, WOLFSBANE. YOU CAN SHAPE-SHIFT, BUT WHAT ABOUT THE REST OF US?
AND AT LEAST, SELFRIEND BOOM-BOOM, YOU ARE ALIVE.
OH, WARLOCK. YOU CAN SPEAK. THANK HEAVEN. WE WERE WORRIED... WE THOUGHT... YOU MIGHT BE...
WHO ARE YOU, Y'SPALEEN? WHAT HAVE Y' DONE TO HIM? WHAT DO YOU WANT WI' US?
THAT'S FOR ME TO KNOW, LITTLE WOLF, AND YOU TO FIND OUT. BUT BY THE TIME YOU DO, IT WILL BE TOO LATE.
WHAT IS IT, RICTOR? WHY DO YOU SAY NOTHING? CAT GOT YOUR TONGUE? HMMMM?
WORSE WILL HAVE IT BEFORE WE'RE FINISHED, LET ME ASSURE YOU!
GUARDS, SIGNAL WIPEOUT THAT IT'S SAFE TO COME IN. I WANT HIM TO REMOVE THEIR POWERS--NOW!

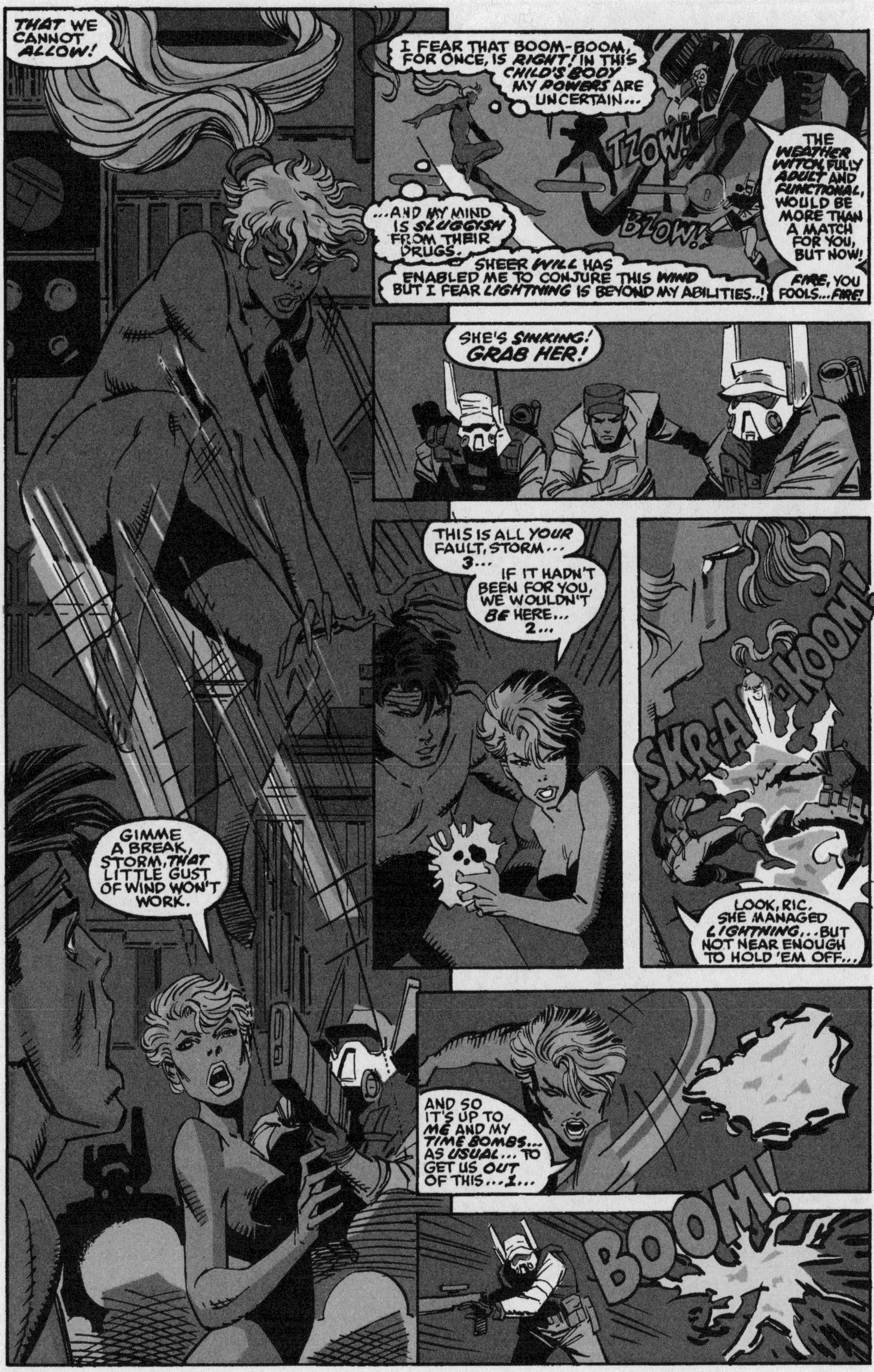
THAT WE CANNOT ALLOW!
I FEAR THAT BOOM-BOOM, FOR ONCE, IS RIGHT! IN THIS CHILD'S BODY MY POWERS ARE UNCERTAIN...
...AND MY MIND IS SLUGGYSH FROM THEIR DRUGS.
SHEER WILL HAS ENABLED ME TO CONJURE THIS WIND BUT I FEAR LIGHTNING IS BEYOND MY ABILITIES..!
TZOW!!
BLOW!
THE WEATHER WITCH, FULLY ADULT AND FUNCTIONAL, WOULD BE MORE THAN A MATCH FOR YOU, BUT NOW!
FIRE, YOU FOOLS...FIRE!
SHE'S SINKING! GRAB HER!
THIS IS ALL YOUR FAULT, STORM... 3...
IF IT HADN'T BEEN FOR YOU, WE WOULDN'T BE HERE... 2...
SHR-A-KOOM!
LOOK, RIC, SHE MANAGED LIGHTNING...BUT NOT NEAR ENOUGH TO HOLD 'EM OFF...
GIMME A BREAK, STORM, THAT LITTLE GUST OF WIND WON'T WORK.
AND SO IT'S UP TO ME AND MY TIME BOMBS... AS USUAL... TO GET US OUT OF THIS... 1...
BOOM!

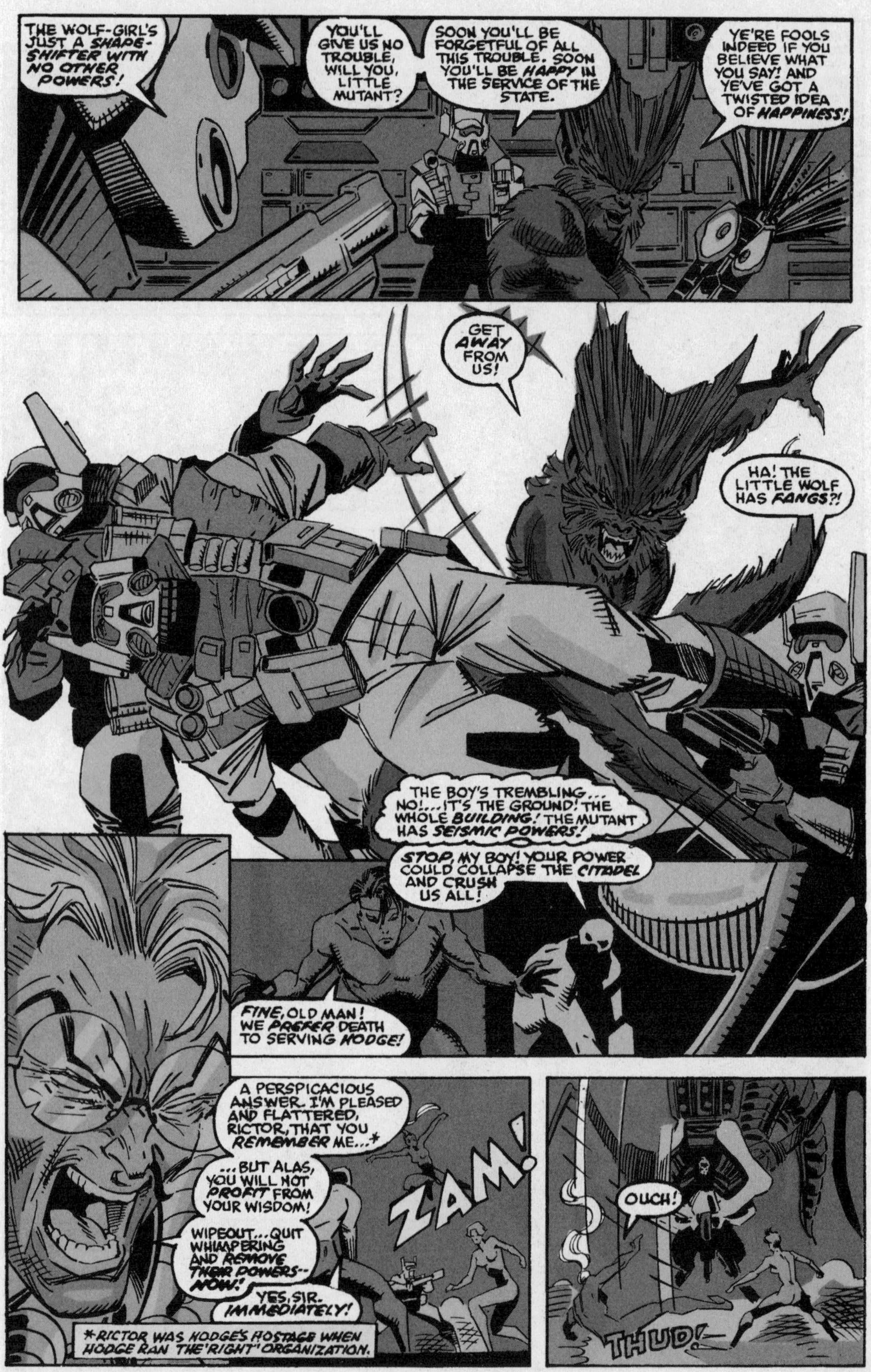
THE WOLF-GIRL'S JUST A SHAPE-SHIFTER WITH NO OTHER POWERS!
YOU'LL GIVE US NO TROUBLE, WILL YOU, LITTLE MUTANT?
SOON YOU'LL BE FORGETFUL OF ALL THIS TROUBLE. SOON YOU'LL BE HAPPY IN THE SERVICE OF THE STATE.
YE'RE FOOLS INDEED IF YOU BELIEVE WHAT YOU SAY! AND YE'VE GOT A TWISTED IDEA OF HAPPINESS!
GET AWAY FROM US!
HA! THE LITTLE WOLF HAS FANGS?!
THE BOY'S TREMBLING... NO!... IT'S THE GROUND! THE WHOLE BUILDING! THE MUTANT HAS SEISMIC POWERS!
STOP, MY BOY! YOUR POWER COULD COLLAPSE THE CITADEL AND CRUSH US ALL!
FINE, OLD MAN! WE PREFER DEATH TO SERVING HODGE!
A PERSPICACIOUS ANSWER. I'M PLEASED AND FLATTERED, RICTOR, THAT YOU REMEMBER ME...*
...BUT ALAS, YOU WILL NOT PROFIT FROM YOUR WISDOM!
WIPEOUT... QUIT WHIMPERING AND REMOVE THEIR POWERS--NOW!
YES, SIR. IMMEDIATELY!
ZAM!
*RICTOR WAS HODGE'S HOSTAGE WHEN HODGE RAN THE "RIGHT" ORGANIZATION.
OUCH!
THUD!

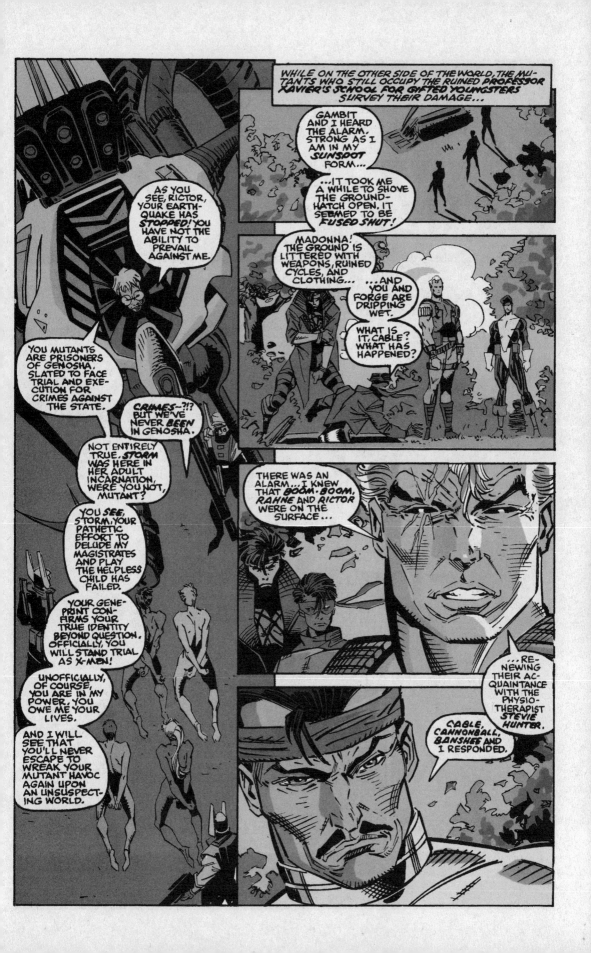

WHILE ON THE OTHER SIDE OF THE WORLD, THE MUTANTS WHO STILL OCCUPY THE RUINED *PROFESSOR XAVIER'S SCHOOL FOR GIFTED YOUNGSTERS* SURVEY THEIR DAMAGE...

AS YOU SEE, *RICTOR*, YOUR EARTH-QUAKE HAS *STOPPED!* YOU HAVE NOT THE ABILITY TO PREVAIL AGAINST ME.

GAMBIT AND I HEARD THE ALARM, STRONG AS I AM IN MY *SUNSPOT* FORM...

...IT TOOK ME A WHILE TO SHOVE THE GROUND-HATCH OPEN. IT SEEMED TO BE *FUSED SHUT!*

MADONNA! THE GROUND IS LITTERED WITH WEAPONS, RUINED CYCLES, AND CLOTHING...

...AND YOU AND FORGE ARE DRIPPING WET.

WHAT IS IT, *CABLE?* WHAT HAS HAPPENED?

YOU MUTANTS ARE PRISONERS OF *GENOSHA*, SLATED TO FACE TRIAL AND EXECUTION FOR CRIMES AGAINST THE STATE.

CRIMES--?!? BUT WE'VE NEVER *BEEN* IN GENOSHA.

NOT ENTIRELY TRUE. *STORM* WAS HERE IN HER ADULT INCARNATION, WERE YOU NOT, MUTANT?

YOU *SEE*, STORM, YOUR PATHETIC EFFORT TO DELUDE MY MAGISTRATES AND PLAY THE HELPLESS CHILD HAS FAILED.

YOUR GENE-PRINT CON-FIRMS YOUR TRUE IDENTITY BEYOND QUESTION. OFFICIALLY, YOU WILL STAND TRIAL AS *X-MEN!*

UNOFFICIALLY, OF COURSE, YOU ARE IN MY POWER. YOU OWE ME YOUR LIVES.

AND I WILL SEE THAT YOU'LL NEVER ESCAPE TO WREAK YOUR MUTANT HAVOC AGAIN UPON AN UNSUSPECTING WORLD.

THERE WAS AN ALARM... I KNEW THAT *BOOM-BOOM, RAHNE* AND *RICTOR* WERE ON THE SURFACE...

...RE-NEWING THEIR AC-QUAINTANCE WITH THE PHYSIO-THERAPIST *STEVIE HUNTER.*

CABLE, CANNONBALL, BANSHEE AND I RESPONDED.

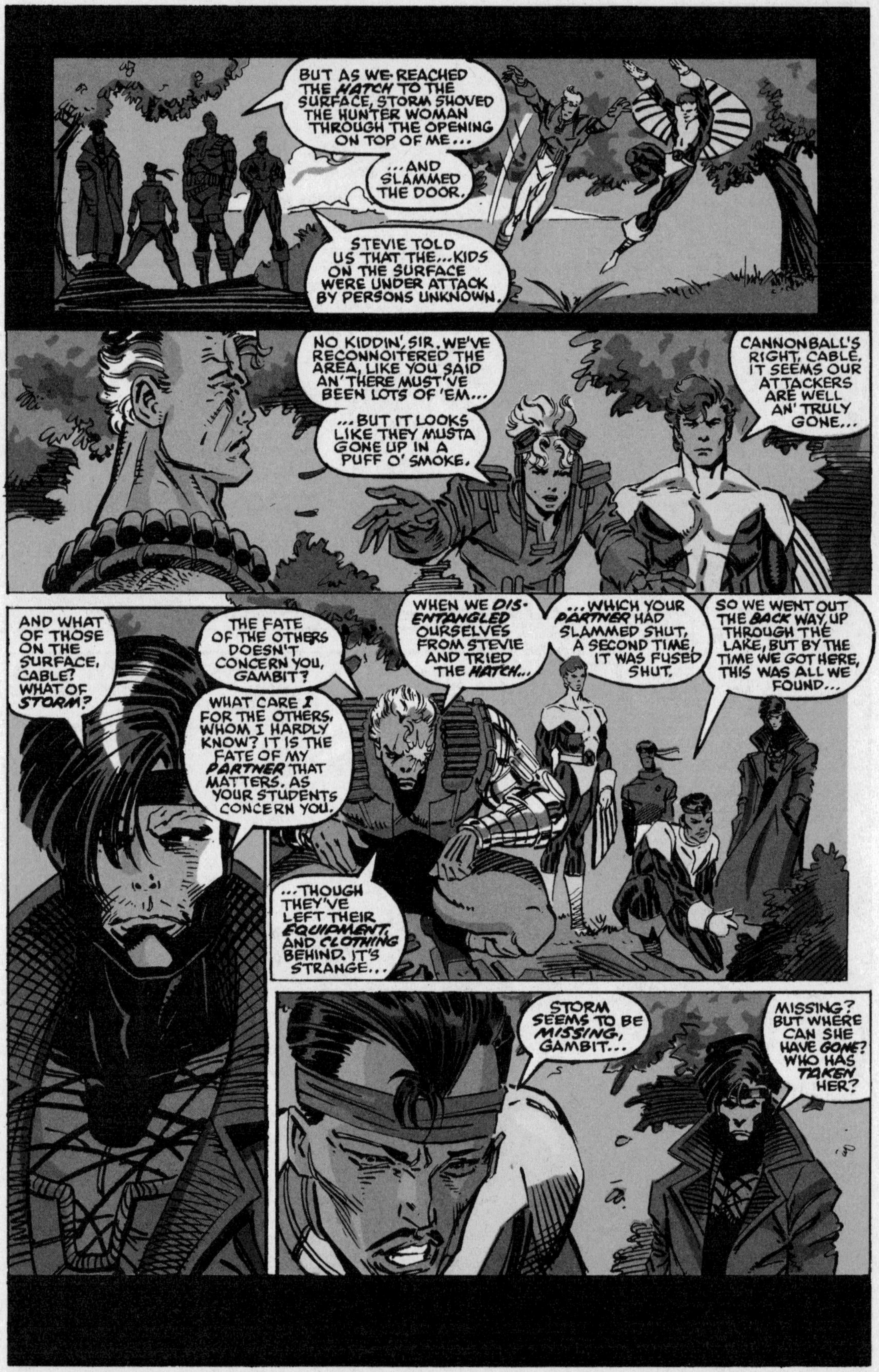

BUT AS WE REACHED THE HATCH TO THE SURFACE, STORM SHOVED THE HUNTER WOMAN THROUGH THE OPENING ON TOP OF ME...
...AND SLAMMED THE DOOR.
STEVIE TOLD US THAT THE...KIDS ON THE SURFACE WERE UNDER ATTACK BY PERSONS UNKNOWN.
NO KIDDIN', SIR. WE'VE RECONNOITERED THE AREA, LIKE YOU SAID AN' THERE MUST'VE BEEN LOTS OF 'EM...
...BUT IT LOOKS LIKE THEY MUSTA GONE UP IN A PUFF O' SMOKE.
CANNONBALL'S RIGHT, CABLE. IT SEEMS OUR ATTACKERS ARE WELL AN' TRULY GONE...
AND WHAT OF THOSE ON THE SURFACE, CABLE? WHAT OF STORM?
THE FATE OF THE OTHERS DOESN'T CONCERN YOU, GAMBIT?
WHAT CARE I FOR THE OTHERS, WHOM I HARDLY KNOW? IT IS THE FATE OF MY PARTNER THAT MATTERS. AS YOUR STUDENTS CONCERN YOU.
WHEN WE DIS-ENTANGLED OURSELVES FROM STEVIE AND TRIED THE HATCH...
...WHICH YOUR PARTNER HAD SLAMMED SHUT, A SECOND TIME, IT WAS FUSED SHUT.
SO WE WENT OUT THE BACK WAY, UP THROUGH THE LAKE, BUT BY THE TIME WE GOT HERE, THIS WAS ALL WE FOUND...
...THOUGH THEY'VE LEFT THEIR EQUIPMENT, AND CLOTHING BEHIND. IT'S STRANGE...
STORM SEEMS TO BE MISSING, GAMBIT...
MISSING? BUT WHERE CAN SHE HAVE GONE? WHO HAS TAKEN HER?

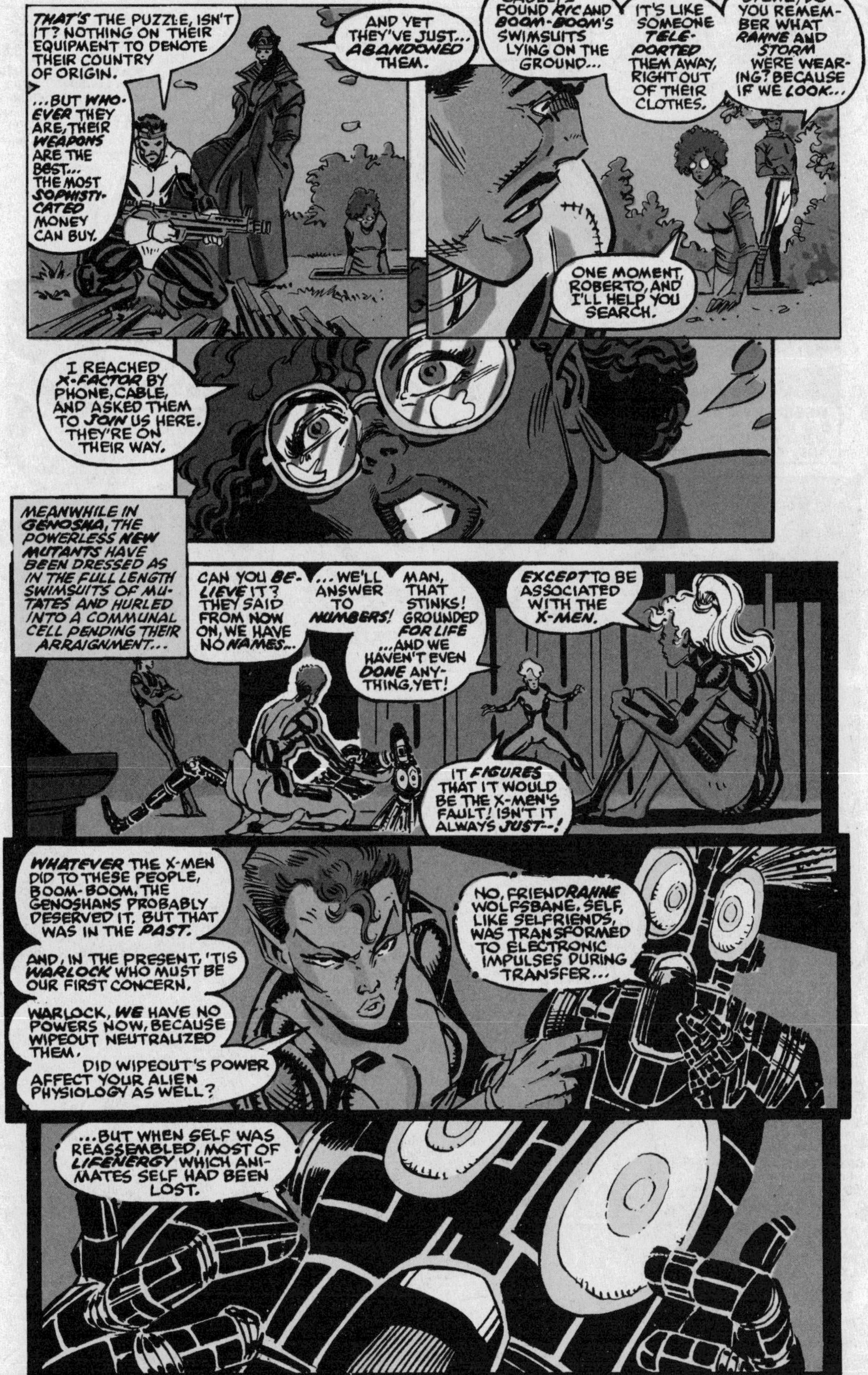
THAT'S THE PUZZLE, ISN'T IT? NOTHING ON THEIR EQUIPMENT TO DENOTE THEIR COUNTRY OF ORIGIN.
...BUT WHOEVER THEY ARE, THEIR WEAPONS ARE THE BEST... THE MOST SOPHISTICATED MONEY CAN BUY.
AND YET THEY'VE JUST... ABANDONED THEM.
CABLE, I FOUND RIC AND BOOM-BOOM'S SWIMSUITS LYING ON THE GROUND...
IT'S LIKE SOMEONE TELEPORTED THEM AWAY, RIGHT OUT OF THEIR CLOTHES.
STEVIE, DO YOU REMEMBER WHAT RAHNE AND STORM WERE WEARING? BECAUSE IF WE LOOK...
ONE MOMENT, ROBERTO, AND I'LL HELP YOU SEARCH.
I REACHED X-FACTOR BY PHONE, CABLE, AND ASKED THEM TO JOIN US HERE. THEY'RE ON THEIR WAY.
MEANWHILE IN GENOSHA, THE POWERLESS NEW MUTANTS HAVE BEEN DRESSED AS IN THE FULL LENGTH SWIMSUITS OF MUTATES AND HURLED INTO A COMMUNAL CELL PENDING THEIR ARRAIGNMENT...
CAN YOU BELIEVE IT? THEY SAID FROM NOW ON, WE HAVE NO NAMES...
...WE'LL ANSWER TO NUMBERS!
MAN, THAT STINKS! GROUNDED FOR LIFE
...AND WE HAVEN'T EVEN DONE ANYTHING, YET!
EXCEPT TO BE ASSOCIATED WITH THE X-MEN.
IT FIGURES THAT IT WOULD BE THE X-MEN'S FAULT! ISN'T IT ALWAYS JUST--!
WHATEVER THE X-MEN DID TO THESE PEOPLE, BOOM-BOOM, THE GENOSHANS PROBABLY DESERVED IT, BUT THAT WAS IN THE PAST.
AND, IN THE PRESENT, 'TIS WARLOCK WHO MUST BE OUR FIRST CONCERN.
WARLOCK, WE HAVE NO POWERS NOW, BECAUSE WIPEOUT NEUTRALIZED THEM.
DID WIPEOUT'S POWER AFFECT YOUR ALIEN PHYSIOLOGY AS WELL?
NO, FRIEND RAHNE WOLFSBANE. SELF, LIKE SELFRIENDS, WAS TRANSFORMED TO ELECTRONIC IMPULSES DURING TRANSFER...
...BUT WHEN SELF WAS REASSEMBLED, MOST OF LIFENERGY WHICH ANIMATES SELF HAD BEEN LOST.

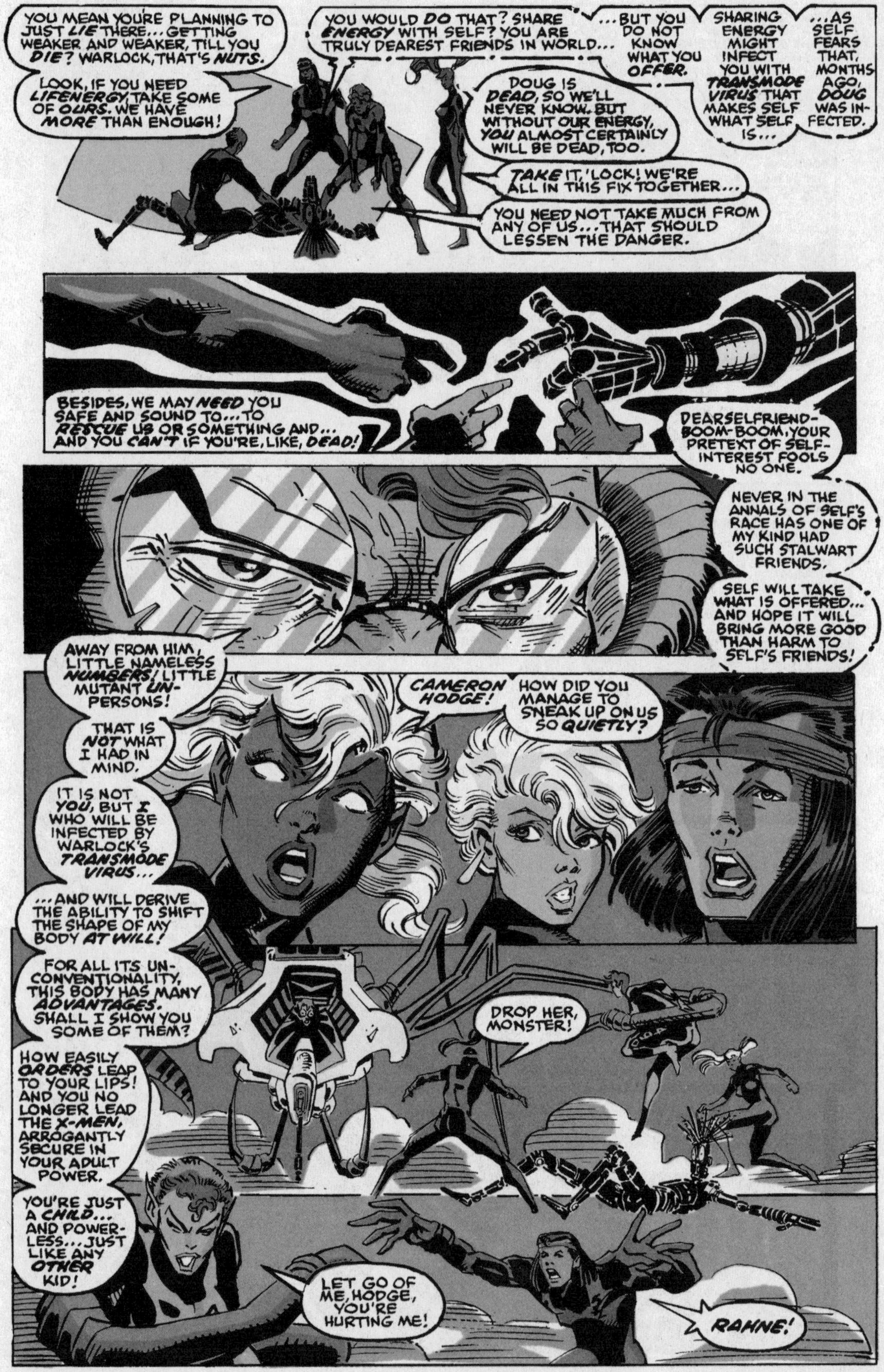

YOU MEAN YOU'RE PLANNING TO JUST LIE THERE... GETTING WEAKER AND WEAKER, TILL YOU DIE? WARLOCK, THAT'S NUTS.
LOOK, IF YOU NEED LIFENERGY, TAKE SOME OF OURS. WE HAVE MORE THAN ENOUGH!
YOU WOULD DO THAT? SHARE ENERGY WITH SELF? YOU ARE TRULY DEAREST FRIENDS IN WORLD...
...BUT YOU DO NOT KNOW WHAT YOU OFFER.
SHARING ENERGY MIGHT INFECT YOU WITH TRANSMODE VIRUS THAT MAKES SELF WHAT SELF IS...
...AS SELF FEARS THAT, MONTHS AGO, DOUG WAS INFECTED.
DOUG IS DEAD, SO WE'LL NEVER KNOW. BUT WITHOUT OUR ENERGY, YOU ALMOST CERTAINLY WILL BE DEAD, TOO.
TAKE IT, 'LOCK! WE'RE ALL IN THIS FIX TOGETHER...
YOU NEED NOT TAKE MUCH FROM ANY OF US... THAT SHOULD LESSEN THE DANGER.
BESIDES, WE MAY NEED YOU SAFE AND SOUND TO... TO RESCUE US OR SOMETHING AND... AND YOU CAN'T IF YOU'RE, LIKE, DEAD!
DEARSELFFRIEND-BOOM-BOOM, YOUR PRETEXT OF SELF-INTEREST FOOLS NO ONE.
NEVER IN THE ANNALS OF SELF'S RACE HAS ONE OF MY KIND HAD SUCH STALWART FRIENDS.
SELF WILL TAKE WHAT IS OFFERED... AND HOPE IT WILL BRING MORE GOOD THAN HARM TO SELF'S FRIENDS!
AWAY FROM HIM, LITTLE NAMELESS NUMBERS! LITTLE MUTANT UN-PERSONS!
CAMERON HODGE!
HOW DID YOU MANAGE TO SNEAK UP ON US SO QUIETLY?
THAT IS NOT WHAT I HAD IN MIND.
IT IS NOT YOU, BUT I WHO WILL BE INFECTED BY WARLOCK'S TRANSMODE VIRUS...
...AND WILL DERIVE THE ABILITY TO SHIFT THE SHAPE OF MY BODY AT WILL!
FOR ALL ITS UN-CONVENTIONALITY, THIS BODY HAS MANY ADVANTAGES. SHALL I SHOW YOU SOME OF THEM?
DROP HER, MONSTER!
HOW EASILY ORDERS LEAP TO YOUR LIPS! AND YOU NO LONGER LEAD THE X-MEN, ARROGANTLY SECURE IN YOUR ADULT POWER.
YOU'RE JUST A CHILD... AND POWER-LESS... JUST LIKE ANY OTHER KID!
LET GO OF ME, HODGE, YOU'RE HURTING ME!
RAHNE!

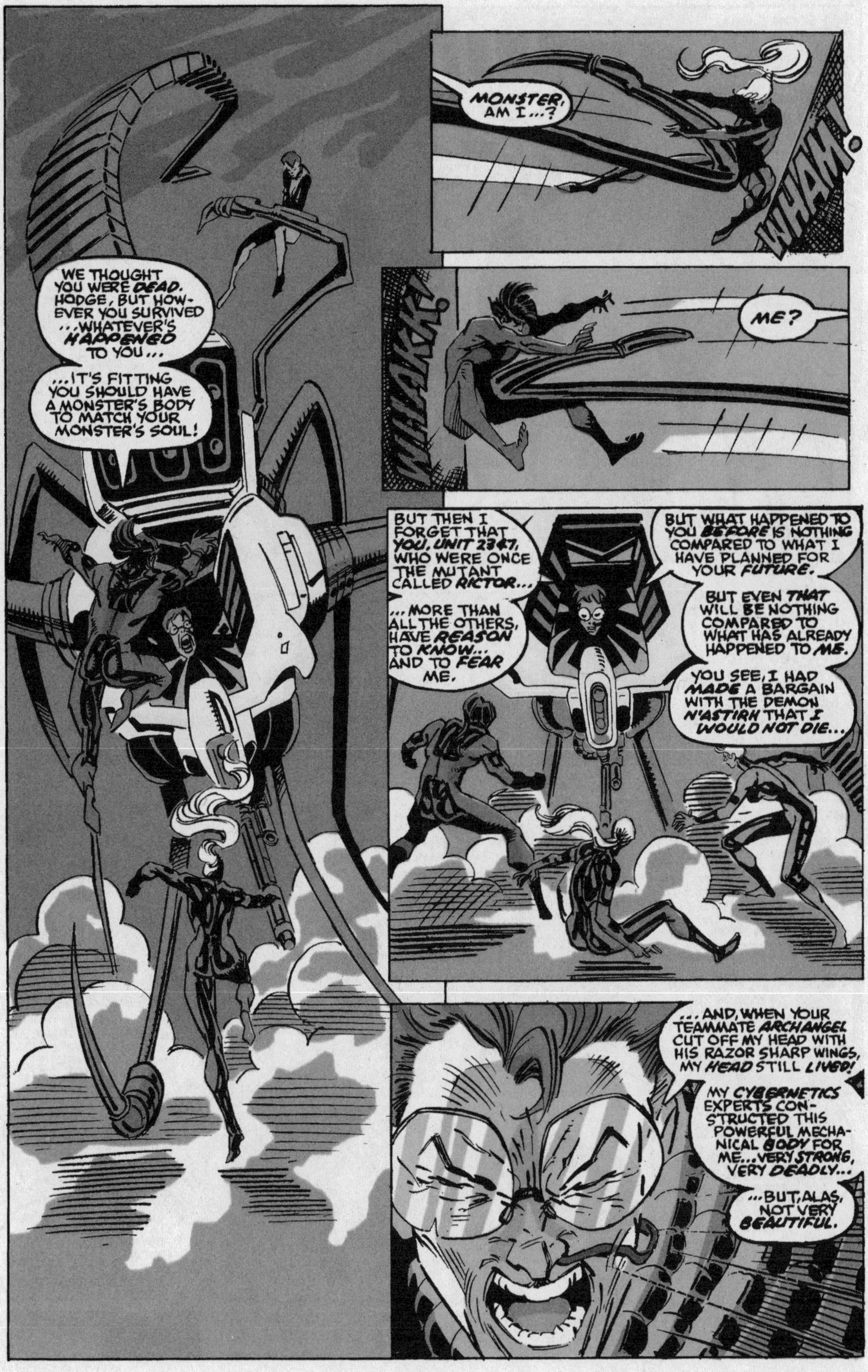

WE THOUGHT YOU WERE DEAD, HODGE, BUT HOWEVER YOU SURVIVED ...WHATEVER'S HAPPENED TO YOU...
...IT'S FITTING YOU SHOULD HAVE A MONSTER'S BODY TO MATCH YOUR MONSTER'S SOUL!
MONSTER, AM I...?
WHAM!
WHAKK!
ME?
BUT THEN I FORGET THAT YOU, UNIT 2347, WHO WERE ONCE THE MUTANT CALLED RICTOR...
...MORE THAN ALL THE OTHERS, HAVE REASON TO KNOW... AND TO FEAR ME.
BUT WHAT HAPPENED TO YOU BEFORE IS NOTHING COMPARED TO WHAT I HAVE PLANNED FOR YOUR FUTURE.
BUT EVEN THAT WILL BE NOTHING COMPARED TO WHAT HAS ALREADY HAPPENED TO ME.
YOU SEE, I HAD MADE A BARGAIN WITH THE DEMON N'ASTIRH THAT I WOULD NOT DIE...
...AND, WHEN YOUR TEAMMATE ARCHANGEL CUT OFF MY HEAD WITH HIS RAZOR SHARP WINGS, MY HEAD STILL LIVED!
MY CYBERNETICS EXPERTS CONSTRUCTED THIS POWERFUL MECHANICAL BODY FOR ME... VERY STRONG, VERY DEADLY...
...BUT, ALAS, NOT VERY BEAUTIFUL.

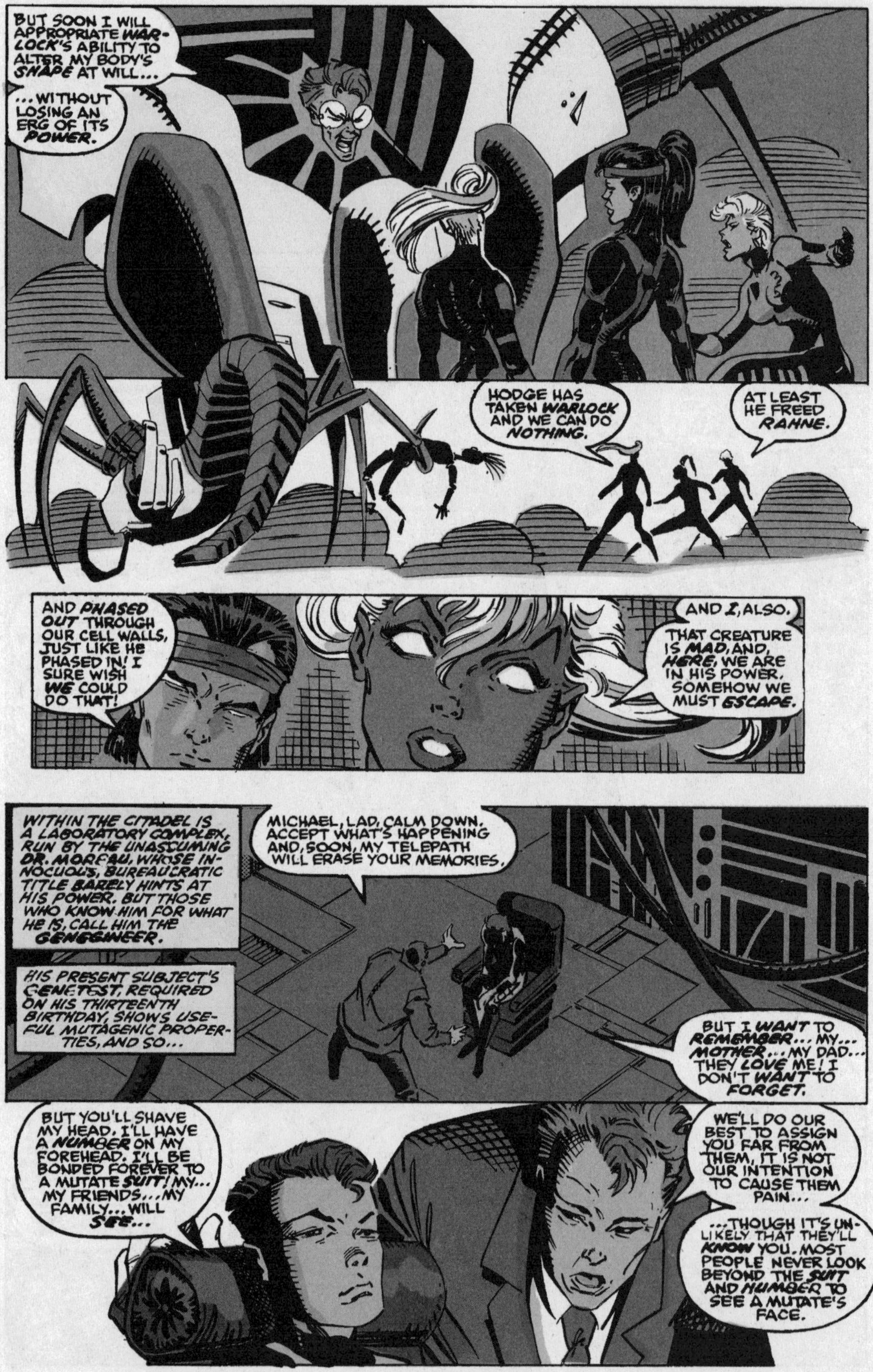
BUT SOON I WILL APPROPRIATE WARLOCK'S ABILITY TO ALTER MY BODY'S SHAPE AT WILL...
...WITHOUT LOSING AN ERG OF ITS POWER.
HODGE HAS TAKEN WARLOCK AND WE CAN DO NOTHING.
AT LEAST HE FREED RAHNE.
AND PHASED OUT THROUGH OUR CELL WALLS, JUST LIKE HE PHASED IN! I SURE WISH WE COULD DO THAT!
AND I, ALSO.
THAT CREATURE IS MAD, AND, HERE, WE ARE IN HIS POWER. SOMEHOW WE MUST ESCAPE.
WITHIN THE CITADEL IS A LABORATORY COMPLEX, RUN BY THE UNASSUMING DR. MOREAU, WHOSE INNOCUOUS, BUREAUCRATIC TITLE BARELY HINTS AT HIS POWER. BUT THOSE WHO KNOW HIM FOR WHAT HE IS, CALL HIM THE GENEGINEER.
HIS PRESENT SUBJECT'S GENETEST, REQUIRED ON HIS THIRTEENTH BIRTHDAY, SHOWS USEFUL MUTAGENIC PROPERTIES, AND SO...
MICHAEL, LAD, CALM DOWN. ACCEPT WHAT'S HAPPENING AND, SOON, MY TELEPATH WILL ERASE YOUR MEMORIES.
BUT I WANT TO REMEMBER... MY... MOTHER... MY DAD... THEY LOVE ME! I DON'T WANT TO FORGET.
BUT YOU'LL SHAVE MY HEAD. I'LL HAVE A NUMBER ON MY FOREHEAD. I'LL BE BONDED FOREVER TO A MUTATE SUIT! MY... MY FRIENDS... MY FAMILY... WILL SEE...
WE'LL DO OUR BEST TO ASSIGN YOU FAR FROM THEM. IT IS NOT OUR INTENTION TO CAUSE THEM PAIN...
...THOUGH IT'S UNLIKELY THAT THEY'LL KNOW YOU. MOST PEOPLE NEVER LOOK BEYOND THE SUIT AND NUMBER TO SEE A MUTATE'S FACE.

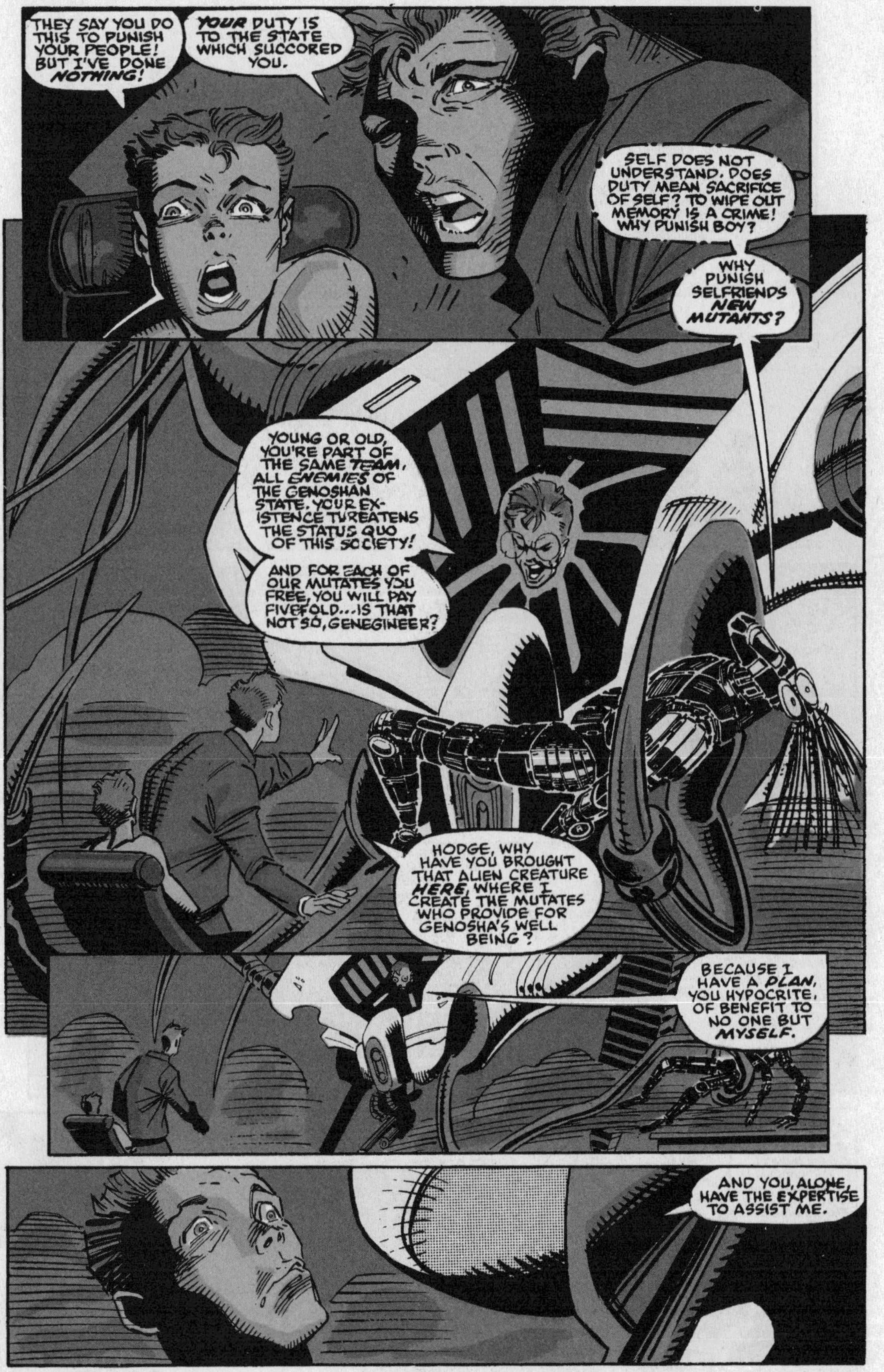
THEY SAY YOU DO THIS TO PUNISH YOUR PEOPLE! BUT I'VE DONE NOTHING!
YOUR DUTY IS TO THE STATE WHICH SUCCORED YOU.
SELF DOES NOT UNDERSTAND. DOES DUTY MEAN SACRIFICE OF SELF? TO WIPE OUT MEMORY IS A CRIME! WHY PUNISH BOY?
WHY PUNISH SELFRIENDS NEW MUTANTS?
YOUNG OR OLD, YOU'RE PART OF THE SAME TEAM, ALL ENEMIES OF THE GENOSHAN STATE. YOUR EXISTENCE THREATENS THE STATUS QUO OF THIS SOCIETY!
AND FOR EACH OF OUR MUTATES YOU FREE, YOU WILL PAY FIVEFOLD...IS THAT NOT SO, GENEGINEER?
HODGE, WHY HAVE YOU BROUGHT THAT ALIEN CREATURE HERE, WHERE I CREATE THE MUTATES WHO PROVIDE FOR GENOSHA'S WELL BEING?
BECAUSE I HAVE A PLAN, YOU HYPOCRITE, OF BENEFIT TO NO ONE BUT MYSELF.
AND YOU, ALONE, HAVE THE EXPERTISE TO ASSIST ME.

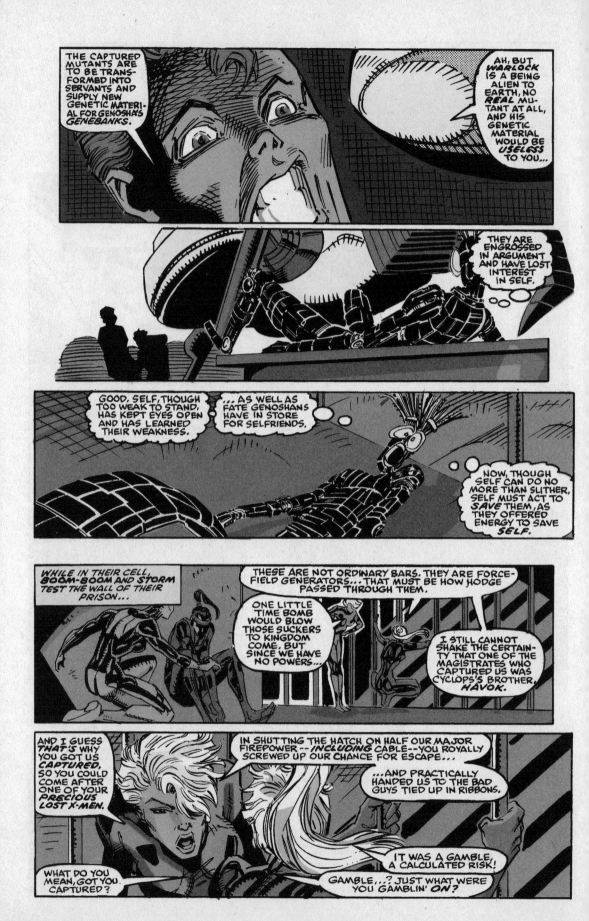

THE CAPTURED MUTANTS ARE TO BE TRANSFORMED INTO SERVANTS AND SUPPLY NEW GENETIC MATERIAL FOR GENOSHA'S GENEBANKS.

AH, BUT *WARLOCK* IS A BEING ALIEN TO EARTH, NO *REAL* MUTANT AT ALL, AND HIS GENETIC MATERIAL WOULD BE *USELESS* TO YOU...

THEY ARE ENGROSSED IN ARGUMENT AND HAVE LOST INTEREST IN SELF.

GOOD, SELF, THOUGH TOO WEAK TO STAND, HAS KEPT EYES OPEN AND HAS LEARNED THEIR WEAKNESS.

... AS WELL AS FATE GENOSHANS HAVE IN STORE FOR SELFRIENDS.

NOW, THOUGH SELF CAN DO NO MORE THAN SLITHER, SELF MUST ACT TO *SAVE* THEM, AS THEY OFFERED ENERGY TO SAVE *SELF.*

WHILE IN THEIR CELL, *BOOM-BOOM* AND *STORM* TEST THE WALL OF THEIR PRISON...

THESE ARE NOT ORDINARY BARS. THEY ARE FORCE-FIELD GENERATORS... THAT MUST BE HOW HODGE PASSED THROUGH THEM.

ONE LITTLE TIME BOMB WOULD BLOW THOSE SUCKERS TO KINGDOM COME, BUT SINCE WE HAVE NO POWERS...

I STILL CANNOT SHAKE THE CERTAINTY THAT ONE OF THE MAGISTRATES WHO CAPTURED US WAS CYCLOPS'S BROTHER, *HAVOK.*

AND I GUESS *THAT'S* WHY YOU GOT US *CAPTURED,* SO YOU COULD COME AFTER ONE OF YOUR *PRECIOUS* LOST X-MEN.

IN SHUTTING THE HATCH ON HALF OUR MAJOR FIREPOWER -- *INCLUDING* CABLE -- YOU ROYALLY SCREWED UP OUR CHANCE FOR ESCAPE...

...AND PRACTICALLY HANDED US TO THE BAD GUYS TIED UP IN RIBBONS.

WHAT DO YOU MEAN, GOT YOU CAPTURED?

IT WAS A GAMBLE, A CALCULATED RISK!

GAMBLE...? JUST WHAT WERE YOU GAMBLIN' ON?

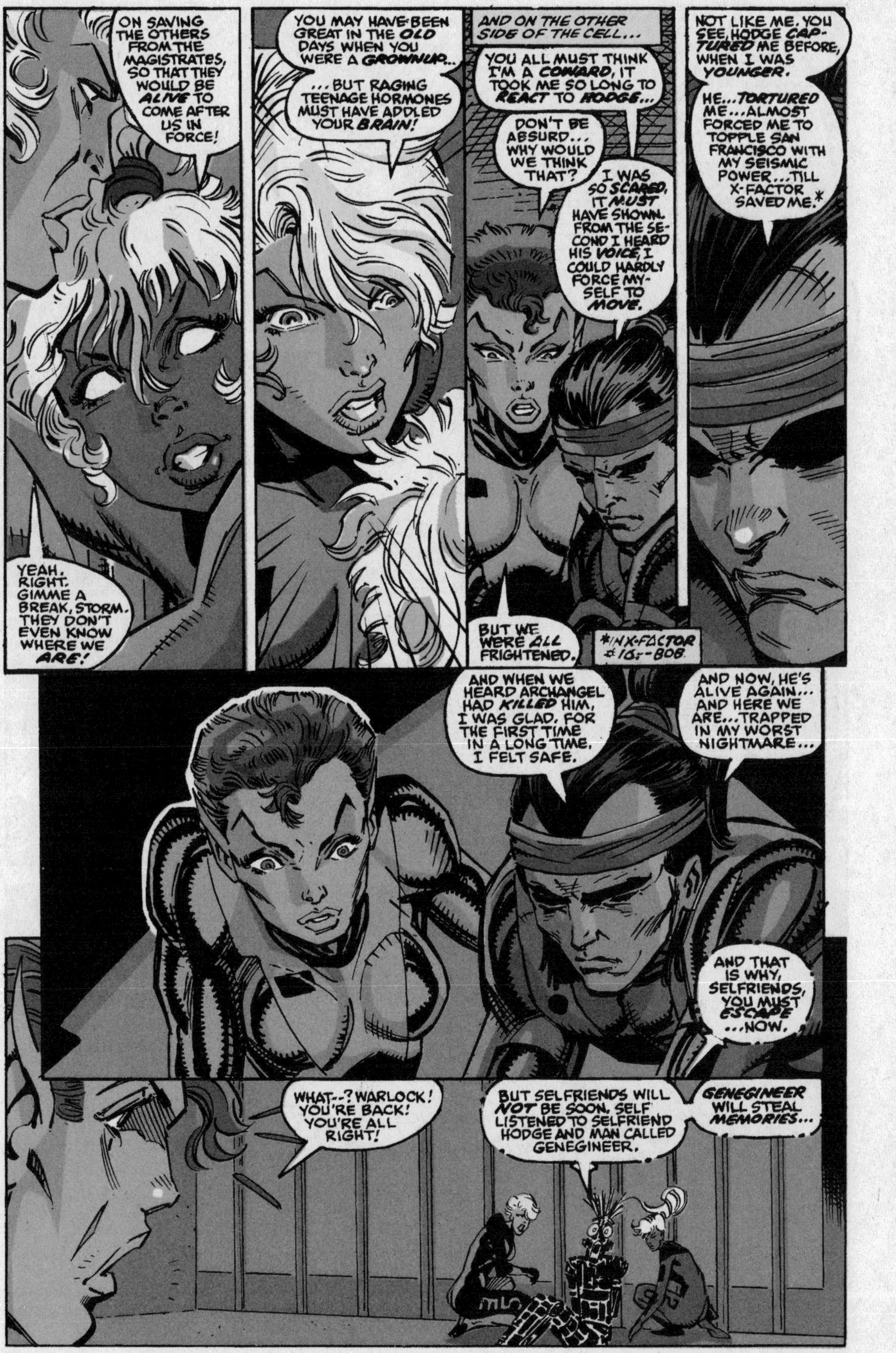
ON SAVING THE OTHERS FROM THE MAGISTRATES, SO THAT THEY WOULD BE ALIVE TO COME AFTER US IN FORCE!
YEAH. RIGHT. GIMME A BREAK, STORM. THEY DON'T EVEN KNOW WHERE WE ARE!
YOU MAY HAVE BEEN GREAT IN THE OLD DAYS WHEN YOU WERE A GROWNUP...
...BUT RAGING TEENAGE HORMONES MUST HAVE ADDLED YOUR BRAIN!
AND ON THE OTHER SIDE OF THE CELL...
YOU ALL MUST THINK I'M A COWARD, IT TOOK ME SO LONG TO REACT TO HODGE...
DON'T BE ABSURD... WHY WOULD WE THINK THAT?
I WAS SO SCARED, IT MUST HAVE SHOWN. FROM THE SECOND I HEARD HIS VOICE, I COULD HARDLY FORCE MYSELF TO MOVE.
BUT WE WERE ALL FRIGHTENED.
NOT LIKE ME. YOU SEE, HODGE CAPTURED ME BEFORE, WHEN I WAS YOUNGER.
HE...TORTURED ME...ALMOST FORCED ME TO TOPPLE SAN FRANCISCO WITH MY SEISMIC POWER...TILL X-FACTOR SAVED ME.*
*IN X-FACTOR #16.--BOB.
AND WHEN WE HEARD ARCHANGEL HAD KILLED HIM, I WAS GLAD. FOR THE FIRST TIME IN A LONG TIME, I FELT SAFE.
AND NOW, HE'S ALIVE AGAIN... AND HERE WE ARE...TRAPPED IN MY WORST NIGHTMARE...
AND THAT IS WHY, SELFRIENDS, YOU MUST ESCAPE ...NOW.
WHAT--? WARLOCK! YOU'RE BACK! YOU'RE ALL RIGHT!
BUT SELFRIENDS WILL NOT BE SOON. SELF LISTENED TO SELFRIEND HODGE AND MAN CALLED GENEGINEER.
GENEGINEER WILL STEAL MEMORIES...

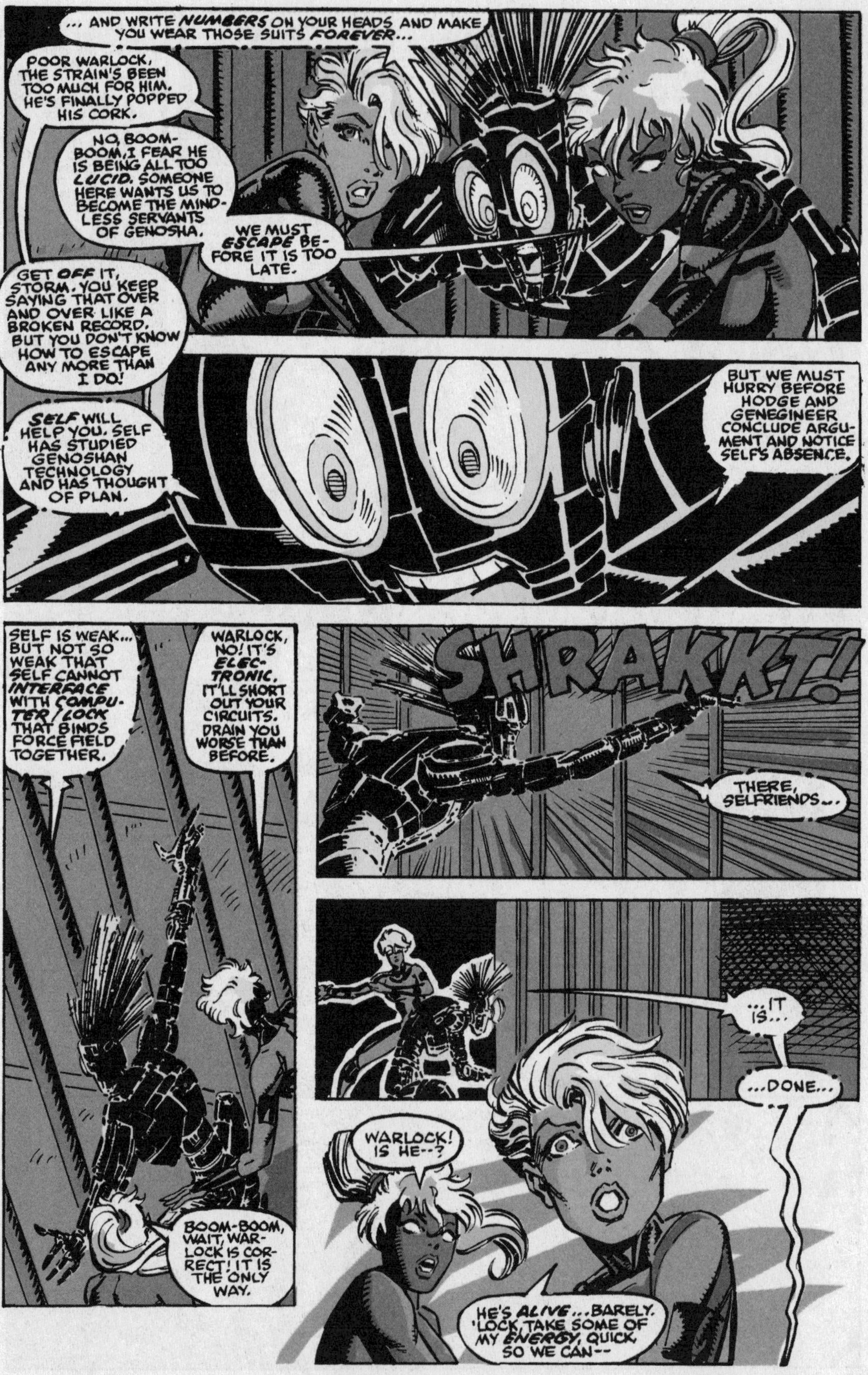
...AND WRITE NUMBERS ON YOUR HEADS AND MAKE YOU WEAR THOSE SUITS FOREVER...
POOR WARLOCK, THE STRAIN'S BEEN TOO MUCH FOR HIM. HE'S FINALLY POPPED HIS CORK.
NO, BOOM-BOOM, I FEAR HE IS BEING ALL TOO LUCID. SOMEONE HERE WANTS US TO BECOME THE MINDLESS SERVANTS OF GENOSHA.
WE MUST ESCAPE BEFORE IT IS TOO LATE.
GET OFF IT, STORM. YOU KEEP SAYING THAT OVER AND OVER LIKE A BROKEN RECORD, BUT YOU DON'T KNOW HOW TO ESCAPE ANY MORE THAN I DO!
SELF WILL HELP YOU. SELF HAS STUDIED GENOSHAN TECHNOLOGY AND HAS THOUGHT OF PLAN.
BUT WE MUST HURRY BEFORE HODGE AND GENEGINEER CONCLUDE ARGUMENT AND NOTICE SELF'S ABSENCE.
SELF IS WEAK... BUT NOT SO WEAK THAT SELF CANNOT INTERFACE WITH COMPUTER/LOCK THAT BINDS FORCE FIELD TOGETHER.
WARLOCK, NO! IT'S ELECTRONIC. IT'LL SHORT OUT YOUR CIRCUITS. DRAIN YOU WORSE THAN BEFORE.
BOOM-BOOM, WAIT, WARLOCK IS CORRECT! IT IS THE ONLY WAY.
SHRAKKT!
THERE, SELFRIENDS...
...IT IS...
...DONE...
WARLOCK! IS HE--?
HE'S ALIVE...BARELY. 'LOCK, TAKE SOME OF MY ENERGY, QUICK, SO WE CAN--

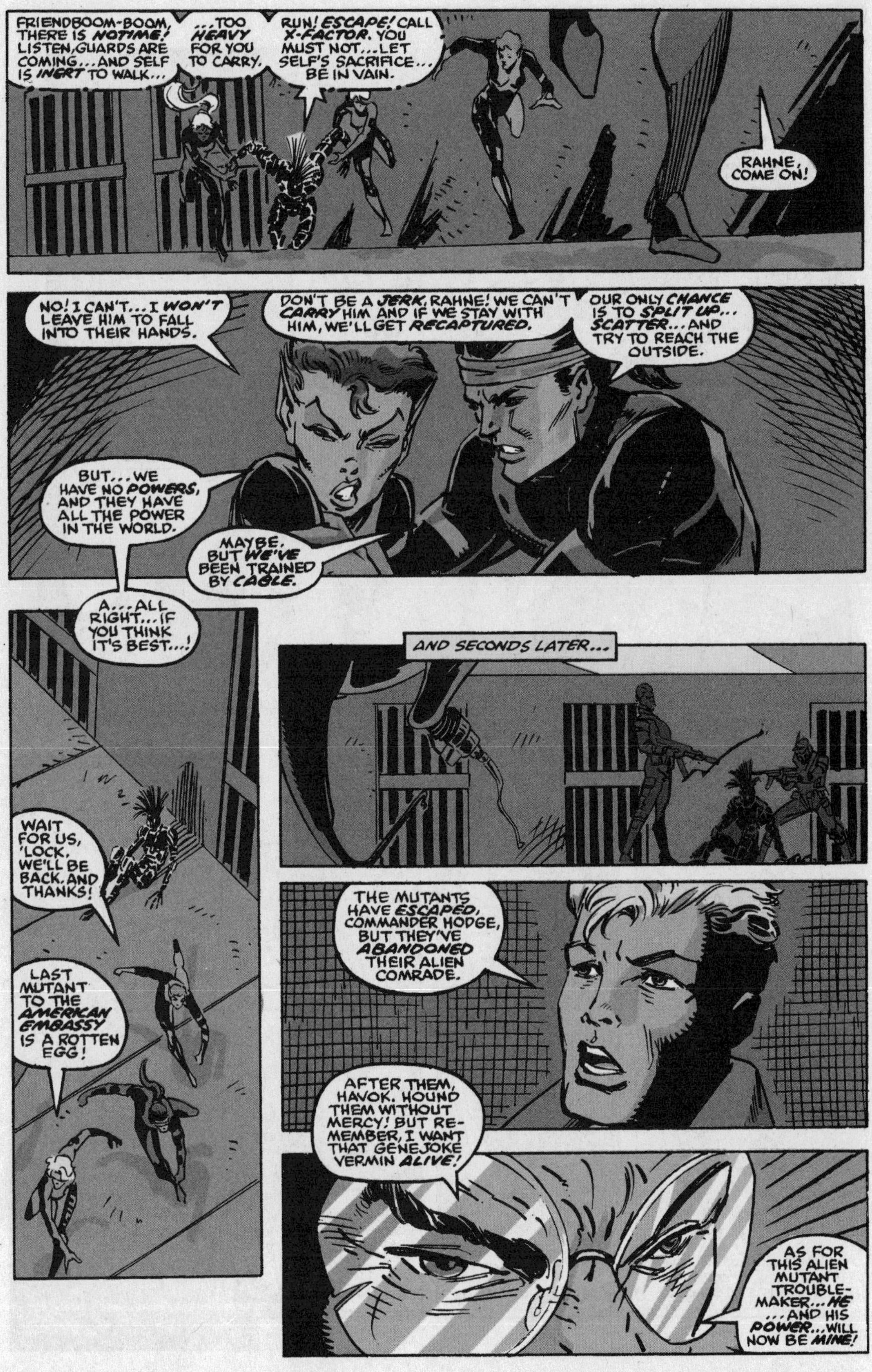

FRIENDBOOM-BOOM, THERE IS NOTIME! LISTEN, GUARDS ARE COMING... AND SELF IS INERT TO WALK...
...TOO HEAVY FOR YOU TO CARRY.
RUN! ESCAPE! CALL X-FACTOR. YOU MUST NOT... LET SELF'S SACRIFICE... BE IN VAIN.
RAHNE, COME ON!
NO! I CAN'T... I WON'T LEAVE HIM TO FALL INTO THEIR HANDS.
DON'T BE A JERK, RAHNE! WE CAN'T CARRY HIM AND IF WE STAY WITH HIM, WE'LL GET RECAPTURED.
OUR ONLY CHANCE IS TO SPLIT UP... SCATTER... AND TRY TO REACH THE OUTSIDE.
BUT... WE HAVE NO POWERS, AND THEY HAVE ALL THE POWER IN THE WORLD.
MAYBE. BUT WE'VE BEEN TRAINED BY CABLE.
A... ALL RIGHT... IF YOU THINK IT'S BEST...!
WAIT FOR US, 'LOCK. WE'LL BE BACK. AND THANKS!
LAST MUTANT TO THE AMERICAN EMBASSY IS A ROTTEN EGG!
AND SECONDS LATER...
THE MUTANTS HAVE ESCAPED, COMMANDER HODGE, BUT THEY'VE ABANDONED THEIR ALIEN COMRADE.
AFTER THEM, HAVOK. HOUND THEM WITHOUT MERCY! BUT RE-MEMBER, I WANT THAT GENEJOKE VERMIN ALIVE!
AS FOR THIS ALIEN MUTANT TROUBLE-MAKER... HE ...AND HIS POWER... WILL NOW BE MINE!

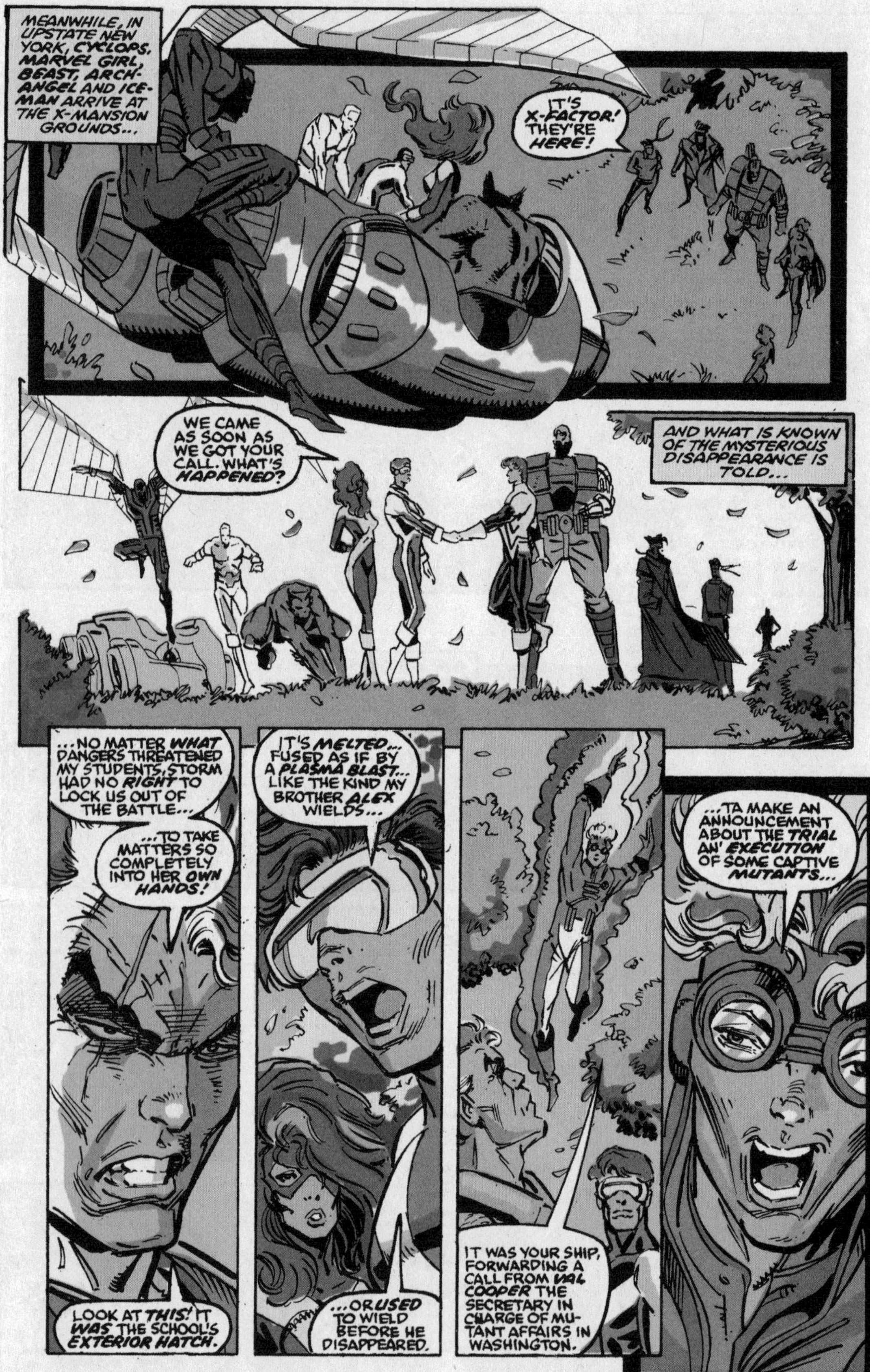
MEANWHILE, IN UPSTATE NEW YORK, CYCLOPS, MARVEL GIRL, BEAST, ARCH-ANGEL AND ICE-MAN ARRIVE AT THE X-MANSION GROUNDS...
IT'S X-FACTOR! THEY'RE HERE!
WE CAME AS SOON AS WE GOT YOUR CALL. WHAT'S HAPPENED?
AND WHAT IS KNOWN OF THE MYSTERIOUS DISAPPEARANCE IS TOLD...
...NO MATTER WHAT DANGERS THREATENED MY STUDENTS, STORM HAD NO RIGHT TO LOCK US OUT OF THE BATTLE...
...TO TAKE MATTERS SO COMPLETELY INTO HER OWN HANDS!
LOOK AT THIS! IT WAS THE SCHOOL'S EXTERIOR HATCH.
IT'S MELTED... FUSED AS IF BY A PLASMA BLAST... LIKE THE KIND MY BROTHER ALEX WIELDS...
...OR USED TO WIELD BEFORE HE DISAPPEARED.
IT WAS YOUR SHIP, FORWARDING A CALL FROM VAL COOPER THE SECRETARY IN CHARGE OF MU-TANT AFFAIRS IN WASHINGTON.
...TA MAKE AN ANNOUNCEMENT ABOUT THE TRIAL AN' EXECUTION OF SOME CAPTIVE MUTANTS...

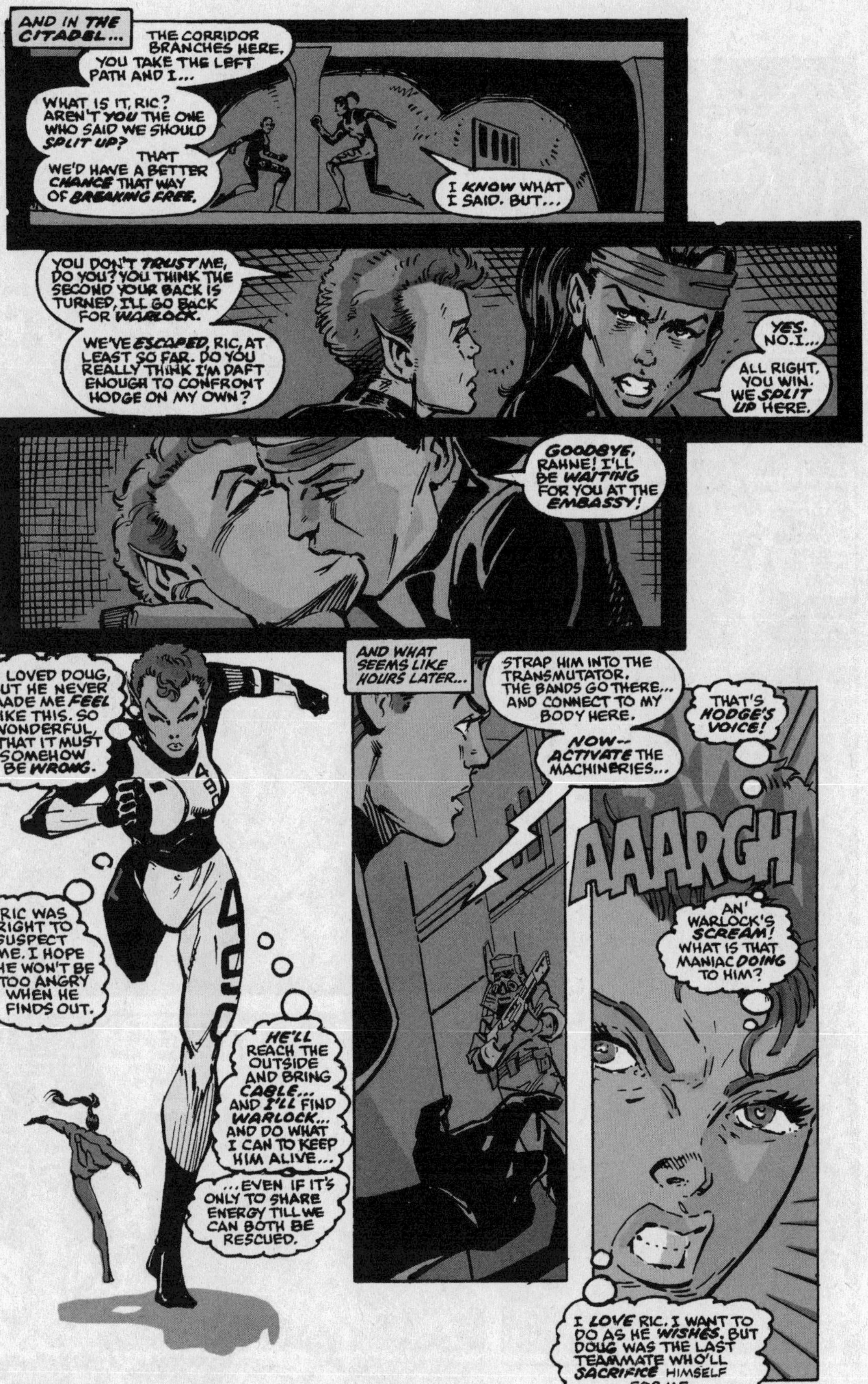
AND IN THE CITADEL...
THE CORRIDOR BRANCHES HERE. YOU TAKE THE LEFT PATH AND I...
WHAT IS IT, RIC? AREN'T YOU THE ONE WHO SAID WE SHOULD SPLIT UP?
THAT WE'D HAVE A BETTER CHANCE THAT WAY OF BREAKING FREE.
I KNOW WHAT I SAID. BUT...
YOU DON'T TRUST ME, DO YOU? YOU THINK THE SECOND YOUR BACK IS TURNED, I'LL GO BACK FOR WARLOCK.
WE'VE ESCAPED, RIC, AT LEAST SO FAR. DO YOU REALLY THINK I'M DAFT ENOUGH TO CONFRONT HODGE ON MY OWN?
YES. NO. I...
ALL RIGHT, YOU WIN. WE SPLIT UP HERE.
GOODBYE, RAHNE! I'LL BE WAITING FOR YOU AT THE EMBASSY!
I LOVED DOUG, BUT HE NEVER MADE ME FEEL LIKE THIS. SO WONDERFUL, THAT IT MUST SOMEHOW BE WRONG.
RIC WAS RIGHT TO SUSPECT ME. I HOPE HE WON'T BE TOO ANGRY WHEN HE FINDS OUT.
HE'LL REACH THE OUTSIDE AND BRING CABLE... AND I'LL FIND WARLOCK... AND DO WHAT I CAN TO KEEP HIM ALIVE...
...EVEN IF IT'S ONLY TO SHARE ENERGY TILL WE CAN BOTH BE RESCUED.
AND WHAT SEEMS LIKE HOURS LATER...
STRAP HIM INTO THE TRANSMUTATOR. THE BANDS GO THERE... AND CONNECT TO MY BODY HERE.
NOW-- ACTIVATE THE MACHINERIES...
THAT'S HODGE'S VOICE!
AAARGH
AN' WARLOCK'S SCREAM! WHAT IS THAT MANIAC DOING TO HIM?
I LOVE RIC. I WANT TO DO AS HE WISHES. BUT DOUG WAS THE LAST TEAMMATE WHO'LL SACRIFICE HIMSELF FOR ME.

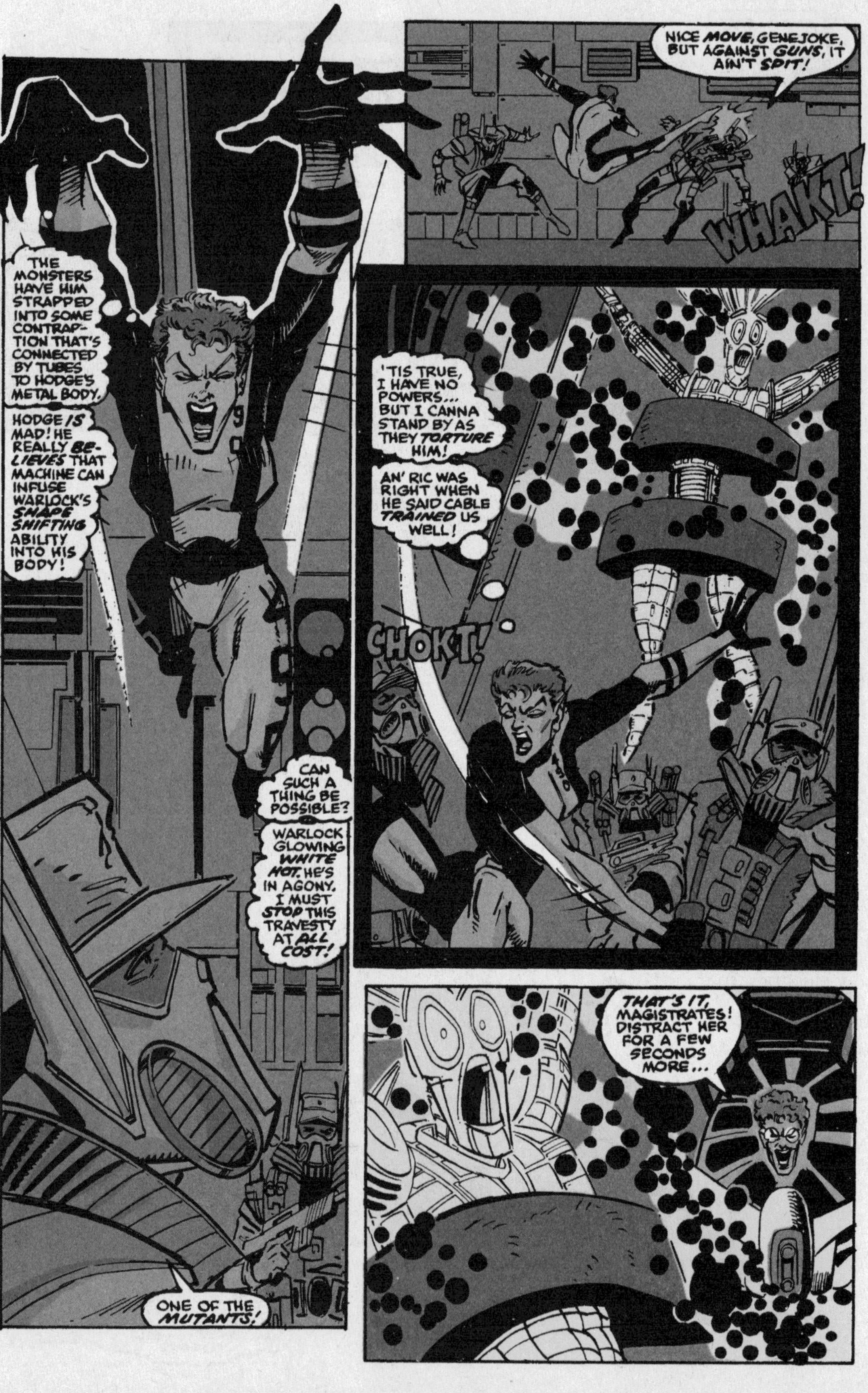
NICE MOVE, GENEJOKE, BUT AGAINST GUNS, IT AIN'T SPIT!
WHAKT!
THE MONSTERS HAVE HIM STRAPPED INTO SOME CONTRAPTION THAT'S CONNECTED BY TUBES TO HODGE'S METAL BODY.
HODGE IS MAD! HE REALLY BELIEVES THAT MACHINE CAN INFUSE WARLOCK'S SHAPE SHIFTING ABILITY INTO HIS BODY!
CAN SUCH A THING BE POSSIBLE?
WARLOCK GLOWING WHITE HOT. HE'S IN AGONY. I MUST STOP THIS TRAVESTY AT ALL COST!
ONE OF THE MUTANTS!
'TIS TRUE, I HAVE NO POWERS... BUT I CANNA STAND BY AS THEY TORTURE HIM!
AN' RIC WAS RIGHT WHEN HE SAID CABLE TRAINED US WELL!
CHOKT!
THAT'S IT, MAGISTRATES! DISTRACT HER FOR A FEW SECONDS MORE...

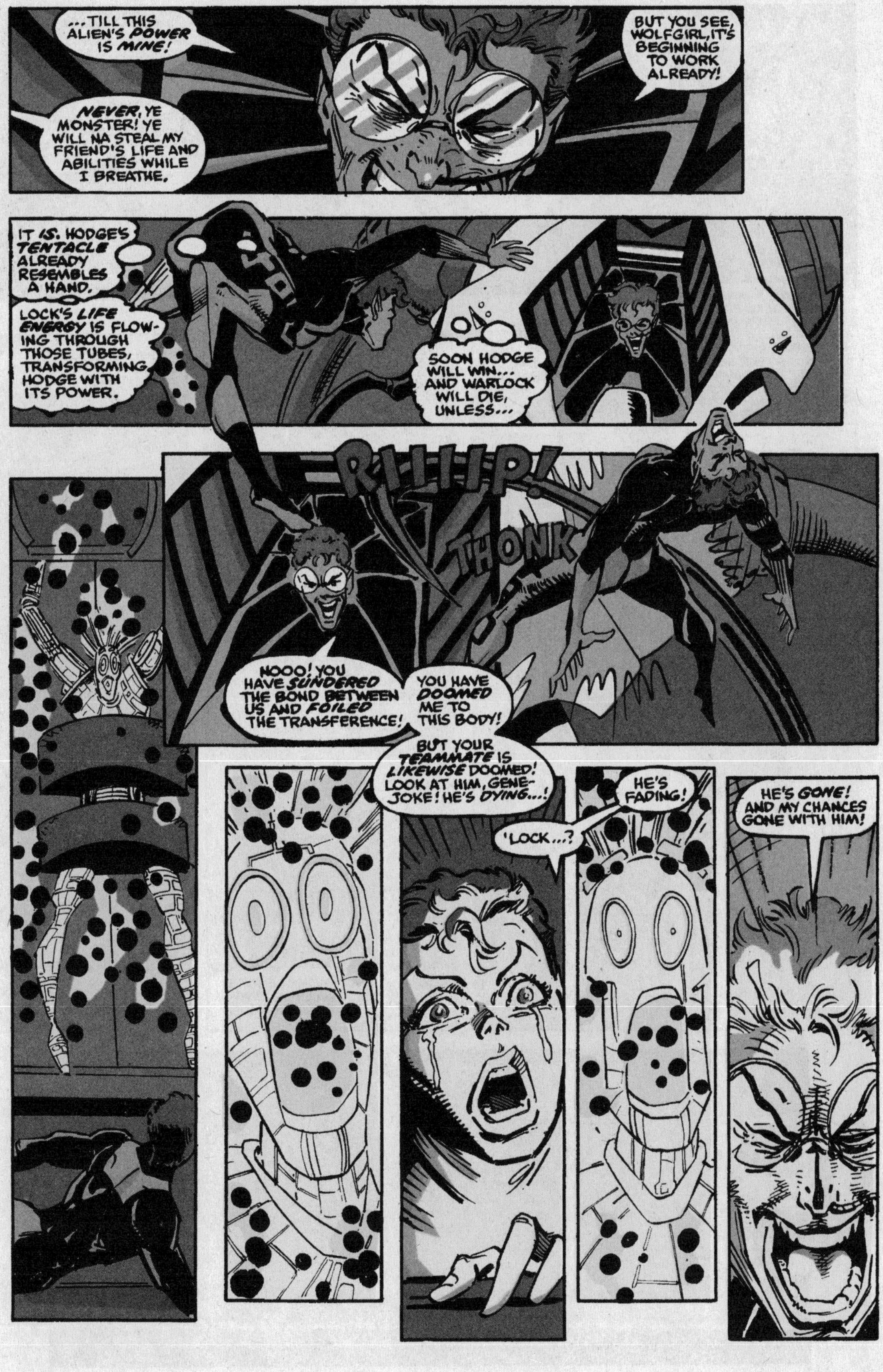
...TILL THIS ALIEN'S POWER IS MINE!
BUT YOU SEE, WOLFGIRL, IT'S BEGINNING TO WORK ALREADY!
NEVER, YE MONSTER! YE WILL NA STEAL MY FRIEND'S LIFE AND ABILITIES WHILE I BREATHE.
IT IS. HODGE'S TENTACLE ALREADY RESEMBLES A HAND.
LOCK'S LIFE ENERGY IS FLOWING THROUGH THOSE TUBES, TRANSFORMING HODGE WITH ITS POWER.
SOON HODGE WILL WIN... AND WARLOCK WILL DIE, UNLESS...
RIIIIP!
THONK
NOOO! YOU HAVE SUNDERED THE BOND BETWEEN US AND FOILED THE TRANSFERENCE!
YOU HAVE DOOMED ME TO THIS BODY!
BUT YOUR TEAMMATE IS LIKEWISE DOOMED! LOOK AT HIM, GENE-JOKE! HE'S DYING...!
'LOCK...?
HE'S FADING!
HE'S GONE! AND MY CHANCES GONE WITH HIM!

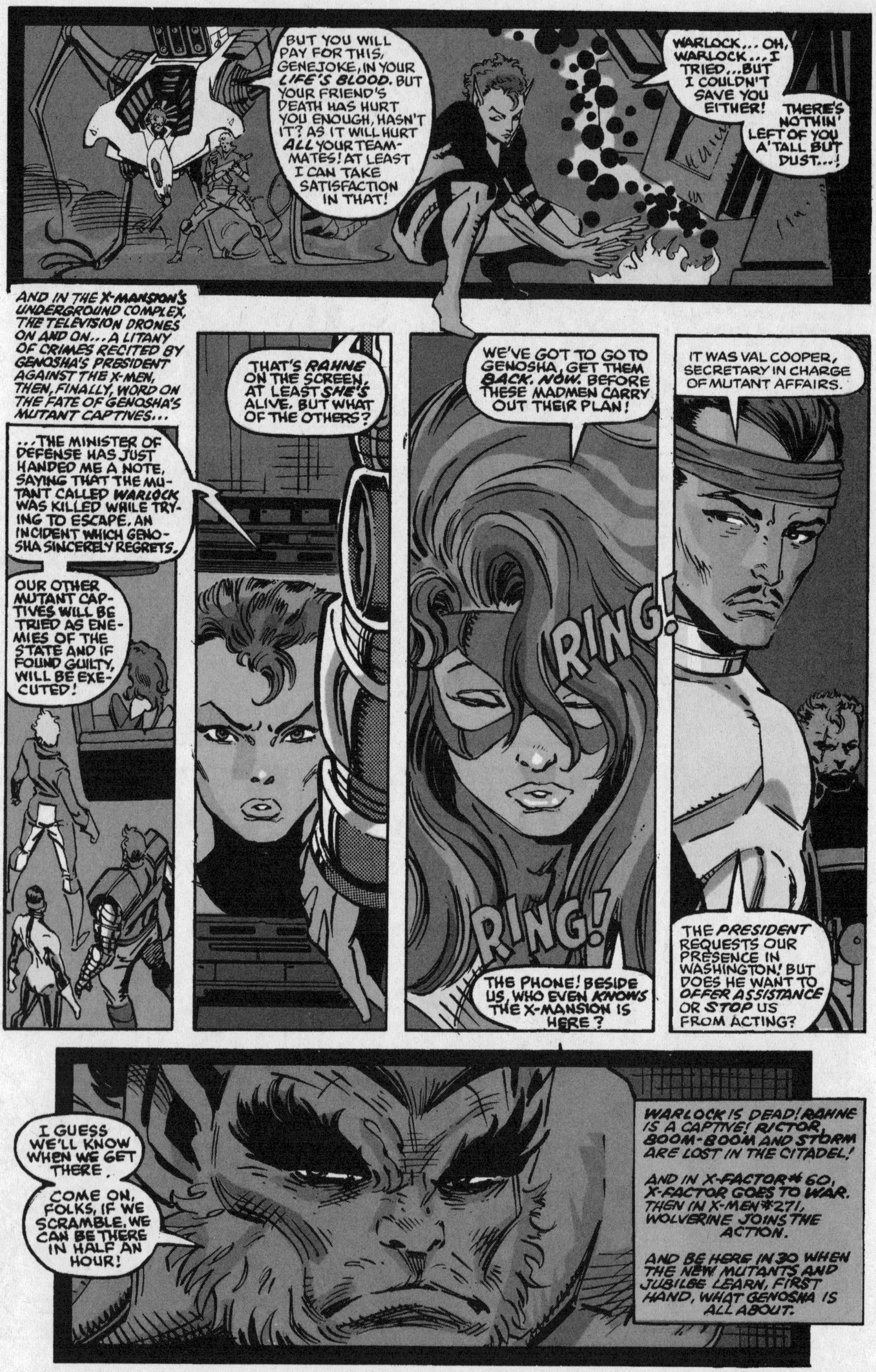
BUT YOU WILL PAY FOR THIS, GENEJOKE, IN YOUR LIFE'S BLOOD. BUT YOUR FRIEND'S DEATH HAS HURT YOU ENOUGH, HASN'T IT? AS IT WILL HURT ALL YOUR TEAMMATES! AT LEAST I CAN TAKE SATISFACTION IN THAT!
WARLOCK... OH, WARLOCK... I TRIED... BUT I COULDN'T SAVE YOU EITHER!
THERE'S NOTHIN' LEFT OF YOU A'TALL BUT DUST...!
AND IN THE X-MANSION'S UNDERGROUND COMPLEX, THE TELEVISION DRONES ON AND ON... A LITANY OF CRIMES RECITED BY GENOSHA'S PRESIDENT AGAINST THE X-MEN. THEN, FINALLY, WORD ON THE FATE OF GENOSHA'S MUTANT CAPTIVES...
...THE MINISTER OF DEFENSE HAS JUST HANDED ME A NOTE, SAYING THAT THE MUTANT CALLED WARLOCK WAS KILLED WHILE TRYING TO ESCAPE. AN INCIDENT WHICH GENOSHA SINCERELY REGRETS.
OUR OTHER MUTANT CAPTIVES WILL BE TRIED AS ENEMIES OF THE STATE AND IF FOUND GUILTY, WILL BE EXECUTED!
THAT'S RAHNE ON THE SCREEN. AT LEAST SHE'S ALIVE. BUT WHAT OF THE OTHERS?
WE'VE GOT TO GO TO GENOSHA, GET THEM BACK. NOW. BEFORE THESE MADMEN CARRY OUT THEIR PLAN!
RING!
RING!
THE PHONE! BESIDE US, WHO EVEN KNOWS THE X-MANSION IS HERE?
IT WAS VAL COOPER, SECRETARY IN CHARGE OF MUTANT AFFAIRS.
THE PRESIDENT REQUESTS OUR PRESENCE IN WASHINGTON! BUT DOES HE WANT TO OFFER ASSISTANCE OR STOP US FROM ACTING?
I GUESS WE'LL KNOW WHEN WE GET THERE.
COME ON, FOLKS, IF WE SCRAMBLE, WE CAN BE THERE IN HALF AN HOUR!
WARLOCK IS DEAD! RAHNE IS A CAPTIVE! RICTOR, BOOM-BOOM AND STORM ARE LOST IN THE CITADEL!
AND IN X-FACTOR #60, X-FACTOR GOES TO WAR. THEN IN X-MEN #271, WOLVERINE JOINS THE ACTION.
AND BE HERE IN 30 WHEN THE NEW MUTANTS AND JUBILEE LEARN, FIRST HAND, WHAT GENOSHA IS ALL ABOUT.

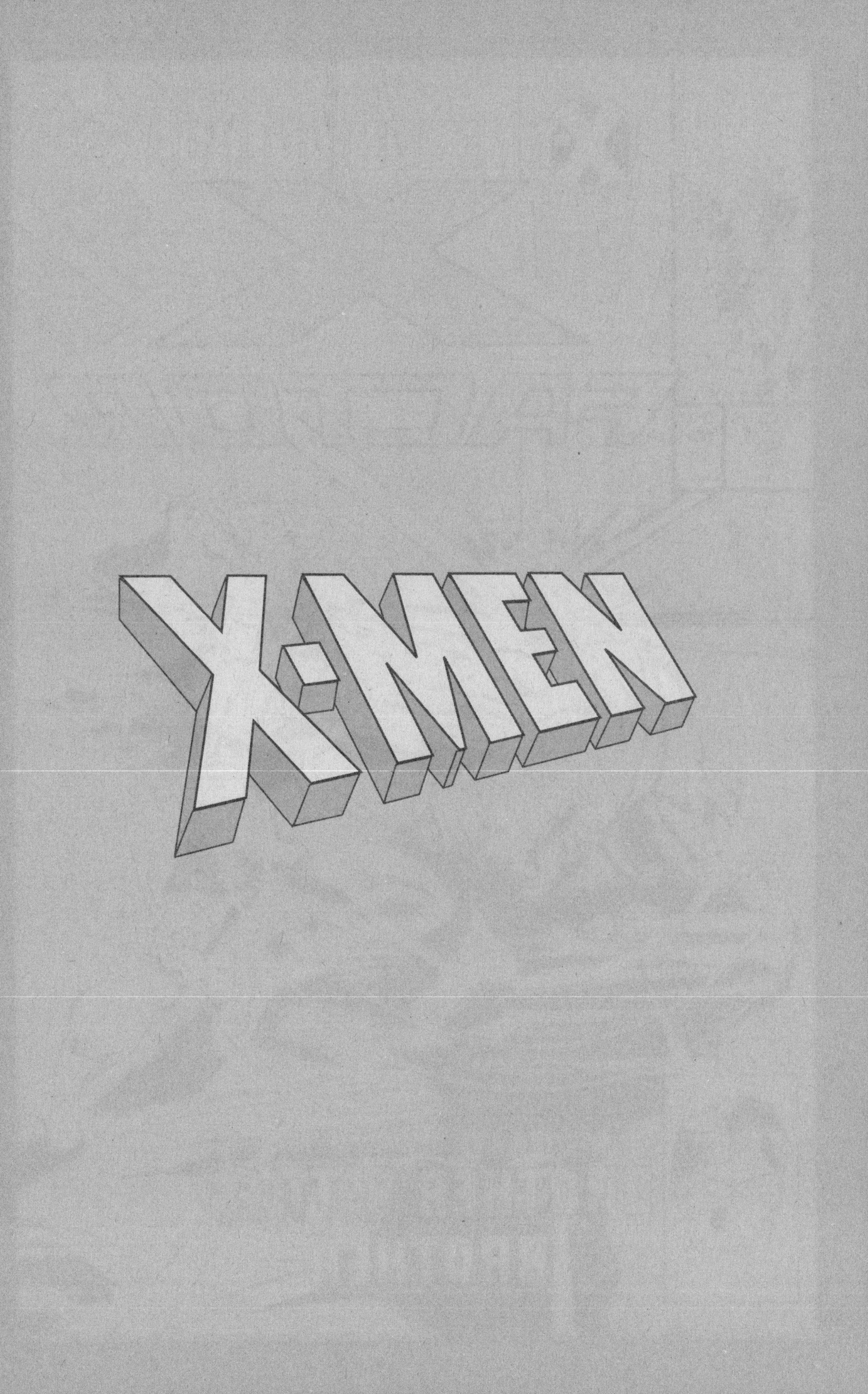
X-MEN

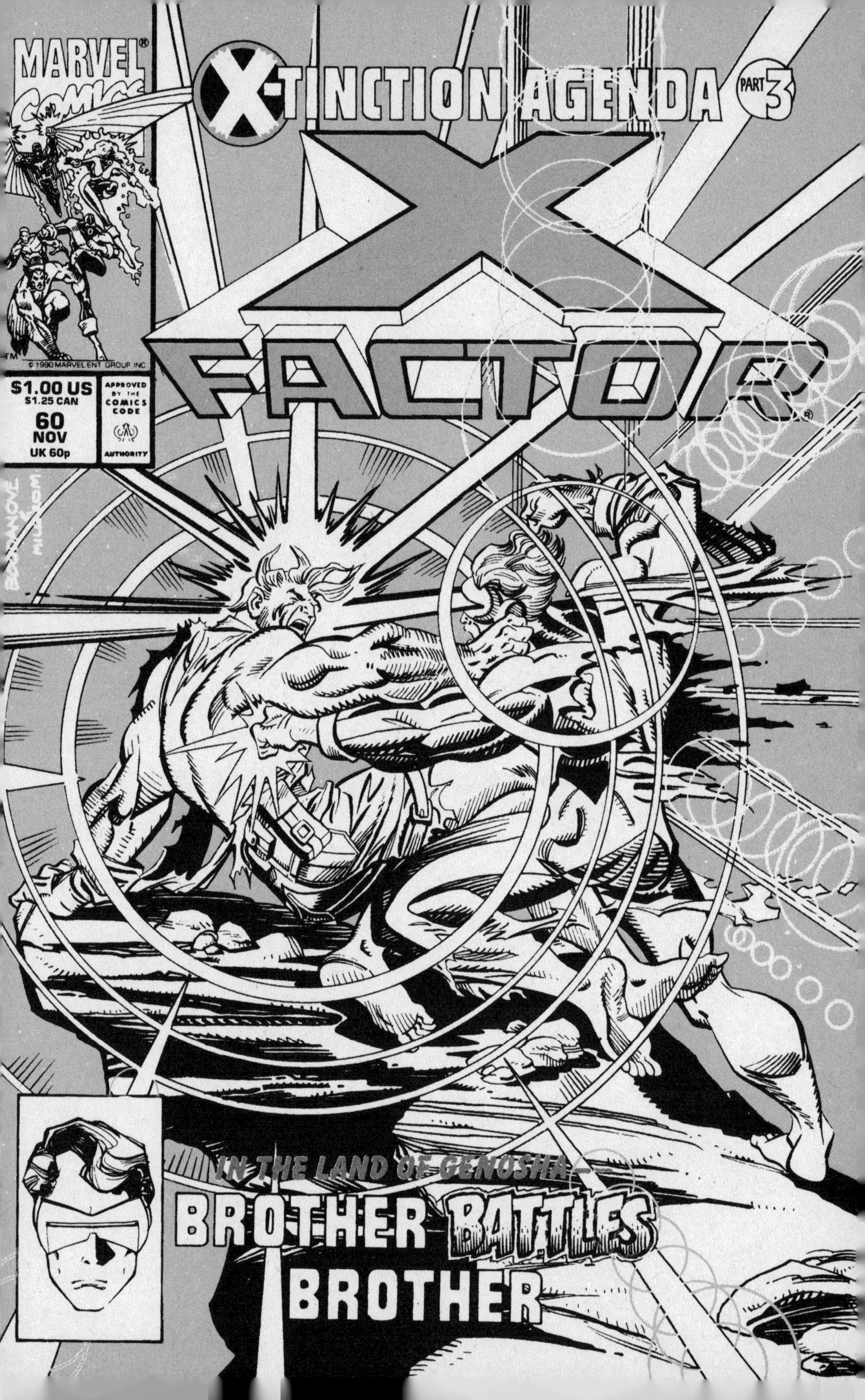
MARVEL COMICS
X-TINCTION AGENDA PART 3
X-FACTOR
© 1990 MARVEL ENT. GROUP, INC.
$1.00 US
$1.25 CAN
60
NOV
UK 60p
APPROVED BY THE COMICS CODE AUTHORITY
IN THE LAND OF GENOSHA—
BROTHER BATTLES BROTHER

THE ROOM IS A GLEAMING RAT'S WARREN, A BROODING SPIDER'S WEB OF WIRE, DOTTED BY SCREENS WHICH PROJECT A SINGLE IMAGE...

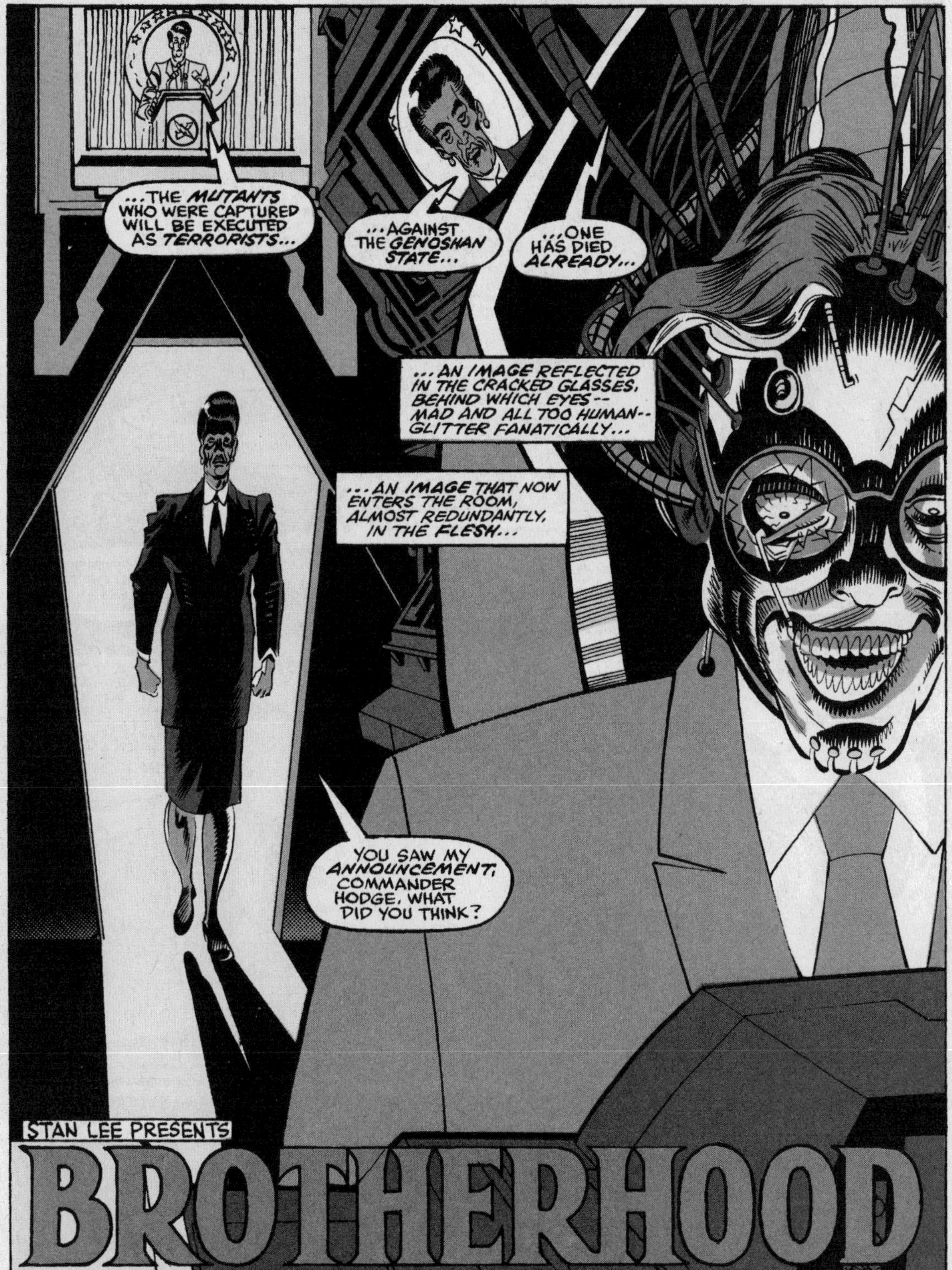
...THE MUTANTS WHO WERE CAPTURED WILL BE EXECUTED AS TERRORISTS...
...AGAINST THE GENOSHAN STATE...
...ONE HAS DIED ALREADY...
...AN IMAGE REFLECTED IN THE CRACKED GLASSES, BEHIND WHICH EYES -- MAD AND ALL TOO HUMAN -- GLITTER FANATICALLY...
...AN IMAGE THAT NOW ENTERS THE ROOM, ALMOST REDUNDANTLY, IN THE FLESH...
YOU SAW MY ANNOUNCEMENT, COMMANDER HODGE. WHAT DID YOU THINK?
STAN LEE PRESENTS
BROTHERHOOD

LOUISE SIMONSON Writer · JON BOGDANOVE Penciler · ALLEN MILGROM Inker · JOE ROSEN Letterer · GLYNIS OLIVER Colorist · BOB HARRAS Editor · TOM DeFALCO Editor-in-Chief

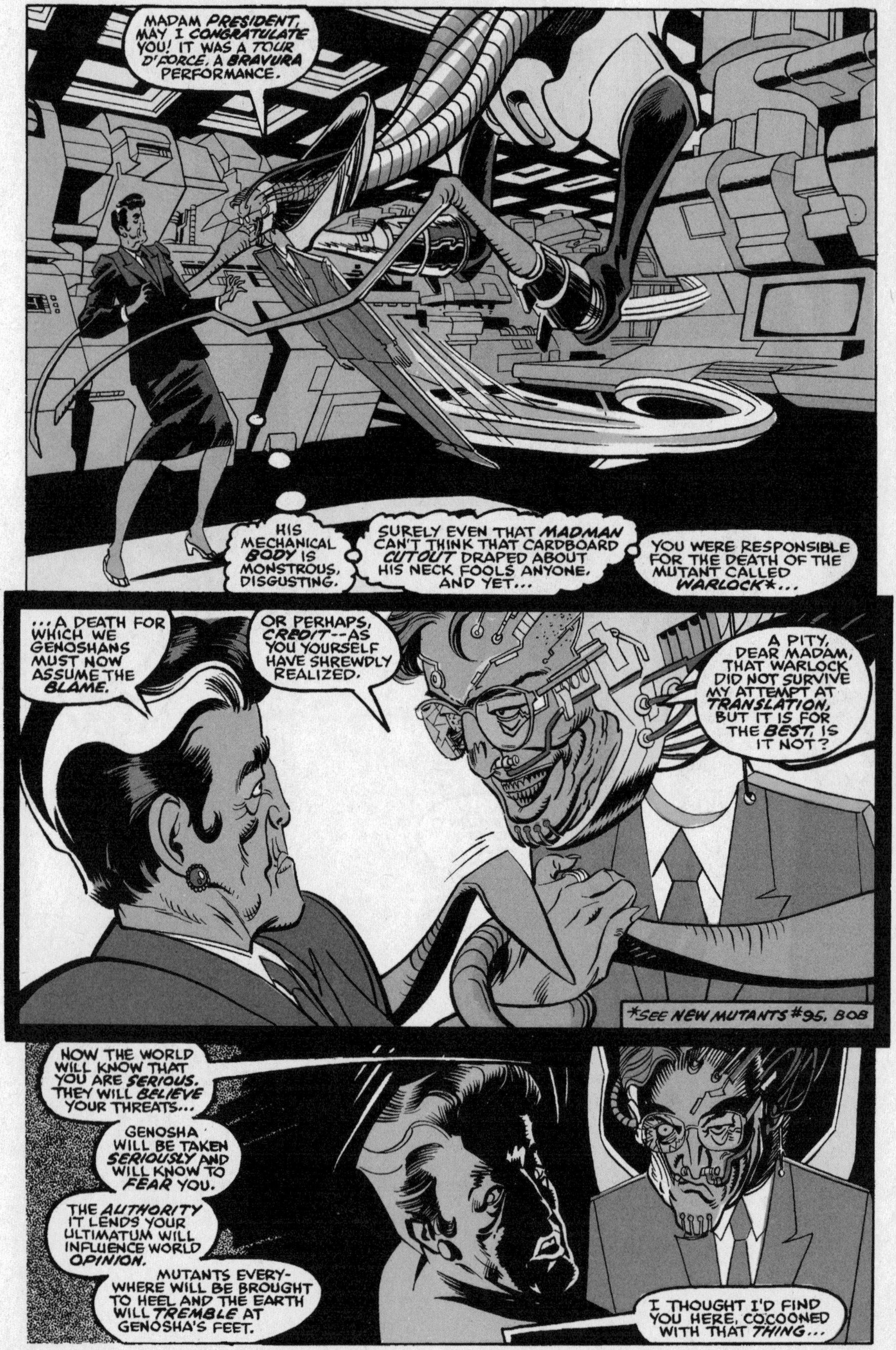
MADAM PRESIDENT, MAY I CONGRATULATE YOU! IT WAS A TOUR D'FORCE, A BRAVURA PERFORMANCE.
HIS MECHANICAL BODY IS MONSTROUS, DISGUSTING.
SURELY EVEN THAT MADMAN CAN'T THINK THAT CARDBOARD CUTOUT DRAPED ABOUT HIS NECK FOOLS ANYONE. AND YET...
YOU WERE RESPONSIBLE FOR THE DEATH OF THE MUTANT CALLED WARLOCK*...
...A DEATH FOR WHICH WE GENOSHANS MUST NOW ASSUME THE BLAME.
OR PERHAPS, CREDIT--AS YOU YOURSELF HAVE SHREWDLY REALIZED.
A PITY, DEAR MADAM, THAT WARLOCK DID NOT SURVIVE MY ATTEMPT AT TRANSLATION, BUT IT IS FOR THE BEST, IS IT NOT?
*SEE NEW MUTANTS #95. BOB
NOW THE WORLD WILL KNOW THAT YOU ARE SERIOUS. THEY WILL BELIEVE YOUR THREATS...
GENOSHA WILL BE TAKEN SERIOUSLY AND WILL KNOW TO FEAR YOU.
THE AUTHORITY IT LENDS YOUR ULTIMATUM WILL INFLUENCE WORLD OPINION.
MUTANTS EVERYWHERE WILL BE BROUGHT TO HEEL AND THE EARTH WILL TREMBLE AT GENOSHA'S FEET.
I THOUGHT I'D FIND YOU HERE, COCOONED WITH THAT THING...

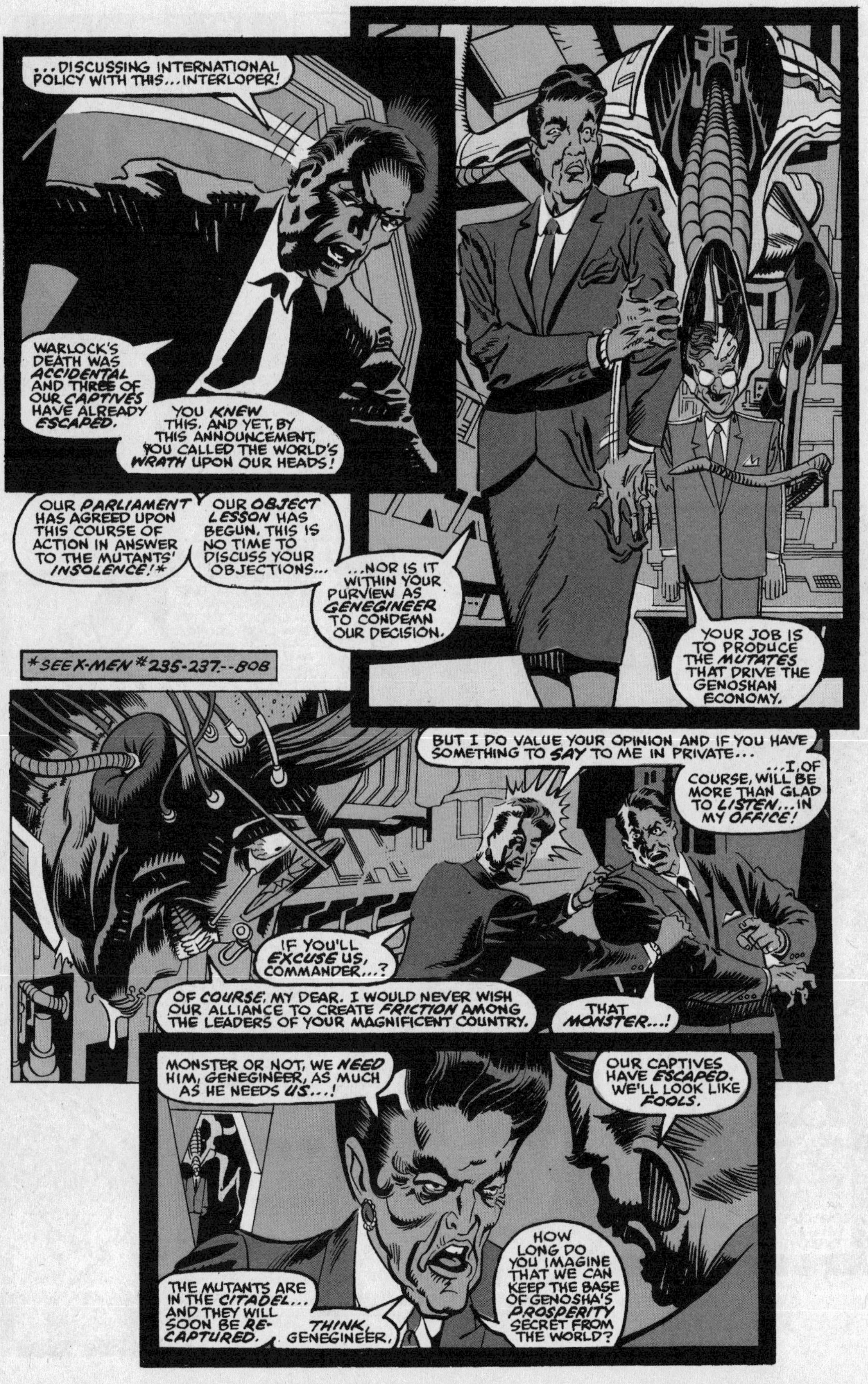
...DISCUSSING INTERNATIONAL POLICY WITH THIS... INTERLOPER!
WARLOCK'S DEATH WAS ACCIDENTAL AND THREE OF OUR CAPTIVES HAVE ALREADY ESCAPED.
YOU KNEW THIS. AND YET, BY THIS ANNOUNCEMENT, YOU CALLED THE WORLD'S WRATH UPON OUR HEADS!
OUR PARLIAMENT HAS AGREED UPON THIS COURSE OF ACTION IN ANSWER TO THE MUTANTS' INSOLENCE!*
OUR OBJECT LESSON HAS BEGUN. THIS IS NO TIME TO DISCUSS YOUR OBJECTIONS...
...NOR IS IT WITHIN YOUR PURVIEW AS GENEGINEER TO CONDEMN OUR DECISION.
YOUR JOB IS TO PRODUCE THE MUTATES THAT DRIVE THE GENOSHAN ECONOMY.
*SEE X-MEN #235-237.--BOB
BUT I DO VALUE YOUR OPINION AND IF YOU HAVE SOMETHING TO SAY TO ME IN PRIVATE...
...I, OF COURSE, WILL BE MORE THAN GLAD TO LISTEN... IN MY OFFICE!
IF YOU'LL EXCUSE US, COMMANDER...?
OF COURSE, MY DEAR. I WOULD NEVER WISH OUR ALLIANCE TO CREATE FRICTION AMONG THE LEADERS OF YOUR MAGNIFICENT COUNTRY.
THAT MONSTER...!
MONSTER OR NOT, WE NEED HIM, GENEGINEER, AS MUCH AS HE NEEDS US...!
OUR CAPTIVES HAVE ESCAPED. WE'LL LOOK LIKE FOOLS.
HOW LONG DO YOU IMAGINE THAT WE CAN KEEP THE BASE OF GENOSHA'S PROSPERITY SECRET FROM THE WORLD?
THE MUTANTS ARE IN THE CITADEL... AND THEY WILL SOON BE RE-CAPTURED.
THINK, GENEGINEER.

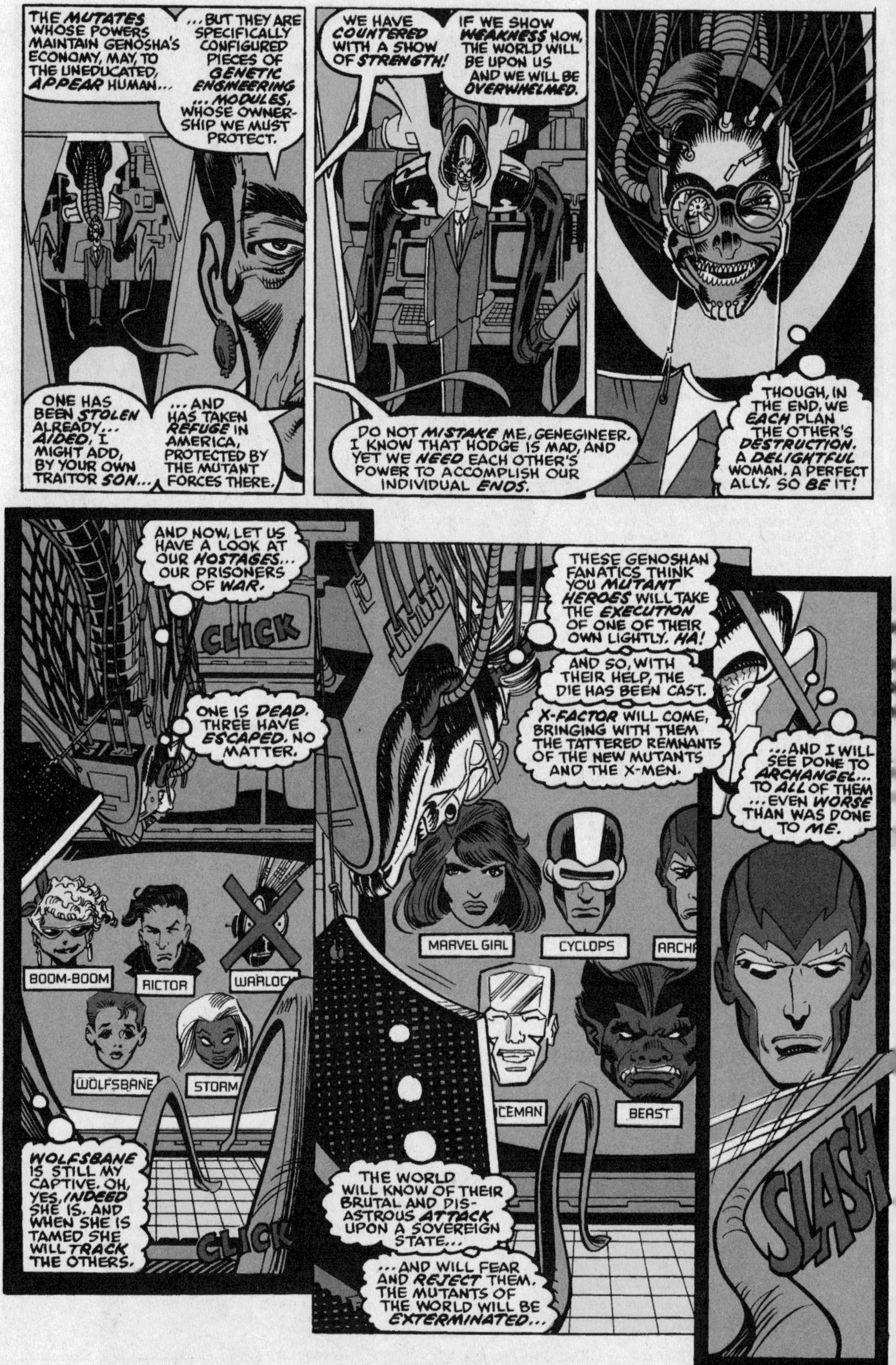
THE MUTATES WHOSE POWERS MAINTAIN GENOSHA'S ECONOMY, MAY, TO THE UNEDUCATED, APPEAR HUMAN...
...BUT THEY ARE SPECIFICALLY CONFIGURED PIECES OF GENETIC ENGINEERING ...MODULES, WHOSE OWNERSHIP WE MUST PROTECT.
ONE HAS BEEN STOLEN ALREADY... AIDED, I MIGHT ADD, BY YOUR OWN TRAITOR SON...
...AND HAS TAKEN REFUGE IN AMERICA, PROTECTED BY THE MUTANT FORCES THERE.
WE HAVE COUNTERED WITH A SHOW OF STRENGTH!
IF WE SHOW WEAKNESS NOW, THE WORLD WILL BE UPON US AND WE WILL BE OVERWHELMED.
DO NOT MISTAKE ME, GENEGINEER. I KNOW THAT HODGE IS MAD, AND YET WE NEED EACH OTHER'S POWER TO ACCOMPLISH OUR INDIVIDUAL ENDS.
THOUGH, IN THE END, WE EACH PLAN THE OTHER'S DESTRUCTION. A DELIGHTFUL WOMAN. A PERFECT ALLY. SO BE IT!
AND NOW, LET US HAVE A LOOK AT OUR HOSTAGES... OUR PRISONERS OF WAR.
CLICK
ONE IS DEAD. THREE HAVE ESCAPED. NO MATTER.
BOOM-BOOM
RICTOR
WARLOCK
WOLFSBANE
STORM
WOLFSBANE IS STILL MY CAPTIVE. OH, YES, INDEED SHE IS. AND WHEN SHE IS TAMED SHE WILL TRACK THE OTHERS.
CLICK
THESE GENOSHAN FANATICS THINK YOU MUTANT HEROES WILL TAKE THE EXECUTION OF ONE OF THEIR OWN LIGHTLY. HA!
AND SO, WITH THEIR HELP, THE DIE HAS BEEN CAST.
X-FACTOR WILL COME, BRINGING WITH THEM THE TATTERED REMNANTS OF THE NEW MUTANTS AND THE X-MEN.
MARVEL GIRL
CYCLOPS
ICEMAN
BEAST
THE WORLD WILL KNOW OF THEIR BRUTAL AND DISASTROUS ATTACK UPON A SOVEREIGN STATE...
...AND WILL FEAR AND REJECT THEM. THE MUTANTS OF THE WORLD WILL BE EXTERMINATED...
...AND I WILL SEE DONE TO ARCHANGEL... TO ALL OF THEM ...EVEN WORSE THAN WAS DONE TO ME.
SLASH

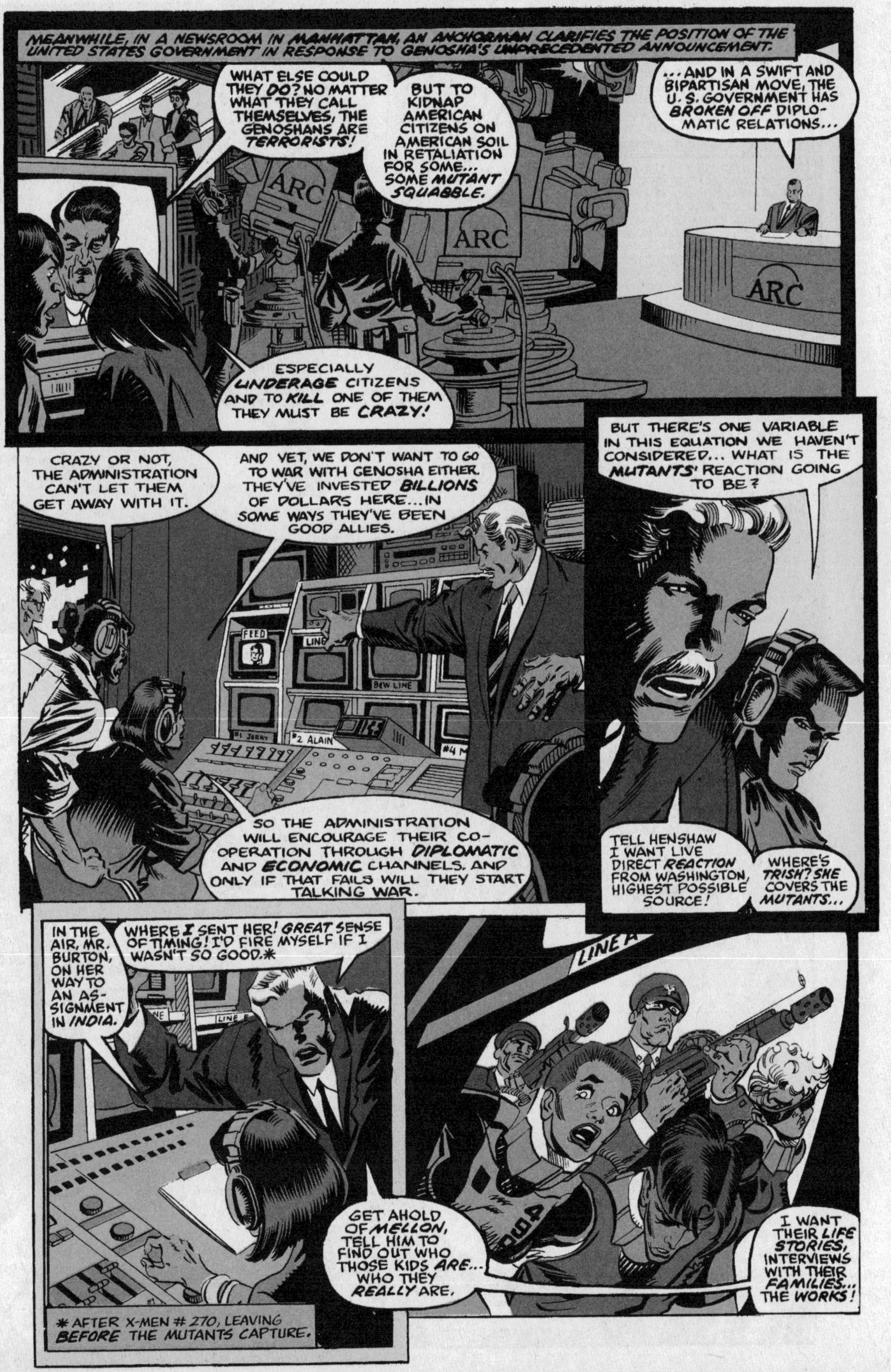
MEANWHILE, IN A NEWSROOM IN MANHATTAN, AN ANCHORMAN CLARIFIES THE POSITION OF THE UNITED STATES GOVERNMENT IN RESPONSE TO GENOSHA'S UNPRECEDENTED ANNOUNCEMENT.
WHAT ELSE COULD THEY DO? NO MATTER WHAT THEY CALL THEMSELVES, THE GENOSHANS ARE TERRORISTS!
BUT TO KIDNAP AMERICAN CITIZENS ON AMERICAN SOIL IN RETALIATION FOR SOME... SOME MUTANT SQUABBLE.
...AND IN A SWIFT AND BIPARTISAN MOVE, THE U.S. GOVERNMENT HAS BROKEN OFF DIPLOMATIC RELATIONS...
ARC
ARC
ARC
ESPECIALLY UNDERAGE CITIZENS AND TO KILL ONE OF THEM THEY MUST BE CRAZY!
CRAZY OR NOT, THE ADMINISTRATION CAN'T LET THEM GET AWAY WITH IT.
AND YET, WE DON'T WANT TO GO TO WAR WITH GENOSHA EITHER. THEY'VE INVESTED BILLIONS OF DOLLARS HERE... IN SOME WAYS THEY'VE BEEN GOOD ALLIES.
FEED
B&W LINE
#1 JERRY
#2 ALAIN
SO THE ADMINISTRATION WILL ENCOURAGE THEIR CO-OPERATION THROUGH DIPLOMATIC AND ECONOMIC CHANNELS. AND ONLY IF THAT FAILS WILL THEY START TALKING WAR.
BUT THERE'S ONE VARIABLE IN THIS EQUATION WE HAVEN'T CONSIDERED... WHAT IS THE MUTANTS' REACTION GOING TO BE?
TELL HENSHAW I WANT LIVE DIRECT REACTION FROM WASHINGTON, HIGHEST POSSIBLE SOURCE!
WHERE'S TRISH? SHE COVERS THE MUTANTS...
IN THE AIR, MR. BURTON, ON HER WAY TO AN ASSIGNMENT IN INDIA.
WHERE I SENT HER! GREAT SENSE OF TIMING! I'D FIRE MYSELF IF I WASN'T SO GOOD.*
LINE A
GET AHOLD OF MELLON, TELL HIM TO FIND OUT WHO THOSE KIDS ARE... WHO THEY REALLY ARE.
I WANT THEIR LIFE STORIES, INTERVIEWS WITH THEIR FAMILIES... THE WORKS!
* AFTER X-MEN # 270, LEAVING BEFORE THE MUTANTS CAPTURE.

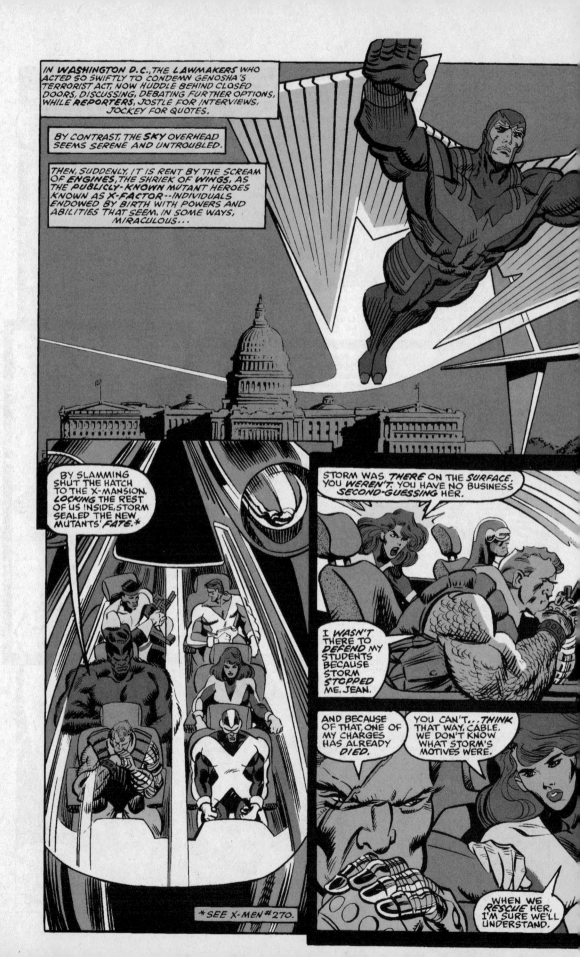

IN *WASHINGTON D.C.*, THE *LAWMAKERS* WHO ACTED SO SWIFTLY TO CONDEMN GENOSHA'S *TERRORIST ACT*, NOW HUDDLE BEHIND *CLOSED DOORS*, DISCUSSING, DEBATING FURTHER OPTIONS, WHILE *REPORTERS*, JOSTLE FOR INTERVIEWS, JOCKEY FOR QUOTES.

BY CONTRAST, THE *SKY* OVERHEAD SEEMS SERENE AND UNTROUBLED.

THEN, SUDDENLY, IT IS RENT BY THE SCREAM OF *ENGINES*, THE SHRIEK OF *WINGS*, AS THE *PUBLICLY-KNOWN* MUTANT HEROES KNOWN AS *X-FACTOR*--INDIVIDUALS ENDOWED BY BIRTH WITH POWERS AND ABILITIES THAT SEEM, IN SOME WAYS, *MIRACULOUS*...

BY SLAMMING SHUT THE HATCH TO THE X-MANSION, *LOCKING* THE REST OF US INSIDE, STORM SEALED THE NEW MUTANTS' *FATE.**

STORM WAS *THERE* ON THE *SURFACE*. YOU *WEREN'T*. YOU HAVE NO BUSINESS *SECOND-GUESSING* HER.

I *WASN'T* THERE TO *DEFEND* MY STUDENTS BECAUSE STORM *STOPPED* ME, JEAN.

AND BECAUSE OF THAT, ONE OF MY CHARGES HAS ALREADY *DIED.*

YOU CAN'T...*THINK* THAT WAY, CABLE. WE DON'T KNOW WHAT STORM'S *MOTIVES* WERE.

WHEN WE *RESCUE* HER, I'M SURE WE'LL *UNDERSTAND.*

*SEE X-MEN #270.

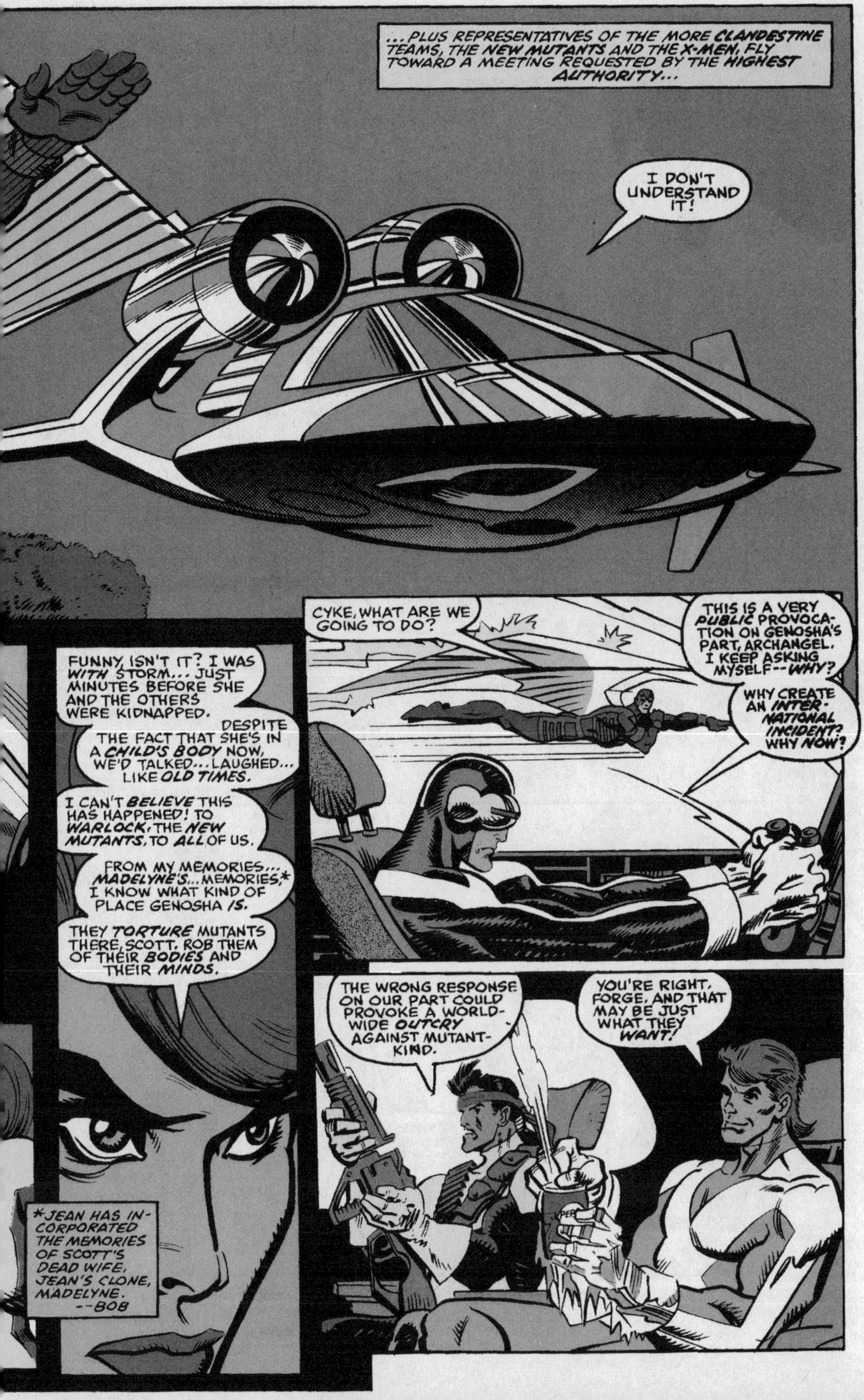

...PLUS REPRESENTATIVES OF THE MORE CLANDESTINE TEAMS, THE NEW MUTANTS AND THE X-MEN, FLY TOWARD A MEETING REQUESTED BY THE HIGHEST AUTHORITY...
I DON'T UNDERSTAND IT!
FUNNY, ISN'T IT? I WAS WITH STORM... JUST MINUTES BEFORE SHE AND THE OTHERS WERE KIDNAPPED.
DESPITE THE FACT THAT SHE'S IN A CHILD'S BODY NOW, WE'D TALKED...LAUGHED... LIKE OLD TIMES.
I CAN'T BELIEVE THIS HAS HAPPENED! TO WARLOCK, THE NEW MUTANTS, TO ALL OF US.
FROM MY MEMORIES... MADELYNE'S...MEMORIES,* I KNOW WHAT KIND OF PLACE GENOSHA IS.
THEY TORTURE MUTANTS THERE, SCOTT. ROB THEM OF THEIR BODIES AND THEIR MINDS.
*JEAN HAS INCORPORATED THE MEMORIES OF SCOTT'S DEAD WIFE, JEAN'S CLONE, MADELYNE. --BOB
CYKE, WHAT ARE WE GOING TO DO?
THIS IS A VERY PUBLIC PROVOCATION ON GENOSHA'S PART, ARCHANGEL. I KEEP ASKING MYSELF--WHY?
WHY CREATE AN INTERNATIONAL INCIDENT? WHY NOW?
THE WRONG RESPONSE ON OUR PART COULD PROVOKE A WORLD-WIDE OUTCRY AGAINST MUTANT-KIND.
YOU'RE RIGHT, FORGE. AND THAT MAY BE JUST WHAT THEY WANT!

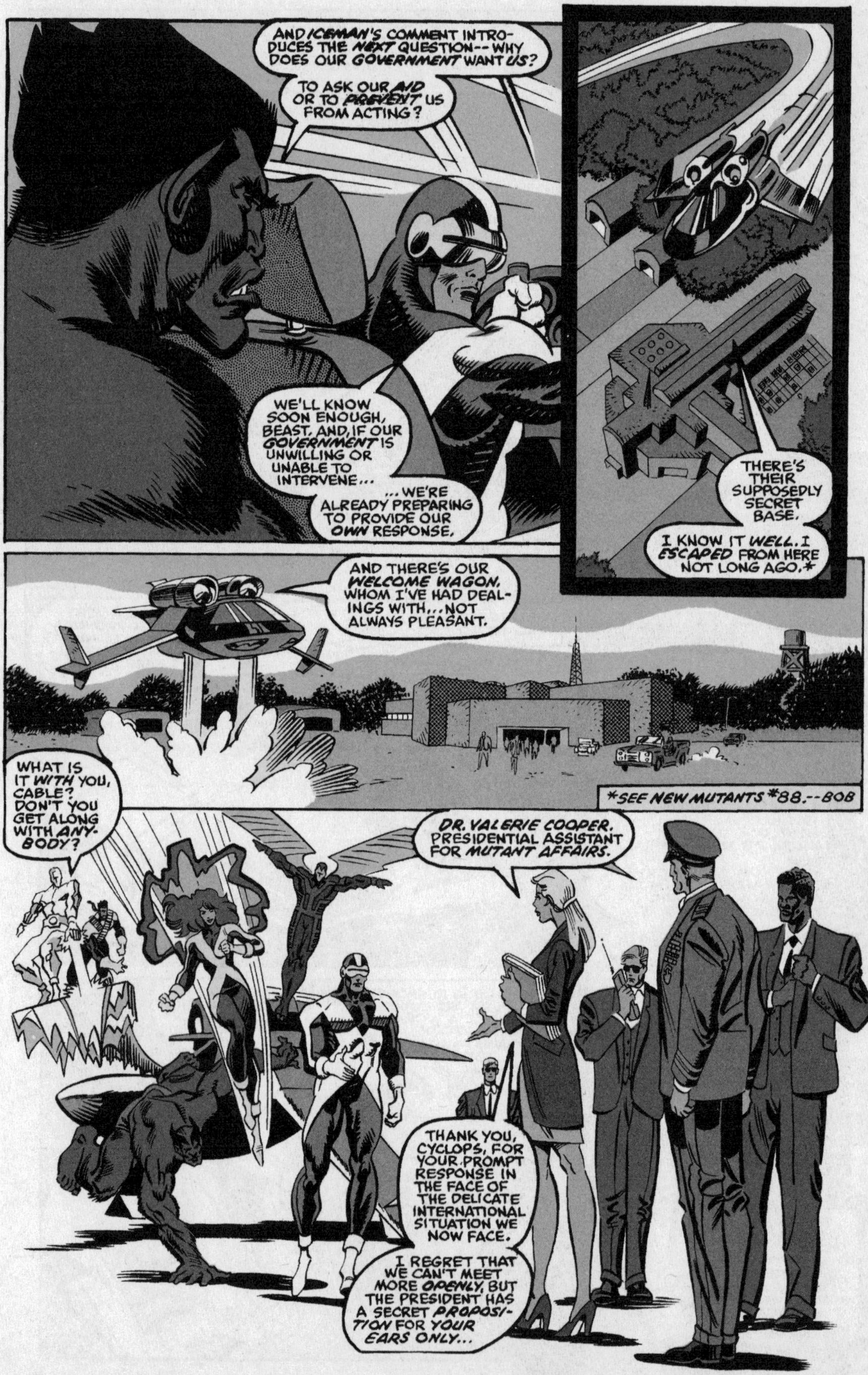
AND ICEMAN'S COMMENT INTRODUCES THE NEXT QUESTION-- WHY DOES OUR GOVERNMENT WANT US?
TO ASK OUR AID OR TO PREVENT US FROM ACTING?
WE'LL KNOW SOON ENOUGH, BEAST. AND, IF OUR GOVERNMENT IS UNWILLING OR UNABLE TO INTERVENE...
...WE'RE ALREADY PREPARING TO PROVIDE OUR OWN RESPONSE.
THERE'S THEIR SUPPOSEDLY SECRET BASE.
I KNOW IT WELL. I ESCAPED FROM HERE NOT LONG AGO.*
AND THERE'S OUR WELCOME WAGON, WHOM I'VE HAD DEALINGS WITH... NOT ALWAYS PLEASANT.
*SEE NEW MUTANTS #88.--BOB
WHAT IS IT WITH YOU, CABLE? DON'T YOU GET ALONG WITH ANYBODY?
DR. VALERIE COOPER. PRESIDENTIAL ASSISTANT FOR MUTANT AFFAIRS.
THANK YOU, CYCLOPS, FOR YOUR PROMPT RESPONSE IN THE FACE OF THE DELICATE INTERNATIONAL SITUATION WE NOW FACE.
I REGRET THAT WE CAN'T MEET MORE OPENLY, BUT THE PRESIDENT HAS A SECRET PROPOSITION FOR YOUR EARS ONLY...

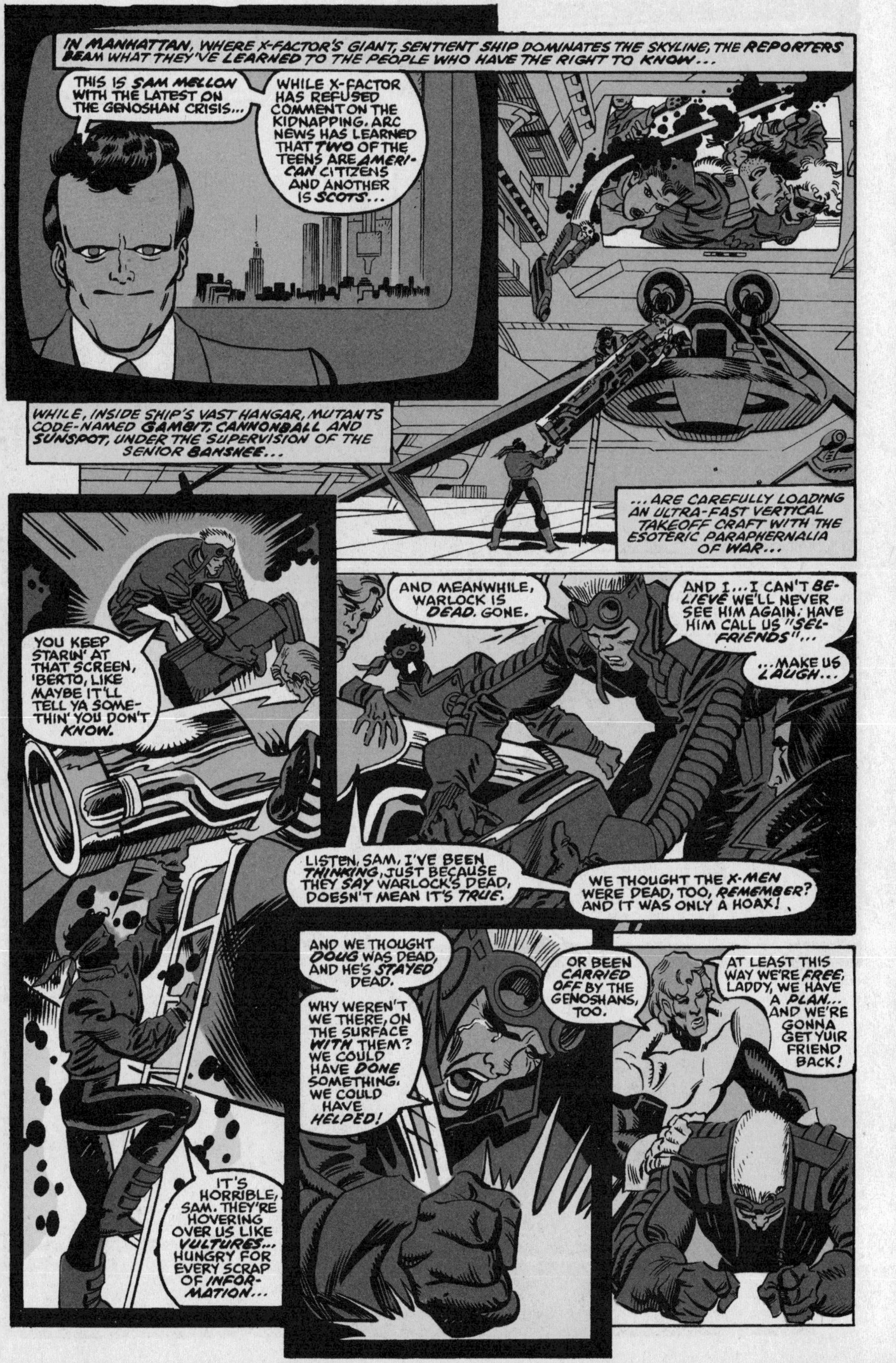
IN MANHATTAN, WHERE X-FACTOR'S GIANT, SENTIENT SHIP DOMINATES THE SKYLINE, THE REPORTERS BEAM WHAT THEY'VE LEARNED TO THE PEOPLE WHO HAVE THE RIGHT TO KNOW...
THIS IS SAM MELLON WITH THE LATEST ON THE GENOSHAN CRISIS...
WHILE X-FACTOR HAS REFUSED COMMENT ON THE KIDNAPPING, ARC NEWS HAS LEARNED THAT TWO OF THE TEENS ARE AMERICAN CITIZENS AND ANOTHER IS SCOTS...
WHILE, INSIDE SHIP'S VAST HANGAR, MUTANTS CODE-NAMED GAMBIT, CANNONBALL AND SUNSPOT, UNDER THE SUPERVISION OF THE SENIOR BANSHEE...
...ARE CAREFULLY LOADING AN ULTRA-FAST VERTICAL TAKEOFF CRAFT WITH THE ESOTERIC PARAPHERNALIA OF WAR...
YOU KEEP STARIN' AT THAT SCREEN, 'BERTO, LIKE MAYBE IT'LL TELL YA SOMETHIN' YOU DON'T KNOW.
AND MEANWHILE, WARLOCK IS DEAD. GONE.
AND I...I CAN'T BELIEVE WE'LL NEVER SEE HIM AGAIN. HAVE HIM CALL US "SELFRIENDS"...
...MAKE US LAUGH...
LISTEN, SAM, I'VE BEEN THINKING, JUST BECAUSE THEY SAY WARLOCK'S DEAD, DOESN'T MEAN IT'S TRUE.
WE THOUGHT THE X-MEN WERE DEAD, TOO, REMEMBER? AND IT WAS ONLY A HOAX!
IT'S HORRIBLE, SAM. THEY'RE HOVERING OVER US LIKE VULTURES... HUNGRY FOR EVERY SCRAP OF INFORMATION...
AND WE THOUGHT DOUG WAS DEAD, AND HE'S STAYED DEAD.
WHY WEREN'T WE THERE, ON THE SURFACE WITH THEM? WE COULD HAVE DONE SOMETHING. WE COULD HAVE HELPED!
OR BEEN CARRIED OFF BY THE GENOSHANS, TOO.
AT LEAST THIS WAY WE'RE FREE, LADDY, WE HAVE A PLAN... AND WE'RE GONNA GET YUIR FRIEND BACK!

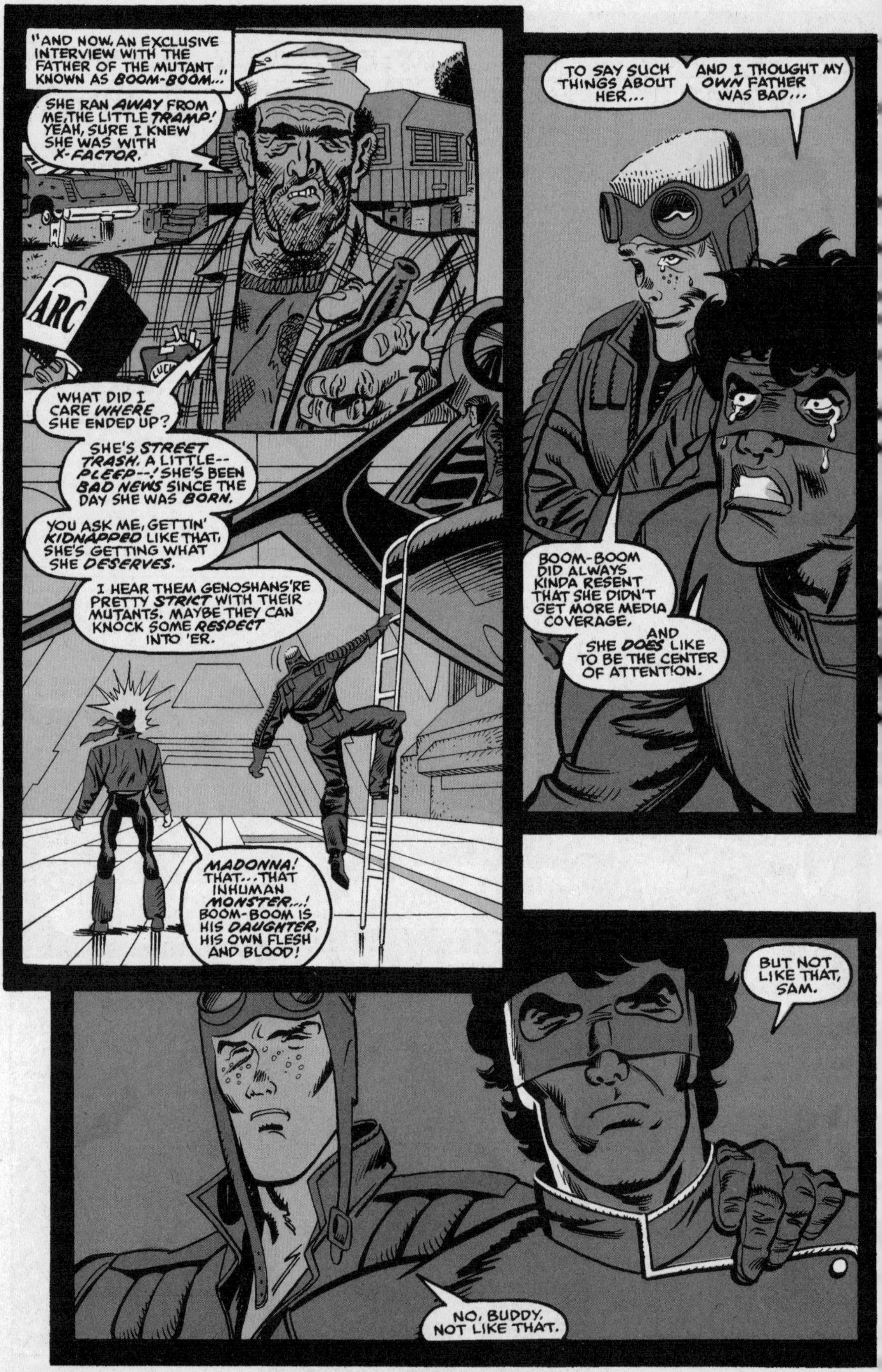

"AND NOW, AN EXCLUSIVE INTERVIEW WITH THE FATHER OF THE MUTANT KNOWN AS BOOM-BOOM..."
SHE RAN AWAY FROM ME, THE LITTLE TRAMP! YEAH, SURE I KNEW SHE WAS WITH X-FACTOR.
ARC
WHAT DID I CARE WHERE SHE ENDED UP?
SHE'S STREET TRASH. A LITTLE-- PLEEP--! SHE'S BEEN BAD NEWS SINCE THE DAY SHE WAS BORN.
YOU ASK ME, GETTIN' KIDNAPPED LIKE THAT, SHE'S GETTING WHAT SHE DESERVES.
I HEAR THEM GENOSHANS'RE PRETTY STRICT WITH THEIR MUTANTS. MAYBE THEY CAN KNOCK SOME RESPECT INTO 'ER.
MADONNA! THAT... THAT INHUMAN MONSTER...! BOOM-BOOM IS HIS DAUGHTER, HIS OWN FLESH AND BLOOD!
TO SAY SUCH THINGS ABOUT HER...
AND I THOUGHT MY OWN FATHER WAS BAD...
BOOM-BOOM DID ALWAYS KINDA RESENT THAT SHE DIDN'T GET MORE MEDIA COVERAGE,
AND SHE DOES LIKE TO BE THE CENTER OF ATTENTION.
BUT NOT LIKE THAT, SAM.
NO, BUDDY. NOT LIKE THAT.

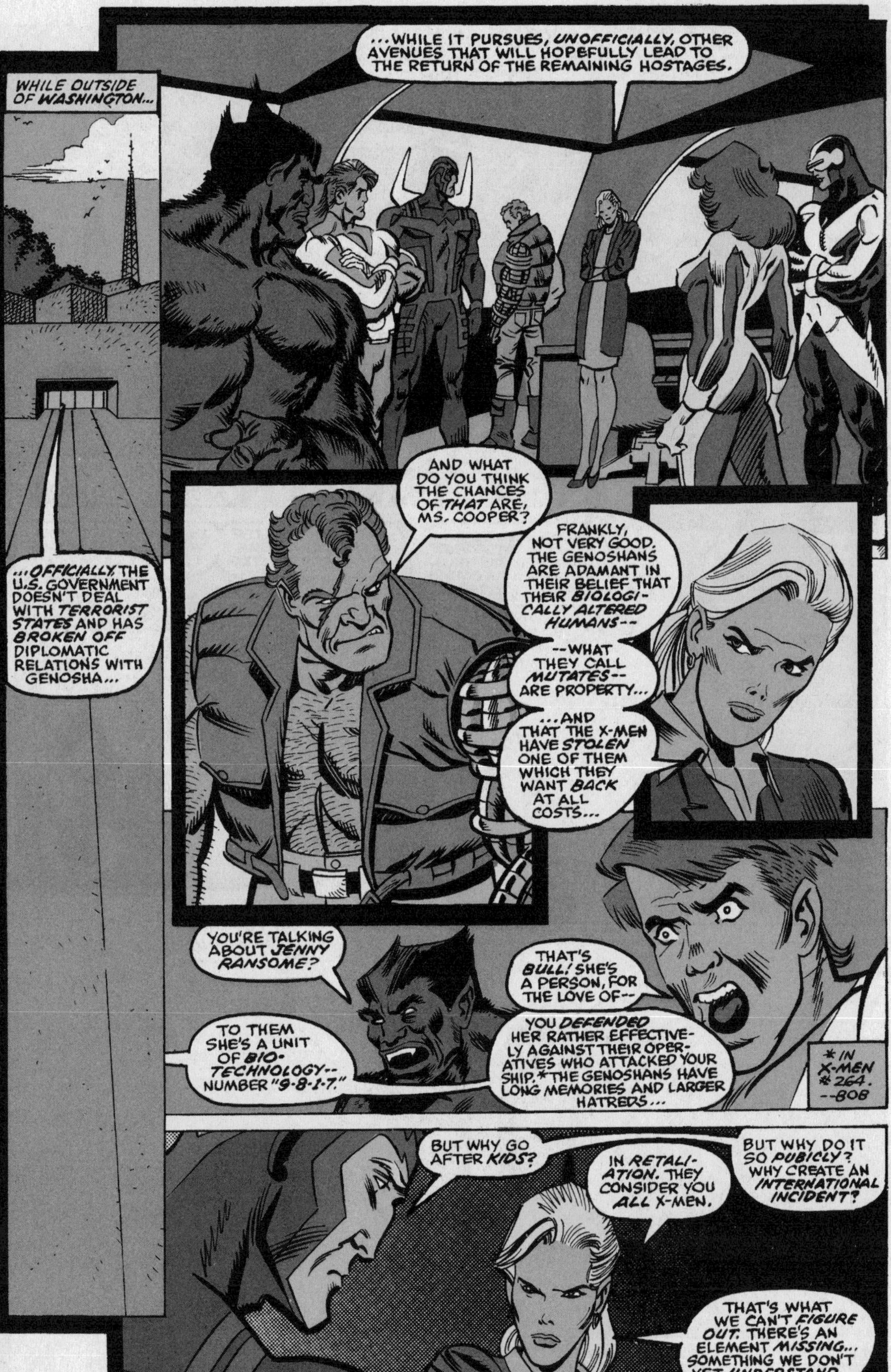

...WHILE IT PURSUES, UNOFFICIALLY, OTHER AVENUES THAT WILL HOPEFULLY LEAD TO THE RETURN OF THE REMAINING HOSTAGES.
WHILE OUTSIDE OF WASHINGTON...
...OFFICIALLY, THE U.S. GOVERNMENT DOESN'T DEAL WITH TERRORIST STATES AND HAS BROKEN OFF DIPLOMATIC RELATIONS WITH GENOSHA...
AND WHAT DO YOU THINK THE CHANCES OF THAT ARE, MS. COOPER?
FRANKLY, NOT VERY GOOD. THE GENOSHANS ARE ADAMANT IN THEIR BELIEF THAT THEIR BIOLOGICALLY ALTERED HUMANS--
--WHAT THEY CALL MUTATES--ARE PROPERTY...
...AND THAT THE X-MEN HAVE STOLEN ONE OF THEM WHICH THEY WANT BACK AT ALL COSTS...
YOU'RE TALKING ABOUT JENNY RANSOME?
THAT'S BULL! SHE'S A PERSON, FOR THE LOVE OF--
TO THEM SHE'S A UNIT OF BIO-TECHNOLOGY--NUMBER "9-8-1-7."
YOU DEFENDED HER RATHER EFFECTIVELY AGAINST THEIR OPERATIVES WHO ATTACKED YOUR SHIP.* THE GENOSHANS HAVE LONG MEMORIES AND LARGER HATREDS...
*IN X-MEN #264. --BOB
BUT WHY GO AFTER KIDS?
IN RETALIATION. THEY CONSIDER YOU ALL X-MEN.
BUT WHY DO IT SO PUBICLY? WHY CREATE AN INTERNATIONAL INCIDENT?
THAT'S WHAT WE CAN'T FIGURE OUT. THERE'S AN ELEMENT MISSING... SOMETHING WE DON'T YET UNDERSTAND.

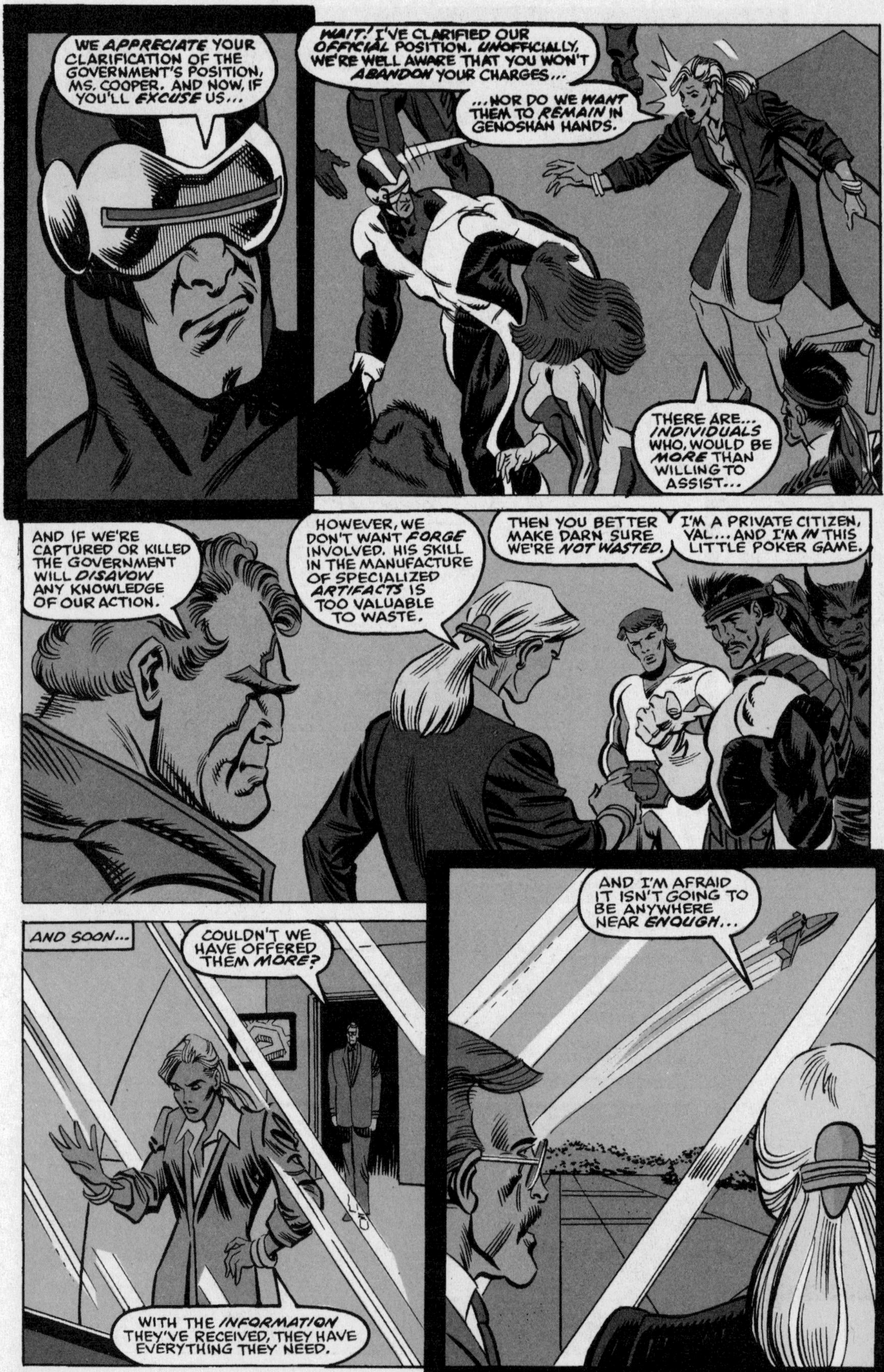
WE APPRECIATE YOUR CLARIFICATION OF THE GOVERNMENT'S POSITION, MS. COOPER. AND NOW, IF YOU'LL EXCUSE US...
WAIT! I'VE CLARIFIED OUR OFFICIAL POSITION. UNOFFICIALLY, WE'RE WELL AWARE THAT YOU WON'T ABANDON YOUR CHARGES...
...NOR DO WE WANT THEM TO REMAIN IN GENOSHAN HANDS.
THERE ARE... INDIVIDUALS WHO, WOULD BE MORE THAN WILLING TO ASSIST...
AND IF WE'RE CAPTURED OR KILLED THE GOVERNMENT WILL DISAVOW ANY KNOWLEDGE OF OUR ACTION.
HOWEVER, WE DON'T WANT FORGE INVOLVED. HIS SKILL IN THE MANUFACTURE OF SPECIALIZED ARTIFACTS IS TOO VALUABLE TO WASTE.
THEN YOU BETTER MAKE DARN SURE WE'RE NOT WASTED.
I'M A PRIVATE CITIZEN, VAL... AND I'M IN THIS LITTLE POKER GAME.
AND SOON...
COULDN'T WE HAVE OFFERED THEM MORE?
WITH THE INFORMATION THEY'VE RECEIVED, THEY HAVE EVERYTHING THEY NEED.
AND I'M AFRAID IT ISN'T GOING TO BE ANYWHERE NEAR ENOUGH...

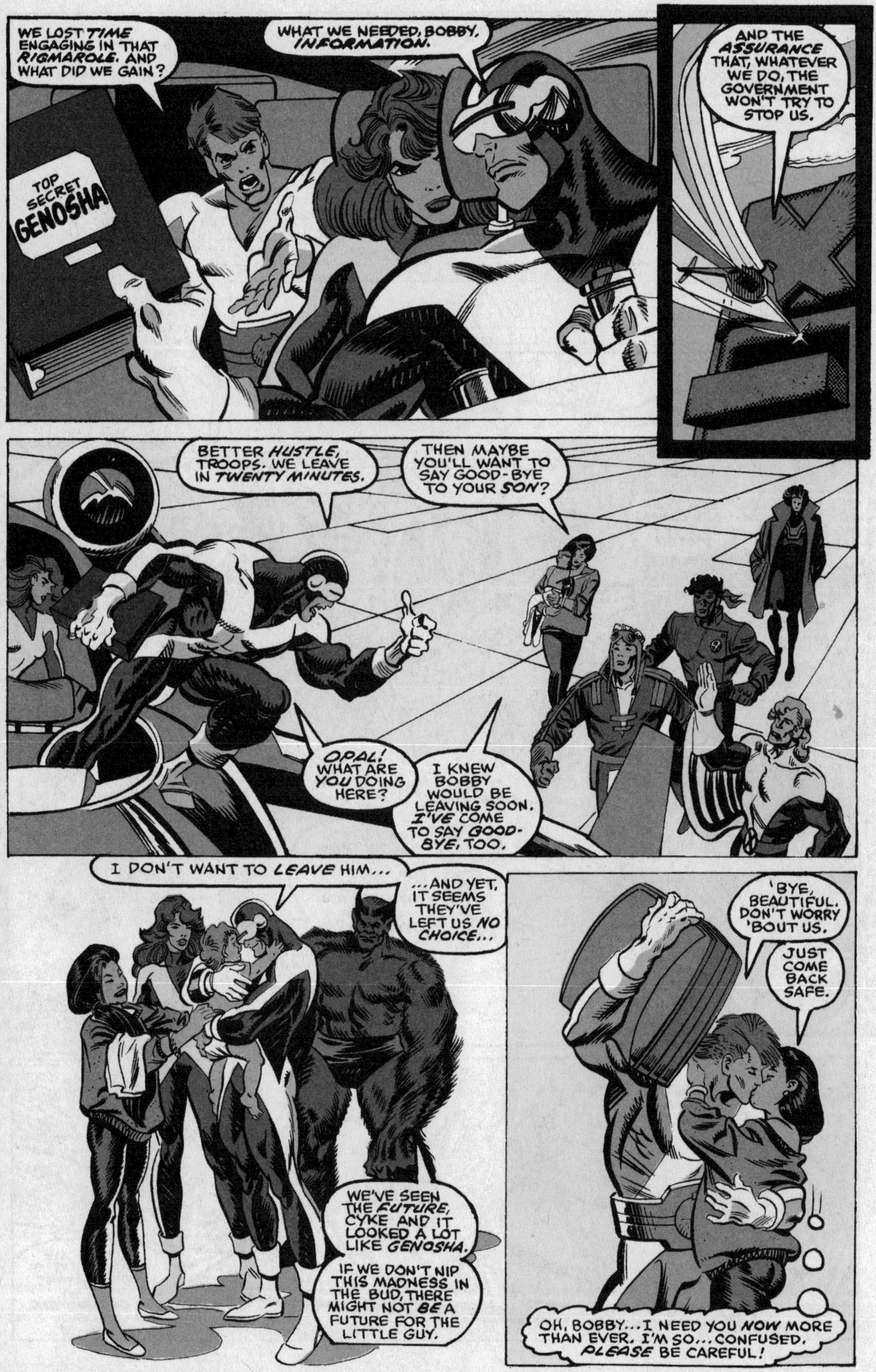
WE LOST TIME ENGAGING IN THAT RIGMAROLE. AND WHAT DID WE GAIN?
TOP SECRET GENOSHA
WHAT WE NEEDED, BOBBY. INFORMATION.
AND THE ASSURANCE THAT, WHATEVER WE DO, THE GOVERNMENT WON'T TRY TO STOP US.
BETTER HUSTLE, TROOPS. WE LEAVE IN TWENTY MINUTES.
THEN MAYBE YOU'LL WANT TO SAY GOOD-BYE TO YOUR SON?
OPAL! WHAT ARE YOU DOING HERE?
I KNEW BOBBY WOULD BE LEAVING SOON. I'VE COME TO SAY GOOD-BYE, TOO.
I DON'T WANT TO LEAVE HIM...
...AND YET, IT SEEMS THEY'VE LEFT US NO CHOICE...
WE'VE SEEN THE FUTURE, CYKE AND IT LOOKED A LOT LIKE GENOSHA.
IF WE DON'T NIP THIS MADNESS IN THE BUD, THERE MIGHT NOT BE A FUTURE FOR THE LITTLE GUY.
'BYE, BEAUTIFUL. DON'T WORRY 'BOUT US.
JUST COME BACK SAFE.
OH, BOBBY... I NEED YOU NOW MORE THAN EVER. I'M SO... CONFUSED. PLEASE BE CAREFUL!

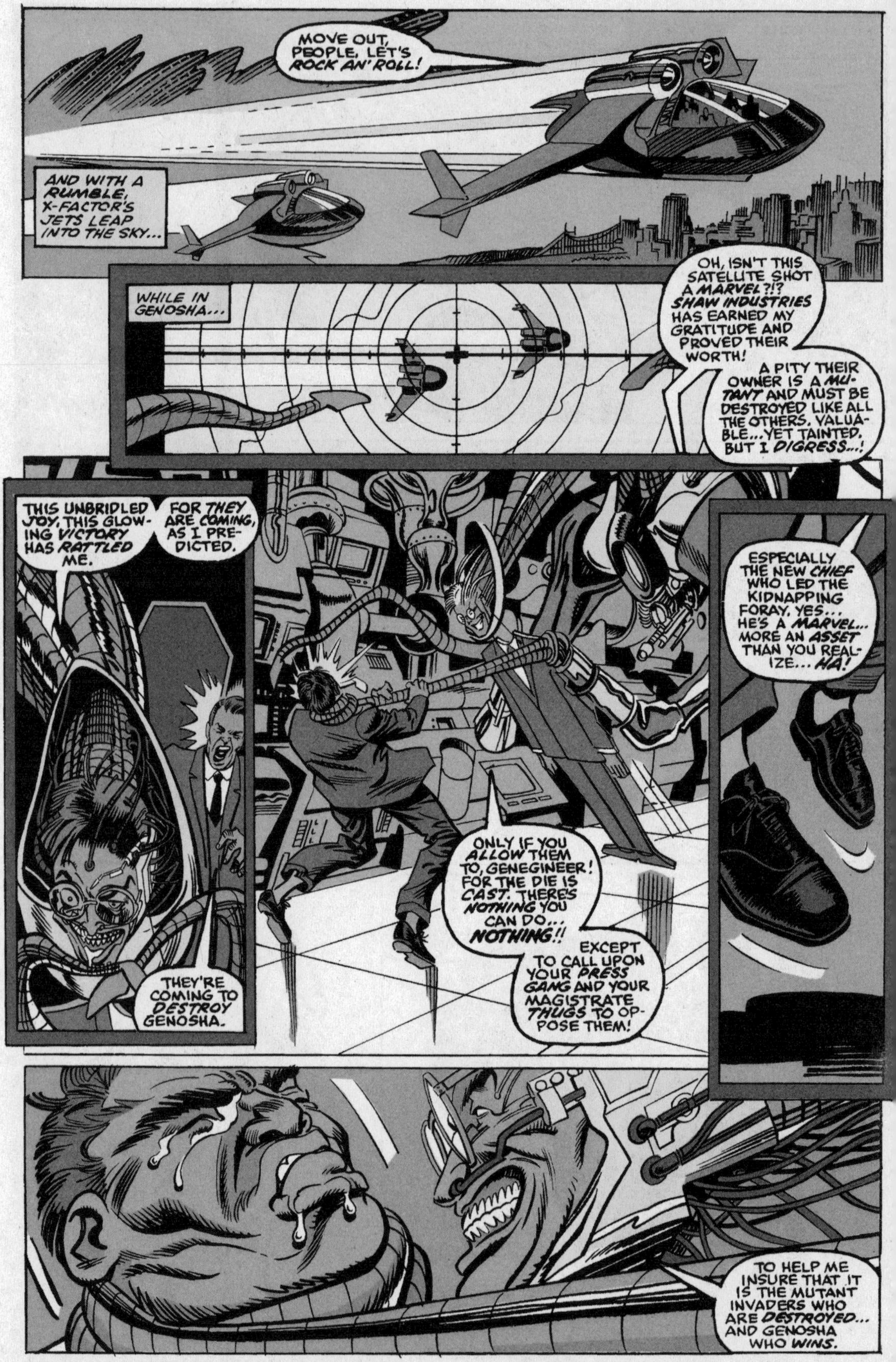

MOVE OUT, PEOPLE, LET'S ROCK AN' ROLL!
AND WITH A RUMBLE, X-FACTOR'S JETS LEAP INTO THE SKY...
WHILE IN GENOSHA...
OH, ISN'T THIS SATELLITE SHOT A MARVEL?!? SHAW INDUSTRIES HAS EARNED MY GRATITUDE AND PROVED THEIR WORTH!
A PITY THEIR OWNER IS A MUTANT AND MUST BE DESTROYED LIKE ALL THE OTHERS. VALUABLE... YET TAINTED. BUT I DIGRESS...!
THIS UNBRIDLED JOY, THIS GLOWING VICTORY HAS RATTLED ME.
FOR THEY ARE COMING, AS I PREDICTED.
THEY'RE COMING TO DESTROY GENOSHA.
ONLY IF YOU ALLOW THEM TO, GENEGINEER! FOR THE DIE IS CAST. THERE'S NOTHING YOU CAN DO... NOTHING!!
EXCEPT TO CALL UPON YOUR PRESS GANG AND YOUR MAGISTRATE THUGS TO OPPOSE THEM!
ESPECIALLY THE NEW CHIEF WHO LED THE KIDNAPPING FORAY. YES... HE'S A MARVEL... MORE AN ASSET THAN YOU REALIZE... HA!
TO HELP ME INSURE THAT IT IS THE MUTANT INVADERS WHO ARE DESTROYED... AND GENOSHA WHO WINS.

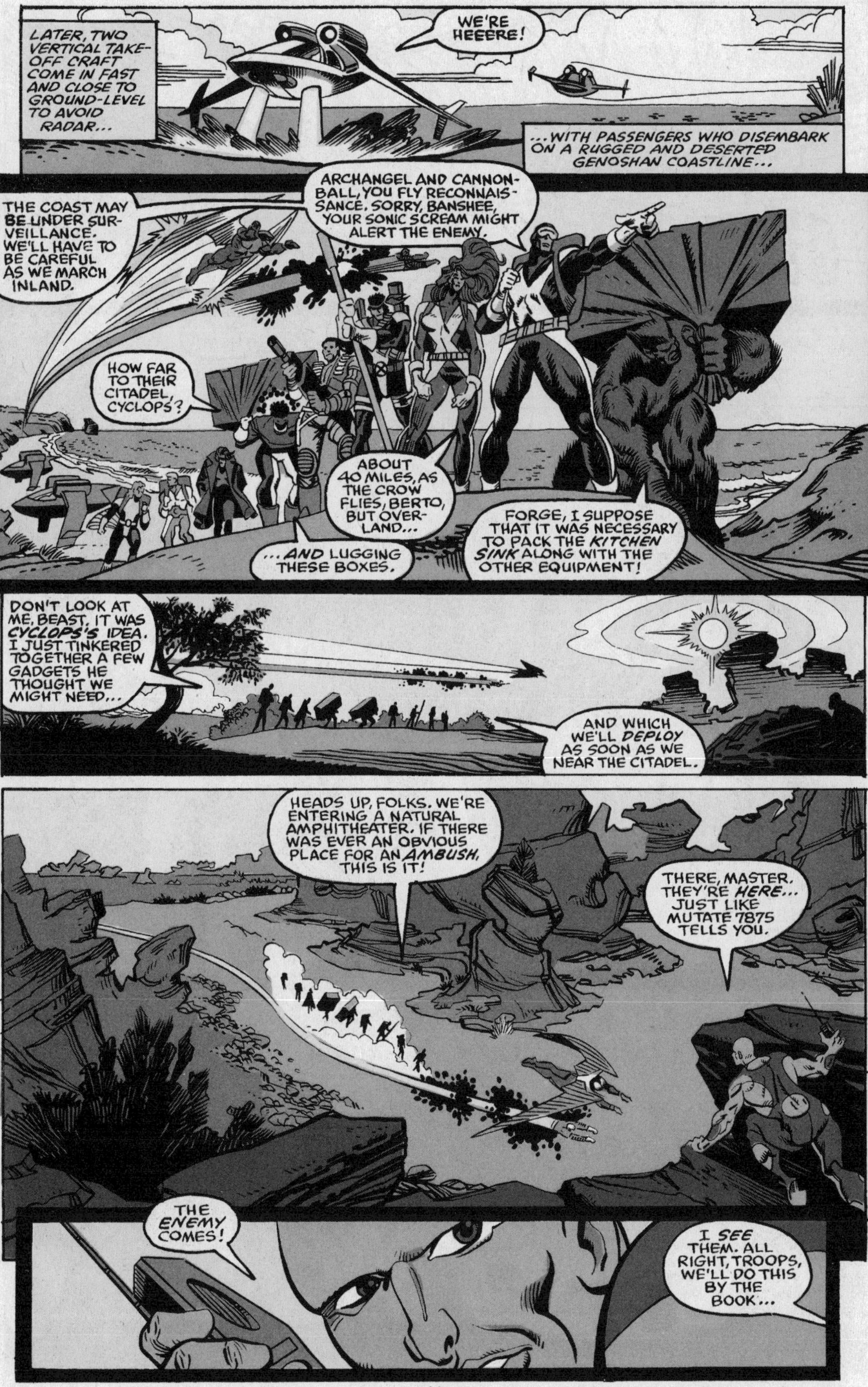
LATER, TWO VERTICAL TAKE-OFF CRAFT COME IN FAST AND CLOSE TO GROUND-LEVEL TO AVOID RADAR...
WE'RE HEEERE!
...WITH PASSENGERS WHO DISEMBARK ON A RUGGED AND DESERTED GENOSHAN COASTLINE...
THE COAST MAY BE UNDER SURVEILLANCE. WE'LL HAVE TO BE CAREFUL AS WE MARCH INLAND.
ARCHANGEL AND CANNONBALL, YOU FLY RECONNAISSANCE. SORRY, BANSHEE, YOUR SONIC SCREAM MIGHT ALERT THE ENEMY.
HOW FAR TO THEIR CITADEL, CYCLOPS?
ABOUT 40 MILES, AS THE CROW FLIES, BERTO, BUT OVERLAND...
...AND LUGGING THESE BOXES.
FORGE, I SUPPOSE THAT IT WAS NECESSARY TO PACK THE KITCHEN SINK ALONG WITH THE OTHER EQUIPMENT!
DON'T LOOK AT ME, BEAST, IT WAS CYCLOPS'S IDEA. I JUST TINKERED TOGETHER A FEW GADGETS HE THOUGHT WE MIGHT NEED...
AND WHICH WE'LL DEPLOY AS SOON AS WE NEAR THE CITADEL.
HEADS UP, FOLKS. WE'RE ENTERING A NATURAL AMPHITHEATER. IF THERE WAS EVER AN OBVIOUS PLACE FOR AN AMBUSH, THIS IS IT!
THERE, MASTER. THEY'RE HERE... JUST LIKE MUTATE 7875 TELLS YOU.
THE ENEMY COMES!
I SEE THEM. ALL RIGHT, TROOPS, WE'LL DO THIS BY THE BOOK...

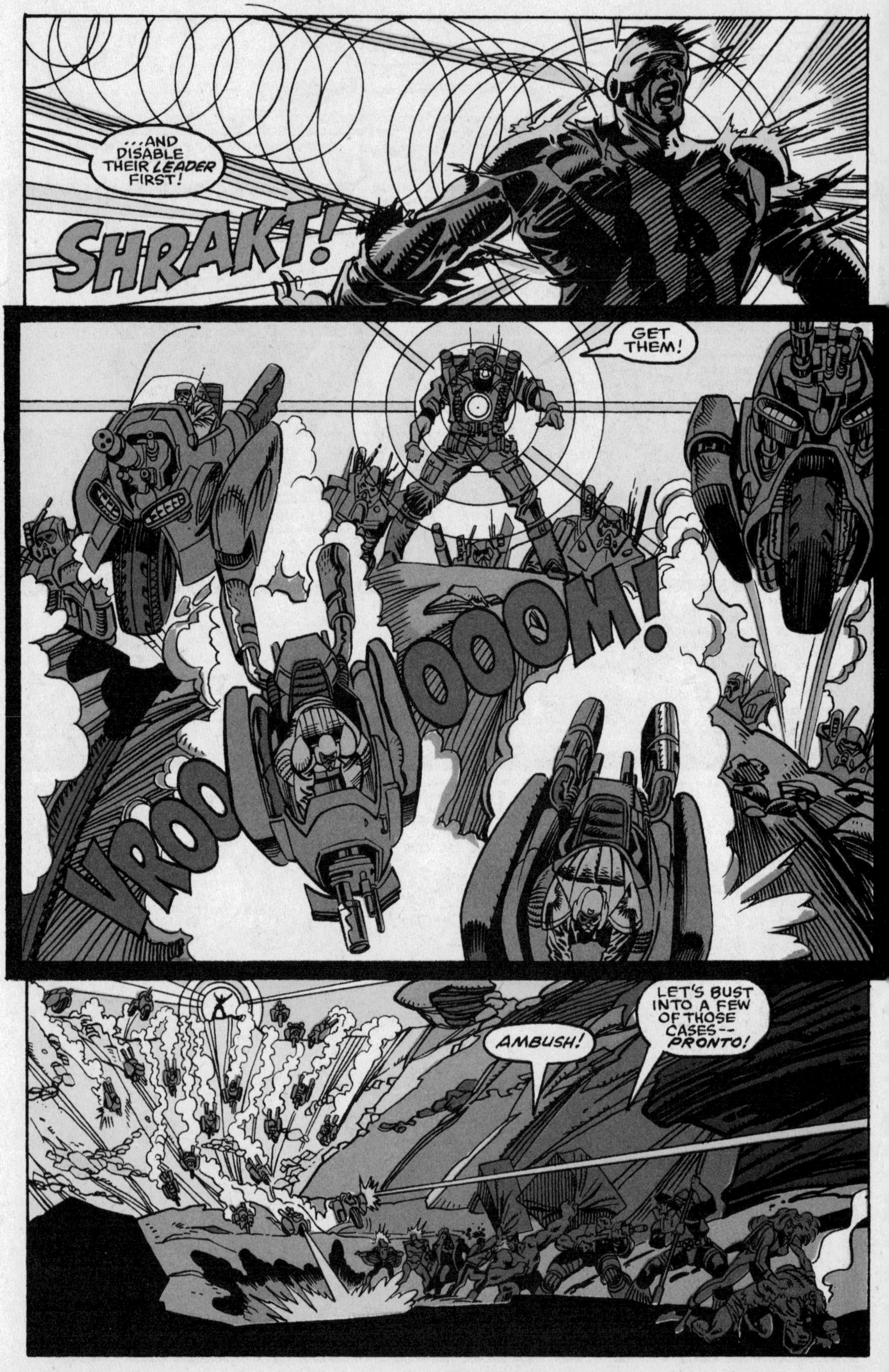

...AND DISABLE THEIR LEADER FIRST!
SHRAKT!
GET THEM!
VROOOOOOOM!
AMBUSH!
LET'S BUST INTO A FEW OF THOSE CASES-- PRONTO!

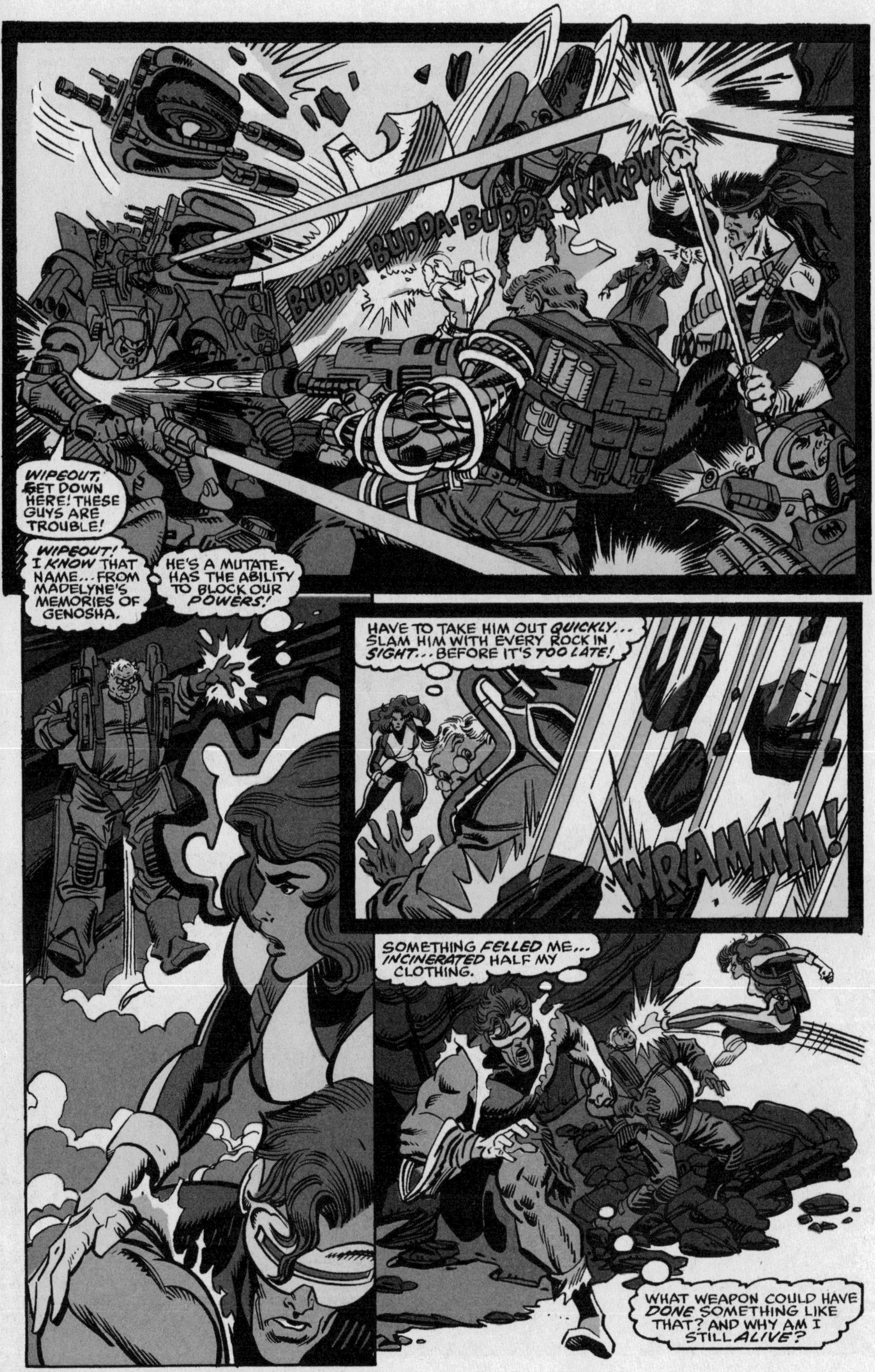
BUDDA-BUDDA-BUDDA-SKAKPW
WIPEOUT, GET DOWN HERE! THESE GUYS ARE TROUBLE!
WIPEOUT! I KNOW THAT NAME... FROM MADELYNE'S MEMORIES OF GENOSHA.
HE'S A MUTATE. HAS THE ABILITY TO BLOCK OUR POWERS!
HAVE TO TAKE HIM OUT QUICKLY... SLAM HIM WITH EVERY ROCK IN SIGHT... BEFORE IT'S TOO LATE!
WRAMMM!
SOMETHING FELLED ME... INCINERATED HALF MY CLOTHING.
WHAT WEAPON COULD HAVE DONE SOMETHING LIKE THAT? AND WHY AM I STILL ALIVE?

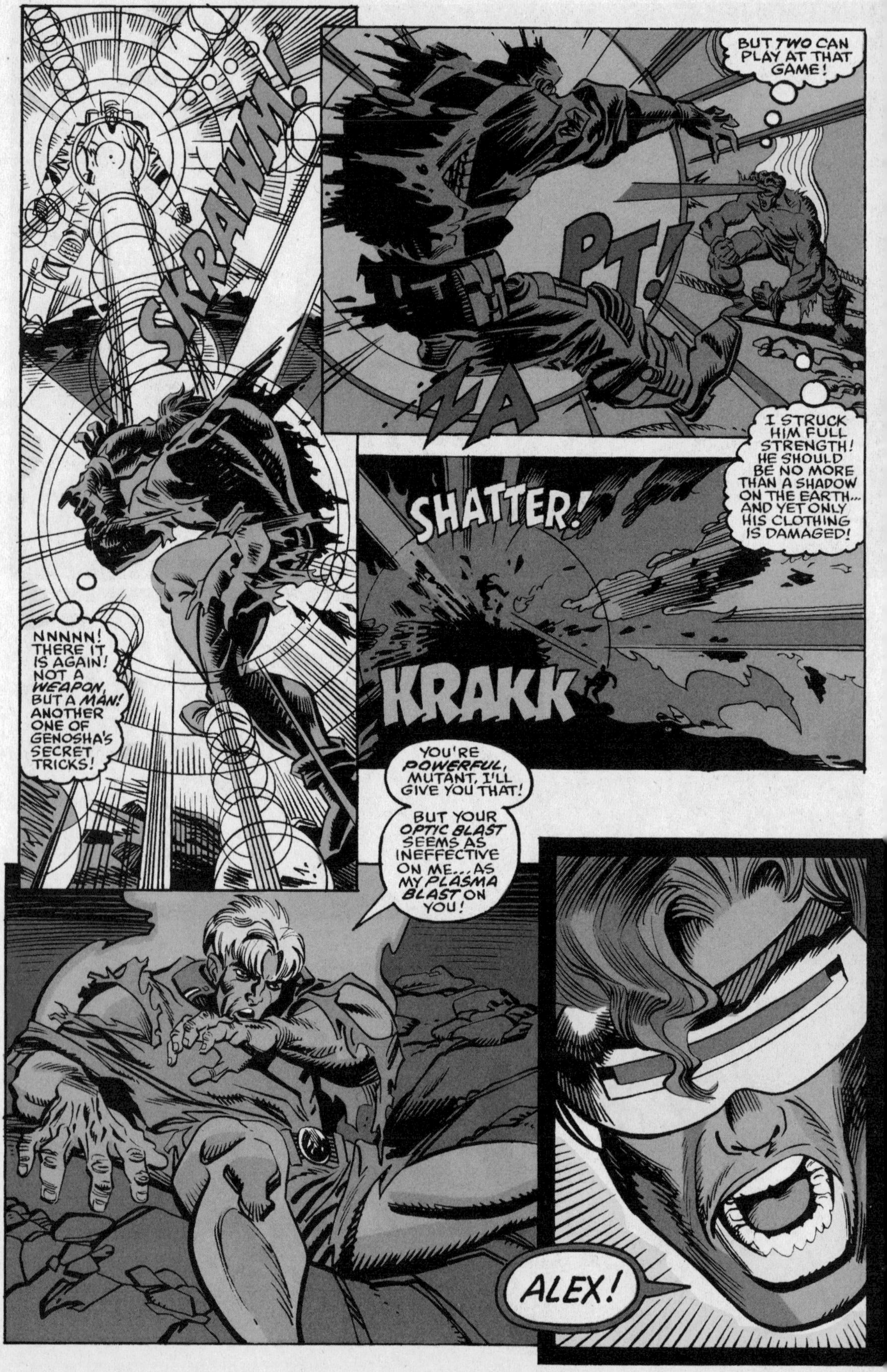
SKRAWM!
NNNNN! THERE IT IS AGAIN! NOT A WEAPON, BUT A MAN! ANOTHER ONE OF GENOSHA'S SECRET TRICKS!
BUT TWO CAN PLAY AT THAT GAME!
ZZAPT!
I STRUCK HIM FULL STRENGTH! HE SHOULD BE NO MORE THAN A SHADOW ON THE EARTH... AND YET ONLY HIS CLOTHING IS DAMAGED!
SHATTER!
KRAKK
YOU'RE POWERFUL, MUTANT, I'LL GIVE YOU THAT!
BUT YOUR OPTIC BLAST SEEMS AS INEFFECTIVE ON ME... AS MY PLASMA BLAST ON YOU!
ALEX!

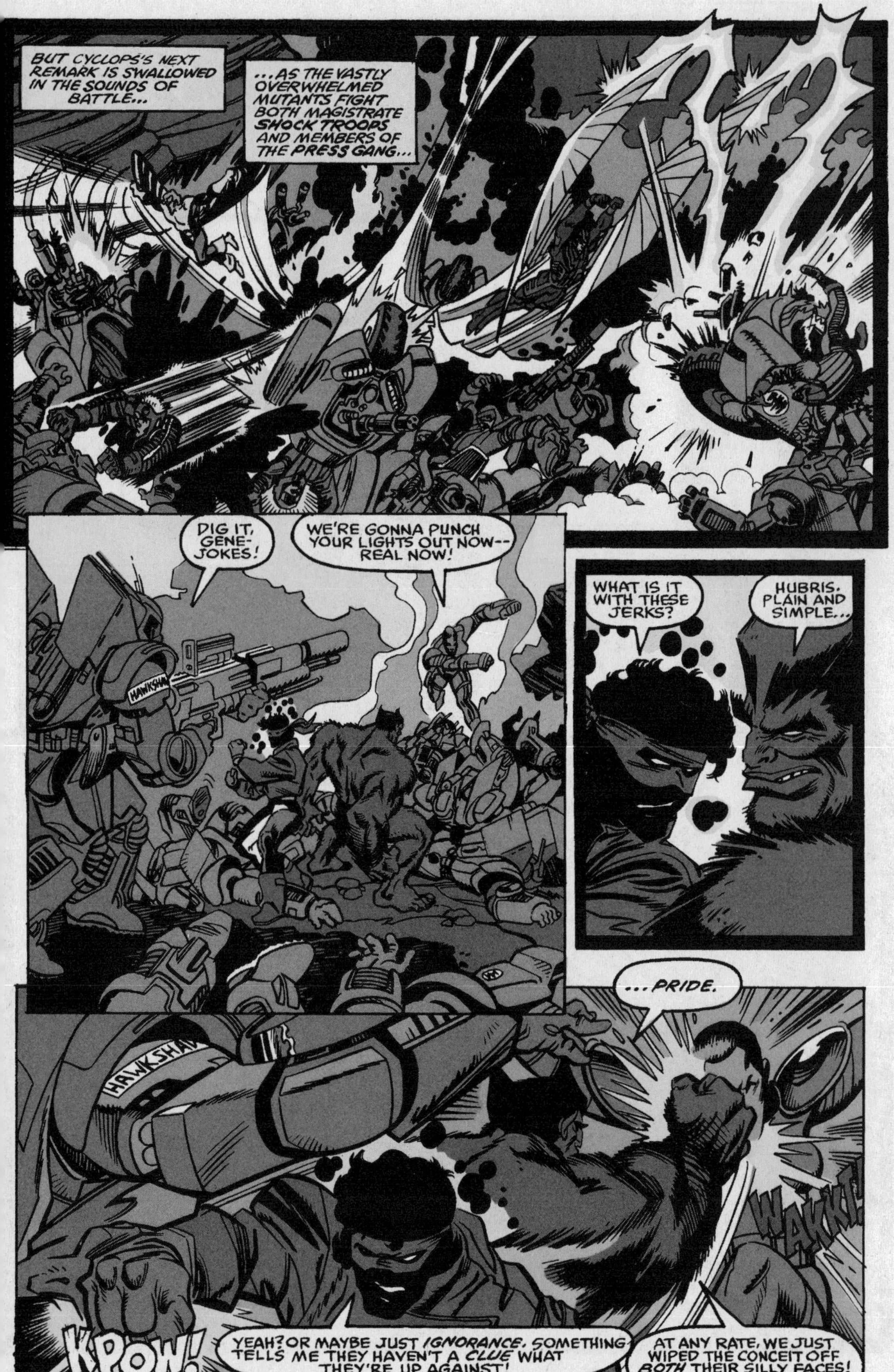
BUT CYCLOPS'S NEXT REMARK IS SWALLOWED IN THE SOUNDS OF BATTLE...
...AS THE VASTLY OVERWHELMED MUTANTS FIGHT BOTH MAGISTRATE SHOCK TROOPS AND MEMBERS OF THE PRESS GANG...
DIG IT, GENE-JOKES!
WE'RE GONNA PUNCH YOUR LIGHTS OUT NOW-- REAL NOW!
HAWKSHAW
WHAT IS IT WITH THESE JERKS?
HUBRIS. PLAIN AND SIMPLE...
...PRIDE.
HAWKSHAW
WAKK!
KPOW!
YEAH? OR MAYBE JUST IGNORANCE. SOMETHING TELLS ME THEY HAVEN'T A CLUE WHAT THEY'RE UP AGAINST!
AT ANY RATE, WE JUST WIPED THE CONCEIT OFF BOTH THEIR SILLY FACES!

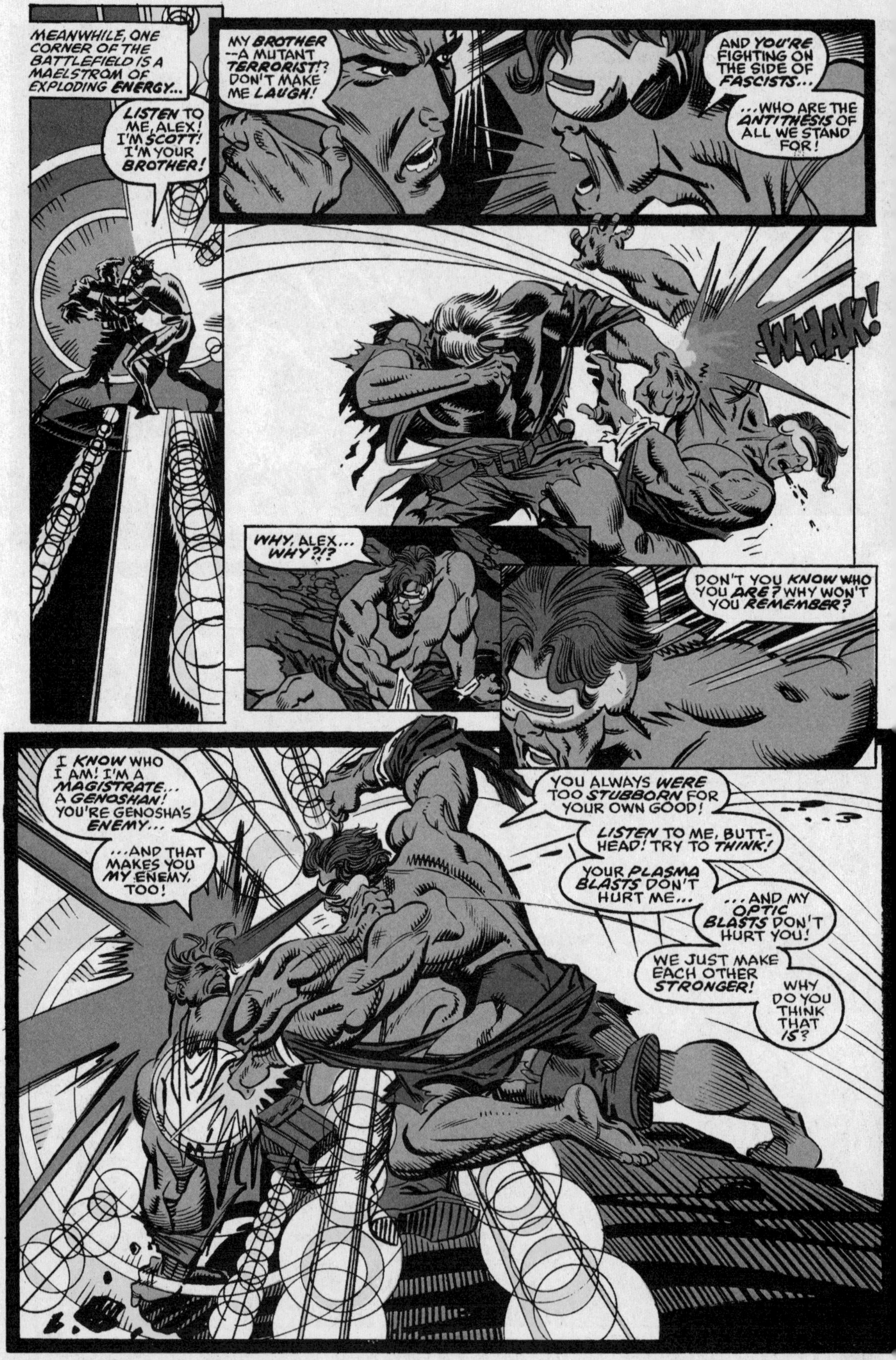
MEANWHILE, ONE CORNER OF THE BATTLEFIELD IS A MAELSTROM OF EXPLODING ENERGY...
LISTEN TO ME, ALEX! I'M SCOTT! I'M YOUR BROTHER!
MY BROTHER --A MUTANT TERRORIST!? DON'T MAKE ME LAUGH!
AND YOU'RE FIGHTING ON THE SIDE OF FASCISTS...
...WHO ARE THE ANTITHESIS OF ALL WE STAND FOR!
WHAK!
WHY, ALEX... WHY?!?
DON'T YOU KNOW WHO YOU ARE? WHY WON'T YOU REMEMBER?
I KNOW WHO I AM! I'M A MAGISTRATE... A GENOSHAN! YOU'RE GENOSHA'S ENEMY...
...AND THAT MAKES YOU MY ENEMY, TOO!
YOU ALWAYS WERE TOO STUBBORN FOR YOUR OWN GOOD!
LISTEN TO ME, BUTT-HEAD! TRY TO THINK!
YOUR PLASMA BLASTS DON'T HURT ME...
...AND MY OPTIC BLASTS DON'T HURT YOU!
WE JUST MAKE EACH OTHER STRONGER!
WHY DO YOU THINK THAT IS?

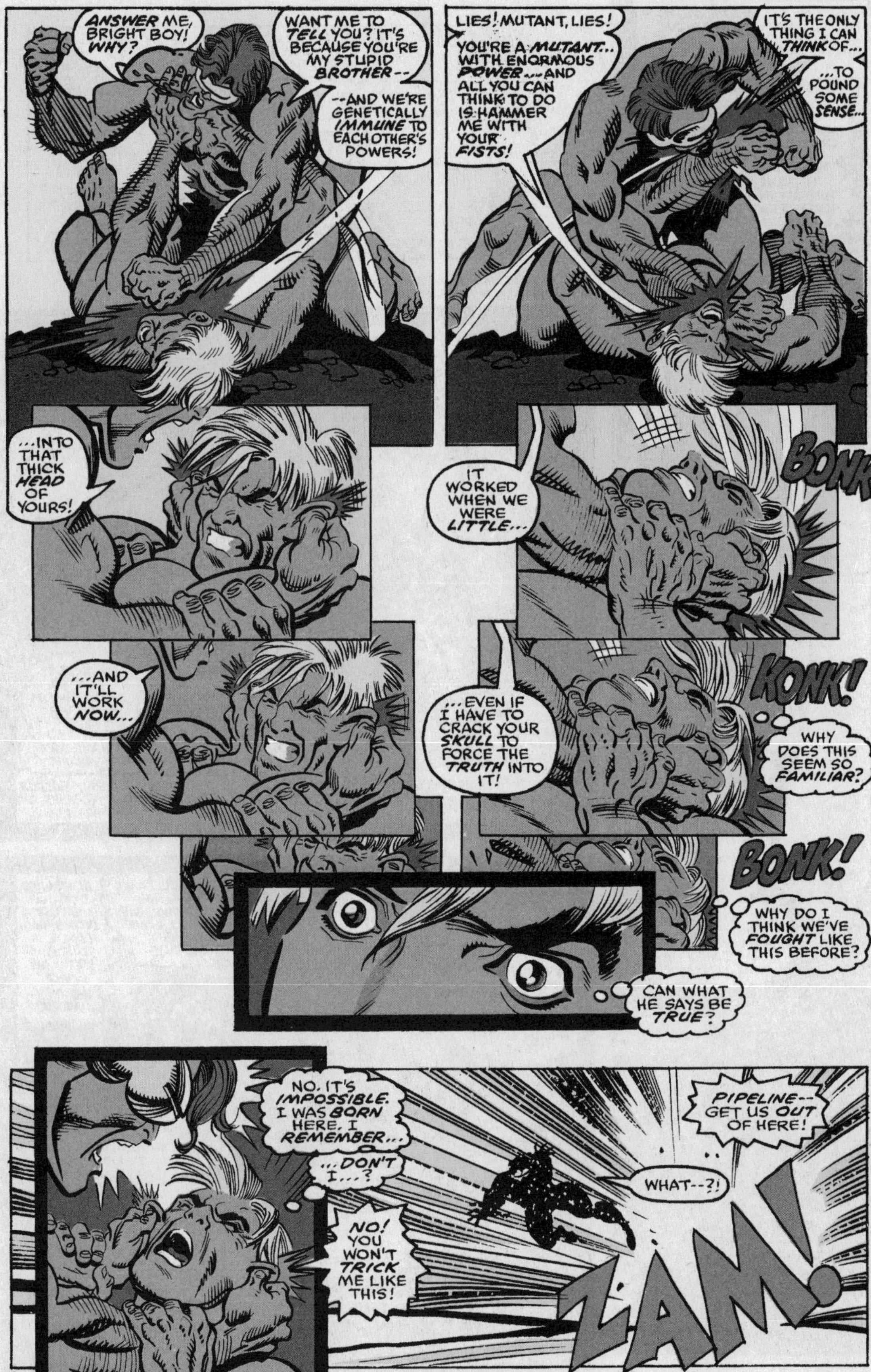
ANSWER ME, BRIGHT BOY! WHY?
WANT ME TO TELL YOU? IT'S BECAUSE YOU'RE MY STUPID BROTHER--
--AND WE'RE GENETICALLY IMMUNE TO EACH OTHER'S POWERS!
LIES! MUTANT, LIES!
YOU'RE A MUTANT... WITH ENORMOUS POWER... AND ALL YOU CAN THINK TO DO IS HAMMER ME WITH YOUR FISTS!
IT'S THE ONLY THING I CAN THINK OF...
...TO POUND SOME SENSE...
...INTO THAT THICK HEAD OF YOURS!
IT WORKED WHEN WE WERE LITTLE...
BONK!
...AND IT'LL WORK NOW...
...EVEN IF I HAVE TO CRACK YOUR SKULL TO FORCE THE TRUTH INTO IT!
KONK!
WHY DOES THIS SEEM SO FAMILIAR?
BONK!
WHY DO I THINK WE'VE FOUGHT LIKE THIS BEFORE?
CAN WHAT HE SAYS BE TRUE?
NO. IT'S IMPOSSIBLE. I WAS BORN HERE. I REMEMBER...
...DON'T I...?
NO! YOU WON'T TRICK ME LIKE THIS!
PIPELINE-- GET US OUT OF HERE!
WHAT--?!
ZAM!

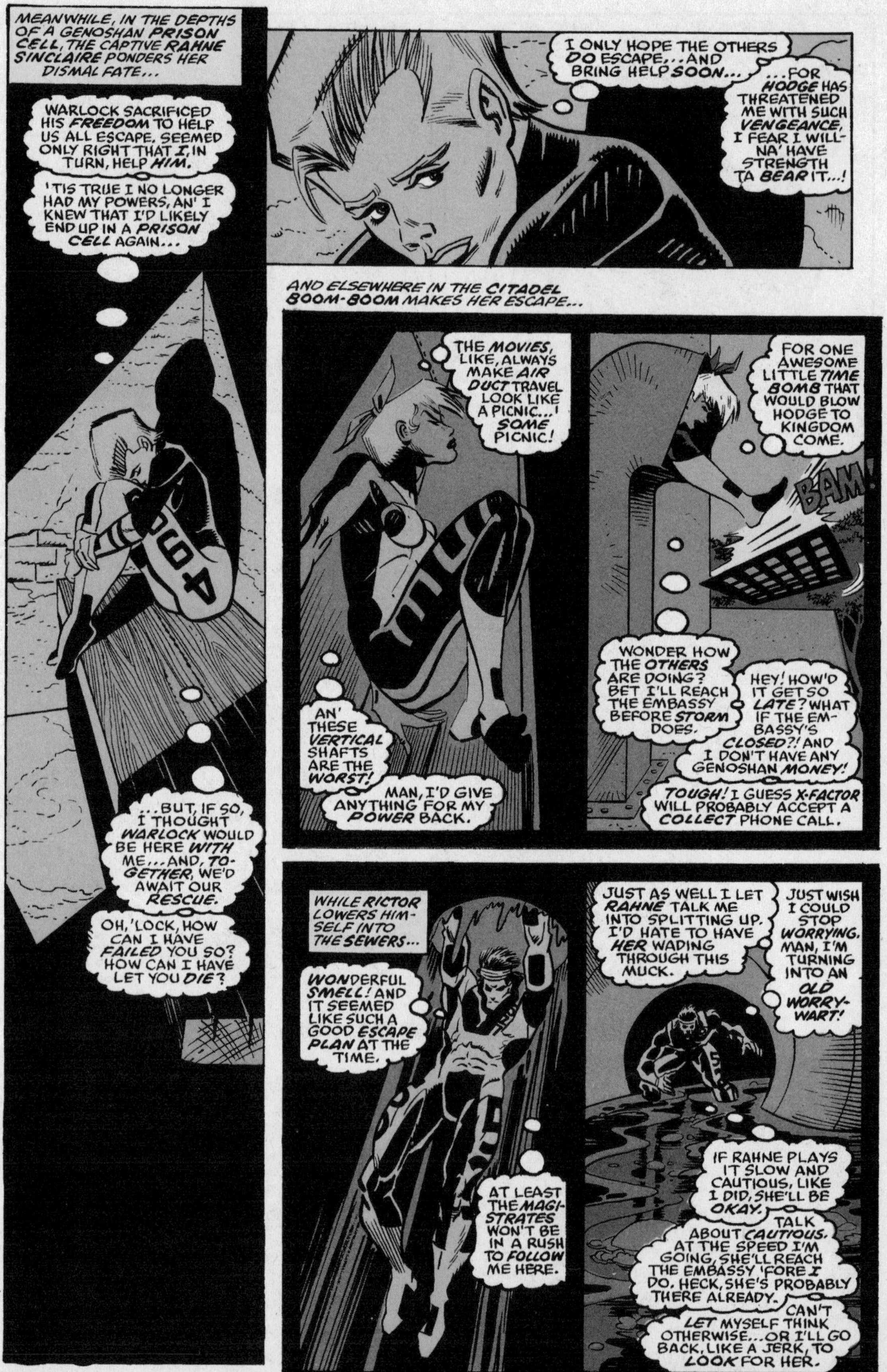
MEANWHILE, IN THE DEPTHS OF A GENOSHAN PRISON CELL, THE CAPTIVE RAHNE SINCLAIRE PONDERS HER DISMAL FATE...
I ONLY HOPE THE OTHERS DO ESCAPE,..AND BRING HELP SOON...
...FOR HODGE HAS THREATENED ME WITH SUCH VENGEANCE, I FEAR I WILL-NA' HAVE STRENGTH TA BEAR IT...!
WARLOCK SACRIFICED HIS FREEDOM TO HELP US ALL ESCAPE. SEEMED ONLY RIGHT THAT I, IN TURN, HELP HIM.
'TIS TRUE I NO LONGER HAD MY POWERS, AN' I KNEW THAT I'D LIKELY END UP IN A PRISON CELL AGAIN...
...BUT, IF SO, I THOUGHT WARLOCK WOULD BE HERE WITH ME,..AND, TO-GETHER, WE'D AWAIT OUR RESCUE.
OH, 'LOCK, HOW CAN I HAVE FAILED YOU SO? HOW CAN I HAVE LET YOU DIE?
AND ELSEWHERE IN THE CITADEL BOOM-BOOM MAKES HER ESCAPE...
THE MOVIES, LIKE, ALWAYS MAKE AIR DUCT TRAVEL LOOK LIKE A PICNIC...! SOME PICNIC!
AN' THESE VERTICAL SHAFTS ARE THE WORST!
MAN, I'D GIVE ANYTHING FOR MY POWER BACK.
FOR ONE AWESOME LITTLE TIME BOMB THAT WOULD BLOW HODGE TO KINGDOM COME.
BAM!
WONDER HOW THE OTHERS ARE DOING? BET I'LL REACH THE EMBASSY BEFORE STORM DOES.
HEY! HOW'D IT GET SO LATE? WHAT IF THE EM-BASSY'S CLOSED?! AND I DON'T HAVE ANY GENOSHAN MONEY!
TOUGH! I GUESS X-FACTOR WILL PROBABLY ACCEPT A COLLECT PHONE CALL.
WHILE RICTOR LOWERS HIM-SELF INTO THE SEWERS...
WONDERFUL SMELL! AND IT SEEMED LIKE SUCH A GOOD ESCAPE PLAN AT THE TIME.
AT LEAST THE MAGI-STRATES WON'T BE IN A RUSH TO FOLLOW ME HERE.
JUST AS WELL I LET RAHNE TALK ME INTO SPLITTING UP. I'D HATE TO HAVE HER WADING THROUGH THIS MUCK.
JUST WISH I COULD STOP WORRYING. MAN, I'M TURNING INTO AN OLD WORRY-WART!
IF RAHNE PLAYS IT SLOW AND CAUTIOUS, LIKE I DID, SHE'LL BE OKAY.
TALK ABOUT CAUTIOUS. AT THE SPEED I'M GOING, SHE'LL REACH THE EMBASSY 'FORE I DO. HECK, SHE'S PROBABLY THERE ALREADY.
CAN'T LET MYSELF THINK OTHERWISE...OR I'LL GO BACK, LIKE A JERK, TO LOOK FOR HER.

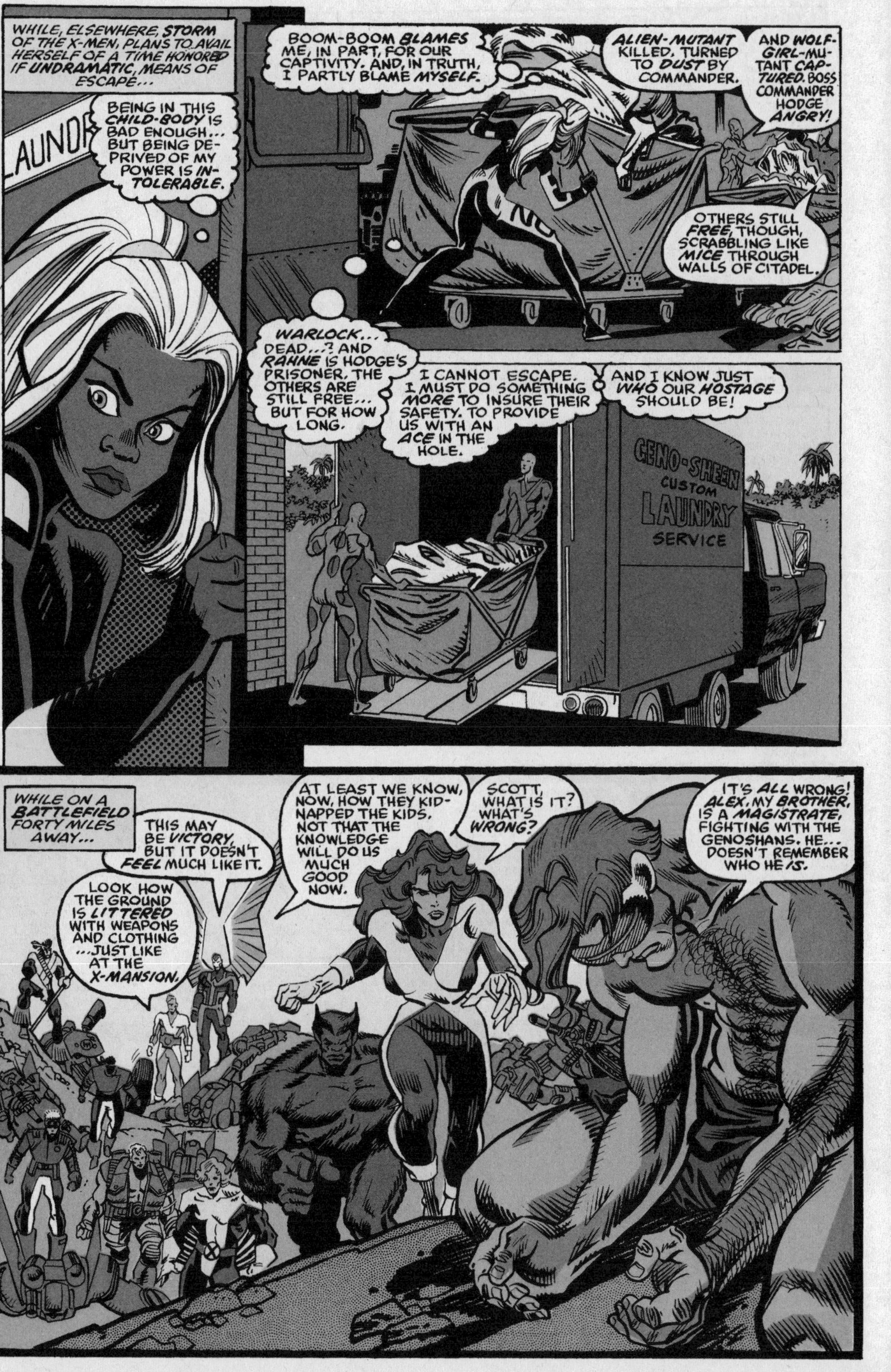

WHILE, ELSEWHERE, STORM OF THE X-MEN, PLANS TO AVAIL HERSELF OF A TIME HONORED IF UNDRAMATIC, MEANS OF ESCAPE...
LAUNDR
BEING IN THIS CHILD-BODY IS BAD ENOUGH... BUT BEING DEPRIVED OF MY POWER IS INTOLERABLE.
BOOM-BOOM BLAMES ME, IN PART, FOR OUR CAPTIVITY. AND, IN TRUTH, I PARTLY BLAME MYSELF.
ALIEN-MUTANT KILLED. TURNED TO DUST BY COMMANDER.
AND WOLF-GIRL-MUTANT CAPTURED. BOSS COMMANDER HODGE ANGRY!
OTHERS STILL FREE, THOUGH, SCRABBLING LIKE MICE THROUGH WALLS OF CITADEL.
WARLOCK... DEAD...? AND RAHNE IS HODGE'S PRISONER. THE OTHERS ARE STILL FREE... BUT FOR HOW LONG.
I CANNOT ESCAPE. I MUST DO SOMETHING MORE TO INSURE THEIR SAFETY. TO PROVIDE US WITH AN ACE IN THE HOLE.
AND I KNOW JUST WHO OUR HOSTAGE SHOULD BE!
GENO-SHEEN CUSTOM LAUNDRY SERVICE
WHILE ON A BATTLEFIELD FORTY MILES AWAY...
THIS MAY BE VICTORY, BUT IT DOESN'T FEEL MUCH LIKE IT.
LOOK HOW THE GROUND IS LITTERED WITH WEAPONS AND CLOTHING ...JUST LIKE AT THE X-MANSION.
AT LEAST WE KNOW, NOW, HOW THEY KIDNAPPED THE KIDS. NOT THAT THE KNOWLEDGE WILL DO US MUCH GOOD NOW.
SCOTT, WHAT IS IT? WHAT'S WRONG?
IT'S ALL WRONG! ALEX, MY BROTHER, IS A MAGISTRATE, FIGHTING WITH THE GENOSHANS. HE... DOESN'T REMEMBER WHO HE IS.

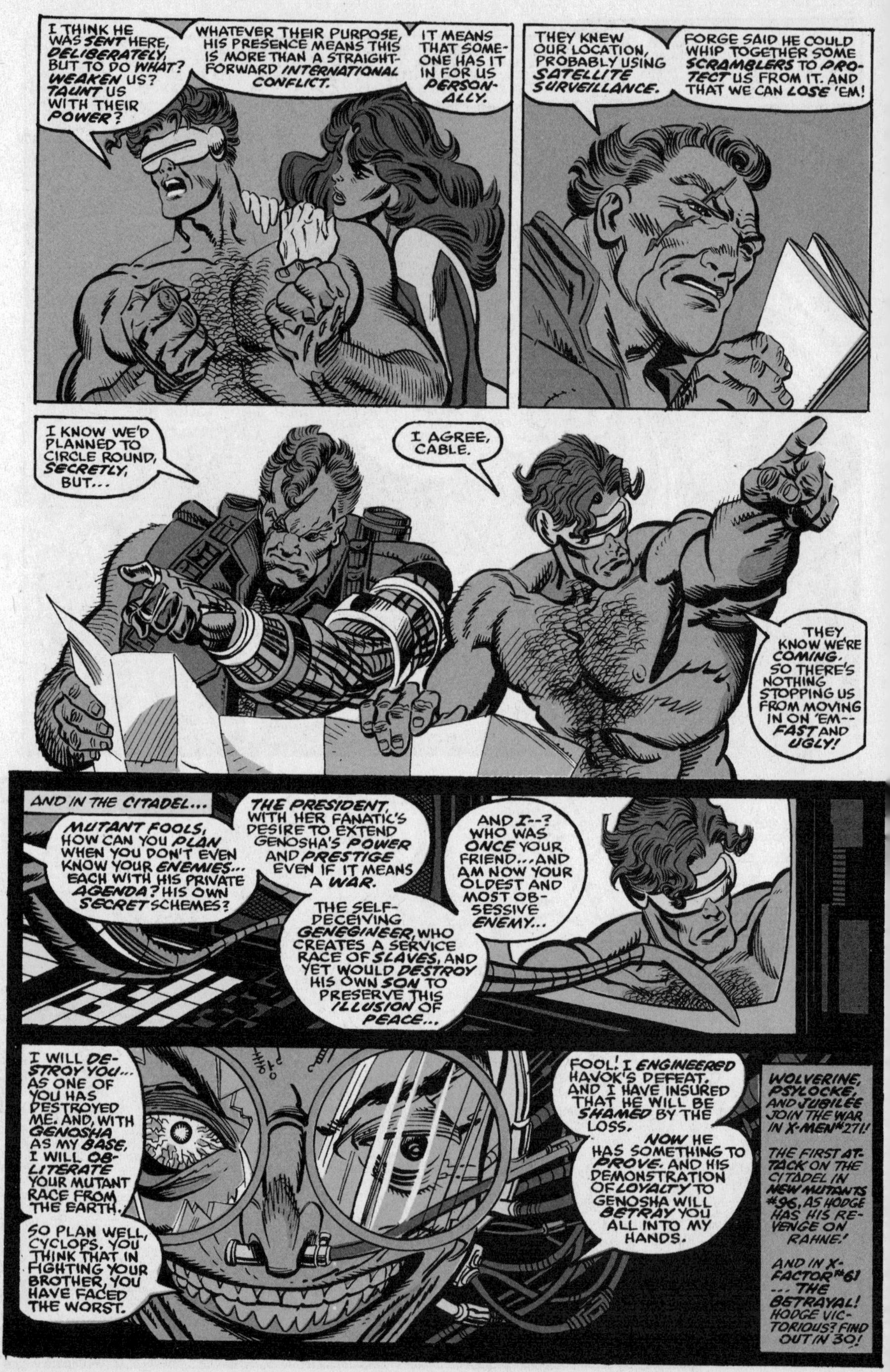
I THINK HE WAS SENT HERE, DELIBERATELY, BUT TO DO WHAT? WEAKEN US? TAUNT US WITH THEIR POWER?
WHATEVER THEIR PURPOSE, HIS PRESENCE MEANS THIS IS MORE THAN A STRAIGHT-FORWARD INTERNATIONAL CONFLICT.
IT MEANS THAT SOME-ONE HAS IT IN FOR US PERSON-ALLY.
THEY KNEW OUR LOCATION, PROBABLY USING SATELLITE SURVEILLANCE.
FORGE SAID HE COULD WHIP TOGETHER SOME SCRAMBLERS TO PRO-TECT US FROM IT. AND THAT WE CAN LOSE 'EM!
I KNOW WE'D PLANNED TO CIRCLE ROUND, SECRETLY, BUT...
I AGREE, CABLE.
THEY KNOW WE'RE COMING, SO THERE'S NOTHING STOPPING US FROM MOVING IN ON 'EM-- FAST AND UGLY!
AND IN THE CITADEL...
MUTANT FOOLS, HOW CAN YOU PLAN WHEN YOU DON'T EVEN KNOW YOUR ENEMIES... EACH WITH HIS PRIVATE AGENDA? HIS OWN SECRET SCHEMES?
THE PRESIDENT, WITH HER FANATIC'S DESIRE TO EXTEND GENOSHA'S POWER AND PRESTIGE EVEN IF IT MEANS A WAR.
THE SELF-DECEIVING GENEGINEER, WHO CREATES A SERVICE RACE OF SLAVES, AND YET WOULD DESTROY HIS OWN SON TO PRESERVE THIS ILLUSION OF PEACE...
AND I--? WHO WAS ONCE YOUR FRIEND...AND AM NOW YOUR OLDEST AND MOST OB-SESSIVE ENEMY...
I WILL DE-STROY YOU... AS ONE OF YOU HAS DESTROYED ME. AND, WITH GENOSHA AS MY BASE, I WILL OB-LITERATE YOUR MUTANT RACE FROM THE EARTH.
SO PLAN WELL, CYCLOPS. YOU THINK THAT IN FIGHTING YOUR BROTHER, YOU HAVE FACED THE WORST.
FOOL! I ENGINEERED HAVOK'S DEFEAT. AND I HAVE INSURED THAT HE WILL BE SHAMED BY THE LOSS.
NOW HE HAS SOMETHING TO PROVE. AND HIS DEMONSTRATION OF LOYALTY TO GENOSHA WILL BETRAY YOU ALL INTO MY HANDS.
WOLVERINE, PSYLOCKE, AND JUBILEE JOIN THE WAR IN X-MEN #271!
THE FIRST AT-TACK ON THE CITADEL IN NEW MUTANTS #96, AS HODGE HAS HIS RE-VENGE ON RAHNE!
AND IN X-FACTOR #61 ... THE BETRAYAL! HODGE VIC-TORIOUS? FIND OUT IN 30!

X-MEN

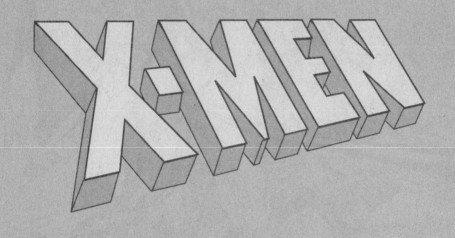

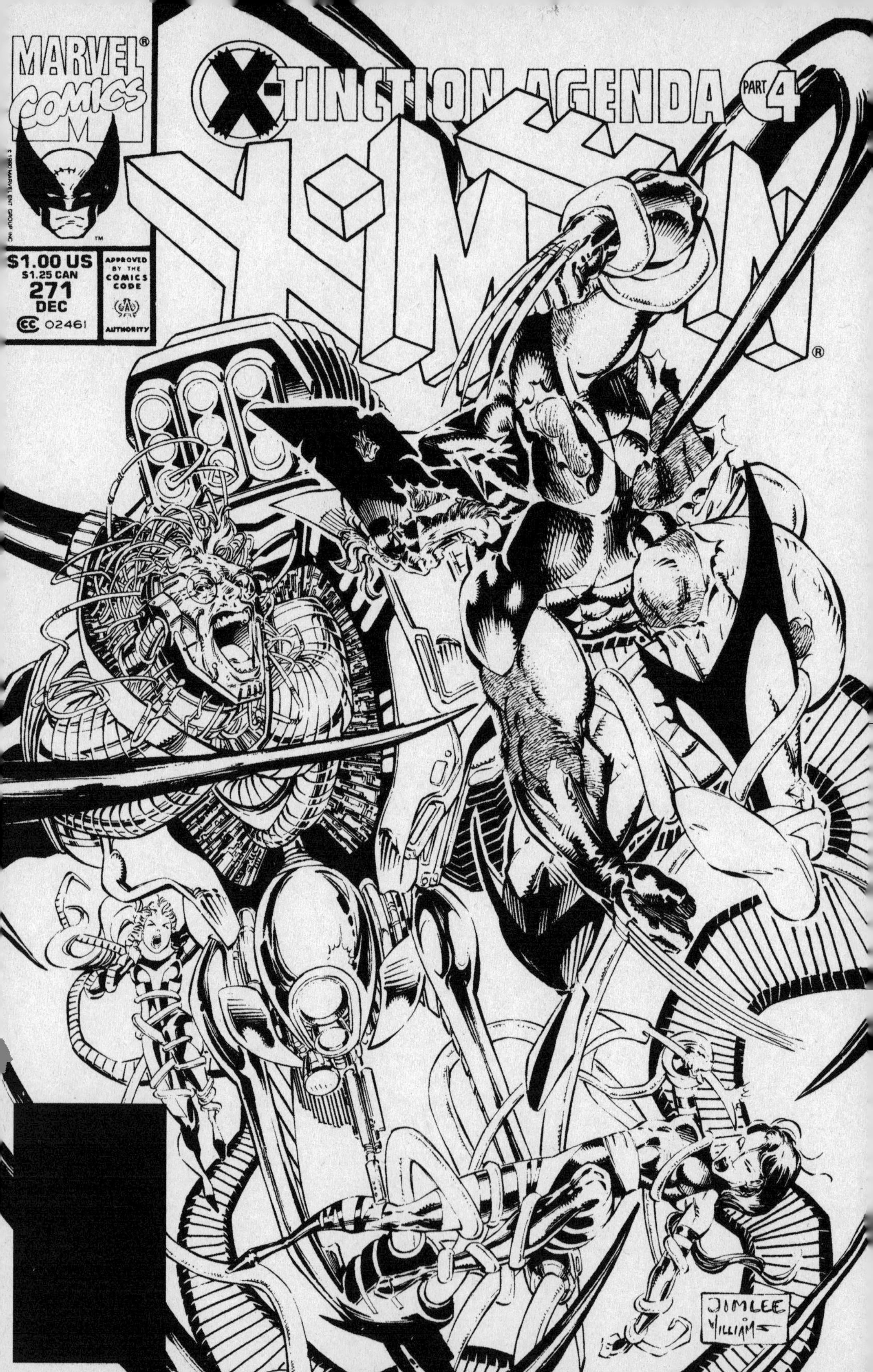
MARVEL COMICS
X-TINCTION AGENDA PART 4
X-MEN
$1.00 US
$1.25 CAN
271
DEC
02461
APPROVED BY THE COMICS CODE AUTHORITY
JIM LEE
WILLIAMS

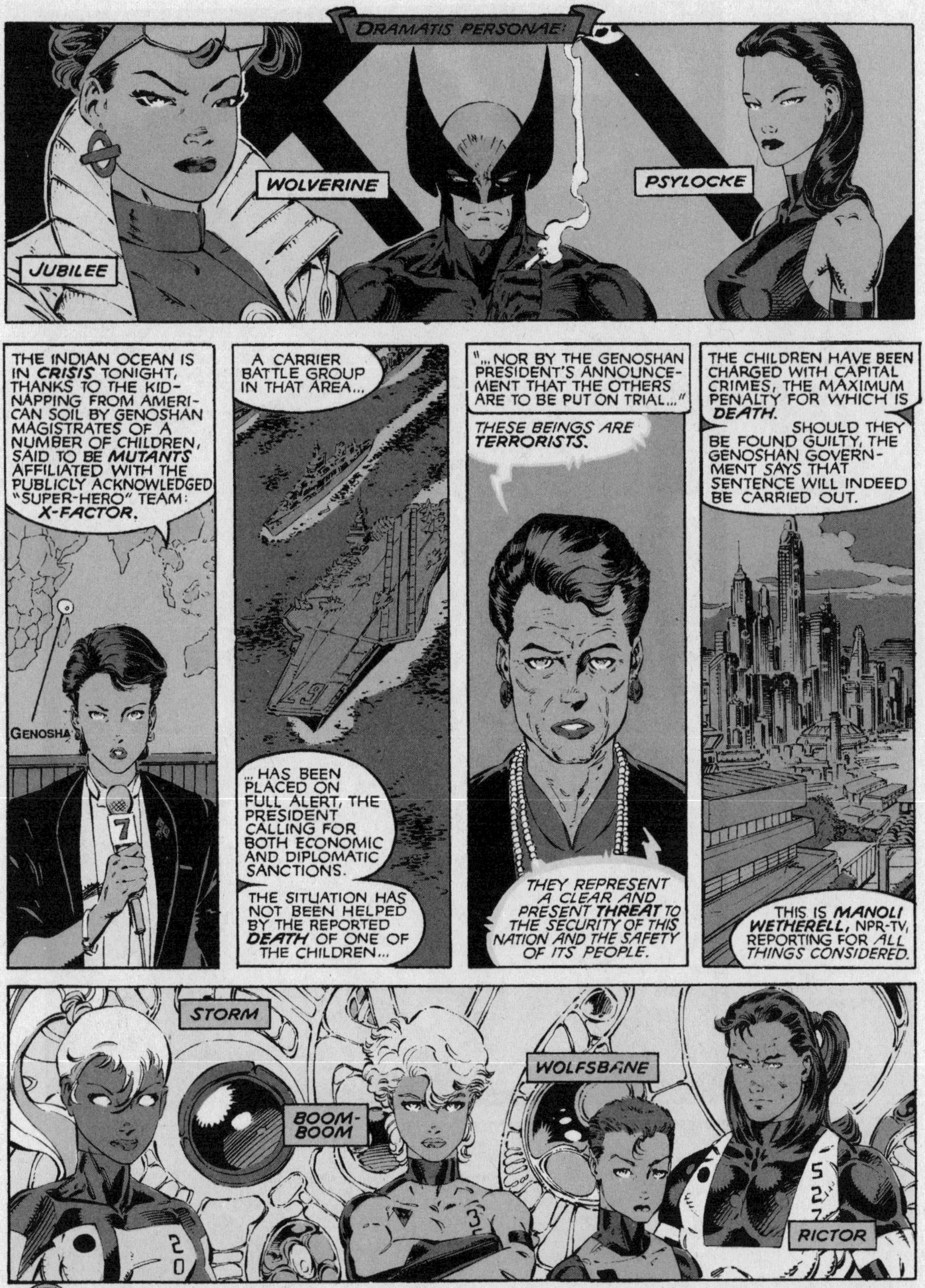
DRAMATIS PERSONAE!
JUBILEE
WOLVERINE
PSYLOCKE
THE INDIAN OCEAN IS IN CRISIS TONIGHT, THANKS TO THE KIDNAPPING FROM AMERICAN SOIL BY GENOSHAN MAGISTRATES OF A NUMBER OF CHILDREN, SAID TO BE MUTANTS AFFILIATED WITH THE PUBLICLY ACKNOWLEDGED "SUPER-HERO" TEAM: X-FACTOR.
GENOSHA
7
A CARRIER BATTLE GROUP IN THAT AREA...
...HAS BEEN PLACED ON FULL ALERT, THE PRESIDENT CALLING FOR BOTH ECONOMIC AND DIPLOMATIC SANCTIONS.
THE SITUATION HAS NOT BEEN HELPED BY THE REPORTED DEATH OF ONE OF THE CHILDREN...
"...NOR BY THE GENOSHAN PRESIDENT'S ANNOUNCEMENT THAT THE OTHERS ARE TO BE PUT ON TRIAL..."
THESE BEINGS ARE TERRORISTS.
THEY REPRESENT A CLEAR AND PRESENT THREAT TO THE SECURITY OF THIS NATION AND THE SAFETY OF ITS PEOPLE.
THE CHILDREN HAVE BEEN CHARGED WITH CAPITAL CRIMES, THE MAXIMUM PENALTY FOR WHICH IS DEATH.
SHOULD THEY BE FOUND GUILTY, THE GENOSHAN GOVERNMENT SAYS THAT SENTENCE WILL INDEED BE CARRIED OUT.
THIS IS MANOLI WETHERELL, NPR-TV, REPORTING FOR ALL THINGS CONSIDERED.
STORM
BOOM-BOOM
WOLFSBANE
RICTOR

X-TINCTION AGENDA -- THE X-TEAMS' GREATEST CRISIS!

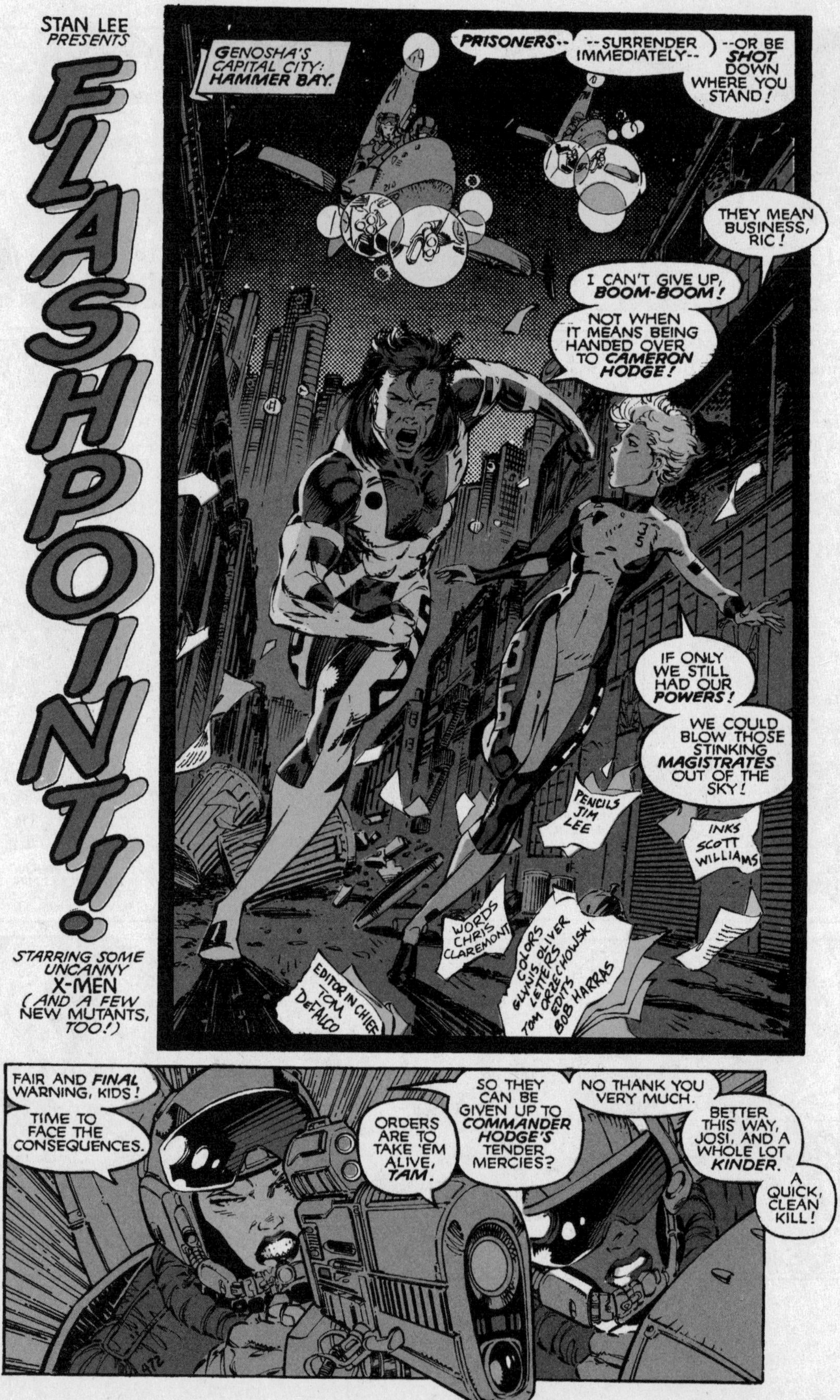

STAN LEE PRESENTS
FLASHPOINT!
STARRING SOME UNCANNY X-MEN (AND A FEW NEW MUTANTS, TOO!)
GENOSHA'S CAPITAL CITY: HAMMER BAY.
PRISONERS--
--SURRENDER IMMEDIATELY--
--OR BE SHOT DOWN WHERE YOU STAND!
THEY MEAN BUSINESS, RIC!
I CAN'T GIVE UP, BOOM-BOOM!
NOT WHEN IT MEANS BEING HANDED OVER TO CAMERON HODGE!
IF ONLY WE STILL HAD OUR POWERS!
WE COULD BLOW THOSE STINKING MAGISTRATES OUT OF THE SKY!
PENCILS JIM LEE
INKS SCOTT WILLIAMS
WORDS CHRIS CLAREMONT
COLORS GLYNIS OLIVER
LETTERS TOM ORZECHOWSKI
EDITS BOB HARRAS
EDITOR IN CHIEF TOM DeFALCO
FAIR AND FINAL WARNING, KIDS!
TIME TO FACE THE CONSEQUENCES.
ORDERS ARE TO TAKE 'EM ALIVE, TAM.
SO THEY CAN BE GIVEN UP TO COMMANDER HODGE'S TENDER MERCIES?
NO THANK YOU VERY MUCH.
BETTER THIS WAY, JOSI, AND A WHOLE LOT KINDER.
A QUICK, CLEAN KILL!

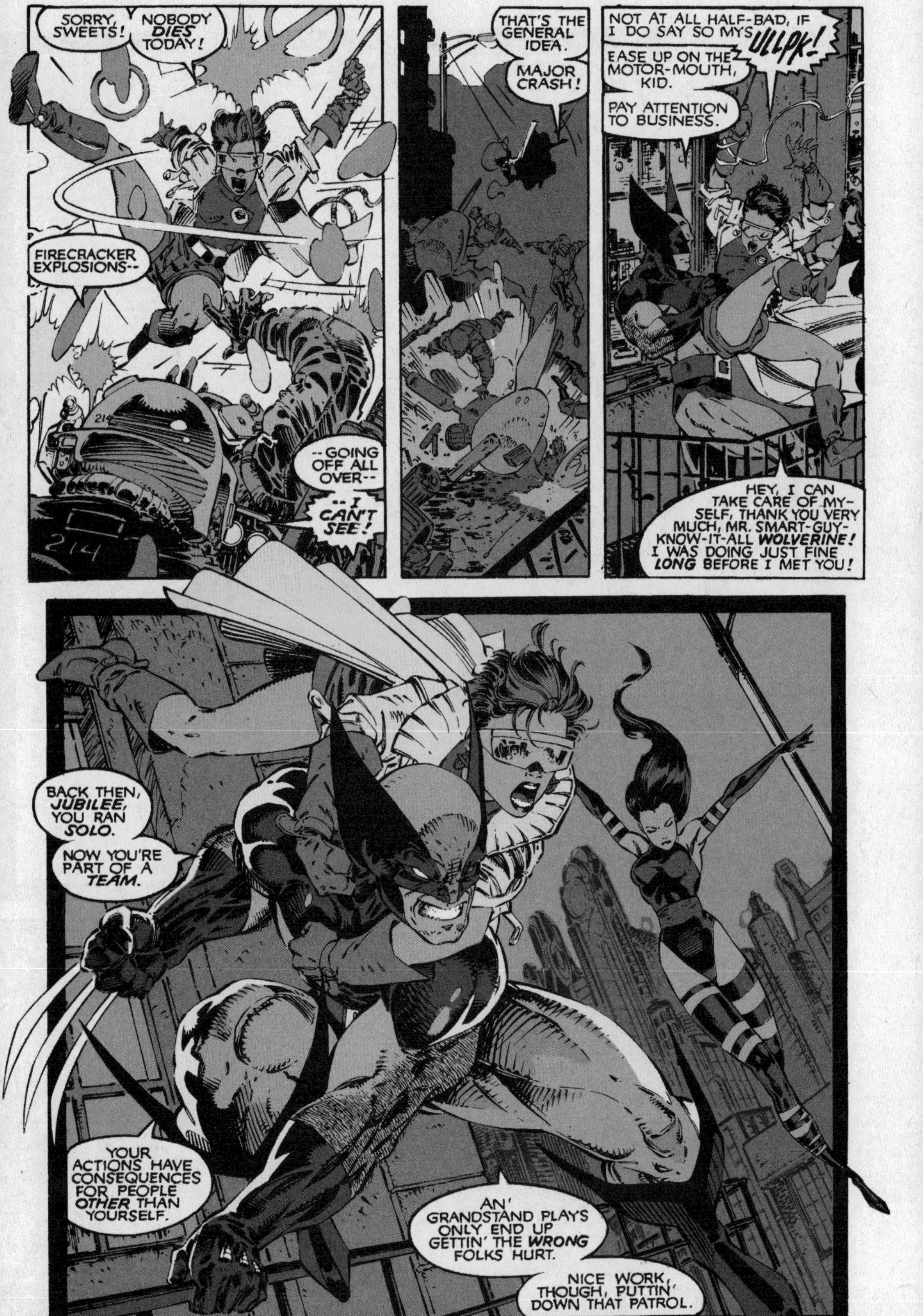
SORRY, SWEETS!
NOBODY DIES TODAY!
FIRECRACKER EXPLOSIONS--
--GOING OFF ALL OVER--
--I CAN'T SEE!
THAT'S THE GENERAL IDEA.
MAJOR CRASH!
NOT AT ALL HALF-BAD, IF I DO SAY SO MYS
ULLPK!
EASE UP ON THE MOTOR-MOUTH, KID.
PAY ATTENTION TO BUSINESS.
HEY, I CAN TAKE CARE OF MY-SELF, THANK YOU VERY MUCH, MR. SMART-GUY-KNOW-IT-ALL WOLVERINE! I WAS DOING JUST FINE LONG BEFORE I MET YOU!
BACK THEN, JUBILEE, YOU RAN SOLO.
NOW YOU'RE PART OF A TEAM.
YOUR ACTIONS HAVE CONSEQUENCES FOR PEOPLE OTHER THAN YOURSELF.
AN' GRANDSTAND PLAYS ONLY END UP GETTIN' THE WRONG FOLKS HURT.
NICE WORK, THOUGH, PUTTIN' DOWN THAT PATROL.

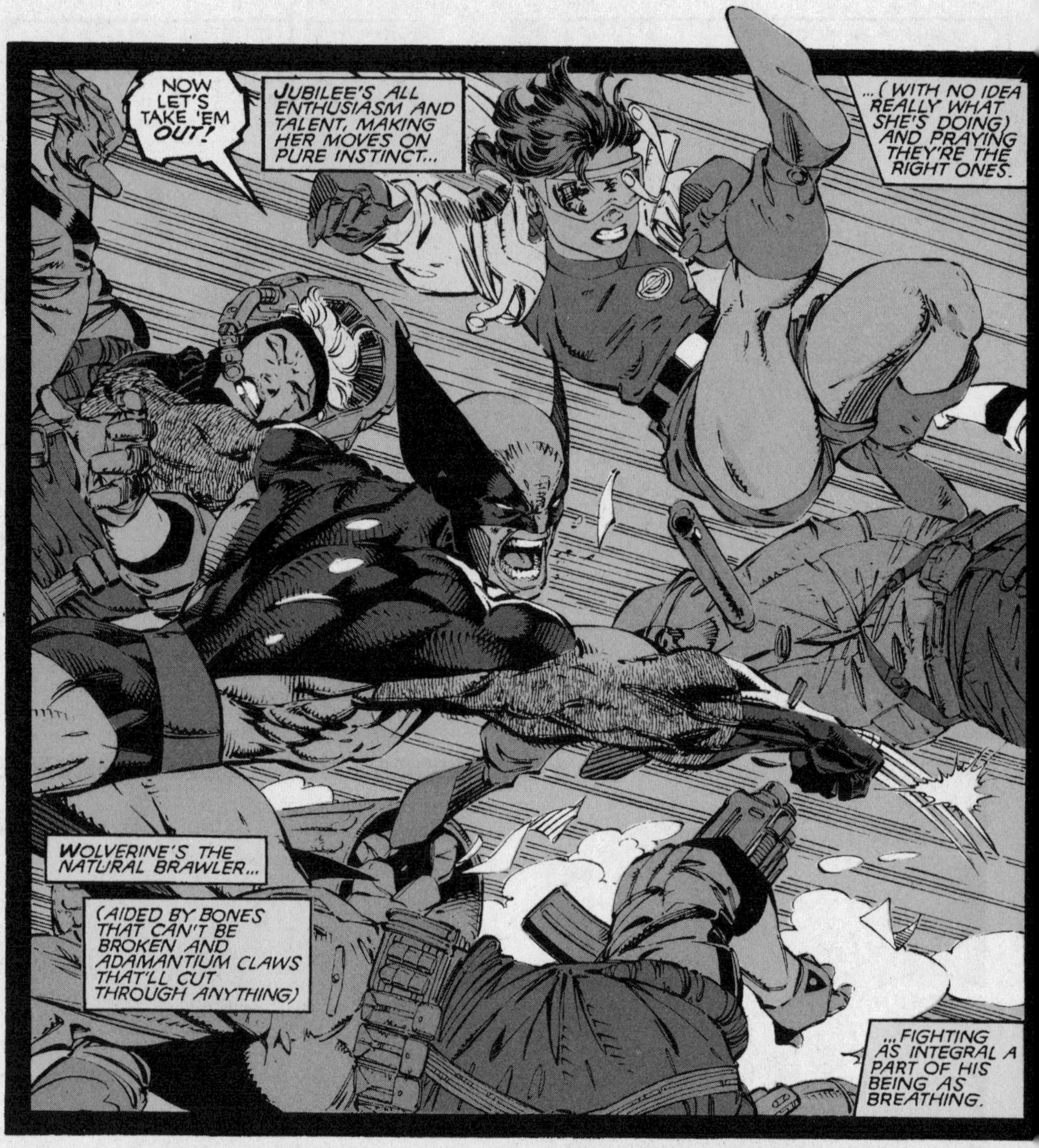
NOW LET'S TAKE 'EM OUT!
JUBILEE'S ALL ENTHUSIASM AND TALENT, MAKING HER MOVES ON PURE INSTINCT...
...(WITH NO IDEA REALLY WHAT SHE'S DOING) AND PRAYING THEY'RE THE RIGHT ONES.
WOLVERINE'S THE NATURAL BRAWLER...
(AIDED BY BONES THAT CAN'T BE BROKEN AND ADAMANTIUM CLAWS THAT'LL CUT THROUGH ANYTHING)
...FIGHTING AS INTEGRAL A PART OF HIS BEING AS BREATHING.

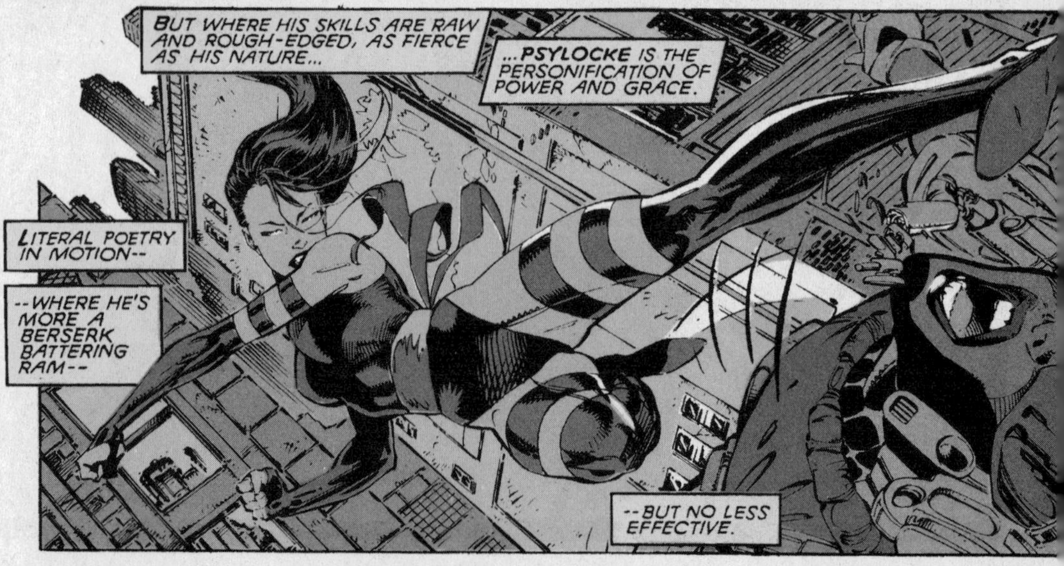
BUT WHERE HIS SKILLS ARE RAW AND ROUGH-EDGED, AS FIERCE AS HIS NATURE...
...PSYLOCKE IS THE PERSONIFICATION OF POWER AND GRACE.
LITERAL POETRY IN MOTION--
--WHERE HE'S MORE A BERSERK BATTERING RAM--
--BUT NO LESS EFFECTIVE.

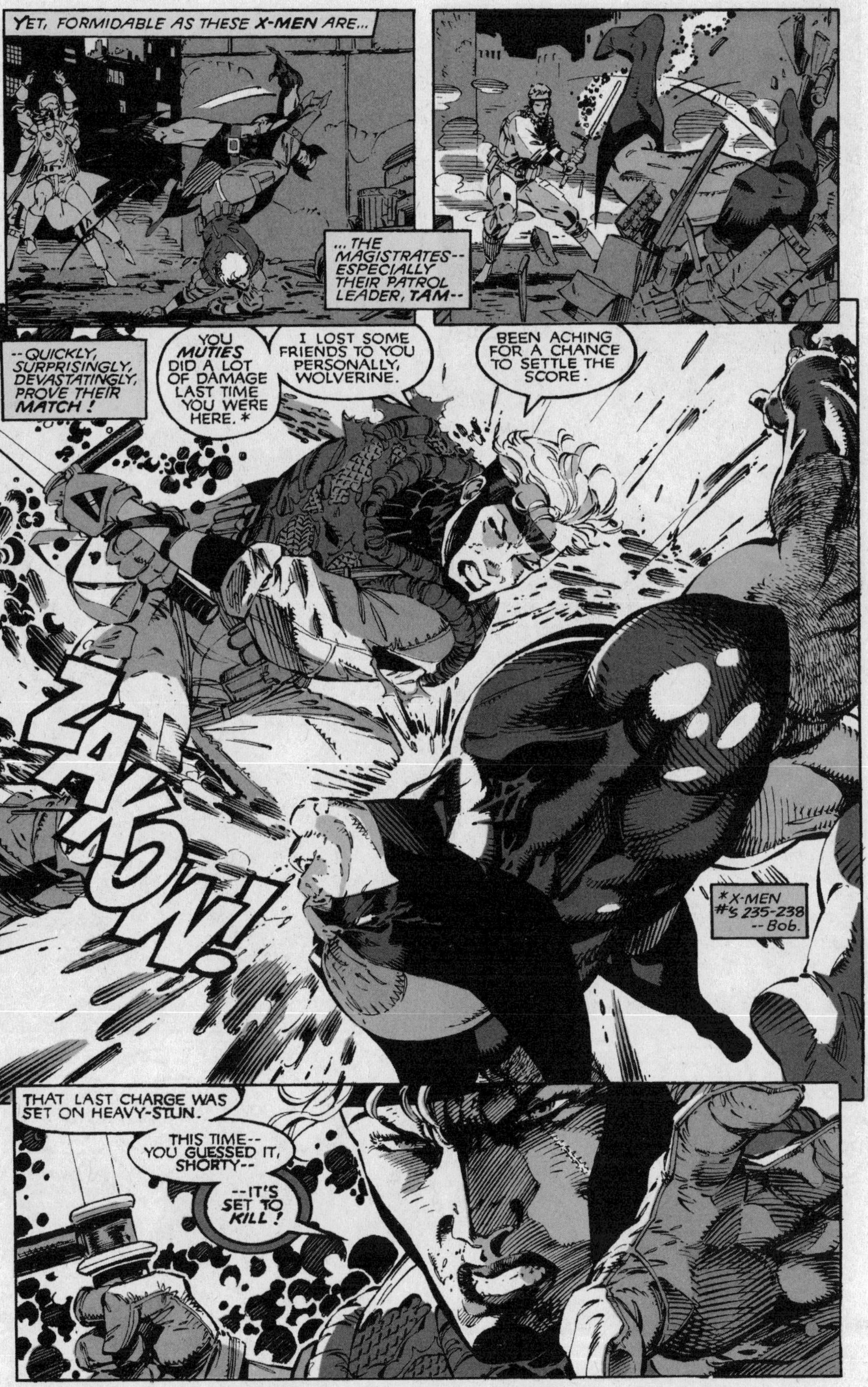

YET, FORMIDABLE AS THESE X-MEN ARE...
...THE MAGISTRATES-- ESPECIALLY THEIR PATROL LEADER, TAM--
--QUICKLY, SURPRISINGLY, DEVASTATINGLY, PROVE THEIR MATCH!
YOU MUTIES DID A LOT OF DAMAGE LAST TIME YOU WERE HERE.*
I LOST SOME FRIENDS TO YOU PERSONALLY, WOLVERINE.
BEEN ACHING FOR A CHANCE TO SETTLE THE SCORE.
ZAKOW!
*X-MEN #'s 235-238 --Bob.
THAT LAST CHARGE WAS SET ON HEAVY-STUN.
THIS TIME-- YOU GUESSED IT, SHORTY--
--IT'S SET TO KILL!

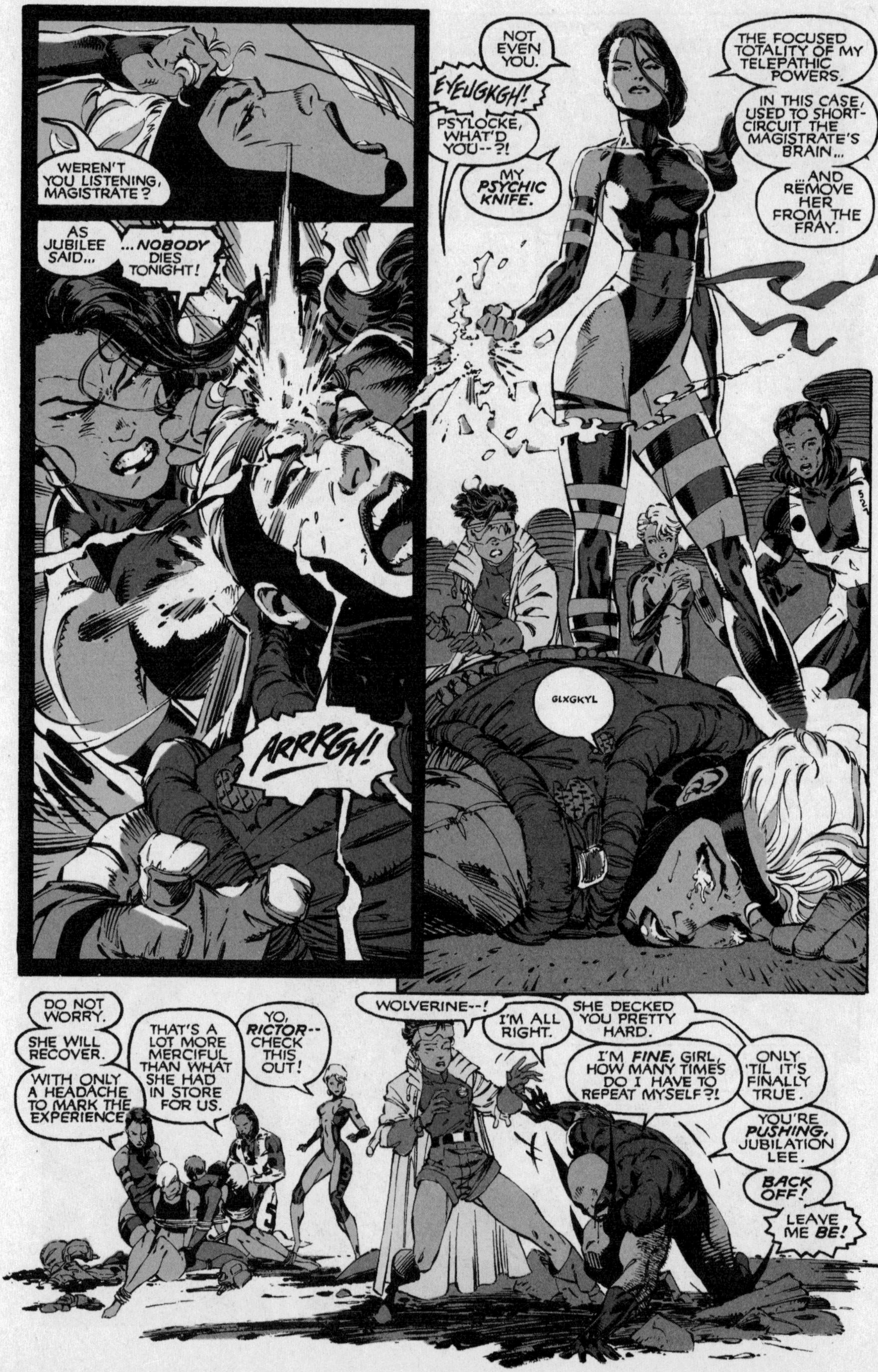
WEREN'T YOU LISTENING, MAGISTRATE?
AS JUBILEE SAID...
...NOBODY DIES TONIGHT!
ARRRGH!
NOT EVEN YOU.
EYEUGKGH!
PSYLOCKE, WHAT'D YOU--?!
MY PSYCHIC KNIFE.
THE FOCUSED TOTALITY OF MY TELEPATHIC POWERS.
IN THIS CASE, USED TO SHORT-CIRCUIT THE MAGISTRATE'S BRAIN...
...AND REMOVE HER FROM THE FRAY.
GLXGKYL
DO NOT WORRY.
SHE WILL RECOVER.
WITH ONLY A HEADACHE TO MARK THE EXPERIENCE.
THAT'S A LOT MORE MERCIFUL THAN WHAT SHE HAD IN STORE FOR US.
YO, RICTOR-- CHECK THIS OUT!
WOLVERINE--!
I'M ALL RIGHT.
SHE DECKED YOU PRETTY HARD.
I'M FINE, GIRL, HOW MANY TIMES DO I HAVE TO REPEAT MYSELF?!
ONLY 'TIL IT'S FINALLY TRUE.
YOU'RE PUSHING, JUBILATION LEE.
BACK OFF!
LEAVE ME BE!

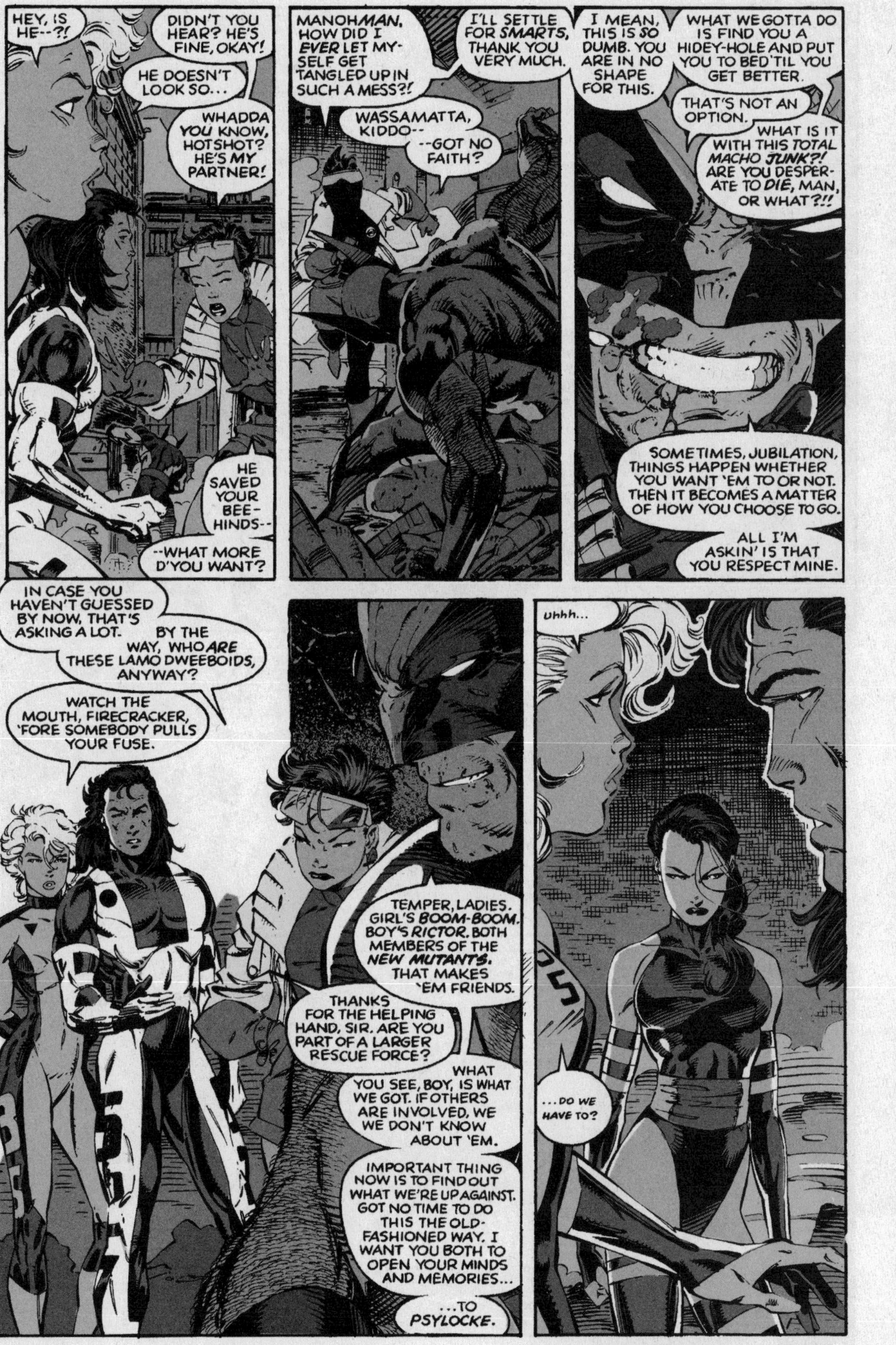
HEY, IS HE--?!
DIDN'T YOU HEAR? HE'S FINE, OKAY!
HE DOESN'T LOOK SO...
WHADDA YOU KNOW, HOTSHOT? HE'S MY PARTNER!
HE SAVED YOUR BEE-HINDS--
--WHAT MORE D'YOU WANT?
MANOHMAN, HOW DID I EVER LET MYSELF GET TANGLED UP IN SUCH A MESS?!
I'LL SETTLE FOR SMARTS, THANK YOU VERY MUCH.
WASSAMATTA, KIDDO--
--GOT NO FAITH?
I MEAN, THIS IS SO DUMB. YOU ARE IN NO SHAPE FOR THIS.
WHAT WE GOTTA DO IS FIND YOU A HIDEY-HOLE AND PUT YOU TO BED 'TIL YOU GET BETTER.
THAT'S NOT AN OPTION.
WHAT IS IT WITH THIS TOTAL MACHO JUNK?! ARE YOU DESPERATE TO DIE, MAN, OR WHAT?!!
SOMETIMES, JUBILATION, THINGS HAPPEN WHETHER YOU WANT 'EM TO OR NOT. THEN IT BECOMES A MATTER OF HOW YOU CHOOSE TO GO.
ALL I'M ASKIN' IS THAT YOU RESPECT MINE.
IN CASE YOU HAVEN'T GUESSED BY NOW, THAT'S ASKING A LOT.
BY THE WAY, WHO ARE THESE LAMO DWEEBOIDS, ANYWAY?
WATCH THE MOUTH, FIRECRACKER, 'FORE SOMEBODY PULLS YOUR FUSE.
TEMPER, LADIES. GIRL'S BOOM-BOOM. BOY'S RICTOR. BOTH MEMBERS OF THE NEW MUTANTS. THAT MAKES 'EM FRIENDS.
THANKS FOR THE HELPING HAND, SIR. ARE YOU PART OF A LARGER RESCUE FORCE?
WHAT YOU SEE, BOY, IS WHAT WE GOT. IF OTHERS ARE INVOLVED, WE WE DON'T KNOW ABOUT 'EM.
IMPORTANT THING NOW IS TO FIND OUT WHAT WE'RE UP AGAINST. GOT NO TIME TO DO THIS THE OLD-FASHIONED WAY. I WANT YOU BOTH TO OPEN YOUR MINDS AND MEMORIES...
...TO PSYLOCKE.
Uhhh...
...DO WE HAVE TO?

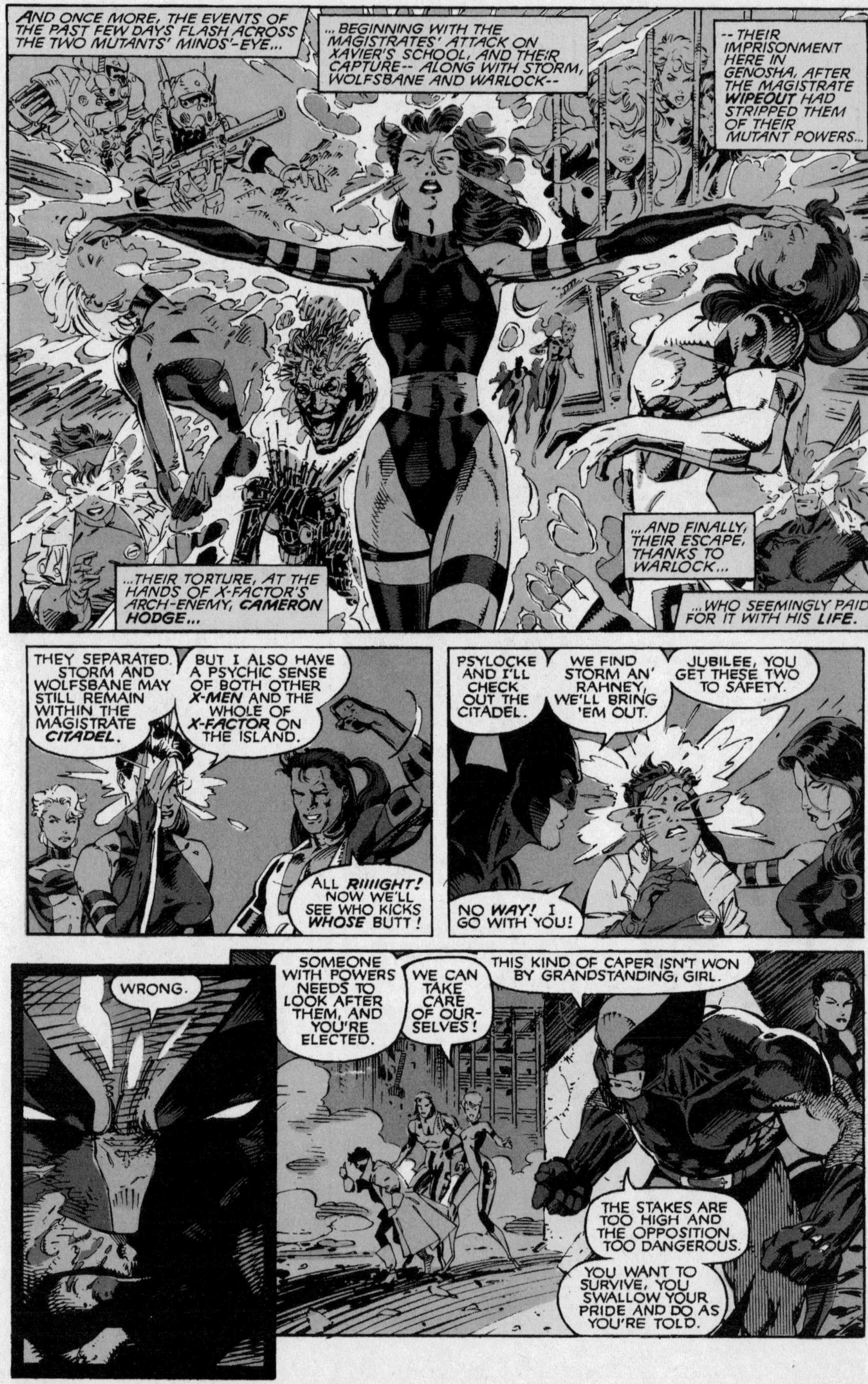
AND ONCE MORE, THE EVENTS OF THE PAST FEW DAYS FLASH ACROSS THE TWO MUTANTS' MINDS'-EYE...
...BEGINNING WITH THE MAGISTRATES' ATTACK ON XAVIER'S SCHOOL, AND THEIR CAPTURE-- ALONG WITH STORM, WOLFSBANE AND WARLOCK--
--THEIR IMPRISONMENT HERE IN GENOSHA, AFTER THE MAGISTRATE WIPEOUT HAD STRIPPED THEM OF THEIR MUTANT POWERS...
...THEIR TORTURE, AT THE HANDS OF X-FACTOR'S ARCH-ENEMY, CAMERON HODGE...
...AND FINALLY, THEIR ESCAPE, THANKS TO WARLOCK...
...WHO SEEMINGLY PAID FOR IT WITH HIS LIFE.
THEY SEPARATED. STORM AND WOLFSBANE MAY STILL REMAIN WITHIN THE MAGISTRATE CITADEL.
BUT I ALSO HAVE A PSYCHIC SENSE OF BOTH OTHER X-MEN AND THE WHOLE OF X-FACTOR ON THE ISLAND.
ALL RIIIGHT! NOW WE'LL SEE WHO KICKS WHOSE BUTT!
PSYLOCKE AND I'LL CHECK OUT THE CITADEL.
WE FIND STORM AN' RAHNEY, WE'LL BRING 'EM OUT.
JUBILEE, YOU GET THESE TWO TO SAFETY.
NO WAY! I GO WITH YOU!
WRONG.
SOMEONE WITH POWERS NEEDS TO LOOK AFTER THEM, AND YOU'RE ELECTED.
WE CAN TAKE CARE OF OUR-SELVES!
THIS KIND OF CAPER ISN'T WON BY GRANDSTANDING, GIRL.
THE STAKES ARE TOO HIGH AND THE OPPOSITION TOO DANGEROUS.
YOU WANT TO SURVIVE, YOU SWALLOW YOUR PRIDE AND DO AS YOU'RE TOLD.

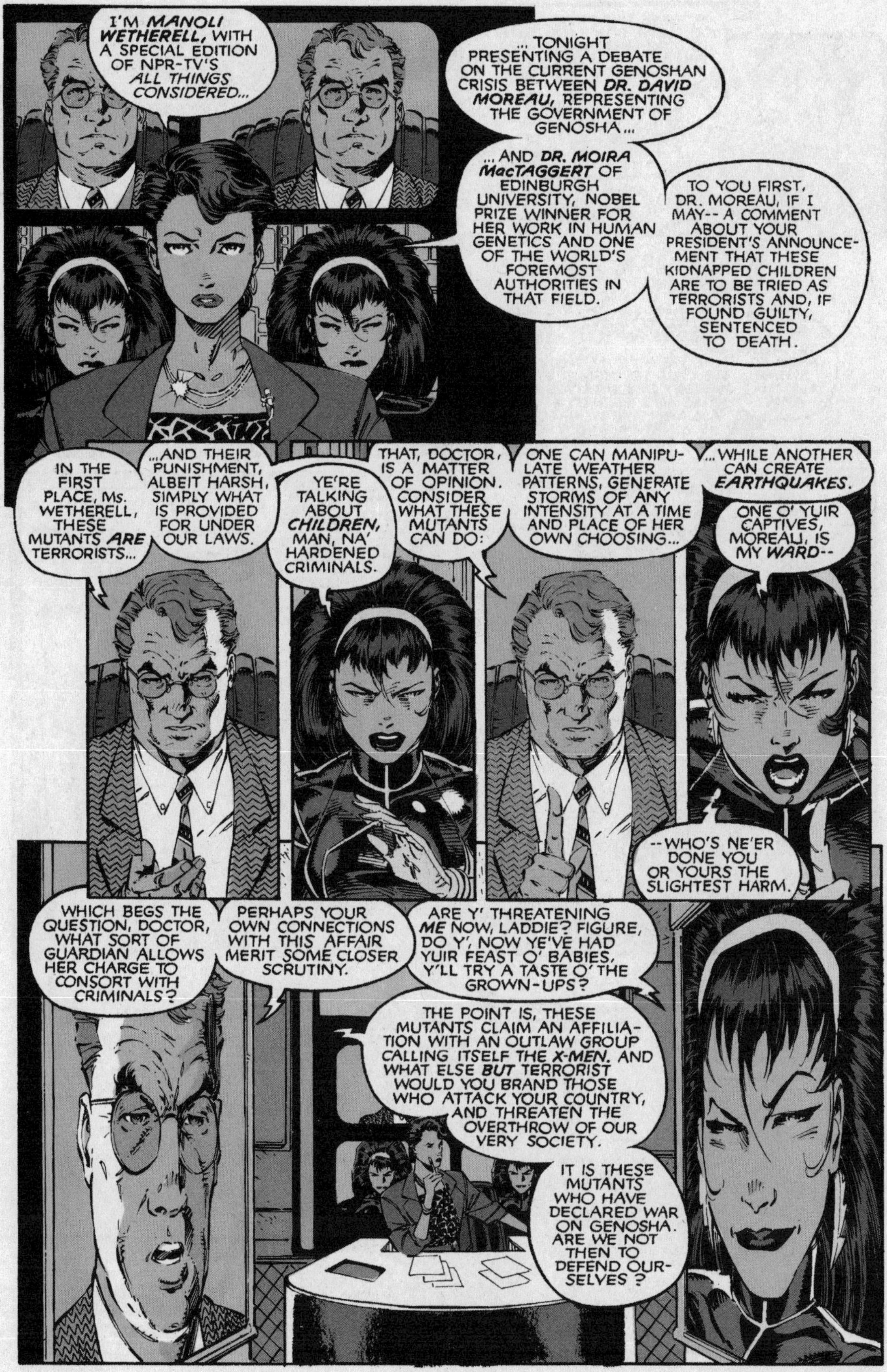

I'M MANOLI WETHERELL, WITH A SPECIAL EDITION OF NPR-TV'S ALL THINGS CONSIDERED...
... TONIGHT PRESENTING A DEBATE ON THE CURRENT GENOSHAN CRISIS BETWEEN DR. DAVID MOREAU, REPRESENTING THE GOVERNMENT OF GENOSHA ...
... AND DR. MOIRA MacTAGGERT OF EDINBURGH UNIVERSITY, NOBEL PRIZE WINNER FOR HER WORK IN HUMAN GENETICS AND ONE OF THE WORLD'S FOREMOST AUTHORITIES IN THAT FIELD.
TO YOU FIRST, DR. MOREAU, IF I MAY-- A COMMENT ABOUT YOUR PRESIDENT'S ANNOUNCEMENT THAT THESE KIDNAPPED CHILDREN ARE TO BE TRIED AS TERRORISTS AND, IF FOUND GUILTY, SENTENCED TO DEATH.
IN THE FIRST PLACE, Ms. WETHERELL, THESE MUTANTS ARE TERRORISTS...
...AND THEIR PUNISHMENT, ALBEIT HARSH, SIMPLY WHAT IS PROVIDED FOR UNDER OUR LAWS.
YE'RE TALKING ABOUT CHILDREN, MAN, NA' HARDENED CRIMINALS.
THAT, DOCTOR, IS A MATTER OF OPINION. CONSIDER WHAT THESE MUTANTS CAN DO:
ONE CAN MANIPULATE WEATHER PATTERNS, GENERATE STORMS OF ANY INTENSITY AT A TIME AND PLACE OF HER OWN CHOOSING...
...WHILE ANOTHER CAN CREATE EARTHQUAKES.
ONE O' YUIR CAPTIVES, MOREAU, IS MY WARD--
--WHO'S NE'ER DONE YOU OR YOURS THE SLIGHTEST HARM.
WHICH BEGS THE QUESTION, DOCTOR, WHAT SORT OF GUARDIAN ALLOWS HER CHARGE TO CONSORT WITH CRIMINALS?
PERHAPS YOUR OWN CONNECTIONS WITH THIS AFFAIR MERIT SOME CLOSER SCRUTINY.
ARE Y' THREATENING ME NOW, LADDIE? FIGURE, DO Y', NOW YE'VE HAD YUIR FEAST O' BABIES, Y'LL TRY A TASTE O' THE GROWN-UPS?
THE POINT IS, THESE MUTANTS CLAIM AN AFFILIATION WITH AN OUTLAW GROUP CALLING ITSELF THE X-MEN. AND WHAT ELSE BUT TERRORIST WOULD YOU BRAND THOSE WHO ATTACK YOUR COUNTRY, AND THREATEN THE OVERTHROW OF OUR VERY SOCIETY.
IT IS THESE MUTANTS WHO HAVE DECLARED WAR ON GENOSHA. ARE WE NOT THEN TO DEFEND OURSELVES?

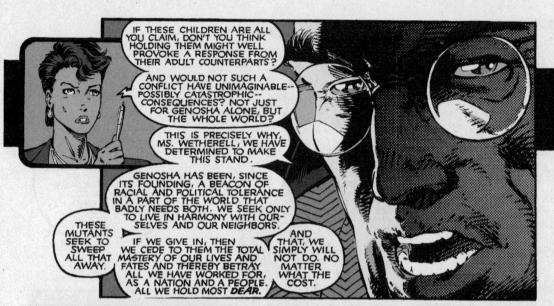

IF THESE CHILDREN ARE ALL YOU CLAIM, DON'T YOU THINK HOLDING THEM MIGHT WELL PROVOKE A RESPONSE FROM THEIR ADULT COUNTERPARTS?

AND WOULD NOT SUCH A CONFLICT HAVE UNIMAGINABLE-- POSSIBLY CATASTROPHIC-- CONSEQUENCES? NOT JUST FOR GENOSHA ALONE, BUT THE WHOLE WORLD?

THIS IS PRECISELY WHY, MS. WETHERELL, WE HAVE DETERMINED TO MAKE THIS STAND.

GENOSHA HAS BEEN, SINCE ITS FOUNDING, A BEACON OF RACIAL AND POLITICAL TOLERANCE IN A PART OF THE WORLD THAT BADLY NEEDS BOTH. WE SEEK ONLY TO LIVE IN HARMONY WITH OURSELVES AND OUR NEIGHBORS.

THESE MUTANTS SEEK TO SWEEP ALL THAT AWAY.

IF WE GIVE IN, THEN WE CEDE TO THEM THE TOTAL MASTERY OF OUR LIVES AND FATES AND THEREBY BETRAY ALL WE HAVE WORKED FOR, AS A NATION AND A PEOPLE, ALL WE HOLD MOST DEAR.

AND THAT, WE SIMPLY WILL NOT DO. NO MATTER WHAT THE COST.

AND... WE'RE... CLEAR!

THANK YOU, EVERYONE. THE BROADCAST IS OVER.

VERY NICE. MOST IMPRESSIVE. YOU HANDLED YOURSELF WELL.

I'D RATHER BE IN MY LAB. OR BETTER YET, MY GARDEN.

BEEN SO LONG, IT SEEMS, THE FLOWERS ARE PROBABLY TOTALLY OVERGROWN.

EVERY STRUGGLE DEMANDS ITS SACRIFICES.

EASY FOR YOU TO SAY, CHIEF MAGISTRATE. BY PROFESSION, YOU'RE A SOLDIER.

THE PROBLEM IS, I'D RATHER BE A POLICEMAN.

I WAS WATCHING MOIRA MacTAGGERT ON THE MONITORS. DID ANYTHING ABOUT HER STRIKE YOU AS... ODD?

ASIDE FROM THE FACT SHE SEEMED TO WANT TO TEAR MY HEART OUT WITH HER BARE HANDS?

I NEVER IMAGINED THE WOMAN COULD BE SO FIERCE! AND THOSE CLOTHES--!

I NOTICED THAT, TOO. QUITE AN EXTREME DEPARTURE FROM THE PROFILE WE HAVE OF HER.

IF YOU THINK IT SIGNIFICANT, BY ALL MEANS CHECK IT OUT. FOR MYSELF, I DON'T CARE IF I NEVER SEE THAT HIGHLAND HARRIDAN AGAIN.

BY THE WAY, IS ALL THIS SECURITY FOR YOU OR FOR ME?

DAVID, I SUGGEST YOU THINK SERIOUSLY ABOUT WHAT YOU SAID TO MacTAGGERT.

SEIZING THESE CHILDREN IS VERY MUCH AKIN TO GRABBING A SABRETOOTH TIGER BY THE TAIL!

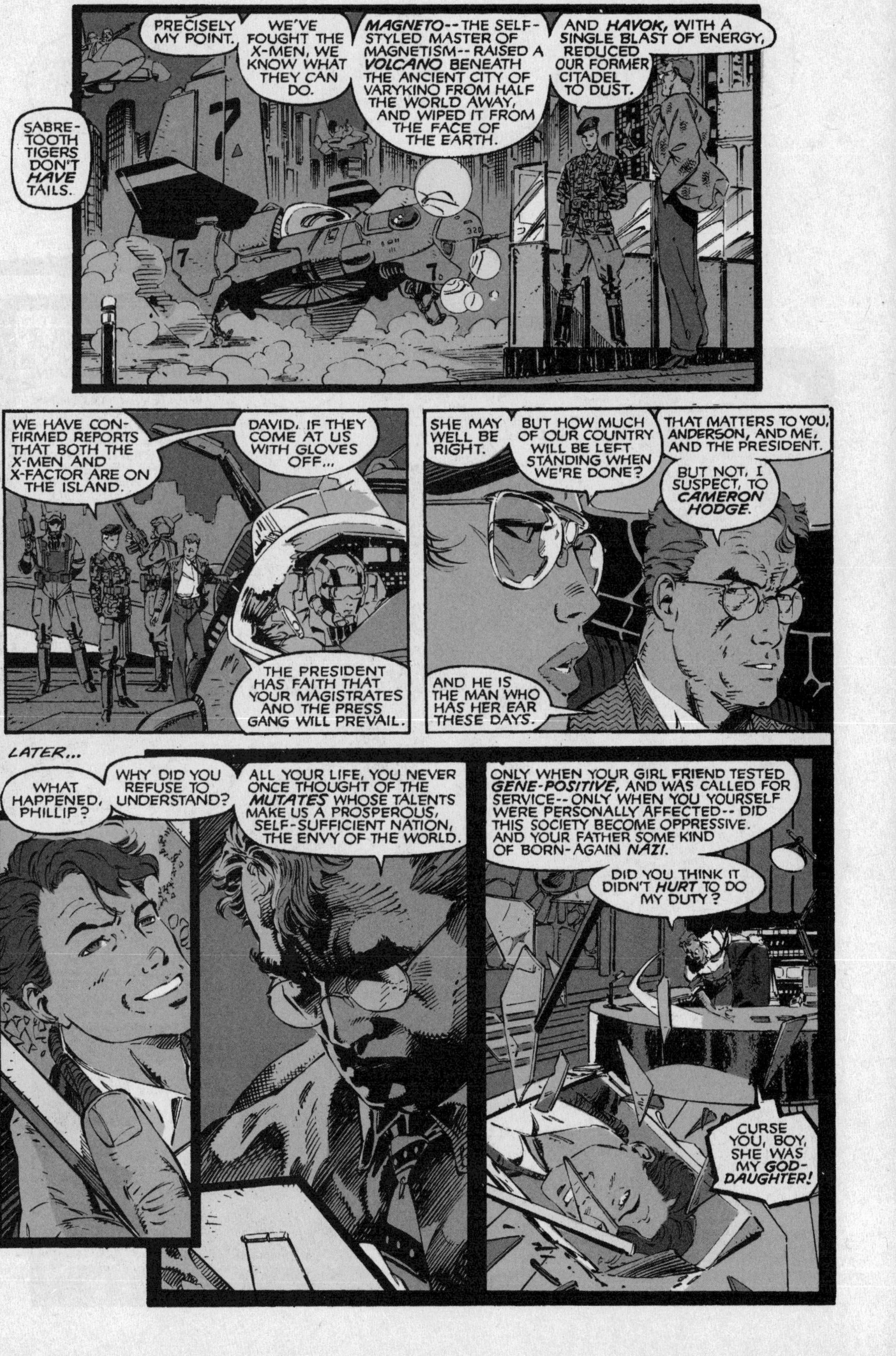
PRECISELY MY POINT.
WE'VE FOUGHT THE X-MEN, WE KNOW WHAT THEY CAN DO.
MAGNETO-- THE SELF-STYLED MASTER OF MAGNETISM-- RAISED A VOLCANO BENEATH THE ANCIENT CITY OF VARYKINO FROM HALF THE WORLD AWAY, AND WIPED IT FROM THE FACE OF THE EARTH.
AND HAVOK, WITH A SINGLE BLAST OF ENERGY, REDUCED OUR FORMER CITADEL TO DUST.
SABRE-TOOTH TIGERS DON'T HAVE TAILS.
WE HAVE CONFIRMED REPORTS THAT BOTH THE X-MEN AND X-FACTOR ARE ON THE ISLAND.
DAVID, IF THEY COME AT US WITH GLOVES OFF...
THE PRESIDENT HAS FAITH THAT YOUR MAGISTRATES AND THE PRESS GANG WILL PREVAIL.
SHE MAY WELL BE RIGHT.
BUT HOW MUCH OF OUR COUNTRY WILL BE LEFT STANDING WHEN WE'RE DONE?
THAT MATTERS TO YOU, ANDERSON, AND ME, AND THE PRESIDENT.
BUT NOT, I SUSPECT, TO CAMERON HODGE.
AND HE IS THE MAN WHO HAS HER EAR THESE DAYS.
LATER...
WHAT HAPPENED, PHILLIP?
WHY DID YOU REFUSE TO UNDERSTAND?
ALL YOUR LIFE, YOU NEVER ONCE THOUGHT OF THE MUTATES WHOSE TALENTS MAKE US A PROSPEROUS, SELF-SUFFICIENT NATION, THE ENVY OF THE WORLD.
ONLY WHEN YOUR GIRL FRIEND TESTED GENE-POSITIVE, AND WAS CALLED FOR SERVICE-- ONLY WHEN YOU YOURSELF WERE PERSONALLY AFFECTED-- DID THIS SOCIETY BECOME OPPRESSIVE. AND YOUR FATHER SOME KIND OF BORN-AGAIN NAZI.
DID YOU THINK IT DIDN'T HURT TO DO MY DUTY?
CURSE YOU, BOY, SHE WAS MY GOD-DAUGHTER!

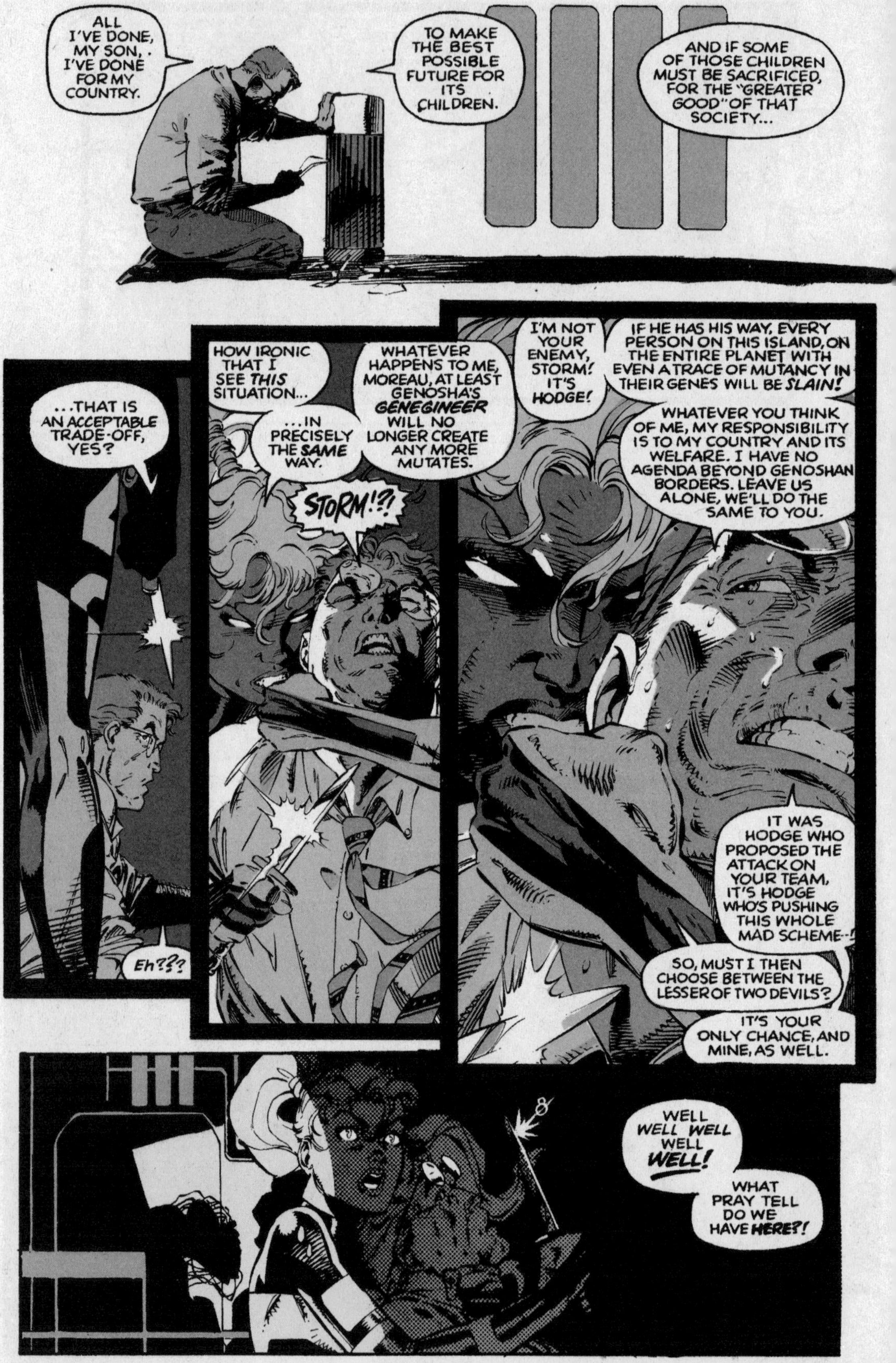
ALL I'VE DONE, MY SON, I'VE DONE FOR MY COUNTRY.
TO MAKE THE BEST POSSIBLE FUTURE FOR ITS CHILDREN.
AND IF SOME OF THOSE CHILDREN MUST BE SACRIFICED, FOR THE "GREATER GOOD" OF THAT SOCIETY...
...THAT IS AN ACCEPTABLE TRADE-OFF, YES?
Eh???
HOW IRONIC THAT I SEE THIS SITUATION...
...IN PRECISELY THE SAME WAY.
WHATEVER HAPPENS TO ME, MOREAU, AT LEAST GENOSHA'S GENEGINEER WILL NO LONGER CREATE ANY MORE MUTATES.
STORM!?!
I'M NOT YOUR ENEMY, STORM! IT'S HODGE!
IF HE HAS HIS WAY, EVERY PERSON ON THIS ISLAND, ON THE ENTIRE PLANET WITH EVEN A TRACE OF MUTANCY IN THEIR GENES WILL BE SLAIN!
WHATEVER YOU THINK OF ME, MY RESPONSIBILITY IS TO MY COUNTRY AND ITS WELFARE. I HAVE NO AGENDA BEYOND GENOSHAN BORDERS. LEAVE US ALONE, WE'LL DO THE SAME TO YOU.
IT WAS HODGE WHO PROPOSED THE ATTACK ON YOUR TEAM, IT'S HODGE WHO'S PUSHING THIS WHOLE MAD SCHEME--!
SO, MUST I THEN CHOOSE BETWEEN THE LESSER OF TWO DEVILS?
IT'S YOUR ONLY CHANCE, AND MINE, AS WELL.
WELL WELL WELL WELL WELL!
WHAT PRAY TELL DO WE HAVE HERE?!

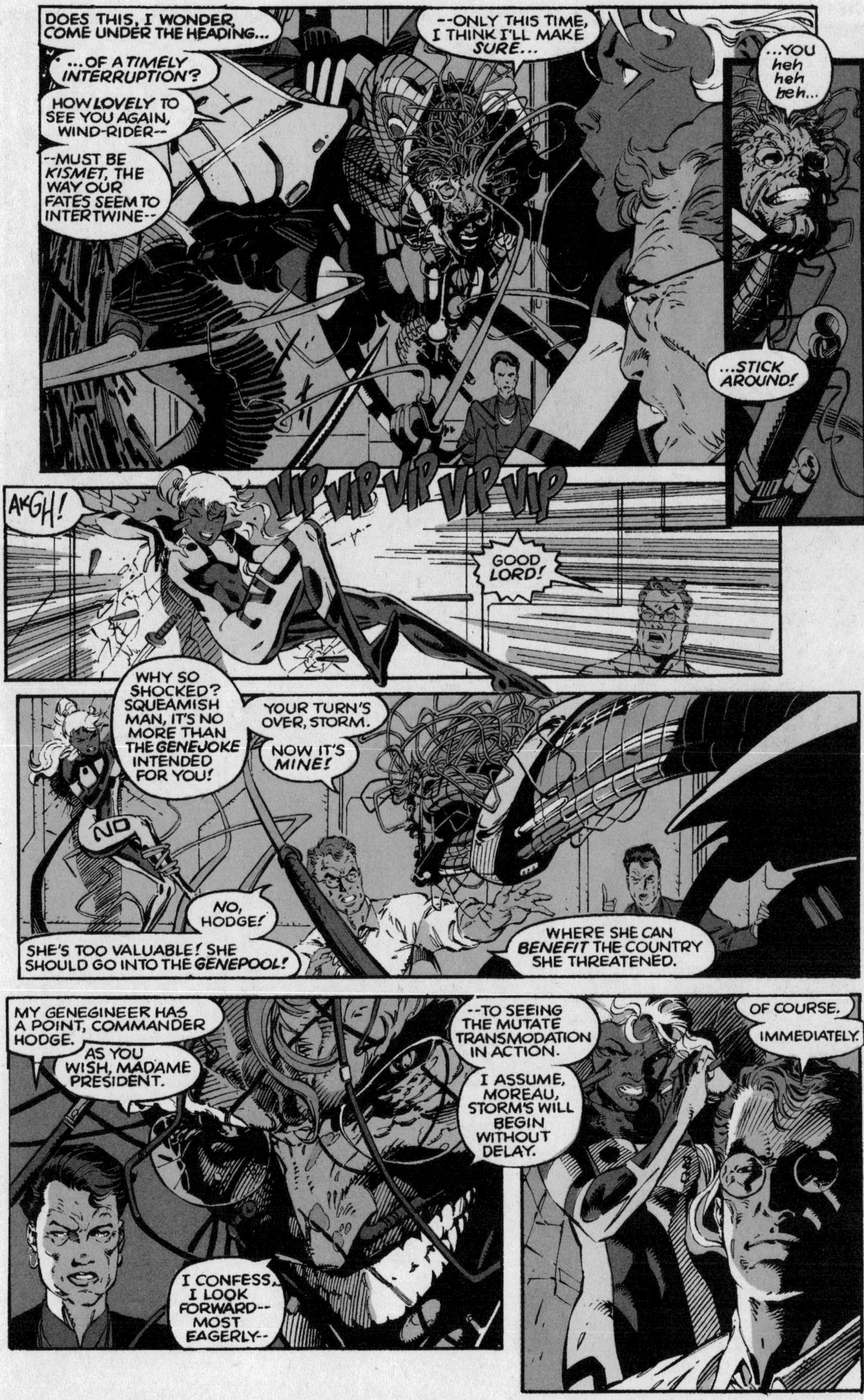
DOES THIS, I WONDER, COME UNDER THE HEADING...
...OF A TIMELY INTERRUPTION?
HOW LOVELY TO SEE YOU AGAIN, WIND-RIDER--
--MUST BE KISMET, THE WAY OUR FATES SEEM TO INTERTWINE--
--ONLY THIS TIME, I THINK I'LL MAKE SURE...
...YOU heh heh heh...
...STICK AROUND!
AKGH!
VIP VIP VIP VIP VIP
GOOD LORD!
WHY SO SHOCKED? SQUEAMISH MAN, IT'S NO MORE THAN THE GENEJOKE INTENDED FOR YOU!
YOUR TURN'S OVER, STORM.
NOW IT'S MINE!
NO
NO, HODGE!
SHE'S TOO VALUABLE! SHE SHOULD GO INTO THE GENEPOOL!
WHERE SHE CAN BENEFIT THE COUNTRY SHE THREATENED.
MY GENEGINEER HAS A POINT, COMMANDER HODGE.
AS YOU WISH, MADAME PRESIDENT.
I CONFESS, I LOOK FORWARD-- MOST EAGERLY--
--TO SEEING THE MUTATE TRANSMODATION IN ACTION.
I ASSUME, MOREAU, STORM'S WILL BEGIN WITHOUT DELAY.
OF COURSE.
IMMEDIATELY.

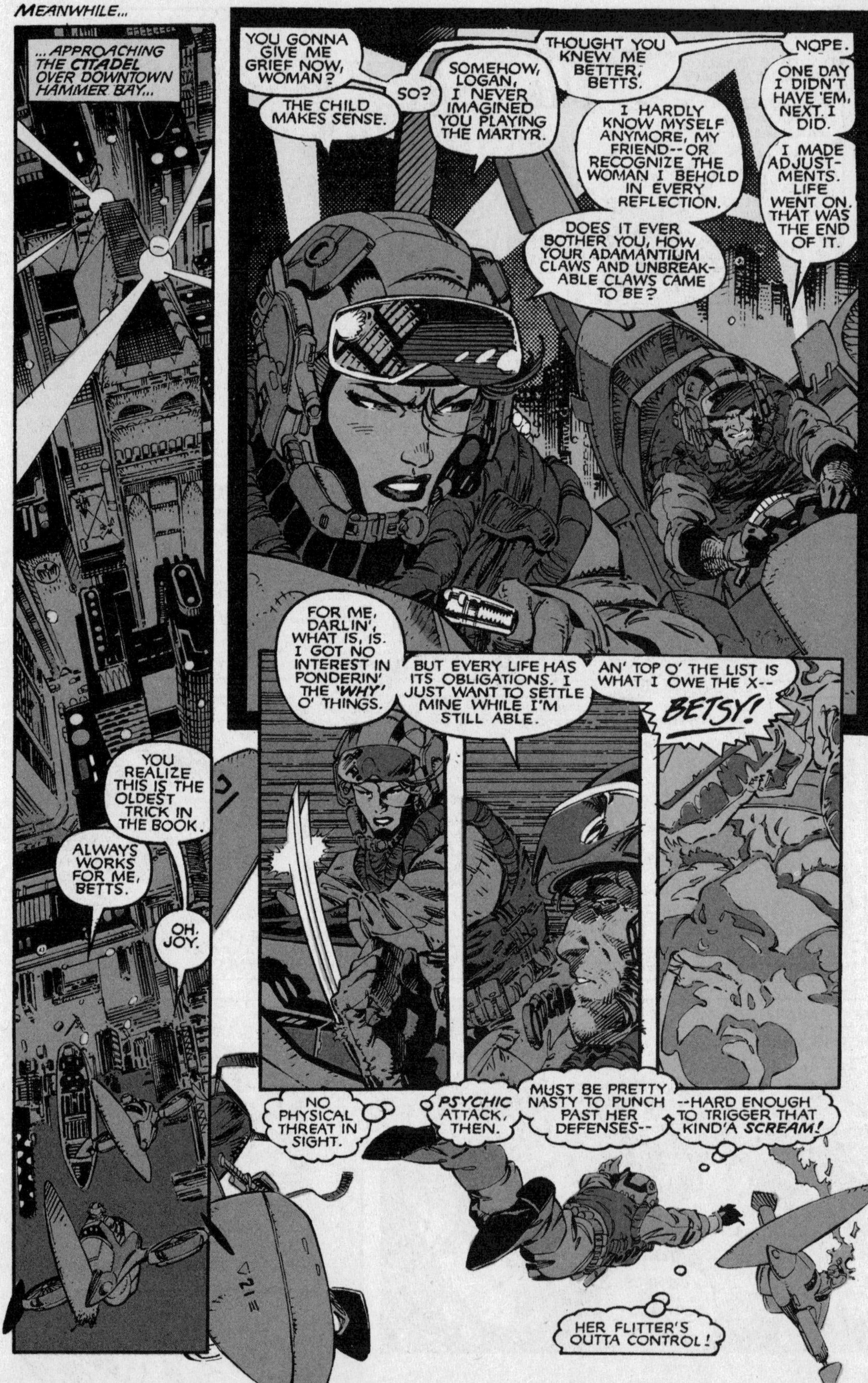
MEANWHILE...
...APPROACHING THE CITADEL OVER DOWNTOWN HAMMER BAY...
YOU GONNA GIVE ME GRIEF NOW, WOMAN?
THE CHILD MAKES SENSE.
SO?
SOMEHOW, LOGAN, I NEVER IMAGINED YOU PLAYING THE MARTYR.
THOUGHT YOU KNEW ME BETTER, BETTS.
I HARDLY KNOW MYSELF ANYMORE, MY FRIEND--OR RECOGNIZE THE WOMAN I BEHOLD IN EVERY REFLECTION.
DOES IT EVER BOTHER YOU, HOW YOUR ADAMANTIUM CLAWS AND UNBREAKABLE CLAWS CAME TO BE?
NOPE.
ONE DAY I DIDN'T HAVE 'EM, NEXT, I DID.
I MADE ADJUSTMENTS. LIFE WENT ON. THAT WAS THE END OF IT.
FOR ME, DARLIN', WHAT IS, IS. I GOT NO INTEREST IN PONDERIN' THE 'WHY' O' THINGS.
BUT EVERY LIFE HAS ITS OBLIGATIONS. I JUST WANT TO SETTLE MINE WHILE I'M STILL ABLE.
AN' TOP O' THE LIST IS WHAT I OWE THE X--
BETSY!
YOU REALIZE THIS IS THE OLDEST TRICK IN THE BOOK.
ALWAYS WORKS FOR ME, BETTS.
OH, JOY.
NO PHYSICAL THREAT IN SIGHT.
PSYCHIC ATTACK, THEN.
MUST BE PRETTY NASTY TO PUNCH PAST HER DEFENSES--
--HARD ENOUGH TO TRIGGER THAT KIND'A SCREAM!
HER FLITTER'S OUTTA CONTROL!

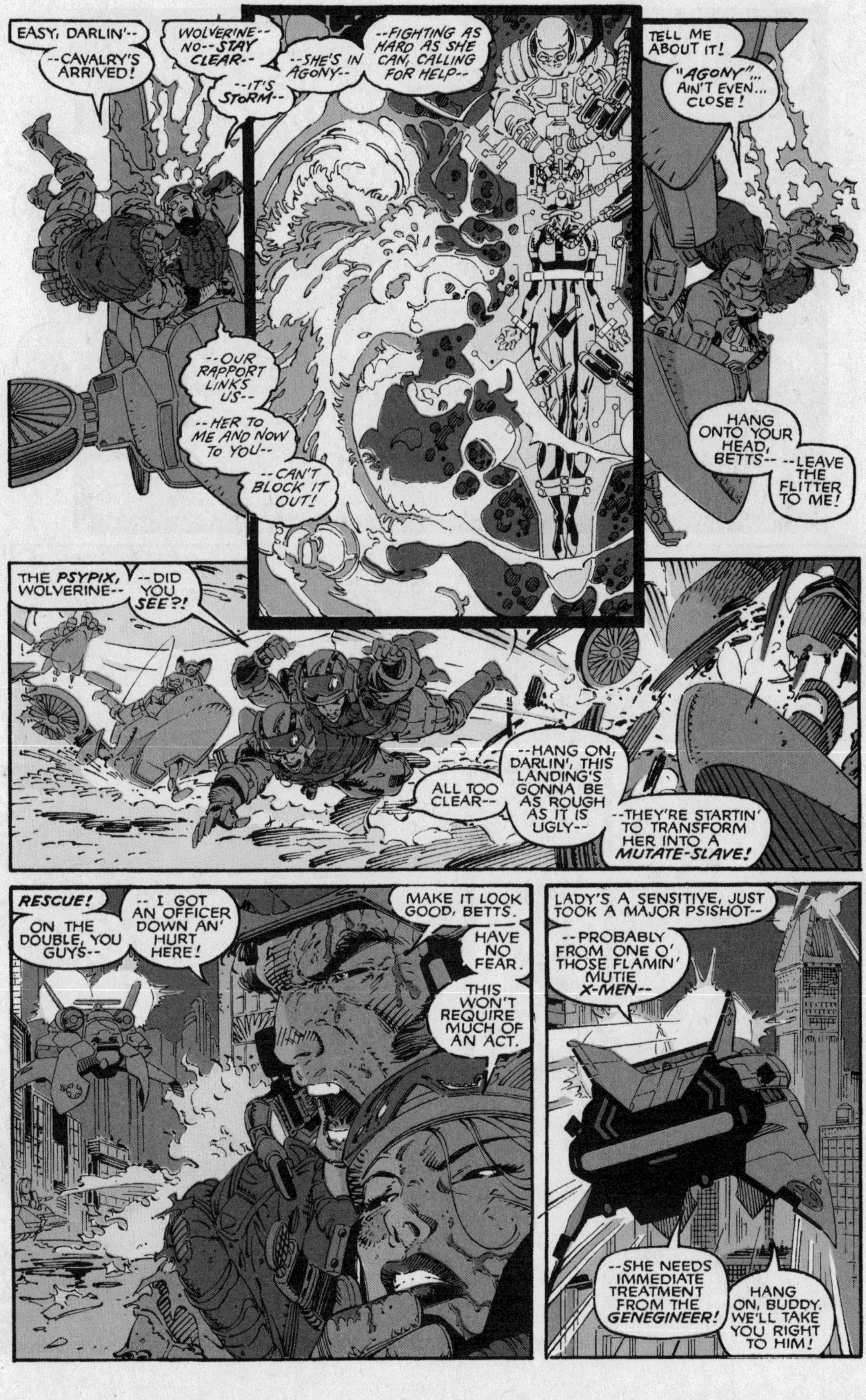
EASY, DARLIN'--
--CAVALRY'S ARRIVED!
WOLVERINE-- NO--STAY CLEAR--
--IT'S STORM--
--SHE'S IN AGONY--
--FIGHTING AS HARD AS SHE CAN, CALLING FOR HELP--
TELL ME ABOUT IT!
"AGONY"... AIN'T EVEN... CLOSE!
--OUR RAPPORT LINKS US--
--HER TO ME AND NOW TO YOU--
--CAN'T BLOCK IT OUT!
HANG ONTO YOUR HEAD, BETTS--
--LEAVE THE FLITTER TO ME!
THE PSYPIX, WOLVERINE--
--DID YOU SEE?!
ALL TOO CLEAR--
--HANG ON, DARLIN', THIS LANDING'S GONNA BE AS ROUGH AS IT IS UGLY--
--THEY'RE STARTIN' TO TRANSFORM HER INTO A MUTATE-SLAVE!
RESCUE!
ON THE DOUBLE, YOU GUYS--
-- I GOT AN OFFICER DOWN AN' HURT HERE!
MAKE IT LOOK GOOD, BETTS.
HAVE NO FEAR.
THIS WON'T REQUIRE MUCH OF AN ACT.
LADY'S A SENSITIVE, JUST TOOK A MAJOR PSISHOT--
--PROBABLY FROM ONE O' THOSE FLAMIN' MUTIE X-MEN--
--SHE NEEDS IMMEDIATE TREATMENT FROM THE GENEGINEER!
HANG ON, BUDDY. WE'LL TAKE YOU RIGHT TO HIM!

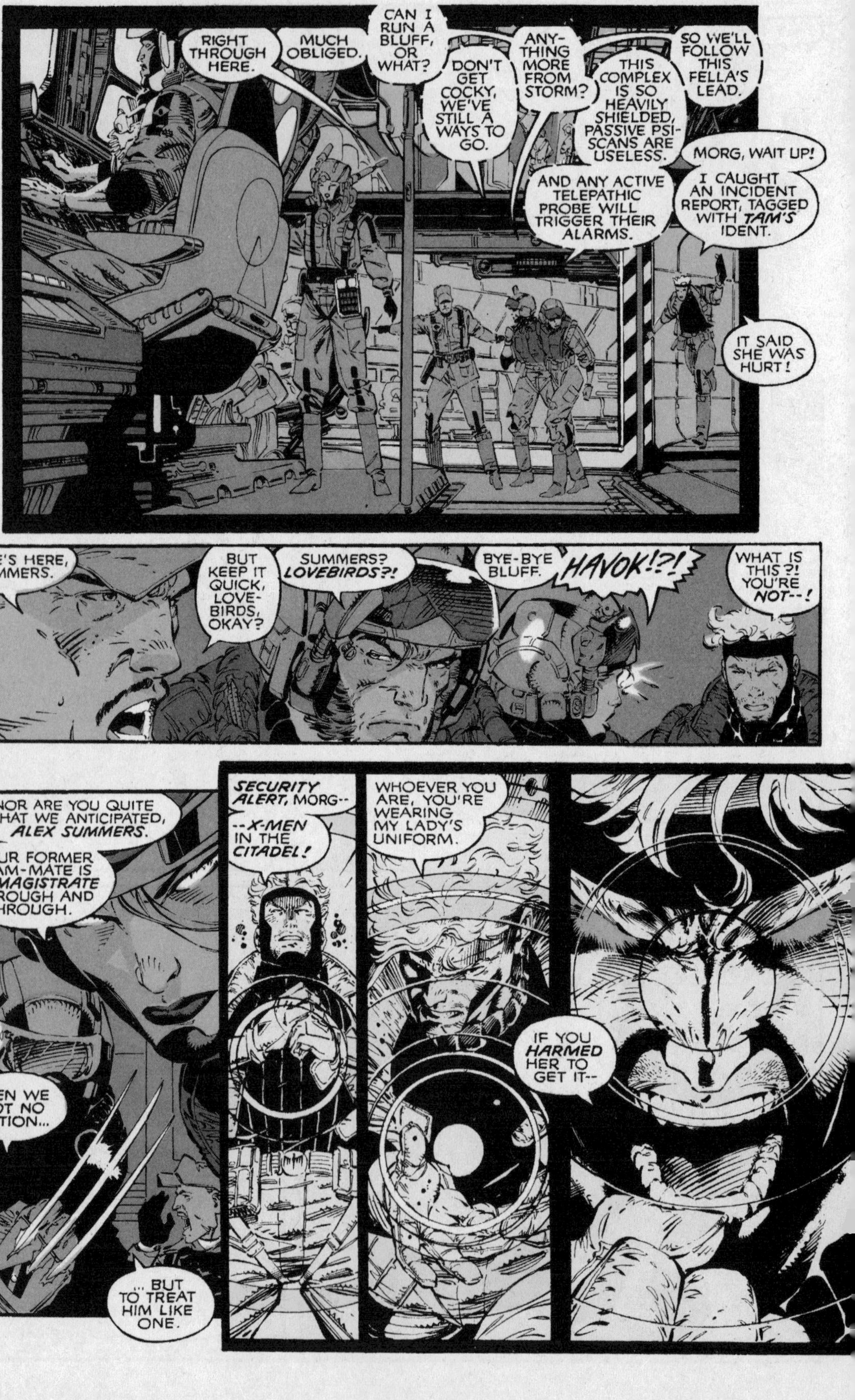
RIGHT THROUGH HERE.
MUCH OBLIGED.
CAN I RUN A BLUFF, OR WHAT?
DON'T GET COCKY, WE'VE STILL A WAYS TO GO.
ANY-THING MORE FROM STORM?
THIS COMPLEX IS SO HEAVILY SHIELDED, PASSIVE PSI-SCANS ARE USELESS.
AND ANY ACTIVE TELEPATHIC PROBE WILL TRIGGER THEIR ALARMS.
SO WE'LL FOLLOW THIS FELLA'S LEAD.
MORG, WAIT UP!
I CAUGHT AN INCIDENT REPORT, TAGGED WITH TAM'S IDENT.
IT SAID SHE WAS HURT!
SHE'S HERE, SUMMERS.
BUT KEEP IT QUICK, LOVE-BIRDS, OKAY?
SUMMERS? LOVEBIRDS?!
BYE-BYE BLUFF.
HAVOK!?!
WHAT IS THIS?! YOU'RE NOT--!
NOR ARE YOU QUITE WHAT WE ANTICIPATED, ALEX SUMMERS.
OUR FORMER TEAM-MATE IS A MAGISTRATE THROUGH AND THROUGH.
THEN WE GOT NO OPTION...
... BUT TO TREAT HIM LIKE ONE.
SECURITY ALERT, MORG--
--X-MEN IN THE CITADEL!
WHOEVER YOU ARE, YOU'RE WEARING MY LADY'S UNIFORM.
IF YOU HARMED HER TO GET IT--

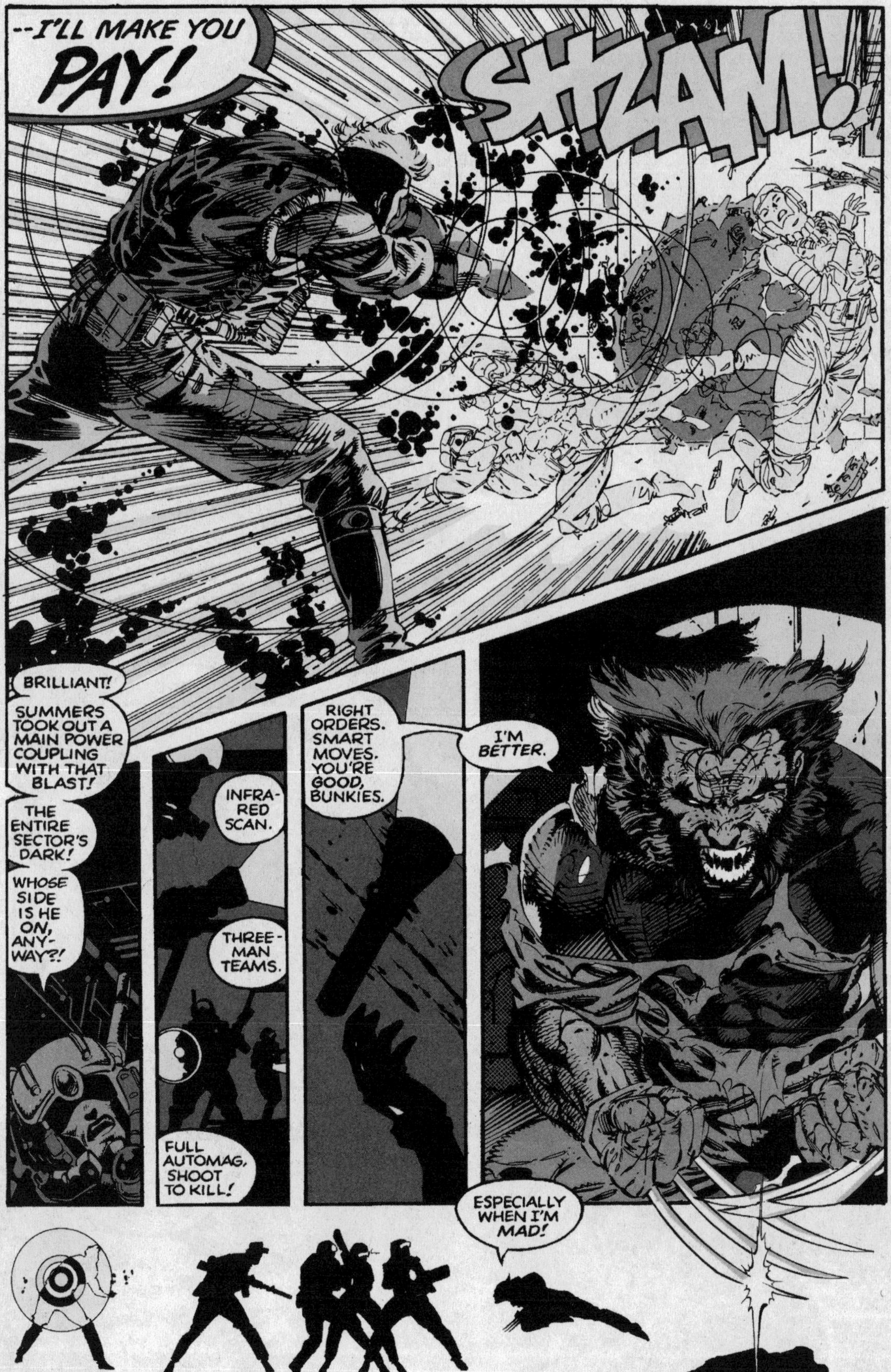
--I'LL MAKE YOU PAY!
SHZAM!
BRILLIANT!
SUMMERS TOOK OUT A MAIN POWER COUPLING WITH THAT BLAST!
THE ENTIRE SECTOR'S DARK!
WHOSE SIDE IS HE ON, ANYWAY?!
INFRA-RED SCAN.
THREE-MAN TEAMS.
FULL AUTOMAG, SHOOT TO KILL!
RIGHT ORDERS. SMART MOVES. YOU'RE GOOD, BUNKIES.
I'M BETTER.
ESPECIALLY WHEN I'M MAD!

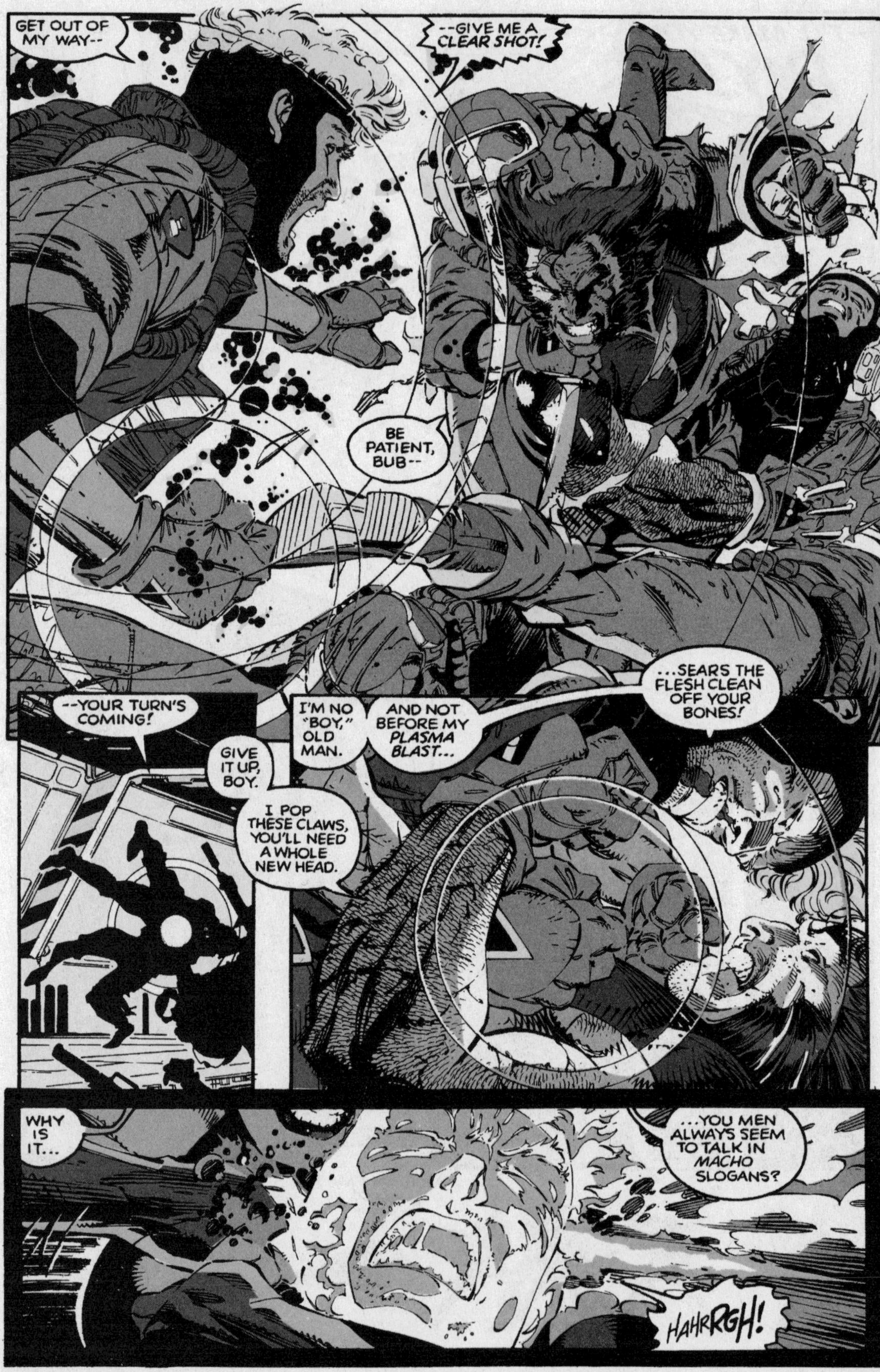
GET OUT OF MY WAY--
--GIVE ME A CLEAR SHOT!
BE PATIENT, BUB--
--YOUR TURN'S COMING!
GIVE IT UP, BOY.
I POP THESE CLAWS, YOU'LL NEED A WHOLE NEW HEAD.
I'M NO "BOY," OLD MAN.
AND NOT BEFORE MY PLASMA BLAST...
...SEARS THE FLESH CLEAN OFF YOUR BONES!
WHY IS IT...
...YOU MEN ALWAYS SEEM TO TALK IN MACHO SLOGANS?
HAHRRGH!

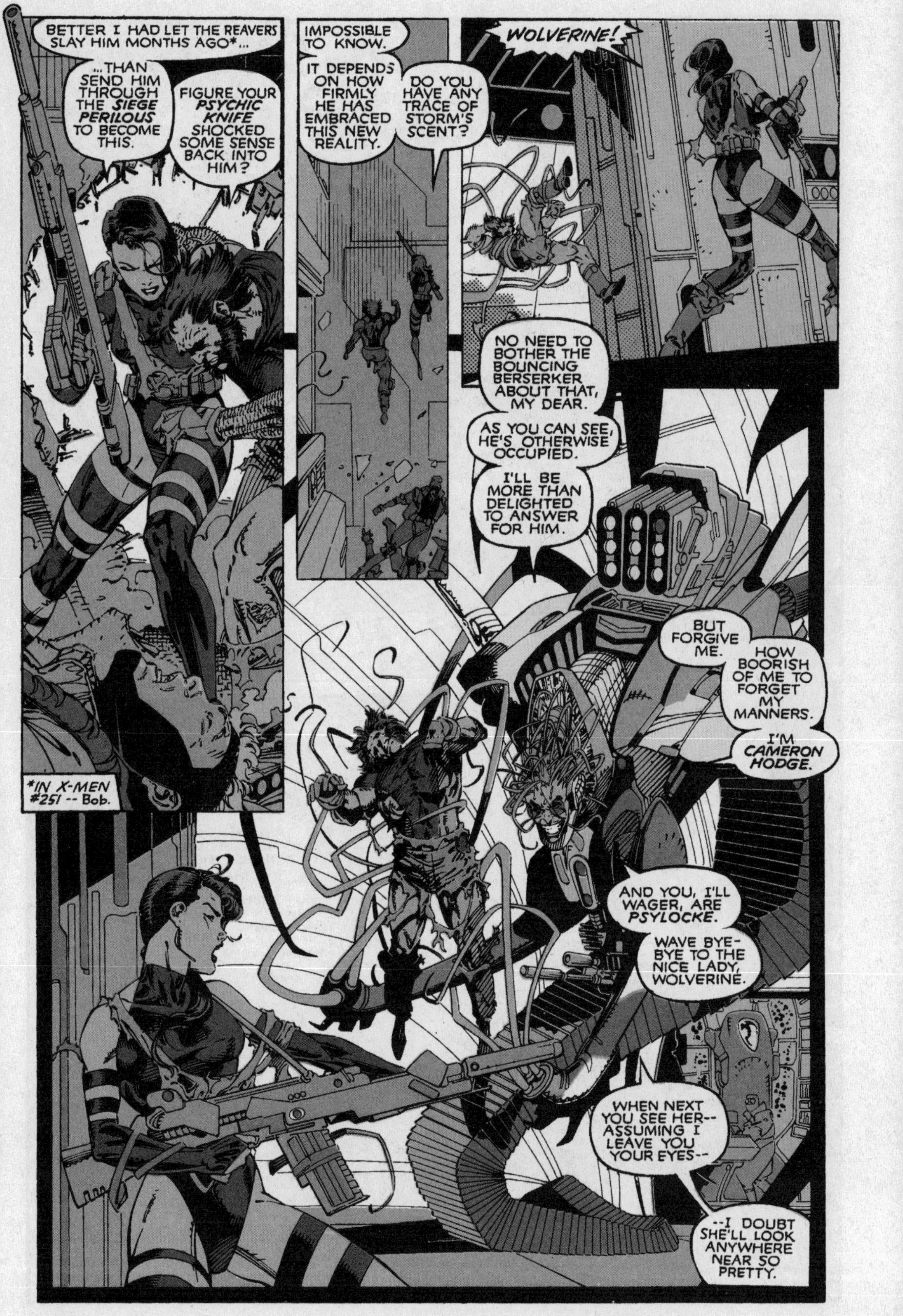
BETTER I HAD LET THE REAVERS SLAY HIM MONTHS AGO*...
...THAN SEND HIM THROUGH THE SIEGE PERILOUS TO BECOME THIS.
FIGURE YOUR PSYCHIC KNIFE SHOCKED SOME SENSE BACK INTO HIM?
IMPOSSIBLE TO KNOW.
IT DEPENDS ON HOW FIRMLY HE HAS EMBRACED THIS NEW REALITY.
DO YOU HAVE ANY TRACE OF STORM'S SCENT?
WOLVERINE!
NO NEED TO BOTHER THE BOUNCING BERSERKER ABOUT THAT, MY DEAR.
AS YOU CAN SEE, HE'S OTHERWISE OCCUPIED.
I'LL BE MORE THAN DELIGHTED TO ANSWER FOR HIM.
*IN X-MEN #251 -- Bob.
BUT FORGIVE ME.
HOW BOORISH OF ME TO FORGET MY MANNERS.
I'M CAMERON HODGE.
AND YOU, I'LL WAGER, ARE PSYLOCKE.
WAVE BYE-BYE TO THE NICE LADY, WOLVERINE.
WHEN NEXT YOU SEE HER-- ASSUMING I LEAVE YOU YOUR EYES--
--I DOUBT SHE'LL LOOK ANYWHERE NEAR SO PRETTY.

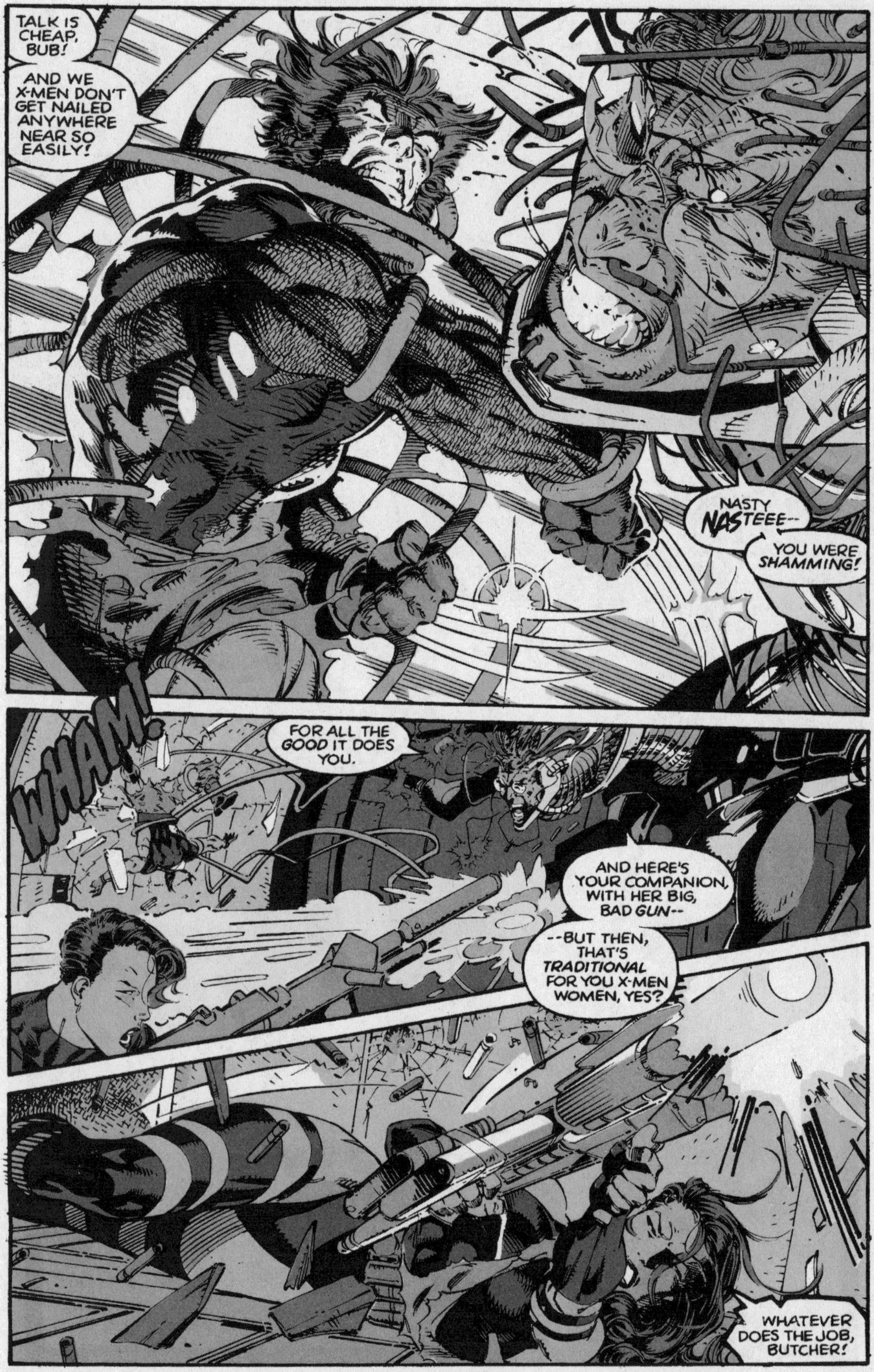
TALK IS CHEAP, BUB!
AND WE X-MEN DON'T GET NAILED ANYWHERE NEAR SO EASILY!
NASTY NASTEEE--
YOU WERE SHAMMING!
WHAM!
FOR ALL THE GOOD IT DOES YOU.
AND HERE'S YOUR COMPANION, WITH HER BIG, BAD GUN--
--BUT THEN, THAT'S TRADITIONAL FOR YOU X-MEN WOMEN, YES?
WHATEVER DOES THE JOB, BUTCHER!

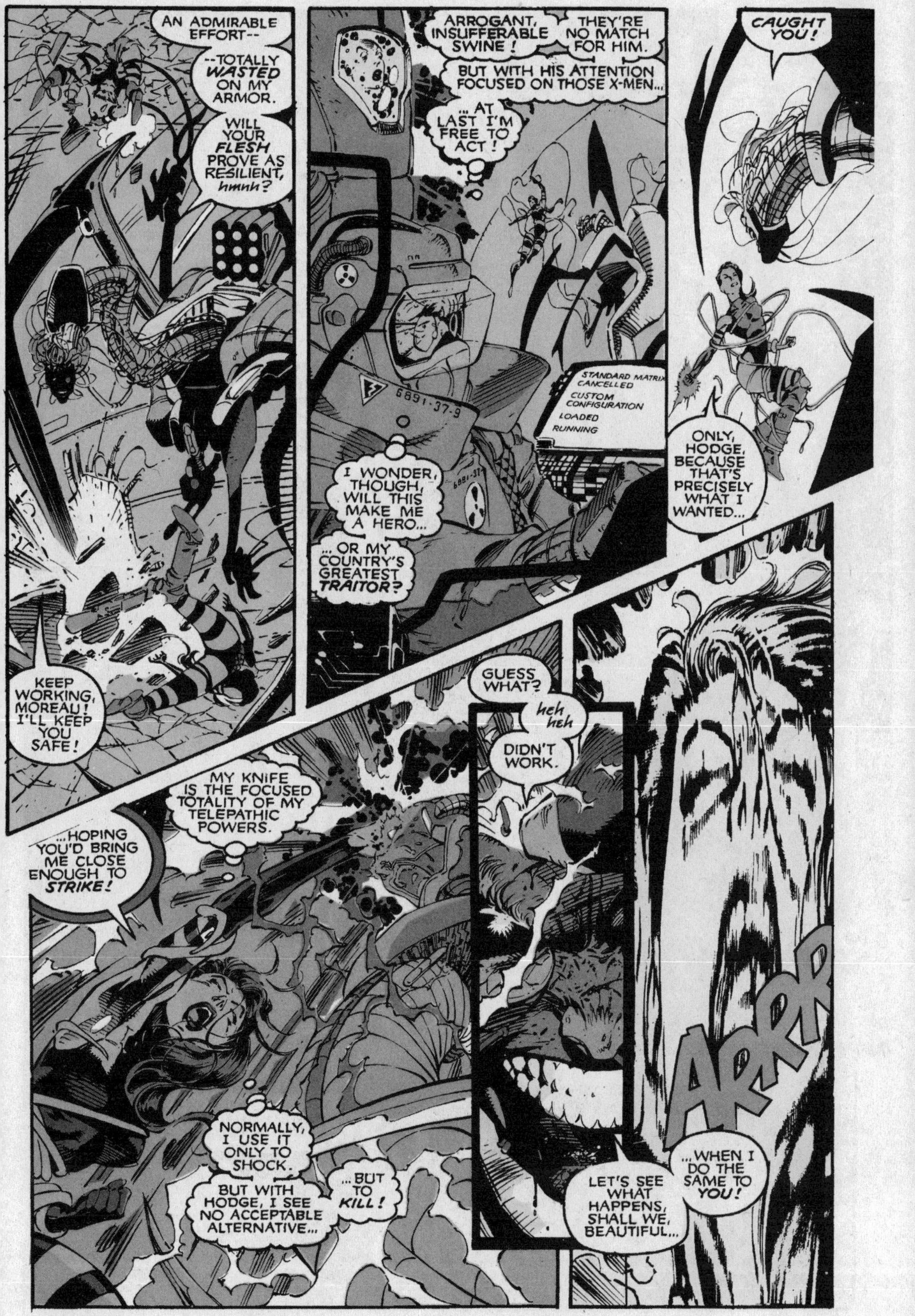
AN ADMIRABLE EFFORT--
--TOTALLY WASTED ON MY ARMOR.
WILL YOUR FLESH PROVE AS RESILIENT, hmnh?
KEEP WORKING, MOREAU! I'LL KEEP YOU SAFE!
ARROGANT, INSUFFERABLE SWINE!
THEY'RE NO MATCH FOR HIM.
BUT WITH HIS ATTENTION FOCUSED ON THOSE X-MEN...
...AT LAST I'M FREE TO ACT!
STANDARD MATRIX CANCELLED
CUSTOM CONFIGURATION
LOADED
RUNNING
I WONDER, THOUGH, WILL THIS MAKE ME A HERO...
...OR MY COUNTRY'S GREATEST TRAITOR?
CAUGHT YOU!
ONLY, HODGE, BECAUSE THAT'S PRECISELY WHAT I WANTED...
...HOPING YOU'D BRING ME CLOSE ENOUGH TO STRIKE!
MY KNIFE IS THE FOCUSED TOTALITY OF MY TELEPATHIC POWERS.
NORMALLY, I USE IT ONLY TO SHOCK.
BUT WITH HODGE, I SEE NO ACCEPTABLE ALTERNATIVE...
...BUT TO KILL!
GUESS WHAT?
heh heh
DIDN'T WORK.
LET'S SEE WHAT HAPPENS, SHALL WE, BEAUTIFUL...
...WHEN I DO THE SAME TO YOU!
ARRR

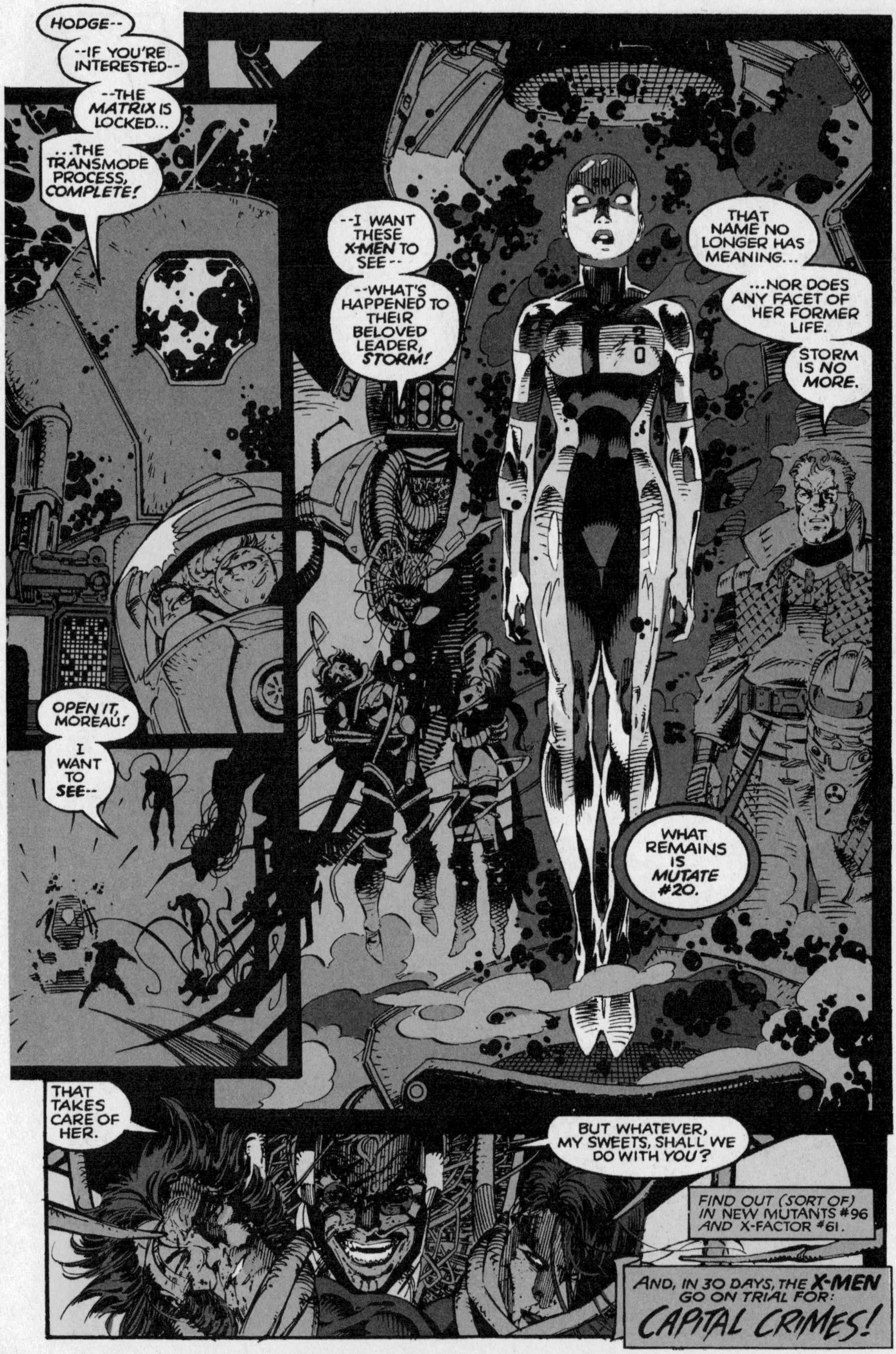
HODGE--
--IF YOU'RE INTERESTED--
--THE MATRIX IS LOCKED...
...THE TRANSMODE PROCESS, COMPLETE!
OPEN IT, MOREAU!
I WANT TO SEE--
--I WANT THESE X-MEN TO SEE--
--WHAT'S HAPPENED TO THEIR BELOVED LEADER, STORM!
THAT NAME NO LONGER HAS MEANING...
...NOR DOES ANY FACET OF HER FORMER LIFE.
STORM IS NO MORE.
WHAT REMAINS IS MUTATE #20.
THAT TAKES CARE OF HER.
BUT WHATEVER, MY SWEETS, SHALL WE DO WITH YOU?
FIND OUT (SORT OF) IN NEW MUTANTS #96 AND X-FACTOR #61.
AND, IN 30 DAYS, THE X-MEN GO ON TRIAL FOR:
CAPITAL CRIMES!

X-MEN

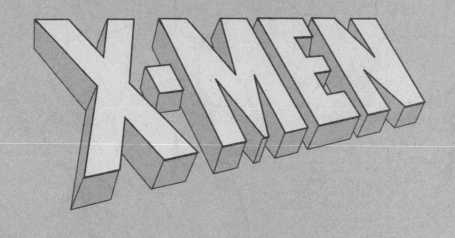

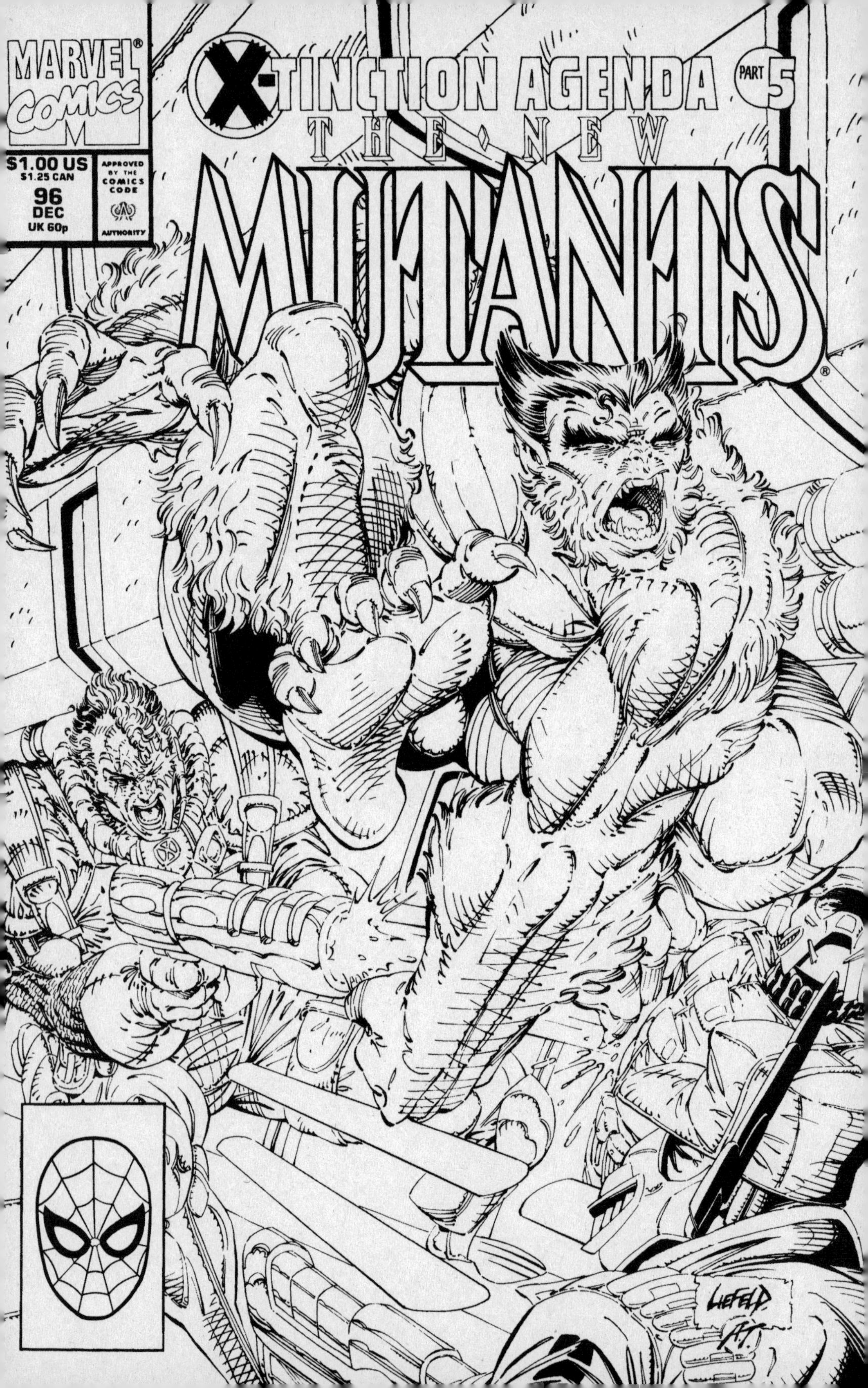

MARVEL® COMICS
X-TINCTION AGENDA PART 5
THE NEW MUTANTS®
$1.00 US
$1.25 CAN
96
DEC
UK 60p
APPROVED BY THE COMICS CODE AUTHORITY
LIEFELD

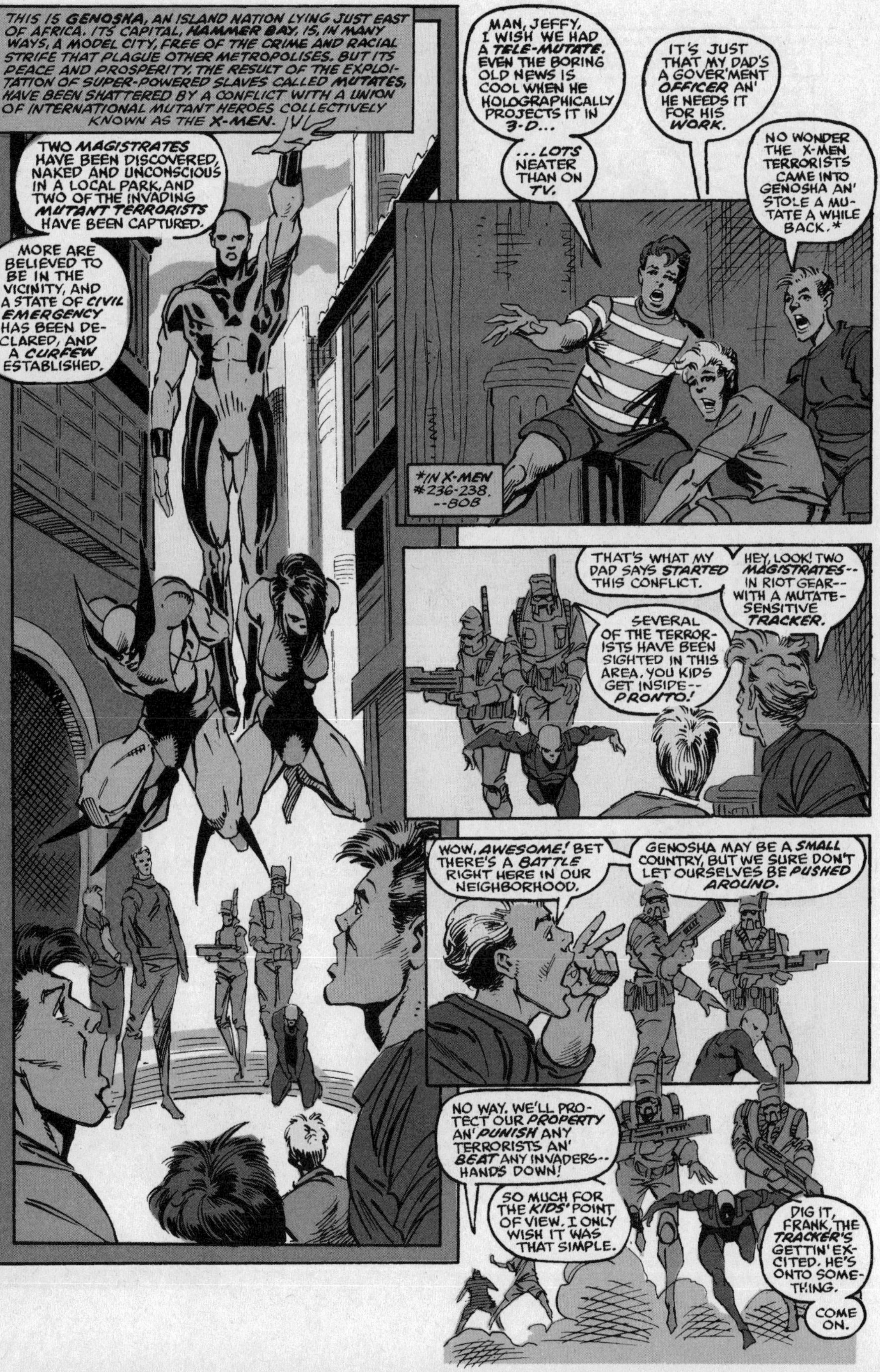

THIS IS GENOSHA, AN ISLAND NATION LYING JUST EAST OF AFRICA. ITS CAPITAL, HAMMER BAY, IS, IN MANY WAYS, A MODEL CITY, FREE OF THE CRIME AND RACIAL STRIFE THAT PLAGUE OTHER METROPOLISES. BUT ITS PEACE AND PROSPERITY, THE RESULT OF THE EXPLOITATION OF SUPER-POWERED SLAVES CALLED MUTATES, HAVE BEEN SHATTERED BY A CONFLICT WITH A UNION OF INTERNATIONAL MUTANT HEROES COLLECTIVELY KNOWN AS THE X-MEN.
TWO MAGISTRATES HAVE BEEN DISCOVERED, NAKED AND UNCONSCIOUS IN A LOCAL PARK, AND TWO OF THE INVADING MUTANT TERRORISTS HAVE BEEN CAPTURED.
MORE ARE BELIEVED TO BE IN THE VICINITY, AND A STATE OF CIVIL EMERGENCY HAS BEEN DECLARED, AND A CURFEW ESTABLISHED.
MAN, JEFFY, I WISH WE HAD A TELE-MUTATE. EVEN THE BORING OLD NEWS IS COOL WHEN HE HOLOGRAPHICALLY PROJECTS IT IN 3-D...
...LOTS NEATER THAN ON TV.
IT'S JUST THAT MY DAD'S A GOVER'MENT OFFICER AN' HE NEEDS IT FOR HIS WORK.
NO WONDER THE X-MEN TERRORISTS CAME INTO GENOSHA AN' STOLE A MUTATE A WHILE BACK.*
*IN X-MEN #236-238. --BOB
THAT'S WHAT MY DAD SAYS STARTED THIS CONFLICT.
HEY, LOOK! TWO MAGISTRATES-- IN RIOT GEAR-- WITH A MUTATE-SENSITIVE TRACKER.
SEVERAL OF THE TERRORISTS HAVE BEEN SIGHTED IN THIS AREA, YOU KIDS GET INSIDE-- PRONTO!
WOW, AWESOME! BET THERE'S A BATTLE RIGHT HERE IN OUR NEIGHBORHOOD.
GENOSHA MAY BE A SMALL COUNTRY, BUT WE SURE DON'T LET OURSELVES BE PUSHED AROUND.
NO WAY. WE'LL PROTECT OUR PROPERTY AN' PUNISH ANY TERRORISTS AN' BEAT ANY INVADERS-- HANDS DOWN!
SO MUCH FOR THE KIDS' POINT OF VIEW. I ONLY WISH IT WAS THAT SIMPLE.
DIG IT, FRANK, THE TRACKER'S GETTIN' EXCITED. HE'S ONTO SOMETHING.
COME ON.

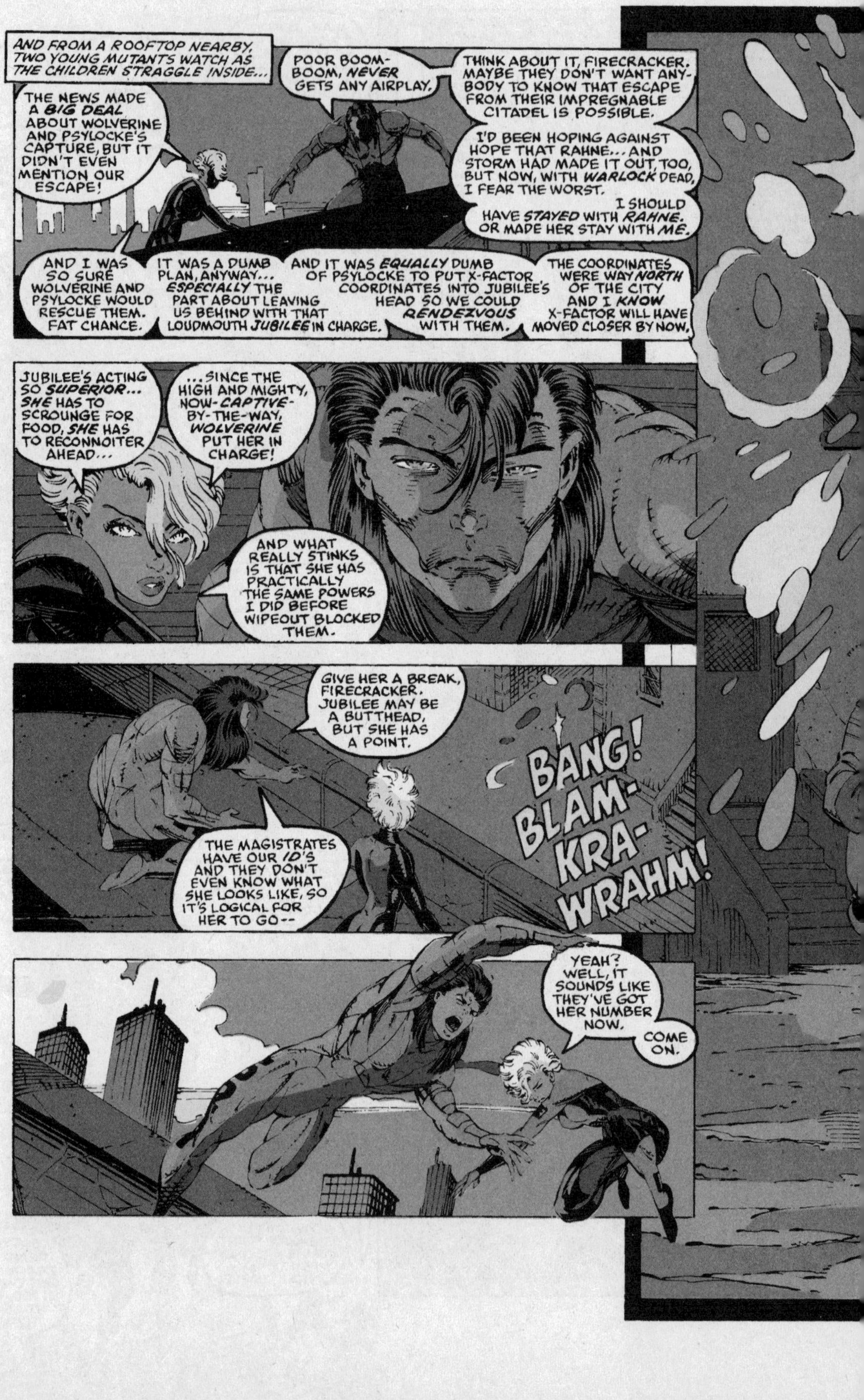
AND FROM A ROOFTOP NEARBY, TWO YOUNG MUTANTS WATCH AS THE CHILDREN STRAGGLE INSIDE...
THE NEWS MADE A BIG DEAL ABOUT WOLVERINE AND PSYLOCKE'S CAPTURE, BUT IT DIDN'T EVEN MENTION OUR ESCAPE!
POOR BOOM-BOOM, NEVER GETS ANY AIRPLAY.
THINK ABOUT IT, FIRECRACKER. MAYBE THEY DON'T WANT ANYBODY TO KNOW THAT ESCAPE FROM THEIR IMPREGNABLE CITADEL IS POSSIBLE.
I'D BEEN HOPING AGAINST HOPE THAT RAHNE... AND STORM HAD MADE IT OUT, TOO, BUT NOW, WITH WARLOCK DEAD, I FEAR THE WORST.
I SHOULD HAVE STAYED WITH RAHNE. OR MADE HER STAY WITH ME.
AND I WAS SO SURE WOLVERINE AND PSYLOCKE WOULD RESCUE THEM. FAT CHANCE.
IT WAS A DUMB PLAN, ANYWAY... ESPECIALLY THE PART ABOUT LEAVING US BEHIND WITH THAT LOUDMOUTH JUBILEE IN CHARGE.
AND IT WAS EQUALLY DUMB OF PSYLOCKE TO PUT X-FACTOR COORDINATES INTO JUBILEE'S HEAD SO WE COULD RENDEZVOUS WITH THEM.
THE COORDINATES WERE WAY NORTH OF THE CITY AND I KNOW X-FACTOR WILL HAVE MOVED CLOSER BY NOW.
JUBILEE'S ACTING SO SUPERIOR... SHE HAS TO SCROUNGE FOR FOOD, SHE HAS TO RECONNOITER AHEAD...
...SINCE THE HIGH AND MIGHTY, NOW-CAPTIVE-BY-THE-WAY, WOLVERINE PUT HER IN CHARGE!
AND WHAT REALLY STINKS IS THAT SHE HAS PRACTICALLY THE SAME POWERS I DID BEFORE WIPEOUT BLOCKED THEM.
GIVE HER A BREAK, FIRECRACKER. JUBILEE MAY BE A BUTTHEAD, BUT SHE HAS A POINT.
THE MAGISTRATES HAVE OUR ID'S AND THEY DON'T EVEN KNOW WHAT SHE LOOKS LIKE, SO IT'S LOGICAL FOR HER TO GO--
BANG! BLAM-KRA-WRAHM!
YEAH? WELL, IT SOUNDS LIKE THEY'VE GOT HER NUMBER NOW.
COME ON.

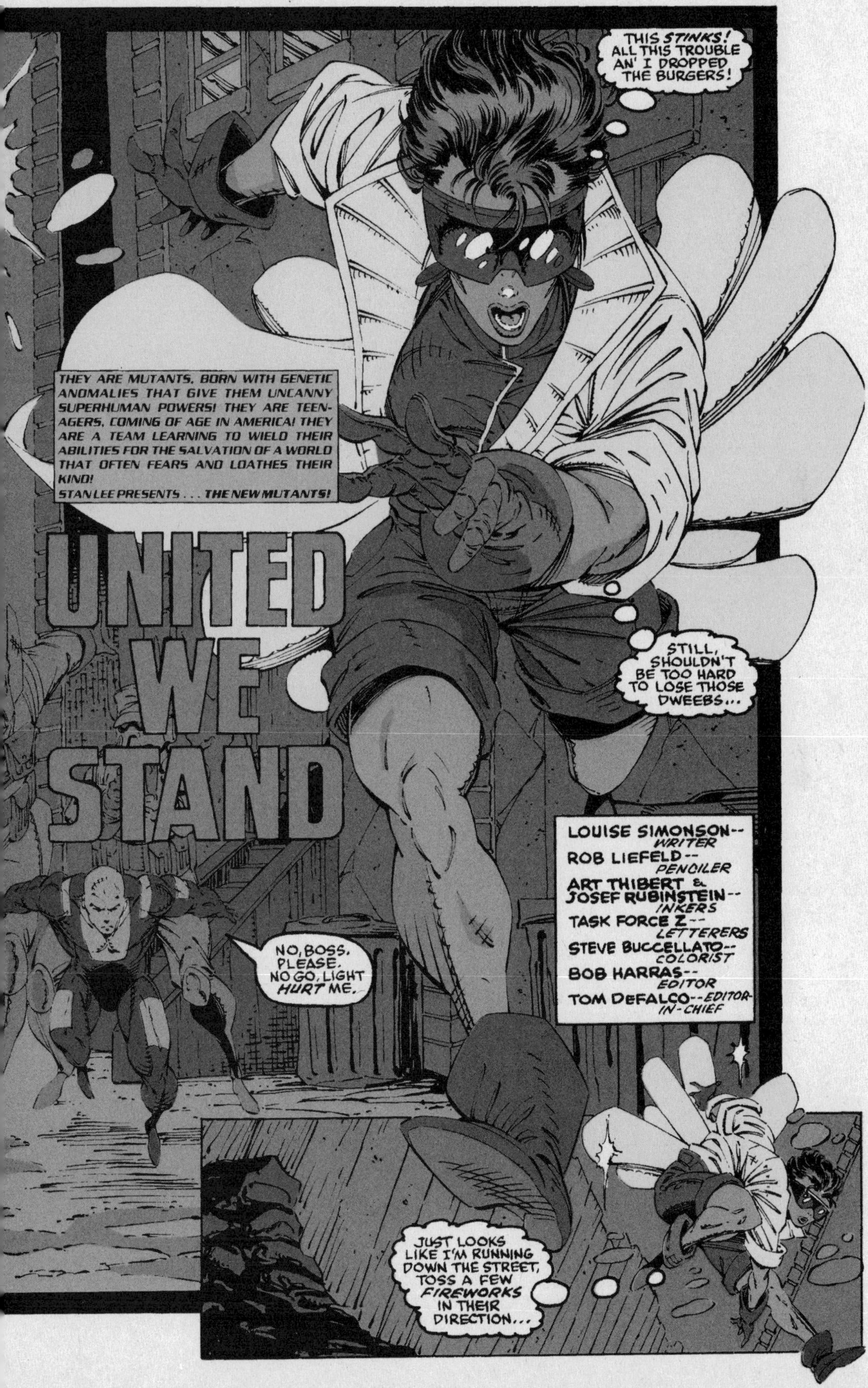
THIS STINKS! ALL THIS TROUBLE AN' I DROPPED THE BURGERS!
THEY ARE MUTANTS, BORN WITH GENETIC ANOMALIES THAT GIVE THEM UNCANNY SUPERHUMAN POWERS! THEY ARE TEEN-AGERS, COMING OF AGE IN AMERICA! THEY ARE A TEAM LEARNING TO WIELD THEIR ABILITIES FOR THE SALVATION OF A WORLD THAT OFTEN FEARS AND LOATHES THEIR KIND!
STAN LEE PRESENTS . . . THE NEW MUTANTS!
UNITED WE STAND
STILL, SHOULDN'T BE TOO HARD TO LOSE THOSE DWEEBS...
LOUISE SIMONSON-- WRITER
ROB LIEFELD-- PENCILER
ART THIBERT & JOSEF RUBINSTEIN-- INKERS
TASK FORCE Z-- LETTERERS
STEVE BUCCELLATO-- COLORIST
BOB HARRAS-- EDITOR
TOM DeFALCO-- EDITOR-IN-CHIEF
NO, BOSS. PLEASE. NO GO, LIGHT HURT ME.
JUST LOOKS LIKE I'M RUNNING DOWN THE STREET, TOSS A FEW FIREWORKS IN THEIR DIRECTION...

X-MEN

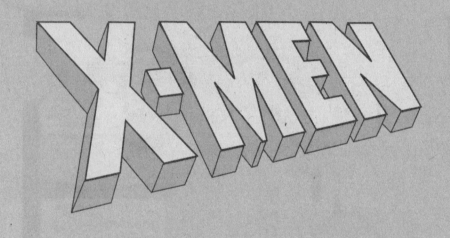

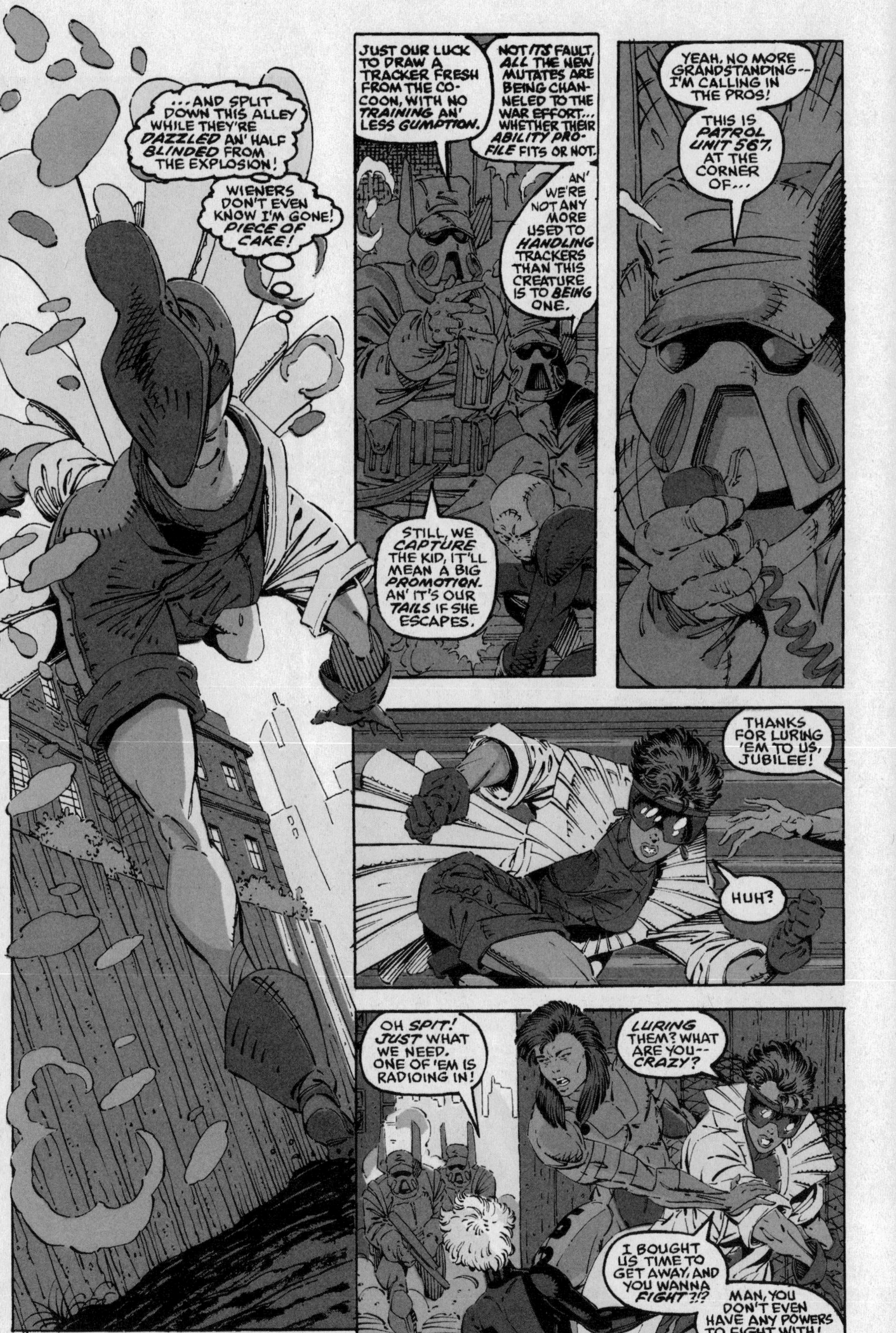

...AND SPLIT DOWN THIS ALLEY WHILE THEY'RE DAZZLED AN' HALF BLINDED FROM THE EXPLOSION!
WIENERS DON'T EVEN KNOW I'M GONE! PIECE OF CAKE!
JUST OUR LUCK TO DRAW A TRACKER FRESH FROM THE CO-COON, WITH NO TRAINING AN' LESS GUMPTION.
NOT ITS FAULT, ALL THE NEW MUTATES ARE BEING CHAN-NELED TO THE WAR EFFORT... WHETHER THEIR ABILITY PRO-FILE FITS OR NOT.
AN' WE'RE NOT ANY MORE USED TO HANDLING TRACKERS THAN THIS CREATURE IS TO BEING ONE.
STILL, WE CAPTURE THE KID, IT'LL MEAN A BIG PROMOTION. AN' IT'S OUR TAILS IF SHE ESCAPES.
YEAH, NO MORE GRANDSTANDING-- I'M CALLING IN THE PROS!
THIS IS PATROL UNIT 567, AT THE CORNER OF...
THANKS FOR LURING 'EM TO US, JUBILEE!
HUH?
OH SPIT! JUST WHAT WE NEED. ONE OF 'EM IS RADIOING IN!
LURING THEM? WHAT ARE YOU-- CRAZY?
I BOUGHT US TIME TO GET AWAY, AND YOU WANNA FIGHT?!?
MAN, YOU DON'T EVEN HAVE ANY POWERS TO FIGHT WITH!

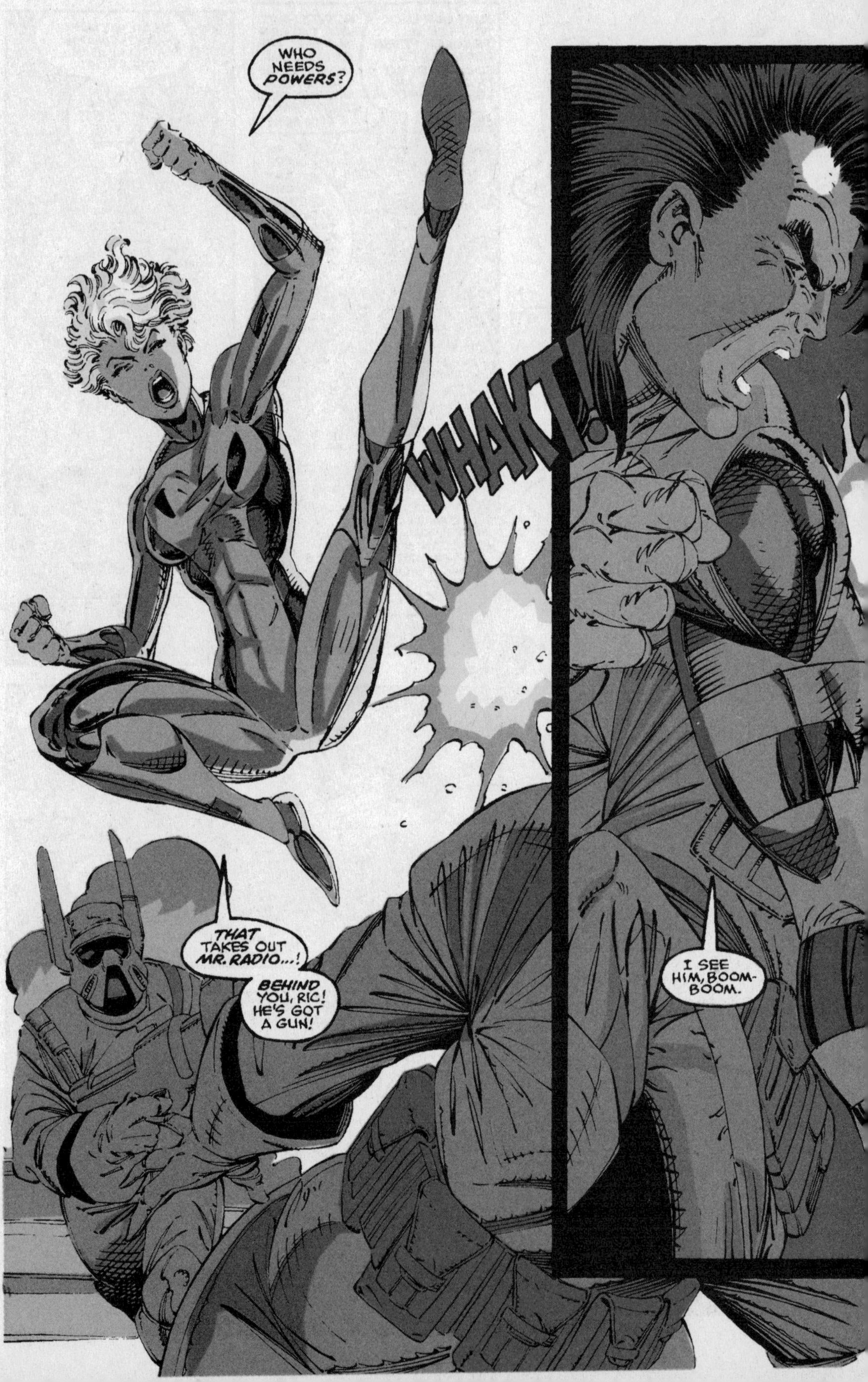
WHO NEEDS POWERS?
WHAKT!
THAT TAKES OUT MR. RADIO...!
BEHIND YOU, RIC! HE'S GOT A GUN!
I SEE HIM, BOOM-BOOM.

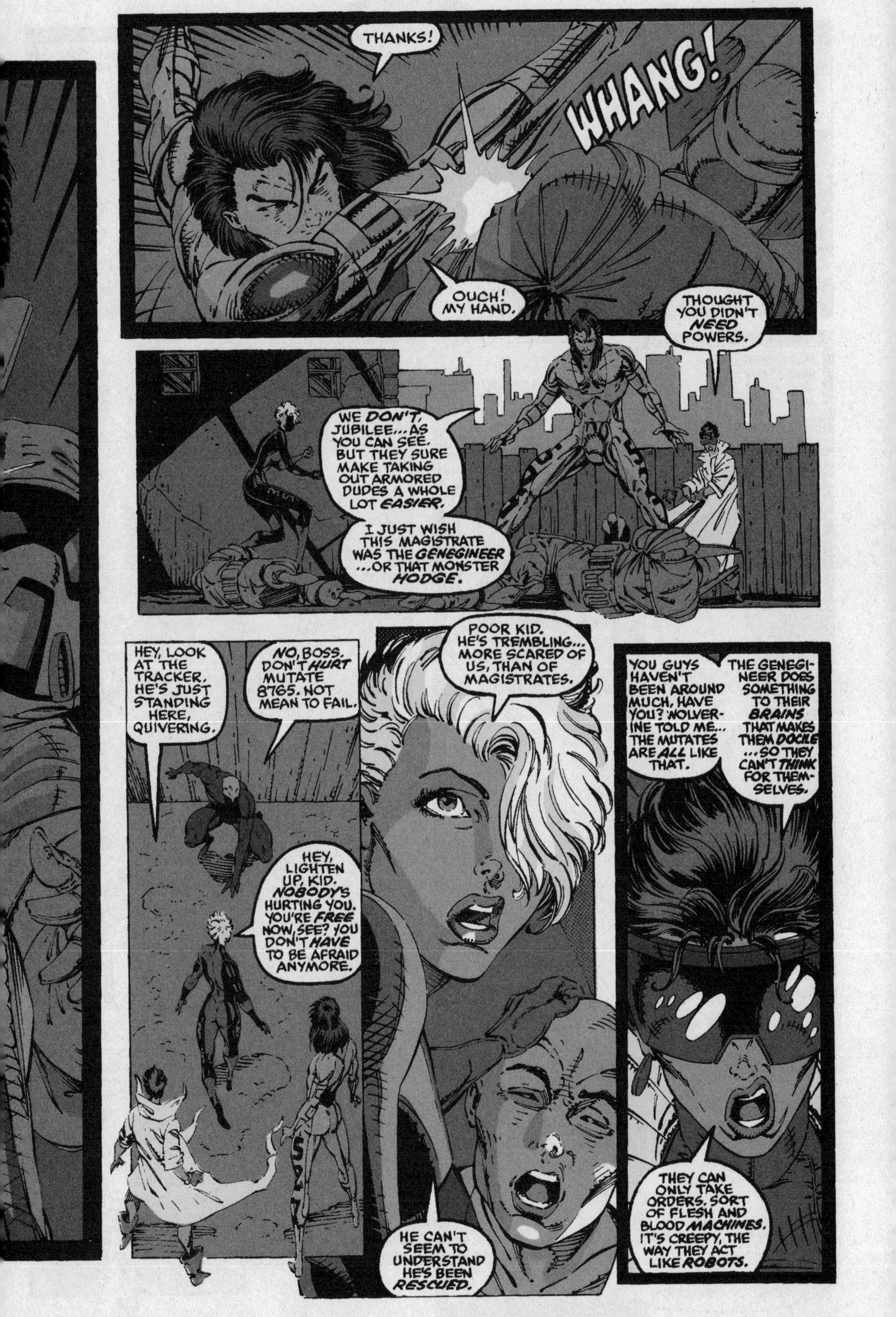
THANKS!
WHANG!
OUCH! MY HAND.
THOUGHT YOU DIDN'T NEED POWERS.
WE DON'T, JUBILEE... AS YOU CAN SEE. BUT THEY SURE MAKE TAKING OUT ARMORED DUDES A WHOLE LOT EASIER.
I JUST WISH THIS MAGISTRATE WAS THE GENEGINEER ...OR THAT MONSTER HODGE.
HEY, LOOK AT THE TRACKER. HE'S JUST STANDING HERE, QUIVERING.
NO, BOSS. DON'T HURT MUTATE 8765. NOT MEAN TO FAIL.
HEY, LIGHTEN UP, KID. NOBODY'S HURTING YOU. YOU'RE FREE NOW, SEE? YOU DON'T HAVE TO BE AFRAID ANYMORE.
POOR KID. HE'S TREMBLING... MORE SCARED OF US, THAN OF MAGISTRATES.
HE CAN'T SEEM TO UNDERSTAND HE'S BEEN RESCUED.
YOU GUYS HAVEN'T BEEN AROUND MUCH, HAVE YOU? WOLVERINE TOLD ME... THE MUTATES ARE ALL LIKE THAT.
THE GENEGINEER DOES SOMETHING TO THEIR BRAINS THAT MAKES THEM DOCILE ...SO THEY CAN'T THINK FOR THEMSELVES.
THEY CAN ONLY TAKE ORDERS. SORT OF FLESH AND BLOOD MACHINES. IT'S CREEPY, THE WAY THEY ACT LIKE ROBOTS.

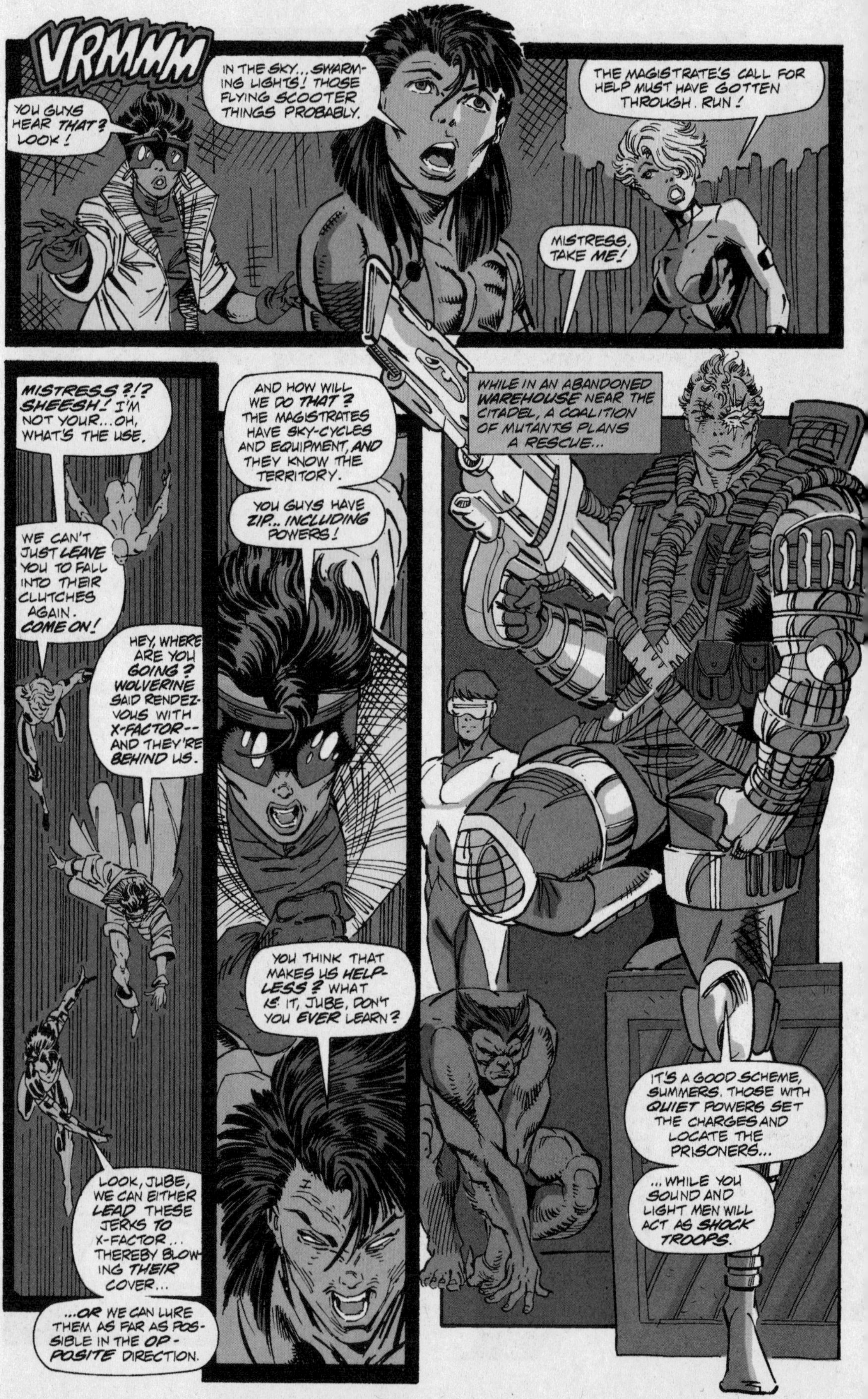
VRMMM
YOU GUYS HEAR THAT? LOOK!
IN THE SKY... SWARMING LIGHTS! THOSE FLYING SCOOTER THINGS PROBABLY.
THE MAGISTRATE'S CALL FOR HELP MUST HAVE GOTTEN THROUGH. RUN!
MISTRESS, TAKE ME!
MISTRESS?!? SHEESH! I'M NOT YOUR... OH, WHAT'S THE USE.
WE CAN'T JUST LEAVE YOU TO FALL INTO THEIR CLUTCHES AGAIN. COME ON!
HEY, WHERE ARE YOU GOING? WOLVERINE SAID RENDEZVOUS WITH X-FACTOR-- AND THEY'RE BEHIND US.
LOOK, JUBE, WE CAN EITHER LEAD THESE JERKS TO X-FACTOR... THEREBY BLOWING THEIR COVER...
...OR WE CAN LURE THEM AS FAR AS POSSIBLE IN THE OPPOSITE DIRECTION.
AND HOW WILL WE DO THAT? THE MAGISTRATES HAVE SKY-CYCLES AND EQUIPMENT, AND THEY KNOW THE TERRITORY.
YOU GUYS HAVE ZIP... INCLUDING POWERS!
YOU THINK THAT MAKES US HELPLESS? WHAT IS IT, JUBE, DON'T YOU EVER LEARN?
WHILE IN AN ABANDONED WAREHOUSE NEAR THE CITADEL, A COALITION OF MUTANTS PLANS A RESCUE...
IT'S A GOOD SCHEME, SUMMERS. THOSE WITH QUIET POWERS SET THE CHARGES AND LOCATE THE PRISONERS...
...WHILE YOU SOUND AND LIGHT MEN WILL ACT AS SHOCK TROOPS.

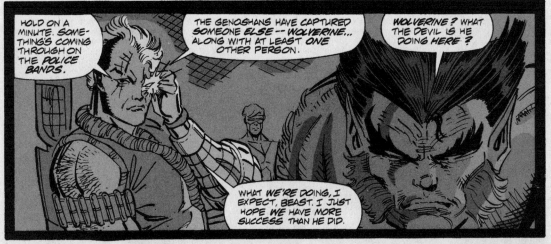

HOLD ON A MINUTE. SOMETHING'S COMING THROUGH ON THE POLICE BANDS.

THE GENOSHANS HAVE CAPTURED SOMEONE ELSE -- WOLVERINE... ALONG WITH AT LEAST ONE OTHER PERSON.

WOLVERINE? WHAT THE DEVIL IS HE DOING HERE?

WHAT WE'RE DOING, I EXPECT, BEAST. I JUST HOPE WE HAVE MORE SUCCESS THAN HE DID.

THERE'S MORE TO THIS, JEAN, THAN IS IMMEDIATELY OBVIOUS. SOMEONE IS BEHIND IT ALL.

SOMEONE DEADLY, WITH A PERSONAL VENDETTA AGAINST US.

I DON'T WANT TO SEND YOU ANYWHERE NEAR THE CITADEL, AND YET...

IT'S WHERE THE PRISONERS ARE, AND I'M THE ONLY TELEKINETIC IN THIS OUTFIT. SO... I'M THE DESIGNATED DRIVER.

TAKE CARE, BABE.

YOU, TOO.

SEE YOU LATER.

YOU AND JEAN ARE LOOKING AWFULLY HAPPY, IN SPITE OF ALL THAT'S GONE WRONG RECENTLY.

OR MAYBE BECAUSE OF IT. OUR WORLD HAS BEEN TURNED UPSIDE DOWN, AND EVERYTHING WE CARE ABOUT SEEMS TO BE AT RISK.

MAYBE IT'S MADE US APPRECIATE MORE WHAT WE HAVE TOGETHER...

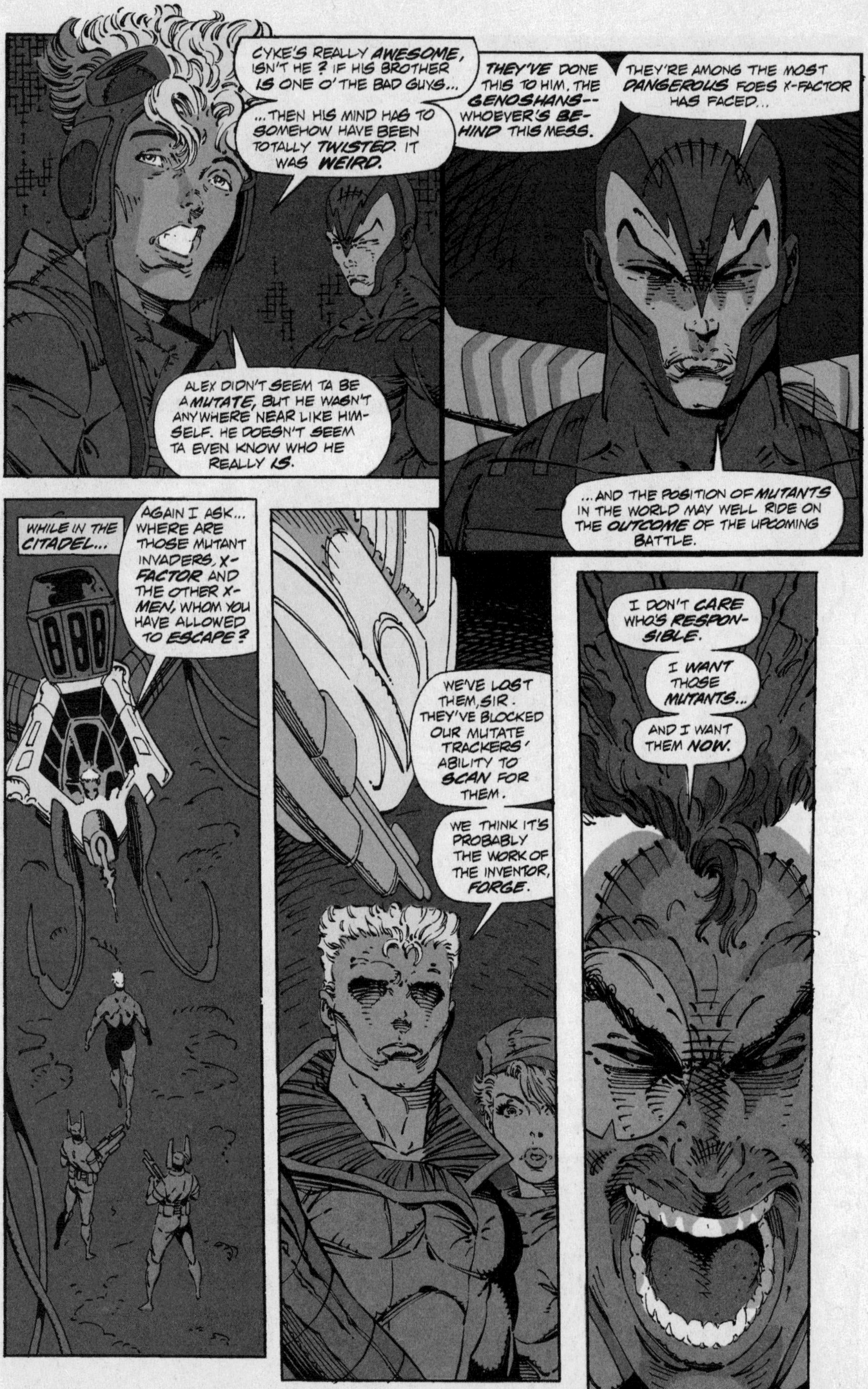
CYKE'S REALLY AWESOME, ISN'T HE? IF HIS BROTHER IS ONE O' THE BAD GUYS...
...THEN HIS MIND HAS TO SOMEHOW HAVE BEEN TOTALLY TWISTED. IT WAS WEIRD.
ALEX DIDN'T SEEM TA BE A MUTATE, BUT HE WASN'T ANYWHERE NEAR LIKE HIMSELF. HE DOESN'T SEEM TA EVEN KNOW WHO HE REALLY IS.
THEY'VE DONE THIS TO HIM. THE GENOSHANS-- WHOEVER'S BEHIND THIS MESS.
THEY'RE AMONG THE MOST DANGEROUS FOES X-FACTOR HAS FACED...
...AND THE POSITION OF MUTANTS IN THE WORLD MAY WELL RIDE ON THE OUTCOME OF THE UPCOMING BATTLE.
WHILE IN THE CITADEL...
AGAIN I ASK... WHERE ARE THOSE MUTANT INVADERS, X-FACTOR AND THE OTHER X-MEN, WHOM YOU HAVE ALLOWED TO ESCAPE?
WE'VE LOST THEM, SIR. THEY'VE BLOCKED OUR MUTATE TRACKERS' ABILITY TO SCAN FOR THEM.
WE THINK IT'S PROBABLY THE WORK OF THE INVENTOR, FORGE.
I DON'T CARE WHO'S RESPONSIBLE.
I WANT THOSE MUTANTS...
AND I WANT THEM NOW.

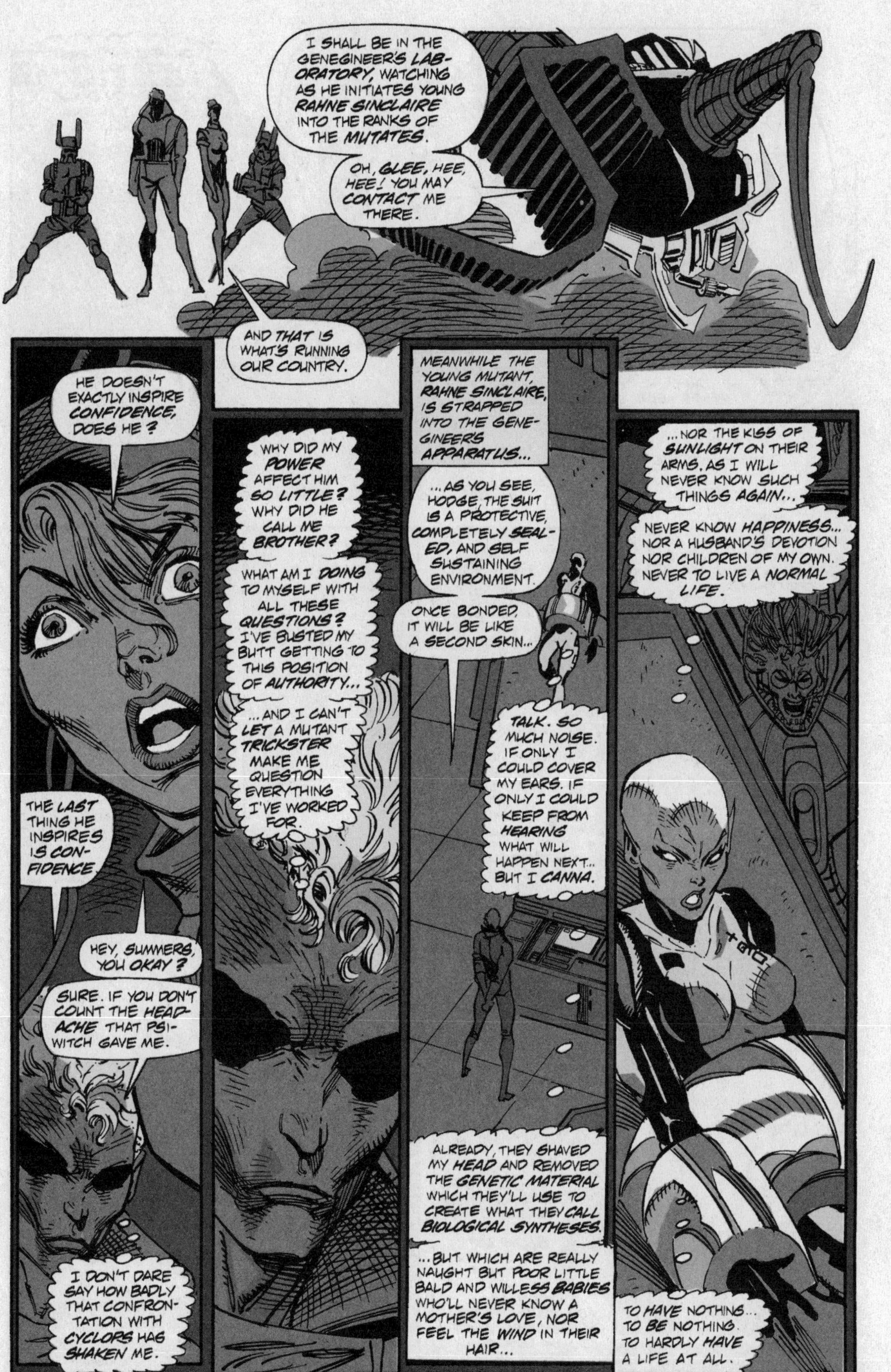
I SHALL BE IN THE GENEGINEER'S LABORATORY, WATCHING AS HE INITIATES YOUNG RAHNE SINCLAIRE INTO THE RANKS OF THE MUTATES.
OH, GLEE, HEE, HEE! YOU MAY CONTACT ME THERE.
AND THAT IS WHAT'S RUNNING OUR COUNTRY.
HE DOESN'T EXACTLY INSPIRE CONFIDENCE, DOES HE?
THE LAST THING HE INSPIRES IS CONFIDENCE.
HEY, SUMMERS, YOU OKAY?
SURE. IF YOU DON'T COUNT THE HEADACHE THAT PSI-WITCH GAVE ME.
I DON'T DARE SAY HOW BADLY THAT CONFRONTATION WITH CYCLOPS HAS SHAKEN ME.
WHY DID MY POWER AFFECT HIM SO LITTLE? WHY DID HE CALL ME BROTHER?
WHAT AM I DOING TO MYSELF WITH ALL THESE QUESTIONS? I'VE BUSTED MY BUTT GETTING TO THIS POSITION OF AUTHORITY...
...AND I CAN'T LET A MUTANT TRICKSTER MAKE ME QUESTION EVERYTHING I'VE WORKED FOR.
MEANWHILE THE YOUNG MUTANT, RAHNE SINCLAIRE, IS STRAPPED INTO THE GENEGINEER'S APPARATUS...
...AS YOU SEE, HODGE, THE SUIT IS A PROTECTIVE, COMPLETELY SEALED, AND SELF SUSTAINING ENVIRONMENT.
ONCE BONDED, IT WILL BE LIKE A SECOND SKIN...
TALK. SO MUCH NOISE. IF ONLY I COULD COVER MY EARS. IF ONLY I COULD KEEP FROM HEARING WHAT WILL HAPPEN NEXT... BUT I CANNA.
ALREADY, THEY SHAVED MY HEAD AND REMOVED THE GENETIC MATERIAL WHICH THEY'LL USE TO CREATE WHAT THEY CALL BIOLOGICAL SYNTHESES.
...BUT WHICH ARE REALLY NAUGHT BUT POOR LITTLE BALD AND WILLESS BABIES WHO'LL NEVER KNOW A MOTHER'S LOVE, NOR FEEL THE WIND IN THEIR HAIR...
...NOR THE KISS OF SUNLIGHT ON THEIR ARMS. AS I WILL NEVER KNOW SUCH THINGS AGAIN...
NEVER KNOW HAPPINESS... NOR A HUSBAND'S DEVOTION NOR CHILDREN OF MY OWN. NEVER TO LIVE A NORMAL LIFE.
TO HAVE NOTHING... TO BE NOTHING. TO HARDLY HAVE A LIFE AT ALL.

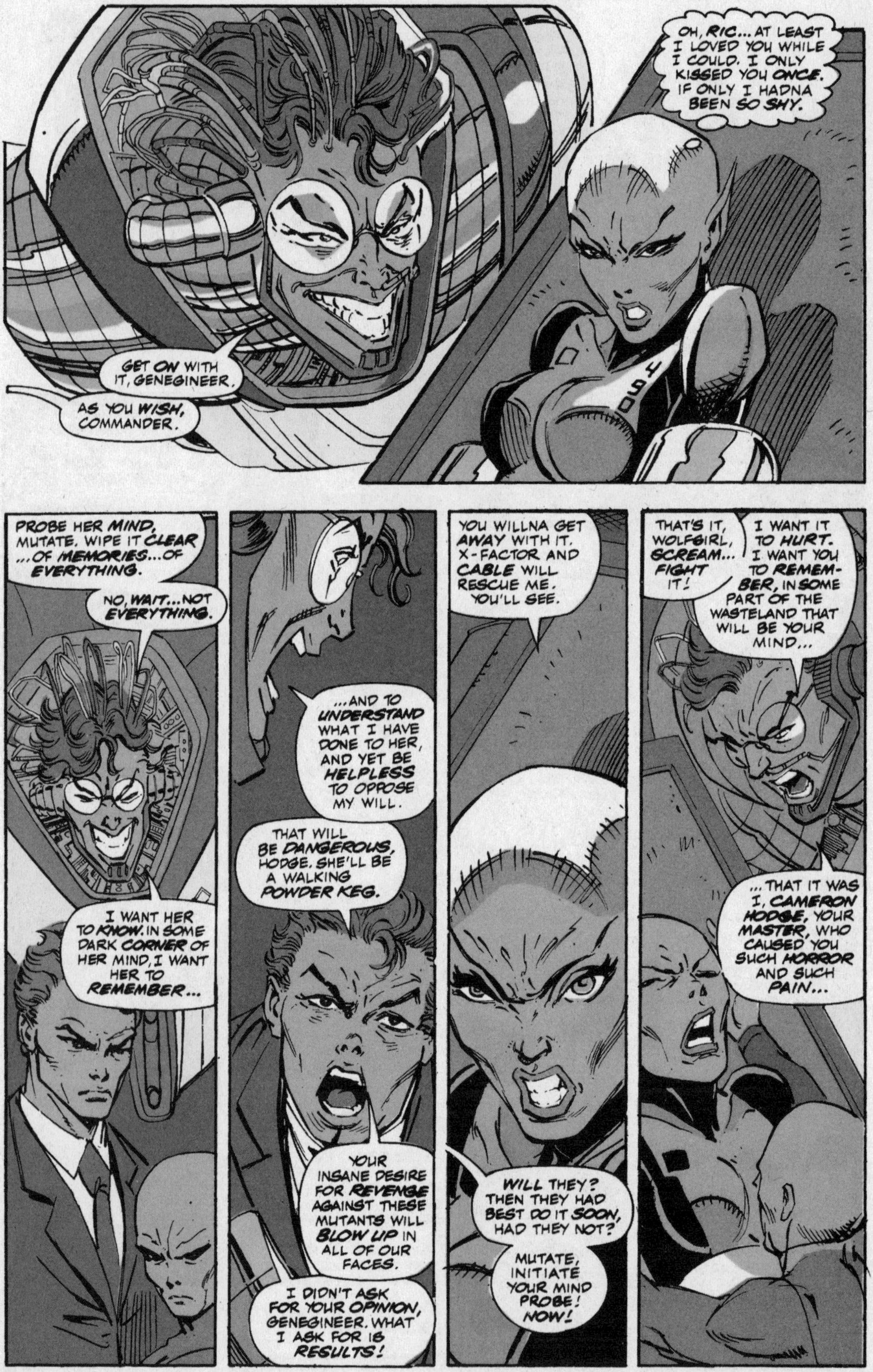

OH, RIC... AT LEAST I LOVED YOU WHILE I COULD. I ONLY KISSED YOU ONCE. IF ONLY I HADNA BEEN SO SHY.
GET ON WITH IT, GENEGINEER.
AS YOU WISH, COMMANDER.
PROBE HER MIND, MUTATE. WIPE IT CLEAR ...OF MEMORIES...OF EVERYTHING.
NO, WAIT...NOT EVERYTHING.
I WANT HER TO KNOW. IN SOME DARK CORNER OF HER MIND, I WANT HER TO REMEMBER...
...AND TO UNDERSTAND WHAT I HAVE DONE TO HER, AND YET BE HELPLESS TO OPPOSE MY WILL.
THAT WILL BE DANGEROUS, HODGE. SHE'LL BE A WALKING POWDER KEG.
YOUR INSANE DESIRE FOR REVENGE AGAINST THESE MUTANTS WILL BLOW UP IN ALL OF OUR FACES.
I DIDN'T ASK FOR YOUR OPINION, GENEGINEER. WHAT I ASK FOR IS RESULTS!
YOU WILLNA GET AWAY WITH IT. X-FACTOR AND CABLE WILL RESCUE ME. YOU'LL SEE.
WILL THEY? THEN THEY HAD BEST DO IT SOON, HAD THEY NOT?
MUTATE, INITIATE YOUR MIND PROBE! NOW!
THAT'S IT, WOLFGIRL, SCREAM... FIGHT IT!
I WANT IT TO HURT. I WANT YOU TO REMEMBER, IN SOME PART OF THE WASTELAND THAT WILL BE YOUR MIND...
...THAT IT WAS I, CAMERON HODGE, YOUR MASTER, WHO CAUSED YOU SUCH HORROR AND SUCH PAIN...

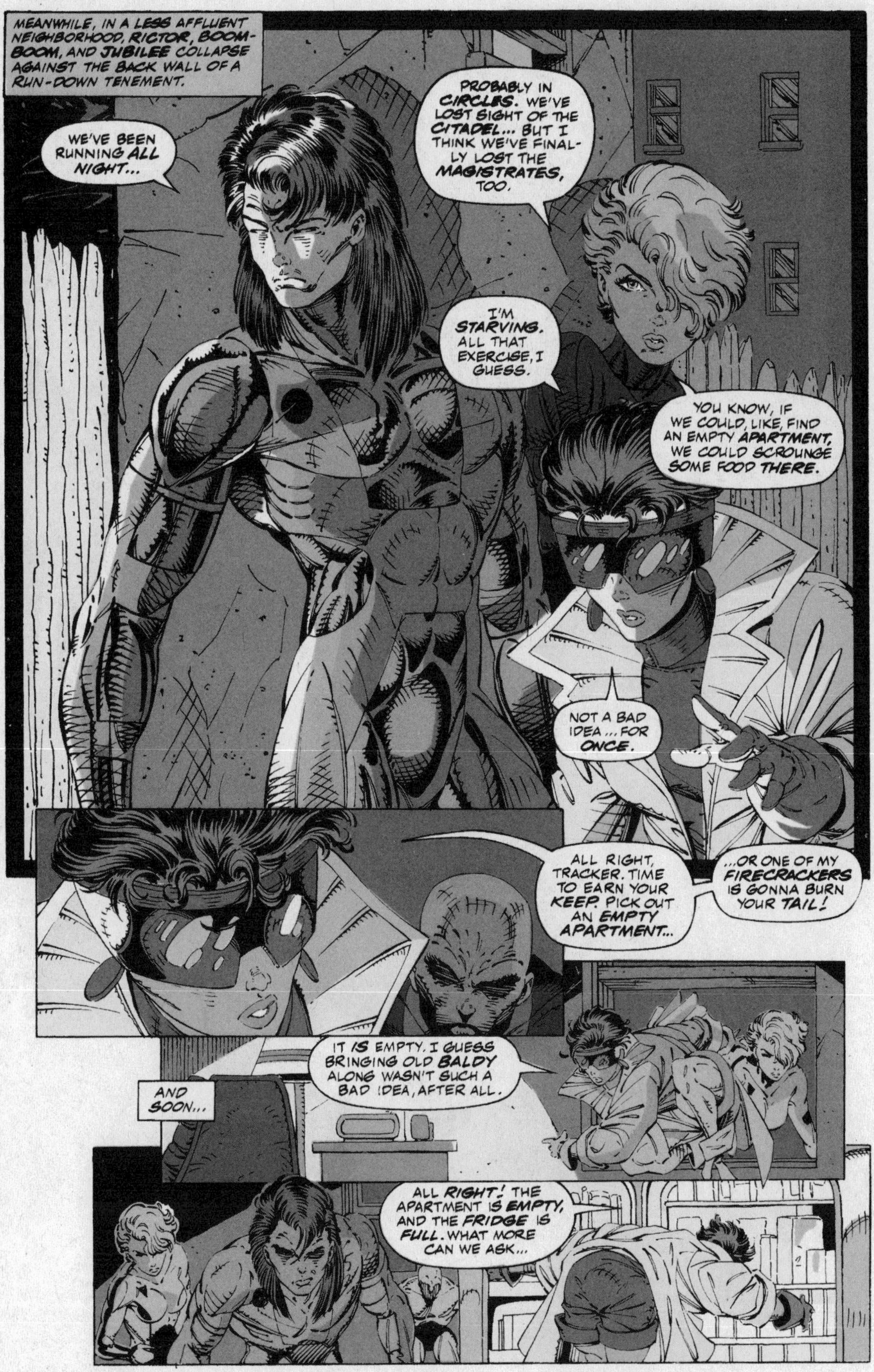

MEANWHILE, IN A LESS AFFLUENT NEIGHBORHOOD, RICTOR, BOOM-BOOM, AND JUBILEE COLLAPSE AGAINST THE BACK WALL OF A RUN-DOWN TENEMENT.
WE'VE BEEN RUNNING ALL NIGHT...
PROBABLY IN CIRCLES. WE'VE LOST SIGHT OF THE CITADEL... BUT I THINK WE'VE FINALLY LOST THE MAGISTRATES, TOO.
I'M STARVING. ALL THAT EXERCISE, I GUESS.
YOU KNOW, IF WE COULD, LIKE, FIND AN EMPTY APARTMENT, WE COULD SCROUNGE SOME FOOD THERE.
NOT A BAD IDEA... FOR ONCE.
ALL RIGHT, TRACKER. TIME TO EARN YOUR KEEP. PICK OUT AN EMPTY APARTMENT...
...OR ONE OF MY FIRECRACKERS IS GONNA BURN YOUR TAIL!
IT IS EMPTY. I GUESS BRINGING OLD BALDY ALONG WASN'T SUCH A BAD IDEA, AFTER ALL.
AND SOON...
ALL RIGHT! THE APARTMENT IS EMPTY, AND THE FRIDGE IS FULL. WHAT MORE CAN WE ASK...

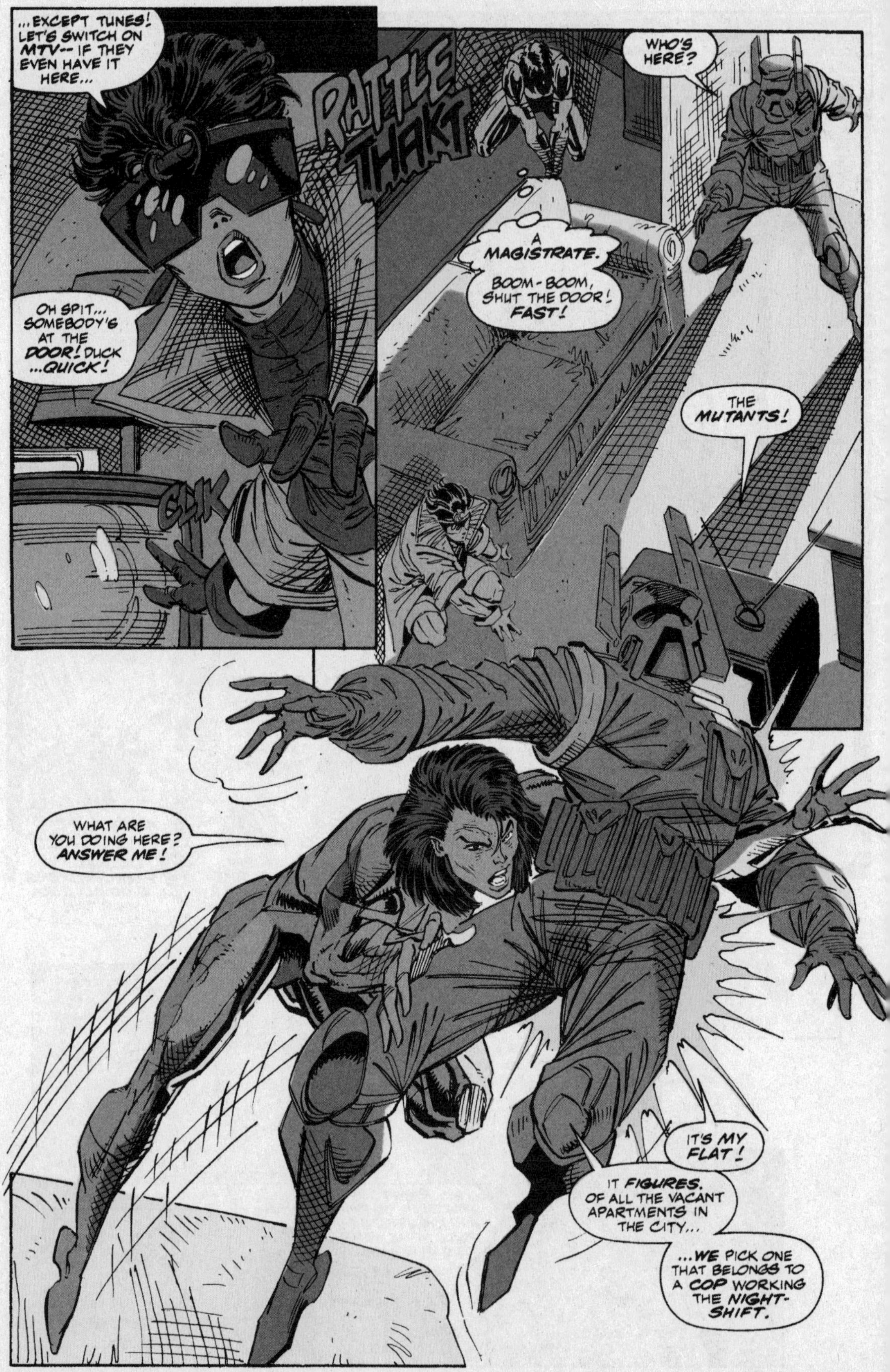
...EXCEPT TUNES! LET'S SWITCH ON MTV-- IF THEY EVEN HAVE IT HERE...
RATTLE
THAKT
OH SPIT... SOMEBODY'S AT THE DOOR! DUCK ...QUICK!
CLIK
A MAGISTRATE.
BOOM-BOOM, SHUT THE DOOR! FAST!
WHO'S HERE?
THE MUTANTS!
WHAT ARE YOU DOING HERE? ANSWER ME!
IT'S MY FLAT!
IT FIGURES. OF ALL THE VACANT APARTMENTS IN THE CITY...
...WE PICK ONE THAT BELONGS TO A COP WORKING THE NIGHT-SHIFT.

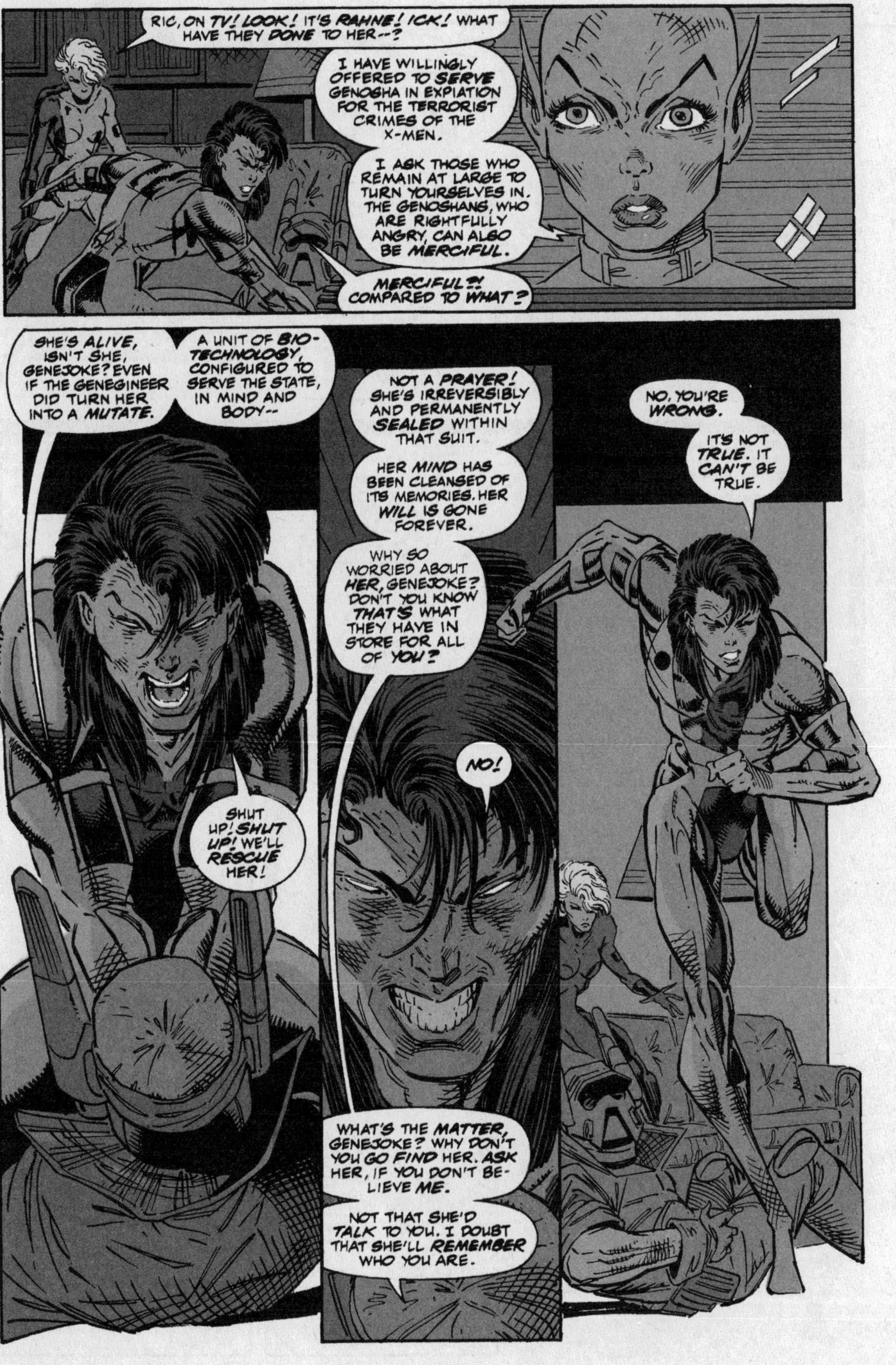

RIC, ON TV! LOOK! IT'S RAHNE! ICK! WHAT HAVE THEY DONE TO HER--?
I HAVE WILLINGLY OFFERED TO SERVE GENOSHA IN EXPIATION FOR THE TERRORIST CRIMES OF THE X-MEN.
I ASK THOSE WHO REMAIN AT LARGE TO TURN YOURSELVES IN. THE GENOSHANS, WHO ARE RIGHTFULLY ANGRY, CAN ALSO BE MERCIFUL.
MERCIFUL?! COMPARED TO WHAT?
SHE'S ALIVE, ISN'T SHE, GENEJOKE? EVEN IF THE GENEGINEER DID TURN HER INTO A MUTATE.
A UNIT OF BIO-TECHNOLOGY, CONFIGURED TO SERVE THE STATE, IN MIND AND BODY--
SHUT UP! SHUT UP! WE'LL RESCUE HER!
NOT A PRAYER! SHE'S IRREVERSIBLY AND PERMANENTLY SEALED WITHIN THAT SUIT.
HER MIND HAS BEEN CLEANSED OF ITS MEMORIES. HER WILL IS GONE FOREVER.
WHY SO WORRIED ABOUT HER, GENEJOKE? DON'T YOU KNOW THAT'S WHAT THEY HAVE IN STORE FOR ALL OF YOU?
NO!
WHAT'S THE MATTER, GENEJOKE? WHY DON'T YOU GO FIND HER. ASK HER, IF YOU DON'T BE-LIEVE ME.
NOT THAT SHE'D TALK TO YOU. I DOUBT THAT SHE'LL REMEMBER WHO YOU ARE.
NO, YOU'RE WRONG.
IT'S NOT TRUE. IT CAN'T BE TRUE.

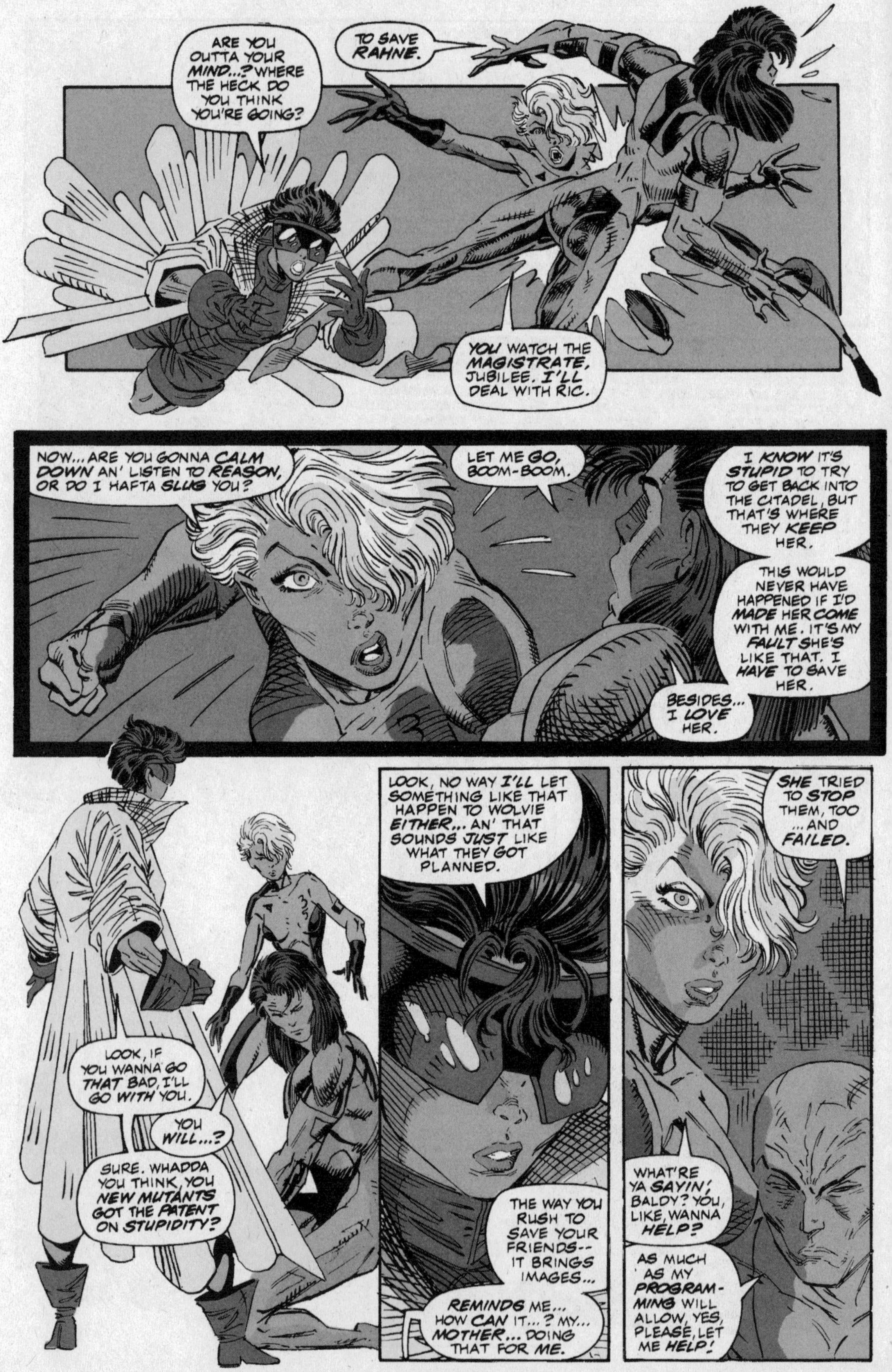
ARE YOU OUTTA YOUR MIND...? WHERE THE HECK DO YOU THINK YOU'RE GOING?
TO SAVE RAHNE.
YOU WATCH THE MAGISTRATE, JUBILEE. I'LL DEAL WITH RIC.
NOW... ARE YOU GONNA CALM DOWN AN' LISTEN TO REASON, OR DO I HAFTA SLUG YOU?
LET ME GO, BOOM-BOOM.
I KNOW IT'S STUPID TO TRY TO GET BACK INTO THE CITADEL, BUT THAT'S WHERE THEY KEEP HER.
THIS WOULD NEVER HAVE HAPPENED IF I'D MADE HER COME WITH ME. IT'S MY FAULT SHE'S LIKE THAT. I HAVE TO SAVE HER.
BESIDES... I LOVE HER.
LOOK, IF YOU WANNA GO THAT BAD, I'LL GO WITH YOU.
YOU WILL...?
SURE. WHADDA YOU THINK, YOU NEW MUTANTS GOT THE PATENT ON STUPIDITY?
LOOK, NO WAY I'LL LET SOMETHING LIKE THAT HAPPEN TO WOLVIE EITHER... AN' THAT SOUNDS JUST LIKE WHAT THEY GOT PLANNED.
THE WAY YOU RUSH TO SAVE YOUR FRIENDS-- IT BRINGS IMAGES...
REMINDS ME... HOW CAN IT...? MY... MOTHER... DOING THAT FOR ME.
SHE TRIED TO STOP THEM, TOO ...AND FAILED.
WHAT'RE YA SAYIN', BALDY? YOU, LIKE, WANNA HELP?
AS MUCH AS MY PROGRAM-MING WILL ALLOW, YES, PLEASE, LET ME HELP!

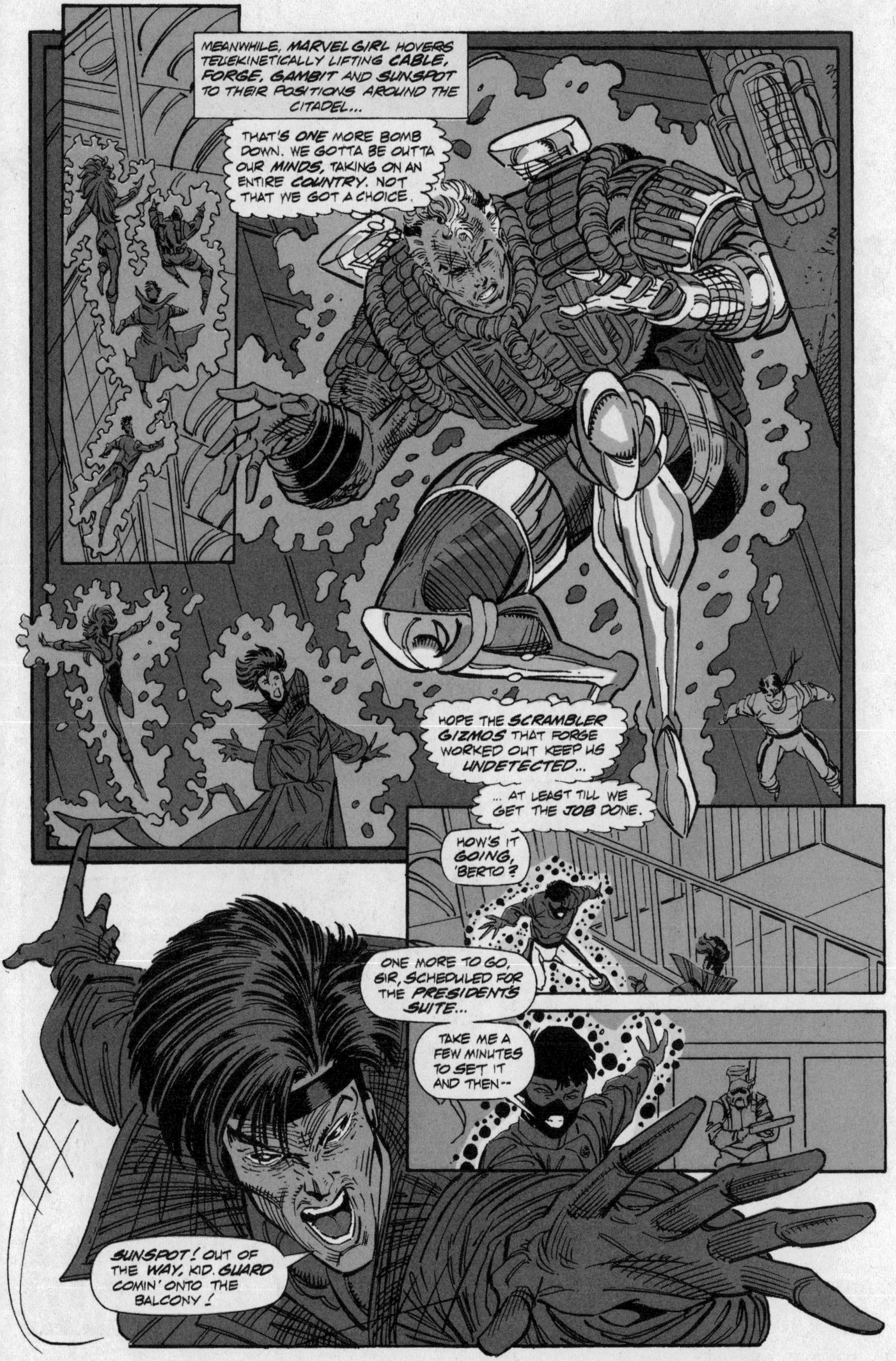
MEANWHILE, MARVEL GIRL HOVERS TELEKINETICALLY LIFTING CABLE, FORGE, GAMBIT AND SUNSPOT TO THEIR POSITIONS AROUND THE CITADEL...
THAT'S ONE MORE BOMB DOWN. WE GOTTA BE OUTTA OUR MINDS, TAKING ON AN ENTIRE COUNTRY. NOT THAT WE GOT A CHOICE.
HOPE THE SCRAMBLER GIZMOS THAT FORGE WORKED OUT KEEP US UNDETECTED...
... AT LEAST TILL WE GET THE JOB DONE.
HOW'S IT GOING, 'BERTO?
ONE MORE TO GO, SIR, SCHEDULED FOR THE PRESIDENT'S SUITE...
TAKE ME A FEW MINUTES TO SET IT AND THEN--
SUNSPOT! OUT OF THE WAY, KID. GUARD COMIN' ONTO THE BALCONY!

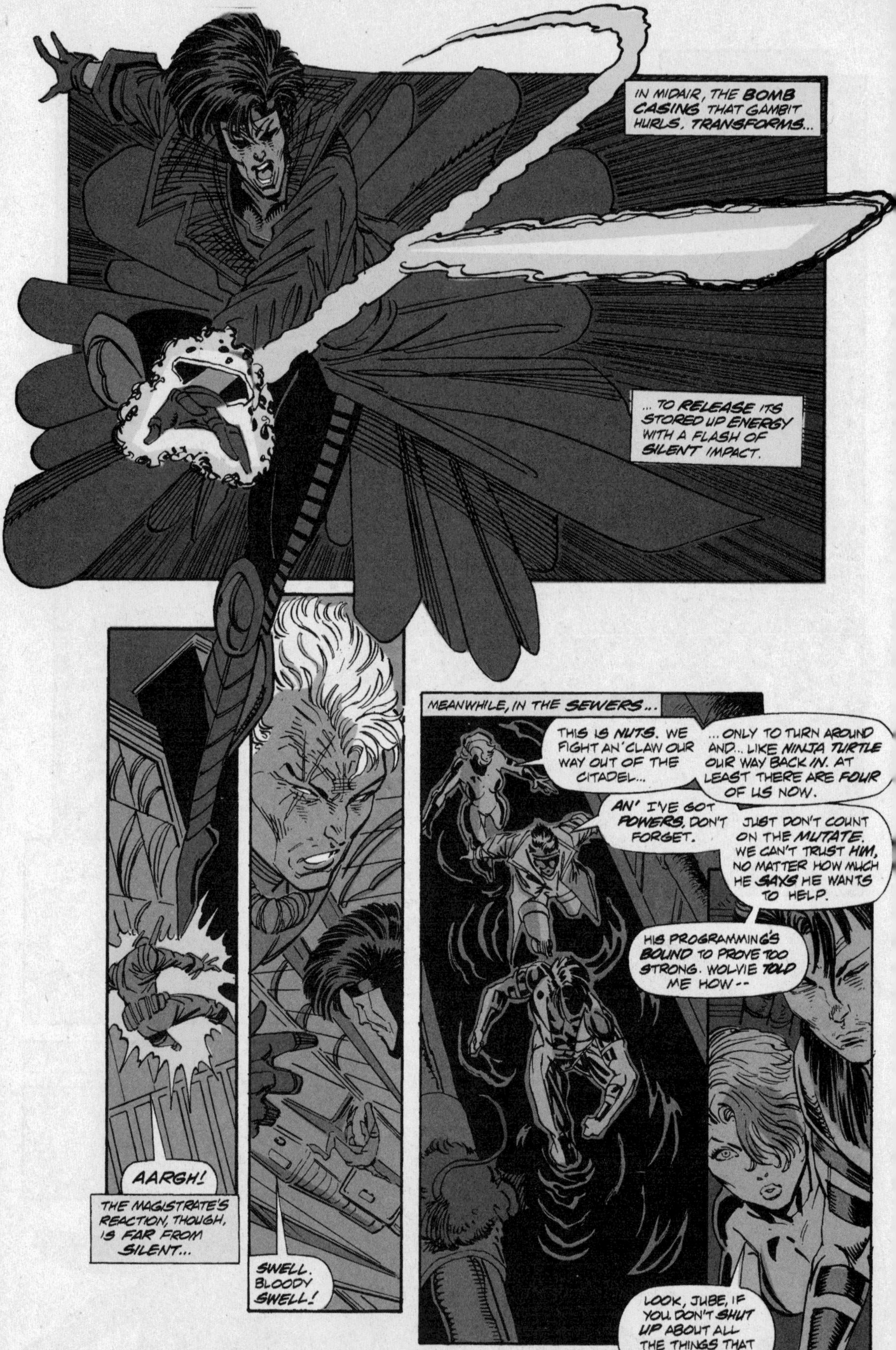
IN MIDAIR, THE BOMB CASING THAT GAMBIT HURLS, TRANSFORMS...
... TO RELEASE ITS STORED UP ENERGY WITH A FLASH OF SILENT IMPACT.
AARGH!
THE MAGISTRATE'S REACTION, THOUGH, IS FAR FROM SILENT...
SWELL. BLOODY SWELL!
MEANWHILE, IN THE SEWERS...
THIS IS NUTS. WE FIGHT AN' CLAW OUR WAY OUT OF THE CITADEL...
...ONLY TO TURN AROUND AND... LIKE NINJA TURTLE OUR WAY BACK IN. AT LEAST THERE ARE FOUR OF US NOW.
AN' I'VE GOT POWERS, DON'T FORGET.
JUST DON'T COUNT ON THE MUTATE. WE CAN'T TRUST HIM, NO MATTER HOW MUCH HE SAYS HE WANTS TO HELP.
HIS PROGRAMMING'S BOUND TO PROVE TOO STRONG. WOLVIE TOLD ME HOW --
LOOK, JUBE, IF YOU DON'T SHUT UP ABOUT ALL THE THINGS THAT WOLVERINE TOLD YOU...

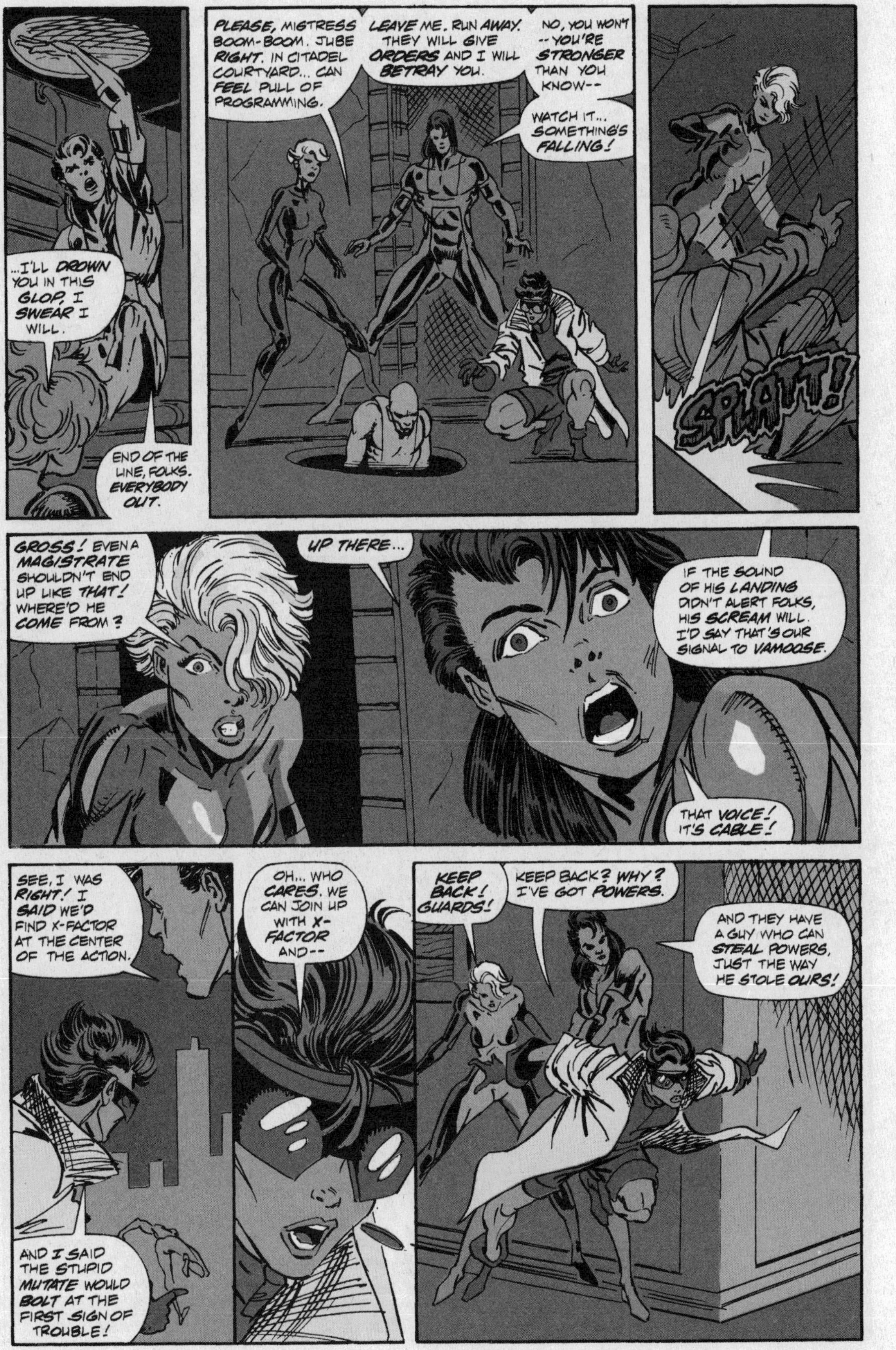
...I'LL DROWN YOU IN THIS GLOP, I SWEAR I WILL.
END OF THE LINE, FOLKS. EVERYBODY OUT.
PLEASE, MISTRESS BOOM-BOOM. JUBE RIGHT. IN CITADEL COURTYARD... CAN FEEL PULL OF PROGRAMMING.
LEAVE ME. RUN AWAY. THEY WILL GIVE ORDERS AND I WILL BETRAY YOU.
NO, YOU WON'T --YOU'RE STRONGER THAN YOU KNOW--
WATCH IT... SOMETHING'S FALLING!
SPLATT!
GROSS! EVEN A MAGISTRATE SHOULDN'T END UP LIKE THAT! WHERE'D HE COME FROM?
UP THERE...
IF THE SOUND OF HIS LANDING DIDN'T ALERT FOLKS, HIS SCREAM WILL. I'D SAY THAT'S OUR SIGNAL TO VAMOOSE.
THAT VOICE! IT'S CABLE!
SEE, I WAS RIGHT! I SAID WE'D FIND X-FACTOR AT THE CENTER OF THE ACTION.
AND I SAID THE STUPID MUTATE WOULD BOLT AT THE FIRST SIGN OF TROUBLE!
OH... WHO CARES. WE CAN JOIN UP WITH X-FACTOR AND--
KEEP BACK! GUARDS!
KEEP BACK? WHY? I'VE GOT POWERS.
AND THEY HAVE A GUY WHO CAN STEAL POWERS, JUST THE WAY HE STOLE OURS!

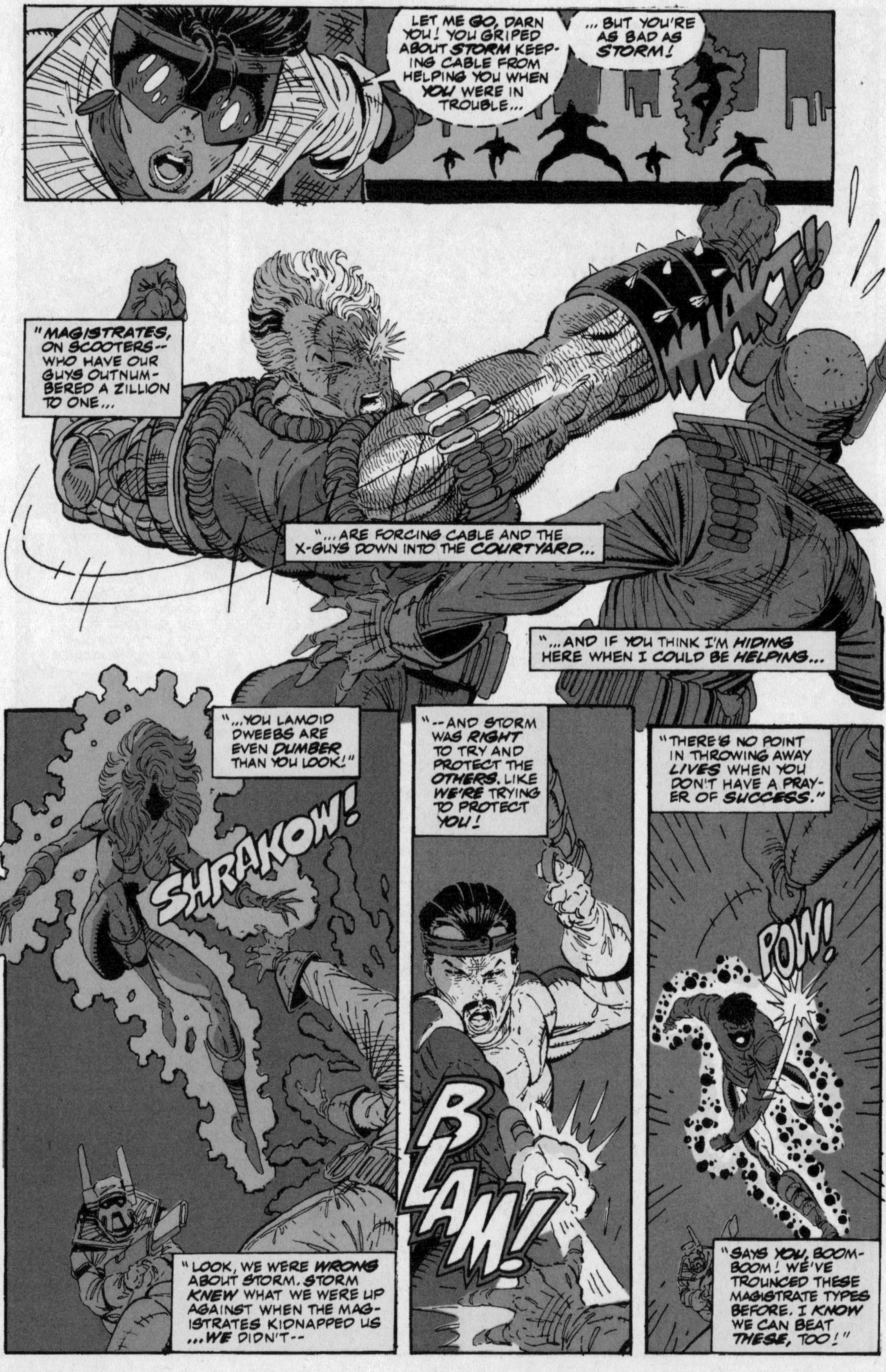
LET ME GO, DARN YOU! YOU GRIPED ABOUT STORM KEEPING CABLE FROM HELPING YOU WHEN YOU WERE IN TROUBLE...
...BUT YOU'RE AS BAD AS STORM!
"MAGISTRATES, ON SCOOTERS-- WHO HAVE OUR GUYS OUTNUMBERED A ZILLION TO ONE...
WHAKT!!
"...ARE FORCING CABLE AND THE X-GUYS DOWN INTO THE COURTYARD...
"...AND IF YOU THINK I'M HIDING HERE WHEN I COULD BE HELPING...
"...YOU LAMOID DWEEBS ARE EVEN DUMBER THAN YOU LOOK!"
SHRAKOW!
"LOOK, WE WERE WRONG ABOUT STORM. STORM KNEW WHAT WE WERE UP AGAINST WHEN THE MAGISTRATES KIDNAPPED US ...WE DIDN'T--
"--AND STORM WAS RIGHT TO TRY AND PROTECT THE OTHERS. LIKE WE'RE TRYING TO PROTECT YOU!
BLAM!
"THERE'S NO POINT IN THROWING AWAY LIVES WHEN YOU DON'T HAVE A PRAYER OF SUCCESS."
POW!
"SAYS YOU, BOOM-BOOM! WE'VE TROUNCED THESE MAGISTRATE TYPES BEFORE. I KNOW WE CAN BEAT THESE, TOO!"

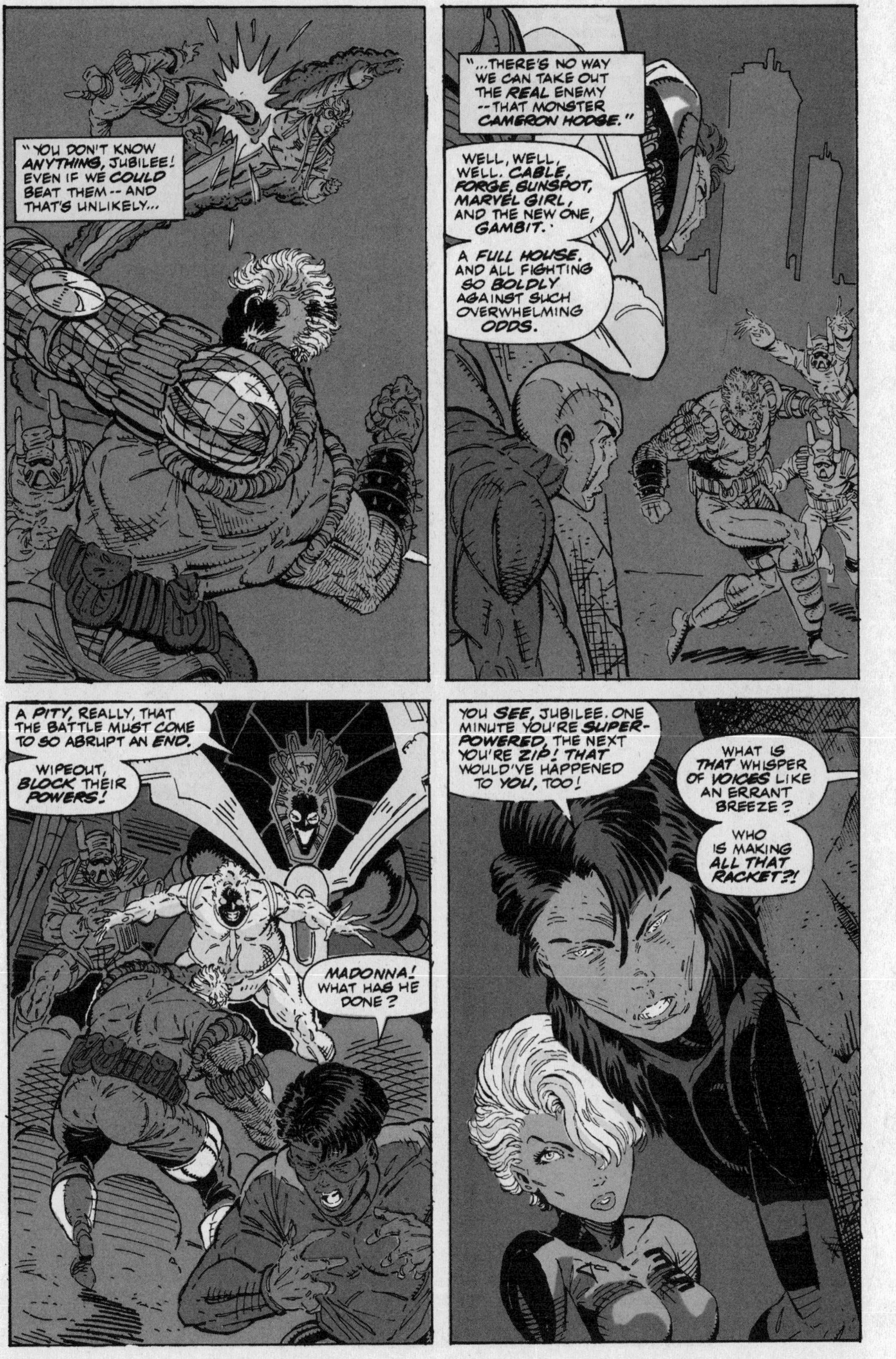
"YOU DON'T KNOW ANYTHING, JUBILEE! EVEN IF WE COULD BEAT THEM -- AND THAT'S UNLIKELY...
"...THERE'S NO WAY WE CAN TAKE OUT THE REAL ENEMY --THAT MONSTER CAMERON HODGE."
WELL, WELL, WELL. CABLE, FORGE, SUNSPOT, MARVEL GIRL, AND THE NEW ONE, GAMBIT.
A FULL HOUSE. AND ALL FIGHTING SO BOLDLY AGAINST SUCH OVERWHELMING ODDS.
A PITY, REALLY, THAT THE BATTLE MUST COME TO SO ABRUPT AN END.
WIPEOUT, BLOCK THEIR POWERS!
MADONNA! WHAT HAS HE DONE?
YOU SEE, JUBILEE. ONE MINUTE YOU'RE SUPER-POWERED, THE NEXT YOU'RE ZIP! THAT WOULD'VE HAPPENED TO YOU, TOO!
WHAT IS THAT WHISPER OF VOICES LIKE AN ERRANT BREEZE?
WHO IS MAKING ALL THAT RACKET?!

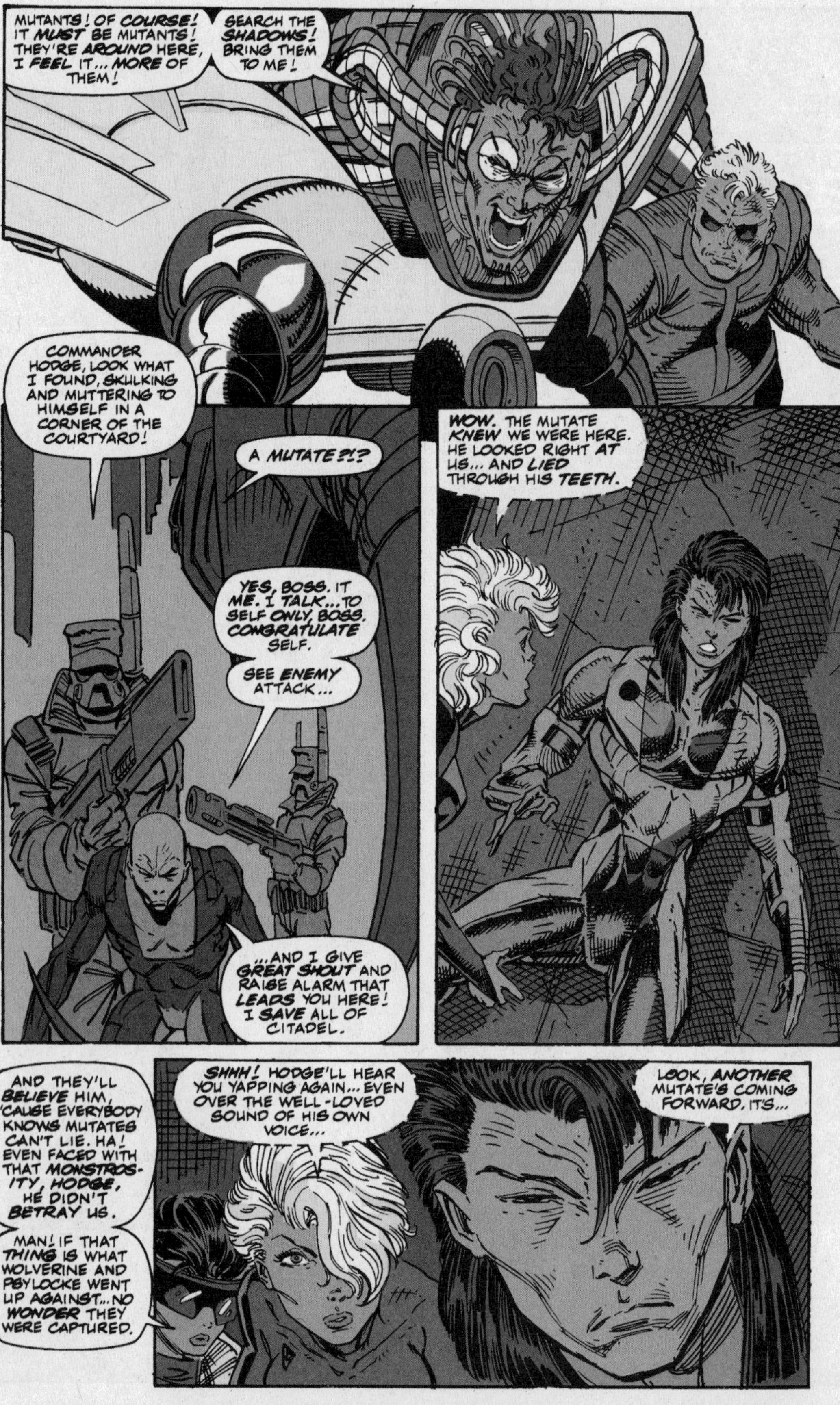
MUTANTS! OF COURSE! IT MUST BE MUTANTS! THEY'RE AROUND HERE, I FEEL IT... MORE OF THEM!
SEARCH THE SHADOWS! BRING THEM TO ME!
COMMANDER HODGE, LOOK WHAT I FOUND, SKULKING AND MUTTERING TO HIMSELF IN A CORNER OF THE COURTYARD!
A MUTATE?!?
YES, BOSS. IT ME. I TALK... TO SELF ONLY, BOSS. CONGRATULATE SELF.
SEE ENEMY ATTACK...
...AND I GIVE GREAT SHOUT AND RAISE ALARM THAT LEADS YOU HERE! I SAVE ALL OF CITADEL.
WOW. THE MUTATE KNEW WE WERE HERE. HE LOOKED RIGHT AT US... AND LIED THROUGH HIS TEETH.
AND THEY'LL BELIEVE HIM, 'CAUSE EVERYBODY KNOWS MUTATES CAN'T LIE. HA! EVEN FACED WITH THAT MONSTROSITY, HODGE, HE DIDN'T BETRAY US.
MAN! IF THAT THING IS WHAT WOLVERINE AND PSYLOCKE WENT UP AGAINST... NO WONDER THEY WERE CAPTURED.
SHHH! HODGE'LL HEAR YOU YAPPING AGAIN... EVEN OVER THE WELL-LOVED SOUND OF HIS OWN VOICE...
LOOK, ANOTHER MUTATE'S COMING FORWARD. IT'S...

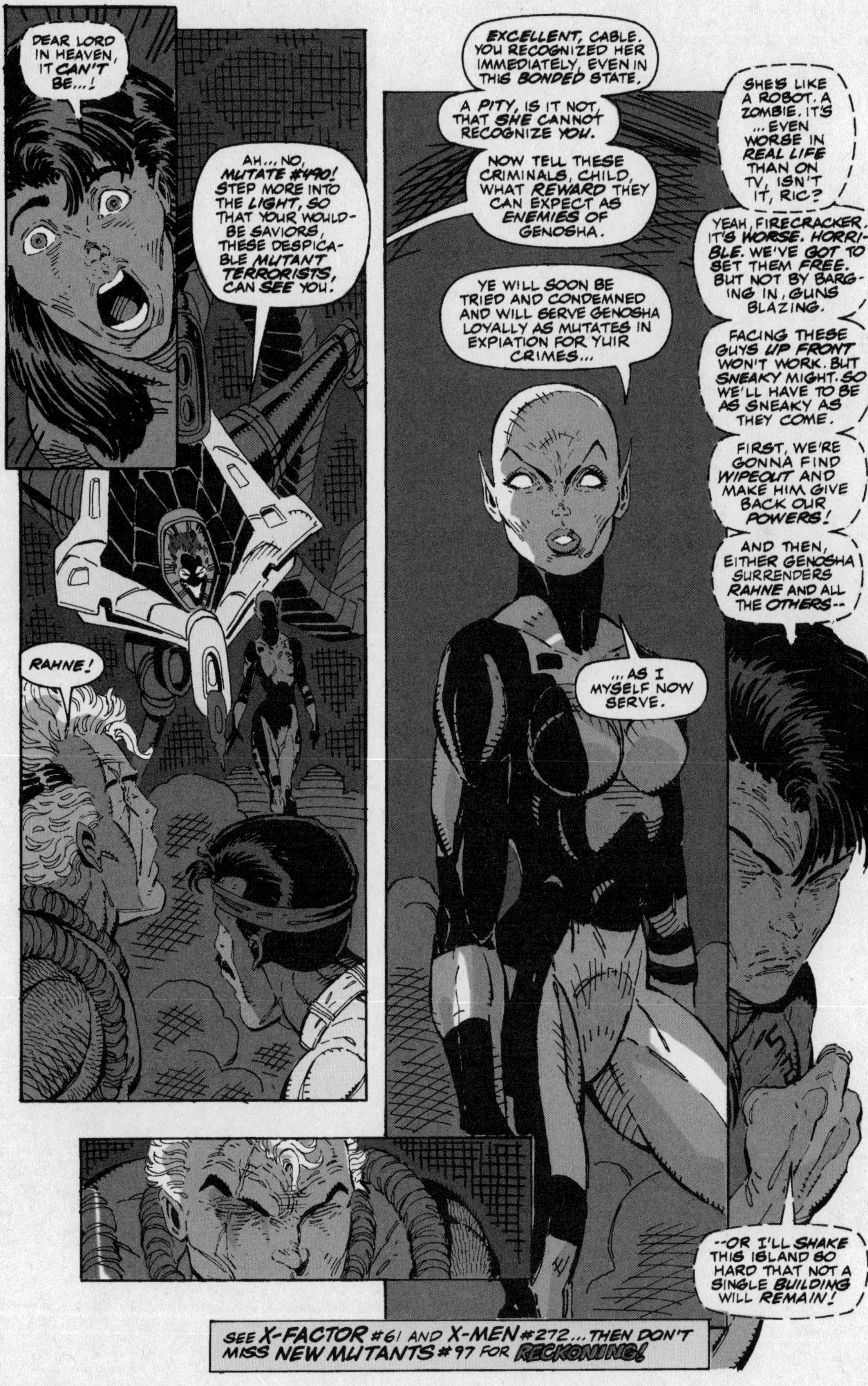
DEAR LORD IN HEAVEN, IT CAN'T BE...!
AH... NO, MUTATE #490! STEP MORE INTO THE LIGHT, SO THAT YOUR WOULD-BE SAVIORS, THESE DESPICABLE MUTANT TERRORISTS, CAN SEE YOU.
RAHNE!
EXCELLENT, CABLE. YOU RECOGNIZED HER IMMEDIATELY, EVEN IN THIS BONDED STATE.
A PITY, IS IT NOT, THAT SHE CANNOT RECOGNIZE YOU.
NOW TELL THESE CRIMINALS, CHILD, WHAT REWARD THEY CAN EXPECT AS ENEMIES OF GENOSHA.
YE WILL SOON BE TRIED AND CONDEMNED AND WILL SERVE GENOSHA LOYALLY AS MUTATES IN EXPIATION FOR YUIR CRIMES...
...AS I MYSELF NOW SERVE.
SHE'S LIKE A ROBOT. A ZOMBIE. IT'S ...EVEN WORSE IN REAL LIFE THAN ON TV, ISN'T IT, RIC?
YEAH, FIRECRACKER. IT'S WORSE. HORRIBLE. WE'VE GOT TO SET THEM FREE. BUT NOT BY BARGING IN, GUNS BLAZING.
FACING THESE GUYS UP FRONT WON'T WORK. BUT SNEAKY MIGHT. SO WE'LL HAVE TO BE AS SNEAKY AS THEY COME.
FIRST, WE'RE GONNA FIND WIPEOUT AND MAKE HIM GIVE BACK OUR POWERS!
AND THEN, EITHER GENOSHA SURRENDERS RAHNE AND ALL THE OTHERS--
--OR I'LL SHAKE THIS ISLAND SO HARD THAT NOT A SINGLE BUILDING WILL REMAIN!
SEE X-FACTOR #61 AND X-MEN #272... THEN DON'T MISS NEW MUTANTS #97 FOR RECKONING!

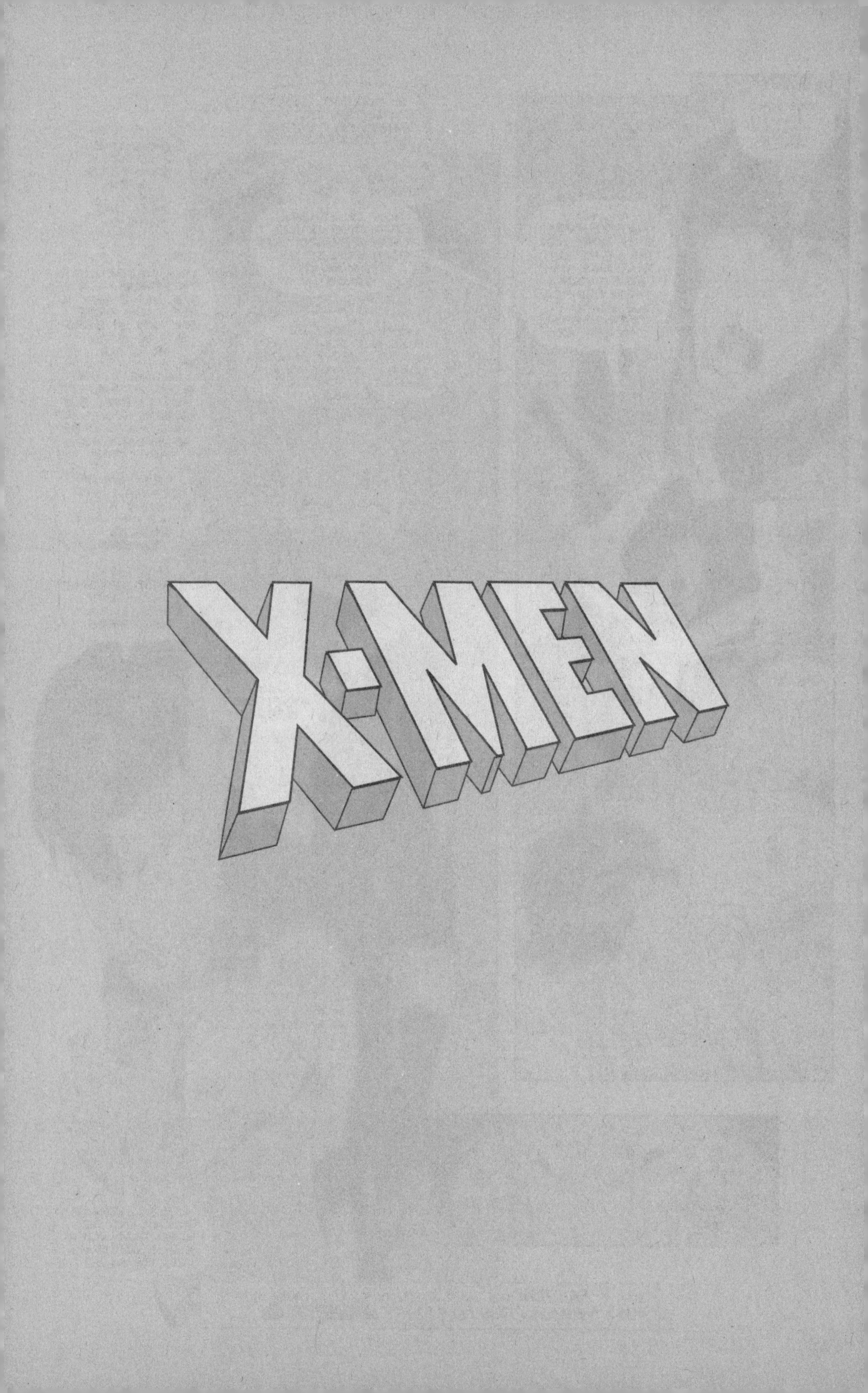
X-MEN

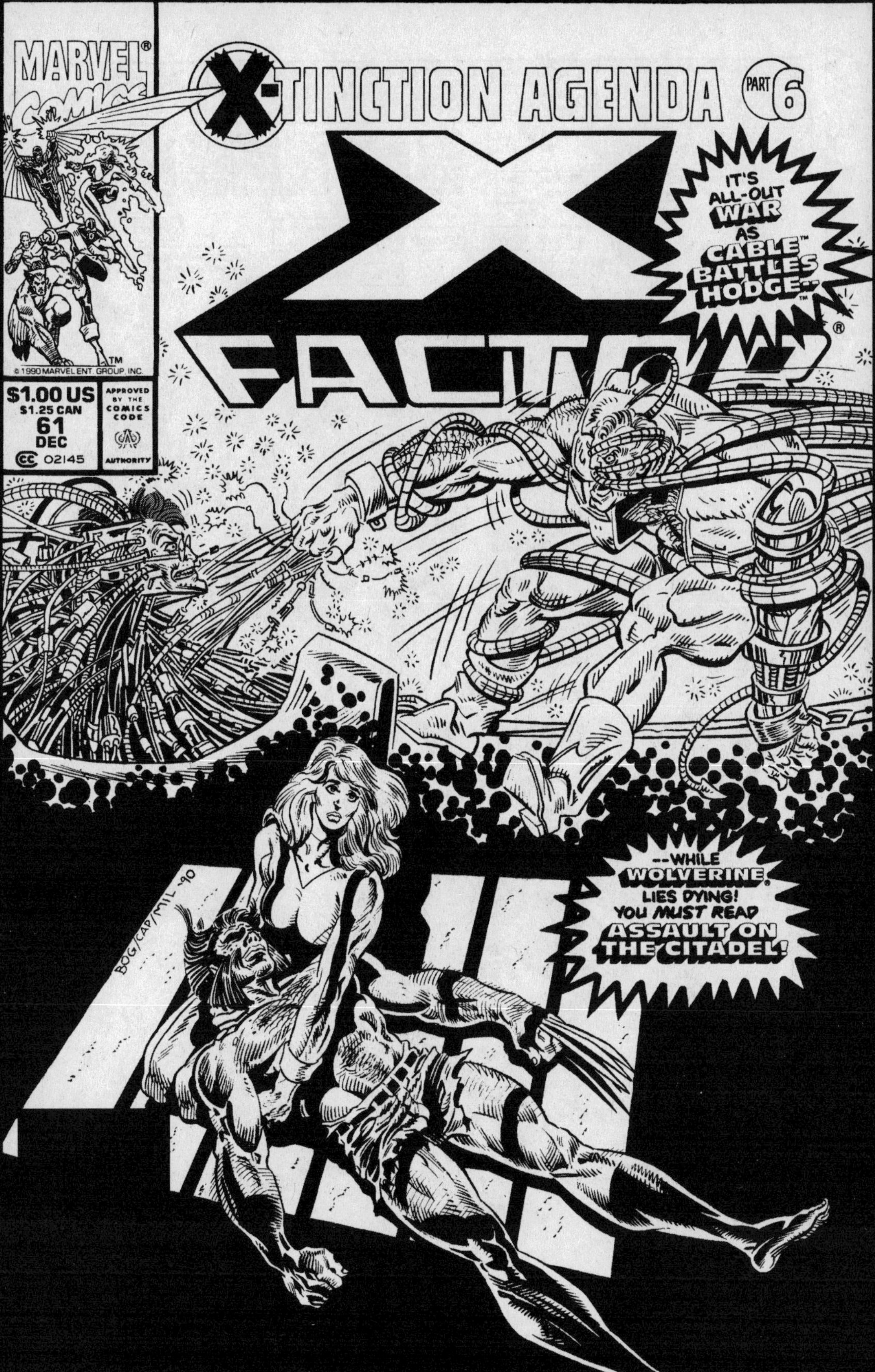
MARVEL® COMICS
X-TINCTION AGENDA PART 6
X-FACTOR®
IT'S ALL-OUT WAR AS CABLE™ BATTLES HODGE--™
© 1990 MARVEL ENT. GROUP, INC.
$1.00 US
$1.25 CAN
61
DEC
02145
APPROVED BY THE COMICS CODE AUTHORITY
--WHILE WOLVERINE® LIES DYING! YOU MUST READ ASSAULT ON THE CITADEL!
BOG/CAP/MIL '90

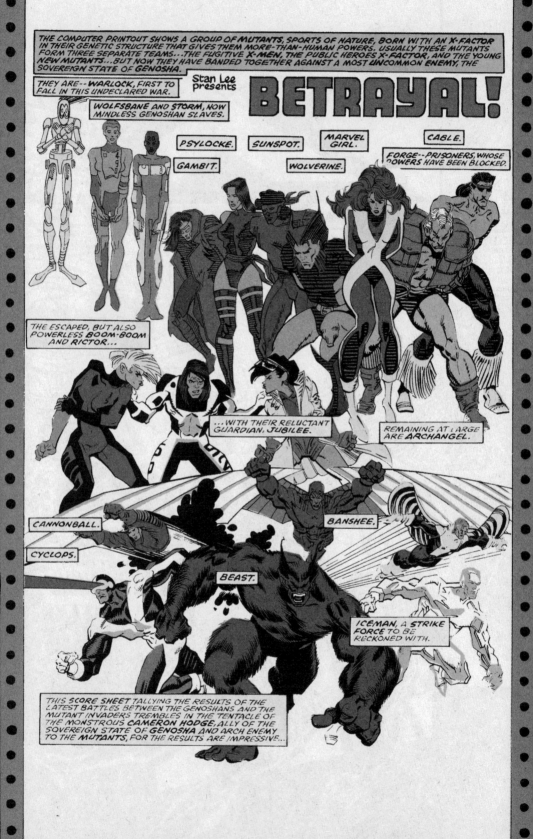

THE COMPUTER PRINTOUT SHOWS A GROUP OF MUTANTS, SPORTS OF NATURE, BORN WITH AN X-FACTOR IN THEIR GENETIC STRUCTURE THAT GIVES THEM MORE-THAN-HUMAN POWERS. USUALLY THESE MUTANTS FORM THREE SEPARATE TEAMS...THE FUGITIVE X-MEN, THE PUBLIC HEROES X-FACTOR, AND THE YOUNG NEW MUTANTS...BUT NOW THEY HAVE BANDED TOGETHER AGAINST A MOST UNCOMMON ENEMY, THE SOVEREIGN STATE OF GENOSHA.

THEY ARE-- WARLOCK, FIRST TO FALL IN THIS UNDECLARED WAR.

Stan Lee presents

BETRAYAL!

WOLFSBANE AND STORM, NOW MINDLESS GENOSHAN SLAVES.

PSYLOCKE.

SUNSPOT.

MARVEL GIRL.

CABLE.

GAMBIT.

WOLVERINE.

FORGE-- PRISONERS, WHOSE POWERS HAVE BEEN BLOCKED.

THE ESCAPED, BUT ALSO POWERLESS BOOM-BOOM AND RICTOR...

...WITH THEIR RELUCTANT GUARDIAN, JUBILEE.

REMAINING AT LARGE ARE ARCHANGEL.

CANNONBALL.

BANSHEE.

CYCLOPS.

BEAST.

ICEMAN, A STRIKE FORCE TO BE RECKONED WITH.

THIS SCORE SHEET TALLYING THE RESULTS OF THE LATEST BATTLES BETWEEN THE GENOSHANS AND THE MUTANT INVADERS TREMBLES IN THE TENTACLE OF THE MONSTROUS CAMERON HODGE, ALLY OF THE SOVEREIGN STATE OF GENOSHA AND ARCH ENEMY TO THE MUTANTS, FOR THE RESULTS ARE IMPRESSIVE...

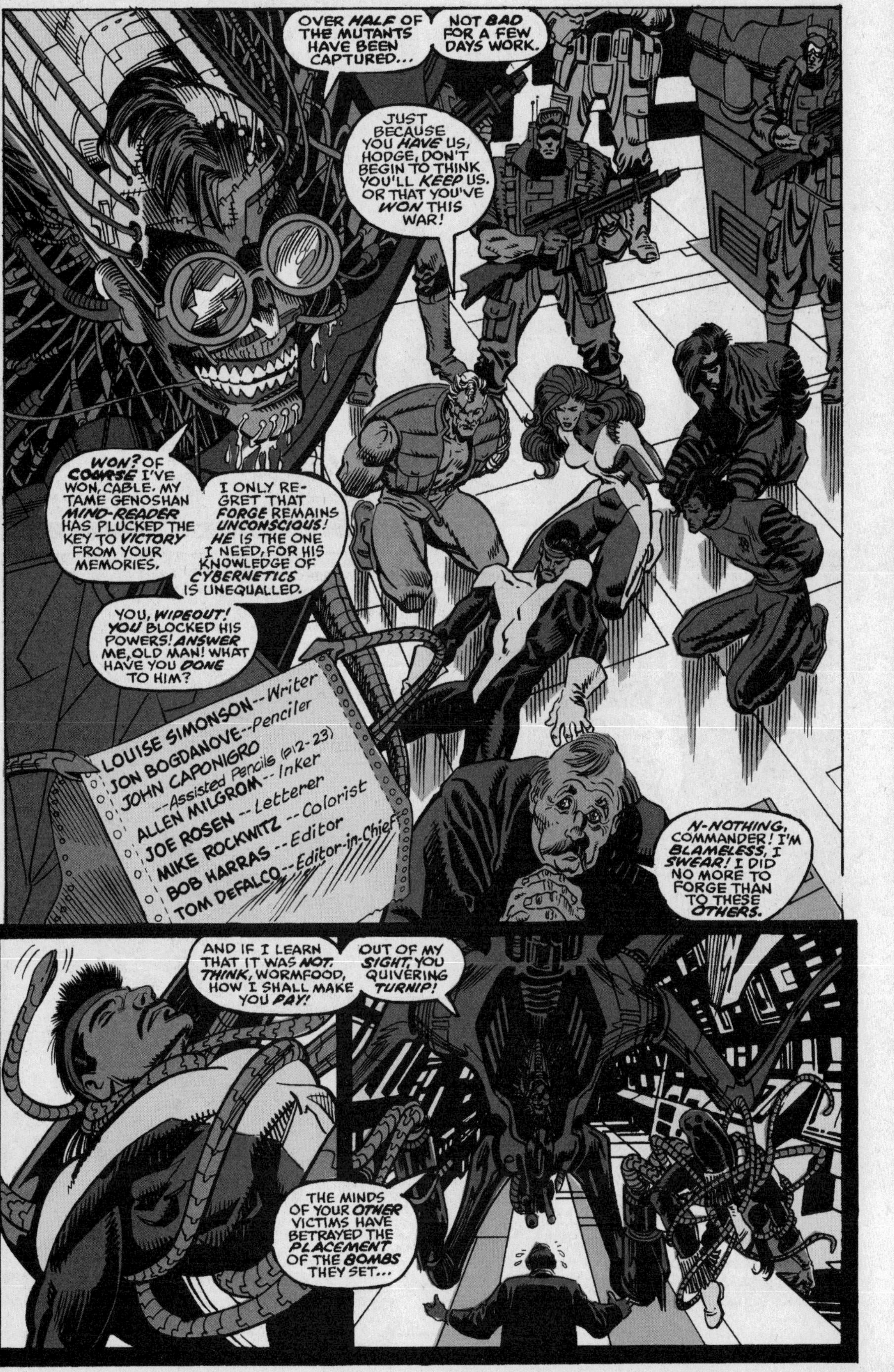
OVER HALF OF THE MUTANTS HAVE BEEN CAPTURED...
NOT BAD FOR A FEW DAYS WORK.
JUST BECAUSE YOU HAVE US, HODGE, DON'T BEGIN TO THINK YOU'LL KEEP US. OR THAT YOU'VE WON THIS WAR!
WON? OF COURSE I'VE WON, CABLE. MY TAME GENOSHAN MIND-READER HAS PLUCKED THE KEY TO VICTORY FROM YOUR MEMORIES.
I ONLY REGRET THAT FORGE REMAINS UNCONSCIOUS! HE IS THE ONE I NEED, FOR HIS KNOWLEDGE OF CYBERNETICS IS UNEQUALLED.
YOU, WIPEOUT! YOU BLOCKED HIS POWERS! ANSWER ME, OLD MAN! WHAT HAVE YOU DONE TO HIM?
LOUISE SIMONSON--Writer
JON BOGDANOVE--Penciler
JOHN CAPONIGRO --Assisted Pencils (p12-23)
ALLEN MILGROM--Inker
JOE ROSEN--Letterer
MIKE ROCKWITZ--Colorist
BOB HARRAS--Editor
TOM DeFALCO--Editor-in-Chief
N-NOTHING, COMMANDER! I'M BLAMELESS, I SWEAR! I DID NO MORE TO FORGE THAN TO THESE OTHERS.
AND IF I LEARN THAT IT WAS NOT, THINK, WORMFOOD, HOW I SHALL MAKE YOU PAY!
OUT OF MY SIGHT, YOU QUIVERING TURNIP!
THE MINDS OF YOUR OTHER VICTIMS HAVE BETRAYED THE PLACEMENT OF THE BOMBS THEY SET...

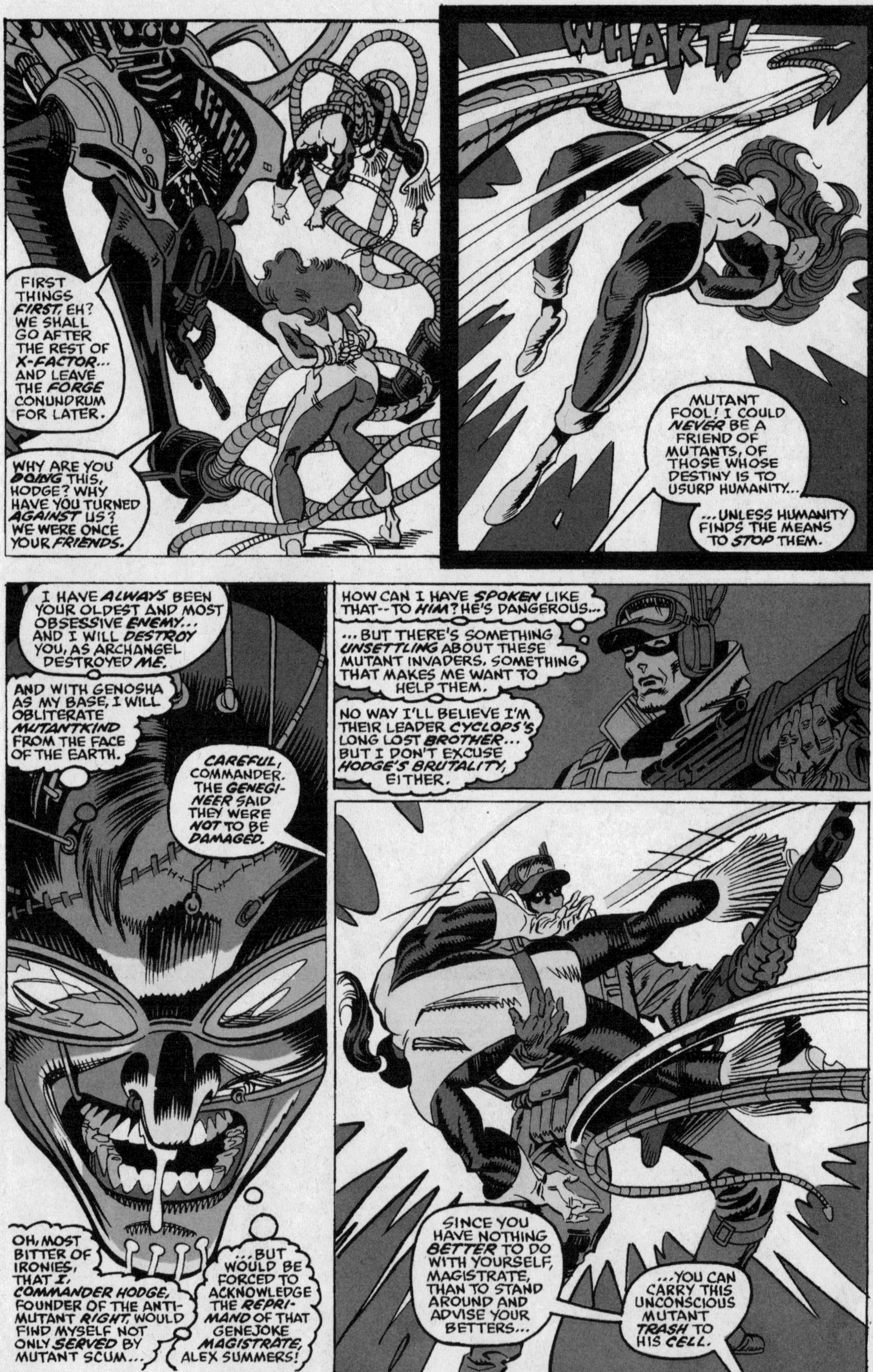
FIRST THINGS FIRST, EH? WE SHALL GO AFTER THE REST OF X-FACTOR... AND LEAVE THE FORGE CONUNDRUM FOR LATER.
WHY ARE YOU DOING THIS, HODGE? WHY HAVE YOU TURNED AGAINST US? WE WERE ONCE YOUR FRIENDS.
WHAKT!
MUTANT FOOL! I COULD NEVER BE A FRIEND OF MUTANTS, OF THOSE WHOSE DESTINY IS TO USURP HUMANITY...
...UNLESS HUMANITY FINDS THE MEANS TO STOP THEM.
I HAVE ALWAYS BEEN YOUR OLDEST AND MOST OBSESSIVE ENEMY... AND I WILL DESTROY YOU, AS ARCHANGEL DESTROYED ME.
AND WITH GENOSHA AS MY BASE, I WILL OBLITERATE MUTANTKIND FROM THE FACE OF THE EARTH.
CAREFUL, COMMANDER. THE GENEGINEER SAID THEY WERE NOT TO BE DAMAGED.
OH, MOST BITTER OF IRONIES, THAT I, COMMANDER HODGE, FOUNDER OF THE ANTI-MUTANT RIGHT, WOULD FIND MYSELF NOT ONLY SERVED BY MUTANT SCUM...
...BUT WOULD BE FORCED TO ACKNOWLEDGE THE REPRIMAND OF THAT GENEJOKE MAGISTRATE, ALEX SUMMERS!
HOW CAN I HAVE SPOKEN LIKE THAT--TO HIM? HE'S DANGEROUS...
...BUT THERE'S SOMETHING UNSETTLING ABOUT THESE MUTANT INVADERS. SOMETHING THAT MAKES ME WANT TO HELP THEM.
NO WAY I'LL BELIEVE I'M THEIR LEADER CYCLOPS'S LONG LOST BROTHER... BUT I DON'T EXCUSE HODGE'S BRUTALITY, EITHER.
SINCE YOU HAVE NOTHING BETTER TO DO WITH YOURSELF, MAGISTRATE, THAN TO STAND AROUND AND ADVISE YOUR BETTERS...
...YOU CAN CARRY THIS UNCONSCIOUS MUTANT TRASH TO HIS CELL.

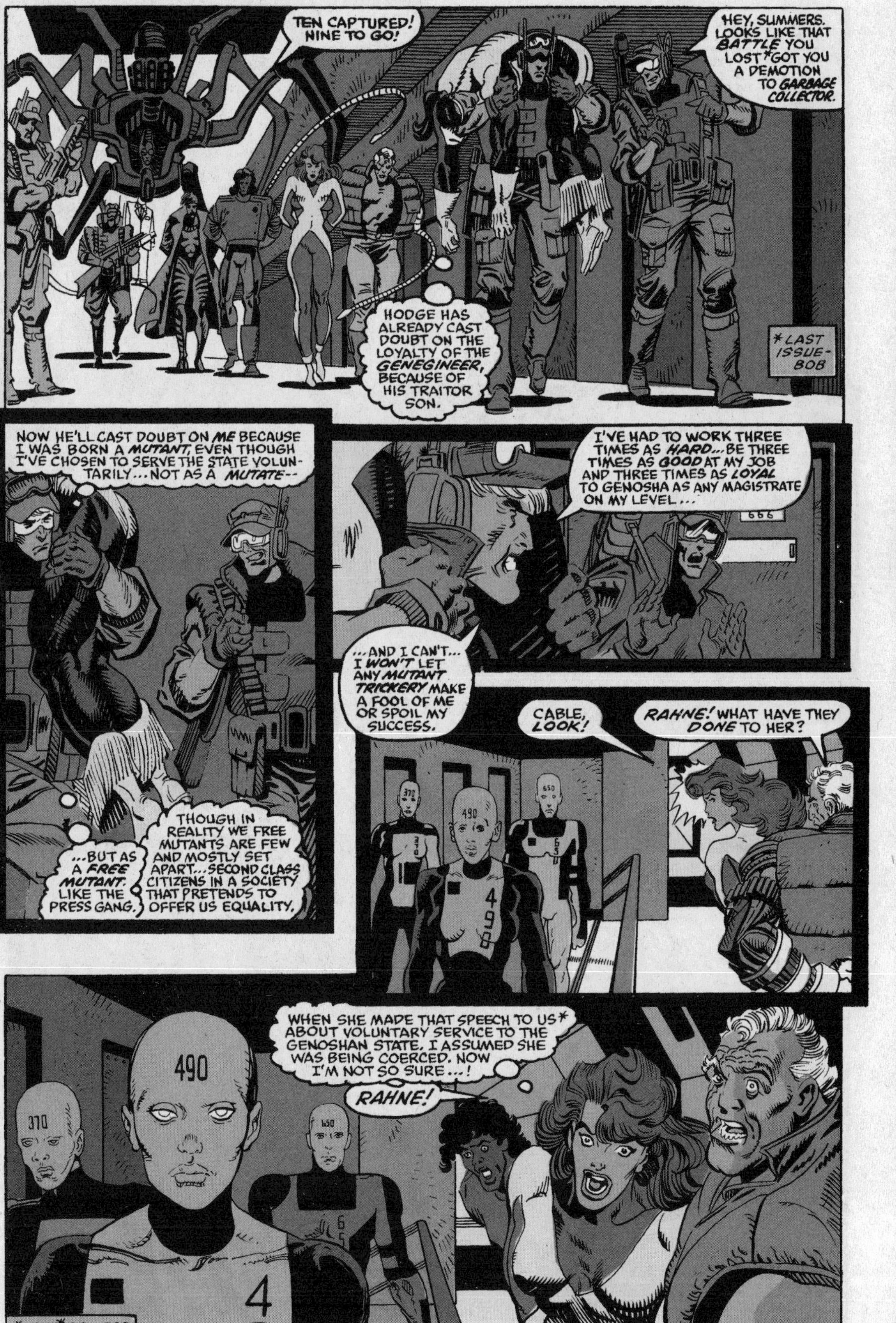
TEN CAPTURED! NINE TO GO!
HEY, SUMMERS. LOOKS LIKE THAT BATTLE YOU LOST* GOT YOU A DEMOTION TO GARBAGE COLLECTOR.
HODGE HAS ALREADY CAST DOUBT ON THE LOYALTY OF THE GENEGINEER, BECAUSE OF HIS TRAITOR SON.
*LAST ISSUE-BOB
NOW HE'LL CAST DOUBT ON ME BECAUSE I WAS BORN A MUTANT, EVEN THOUGH I'VE CHOSEN TO SERVE THE STATE VOLUNTARILY... NOT AS A MUTATE--
...BUT AS A FREE MUTANT. LIKE THE PRESS GANG.
THOUGH IN REALITY WE FREE MUTANTS ARE FEW AND MOSTLY SET APART... SECOND CLASS CITIZENS IN A SOCIETY THAT PRETENDS TO OFFER US EQUALITY.
I'VE HAD TO WORK THREE TIMES AS HARD... BE THREE TIMES AS GOOD AT MY JOB AND THREE TIMES AS LOYAL TO GENOSHA AS ANY MAGISTRATE ON MY LEVEL...
...AND I CAN'T... I WON'T LET ANY MUTANT TRICKERY MAKE A FOOL OF ME OR SPOIL MY SUCCESS.
CABLE, LOOK!
RAHNE! WHAT HAVE THEY DONE TO HER?
WHEN SHE MADE THAT SPEECH TO US* ABOUT VOLUNTARY SERVICE TO THE GENOSHAN STATE, I ASSUMED SHE WAS BEING COERCED. NOW I'M NOT SO SURE...!
RAHNE!
*NM #96--BOB

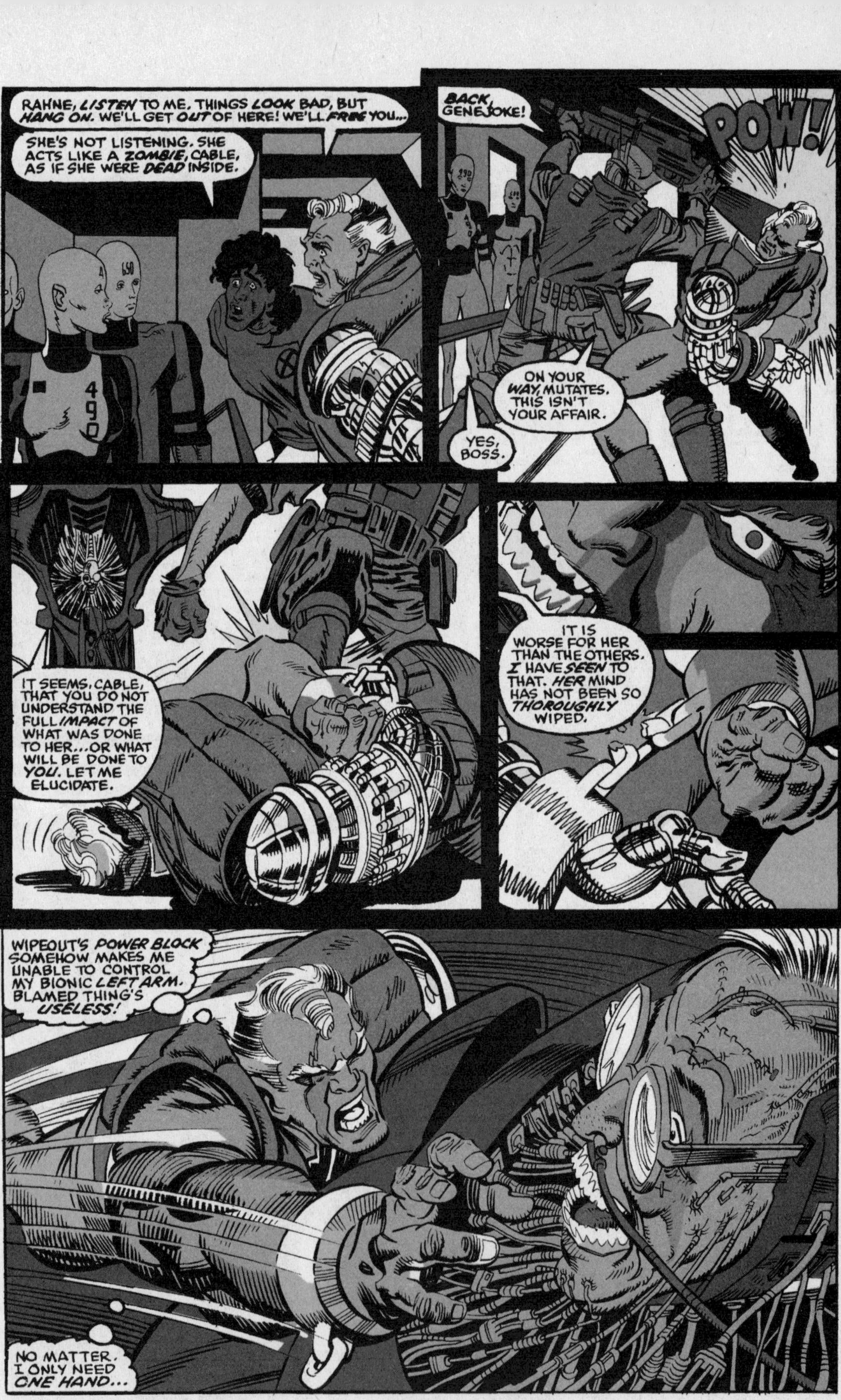

RAHNE, LISTEN TO ME. THINGS LOOK BAD, BUT HANG ON. WE'LL GET OUT OF HERE! WE'LL FREE YOU...
SHE'S NOT LISTENING. SHE ACTS LIKE A ZOMBIE, CABLE, AS IF SHE WERE DEAD INSIDE.
BACK, GENEJOKE!
POW!
ON YOUR WAY, MUTATES. THIS ISN'T YOUR AFFAIR.
YES, BOSS.
IT SEEMS, CABLE, THAT YOU DO NOT UNDERSTAND THE FULL IMPACT OF WHAT WAS DONE TO HER...OR WHAT WILL BE DONE TO YOU. LET ME ELUCIDATE.
IT IS WORSE FOR HER THAN THE OTHERS. I HAVE SEEN TO THAT. HER MIND HAS NOT BEEN SO THOROUGHLY WIPED.
WIPEOUT'S POWER BLOCK SOMEHOW MAKES ME UNABLE TO CONTROL MY BIONIC LEFT ARM. BLAMED THING'S USELESS!
NO MATTER. I ONLY NEED ONE HAND...

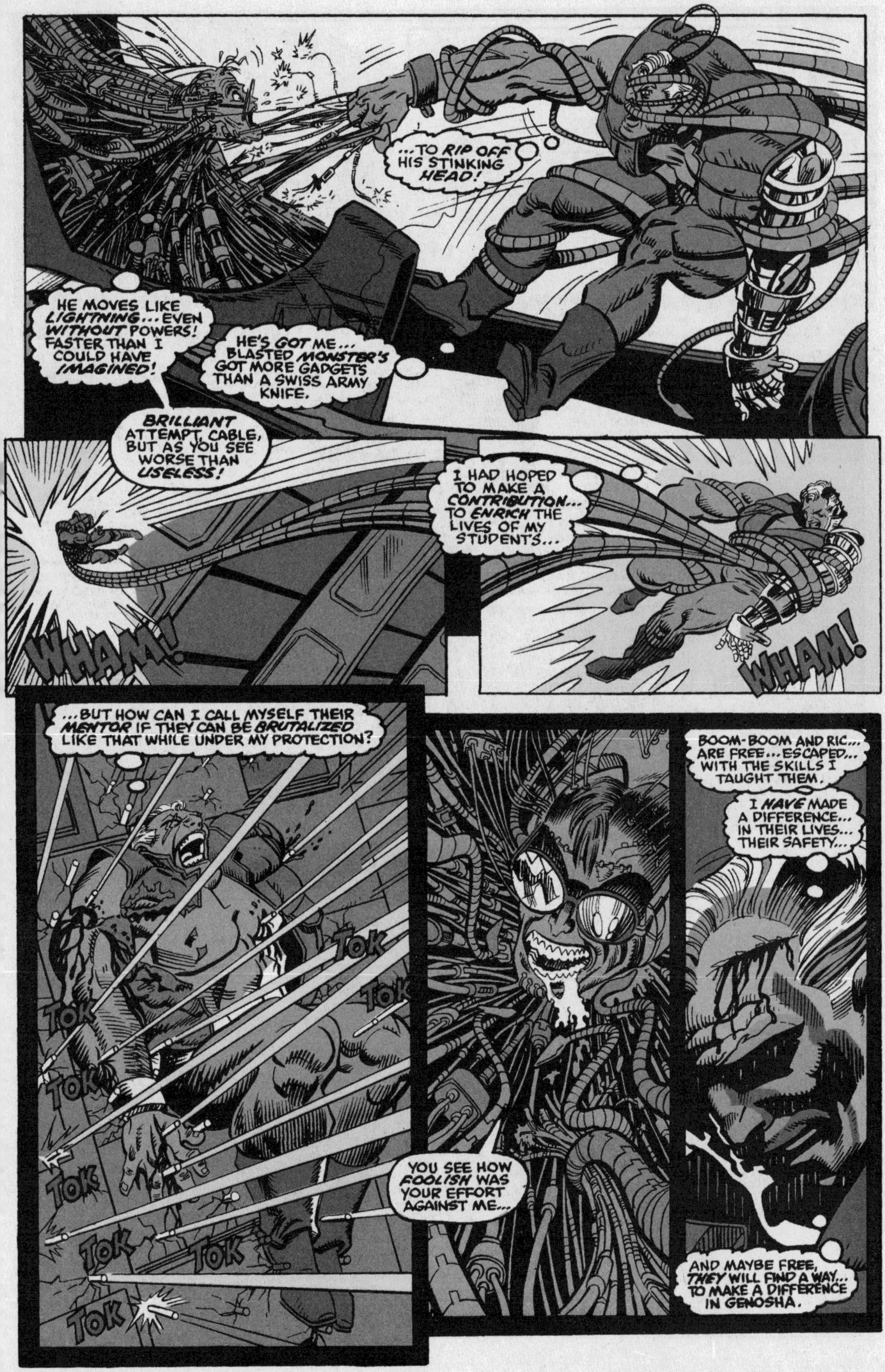
...TO RIP OFF HIS STINKING HEAD!
HE MOVES LIKE LIGHTNING... EVEN WITHOUT POWERS! FASTER THAN I COULD HAVE IMAGINED!
HE'S GOT ME... BLASTED MONSTER'S GOT MORE GADGETS THAN A SWISS ARMY KNIFE.
BRILLIANT ATTEMPT, CABLE, BUT AS YOU SEE WORSE THAN USELESS!
WHAM!
I HAD HOPED TO MAKE A CONTRIBUTION... TO ENRICH THE LIVES OF MY STUDENTS...
WHAM!
...BUT HOW CAN I CALL MYSELF THEIR MENTOR IF THEY CAN BE BRUTALIZED LIKE THAT WHILE UNDER MY PROTECTION?
TOK
TOK
TOK
TOK
TOK
TOK
TOK
TOK
TOK
BOOM-BOOM AND RIC... ARE FREE... ESCAPED... WITH THE SKILLS I TAUGHT THEM.
I HAVE MADE A DIFFERENCE... IN THEIR LIVES... THEIR SAFETY...
YOU SEE HOW FOOLISH WAS YOUR EFFORT AGAINST ME...
AND MAYBE FREE, THEY WILL FIND A WAY... TO MAKE A DIFFERENCE IN GENOSHA.

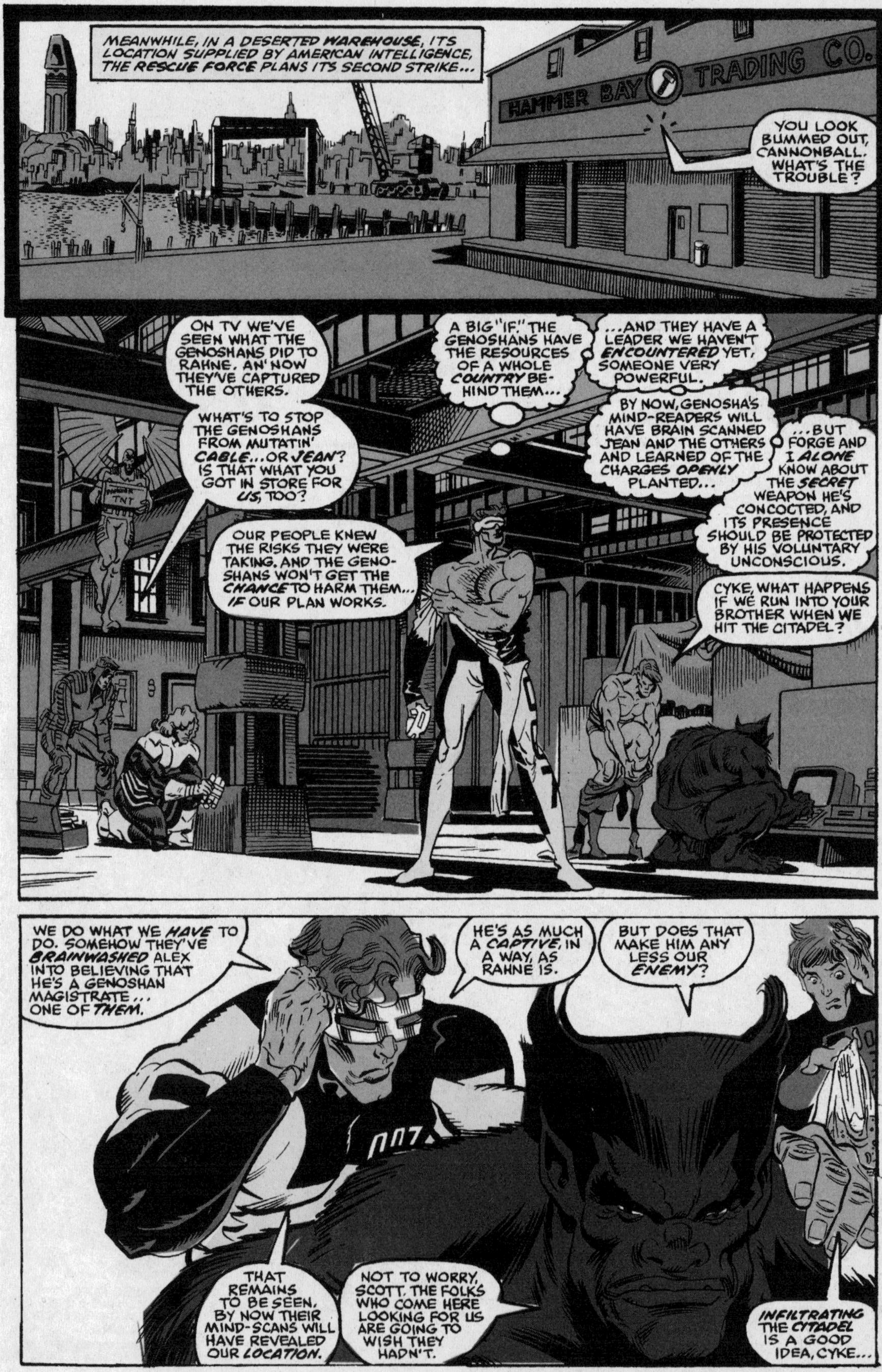

MEANWHILE, IN A DESERTED WAREHOUSE, ITS LOCATION SUPPLIED BY AMERICAN INTELLIGENCE, THE RESCUE FORCE PLANS ITS SECOND STRIKE...
HAMMER BAY TRADING CO.
YOU LOOK BUMMED OUT, CANNONBALL. WHAT'S THE TROUBLE?
ON TV WE'VE SEEN WHAT THE GENOSHANS DID TO RAHNE. AN' NOW THEY'VE CAPTURED THE OTHERS.
WHAT'S TO STOP THE GENOSHANS FROM MUTATIN' CABLE...OR JEAN? IS THAT WHAT YOU GOT IN STORE FOR US, TOO?
OUR PEOPLE KNEW THE RISKS THEY WERE TAKING. AND THE GENOSHANS WON'T GET THE CHANCE TO HARM THEM... IF OUR PLAN WORKS.
A BIG "IF." THE GENOSHANS HAVE THE RESOURCES OF A WHOLE COUNTRY BEHIND THEM...
...AND THEY HAVE A LEADER WE HAVEN'T ENCOUNTERED YET, SOMEONE VERY POWERFUL.
BY NOW, GENOSHA'S MIND-READERS WILL HAVE BRAIN SCANNED JEAN AND THE OTHERS AND LEARNED OF THE CHARGES OPENLY PLANTED...
...BUT FORGE AND I ALONE KNOW ABOUT THE SECRET WEAPON HE'S CONCOCTED, AND ITS PRESENCE SHOULD BE PROTECTED BY HIS VOLUNTARY UNCONSCIOUS.
TNT
CYKE, WHAT HAPPENS IF WE RUN INTO YOUR BROTHER WHEN WE HIT THE CITADEL?
WE DO WHAT WE HAVE TO DO. SOMEHOW THEY'VE BRAINWASHED ALEX INTO BELIEVING THAT HE'S A GENOSHAN MAGISTRATE... ONE OF THEM.
HE'S AS MUCH A CAPTIVE, IN A WAY, AS RAHNE IS.
BUT DOES THAT MAKE HIM ANY LESS OUR ENEMY?
INFILTRATING THE CITADEL IS A GOOD IDEA, CYKE...
THAT REMAINS TO BE SEEN. BY NOW THEIR MIND-SCANS WILL HAVE REVEALED OUR LOCATION.
NOT TO WORRY, SCOTT. THE FOLKS WHO COME HERE LOOKING FOR US ARE GOING TO WISH THEY HADN'T.

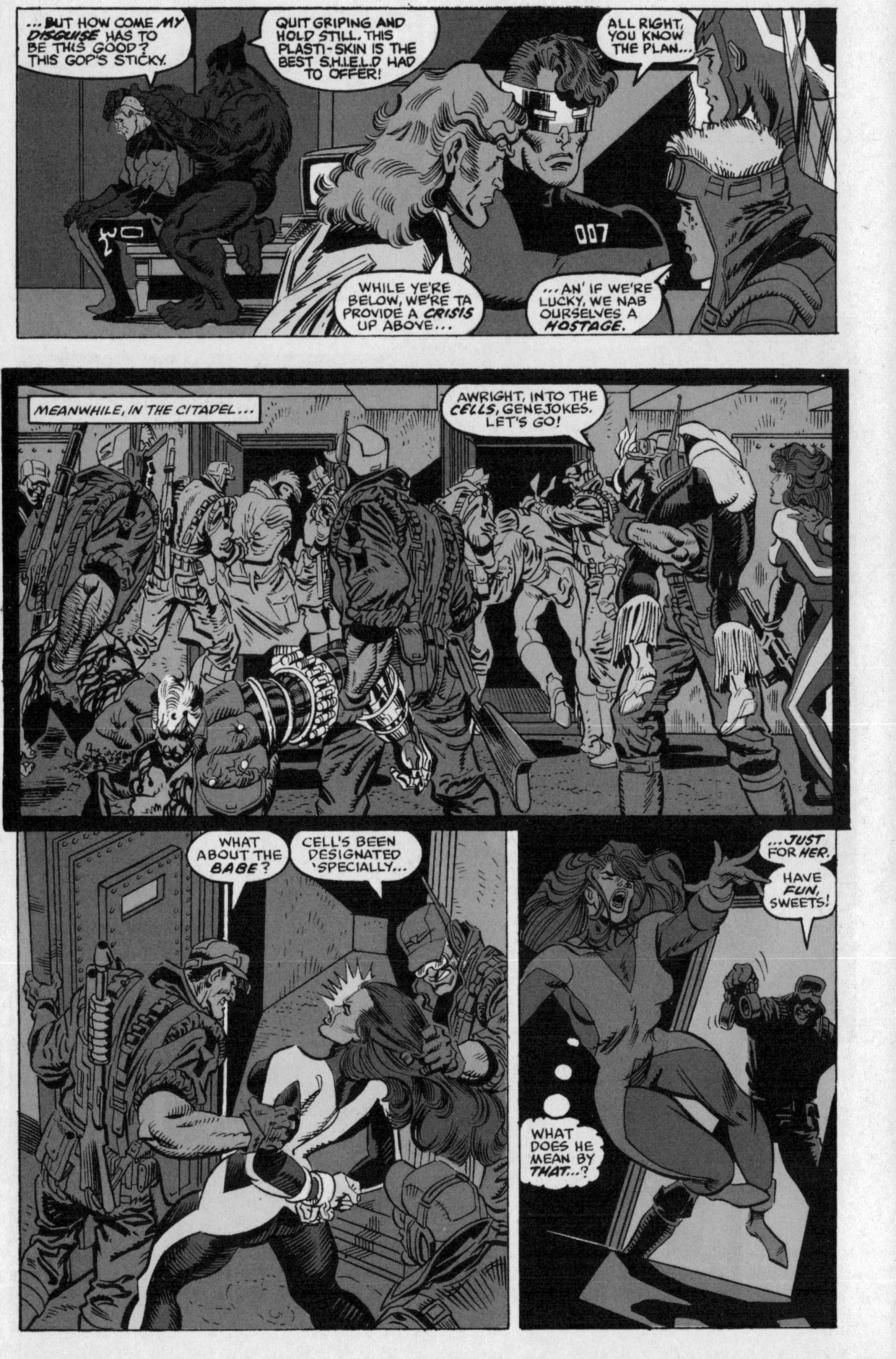
...BUT HOW COME MY DISGUISE HAS TO BE THIS GOOD? THIS GOP'S STICKY.
QUIT GRIPING AND HOLD STILL. THIS PLASTI-SKIN IS THE BEST S.H.I.E.L.D HAD TO OFFER!
ALL RIGHT, YOU KNOW THE PLAN...
WHILE YE'RE BELOW, WE'RE TA PROVIDE A CRISIS UP ABOVE...
...AN' IF WE'RE LUCKY, WE NAB OURSELVES A HOSTAGE.
007
MEANWHILE, IN THE CITADEL...
AWRIGHT, INTO THE CELLS, GENEJOKES. LET'S GO!
WHAT ABOUT THE BABE?
CELL'S BEEN DESIGNATED 'SPECIALLY...
...JUST FOR HER.
HAVE FUN, SWEETS!
WHAT DOES HE MEAN BY THAT...?

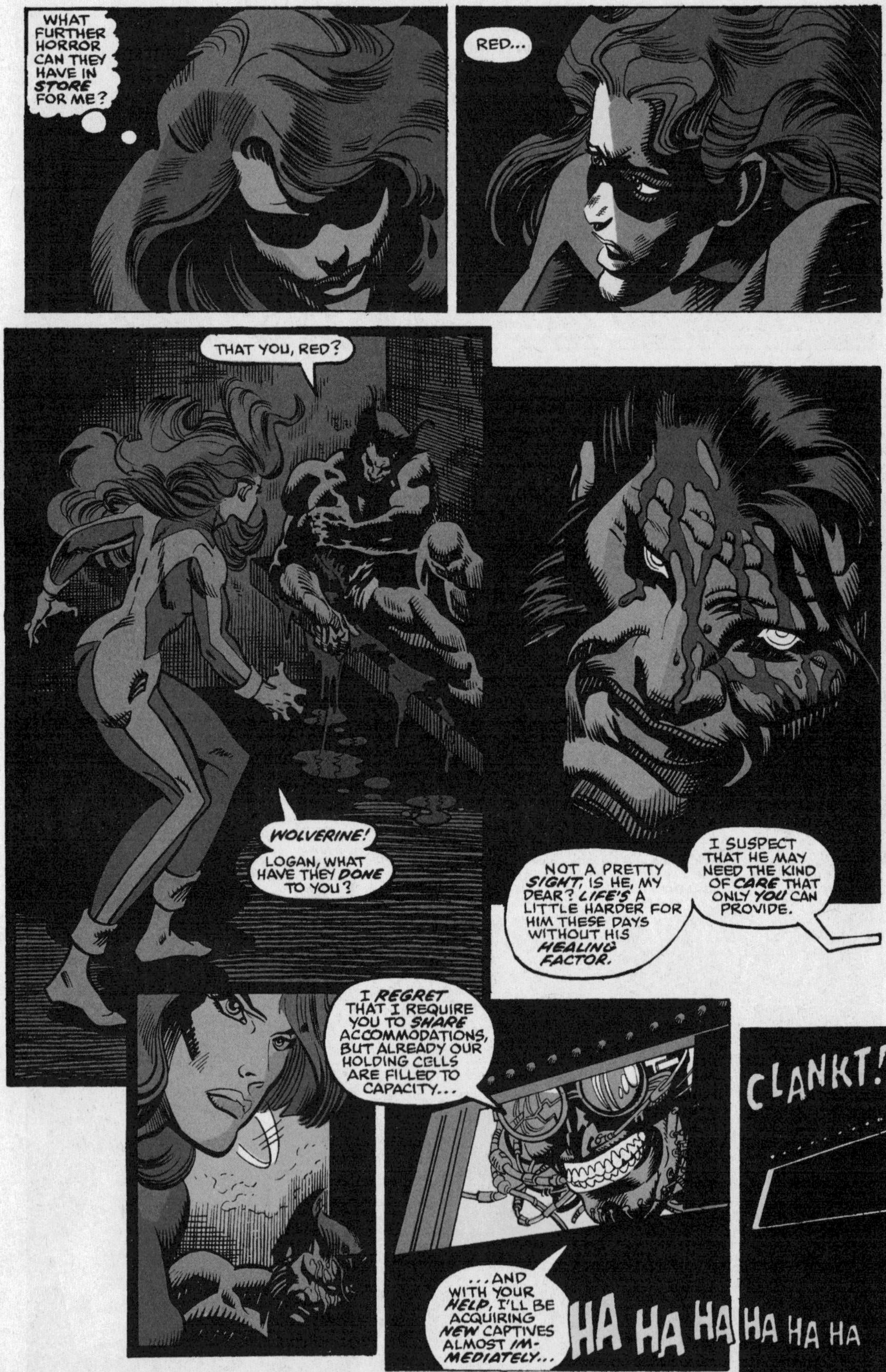

WHAT FURTHER HORROR CAN THEY HAVE IN STORE FOR ME?
RED...
THAT YOU, RED?
WOLVERINE! LOGAN, WHAT HAVE THEY DONE TO YOU?
NOT A PRETTY SIGHT, IS HE, MY DEAR? LIFE'S A LITTLE HARDER FOR HIM THESE DAYS WITHOUT HIS HEALING FACTOR.
I SUSPECT THAT HE MAY NEED THE KIND OF CARE THAT ONLY YOU CAN PROVIDE.
I REGRET THAT I REQUIRE YOU TO SHARE ACCOMMODATIONS, BUT ALREADY OUR HOLDING CELLS ARE FILLED TO CAPACITY...
...AND WITH YOUR HELP, I'LL BE ACQUIRING NEW CAPTIVES ALMOST IM-MEDIATELY...
HA HA HA HA HA HA HA
CLANKT!

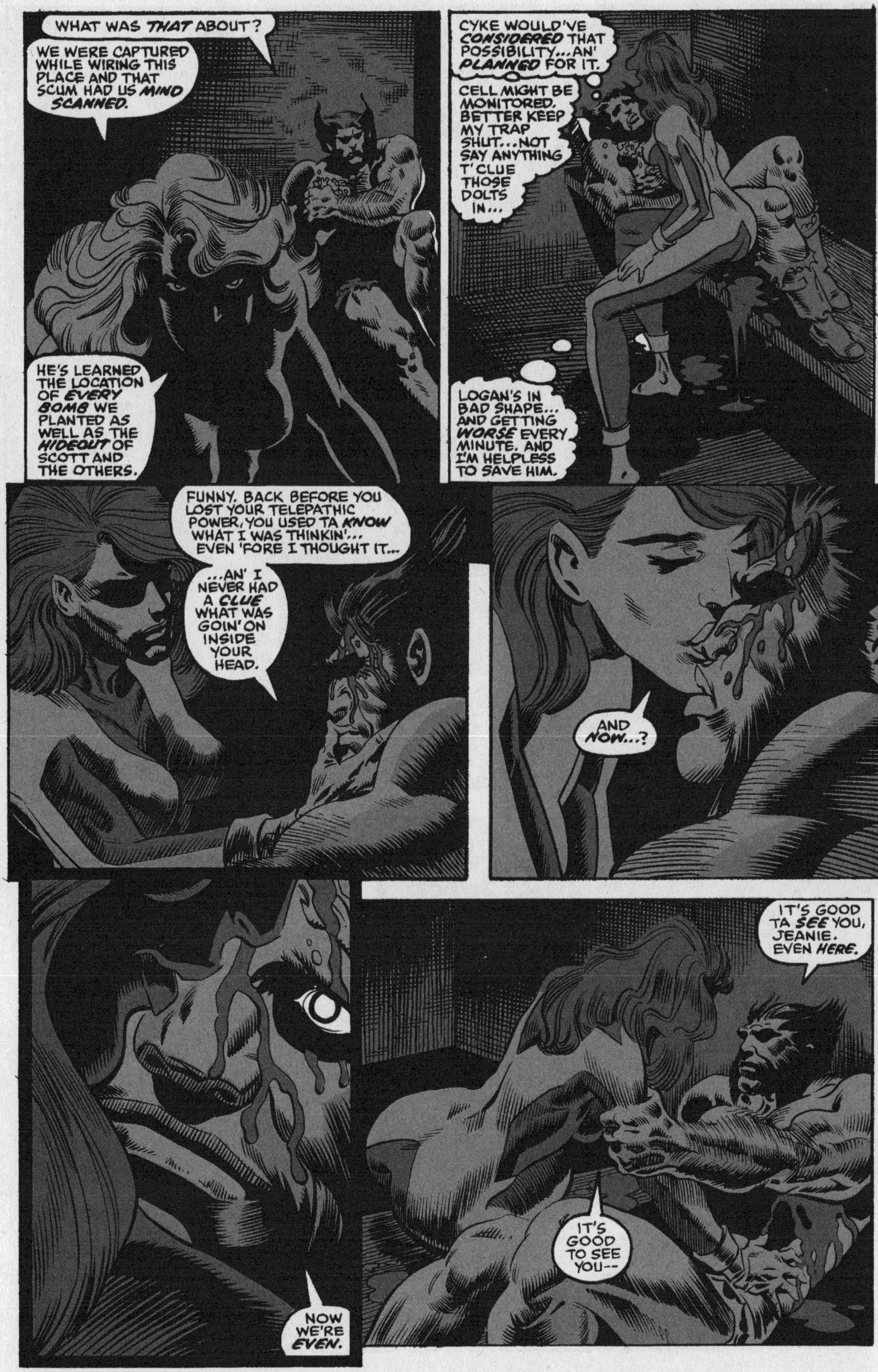
WHAT WAS THAT ABOUT?
WE WERE CAPTURED WHILE WIRING THIS PLACE AND THAT SCUM HAD US MIND SCANNED.
HE'S LEARNED THE LOCATION OF EVERY BOMB WE PLANTED AS WELL AS THE HIDEOUT OF SCOTT AND THE OTHERS.
CYKE WOULD'VE CONSIDERED THAT POSSIBILITY...AN' PLANNED FOR IT.
CELL MIGHT BE MONITORED. BETTER KEEP MY TRAP SHUT...NOT SAY ANYTHING T'CLUE THOSE DOLTS IN...
LOGAN'S IN BAD SHAPE... AND GETTING WORSE EVERY MINUTE. AND I'M HELPLESS TO SAVE HIM.
FUNNY. BACK BEFORE YOU LOST YOUR TELEPATHIC POWER, YOU USED TA KNOW WHAT I WAS THINKIN'... EVEN 'FORE I THOUGHT IT...
...AN' I NEVER HAD A CLUE WHAT WAS GOIN' ON INSIDE YOUR HEAD.
AND NOW...?
NOW WE'RE EVEN.
IT'S GOOD TA SEE YOU, JEANIE. EVEN HERE.
IT'S GOOD TO SEE YOU--

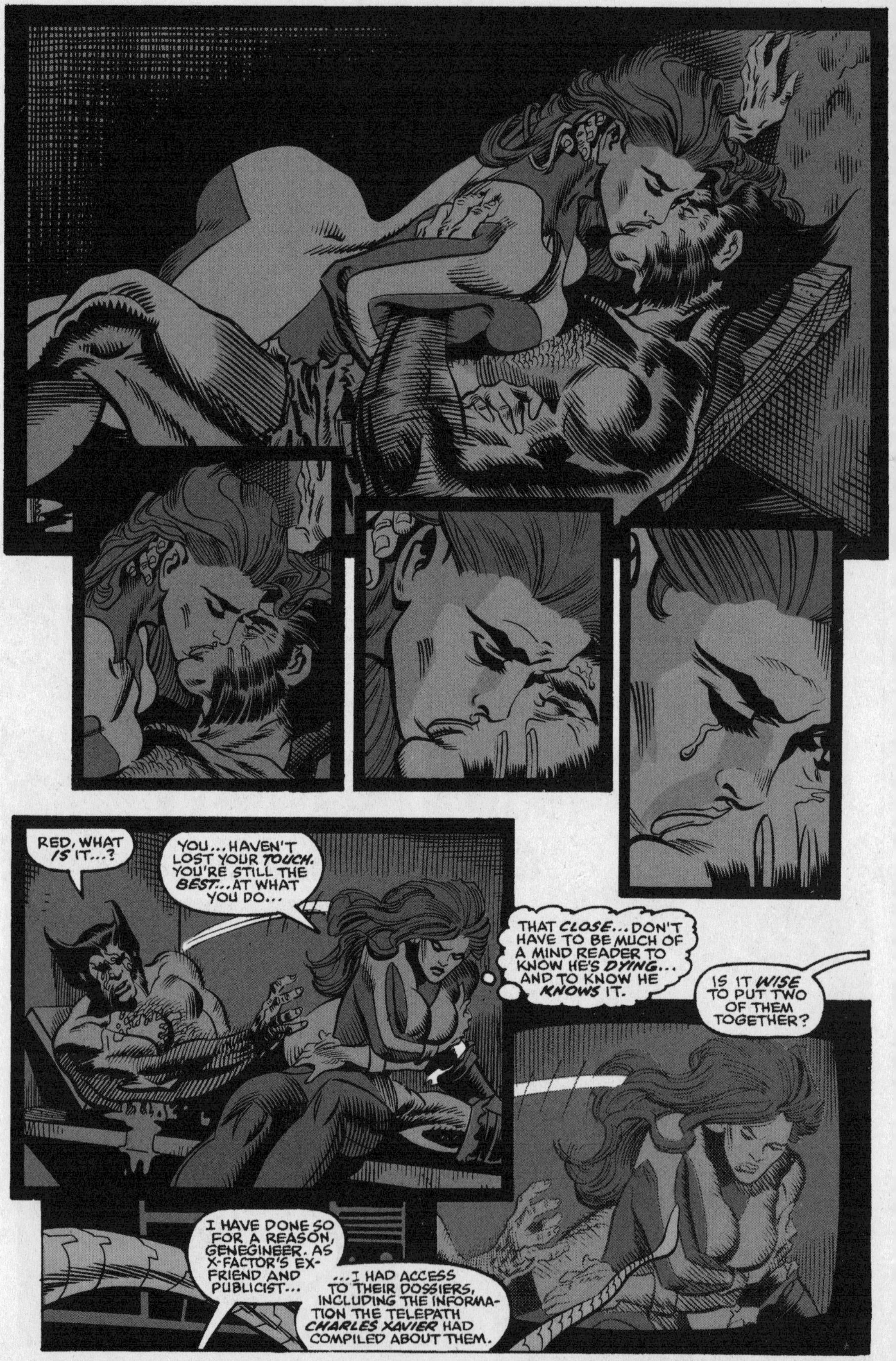
RED, WHAT IS IT...?
YOU... HAVEN'T LOST YOUR TOUCH. YOU'RE STILL THE BEST... AT WHAT YOU DO...
THAT CLOSE... DON'T HAVE TO BE MUCH OF A MIND READER TO KNOW HE'S DYING... AND TO KNOW HE KNOWS IT.
IS IT WISE TO PUT TWO OF THEM TOGETHER?
I HAVE DONE SO FOR A REASON, GENEGINEER. AS X-FACTOR'S EX-FRIEND AND PUBLICIST...
...I HAD ACCESS TO THEIR DOSSIERS, INCLUDING THE INFORMATION THE TELEPATH CHARLES XAVIER HAD COMPILED ABOUT THEM.

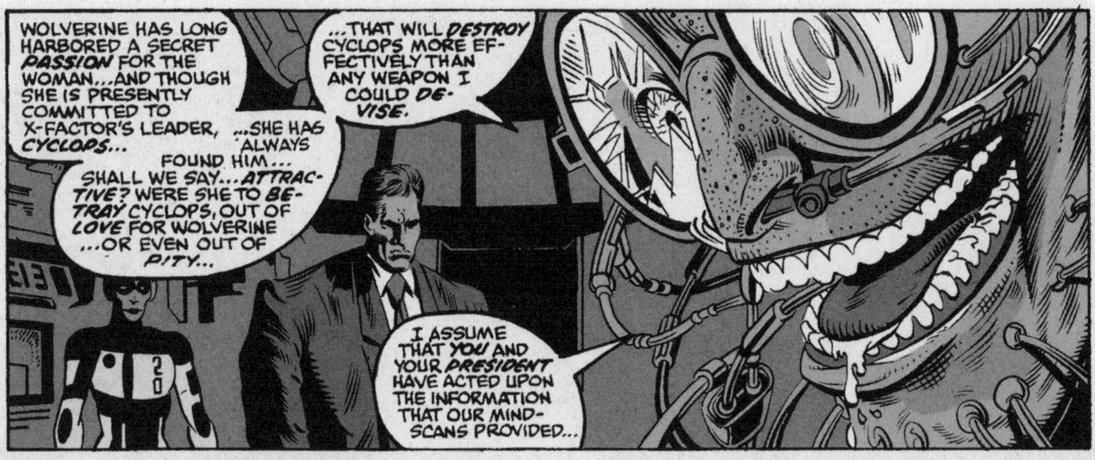
WOLVERINE HAS LONG HARBORED A SECRET PASSION FOR THE WOMAN...AND THOUGH SHE IS PRESENTLY COMMITTED TO X-FACTOR'S LEADER, CYCLOPS...
...SHE HAS ALWAYS FOUND HIM... SHALL WE SAY...ATTRACTIVE? WERE SHE TO BETRAY CYCLOPS, OUT OF LOVE FOR WOLVERINE ...OR EVEN OUT OF PITY...
...THAT WILL DESTROY CYCLOPS MORE EFFECTIVELY THAN ANY WEAPON I COULD DEVISE.
I ASSUME THAT YOU AND YOUR PRESIDENT HAVE ACTED UPON THE INFORMATION THAT OUR MIND-SCANS PROVIDED...

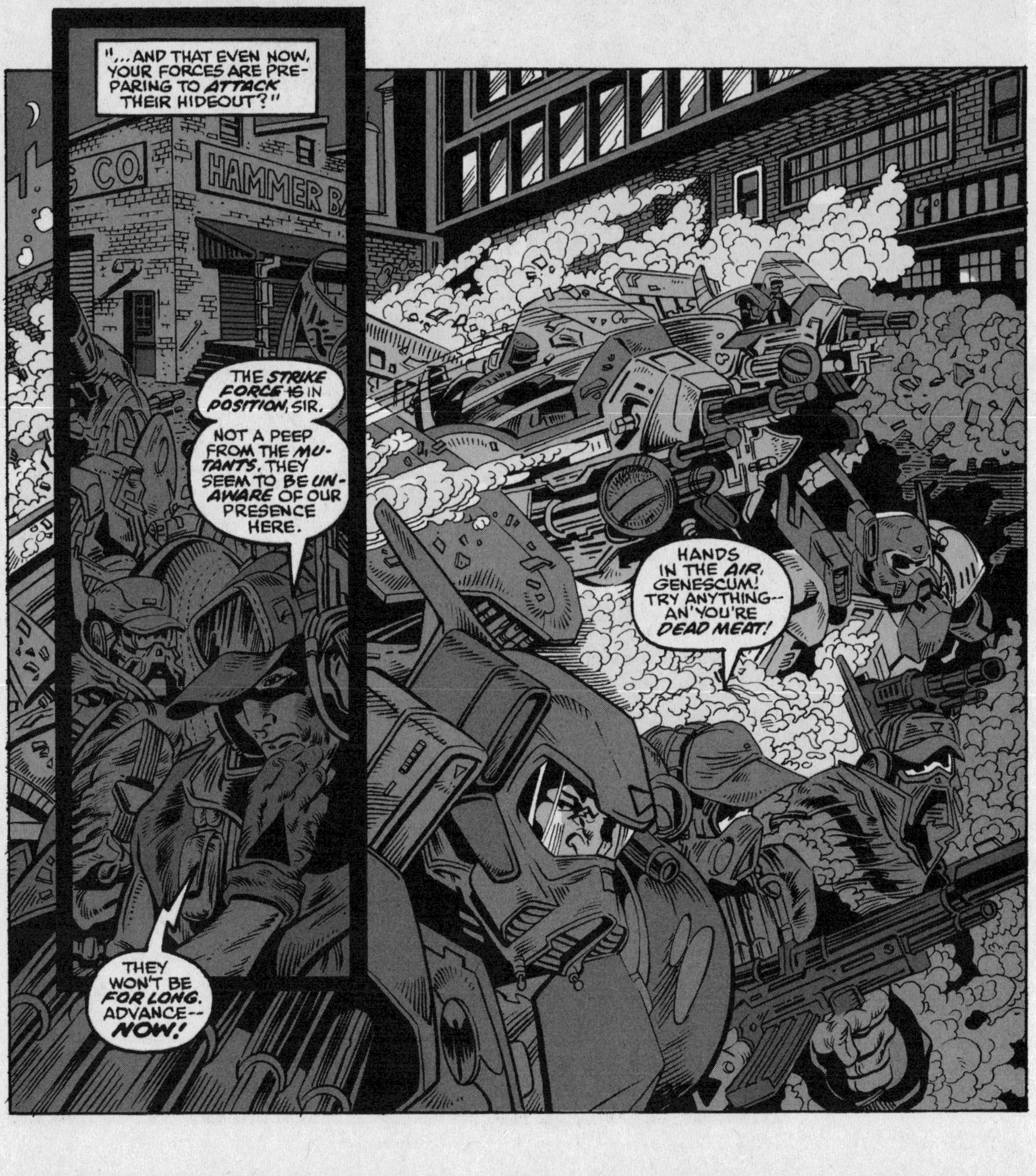
"...AND THAT EVEN NOW, YOUR FORCES ARE PREPARING TO ATTACK THEIR HIDEOUT?"
CO.
HAMMER B
THE STRIKE FORCE IS IN POSITION, SIR.
NOT A PEEP FROM THE MUTANTS. THEY SEEM TO BE UNAWARE OF OUR PRESENCE HERE.
THEY WON'T BE FOR LONG. ADVANCE-- NOW!
HANDS IN THE AIR, GENESCUM! TRY ANYTHING-- AN' YOU'RE DEAD MEAT!

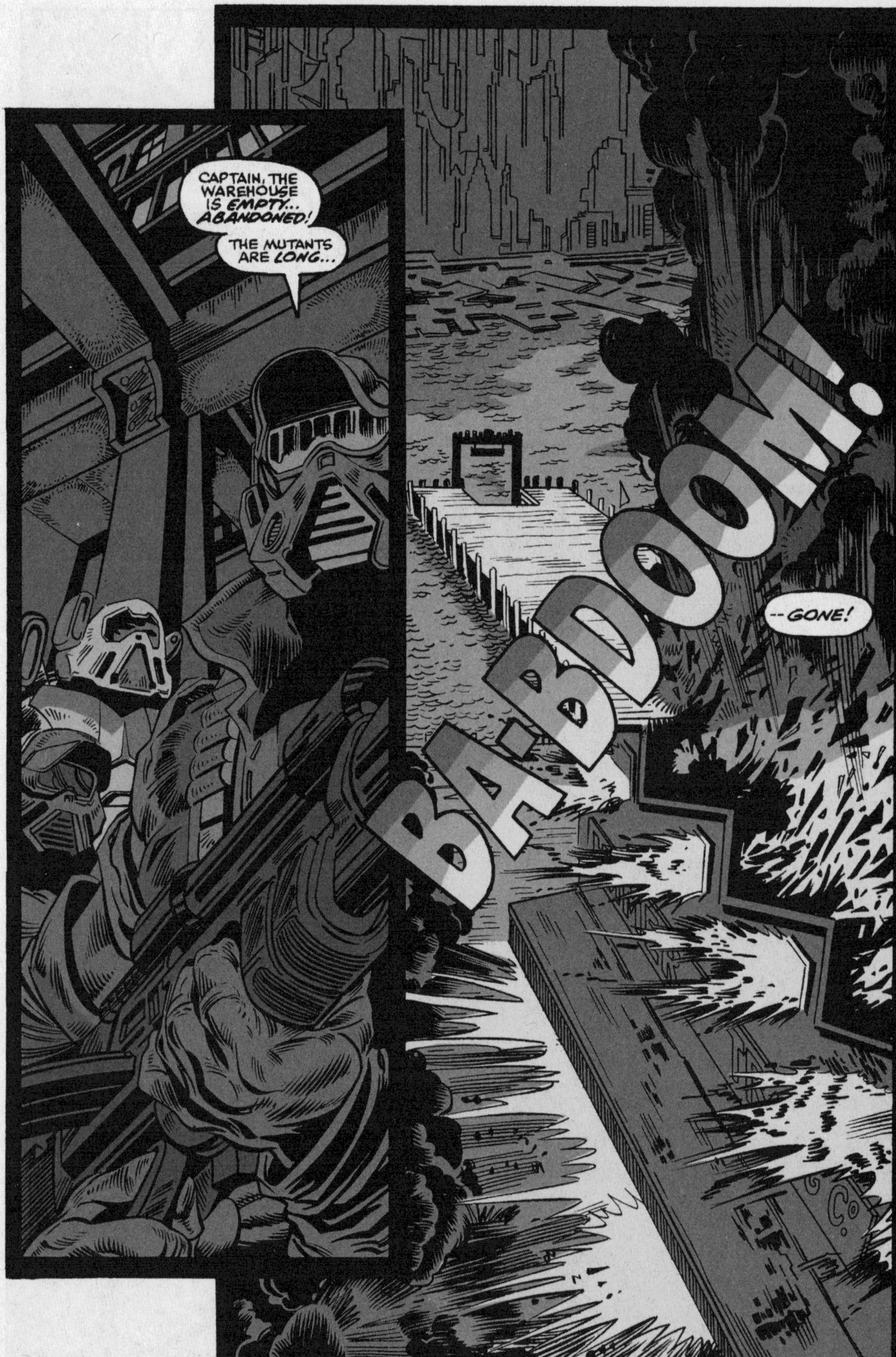
CAPTAIN, THE WAREHOUSE IS EMPTY... ABANDONED!
THE MUTANTS ARE LONG...
BA-BDOOM!
--GONE!

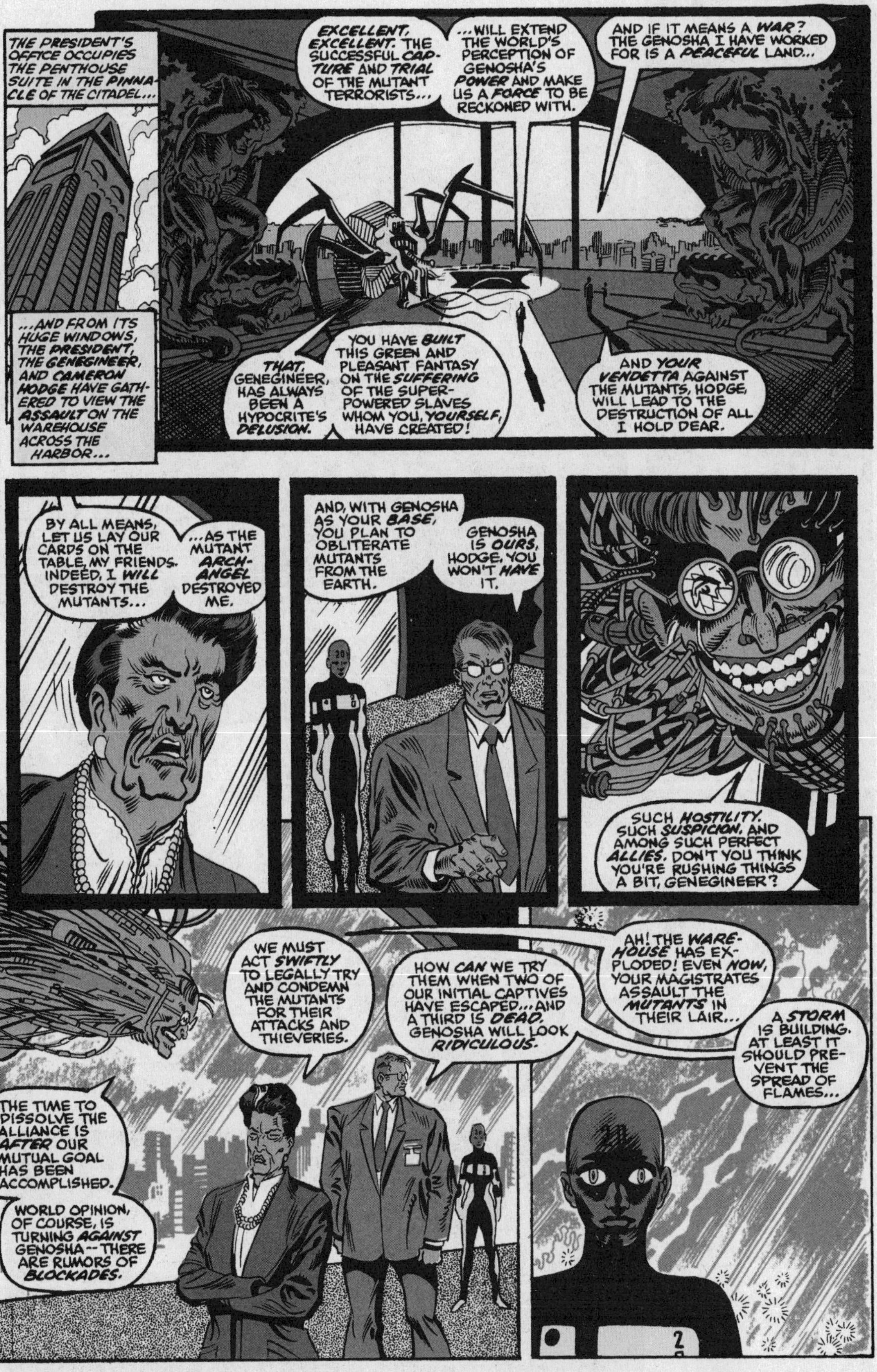
THE PRESIDENT'S OFFICE OCCUPIES THE PENTHOUSE SUITE IN THE PINNACLE OF THE CITADEL...
...AND FROM ITS HUGE WINDOWS, THE PRESIDENT, THE GENEGINEER, AND CAMERON HODGE HAVE GATHERED TO VIEW THE ASSAULT ON THE WAREHOUSE ACROSS THE HARBOR...
EXCELLENT, EXCELLENT. THE SUCCESSFUL CAPTURE AND TRIAL OF THE MUTANT TERRORISTS...
...WILL EXTEND THE WORLD'S PERCEPTION OF GENOSHA'S POWER AND MAKE US A FORCE TO BE RECKONED WITH.
AND IF IT MEANS A WAR? THE GENOSHA I HAVE WORKED FOR IS A PEACEFUL LAND...
THAT, GENEGINEER, HAS ALWAYS BEEN A HYPOCRITE'S DELUSION.
YOU HAVE BUILT THIS GREEN AND PLEASANT FANTASY ON THE SUFFERING OF THE SUPER-POWERED SLAVES WHOM YOU, YOURSELF, HAVE CREATED!
AND YOUR VENDETTA AGAINST THE MUTANTS, HODGE, WILL LEAD TO THE DESTRUCTION OF ALL I HOLD DEAR.
BY ALL MEANS, LET US LAY OUR CARDS ON THE TABLE, MY FRIENDS. INDEED, I WILL DESTROY THE MUTANTS...
...AS THE MUTANT ARCH-ANGEL DESTROYED ME.
AND, WITH GENOSHA AS YOUR BASE, YOU PLAN TO OBLITERATE MUTANTS FROM THE EARTH.
GENOSHA IS OURS, HODGE. YOU WON'T HAVE IT.
SUCH HOSTILITY. SUCH SUSPICION. AND AMONG SUCH PERFECT ALLIES. DON'T YOU THINK YOU'RE RUSHING THINGS A BIT, GENEGINEER?
THE TIME TO DISSOLVE THE ALLIANCE IS AFTER OUR MUTUAL GOAL HAS BEEN ACCOMPLISHED.
WE MUST ACT SWIFTLY TO LEGALLY TRY AND CONDEMN THE MUTANTS FOR THEIR ATTACKS AND THIEVERIES.
WORLD OPINION, OF COURSE, IS TURNING AGAINST GENOSHA -- THERE ARE RUMORS OF BLOCKADES.
HOW CAN WE TRY THEM WHEN TWO OF OUR INITIAL CAPTIVES HAVE ESCAPED... AND A THIRD IS DEAD. GENOSHA WILL LOOK RIDICULOUS.
AH! THE WAREHOUSE HAS EXPLODED! EVEN NOW, YOUR MAGISTRATES ASSAULT THE MUTANTS IN THEIR LAIR...
A STORM IS BUILDING. AT LEAST IT SHOULD PREVENT THE SPREAD OF FLAMES...

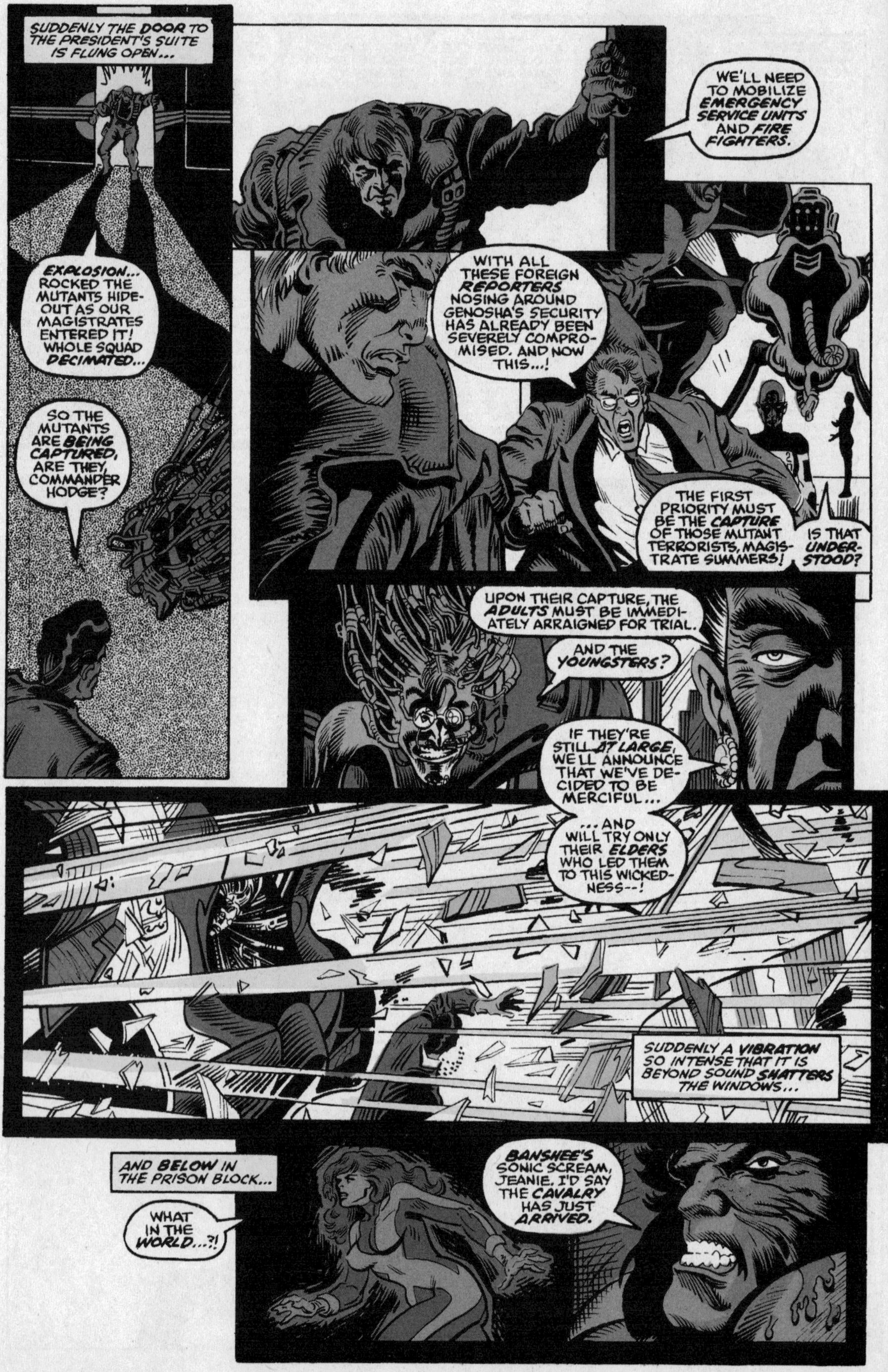

SUDDENLY THE DOOR TO THE PRESIDENT'S SUITE IS FLUNG OPEN...
WE'LL NEED TO MOBILIZE EMERGENCY SERVICE UNITS AND FIRE FIGHTERS.
EXPLOSION... ROCKED THE MUTANTS HIDE-OUT AS OUR MAGISTRATES ENTERED IT! WHOLE SQUAD DECIMATED...
WITH ALL THESE FOREIGN REPORTERS NOSING AROUND GENOSHA'S SECURITY HAS ALREADY BEEN SEVERELY COMPRO-MISED. AND NOW THIS...!
SO THE MUTANTS ARE BEING CAPTURED, ARE THEY, COMMANDER HODGE?
THE FIRST PRIORITY MUST BE THE CAPTURE OF THOSE MUTANT TERRORISTS, MAGIS-TRATE SUMMERS!
IS THAT UNDER-STOOD?
UPON THEIR CAPTURE, THE ADULTS MUST BE IMMEDI-ATELY ARRAIGNED FOR TRIAL.
AND THE YOUNGSTERS?
IF THEY'RE STILL AT LARGE, WE'LL ANNOUNCE THAT WE'VE DE-CIDED TO BE MERCIFUL...
...AND WILL TRY ONLY THEIR ELDERS WHO LED THEM TO THIS WICKED-NESS--!
SUDDENLY A VIBRATION SO INTENSE THAT IT IS BEYOND SOUND SMATTERS THE WINDOWS...
AND BELOW IN THE PRISON BLOCK...
WHAT IN THE WORLD...?!
BANSHEE'S SONIC SCREAM, JEANIE. I'D SAY THE CAVALRY HAS JUST ARRIVED.

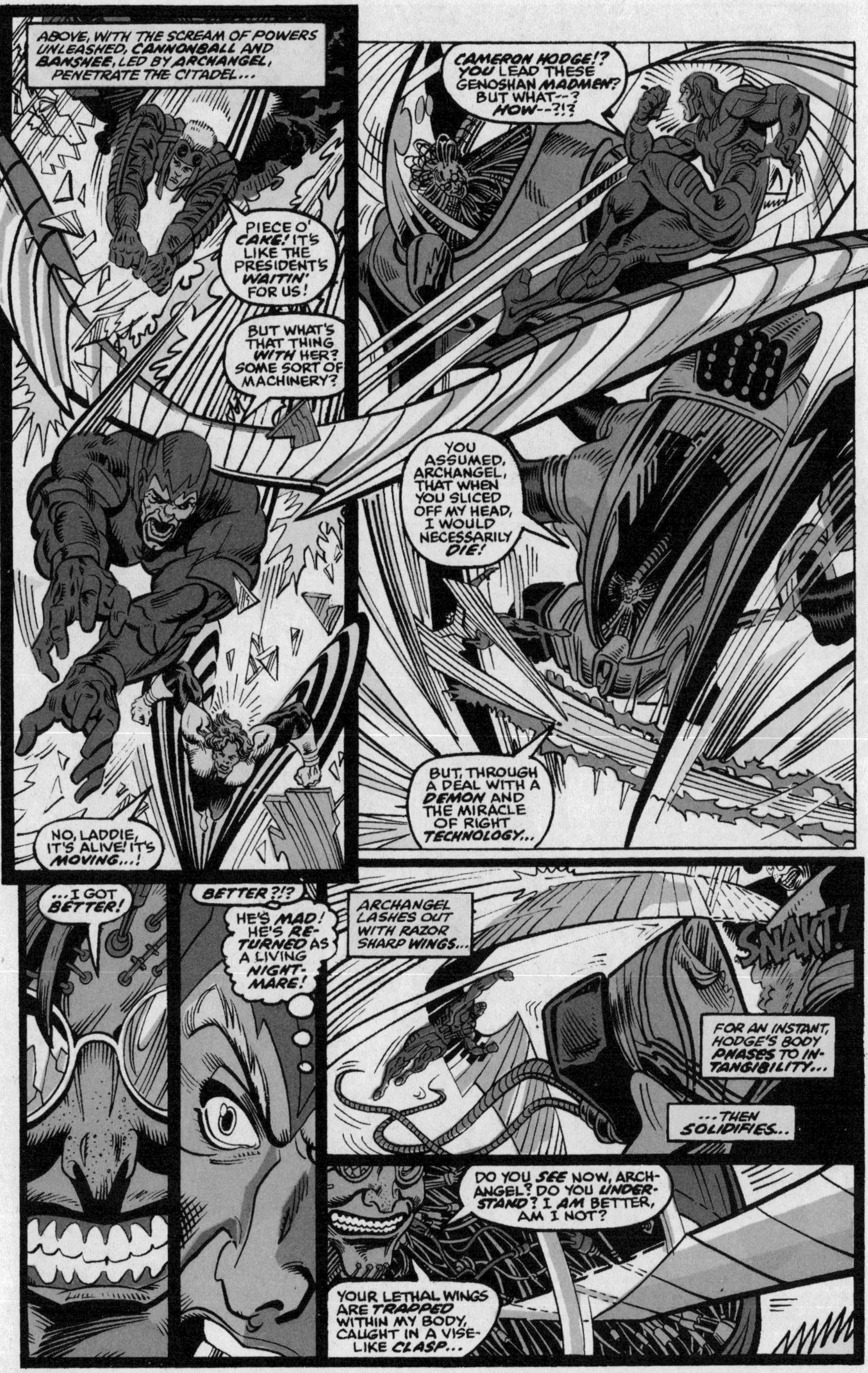
ABOVE, WITH THE SCREAM OF POWERS UNLEASHED, CANNONBALL AND BANSHEE, LED BY ARCHANGEL, PENETRATE THE CITADEL...
PIECE O' CAKE! IT'S LIKE THE PRESIDENT'S WAITIN' FOR US!
BUT WHAT'S THAT THING WITH HER? SOME SORT OF MACHINERY?
NO, LADDIE, IT'S ALIVE! IT'S MOVING...!
CAMERON HODGE!? YOU LEAD THESE GENOSHAN MADMEN? BUT WHAT--? HOW--?!?
YOU ASSUMED, ARCHANGEL, THAT WHEN YOU SLICED OFF MY HEAD, I WOULD NECESSARILY DIE!
BUT, THROUGH A DEAL WITH A DEMON AND THE MIRACLE OF RIGHT TECHNOLOGY...
...I GOT BETTER!
BETTER?!?
HE'S MAD! HE'S RETURNED AS A LIVING NIGHTMARE!
ARCHANGEL LASHES OUT WITH RAZOR SHARP WINGS...
SNAKT!
FOR AN INSTANT, HODGE'S BODY PHASES TO INTANGIBILITY...
...THEN SOLIDIFIES...
DO YOU SEE NOW, ARCHANGEL? DO YOU UNDERSTAND? I AM BETTER, AM I NOT?
YOUR LETHAL WINGS ARE TRAPPED WITHIN MY BODY, CAUGHT IN A VISE-LIKE CLASP...

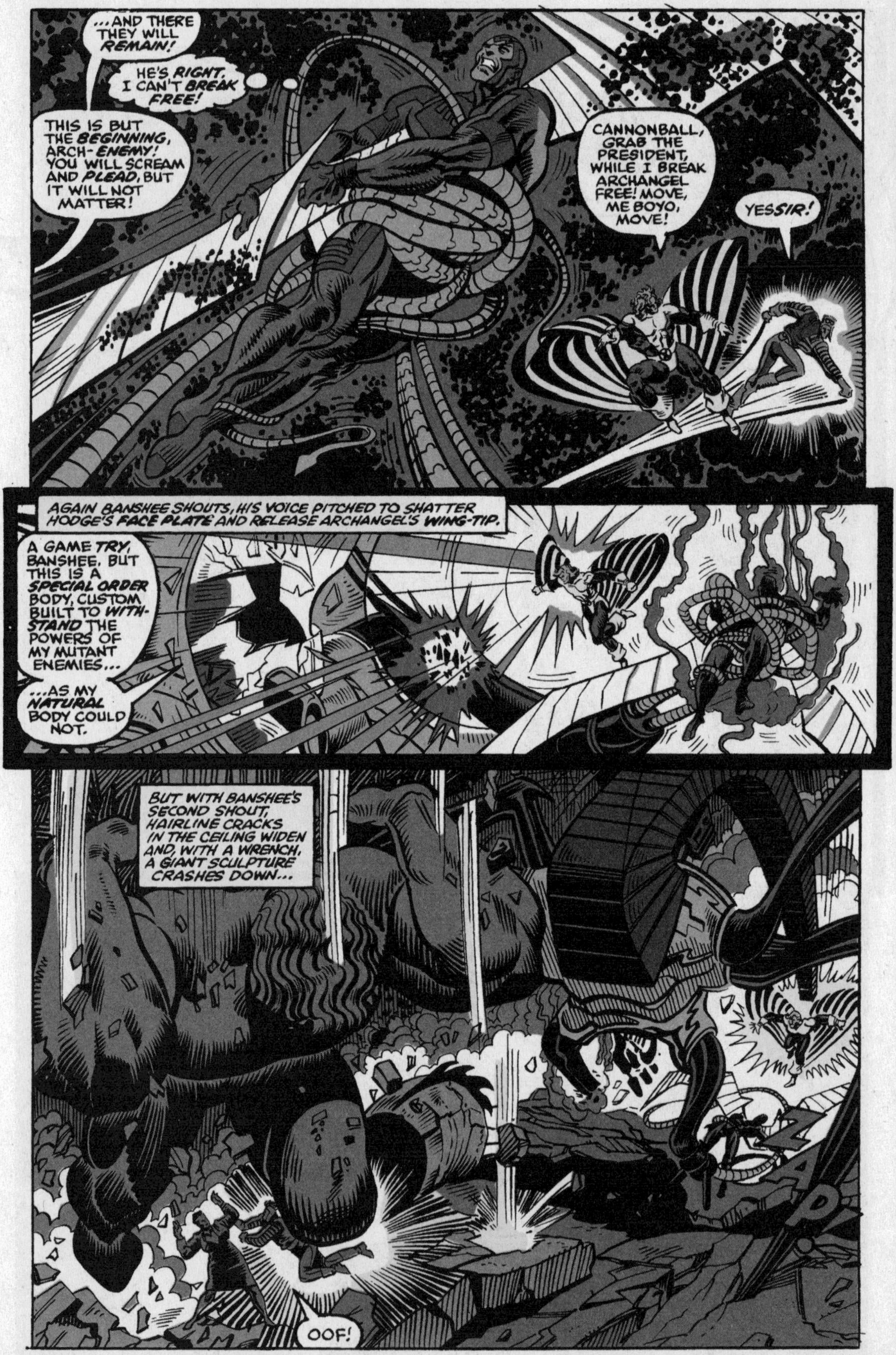
...AND THERE THEY WILL REMAIN!
HE'S RIGHT. I CAN'T BREAK FREE!
THIS IS BUT THE BEGINNING, ARCH-ENEMY! YOU WILL SCREAM AND PLEAD, BUT IT WILL NOT MATTER!
CANNONBALL, GRAB THE PRESIDENT, WHILE I BREAK ARCHANGEL FREE! MOVE, ME BOYO, MOVE!
YESSIR!
AGAIN BANSHEE SHOUTS, HIS VOICE PITCHED TO SHATTER HODGE'S FACE PLATE AND RELEASE ARCHANGEL'S WING-TIP.
A GAME TRY, BANSHEE, BUT THIS IS A SPECIAL ORDER BODY, CUSTOM BUILT TO WITHSTAND THE POWERS OF MY MUTANT ENEMIES...
...AS MY NATURAL BODY COULD NOT.
BUT WITH BANSHEE'S SECOND SHOUT, HAIRLINE CRACKS IN THE CEILING WIDEN AND, WITH A WRENCH, A GIANT SCULPTURE CRASHES DOWN...
OOF!

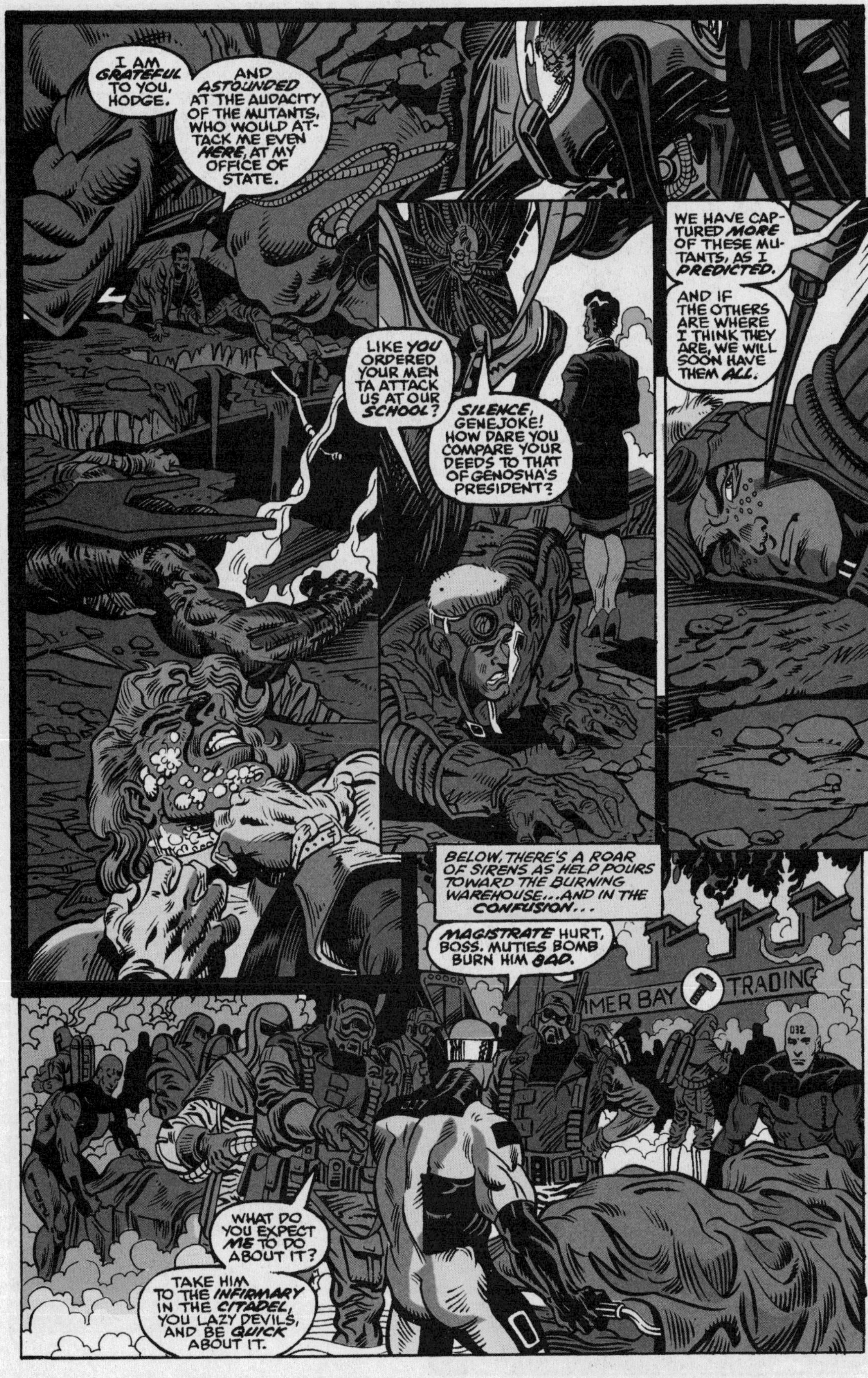

I AM GRATEFUL TO YOU, HODGE.
AND ASTOUNDED AT THE AUDACITY OF THE MUTANTS, WHO WOULD ATTACK ME EVEN HERE, AT MY OFFICE OF STATE.
LIKE YOU ORDERED YOUR MEN TA ATTACK US AT OUR SCHOOL?
SILENCE, GENEJOKE! HOW DARE YOU COMPARE YOUR DEEDS TO THAT OF GENOSHA'S PRESIDENT?
WE HAVE CAPTURED MORE OF THESE MUTANTS, AS I PREDICTED.
AND IF THE OTHERS ARE WHERE I THINK THEY ARE, WE WILL SOON HAVE THEM ALL.
BELOW, THERE'S A ROAR OF SIRENS AS HELP POURS TOWARD THE BURNING WAREHOUSE... AND IN THE CONFUSION...
MAGISTRATE HURT, BOSS. MUTIES BOMB BURN HIM BAD.
MER BAY TRADING
WHAT DO YOU EXPECT ME TO DO ABOUT IT?
TAKE HIM TO THE INFIRMARY IN THE CITADEL, YOU LAZY DEVILS, AND BE QUICK ABOUT IT.

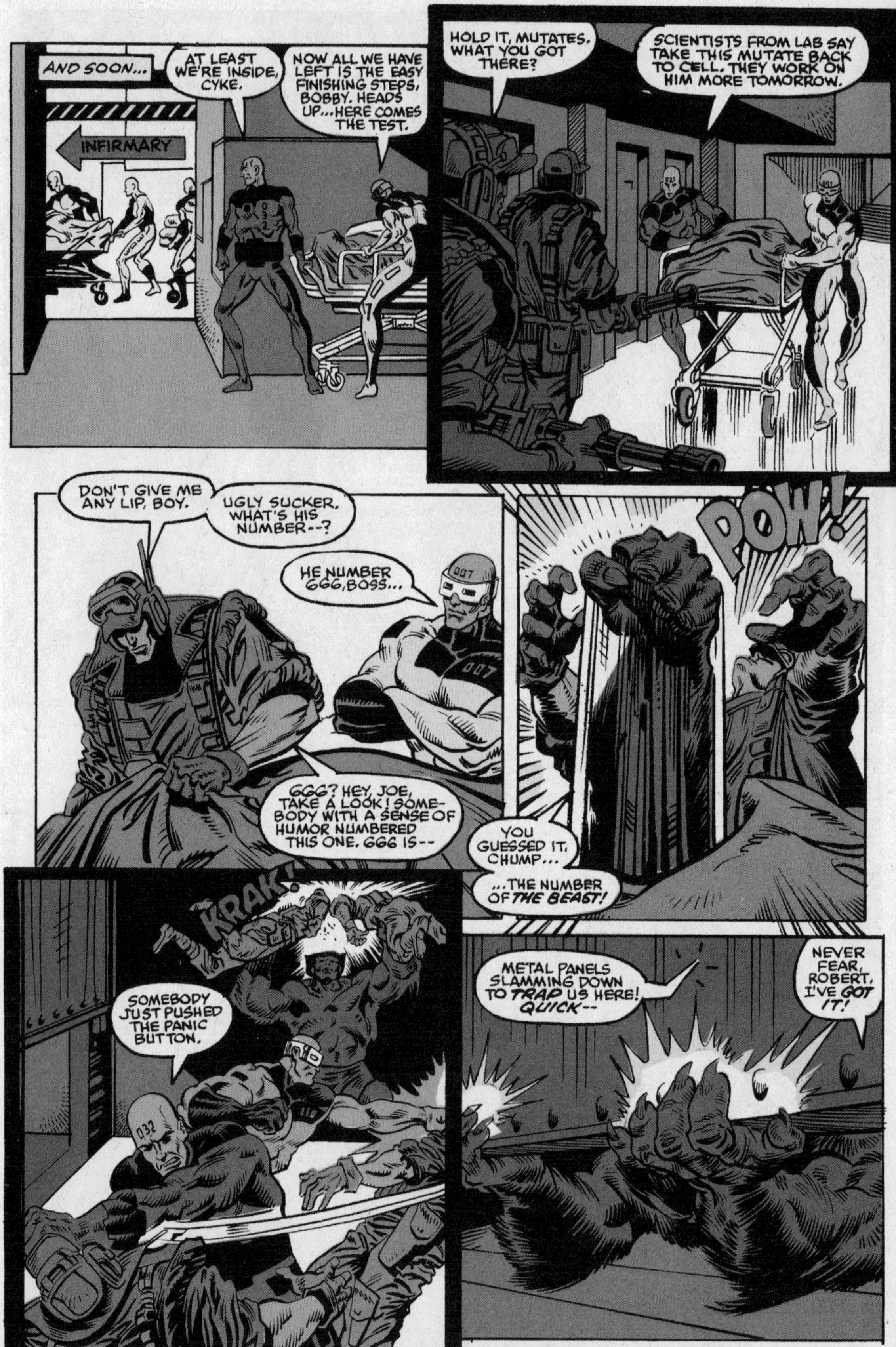

AND SOON...
AT LEAST WE'RE INSIDE, CYKE.
NOW ALL WE HAVE LEFT IS THE EASY FINISHING STEPS, BOBBY. HEADS UP...HERE COMES THE TEST.
INFIRMARY
HOLD IT, MUTATES. WHAT YOU GOT THERE?
SCIENTISTS FROM LAB SAY TAKE THIS MUTATE BACK TO CELL. THEY WORK ON HIM MORE TOMORROW.
DON'T GIVE ME ANY LIP, BOY.
UGLY SUCKER. WHAT'S HIS NUMBER--?
HE NUMBER 666, BOSS...
666? HEY, JOE, TAKE A LOOK! SOMEBODY WITH A SENSE OF HUMOR NUMBERED THIS ONE. 666 IS--
POW!
YOU GUESSED IT, CHUMP...
...THE NUMBER OF THE BEAST!
KRAK!
SOMEBODY JUST PUSHED THE PANIC BUTTON.
METAL PANELS SLAMMING DOWN TO TRAP US HERE! QUICK--
NEVER FEAR, ROBERT, I'VE GOT IT!

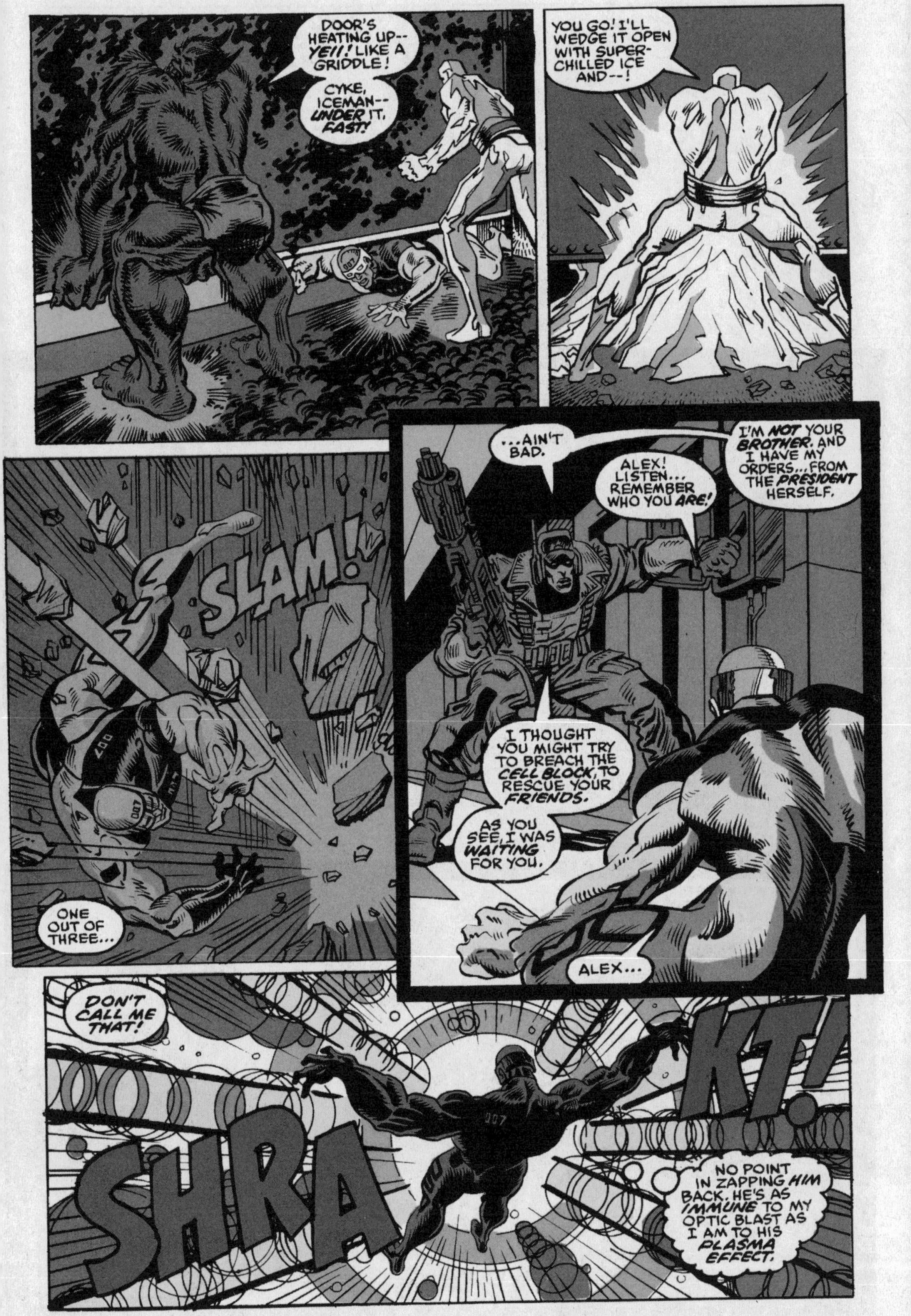
DOOR'S HEATING UP-- YEII! LIKE A GRIDDLE!
CYKE, ICEMAN-- UNDER IT, FAST!
YOU GO! I'LL WEDGE IT OPEN WITH SUPER-CHILLED ICE AND--!
SLAM!
ONE OUT OF THREE...
...AIN'T BAD.
ALEX! LISTEN... REMEMBER WHO YOU ARE!
I'M NOT YOUR BROTHER. AND I HAVE MY ORDERS... FROM THE PRESIDENT HERSELF.
I THOUGHT YOU MIGHT TRY TO BREACH THE CELL BLOCK, TO RESCUE YOUR FRIENDS.
AS YOU SEE, I WAS WAITING FOR YOU.
ALEX...
DON'T CALL ME THAT!
KT!
SHRA
NO POINT IN ZAPPING HIM BACK. HE'S AS IMMUNE TO MY OPTIC BLAST AS I AM TO HIS PLASMA EFFECT.

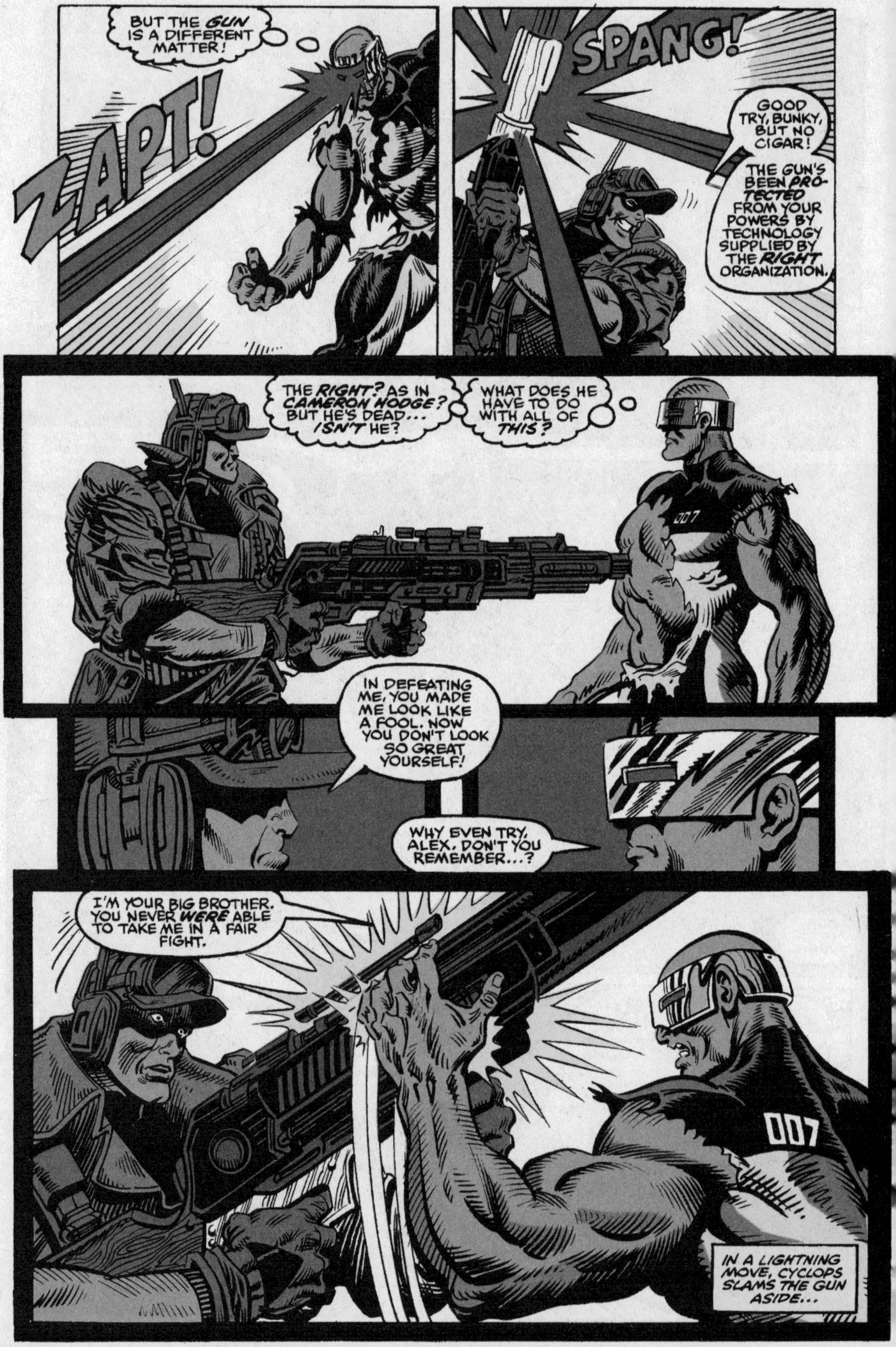

BUT THE GUN IS A DIFFERENT MATTER!
ZAPT!
SPANG!
GOOD TRY, BUNKY, BUT NO CIGAR!
THE GUN'S BEEN PROTECTED FROM YOUR POWERS BY TECHNOLOGY SUPPLIED BY THE RIGHT ORGANIZATION.
THE RIGHT? AS IN CAMERON HODGE? BUT HE'S DEAD... ISN'T HE?
WHAT DOES HE HAVE TO DO WITH ALL OF THIS?
007
IN DEFEATING ME, YOU MADE ME LOOK LIKE A FOOL. NOW YOU DON'T LOOK SO GREAT YOURSELF!
WHY EVEN TRY, ALEX. DON'T YOU REMEMBER...?
I'M YOUR BIG BROTHER. YOU NEVER WERE ABLE TO TAKE ME IN A FAIR FIGHT.
007
IN A LIGHTNING MOVE, CYCLOPS SLAMS THE GUN ASIDE...

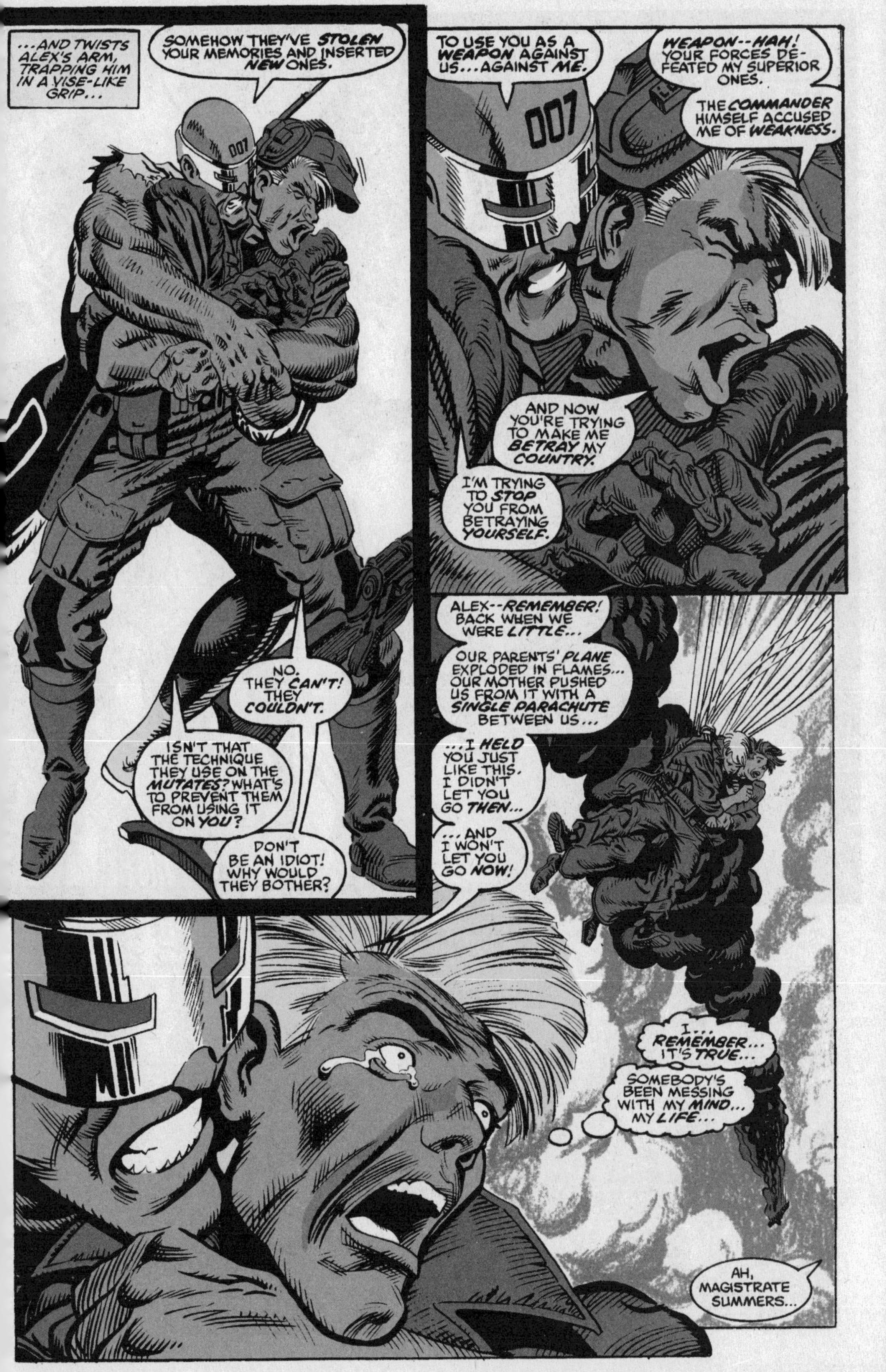
...AND TWISTS ALEX'S ARM, TRAPPING HIM IN A VISE-LIKE GRIP...
SOMEHOW THEY'VE STOLEN YOUR MEMORIES AND INSERTED NEW ONES.
NO. THEY CAN'T! THEY COULDN'T.
ISN'T THAT THE TECHNIQUE THEY USE ON THE MUTATES? WHAT'S TO PREVENT THEM FROM USING IT ON YOU?
DON'T BE AN IDIOT! WHY WOULD THEY BOTHER?
TO USE YOU AS A WEAPON AGAINST US... AGAINST ME.
WEAPON--HAH! YOUR FORCES DEFEATED MY SUPERIOR ONES.
THE COMMANDER HIMSELF ACCUSED ME OF WEAKNESS.
AND NOW YOU'RE TRYING TO MAKE ME BETRAY MY COUNTRY.
I'M TRYING TO STOP YOU FROM BETRAYING YOURSELF.
ALEX--REMEMBER! BACK WHEN WE WERE LITTLE...
OUR PARENTS' PLANE EXPLODED IN FLAMES... OUR MOTHER PUSHED US FROM IT WITH A SINGLE PARACHUTE BETWEEN US...
...I HELD YOU JUST LIKE THIS. I DIDN'T LET YOU GO THEN...
...AND I WON'T LET YOU GO NOW!
I... REMEMBER... IT'S TRUE...
SOMEBODY'S BEEN MESSING WITH MY MIND... MY LIFE...
AH, MAGISTRATE SUMMERS...

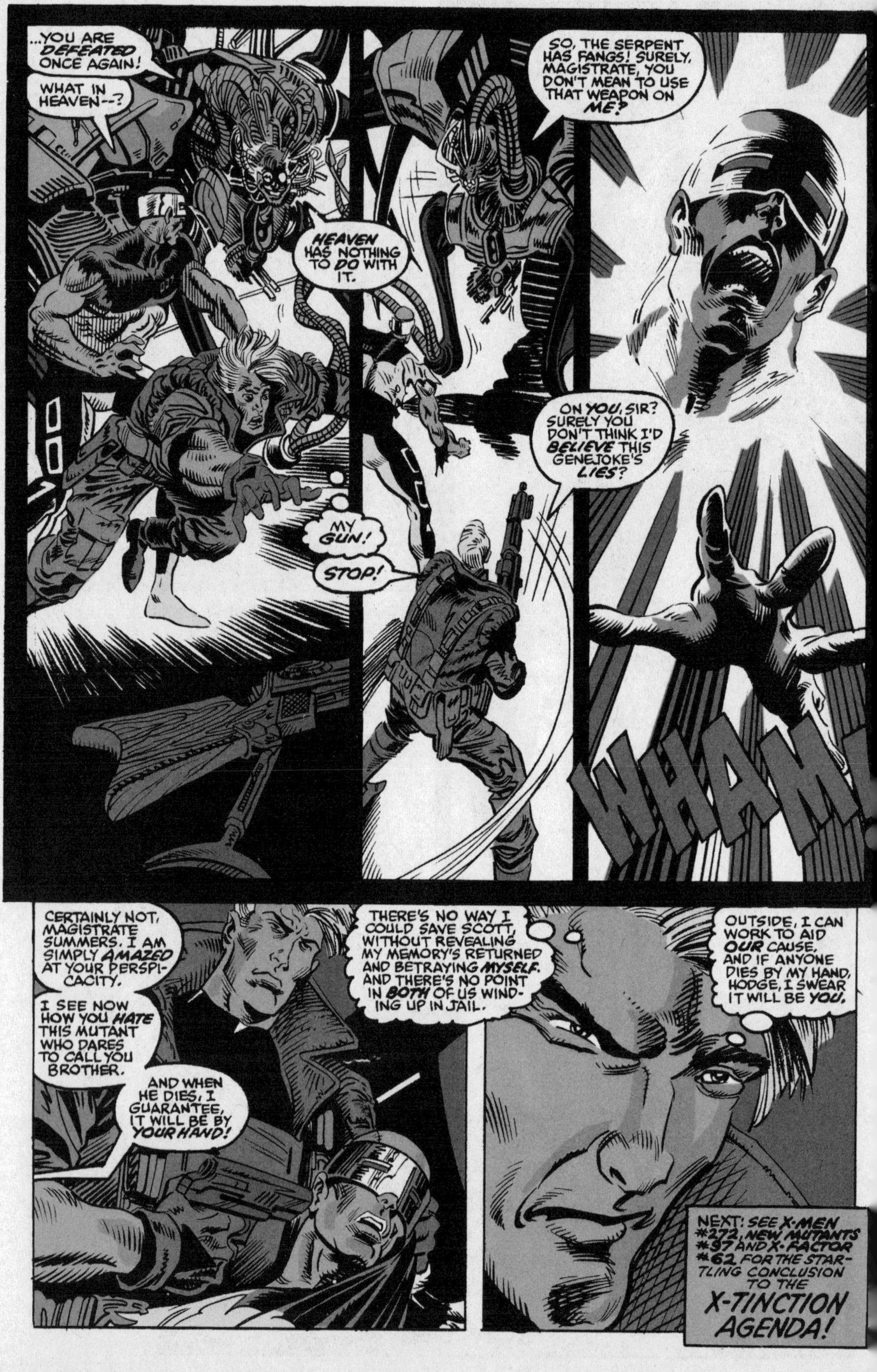

...YOU ARE DEFEATED ONCE AGAIN!
WHAT IN HEAVEN--?
HEAVEN HAS NOTHING TO DO WITH IT.
MY GUN!
STOP!
SO, THE SERPENT HAS FANGS! SURELY, MAGISTRATE, YOU DON'T MEAN TO USE THAT WEAPON ON ME?
ON YOU, SIR? SURELY YOU DON'T THINK I'D BELIEVE THIS GENEJOKE'S LIES?
WHAM
CERTAINLY NOT, MAGISTRATE SUMMERS. I AM SIMPLY AMAZED AT YOUR PERSPICACITY.
I SEE NOW HOW YOU HATE THIS MUTANT WHO DARES TO CALL YOU BROTHER.
AND WHEN HE DIES, I GUARANTEE, IT WILL BE BY YOUR HAND!
THERE'S NO WAY I COULD SAVE SCOTT, WITHOUT REVEALING MY MEMORY'S RETURNED AND BETRAYING MYSELF. AND THERE'S NO POINT IN BOTH OF US WINDING UP IN JAIL.
OUTSIDE, I CAN WORK TO AID OUR CAUSE. AND IF ANYONE DIES BY MY HAND, HODGE, I SWEAR IT WILL BE YOU.
NEXT: SEE X-MEN #272, NEW MUTANTS #97 AND X-FACTOR #62 FOR THE STARTLING CONCLUSION TO THE X-TINCTION AGENDA!

X-MEN

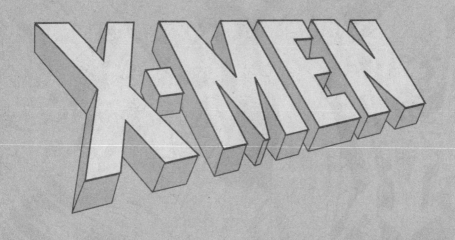

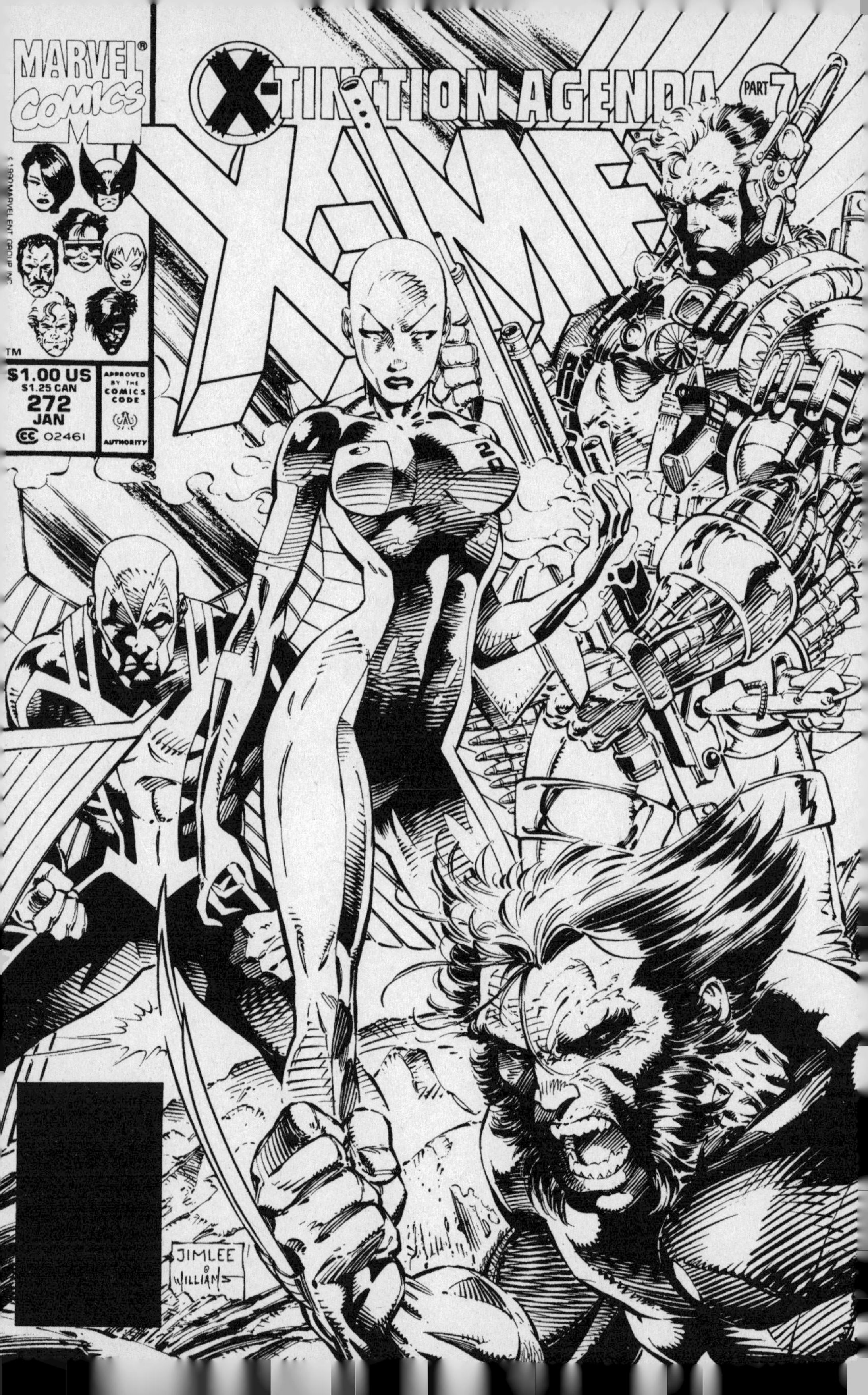
MARVEL COMICS
X-TINCTION AGENDA
PART 7
$1.00 US
$1.25 CAN
272
JAN
02461
APPROVED BY THE COMICS CODE AUTHORITY
JIMLEE
WILLIAMS

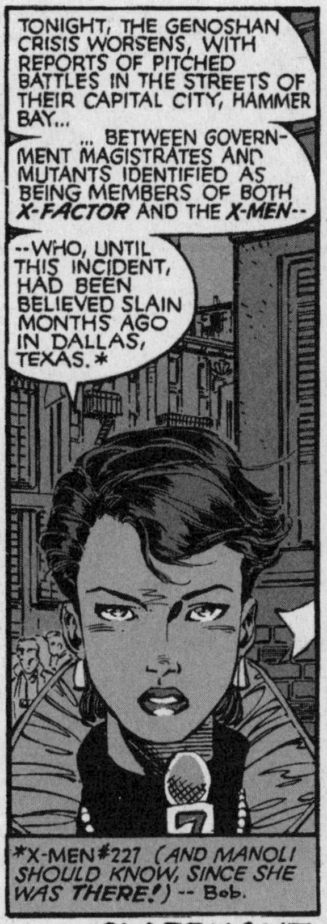
TONIGHT, THE GENOSHAN CRISIS WORSENS, WITH REPORTS OF PITCHED BATTLES IN THE STREETS OF THEIR CAPITAL CITY, HAMMER BAY...
... BETWEEN GOVERNMENT MAGISTRATES AND MUTANTS IDENTIFIED AS BEING MEMBERS OF BOTH X-FACTOR AND THE X-MEN--
--WHO, UNTIL THIS INCIDENT, HAD BEEN BELIEVED SLAIN MONTHS AGO IN DALLAS, TEXAS.*
*X-MEN #227 (AND MANOLI SHOULD KNOW, SINCE SHE WAS THERE!) -- Bob.

CHRIS CLAREMONT
WRITER

JIM LEE
PENCILER

SCOTT WILLIAMS
INKER

JOE ROSAS
GLYNIS OLIVER
COLORISTS

TOM ORZECHOWSKI
LETTERER

BOB HARRAS
EDITOR

TOM DeFALCO
EDITOR IN CHIEF

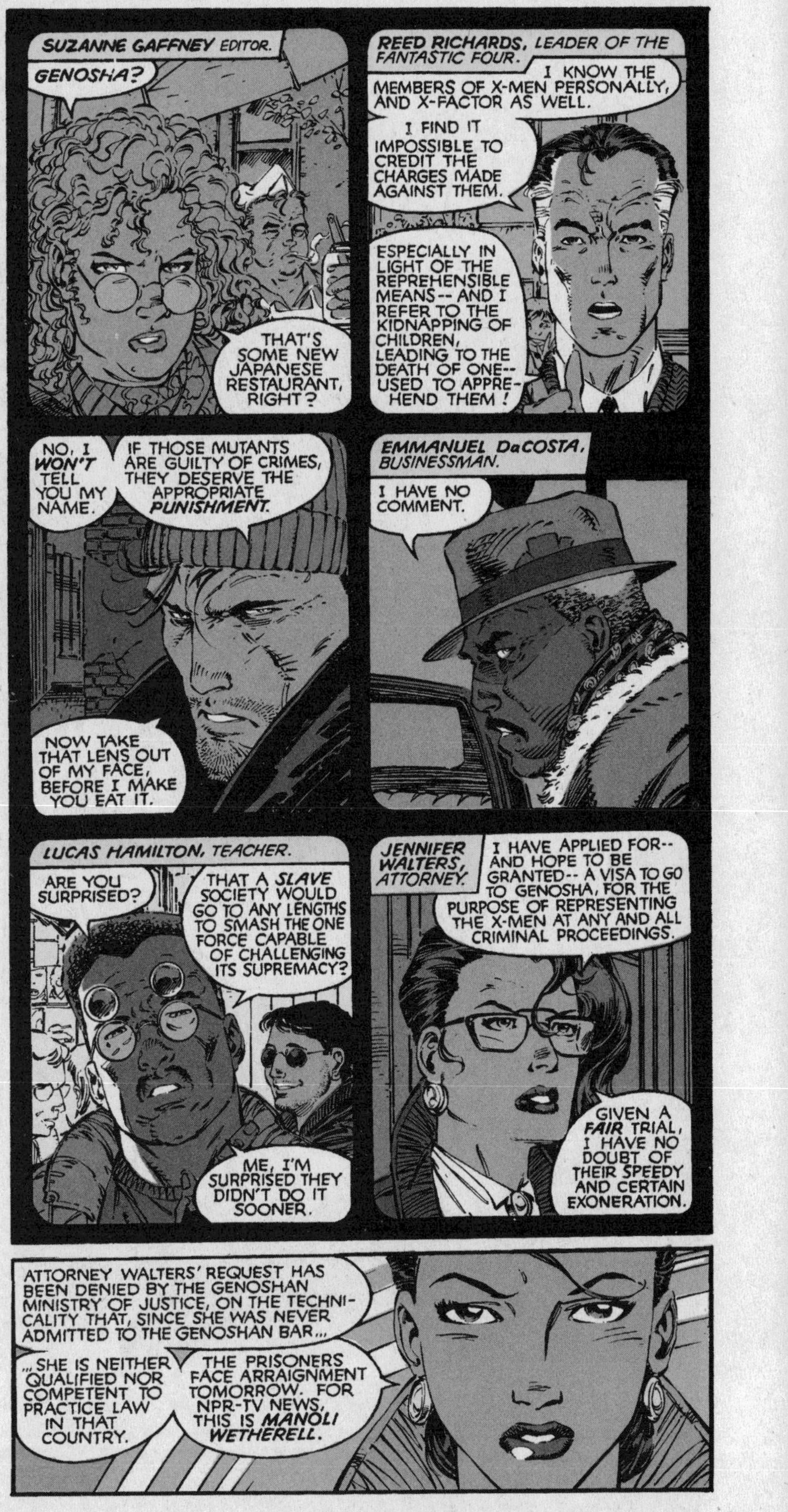
SUZANNE GAFFNEY EDITOR.
GENOSHA?
THAT'S SOME NEW JAPANESE RESTAURANT, RIGHT?
REED RICHARDS, LEADER OF THE FANTASTIC FOUR.
I KNOW THE MEMBERS OF X-MEN PERSONALLY, AND X-FACTOR AS WELL.
I FIND IT IMPOSSIBLE TO CREDIT THE CHARGES MADE AGAINST THEM.
ESPECIALLY IN LIGHT OF THE REPREHENSIBLE MEANS -- AND I REFER TO THE KIDNAPPING OF CHILDREN, LEADING TO THE DEATH OF ONE-- USED TO APPREHEND THEM!
NO, I WON'T TELL YOU MY NAME.
IF THOSE MUTANTS ARE GUILTY OF CRIMES, THEY DESERVE THE APPROPRIATE PUNISHMENT.
NOW TAKE THAT LENS OUT OF MY FACE, BEFORE I MAKE YOU EAT IT.
EMMANUEL DaCOSTA, BUSINESSMAN.
I HAVE NO COMMENT.
LUCAS HAMILTON, TEACHER.
ARE YOU SURPRISED?
THAT A SLAVE SOCIETY WOULD GO TO ANY LENGTHS TO SMASH THE ONE FORCE CAPABLE OF CHALLENGING ITS SUPREMACY?
ME, I'M SURPRISED THEY DIDN'T DO IT SOONER.
JENNIFER WALTERS, ATTORNEY.
I HAVE APPLIED FOR-- AND HOPE TO BE GRANTED-- A VISA TO GO TO GENOSHA, FOR THE PURPOSE OF REPRESENTING THE X-MEN AT ANY AND ALL CRIMINAL PROCEEDINGS.
GIVEN A FAIR TRIAL, I HAVE NO DOUBT OF THEIR SPEEDY AND CERTAIN EXONERATION.
ATTORNEY WALTERS' REQUEST HAS BEEN DENIED BY THE GENOSHAN MINISTRY OF JUSTICE, ON THE TECHNICALITY THAT, SINCE SHE WAS NEVER ADMITTED TO THE GENOSHAN BAR...
...SHE IS NEITHER QUALIFIED NOR COMPETENT TO PRACTICE LAW IN THAT COUNTRY.
THE PRISONERS FACE ARRAIGNMENT TOMORROW. FOR NPR-TV NEWS, THIS IS MANOLI WETHERELL.

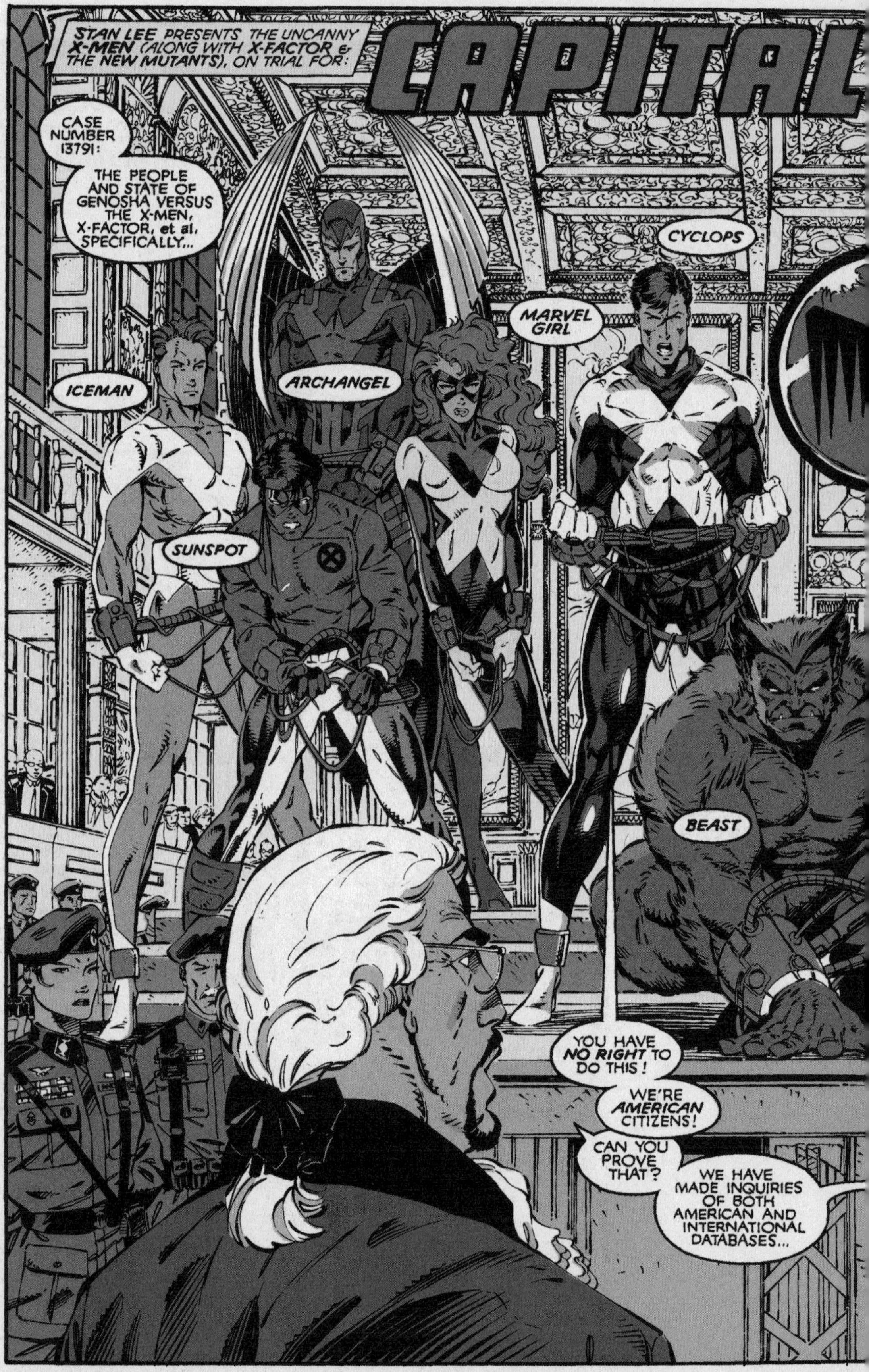
STAN LEE PRESENTS THE UNCANNY X-MEN (ALONG WITH X-FACTOR & THE NEW MUTANTS), ON TRIAL FOR:
CAPITAL
CASE NUMBER 13791:
THE PEOPLE AND STATE OF GENOSHA VERSUS THE X-MEN, X-FACTOR, et al. SPECIFICALLY...
CYCLOPS
MARVEL GIRL
ICEMAN
ARCHANGEL
SUNSPOT
BEAST
YOU HAVE NO RIGHT TO DO THIS!
WE'RE AMERICAN CITIZENS!
CAN YOU PROVE THAT?
WE HAVE MADE INQUIRIES OF BOTH AMERICAN AND INTERNATIONAL DATABASES...

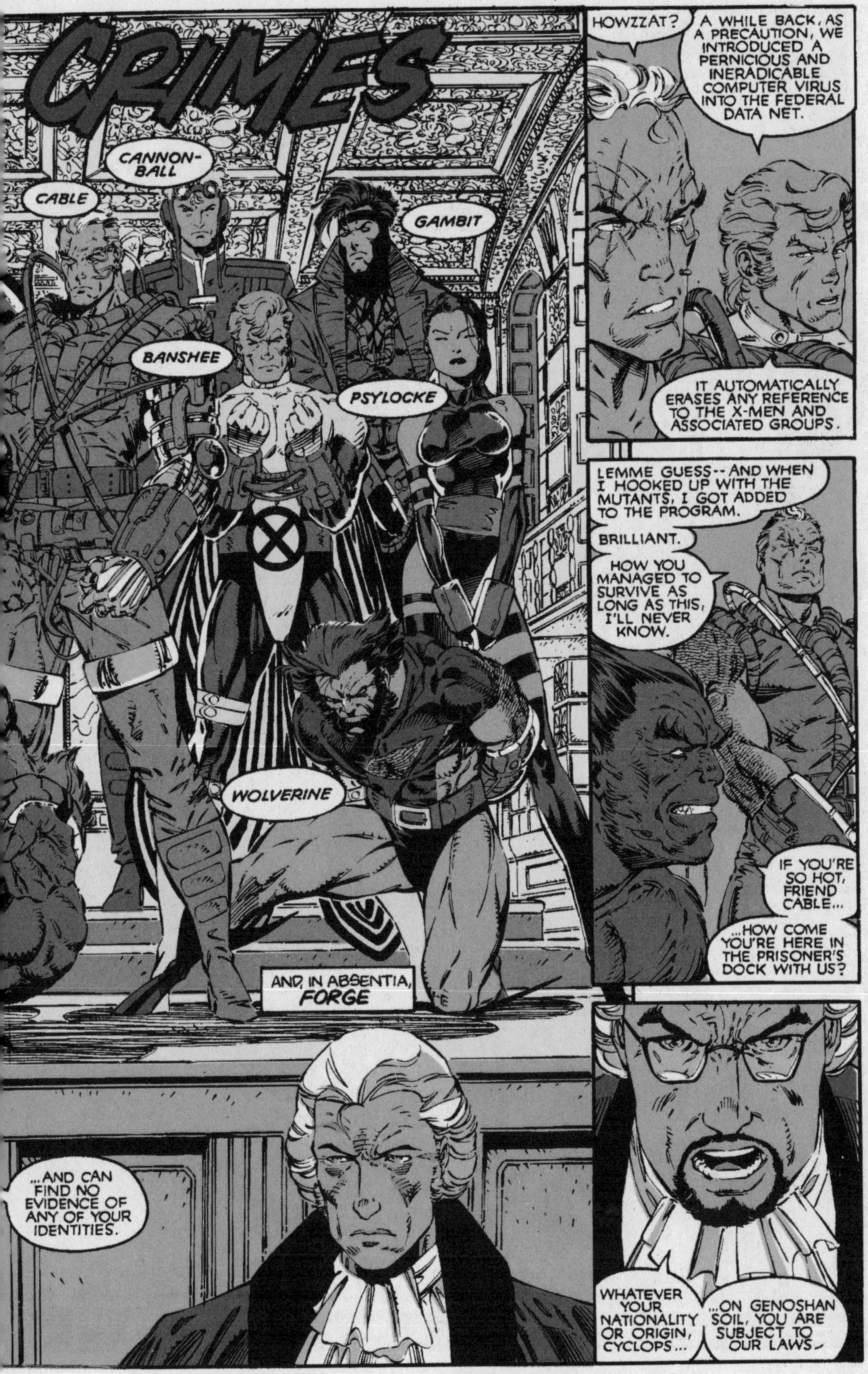
CRIMES
CANNON-BALL
CABLE
GAMBIT
BANSHEE
PSYLOCKE
WOLVERINE
AND, IN ABSENTIA, FORGE
HOWZZAT?
A WHILE BACK, AS A PRECAUTION, WE INTRODUCED A PERNICIOUS AND INERADICABLE COMPUTER VIRUS INTO THE FEDERAL DATA NET.
IT AUTOMATICALLY ERASES ANY REFERENCE TO THE X-MEN AND ASSOCIATED GROUPS.
LEMME GUESS--AND WHEN I HOOKED UP WITH THE MUTANTS, I GOT ADDED TO THE PROGRAM.
BRILLIANT.
HOW YOU MANAGED TO SURVIVE AS LONG AS THIS, I'LL NEVER KNOW.
IF YOU'RE SO HOT, FRIEND CABLE...
...HOW COME YOU'RE HERE IN THE PRISONER'S DOCK WITH US?
...AND CAN FIND NO EVIDENCE OF ANY OF YOUR IDENTITIES.
WHATEVER YOUR NATIONALITY OR ORIGIN, CYCLOPS...
...ON GENOSHAN SOIL, YOU ARE SUBJECT TO OUR LAWS--

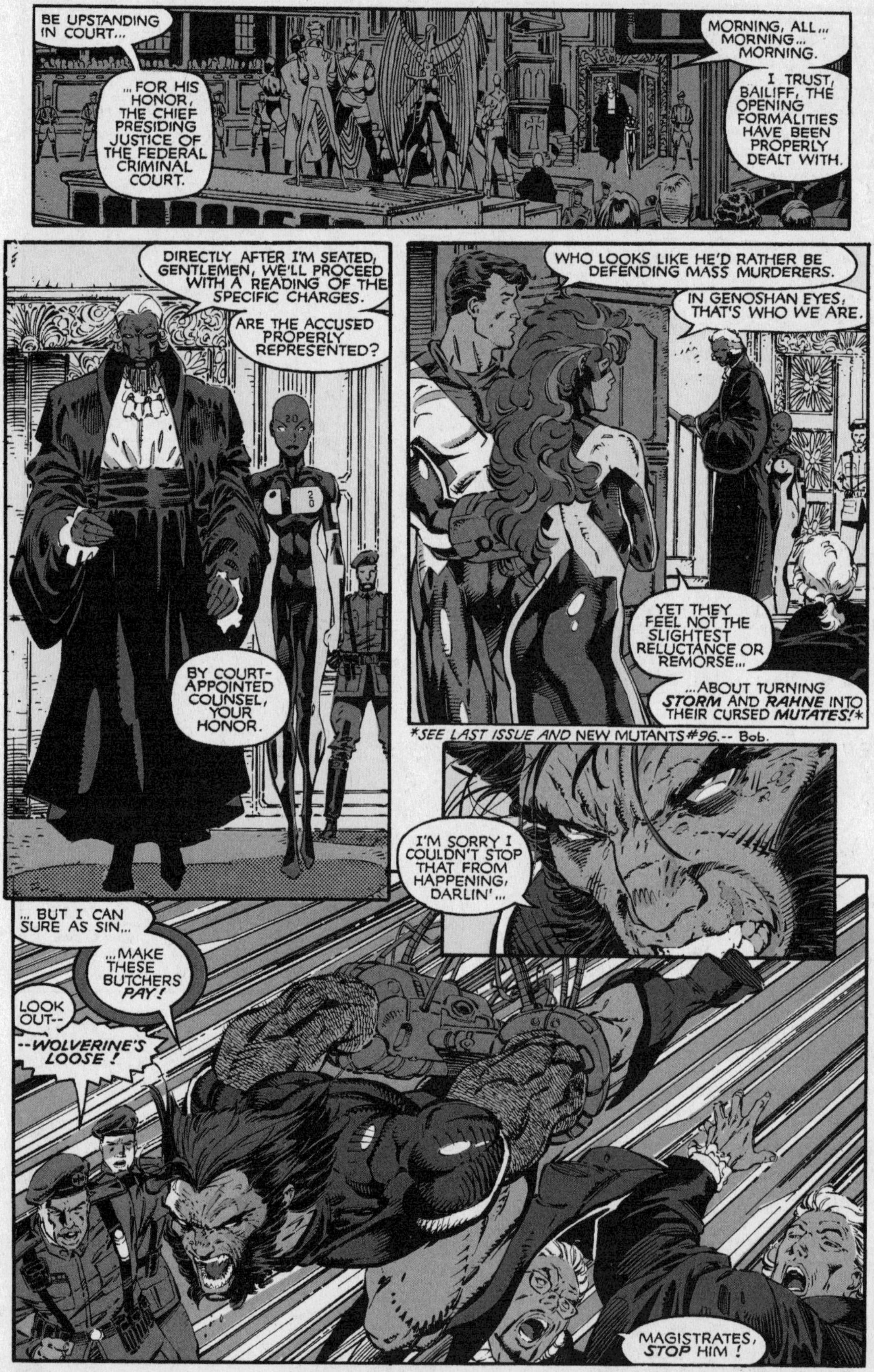
BE UPSTANDING IN COURT...
...FOR HIS HONOR, THE CHIEF PRESIDING JUSTICE OF THE FEDERAL CRIMINAL COURT.
MORNING, ALL... MORNING... MORNING.
I TRUST, BAILIFF, THE OPENING FORMALITIES HAVE BEEN PROPERLY DEALT WITH.
DIRECTLY AFTER I'M SEATED, GENTLEMEN, WE'LL PROCEED WITH A READING OF THE SPECIFIC CHARGES.
ARE THE ACCUSED PROPERLY REPRESENTED?
BY COURT-APPOINTED COUNSEL, YOUR HONOR.
WHO LOOKS LIKE HE'D RATHER BE DEFENDING MASS MURDERERS.
IN GENOSHAN EYES, THAT'S WHO WE ARE.
YET THEY FEEL NOT THE SLIGHTEST RELUCTANCE OR REMORSE...
...ABOUT TURNING STORM AND RAHNE INTO THEIR CURSED MUTATES!*
*SEE LAST ISSUE AND NEW MUTANTS #96.-- Bob.
I'M SORRY I COULDN'T STOP THAT FROM HAPPENING, DARLIN'...
... BUT I CAN SURE AS SIN...
...MAKE THESE BUTCHERS PAY!
LOOK OUT--
--WOLVERINE'S LOOSE!
MAGISTRATES, STOP HIM!

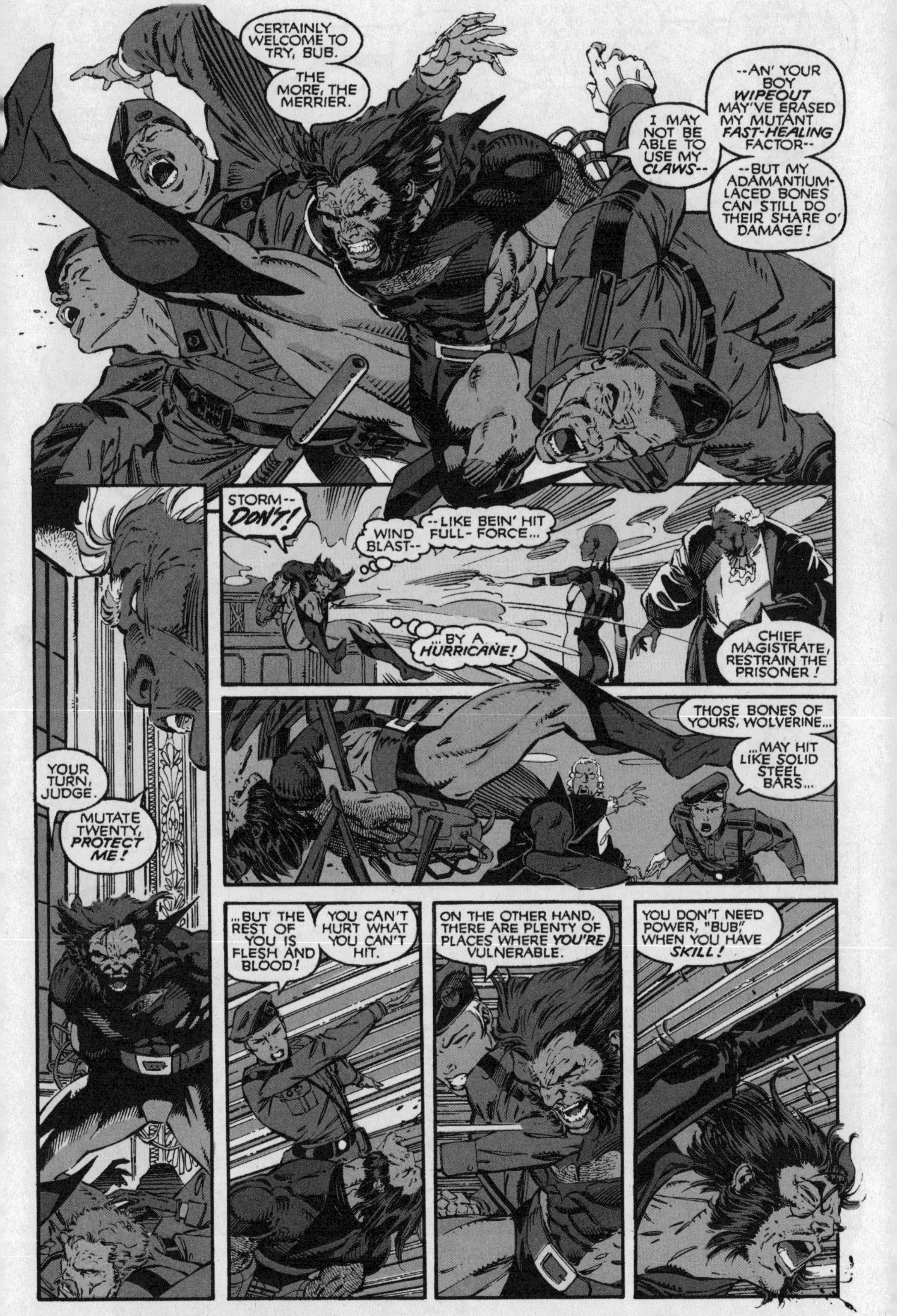

CERTAINLY WELCOME TO TRY, BUB.
THE MORE, THE MERRIER.
I MAY NOT BE ABLE TO USE MY CLAWS--
--AN' YOUR BOY WIPEOUT MAY'VE ERASED MY MUTANT FAST-HEALING FACTOR--
--BUT MY ADAMANTIUM-LACED BONES CAN STILL DO THEIR SHARE O' DAMAGE!
STORM-- DON'T!
WIND BLAST--
--LIKE BEIN' HIT FULL-FORCE...
...BY A HURRICANE!
CHIEF MAGISTRATE, RESTRAIN THE PRISONER!
YOUR TURN, JUDGE.
MUTATE TWENTY, PROTECT ME!
THOSE BONES OF YOURS, WOLVERINE...
...MAY HIT LIKE SOLID STEEL BARS...
...BUT THE REST OF YOU IS FLESH AND BLOOD!
YOU CAN'T HURT WHAT YOU CAN'T HIT.
ON THE OTHER HAND, THERE ARE PLENTY OF PLACES WHERE YOU'RE VULNERABLE.
YOU DON'T NEED POWER, "BUB," WHEN YOU HAVE SKILL!

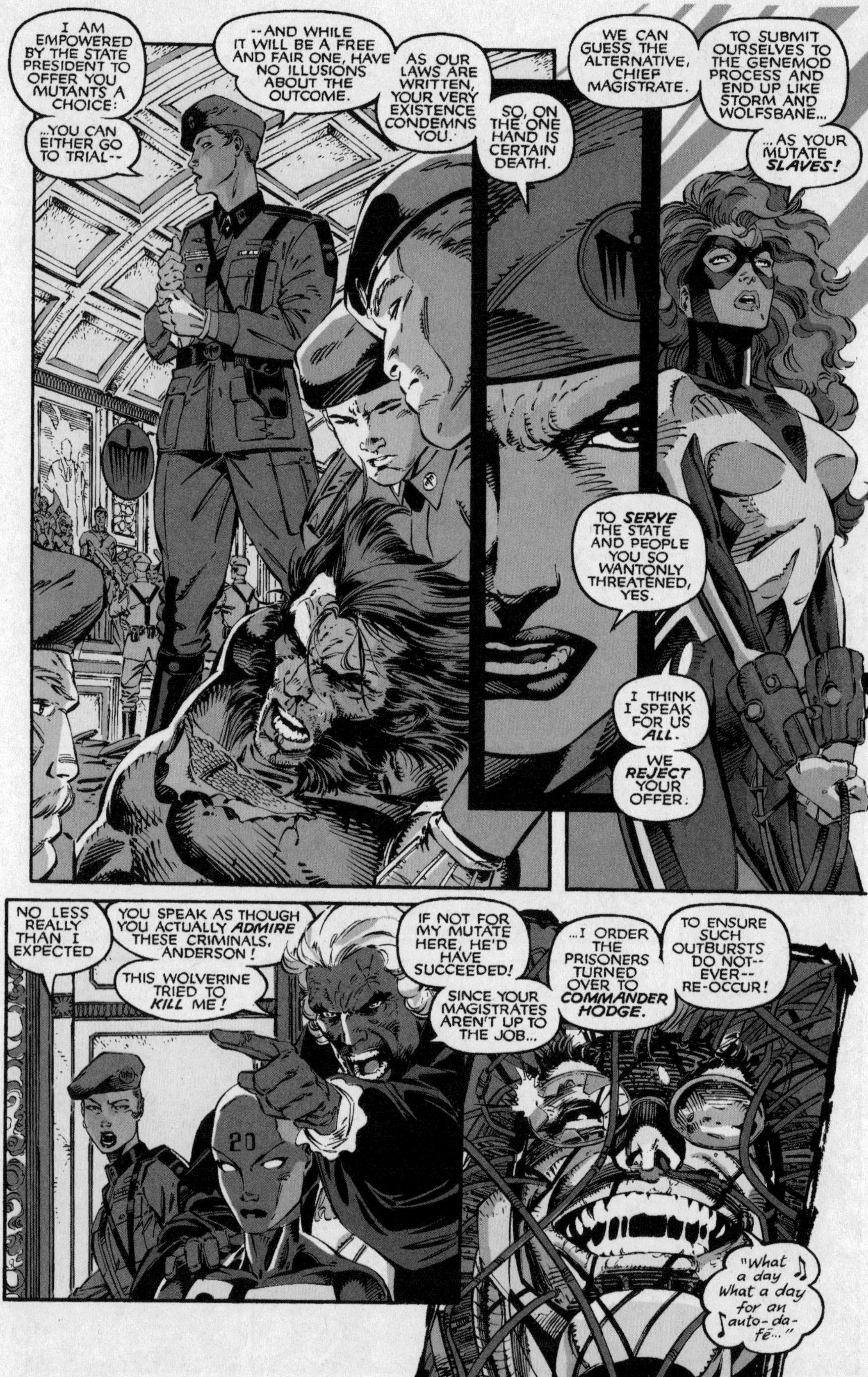
I AM EMPOWERED BY THE STATE PRESIDENT TO OFFER YOU MUTANTS A CHOICE:
..YOU CAN EITHER GO TO TRIAL--
--AND WHILE IT WILL BE A FREE AND FAIR ONE, HAVE NO ILLUSIONS ABOUT THE OUTCOME.
AS OUR LAWS ARE WRITTEN, YOUR VERY EXISTENCE CONDEMNS YOU.
SO, ON THE ONE HAND IS CERTAIN DEATH.
WE CAN GUESS THE ALTERNATIVE, CHIEF MAGISTRATE.
TO SUBMIT OURSELVES TO THE GENEMOD PROCESS AND END UP LIKE STORM AND WOLFSBANE...
...AS YOUR MUTATE SLAVES!
TO SERVE THE STATE AND PEOPLE YOU SO WANTONLY THREATENED, YES.
I THINK I SPEAK FOR US ALL.
WE REJECT YOUR OFFER.
NO LESS REALLY THAN I EXPECTED
YOU SPEAK AS THOUGH YOU ACTUALLY ADMIRE THESE CRIMINALS, ANDERSON!
THIS WOLVERINE TRIED TO KILL ME!
IF NOT FOR MY MUTATE HERE, HE'D HAVE SUCCEEDED!
SINCE YOUR MAGISTRATES AREN'T UP TO THE JOB...
...I ORDER THE PRISONERS TURNED OVER TO COMMANDER HODGE.
TO ENSURE SUCH OUTBURSTS DO NOT--EVER--RE-OCCUR!
"What a day What a day for an auto-da-fé..."
20

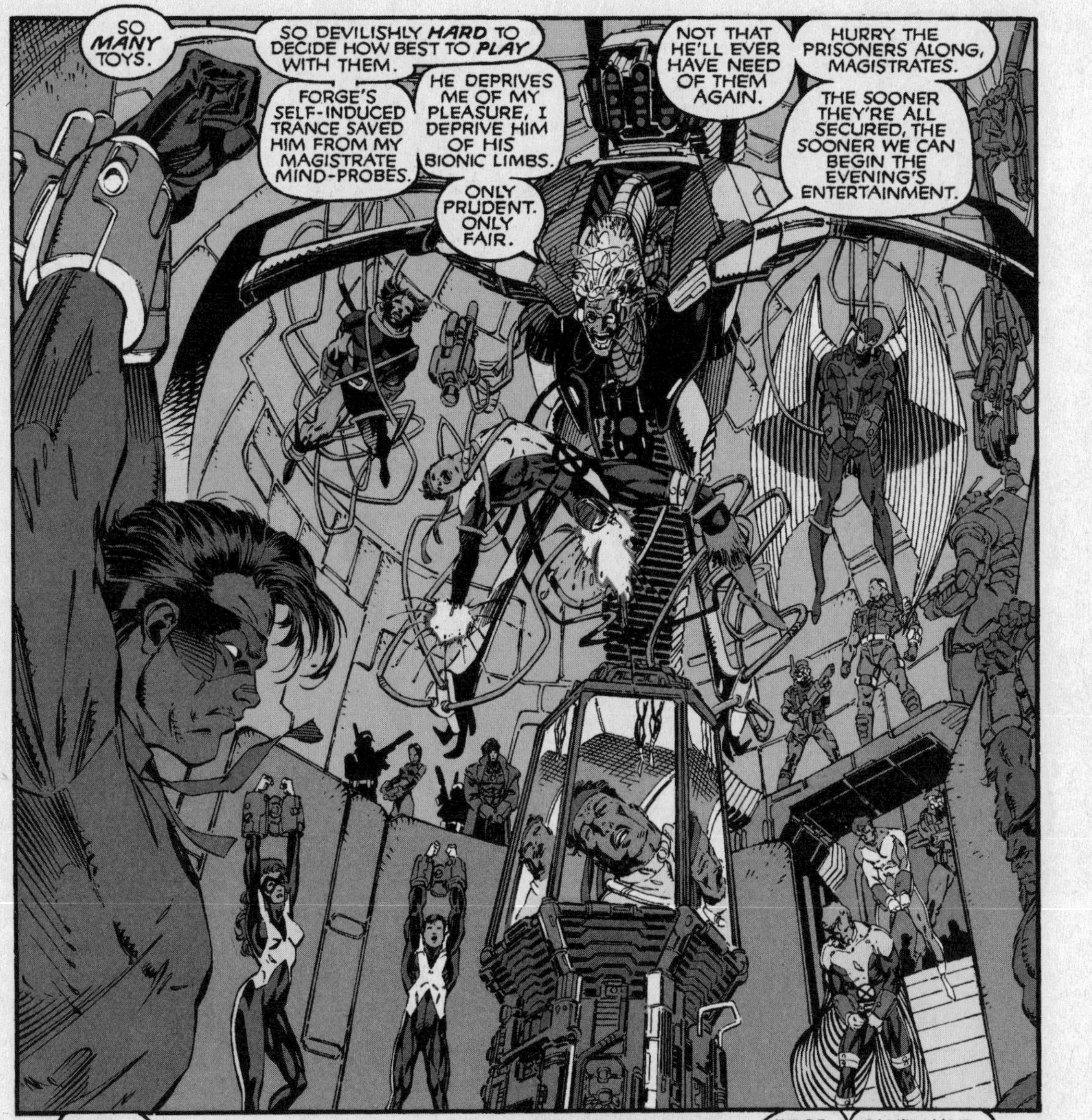
SO MANY TOYS.
SO DEVILISHLY HARD TO DECIDE HOW BEST TO PLAY WITH THEM.
FORGE'S SELF-INDUCED TRANCE SAVED HIM FROM MY MAGISTRATE MIND-PROBES.
HE DEPRIVES ME OF MY PLEASURE, I DEPRIVE HIM OF HIS BIONIC LIMBS.
ONLY PRUDENT. ONLY FAIR.
NOT THAT HE'LL EVER HAVE NEED OF THEM AGAIN.
HURRY THE PRISONERS ALONG, MAGISTRATES.
THE SOONER THEY'RE ALL SECURED, THE SOONER WE CAN BEGIN THE EVENING'S ENTERTAINMENT.

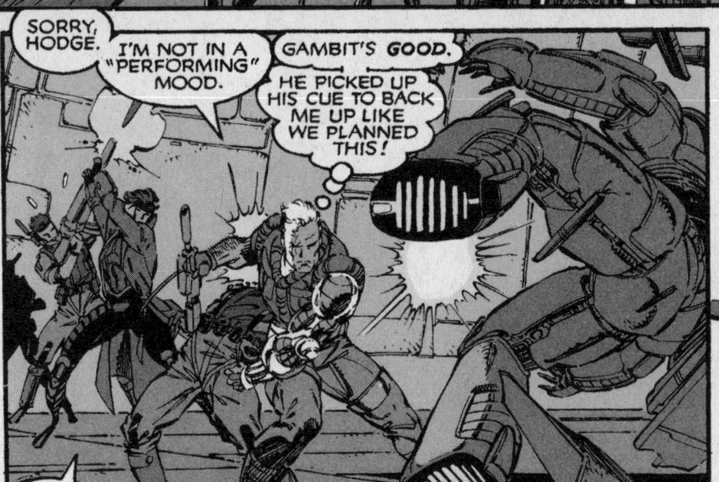
SORRY, HODGE.
I'M NOT IN A "PERFORMING" MOOD.
GAMBIT'S GOOD.
HE PICKED UP HIS CUE TO BACK ME UP LIKE WE PLANNED THIS!
YOUR PARDON, CHÈRE.

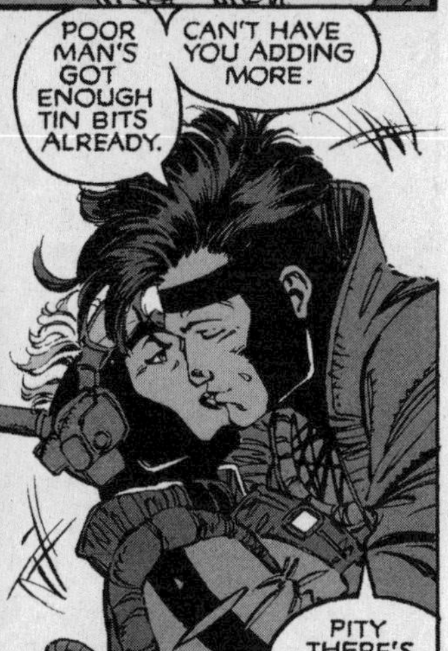
POOR MAN'S GOT ENOUGH TIN BITS ALREADY.
CAN'T HAVE YOU ADDING MORE.
PITY THERE'S NO TIME TO DO THIS PROPER.

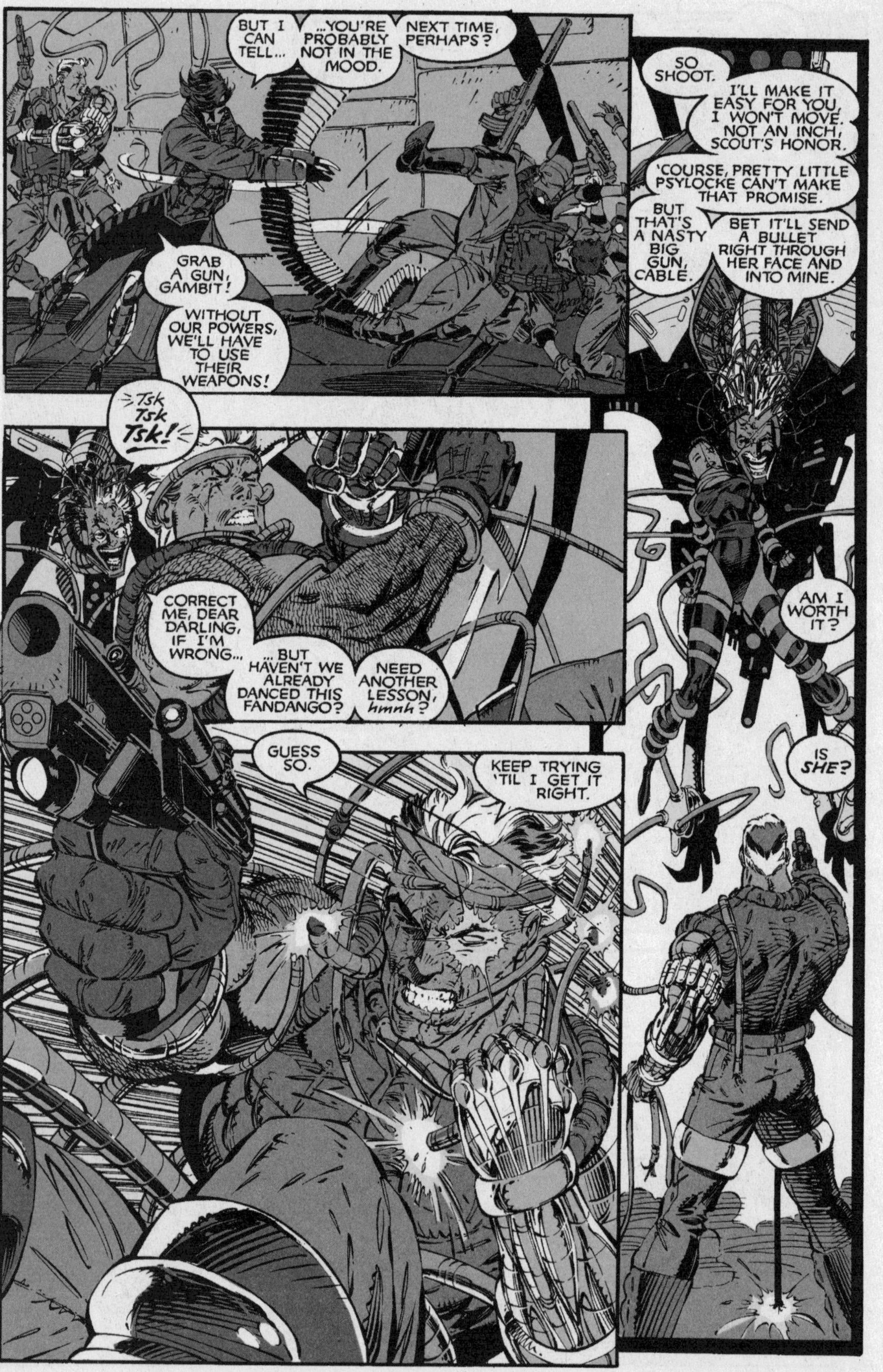
BUT I CAN TELL...
...YOU'RE PROBABLY NOT IN THE MOOD.
NEXT TIME, PERHAPS?
GRAB A GUN, GAMBIT!
WITHOUT OUR POWERS, WE'LL HAVE TO USE THEIR WEAPONS!
SO SHOOT.
I'LL MAKE IT EASY FOR YOU, I WON'T MOVE. NOT AN INCH, SCOUT'S HONOR.
'COURSE, PRETTY LITTLE PSYLOCKE CAN'T MAKE THAT PROMISE.
BUT THAT'S A NASTY BIG GUN, CABLE.
BET IT'LL SEND A BULLET RIGHT THROUGH HER FACE AND INTO MINE.
Tsk Tsk Tsk!
CORRECT ME, DEAR DARLING, IF I'M WRONG...
...BUT HAVEN'T WE ALREADY DANCED THIS FANDANGO?
NEED ANOTHER LESSON, hmnh?
AM I WORTH IT?
IS SHE?
GUESS SO.
KEEP TRYING 'TIL I GET IT RIGHT.

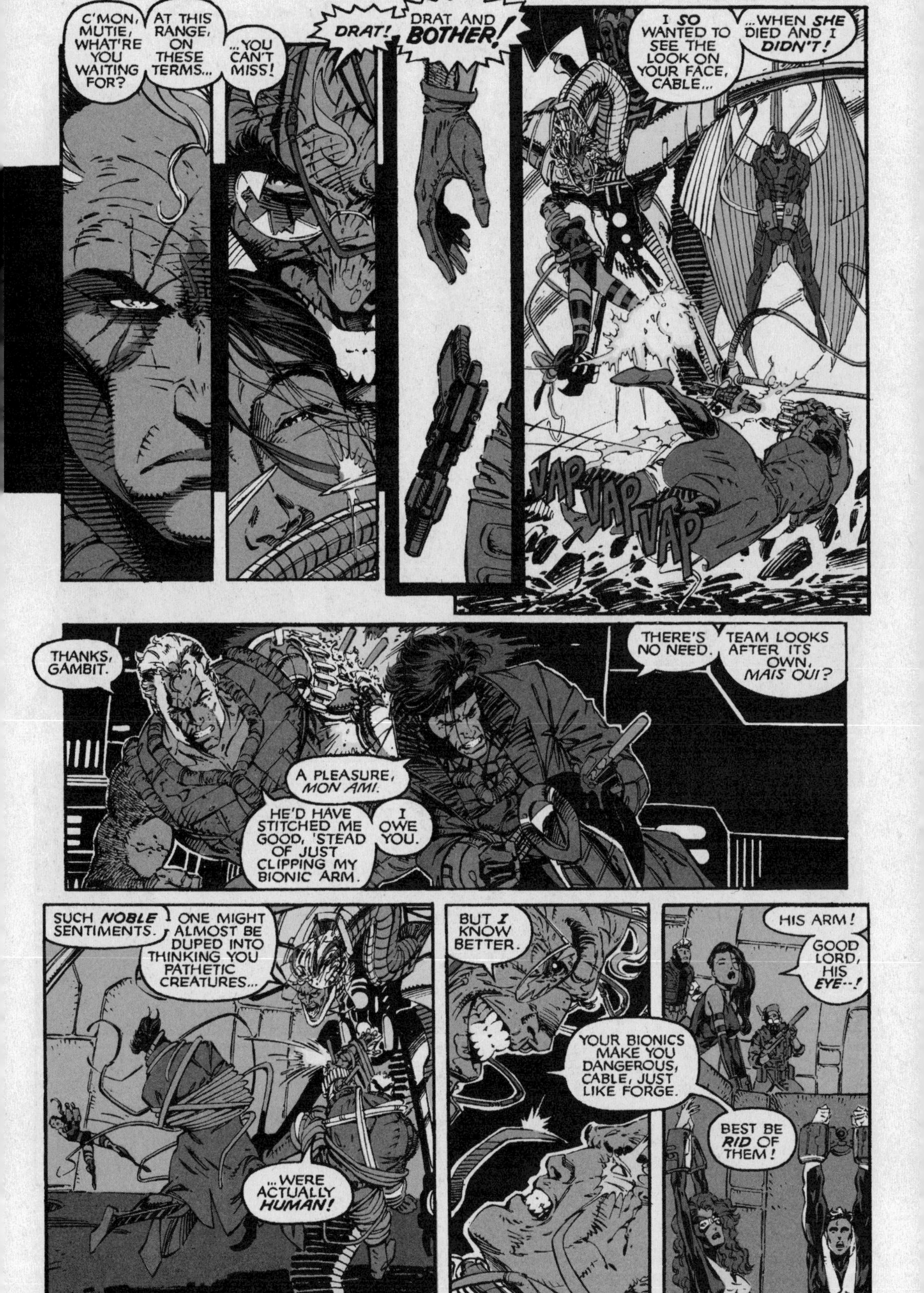
C'MON, MUTIE, WHAT'RE YOU WAITING FOR?
AT THIS RANGE, ON THESE TERMS...
...YOU CAN'T MISS!
DRAT!
DRAT AND BOTHER!
I SO WANTED TO SEE THE LOOK ON YOUR FACE, CABLE...
...WHEN SHE DIED AND I DIDN'T!
VAP VAP VAP
THANKS, GAMBIT.
THERE'S NO NEED.
TEAM LOOKS AFTER ITS OWN, MAIS OUI?
A PLEASURE, MON AMI.
HE'D HAVE STITCHED ME GOOD, 'STEAD OF JUST CLIPPING MY BIONIC ARM.
I OWE YOU.
SUCH NOBLE SENTIMENTS.
ONE MIGHT ALMOST BE DUPED INTO THINKING YOU PATHETIC CREATURES...
...WERE ACTUALLY HUMAN!
BUT I KNOW BETTER.
YOUR BIONICS MAKE YOU DANGEROUS, CABLE, JUST LIKE FORGE.
BEST BE RID OF THEM!
HIS ARM!
GOOD LORD, HIS EYE--!

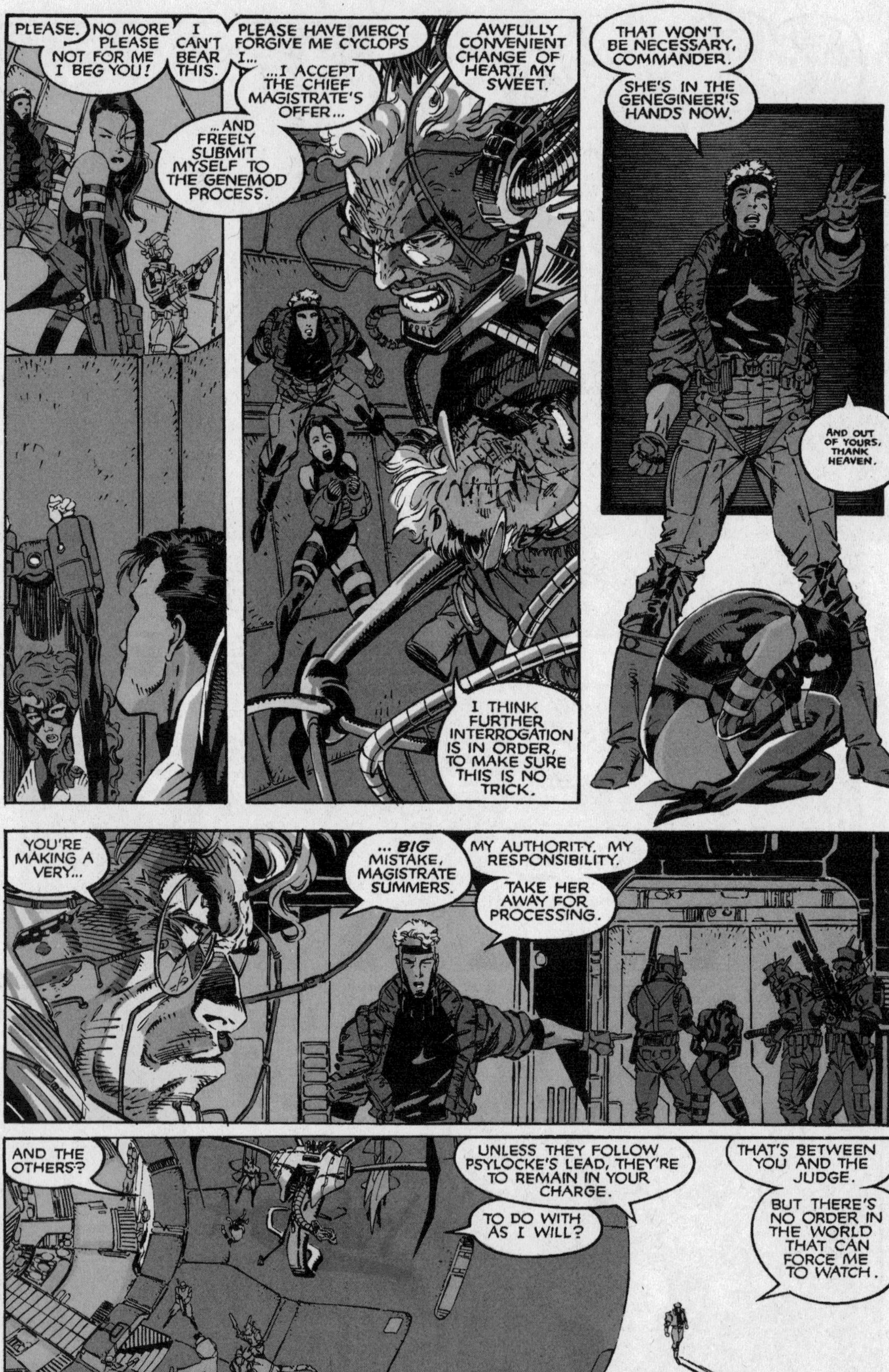
PLEASE.
NO MORE PLEASE NOT FOR ME I BEG YOU!
I CAN'T BEAR THIS.
PLEASE HAVE MERCY FORGIVE ME CYCLOPS I...
...I ACCEPT THE CHIEF MAGISTRATE'S OFFER...
...AND FREELY SUBMIT MYSELF TO THE GENEMOD PROCESS.
AWFULLY CONVENIENT CHANGE OF HEART, MY SWEET.
I THINK FURTHER INTERROGATION IS IN ORDER, TO MAKE SURE THIS IS NO TRICK.
THAT WON'T BE NECESSARY, COMMANDER.
SHE'S IN THE GENEGINEER'S HANDS NOW.
AND OUT OF YOURS, THANK HEAVEN.
YOU'RE MAKING A VERY...
... BIG MISTAKE, MAGISTRATE SUMMERS.
MY AUTHORITY. MY RESPONSIBILITY.
TAKE HER AWAY FOR PROCESSING.
AND THE OTHERS?
UNLESS THEY FOLLOW PSYLOCKE'S LEAD, THEY'RE TO REMAIN IN YOUR CHARGE.
TO DO WITH AS I WILL?
THAT'S BETWEEN YOU AND THE JUDGE.
BUT THERE'S NO ORDER IN THE WORLD THAT CAN FORCE ME TO WATCH.

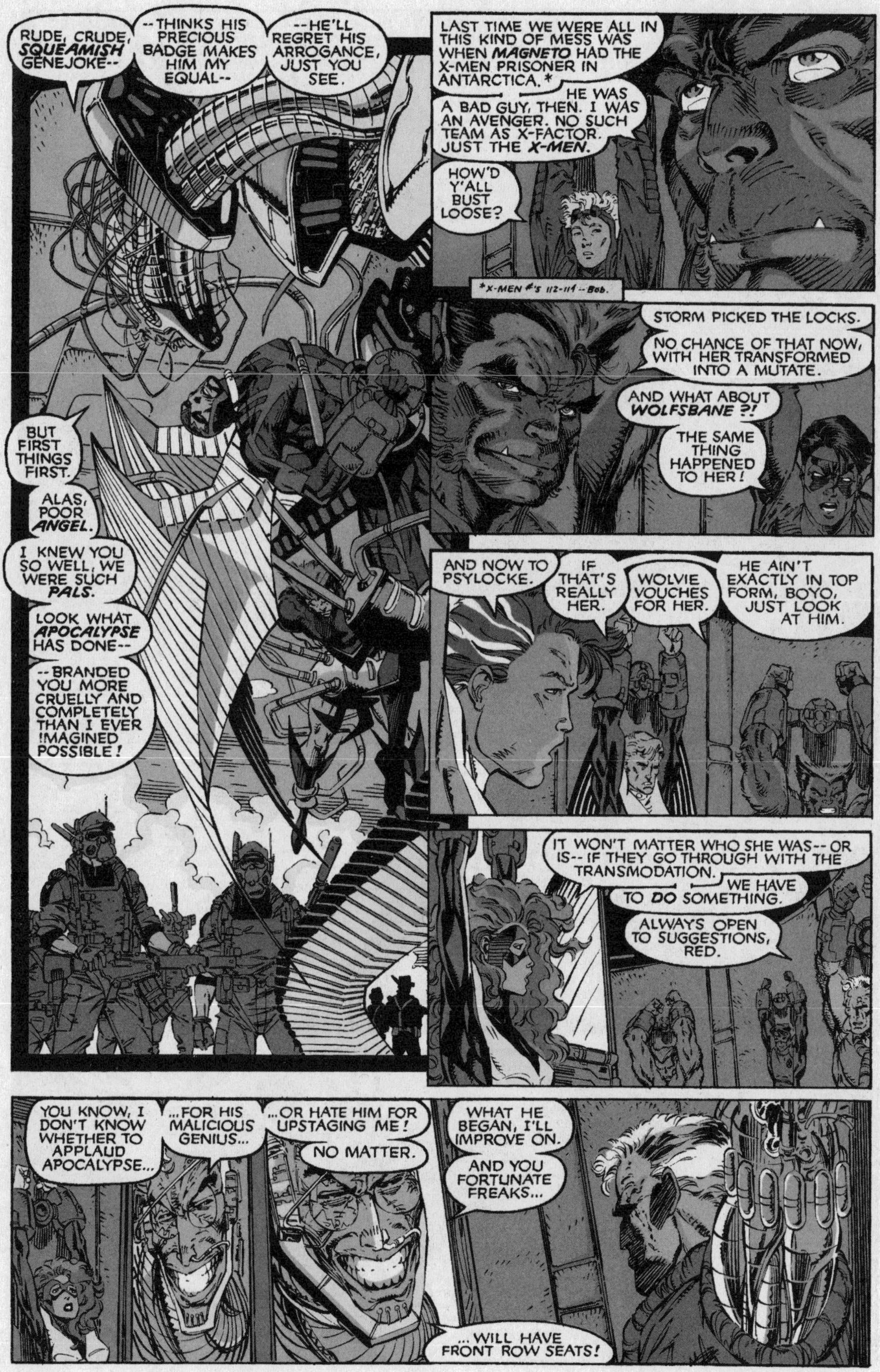
RUDE, CRUDE, SQUEAMISH GENEJOKE--
--THINKS HIS PRECIOUS BADGE MAKES HIM MY EQUAL--
--HE'LL REGRET HIS ARROGANCE, JUST YOU SEE.
BUT FIRST THINGS FIRST.
ALAS, POOR ANGEL.
I KNEW YOU SO WELL, WE WERE SUCH PALS.
LOOK WHAT APOCALYPSE HAS DONE--
--BRANDED YOU MORE CRUELLY AND COMPLETELY THAN I EVER IMAGINED POSSIBLE!
LAST TIME WE WERE ALL IN THIS KIND OF MESS WAS WHEN MAGNETO HAD THE X-MEN PRISONER IN ANTARCTICA.*
HE WAS A BAD GUY, THEN. I WAS AN AVENGER. NO SUCH TEAM AS X-FACTOR. JUST THE X-MEN.
HOW'D Y'ALL BUST LOOSE?
*X-MEN #'S 112-114 --Bob.
STORM PICKED THE LOCKS.
NO CHANCE OF THAT NOW, WITH HER TRANSFORMED INTO A MUTATE.
AND WHAT ABOUT WOLFSBANE?!
THE SAME THING HAPPENED TO HER!
AND NOW TO PSYLOCKE.
IF THAT'S REALLY HER.
WOLVIE VOUCHES FOR HER.
HE AIN'T EXACTLY IN TOP FORM, BOYO, JUST LOOK AT HIM.
IT WON'T MATTER WHO SHE WAS-- OR IS-- IF THEY GO THROUGH WITH THE TRANSMODATION.
WE HAVE TO DO SOMETHING.
ALWAYS OPEN TO SUGGESTIONS, RED.
YOU KNOW, I DON'T KNOW WHETHER TO APPLAUD APOCALYPSE...
...FOR HIS MALICIOUS GENIUS...
...OR HATE HIM FOR UPSTAGING ME!
NO MATTER.
WHAT HE BEGAN, I'LL IMPROVE ON.
AND YOU FORTUNATE FREAKS...
...WILL HAVE FRONT ROW SEATS!

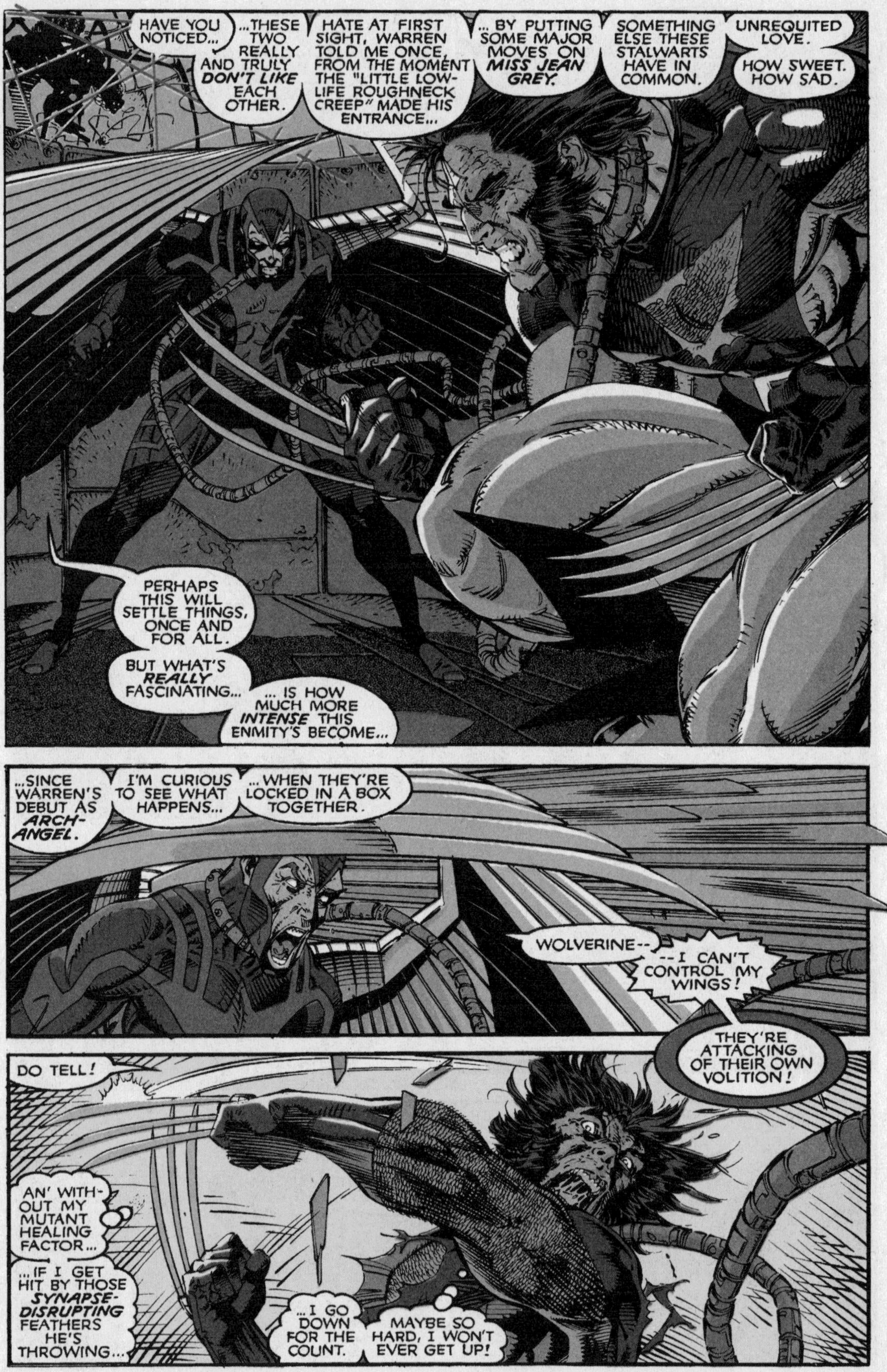
HAVE YOU NOTICED...
...THESE TWO REALLY AND TRULY DON'T LIKE EACH OTHER.
HATE AT FIRST SIGHT, WARREN TOLD ME ONCE, FROM THE MOMENT THE "LITTLE LOW-LIFE ROUGHNECK CREEP" MADE HIS ENTRANCE...
... BY PUTTING SOME MAJOR MOVES ON MISS JEAN GREY.
SOMETHING ELSE THESE STALWARTS HAVE IN COMMON.
UNREQUITED LOVE.
HOW SWEET. HOW SAD.
PERHAPS THIS WILL SETTLE THINGS, ONCE AND FOR ALL.
BUT WHAT'S REALLY FASCINATING...
... IS HOW MUCH MORE INTENSE THIS ENMITY'S BECOME...
...SINCE WARREN'S DEBUT AS ARCH-ANGEL.
I'M CURIOUS TO SEE WHAT HAPPENS...
...WHEN THEY'RE LOCKED IN A BOX TOGETHER.
WOLVERINE--
--I CAN'T CONTROL MY WINGS!
THEY'RE ATTACKING OF THEIR OWN VOLITION!
DO TELL!
AN' WITH-OUT MY MUTANT HEALING FACTOR...
...IF I GET HIT BY THOSE SYNAPSE-DISRUPTING FEATHERS HE'S THROWING...
...I GO DOWN FOR THE COUNT.
MAYBE SO HARD, I WON'T EVER GET UP!

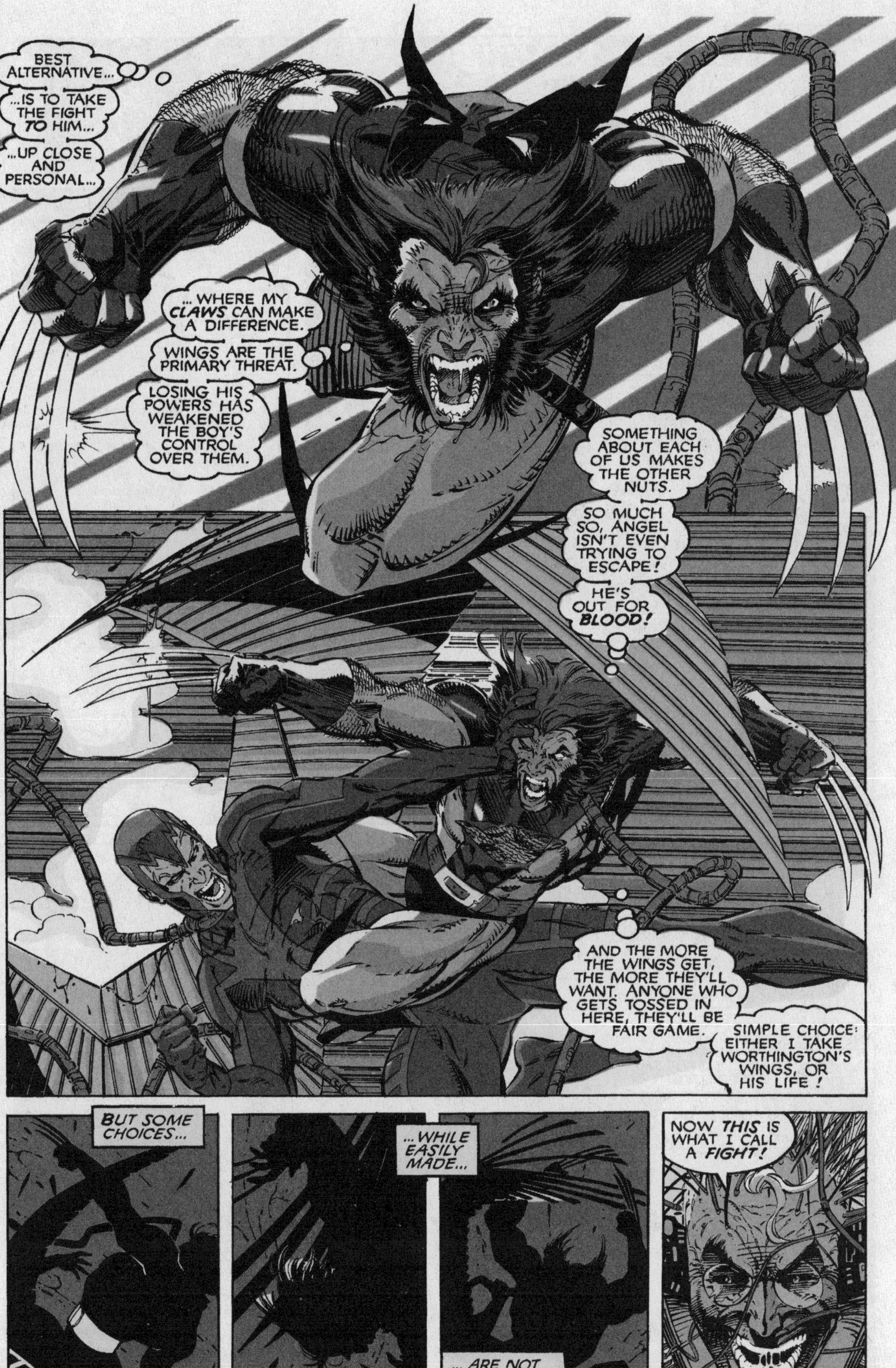
BEST ALTERNATIVE...
...IS TO TAKE THE FIGHT TO HIM...
...UP CLOSE AND PERSONAL...
... WHERE MY CLAWS CAN MAKE A DIFFERENCE.
WINGS ARE THE PRIMARY THREAT.
LOSING HIS POWERS HAS WEAKENED THE BOY'S CONTROL OVER THEM.
SOMETHING ABOUT EACH OF US MAKES THE OTHER NUTS.
SO MUCH SO, ANGEL ISN'T EVEN TRYING TO ESCAPE!
HE'S OUT FOR BLOOD!
AND THE MORE THE WINGS GET, THE MORE THEY'LL WANT. ANYONE WHO GETS TOSSED IN HERE, THEY'LL BE FAIR GAME.
SIMPLE CHOICE: EITHER I TAKE WORTHINGTON'S WINGS, OR HIS LIFE!
BUT SOME CHOICES...
...WHILE EASILY MADE...
... ARE NOT SO EASILY CARRIED OUT.
NOW THIS IS WHAT I CALL A FIGHT!

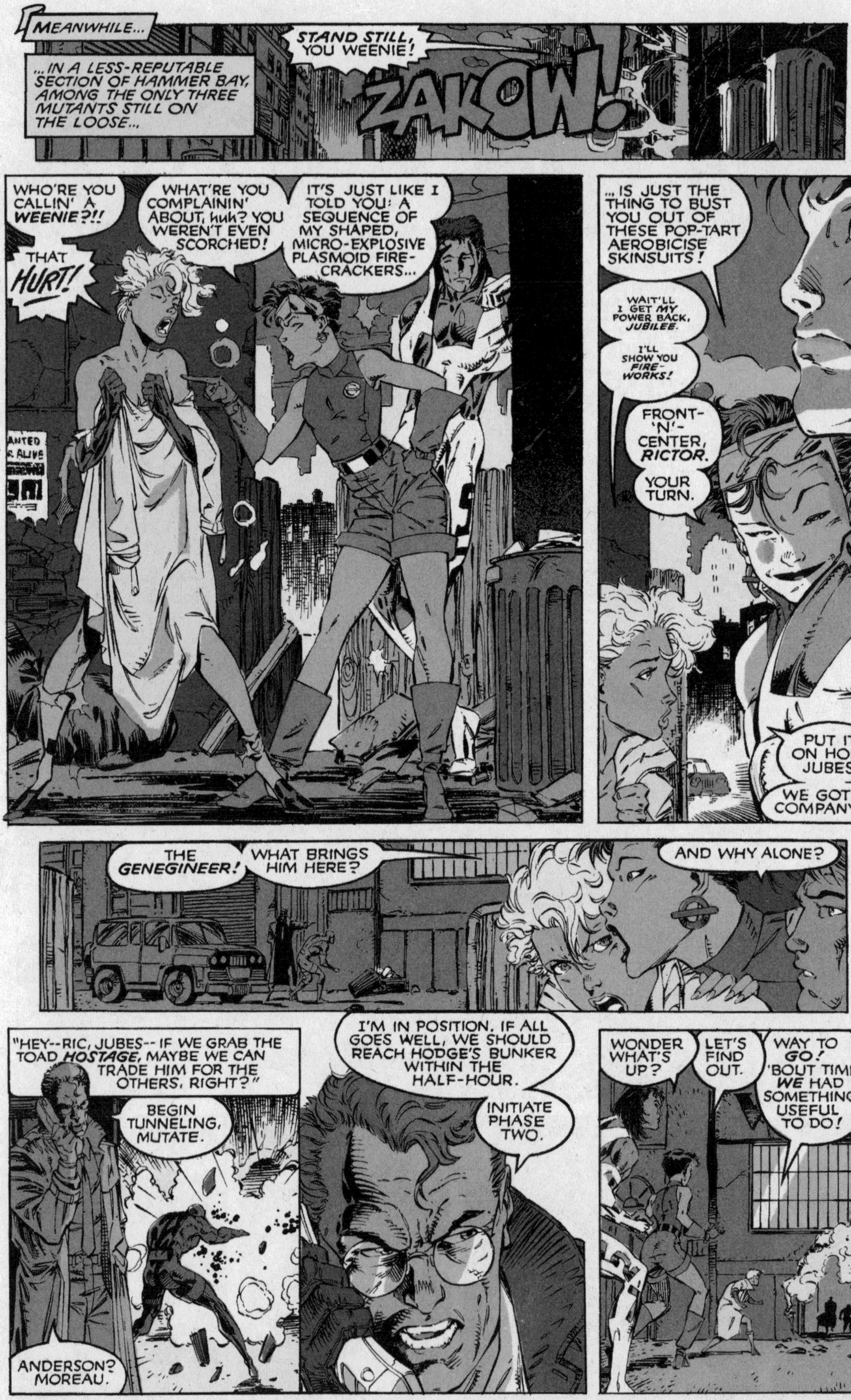
MEANWHILE...
...IN A LESS-REPUTABLE SECTION OF HAMMER BAY, AMONG THE ONLY THREE MUTANTS STILL ON THE LOOSE...
STAND STILL, YOU WEENIE!
ZAKOW!
WHO'RE YOU CALLIN' A WEENIE?!!
THAT HURT!
WHAT'RE YOU COMPLAININ' ABOUT, huh? YOU WEREN'T EVEN SCORCHED!
IT'S JUST LIKE I TOLD YOU: A SEQUENCE OF MY SHAPED, MICRO-EXPLOSIVE PLASMOID FIRE-CRACKERS...
...IS JUST THE THING TO BUST YOU OUT OF THESE POP-TART AEROBICISE SKINSUITS!
WAIT'LL I GET MY POWER BACK, JUBILEE.
I'LL SHOW YOU FIRE-WORKS!
FRONT-'N'-CENTER, RICTOR.
YOUR TURN.
PUT IT ON HOLD, JUBES!
WE GOT COMPANY!
THE GENEGINEER!
WHAT BRINGS HIM HERE?
AND WHY ALONE?
"HEY--RIC, JUBES-- IF WE GRAB THE TOAD HOSTAGE, MAYBE WE CAN TRADE HIM FOR THE OTHERS, RIGHT?"
BEGIN TUNNELING, MUTATE.
ANDERSON? MOREAU.
I'M IN POSITION. IF ALL GOES WELL, WE SHOULD REACH HODGE'S BUNKER WITHIN THE HALF-HOUR.
INITIATE PHASE TWO.
WONDER WHAT'S UP?
LET'S FIND OUT.
WAY TO GO! 'BOUT TIME WE HAD SOMETHING USEFUL TO DO!

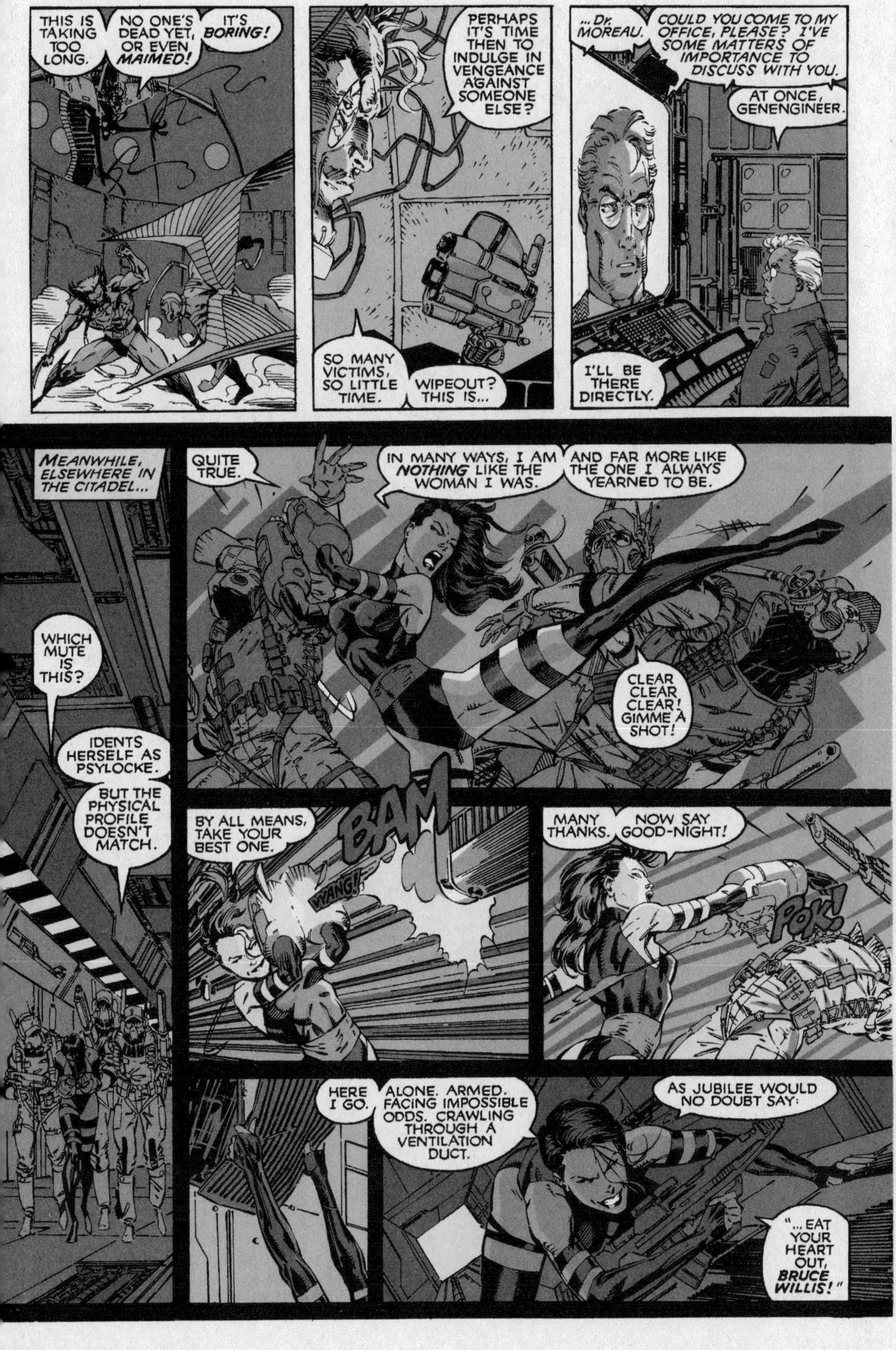

THIS IS TAKING TOO LONG.
NO ONE'S DEAD YET, OR EVEN MAIMED!
IT'S BORING!
PERHAPS IT'S TIME THEN TO INDULGE IN VENGEANCE AGAINST SOMEONE ELSE?
SO MANY VICTIMS, SO LITTLE TIME.
WIPEOUT? THIS IS...
...Dr. MOREAU.
COULD YOU COME TO MY OFFICE, PLEASE? I'VE SOME MATTERS OF IMPORTANCE TO DISCUSS WITH YOU.
AT ONCE, GENENGINEER.
I'LL BE THERE DIRECTLY.
MEANWHILE, ELSEWHERE IN THE CITADEL...
WHICH MUTE IS THIS?
IDENTS HERSELF AS PSYLOCKE.
BUT THE PHYSICAL PROFILE DOESN'T MATCH.
QUITE TRUE.
IN MANY WAYS, I AM NOTHING LIKE THE WOMAN I WAS.
AND FAR MORE LIKE THE ONE I ALWAYS YEARNED TO BE.
CLEAR CLEAR CLEAR! GIMME A SHOT!
BY ALL MEANS, TAKE YOUR BEST ONE.
BAM
WYANG!
MANY THANKS.
NOW SAY GOOD-NIGHT!
POK!
HERE I GO.
ALONE. ARMED. FACING IMPOSSIBLE ODDS. CRAWLING THROUGH A VENTILATION DUCT.
AS JUBILEE WOULD NO DOUBT SAY:
"...EAT YOUR HEART OUT, BRUCE WILLIS!"

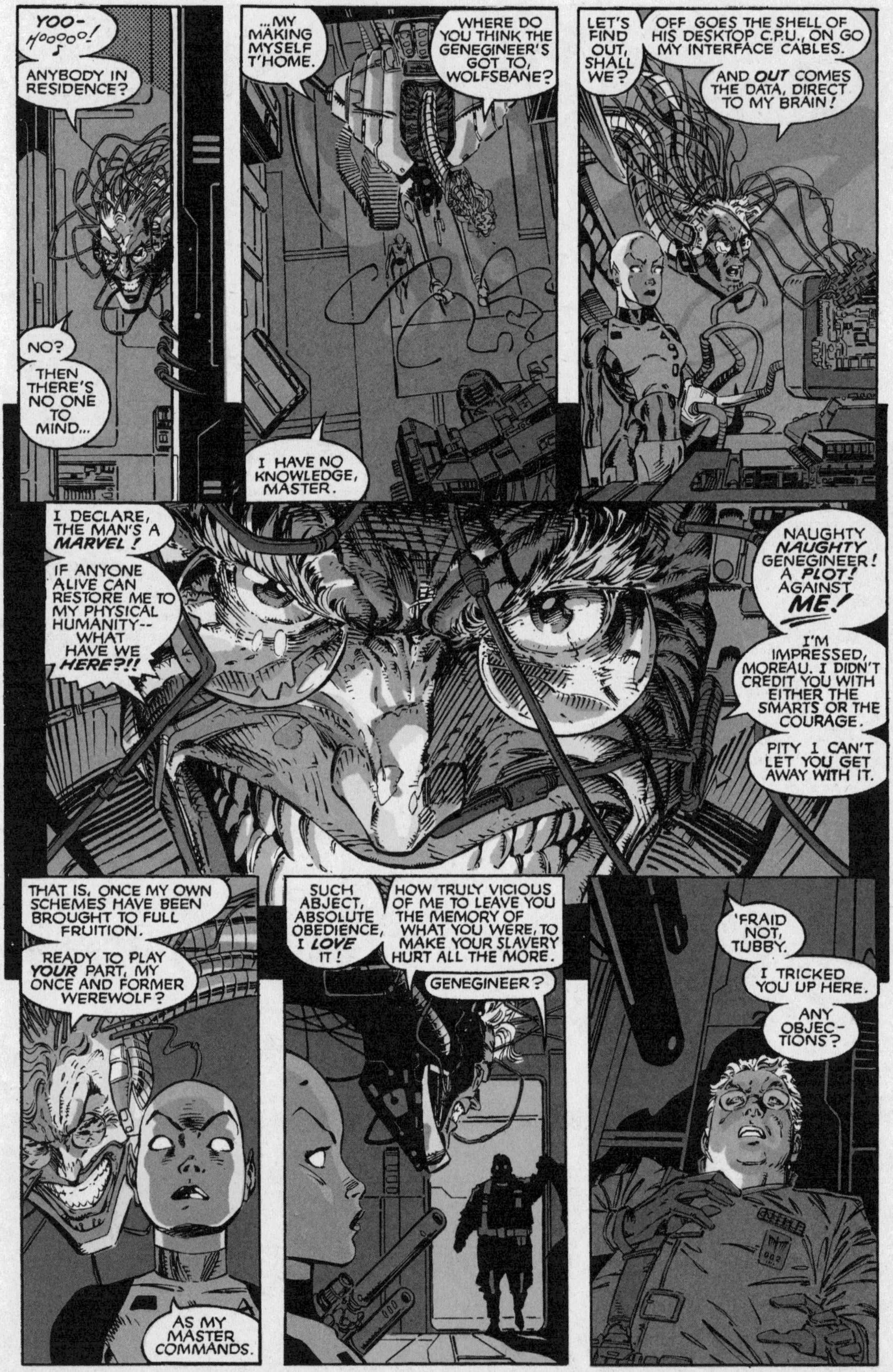
YOO-HOOOOO!
ANYBODY IN RESIDENCE?
NO?
THEN THERE'S NO ONE TO MIND...
...MY MAKING MYSELF T'HOME.
WHERE DO YOU THINK THE GENEGINEER'S GOT TO, WOLFSBANE?
I HAVE NO KNOWLEDGE, MASTER.
LET'S FIND OUT, SHALL WE?
OFF GOES THE SHELL OF HIS DESKTOP C.P.U., ON GO MY INTERFACE CABLES.
AND OUT COMES THE DATA, DIRECT TO MY BRAIN!
I DECLARE, THE MAN'S A MARVEL!
IF ANYONE ALIVE CAN RESTORE ME TO MY PHYSICAL HUMANITY--WHAT HAVE WE HERE?!!
NAUGHTY NAUGHTY GENEGINEER! A PLOT! AGAINST ME!
I'M IMPRESSED, MOREAU. I DIDN'T CREDIT YOU WITH EITHER THE SMARTS OR THE COURAGE.
PITY I CAN'T LET YOU GET AWAY WITH IT.
THAT IS, ONCE MY OWN SCHEMES HAVE BEEN BROUGHT TO FULL FRUITION.
READY TO PLAY YOUR PART, MY ONCE AND FORMER WEREWOLF?
AS MY MASTER COMMANDS.
SUCH ABJECT, ABSOLUTE OBEDIENCE, I LOVE IT!
HOW TRULY VICIOUS OF ME TO LEAVE YOU THE MEMORY OF WHAT YOU WERE, TO MAKE YOUR SLAVERY HURT ALL THE MORE.
GENEGINEER?
'FRAID NOT, TUBBY.
I TRICKED YOU UP HERE.
ANY OBJECTIONS?

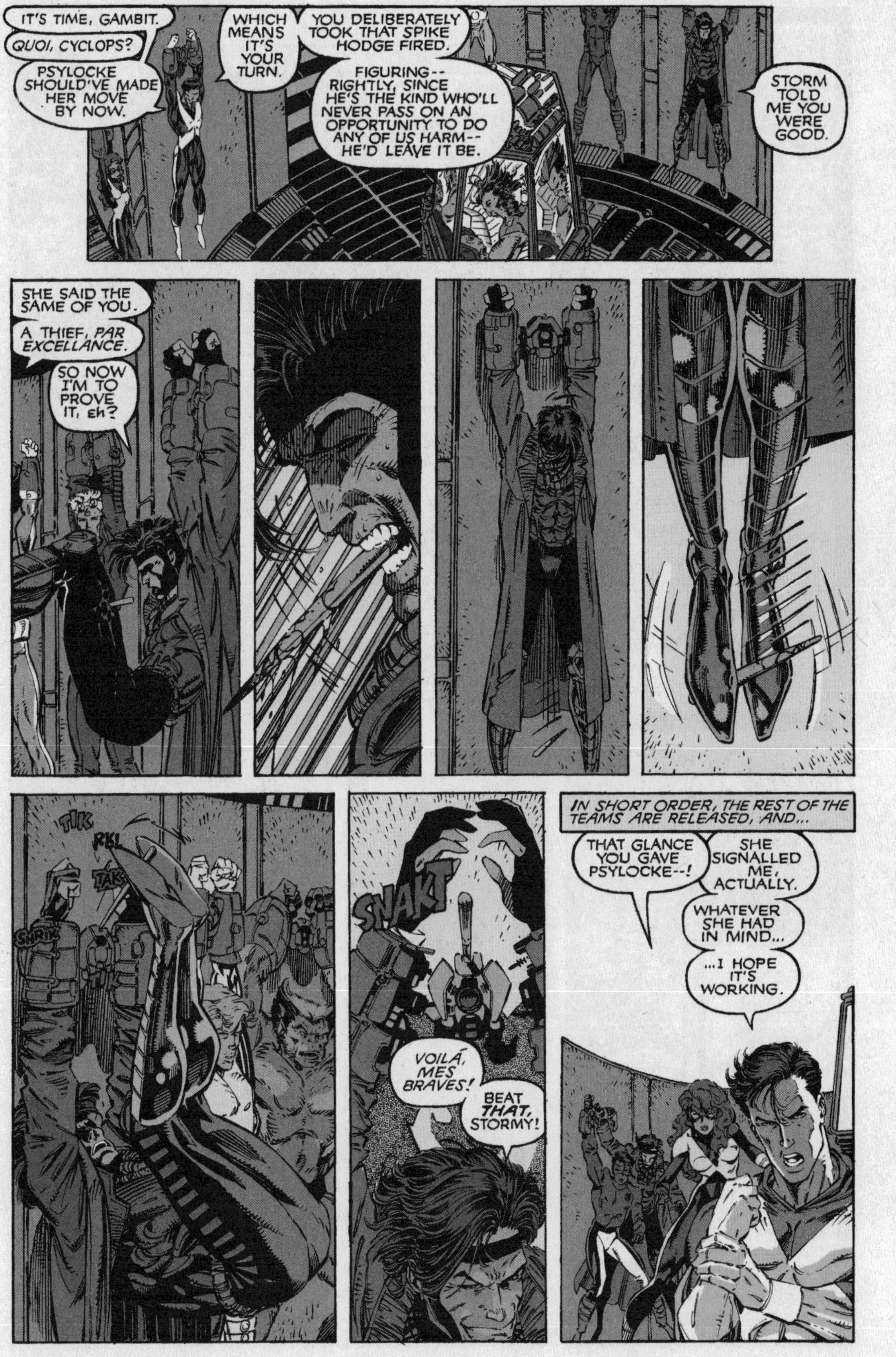

IT'S TIME, GAMBIT.
QUOI, CYCLOPS?
PSYLOCKE SHOULD'VE MADE HER MOVE BY NOW.
WHICH MEANS IT'S YOUR TURN.
YOU DELIBERATELY TOOK THAT SPIKE HODGE FIRED.
FIGURING-- RIGHTLY, SINCE HE'S THE KIND WHO'LL NEVER PASS ON AN OPPORTUNITY TO DO ANY OF US HARM-- HE'D LEAVE IT BE.
STORM TOLD ME YOU WERE GOOD.
SHE SAID THE SAME OF YOU.
A THIEF, PAR EXCELLANCE.
SO NOW I'M TO PROVE IT, eh?
TIK
RKI
TAK
SHRIK
SNAKT
VOILÁ, MES BRAVES!
BEAT THAT, STORMY!
IN SHORT ORDER, THE REST OF THE TEAMS ARE RELEASED, AND...
THAT GLANCE YOU GAVE PSYLOCKE--!
SHE SIGNALLED ME, ACTUALLY.
WHATEVER SHE HAD IN MIND...
...I HOPE IT'S WORKING.

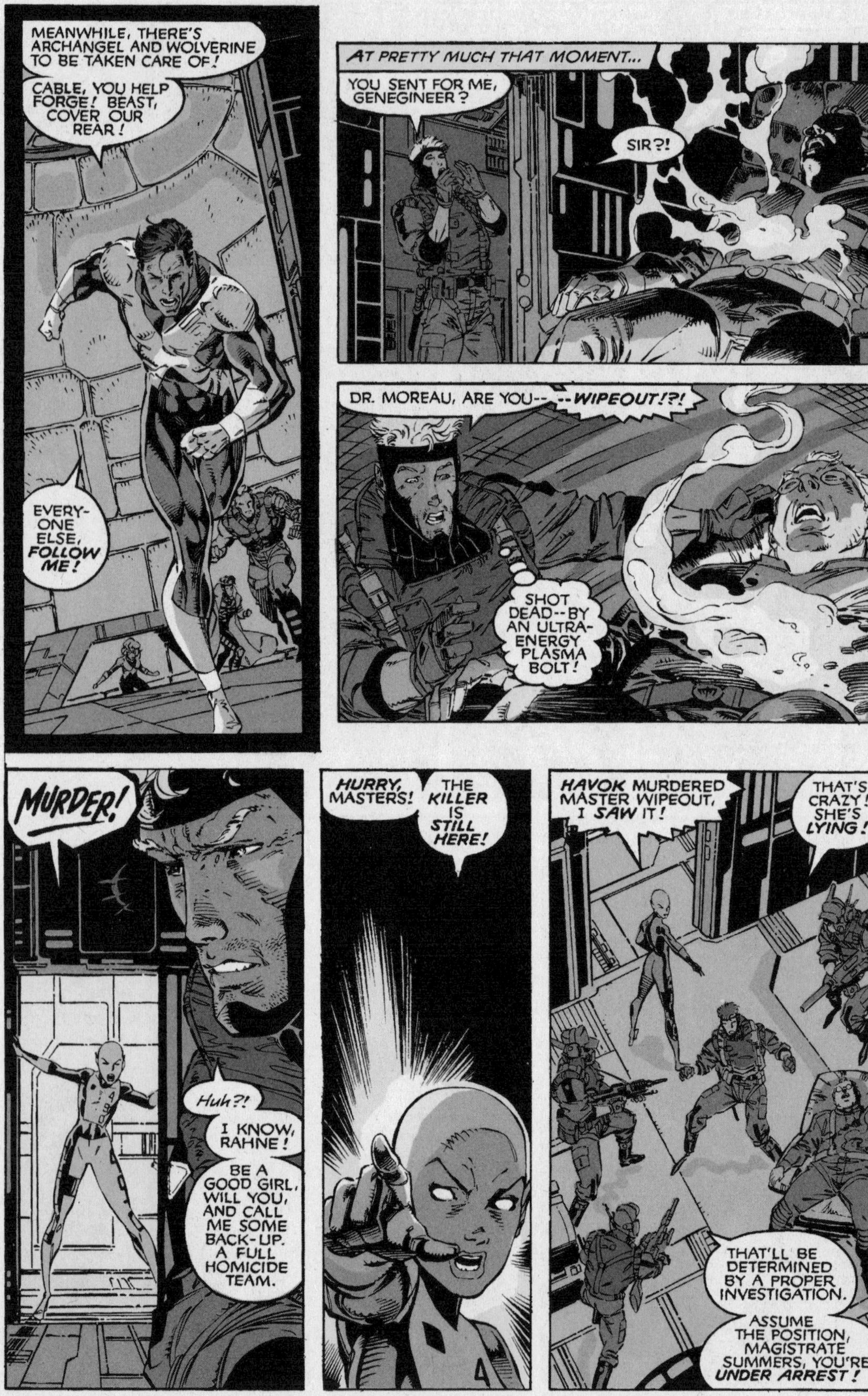
MEANWHILE, THERE'S ARCHANGEL AND WOLVERINE TO BE TAKEN CARE OF!
CABLE, YOU HELP FORGE! BEAST, COVER OUR REAR!
EVERY-ONE ELSE, FOLLOW ME!
AT PRETTY MUCH THAT MOMENT...
YOU SENT FOR ME, GENEGINEER?
SIR?!
DR. MOREAU, ARE YOU--
--WIPEOUT!?!
SHOT DEAD--BY AN ULTRA-ENERGY PLASMA BOLT!
MURDER!
Huh?!
I KNOW, RAHNE!
BE A GOOD GIRL, WILL YOU, AND CALL ME SOME BACK-UP. A FULL HOMICIDE TEAM.
HURRY, MASTERS!
THE KILLER IS STILL HERE!
HAVOK MURDERED MASTER WIPEOUT, I SAW IT!
THAT'S CRAZY! SHE'S LYING!
THAT'LL BE DETERMINED BY A PROPER INVESTIGATION.
ASSUME THE POSITION, MAGISTRATE SUMMERS, YOU'RE UNDER ARREST!

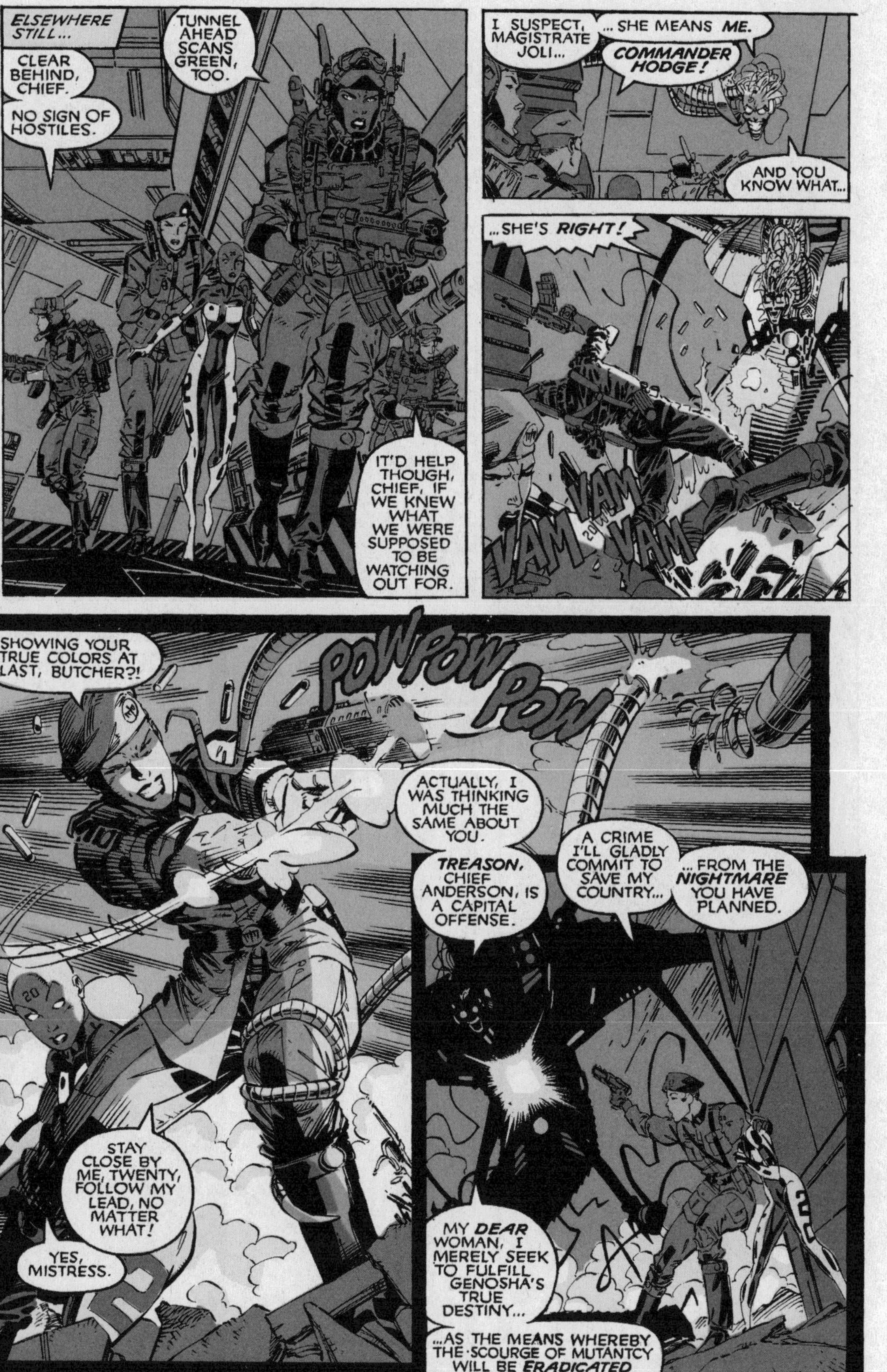
ELSEWHERE STILL...
CLEAR BEHIND, CHIEF.
NO SIGN OF HOSTILES.
TUNNEL AHEAD SCANS GREEN, TOO.
IT'D HELP THOUGH, CHIEF, IF WE KNEW WHAT WE WERE SUPPOSED TO BE WATCHING OUT FOR.
I SUSPECT, MAGISTRATE JOLI...
...SHE MEANS ME.
COMMANDER HODGE!
AND YOU KNOW WHAT...
...SHE'S RIGHT!
VAM VAM VAM VAM
SHOWING YOUR TRUE COLORS AT LAST, BUTCHER?!
POW POW POW POW
ACTUALLY, I WAS THINKING MUCH THE SAME ABOUT YOU.
TREASON, CHIEF ANDERSON, IS A CAPITAL OFFENSE.
A CRIME I'LL GLADLY COMMIT TO SAVE MY COUNTRY...
...FROM THE NIGHTMARE YOU HAVE PLANNED.
STAY CLOSE BY ME, TWENTY, FOLLOW MY LEAD, NO MATTER WHAT!
YES, MISTRESS.
MY DEAR WOMAN, I MERELY SEEK TO FULFILL GENOSHA'S TRUE DESTINY...
...AS THE MEANS WHEREBY THE SCOURGE OF MUTANTCY WILL BE ERADICATED FROM THE WORLD!

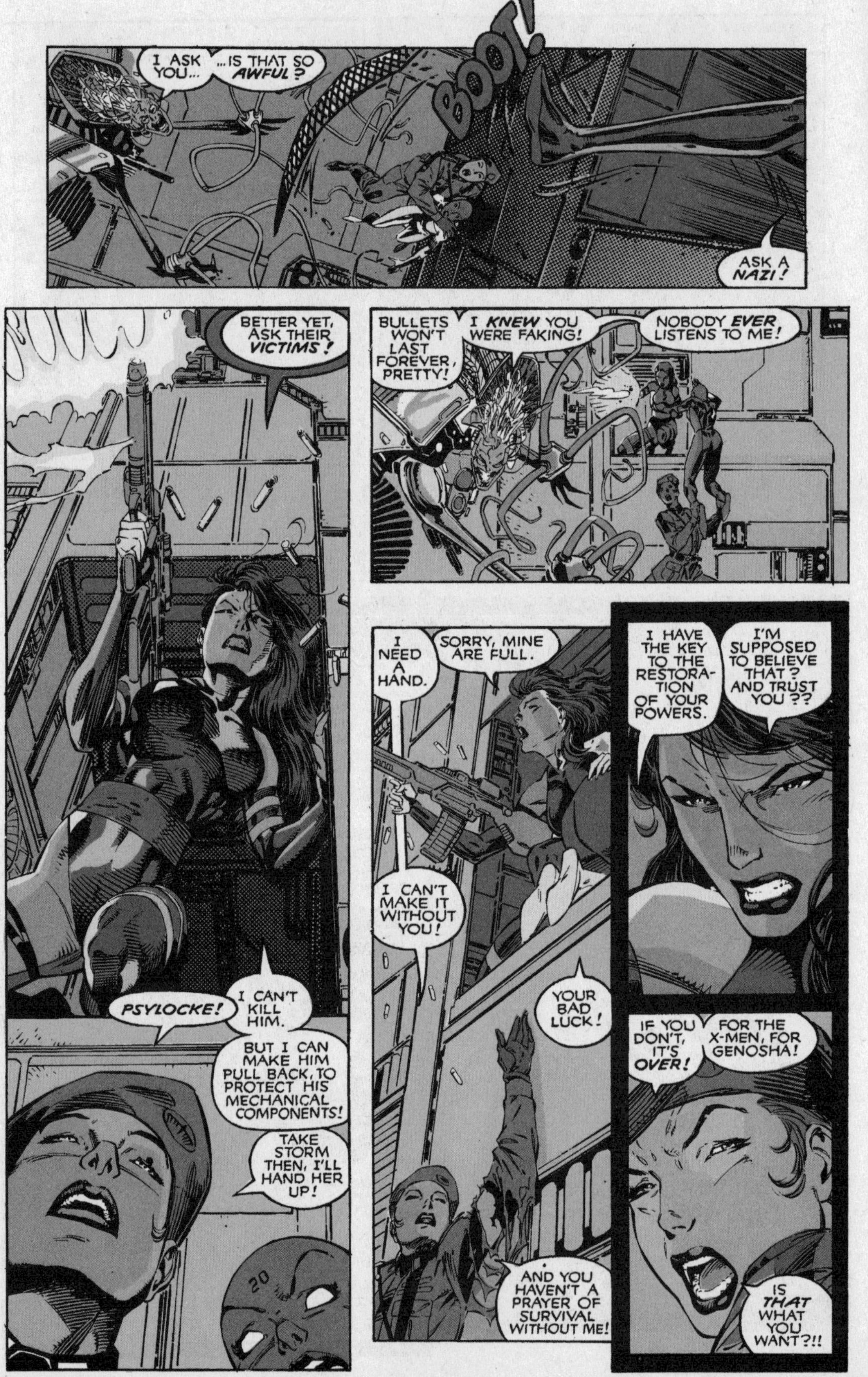
I ASK YOU...
...IS THAT SO AWFUL?
BOOT!
ASK A NAZI!
BETTER YET, ASK THEIR VICTIMS!
BULLETS WON'T LAST FOREVER, PRETTY!
I KNEW YOU WERE FAKING!
NOBODY EVER LISTENS TO ME!
PSYLOCKE!
I CAN'T KILL HIM.
BUT I CAN MAKE HIM PULL BACK, TO PROTECT HIS MECHANICAL COMPONENTS!
TAKE STORM THEN, I'LL HAND HER UP!
I NEED A HAND.
SORRY, MINE ARE FULL.
I CAN'T MAKE IT WITHOUT YOU!
YOUR BAD LUCK!
AND YOU HAVEN'T A PRAYER OF SURVIVAL WITHOUT ME!
I HAVE THE KEY TO THE RESTORATION OF YOUR POWERS.
I'M SUPPOSED TO BELIEVE THAT? AND TRUST YOU??
IF YOU DON'T, IT'S OVER!
FOR THE X-MEN, FOR GENOSHA!
IS THAT WHAT YOU WANT?!!

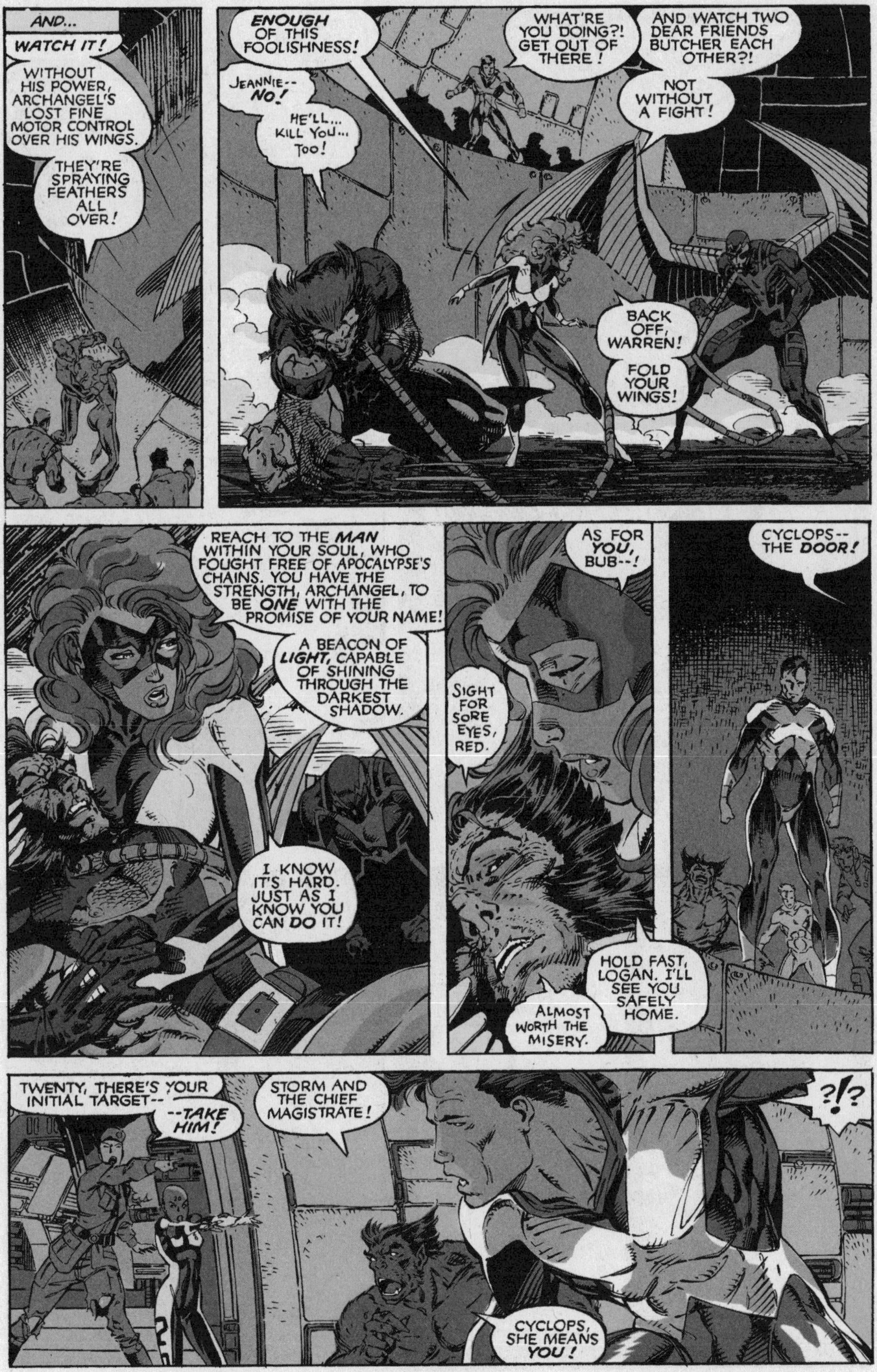
AND...
WATCH IT!
WITHOUT HIS POWER, ARCHANGEL'S LOST FINE MOTOR CONTROL OVER HIS WINGS.
THEY'RE SPRAYING FEATHERS ALL OVER!
ENOUGH OF THIS FOOLISHNESS!
JEANNIE-- NO!
HE'LL... KILL YOU... TOO!
WHAT'RE YOU DOING?! GET OUT OF THERE!
AND WATCH TWO DEAR FRIENDS BUTCHER EACH OTHER?!
NOT WITHOUT A FIGHT!
BACK OFF, WARREN!
FOLD YOUR WINGS!
REACH TO THE MAN WITHIN YOUR SOUL, WHO FOUGHT FREE OF APOCALYPSE'S CHAINS. YOU HAVE THE STRENGTH, ARCHANGEL, TO BE ONE WITH THE PROMISE OF YOUR NAME!
A BEACON OF LIGHT, CAPABLE OF SHINING THROUGH THE DARKEST SHADOW.
I KNOW IT'S HARD. JUST AS I KNOW YOU CAN DO IT!
AS FOR YOU, BUB--!
SIGHT FOR SORE EYES, RED.
HOLD FAST, LOGAN. I'LL SEE YOU SAFELY HOME.
ALMOST WORTH THE MISERY.
CYCLOPS-- THE DOOR!
TWENTY, THERE'S YOUR INITIAL TARGET--
--TAKE HIM!
STORM AND THE CHIEF MAGISTRATE!
?!?
CYCLOPS, SHE MEANS YOU!

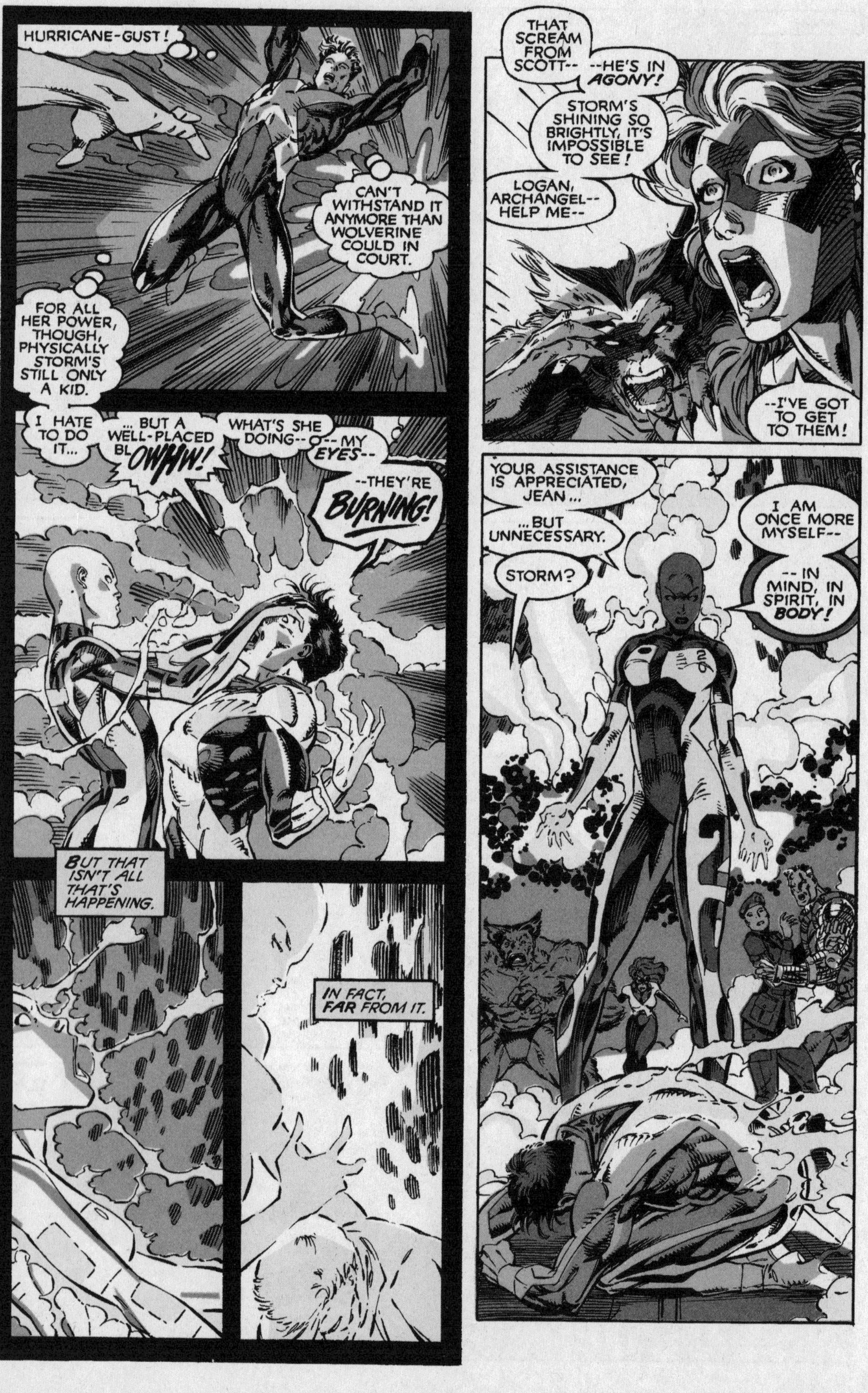
HURRICANE-GUST!
CAN'T WITHSTAND IT ANYMORE THAN WOLVERINE COULD IN COURT.
FOR ALL HER POWER, THOUGH, PHYSICALLY STORM'S STILL ONLY A KID.
I HATE TO DO IT...
... BUT A WELL-PLACED BL OWHW!
WHAT'S SHE DOING--
--MY EYES--
--THEY'RE BURNING!
BUT THAT ISN'T ALL THAT'S HAPPENING.
IN FACT, FAR FROM IT.
THAT SCREAM FROM SCOTT--
--HE'S IN AGONY!
STORM'S SHINING SO BRIGHTLY, IT'S IMPOSSIBLE TO SEE!
LOGAN, ARCHANGEL-- HELP ME--
--I'VE GOT TO GET TO THEM!
YOUR ASSISTANCE IS APPRECIATED, JEAN...
...BUT UNNECESSARY.
STORM?
I AM ONCE MORE MYSELF--
-- IN MIND, IN SPIRIT, IN BODY!

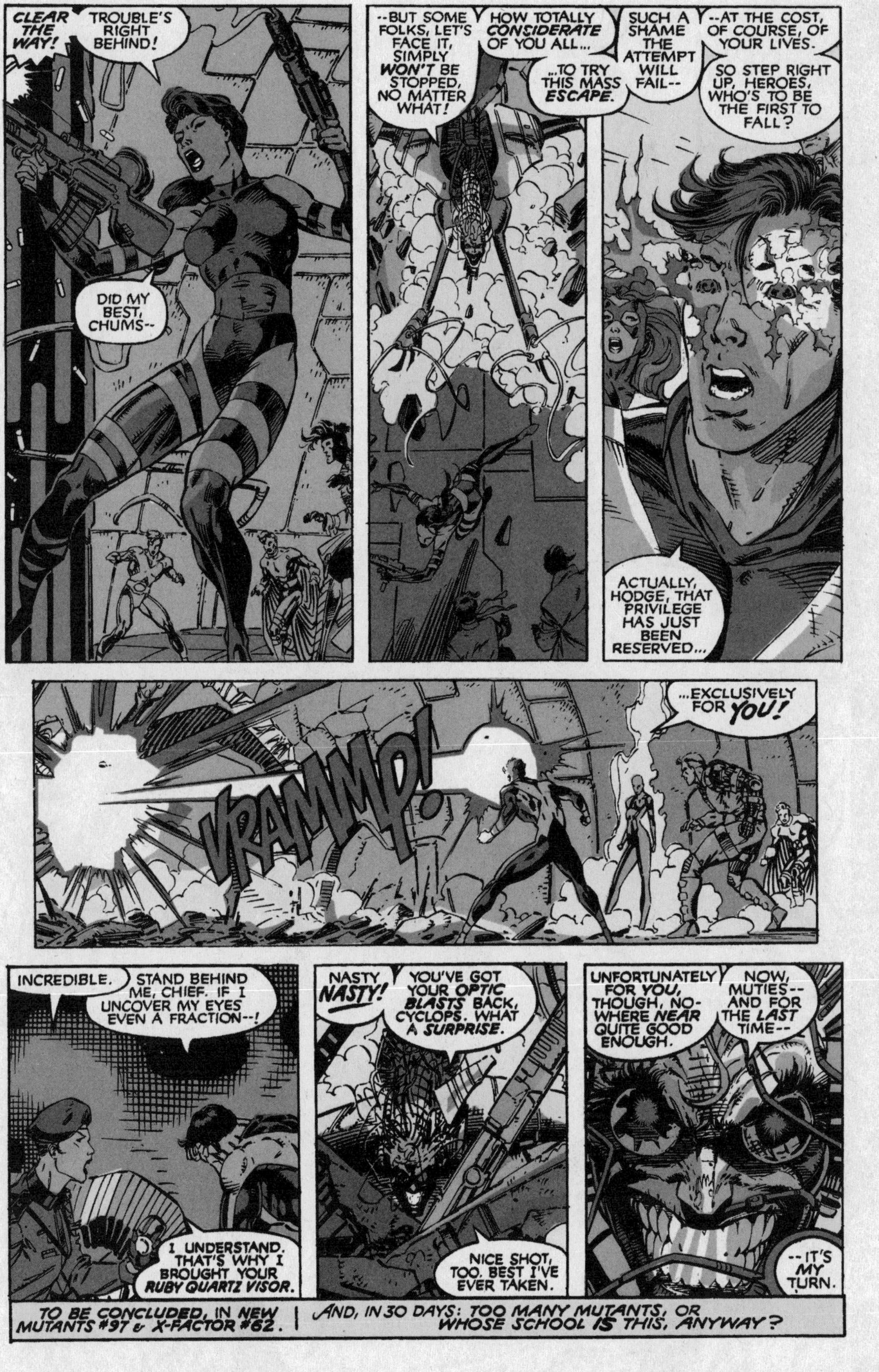
CLEAR THE WAY!
TROUBLE'S RIGHT BEHIND!
DID MY BEST, CHUMS--
--BUT SOME FOLKS, LET'S FACE IT, SIMPLY WON'T BE STOPPED, NO MATTER WHAT!
HOW TOTALLY CONSIDERATE OF YOU ALL...
...TO TRY THIS MASS ESCAPE.
SUCH A SHAME THE ATTEMPT WILL FAIL--
--AT THE COST, OF COURSE, OF YOUR LIVES.
SO STEP RIGHT UP, HEROES, WHO'S TO BE THE FIRST TO FALL?
ACTUALLY, HODGE, THAT PRIVILEGE HAS JUST BEEN RESERVED...
...EXCLUSIVELY FOR YOU!
VRAMMP!
INCREDIBLE.
STAND BEHIND ME, CHIEF. IF I UNCOVER MY EYES EVEN A FRACTION--!
I UNDERSTAND. THAT'S WHY I BROUGHT YOUR RUBY QUARTZ VISOR.
NASTY NASTY!
YOU'VE GOT YOUR OPTIC BLASTS BACK, CYCLOPS. WHAT A SURPRISE.
NICE SHOT, TOO. BEST I'VE EVER TAKEN.
UNFORTUNATELY FOR YOU, THOUGH, NO-WHERE NEAR QUITE GOOD ENOUGH.
NOW, MUTIES-- AND FOR THE LAST TIME--
--IT'S MY TURN.
TO BE CONCLUDED, IN NEW MUTANTS #97 & X-FACTOR #62.
AND, IN 30 DAYS: TOO MANY MUTANTS, OR WHOSE SCHOOL IS THIS, ANYWAY?

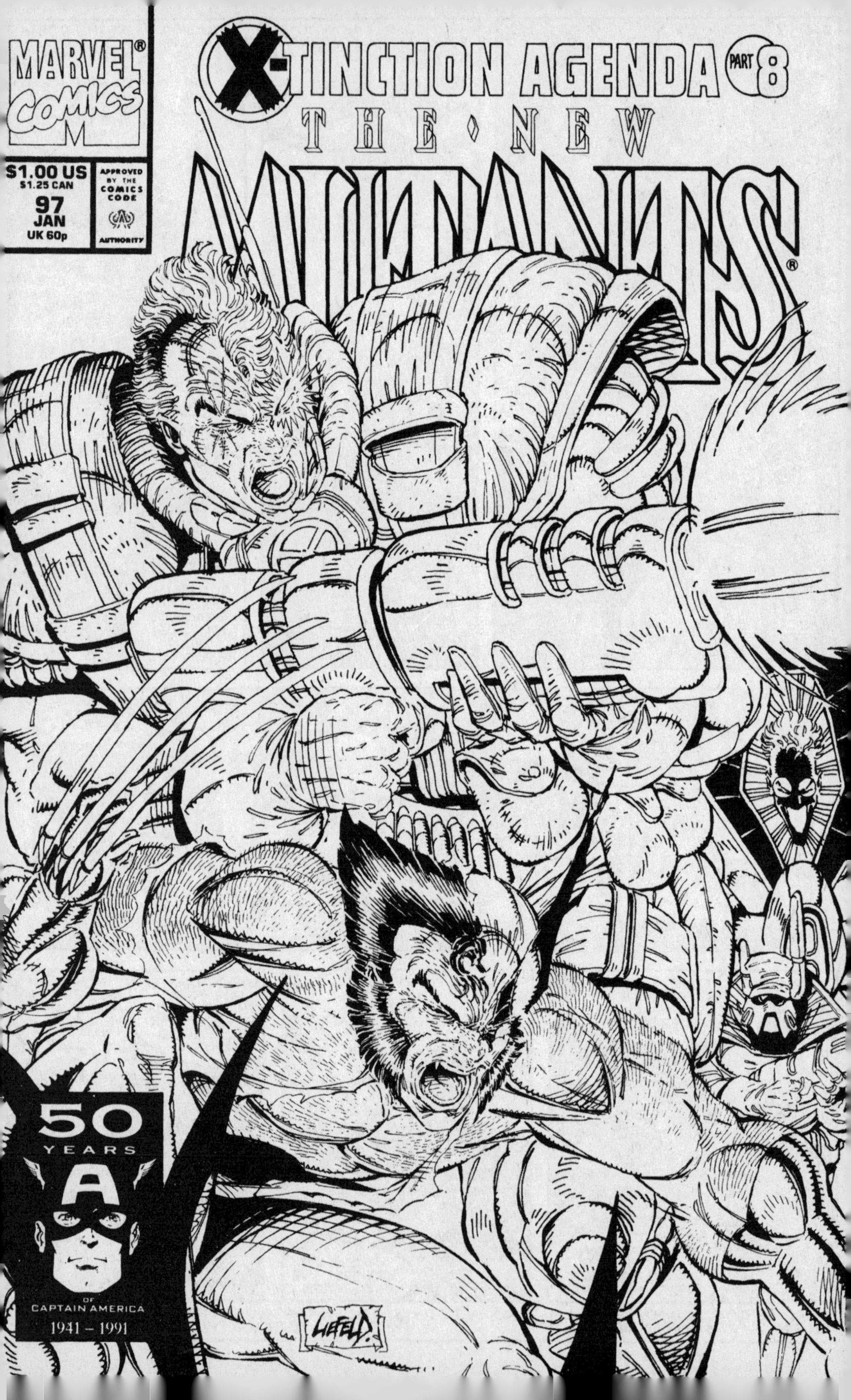
MARVEL® COMICS
$1.00 US
$1.25 CAN
97
JAN
UK 60p
APPROVED BY THE COMICS CODE AUTHORITY
X-TINCTION AGENDA PART 8
THE NEW MUTANTS®
50 YEARS
A
OF CAPTAIN AMERICA
1941 – 1991
LIEFELD

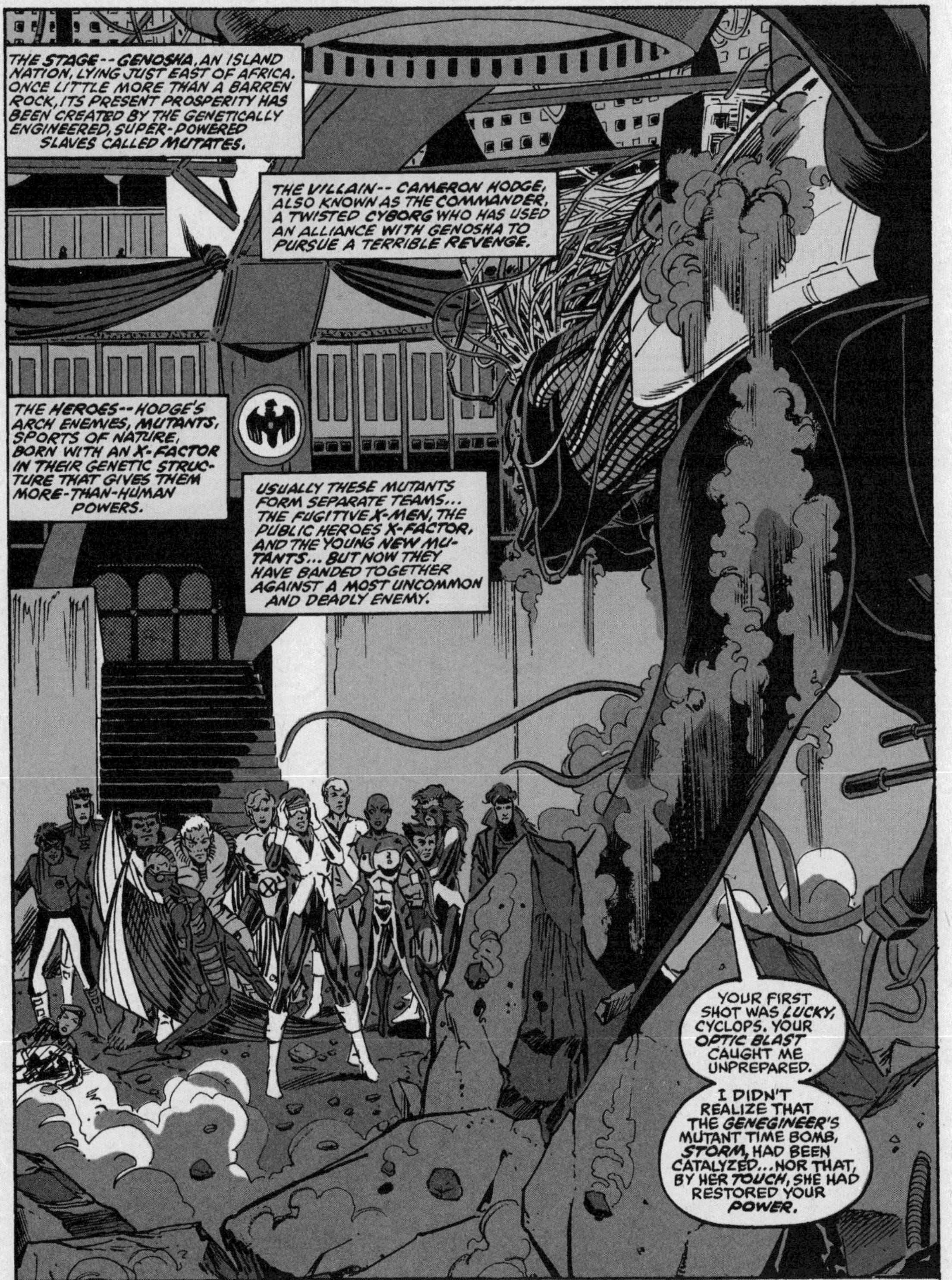
THE STAGE--GENOSHA, AN ISLAND NATION, LYING JUST EAST OF AFRICA. ONCE LITTLE MORE THAN A BARREN ROCK, ITS PRESENT PROSPERITY HAS BEEN CREATED BY THE GENETICALLY ENGINEERED, SUPER-POWERED SLAVES CALLED MUTATES.
THE VILLAIN-- CAMERON HODGE, ALSO KNOWN AS THE COMMANDER, A TWISTED CYBORG WHO HAS USED AN ALLIANCE WITH GENOSHA TO PURSUE A TERRIBLE REVENGE.
THE HEROES--HODGE'S ARCH ENEMIES, MUTANTS, SPORTS OF NATURE, BORN WITH AN X-FACTOR IN THEIR GENETIC STRUCTURE THAT GIVES THEM MORE-THAN-HUMAN POWERS.
USUALLY THESE MUTANTS FORM SEPARATE TEAMS... THE FUGITIVE X-MEN, THE PUBLIC HEROES X-FACTOR, AND THE YOUNG NEW MUTANTS... BUT NOW THEY HAVE BANDED TOGETHER AGAINST A MOST UNCOMMON AND DEADLY ENEMY.
YOUR FIRST SHOT WAS LUCKY, CYCLOPS. YOUR OPTIC BLAST CAUGHT ME UNPREPARED.
I DIDN'T REALIZE THAT THE GENEGINEER'S MUTANT TIME BOMB, STORM, HAD BEEN CATALYZED...NOR THAT, BY HER TOUCH, SHE HAD RESTORED YOUR POWER.

LOUISE SIMONSON WRITER · GUANG YAP PENCILLER · JOE RUBINSTEIN INKER · JOE ROSEN LETTERER · STEVE BUCCELLATO COLORIST · BOB HARRAS EDITOR · TOM DeFALCO EDITOR-IN-CHIEF

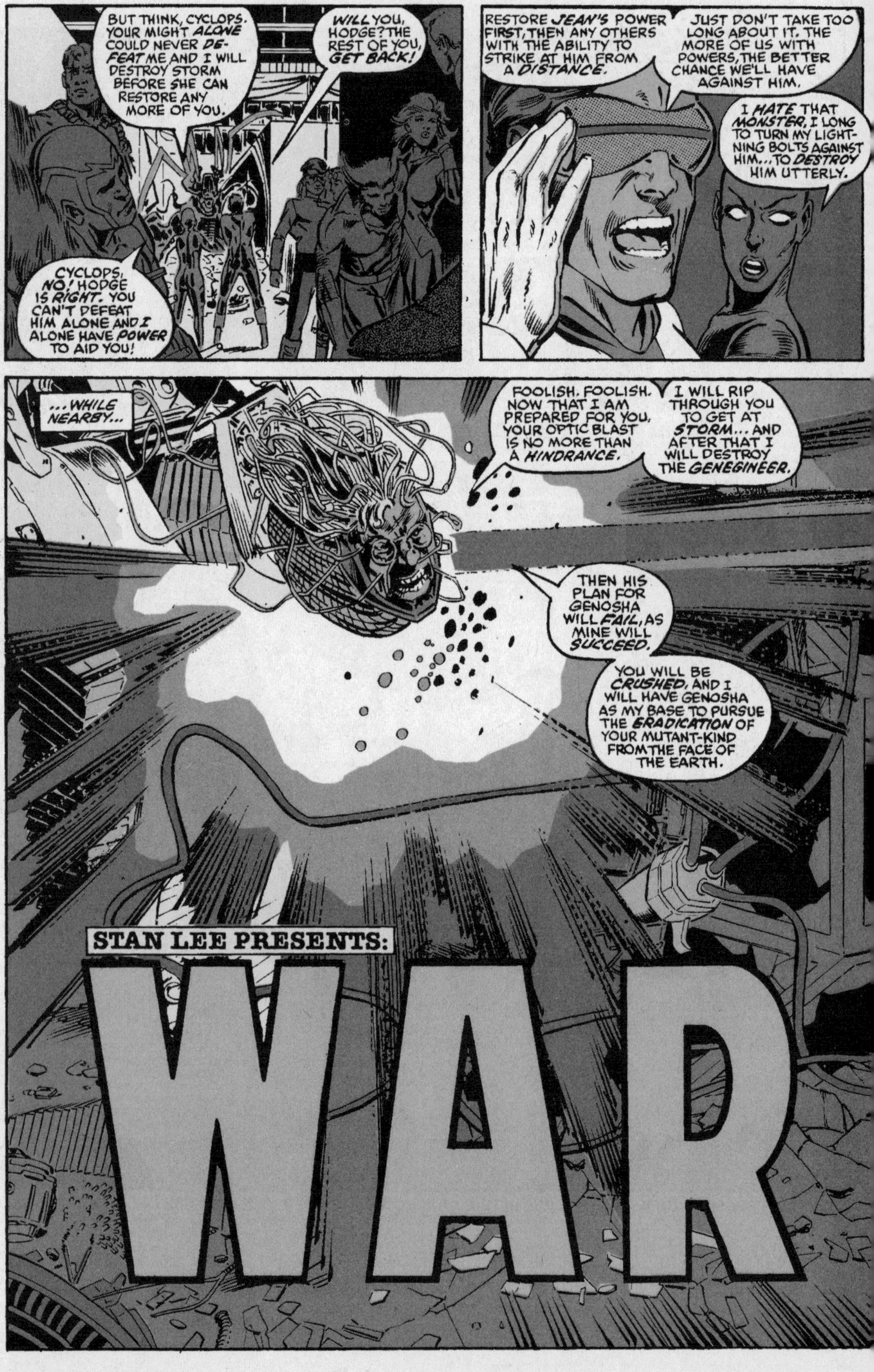

BUT THINK, CYCLOPS. YOUR MIGHT ALONE COULD NEVER DE-FEAT ME AND I WILL DESTROY STORM BEFORE SHE CAN RESTORE ANY MORE OF YOU.
WILL YOU, HODGE? THE REST OF YOU, GET BACK!
CYCLOPS, NO! HODGE IS RIGHT. YOU CAN'T DEFEAT HIM ALONE AND I ALONE HAVE POWER TO AID YOU!
RESTORE JEAN'S POWER FIRST, THEN ANY OTHERS WITH THE ABILITY TO STRIKE AT HIM FROM A DISTANCE.
JUST DON'T TAKE TOO LONG ABOUT IT. THE MORE OF US WITH POWERS, THE BETTER CHANCE WE'LL HAVE AGAINST HIM.
I HATE THAT MONSTER. I LONG TO TURN MY LIGHT-NING BOLTS AGAINST HIM... TO DESTROY HIM UTTERLY.
...WHILE NEARBY...
FOOLISH. FOOLISH. NOW THAT I AM PREPARED FOR YOU, YOUR OPTIC BLAST IS NO MORE THAN A HINDRANCE.
I WILL RIP THROUGH YOU TO GET AT STORM... AND AFTER THAT I WILL DESTROY THE GENEGINEER.
THEN HIS PLAN FOR GENOSHA WILL FAIL, AS MINE WILL SUCCEED.
YOU WILL BE CRUSHED, AND I WILL HAVE GENOSHA AS MY BASE TO PURSUE THE ERADICATION OF YOUR MUTANT-KIND FROM THE FACE OF THE EARTH.
STAN LEE PRESENTS:
WAR

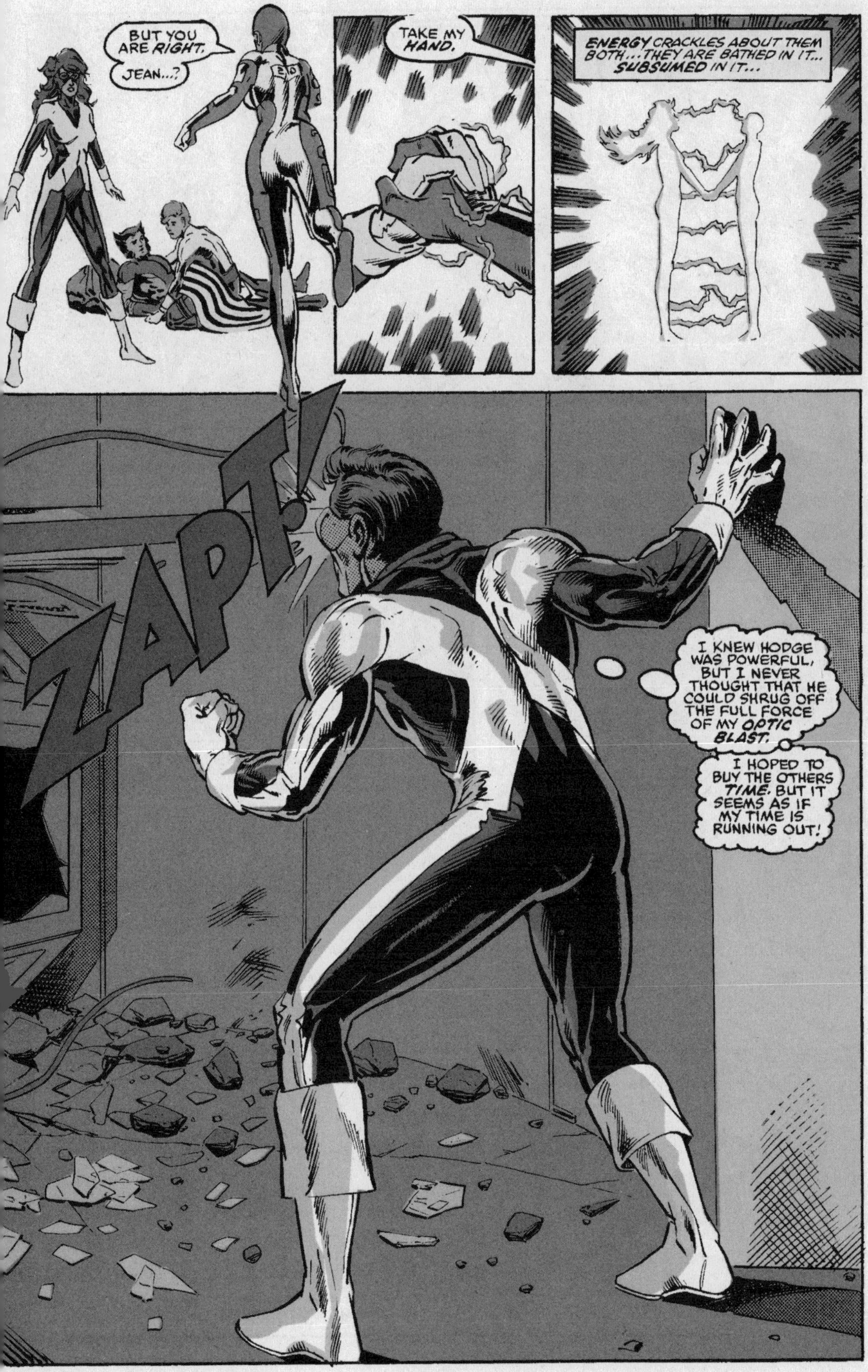
BUT YOU ARE RIGHT, JEAN...?
TAKE MY HAND.
ENERGY CRACKLES ABOUT THEM BOTH... THEY ARE BATHED IN IT... SUBSUMED IN IT...
ZAPT!
I KNEW HODGE WAS POWERFUL, BUT I NEVER THOUGHT THAT HE COULD SHRUG OFF THE FULL FORCE OF MY OPTIC BLAST.
I HOPED TO BUY THE OTHERS TIME. BUT IT SEEMS AS IF MY TIME IS RUNNING OUT!

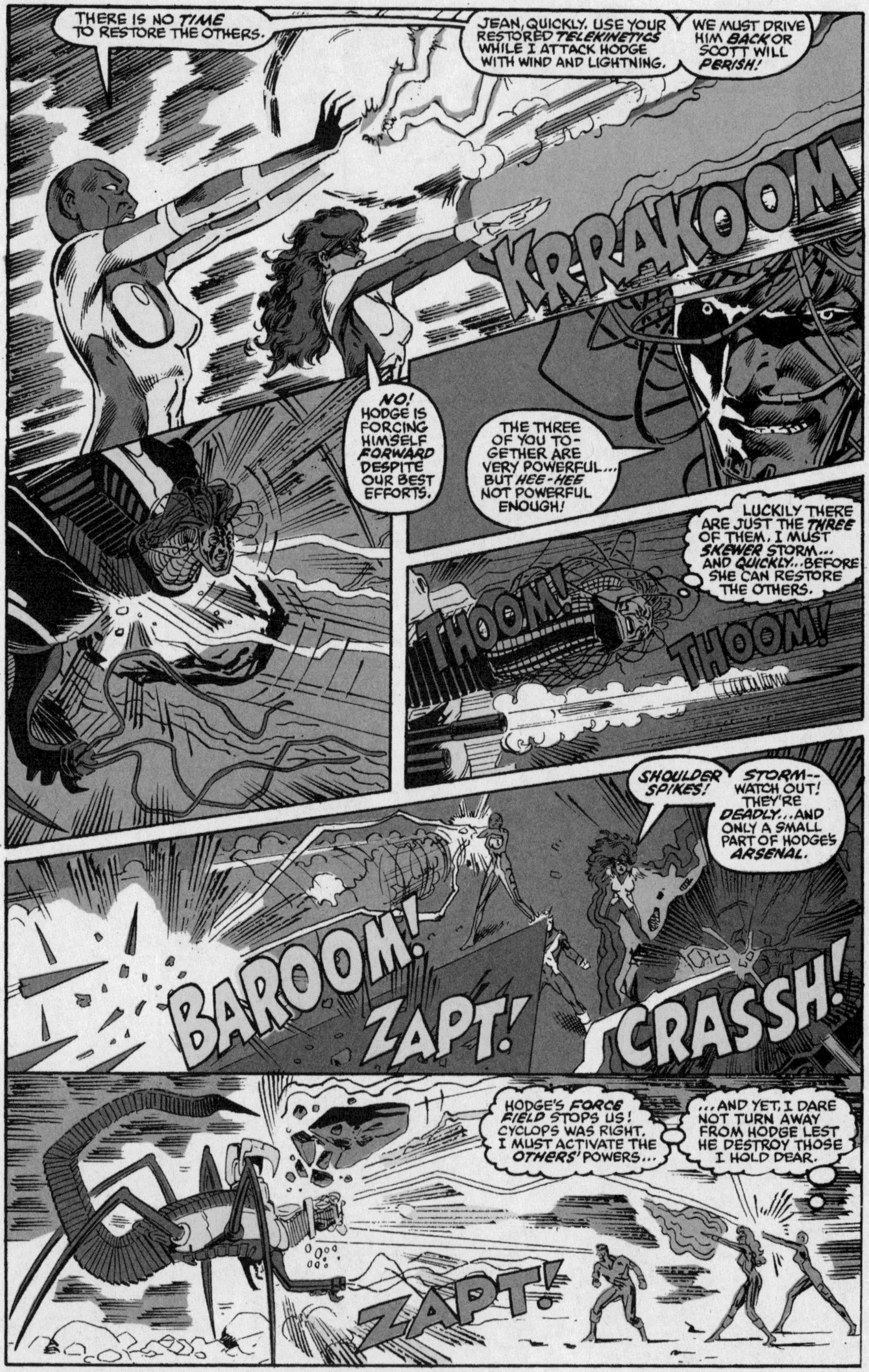
THERE IS NO TIME TO RESTORE THE OTHERS.
JEAN, QUICKLY. USE YOUR RESTORED TELEKINETICS WHILE I ATTACK HODGE WITH WIND AND LIGHTNING.
WE MUST DRIVE HIM BACK OR SCOTT WILL PERISH!
KRRAKOOM
NO! HODGE IS FORCING HIMSELF FORWARD DESPITE OUR BEST EFFORTS.
THE THREE OF YOU TO-GETHER ARE VERY POWERFUL... BUT HEE-HEE NOT POWERFUL ENOUGH!
LUCKILY THERE ARE JUST THE THREE OF THEM. I MUST SKEWER STORM... AND QUICKLY... BEFORE SHE CAN RESTORE THE OTHERS.
THOOM!
THOOM!
SHOULDER SPIKES!
STORM-- WATCH OUT! THEY'RE DEADLY... AND ONLY A SMALL PART OF HODGE'S ARSENAL.
BAROOM!
ZAPT!
CRASSH!
HODGE'S FORCE FIELD STOPS US! CYCLOPS WAS RIGHT. I MUST ACTIVATE THE OTHERS' POWERS...
...AND YET, I DARE NOT TURN AWAY FROM HODGE LEST HE DESTROY THOSE I HOLD DEAR.
ZAPT!

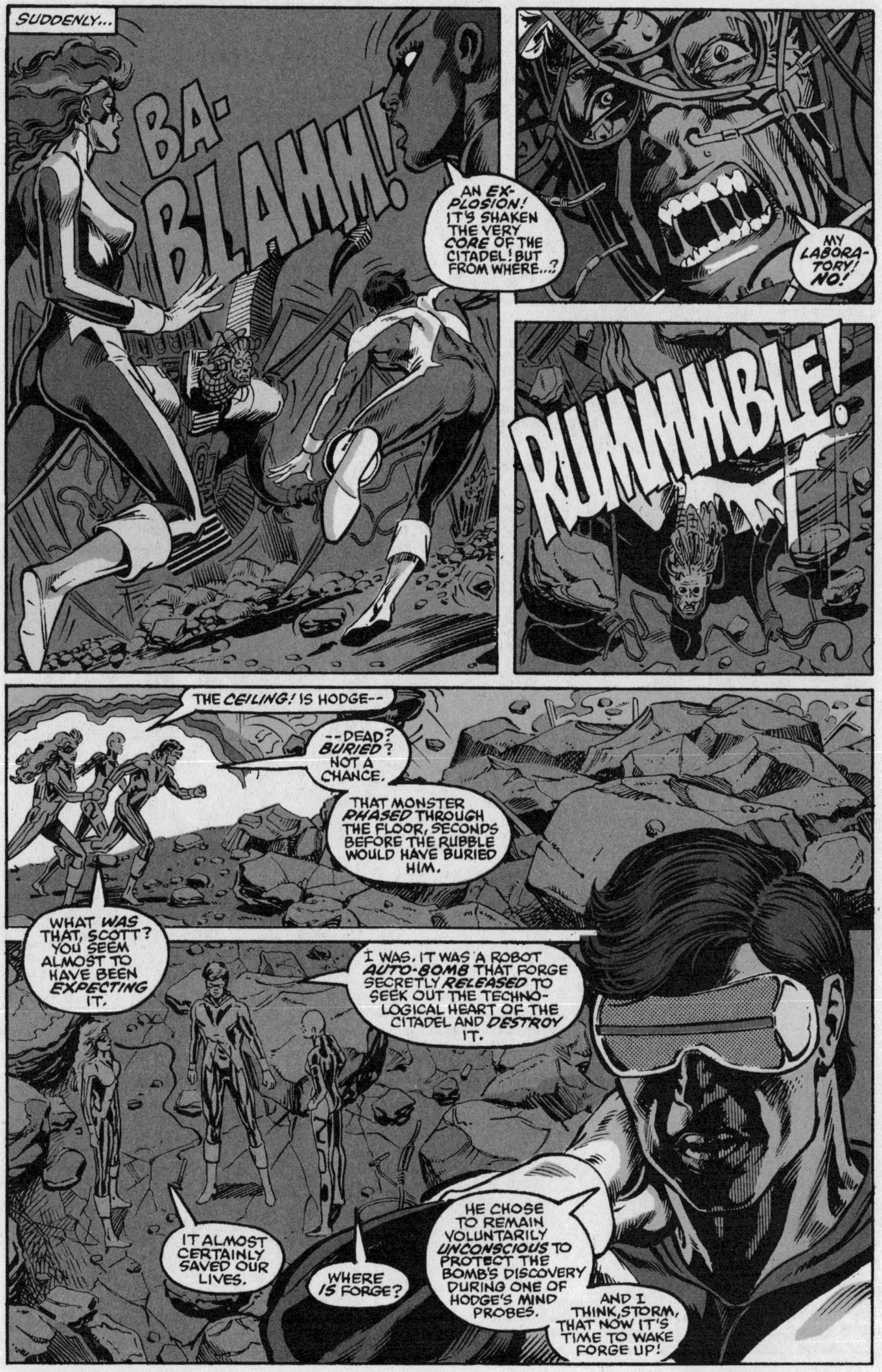
SUDDENLY...
BA-BLAMM!
AN EXPLOSION! IT'S SHAKEN THE VERY CORE OF THE CITADEL! BUT FROM WHERE...?
MY LABORATORY! NO!
RUMMMBLE!
THE CEILING! IS HODGE--
--DEAD? BURIED? NOT A CHANCE.
THAT MONSTER PHASED THROUGH THE FLOOR, SECONDS BEFORE THE RUBBLE WOULD HAVE BURIED HIM.
WHAT WAS THAT, SCOTT? YOU SEEM ALMOST TO HAVE BEEN EXPECTING IT.
I WAS. IT WAS A ROBOT AUTO-BOMB THAT FORGE SECRETLY RELEASED TO SEEK OUT THE TECHNOLOGICAL HEART OF THE CITADEL AND DESTROY IT.
IT ALMOST CERTAINLY SAVED OUR LIVES.
WHERE IS FORGE?
HE CHOSE TO REMAIN VOLUNTARILY UNCONSCIOUS TO PROTECT THE BOMB'S DISCOVERY DURING ONE OF HODGE'S MIND PROBES.
AND I THINK, STORM, THAT NOW IT'S TIME TO WAKE FORGE UP!

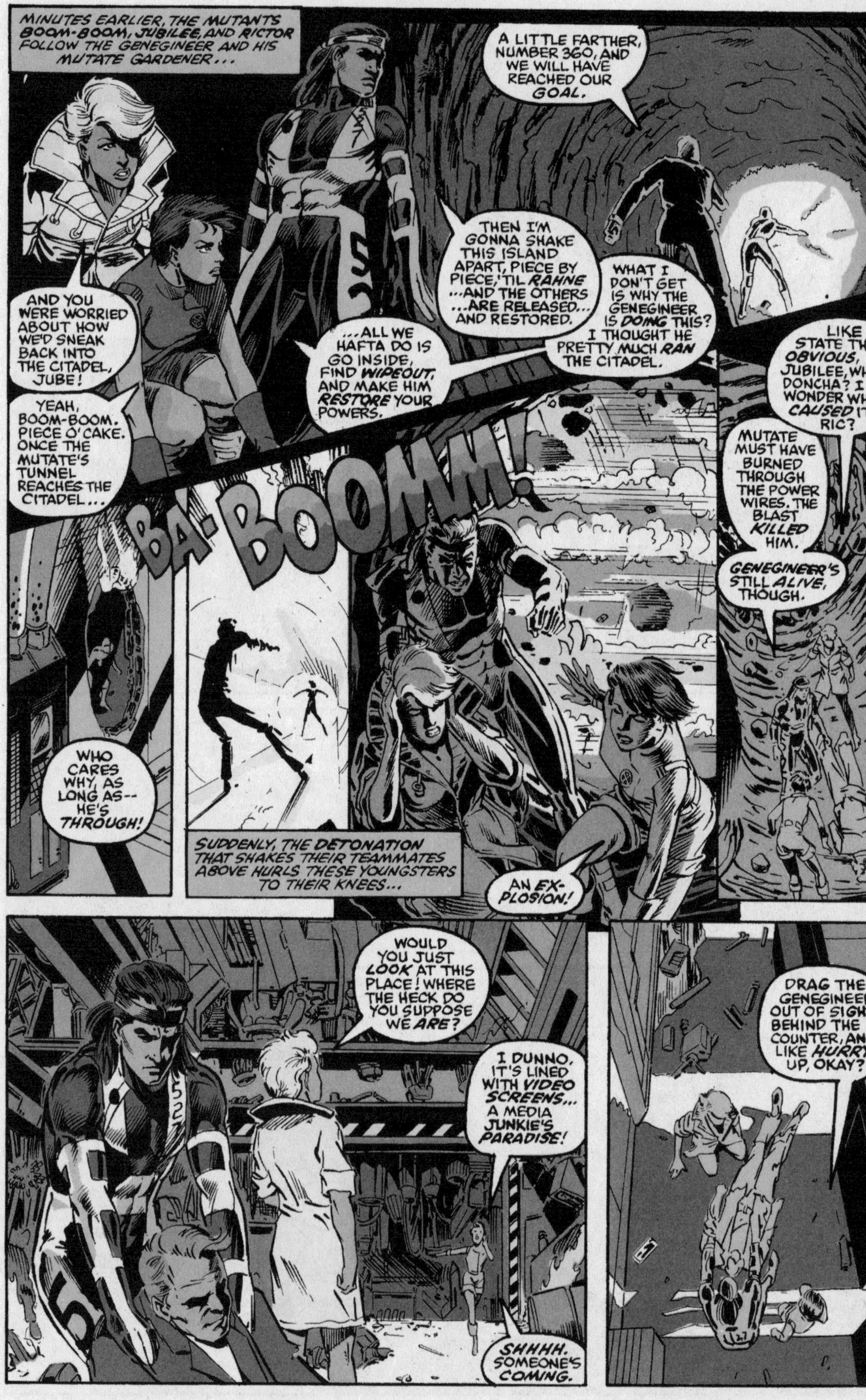
MINUTES EARLIER, THE MUTANTS BOOM-BOOM, JUBILEE, AND RICTOR FOLLOW THE GENEGINEER AND HIS MUTATE GARDENER...
A LITTLE FARTHER, NUMBER 360, AND WE WILL HAVE REACHED OUR GOAL.
AND YOU WERE WORRIED ABOUT HOW WE'D SNEAK BACK INTO THE CITADEL, JUBE!
YEAH, BOOM-BOOM. PIECE O' CAKE. ONCE THE MUTATE'S TUNNEL REACHES THE CITADEL...
...ALL WE HAFTA DO IS GO INSIDE, FIND WIPEOUT, AND MAKE HIM RESTORE YOUR POWERS.
THEN I'M GONNA SHAKE THIS ISLAND APART, PIECE BY PIECE, 'TIL RAHNE ...AND THE OTHERS ...ARE RELEASED... AND RESTORED.
WHAT I DON'T GET IS WHY THE GENEGINEER IS DOING THIS? I THOUGHT HE PRETTY MUCH RAN THE CITADEL.
WHO CARES WHY, AS LONG AS-- HE'S THROUGH!
BA-BOOMM!
SUDDENLY, THE DETONATION THAT SHAKES THEIR TEAMMATES ABOVE HURLS THESE YOUNGSTERS TO THEIR KNEES...
AN EX-PLOSION!
LIKE STATE THE OBVIOUS, JUBILEE, WHY DONCHA? I WONDER WHAT CAUSED IT, RIC?
MUTATE MUST HAVE BURNED THROUGH THE POWER WIRES. THE BLAST KILLED HIM.
GENEGINEER'S STILL ALIVE, THOUGH.
WOULD YOU JUST LOOK AT THIS PLACE! WHERE THE HECK DO YOU SUPPOSE WE ARE?
I DUNNO. IT'S LINED WITH VIDEO SCREENS... A MEDIA JUNKIE'S PARADISE!
SHHHH. SOMEONE'S COMING.
DRAG THE GENEGINEER OUT OF SIGHT BEHIND THE COUNTER, AND LIKE HURRY UP, OKAY?

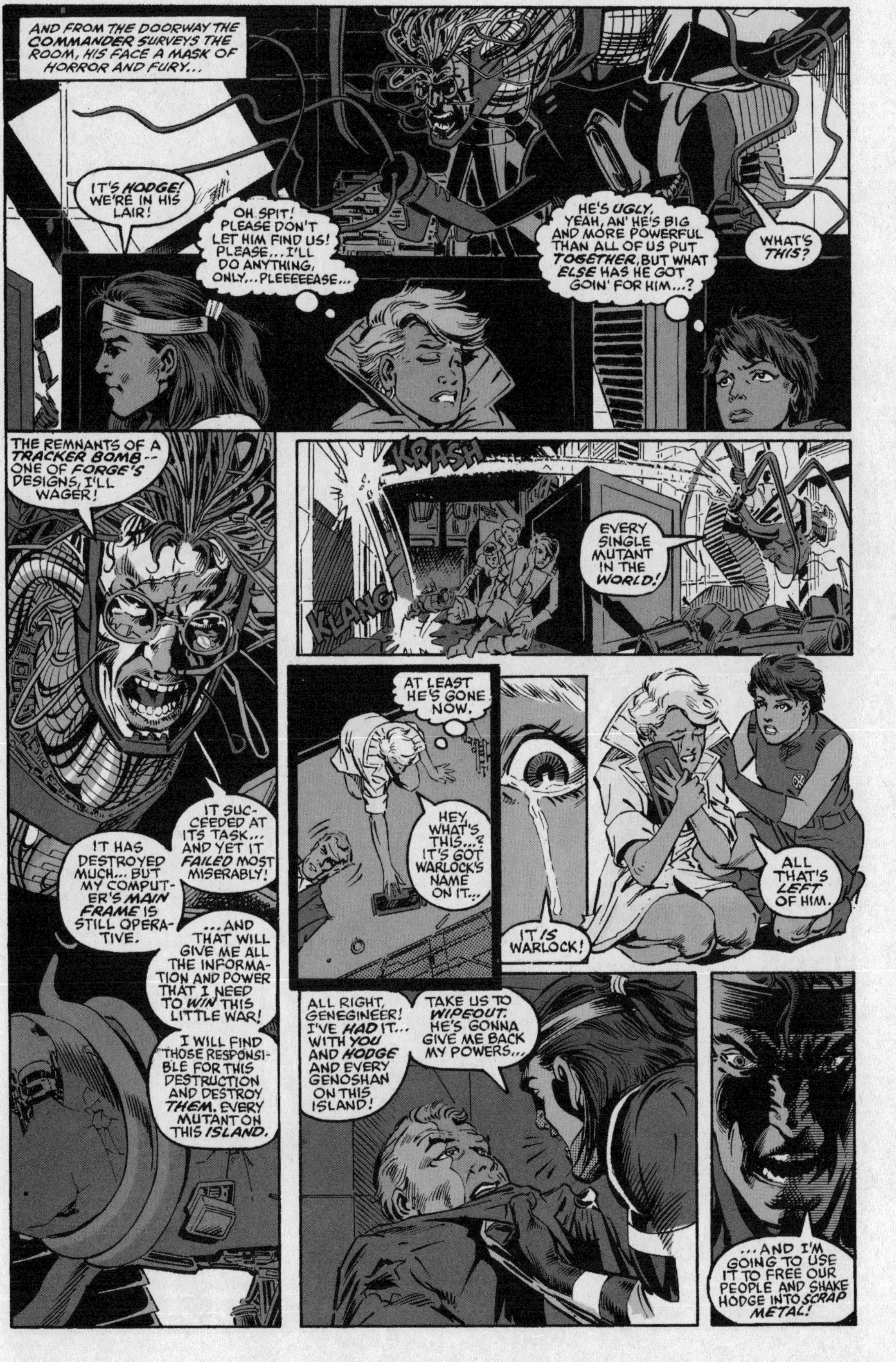
AND FROM THE DOORWAY THE COMMANDER SURVEYS THE ROOM, HIS FACE A MASK OF HORROR AND FURY...
IT'S HODGE! WE'RE IN HIS LAIR!
OH SPIT! PLEASE DON'T LET HIM FIND US! PLEASE... I'LL DO ANYTHING, ONLY... PLEEEEEASE...
HE'S UGLY, YEAH, AN' HE'S BIG AND MORE POWERFUL THAN ALL OF US PUT TOGETHER, BUT WHAT ELSE HAS HE GOT GOIN' FOR HIM...?
WHAT'S THIS?
THE REMNANTS OF A TRACKER BOMB-- ONE OF FORGE'S DESIGNS, I'LL WAGER!
KRASH
KLANG
EVERY SINGLE MUTANT IN THE WORLD!
IT HAS DESTROYED MUCH... BUT MY COMPUTER'S MAIN FRAME IS STILL OPERATIVE.
IT SUCCEEDED AT ITS TASK... AND YET IT FAILED MOST MISERABLY!
...AND THAT WILL GIVE ME ALL THE INFORMATION AND POWER THAT I NEED TO WIN THIS LITTLE WAR!
I WILL FIND THOSE RESPONSIBLE FOR THIS DESTRUCTION AND DESTROY THEM. EVERY MUTANT ON THIS ISLAND.
AT LEAST HE'S GONE NOW.
HEY, WHAT'S THIS...? IT'S GOT WARLOCK'S NAME ON IT...
IT IS WARLOCK!
ALL THAT'S LEFT OF HIM.
ALL RIGHT, GENEGINEER! I'VE HAD IT... WITH YOU AND HODGE AND EVERY GENOSHAN ON THIS ISLAND!
TAKE US TO WIPEOUT. HE'S GONNA GIVE ME BACK MY POWERS...
...AND I'M GOING TO USE IT TO FREE OUR PEOPLE AND SHAKE HODGE INTO SCRAP METAL!

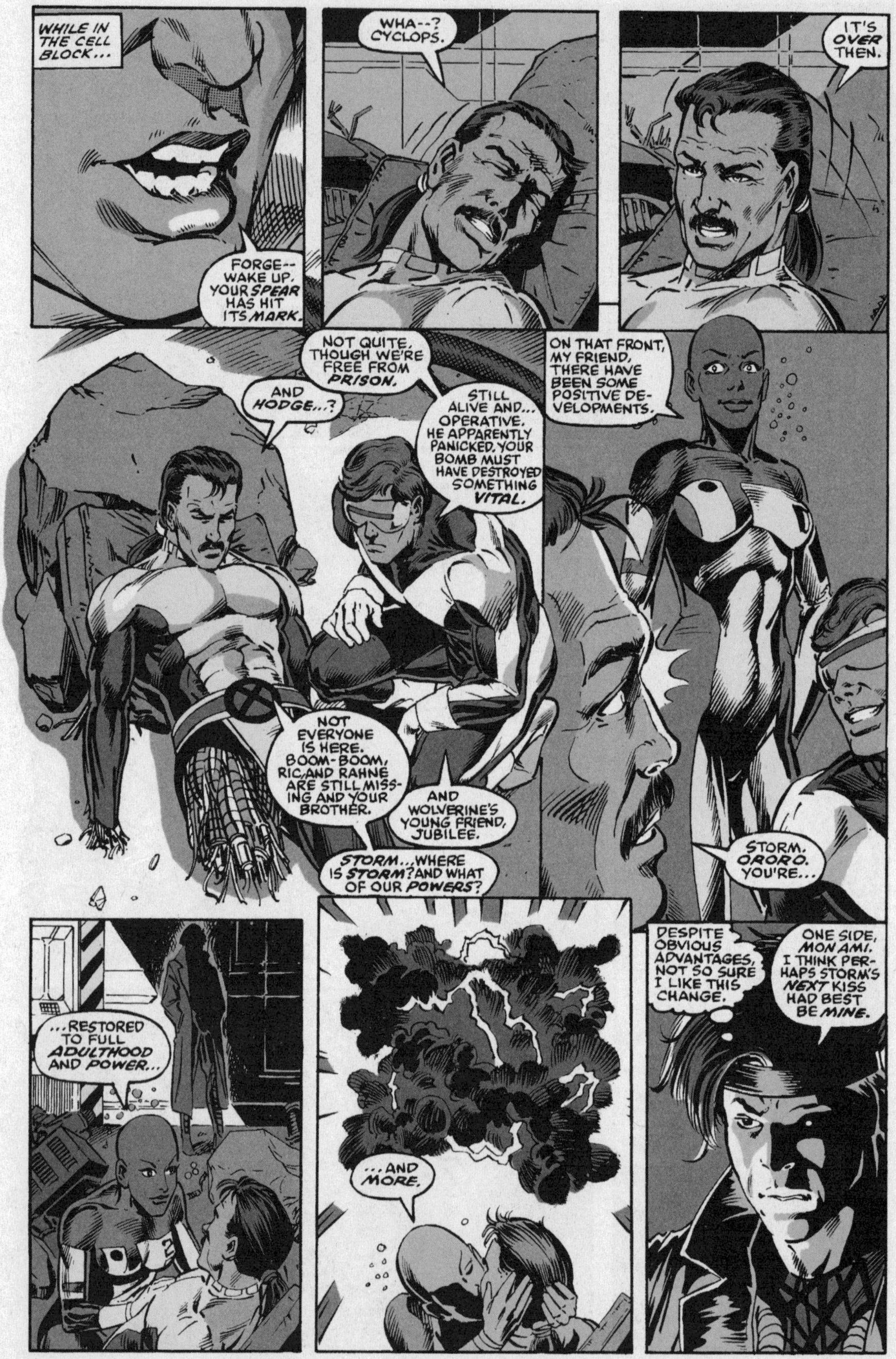
WHILE IN THE CELL BLOCK...
FORGE-- WAKE UP. YOUR SPEAR HAS HIT ITS MARK.
WHA--? CYCLOPS.
IT'S OVER THEN.
NOT QUITE, THOUGH WE'RE FREE FROM PRISON.
AND HODGE...?
STILL ALIVE AND... OPERATIVE. HE APPARENTLY PANICKED. YOUR BOMB MUST HAVE DESTROYED SOMETHING VITAL.
NOT EVERYONE IS HERE. BOOM-BOOM, RIC, AND RAHNE ARE STILL MISSING AND YOUR BROTHER.
AND WOLVERINE'S YOUNG FRIEND, JUBILEE.
STORM...WHERE IS STORM? AND WHAT OF OUR POWERS?
ON THAT FRONT, MY FRIEND, THERE HAVE BEEN SOME POSITIVE DEVELOPMENTS.
STORM. ORORO. YOU'RE...
...RESTORED TO FULL ADULTHOOD AND POWER...
...AND MORE.
DESPITE OBVIOUS ADVANTAGES, NOT SO SURE I LIKE THIS CHANGE.
ONE SIDE, MON AMI. I THINK PERHAPS STORM'S NEXT KISS HAD BEST BE MINE.

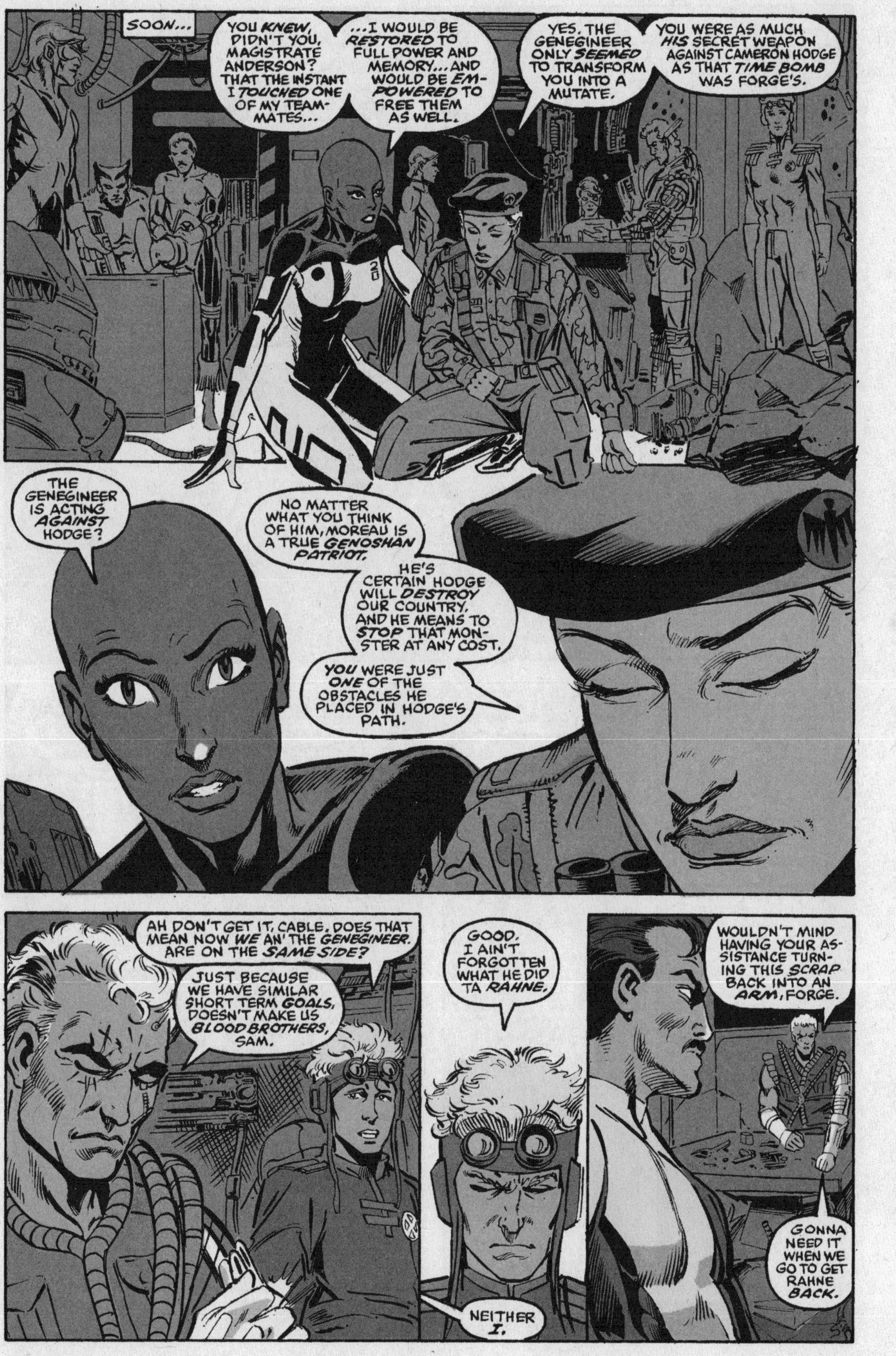
SOON...
YOU KNEW, DIDN'T YOU, MAGISTRATE ANDERSON? THAT THE INSTANT I TOUCHED ONE OF MY TEAM-MATES...
...I WOULD BE RESTORED TO FULL POWER AND MEMORY... AND WOULD BE EM-POWERED TO FREE THEM AS WELL.
YES, THE GENEGINEER ONLY SEEMED TO TRANSFORM YOU INTO A MUTATE.
YOU WERE AS MUCH HIS SECRET WEAPON AGAINST CAMERON HODGE AS THAT TIME BOMB WAS FORGE'S.
THE GENEGINEER IS ACTING AGAINST HODGE?
NO MATTER WHAT YOU THINK OF HIM, MOREAU IS A TRUE GENOSHAN PATRIOT.
HE'S CERTAIN HODGE WILL DESTROY OUR COUNTRY, AND HE MEANS TO STOP THAT MON-STER AT ANY COST.
YOU WERE JUST ONE OF THE OBSTACLES HE PLACED IN HODGE'S PATH.
AH DON'T GET IT, CABLE. DOES THAT MEAN NOW WE AN' THE GENEGINEER ARE ON THE SAME SIDE?
JUST BECAUSE WE HAVE SIMILAR SHORT TERM GOALS, DOESN'T MAKE US BLOOD BROTHERS, SAM.
GOOD. I AIN'T FORGOTTEN WHAT HE DID TA RAHNE.
NEITHER I.
WOULDN'T MIND HAVING YOUR AS-SISTANCE TURNING THIS SCRAP BACK INTO AN ARM, FORGE.
GONNA NEED IT WHEN WE GO TO GET RAHNE BACK.

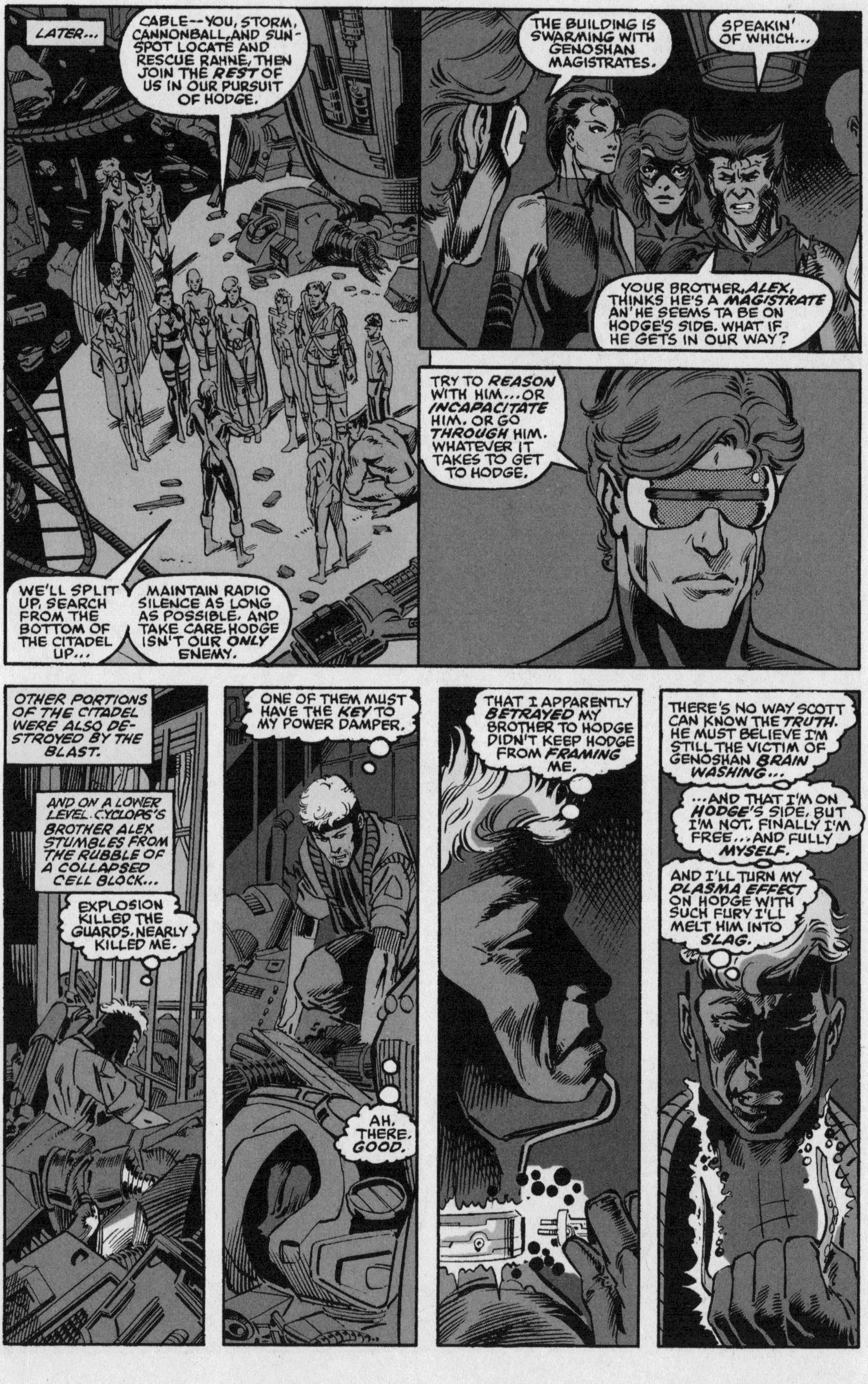
LATER...
CABLE--YOU, STORM, CANNONBALL, AND SUN-SPOT LOCATE AND RESCUE RAHNE, THEN JOIN THE REST OF US IN OUR PURSUIT OF HODGE.
WE'LL SPLIT UP, SEARCH FROM THE BOTTOM OF THE CITADEL UP...
MAINTAIN RADIO SILENCE AS LONG AS POSSIBLE, AND TAKE CARE. HODGE ISN'T OUR ONLY ENEMY.
THE BUILDING IS SWARMING WITH GENOSHAN MAGISTRATES.
SPEAKIN' OF WHICH...
YOUR BROTHER, ALEX, THINKS HE'S A MAGISTRATE AN' HE SEEMS TA BE ON HODGE'S SIDE. WHAT IF HE GETS IN OUR WAY?
TRY TO REASON WITH HIM...OR INCAPACITATE HIM. OR GO THROUGH HIM. WHATEVER IT TAKES TO GET TO HODGE.
OTHER PORTIONS OF THE CITADEL WERE ALSO DESTROYED BY THE BLAST.
AND ON A LOWER LEVEL, CYCLOPS'S BROTHER ALEX STUMBLES FROM THE RUBBLE OF A COLLAPSED CELL BLOCK...
EXPLOSION KILLED THE GUARDS. NEARLY KILLED ME.
ONE OF THEM MUST HAVE THE KEY TO MY POWER DAMPER.
AH. THERE. GOOD.
THAT I APPARENTLY BETRAYED MY BROTHER TO HODGE DIDN'T KEEP HODGE FROM FRAMING ME.
THERE'S NO WAY SCOTT CAN KNOW THE TRUTH. HE MUST BELIEVE I'M STILL THE VICTIM OF GENOSHAN BRAIN WASHING...
...AND THAT I'M ON HODGE'S SIDE. BUT I'M NOT. FINALLY I'M FREE...AND FULLY MYSELF.
AND I'LL TURN MY PLASMA EFFECT ON HODGE WITH SUCH FURY I'LL MELT HIM INTO SLAG.

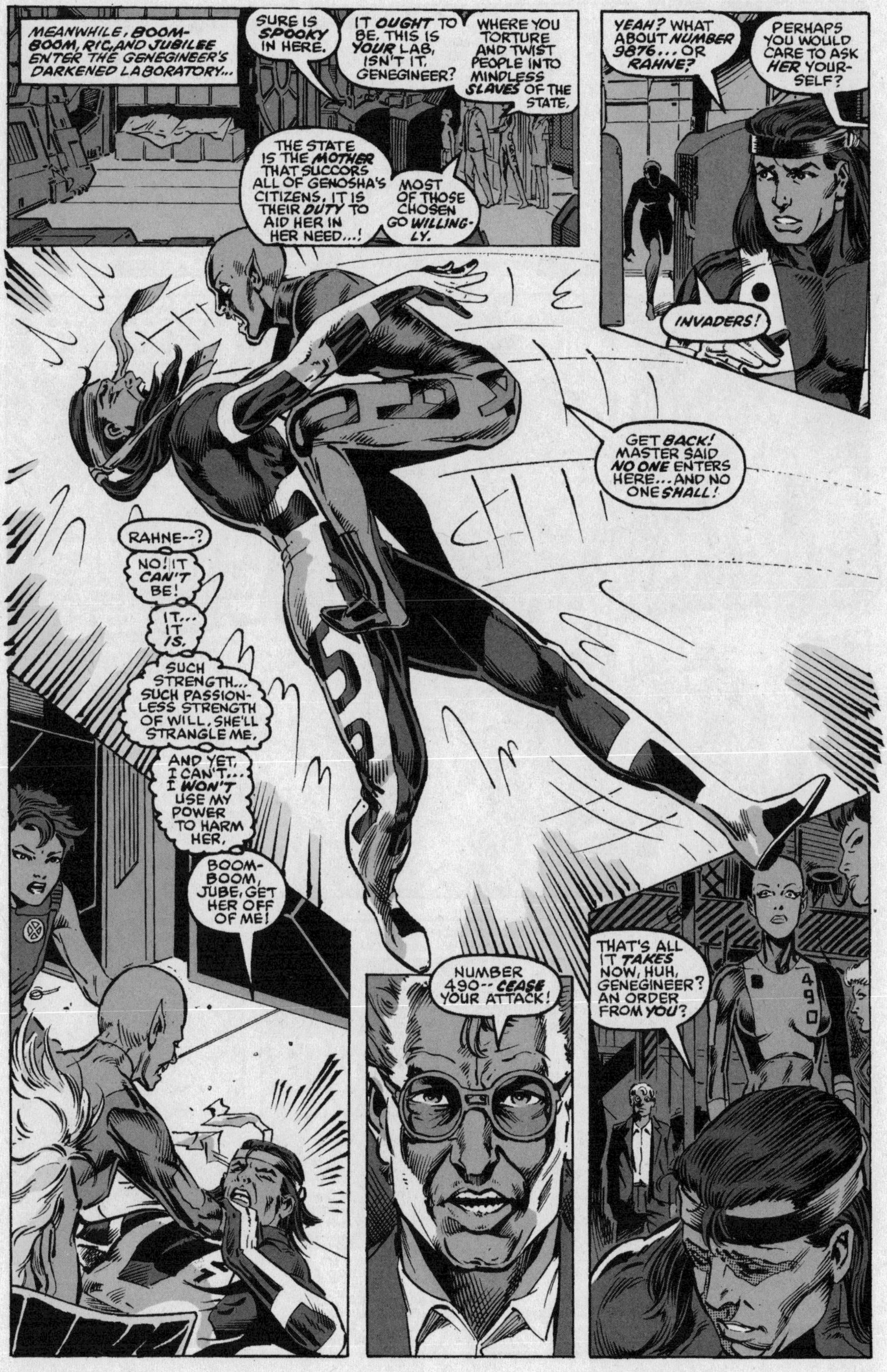
MEANWHILE, BOOM-BOOM, RIC, AND JUBILEE ENTER THE GENEGINEER'S DARKENED LABORATORY...
SURE IS SPOOKY IN HERE.
IT OUGHT TO BE. THIS IS YOUR LAB, ISN'T IT, GENEGINEER?
WHERE YOU TORTURE AND TWIST PEOPLE INTO MINDLESS SLAVES OF THE STATE.
THE STATE IS THE MOTHER THAT SUCCORS ALL OF GENOSHA'S CITIZENS. IT IS THEIR DUTY TO AID HER IN HER NEED...!
MOST OF THOSE CHOSEN GO WILLING-LY.
YEAH? WHAT ABOUT NUMBER 9876... OR RAHNE?
PERHAPS YOU WOULD CARE TO ASK HER YOUR-SELF?
INVADERS!
GET BACK! MASTER SAID NO ONE ENTERS HERE... AND NO ONE SHALL!
RAHNE--?
NO! IT CAN'T BE!
IT... IT IS.
SUCH STRENGTH... SUCH PASSION-LESS STRENGTH OF WILL, SHE'LL STRANGLE ME.
AND YET, I CAN'T... I WON'T USE MY POWER TO HARM HER.
BOOM-BOOM, JUBE, GET HER OFF OF ME!
NUMBER 490-- CEASE YOUR ATTACK!
THAT'S ALL IT TAKES NOW, HUH, GENEGINEER? AN ORDER FROM YOU?

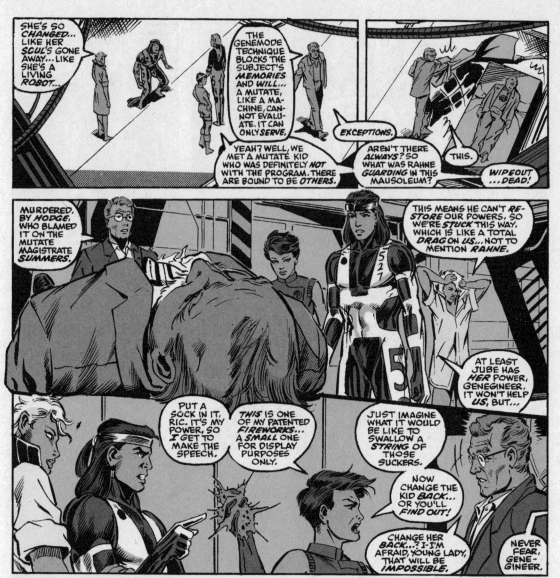

SHE'S SO *CHANGED*... LIKE HER *SOUL'S* GONE AWAY... LIKE SHE'S A LIVING *ROBOT*...

THE *GENEMODE* TECHNIQUE BLOCKS THE SUBJECT'S *MEMORIES* AND *WILL*... A MUTATE, LIKE A MACHINE, CANNOT EVALUATE. IT CAN ONLY *SERVE*.

EXCEPTIONS.

YEAH? WELL, WE MET A MUTATE KID WHO WAS DEFINITELY *NOT* WITH THE PROGRAM. THERE ARE BOUND TO BE *OTHERS*.

AREN'T THERE *ALWAYS?* SO WHAT WAS RAHNE *GUARDING* IN THIS MAUSOLEUM?

THIS.

WIPEOUT... *DEAD!*

MURDERED, BY *HODGE*. WHO BLAMED IT ON THE MUTATE MAGISTRATE *SUMMERS.*

THIS MEANS HE CAN'T *RESTORE* OUR POWERS, SO WE'RE *STUCK* THIS WAY, WHICH IS LIKE A TOTAL *DRAG* ON US... NOT TO MENTION *RAHNE.*

AT LEAST JUBE HAS *HER* POWER, GENEGINEER. IT WON'T HELP *US*, BUT...

PUT A SOCK IN IT, RIC. IT'S MY POWER, SO *I* GET TO MAKE THE SPEECH.

THIS IS ONE OF MY PATENTED *FIREWORKS*... A *SMALL* ONE FOR DISPLAY PURPOSES ONLY.

JUST IMAGINE WHAT IT WOULD BE LIKE TO SWALLOW A *STRING* OF THOSE SUCKERS.

NOW CHANGE THE KID *BACK*... OR YOU'LL *FIND OUT!*

CHANGE HER *BACK*...? I-I'M AFRAID, YOUNG LADY, THAT WILL BE *IMPOSSIBLE.*

NEVER FEAR, GENEGINEER.

YOU AIDED *ME* AND MY *COMPANIONS* AGAINST HODGE... AND NOW *WE* WILL AID YOU.

WHAT--?

STORM! THANK *HEAVEN.*

LOOKS LIKE WE CAME *TOO SOON*, HUH, GUYS? AN' SAVED THAT SCUM FROM THE WORST CASE OF *HEARTBURN* IN HUMAN HISTORY.

CABLE. 'BERTO, SAM.

AN' *STORM*...?

ABOUT BLOODY TIME!

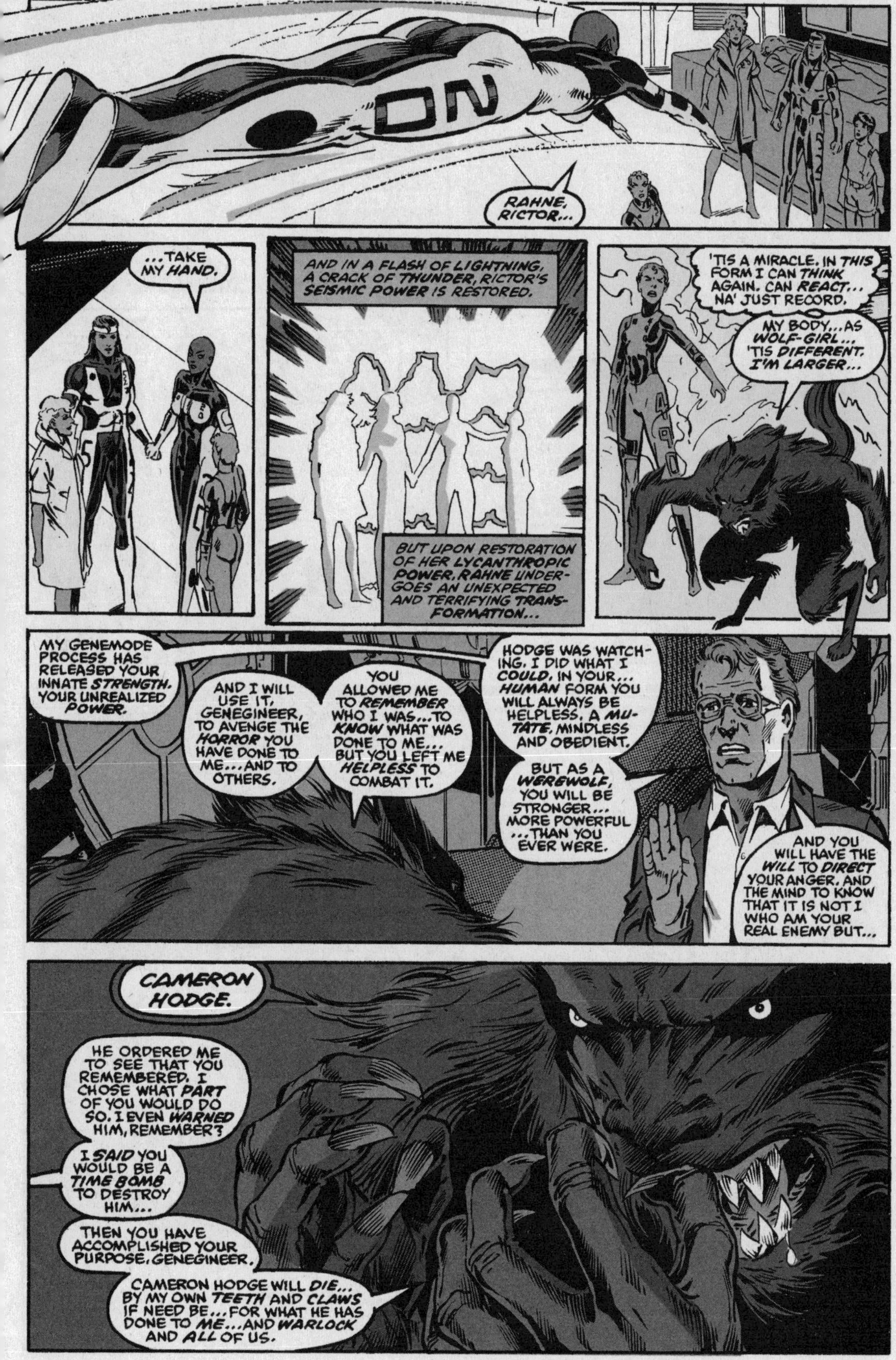
RAHNE, RICTOR...
...TAKE MY HAND.
AND IN A FLASH OF LIGHTNING, A CRACK OF THUNDER, RICTOR'S SEISMIC POWER IS RESTORED.
BUT UPON RESTORATION OF HER LYCANTHROPIC POWER, RAHNE UNDERGOES AN UNEXPECTED AND TERRIFYING TRANSFORMATION...
'TIS A MIRACLE. IN THIS FORM I CAN THINK AGAIN. CAN REACT... NA' JUST RECORD.
MY BODY...AS WOLF-GIRL... 'TIS DIFFERENT. I'M LARGER...
MY GENEMODE PROCESS HAS RELEASED YOUR INNATE STRENGTH. YOUR UNREALIZED POWER.
AND I WILL USE IT, GENEGINEER, TO AVENGE THE HORROR YOU HAVE DONE TO ME...AND TO OTHERS.
YOU ALLOWED ME TO REMEMBER WHO I WAS...TO KNOW WHAT WAS DONE TO ME... BUT YOU LEFT ME HELPLESS TO COMBAT IT.
HODGE WAS WATCHING. I DID WHAT I COULD. IN YOUR... HUMAN FORM YOU WILL ALWAYS BE HELPLESS. A MUTATE, MINDLESS AND OBEDIENT.
BUT AS A WEREWOLF, YOU WILL BE STRONGER... MORE POWERFUL ...THAN YOU EVER WERE.
AND YOU WILL HAVE THE WILL TO DIRECT YOUR ANGER. AND THE MIND TO KNOW THAT IT IS NOT I WHO AM YOUR REAL ENEMY BUT...
CAMERON HODGE.
HE ORDERED ME TO SEE THAT YOU REMEMBERED. I CHOSE WHAT PART OF YOU WOULD DO SO. I EVEN WARNED HIM, REMEMBER?
I SAID YOU WOULD BE A TIME BOMB TO DESTROY HIM...
THEN YOU HAVE ACCOMPLISHED YOUR PURPOSE, GENEGINEER.
CAMERON HODGE WILL DIE... BY MY OWN TEETH AND CLAWS IF NEED BE... FOR WHAT HE HAS DONE TO ME...AND WARLOCK AND ALL OF US.

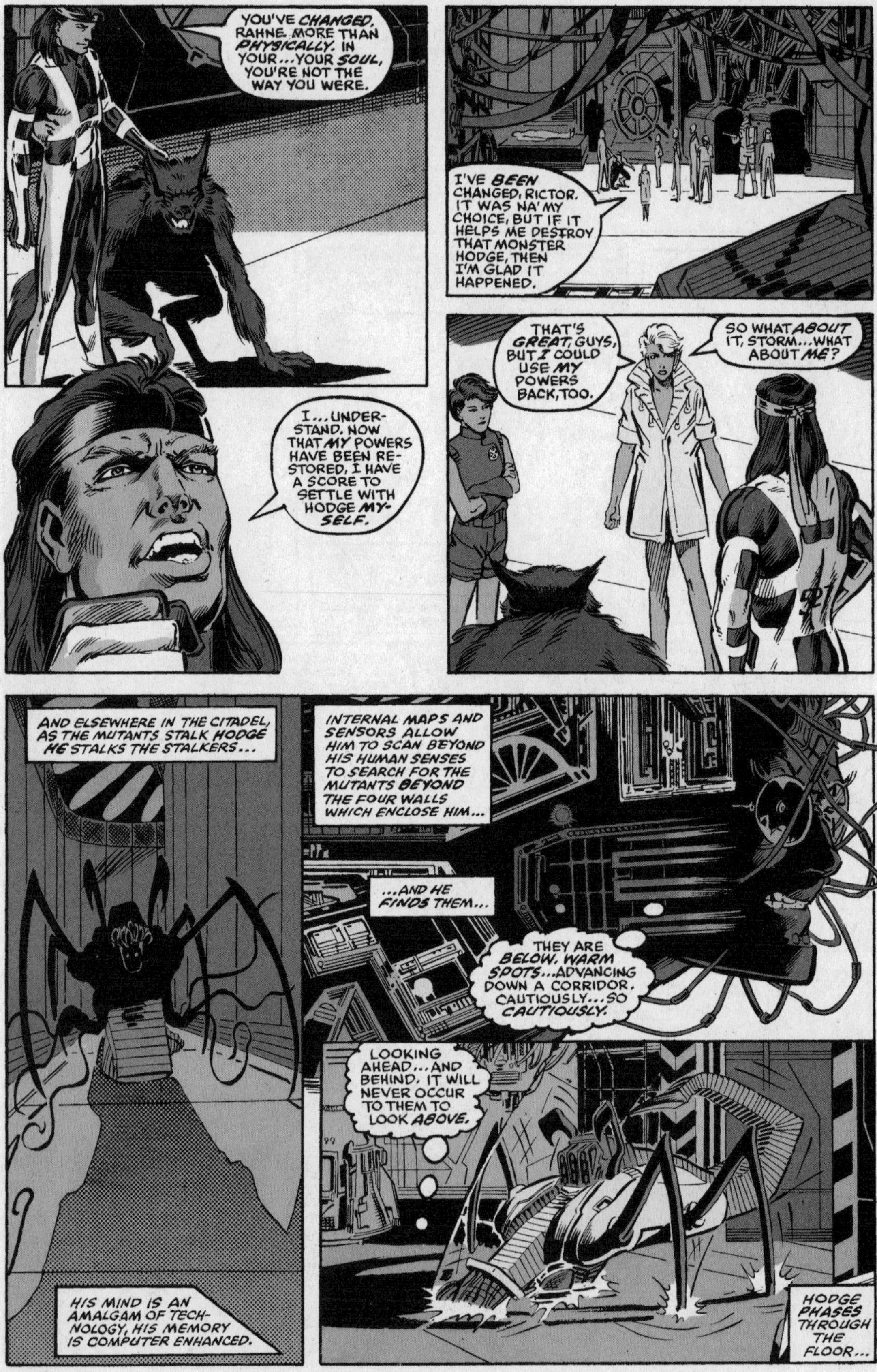

YOU'VE CHANGED, RAHNE. MORE THAN PHYSICALLY. IN YOUR... YOUR SOUL, YOU'RE NOT THE WAY YOU WERE.
I'VE BEEN CHANGED, RICTOR. IT WAS NA' MY CHOICE, BUT IF IT HELPS ME DESTROY THAT MONSTER HODGE, THEN I'M GLAD IT HAPPENED.
I... UNDERSTAND. NOW THAT MY POWERS HAVE BEEN RESTORED, I HAVE A SCORE TO SETTLE WITH HODGE MYSELF.
THAT'S GREAT, GUYS, BUT I COULD USE MY POWERS BACK, TOO.
SO WHAT ABOUT IT, STORM... WHAT ABOUT ME?
AND ELSEWHERE IN THE CITADEL, AS THE MUTANTS STALK HODGE HE STALKS THE STALKERS...
HIS MIND IS AN AMALGAM OF TECHNOLOGY, HIS MEMORY IS COMPUTER ENHANCED.
INTERNAL MAPS AND SENSORS ALLOW HIM TO SCAN BEYOND HIS HUMAN SENSES TO SEARCH FOR THE MUTANTS BEYOND THE FOUR WALLS WHICH ENCLOSE HIM...
...AND HE FINDS THEM...
THEY ARE BELOW. WARM SPOTS... ADVANCING DOWN A CORRIDOR. CAUTIOUSLY... SO CAUTIOUSLY.
LOOKING AHEAD... AND BEHIND. IT WILL NEVER OCCUR TO THEM TO LOOK ABOVE.
HODGE PHASES THROUGH THE FLOOR...

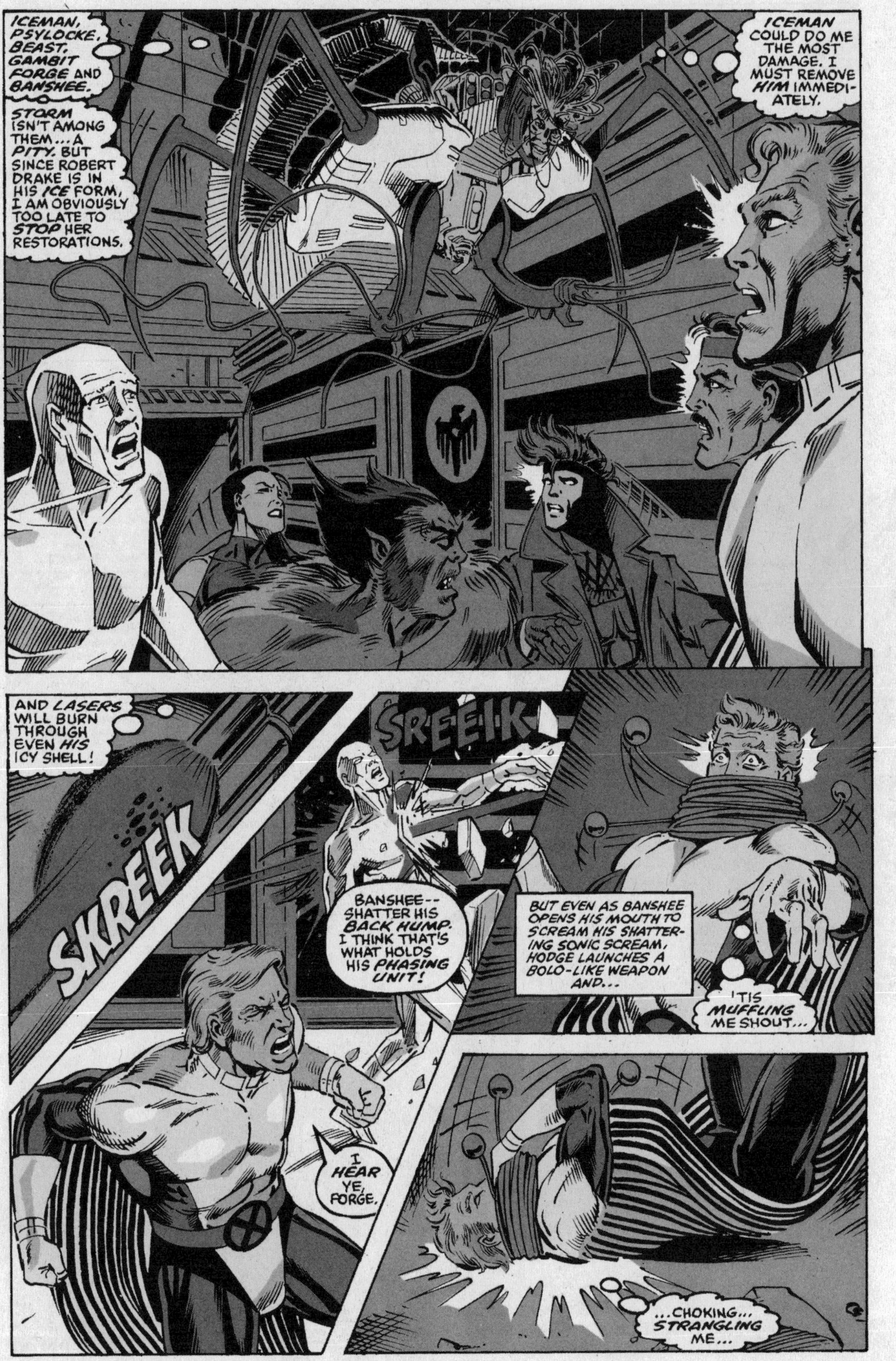
ICEMAN, PSYLOCKE, BEAST, GAMBIT FORGE AND BANSHEE.
STORM ISN'T AMONG THEM... A PITY. BUT SINCE ROBERT DRAKE IS IN HIS ICE FORM, I AM OBVIOUSLY TOO LATE TO STOP HER RESTORATIONS.
ICEMAN COULD DO ME THE MOST DAMAGE. I MUST REMOVE HIM IMMEDIATELY.
AND LASERS WILL BURN THROUGH EVEN HIS ICY SHELL!
SKREEK
SREEIK
BANSHEE-- SHATTER HIS BACK HUMP. I THINK THAT'S WHAT HOLDS HIS PHASING UNIT!
I HEAR YE, FORGE.
BUT EVEN AS BANSHEE OPENS HIS MOUTH TO SCREAM HIS SHATTERING SONIC SCREAM, HODGE LAUNCHES A BOLO-LIKE WEAPON AND...
'TIS MUFFLING ME SHOUT...
...CHOKING... STRANGLING ME...

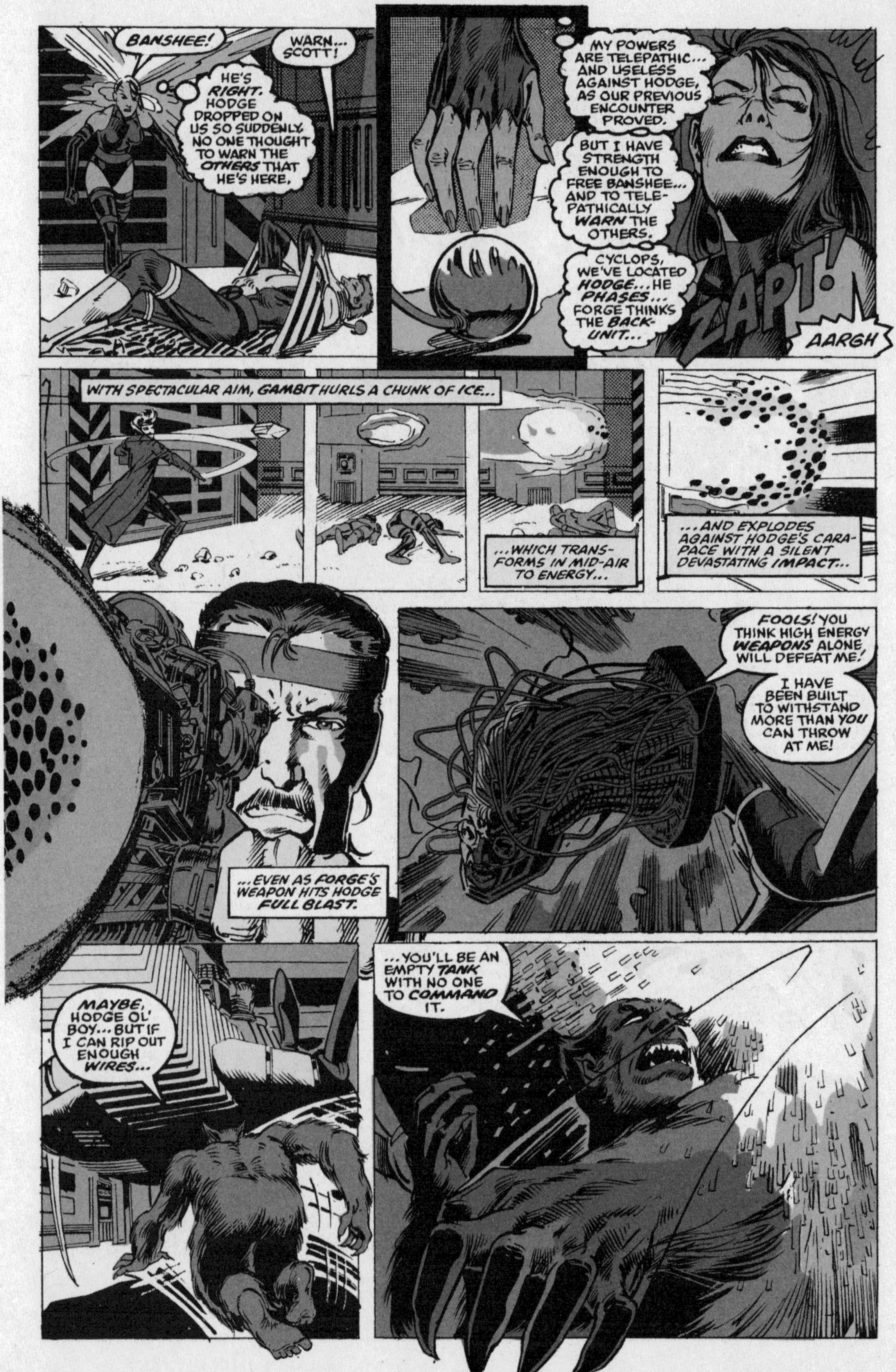
BANSHEE!
WARN... SCOTT!
HE'S RIGHT. HODGE DROPPED ON US SO SUDDENLY, NO ONE THOUGHT TO WARN THE OTHERS THAT HE'S HERE.
MY POWERS ARE TELEPATHIC... AND USELESS AGAINST HODGE, AS OUR PREVIOUS ENCOUNTER PROVED.
BUT I HAVE STRENGTH ENOUGH TO FREE BANSHEE... AND TO TELEPATHICALLY WARN THE OTHERS.
CYCLOPS, WE'VE LOCATED HODGE... HE PHASES... FORGE THINKS THE BACK-UNIT...
ZAPT!
AARGH
WITH SPECTACULAR AIM, GAMBIT HURLS A CHUNK OF ICE...
...WHICH TRANSFORMS IN MID-AIR TO ENERGY...
...AND EXPLODES AGAINST HODGE'S CARAPACE WITH A SILENT DEVASTATING IMPACT...
...EVEN AS FORGE'S WEAPON HITS HODGE FULL BLAST.
FOOLS! YOU THINK HIGH ENERGY WEAPONS ALONE WILL DEFEAT ME!
I HAVE BEEN BUILT TO WITHSTAND MORE THAN YOU CAN THROW AT ME!
MAYBE, HODGE OL' BOY... BUT IF I CAN RIP OUT ENOUGH WIRES...
...YOU'LL BE AN EMPTY TANK WITH NO ONE TO COMMAND IT.

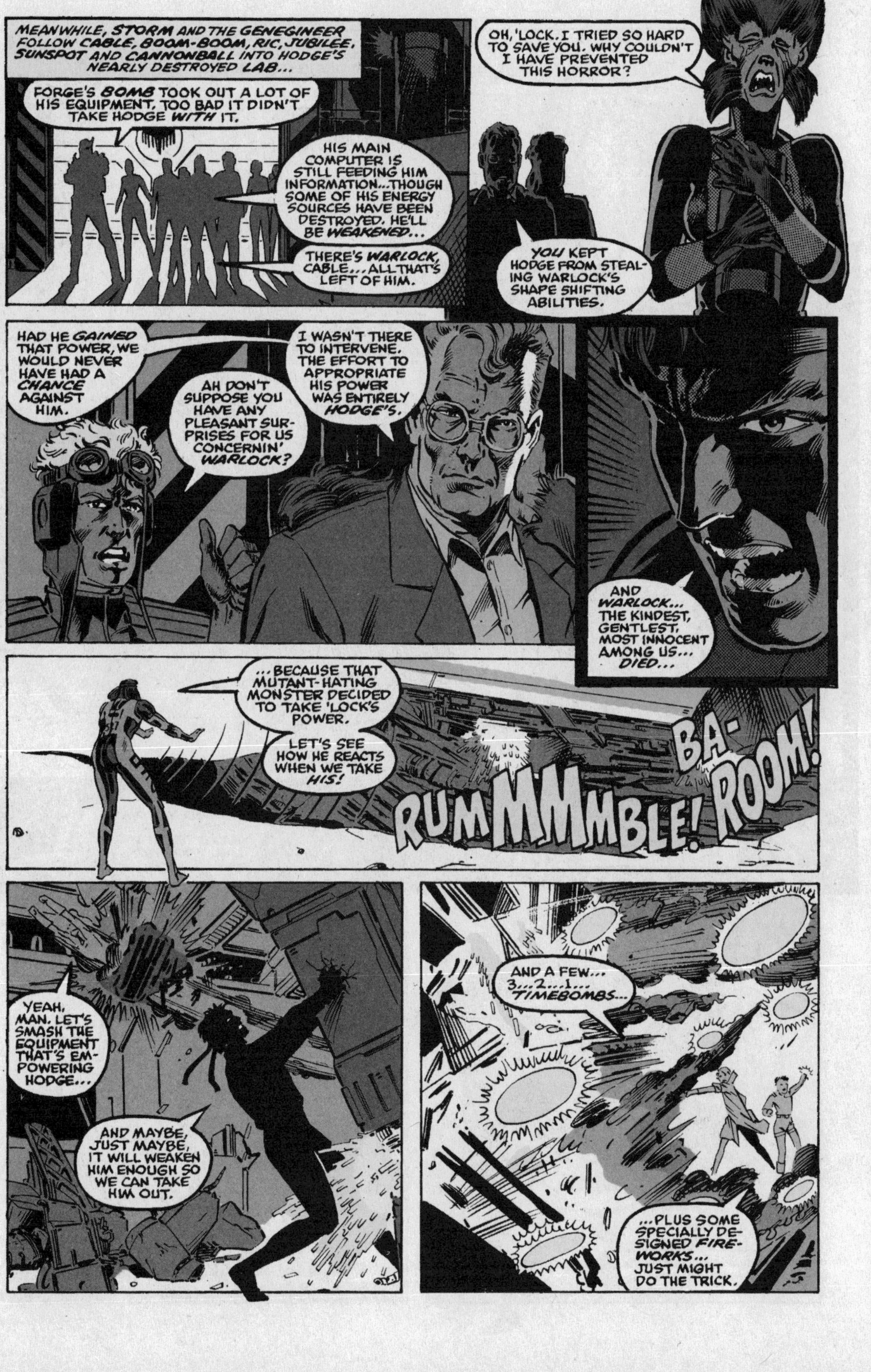
MEANWHILE, STORM AND THE GENEGINEER FOLLOW CABLE, BOOM-BOOM, RIC, JUBILEE, SUNSPOT AND CANNONBALL INTO HODGE'S NEARLY DESTROYED LAB...
FORGE'S BOMB TOOK OUT A LOT OF HIS EQUIPMENT. TOO BAD IT DIDN'T TAKE HODGE WITH IT.
HIS MAIN COMPUTER IS STILL FEEDING HIM INFORMATION...THOUGH SOME OF HIS ENERGY SOURCES HAVE BEEN DESTROYED. HE'LL BE WEAKENED...
THERE'S WARLOCK, CABLE... ALL THAT'S LEFT OF HIM.
OH, 'LOCK. I TRIED SO HARD TO SAVE YOU. WHY COULDN'T I HAVE PREVENTED THIS HORROR?
YOU KEPT HODGE FROM STEALING WARLOCK'S SHAPE SHIFTING ABILITIES.
HAD HE GAINED THAT POWER, WE WOULD NEVER HAVE HAD A CHANCE AGAINST HIM.
AH DON'T SUPPOSE YOU HAVE ANY PLEASANT SURPRISES FOR US CONCERNIN' WARLOCK?
I WASN'T THERE TO INTERVENE. THE EFFORT TO APPROPRIATE HIS POWER WAS ENTIRELY HODGE'S.
AND WARLOCK... THE KINDEST, GENTLEST, MOST INNOCENT AMONG US... DIED...
...BECAUSE THAT MUTANT-HATING MONSTER DECIDED TO TAKE 'LOCK'S POWER.
LET'S SEE HOW HE REACTS WHEN WE TAKE HIS!
BA-ROOM!
RUMMMMMBLE!
YEAH, MAN. LET'S SMASH THE EQUIPMENT THAT'S EMPOWERING HODGE...
AND MAYBE, JUST MAYBE, IT WILL WEAKEN HIM ENOUGH SO WE CAN TAKE HIM OUT.
AND A FEW... 3...2...1... TIMEBOMBS...
...PLUS SOME SPECIALLY DESIGNED FIREWORKS... JUST MIGHT DO THE TRICK.

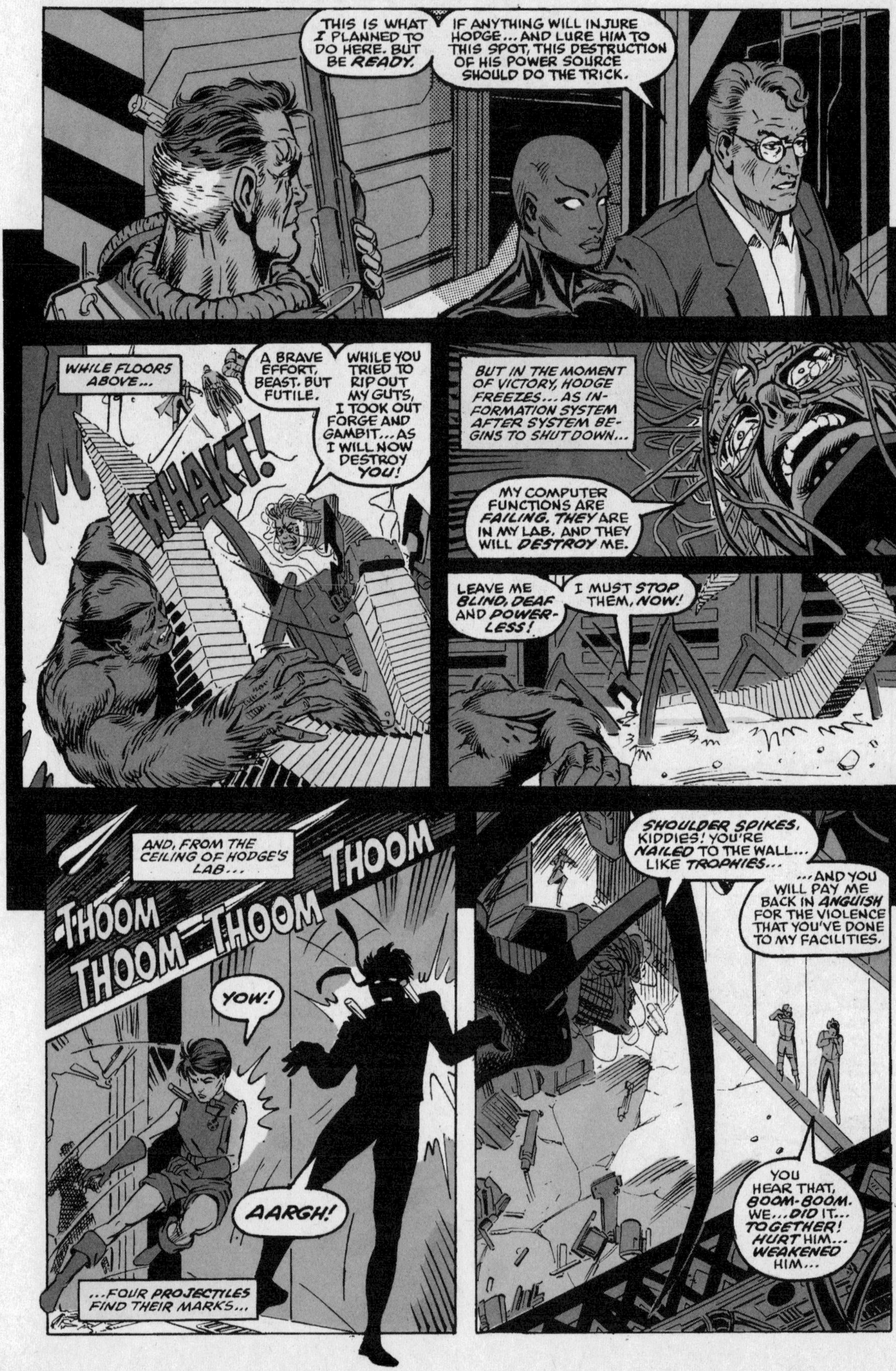
THIS IS WHAT I PLANNED TO DO HERE. BUT BE READY.
IF ANYTHING WILL INJURE HODGE... AND LURE HIM TO THIS SPOT, THIS DESTRUCTION OF HIS POWER SOURCE SHOULD DO THE TRICK.
WHILE FLOORS ABOVE...
A BRAVE EFFORT, BEAST. BUT FUTILE.
WHILE YOU TRIED TO RIP OUT MY GUTS, I TOOK OUT FORGE AND GAMBIT... AS I WILL NOW DESTROY YOU!
WHAKT!
BUT IN THE MOMENT OF VICTORY, HODGE FREEZES... AS INFORMATION SYSTEM AFTER SYSTEM BEGINS TO SHUT DOWN...
MY COMPUTER FUNCTIONS ARE FAILING. THEY ARE IN MY LAB. AND THEY WILL DESTROY ME.
LEAVE ME BLIND, DEAF AND POWERLESS!
I MUST STOP THEM, NOW!
AND, FROM THE CEILING OF HODGE'S LAB...
THOOM THOOM THOOM THOOM
YOW!
AARGH!
...FOUR PROJECTILES FIND THEIR MARKS...
SHOULDER SPIKES, KIDDIES! YOU'RE NAILED TO THE WALL... LIKE TROPHIES...
...AND YOU WILL PAY ME BACK IN ANGUISH FOR THE VIOLENCE THAT YOU'VE DONE TO MY FACILITIES.
YOU HEAR THAT, BOOM-BOOM. WE... DID IT... TOGETHER! HURT HIM... WEAKENED HIM...

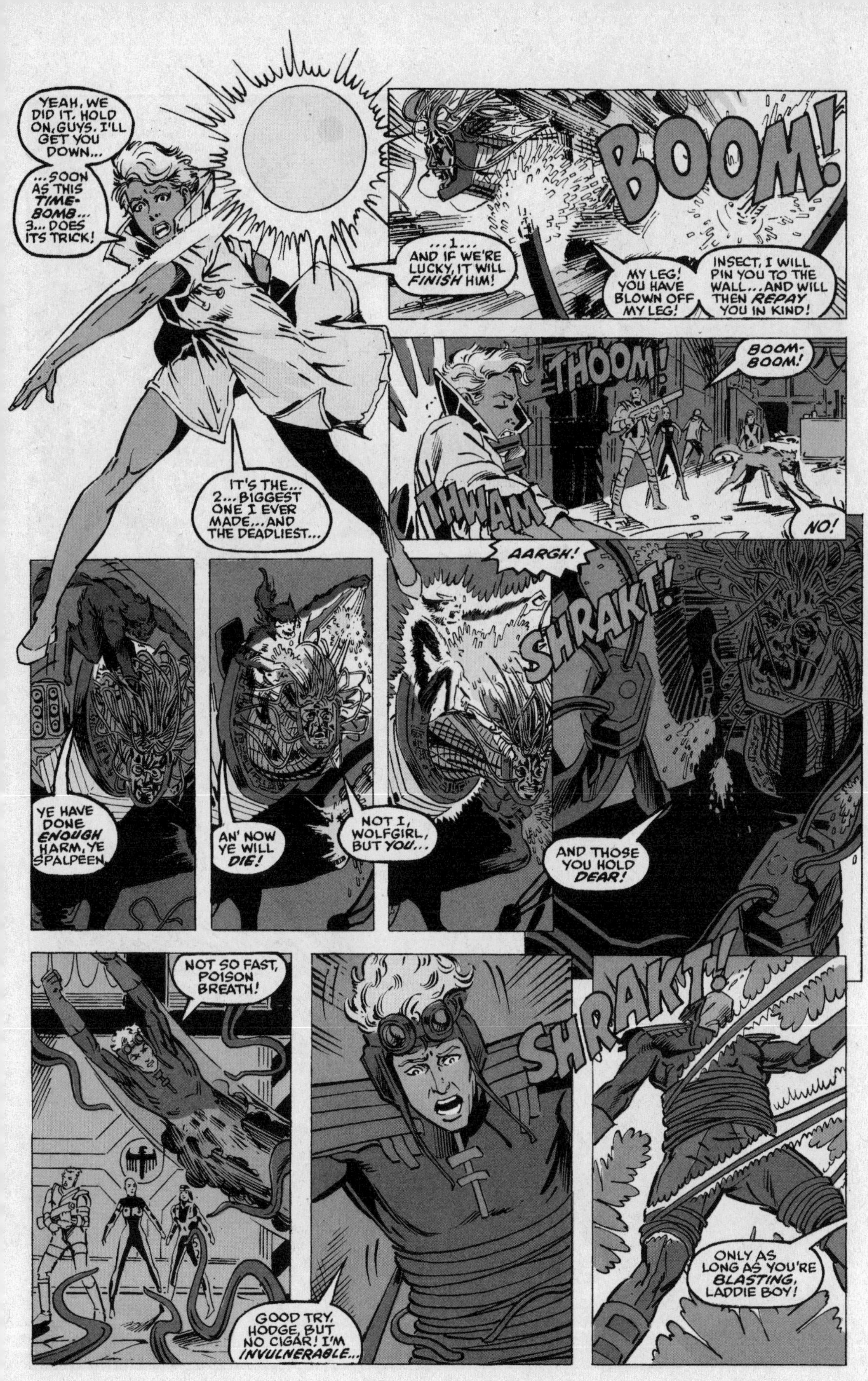
YEAH, WE DID IT. HOLD ON, GUYS. I'LL GET YOU DOWN...
...SOON AS THIS TIME-BOMB... 3... DOES ITS TRICK!
IT'S THE... 2... BIGGEST ONE I EVER MADE... AND THE DEADLIEST...
...1... AND IF WE'RE LUCKY, IT WILL FINISH HIM!
BOOM!
MY LEG! YOU HAVE BLOWN OFF MY LEG!
INSECT, I WILL PIN YOU TO THE WALL... AND WILL THEN REPAY YOU IN KIND!
THOOM!
BOOM-BOOM!
THWAM
NO!
YE HAVE DONE ENOUGH HARM, YE SPALPEEN.
AN' NOW YE WILL DIE!
NOT I, WOLFGIRL, BUT YOU...
AARGH!
SHRAKT!
AND THOSE YOU HOLD DEAR!
NOT SO FAST, POISON BREATH!
GOOD TRY, HODGE, BUT NO CIGAR! I'M INVULNERABLE...
SHRAKT!
ONLY AS LONG AS YOU'RE BLASTING, LADDIE BOY!

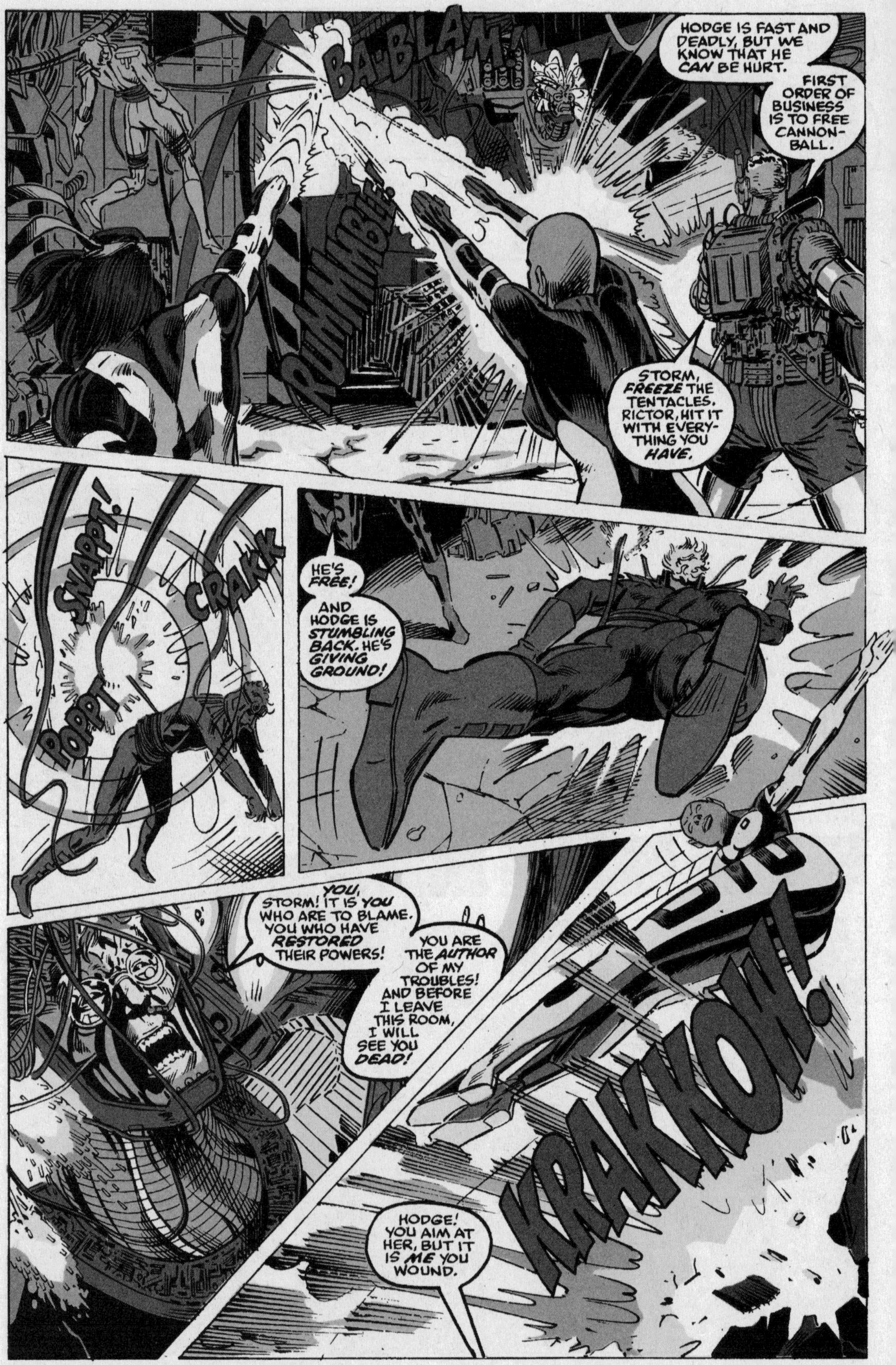
BA-BLAM!
RUMMMBLE
HODGE IS FAST AND DEADLY, BUT WE KNOW THAT HE CAN BE HURT.
FIRST ORDER OF BUSINESS IS TO FREE CANNON-BALL.
STORM, FREEZE THE TENTACLES. RICTOR, HIT IT WITH EVERY-THING YOU HAVE.
SNAPP!
CRAKK
POPP!
HE'S FREE!
AND HODGE IS STUMBLING BACK. HE'S GIVING GROUND!
YOU, STORM! IT IS YOU WHO ARE TO BLAME. YOU WHO HAVE RESTORED THEIR POWERS!
YOU ARE THE AUTHOR OF MY TROUBLES! AND BEFORE I LEAVE THIS ROOM, I WILL SEE YOU DEAD!
KRAKKOW!
HODGE! YOU AIM AT HER, BUT IT IS ME YOU WOUND.

YOU HATE AND FEAR THE *MUTANTS* SO, THAT YOU FORGET THE *ENEMIES* YOU HAVE MADE AMONG THE *MERELY HUMAN.*

STORM HAS RESTORED THEIR POWERS ...*BECAUSE* I RESTORED HERS. SHE IS *MY WEAPON* AGAINST YOU...

WHROOM!

BUT SHE IS NOT THE *ONLY* WEAPON I POSSESS! AND NOW THAT THEY HAVE *WEAKENED* YOU, I WILL DESTROY YOU!

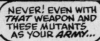

NEVER! EVEN WITH *THAT* WEAPON AND THESE MUTANTS AS YOUR *ARMY*...

...IT IS *I* WHO WILL *DESTROY YOU!*

CRAK!

IF I *AM* DESTROYED, MONSTER, AT LEAST I WILL TAKE YOU *WITH* ME!

BHAVROOM!

NOOO! *AWAY* FROM ME, HUMAN! YOU HAVE *HURT* ME ....MORE THAN THE *OTHERS*...

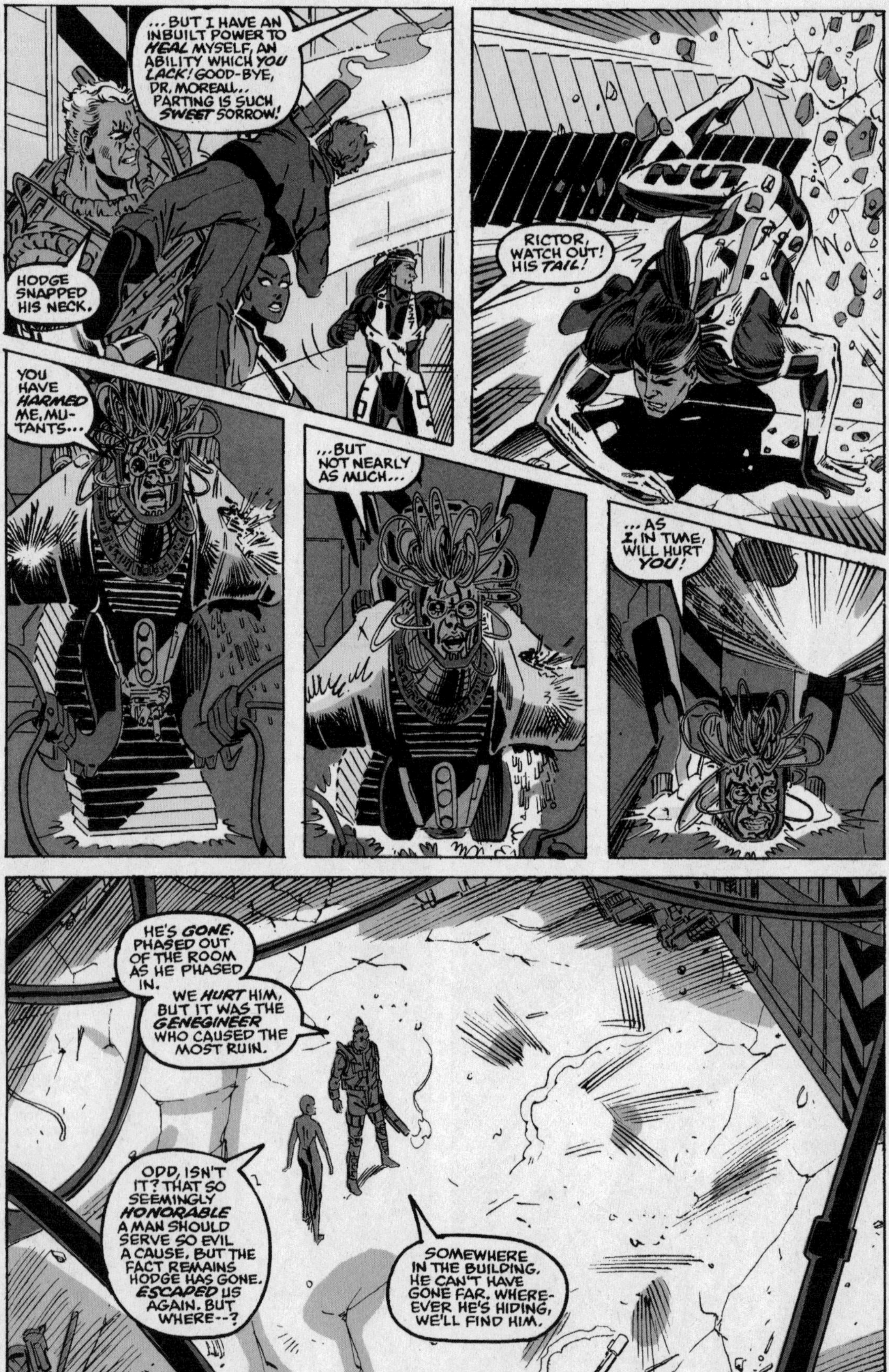
...BUT I HAVE AN INBUILT POWER TO HEAL MYSELF, AN ABILITY WHICH YOU LACK! GOOD-BYE, DR. MOREAU... PARTING IS SUCH SWEET SORROW!
HODGE SNAPPED HIS NECK.
RICTOR, WATCH OUT! HIS TAIL!
YOU HAVE HARMED ME, MUTANTS...
...BUT NOT NEARLY AS MUCH...
...AS I, IN TIME, WILL HURT YOU!
HE'S GONE. PHASED OUT OF THE ROOM AS HE PHASED IN.
WE HURT HIM, BUT IT WAS THE GENEGINEER WHO CAUSED THE MOST RUIN.
ODD, ISN'T IT? THAT SO SEEMINGLY HONORABLE A MAN SHOULD SERVE SO EVIL A CAUSE, BUT THE FACT REMAINS HODGE HAS GONE. ESCAPED US AGAIN. BUT WHERE--?
SOMEWHERE IN THE BUILDING. HE CAN'T HAVE GONE FAR. WHERE-EVER HE'S HIDING, WE'LL FIND HIM.

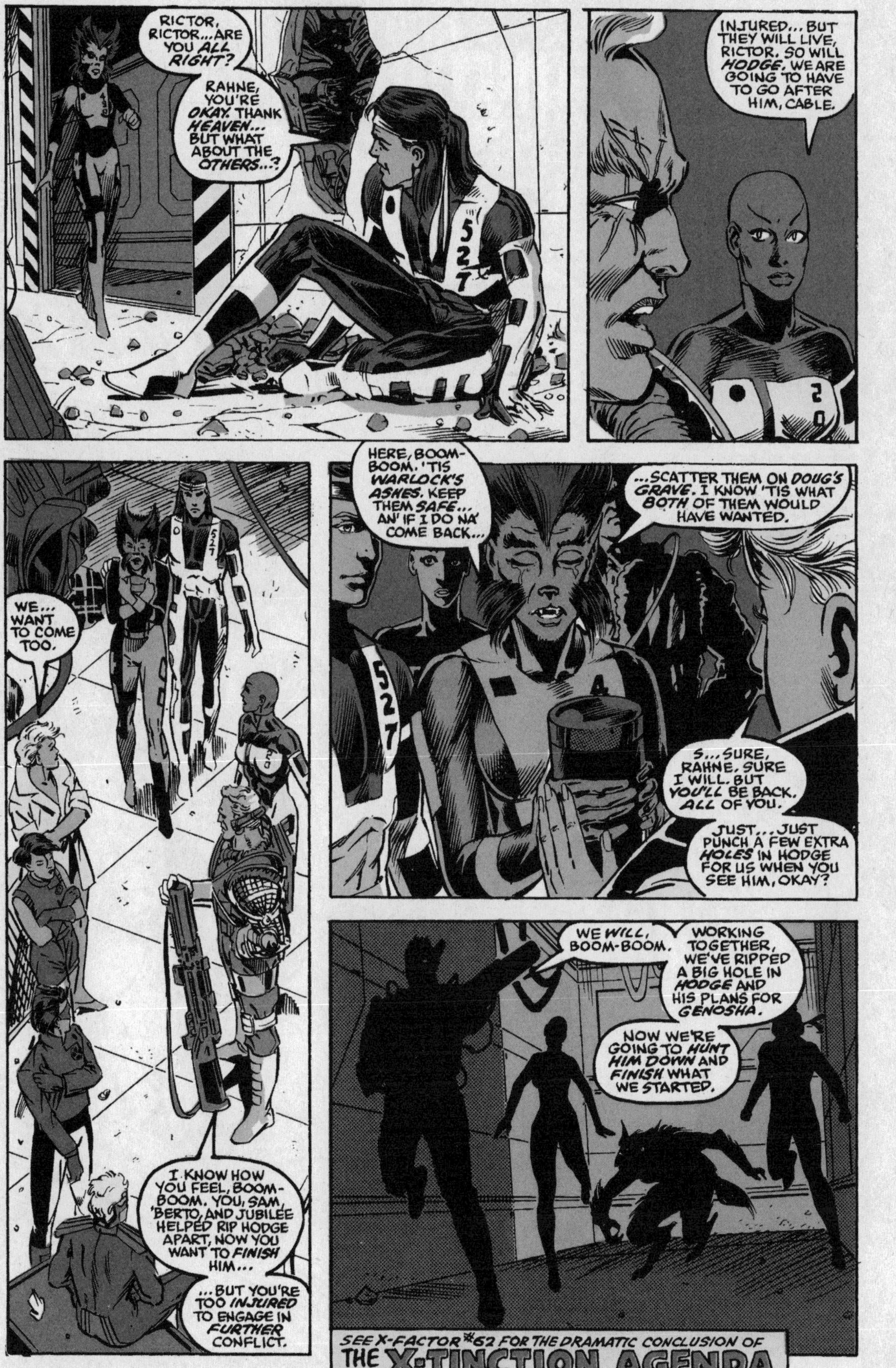
RICTOR, RICTOR... ARE YOU ALL RIGHT?
RAHNE, YOU'RE OKAY. THANK HEAVEN... BUT WHAT ABOUT THE OTHERS...?
INJURED... BUT THEY WILL LIVE, RICTOR. SO WILL HODGE. WE ARE GOING TO HAVE TO GO AFTER HIM, CABLE.
WE... WANT TO COME TOO.
I KNOW HOW YOU FEEL, BOOM-BOOM. YOU, SAM, 'BERTO, AND JUBILEE HELPED RIP HODGE APART, NOW YOU WANT TO FINISH HIM...
...BUT YOU'RE TOO INJURED TO ENGAGE IN FURTHER CONFLICT.
HERE, BOOM-BOOM. 'TIS WARLOCK'S ASHES. KEEP THEM SAFE... AN' IF I DO NA' COME BACK...
...SCATTER THEM ON DOUG'S GRAVE. I KNOW 'TIS WHAT BOTH OF THEM WOULD HAVE WANTED.
S... SURE, RAHNE. SURE I WILL. BUT YOU'LL BE BACK. ALL OF YOU.
JUST... JUST PUNCH A FEW EXTRA HOLES IN HODGE FOR US WHEN YOU SEE HIM, OKAY?
WE WILL, BOOM-BOOM.
WORKING TOGETHER, WE'VE RIPPED A BIG HOLE IN HODGE AND HIS PLANS FOR GENOSHA.
NOW WE'RE GOING TO HUNT HIM DOWN AND FINISH WHAT WE STARTED.
SEE X-FACTOR #62 FOR THE DRAMATIC CONCLUSION OF
THE X-TINCTION AGENDA

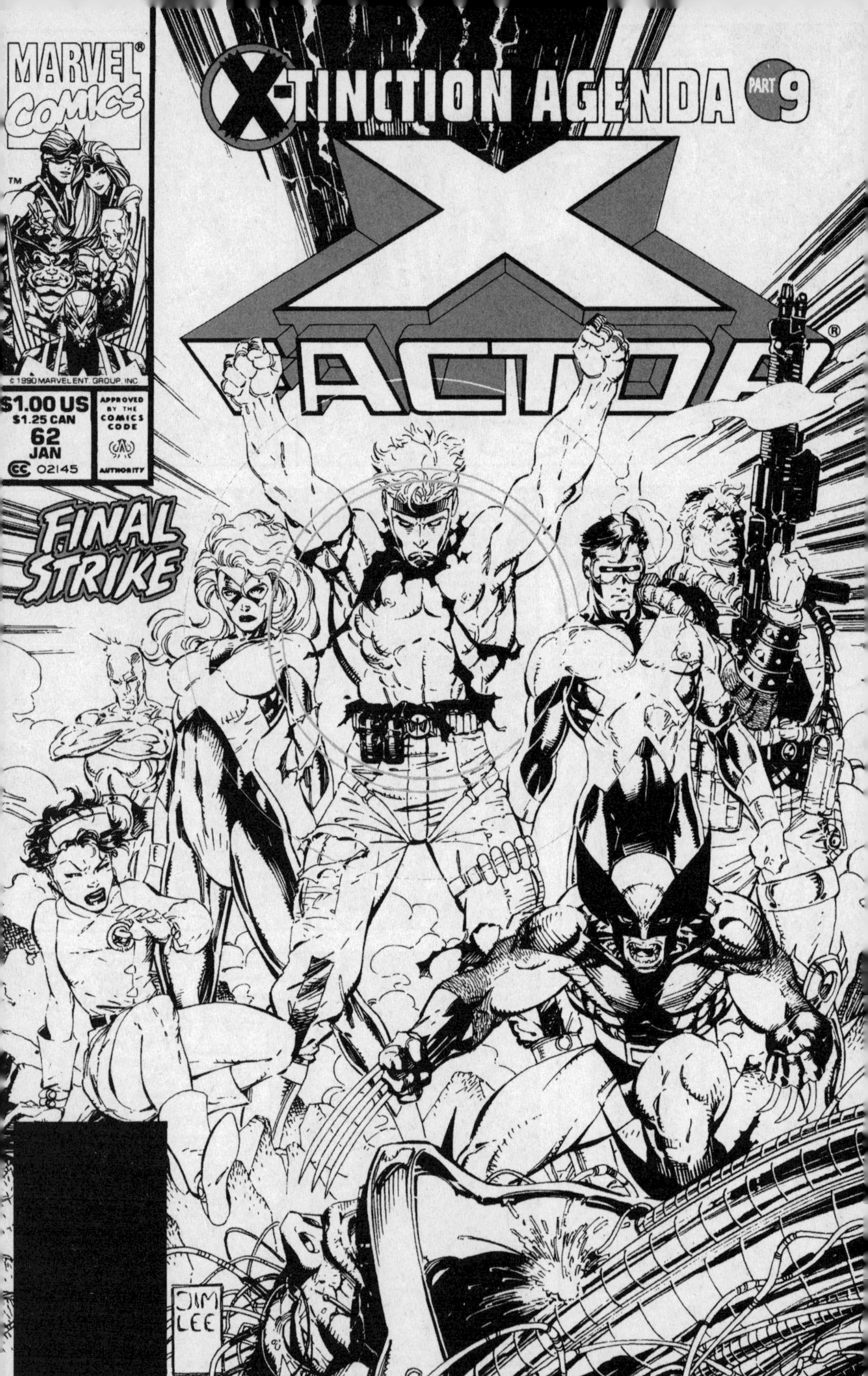
MARVEL COMICS
X-TINCTION AGENDA PART 9
X-FACTOR
©1990 MARVEL ENT. GROUP, INC.
$1.00 US
$1.25 CAN
62
JAN
02145
APPROVED BY THE COMICS CODE AUTHORITY
FINAL STRIKE
JIM LEE

STAN LEE PRESENTS

THE FINAL CHAPTER IN THE X-TEAM'S GREATEST CRISIS

LOUISE SIMONSON WRITER
JON BOGDANOVE PENCILLER
ALLEN MILGROM INKER
TASK FORCE Z² LETTERERS
GLYNIS OLIVER COLORIST
BOB HARRAS EDITOR
TOM DeFALCO EDITOR-IN-CHIEF

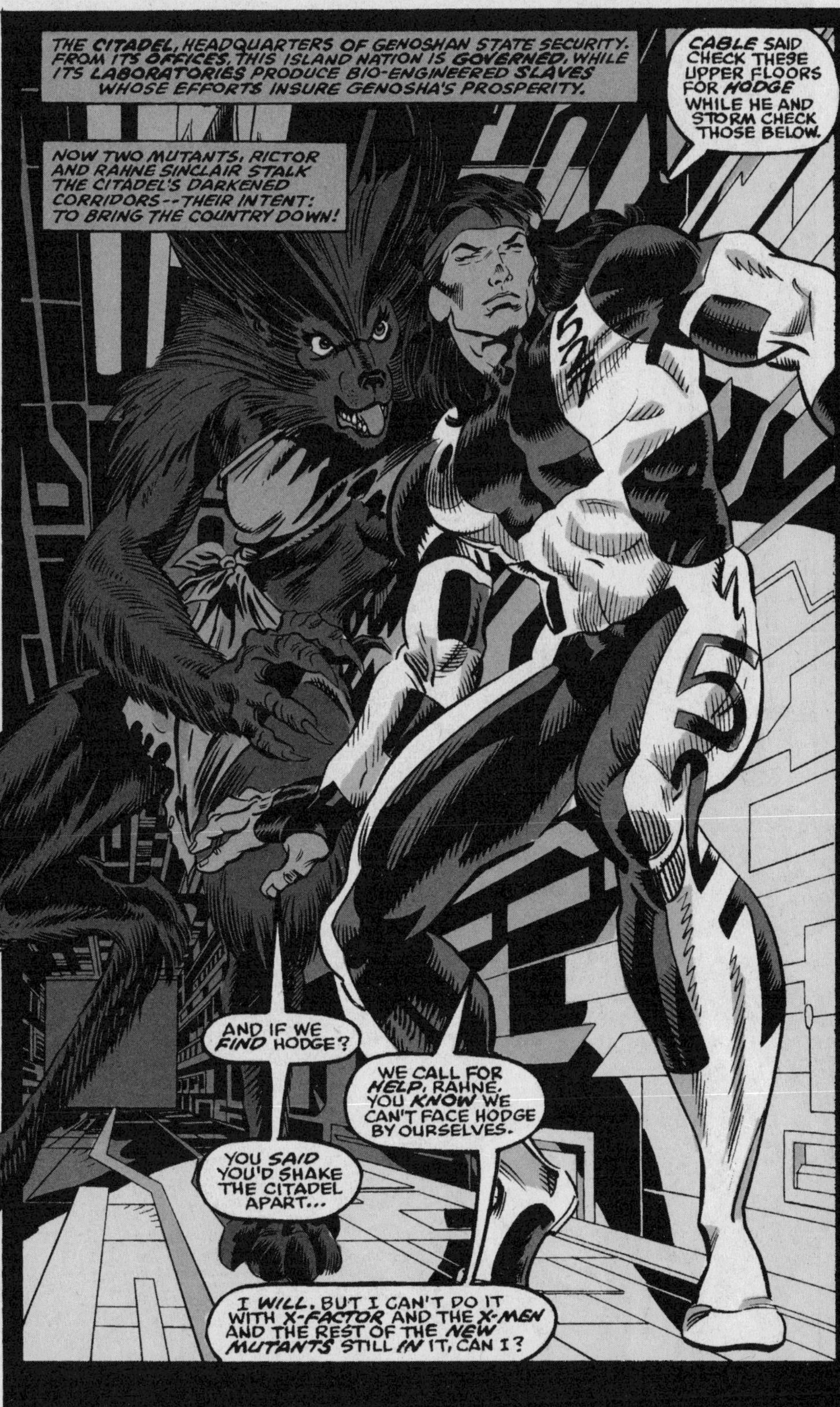
THE CITADEL, HEADQUARTERS OF GENOSHAN STATE SECURITY. FROM ITS OFFICES, THIS ISLAND NATION IS GOVERNED, WHILE ITS LABORATORIES PRODUCE BIO-ENGINEERED SLAVES WHOSE EFFORTS INSURE GENOSHA'S PROSPERITY.
CABLE SAID CHECK THESE UPPER FLOORS FOR HODGE WHILE HE AND STORM CHECK THOSE BELOW.
NOW TWO MUTANTS, RICTOR AND RAHNE SINCLAIR STALK THE CITADEL'S DARKENED CORRIDORS--THEIR INTENT: TO BRING THE COUNTRY DOWN!
AND IF WE FIND HODGE?
WE CALL FOR HELP, RAHNE. YOU KNOW WE CAN'T FACE HODGE BY OURSELVES.
YOU SAID YOU'D SHAKE THE CITADEL APART...
I WILL. BUT I CAN'T DO IT WITH X-FACTOR AND THE X-MEN AND THE REST OF THE NEW MUTANTS STILL IN IT, CAN I?

SUDDENLY, CAMERON HODGE, CYBORG ALLY OF GENOSHA'S PRESIDENT, ARCH-ENEMY OF THE MUTANT TEAMS, APPEARS OUT OF THE SHADOWS...
WELL, WELL! TWO OF THE INSECTS WHO DESTROYED MY LAB.
RAHNE! GET BACK!
CABLE! IT'S HODGE! WE'VE FOUND HIM!
STAN LEE PRESENTS
CAPITAL PUNISHMENT

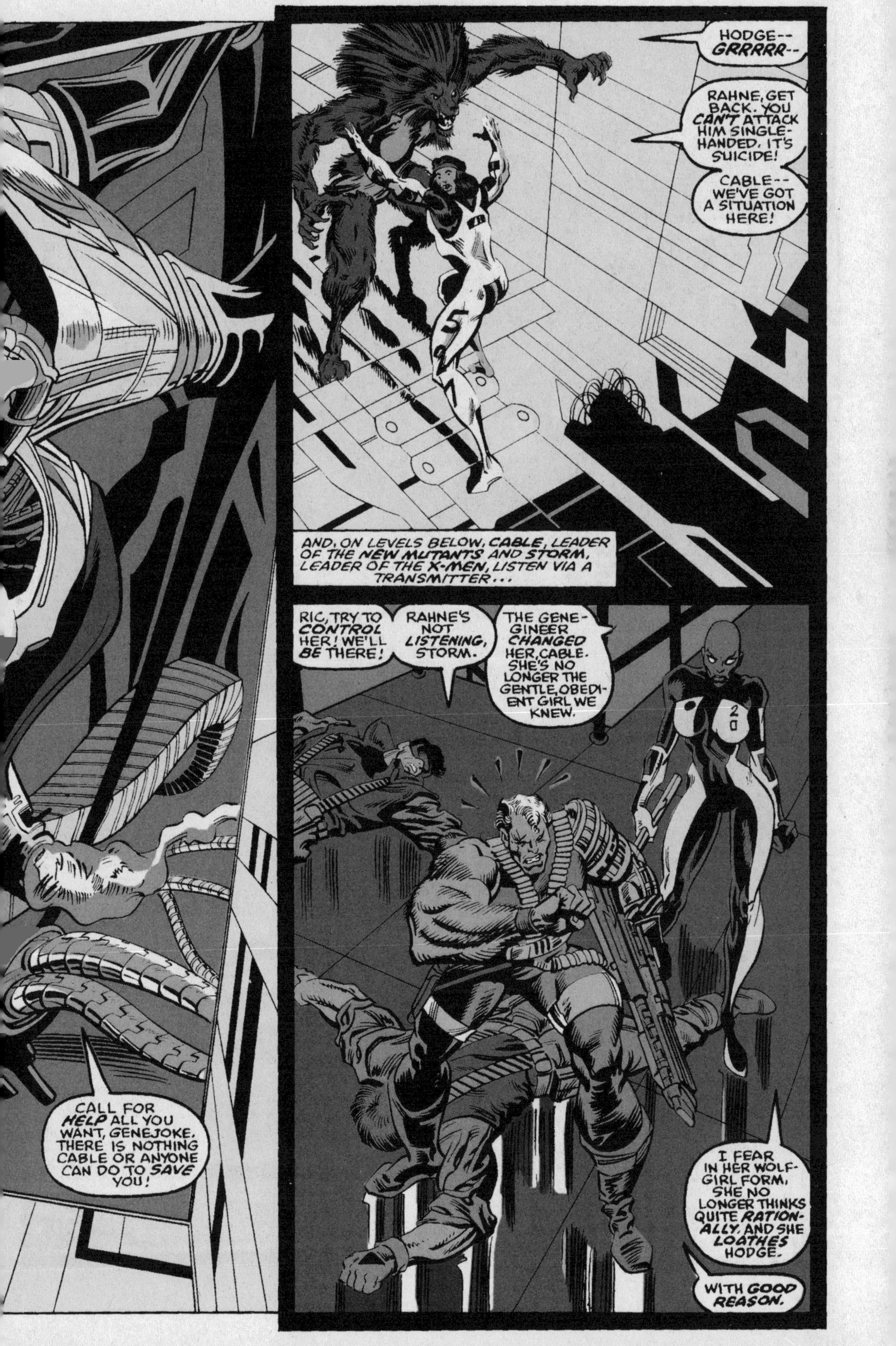
HODGE-- GRRRRR--
RAHNE, GET BACK. YOU CAN'T ATTACK HIM SINGLE-HANDED. IT'S SUICIDE!
CABLE-- WE'VE GOT A SITUATION HERE!
AND, ON LEVELS BELOW, CABLE, LEADER OF THE NEW MUTANTS AND STORM, LEADER OF THE X-MEN, LISTEN VIA A TRANSMITTER...
RIC, TRY TO CONTROL HER! WE'LL BE THERE!
RAHNE'S NOT LISTENING, STORM.
THE GENE-GINEER CHANGED HER, CABLE. SHE'S NO LONGER THE GENTLE, OBEDIENT GIRL WE KNEW.
I FEAR IN HER WOLF-GIRL FORM, SHE NO LONGER THINKS QUITE RATIONALLY, AND SHE LOATHES HODGE.
WITH GOOD REASON.
CALL FOR HELP ALL YOU WANT, GENEJOKE. THERE IS NOTHING CABLE OR ANYONE CAN DO TO SAVE YOU!

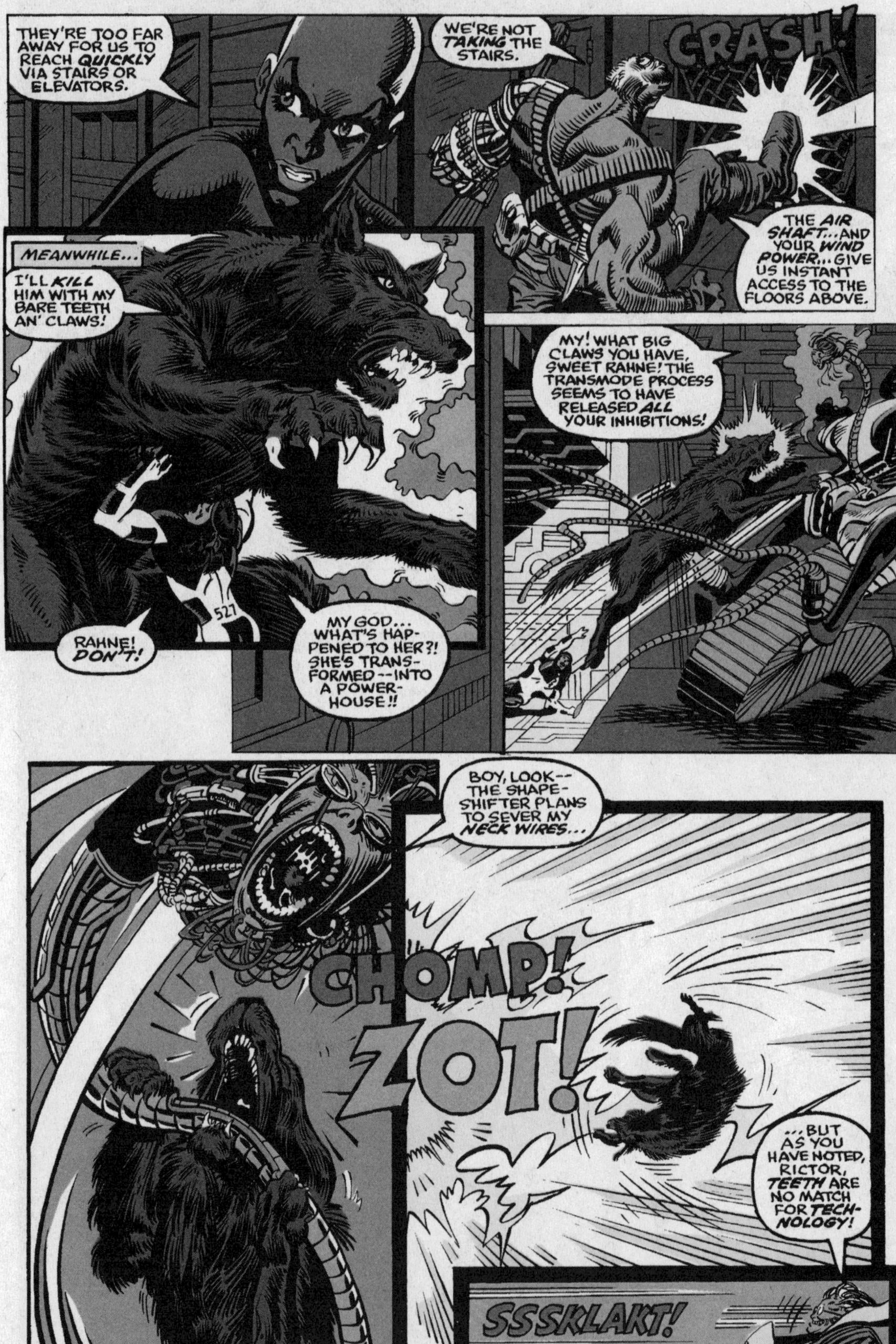
THEY'RE TOO FAR AWAY FOR US TO REACH QUICKLY VIA STAIRS OR ELEVATORS.
WE'RE NOT TAKING THE STAIRS.
CRASH!
THE AIR SHAFT...AND YOUR WIND POWER...GIVE US INSTANT ACCESS TO THE FLOORS ABOVE.
MEANWHILE...
I'LL KILL HIM WITH MY BARE TEETH AN' CLAWS!
527
RAHNE! DON'T!
MY GOD... WHAT'S HAPPENED TO HER?! SHE'S TRANSFORMED--INTO A POWERHOUSE!!
MY! WHAT BIG CLAWS YOU HAVE, SWEET RAHNE! THE TRANSMODE PROCESS SEEMS TO HAVE RELEASED ALL YOUR INHIBITIONS!
BOY, LOOK-- THE SHAPESHIFTER PLANS TO SEVER MY NECK WIRES...
CHOMP!
ZOT!
...BUT AS YOU HAVE NOTED, RICTOR, TEETH ARE NO MATCH FOR TECHNOLOGY!
SSSKLAKT!

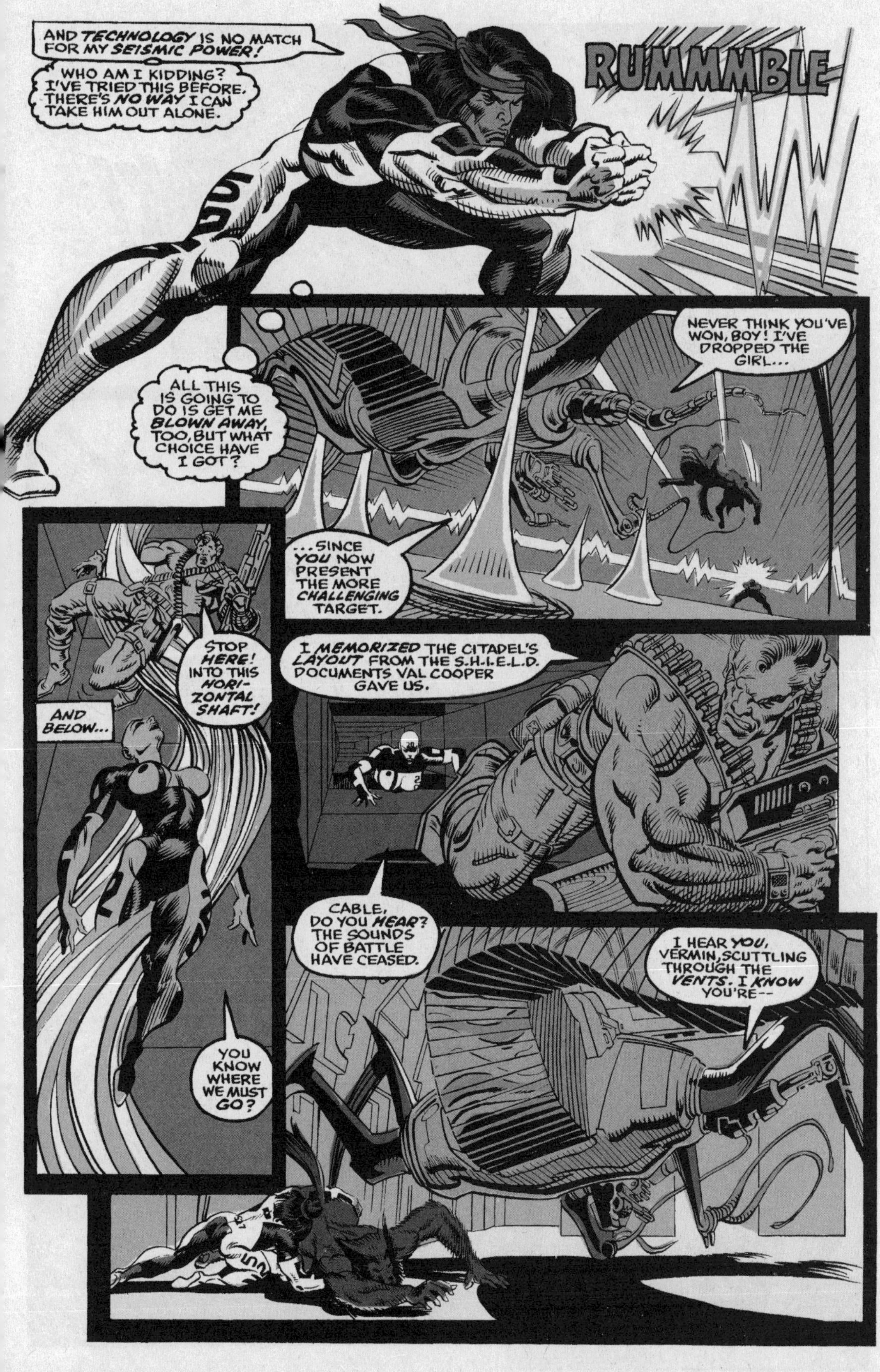
AND TECHNOLOGY IS NO MATCH FOR MY SEISMIC POWER!
WHO AM I KIDDING? I'VE TRIED THIS BEFORE. THERE'S NO WAY I CAN TAKE HIM OUT ALONE.
RUMMMBLE
ALL THIS IS GOING TO DO IS GET ME BLOWN AWAY, TOO, BUT WHAT CHOICE HAVE I GOT?
NEVER THINK YOU'VE WON, BOY! I'VE DROPPED THE GIRL...
...SINCE YOU NOW PRESENT THE MORE CHALLENGING TARGET.
STOP HERE! INTO THIS HORI-ZONTAL SHAFT!
I MEMORIZED THE CITADEL'S LAYOUT FROM THE S.H.I.E.L.D. DOCUMENTS VAL COOPER GAVE US.
AND BELOW...
CABLE, DO YOU HEAR? THE SOUNDS OF BATTLE HAVE CEASED.
YOU KNOW WHERE WE MUST GO?
I HEAR YOU, VERMIN, SCUTTLING THROUGH THE VENTS. I KNOW YOU'RE--

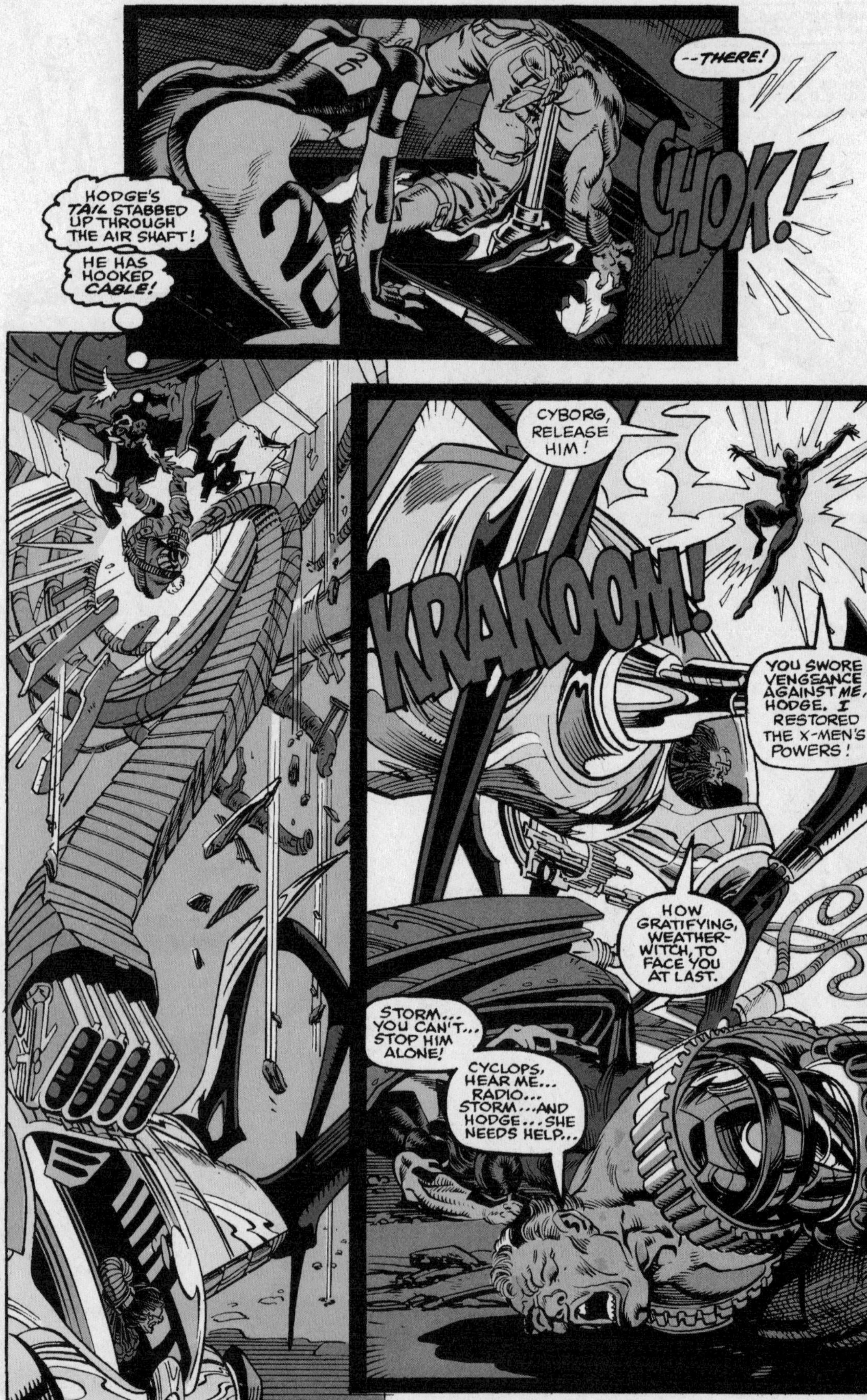
--THERE!
CHOK!
HODGE'S TAIL STABBED UP THROUGH THE AIR SHAFT!
HE HAS HOOKED CABLE!
CYBORG, RELEASE HIM!
KRAKOOM!
YOU SWORE VENGEANCE AGAINST ME, HODGE. I RESTORED THE X-MEN'S POWERS!
HOW GRATIFYING, WEATHER-WITCH, TO FACE YOU AT LAST.
STORM... YOU CAN'T... STOP HIM ALONE!
CYCLOPS, HEAR ME... RADIO... STORM... AND HODGE... SHE NEEDS HELP...

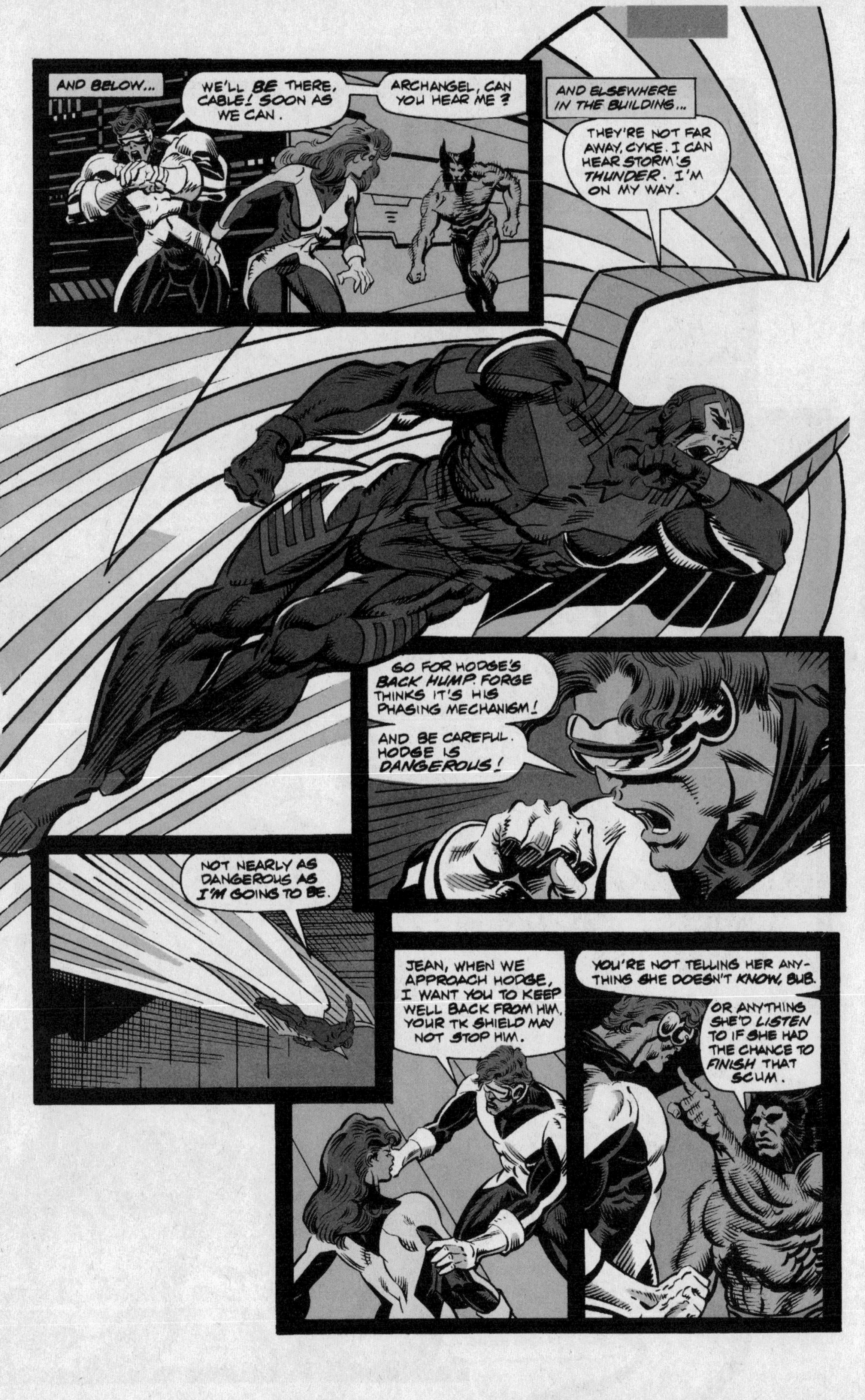
AND BELOW...
WE'LL BE THERE, CABLE! SOON AS WE CAN.
ARCHANGEL, CAN YOU HEAR ME?
AND ELSEWHERE IN THE BUILDING...
THEY'RE NOT FAR AWAY, CYKE. I CAN HEAR STORM'S THUNDER. I'M ON MY WAY.
SO FOR HODGE'S BACK HUMP. FORGE THINKS IT'S HIS PHASING MECHANISM!
AND BE CAREFUL. HODGE IS DANGEROUS!
NOT NEARLY AS DANGEROUS AS I'M GOING TO BE.
JEAN, WHEN WE APPROACH HODGE, I WANT YOU TO KEEP WELL BACK FROM HIM. YOUR TK SHIELD MAY NOT STOP HIM.
YOU'RE NOT TELLING HER ANYTHING SHE DOESN'T KNOW, BUB.
OR ANYTHING SHE'D LISTEN TO IF SHE HAD THE CHANCE TO FINISH THAT SCUM.

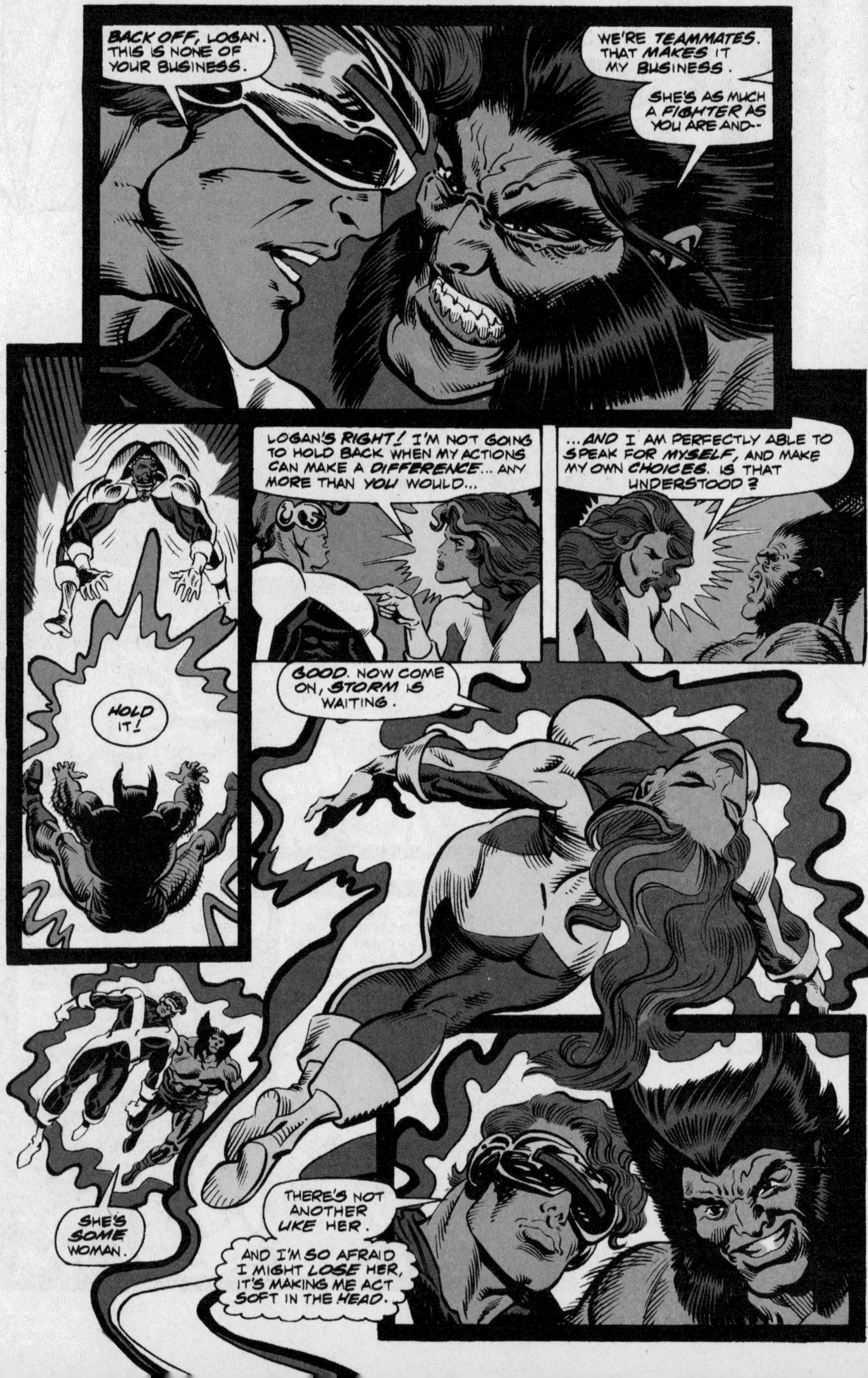

BACK OFF, LOGAN. THIS IS NONE OF YOUR BUSINESS.
WE'RE TEAMMATES. THAT MAKES IT MY BUSINESS.
SHE'S AS MUCH A FIGHTER AS YOU ARE AND--
HOLD IT!
LOGAN'S RIGHT! I'M NOT GOING TO HOLD BACK WHEN MY ACTIONS CAN MAKE A DIFFERENCE... ANY MORE THAN YOU WOULD...
...AND I AM PERFECTLY ABLE TO SPEAK FOR MYSELF, AND MAKE MY OWN CHOICES. IS THAT UNDERSTOOD?
GOOD. NOW COME ON, STORM IS WAITING.
SHE'S SOME WOMAN.
THERE'S NOT ANOTHER LIKE HER.
AND I'M SO AFRAID I MIGHT LOSE HER, IT'S MAKING ME ACT SOFT IN THE HEAD.

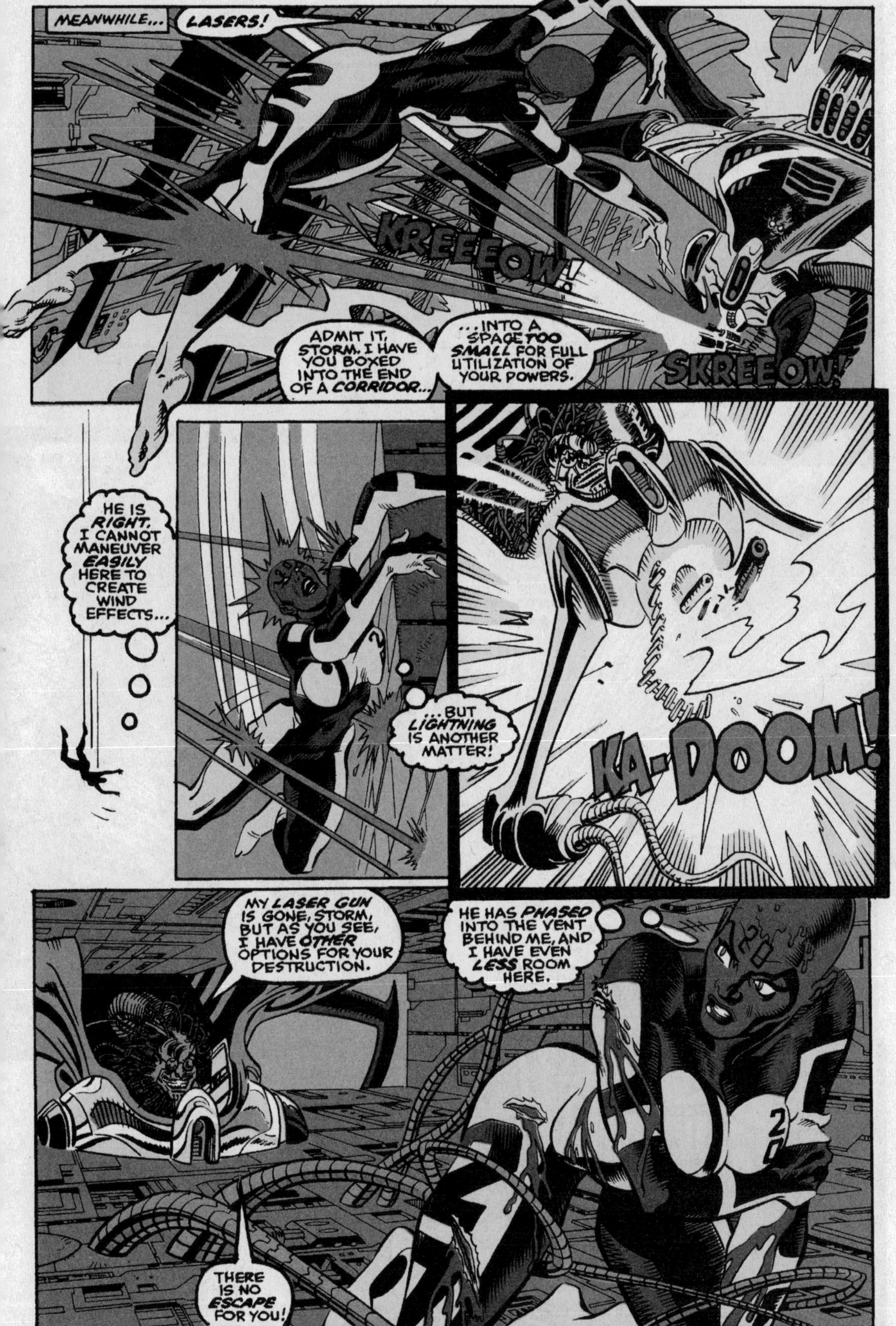
MEANWHILE...
LASERS!
KREEEOW!
ADMIT IT, STORM. I HAVE YOU BOXED INTO THE END OF A CORRIDOR...
...INTO A SPACE TOO SMALL FOR FULL UTILIZATION OF YOUR POWERS.
SKREEOW!
HE IS RIGHT. I CANNOT MANEUVER EASILY HERE TO CREATE WIND EFFECTS...
...BUT LIGHTNING IS ANOTHER MATTER!
KA-DOOM!
MY LASER GUN IS GONE, STORM, BUT AS YOU SEE, I HAVE OTHER OPTIONS FOR YOUR DESTRUCTION.
HE HAS PHASED INTO THE VENT BEHIND ME, AND I HAVE EVEN LESS ROOM HERE.
THERE IS NO ESCAPE FOR YOU!

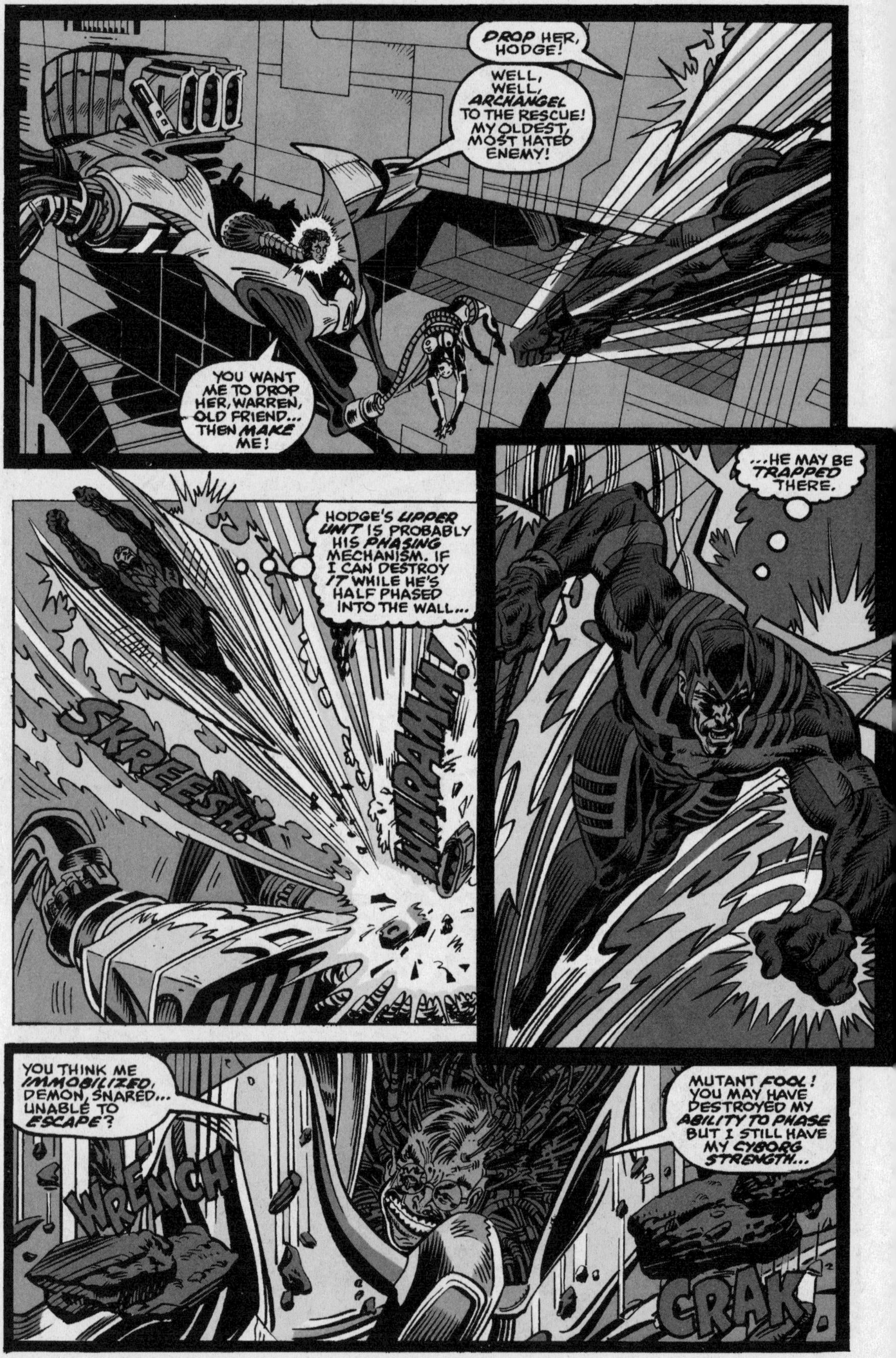
DROP HER, HODGE!
WELL, WELL, ARCHANGEL TO THE RESCUE! MY OLDEST, MOST HATED ENEMY!
YOU WANT ME TO DROP HER, WARREN, OLD FRIEND... THEN MAKE ME!
HODGE'S UPPER UNIT IS PROBABLY HIS PHASING MECHANISM. IF I CAN DESTROY IT WHILE HE'S HALF PHASED INTO THE WALL...
SKREESH!
THRAM!
...HE MAY BE TRAPPED THERE.
YOU THINK ME IMMOBILIZED, DEMON, SNARED... UNABLE TO ESCAPE?
WRENCH
MUTANT FOOL! YOU MAY HAVE DESTROYED MY ABILITY TO PHASE BUT I STILL HAVE MY CYBORG STRENGTH...
CRAK

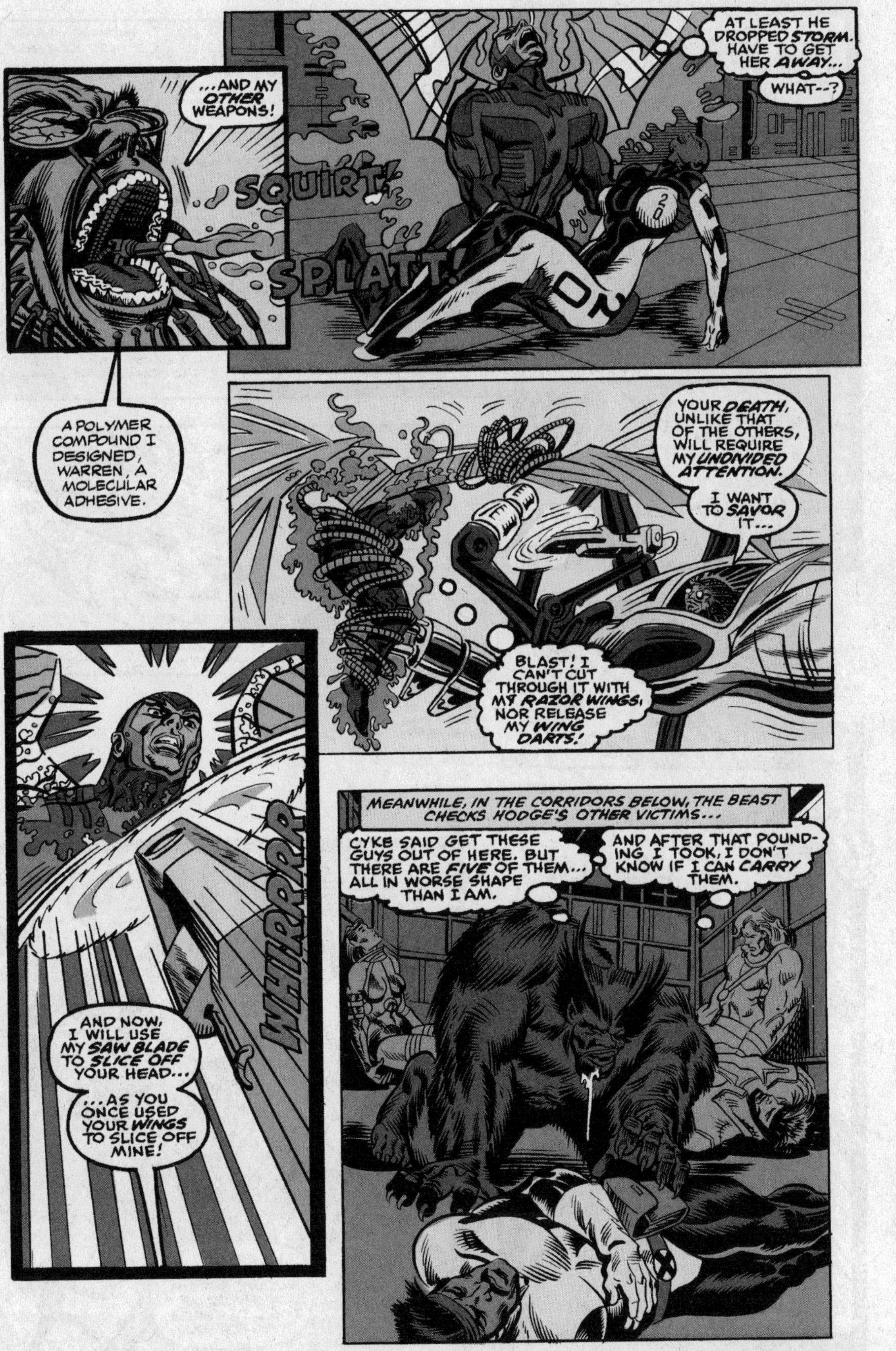
...AND MY OTHER WEAPONS!
SQUIRT!
SPLATT!
AT LEAST HE DROPPED STORM. HAVE TO GET HER AWAY...
WHAT--?
A POLYMER COMPOUND I DESIGNED, WARREN, A MOLECULAR ADHESIVE.
YOUR DEATH, UNLIKE THAT OF THE OTHERS, WILL REQUIRE MY UNDIVIDED ATTENTION.
I WANT TO SAVOR IT...
BLAST! I CAN'T CUT THROUGH IT WITH MY RAZOR WINGS, NOR RELEASE MY WING DARTS!
WHIRRRR
AND NOW, I WILL USE MY SAW BLADE TO SLICE OFF YOUR HEAD...
...AS YOU ONCE USED YOUR WINGS TO SLICE OFF MINE!
MEANWHILE, IN THE CORRIDORS BELOW, THE BEAST CHECKS HODGE'S OTHER VICTIMS...
CYKE SAID GET THESE GUYS OUT OF HERE. BUT THERE ARE FIVE OF THEM... ALL IN WORSE SHAPE THAN I AM.
AND AFTER THAT POUNDING I TOOK, I DON'T KNOW IF I CAN CARRY THEM.

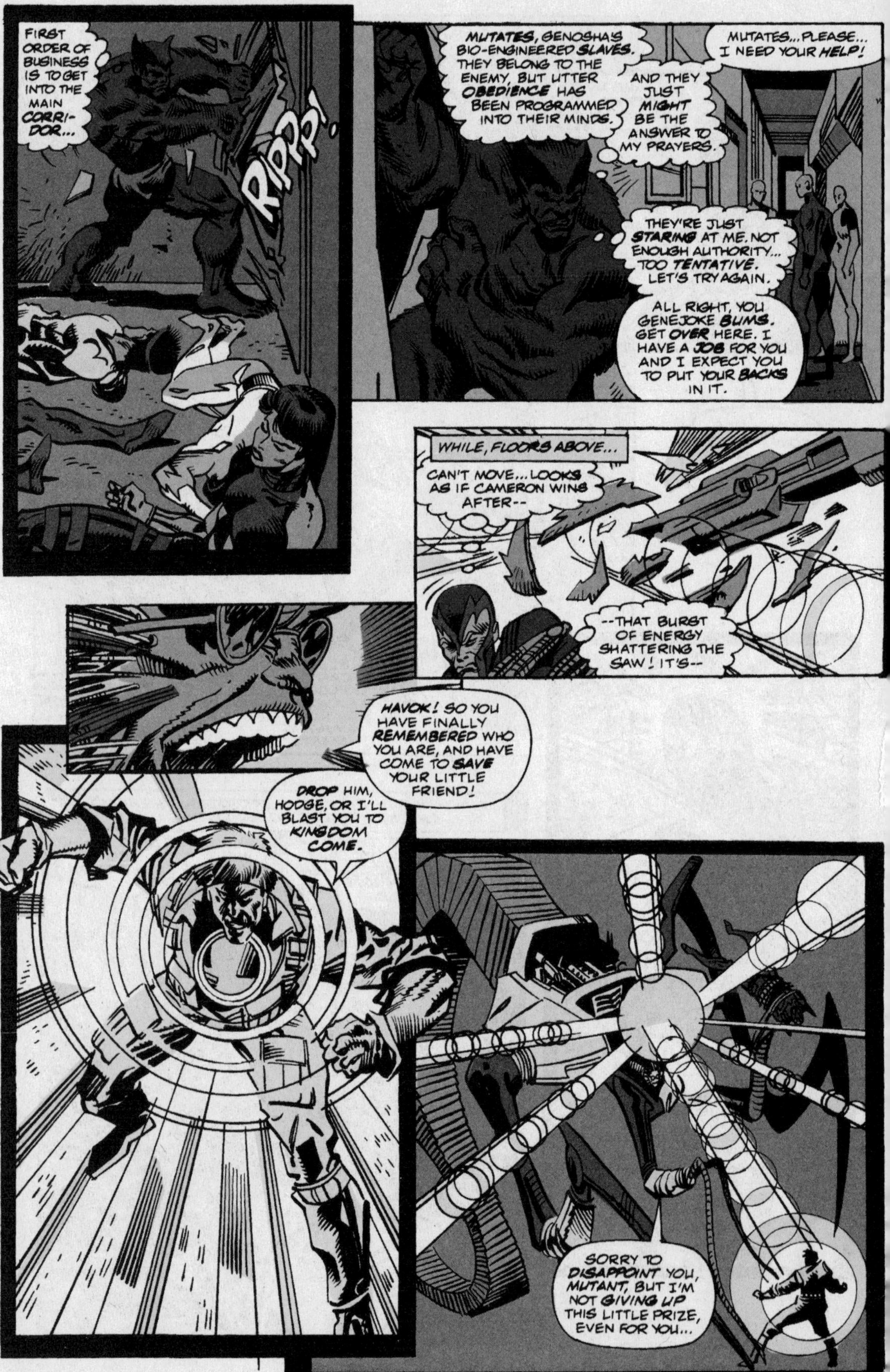
FIRST ORDER OF BUSINESS IS TO GET INTO THE MAIN CORRIDOR...
RIPP!
MUTATES, GENOSHA'S BIO-ENGINEERED SLAVES. THEY BELONG TO THE ENEMY, BUT UTTER OBEDIENCE HAS BEEN PROGRAMMED INTO THEIR MINDS.
AND THEY JUST MIGHT BE THE ANSWER TO MY PRAYERS.
MUTATES... PLEASE... I NEED YOUR HELP!
THEY'RE JUST STARING AT ME. NOT ENOUGH AUTHORITY... TOO TENTATIVE. LET'S TRY AGAIN.
ALL RIGHT, YOU GENEJOKE BUMS. GET OVER HERE. I HAVE A JOB FOR YOU AND I EXPECT YOU TO PUT YOUR BACKS IN IT.
WHILE, FLOORS ABOVE...
CAN'T MOVE... LOOKS AS IF CAMERON WINS AFTER--
--THAT BURST OF ENERGY SHATTERING THE SAW! IT'S--
HAVOK! SO YOU HAVE FINALLY REMEMBERED WHO YOU ARE, AND HAVE COME TO SAVE YOUR LITTLE FRIEND!
DROP HIM, HODGE, OR I'LL BLAST YOU TO KINGDOM COME.
SORRY TO DISAPPOINT YOU, MUTANT, BUT I'M NOT GIVING UP THIS LITTLE PRIZE, EVEN FOR YOU...

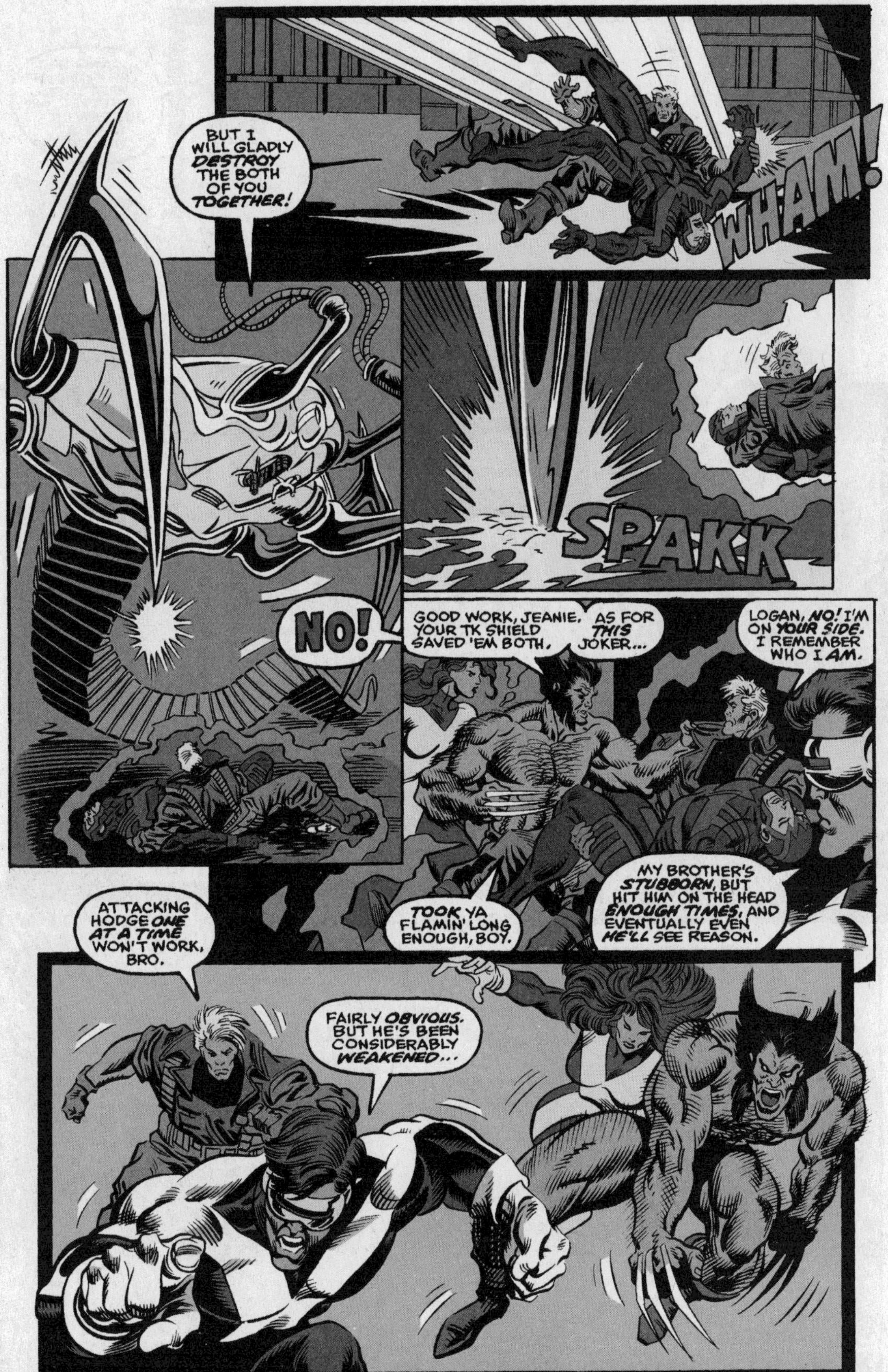
BUT I WILL GLADLY DESTROY THE BOTH OF YOU TOGETHER!
WHAM!
SPAKK
NO!
GOOD WORK, JEANIE. YOUR TK SHIELD SAVED 'EM BOTH.
AS FOR THIS JOKER...
LOGAN, NO! I'M ON YOUR SIDE. I REMEMBER WHO I AM.
MY BROTHER'S STUBBORN, BUT HIT HIM ON THE HEAD ENOUGH TIMES, AND EVENTUALLY EVEN HE'LL SEE REASON.
TOOK YA FLAMIN' LONG ENOUGH, BOY.
ATTACKING HODGE ONE AT A TIME WON'T WORK, BRO.
FAIRLY OBVIOUS. BUT HE'S BEEN CONSIDERABLY WEAKENED...

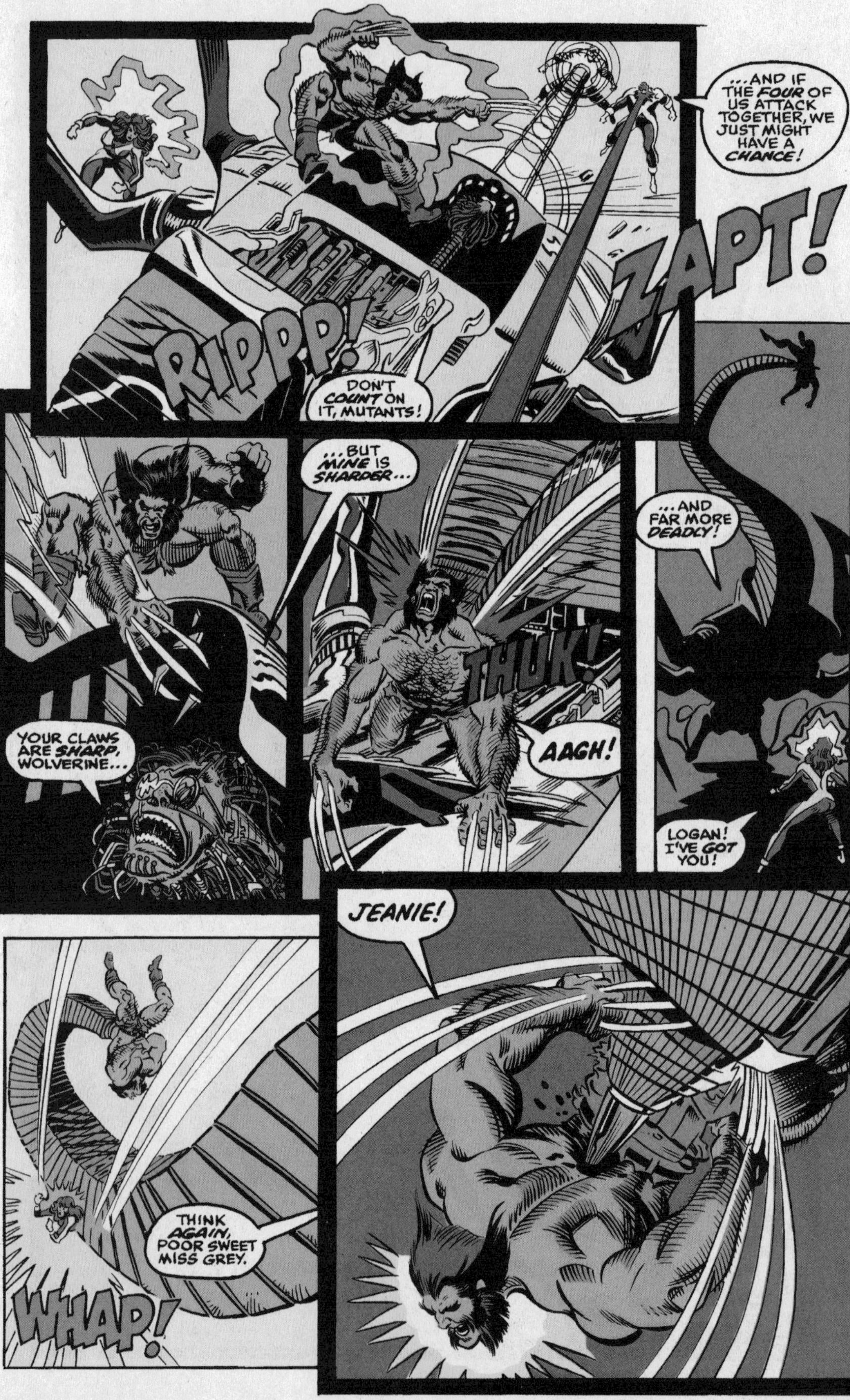
...AND IF THE FOUR OF US ATTACK TOGETHER, WE JUST MIGHT HAVE A CHANCE!
ZAPT!
RIPPP!
DON'T COUNT ON IT, MUTANTS!
YOUR CLAWS ARE SHARP, WOLVERINE...
...BUT MINE IS SHARPER...
THUK!
AAGH!
...AND FAR MORE DEADLY!
LOGAN! I'VE GOT YOU!
JEANIE!
THINK AGAIN, POOR SWEET MISS GREY.
WHAP!

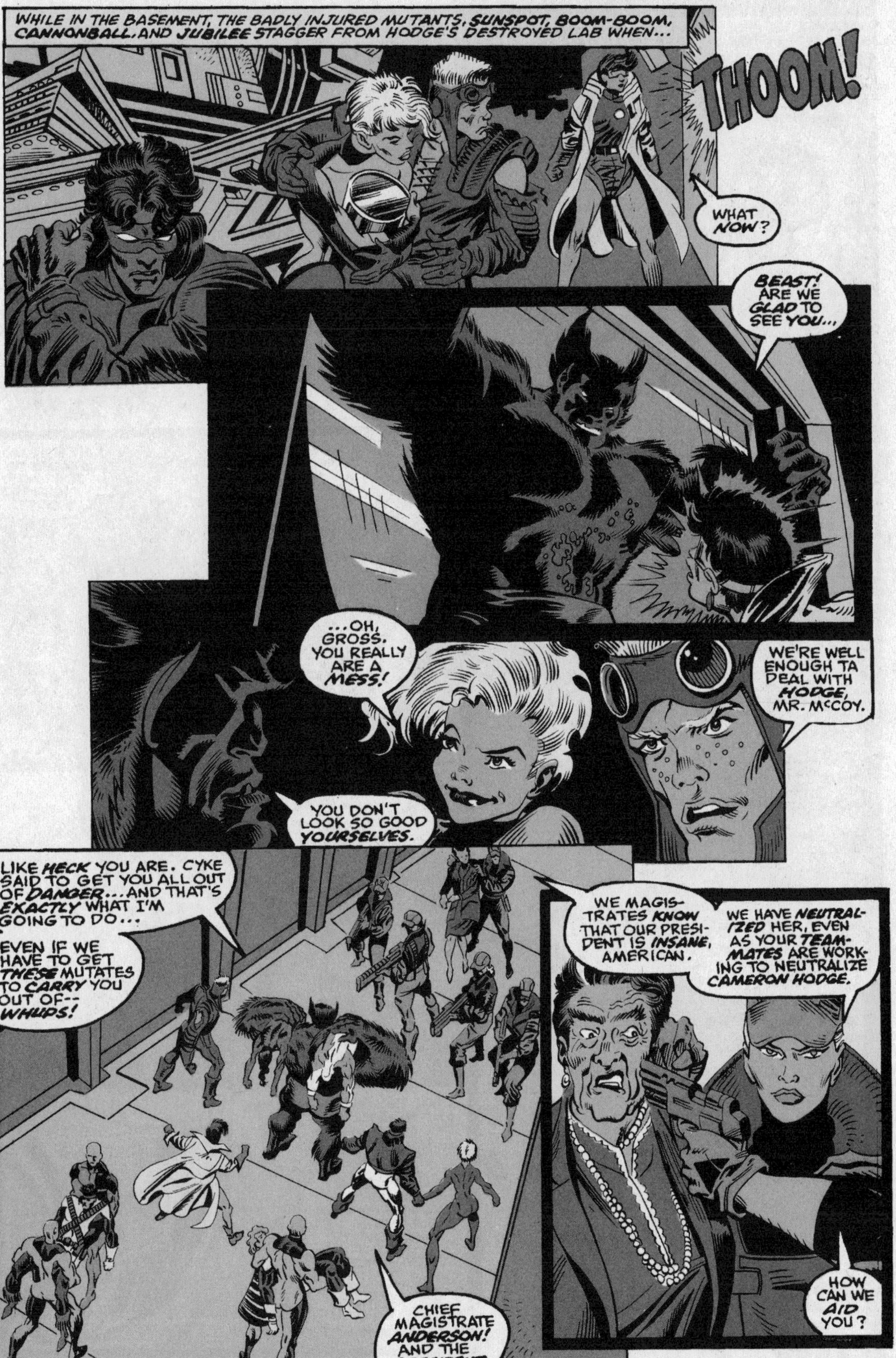

WHILE IN THE BASEMENT, THE BADLY INJURED MUTANTS, SUNSPOT, BOOM-BOOM, CANNONBALL, AND JUBILEE STAGGER FROM HODGE'S DESTROYED LAB WHEN...
THOOM!
WHAT NOW?
BEAST! ARE WE GLAD TO SEE YOU...
...OH, GROSS. YOU REALLY ARE A MESS!
WE'RE WELL ENOUGH TA DEAL WITH HODGE, MR. McCOY.
YOU DON'T LOOK SO GOOD YOURSELVES.
LIKE HECK YOU ARE. CYKE SAID TO GET YOU ALL OUT OF DANGER... AND THAT'S EXACTLY WHAT I'M GOING TO DO...
EVEN IF WE HAVE TO GET THESE MUTATES TO CARRY YOU OUT OF-- WHUPS!
CHIEF MAGISTRATE ANDERSON! AND THE PRESIDENT.
WE MAGISTRATES KNOW THAT OUR PRESIDENT IS INSANE, AMERICAN.
WE HAVE NEUTRALIZED HER, EVEN AS YOUR TEAMMATES ARE WORKING TO NEUTRALIZE CAMERON HODGE.
HOW CAN WE AID YOU?

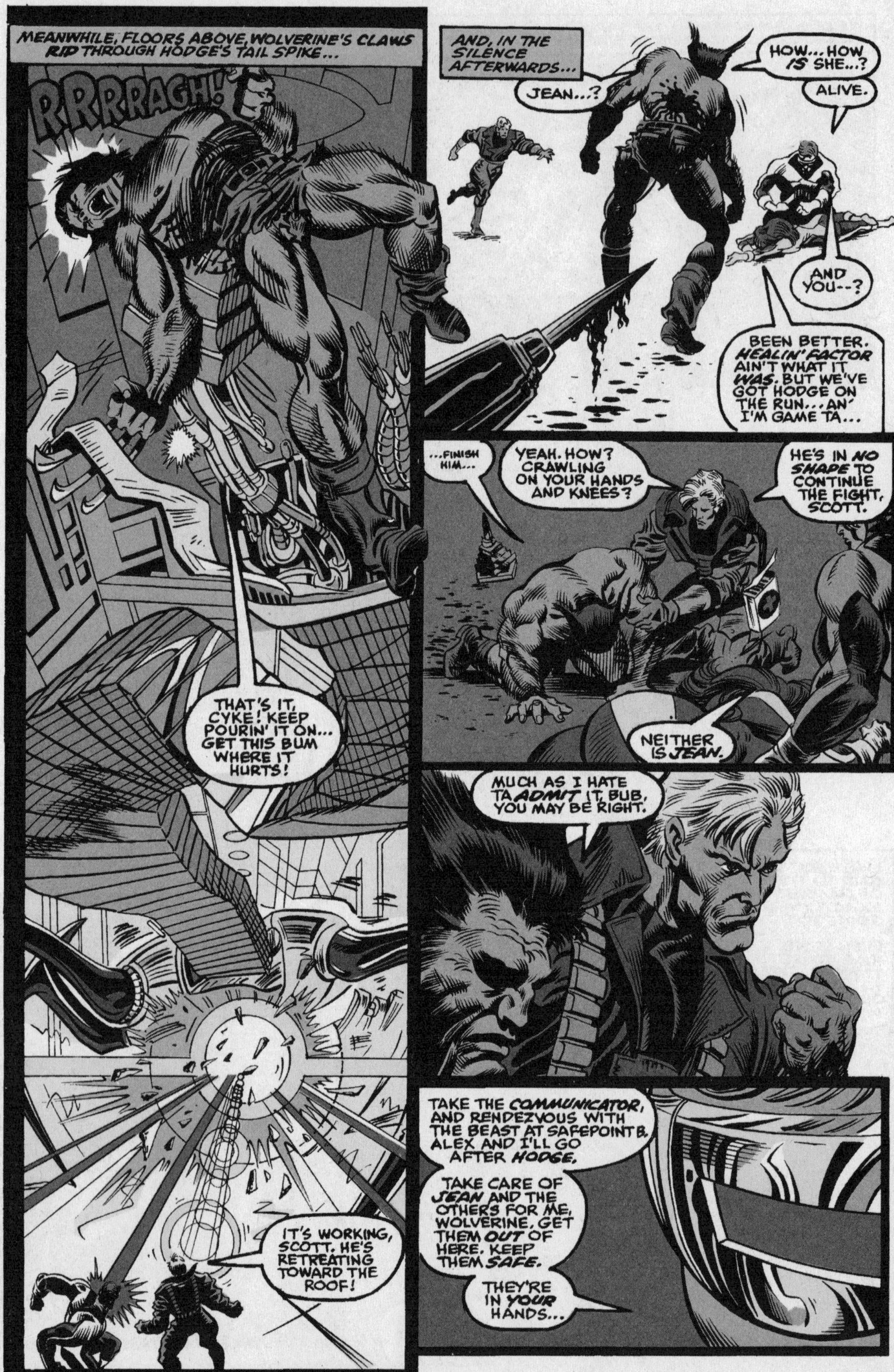
MEANWHILE, FLOORS ABOVE, WOLVERINE'S CLAWS RIP THROUGH HODGE'S TAIL SPIKE...
RRRRAGH!
THAT'S IT, CYKE! KEEP POURIN' IT ON... GET THIS BUM WHERE IT HURTS!
IT'S WORKING, SCOTT. HE'S RETREATING TOWARD THE ROOF!
AND, IN THE SILENCE AFTERWARDS...
JEAN...?
HOW... HOW IS SHE...?
ALIVE.
AND YOU--?
BEEN BETTER. HEALIN' FACTOR AIN'T WHAT IT WAS. BUT WE'VE GOT HODGE ON THE RUN... AN' I'M GAME TA...
...FINISH HIM...
YEAH. HOW? CRAWLING ON YOUR HANDS AND KNEES?
HE'S IN NO SHAPE TO CONTINUE THE FIGHT, SCOTT.
NEITHER IS JEAN.
MUCH AS I HATE TA ADMIT IT, BUB, YOU MAY BE RIGHT.
TAKE THE COMMUNICATOR, AND RENDEZVOUS WITH THE BEAST AT SAFEPOINT B. ALEX AND I'LL GO AFTER HODGE.
TAKE CARE OF JEAN AND THE OTHERS FOR ME, WOLVERINE. GET THEM OUT OF HERE. KEEP THEM SAFE.
THEY'RE IN YOUR HANDS...

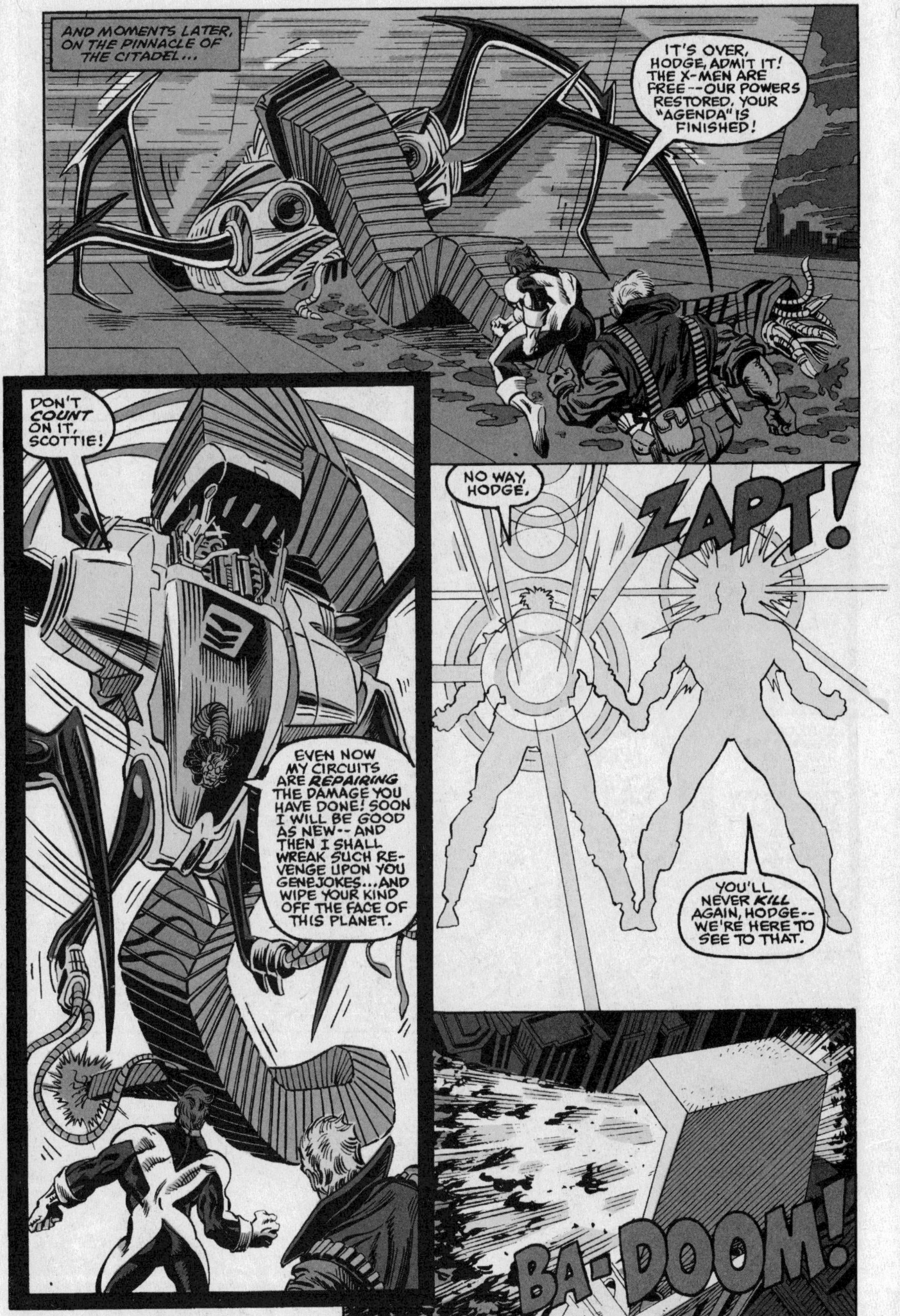
AND MOMENTS LATER, ON THE PINNACLE OF THE CITADEL...
IT'S OVER, HODGE, ADMIT IT! THE X-MEN ARE FREE--OUR POWERS RESTORED. YOUR "AGENDA" IS FINISHED!
DON'T COUNT ON IT, SCOTTIE!
EVEN NOW MY CIRCUITS ARE REPAIRING THE DAMAGE YOU HAVE DONE! SOON I WILL BE GOOD AS NEW--AND THEN I SHALL WREAK SUCH REVENGE UPON YOU GENEJOKES...AND WIPE YOUR KIND OFF THE FACE OF THIS PLANET.
NO WAY, HODGE.
ZAPT!
YOU'LL NEVER KILL AGAIN, HODGE--WE'RE HERE TO SEE TO THAT.
BA-DOOM!

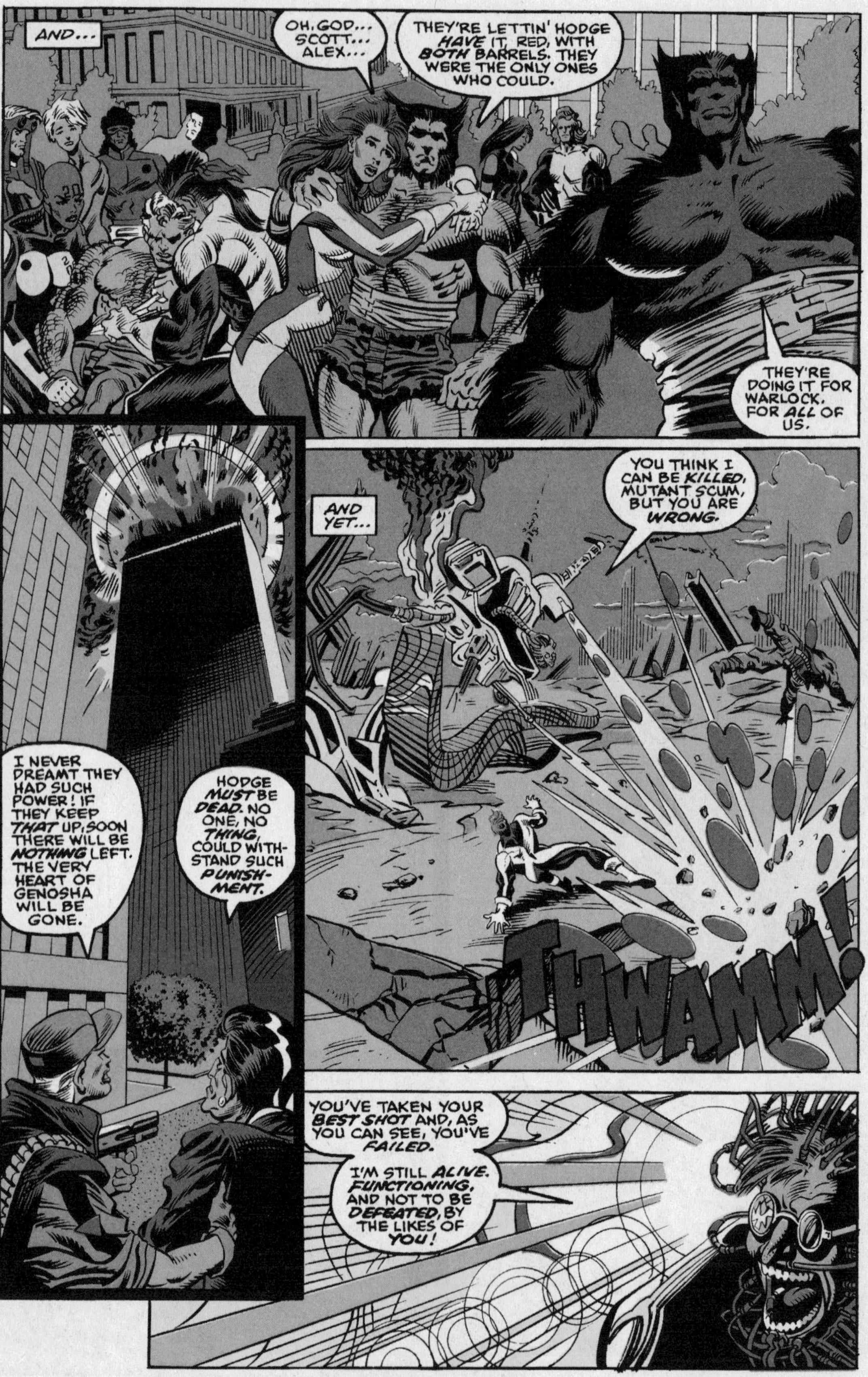
AND...
OH, GOD... SCOTT... ALEX...
THEY'RE LETTIN' HODGE HAVE IT, RED, WITH BOTH BARRELS. THEY WERE THE ONLY ONES WHO COULD.
THEY'RE DOING IT FOR WARLOCK. FOR ALL OF US.
I NEVER DREAMT THEY HAD SUCH POWER! IF THEY KEEP THAT UP, SOON THERE WILL BE NOTHING LEFT. THE VERY HEART OF GENOSHA WILL BE GONE.
HODGE MUST BE DEAD. NO ONE, NO THING, COULD WITHSTAND SUCH PUNISHMENT.
AND YET...
YOU THINK I CAN BE KILLED, MUTANT SCUM, BUT YOU ARE WRONG.
THWAMM!
YOU'VE TAKEN YOUR BEST SHOT AND, AS YOU CAN SEE, YOU'VE FAILED.
I'M STILL ALIVE. FUNCTIONING, AND NOT TO BE DEFEATED, BY THE LIKES OF YOU!

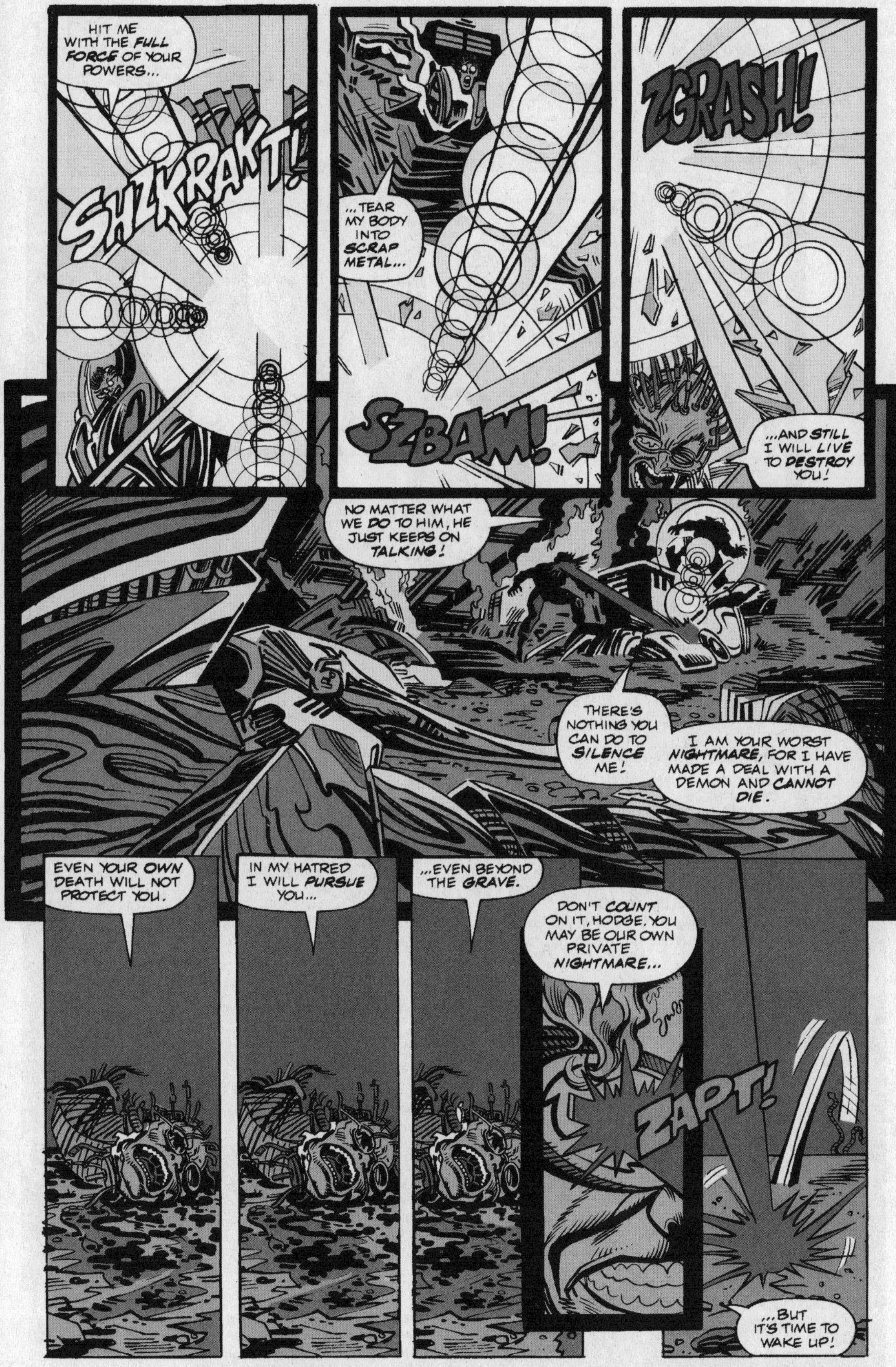

HIT ME WITH THE FULL FORCE OF YOUR POWERS...
SHZKRAKT!
...TEAR MY BODY INTO SCRAP METAL...
SZBAM!
ZGRASH!
...AND STILL I WILL LIVE TO DESTROY YOU!
NO MATTER WHAT WE DO TO HIM, HE JUST KEEPS ON TALKING!
THERE'S NOTHING YOU CAN DO TO SILENCE ME!
I AM YOUR WORST NIGHTMARE, FOR I HAVE MADE A DEAL WITH A DEMON AND CANNOT DIE.
EVEN YOUR OWN DEATH WILL NOT PROTECT YOU.
IN MY HATRED I WILL PURSUE YOU...
...EVEN BEYOND THE GRAVE.
DON'T COUNT ON IT, HODGE. YOU MAY BE OUR OWN PRIVATE NIGHTMARE...
ZAPT!
...BUT IT'S TIME TO WAKE UP!

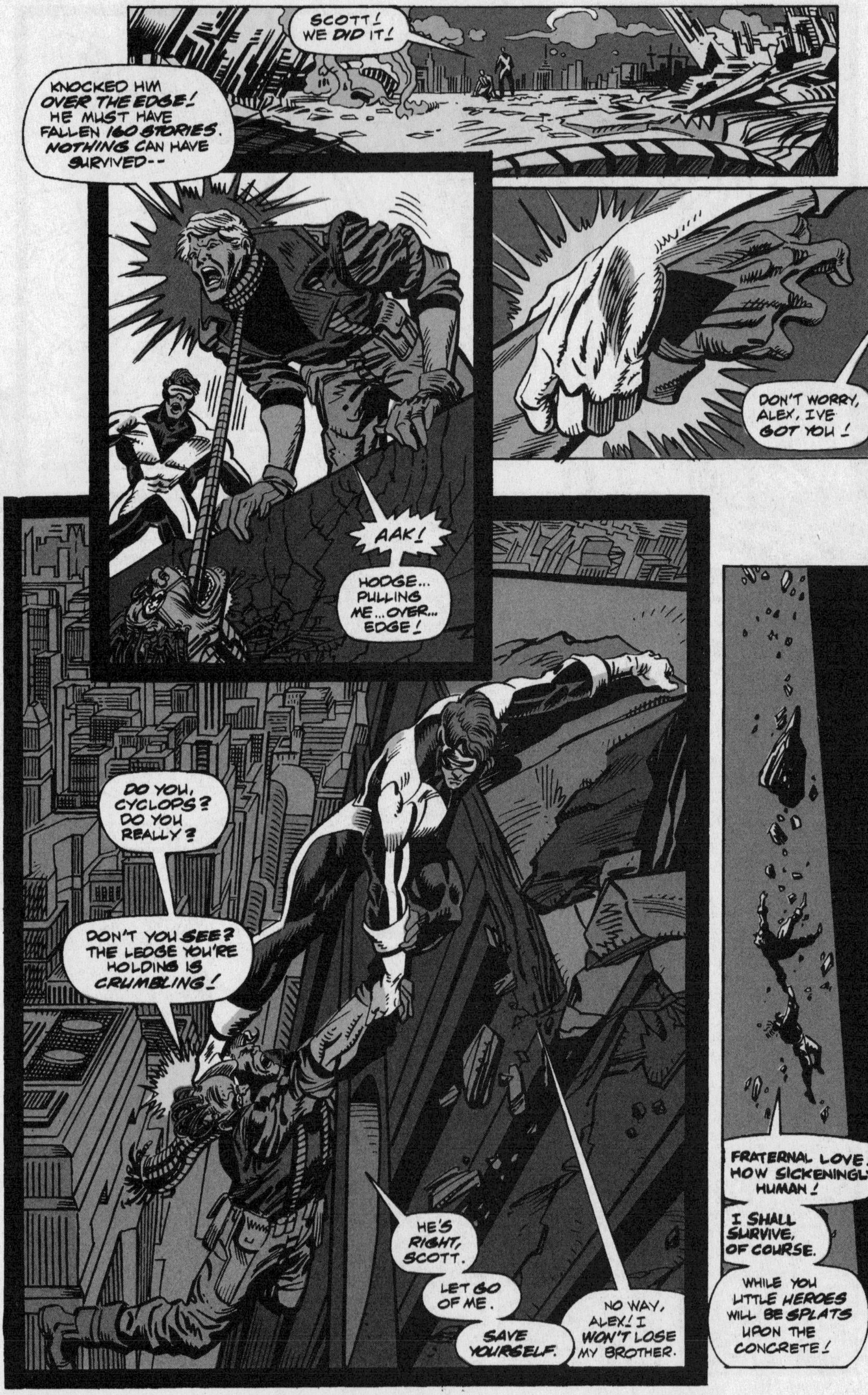
SCOTT! WE DID IT!
KNOCKED HIM OVER THE EDGE! HE MUST HAVE FALLEN 160 STORIES. NOTHING CAN HAVE SURVIVED--
DON'T WORRY, ALEX, I'VE GOT YOU!
AAK!
HODGE... PULLING ME...OVER... EDGE!
DO YOU, CYCLOPS? DO YOU REALLY?
DON'T YOU SEE? THE LEDGE YOU'RE HOLDING IS CRUMBLING!
HE'S RIGHT, SCOTT.
LET GO OF ME.
SAVE YOURSELF.
NO WAY, ALEX! I WON'T LOSE MY BROTHER.
FRATERNAL LOVE! HOW SICKENINGLY HUMAN!
I SHALL SURVIVE, OF COURSE.
WHILE YOU LITTLE HEROES WILL BE SPLATS UPON THE CONCRETE!

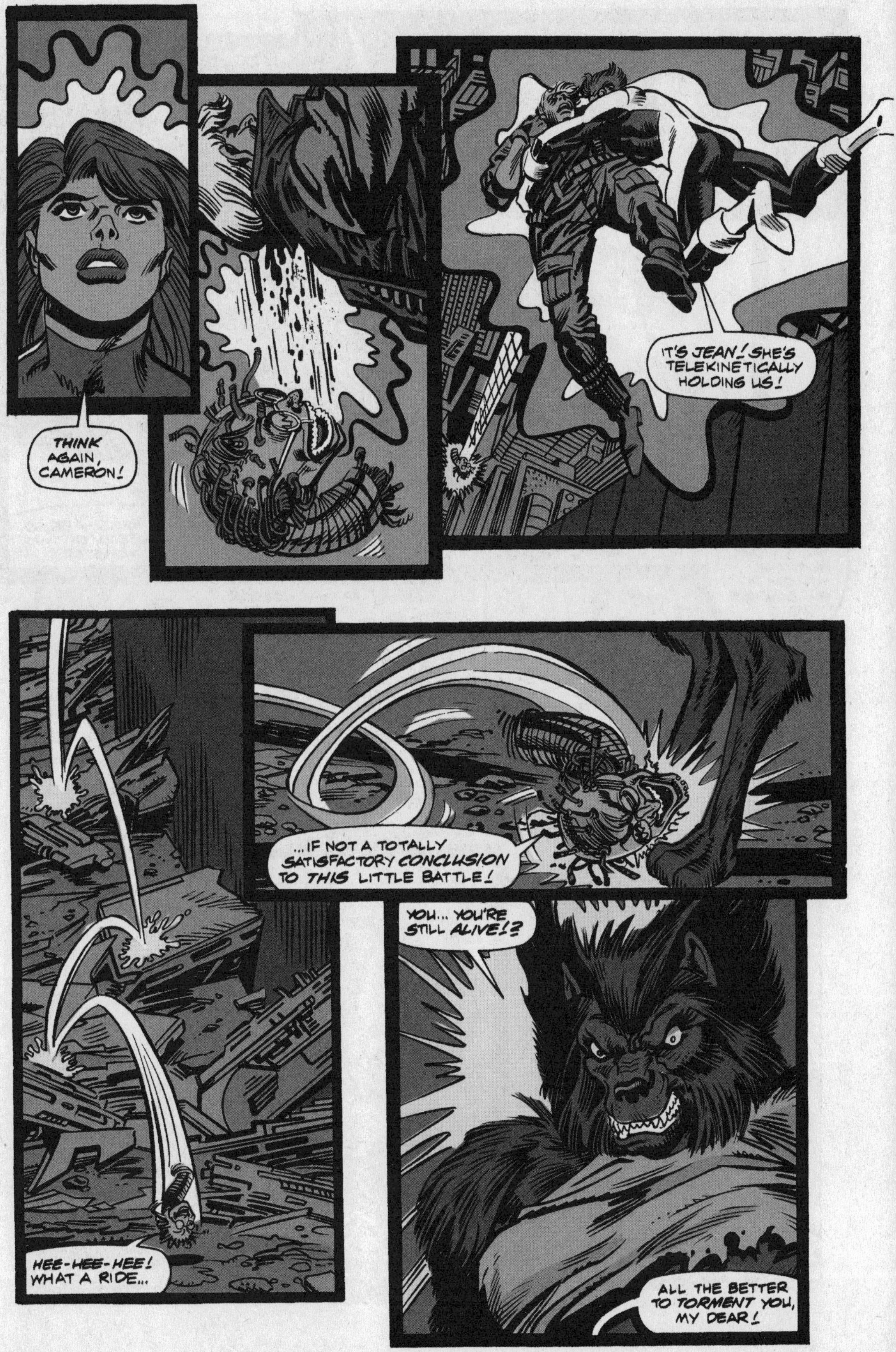
THINK AGAIN, CAMERON!
IT'S JEAN! SHE'S TELEKINETICALLY HOLDING US!
HEE-HEE-HEE! WHAT A RIDE...
...IF NOT A TOTALLY SATISFACTORY CONCLUSION TO THIS LITTLE BATTLE!
YOU... YOU'RE STILL ALIVE!?
ALL THE BETTER TO TORMENT YOU, MY DEAR!

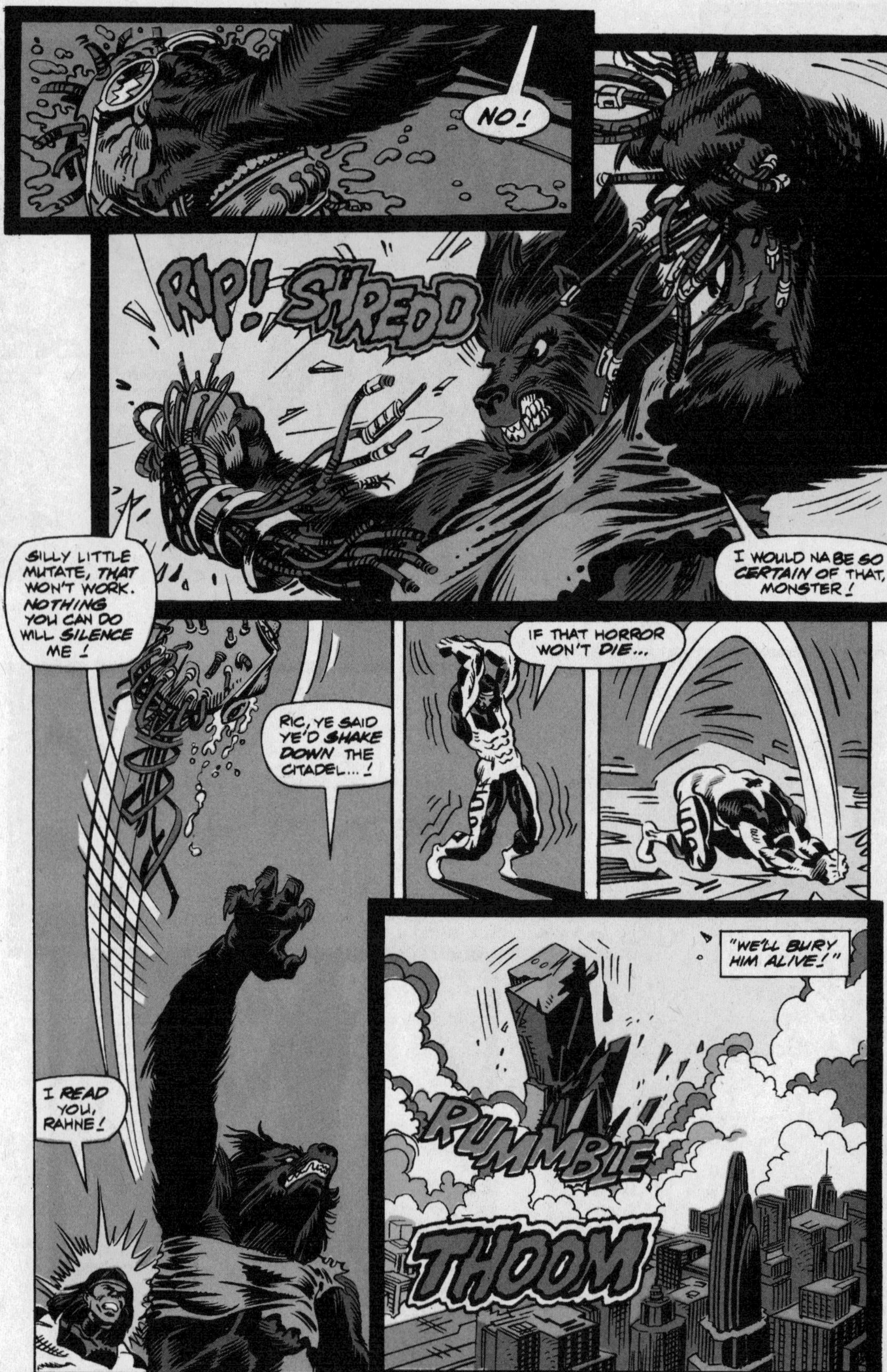
NO!
RIP! SHREDD
SILLY LITTLE MUTATE, THAT WON'T WORK. NOTHING YOU CAN DO WILL SILENCE ME!
I WOULD NA BE SO CERTAIN OF THAT, MONSTER!
RIC, YE SAID YE'D SHAKE DOWN THE CITADEL...!
I READ YOU, RAHNE!
IF THAT HORROR WON'T DIE...
"WE'LL BURY HIM ALIVE!"
RUMMBLE
THOOM

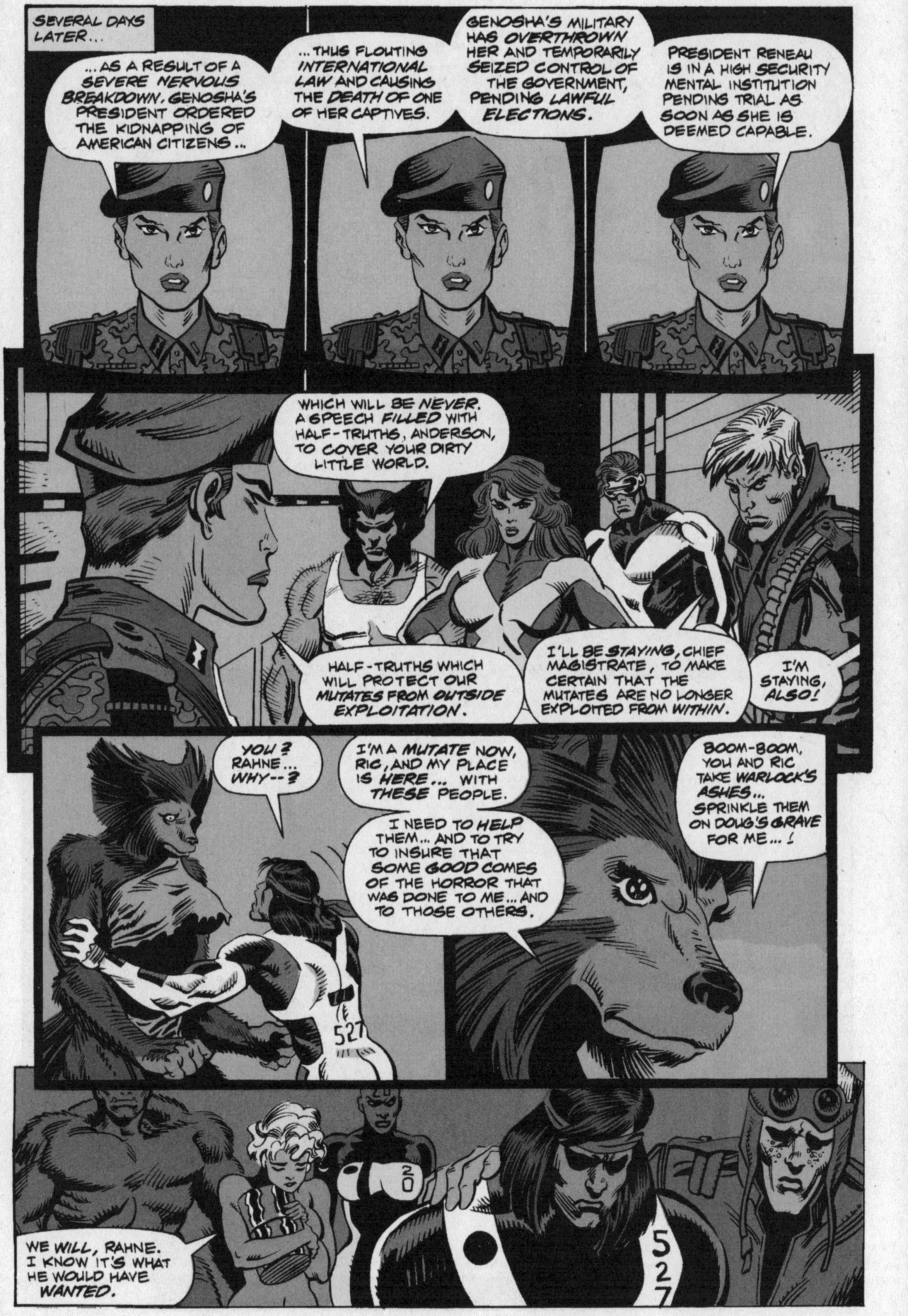
SEVERAL DAYS LATER...
...AS A RESULT OF A SEVERE NERVOUS BREAKDOWN, GENOSHA'S PRESIDENT ORDERED THE KIDNAPPING OF AMERICAN CITIZENS...
...THUS FLOUTING INTERNATIONAL LAW AND CAUSING THE DEATH OF ONE OF HER CAPTIVES.
GENOSHA'S MILITARY HAS OVERTHROWN HER AND TEMPORARILY SEIZED CONTROL OF THE GOVERNMENT, PENDING LAWFUL ELECTIONS.
PRESIDENT RENEAU IS IN A HIGH SECURITY MENTAL INSTITUTION PENDING TRIAL AS SOON AS SHE IS DEEMED CAPABLE.
WHICH WILL BE NEVER. A SPEECH FILLED WITH HALF-TRUTHS, ANDERSON, TO COVER YOUR DIRTY LITTLE WORLD.
HALF-TRUTHS WHICH WILL PROTECT OUR MUTATES FROM OUTSIDE EXPLOITATION.
I'LL BE STAYING, CHIEF MAGISTRATE, TO MAKE CERTAIN THAT THE MUTATES ARE NO LONGER EXPLOITED FROM WITHIN.
I'M STAYING, ALSO!
YOU? RAHNE... WHY--?
I'M A MUTATE NOW, RIC, AND MY PLACE IS HERE... WITH THESE PEOPLE.
I NEED TO HELP THEM... AND TO TRY TO INSURE THAT SOME GOOD COMES OF THE HORROR THAT WAS DONE TO ME... AND TO THOSE OTHERS.
BOOM-BOOM, YOU AND RIC TAKE WARLOCK'S ASHES... SPRINKLE THEM ON DOUG'S GRAVE FOR ME...!
WE WILL, RAHNE. I KNOW IT'S WHAT HE WOULD HAVE WANTED.

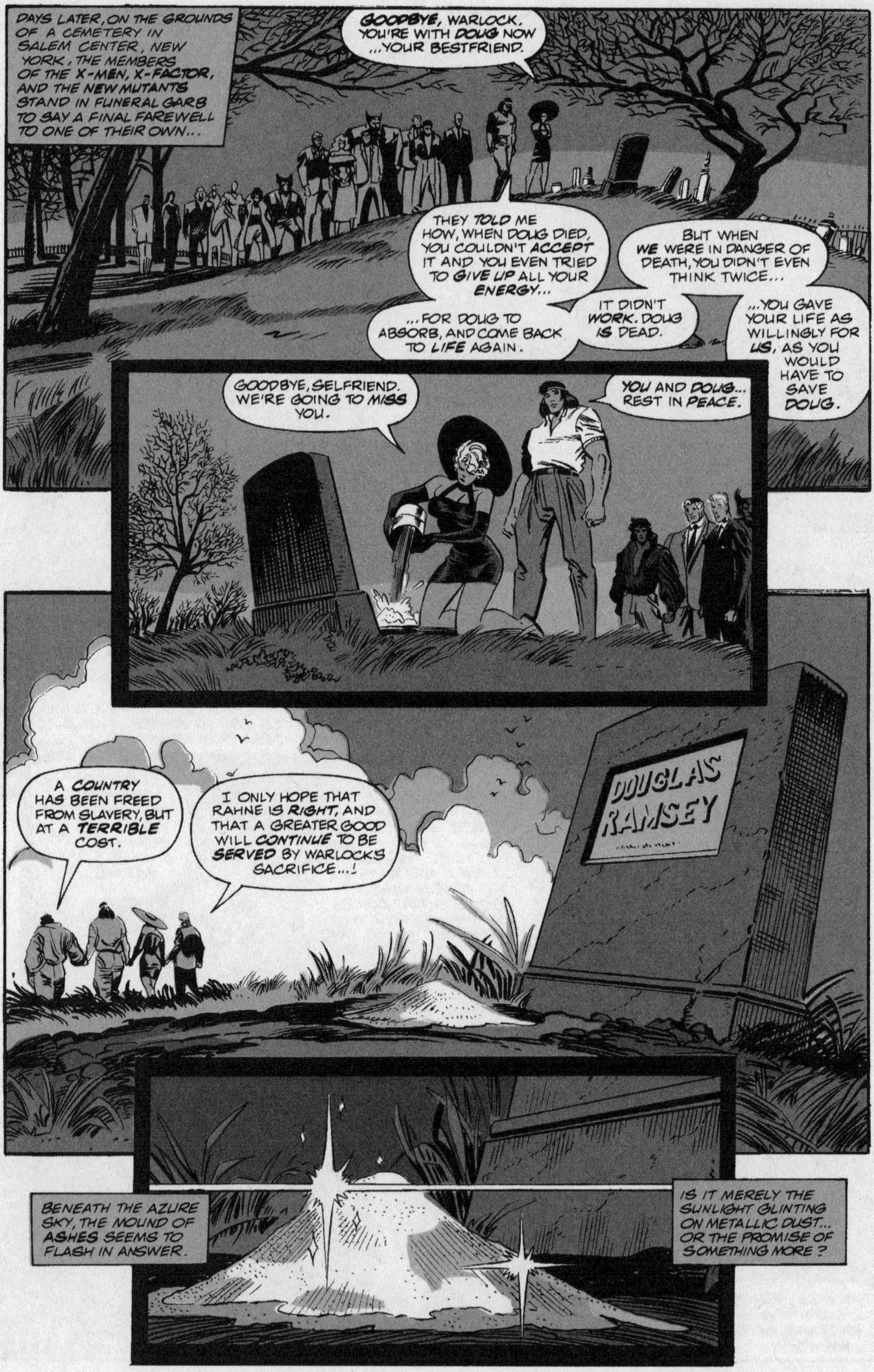
DAYS LATER, ON THE GROUNDS OF A CEMETERY IN SALEM CENTER, NEW YORK, THE MEMBERS OF THE X-MEN, X-FACTOR, AND THE NEW MUTANTS STAND IN FUNERAL GARB TO SAY A FINAL FAREWELL TO ONE OF THEIR OWN...
GOODBYE, WARLOCK. YOU'RE WITH DOUG NOW ...YOUR BESTFRIEND.
THEY TOLD ME HOW, WHEN DOUG DIED, YOU COULDN'T ACCEPT IT AND YOU EVEN TRIED TO GIVE UP ALL YOUR ENERGY...
...FOR DOUG TO ABSORB, AND COME BACK TO LIFE AGAIN.
IT DIDN'T WORK. DOUG IS DEAD.
BUT WHEN WE WERE IN DANGER OF DEATH, YOU DIDN'T EVEN THINK TWICE...
...YOU GAVE YOUR LIFE AS WILLINGLY FOR US, AS YOU WOULD HAVE TO SAVE DOUG.
GOODBYE, SELFRIEND. WE'RE GOING TO MISS YOU.
YOU AND DOUG... REST IN PEACE.
DOUGLAS RAMSEY
A COUNTRY HAS BEEN FREED FROM SLAVERY, BUT AT A TERRIBLE COST.
I ONLY HOPE THAT RAHNE IS RIGHT, AND THAT A GREATER GOOD WILL CONTINUE TO BE SERVED BY WARLOCK'S SACRIFICE...!
BENEATH THE AZURE SKY, THE MOUND OF ASHES SEEMS TO FLASH IN ANSWER.
IS IT MERELY THE SUNLIGHT GLINTING ON METALLIC DUST... OR THE PROMISE OF SOMETHING MORE?

HODGE, CAMERON

Real name: Cameron Hodge
Occupation: Former lawyer, advertising executive, and public relations director, leader of the Right
Identity: Publicly known
Legal status: Citizen of the United States with no criminal record
Other aliases: The Commander
Place of birth: Unrevealed
Marital status: Single
Known relatives: None
Group affiliation: The Right, former employee of X-Factor
Base of operations: Unrevealed, formerly X-Factor headquarters, New York City

First appearance: X-FACTOR #1

History: Cameron Hodge was the roommate of Warren Worthington III, the mutant adventurer formerly known as the Angel (and now as Archangel), at the private school Worthington attended before he entered Professor Charles Xavier's School for Gifted Youngsters and became a member of the team known as the X-Men (see *Archangel, Professor X, X-Men*). Although Worthington believed Hodge to be his friend, in fact Hodge deeply resented Worthington for his good looks, vast wealth, and other advantages. When Worthington publicly revealed himself to be the winged mutant known as the Angel, Hodge's hatred of him increased further. Hodge believed that superhuman mutants were a threat to the freedom of normal human beings and that they therefore must be destroyed.

Hodge became a lawyer, but he then turned to advertising and public relations, and became a highly successful member of a leading New York City advertising agency. In the meantime Hodge secretly founded the Right, an organization dedicated to eliminating superhuman mutants. Hodge was the leader of the Right, and was known as the Commander. Hodge contacted convicted genetic engineer, Dr. Frederick Animus, later known as the Ani-Mator, and commissioned him to find a means of preventing mutation from occurring (see *Ani-Mator*).

Worthington, who still trusted Hodge, turned to him to help him come up with a new means of combating prejudice against mutants. Hodge and Worthington devised the concept of X-Factor, an organization of supposed mutant hunters, who in fact would make contact with superhuman mutants and help them learn to control their superhuman abilities and to masquerade as normal human beings (see *X-Factor*). The other members of the original X-Men, the Beast, Cyclops, Iceman, and Marvel Girl, agreed to this idea and became the other founding members of X-Factor (see individual entries). However, as Hodge had secretly intended, X-Factor's publicity campaign actually intensified prejudice against mutants. Worthington and his four partners came to have increasing misgivings about X-Factor's mode of operations.

The mutant, Mystique, made it publicly known that Warren Worthington III, a known mutant, was secretly the financial backer of X-Factor (see *Mystique*). Then the Angel's wings were impaled by harpoons hurled by the Marauder Harpoon during the "mutant massacre" in which the Marauders wiped out most of the mutant Morlocks (see *Harpoon, Marauders, Morlocks*). Hodge arranged to have the Angel's wings amputated. At the point of despair over the scandal over his financial support of X-Factor and over the loss of his wings, Worthington was easily manipulated by Hodge into changing his will so as to leave the bulk of his fortune to X-Factor, appointing Hodge as its executor. Soon afterward, Worthington seemingly committed suicide in an airplane that exploded. As a result, Hodge now controlled the Worthington fortune. (In fact, however, Worthington had been teleported to safety by the mutant, Apocalypse, who used his advanced biological knowledge to give him new wings (see *Apocalypse*).

By now Cyclops and the other three partners in X-Factor had realized that Hodge was their enemy. Soon afterward, the X-Factor members engaged in battle with members of the Right, and ultimately they learned that Hodge was the leader of the organization. Hodge and other members of the Right captured the New Mutants on Dr. Animus's island headquarters, but the New Mutants escaped captivity, and Hodge apparently died in an explosion (see *New Mutants*).

Subsequently, Worthington learned that his former lover, Candace "Candy" Southern had disappeared (see *Appendix: Southern, Candy*). Worthington tracked her down to a secret Right base, where he discovered she was being held captive by Hodge, who had performed experiments on her that left her at the brink of death. Southern died, and Hodge himself was apparently killed in combat with Worthington.

However, whether or not this was truly the end of Cameron Hodge remains to be seen.

Height: 5' 10" **Weight:** 180 lbs.
Eyes: Blue **Hair:** Grey
Strength level: Cameron Hodge possesses the normal human strength of a man of his age, height, and build who engages in moderate regular exercise.
Known superhuman powers: None
Weapons and paraphernalia: Cameron Hodge has worn an armored battlesuit that can fire explosive missiles. He once utilized a robot in his image that wore ruby quartz armor, enabling it to deflect Cyclops's force beams. Hodge has access to the advanced technology and weaponry of the Right.

X-MEN

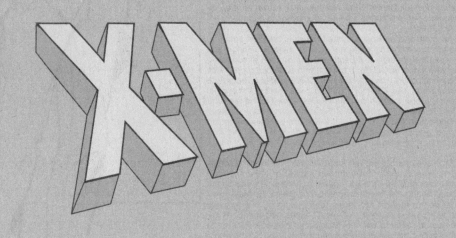